The series Lecture Notes in Computer Science (LNCS), including its subseries Lecture Notes in Artificial Intelligence (LNAI) and Lecture Notes in Bioinformatics (LNBI), has established itself as a medium for the publication of new developments in computer science and information technology research, teaching, and education.

LNCS enjoys close cooperation with the computer science R & D community, the series counts many renowned academics among its volume editors and paper authors, and collaborates with prestigious societies. Its mission is to serve this international community by providing an invaluable service, mainly focused on the publication of conference and workshop proceedings and postproceedings. LNCS commenced publication in 1973.

Guang Yang · Ehsan Adeli · Marleen de Bruijne ·
Bartłomiej W. Papież · Stefanie Speidel ·
Pallavi Tiwari · Guoyan Zheng ·
Mohammad Yaqub · Qi Dou · Islem Rekik
Editors

Medical Image Computing and Computer Assisted Intervention – MICCAI 2026

29th International Conference
Strasbourg, France, September 27 – October 1, 2026
Proceedings, Part XVI

Springer

Editors
Guang Yang
Imperial College London
London, UK

Ehsan Adeli
Stanford University
Palo Alto, CA, USA

Marleen de Bruijne
Erasmus MC
Rotterdam, The Netherlands

Department of Computer Science
University of Copenhagen
Copenhagen, Denmark

Bartłomiej W. Papież
University of Oxford
Oxford, UK

Pallavi Tiwari
University of Wisconsin-Madison
Madison, WI, USA

Stefanie Speidel
TU Dresden/German Cancer Research Center
Dresden, Sachsen, Germany

Mohammad Yaqub
Mohamed bin Zayed University of Artificial Intelligence
Abu Dhabi, United Arab Emirates

Guoyan Zheng
Shanghai Jiao Tong University
Shanghai, China

Islem Rekik
Imperial College London
London, UK

Qi Dou
The Chinese University of Hong Kong
Hong Kong, Hong Kong

ISSN 0302-9743 ISSN 1611-3349 (electronic)
Lecture Notes in Computer Science
ISBN 978-3-032-38235-1 ISBN 978-3-032-38236-8 (eBook)
https://doi.org/10.1007/978-3-032-38236-8

This Springer imprint is published by the registered company Springer Nature Switzerland AG
The registered company address is: Gewerbestrasse 11, 6330 Cham, Switzerland

Preface

We are delighted to present the proceedings of the 29th International Conference on Medical Image Computing and Computer Assisted Intervention (MICCAI 2026), held in Strasbourg, France on September 27 – October 1, 2026. Following the missed opportunity to gather in Strasbourg in 2021, it was especially joyful to finally welcome the MICCAI community to this wonderful city. Beyond its remarkable cultural heritage, Strasbourg is a vibrant European capital shaped by the exchange of ideas across borders and disciplines. It has also fostered a thriving interdisciplinary research ecosystem in which artificial intelligence, medical imaging, engineering, and clinical sciences come together, perfectly reflecting the collaborative spirit and foundations of MICCAI.

The conference featured a broad programme of satellite events on September 27 and October 1, comprising 112 workshops, tutorials, and challenges. This year also marked an important milestone for the Clinical Translation in Medical Image Computing and Computer Assisted Intervention conference (CLINICCAI), whose fifth edition was held on September 29. For the first time, CLINICCAI was organized in close collaboration with the MICCAI Organizing Committee rather than as an independent event, further reinforcing MICCAI's commitment to clinical translation and engagement. Open science remained another important area of focus, with the conference hosting its second Open Data Session on September 30.

MICCAI 2026 set a new record for submissions, with a 25% increase compared with 2025. We received 4,601 full submissions, of which 4,402 advanced to full review. After review, 1,167 papers were accepted for presentation, representing an acceptance rate of approximately 27%. One hundred and ninety-nine papers were desk-rejected because they did not comply with the submission guidelines, including papers with unverifiable references and papers that violated the double-submission rules. The final accepted papers comprise the 19 volumes of the Lecture Notes in Computer Science (LNCS) proceedings, as follows:

- Part I, LNCS Volume 16878: Adapting Foundation Models for Medical Imaging: Large Vision and Language Models (I)
- Part II, LNCS Volume 16879: Adapting Foundation Models for Medical Imaging: Large Vision and Language Models (II)
- Part III, LNCS Volume 16880: Efficient Learning Strategies in Medical Imaging
- Part IV, LNCS Volume 16881: Domain Adaptation and Generalization in Medical Imaging
- Part V, LNCS Volume 16882: Trustworthy, Explainable, and Responsible Medical AI
- Part VI, LNCS Volume 16883: Medical Image Segmentation (I)
- Part VII, LNCS Volume 16884: Medical Image Segmentation (II)
- Part VIII, LNCS Volume 16885: Computer-Aided Diagnosis (I)
- Part IX, LNCS Volume 16886: Computer-Aided Diagnosis (II)
- Part X, LNCS Volume 16887: Longitudinal Modeling, Staging, and Prognosis

- Part XI, LNCS Volume 16888: Image Reconstruction and Image Enhancement
- Part XII, LNCS Volume 16889: Medical Image Registration; Shape Analysis
- Part XIII, LNCS Volume 16890: Medical Image Synthesis and Super-resolution
- Part XIV, LNCS Volume 16891: Computational Pathology; Microscopic Imaging
- Part XV, LNCS Volume 16892: Surgical Data Science and Scene Understanding
- Part XVI, LNCS Volume 16893: Image-Guided Surgery and Intervention
- Part XVII, LNCS Volume 16894: Neuroimaging and Brain-Computer Interfaces
- Part XVIII, LNCS Volume 16895: Benchmarking Datasets and Methods; Clinical Applications
- Part XIX, LNCS Volume 16896: Emerging Techniques and Applications

The papers for the proceedings were selected through a rigorous double-blind peer-review process in which submissions received three reviews each on average. The MICCAI 2026 Program Committee (PC) consisted of 244 Area Chairs (ACs) and over 3,900 scientific reviewers, representing 71 countries across all major continents. About a quarter (23%) of the ACs self-identified as women. Each area chair managed the review of roughly 33 papers, and the average workload was four papers per reviewer. Area chairs and reviewers were selected following public calls to the community and were vetted by the program chairs. As in the past, the Microsoft Conference Management Toolkit (CMT) was used for paper management and organization of the overall review process. The Toronto Paper Matching System (TPMS) was again employed to help ensure that papers were evaluated by area chairs and reviewers with the appropriate expertise. While a special effort was made this year to improve the quality of paper matches by reworking both the TPMS formulae and the CMT categorization of papers and PC member profiles, we recognize the ongoing challenge of securing high-quality reviews in the face of ever-increasing submission numbers.

Based on the double-blind reviews, area chairs' recommendations, and program chairs' decisions, 9% (376) of papers were provisionally accepted without rebuttal, 51% (2255) were rejected, and 40% (1771) proceeded to the rebuttal stage. Final decisions were made based on all available information, including paper screening, adherence to the author submission guidelines, reviews, rebuttals, 2–3 independent meta-reviews, communications during the review process, and, in some cases, additional assessment by the program chairs. A dedicated team was formed to enforce the dual-submission policy. The program committee scrutinized papers flagged during review, manuscripts of special interest, potential cases of plagiarism, and appeals from authors. The committee was particularly attentive to indications of Large Language Model (LLM) misuse in both submissions and reviews, an increasingly vexing issue not only at MICCAI but also in science more generally.

The 1,167 accepted papers that constituted this year's scientific program originated from 48 countries. Almost 80% of these papers came from the following five countries, as identified by the first author's affiliation: China, including Hong Kong SAR and Macao SAR (547); the USA (141); South Korea (95); the UK (68); and Germany (63). The next five countries, in descending order of the number of accepted papers, were Canada (29), France (29), Australia (28), India (24), and the United Arab Emirates (18), highlighting MICCAI's continuing efforts to broaden its global impact.

To build the program of 153 podium presentations, accepted papers were first clustered by technical theme. For each theme, oral presentation candidates were chosen from the papers that received overwhelming enthusiasm from the area chairs and reviewers. These candidates were then narrowed down to the final list by ensuring that the program represented the range of technical contributions and clinical applications covered by the papers and reflected both geographic and demographic inclusivity among its presenters. Among the 153 presentations, 99 were selected as long oral presentations and 54 as spotlight presentations (short talks). The distinction between oral and spotlight presentations was not meant to reflect a difference in technical quality or contribution. These assignments were made primarily based on programming considerations, thematic balance, session structure, and time constraints. All of these papers were recognized by the reviewers and area chairs as having strong potential for clinical translation, making significant contributions to both the technical and clinical communities, or advancing the field through the release of open-source code and publicly available datasets.

MICCAI 2026 was organized around two overarching themes. The first, From Concept to Clinical Impact, emphasized the translational trajectory of MICCAI methods from foundational research to robust deployable systems that improve clinical decision-making and patient care. To support this theme, we strengthened engagement with industry, healthcare providers, and technology partners through dedicated panels, translational showcases, and structured mentoring activities in close collaboration with the MICCAI Student Board and leading experts across academia and industry.

The second theme, Connected Communities and Global Collaboration, reflected MICCAI's long-standing role as an international forum that brings together diverse research communities across continents. It focused on strengthening collaboration across established and emerging ecosystems, fostering inclusivity, and improving access across career stages and regions. Targeted mentoring initiatives supported early-career researchers in scientific writing, submission strategy, and rebuttal preparation, while additional programs broadened participation from underrepresented and resource-constrained communities.

MICCAI 2026 also emphasized the translation of research into real-world healthcare deployment. Dedicated sessions addressed clinical challenges, data governance, and responsible AI, including privacy, regulatory constraints, and reproducibility. A key focus was strengthening collaboration between academia, hospitals, industry, and startups to accelerate clinical translation.

In addition, MICCAI 2026 promoted an innovation-oriented ecosystem connecting researchers, clinicians, and industry stakeholders. This included an expanded Startup Village, industry showcases, mentoring sessions, and entrepreneurship activities that supported technology transfer and new collaborations. Complementary workshops, hackathons, and thematic schools extended engagement beyond the conference. Through these efforts, MICCAI 2026 reinforced its role as the leading global forum for medical image computing and computer-assisted intervention while accelerating clinical impact and strengthening collaboration across the healthcare AI ecosystem.

To further the mission of enhancing inclusion at MICCAI, we offered travel grants to candidates from lower- and middle-income countries as well as from countries historically underrepresented in the MICCAI community, including those from Africa, Asia, and Latin America. We also provided partial support to additional participants through the MICCAI Society Registration Grants. Funding was made possible by generous support from the MICCAI Society, donations from individual groups within the MICCAI community, and financial support from non-commercial sponsors. Support for US-based students and early-career investigators was provided by the National Institute of Biomedical Imaging and Bioengineering of the National Institutes of Health (NIH) under Award Number R13EB035922. The content expressed in written conference materials or publications and by speakers and moderators does not necessarily reflect the official policies of the NIH; nor does mention of trade names, commercial practices, or organizations imply endorsement by the U.S. Government.

A meeting of MICCAI's scale and impact is only possible through the collective dedication and tireless efforts of many individuals, most notably the members of this year's organizing committees. While every member played a vital role, we would like to especially recognize several key contributors. The Workshops Committee (Xiu Wang, Sophia Bano, Shadi Albarqouni, and Chunfeng Lian), Tutorials Committee (Andrea Lara and Anees Kazi), and Challenges Committee (Olivier Colliot, Moi Hoon Yap, Ulas Bagci, Annika Reinke, Gorkem Durak, and Charlotte Godard) reviewed a total of 191 satellite event proposals and assembled a diverse, high-quality program. We are particularly grateful to our Satellite Program Committee (Spyridon Bakas, Ghada Zamzmi, and Xiaoxiao Li) for skillfully coordinating the 112 accepted satellite events into a cohesive and well-structured program. The Panel Committee, headed by Tanveer Syeda-Mahmood, established a strong panel that facilitated in-depth discussions of our conference themes. The Student Committee, under the leadership of Camila Gonzalez and Numan Saeed, introduced a new and impactful program that further enriched the participation and engagement of students and early-career researchers.

We also appreciate the exemplary work of our Outreach & Sponsorship Team: Angelica Aviles Rivero, Rachid Jennane, Mohammad Yaqub, Nassir Navab, Lina Chato, Mohammed Almasni, Ilkay Oksuz, Muhammad Rushdi, Shereen Fouad, Alaa Alkaysi, and Salma Hassan, for their efforts in securing financial support for the conference despite the challenging economic climate and helping to further expand MICCAI's reach into underrepresented regions. Joseph Chin-Chi Kuo, Farouk Dako, Shahrukh Hashmi, Rafat Damseh, and Michael B. Wallace, together with the CLINICCAI Program Committee, ensured the continued success of CLINICCAI as a distinctive flagship of MICCAI. Martijn P.A. Starmans, Apostolia Tsirikoglou, Lidia Garrucho Moras, and Kaouther Mouheb provided distinguished leadership in advancing the Open Data Initiative.

A tremendous amount of work was carried out by the Local Organizing Committee, chaired by Caroline Essert, whose commitment and meticulous attention to every detail were critical to the smooth execution of the meeting. We are also grateful to the team of Student Volunteers, led by Jonas Mehtali, for their enthusiasm and dedication in organizing the student activities that complemented the scientific program and helped build a vibrant and cohesive student community. We are deeply grateful to our local supporting institutions: the University of Strasbourg, ICube Institute, ITI HealthTech, and ENACT Cluster, for their generous contributions to and support for the conference. We also wish to extend our heartfelt thanks to the City of Strasbourg and the team at the Convention Centre of Strasbourg, led by Ramona Fischer and Anne Knaus, whose dedication, professionalism, and unwavering support made it possible to bring MICCAI 2026 to France.

We would also like to express our sincere appreciation to Geng Chen, our Publication Chair, for his outstanding efforts in overseeing the preparation and production of the conference proceedings. His professionalism, efficiency, and meticulous attention to detail ensured the timely and high-quality publication of the scientific program. Our heartfelt thanks also go to our Keynote Chairs: Min Xu, Michael Brady, and Nassir Navab, for assembling an exceptional keynote program that brought together internationally renowned leaders whose inspiring talks helped shape the scientific discussions and vision of MICCAI 2026. We are deeply grateful to our Equity, Diversity & Inclusion Chairs: Celia Cintas, Esther Puyol-Antón, Aamna Al Shehhi, and Jihad Zahir, for their dedication to fostering a welcoming, inclusive, and diverse conference environment. Their initiatives and thoughtful leadership strengthened our commitment to ensuring that MICCAI remains an open, supportive, and accessible community for researchers from all backgrounds. In addition, we sincerely thank our Career Development and Mentorship Chairs: Antonio Porras, Baiying Lei, and Anees Kazi, for their commitment to supporting the professional growth of our community. Through the organization of mentorship activities and career development initiatives, they created valuable opportunities for students, early-career researchers, and emerging leaders to connect, learn, and thrive within the MICCAI community.

We would also like to express our sincere gratitude to the MICCAI Society Board of Directors and, in particular, to its President, Marius George Linguraru, and former President, Caroline Essert, for their support and constructive feedback. We gratefully acknowledge the contributions of the MICCAI Society secretariat personnel: Janette Wallace and Johanne Langford, who oversaw logistics and budgets, and Diana Cunningham and John Baxter, who provided timely conference announcements in the MICCAI Society newsletters and MICCAI Morning issues. The proficient on-site organization of the conference, including budget management and event operations, was the commendable work of our Professional Conference Organizer, Dekon Congress & Tourism, led by Mehmet Eldegez.

The proceedings of MICCAI 2026 are the fruit of the extraordinary work of our entire community. We would like to give special recognition to Kitty Wong, the MICCAI Submission System Manager, and express our deepest gratitude for her unwavering dedication and exceptional support throughout every stage of the conference organization. From managing the submission and review system to coordinating countless operational details behind the scenes, Kitty has consistently gone above and beyond to ensure that every aspect of the process runs smoothly and efficiently. Her professionalism, responsiveness, meticulous attention to detail, and tireless commitment have been instrumental in making the review process and conference organization a success. Kitty's dedication, patience, and positive spirit are invaluable assets to the MICCAI community. We have been truly fortunate to work alongside her, and the conference would simply not have been possible without her extraordinary efforts. On behalf of the entire MICCAI community, we extend our heartfelt appreciation and sincere thanks for everything she has done.

We are especially grateful to the members of the Program Committee team for their dedication and tremendous efforts throughout the conference preparations, from planning and paper review to decision-making and handling countless emails. It was certainly challenging, but also immensely rewarding! Our warmest congratulations and sincere thanks go to all our ACs and reviewers for their outstanding work and for meeting every deadline. Most importantly, we extend our deepest appreciation to all the authors for the time, creativity, and effort they invested in preparing their manuscripts and supporting the conference through their submissions. The success of MICCAI 2026 is a direct reflection of the exceptional quality of the work presented at the meeting. Heartfelt congratulations to all our authors and contributors on their outstanding achievements!

In closing, we once again thank every individual and team involved in organizing MICCAI 2026. Their inspiring dedication, professionalism, enthusiasm, and collaborative spirit made this year's conference a truly outstanding and memorable occasion. We hope you thoroughly enjoyed MICCAI 2026 and your time with us in Strasbourg. We now look forward with great excitement to reuniting with the MICCAI community next year in Auckland, New Zealand, for MICCAI 2027!

September 2026

Guang Yang
Ehsan Adeli
Marleen de Bruijne
Bartłomiej W. Papież
Stefanie Speidel
Pallavi Tiwari
Guoyan Zheng
MICCAI 2026 Program Chairs

Mohammad Yaqub
Islem Rekik
Qi Dou
MICCAI 2026 General Chairs

Organization

General Chairs

Mohammad Yaqub	Mohamed bin Zayed University of Artificial Intelligence, UAE
Islem Rekik	Imperial College London, UK
Qi Dou	Chinese University of Hong Kong, China

Program Chairs

Guang Yang (Lead)	Imperial College London, UK
Ehsan Adeli	Stanford University, USA
Marleen de Bruijne	Erasmus MC, Netherlands and University of Copenhagen, Denmark
Bartłomiej W. Papież	University of Oxford, UK
Stefanie Speidel	TU Dresden & German Cancer Research Center, Germany
Pallavi Tiwari	University of Wisconsin–Madison, USA
Guoyan Zheng	Shanghai Jiao Tong University, China

Satellite Event Committee

Spyridon Bakas (Lead)	Indiana University, USA
Xiaoxiao Li	University of British Columbia, Canada
Ghada Zamzmi	HeartFlow, USA

Workshop Committee

Xiu Wang (Lead)	University of Sydney, Australia
Sophia Bano	University College London, UK
Shadi Albarqouni	University of Bonn, Germany
Chunfeng Lian	Xi'an Jiaotong University, China

Challenges Committee

Olivier Colliot (Lead)	French National Centre for Scientific Research, France
Moi Hoon Yap	Manchester Metropolitan University, UK
Ulas Bagci	Northwestern University, USA
Annika Reinke	Heidelberg University, Germany
Charlotte Godard	Paris Brain Institute, France
Gorkem Durak	Northwestern University, USA
Lena Maier-Hein (Advisor)	Heidelberg University, Germany

Tutorials Committee

Andrea Lara (Lead)	Universidad Galileo, Guatemala
Anees Kazi	Harvard Medical School, USA

MICCAI-Clinical (CLINICCAI) Committee

Joseph Chin-Chi Kuo (Lead)	China Medical University Hospital, China
Farouk Dako	University of Pennsylvania, USA
Shahrukh Hashmi	Department of Health, Abu Dhabi, UAE
Rafat Damseh	United Arab Emirates University, UAE
Michael B. Wallace	Mayo Clinic, USA
Tausifa Jan Saleem	Mohamed bin Zayed University of Artificial Intelligence, UAE

Publication Committee

Geng Chen	Northwestern Polytechnical University, China

Keynote Committee

Min Xu (Lead)	Carnegie Mellon University, USA
Michael Brady	Oxford Clinical Diagnostic Centre, UK
Nassir Navab	Technical University of Munich, Germany

Sponsorship Committee

Angelica Aviles Rivero (Lead)	Tsinghua University, China
Rachid Jennane	University of Orléans, France
Nassir Navab	Technical University of Munich, Germany
Mohammad Yaqub	Mohamed bin Zayed University of Artificial Intelligence, UAE

Outreach Committee

Lina Chato (Lead)	University of South Dakota, USA
Mohammed Almasni	Sejong University, South Korea
Mohamed Mabrok	Qatar University, Qatar
Ilkay Oksuz	Istanbul Technical University, Turkey
Muhammad Rushdi	Cairo University, Egypt
Shereen Fouad	Aston University, UK
Alaa Alkaysi	University of Technology-Iraq, Iraq

Open Data Committee

Martijn P. A. Starmans (Lead)	Erasmus MC, Netherlands
Apostolia Tsirikoglou	Karolinska Institutet, Sweden
Kaouther Mouheb	Erasmus MC, Netherlands
Lidia Garrucho Moras	Universitat de Barcelona, Spain

Students Committee

Camila Gonzalez (Lead)	Stanford University, USA
Numan Saeed	Mohamed bin Zayed University of Artificial Intelligence, UAE

Equity, Diversity and Inclusion Committee

Celia Cintas (Lead)	IBM, USA
Esther Puyol-Antón	King's College London and Heartflow, UK
Aamna Al Shehhi	Khalifa University, UAE

Jihad Zahir	Cadi Ayyad University, Morocco
Baoru Huang	Imperial College London, UK

Career Development and Mentorship Committee

Antonio Porras (Lead)	University of Chicago, USA
Baiying Lei	Shenzhen University, China
Anees Kazi	Harvard Medical School, USA

Local Organizers

Caroline Essert (Lead)	University of Strasbourg, France
Aamna Al Shehhi	Khalifa University, UAE
Omar Alkadi	University of Jordan, Jordan
Shadab Khan	ADIA Lab, UAE
Mai Ahmed Shaaban	Mohamed bin Zayed University of Artificial Intelligence, UAE
Ibrahim Almakky	Mohamed bin Zayed University of Artificial Intelligence, UAE
Numan Saeed	Mohamed bin Zayed University of Artificial Intelligence, UAE
Shahad Hardan	Mohamed bin Zayed University of Artificial Intelligence, UAE
Salma Hassan	Mohamed bin Zayed University of Artificial Intelligence, UAE
Mostafa Salem	Mohamed bin Zayed University of Artificial Intelligence, UAE
Tausifa Jan Saleem	Mohamed bin Zayed University of Artificial Intelligence, UAE
Dwarikanath Mahapatra	Khalifa University, UAE
Yutong Xie	Mohamed bin Zayed University of Artificial Intelligence, UAE
Asif Hanif	Mohamed bin Zayed University of Artificial Intelligence, UAE
Mohammad Yaqub	Mohamed bin Zayed University of Artificial Intelligence, UAE

Program Committee (Area Chairs)

Sharib Ali	University of Leeds, UK
Syed Anwar	Children's National Hospital, USA
Pablo Arbelaez	Universidad de los Andes, Colombia
Ulas Bagci	Northwestern University, USA
Abhirup Banerjee	University of Oxford, UK
Joao Barreto	University of Coimbra, Portugal
Neslihan Bayramoglu	University of Oulu, Finland
Cosmin Bercea	Technical University of Munich and Helmholtz AI and Helmholtz Center Munich, Germany
Alaa Bessadok	Université de Carthage, Tunisia
Binod Bhattarai	University of Aberdeen, UK
Benjamin Billot	Inria, France
Ryoma Bise	Kyushu University, Japan
Federico Bolelli	Università degli Studi di Modena e Reggio Emilia, Italy
Katharina Breininger	Center for AI and Data Science, University of Würzburg, Germany
Esther Bron	Erasmus MC, Netherlands
Mariano Cabezas	Universitat de Girona, Spain
Peng Cao	Northeastern University, China
Cheng Chen	University of Hong Kong, China
Hao Chen	Hong Kong University of Science and Technology, China
Jianan Chen	University College London, UK
Xin Chen	University of Nottingham, UK
Zhaolin Chen	Monash University, Australia
Zhen Chen	Hong Kong Polytechnic University, China
Jun Cheng	Institute for Infocomm Research, A*STAR, Singapore
Li Cheng	University of Alberta, Canada
Toby Collins	IRCAD, France
Kang Dang	Xi'an Jiaotong-Liverpool University, China
Behdad Dashtbozorg	Netherlands Cancer Institute, Netherlands
Elena De Momi	Politecnico di Milano, Italy
Ruining Deng	Weill Cornell Medicine, USA
Christian Desrosiers	École de technologie supérieure, Canada
Blake Dewey	Johns Hopkins University, USA
Jose Dolz	ETS Montreal, Canada
Reuben Dorent	Inria, France
Niharika D'Souza	IBM Research, USA

Dmitry V. Dylov	Computational Imaging Laboratory, Russia
Roy Eagleson	Western University, Canada
Mostafa El Habib Daho	University of Western Brittany, France
Huihui Fang	Nanyang Technological University, Singapore
Azade Farshad	ELLIS Institute Finland and Aalto University, Finland and Technical University of Munich, Germany
Huazhu Fu	IAIC, A*STAR, Singapore
Jin Kyu Gahm	Pusan National University, South Korea
Yue Gao	Tsinghua University, China
Zhifan Gao	Sun Yat-sen University, China
Zongyuan Ge	Monash University, Australia
Guido Gerig	New York University, USA
Elodie Germani	Université de Rennes, France
Ricardo Gonzales	Harvard Medical School, USA
Camila Gonzalez	Medical University of Vienna, Austria
Karthik Gopinath	Heartflow, USA
Pietro Gori	Télécom Paris, France
Pengfei Guo	NVIDIA, USA
Xueqi Guo	Siemens Healthineers, USA
Prashnna Gyawali	West Virginia University, USA
Ilker Hacihaliloglu	University of British Columbia, Canada
Xiangmin Han	Tsinghua University, China
Yuting He	Case Western Reserve University, USA
Monica Hernandez	University of Zaragoza, Spain
Yi Hong	Shanghai Jiao Tong University, China
Benjamin Hou	Imperial College London, UK
Dan Hu	University of North Carolina at Chapel Hill, USA
Xiaoling Hu	Harvard Medical School, USA
Baoru Huang	University of Liverpool, UK
Junzhou Huang	University of Texas at Arlington, USA
Yuankai Huo	Vanderbilt University, USA
Jana Hutter	King's College London, UK
Abdullah-Al-Zubaer Imran	University of Kentucky, USA
Mohammad Jafari	Amazon, Canada
Amir Jamaludin	University of Oxford, UK
Won-Ki Jeong	Korea University, South Korea
Meirui Jiang	Ant Group, China
Tingting Jiang	Peking University, China
Zhifan Jiang	Children's National Hospital, USA
Zhongliang Jiang	University of Hong Kong, China
Dakai Jin	Alibaba USA Inc., USA

Julio Silva-Rodríguez	ETH Zurich, Switzerland
Vivek Singh	Siemens Healthineers, USA
Kevin Smith	KTH Royal Institute of Technology, Sweden
Yang Song	University of New South Wales, Australia
Youyi Song	China Pharmaceutical University, China
Sahar Soussa	Nile University, Egypt
Rachel Sparks	King's College London, UK
Vinkle Srivastav	IIT Madras, India
Ruisheng Su	Eindhoven University of Technology, Netherlands
Carole Sudre	University College London, UK
Yao Sui	Peking University, China
Kyung Sung	University of California, Los Angeles, USA
Tanveer Syeda-Mahmood	IBM Research, USA
Tao Tan	Macao Polytechnic University, China
Xiaoying Tang	Southern University of Science and Technology, China
Yucheng Tang	NVIDIA, USA
Zhenyu Tang	Beihang University, China
Qian Tao	Delft University of Technology, Netherlands
Austin Tapp	Children's National Hospital, USA
Lin Tian	Harvard Medical School and Massachusetts General Hospital, USA
Martin Urschler	Medical University of Graz, Austria
Maria Vakalopoulou	CentraleSupélec, France
María del C. Valdés Hernández	University of Edinburgh, UK
Fons van der Sommen	Eindhoven University of Technology, Netherlands
Francisco Vasconcelos	University College London, UK
Harini Veeraraghavan	Memorial Sloan Kettering Cancer Center, USA
Archana Venkataraman	Johns Hopkins University, USA
Sulaiman Vesal	Stanford University, USA
Christian Wachinger	Technical University of Munich, Germany
Changmiao Wang	Shenzhen Research Institute of Big Data, China
Chengjia Wang	Heriot-Watt University, UK
Hong Wang	Xi'an Jiaotong University, China
Manning Wang	Fudan University, China
Puyang Wang	Ant Group, USA
Shujun Wang	Hong Kong Polytechnic University, China
Shuo Wang	Fudan University, China
Xiaosong Wang	Shanghai AI Laboratory, China
Yaqi Wang	Hangzhou Dianzi University, China
Donglai Wei	Boston College, USA
Thomas Wendler	University Hospital Augsburg, Germany

Bryan Williams	Lancaster University, UK
Ken C.L. Wong	IBM Research – Almaden Research Center, USA
Jonghye Woo	Massachusetts General Hospital and Harvard Medical School, USA
Ye Wu	Nanjing University of Science and Technology, China
Yicheng Wu	Imperial College London, UK
Yong Xia	Northwestern Polytechnical University, China
Yiming Xiao	Concordia University, Canada
Fuyong Xing	University of Colorado, Denver, USA
Xiaohan Xing	Stanford University, USA
Xuanang Xu	Yale University, USA
Yan Xu	Beihang University, China
Yanwu Xu	South China University of Technology, China
Yanyu Xu	Shandong University, China
Zhe Xu	Columbia University, USA
Wufeng Xue	Shenzhen University, China
Ke Yan	Alibaba DAMO Academy, China
Zengqiang Yan	Huazhong University of Science and Technology, China
Jiancheng Yang	ELLIS Institute Finland and Aalto University, Finland
Qiushi Yang	City University of Hong Kong, China
Yanwu Yang	University of Tübingen and Max Planck Institute of Intelligent Systems, Germany
Jiawen Yao	DAMO Academy, Alibaba Group, China
Qingsong Yao	Stanford University, USA
Dong Hye Ye	Georgia State University, USA
Zhaozheng Yin	Stony Brook University, USA
Chenyu You	Stony Brook University, USA
Lequan Yu	University of Hong Kong, China
Fatemeh Zabihollahy	University of Toronto, Canada
Fan Zhang	University of Electronic Science and Technology of China, China
Jianpeng Zhang	Alibaba DAMO Academy, China
Jiong Zhang	Nanjing University, China
Lichi Zhang	Shanghai Jiao Tong University, China
Xiaofan Zhang	Shanghai Jiao Tong University, China
Yi Zhang	Sichuan University, China
Yizhe Zhang	Nanjing University of Science and Technology, China
Fenqiang Zhao	DAMO Academy, Alibaba Group, China
He Zhao	University of Liverpool, UK

Lin Zhao	New Jersey Institute of Technology, USA
Qingyu Zhao	Weill Cornell Medicine, USA
Rongchang Zhao	Central South University, China
Yitian Zhao	Cixi Institute of Biomedical Engineering, Ningbo Institute of Industrial Technology, Chinese Academy of Sciences, China
Yefeng Zheng	Westlake University, China
Yushan Zheng	Beihang University, China
Zichun Zhong	Wayne State University, USA
Bo Zhou	Northwestern University, USA
Luping Zhou	University of Sydney, Australia
Qin Zhou	East China University of Science and Technology, China
Tianfei Zhou	Beijing Institute of Technology, China
Yan-Jie Zhou	DAMO Academy, Alibaba Group, China
Yi Zhou	Southeast University, China
Yuyin Zhou	University of California, Santa Cruz, USA
Zongwei Zhou	Johns Hopkins University, USA
Meilu Zhu	University of Hong Kong, China
Veronika Zimmer	Technical University of Munich and Siemens Healthineers, Germany
Ke Zou	Sichuan University, China
Lianrui Zuo	Vanderbilt University, USA

Outstanding Area Chairs

Carole Sudre	University College London, UK
Lianrui Zuo	Vanderbilt University, USA
Mostafa El Habib Daho	University of Western Brittany, France

Outstanding Reviewers

Yunlong He	Télécom Paris, France
Julius Hense	TU Berlin, Germany
Arthur Longuefosse	RIKEN, Japan
Johanna Müller	Friedrich-Alexander-Universität Erlangen-Nürnberg, Germany
Aminu Musa	Federal University Dutse, Nigeria
Andreas Østvik	Norwegian University of Science and Technology, Norway

Nathan Painchaud	CREATIS, France
Luca Parolari	University of Padua, Italy
Mostafa Salem	Mohamed bin Zayed University of Artificial Intelligence, UAE
Weirong Wang	Hangzhou Institute for Advanced Study, University of Chinese Academy of Sciences, China

Honorable Mentions (Reviewers)

Marwan Abbas	Mayo Clinic, USA
Jaesin Ahn	Kyungpook National University, South Korea
Michel Antunes	Smith & Nephew, Portugal
Alberto Arrigoni	Istituto di Ricerche Farmacologiche Mario Negri IRCCS, Italy
Shreeram Athreya	University of California, Los Angeles, USA
Johannes Brandt	Technische Universität München, Germany
Salvatore Calcagno	University of Catania, Italy
Liane Canas	King's College London, UK
Lara Cavinato	Politecnico di Milano, Italy
Satrajit Chakrabarty	GE HealthCare, USA
Dongdong Chen	Anhui University, China
Weihao Cheng	Hangzhou Dianzi University, China
Olivier Colliot	CNRS, France
Pierrick Coupé	CNRS and University of Bordeaux, France
Jürgen Dammers	Forschungszentrum Jülich, Germany
Sanuwani Dayarathna	Monash University, Australia
Lei Deng	Central South University, China
Wenting Duan	University of Lincoln, UK
Ertunc Erdil	ETH Zurich, Switzerland
Yannik Frisch	University of Heidelberg, Germany
Boxun Fu	Xidian University, China
Adrian Galdran	Universitat Pompeu Fabra, Spain
Fei Gao	University of Science and Technology of China, China
Haifan Gong	University of Pennsylvania, USA
Alvaro Gonzalez-Jimenez	University Hospital of Basel, Switzerland
Valerio Guarrasi	Università Campus Bio-Medico di Roma, Italy
Diandian Guo	Chinese University of Hong Kong, China
Arnela Hadzic	Medical University of Graz, Austria

Salma Hassan	Mohamed Bin Zayed University of Artificial Intelligence, UAE
Dongdong He	Harbin Institute of Technology, China
Da-Woon Heo	Korea University, South Korea
Mariko Isogawa	Keio University, Japan
Ji-Hoon Jeong	Sungkyunkwan University, South Korea
Zhuoyun Jiang	University of Shanghai for Science and Technology, China
Shuo Jiang	Hangzhou Dianzi University, China
Amelia Jiménez-Sánchez	Universitat de Barcelona, Spain
Erwan Kerrien	Inria, France
Abbas Khan	Queen Mary University of London, UK
Young-Gon Kim	Seoul National University Hospital, South Korea
Youngwoo Kim	Kumoh National Institute of Technology, South Korea
Ender Konukoglu	ETH Zurich, Switzerland
Naveen Kumar Kummari	Mohamed bin Zayed University of Artificial Intelligence, UAE
Frank Langbein	Cardiff University, UK
François Lecomte-Denis	Inria, France
Won Hee Lee	Kyung Hee University, South Korea
Huiqi Li	Beijing Institute of Technology, China
Jun Li	Technical University of Munich, Germany
Miao Li	Tsinghua University, China
Ruizhe Li	University of Nottingham, UK
Simone Lionetti	Lucerne University of Applied Sciences and Arts, Switzerland
Feng Liu	University of Queensland, Australia
Andrea Loddo	University of Cagliari, Italy
Angela Lombardi	Politecnico di Bari, Italy
Luca Lumetti	University of Modena and Reggio Emilia, Italy
Huoling Luo	Shenzhen University of Information Technology, China
Ngoc Ly	University of Science-VNUHCM, Vietnam
Jamie McClelland	University College London, UK
Martin Menten	Technical University of Munich, Germany
Klaus Mueller	Stony Brook University, USA
Favour Nerrise	Stanford University, USA
Ahmad P. Tafti	University of Pittsburgh, USA
Yongsheng Pan	Northwestern Polytechnical University, China
Mario Parreno Centeno	Oulu University, Finland
Kelly Payette	University Children's Hospital Zurich, Switzerland

Yoon Seok Yang	SUNY Korea, South Korea
Chunzhi Yi	Harbin Institute of Technology, China
Kyungho Yoon	Yonsei University, South Korea
Han Yu	Nanjing University of Posts and Telecommunications, China
Zheng Yu	University of Adelaide, Australia
Mariam Zabihi	University College London, UK
Stefan Zachow	Zuse Institute Berlin, Germany
Qing Zhang	East China Normal University, China
Wanjun Zhang	Henan University, China
Shilun Zhao	ShanghaiTech University, China
Lujia Zhong	University of Southern California, USA
Jiayuan Zhu	University of Oxford, UK

Mentorship Program (Mentors)

Ekaterina Antipushina	Applied AI Institute, Russia
Stephen Aylward	NVIDIA, USA
Rotimi-Williams Bello	Tshwane University of Technology, South Africa
Mariano Cabezas Grebol	Macquarie University, Australia
Zhen Chen	Hong Kong Polytechnic University, China
Li Cheng	University of Alberta, Canada
Kathleen Curran	University College Dublin, Ireland
Behdad Dashtbozorg	Netherlands Cancer Institute, Netherlands
Kanchana Devanathan	Vanderbilt University, USA
Qi Dou	Chinese University of Hong Kong, China
Niharika Dsouza	IBM Research, USA
Mohammad Eslami	Harvard Medical School, USA
Caroline Essert	University of Strasbourg, France
Ruogu Fang	University of Florida, USA
Huazhu Fu	Institute of Advanced Intelligence and Computing, A*STAR, Singapore
Zhifan Gao	Sun Yat-sen University, China
Zulqarnain Gilani	Edith Cowan University and University of Western Australia, Australia
Polat Goktas	Sabanci University, Turkey
Leo Joskowicz	Hebrew University of Jerusalem, Israel
Bernhard Kainz	Friedrich-Alexander-Universität Erlangen-Nürnberg, Germany and Imperial College London, UK
Neerav Karani	QuantCo, USA

Karim Lekadir	Icrea and Universitat de Barcelona, Spain
Xiaoxiao Li	University of British Columbia, Canada
Guiqiu Liao	University of Pennsylvania, USA
Marius George Linguraru	Children's National Hospital, USA
Peirong Liu	Johns Hopkins University, USA
Siladittya Manna	Hong Kong Baptist University, China
Tommaso Mansi	Janssen R&D Data Science, USA
Qingjie Meng	University of Birmingham, UK
Nassir Navab	Technical University of Munich, Germany
Roseline Ogundokun	Redeemer's University, Nigeria
Mohammad Rizwan	Hammond Chemicals, UK
Divya Saleela	University of Southampton, UK
Julia Schnabel	Computational Imaging and AI in Medicine, Germany
Bella Specktor Fadida	University of Haifa, Israel
Kyung Sung	University of California, Los Angeles, USA
Mathias Unberath	Johns Hopkins University, USA
Archana Venkataraman	Boston University, USA
Shandong Wu	University of Pittsburgh, USA
Fuyong Xing	University of Colorado Denver, USA
Jiancheng (JC) Yang	ELLIS Institute Finland and Aalto University, Finland
Le Zhang	University of Birmingham, UK
Rongchang Zhao	Central South University, China
S. Kevin Zhou	Institute of Computing Technology, China
Lei Zhu	Hong Kong University of Science and Technology, Guangzhou, China
Maria A. Zuluaga	EURECOM, France

Additional Reviewers

Abdullah
Marwan Abbas
Syed Farhan Abbas
Hamid Abbasi
Gabriele Abbate
Zeinab Abboud
Nassib Abdallah
Lamiaa Abdel-Hamid
Abeer Abdelhamid
Kumar Abhishek
Farhan Fuad Abir
Purang Abolmaesumi
Mohammad Mahdi Abootorabi
Mansour Abtahi
Jumana Abu-Khalaf
Titipat Achakulvisut
Ashok Vardhan Addala
Hamidreza Aftabi
Akshay Agarwal
Oktay Agcaoglu
Aarush Aggarwal
Zahra Aghaloo

Shashank Agnihotri
Antonio Agudo
Marco Agus
Sakib Ahammed
Artur Aharonyan
Raha Ahmadi
Seyed-Ahmad Ahmadi
Sheraz Ahmed
Euijoon Ahn
Jaesin Ahn
Suhyun Ahn
Antti Ahola
Happiness Aigbogun
Aroof Aimen
Naren Akash
Elif Ecem Akbaba
Younes Akbari
Faranak Akbarifar
Emre Akbas
Muhammad Usman Akram
Mumu Aktar
Tanya Akumu
Dawood Al Chanti
Wafa Al Ghallabi
Mugahed A. Al-antari
Khaoula Alaoui Belghiti
Abbas Alatrany
Baidaa Al-Bander
Chadi Albitar
Abdalrahman Alblwi
Julia Alekseenko
Daniel Alexander
Felicia Alfano
Saghir Alfasly
Walid Al-Haidri
Hassan Alhajj
Danish Ali
Hazrat Ali
Kausar Ali
Mansoor Ali
Adamu Ali-Gombe
Farouq Aliyu
Omar Al-Kadi
Mohammad Alkhatib
Ahmed Alksas
Erwin Alles
Mohammed Al-masni
Ahmed Al-Qurri
Arwa Alrubaian
Mohammad Alsharid
Pablo Alvarez
Charlems Alvarez-Jimenez
Jennifer Alvén
Jakob Ambsdorf
Ankit Amrutkar
Dayeong An
Delin An
Haill An
Jinseo An
Jonghoon An
Sion An
Rishi Ananth
Dimitrios Anastasiou
Wang Anbang
Gustavo Andrade-Miranda
Vincent Andrearczyk
Naga Surya Sandeep Angara
Fatai Anifowose
Anna Anikina
André Anjos
Faizanuddin Ansari
Ekaterina Antipushina
Michela Antonelli
Michel Antunes
Kian Anvari Hamedani
Yunke Ao
Yoshimitsu Aoki
Erchan Aptoula
Madhu Aravindan
Ignacio Arganda-Carreras
Tomas Arias-Vergara
Mikel Ariz
Mehak Arora
Ahmad Arrabi
Alberto Arrigoni
Muhammad Waqas Arshad
Sai Susmitha Arvapalli
Mohammad Asadi
Yuta Asano
John Ashburner

Tajamul Ashraf
Pooya Ashtari
Mehdi Astaraki
Arda Atalık
Chinmayee Athalye
Thomas Athey
Shreeram Athreya
Indriyati Atmosukarto
Mohammad Atwany
Benjamin Aubert
Marc Aubreville
Mehmet Yigit Avci
Paolo Avesani
Jordina Aviles Verdera
Navchetan Awasthi
Suyash Awate
Ishak Ayad
Orhun Utku Aydin
Ilhan Aytutuldu
Lev Ayzenberg
Puria Azadi Moghadam
Faiza Azhar
Mohammad Saber Azimi
Abu Zahid Bin Aziz
Iyad Ba Gari
Hyeon-Min Bae
Jongduk Baek
Seung Baek
Seunghun Baek
Priyanka Bagade
Negin Baghbanzadeh
Ali Bahari Malayeri
Mohammed Baharoon
Harrison Bai
Jieyun Bai
Long Bai
Wenjia Bai
Xiangzhi Bai
Xiaoyu Bai
Xuguang Bai
Yunhao Bai
Ujjwal Baid
Chandrajit Bajaj
Ghassen Baklouti
Shreyan Bakshi
Yoganand Balagurunathan
Guha Balakrishnan
Shidin Balakrishnan
Shafa Balaram
Abdourahmane Balde
Vishnu Vardhan Baligodugula
Yutong Ban
Imon Banerjee
Oishi Banerjee
Soumyanil Banerjee
Chandan Ganesh Bangalore Yogananda
David Bani-Harouni
Fangxun Bao
Rina Bao
Shunxing Bao
D M Bappy
Catarina Barata
Payam Barnaghi
Juan Barragan Noguera
Hritam Basak
Soumen Basu
Tanmay Basu
Deepti R Bathula
Dheerendranath Battalapalli
Matthew Baugh
Christoph Baur
Simon Baur
Nourhan Bayasi
Mahdi Bayat
Siming Bayer
Roza Bayrak
Clément Beitone
Soufiane Belharbi
Giovanni Bellitto
Rotimi-Williams Bello
Dafna Ben Bashat
Andreas Bender
Sean Benson
Jamal Bentahar
Mariana Bento
Jose Bernal
Olivier Bernard
Gabriel Bernardino
Richard Bethlehem
Can Deniz Bezek

Riddhish Bhalodia
Rahul Bhardwaj
Nithya Bhasker
Divya Bhatia
Deblina Bhattacharjee
Sourav Bhattacharjee
Ning Bi
Yuan Bi
Diego Biagini
Cheng Bian
Wanyu Bian
Zhangxing Bian
Khawaja Bilal
Harald Binder
Nur Suriza Syazwany
Binti Ahmad Nizam
Kyriaki-Margarita Bintsi
Kimberley Bird
Manuel Birlo
George Biros
Alceu Bissoto
Soma Biswas
David Black
Matthew Blackledge
Nathan Blake
Yuntian Bo
Sudhakavya Bodapati Venkata
Lea Bogensperger
Patrick Bolan
Christopher Boland
Vanessa Borst
Marc Boubnovski Martell
Said Boumaraf
Anis Bourou
Alexandre Bousse
Arnaud Boutillon
Nicolas Boutry
Maria Boyko
Rowan Bradbury
Abdelbasset Brahim
Johannes Brandt
Kit Bransby
Laura Brattain
Diego Bravo
Ali Braytee
Keno Bressem
Christopher Bridge
Ricardo Brioso
Tom Brosch
James Brown
Ekaterina Brui
David Brundage
Michal Brzus
Zhenyu Bu
Lukas Buess
Katja Bühler
Doanh Cao Bui
Nhat-Tan Bui
Phuoc-Nguyen Bui
Christina Bukas
Junghyun Bum
Valay Bundele
Arianna Bunnell
Ninon Burgos
Nikolay Burlutskiy
Yunsu Byeon
Ji Young Byun
Alessandro Cacciatore
Francisco Caetano
Noa Cahan
Chengfei Cai
Jiushen Cai
Kunyan Cai
Linghan Cai
Lishan Cai
Tongan Cai
Weidong Cai
Zemin Cai
Zhuotong Cai
Zongyou Cai
Salvatore Calcagno
Ross Callaghan
Lilian Calvet
Duy-Cat Can
Pere Canals
Liane Canas
Antonio Candito
Bo Cao
Chao Cao
Guogang Cao

Jianfeng Cao
Kangyang Cao
Rui Cao
Shuang Cao
Tian Cao
Yankun Cao
Zhenjie Cao
Daniel Capellán-Martín
Aaron Carass
Ionut Cardei
Paula Cárdenas
Luca Carlini
Owen Carmichael
Diedre Carmo
Patrick Carnahan
Gustavo Carneiro
Anna Caroli
Hector Carrion
Jacob Carse
Adrià Casamitjana
Alessandro Casella
Eduardo Castañeda
Philippe C. Cattin
Thiago Cavalcanti
Lara Cavinato
Alberto Mario Ceballos-Arroyo
Stefano Cerri
Dong-Kyu Chae
Han Joo Chae
Shurong Chai
Krishna Chaitanya
Satrajit Chakrabarty
Souradeep Chakraborty
Chi Kwan Chan
Trevor Chan
Wei Xuan Chan
Weng Ian Chan
Wing Chi Chan
Yi Hao Chan
Deeph Chana
Dibaloke Chanda
Shekhar Chandra
Heyou Chang
Qing Chang
Yao-Jen Chang
Yue Changpeng
Pradyumna Chari
Masoud Charkhabi
Rajdeep Chatterjee
Sudhanya Chatterjee
Pratik Chattopadhyay
Soumitri Chattopadhyay
Gustavo Ramon Chau Loo Kung
Muhammad Faizyab Ali Chaudhary
Joohi Chauhan
Joël Chavas
Levy Chaves
Tongtong Che
Yiming Che
Bohao Chen
Bolin Chen
Boyu Chen
Changfang Chen
Chu Chen
Chuan Chen
Cunjian Chen
Dehua Chen
Dongdong Chen
Duoyou Chen
Fuqiang Chen
Geng Chen
Guannan Chen
Hairui Chen
Han Chen
Hongbo Chen
Hsiang-Ting Chen
Huan-Yu Chen
Hung-Hsuan Chen
Jiabao Chen
Jiangning Chen
Jiayi Chen
Jiazhou Chen
Jie Chen
Jieneng Chen
Jixiang Chen
Jun Chen
Junxiang Chen
Junzhou Chen
Kai Chen
Kanghao Chen

Kevin Chen
Li Chen
Lifang Chen
Ling Chen
Lingyu Chen
Lixuan Chen
Ma Chen
Minheng Chen
Peikai Chen
Peilin Chen
Pingyi Chen
Qi Chen
Qiang Chen
Qingchao Chen
Shaobin Chen
Shengchao Chen
Shengjia Chen
Shijing Chen
Tao Chen
Tong Chen
Wanwen Chen
Wanyi Chen
Wei Chen
Weijie Chen
Wenting Chen
Wenxuan Chen
Xiang Chen
Xiaohua Chen
Xiaoyang Chen
Xin Chen
Xizi Chen
Xueli Chen
Yaowen Chen
Yaqian Chen
Yaxi Chen
Yifei Chen
Yihong Chen
Yiliang Chen
Yiming Chen
Yinda Chen
Yingyu Chen
Yinran Chen
Yixiong Chen
Yong Chen
Yu Chen
Yuanyuan Chen
Yufei Chen
Yuhang Chen
Zhanghao Chen
Zhaojin Chen
Zhaomin Chen
Zhaozheng Chen
Zhennong Chen
Zhenqin Chen
Zhi Chen
Zhihao Chen
Zhong Chen
Zifan Chen
Zihao Chen
Zijiao Chen
Ziyang Chen
Chang-Chieh Cheng
Chun-Wun Cheng
Chunyang Cheng
Jiale Cheng
Jian Cheng
Jianhong Cheng
Jing Cheng
Junfu Cheng
Junlong Cheng
Kun Cheng
Pujin Cheng
Teng Cheng
Weihao Cheng
Xinxing Cheng
Yanqi Cheng
Zihan Cheng
Daeyoung Cheon
Farida Cheriet
Teja Krishna Cherukuri
James Chung-Wai Cheung
Ka Chun Cheung
Matt Cheung
Anju Chhetri
Mark Chiew
Philip Chikontwe
Ching-Hao Chiu
Hyuna Cho
Jaejin Cho
Jaeyoung Cho

Minji Cho
Sue Min Cho
Yeong-Jun Cho
Tomáš Chobola
Changyong Choi
Gyuho Choi
Hanseung Choi
Hyoungshin Choi
Jang-Hwan Choi
Jin Woo Choi
Kyu Sung Choi
Sang-Il Choi
Woohyeok Choi
Wookjin Choi
Yangsean Choi
Yujin Choi
Kyobin Choo
Omar Choudhry
Argyrios Christodoulidis
Dimosthenis Chrysochoou
Lingyang Chu
Yuetan Chu
Artur Chudzik
Il Yong Chun
Albert Chung
Minyoung Chung
Pau-Choo Chung
Woojin Chung
Yunsung Chung
Nikhil Churamani
Konrad Ciecierski
Ozkan Cigdem
Catalin Ciobirca
Allison Clement
Dana Cobzas
Paulo Jorge Coelho
Olivier Colliot
Chao Cong
Cong Cong
William Consagra
Pierre-Henri Conze
Tim Cootes
Hélène Corbaz
Valentina Corbetta
Baris Coskunuzer
Stephane Cotin
Pierrick Coupé
Francesco Cremonesi
Alessandro Crimi
Ines Alejandro Cruz Guerrero
Angel Cruz-Roa
Beilei Cui
Hengfei Cui
Jian Cui
Jianan Cui
Jiaqi Cui
Mengmeng Cui
Ruize Cui
Wenhui Cui
Xiaoxiao Cui
Zhe Cui
Sasa Cukovic
Tolga Cukur
Kelvin Cunha
Ariel Curiale
Yudha Raja Singam D.
Mohamad Dabboussi
Lavsen Dahal
Rema Daher
Di Dai
Guowei Dai
Ling Dai
Linrui Dai
Wei Dai
Weicheng Dai
Connor Daly
Salma Dammak
Jürgen Dammers
Rafat Damseh
Corentin Dancette
Iman Dandapath
Danilo Danese
Min Dang
Trung Dang
Meghal Dani
Bilel Daoud
Salman Ul Hassan Dar
Eleonora D'Arnese
Abhijit Das
Badhan Kumar Das

Debanjan Das
Dhritiman Das
Debashis Das Chakladar
Muhammed Furkan Dasdelen
Soma Dasgupta
Christos Davatzikos
Muhammad Dawood
Tareen Dawood
Sanuwani Dayarathna
Akshay Daydar
Laura Daza
Ezequiel de la Rosa
Swakshar Deb
Charles Delahunt
Herve Delingette
Başar Demir
Ugur Demir
Omer Demirel
Botao Deng
Chao Deng
Lei Deng
Liang-Jian Deng
Qingxin Deng
Xiang Deng
Yingjiao Deng
Yu Deng
Zhipeng Deng
Zhiwei Deng
Zhongying Deng
Elena Denisova
Cem Deniz
Felix Denzinger
Adrien Depeursinge
Kanchana Devanathan
Alina Devkota
Dipayan Dewan
Samrat Kumar Dey
Swarnava Dey
Manish Dhakal
Sobhan Dhara
Jennifer Dhont
Mariachiara Di Cosmo
Théo Di Piazza
Francesco Di Salvo
Roberto Di Via
Yueqin Diao
Jouke Dijkstra
Avtantil Dimitriadis
Sadia Din
Guanqun Ding
Han Ding
Kexin Ding
Qiaoqiao Ding
Rizhi Ding
Saisai Ding
Tianyi Ding
Xiaohuan Ding
Xinpeng Ding
Ying Ding
Kerol Djoumessi
Ha Thanh Do
Hyungrok Do
Daniel Dobkin
Sebastian Doerrich
Mischa Dombrowski
Aimei Dong
Di Dong
Fangfang Dong
Haoyu Dong
Hexin Dong
Mengjin Dong
Min Dong
Shoubin Dong
Siyuan Dong
Xiuyu Dong
Yafei Dong
Yihong Dong
Zhengyuan Dong
Zijian Dong
Jonathan Donnelly
Gianfranco Doretto
Zolnamar Dorjsembe
Haoran Dou
Shuguang Dou
Yimeng Dou
Yulong Dou
Hassen Drira
Anghong Du
Chenhe Du
Dongyang Du

Hao Du
Honghui Du
Ji Du
Jiawei Du
Jie Du
Lei Du
Penghui Du
Shaoyi Du
Siyi Du
Tianming Du
Yao Du
Ye Du
Yuetian Du
Yuexi Du
Dingna Duan
Jinming Duan
Peiyu Duan
Wenting Duan
Yaofei Duan
Kauê Duarte
Thomas Duboudin
David Dueñas Gaviria
Benoit Dufumier
Felix Dülmer
Andrea Dunn Beltran
Fatih Duran
Nicholas Durr
Tapas Dutta
Nicha Dvornek
Jagan Mohan Reddy Dwarampudi
Witold Dyrka
Obed Dzikunu
Oleh Dzyubachyk
Chamira Edussooriya
Aniek Eijpe
Favour Ekong
Nafie El Amrani
Sidaty El Hadramy
Marawan Elbatel
Abdussalam Elhanashi
Mohamed Elmanna
Mohamed Elsharkawy
Mohamed Elshrif
Daniel Elson
Eyad Elyan
Noha El-Zehiry
Taha Emre
Sandy Engelhardt
Ertunc Erdil
Marius Erdt
Ayhan Can Erdur
Franciskus Xaverius Erick
Alina Ermilova
Ilker Ersoy
Dennis Eschweiler
Meltem Esengönül
Mohammad Eslami
Nazila Esmaeili
Parhom Esmaeili
Elyar Esmaeilzadeh
Shahrooz Faghihroohi
Alexandre Falcao
Chao Fan
Di Fan
Jianan Fan
Jiansong Fan
Kailong Fan
Liang Fan
Mengchen Fan
Wenrui Fan
Xiaoya Fan
Xiaoyao Fan
Xin Fan
Xinqi Fan
Yubo Fan
Yuheng Fan
Zhiting Fan
Zipei Fan
Fen Fang
Hao Fang
Songke Fang
Wei Fang
Xi Fang
Yingying Fang
Yuqi Fang
Zhenghan Fang
Aly Farag
Somayeh Farahani
Manel Farhat
Andreia Faria

Aiman Farooq
Hasan Farooq
Muhammad Ali Farooq
Muhammad Umar Farooq
Syed Hasib Akhter Faruqui
Giuseppe Fasano
Jamil Fayyad
Botond Fazekas
Edoardo Fazzari
Maximilian Fehrentz
Manman Fei
Yuchen Fei
Paula Feldman
Lina Felsner
Chaolu Feng
Jing Feng
Jun Feng
Ming Feng
Siwei Feng
Siyang Feng
Yidan Feng
Yushi Feng
Zehui Feng
Zetian Feng
Zishun Feng
Philipp Feodorovici
Aasa Feragen
Abdesselam Ferdi
Tharindu Fernando
André Ferreira
Jean Feydy
Leo Fillioux
Marten Finck
Maria Chiara Fiorentino
Alessio Fiorin
Paul Fischer
Stefan Fischer
Roman Flepp
Kyriakos Flouris
Stefano Fogarollo
Bernhard Föllmer
A Fong
Fahimeh Fooladgar
Nils Daniel Forkert
Jean-Rassaire Fouefack
Joris Fournel
Kevin François-Bouaou
Moti Freiman
Michael Friebe
Christoph Friedrich
Paul Friedrich
Yannik Frisch
Baochen Fu
Boxun Fu
Jia Fu
Jingru Fu
Qifan Fu
Rong Fu
Suzhong Fu
Xiangling Fu
Xueming Fu
Yibing Fu
Yingji Fu
Yu Fu
Yuxuan Fu
Zeyu Fu
Moritz Fuchs
Hiroshi Fujita
Florian Fürnrohr
Ryo Furukawa
Michael Gadermayr
Fasil Gadjimuradov
Emilien Gadoux
Miruna-Alexandra Gafencu
Laurent Gajny
Efstathios Galanakis
Adrian Galdran
Gurur Gamgam
Haitao Gan
Yu Gan
Iyyakutti Iyappan Ganapathi
Vaibhav Gandhi
Aniruddha Ganguly
Chang Gao
Cong Gao
Fei Gao
Rui Gao
Shangqi Gao
Shuo Gao
Weiwei Gao

Xiaoru Gao
Xinbo Gao
Xingyu Gao
Yajun Gao
Yang Gao
Yao Gao
Yaozong Gao
Yi Gao
Yibo Gao
Yifan Gao
Yuan Gao
Yurui Gao
Zeyu Gao
Zheyao Gao
Zhirui Gao
Zhuangzhi Gao
Mengxi Gao
Utpal Garain
Alvaro Garcia-Tornel Garcia-Camba
Gautam Gare
Gaurav Garg
Eleftherios Garyfallidis
Sergios Gatidis
Ioannis Gatopoulos
Romane Gauriau
Rongjun Ge
Ruiquan Ge
Yuyan Ge
Haixiao Geng
Konstantinos Georgas
Ajo George
Yasmeen George
Beerend Gerats
Negin Ghamsarian
Yazan Gharaibeh
Mohammed Amine Gharsallaoui
Ghazal Ghazaei
Madhusudan Ghosh
Shantanu Ghosh
Yongha Gi
Debora Gil
Simon Ging
Rémi Giraud
Tristan Glatard
Ben Glocker
Patrick Godau
Bharti Goel
Wesley Gohn
Polina Golland
Alberto Gomez
Catalina Gomez
Santiago Gómez Hernández
Estibaliz Gómez-de-Mariscal
Haifan Gong
Wei Gong
Xun Gong
Md Raihan Goni
German Gonzalez
Cristina González
Ines Gonzalez Pepe
Jesus Gonzalez Riveros
Alvaro Gonzalez-Jimenez
Sharath Gopal
Shekoufeh Gorgi Zadeh
Mikhail Gorodnichev
Subrahmanyam Gorthi
Michael Götz
Shuiping Gou
Maged Goubran
Darshana Govind
Shreyank Gowda
Aman Goyal
Puneet Goyal
Robert Graf
Costantino Grana
Eric Granger
Jason Granstedt
Vicente Grau
Thomas Grenier
Clément Grisi
Fabian Gröger
Michal Grzeszczyk
Fei Gu
Feng Gu
Jinchen Gu
Leslie Gu
Qiangqiang Gu
Ran Gu
Xue Gu
Yannian Gu

Yi Gu
Yuanyuan Gu
Yun Gu
Haoyue Guan
Qingji Guan
Valerio Guarrasi
Luis Guayacan
Houssem-Eddine Gueziri
Luying Gui
Halil Gulluk
Malitha Gunawardhana
Ayse Gungor
Manuel Günther
Changlu Guo
Diandian Guo
Fei Guo
Fumin Guo
Guangyu Guo
Heng Guo
Hongbo Guo
Jia Guo
Jiayu Guo
Jixiang Guo
Jun Guo
Lijun Guo
Wenzhangzhi Guo
Xiaojuan Guo
Yanfei Guo
Yong Guo
Zaiyang Guo
Zuwei Guo
Ankur Gupta
Gagan Gupta
Sukrit Gupta
Kali Gürkahraman
Boris Gutman
Carmen Guzman-Garcia
Seunghyun Gwak
Sung Min Ha
Stathis Hadjidemetriou
Arnela Hadzic
Ibrahim Hadzic
Ida Häggström
James Hahn
Justin Haldar
Verena Jasmin Hallitschke
Ghassan Hamarneh
Emadeldeen Hamdan
Abdullah Hamdi
Donghee Han
Hu Han
Hua Han
Hyunkyung Han
Ji Yong Han
Jingxin Han
Jinyoung Han
John Han
Kangfu Han
Luyi Han
Seokmin Han
Xian-Hua Han
Xiao Han
Xiaodong Han
Xu Han
Yoseob Han
Yuqiang Han
Jonny Hancox
Asif Hanif
Muhammad Abdullah Hanif
Hartmut Häntze
Degan Hao
Huaying Hao
Jilei Hao
Jing Hao
Qin Hao
Shuang Hao
Teqi Hao
Xinyu Hao
Yingqi Hao
Nazim Haouchine
Shahad Hardan
Mohamed Harmanani
Mahade Hasan
Mahmudul Hasan
Sam Hashemi
Sara Hashemi
Anam Hashmi
Marta Hasny
Ghulam Mubashar Hassan
Salma Hassan

Charles Hatt
Hideaki Hayashi
Mansoor Hayat
Savannah Hays
Along He
Chloe He
Dinglun He
Dongdong He
Hangzhou He
Hongliang He
Huiguang He
Lei He
Linchao He
Mengshen He
Mengxian He
Runlong He
Sheng He
Xinzi He
Xuelei He
Yimeng He
Ying He
Yongjun He
Yunlong He
Zhenqi He
Zhibin He
Ziyang He
Moein Heidari
Jonas Hein
Mattias Heinrich
Jon Heiselman
Halil Helvaci
Anja Hennemuth
Julius Hense
Chanyeong Heo
Da-Woon Heo
Juampablo Heras Rivera
Lisa Herzog
Risa Higashita
Adam Hilbert
Meva Himmetoglu
Carlos Hinojosa
Florian Hinterwimmer
Rebecca Hisey
Md Hasibul Husain Hisham
David Ho
Edmond S. L. Ho
Ming-Yang Ho
Ngoc Huynh Ho
Matthew Holden
Felix Holm
Gregory Holste
Charmgil Hong
Jaeseong Hong
Pa Hong
Qingqi Hong
Sungrae Hong
Xiaoming Hong
Yang Hong
Nicolas Honnorat
Hidekata Hontani
Amir Hooshiar
Md. Enamul Hoq
Mobarak Hoque
Md Belayat Hossain
Tonmoy Hossain
Md Azam Hossain
Golriz Hosseinimanesh
Junlin Hou
Qingshan Hou
Rui Hou
Wenguang Hou
Xiangjian Hou
Yucun Hou
Prantik Howlader
Cheyu Hsu
Chih-Chung Hsu
William Hsu
Anjun Hu
Chuanfei Hu
Haigen Hu
Hao Hu
Huawen Hu
Jinlong Hu
Jisu Hu
Junjie Hu
Kai Hu
Liwei Hu
Ming Hu
Qiang Hu
Renjiu Hu

Shiang Hu
Shishuai Hu
Taiyuan Hu
Wei Hu
Xi Yuan Hu
Xingcan Hu
Yang Hu
Yibo Hu
Yuqi Hu
Zhangfeng Hu
Zhehao Hu
Zhisen Hu
Shengyi Hua
Zheang Huai
Bangyan Huang
Bin Huang
Bingsheng Huang
Cheng Huang
Chun-Rong Huang
Dianye Huang
Guantian Huang
Haolin Huang
Jiahao Huang
Jiahui Huang
Jiaju Huang
Jiaxing Huang
Jinghan Huang
Kai Huang
Kaiwen Huang
Kaizhu Huang
Le Huang
Luojie Huang
Peixiang Huang
Ruobing Huang
Shiqi Huang
Shuo Huang
Siyi Huang
Tianqi Huang
Wei Huang
Weimin Huang
Weitian Huang
Wenhui Huang
Wenli Huang
Wenqi Huang
Xingyu Huang
Xinrui Huang
Yan Huang
Yanyan Huang
Yaping Huang
Yi Huang
Yigeng Huang
Yi-Jie Huang
Yijin Huang
Yiming Huang
Ying Huang
Yongqiang Huang
Yuhao Huang
Yunzhi Huang
Zhe Huang
Zhen Huang
Zheng Huang
Zhenxing Huang
Zhi-An Huang
Zixuan Huang
Arnaud Huaulmé
Charmayne Hughes
Michael Hughes
Edward Hui
Hui Hui
Jiayu Huo
Mohammad Arafat Hussain
Muhammad Ishfaq Hussain
Tanveer Hussain
Yasir Hussain
Seong Jae Hwang
Sunil Hwang
Yechan Hwang
Yunseob Hwang
Bulat Ibragimov
Kamil Ibragimov
Mahmoud Ibrahim
Ilknur Icke
Azeez Idris
Mudassir Iftikhar
Kay Igwe
Efe Ilicak
Alfredo Illanes
Abdul-Mojeed Ilyas
Talha Ilyas
Hyeonseung Im

Sunghoon Im
Baris Imre
Veera Venkata Raghunath Indugu
Radu Tudor Ionescu
Asim Iqbal
Amanda Isaac
Md Saiful Islam
Mariko Isogawa
Koichi Ito
Hayato Itoh
Krithika Iyer
Athira Jacob
Mathews Jacob
Kshitij Jadhav
Mohit Jain
Pankaj Jain
Bushra Jalil
Mahtab Jamali
Amoon Jamzad
Beakcheol Jang
Boa Jang
Han Jang
Hyensoo Jang
Ikbeom Jang
Pierre Jannin
Vincent Jaouen
Ronnachai Jaroensri
Tim Jaspers
Alexander Jaus
Nivetha Jayakumar
Umarani Jayaraman
Niyonteze Jean De Dieu
Hana Jebril
Ahmadreza Jeddi
Duhee Jeon
Yongjun Jeon
Young Seok Jeon
Hwihun Jeong
Ji-Hoon Jeong
Jiwoong Jeong
Minjae Jeong
Rathinaraja Jeyaraj
Ranjeet Ranjan Jha
Changkai Ji
Jianhang Ji
Zexin Ji
Dengqiang Jia
Fucang Jia
Junhao Jia
Qi Jia
Tong Jia
Xibin Jia
Zhenge Jia
Bailiang Jian
Jia-Xian Jian
Benxiang Jiang
Bo Jiang
Dengrong Jiang
Hao Jiang
Haojun Jiang
Haotian Jiang
Hongxu Jiang
Juntao Jiang
Lihong Jiang
Ning Jiang
Peilin Jiang
Shancheng Jiang
Shuo Jiang
Wei Jiang
Weili Jiang
Wenbo Jiang
Wenchao Jiang
Wenhao Jiang
Xi Jiang
Xiajun Jiang
Xiaoyi Jiang
Yishan Jiang
Yiwen Jiang
Yufeng Jiang
Yuming Jiang
Yuncheng Jiang
Yuxian Jiang
Zhuoyun Jiang
Yining Jiao
Betshrine Rachel Jibinsingh
Amelia Jiménez-Sánchez
Kudirat Jimoh
Lingbo Jin
Qiyu Jin
Qunchao Jin

Rui Jin
Tao Jin
Yili Jin
Yueming Jin
Ze Jin
Bin Jing
Peiyuan Jing
Sanghyun Jo
Matjaz Jogan
Craig Jones
Gihun Joo
Anand Joshi
Shantanu Joshi
Leo Joskowicz
Samuel Joutard
Ce Ju
Lie Ju
Guil Jung
Heechul Jung
Jay Hwasung Jung
Juho Jung
Julip Jung
Kyu-Hwan Jung
Seung-Won Jung
Wonsik Jung
Sreekanth K Manikandan
Mounir Kaaniche
Twaha Kabika
Ashad Kabir
Krish Kabra
Takeaki Kadota
Ali Kafaei Zad Tehrani
Sevgi Kafali
Joshua Kaggie
Fredrik Kahl
Johannes Kaiser
John Kalafut
Niveditha Kalavakonda
Joanna Kaleta
John Kalkhof
Grigorios Kalliatakis
Odysseus Kaloidas
Panagiotis Kalozoumis
Tae-Eui Kam
Sreeram Kamabattula
Sharif Amit Kamran
Shichao Kan
Bhavik Kanekar
Dong Un Kang
June Kang
Junghwa Kang
Luoyao Kang
Ming Kang
Mingon Kang
Myeongkyun Kang
Qingbo Kang
Solha Kang
Praveenkumar Kanithi
Arunkumar Kannan
Madhavi Kannan
Dmitrii Kaplun
Saarthak Kapse
Siddhartha Kapuria
Aupendu Kar
Mokshagna Sai Teja Karanam
Amirhossein Kardoost
Yasmin Kassim
Tushar Kataria
Alexander Katzmann
Gurwinder Kaur
Eiryo Kawakami
Ali Kazemi
Mohammad Mahdi Kazemi Esfeh
Jing Ke
Xiao Ke
Razmig Kechichian
Tanzila Kehkashan
Matthias Keicher
Noam Keidar
Ayse Keles
Connah Kendrick
Roshan Kenia
Erwan Kerrien
Sara Ketabi
Nabeel Khalid
Sirvan Khalighi
Abbas Khan
Abdul Rehman Khan
Misaal Khan
Muhammad Irfan Khan

Muneeb Khan
Naimul Khan
Saba Khan
Shadab Khan
Sheheryar Khan
Sulaiman Khan
Ufaq Khan
Ziaullah Khan
Pulkit Khandelwal
Mahdieh Khanmohammadi
Rezkellah Noureddine Khiati
Julien Khlaut
Prathamesh Pradeep Khole
Hee Guan Khor
Mahapara Khurshid
Behnam Kiani Kalejahi
Tomohiro Kikuchi
Boah Kim
Bryan Sangwoo Kim
Byeong Soo Kim
Byung Hyung Kim
Byung-Hoon Kim
Chanyoung Kim
Daeseung Kim
Dohyun Kim
Harim Kim
Heejong Kim
Ho Heon Kim
Hongin Kim
Hye Ryun Kim
Hyeongsub Kim
Hyunmin Kim
Jeongin Kim
Jiehyun Kim
Jin Kim
Jinman Kim
Jonghun Kim
Jongwoo Kim
June Sic Kim
Junmo Kim
Junyeong Kim
Ka Young Kim
Kiduk Kim
Kyeong Ho Kim
Kyungsu Kim
Kyuri Kim
Mansu Kim
Minjun Kim
Minwoo Kim
Namkug Kim
Sanghyuk Kim
Sangwook Kim
Seongjun Kim
Sihwan Kim
So Hyun Kim
Songsoo Kim
Soopil Kim
Suhyeon Kim
Sunghun Kim
Taehun Kim
Taek Min Kim
Young-Gon Kim
Young-Min Kim
Youngwoo Kim
Yunsoo Kim
Alvin Kimbowa
Scott Kinder
Kaleab Kinfu
Andrew King
Miranda Kirby
Yannick Kirchhoff
Maxim Kireev
Tristan Kirscher
Gabriel Kiss
Itaru Kitahara
Yoshiro Kitamura
Klaus-Rudolf Kladny
Jens Kleesiek
Tobias Klinder
Vladimir Klinshov
Hannah Kniesel
Hanbin Ko
Seonghyeon Ko
Kazuma Kobayashi
Erich Kobler
Lisa Koch
Ryoichi Koga
Tatsuki Koike
Taha Koleilat
Satoshi Kondo

Praneeta R Konduri
Fanwei Kong
Jindi Kong
Ming Kong
Yan Kong
Youyong Kong
Anastasia Konik
Mirko Konstantin
Ender Konukoglu
Aishik Konwer
Nicholas Konz
Myoung-Wan Koo
Ivica Kopriva
Yilmaz Korkmaz
Kivanc Kose
Niklas Koser
Shyam Reddy Kotha
Konstantinos Koukoutegos
Deepika Koundal
Adam Krawczyk
Zuzanna Krawczyk-Borysiak
Julian Kreimeier
Anithapriya Krishnan
Deepa Krishnaswamy
Felix Krones
Frithjof Kruggel
Alexander Krull
Henry Krumb
Dongyang Kuang
Hulin Kuang
Dariusz Kucharski
Thomas Kuestner
Thijs Kuipers
Harshita Kukreja
Joshua Kulasingham
Aleksandra Kulbaka
Pranav Kulkarni
Abhay Kumar
Ashwin Kumar
Harshit Kumar
Nishant Kumar
Sandeep Kumar
Snehil Kumar
Nagendra Kumar
Naveen Kumar Kummari
Shinjini Kundu
Soumya Kundu
Manuela Kunz
Po-Chih Kuo
Tahsin Kurc
Nikhil Cherian Kurian
Semen Kurkin
Vinod Kurmi
Rafsanjany Kushol
Jin Tae Kwak
Hyeokjin Kwon
Jii Kwon
Jong Kwon
Junmo Kwon
Sunyoung Kwon
Jan Kybic
Agnieszka Lach
Chih Lai
Songning Lai
Taotao Lai
Hala Lamdouar
Hengrong Lan
Qizhen Lan
Tianzhong Lan
Yinyu Lan
Bennett Landman
Frank Langbein
Georg Langs
Qicheng Lao
Othmane Laousy
Andrea Lara
Bianca Lassen-Schmidt
Patricia Lasserre
Sarah Latus
Wai Tak Lau
Shlomi Laufer
Max-Heinrich Laves
Aonghus Lawlor
Scindhiya Laxmi
Duc Tai Le
Loic Le Folgoc
François Lecomte-Denis
Maria Ledesma-Carbayo
Brian Lee
Bumshik Lee

Dongheon Lee
Euijong Lee
Eungjoo Lee
Gyeongmin Lee
Hansang Lee
Hoi Leong Lee
Hong Joo Lee
Hyeonjun Lee
Hyun Gyu Lee
Hyungyung Lee
Hyunyeol Lee
Jaeho Lee
Jaesung Lee
Jangho Lee
Jiyang Lee
Jonghyun Lee
Jongmin Lee
Jong-Min Lee
Jooho Lee
Ju Hwan Lee
Jungwook Lee
Junhyeok Lee
Junseok Lee
Min Hun Lee
Minsik Lee
Moon Hwan Lee
Sanghyuck Lee
Sangmin Lee
Sangyoon Lee
Seoyoung Lee
Seungeun Lee
Sing Chun Lee
Won Hee Lee
Woonghee Lee
Youngjoon Lee
Yugyung Lee
Yurim Lee
Antoine Legouhy
Long Lei
Minglong Lei
Xuan Lei
Yiming Lei
Karoline Leiberg
Nick Lemke
Yilin Leng
Matthias Lenga
Dimitrios Lenis
Gabriel Lepetit-Aimon
Carson Leung
Meir Levi
Michael Levine
Ao Li
Bin Li
Binghua Li
Bo Li
Chao Li
Chaoyi Li
Cheng Li
Chengkun Li
Chengyin Li
Chentao Li
Chuanpu Li
Cynthia Xinran Li
Dawei Li
Fan Li
Feng Li
Frank Li
Guang Li
Guanya Li
Guoshi Li
Haifang Li
Haiqing Li
Haitao Li
Han Li
Hanyu Li
Hao Li
Haofeng Li
Haojin Li
Haoshen Li
Haoxiang Li
He Li
Heng Li
Hongming Li
Hongshuo Li
Hongyu Li
Hongzhao Li
Huiqi Li
Jiafeng Li
Jialin Li
Jialu Li

Jiapeng Li
Jiawen Li
Jihe Li
Jincheng Li
Jingming Li
Jinpeng Li
Jun Li
Juncheng Li
Junjian Li
Jupeng Li
Kaiwen Li
Kaiyan Li
Kang Li
Kehan Li
Kun Li
Lei Li
Lin Li
Ling Li
Miao Li
Min Li
Peng Li
Qi Li
Qiaoxin Li
Qingli Li
Qingya Li
Qiyue Li
Rui Li
Ruiyang Li
Ruizhe Li
Ruocheng Li
Sanqian Li
Shaowei Li
Shibo Li
Shiwei Li
Shuaibo Li
Shumeng Li
Shusheng Li
Sijia Li
Siqi Li
Tao Li
Teng Li
Tiansong Li
Weiling Li
Wen Li
Wenbo Li
Wenxuan Li
Wenxue Li
Xiang Li
Xiangchen Li
Xiangyu Li
Xiaomeng Li
Xiaoxiao Li
Xiao-Xin Li
Xiaoye Li
Xieji Li
Xing Li
Xinshan Li
Xinyue Li
Xue Li
Xueshen Li
Xuesong Li
Xueyang Li
Yang Li
Yaoqian Li
Yaxuan Li
Ye Li
Yicong Li
Yidi Li
Yijie Li
Yijin Li
Yingshu Li
Yingtai Li
Yinsheng Li
Yiping Li
Yiran Li
Yitong Li
Yonghong Li
Yuchen Li
Yudong Li
Yuheng Li
Yutong Li
Zhe Li
Zhen Li
Zhenghong Li
Zhenping Li
Zhiyuan Li
Zhjin Li
Zhuoan Li
Zi Li
Zihan Li

Ziyu Li
Zuoyong Li
Chenyu Lian
Sheng Lian
Dong Liang
Huanwen Liang
Jianwen Liang
Junjie Liang
Kewei Liang
Li Liang
Wei Liang
Xiaokun Liang
Xinglong Liang
Yixiong Liang
Yongjie Liang
Yuxuan Liang
Zhichao Liang
Guiqiu Liao
Wei Liao
Weicheng Liao
Xiangyun Liao
Zehui Liao
Andrzej Liebert
Gilbert Lim
Min Hyuk Lim
Michelle Espranita Liman
Bowen Lin
Che Lin
Fengming Lin
Fuchun Lin
Haoneng Lin
Jhih-Yuan Lin
Jianxin Lin
Junjie Lin
Nan Lin
Rizhong Lin
Runjia Lin
Tianyu Lin
Tong Lin
Weiping Lin
Wenjun Lin
Xian Lin
Yi Lin
Ying-Chih Lin
Yiqun Lin
Yiwei Lin
Yiyang Lin
Youn-Long Lin
Zehui Lin
Haibin Ling
Simone Lionetti
A.J. Lisowska
Ciro Listone
Mattia Litrico
Baodi Liu
Chang Liu
Che Liu
Chen Liu
Cheng Liu
Chenxi Liu
Chenyu Liu
Chunwei Liu
Congcong Liu
Dichao Liu
Fangyi Liu
Feihong Liu
Feng Liu
Fengbei Liu
Fenglin Liu
Han Liu
Hao Liu
Hengjie Liu
Hengyan Liu
Hong Liu
Hongying Liu
Huan Liu
Hui Liu
Jiahe Liu
Jiameng Liu
Jianlei Liu
Jiaxiang Liu
Jiaxuan Liu
Jie Liu
Jin Liu
Jinchao Liu
Jingsong Liu
Jingxin Liu
Jingyu Liu
Jinyuan Liu
Jiquan Liu

Jiyao Liu
Juan Liu
Jun Liu
Junqi Liu
Kang Liu
Lei Liu
Li Liu
Linjie Liu
Mengjun Liu
Mengting Liu
Mianxin Liu
Mingsi Liu
Mingtian Liu
Mingxin Liu
Mingxuan Liu
Mingyuan Liu
Peng Liu
Quanying Liu
Ruishan Liu
Runhao Liu
Shangwang Liu
Shengfeng Liu
Shengyuan Liu
Shu Liu
Shuting Liu
Sidong Liu
Tiantian Liu
Ting Liu
Tingwei Liu
Wei Liu
Wenjian Liu
Wenzheng Liu
Xiabi Liu
Xianjing Liu
Xiaohua Liu
Xiaoyue Liu
Xinyu Liu
Xixi Liu
Xuan Liu
Xueli Liu
Xueyu Liu
Yajun Liu
Yan Liu
Yanbei Liu
Yang Liu
Yanzhen Liu
Yihao Liu
Yikang Liu
Yiming Liu
Yingcheng Liu
Yiqing Liu
Yu Liu
Yuanye Liu
Yuhang Liu
Yunbi Liu
Yuxi Liu
Yuxiao Liu
Yuxuan Liu
Zeyu Liu
Zhe Liu
Zhentao Liu
Zhenyu Liu
Zhi Liu
Zhiyuan Liu
Zhu Liu
Ziteng Liu
Ziwen Liu
Zuozhu Liu
Andrea Loddo
Ojaswita Lokre
Andreas Lolos
Angela Lombardi
Bining Long
Jiake Long
Lifan Long
Ziyang Long
Arthur Longuefosse
Renaud Lopes
Miguel López-Pérez
Marco Lorenzi
Meng Lou
Wei Lou
Yiwei Lou
Marta Lovino
Chenggang Lu
Chenyang Lu
Chunyao Lu
Donghuan Lu
Hengfa Lu
Jiacheng Lu

Jingfeng Lu
Li Lu
Lin Lu
Shuai Lu
Wenjing Lu
Yao Lu
Yifan Lu
Yuhuan Lu
Zhengda Lu
Zhicheng Lu
Zhihe Lu
Zhixiang Lu
Zilin Lu
Ziqian Lu
Haijing Luan
Xiao Luan
Luca Lumetti
Chen Luo
Guibo Luo
Haozhe Luo
Huoling Luo
Jiajie Luo
Ma Luo
Mingyuan Luo
Qinxuan Luo
Tao Luo
Xiaoling Luo
Xin Luo
Xinzhe Luo
Xuexiong Luo
Ye Luo
Yiwen Luo
Yong Luo
Yu Luo
Zhiming Luo
Zihao Luo
Marie Luong
Xingguo Lv
Buntheng Ly
Ngoc Ly
Son Ly
Donghang Lyu
Ilwoo Lyu
Jun Lyu
Mengye Lyu
Qing Lyu
Yanjun Lyu
Yiheng Lyu
Yilin Lyu
Vivek M
Meharban M S
Sharath M S
Deeksha M Shama
Changsheng Ma
Da Ma
Gengchen Ma
He Ma
Hehuan Ma
Jiaxin Ma
Jun Ma
Junbo Ma
Lei Ma
Ling Ma
Liyan Ma
Qi Ma
Qiang Ma
Shixing Ma
Tai Ma
Tengfei Ma
Wei Ma
Xiangyuan Ma
Xiaodong Ma
Xinke Ma
Xinyu Ma
Xiyao Ma
Yuefeng Ma
Yutao Ma
Zihan Ma
Lennart Maack
Mohamed Mabrok
Julia Machnio
Frederik Maes
Nooshin Maghsoodi
Amirreza Mahbod
Mohammed Mahmoud
Md Ishtyaq Mahmud
Amulya Kumar Mahto
Andreas Maier
Klaus H. Maier-Hein
Boris Mailhe

Aamir Malik
Hashmat Shadab Malik
Norberto Malpica
Richa Malviya Dutta
Michail Mamalakis
Jan Emily Mangulabnan
Merry Mani
Ali Mansouri
Yiji Mao
Arooba Maqsood
Vincenzo Marcianò
Jan Margeta
Umar Marikkar
Brett Marinelli
Zdravko Marinov
Jose Diogo Marques dos Santos
Pablo Márquez Neila
Carsten Marr
Yassine Marrakchi
Nicolas Martin
Thomas Martinetz
Fabio Martínez
Maria Martini
Queralt Martín-Saladich
Pierre Marza
Axel Masquelin
Yoshitaka Masutani
Tejas Sudharshan Mathai
Raji Mathew
Prateek Mathur
Sasan Matinfar
Hiroki Matsuzaki
Petr Matula
Lev Matveev
Dimitrios Mavroeidis
Perla Mayo
Badhan Mazumder
Ashery Mbilinyi
Jamie McClelland
Niccolo McConnell
Yasamin Medghalchi
Pau Medrano-Gracia
Mostafa Mehdipour Ghazi
Raghav Mehta
Jonas Mehtali
Liye Mei
Siyuan Mei
Erik Meijering
M S Mekala
Alaa Melek
Alexandre Mello
Cai Meng
Hui Meng
Jia Meng
Mingyuan Meng
Nan Meng
Runqi Meng
Yan Meng
Zhu Meng
Zijie Meng
Martin Menten
Engelbert Mephu Nguifo
Talha Meraj
Dorit Merhof
Weiming Mi
Dong Miao
Juzheng Miao
Yao Miao
Filippo Michelotti
Leo Milecki
Dongbo Min
Hyun-Seok Min
Zhe Min
Wenlong Ming
Duy Minh Ho Nguyen
Davneet Minhas
Giulio Minore
Daniel Minsky
Qazaleh Mirsharif
Ghazaleh Mirzaee
Leo Misera
Rashika Mishra
Suraj Mishra
Virendra Mishra
Sampa Misra
Tadashi Miyamoto
Tadahaya Mizuno
Marc Modat
C. Krishna Mohan
Sovesh Mohapatra

Ramtin Mojtahedi
Marc Molina van den Bosch
Hendrik Möller
Joyanta Jyoti Mondal
Sumita Mondal
Sidratul Montaha
Javier A. Montoya-Zegarra
Jong Hak Moon
Ashkan Moradi
Saed Moradi
José Morano
Laurin Mordhorst
Alejandra Moreno Tarazona
Carlos Moreno-Garcia
Kensaku Mori
Henrique Morimitsu
Matteo Moro
Ken'ichi Morooka
Aliasghar Mortazi
Mayar Mostafa
Lei Mou
Lichao Mou
Tian Mou
Simmi Mourya
Samir Moustafa
Nan Mu
Wei Mu
Klaus Mueller
Pritam Mukherjee
Anirban Mukhopadhyay
Henning Müller
Johanna Müller
Philip Müller
Sarah Müller
Marion Mundt
Nusrat Munia
Asbjørn Munk
Aminu Musa
Toufiq Musah
Przemyslaw Musialski
Vit Musil
Saif Musluh
Yasmine Mustafa
Pushkar Mutha
Inye Na
Shahabedin Nabavi
Saad Nadeem
Roman Naeem
Manas Nag
Hajime Nagahara
Reza Naghne
Md Jaber Al Nahian
Toshiya Nakaguchi
Sahil Nalawade
Woo-Jeoung Nam
Khashayar Namdar
Nandakishor Nandakishor
Vittoria Nardone
André Nascimento
Sarah Nassar
Yassine Nasser
Rodrigo Nava
Deepak Ranjan Nayak
Herve Nicolas Nbonsou Tegang
Giacomo Nebbia
Sven Nebelung
Fnu Neha
Omid Nejatimanzari
Iman Nematollahi
Alberto Neri
Favour Nerrise
Sara Neves Silva
Jacob Newman
Alasdair Newson
Cuong Ngo
Binh Nguyen
Huy Nguyen
Khoa Nguyen
Tan Nguyen
Tan-Cong Nguyen
Tri-Thien Nguyen
Trong-Thuan Nguyen
Phi Nguyễn
Thanh Nguyen-Duc
Chang Ni
Jun Ni
Ke Ni
Shuo Ni
Hannes Nickisch
Jingxin Nie

Weizhi Nie
Xinyu Nie
Maximilian Nielsen
Andreas Nienkötter
Aditya Nigam
Dmitry Nikolaev
Emmanouil Nikolakakis
Guochen Ning
Junzhi Ning
Wenbo Ning
Xiaolin Ning
Zeeshan Nisar
Kazuya Nishimura
Sijie Niu
Usma Niyaz
Vincent Noblet
Shahryar Noei
Jeonghyun Noh
Junhyug Noh
Wonjong Noh
Fuad Noman
Anass Nouri
Alexey Novikov
Franciszek Nowak
Hanung Nugroho
Felix Nützel
Chinedu Nwoye
Emilio Ochoa
Gilberto Ochoa-Ruiz
Samuel Ofosu Mensah
Marzieh Oghbaie
Roseline Ogundokun
Hyun-Jic Oh
Ji-Hun Oh
Kwanseok Oh
Sang-Il Oh
Seong Je Oh
Sewook Oh
Ajibola Oladokun
Oluwole Olajide
Laura Oliva Maza
Sara Oliveira
Antoine Olivier
Juan Olmos
Blessing Olorunfemi
Jimena Olveres
Doruk Oner
John Onofrey
Eliza Orasanu
Alexei Ossadtchi
Andreas Østvik
Yoshito Otake
Yafei Ou
Mehdi Ounissi
Nora Ouzir
Utku Ozbulak
Gökhan Özbulak
Caner Ozer
Kutsev Ozyoruk
Andre Pacheco
Suraj Pai
Nathan Painchaud
Eduardo Pais Pooch
Ashkan Pakzad
Aditya Pal
Basudha Pal
Subhash Pal
Balamurugan Palaniappan
Christoph Palm
Naveen Paluru
Viswanath Pamulakanty Sudarshan
Fei Pan
Haoyu Pan
Meihong Pan
Qingtao Pan
Wentao Pan
Xiang Pan
Xinlei Pan
Yongsheng Pan
Eleftheria Panagiotaki
Manish Pandey
Egor Panfilov
Fengqian Pang
Haowen Pang
Kaifeng Pang
Xintao Pang
Yunkui Pang
Hsing-Kuo Pao
Tasos Papastylianou
Ganesh Paramasivam

Jay Paranjape
Abhijeet Parida
Sourav Parija
Chae Jung Park
Chunsu Park
Doohyun Park
Doyoung Park
Heejung Park
Hogun Park
Ho-Min Park
Hyejin Park
Hyoung Suk Park
Hyunjin Park
Jonggwon Park
Joon Sik Park
Joonhyuk Park
Juyoun Park
Robin Park
Sung-Hong Park
Wonjung Park
Luca Parolari
Mario Parreno Centeno
Srivibha Parthasarathy
Akshay Paruchuri
Andrea Passerini
Srivathsa Pasumarthi
Oankar Patil
Shubham Patil
Arijit Patra
Mayank Patwari
Angshuman Paul
Riti Paul
Ruben Pauwels
Kelly Payette
Nicolo Pecco
João Pedrosa
Jialun Pei
Yuchen Pei
Yuru Pei
Himashi Peiris
Chantal Pellegrini
Akila Pemasiri
Jiachuan Peng
Jie Peng
Liangrui Peng
Linkai Peng
Tingying Peng
Xiaoling Peng
Yanjun Peng
Yige Peng
Yunsong Peng
Zelin Peng
Zhihao Peng
Matteo Pennisi
Jacob Peoples
Sergio Pereira
Alessandro Perelli
Alejandra Perez
Paula Andrea Pérez-Toro
Matthias Perkonigg
Daniele Perlo
Terry Peters
Eike Petersen
Simon Pezold
Elisabeth Pfaehler
Micha Pfeiffer
Duy Khoa Pham
Dzung Pham
Trong Thang Pham
Van-Nguyen Pham
Tanmoy Sarkar Pias
Tomasz Pieciak
Omar Piña-Ramirez
Thomas Pinetz
Stefan Ploner
Gasper Podobnik
Eleonora Poeta
Kilian Pohl
Sandesh Pokhrel
Isabella Poles
Robert Policelli
Giuseppe Pontillo
Aloys Portafaix
Michael Potter
Nakul Poudel
Pranav Poudel
Lighittha PR
Chinmay Prabhakar
John Prada
Raphael Prevost

Federica Proietto Salanitri
Yao Pu
Sergi Pujades
Vineet Punyamoorty
Elodie Puybareau
Melika Qahqaie
Ashwaq Qasem
Adnan Qayyum
Kehan Qi
Liangce Qi
Lin Qi
Quan Qi
Shile Qi
Xiaoran Qi
Yaolei Qi
Chen Qian
Xusheng Qian
Yan Qiang
Maoying Qiao
Yanyuan Qiao
Chendong Qin
Fangbo Qin
Feiwei Qin
Genggeng Qin
Jiaolong Qin
Yi Qin
Linbo Qing
Jie Qiu
Junlai Qiu
Liang Qiu
Shi Qiu
Shihan Qiu
Song Qiu
Xingyu Qiu
Xinmei Qiu
Zhike Qiu
Tran Minh Quan
Ningfeng Que
Sandro Queirós
Willmer Rafell Quiñones Robles
Sharon Quispe
Neeraja R.
Sinyoung Ra
Akm Shahariar Azad Rabby
Hamid R. Rabiee
Daniel Racoceanu
Alicja Rączkowska
Lavdie Rada
Dharini Raghavan
Chandravardhan Singh Raghaw
Matthew Ragoza
Maqsudur Rahman
Md Mostafijur Rahman
Muhammad Mahboob Ur Rahman
Sowad Rahman
Tarek Rahman
Wahyu Rahmaniar
Shyam Nandan Rai
Sudarshan Rajagopalan
Ajitha Rajan
Santhiya Rajan
Jagath Rajapakse
João Ramalhinho
Jayroop Ramesh
Ruisheng Ran
Amin Ranem
Aneesh Rangnekar
Asha Rani
Rakesh Ranjan
Amog Rao
Carolina Raposo
Essam Rashed
Hatem Rashwan
Sebastian Rassmann
Sparsh Rastogi
Lakmali Nadeesha Kumari Rathukohe Mudiyanselage
Mahesh Raveendranatha Panicker
Keerthi Sravan Ravi
Sadhana Ravikumar
Vikram Ravindra
Yogesh Rawat
Manahil Raza
Imran Razzak
Divya D Reddy
Mourad Rehali
Abdul Rehman
Paolo Remagnino
Samuel Remedios
Moritz Rempe

Ge Ren
Qin Ren
Sijie Ren
Siyang Ren
Tianyi Ren
Yudan Ren
Yuyang Ren
Zehua Ren
Zhihang Ren
David Restrepo
Mauricio Reyes
Abel Reyes-Angulo
Hadrien Reynaud
Hayley Reynolds
Thiago Rezende
Eman Rezk
Helena Ribeiro Torres
Anne-Marie Rickmann
Bastian Rieck
Brandalyn Riedel
Isabel Rio-Torto
Jens Rittscher
Duhyun Ro
Youngmin Ro
Charlotte Robert
Harry Robertshaw
Robert Robinson
Jessica Rodgers
Ranga Rodrigo
Antonio Rodriguez-Sanchez
Harry Rogers
Maximilian Rokuss
Eduardo Romero
Ali Roozbehi
Timo Ropinski
Pooneh Roshanitabrizi
Paul Rosin
Holger Roth
Rahimeh Rouhi
Gideon Rouwendaal
Saikat Roy
Dan Ruan
Josué Ruano-Balseca
Mathieu Rubeaux
Nejung Rue
Filippo Ruffini
Danny Ruijters
Josef Lorenz Rumberger
Hosuk Ryou
Hoe Sung Ryu
Kanghyun Ryu
Andrzej Rzepiela
J. S.
Muralikrishna S. N.
Sowmya S Sundaram
Armin Saadat
Sari Saba-Sadiya
Amirhossein Sabour
Maziar Sabouri
Bhuvan Sachdeva
Ario Sadafi
Binesh Sadanandan
Amir Reza Sadri
Fahad Saeed
Shaheer Saeed
Faezeh Safari
Aon Safdar
Monjoy Saha
Pramit Saha
Farhang Sahba
Heba Sailem
Simone Saitta
Md Sajid
Shadman Sakib
Soorena Salari
Divya Saleela
Afsah Saleem
Tausifa Jan Saleem
Md Sirajus Salekin
Mostafa Salem
Emmanuelle Salin
Samuele Salti
Md Samiullah
Karen Sanchez
Alejandro Sanchez Guinea
Ricardo Sanchez-Matilla
Yudi Sang
Sara Sangalli
Daniel Santak Wolf
Caio Santana

Ruggiero Santeramo
Ainkaran Santhirasekaram
Carlos Santiago
Alice Santilli
Nishchal Sapkota
Parham Saremi
Rachana Sathish
Sandra Emi Sato Imuro
Olivier Saut
Shier Nee Saw
Christian Schiffer
Robin Schirrmeister
Alexander Schlaefer
Adam Schmidt
Julia Schnabel
Till Schnabel
Daniel Scholz
Daan Schouten
Sebastian Schröder
Peter Schüffler
Johannes Schuiki
Nico Schulthess
Jeanette Schulz-Menger
Assaf Schuster
Davide Scorza
Michaël Sdika
Thalia Seale
Kyle See
Philipp Seeböck
Lalithkumar Seenivasan
Matthias Seibold
Alexander Seitel
Yang Sejung
Alexander Selivanov
Raghavendra Selvan
Jothiraj Selvaraj
Ilia Semenkov
Ahmet Sen
Sourya Sengupta
Thilo Sentker
Chang Wook Seo
Hyewon Seo
Sumin Seo
Yuri Seo
Maxime Sermesant
Manuel Serna-Aguilera
Giuseppe Serra
Carmen Serrano
Xavier Sevillano
Marvin Seyfarth
Qingrui Sha
Tianming Sha
Mai A. Shaaban
Nazmus Shakib Shadin
Ahmed Shaffie
Hina Shah
Jay Shah
Keyur Devendra Shah
Nisarg Shah
Nagur Shareef Shaik
Nazim Shaikh
S. Shailja
Amit Shakya
Mahesh Shakya
Nina Shamsi
Niyas Shamsudeen Kutty
Caifeng Shan
Jiwei Shan
Shanshan Shan
Yixin Shan
Dattesh Dayanand Shanbhag
Jiang Shang
Yeqin Shao
Maxim Sharaev
Lalith Sharan
Ajay Sharma
Saurav Sharma
Vanshali Sharma
Varsha Sharma
Furqan Shaukat
Mona Sheikh Zeinoddin
Ao Shen
Chen Shen
Gang Shen
Hualei Shen
Linlin Shen
Wei Shen
Xiang-Jun Shen
Xinke Shen
Yi Shen

Yiqing Shen
Zhenrong Shen
Zhiqiang Shen
Hongwei Sheng
Yi Sheng
John Shepherd
Bo Shi
Enze Shi
Hang Shi
Haoyuan Shi
Hongjian Shi
Jian Shi
Jiayang Shi
Jun Shi
Kangdi Shi
Peng Shi
Pengcheng Shi
Ruohua Shi
Shuo Shi
Xiaoshuang Shi
Xiaoyu Shi
Yaying Shi
Yi Shi
Yinghuan Shi
Yiyu Shi
Zhan Shi
Shu-Fu Shih
Takuro Shimaya
Jaeseung Shin
Jitae Shin
Seung Yeon Shin
Rakesh Shiradkar
Tamir Shor
David Shorthouse
Hongchao Shu
Jie Shu
Yucheng Shu
Ananya Shukla
Ankita Shukla
Md Rezowan Hossain Ferdous Shuvo
Weixin Si
Rosa Sicilia
Md. Saiful Bari Siddiqui
Sidi Mohamed Sid'El Moctar
Alberto Signoroni
Wilson Silva
Margarida Silveira
Jaeyoon Sim
Ivor Simpson
Zachary Sims
Amritpal Singh
Azad Singh
Dinesh Singh
Karanpartap Singh
Aniruddha Sinha
Ayushi Sinha
Vasilis Siomos
Raviteja Sista
Ssharvien Kumar Sivakumar
Elena Sizikova
Luka Škrlj
Gregory Slabaugh
Dane Smith
Weronika Smolak-Dyżewska
Tiffany Y So
Rajath Soans
Roger Soberanis-Mukul
Paolo Soda
Maina Sogabe
Maëlys Solal
Elanchezhian Somasundaram
Moo Hyun Son
Seungyeon Son
Anthony Song
Haojie Song
Hong Song
Hyunwoo Song
Pei-Cheng Song
Qi Song
Ruoxian Song
Shuang Song
Sifan Song
Tao Song
Xiao Song
Yantao Song
Yiran Song
Yu Song
Yucheng Song
Zhiwei Song
Zhiying Song

Zhiyun Song
Tananun Songdechakraiwut
Kristine Sørensen
Mazen Soufi
Raissa Souza
Roberto Souza
Georgia Sovatzidi
Michal Španěl
Bella Specktor Fadida
William Speier
Ziga Spiclin
Jon Sporring
Przemysław Spurek
Pradeeba Sridar
Anuj Srivastava
Lawrence Staib
Emma Stanley
Martijn Starmans
Johannes Stegmaier
Jan Steinbrener
Nil Stolt-Ansó
Skylar Stolte
Duncan Stothers
Joshua Stough
Robin Strand
Eric Strobl
Jérémie Stym-Popper
Martin Styner
Bo Su
Fei Su
Jiawei Su
Juntao Su
Weifeng Su
Yao Su
Barathi Subramanian
Hongyiel Suh
Julian Suk
K. M. Arefeen Sultan
Muhammad Ahmad Sultan
Nurjahan Sultana
Waqas Sultani
Chao Sun
Diya Sun
Dongbiao Sun
Guanqun Sun
Jiajun Sun
Jian Sun
Jianqi Sun
Jiarui Sun
Jindong Sun
Kaicong Sun
Minghao Sun
Roger Sun
Rui Sun
Ruiqing Sun
Shangquan Sun
Shoukun Sun
Shuifa Sun
Song Sun
Susu Sun
Xia Sun
Xiaowu Sun
Xiaoxue Sun
Xuebin Sun
Yan Sun
Yifei Sun
Yihua Sun
Yiran Sun
Yongheng Sun
Zhaoyi Sun
Zhe Sun
Zhenglong Sun
Zhichao Sun
Zhongxiang Sun
Zijun Sun
Vaanathi Sundaresan
Nak-Jun Sung
Elifnur Sunger
Hanna Suominen
Akara Supratak
Kadambari Suryavanshi
Krunal Suthar
Mohammod Naimul Islam Suvon
Zaneta Swiderska-Chadaj
Tomasz Szczepański
Shabana Tabassum
Sairam Tabibu
Ahmad P. Tafti
Behrad Taghibeyglou
Pablo Tahoces

Riccardo Taiello
Razane Tajeddine
Divyanshu Tak
Eichi Takaya
Saori Takeyama
Shumpei Takezaki
Hugues Talbot
Roger Tam
Utkarsh Tambe
Jose Tamez-Peña
Jeremy Tan
Kaiwen Tan
Shan Tan
Shuangyi Tan
Weimin Tan
Wenjun Tan
Xiaoyu Tan
Arthur Tang
Feilong Tang
Fenghe Tang
Haifeng Tang
Hao Tang
He Tang
Huadong Tang
Jianbo Tang
Jin Tang
Jinshan Tang
Kaibo Tang
Lingzhi Tang
Ming Tang
Shiqin Tang
Yilin Tang
Yucheng Tang
Yuxian Tang
Zhenzhou Tang
Zihao Tang
Michael Tanzer
Tianli Tao
Wenzheng Tao
Yitian Tao
Mickael Tardy
Sansiri Tarnpradab
Giacomo Tarroni
Virginia Tasso
Vasiliki Tassopoulou
Wallapak Tavanapong
Thomas Tavolara
Soroosh Tayebi Arasteh
Gbègninougbo Aurel Davy
Tchokponhoue
Kartikay Tehlan
Lin Teng
Atsushi Teramoto
Rafeek Thahakoya
Antoine Theberge
Sarina Thomas
Peter Thompson
Jacob Thrasher
Sai Natarajan Thrissur Ranganathan
Cristiana Tiago
Jiyu Tian
Qingyao Tian
Qiyuan Tian
Xuanyu Tian
Yibin Tian
Yun Tian
Vijay Srinivas Tida
Zumnan Timbi
Chee-Ming Ting
Fung Fung Ting
Aleksei Tiulpin
Yuta Tokuoka
Santiago Toledo-Cortés
Paulina Tomaszewska
Lyuyang Tong
Shao Tong
Akif Tosun
Nicolas Toussaint
Henry Tregidgo
Georgios Triantafyllou
Eleftherios Trivizakis
Jakob Troidl
Daniel Truhn
Tuan Truong
Liyun Tu
Puxun Tu
Jason Turuwhenua
Aayush Tyagi
Mrinal Tyagi
Georgios Tziritas

Kwang-Hyun Uhm
Constantin Ulrich
Ilkay Ulusoy
Rao Umer
Tamas Ungi
Saritha Unnikrishnan
Eneko Uruñuela
Fatmatulzehra Uslu
Muhammad Usman
Hristina Uzunova
Sami Väänänen
Anil Kumar Vadathya
Theodoros Vagenas
Puru Vaish
Vanya Valindria
Juan Miguel Valverde
Gijs van Tulder
Henk van Voorst
Jef Vandemeulebroucke
Joris Vankerschaver
Juan Vargas Garcia
Bino Varghese
Hooman Vaseli
Rajat Vashistha
Michael Vasilakakis
Neil Vaughan
S. Swaroop Vedula
Jai Prakash Veerla
Danush Kumar Venkatesh
Vikram Venkatraghavan
Tom Vercauteren
Manisha Verma
Mitko Veta
Pierre-Frederic Villard
Pk Vinod
Thanaporn Viriyasaranon
Christiaan Viviers
Hung Vo
Wolf-Dieter Vogl
Anh Vu
Truong Vu
Milos Vukadinovic
Kushal Vyas
Assefa Wahd
Victor Wåhlstrand
Gordon Waiter
Zuzanna Wakefield-Skórniewska
Christian Wallraven
Ricky Walsh
Cheng Wan
Kaiwen Wan
Liang Wan
Shouhong Wan
Xiaohua Wan
Zhiyu Wan
Zishuo Wan
Alan Wang
An Wang
Baizhi Wang
Bin Wang
Bo Wang
Bomin Wang
Changfei Wang
Changjian Wang
Chaoqun Wang
Cheng Wang
Chengkai Wang
Chenglong Wang
Chengyan Wang
Chenhui Wang
Chong Wang
Chunjiang Wang
Chunliang Wang
Cong Wang
Congcong Wang
Dekui Wang
Di Wang
Dongang Wang
Fangyijie Wang
Fanwen Wang
Fuying Wang
Guangzhi Wang
Guoan Wang
Guotai Wang
Haifeng Wang
Hao Wang
Haolin Wang
Haoyu Wang
Hongpeng Wang
Hongqiu Wang

Huanqin Wang
Huayu Wang
Huitao Wang
Janet Wang
Jiacheng Wang
Jiahao Wang
Jian Wang
Jiazhen Wang
Jiazheng Wang
Jihang Wang
Jinfeng Wang
Jinhao Wang
Jixin Wang
Jiyao Wang
Juan Wang
Jueqi Wang
Jui-Kai Wang
Junyi Wang
Junze Wang
Kai Wang
Kailing Wang
Kaini Wang
Lehan Wang
Lei Wang
Li Rong Wang
Liansheng Wang
Lifang Wang
Lihui Wang
Lin Wang
Linwei Wang
Lipo Wang
Lituan Wang
Lu Wang
Luo Wang
Luoyu Wang
Meili Wang
Meng Wang
Mengxiao Wang
Mingliang Wang
Peng Wang
Pingping Wang
Qian Wang
Qianqian Wang
Qijie Wang
Qingying Wang
Qiuli Wang
Rongfang Wang
Rongsheng Wang
Rui Wang
Ruiqi Wang
Ruixuan Wang
Runmin Wang
Sen Wang
Shangfei Wang
Shiru Wang
Shuangyi Wang
Shuhui Wang
Shuihua Wang
Shuo Wang
Sihan Wang
Tao Wang
Tianyu Wang
Tony Wang
Wei Wang
Weichung Wang
Weirong Wang
Xi Wang
Xin Wang
Xingce Wang
Xingyue Wang
Xinkai Wang
Xinyu Wang
Yan Wang
Yi Wang
Yifan Wang
Yifeng Wang
Yihui Wang
Yinghui Wang
Yingni Wang
Yipei Wang
Yiqing Wang
Yiying Wang
Yonghao Wang
Yu Wang
Yuli Wang
Yulin Wang
Yuqi Wang
Zesong Wang
Zhewei Wang
Zhihui Wang

Zhisong Wang
Zhiyan Wang
Zhonghua Wang
Zhou Wang
Zi Wang
Zichen Wang
Zihao Wang
Zipei Wang
Ziyi Wang
Ziyue Wang
Zizhou Wang
Zuhui Wang
Talha Waqas
Tyler Ward
Simon Warfield
Valentine Wargnier Dauchelle
William Warner
Azmine Toushik Wasi
Saad Wazir
Michael Wehrli
Chen Wei
Dong Wei
Guangshun Wei
Hao Wei
Jia Wei
Jie Wei
Linda Wei
Qijie Wei
Ruofeng Wei
Shuwen Wei
Xinjian Wei
Yongbin Wei
Zechen Wei
Ziquan Wei
Jonas Weidner
Michael Wels
Xuyun Wen
Yannuo Wen
Zheyu Wen
Cui Wenju
Philipp Wesp
Kithmin Wickremasinghe
Brady Williamson
Matthias Wilms
Paul Wilson
Eric Wisotzky
Adam Wittek
Marek Wodzinski
Ivo Wolf
Julia Wolleb
Jelmer Wolterink
Dong-Ok Won
Ji Hye Won
Jongjun Won
Bryan Wong
Chun Kit Wong
Joshua Wong
Kitty Wong
Anna Woodard
Mckell Woodland
Stefan Wörz
Beining Wu
Chao Wu
Chengchuan Wu
Chengyu Wu
Chenwei Wu
Cong Wu
Dan Wu
Donghan Wu
Feng Wu
Fuping Wu
Fuzhi Wu
Guoqing Wu
Han Wu
Hao Wu
Honghan Wu
Ji Wu
Jiamin Wu
Jianghao Wu
Jie Ying Wu
Jinlin Wu
Junde Wu
Junyang Wu
Lei Wu
Luohong Wu
Mengqi Wu
Ming Wu
Nian Wu
Qian Wu
Qing Wu

Rong Wu
Ruifan Wu
Ruiqi Wu
Ruoyou Wu
Shaoju Wu
Shaoxuan Wu
Shibin Wu
Shuang Wu
Shuqiong Wu
Taoyu Wu
Victoria Wu
Wei Wu
Weiyi Wu
Wenjun Wu
Wenxia Wu
Wenxuan Wu
Xiangcen Wu
Xiangjun Wu
Xiao Wu
Xinyao Wu
Yanlin Wu
Yihang Wu
Yinhao Wu
Yinzhe Wu
Yongfei Wu
Yonghuang Wu
Yujia Wu
Yunheng Wu
Yu-Te Wu
Zhaolong Wu
Zhengwang Wu
Zhijian Wu
Zhiying Wu
Zhuoyu Wu
Zihao Wu
Zijian Wu
Joris Wuts
Julian Wyatt
Magdalena Wysocki
Haoran Xi
Nan Xi
Pengcheng Xi
Xiaoming Xi
Chao Xia
Chen Xia
Jianan Xia
Mingze Xia
Qing Xia
Tian Xia
Weihao Xia
Weiran Xia
Yihao Xia
Jinhai Xiang
Lei Xiang
Nan Xiang
Tiange Xiang
Tianqi Xiang
Bin Xiao
Deqiang Xiao
Furen Xiao
Jingjing Xiao
Li Xiao
Pan Xiao
Ruolin Xiao
Sa Xiao
Bin Xie
Fengbo Xie
Guo-Sen Xie
Hai Xie
Hao Xie
Housheng Xie
Jianyang Xie
Kangxian Xie
Kunzi Xie
Long Xie
Shiyu Xie
Sihong Xie
Xingyu Xie
Yining Xie
Yiting Xie
Yutong Xie
Zhaoheng Xie
Jack Xin
Jiayi Xin
Changda Xing
Fangxu Xing
Jiarui Xing
Shuwei Xing
Ying Xing
Yucheng Xing

Yuxiang Xing
Zhaohu Xing
Conghao Xiong
Hao Xiong
Honglin Xiong
Huimin Xiong
Sijie Xiong
Xiangyu Xiong
Xinyu Xiong
Yujian Xiong
Zicheng Xiong
Chenchen Xu
Chenfan Xu
Chuankai Xu
Dexuan Xu
Di Xu
Dunyuan Xu
Fangqiang Xu
Gelei Xu
Geng-Xin Xu
Guoping Xu
Hao Xu
Hongming Xu
Jialang Xu
Jiangchang Xu
Jianwei Xu
Jiaqi Xu
Jiashu Xu
Jiaxing Xu
Jinjing Xu
Jun Xu
Junlin Xu
Lei Xu
Lijian Xu
Lina Xu
Mengya Xu
Min Xu
Pengcheng Xu
Qing Xu
Rui Xu
Ruru Xu
Weixin Xu
Xiaowei Xu
Xinran Xu
Xiuyuan Xu
Xuan Xu
Yiwen Xu
Yongchao Xu
Yunqiu Xu
Zhuowei Xu
Ziang Xu
Zibo Xu
Zikang Xu
Ziyue Xu
Cheng Xue
Hui Xue
Jie Xue
Nian Xue
Peng Xue
Rundong Xue
Xiaofei Xue
Yunzhe Xue
Siyi Xun
Yue Xun
Goshiro Yamamoto
Yu Yamaoka
Amine Yamlahi
Bingjie Yan
Chongzhe Yan
Fang Yan
Fanzhe Yan
Jingwen Yan
Junyu Yan
Rui Yan
Siyuan Yan
Tianyi Yan
Yan Yan
Yige Yan
Zhiling Yan
Zhonghao Yan
Zipei Yan
Baoyao Yang
Chen Yang
Chunna Yang
Dong Yang
Fan Yang
Guang Yang
Guangqian Yang
Guangzhengao Yang
Guanyu Yang

Hongjia Yang
Hongxi Yang
Hongxu Yang
Hsin-Jung Yang
Huanqi Yang
Hyeonsik Yang
Hyung-Jeong Yang
Jiachen Yang
Jianhua Yang
Jiaqi Yang
Jiewen Yang
Jijiang Yang
Jin Yang
Junlin Yang
Kaiwen Yang
Kaixiang Yang
Ke Yang
Lei Yang
Litao Yang
Liutao Yang
Long Yang
Peng Yang
Qian Yang
Qianye Yang
Shu Yang
Shuo Yang
Shuojue Yang
Sicheng Yang
Sooyoung Yang
Su Yang
Wanqi Yang
Wei Yang
Xiaochen Yang
Xiaofei Yang
Xiaofeng Yang
Xikai Yang
Xin Yang
Xinnian Yang
Xinyi Yang
Xuan Yang
Yiguang Yang
Yijun Yang
Yingyu Yang
Yoon Seok Yang
Yun Yang
Yuxuan Yang
Zefan Yang
Zekang Yang
Zhaocan Yang
Zhenhong Yang
Zhidong Yang
Zhiwei Yang
Zhiwen Yang
Zijiang Yang
Zixin Yang
Ziyuan Yang
Zongbao Yang
Berrin Yanikoglu
Chenglin Yao
Haoran Yao
Linlin Yao
Tianyuan Yao
Xiaohui Yao
Zhao Yao
Milad Yazdani
Chenfei Ye
Chengze Ye
Chuyang Ye
Jiayu Ye
Johan Ye
Jong Chul Ye
Kangqing Ye
Meng Ye
Shuchang Ye
Xuesong Ye
Xujiong Ye
Yiwen Ye
Yubo Ye
Zhaoyi Ye
Yousef Yeganeh
Varduhi Yeghiazaryan
Chun-Hsiao Yeh
Chunzhi Yi
Huahui Yi
Jirong Yi
Mun Yi
Murong Yi
Weixi Yi
Xin Yi
Yuhao Yi

Zhenyu Yi
Rüveyda Yilmaz
Wen-Wai Yim
Chong Yin
Jiahui Yin
Ming Yin
Pengshuai Yin
Xuefei Yin
Yi Yin
Yunfei Yin
Zihan Yin
Haochao Ying
Qichao Ying
Jay Yoo
Min Kyoon Yoo
Seok Bong Yoo
Yongseon Yoo
Youngjin Yoo
Dan Yoon
Jihun Yoon
Kyungho Yoon
Siyeop Yoon
Susik Yoon
Weiqiu You
Xin You
Khalid Youssef
Andrew Yu
Boxiao Yu
Chaohui Yu
Chengjin Yu
Dahui Yu
De Yu
Fanyang Yu
Han Yu
Jiejiang Yu
Jin-Gang Yu
Jinhua Yu
Mingyang Yu
Qinji Yu
Qinkai Yu
Tingting Yu
Xiangchun Yu
Xiaopeng Yu
Xiaowei Yu
Yang Yu
Yanxuan Yu
Yi Yu
Zhen Yu
Zheng Yu
Ziqi Yu
Cheng Yuan
Gang Yuan
Haoyue Yuan
Jie Yuan
Kun Yuan
Manman Yuan
Mingze Yuan
Xiaohan Yuan
Xinrui Yuan
Yuchen Yuan
Zhouhang Yuan
Novanto Yudistira
Jiangbei Yue
Jiaxin Yue
Peiyan Yue
Boxiang Yun
Juseung Yun
Seong Dae Yun
Ka Yung
Chang Yuwen
Elizabeth Yuwono
Mariam Zabihi
Stefan Zachow
Anas Zafar
Abdelrahman Zaian
Nayyar Zaidi
Fahim Ahmed Zaman
Omar Zamzam
Alexey Zaytsev
Rachid Zeghlache
Ramy Zeineldin
Dong Zeng
Guangjian Zeng
Hongye Zeng
Hui Zeng
Jiajun Zeng
Na Zeng
Pinxian Zeng
Qi Zeng
Qingjie Zeng

Qingyuan Zeng
Shuang Zeng
Tianyi Zeng
Xinyi Zeng
Zhitao Zeng
Ruyi Zha
Xinbei Zha
Yongping Zhai
Aiying Zhang
Baochang Zhang
Bingbing Zhang
Chen Zhang
Chensheng Zhang
Chenxi Zhang
Chuanhao Zhang
Chujie Zhang
Dan Zhang
Dexun Zhang
Dingzhong Zhang
Dong Zhang
Fan Zhang
Feifei Zhang
Francis Xiatian Zhang
Gengwei Zhang
Gongyu Zhang
Guoning Zhang
Haixian Zhang
Han Zhang
Hang Zhang
Hanrong Zhang
Hanwen Zhang
Hanxiao Zhang
Hanyuan Zhang
Hao Zhang
Haochen Zhang
Haofeng Zhang
Haosen Zhang
Haoyue Zhang
Hongyuan Zhang
Huahui Zhang
Hui Zhang
Huihuang Zhang
Jiajin Zhang
Jianhai Zhang
Jianjia Zhang
Jiansong Zhang
Jianwei Zhang
Jiaqing Zhang
Jiazhen Zhang
Jing Zhang
Jingyang Zhang
Jintan Zhang
Jinwei Zhang
Kai Zhang
Ke Zhang
Kun Zhang
Kunyu Zhang
Le Zhang
Lei Zhang
Li Zhang
Lihe Zhang
Lin Zhang
Lingtong Zhang
Ling-Xiao Zhang
Liping Zhang
Lu Zhang
Miaomiao Zhang
Minghui Zhang
Minqing Zhang
Molin Zhang
Nan Zhang
Peng Zhang
Pingping Zhang
Qi Zhang
Qianni Zhang
Qibin Zhang
Qing Zhang
Rongzhao Zhang
Ruicheng Zhang
Ruipeng Zhang
Shipeng Zhang
Shu Zhang
Shuai Zhang
Shuaitong Zhang
Shugang Zhang
Song Zhang
Songyao Zhang
Teng Zhang
Tengda Zhang
Tianqiao Zhang

Tianyu Zhang
Ting Zhang
Tongxu Zhang
Wanjun Zhang
Wei Zhang
Weihang Zhang
Weitong Zhang
Weiwen Zhang
Weiyi Zhang
Wengfeng Zhang
Wenhua Zhang
Wenhui Zhang
Wenjie Zhang
Xiao Zhang
Xiaodong Zhang
Xiaoman Zhang
Xiaoming Zhang
Xiaorui Zhang
Xin Zhang
Xingpeng Zhang
Xuhong Zhang
Yanan Zhang
Yanchao Zhang
Yanteng Zhang
Ye Zhang
Yi Zhang
Yichi Zhang
Yijia Zhang
Yikun Zhang
Yilan Zhang
Yinglin Zhang
Yingying Zhang
You Zhang
Yu Zhang
Yuan Zhang
Yuanwang Zhang
Yubo Zhang
Yudong Zhang
Yue Zhang
Yuelin Zhang
Yuhan Zhang
Yukun Zhang
Yundi Zhang
Yunyan Zhang
Yuyao Zhang
Zeng Zhang
Zeyu Zhang
Zheng Zhang
Zhenxuan Zhang
Zheyuan Zhang
Zhuoneng Zhang
Zichen Zhang
Zijie Zhang
Zijun Zhang
Ziyu Zhang
Zuyu Zhang
Beidi Zhao
Bin Zhao
Bokai Zhao
Chen Zhao
Chongyue Zhao
Fengjun Zhao
Jianhui Zhao
Jichao Zhao
Jun Zhao
Junyong Zhao
Lei Zhao
Li Zhao
Meng Zhao
Na Zhao
Puyang Zhao
Qi Zhao
Shilun Zhao
Weibing Zhao
Weiqin Zhao
Wenbo Zhao
Wenjie Zhao
Wenzhao Zhao
Xiaowei Zhao
Xingzhong Zhao
Xinkai Zhao
Yang Zhao
Yawu Zhao
Yi Zhao
Yidong Zhao
Yijun Zhao
Yue Zhao
Yujing Zhao
Zhicheng Zhao
Zhihao Zhao

Zihao Zhao
Ziwei Zhao
Zixu Zhao
Bo Zhao
Boyun Zheng
Fudan Zheng
Hao Zheng
Jialun Zheng
Jieyu Zheng
Minghang Zheng
Qingqing Zheng
Shenhai Zheng
Shuai Zheng
Yalin Zheng
Yifan Zheng
Yijiang Zheng
Ying Zheng
Yubin Zheng
Aocheng Zhong
Chunlin Zhong
Gaoyan Zhong
Haiqin Zhong
Jian Zhong
Jia-Xing Zhong
Jiayang Zhong
Liang Zhong
Lujia Zhong
Tao Zhong
Wenqi Zhong
Xinliu Zhong
Xinyun Zhong
Yuan Zhong
Feixiang Zhou
Guangquan Zhou
Hangqi Zhou
Hao Zhou
Haoyin Zhou
Huajun Zhou
Jun Zhou
Kang Zhou
Lei Zhou
Linkuan Zhou
Longxi Zhou
Meihua Zhou
Meng Zhou
Mo Zhou
Nan Zhou
Qian Zhou
Qifeng Zhou
Quan Zhou
Ran Zhou
Rong Zhou
Ruixi Zhou
Shihao Zhou
Shuo Zhou
Sijin Zhou
Tao Zhou
Wei Zhou
Wu Zhou
Xiaobing Zhou
Xinrui Zhou
Xueying Zhou
Yao Zhou
Yaxuan Zhou
Youjia Zhou
Yuan Zhou
Yuanpin Zhou
Yubo Zhou
Yue Zhou
Yufei Zhou
Zhen Zhou
Zhengbo Zhou
Zhengchao Zhou
Zhenghua Zhou
Zhenhuan Zhou
Zijian Zhou
Zirui Zhou
Ziteng Zhou
Ziyu Zhou
Chunzheng Zhu
Congcong Zhu
Hancan Zhu
Hengde Zhu
Heqin Zhu
Hongjie Zhu
Jianfei Zhu
Jiayuan Zhu
Jinghua Zhu
Junchao Zhu
Lei Zhu

Lijing Zhu
Mu Zhu
Ning Zhu
Pengli Zhu
Shenghao Zhu
Simeng Zhu
Xiaohui Zhu
Xiliang Zhu
Xun Zhu
Yi Zhu
Yinghao Zhu
Yinheng Zhu
Yitao Zhu
Yuanyi Zhu
Yuanzhuo Zhu
Yuemin Zhu
Yunzheng Zhu
Zhanshi Zhu
Zhengjie Zhu
Zhiqin Zhu
Zhu Zhu
Zirui Zhu
Luoting Zhuang
Mingrui Zhuang
Yipeng Zhuang
Zhemin Zhuang
Li Zhuo
Yupeng Zhuo
Muhammad Zia Ur Rehman
Arif Hassan Zidan
Alexander Ziller
David Zimmerer
Kpêtchéhoué Merveille Santi Zinsou
Lilla Zöllei
Fangrong Zong
Dongmian Zou
Sarah Zou
Shihao Zou
Xinrui Zou
Yunmin Zou
Ziyun Zou
Maria A. Zuluaga
Wenbin Zuo
Gerald Zwettler

Contents

Image-Guided Surgery and Intervention

Image-Guided Surgery and Intervention

A Deep Learning Surrogate Model for Microwave Thermal Ablation: From Preoperative Planning to Intraoperative Re-planning

Ilias Nahmed(✉), Francesco Dettori, Michel Duprez, Pablo Alvarez, and Stéphane Cotin

Université de Strasbourg, CNRS, Inria, ICube, F-67000 Strasbourg, France
ilias.nahmed@inria.fr

Abstract. With the increasing interest in thermal ablation therapies, patient-specific predictive simulations have become crucial for improving both preoperative planning and intraoperative corrections. Planning strategies typically rely on the solution of an inverse problem, yet high-fidelity finite element simulations remain computationally prohibitive when embedded within an optimization loop under strict clinical time constraints. In this work, we introduce a real-time deep learning surrogate model for predicting liver microwave ablation outcomes, trained exclusively on synthetic data and personalized through 3D perfusion maps that encode patient anatomy and local perfusion rates. This surrogate model takes as input the antenna position, power and ablation duration, and outputs the predicted necrosis volume within a few milliseconds. Once integrated into an optimization loop, it becomes possible to propose antenna trajectories and ablation settings that maximize tumor coverage while minimizing damage to healthy tissue. We demonstrate this on clinical data via a physics-based optimization framework that computes optimal ablation parameters in under 2 min, critical for preoperative planning or intraoperative re-planning in microwave ablation. The surrogate model was validated on *in vivo* pre-clinical data where it achieved an average Dice coefficient of 0.82 for necrosis mask prediction.

Keywords: thermal ablation · simulation · planning · surrogate model

1 Introduction

Over the last decades, percutaneous thermal ablation has emerged as a primary minimally invasive alternative to surgical resection [11]. While Radiofrequency Ablation (RFA) has long been the dominant modality, Microwave Ablation (MWA) is increasingly preferred for large tumors due to its ability to generate higher temperatures and larger ablation zones within shorter treatment

G. Yang et al. (Eds.): MICCAI 2026, LNCS 16893, pp. 3–12, 2027.
https://doi.org/10.1007/978-3-032-38236-8_1

times [16]. Ablation outcomes in MWA depend on both intervention-dependent factors (*e.g.* microwave generator power, ablation duration and antenna geometry) and patient-specific variables (*e.g.* tumor proximity to vessels, dielectric and thermal properties). Yet, in practice, clinicians plan MWA parameters following manufacturer-provided charts, which ignore patient-dependent factors and therefore often overestimate ablation sizes. This is particularly important when ablating highly-perfused organs such as the liver or kidney [6,18], where nearby vessels cause temperature loss via advection, *i.e.* the heat-sink effect.

To mitigate these limitations, computational models have been proposed to simulate ablation outcomes [2,14]. Although these models demonstrate superior accuracy over geometric approximations [5,10], their clinical utility is hindered by the prohibitive computational cost of the numerical schemes (*e.g.* finite element method (FEM)) used to solve the underlying partial differential equations (PDEs). This limitation gets further amplified in MWA planning or intraoperative guidance scenarios, where multiple simulations (potentially hundreds) are required for solving the associated inverse problems. Consequently, there is a need for efficient strategies that approximate these outcomes in the shortest possible amount of time.

Recently, surrogate models based on physics-guided neural networks have emerged as a computationally efficient solution, enabling lesion-extent prediction in milliseconds. Such developments include deep networks based on U-Net architectures [13], neural cellular automata [8], and DeepONet-style operator learning [9]. However, these existing frameworks focus on RFA applications, where power control is not possible, and optimization is essentially restricted to probe placement. In contrast, MWA outcomes are strongly sensitive to ablation power and duration [12], requiring these additional control variables to be optimized for improved conformity between the predicted ablation zone and the clinical target. Current methods also often neglect patient-specific vascularization, which influence has been identified as key in the heat-sink effect [4].

In this work, we propose a deep learning surrogate model for liver MWA outcome prediction. The model is conditioned on both intervention- and patient-specific parameters, and outputs 3D thermal damage maps and ablation zones in milliseconds. We demonstrate its potential for inverse problem-solving in MWA through two clinical applications: (i) an end-to-end physics-based MWA planning solution and (ii) an intraoperative MWA re-planning solution for optimizing ablation parameters after antenna misplacement. To ensure generalization without requiring vast clinical datasets, the network is trained exclusively on simulated MW ablations performed on synthetic anatomies, including tumors and vascular structures. To our knowledge, this is the first study to provide a real-time deep learning surrogate for MWA outcome prediction, enabling optimization-based personalization within clinical time constraints.

2 Methods

2.1 Computational Model for Microwave Ablation Simulation

Heat distribution and thermal evolution during MWA is typically modeled using Pennes' Bioheat equation [14]. Disregarding metabolic effects, it reads

$$\rho C \frac{\partial T}{\partial t} = \nabla \cdot (\kappa \nabla T) - \rho_b C_b \omega_b (T - T_b) + Q_{\text{ext}}, \tag{1}$$

where ρ, C, T, ρ_b, C_b and T_b denote the tissue density (kg/m^3), specific heat capacity (J/kg/K) and temperature (K) of the tissue, and for the blood entering the tissue respectively. κ represents the thermal conductivity (W/m/K), ω_b is the blood perfusion rate (1/s) that allows modeling the heat sink effect and Q_{ext} is the external heat source.

The external heat source Q_{ext} represents the thermal energy absorbed by the tissue during MWA. It is related to the electric field intensity $\boldsymbol{E}$ (V/m) of the propagating microwaves and the tissue's electric conductivity σ (S/m) by:

$$Q_{ext} = \frac{1}{2} \sigma \langle \boldsymbol{E}, \boldsymbol{E}^* \rangle. \tag{2}$$

The electric field intensity $\boldsymbol{E}$ is the solution to the microwave propagation problem described by the frequency domain Maxwell equations:

$$\nabla \times \mu_r^{-1} (\nabla \times \boldsymbol{E}) - k_0^2 (\varepsilon_r - j \frac{\sigma}{\omega \varepsilon_0}) \boldsymbol{E} = 0, \tag{3}$$

where ω is the angular frequency (rad/s), μ_r is the relative permeability, ε_r is the relative permittivity, ε_0 is the permittivity in vacuum (F/m), and k_0 is the propagation constant in vacuum (1/m).

We solved the coupled system of PDEs using a FE numerical scheme implemented on FEniCSx [1], with boundary conditions appropriate for MWA and a computational reduction strategy described in our previous work [10]. Finally, we use the Arrhenius model to compute tissue damage and necrosis maps.

2.2 Deep Learning Surrogate Model

We introduce a supervised deep learning surrogate model to achieve clinically compatible computation times. Instead of adopting a physics-informed neural network (PINN) formulation where the governing PDEs are embedded directly into the loss, we rely on a fully supervised approach. Indeed, the coupled electromagnetic–thermal problem described above would make a PINN approach particularly intricate and computationally expensive. By contrast, once trained, our network can be deployed without per-case retraining.

Inputs/Outputs: The network processes both spatial and procedural inputs, consisting of a 3D volumetric perfusion map encoding both anatomy and voxel wise perfusion, along with an oriented 3D Gaussian heatmap representing the

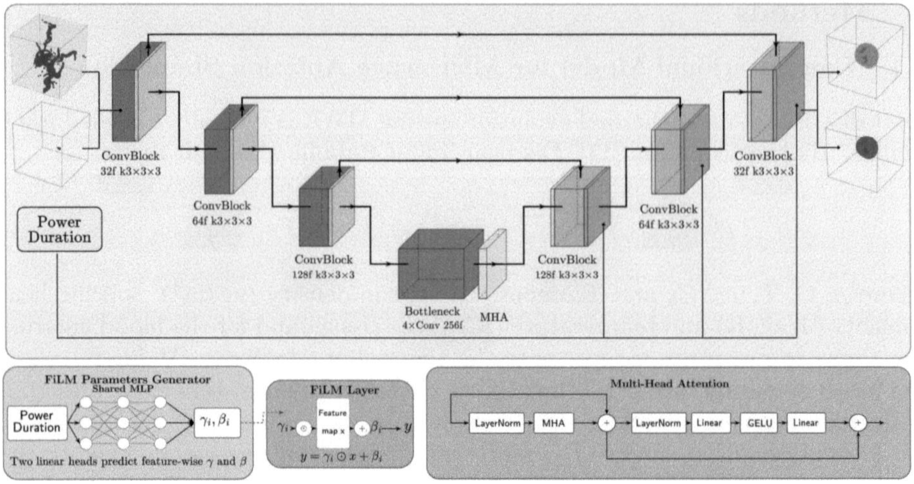

Fig. 1. Overview of the proposed 3D U-Net architecture with FiLM and MHA blocks.

antenna tip and insertion axis. Since the Pennes bioheat equation is highly sensitive to the perfusion parameter [4], explicitly incorporating it into the input is essential for accurate predictions. The network jointly predicts a 3D thermal damage map and a binary necrosis mask.

Architecture: The network is based on a 3D U-Net with feature-wise linear modulation (FiLM) layers and a multi-head self-attention layer (Fig. 1). The encoder consists of three downsampling stages (3^3 convolutions, group normalization and leaky ReLU activations) with channels progressively increasing from 32 to 256. The decoder mirrors this structure, using transposed convolutions for upsampling and skip connections. A bottleneck of four convolutional blocks (256 channels) is followed by a multi-head self-attention block to capture long-range spatial interactions. The procedural parameters (power and duration) are injected at each decoder level via small MLPs that map these inputs to scale and bias vectors modulating the FiLM layers. Finally, a 1^3 convolution layer produces the two output volumes.

Loss Function: The network is supervised on both thermal injury and ablation zone maps through the following loss function:

$$\mathcal{L} = w_1 \mathrm{MSE}(D_{\mathrm{target}}, D_{\mathrm{pred}}) + w_2 \left(1 - \frac{2\,|M_{\mathrm{target}} \cap M_{\mathrm{pred}}|}{|M_{\mathrm{target}} \cup M_{\mathrm{pred}}|}\right) \tag{4}$$

where D_{target} and D_{pred} denote the target and predicted damage maps, M_{target} and M_{pred} denote the target and predicted ablation masks, and w_1, w_2 are empirically-tuned weighting factors. The supervision over the damage map complements the discrete necrosis map with smooth information of thermal injury. This is the rationale we used for keeping both quantities in the network's output.

2.3 Synthetic Dataset Generation

The network is trained only once on a large and diverse computer-generated dataset. By exposing the model to a sufficiently rich distribution of anatomical configurations, perfusion maps, and procedural parameters, we promote generalization across patients and clinical scenarios without requiring per-case retraining. This design enables fast inference at deployment while retaining the predictive fidelity of the underlying physics-based simulations.

The generated dataset consisted of 2400 samples derived from 1200 synthetic perfusion map volumes. For each sample, two randomly generated curved trajectories traversed the volume of interest to represent the portal vein and the vena cava. Additional branches were randomly generated from these primary trajectories to approximate hepatic vascular trees. Each vessel segment was dilated to radii sampled from a normal distribution based on physiological literature [3]. These vessels structures were assigned a perfusion value of 0.2 s^{-1} [4], while the remaining healthy tissue was assigned values ranging from 0.015 to 0.075 s^{-1}. Finally, for each volume, a tumor with irregular boundaries was generated and assigned a perfusion value 1.5 times of the healthy tissue perfusion [17].

MWA simulations were performed (see Sect. 2.1) with and without tumors, with antenna configurations sampled in the vicinity of the tumor center. Ablation parameters were varied to avoid the need for per-patient or per-procedure retraining, with power levels ranging from 30 to 100 W and durations from 180 to 500 s. The dataset was split into 85% for training and 15% for validation.

2.4 Clinically-Motivated Inverse Problem-Solving

In clinical practice, the antenna insertion direction is chosen carefully to maximize ablation outcome and avoid critical structures. Before MWA, this choice relies either on clinical expertise and/or geometric planning tools to minimize insertion risk given the patient's anatomy [7]. During MWA, because of human error, there is no guarantee that the insertion direction will match the planned path and antenna misplacement can occur. In both cases, it is necessary to find optimal ablation parameters appropriate for the tumor under treatment, and given the antenna insertion direction. Here, we propose solutions to these two clinical contexts by efficiently solving the following minimization problem:

$$\arg\min_{P,T,t} \ \lambda_1 \left(1 - \frac{|M_{\text{tumor}} \cap A_{\text{pred}}|}{|M_{\text{tumor}}|}\right) + \lambda_2 \left(1 - \frac{2\,|M_{\text{tumor}} \cap A_{\text{pred}}|}{|M_{\text{tumor}} \cup A_{\text{pred}}|}\right), \quad (5)$$

where $A_{\text{pred}}(P, T, \boldsymbol{t})$ is the ablation zone predicted by our surrogate model for a given power P, ablation duration T and antenna translation along its axis $\boldsymbol{t}$, M_{tumor} is the target tumor mask, λ_1, λ_2 are empirically-tuned weighting factors.

The first term maximizes tumor coverage ($|M_{\text{tumor}} \cap A_{\text{pred}}|/|M_{\text{tumor}}|$), while the second minimizes damage to nearby structures via the Dice Similarity Coefficient (DSC) ($2\ |M_{\text{tumor}} \cap A_{\text{pred}}|/|M_{\text{tumor}} \cup A_{\text{pred}}|$). We solved (5) using the CMA-ES genetic algorithm, with a population size of 15 and 500 maximum iterations.

End-to-End Preoperative MWA Planning Solution: Following [7], the algorithm finds a feasible antenna trajectory satisfying geometric and clinical constraints, including rib avoidance and protection of adjacent organs. In contrast to [7] that relied on a custom genetic algorithm, we employ a standard NSGA-II implementation to reduce optimization overhead. Using the geometrically optimized insertion direction, the algorithm determines the optimal antenna tip position along with ablation power and duration.

Intraoperative MWA Re-planning Solution: We build upon our previous work where we compensated for antenna misplacement during MWA without antenna reinsertion by adjusting power, duration, and axial translation [10]. Here, thanks to our surrogate model, the algorithm can identify new ablation parameters after antenna misplacement within 30 s, which significantly enhances the clinical feasibility of such a re-planning solution.

3 Results and Discussion

3.1 Evaluation of the Surrogate Model

We evaluated the surrogate model's performance in three scenarios: (i) FE simulations on synthetic anatomies, (ii) FE simulations on patient anatomies, and (iii) *in vivo* porcine ablation experiments, with the approval of the local ethics committee. In addition, an ablation study of key network components was also conducted, including a variant using only FiLM layers (NN_F) and a simplified baseline (NN_B) without FiLM layers where power and duration inputs are passed directly to the bottleneck as additional channels. These results are summarized in Table 1.

Table 1. Evaluation of ablation predictions for the surrogate model (NN) and its variants. Average runtimes and DSCs are reported for the three scenarios.

	FE & synth. anatomies	**FE & patient anatomies**	**Porcine *in vivo* experiments**			**Avg. Runtime**
			Abl. 1	**Abl. 2**	**Abl. 3**	
FE	-	-	0.83	0.83	0.80	$\sim$ 260 s
NN	0.94 ± 0.1	0.94 ± 0.1	0.81	0.85	0.78	$\sim$ 2.8 ms
NN_F	0.94 ± 0.1	0.94 ± 0.1	0.80	0.84	0.77	$\sim$ 2.8 ms
NN_B	0.93 ± 0.1	0.93 ± 0.1	0.80	0.84	0.73	$\sim$ 2.4 ms

In the first scenario, synthetic anatomies similar to the training set were used for evaluation. The surrogate model demonstrated high accuracy with an average DSC of 0.94 on the predicted ablation zones. In the second scenario, real patient anatomies extracted from the 3D-IRCADb-01 database [15] were used to evaluate the model. Using FE simulations with varying ablation parameters, one ablation was performed for each volume, resulting in a dataset of 123 volumes of size $100 \times 100 \times 100$. The model maintained robust performance with an average DSC of 0.94, indicating strong generalization to real-patient anatomical structures despite being trained exclusively on synthetic data. Finally, in the third scenario consisting of three *in vivo* porcine ablations, we compared both the FE simulation and the surrogate model predictions against manually segmented lesions. The predicted ablation zones showed close agreement with experimental observations in shape and volume, yielding average DSCs of 0.82 across experiments, consistent with FE simulations. This is illustrated in Fig. 2 via 2D and 3D comparisons of the ground truth ablation zone against both FE and surrogate model outcomes.

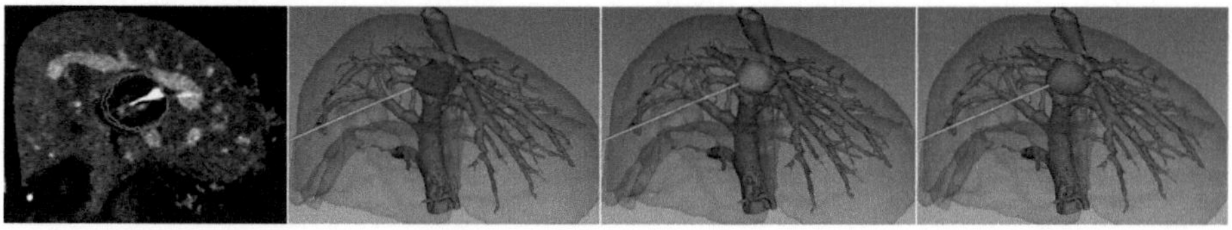

Fig. 2. Ablation zone predictions for one *in vivo* porcine experiment. Ablation zones corresponding to the ground truth (blue), FE prediction (magenta) and surrogate model prediction (green) are shown on a CT slice and 3D reconstructions of the liver.

In terms of computational efficiency, the average runtime for a single FE simulation was approximately 260 s, whereas the surrogate model required only 2.8 ms per inference. While performance was comparable across network variants, our ablation study indicates that FiLM and self-attention layers enhance generalization, a benefit most evident in the *in vivo* evaluation. Overall, these results indicate that the proposed surrogate model achieves near-FE accuracy while reducing computational cost by nearly five orders of magnitude.

3.2 Evaluation of the MWA Planning and Re-planning Solutions

The planning solution proposed in Sect. 2.4 was evaluated using real patient tumors. Only tumors treatable with a single ablation (below 40 mL including 5 mm safety margin) and lying inside the liver were considered, resulting in a total of 112 tumors. Because no clinical ground truth exists for these cases, we evaluated our method by comparing it against a standard clinical baseline. First, we performed geometric planning to determine antenna placement and used manufacturer-provided charts to select the corresponding power and duration. The surrogate model was then employed to compare the ablation outcomes of this baseline approach against our proposed optimization solution.

On the 112 tumors, the average DSC was improved from 0.62 ± 0.12 to 0.80 ± 0.07 when using optimal parameters, which substantially increases healthy tissue preservation. Likewise, the coverage was improved from an average of 0.58 ± 0.11 to 0.90 ± 0.09. Suboptimal coverage occurred primarily in tumors with elongated shapes or near the 40 mL limit, which would likely require more

Table 2. Evaluation of MWA re-planning solution. Mean relative retrieval errors for power and antenna translation for re-planning solutions based on FE and the surrogate model (NN), for three porcine *in vivo* experiments and 100 distinct initial conditions.

Experiment	Power (FE)	Power (NN)	Trans. (FE)	Trans. (NN)
Ablation 1	2.3% ±0.0%	2.6% ±0.2%	0.5% ±0.0%	0.8% ±0.0%
Ablation 2	2.3% ±0.0%	3.3% ±0.4%	2.1% ±0.0%	0.1% ±0.0%
Ablation 3	4.7% ±0.0%	4.1% ±0.4%	1.1% ±0.0%	0.1% ±0.0%

than one ablation. Nevertheless, even in these challenging cases, the proposed physics-informed planning strategy significantly outperformed a geometry-based planning approach. The algorithm found optimal solutions in less than 2 min, including at least 30 s for the geometric planning optimization. Regarding the intraoperative re-planning solution, we followed the evaluation protocol from our previous work [10]. For an *in vivo* ablation experiment with known ablation parameters, we artificially shift the antenna tip along its axis, and use the *in vivo* ablation as tumor target to solve (5). The relative errors of optimal to known ablation parameters are reported in Table 2. The proposed solution achieved results consistent to our previously proposed FE-based re-planning solution [10], but at a fraction of the time: the total optimization time was reduced from more than 50 min to approximately 30 s.

4 Conclusion

This work presents a deep learning surrogate model for predicting MWA outcomes. By leveraging a 3D U-Net architecture enhanced with FiLM conditioning and self-attention, the model effectively encodes 3D perfusion maps and procedural ablation parameters to provide patient-specific predictions in real-time. Although trained exclusively on synthetic data, the model demonstrated remarkable generalization to both *in vivo* porcine experiments and human anatomies, achieving an average DSC of 0.82 on pre-clinical data. Due to its training on a wide range of power settings and physiological conditions, the model adapts well to patient-specific variables, requiring retraining only if new antenna hardware is introduced. In the context of MWA planning, by identifying optimal, tumor-covering ablation parameters in under 2 min, our work demonstrates significant potential for clinical translation. And while our work has focused on liver MWA, our approach remains generic and extensible to other organs. Further, by priorizing classical optimization over black-box approaches, we promote interpretability: in the last iterations of the optimization loop, the surrogate model can be replaced with the FE solution to compensate for model errors. This strategy enhances reliability, a key feature for clinical applications.

A primary limitation of this work lies in its focus on single-probe configurations, whereas large or irregular tumors may require the simultaneous or sequential use of multiple antennas. Future research will extend the framework to account for cumulative thermal effects and overlapping necrosis zones. Such advancements will likely require architectural modifications to the network to handle the non-linear interactions between multiple electromagnetic sources.

Acknowledgments. This work was funded by the MEDITWIN Bpifrance i-Demo project as part of the France 2030 program. The authors would like to thank Dr. Juan Verde and the *Institut Hospitalo-Universitaire (IHU)* of Strasbourg for their support.

Disclosure of Interests. The authors have no conflict of interest to declare.

References

1. Baratta, I.A., et al: DOLFINx: the next generation FEniCS problem solving environment. preprint (2023). https://doi.org/10.5281/zenodo.10447666
2. Bošković, N., Radmilović-Radjenović, M., Radjenović, B.: Finite element analysis of microwave tumor ablation based on open-source software components. Mathematics **11**(12), 2654 (2023). https://doi.org/10.3390/math11122654
3. Debbaut, C., et al.: Analyzing the human liver vascular architecture by combining vascular corrosion casting and micro-CT scanning: a feasibility study. J. Anat. **224**(4), 509–517 (2014). https://doi.org/10.1111/joa.12156
4. Dettori, F., Nahmed, I., Duprez, M., Verde, J., Alvarez, P., Cotin, S.: Personalization of liver microwave ablation simulation. Int. J. Comput. Assist. Radiol. Surg. (2026). https://doi.org/10.1007/s11548-026-03712-1
5. Heshmat, A., et al.: Using patient-specific 3D modeling and simulations to optimize microwave ablation therapy for liver cancer. Cancers **16**(11), 2095 (2024). https://doi.org/10.3390/cancers16112095
6. Ku, M.-C., Fernández-Seara, M.A., Kober, F., Niendorf, T.: Noninvasive renal perfusion measurement using arterial spin labeling (ASL) MRI: basic concept. In: Pohlmann, A., Niendorf, T. (eds.) Preclinical MRI of the Kidney. MMB, vol. 2216, pp. 229–239. Springer, New York (2021). https://doi.org/10.1007/978-1-0716-0978-1_13
7. Lukes, A., Bale, R., Freysinger, W.: Automatic trajectory planning for stereotactic radiofrequency ablation in non-discrete search space . https://doi.org/10.1007/s11548-025-03386-1
8. Mehtali, J., Verde, J.M., Essert, C.: C-NCA: chained neural cellular automata for fast and accurate thermal ablation estimation. In: Proceedings of Medical Image Computing and Computer Assisted Intervention - MICCAI 2025, vol. LNCS 15963. Springer Nature Switzerland (2025)
9. Meister, F., et al.: Fast automatic liver tumor radiofrequency ablation planning via learned physics model. In: Wang, L., Dou, Q., Fletcher, P.T., Speidel, S., Li, S. (eds.) Medical Image Computing and Computer Assisted Intervention – MICCAI 2022, pp. 167–176. Springer Nature Switzerland. https://doi.org/10.1007/978-3-031-16449-1_17
10. Nahmed, I., Dettori, F., Verde, J., Duprez, M., Alvarez, P., Cotin, S.: A digital twin for microwave liver treatment replanning. Int. J. Comput. Assist. Radiol. Surg. (2026). https://doi.org/10.1007/s11548-026-03641-z
11. Poulou, L.S.: Percutaneous microwave ablation vs radiofrequency ablation in the treatment of hepatocellular carcinoma. World J. Hepatol. **7**(8), 1054 (2015). https://doi.org/10.4254/wjh.v7.i8.1054

12. Qiao, H., Sohail, A., Kim, P., Hübner, F., Vogl, T.J.: Intelligent ensemble learning-enhanced finite element modeling for precision thermal ablation in cancer therapy. Comput. Methods Programs Biomed. **274**, 109157 (2026). https://doi.org/10.1016/j.cmpb.2025.109157
13. Shin, M., et al.: PhysRFANet: physics-guided neural network for real-time prediction of thermal effect during radiofrequency ablation treatment **138**, 109349. https://doi.org/10.1016/j.engappai.2024.109349
14. Singh, S., Melnik, R.: Thermal ablation of biological tissues in disease treatment: a review of computational models and future directions. Electromagn. Biol. Med. **39**(2), 49–88 (2020). https://doi.org/10.1080/15368378.2020.1741383
15. Soler, L., et al.: 3D image reconstruction for comparison of algorithm database: a patient-specific anatomical and medical image database. Tech. rep., IRCAD, Strasbourg, France (2010). https://www.ircad.fr/research/data-sets/liver-segmentation-3d-ircadb-01/
16. Sugimoto, K., et al.: Microwave ablation vs. single-needle radiofrequency ablation for the treatment of HCC up to 4 cm: a randomized-controlled trial. JHEP Rep. **7**(1), 101269 (2025). https://doi.org/10.1016/j.jhepr.2024.101269
17. Wang, Y., Hobbs, B.P., Ng, C.S.: CT perfusion characteristics identify metastatic sites in liver. Biomed. Res. Int. (2015). https://doi.org/10.1155/2015/120749
18. Winokur, R.S., et al.: Characterization of in vivo ablation zones following percutaneous microwave ablation of the liver with two commercially available devices: are manufacturer published reference values useful? J. Vasc. Interv. Radiol. **25**(12), 1939-1946.e1 (2014). https://doi.org/10.1016/j.jvir.2014.08.014

Agent-Guided Relational Concept Discovery: Toward Interpretable Surgical Margin Assessment

Nooshin Maghsoodi(✉), Amoon Jamzad, Robert Policelli, Mohammad Farahmand, Dilakshan Srikanthan, Martin Kaufmann, Kevin Y. M. Ren, Shaila Merchant, Sonal Varma, Ross Walker, Doug McKay, John Rudan, Gabor Fichtinger, and Parvin Mousavi

Queen's University, Kingston, ON, Canada
nooshin.maghsoodi@queensu.ca

Abstract. Deep learning models can effectively use Rapid Evaporative Ionization Mass Spectrometry (REIMS) data for surgical margin assessment. However, their clinical adoption remains challenging due to limited generalization to operating room conditions. This difficulty arises because models are typically trained on labeled spectra collected from resected tissue samples, while they must operate on noisy, unlabeled data acquired directly during surgery. In addition, the black-box nature of deep learning models makes it difficult to understand and systematically improve their behavior. Concept-based learning offers a promising way to address these challenges by mapping raw measurements to human-understandable concepts. However, supervised concept-based approaches rely on concept annotations, which are difficult to obtain in complex mass spectrometry workflows. We propose Agent-Guided Concept Discovery, a framework that learns meaningful concepts directly from data without requiring predefined concept labels. During training, a reasoning agent refines semantic descriptions of the learned concepts and adaptively adjusts their weight based on diagnostic relevance. These concepts are further grounded using a biochemical knowledge graph to ensure consistency with known metabolic relationships. Across Skin and Breast Cancer datasets, our model improves balanced accuracy and sensitivity over the baseline. In a representative intraoperative case, it shows fewer false positives, indicating better generalization to surgical conditions.

Keywords: Agentic AI · Concept Learning · Mass Spectrometry

1 Introduction

Achieving clear surgical margins has a significant impact on cancer outcomes. Negative margins indicate that no malignant cells remain at the boundary of the excised tissue, suggesting that the tumor has been fully removed and reducing the risk of residual disease. Today, margin status is typically determined

G. Yang et al. (Eds.): MICCAI 2026, LNCS 16893, pp. 13–22, 2027.
https://doi.org/10.1007/978-3-032-38236-8_2

postoperatively by histopathology, leaving no opportunity for intraoperative adjustment. In contrast, real-time margin assessment allows surgeons to course-correct during resection, both avoiding cutting through the tumor and minimizing unnecessary removal of healthy tissue [10]. Rapid Evaporative Ionization Mass Spectrometry (REIMS) enables intraoperative feedback by providing instantaneous metabolomic profiles from cauterized tissue, which can be classified using machine learning to identify cancer at the point of incision [1].

Prior works have explored multiple strategies to improve REIMS-based margin assessment, including Bayesian neural networks for uncertainty estimation and image-based representations of mass spectra [6,8]. More recently, a foundation model pretrained on large-scale tandem mass spectrometry data, Deep Representations Empowering the Annotation of Mass Spectra (DreaMS) [5], has been proposed and later adapted for REIMS applications [7]. However, fine-tuning this foundation model on small, labeled ex vivo REIMS datasets risks overfitting and limits generalization to noisy intraoperative data. Moreover, despite strong performance, these models largely remain black boxes, offering limited insight into the biochemical drivers of their predictions.

Concept-based learning offers a promising alternative to purely end-to-end classification. Rather than mapping raw spectra directly to diagnostic labels, these models introduce an intermediate representation composed of human-understandable variables [13]. Related approaches further show how such high-level concepts can provide meaningful evidence for interpreting model behavior and predictions [12,17]. However, existing supervised frameworks depend on manually defined concept annotations, which are impractical in complex mass spectrometry workflows.

To address these challenges, we propose Agent-Guided Relational Concept Discovery, a framework for interpretable surgical margin assessment. We introduce a reasoning-agent-in-the-loop training framework that enables automatic discovery of discriminative concepts without requiring concept annotations. The agent analyzes shared spectral patterns, assigns semantic descriptions, and adaptively adjusts the relevance of concepts. These concepts are further grounded using a knowledge graph to ensure consistency with established metabolic pathways. Our main contributions are summarized as follows:

1. *Agent-Guided Concept Discovery without Supervision.* A reasoning agent is incorporated into the training loop to help the model discover and refine meaningful latent representations from embeddings without requiring manual annotations. This is achieved through two key contributions below.
2. *Relational Concept Modeling via Knowledge Graph Construction.* The agent receives the most informative spectral patterns associated with each learned concept and then queries metabolic databases to ground these concepts in biological knowledge. These links generate a knowledge graph connecting concepts to metabolites, pathways, and tissue states, which evolves during training to capture relationships and support more consistent agent feedback.
3. *Reasoning-Driven Concept Weight Optimization.* During training, the agent aggregates supporting evidence to provide feedback on the relevance of the

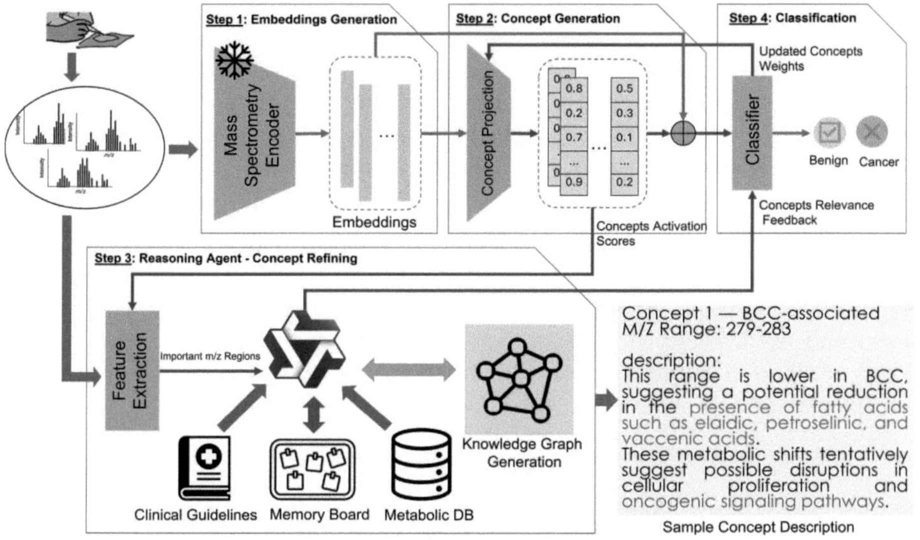

Fig. 1. REIMS spectra are encoded to obtain latent embeddings, which are mapped to concept activations. Samples with high concept activation are analyzed to identify discriminative spectral features. A reasoning agent integrates this information with biochemical knowledge bases to ground the learned concepts, construct a relational knowledge graph, and iteratively refine concepts during training.

learned concepts. This feedback is incorporated into an auxiliary alignment loss, which guides the learning of the concept weights.

2 Materials and Methods

2.1 Data

Ex Vivo Data: Ex vivo REIMS spectra were collected from two surgical oncology cohorts at Kingston Health Sciences Center under institutional ethics approval, with written informed consent obtained from all participants. The basal cell carcinoma (BCC) dataset includes 693 annotated burns from 91 patients (252 tumors, 441 benign), acquired from freshly excised specimens. The breast cancer dataset comprises 144 ex vivo burns from 11 patients (41 tumors, 103 benign), sampled from malignant tissue and adjacent benign parenchyma using the same REIMS protocol.

Intraoperative Data: Intraoperative data were collected during a breast-conserving surgery. Over a 27-min procedure, 1,616 spectra were recorded at 1 Hz and labeled using intraoperative surgical annotations.

2.2 Proposed Model

Figure 1 provides an overview of the proposed framework and its main components. The model is designed to jointly perform surgical margin classification while learning interpretable concepts based on a biochemical knowledge base. The overall pipeline consists of the following components.

Step 1: Embedding Generation via Foundation Model. In the first step, we use the DreaMS foundation model [5] to process raw REIMS spectra. Due to the limited size of our labeled REIMS dataset, the DreaMS parameters are kept frozen and used solely as a feature extractor. For each input spectrum x_i, the model produces a d-dimensional embedding, z_i, which serves as the input to the concept embedding layer.

$$z_i = f_{\text{DreaMS}}(x_i) \in \mathbb{R}^d. \tag{1}$$

Step 2: Concept Embedding Layer. The embedding z_i is mapped to a set of K latent concepts through a learnable linear projection layer, forming an explicit concept bottleneck. Each concept k is parameterized by a weight vector w_k and a bias term b_k. For sample i, the projection first produces an unbounded concept activation score s_{ik}:

$$s_{ik} = w_k^\top z_i + b_k, \qquad p_{ik} = \sigma(s_{ik}). \tag{2}$$

Since s_{ik} is unbounded, its scale may vary across concepts and samples. Therefore, s_{ik} is passed through a sigmoid function to obtain the bounded activation value p_{ik}. These bounded values p_{ik} are only for ranking spectra for feature extraction, whereas the classifier uses the corresponding unbounded logits to preserve information.

To encourage separation between concept directions, the concept vectors $\{w_k\}_{k=1}^K$ are initialized using a cosine-similarity-based criterion. This initialization discourages highly similar concept vectors at the start of training, reducing redundancy in the initial concept space while allowing related concepts to become correlated during optimization when supported by the data.

Step 3: Reasoning Agent for Concept Refinement. To convert concept activations into biologically meaningful representations, we integrate a reasoning agent into the training loop.

Discriminative Spectral Region Identification. Each mass spectrum represents ion intensity over mass-to-charge ratios, denoted by m/z. Since cancer and normal tissues can differ in molecular composition, they may show distinct intensity patterns across specific m/z regions. The feature extraction module associates each learned concept with discriminative m/z ranges by contrasting spectra with high and low concept activation scores. Thus, concepts that were initially numerical parameters in Step 2 become linked to interpretable m/z regions.

Biochemical Grounding. The agent analyzes the identified m/z regions by querying biochemical knowledge bases to retrieve candidate metabolites and pathways. We use RaMP [2,18] as the primary resource, which integrates metabolite identifiers, pathways, and chemical annotations across curated databases. The agent is additionally guided by text-based domain guidelines distilled from free biochemical and clinical resources and the literature [3,9,11,16].

Memory and Knowledge Graph Construction. The agent maintains an external memory that records concept information across epochs, including associated m/z regions, relevance feedback, and classification outcomes. For each candidate concept, overlapping concepts from previous epochs are retrieved and provided to the LLM to improve the consistency of feedback. The agent also updates a concept-level knowledge graph that links concepts to metabolites, pathways, and tissue pathological states, thereby supporting biological interpretation and concept refinement.

Description and Relevance Feedback. Based on this analysis, the agent provides (i) *textual descriptions* that associate concepts with putative metabolic classes, and (ii) *concept relevance* as directional feedback (*more relevant, less relevant*) based on biochemical consistency, historical trends from the memory board, and impact on classification.

Step 4: Agent-Guided Concept Alignment Loss. As mentioned, the model discovers K meaningful concepts from the training data. However, in biochemical analysis, different spectral patterns or m/z regions contribute unequally to tissue characterization and diagnosis [3,11]. Motivated by this, we allow each learned concept to have a distinct weight on the final prediction.

To explicitly control the contribution of each concept, we associate it with a learnable scalar weight parameter α_k. To ensure interpretability and numerical stability, concept weight parameters are constrained to the range $[0,1]$ using a sigmoid reparameterization. The gated concept signal, $\tilde{s}_{ik}$, is then defined as

$$\alpha_k = \sigma(a_k), \quad a_k \in \mathbb{R}, \qquad \tilde{s}_{ik} = \alpha_k \, s_{ik}. \tag{3}$$

The classifier receives both the global embedding and the gated concept signals as input. Specifically, the predicted output for sample i is given by

$$\hat{y}_i = g([\, z_i \;\; \tilde{s}_{i1} \;\; \tilde{s}_{i2} \;\; \dots \;\; \tilde{s}_{iK} \,]), \tag{4}$$

where $g(\cdot)$ represents the classification head. To align the model's use of concepts with the reasoning agent's feedback, we introduce an alignment loss based on a perturbation-based relevance measure inspired by [14]. For each sample i and concept k, we measure the change in the predicted probability when the contribution of concept k is removed from the classifier input.

$$\Delta Y_{ik} = \left| \hat{y}_i - \hat{y}_{i\,(\tilde{s}_{ik} \to 0)} \right| . \tag{5}$$

A larger ΔY_{ik} indicates that the prediction for sample i depends more strongly on concept k.

Based on the reasoning agent's feedback, concepts are grouped into high-relevance concepts $\mathcal{K}_H$ and low-relevance concepts $\mathcal{K}_L$. The sample-level alignment loss is defined as:

$$\mathcal{L}_{\text{align}}^{(i)} = \sum_{k \in \mathcal{K}_H} (1 - \Delta Y_{ik}) + \sum_{k \in \mathcal{K}_L} \Delta Y_{ik}. \tag{6}$$

The alignment loss, $\mathcal{L}_{\text{align}}$, is obtained by averaging $\mathcal{L}_{\text{align}}^{(i)}$ over the batch. The final objective combines classification loss with agent-guided alignment, where $\mathcal{L}_{\text{class}}$ is binary cross-entropy and $\lambda \geq 0$ controls the alignment strength.

$$\mathcal{L}_{\text{total}} = \mathcal{L}_{\text{class}} + \lambda \, \mathcal{L}_{\text{align}}. \tag{7}$$

Table 1. Classification performance (mean ± standard deviation over 30 runs) on REIMS datasets.

Data	Method	Bal. Acc.	Sens.	Spec.	AUROC
Skin Cancer	Transformer	0.74±0.027	**0.72**±0.111	0.76±0.084	0.85±0.015
	DreaMS [5]	0.71±0.034	0.59±0.086	**0.83**±0.054	0.83±0.014
	Our method	**0.76±0.026**	0.70±**0.043**	0.82±**0.031**	**0.86±0.013**
Breast Cancer	Transformer	0.82±0.035	0.78±0.216	0.86±0.062	0.93±0.021
	DreaMS [5]	0.84±0.028	0.80±0.051	0.89±0.026	0.96±0.012
	Our method	**0.87±0.018**	**0.81±0.044**	**0.93±0.024**	**0.98±0.013**

2.3 Experiments

Our experiments consist of the following evaluations: (i) *Classification performance comparison.* We compare the proposed framework against a DreaMS-based baseline that performs classification on foundation model embeddings, on two REIMS mass spectrometry datasets. (ii) *Concept quality evaluation.* We assess interpretability and biological relevance by examining how concept activations vary with hormone receptor status and align with established metabolic pathways. (iii) *Generalization to intraoperative data.* We assess by evaluating performance on an in vivo REIMS case acquired during surgery. (iv) *Ablation studies.* We analyze the contribution of key components by ablating biochemical knowledge base integration and knowledge graph grounding.

Implementation Details. The reasoning agent uses `Qwen2.5-7B-Instruct` as the backbone LLM. Datasets are split into training, validation, and test sets using patient-wise stratification, ensuring no patient overlap between training and test samples. The model learns $K = 8$ concepts and is trained with Adam for up to 40 epochs, using a learning rate of 10^{-3} and a batch size of 32. We set $\lambda = 0.5$ and update the agent every three epochs. Hyperparameters are selected on the validation set. All experiments are repeated 30 times, with results reported as mean and standard deviation. The code and configuration files used in this study are publicly available at: https://github.com/nooshinmaghsoodi/cem-qwen-reims.

3 Results and Discussion

Classification Performance Comparison. The classification results are shown in Table 1. Overall, the proposed model outperforms the DreaMS baseline across both datasets. This indicates that incorporating agent-guided concept embeddings, aimed at improving generalization and interpretability, does not sacrifice classification performance and can even improve it. On the Skin Cancer dataset, we observe an approximate 7% relative improvement in balanced accuracy, along with higher AUROC and a noticeable increase in sensitivity, suggesting improved detection of tumor tissue. Similarly, on the Breast Cancer dataset, our method achieves higher balanced accuracy (0.87) while also improving both sensitivity and specificity.

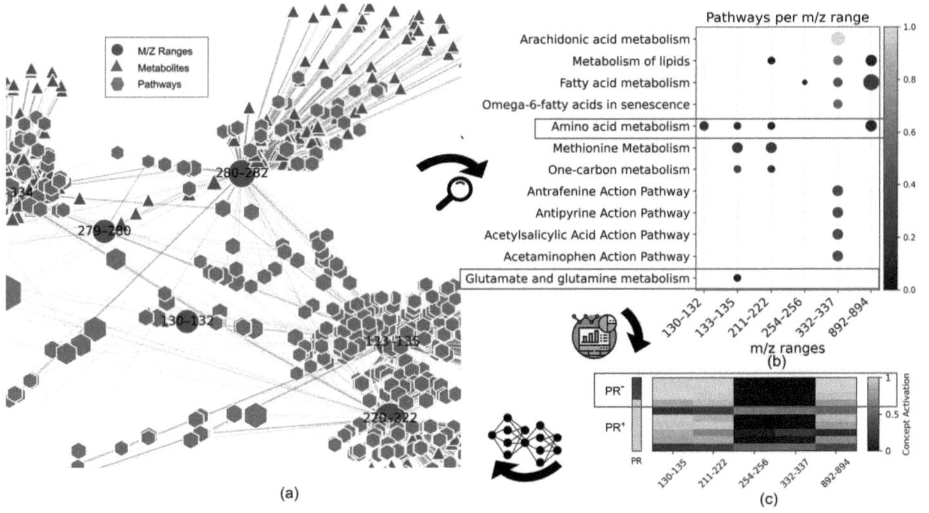

Fig. 2. (a) Breast cancer knowledge graph linking m/z ranges, metabolites, and pathways. (b) Zoomed-in selected pathways for some m/z ranges in (a). (c) Concept activations across tumor samples with their Progesterone Receptor (PR) status.

Clinical Evaluation of Concepts. Figure 2 illustrates how the learned concepts are grounded in biochemical knowledge. Figure 2(a) shows a portion of the Breast Cancer knowledge graph linking informative *m/z* ranges to candidate metabolites and pathways discovered during training. A zoomed-in view from this knowledge graph is shown in Fig. 2(b), highlighting selected m/z ranges and some of their associated pathways, enabling assessment of clinical relevance. We evaluated this relevance by analyzing concept activation scores for tumor samples in the Breast Cancer test set. Figure 2(c) shows the activation of selected concepts together with progesterone receptor (PR) status. Prior studies [4,15] report that PR-negative breast cancers are associated with glutamine metabolism and increased amino acids. Consistent with these findings, Fig. 2(b) highlights amino acid- and glutamine-related pathways linked to the m/z subbands 130–135, 211–222, and 892–894, while Fig. 2(c) shows higher activation of these subbands in PR-negative samples. This consistency supports the biological relevance of the learned concepts and demonstrates the interpretability enabled by the generated knowledge graph.

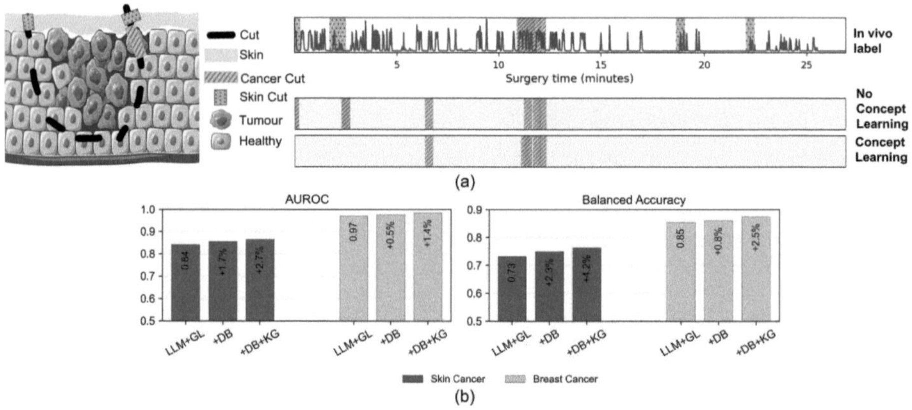

Fig. 3. (a) Intraoperative breast cancer example. The x-axis denotes surgery time. Striped red regions indicate surgeon-noted tumors, while dotted purple regions correspond to skin cuts. (b) Ablation study on both datasets, as metabolic database querying (DB) and knowledge graph reasoning (KG) are added to support the agent + clinical guidelines (GL). Values indicate relative performance gains. (Color figure online)

Generalization to Intraoperative Data. Figure 3(a) shows model predictions on a representative intraoperative breast cancer case with surgeon-provided call-out labels. Stripped red overlaid regions denote the tumor, and dotted purple regions denote the skin cuts during incision. While both models achieve perfect tumor sensitivity, the concept-enhanced model produces fewer false positives than the baseline, particularly in skin regions with tumor-like signatures. This suggests that incorporating biologically aware concepts helps the model better distinguish tumor tissue from skin.

Ablation Study. Ablation study results are shown in Fig. 3(b). In this experiment, components that support the reasoning agent are incrementally added to analyze the effects of the metabolic database and the knowledge graph. Incorporating the metabolic database improves classification performance, with additional gains observed when the knowledge graph is introduced. These effects are more observable on the skin dataset, where the largest relative improvements are observed in balanced accuracy, indicating improved sensitivity to tumor-related spectral patterns. We believe that adding the guideline component alone primarily helps reduce hallucinated semantic explanations generated by the agent.

4 Conclusion

In our proposed framework, an agent operates within the training loop to help the model discover meaningful concepts without explicit concept annotations, aiming to improve interpretability and strengthen generalization. This approach extends models trained on ex vivo data to challenging intraoperative settings while making their decisions easier to understand. The model learns high-level metabolic concepts and directly integrates them into the prediction process, grounding decisions in patterns that remain stable under intraoperative noise. In addition, a dynamically constructed, data-specific knowledge graph reveals underlying biochemical structure and supports iterative interpretation and concept refinement beyond what fixed rule-based systems can provide. A current limitation is the reliance on general metabolic database queries; future work will explore more targeted querying strategies and the integration of gene-level information to further enhance biological specificity and interpretability.

Acknowledgments. This work was supported in part by the Natural Sciences and Engineering Research Council of Canada (NSERC); the Canadian Institutes of Health Research (CIHR); and the Vector Institute. The work of Parvin Mousavi was supported in part by a Canada CIFAR AI Chair and a Canada Research Chair.

Disclosure of Interests. The authors have no competing interests.

References

1. Balog, J., et al.: Intraoperative tissue identification using rapid evaporative ionization mass spectrometry. Sci. Transl. Med. **5**(194), 194ra93–194ra93 (2013)
2. Braisted, J., et al.: RaMP-DB 2.0: a renovated knowledgebase for deriving biological and chemical insight from metabolites, proteins, and genes. Bioinformatics **39**(1), btac726 (2023)
3. Brorsen, L.F., et al.: Metabolomic profiling and accurate diagnosis of basal cell carcinoma by MALDI imaging and machine learning. Exp. Dermatol. **33**(7), e15141 (2024)
4. Budczies, J., et al.: Glutamate enrichment as new diagnostic opportunity in breast cancer. Int. J. Cancer **136**(7), 1619–1628 (2015)

5. Bushuiev, R., Bushuiev, A., Samusevich, R., Brungs, C., Sivic, J., Pluskal, T.: Self-supervised learning of molecular representations from millions of tandem mass spectra using DreaMS. Nat. Biotechnol. **44**(4), 630–640 (2026)
6. Connolly, L., et al.: ImSpect: image-driven self-supervised learning for surgical margin evaluation with mass spectrometry. Int. J. Comput. Assist. Radiol. Surg. **19**(6), 1129–1136 (2024)
7. Farahmand, M., et al.: FACT: foundation model for assessing cancer tissue margins with mass spectrometry. Int. J. Comput. Assist. Radiol. Surg. **20**(6), 1097–1104 (2025)
8. Fooladgar, F., et al.: Uncertainty estimation for margin detection in cancer surgery using mass spectrometry. Int. J. Comput. Assist. Radiol. Surg. **17**(12), 2305–2313 (2022)
9. Fu, Y., et al.: Lipid metabolism in cancer progression and therapeutic strategies. MedComm **2**(1), 27–59 (2021)
10. Jamzad, A., et al.: Improved resection margins in surgical oncology using intraoperative mass spectrometry. In: Martel, A.L., et al. (eds.) MICCAI 2020. LNCS, vol. 12263, pp. 44–53. Springer, Cham (2020). https://doi.org/10.1007/978-3-030-59716-0_5
11. Kaufmann, M., et al.: Testing of rapid evaporative mass spectrometry for histological tissue classification and molecular diagnostics in a multi-site study. Br. J. Cancer **131**, 1298–1308 (2024)
12. Kim, B., et al.: Interpretability beyond feature attribution: quantitative testing with concept activation vectors (TCAV). In: Proceedings of the 35th International Conference on Machine Learning. Proceedings of Machine Learning Research, vol. 80, pp. 2668–2677. PMLR (2018)
13. Koh, P.W., et al.: Concept bottleneck models. In: Proceedings of the 37th International Conference on Machine Learning. Proceedings of Machine Learning Research, vol. 119, pp. 5338–5348. PMLR (2020)
14. Pang, W., Ke, X., Tsutsui, S., Wen, B.: Integrating clinical knowledge into concept bottleneck models. In: Medical Image Computing and Computer Assisted Intervention – MICCAI 2024. Lecture Notes in Computer Science, vol. 15004, pp. 243–253. Springer (2024)
15. Shahnazari, P., Kavousi, K., Khorram Khorshid, H.R., Minuchehr, Z., Goliaei, B., Salek, M., R.: Uncovering subtype-specific metabolic signatures in breast cancer through multimodal integration, attention-based deep learning, and self-organizing maps. Sci. Rep. **15**(1), 21775 (2025)
16. Thomsen, A.A., Rabjerg, M., Marcussen, N., Lund, L., Jensen, O.N.: Mass spectrometry and machine learning for classification and molecular phenotyping of renal cell carcinoma and benign tumors. medRxiv (2026). https://doi.org/10.64898/2026.01.13.26343935
17. Yuksekgonul, M., Wang, M., Zou, J.: Post-hoc concept bottleneck models. In: The Eleventh International Conference on Learning Representations (2023)
18. Zhang, B., Hu, S., Baskin, E., Patt, A., Siddiqui, J.K., Mathé, E.A.: RaMP: a comprehensive relational database of metabolomics pathways for pathway enrichment analysis of genes and metabolites. Metabolites **8**(1), 16 (2018)

All-in-One Augmented Reality Guided Head and Neck Tumor Resection

Yue Yang[1], Matthieu Chabanas[1], Carrie Reale[2], Annie Benson[3], Jason Slagle[2], Matthew Weinger[2], Michael Topf[2], and Jie Ying Wu[1](✉)

[1] Department of Computer Science, Vanderbilt University, Nashville, TN 37235, USA
jieying.wu@vanderbilt.edu
[2] Vanderbilt University Medical Center, Nashville, TN 37232, USA
[3] Department of Biomedical Engineering, Vanderbilt University, Nashville, TN 37235, USA

Abstract. Positive margins are common in head and neck squamous cell carcinoma, yet intraoperative re-resection is often imprecise because margin locations are typically communicated verbally from pathology. We present an all-in-one augmented reality (AR) system that relocalizes positive margins from a resected specimen to the resection bed and visualizes them in situ using HoloLens 2 depth sensing and fully automated markerless surface registration. In a silicone phantom study with six medical trainees, markerless registration achieved target registration errors comparable to a marker-based baseline (median 1.8 mm vs. 1.7 mm; maximum < 4 mm). In a margin relocalization task, AR guidance reduced error from verbal guidance (median 14.2 mm) to a few millimeters (median 3.2 mm), with all AR localizations within 5 mm error. These results support the feasibility of markerless AR margin guidance for more precise intraoperative re-resection.

Keywords: Augmented Reality · Markerless Registration · Head and Neck Cancer · Surgical Margins · Intraoperative Guidance

1 Introduction

Head and neck squamous cell carcinoma (HNSCC) affects hundreds of thousands of patients each year [1] and has one of the highest rates of positive surgical margins among solid tumors [8], contributing to local recurrence and poor outcomes. Intraoperative frozen section analysis is used in over 90% of cases [4], and a positive margin requires the surgeon to re-resect accurately by relocating its position. This is challenging due to complex anatomy and specimen disorientation. In practice, pathologists convey margin locations verbally, which provides only coarse spatial guidance [6]; consequently, re-resections are often imprecise, and only about 20–30% of re-resection specimens contain residual tumor [9].

Augmented reality (AR) head-mounted displays can overlay margin information directly in the surgical field [11]. Prior head-and-neck margin pilots demonstrated feasibility but relied on manual alignment [7,11] or marker-based

G. Yang et al. (Eds.): MICCAI 2026, LNCS 16893, pp. 23–31, 2027.
https://doi.org/10.1007/978-3-032-38236-8_3

registration [2], which can add setup steps, sterile-field clutter, and workflow burden. Recent work on deformable AR guidance for head-and-neck resection focuses on tissue deformation but still requires additional registration cues such as fiducials [13]. In contrast, our focus is specimen-to-resection-bed relocalization of small head-and-neck surfaces using only the AR point-of-view time-of-flight depth sensor for sensing.

Here, we present an all-in-one markerless AR margin guidance system that registers the resected specimen back to the resection bed using geometric data and visualizes positive-margin locations in situ. The technical contribution is an automated AR-only workflow that combines curvature-biased sampling, global alignment, automatic coarse-pose ROI cropping, and point-to-plane iterative closest point (ICP) for small specimen-to-bed registration. We evaluate the system on a silicone face phantom with quantitative registration measurements and a user study with five residents and one medical student, comparing AR-guided versus verbal margin relocation.

2 Methods

As shown in Fig. 1(a), in a phantom scenario, our system relocalizes a positive margin by scanning the specimen, capturing the resection bed with the HoloLens 2 Articulated HAndTracking (AHAT) depth sensor, performing fully automated markerless registration, and rendering the annotated margin in AR. The AHAT sensor also continuously tracks a stylus for quantitative evaluation.

We define right-handed coordinate frames: Head-Mounted Display (HMD) world W, AHAT depth sensor D, resection bed R, specimen scan S, and tool T. A rigid transform from frame X to Y is ${}^{Y}T_{X} \in SE(3)$.

The AR overlay requires placing the specimen scan in the world frame:

$$ {}^{W}T_{S} = {}^{W}T_{D}\,{}^{D}T_{R}\,{}^{R}T_{S} \quad \Leftrightarrow \quad {}^{D}T_{S} = \underbrace{{}^{D}T_{R}}_{T_{DR}}\;\underbrace{{}^{R}T_{S}}_{T_{RS}}, \tag{1} $$

${}^{W}T_{D}$ is provided by HoloLens tracking; ${}^{D}T_{R}$ is known from our depth-fusion reference; and the only unknown is ${}^{R}T_{S}$, estimated by markerless surface registration. Any annotated margin point $\mathbf{x}_S$ is visualized by $\mathbf{x}_W = {}^{W}T_{S}\,\tilde{\mathbf{x}}_S$.

2.1 Resection-Bed and Specimen Surface Acquisition

Resection Bed. The surgeon or resident looks at the exposed cavity for ~3 s while AHAT depth frames are streamed. Each frame is back-projected to 3D and fused into a fixed resection-bed reference frame R using the HMD pose, followed by voxel downsampling and outlier removal to obtain a denoised bed cloud $\mathcal{P}_R = \{\mathbf{p}_i\}_{i=1}^{N_R}$ with normals $\mathbf{n}_{\mathbf{p}_i}$. Because AHAT depth accuracy can vary with surface properties [3], we performed a one-time local depth correction during setup [14]. We used a tracked stylus to sample the local phantom surface. We then paired the nearest AHAT depth points with the stylus contact points, and a least-squares singular value decomposition rigid correction was applied to the cloud.

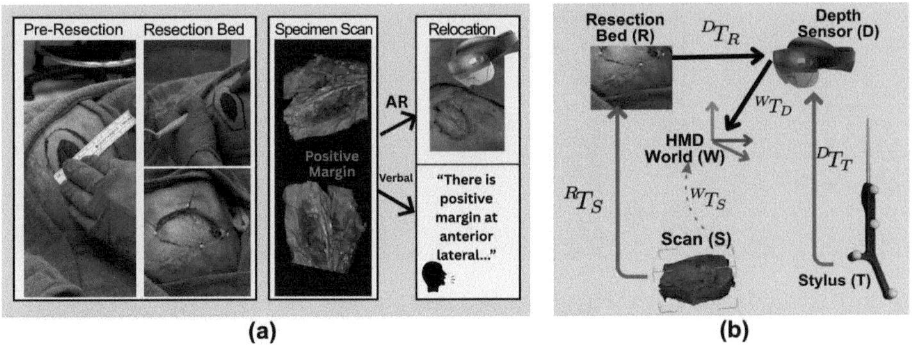

Fig. 1. System pipeline and coordinates: (a) AR-guided vs. traditional margin relocalization workflow. (b) System formulation.

Specimen Scan. The excised specimen is 3D scanned to obtain a point cloud (or mesh sampled to points) $\mathcal{P}_S = \{\mathbf{q}_j\}_{j=1}^{N_S}$ in frame S, along with a margin annotation defined on the scan.

2.2 Fully Automated Markerless Specimen-to-Bed Registration

We eliminate the manual ROI selection required by prior work [14] by (i) improving global registration robustness for small targets (2–4 cm specimens) and (ii) automatically constructing a tight refinement ROI from the coarse pose.

Coarse Global Registration. We compute local curvature scores $k(\cdot)$ on $\mathcal{P}_R$ and $\mathcal{P}_S$, and bias keypoint sampling toward landmark-rich regions:

$$\mathbb{P}(\mathbf{p}_i) \propto \frac{k(\mathbf{p}_i)}{\sum_{m=1}^{N_R} k(\mathbf{p}_m)}. \tag{2}$$

We compute Fast Point Feature Histograms descriptors $\phi(\cdot)$ at sampled points and generate putative correspondences by nearest-neighbor matching in descriptor space [10]:

$$\mathcal{C} = \{(i,j) \mid \|\phi(\mathbf{p}_i) - \phi(\mathbf{q}_j)\| < \tau\}. \tag{3}$$

To tolerate the high outlier rates typical for small anatomical surfaces, we estimate ${}^{R}T_S$ using a TEASER++-style truncated least-squares objective with correspondence weights w_{ij} [12]:

$$\min_{\mathbf{R}\in SO(3),\, \mathbf{t}\in\mathbb{R}^3} \sum_{(i,j)\in\mathcal{C}} w_{ij} \min\Big(\big\|\mathbf{p}_i - (\mathbf{R}\mathbf{q}_j + \mathbf{t})\big\|^2,\ \epsilon^2\Big). \tag{4}$$

As in TEASER++, we use translation-invariant pairwise differences to decouple translation from rotation:

$$\Delta\mathbf{p}_{ik} = \mathbf{p}_i - \mathbf{p}_k, \qquad \Delta\mathbf{q}_{j\ell} = \mathbf{q}_j - \mathbf{q}_\ell, \qquad \Delta\mathbf{p}_{ik} \approx \mathbf{R}\Delta\mathbf{q}_{j\ell} \text{ (inliers)}. \tag{5}$$

This yields a coarse estimate ${}^{R}T_S^{\text{coarse}}$ without any user input.

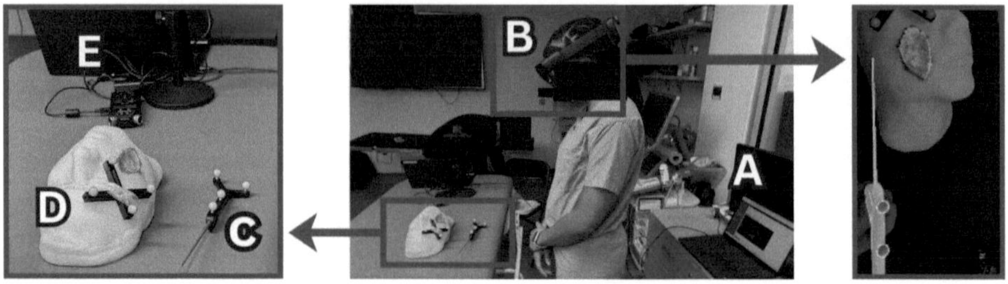

Fig. 2. User study setup: (A) Mixed-reality capture, (B) HMD, (C) tracked stylus, (D) phantom (marker + markerless), (E) close-up mic/camera.

Automatic ROI Construction. Instead of a user-defined ROI, we improved prior work by [14]. Let $\hat{\mathbf{q}}_j = \mathbf{R}^{\text{coarse}}\mathbf{q}_j + \mathbf{t}^{\text{coarse}}$ be specimen points in R. We form Axis-Aligned Bounding Box (AABB)

$$\mathcal{B} = \text{Dilate}\big(\text{AABB}(\{\hat{\mathbf{q}}_j\}),\, m\big), \tag{6}$$

and automatically crop the bed points for ICP:

$$\mathcal{P}_R^{\text{ICP}} = \{\mathbf{p} \in \mathcal{P}_R \mid \mathbf{p} \in \mathcal{B}\}. \tag{7}$$

This focuses computation on the small target structure and prevents false matches elsewhere in the scene, without any manual selection.

Fine Registration. Starting from ${}^{R}T_S^{\text{coarse}}$, we refine with point-to-plane ICP on $\mathcal{P}_R^{\text{ICP}}$ [15]:

$$\min_{\mathbf{R}\in SO(3),\, \mathbf{t}\in\mathbb{R}^3} \sum_{(\mathbf{p},\mathbf{q})\in\mathcal{C}_k} w_{\mathbf{pq}}\Big[\big(\mathbf{R}\mathbf{q}+\mathbf{t}-\mathbf{p}\big)^{\top}\mathbf{n}_{\mathbf{p}}\Big]^2, \tag{8}$$

with robust weights and outlier rejection. The output is ${}^{R}T_S^{\text{final}} \equiv T_{RS}$, used in (1) for AR overlay of the specimen and its annotated positive margin.

We further track a stylus/tool instrumented with retro-reflective markers using the STTAR algorithm [5]. STTAR estimates the tool pose in the AHAT sensor frame as $T_{TS} \equiv {}^{D}T_T$ at runtime. Continuous tool tracking in the world frame is obtained by composing with HMD tracking:

$$T_{TW} \equiv {}^{W}T_T = {}^{W}T_D\,{}^{D}T_T. \tag{9}$$

STTAR reports sub-millimeter accuracy, enabling reliable quantitative evaluation of margin relocalization.

2.3 Evaluation Protocol and Metrics

As shown in Fig. 2, the system was evaluated on a silicone head-and-neck phantom with an artificial cheek tumor resected to create a cavity and specimen. A

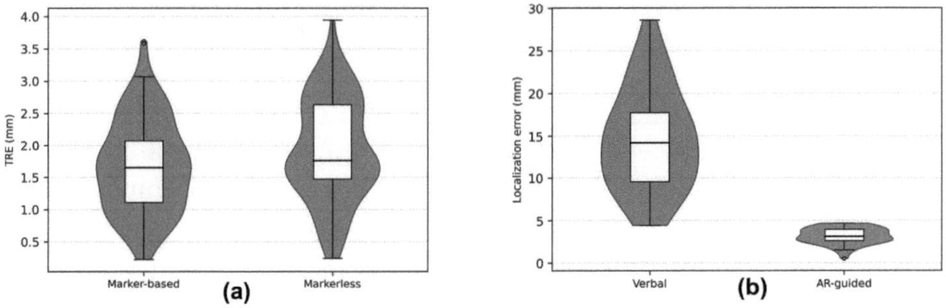

Fig. 3. (a) TRE for marker vs. markerless registration. (b) Margin relocalization error for verbal vs. AR guidance.

structured-light scan provided the specimen model for AR visualization. Participants wore a Microsoft HoloLens 2 and completed two tasks under counterbalanced marker-based and markerless registration conditions. The marker-based baseline used a rigid retro-reflective marker tracked by AR [5]; the markerless condition estimated T_{RS} using the automated pipeline in Sect. 2.2.

Target locations were predefined ink landmarks on the phantom and annotated in the structured-light scan. Similar distractor marks were included to blind participants to the ground-truth locations during verbal localization. Expert stylus touches were used only to digitize reference landmark coordinates and reduce tracking noise.

In the point-matching task, participants touched 19 AR targets on the resection surface with a tracked stylus. Target registration error (TRE) was the Euclidean distance to the corresponding reference landmark. In the margin-relocation task, participants localized six simulated positive margins using either surgeon-scripted verbal guidance simulating the current clinical standard or AR guidance showing a 5 mm green target. We report median, interquartile range, RMSE, maximum/Hausdorff error, and 5 mm coverage (Cov_5). Registration conditions were compared with exact paired Wilcoxon signed-rank tests and rank-biserial effect sizes. Margin-relocation performance was compared using paired t-tests on participant-level medians with Cohen's d_z. NASA-TLX, SUS, and AR-specific ratings were exploratory subjective outcomes.

3 Results

Registration Accuracy. Participants included five ENT trainees (PGY-1 to PGY-5+) and one medical student ($M_{\text{age}} = 30.3$ years, range: 27–33; 4/6 female). All five trainees reported low prior VR/AR experience, whereas the medical student had previously used AR in a work scenario. In the point-matching task, each participant localized 19 targets, yielding 114 point targets per registration method. Figure 3(a) shows the TRE distributions for marker-based and markerless registration, with detailed participant-level metrics reported in Table 1. Across all targets, marker-based and markerless regis-

Table 1. Participant-level and group-level performance. Distances are in mm and Cov_5 is in %.

(a) Registration (point matching): marker-based vs. markerless.

User	Marker-based reg.				Markerless reg.			
	Med [Q1,Q3]	RMSE	Haus	Cov_5	Med [Q1,Q3]	RMSE	Haus	Cov_5
P1	2.4 [1.8,2.7]	2.4	3.6	100.0	2.5 [2.1,2.8]	2.5	3.5	100.0
P2	1.3 [1.1,1.6]	1.4	2.1	100.0	1.7 [1.6,2.1]	1.9	2.8	100.0
P3	1.0 [0.8,1.4]	1.1	1.7	100.0	1.4 [1.1,1.6]	1.4	2.1	100.0
P4	1.9 [1.4,2.0]	1.8	2.6	100.0	2.9 [2.5,3.1]	2.9	3.9	100.0
P5	1.1 [0.7,1.6]	1.2	2.1	100.0	1.6 [1.2,1.7]	1.6	2.7	100.0
P6	2.4 [2.0,2.8]	2.5	3.6	100.0	1.7 [0.9,2.3]	1.9	3.2	100.0
All	1.7 [1.1,2.1]	1.8	3.6	100.0	1.8 [1.5,2.6]	2.1	3.9	100.0

(b) Guidance (margin relocalization): verbal vs. AR.

User	Verbal guidance				AR guidance			
	Med [Q1,Q3]	RMSE	Haus	Cov_5	Med [Q1,Q3]	RMSE	Haus	Cov_5
P1	11.0 [9.4,11.7]	11.2	14.7	0.0	2.5 [2.1,2.8]	2.6	3.6	100.0
P2	13.3 [9.5,16.4]	13.9	19.0	0.0	3.3 [2.7,3.9]	3.3	4.0	100.0
P3	12.6 [6.5,18.0]	14.1	21.4	33.3	3.0 [2.7,3.6]	3.3	4.7	100.0
P4	17.3 [16.0,23.0]	20.3	28.6	0.0	4.4 [4.1,4.4]	4.2	4.6	100.0
P5	9.4 [8.8,13.3]	11.4	16.7	0.0	3.6 [2.9,3.9]	3.4	4.6	100.0
P6	21.9 [17.1,22.5]	20.5	24.9	0.0	2.7 [2.6,2.9]	2.8	3.9	100.0
All	14.2 [9.6,17.8]	15.7	28.6	5.6	3.2 [2.6,3.9]	3.3	4.7	100.0

tration produced similar median TREs (1.7 mm and 1.8 mm, respectively), and both methods achieved 100% 5 mm coverage. A paired Wilcoxon signed-rank test showed no significant difference between registration methods, $p = .31$. These results indicate that the automated depth-only markerless registration achieved accuracy comparable to the fiducial marker-based baseline in this facial specimen setup.

Margin Relocalization Task Performance. Margin relocalization was evaluated using six simulated positive-margin targets per participant, yielding 36 localization attempts per condition. Figure 3(b) shows the localization error distributions for conventional verbal guidance and AR-guided localization, with detailed participant-level metrics reported in Table 1. AR guidance substantially improved margin relocalization accuracy compared with verbal guidance. Across all attempts, the median localization error decreased from 14.2 mm with verbal guidance to 3.2 mm with AR guidance. AR guidance improved participant-level median error for every participant, with a mean paired reduction of 11.0 mm. This improvement was statistically significant, $p = .002$. All AR-guided attempts

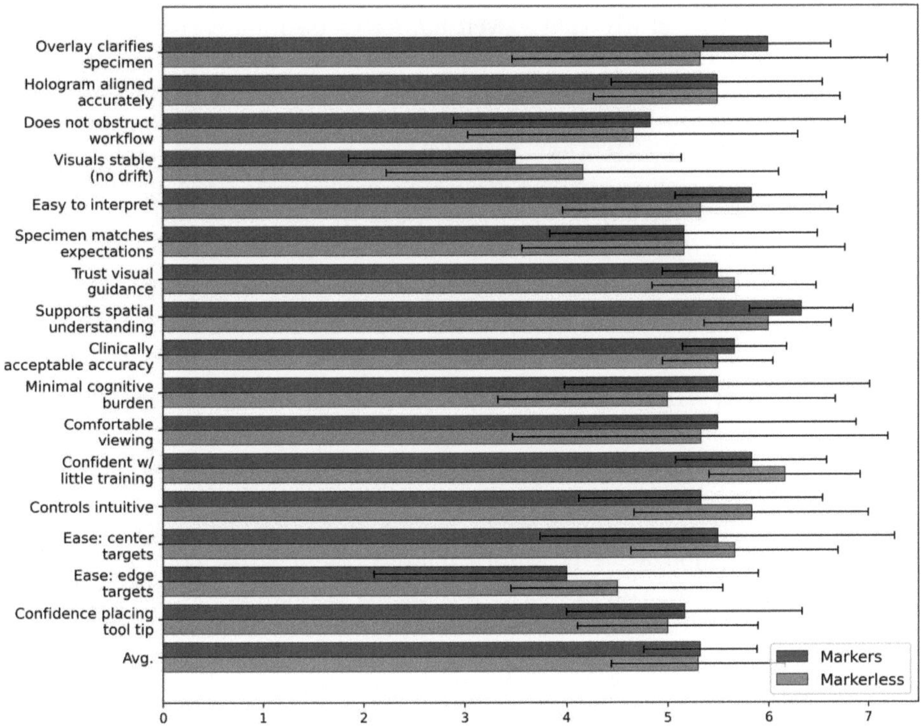

Fig. 4. AR task-specific ratingsAR task-specific ratings

were within 5 mm of the target ($\text{Cov}_5 = 100\%$), whereas only 5.6% of verbal-guided attempts were within 5 mm. Thus, AR guidance reduced a clinically ambiguous verbal relocalization task to consistently sub-5-mm target localization in this phantom setting.

Subjective Questionnaires. We used the six standard NASA-TLX subscales (Mental, Physical, Temporal, Performance, Effort, Frustration). Avg.Score was the mean of the six subscales. Exact paired Wilcoxon signed-rank tests were used to compare Verbal vs. AR guidance within each registration condition ($n = 6$). In the **Markers** condition, AR reduced mental demand compared with verbal guidance ($M = 2.33$, $SD = 1.75$ vs. $M = 4.50$, $SD = 2.07$), $p = .031$. Other TLX subscales and Avg.Score were lower with AR but did not reach significance. In the **Markerless** condition, workload showed a similar trend for Avg.Score ($M = 2.31$, $SD = 1.00$ vs. $M = 3.50$, $SD = 1.11$), $p = .063$, but no subscale was significant. System Usability Scale (SUS) total was similar between registration modes ($M = 73.75$, $SD = 13.49$ for Markers; $M = 70.42$, $SD = 14.00$ for Markerless), $p = .438$, with no significant item-level differences (all $p \geq .159$). In the semi-structured interview, one participant commented on the HMD form factor in relation to existing surgical equipment: "people put our loupes on and off in the OR and I feel like that's even harder to position correctly. And so I think it'd be very easy for someone to put it [HMD] on your head and take it off when scrubbed-in."

Figure 4 summarizes the AR task-specific questionnaire, including the overall average across items (AR Avg). Paired Wilcoxon signed-rank tests were used for each item, with Holm adjustment within the questionnaire family. No item or overall average differed significantly between Markers and Markerless conditions (all $p \geq .157$). AR Avg was nearly identical across conditions ($M = 5.32$, $SD = 0.56$ for Markers; $M = 5.30$, $SD = 0.86$ for Markerless), suggesting that perceived AR task experience was similar with and without fiducial markers.

4 Discussion and Conclusion

We demonstrated an all-in-one AR guidance system for head-and-neck tumor resection that automatically registers a specimen scan to the resection bed and visualizes positive-margin locations in situ. In a controlled phantom study, markerless registration achieved approximately 2 mm TRE, comparable to a marker-based baseline, while AR guidance reduced margin relocalization from centimeter-level error under verbal guidance to a few millimeters. Our system combines lightweight point cloud surface acquisition, automated markerless specimen-to-bed registration, and AR visualization without external RGB-D cameras, fiducial markers, or manual ROI selection. However, our study did not model tissue deformation, bleeding, or specimen shrinkage, and iterative resections were not tested. AHAT depth accuracy and HMD form factor may also vary with surface type and view angle. Finally, the user study included six trainees. Thus, we show that markerless registration can obtain performance comparable to marker-based method, paving the way for future clinical adoption.

Acknowledgments. This work was supported by the National Institutes of Health (NIH) under grant number 1R01EB037685-01. We thank Dr. Michael I. Miga for his contribution.

Disclosure of Interests. The authors have no competing interests in the paper.

References

1. Barsouk, A., Aluru, J.S., Rawla, P., Saginala, K., Barsouk, A.: Epidemiology, risk factors, and prevention of head and neck squamous cell carcinoma. Med. Sci. **11**(2), 42 (2023)
2. Duan, H., et al.: Localization of sentinel lymph nodes using augmented-reality system: a cadaveric feasibility study. Eur. J. Nucl. Med. Mol. Imaging **52**(10), 3643–3652 (2025)
3. Li, H., et al.: EVD surgical guidance with retro-reflective tool tracking and spatial reconstruction using head-mounted augmented reality device. IEEE Trans. Visual Comput. Graph. **31**(9), 6497–6511 (2024)

4. Long, S.M., et al.: Use of intraoperative frozen section to assess final tumor margin status in patients undergoing surgery for oral cavity squamous cell carcinoma. JAMA Otolaryngol. Head Neck Surg. **148**(10), 911–917 (2022)
5. Martin-Gomez, A., et al.: STTAR: surgical tool tracking using off-the-shelf augmented reality head-mounted displays. IEEE Trans. Visual Comput. Graphics **30**(7), 3578–3593 (2023)
6. Nakhleh, R.E.: Quality in surgical pathology communication and reporting. Arch. Pathol. Lab. Med. **135**(11), 1394–1397 (2011)
7. Necker, F.N., Chang, M., Leuze, C., Topf, M.C., Daniel, B.L., Baik, F.M.: Virtual resection specimen interaction using augmented reality holograms to guide margin communication and flap sizing. Otolaryngol. Head Neck Surg. **169**(4), 1083–1085 (2023)
8. Orosco, R.K., et al.: Positive surgical margins in the 10 most common solid cancers. Sci. Rep. **8**(1), 5686 (2018)
9. Prasad, K., et al.: How often is cancer present in oral cavity re-resections after initial positive margins? Laryngoscope **134**(2), 717–724 (2024)
10. Rusu, R.B., Blodow, N., Beetz, M.: Fast point feature histograms (FPFH) for 3D registration. In: IEEE International Conference on Robotics and Automation, pp. 3212–3217. IEEE (2009)
11. Tong, G., et al.: Development of an augmented reality guidance system for head and neck cancer resection. Healthc. Technol. Lett. **11**(2–3), 93–100 (2024)
12. Yang, H., Shi, J., Carlone, L.: Teaser: fast and certifiable point cloud registration. IEEE Trans. Rob. **37**(2), 314–333 (2020)
13. Yang, Q., Li, F., Xu, J., Liu, Z., Sridhar, S., Jin, W., Du, J., Heiselman, J., Miga, M., Topf, M., et al.: Augmented reality-based guidance with deformable registration in head and neck tumor resection. In: International Conference on Medical Image Computing and Computer-Assisted Intervention. pp. 45–54. Springer (2025)
14. Yang, Y., et al.: Markerless augmented reality registration for surgical guidance: a multi-anatomy clinical accuracy study. arXiv preprint arXiv:2511.02086 (2025)
15. Zhang, J., Yao, Y., Deng, B.: Fast and robust iterative closest point. IEEE Trans. Pattern Anal. Mach. Intell. **44**(7), 3450–3466 (2021)

Anatomy-Aware Prediction of Bronchoscopic Accessibility from 3D CT

Linkai Peng[1], Cuiling Sun[2], Bin Wang[1], Jamie Rowell[3], Catherine Gao[3], Oyku Ikizgul[4], Eminenur Sentasci[5], Andrea Bejar[5], Halil Ertugrul Aktas[5], Gorkem Durak[5], Momen Wahidi[3], Christopher Kapp[3], and Ulas Bagci[5(✉)]

[1] Department of Electrical and Computer Engineering, Northwestern University, Evanston, USA
[2] Department of Computer Science, Northwestern University, Evanston, USA
[3] Department of Medicine, Northwestern University, Evanston, USA
[4] Department of Radiology, Istanbul Faculty of Medicine, Istanbul, Turkey
[5] Department of Radiology, Northwestern University, Evanston, USA
ulas.bagci@northwestern.edu

Abstract. Pre-operative planning for bronchoscopy is critical for the diagnosis of lung lesions. Current accessibility assessment relies on subjective manual inspection of CT scans, which is time-consuming and prone to inter-observer variability. In this paper, we formalize bronchoscopy accessibility prediction as a novel supervised learning task and present the first end-to-end framework to address it. We propose an **Anatomy-Aware Mixture-of-Experts (MoE)** model that integrates specialized modules: a CT Expert for local morphological features, a Lobe Expert for anatomical priors, and a Path Geometry Expert that encodes the sequential constraints of the bronchial tree. To support this task, we curated **the first clinical dataset of 438 cases** with pre-operative CT scans and documented procedural outcomes. Experimental results demonstrate that our method achieves an AUROC of 0.8052, significantly outperforming both state-of-the-art baselines and experienced human experts. This work establishes a new benchmark for computer-aided interventional planning in pulmonary medicine. Our data and code will be publicly available at https://nubagcilab.github.io/BronchoAccess/.

Keywords: Mixture of Expert · Bronchoscopy Accessibility · Clinical Planning

1 Introduction

Bronchoscopy is widely used for the diagnosis of pulmonary lesions. Although modern navigation systems assist intra-procedural guidance [6,12], pre-operative accessibility assessment remains largely subjective. As demonstrated in our benchmark, expert bronchoscopists predict a diagnostic procedure with an

G. Yang et al. (Eds.): MICCAI 2026, LNCS 16893, pp. 32–42, 2027.
https://doi.org/10.1007/978-3-032-38236-8_4

AUROC of only 0.5661. This performance highlights the intrinsic difficulty of the task.

Despite its clinical relevance, bronchoscopy accessibility prediction remains underexplored. Prior work has focused on airway segmentation [23,25,26], lesion detection [19], or path planning [5]. While these tasks provide an important basis, they do not directly address procedural accessibility. Existing attempts at outcome prediction rely on handcrafted geometric descriptors and statistical association models without end-to-end supervision [18], failing to capture non-linear interactions between local morphology, anatomical location, and airway complexity. A standardized benchmark for this task is also absent.

To bridge this gap, we first formalize bronchoscopy accessibility prediction as a supervised learning task and curate the first dataset dedicated to this problem. We retrospectively collected 438 clinically verified cases from three medical centers, each with documented procedural outcomes following bronchoscopy for lung lesions. This multi-center cohort provides diverse anatomical variability and realistic clinical distributions.

Building upon this task definition, we propose an anatomy-aware mixture-of-experts (MoE) [20] framework that decomposes accessibility prediction into three components. The CT Expert captures local volumetric context around the lesion. The Lobe Expert encodes anatomical priors reflecting regional variations. The Path Geometry Expert models cumulative geometric constraints along the airway trajectory. These representations are adaptively fused through a gating mechanism that performs case-dependent expert weighting.

To enable systematic evaluation, we further establish the first comprehensive benchmark for bronchoscopy accessibility prediction. The benchmark includes traditional machine learning methods, CT-based deep networks, graph neural networks, and human expert assessment. This benchmark provides a unified evaluation framework for future research on data-driven procedural planning.

Our contributions are three-fold:

1. To address this severely under-studied clinical challenge, we formalize bronchoscopy accessibility prediction as an end-to-end supervised deep learning task. To the best of our knowledge, this work presents the first deep learning application dedicated to predicting functional procedural outcomes directly from pre-operative CT scans.
2. We introduce an anatomy-aware MoE architecture that integrates volumetric imaging, anatomical priors, and airway geometry within a unified model.
3. We establish the first comprehensive benchmark for bronchoscopy accessibility prediction using 438 clinically verified cases and evaluate our framework against diverse computational baselines and human expert assessments.

2 Method

Given CT volume $X \in \mathbb{R}^{H \times W \times D}$, airway tree graph $\mathcal{G} = (\mathcal{V}, \mathcal{E})$, target lesion centroid $\mathbf{c}_N \in \mathbb{R}^3$ and lobe identifier $L \in \{1, \dots, 5\}$, we learn $\mathcal{F} : \{X, \mathcal{G}, \mathbf{c}_N, L\} \rightarrow y$, where $y \in \{0, 1\}$ denotes bronchoscopy accessibility. Our framework decomposes this into three components as shown in Fig. 1.

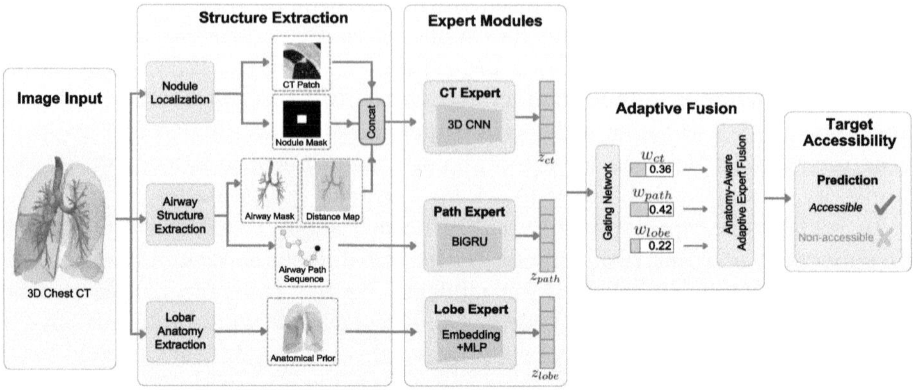

Fig. 1. Overview of the proposed anatomy-aware mixture-of-experts framework for bronchoscopy accessibility prediction.

2.1 Expert Modules

CT Expert. The local structural relationship between the target lesion and the surrounding airway tree plays a central role in bronchoscopy accessibility. CT Expert is formulated to capture the local morphological and spatial relationship between the target lesion and its surrounding airway structures.

We extract a multi-channel 3D patch x comprising the raw CT intensities, a binary lesion mask, and a 3D Euclidean Distance Transform (EDT) [17] of the airway. The lesions are first automatically detected and subsequently verified to ensure consistency with the procedural target. The EDT provides continuous spatial gradients that stabilize learning compared to sparse airway masks. In this way, the model receives an explicit geometric prior reflecting airway accessibility rather than relying solely on implicit learning from intensity patterns.

The multi-channel patch is processed by a custom 3D convolutional encoder. It consists of 4 consecutive residual blocks [8] integrated with squeeze-and-excitation (SE) [10] channel attention. After convolution, a global average pooling layer aggregates the spatial features and a linear layer projects it into a latent embedding $z_{ct} \in \mathbb{R}^d$, where d is the joint feature space dimension.

Lobe Expert. Bronchoscopy difficulty varies across pulmonary lobes due to anatomical differences in branching depth and orientation. To incorporate this anatomical prior, we encode the lobe identity L as a categorical variable and map it into a learnable embedding space via an embedding layer followed by a two-layer MLP: $z_{lobe} = \text{MLP}(\Psi(L))$, $z_{lobe} \in \mathbb{R}^d$. This embedding serves as a global anatomical prior that regularizes the final decision. By encoding lobe identity as a continuous representation, the model can learn structured similarities between lobes rather than treating them as independent categories.

Path Geometry Expert. Accessibility is constrained by cumulative geometric resistance along the airway trajectory from the trachea to the target region. These constraints are sequential and longitudinal in nature, which motivates explicit modeling of the airway trajectory. While the airway tree is naturally a graph, once the navigation path is selected, the data along it forms a one-dimensional ordered sequence of geometric descriptors; we therefore adopt a sequence model rather than a graph neural network. We represent the airway tree as a graph $\mathcal{G}$ derived from the segmented airway and extract the candidate navigation path toward the lesion. For cases with multiple plausible routes, the path with the minimal Euclidean distance to the lesion centroid is selected. Nodes along this path are ordered according to anatomical generation to form a proximal-to-distal sequence. To ensure robustness to segmentation noise, we retain only the largest connected component and remove edges shorter than a predefined physical threshold.

At each node, we compute a set of geometric and topological descriptors, including airway diameter, branching index, curvature, torsion, and relative path length. The ordered feature sequence forms a representation $S = \{\mathbf{s}_1, \ldots, \mathbf{s}_T\}$, where T differs across patients depending on airway depth.

To model longitudinal constraints, we apply a 1-layer bidirectional Gated Recurrent Unit (GRU) [4] over the sequence. The GRU is configured with a hidden size of 128 per direction. The final hidden states from both directions are concatenated and then projected to the joint feature space to obtain a path representation z_{path}. By explicitly modeling the airway as a sequence, this expert captures progressive narrowing, branching accumulation, and distal complexity. This design provides the framework with a topological understanding of accessibility that is complementary to the visual patterns captured by the CT Expert.

2.2 Anatomy-Aware Adaptive Expert Fusion

To handle cross-case heterogeneity, we employ an adaptive mixture-of-experts fusion. A gating network assigns importance weights $\mathbf{w} = [w_{ct}, w_{lobe}, w_{path}]^\top$ to calculate the final fused representation $Z = \sum w_i z_i$. The gating network conditions on case-level anatomical context: target lesion position p, lobe embedding $\Psi(L)$, and graph-level airway statistics g, producing weights via $w = \mathrm{Softmax}(MLP([p; \Psi(L); g]))$. It is implemented as a three-layer MLP with ReLU activations and a final Softmax layer. The fused representation Z is then passed through a classification head to produce the probability of bronchoscopy accessibility $\hat{y} \in [0, 1]$. The entire system is trained using the binary cross-entropy (BCE) loss $\mathcal{L}_{bce}$. To encourage balanced expert utilization, we add an entropy regularization term on the gating weights:

$$\mathcal{L}_{ent} = -\frac{1}{M} \sum_{i=1}^{M} \sum_{j \in \{ct, lobe, path\}} w_{i,j} \log(w_{i,j} + \epsilon), \tag{1}$$

where M denotes the number of samples and ϵ is a small constant for numerical stability. We encourage higher entropy in the gating distribution to avoid degenerate solutions where a single expert dominates across all cases. The total training loss $\mathcal{L}_{total}$ is formulated as: $\mathcal{L}_{total} = \mathcal{L}_{bce} - \lambda\mathcal{L}_{ent}$, where λ is a hyperparameter controlling the regularization strength.

3 Experiments

3.1 Dataset

To fully evaluate the proposed framework, we curated a retrospective multicenter cohort consisting of 438 patients who underwent bronchoscopy for lung lesions. The dataset comprises cases from three clinical centers, including 279 successful procedures and 159 failed attempts. A procedure is labeled successful when diagnostic tissue is confirmed by histopathological analysis of the biopsy sample, which is an objective outcome based on diagnostic yield. Accessibility labels are derived from documented clinical outcomes. All procedures were performed using the same platform to ensure consistency in primary navigation technology across cases. To our knowledge, this is currently the largest dataset reported for outcome-driven bronchoscopy accessibility prediction. The dataset also involves multiple operators and varying device configurations. Although these procedural factors were not explicitly modeled, the multi-center design introduces heterogeneity that reduces systematic bias from a single operator or device type. To ensure robust evaluation, we employ 5-fold cross-validation with patient-level splits.

3.2 Implementations and Compared Methods

For the CT Expert, 3D patches of $128 \times 128 \times 32$ are extracted around the target lesion. Intensity values were clipped to the lung window range and normalized. We used RetinaNet [1,3,14] for lung lesion detection and Naviairway [23] for airway segmentation. All models are trained using AdamW with a learning rate of 1×10^{-3}, batch size 16, and 100 epochs on an NVIDIA A100 GPU. To provide clinical context, 22 clinicians independently assessed accessibility from CT volumes and target locations. Three-level difficulty ratings were mapped to probabilistic scores (0.9, 0.7, 0.4) to compute AUROC and PRAUC. The coefficient λ is set to 0.01. Dropout and weight decay were used during training to prevent overfitting. We compare against conventional machine learning models trained on handcrafted geometric descriptors, CT-based deep networks (ResNet-18 [8], DenseNet-121 [11], EfficientNet-b0 [21], ConvNeXt [16], and Swin Transformer [15]), and graph neural networks (GCN [13], GAT [22], GIN [24], and GraphSAGE [7]) operating on airway topology.

4 Results

4.1 Quantitative Results

Comparison with Diverse Baselines. Table 1 presents the overall comparison across various methods. Conventional machine learning models trained solely on handcrafted geometric features show limited discriminative ability. CT-based deep networks achieve moderate performance, with the best AUROC reaching 0.6333. Graph neural networks slightly improve structural modeling, achieving up to 0.6483 AUROC. Human experts achieve an AUROC of 0.5661, indicating that visual CT inspection alone is insufficient for reliable accessibility estimation.

The proposed anatomy-aware mixture-of-experts model achieves an AUROC of 0.8052 and PR-AUC of 0.8496, significantly outperforming computational baselines and human assessment. These results demonstrate the benefit of explicitly integrating airway trajectory modeling with local imaging cues. Importantly, the proposed model maintains competitive computational efficiency. With 3.83M parameters, it is more lightweight than most CT-based backbone networks while achieving superior predictive performance. This efficiency supports potential integration into pre-procedural planning workflows.

Table 1. Performance comparison of the proposed method against various baseline models. Human assessments were provided by 22 clinicians based on CT volumes and target lesion locations. † indicates statistically significant difference compared with the proposed method (DeLong test, $p < 0.05$).

Input	Method	Acc.	F1	AUROC	PRAUC	Params
Geometric Features	Logistic Regression[9]	0.6136	0.7536	0.5128	0.6897	N/A
	Random Forest[2]	0.5682	0.7031	0.4590	0.5785	N/A
CT Volumes	Densenet121[11]†	0.5909	0.7313	0.5301	0.6543	11.24M
	SwinTransformer[15]†	0.6136	0.7499	0.5418	0.8069	38.50M
	Efficientnetb0[21]†	0.6022	0.7517	0.5725	0.7459	4.69M
	ConvNeXt[16]†	0.6023	0.7482	0.5982	0.7750	31.30M
	Resnet18[8]†	0.5795	0.6185	0.6333	0.7700	33.16M
Airway Graph	GAT[22]†	0.6386	0.7794	0.5767	0.7115	52.35K
	GIN[24]†	0.6265	0.7257	0.5774	0.6782	101.12K
	GraphSage[7]†	0.6203	0.7541	0.5897	0.7129	86.14K
	GCN[13]†	0.6329	0.7752	0.6483	0.7666	51.59K
Human Experts	N/A	0.5272	0.5423	0.5661	0.7434	N/A
Hybrid	**Ours**	**0.8068**	**0.8595**	**0.8052**	**0.8496**	3.83 M

Comparison Under Identical CT Inputs. To ensure that the performance gain does not arise from richer input representations alone, Table 2 compares our model with CT-based deep networks trained on identical multi-channel inputs, including CT intensity, airway distance maps, and lesion masks. Even under this controlled setting, our model maintains a clear advantage. The strongest CNN baseline achieves 0.7310 AUROC, while the proposed method reaches 0.8052 AUROC. This result indicates that architectural decomposition and adaptive expert fusion account for the performance improvement rather than input augmentation alone.

Ablation Study. Table 3 evaluates the contribution of each expert and their combinations. Among single branches, the CT Expert achieves the strongest performance (AUROC 0.7382), confirming that local volumetric context provides a solid baseline. The Path Geometry Expert (0.6040 AUROC) captures meaningful structural constraints along the airway trajectory but remains insufficient alone. The Lobe Expert performs near chance level (0.5513 AUROC), consistent with its role as a global anatomical prior rather than a standalone predictor.

Table 2. Comparison with CT-based deep networks trained using multi-channel volumetric inputs (CT intensity, airway distance transform, and lesion mask). † indicates statistically significant difference compared with the proposed method (DeLong test, $p < 0.05$).

Method	Acc.	F1	AUROC	PRAUC
SwinTransformer† [15]	0.6250	0.7626	0.5243	0.6698
ConvNeXt† [16]	0.6477	0.7438	0.6629	0.7057
Densenet121† [11]	0.6590	0.7058	0.6640	0.7611
Resnet18† [8]	0.6818	0.7586	0.7109	0.7834
Efficientnetb0 [21]	0.6704	0.7819	0.7310	0.8269
Ours	**0.8068**	**0.8595**	**0.8052**	**0.8496**

Pairwise combinations consistently improve over individual modules. Combining CT and Path Experts increases AUROC to 0.7756, demonstrating the complementary effect of trajectory modeling. The full model integrating all three experts achieves the best performance (0.8052 AUROC). We also observe that CT Expert receives higher weights for centrally located lesions, while Path Geometry Expert weights increase for distal and lower-lobe lesions, suggesting anatomically consistent specialization. The gating weights, $\mathbf{w} = [w_{ct}, w_{lobe}, w_{path}]^\top$, thus provide a built-in case-level attribution: for any prediction, $\mathbf{w}$ indicates which anatomical factor drives the decision, offering interpretability without requiring post-hoc explanation methods. These results indicate that bronchoscopy accessibility depends on the joint modeling of local morphology, anatomical context, and cumulative airway geometry rather than any single modality alone.

Table 3. Ablation study evaluating the contribution of each expert module. The full model integrates all experts through adaptive gating.

Lobe Expert	Path Expert	CT Expert	Acc.	F1	AUROC	PRAUC
✓	-	-	0.6190	0.7647	0.5513	0.7030
-	✓	-	0.6310	0.7704	0.6040	0.6665
-	-	✓	0.7500	0.8035	0.7382	0.8028
✓	✓	-	0.7045	0.7968	0.5960	0.6857
✓	-	✓	0.7841	0.8504	0.7477	0.8141
-	✓	✓	0.7500	0.8358	0.7756	0.8030
✓	✓	✓	**0.8068**	**0.8595**	**0.8052**	**0.8496**

4.2 Qualitative Analysis

To further illustrate model behavior, Fig. 2 presents representative cases of true positive, false positive, false negative, and true negative predictions. The red marker indicates the target lesion location, and the airway tree is rendered to visualize the navigational trajectory.

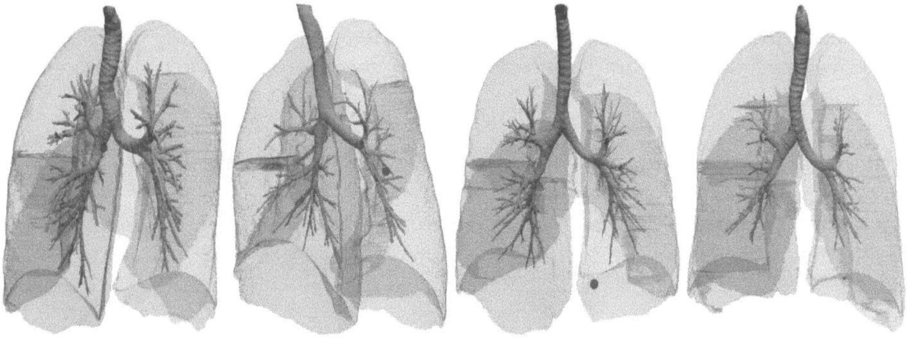

(a) True Positive (b) False Positive (c) False Negative (d) True Negative

Fig. 2. Representative qualitative examples illustrating true positive (TP), false positive (FP), false negative (FN), and true negative (TN) predictions. Airway trees are visualized together with target lesion locations (red markers). (Color figure online)

The true positive case shows a lesion near a well-connected airway branch with sufficient diameter. The false positive case shows a lesion anatomically close to the distal bronchi but with abrupt branching changes along the path, where the CT Expert may overweight local proximity in such cases. The false negative involves a peripheral lesion with limited distal branches, where successful sampling may still occur in practice due to operator expertise or ultra-thin bronchoscopes. The true negative shows a deeply peripheral lesion with sparse connectivity. Overall, accessibility depends on both local lesionairway adjacency and cumulative geometric constraints; clinical execution factors beyond static anatomy also influence outcomes.

5 Conclusion

To the best of our knowledge, this is the first study to systematically formalize bronchoscopy accessibility prediction as a supervised learning problem and to benchmark it against both computational baselines and human expert assessment. The results reveal that this clinically relevant task remains under-explored and difficult under conventional visual evaluation paradigms.

We presented the first learning-based framework for predicting bronchoscopy accessibility directly from pre-procedural CT. The proposed anatomy-aware mixture-of-experts model decomposes accessibility prediction into complementary components. It integrates local volumetric context, global anatomical priors, and sequential airway path geometry within a unified end-to-end architecture.

The experimental results demonstrate that our approach significantly outperforms both state-of-the-art single-modality baselines and experienced human experts. Notably, the model achieves these gains with a lightweight architecture, maintaining low parameter count and computational cost.

By bridging airway topology and functional procedural outcome prediction, this work moves beyond connectivity analysis toward quantitative accessibility assessment. We anticipate that such anatomy-aware modeling may support pre-procedural planning and improve patient selection in bronchoscopy-guided diagnosis.

Acknowledgments. This work was partially supported by NIH R01-HL171376.

Disclosure of Interests. The authors have no competing interests to declare that are relevant to the content of this article.

References

1. Baumgartner, M., Jäger, P.F., Isensee, F., Maier-Hein, K.H.: nndetection: a self-configuring method for medical object detection. In: de Bruijne, M., et al. (eds.) International Conference on Medical Image Computing and Computer-Assisted Intervention, pp. 530–539. Springer (2021). https://doi.org/10.1007/978-3-030-87240-3_51
2. Breiman, L.: Random forests. Mach. Learn. **45**(1), 5–32 (2001)
3. Cardoso, M.J., et al.: MONAI: an open-source framework for deep learning in healthcare. arXiv preprint arXiv:2211.02701 (2022)
4. Cho, K., et al.: Learning phrase representations using RNN encoder–decoder for statistical machine translation. In: Proceedings of the 2014 Conference on Empirical Methods in Natural Language Processing (EMNLP), pp. 1724–1734 (2014)
5. Ciobirca, C., Lango, T., Gruionu, G., Leira, H.O., Gruionu, L., Pastrama, S.: A new procedure for automatic path planning in bronchoscopy. Mater. Today Proc. **5**(13), 26513–26518 (2018)

6. Folch, E.E., et al.: Electromagnetic navigation bronchoscopy for peripheral pulmonary lesions: one-year results of the prospective, multicenter navigate study. J. Thorac. Oncol. **14**(3), 445–458 (2019)
7. Hamilton, W., Ying, Z., Leskovec, J.: Inductive representation learning on large graphs. In: Advances in Neural Information Processing Systems, vol. 30 (2017)
8. He, K., Zhang, X., Ren, S., Sun, J.: Deep residual learning for image recognition. In: Proceedings of the IEEE Conference on Computer Vision and Pattern Recognition, pp. 770–778 (2016)
9. Hosmer Jr, D.W., Lemeshow, S., Sturdivant, R.X.: Applied Logistic Regression. John Wiley & Sons (2013)
10. Hu, J., Shen, L., Sun, G.: Squeeze-and-excitation networks. In: Proceedings of the IEEE Conference on Computer Vision and Pattern Recognition, pp. 7132–7141 (2018)
11. Huang, G., Liu, Z., Van Der Maaten, L., Weinberger, K.Q.: Densely connected convolutional networks. In: Proceedings of the IEEE Conference on Computer Vision and Pattern Recognition, pp. 4700–4708 (2017)
12. Khandhar, S.J., et al.: Electromagnetic navigation bronchoscopy to access lung lesions in 1,000 subjects: first results of the prospective, multicenter navigate study. BMC Pulm. Med. **17**(1), 59 (2017)
13. Kipf, T.N., Welling, M.: Semi-supervised classification with graph convolutional networks. arXiv preprint arXiv:1609.02907 (2016)
14. Lin, T.Y., Goyal, P., Girshick, R., He, K., Dollár, P.: Focal loss for dense object detection. In: Proceedings of the IEEE International Conference on Computer Vision, pp. 2980–2988 (2017)
15. Liu, Z., et al.: Swin transformer: hierarchical vision transformer using shifted windows. In: Proceedings of the IEEE/CVF International Conference on Computer Vision, pp. 10012–10022 (2021)
16. Liu, Z., Mao, H., Wu, C.Y., Feichtenhofer, C., Darrell, T., Xie, S.: A convnet for the 2020s. In: Proceedings of the IEEE/CVF Conference on Computer Vision and Pattern Recognition, pp. 11976–11986 (2022)
17. Meijster, A., Roerdink, J.B., Hesselink, W.H.: A general algorithm for computing distance transforms in linear time. In: Goutsias, J., Vincent, L., Bloomberg, D.S. (eds.) Mathematical Morphology and its Applications to Image and Signal Processing, pp. 331–340. Springer (2000). https://doi.org/10.1007/0-306-47025-X_36
18. Naito, M., Masaki, F., Lisk, R., Tsukada, H., Hata, N.: Predicting reachability to peripheral lesions in transbronchial biopsies using CT-derived geometrical attributes of the bronchial route. Int. J. Comput. Assist. Radiol. Surg. **18**(2), 247–255 (2023)
19. Nasrullah, N., Sang, J., Alam, M.S., Mateen, M., Cai, B., Hu, H.: Automated lung nodule detection and classification using deep learning combined with multiple strategies. Sensors **19**(17), 3722 (2019)
20. Shazeer, N., et al.: Outrageously large neural networks: the sparsely-gated mixture-of-experts layer. arXiv preprint arXiv:1701.06538 (2017)
21. Tan, M., Le, Q.: EfficientNet: rethinking model scaling for convolutional neural networks. In: International Conference on Machine Learning, pp. 6105–6114. PMLR (2019)
22. Veličković, P., Cucurull, G., Casanova, A., Romero, A., Lio, P., Bengio, Y.: Graph attention networks. arXiv preprint arXiv:1710.10903 (2017)
23. Wang, A., Tam, T.C.C., Poon, H.M., Yu, K.C., Lee, W.N.: Naviairway: a bronchiole-sensitive deep learning-based airway segmentation pipeline. arXiv preprint arXiv:2203.04294 (2022)

24. Xu, K., Hu, W., Leskovec, J., Jegelka, S.: How powerful are graph neural networks? arXiv preprint arXiv:1810.00826 (2018)
25. Yang, X., Chen, L., Zheng, Y., Ma, L., Chen, F., Ning, G., Liao, H.: Airway segmentation based on topological structure enhancement using multi-task learning. In: Linguraru, M.G., et al. (eds.) International Conference on Medical Image Computing and Computer-Assisted Intervention, pp. 86–95. Springer (2024). https://doi.org/10.1007/978-3-031-72114-4_9
26. Zhang, M., et al.: Multi-site, multi-domain airway tree modeling. Med. Image Anal. **90**, 102957 (2023)

Anatomy-Aware Standard Plane Localization in 3D Ultrasound with Geometric Constraints

Jianlong Nie[1,2], Xi Ouyang[2], Yuyu Zhou[4], Qi Wan[5], Zhong Xue[2], Xiaohuan Cao[2(✉)], and Dinggang Shen[1,2,3(✉)]

[1] School of Biomedical Engineering and State Key Laboratory of Advanced Medical Materials and Devices, ShanghaiTech University, Shanghai201210, China
Dinggang.Shen@gmail.com
[2] Shanghai United Imaging Intelligence Co. Ltd., Shanghai 200030, China
xiaohuan.cao@uii-ai.com
[3] Shanghai Clinical Research and Trial Center, Shanghai 201210, China
[4] Shanghai United Imaging Healthcare Co. Ltd., Shanghai 201807, China
[5] Wuhan United Imaging Healthcare Co. Ltd., Wuhan 430206, China

Abstract. Standard plane localization is a critical prerequisite in ultrasound scanning for disease diagnosis. Although three-dimensional (3D) ultrasound acquires volumetric data superior to two-dimensional (2D) imaging, manually localizing multiple standard planes simultaneously within 3D volume remains labor-intensive and prone to inter-observer variability. To address this, we propose an anatomy-aware multi-task learning framework with structural prior integration and inter-plane geometric constraints to jointly localize multiple standard planes. To validate the effectiveness and generalizability of our method, we curated a multi-center dataset comprising 800 fetal brain volumes. Our approach outperforms state-of-the-art methods, achieving localization errors of 1.09 mm/3.85°, 1.11 mm/3.93° and 1.20 mm/4.03° on three key standard planes of the fetal brain (i.e., the transventricular plane, the transthalamic plane and the transcerebellar plane, respectively). These findings underscore the method's potential to enhance clinical ultrasound scanning workflows.

Keywords: 3D ultrasound · Fetal brain · Standard plane localization · Multi-task learning · Geometric constraints

1 Introduction

Fetal brain ultrasound, as a non-invasive imaging modality, plays a pivotal role for assessing neurodevelopment and detecting anomalies [3]. Clinical guidelines require acquisition of several standard planes (SPs), including transventricular (TV), transthalamic (TT), and transcerebellar (TC) planes [6] (see Fig. 1). Each of these planes contains key anatomical structures [19]. Although 3D ultrasound

G. Yang et al. (Eds.): MICCAI 2026, LNCS 16893, pp. 43–53, 2027.
https://doi.org/10.1007/978-3-032-38236-8_5

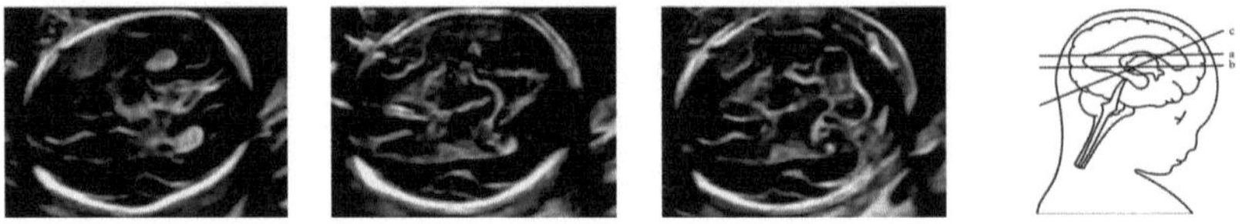

(a) TV plane (b) TT plane (c) TC plane (d) Fetal brain SPs

Fig. 1. Examples of standard planes in 3D fetal brain ultrasound.

enables full brain volume capture and retrospective SP extraction, automated SP localization remains challenging due to poor image quality, large 3D searching space, and high inter-subject anatomical variability. Robust and precise SP localization is essential to boost diagnostic efficiency and to reduce operator dependency.

Existing approaches for standard plane localization in 3D ultrasound can be broadly categorized into two paradigms. The first paradigm treats the task as 2D slice classification, where densely sampled planes are classified using handcrafted features [13] or deep convolutional neural networks [1,2]. To improve the performance, recent studies have incorporated attention mechanisms [9,15] and multi-task learning [4,5]. Additionally, anatomical prior knowledge has been leveraged to enrich feature representations [12,23] or to constrain the searching space [14,18]. However, 2D-based approaches ignore 3D geometric consistency and are sensitive to sampling strategies.

The second paradigm directly estimates continuous plane parameters from the volume [10]. These approaches often employ anatomical landmarks or reference planes to initially restrict the solution space firstly [16,21]. Reinforcement learning [7,22,25] and diffusion models [8] have also been explored to iteratively refine plane estimates. Such multi-stage strategies or iterative optimization are struggling with error propagation, initialization bias and computational cost.

Despite progress, current methods still struggle to achieve robust and precise SP localization that fully exploits the rich anatomical and spatial context embedded within 3D ultrasound volumes. Critically, each SP is defined by specific anatomical structures, thus integrating detailed structural priors holds considerable promise for improving localization accuracy. Moreover, multiple SPs derived from the same fetal organ exhibit well-defined geometric relationships (as shown in Fig. 1(d)). However, Current approaches typically predict them independently, thereby ignoring valuable inter-plane constraints and forgoing opportunities for shared representation learning.

To address these limitations, we propose a unified framework to jointly estimate the parameters of multiple SPs by explicitly integrating anatomical structure information. The main contributions are summarized as follows:

1. We formulate multi-plane localization as a multi-task learning problem, enabling shared representation learning across SPs and thereby enhancing both computational efficiency and inter-plane consistency.

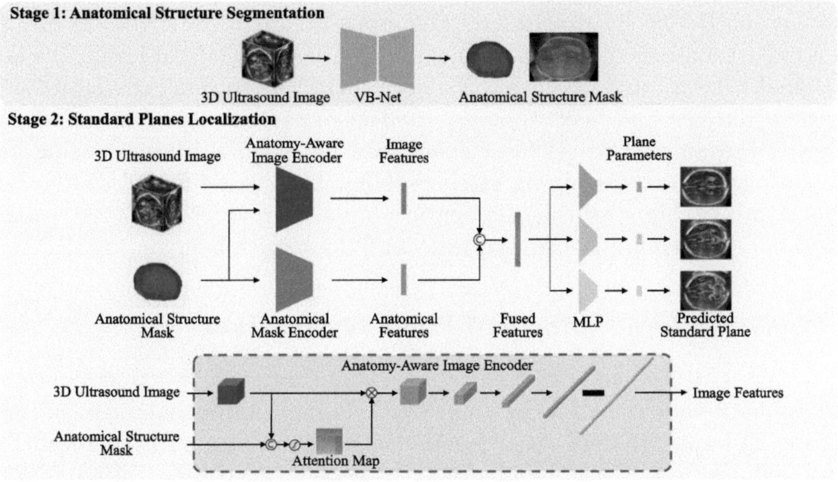

Fig. 2. Overview of our proposed anatomy-aware multi-plane localization framework. The segmentation network (Stage 1) produces an anatomical mask, which is fused with the ultrasound volume for joint multiple plane localization (Stage 2).

2. We incorporate segmentation mask of key anatomical structures not only to guide image feature extraction but also to serve as direct geometric cues for plane parameter prediction.
3. We introduce a novel inter-plane geometric constraint loss to explicitly encodes the known spatial relationships among SPs to regularize the joint prediction process.

2 Method

Our method comprises two sequential stages, as illustrated in Fig. 2. In the first stage, we use a 3D segmentation network to delineate key anatomical structures within the fetal brain ultrasound volume, producing a voxel-wise anatomical mask. In the second stage, we introduce an anatomy-aware localization module for joint localization of the three standard planes of the fetal brain: TV, TT, and TC. Specifically, both the 3D ultrasound volume and the predicted anatomical mask are processed by a multi-task regression network, which simultaneously predicts the parameters of all three planes. This unified design explicitly integrates structural priors to guide accurate and geometrically consistent plane localization.

2.1 Anatomical Structure Segmentation

Standard planes in 3D ultrasound are defined by the presence and spatial arrangement of specific anatomical structures. To encode this prior knowledge, we employ a VB-Net [17] to segment the input 3D ultrasound volume and generate voxel-wise labels of key anatomical structures in the fetal brain. We adopt the original network architecture while optimizing the training configuration for our specific dataset and task. To accommodate our ultrasound dataset, all input volumes are resampled to isotropic spacing of $1.0 \times 1.0 \times 1.0$ mm^3 using linear interpolation. All other training settings follow the coarse model configuration described in [17]. The resulting segmentation mask provides structured anatomical priors for informing the subsequent plane localization stage.

2.2 Anatomy-Aware Standard Plane Localization

To focus computation on anatomically relevant regions, we first compute a bounding box to enclose all foreground voxels in the anatomical mask and apply this cropping jointly to both the original ultrasound volume and the mask. Then, the cropped inputs are processed by two parallel encoders: (1) an anatomy-aware image encoder and (2) an anatomical mask encoder. Their outputs are fused to enable multi-task regression of the three standard plane parameters.

Anatomy-Aware Image Encoder. This encoder processes the cropped ultrasound volume in conjunction with the anatomical mask via a spatial attention mechanism. Initial image features $\mathbf{f}_\mathrm{i}$ are extracted using a 3D $3 \times 3 \times 3$ convolution with batch normalization (BN) and rectified linear unit (ReLU). The initial image features and mask are concatenated and passed through a convolutional subnetwork ($3 \times 3 \times 3$ conv, ReLU, $1 \times 1 \times 1$ conv, and sigmoid) to generate an attention map $\mathbf{A}$. Then, this attention map is element-wise multiplied with the initial image features $\mathbf{f}_\mathrm{i}$. Subsequently, four downsampling steps are applied, each using $2 \times 2 \times 2$ max-pooling (stride 2) and a basic block ($3 \times 3 \times 3$ conv, BN, and ReLU) that doubles feature channels. The final image features $\hat{\mathbf{f}}_\mathrm{i}$ are flattened. This design captures increasingly abstract and context-rich image representations.

Anatomical Mask Encoder. The segmentation mask encodes rich spatial relationships among anatomical structures essential for defining standard planes. To capture inter-structure spatial relationships, we employ a mask encoder with the same architecture as the image encoder but without the attention module, extracting anatomical features $\hat{\mathbf{f}}_\mathrm{m}$ directly from the segmentation mask. The final anatomical features $\hat{\mathbf{f}}_\mathrm{m}$ are flattened.

Feature Fusion and Plane Regression The encoded image features $\hat{\mathbf{f}}_\mathrm{i}$ and anatomical features $\hat{\mathbf{f}}_\mathrm{m}$ are concatenated and fed into a two-layer fully-connected MLP (256 units, ReLU, and 256 units). For standard plane $k \in \{\mathrm{TV}, \mathrm{TT}, \mathrm{TC}\}$, the network outputs a 4-dimensional vector: its first three components are L2-normalized to yield the unit plane normal $\boldsymbol{n}^k$, and the last component gives the signed distance d^k from the origin. Here the origin is set as the center of an ultrasound volume. The multi-task formulation enables shared representation learning across all three planes.

2.3 Loss Function

The total loss function consists of two components: (1) three per-plane regression losses ($\mathcal{L}_{\mathrm{TV}}$, $\mathcal{L}_{\mathrm{TT}}$, $\mathcal{L}_{\mathrm{TC}}$) that penalize errors in normal orientation and distance offset; and (2) two inter-plane geometric constraint losses ($\mathcal{L}_{\mathrm{parallel}}$, $\mathcal{L}_{\mathrm{coplanar}}$) that encode consistent anatomical relationships among the standard planes.

Single Plane Loss. Each standard plane in 3D space is represented by $ax + by + cz = d$. When the coefficients are normalized such that $a^2 + b^2 + c^2 = 1$, the plane's unit normal is given by $\boldsymbol{n} = (a, b, c)$, and the signed distance from the origin to the plane is d.

The single plane loss combines an angular term and a distance term: (1) to emphasize small-angle errors, we use the squared magnitude of the cross product between predicted and ground-truth normals; (2) for the distance offset, we adopt the L_1 loss. The loss for a single plane is formulated as:

$$\mathcal{L}_k = \alpha \cdot \|\boldsymbol{n}_{\mathrm{E}}^k \times \boldsymbol{n}_{\mathrm{G}}^k\|^2 + \beta \cdot |d_{\mathrm{E}}^k - d_{\mathrm{G}}^k|, \tag{1}$$

where $\boldsymbol{n}_{\mathrm{E}}$ and $\boldsymbol{n}_{\mathrm{G}}$ are the predicted and ground-truth unit normals, d_{E} and d_{G} are the corresponding signed distances, $k \in \{\mathrm{TV}, \mathrm{TT}, \mathrm{TC}\}$, and α, β are balancing weights.

Inter-plane Geometric Constraint Loss. Despite inter-subject anatomical variability, the spatial configuration of fetal brain structures imposes consistent geometric relationships among the standard diagnostic planes. Specifically: (1) the TV and TT planes are clinically required to be nearly parallel; and (2) the TC plane is acquired with a slight caudal tilt relative to TV/TT, but its orientation remains anatomically constrained such that the normals of all three planes approximately lie in a common anatomical plane. To enforce these priors, we introduce two geometric constraint losses.

$$\mathcal{L}_{\mathrm{parallel}} = \max\left(0, \cos\left(\tau_{\mathrm{p}}\right) - \boldsymbol{n}_{\mathrm{E}}^{\mathrm{TV}} \cdot \boldsymbol{n}_{\mathrm{E}}^{\mathrm{TT}}\right), \tag{2}$$

where $\boldsymbol{n}_{\mathrm{E}}^{\mathrm{TV}}$ and $\boldsymbol{n}_{\mathrm{E}}^{\mathrm{TT}}$ are the normalized predicted plane normals for the TV and TT planes, respectively, and τ_{p} is the maximum allowable angle deviation in radian.

$$\mathcal{L}_{\mathrm{coplanar}} = \max\left(0, |\boldsymbol{n}_{\mathrm{E}}^{\mathrm{TV}} \cdot \left(\boldsymbol{n}_{\mathrm{E}}^{\mathrm{TT}} \times \boldsymbol{n}_{\mathrm{E}}^{\mathrm{TC}}\right)| - \tau_{\mathrm{c}}\right), \tag{3}$$

where $\boldsymbol{n}_{\mathrm{E}}^{\mathrm{TV}}$, $\boldsymbol{n}_{\mathrm{E}}^{\mathrm{TT}}$ and $\boldsymbol{n}_{\mathrm{E}}^{\mathrm{TC}}$ denote the normalized predicted plane normals for the TV, TT, and TC planes respectively, and τ_{c} is a coplanarity error threshold.

The total loss is the sum of three per-plane losses and two geometric regularizers:

$$\mathcal{L}_{\mathrm{total}} = \lambda_1 \cdot (\mathcal{L}_{\mathrm{TV}} + \mathcal{L}_{\mathrm{TT}} + \mathcal{L}_{\mathrm{TC}}) + \lambda_2 \cdot (\mathcal{L}_{\mathrm{coplanar}} + \mathcal{L}_{\mathrm{parallel}}), \tag{4}$$

where λ_1 and λ_2 balance between three per-plane losses and two inter-plane geometric constraint losses.

3 Experimental Results

3.1 Data Collection and Cohort Characteristics

We constructed a multi-center 3D fetal brain ultrasound dataset comprising 800 volumes from 780 pregnant women in the second trimester. All raw volumes were anonymized, and those with severe artifacts, poor image quality, or incomplete coverage were excluded by experienced sonographers. Data were acquired across four clinical sites. Maternal age ranged from 18 to 46 years.

Annotation was performed using 3D Slicer, where both anatomical structure segmentation mask and standard planes were manually delineated by two trained annotators under sonographer supervision. A two-stage quality control procedure was applied, with ambiguous cases reviewed by senior clinicians to yield consensus ground truth. The dataset was partitioned by patient into training (580), validation (70), and testing (150) sets to prevent data leakage.

3.2 Implementation Details

Our method was implemented in PyTorch and trained on an NVIDIA H20 GPU using the Adam optimizer with a learning rate of 1e-4 and batch size of 96. All volumes were resampled to a uniform spacing of $1.0\times1.0\times1.0\,\text{mm}^3$ and normalized to [0, 1] using min-max normalization. Data augmentation included random translation, rotation, and scaling with a probability of 0.5, applied to the resampled volumes. Subsequently, volumes were cropped to $128\times128\times128$ voxels centered at the image center. The best model for testing was selected in terms of validation performance. Loss weights in Eq. (1) and Eq. (4) were $\alpha = 100.0$, $\beta = 1.0$, $\lambda_1 = 1.0$, $\lambda_2 = 100.0$. Thresholds $\tau_\text{p} = 0.002$ and $\tau_\text{c} = 0.003$ were determined based on statistical analysis of plane orientations in the training cohort and validated on the validation set to ensure generalizability.

3.3 Result Analysis

We evaluate localization accuracy using three metrics: angular deviation (*Ang*), distance error (*Dis*), and Structural Similarity (SSIM) [20]. *Ang* and *Dis* are defined as:

$$Ang = \arccos\left(\frac{\boldsymbol{n}_\text{E}\cdot\boldsymbol{n}_\text{G}}{\|\boldsymbol{n}_\text{E}\|\cdot\|\boldsymbol{n}_\text{G}\|}\right), \tag{5}$$

$$Dis = |d_\text{E} - d_\text{G}|, \tag{6}$$

where $\boldsymbol{n}_\text{E}$ and $\boldsymbol{n}_\text{G}$ are the predicted and ground-truth unit normals, and d_E, d_G are distances from the volume origin.

Inter- and intra-observer variability analysis on 60 random cases validated the reliability of anotations of SPs. High consistency was observed across all

Table 1. Comparison of different methods on SPs localization. ‡ indicates $p < 0.001$, † indicates $p < 0.01$, * indicates $p < 0.05$.

Plane	Metric	Seg	Regress	UDF	RL-US	ITN	Ours
TV	Ang(°)	5.04±3.68‡	5.67±7.40†	7.05±7.41‡	8.29±4.03‡	10.49±6.26‡	**3.85±2.15**
	Dis(mm)	1.42±6.43‡	1.46±1.35‡	1.57±1.26†	2.12±1.81‡	2.56±2.45‡	**1.09±0.85**
	SSIM	0.80±0.12‡	0.79±0.12‡	0.77±0.12‡	0.74±0.14‡	0.70±0.15‡	**0.82±0.11**
TT	Ang(°)	5.03±3.67‡	5.85±7.44‡	7.37±7.92‡	7.05±3.89‡	8.62±5.95‡	**3.93±2.56**
	Dis(mm)	1.57±6.40‡	1.18±1.08‡	1.48±1.37‡	3.31±3.57‡	2.79±2.81‡	**1.11±0.93**
	SSIM	0.81±0.11*	0.80±0.12‡	0.78±0.12‡	0.74±0.14‡	0.72±0.15‡	**0.82±0.11**
TC	Ang(°)	4.10±2.36‡	6.75±7.58‡	8.73±7.46‡	7.95±3.65‡	8.00±4.87‡	**4.03±2.79**
	Dis(mm)	2.24±6.20*	1.30±1.07‡	1.81±1.45‡	2.19±1.74‡	2.65±3.00‡	**1.20±1.00**
	SSIM	0.75±0.12‡	0.75±0.12‡	0.72±0.13‡	0.65±0.15‡	0.66±0.17‡	**0.78±0.12**

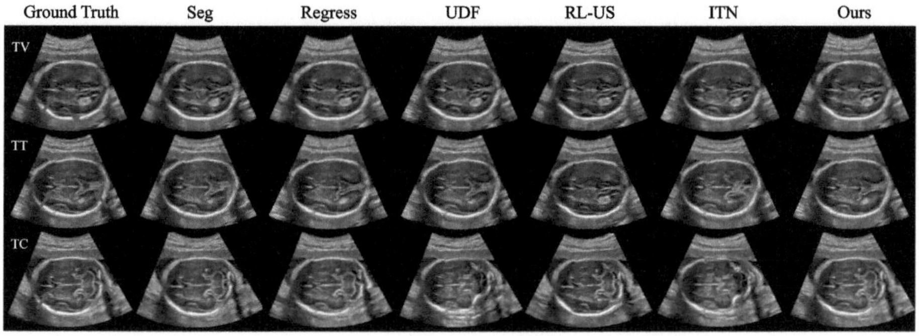

Fig. 3. Visual comparison of SPs localization results of one subject across different methods. Red arrows in the ground truth mark regions with clear inter-method localization discrepancies. (Color figure online)

three SPs (inter-observer: 2.41°–2.43° angular deviation, 0.58–0.79 mm distance error; intra-observer: 2.29°–2.36° in angle, 0.61–1.12 mm in distance), confirming a robust, reliable benchmark for all localization experiments.

We compare our method with five baselines: (1) segmentation-based (Seg), using anatomical structure centroids to predict planes; (2) regression-based (Regress), employing a 3D CNN trained with MSE loss for explicit plane parameters regression; (3) unsigned distance field-based (UDF) [24], extracting planes from predicted distance fields generated by VB-Net; (4) RL-US [21], a reinforcement learning-based ultrasound standard plane localization method; and (5) ITN [11], an iterative transformation network for standard plane detection.

Table 1 reports quantitative results on TV, TT, and TC planes. Paired t-tests confirm our method achieves state-of-the-art performance across most of the metrics, with statistically significant improvement over all competitors. Segmentation-based method shows competitive performance but larger variance,

Table 2. Ablation study for analyzing different components. ∗ means that each column indicates whether the corresponding component is included (✓) or excluded (✗): anatomy-aware attention, anatomical mask encoder, inter-plane geometric constraint loss.

Plane	Metric	Strategies∗			
		(✗ ✓ ✓)	(✓ ✗ ✓)	(✓ ✓ ✗)	(✓ ✓ ✓)
TV	Ang(°)	4.652±2.993	4.623±3.121	4.113±2.352	**3.850±2.153**
	Dis(mm)	1.149±0.872	1.136±0.967	1.148±0.867	**1.085±0.849**
	SSIM	0.805±0.116	0.807±0.118	0.814±0.114	**0.816±0.110**
TT	Ang(°)	4.617±3.004	4.636±3.111	4.250±2.918	**3.929±2.561**
	Dis(mm)	1.112±1.017	1.099±1.012	1.171±1.009	**1.108±0.926**
	SSIM	0.814±0.117	0.815±0.117	0.817±0.114	**0.821±0.109**
TC	Ang(°)	5.273±4.136	5.521±4.479	4.646±3.434	**4.031±2.789**
	Dis(mm)	1.296±1.015	1.368±1.000	1.316±1.018	**1.198±0.997**
	SSIM	0.760±0.123	0.758±0.126	0.768±0.123	**0.784±0.120**

as segmentation failures under poor visualization propagate to localization outliers. Our method can capture inter-structure relationships for consistent predictions. UDF, RL-US, and ITN show higher errors, suggesting implicit representations or reinforcement strategies struggling with clinical precision. Lower variance indicates robustness of our method.

The qualitative visualization in Fig. 3 is fully consistent with quantitative findings. The planes generated by Seg and Regress show higher anatomical consistency with the ground truth than those from UDF, RL-US, and ITN. Specifically, UDF, RL-US and ITN exhibit obvious misalignment of key anatomical landmarks, and detail loss in the TT and TC planes. In contrast, our method achieves near-perfect alignment with the ground truth across all planes.

3.4 Ablation Study

We evaluate component contributions by removing the anatomy-aware attention module, anatomical mask encoder, and inter-plane geometric constraint loss (Table 2). Full model performs best across all planes. Ablation results confirm that both the anatomy-aware attention and mask encoder are critical for integrating anatomical structure information, driving the core performance gain of our framework. Inter-plane geometric constraint loss has smaller but consistent impact across all planes.

3.5 Clinical Biometric Evaluation from SPs

Biometric analysis on testing cases shows that measurements from predicted planes are clinically equivalent to ground truth. Absolute errors are minimal: 0.39±0.38 mm for atrial width of the lateral ventricle in the TV plane, 0.43±0.42 mm for biparietal diameter in the TT plane, and 0.83±0.86 mm for cisterna magna depth in the TC plane. Paired t-tests suggests no significant differences across all planes ($p > 0.05$), validating diagnostic reliability of our method.

4 Conclusion

We have presented a two-stage framework for multiple standard planes localization in 3D fetal brain ultrasound: (1) deep learning segmentation of key anatomical structures, and (2) multi-task regression of standard planes. We explicitly leverage anatomical priors via anatomy-aware image encoding, anatomical structure encoding, and inter-plane geometric constraints. Experiments show our approach outperforms state-of-the-art methods, achieving errors of 1.09–1.20 mm and 3.85°–4.03° across three planes. Limitations include dependency on segmentation quality and potential challenges with rare anatomical anomalies. Future work includes end-to-end training, extending to additional standard planes within the fetal brain, generalizing the framework to standard views of other anatomical structures (e.g., fetal heart and abdomen).

Acknowledgments. This work was supported in part by National Natural Science Foundation of China (grant numbers 82441023, 62131015, U23A20295, 82394432), the China Ministry of Science and Technology (STI2030-Major Projects-2022ZD0209000, STI2030-Major Projects-2022ZD0213100), The Key R&D Program of Guangdong Province, China (grant number 2023B0303040001), HPC Platform of ShanghaiTech University, and National Key R&D Program of China (2024YFF1207103).

Disclosure of Interests. The authors have no competing interests to declare that are relevant to the content of this article.

References

1. Abdillahi, M.A., Baker, M.R., Doğru, A., Buyrukoğlu, S.: Enhanced fetal plane classification in ultrasound imaging via prototypical networks and few-shot learning. J. Imaging Inform. Med., 1–18 (2025)
2. Baumgartner, C.F., Kamnitsas, K., Matthew, J., Smith, S., Kainz, B., Rueckert, D.: Real-time standard scan plane detection and localisation in fetal ultrasound using fully convolutional neural networks. In: Ourselin, S., Joskowicz, L., Sabuncu, M.R., Unal, G., Wells, W. (eds.) MICCAI 2016. LNCS, vol. 9901, pp. 203–211. Springer, Cham (2016). https://doi.org/10.1007/978-3-319-46723-8_24
3. Beyer, T., et al.: What scans we will read: imaging instrumentation trends in clinical oncology. Cancer Imaging **20**(1), 38 (2020)
4. Cai, Y., Sharma, H., Chatelain, P., Noble, J.A.: Multi-task SonoEyeNet: detection of fetal standardized planes assisted by generated sonographer attention maps. In: Frangi, A.F., Schnabel, J.A., Davatzikos, C., Alberola-López, C., Fichtinger, G. (eds.) MICCAI 2018. LNCS, vol. 11070, pp. 871–879. Springer, Cham (2018). https://doi.org/10.1007/978-3-030-00928-1_98

5. Cai, Y., Sharma, H., Chatelain, P., Noble, J.A.: SonoEyeNet: standardized fetal ultrasound plane detection informed by eye tracking. In: 2018 IEEE 15th International Symposium on Biomedical Imaging (ISBI 2018), pp. 1475–1478. IEEE (2018)
6. Fiorentino, M.C., Villani, F.P., Di Cosmo, M., Frontoni, E., Moccia, S.: A review on deep-learning algorithms for fetal ultrasound-image analysis. Med. Image Anal. **83**, 102629 (2023)
7. He, G., et al.: CLP-Net: an advanced artificial intelligence technique for localizing standard planes of cleft lip and palate by three-dimensional ultrasound in the first trimester. BMC Pregnancy Childbirth **25**(1), 10 (2025)
8. Huang, Y., Xu, Y., Dou, H., Deng, J., Yang, X., Zheng, H., Ni, D.: Uncertainty-aware diffusion and reinforcement learning for joint plane localization and anomaly diagnosis in 3D ultrasound. In: Gee, J.C., et al. (eds.) MICCAI 2025. LNCS, vol. 15963. Springer, Cham (2026). https://doi.org/10.1007/978-3-032-04965-0_61
9. Krishna, T.B., Kokil, P.: Automatic identification of fetal biometry planes from ultrasound images: An assistive tool for healthcare professionals. IEEE Sens. J. **24**(24), 42365–42372 (2024)
10. Li, Y., et al.: Standard plane localisation in 3D fetal ultrasound using network with geometric and image loss. Med. Imaging Deep Learn. (2018)
11. Li, Y., et al.: Standard plane detection in 3D fetal ultrasound using an iterative transformation network. In: Frangi, A., Schnabel, J., Davatzikos, C., Alberola-López, C., Fichtinger, G. (eds.) MICCAI 2018. LNCS, vol. 11070. Springer, Cham (2018). https://doi.org/10.1007/978-3-030-00928-1_45
12. Ni, D., et al.: Selective search and sequential detection for standard plane localization in ultrasound. In: Yoshida, H., Warfield, S., Vannier, M.W. (eds.) ABD-MICCAI 2013. LNCS, vol. 8198. Springer, Berlin (2013). https://doi.org/10.1007/978-3-642-41083-3_23
13. Rahmatullah, B., Papageorghiou, A., Noble, J.A.: Automated selection of standardized planes from ultrasound volume. In: Suzuki, K., Wang, F., Shen, D., Yan, P. (eds.) MLMI 2011. LNCS, vol. 7009. Springer, Berlin (2011). https://doi.org/10.1007/978-3-642-24319-6_5
14. Ryou, H., et al.: Automated 3D ultrasound biometry planes extraction for first trimester fetal assessment. In: Wang, L., Adeli, E., Wang, Q., Shi, Y., Suk, HI. (eds.) MLMI 2016. LNCS, vol. 10019. Springer, Cham (2016). https://doi.org/10.1007/978-3-319-47157-0_24
15. Schlemper, J., et al.: Attention-gated networks for improving ultrasound scan plane detection, arXiv preprint (2018). arXiv:1804.05338
16. Schmidt-Richberg, A., et al.: Offset regression networks for view plane estimation in 3D fetal ultrasound. In: Medical Imaging 2019: Image Processing, vol. 10949, pp. 907–912. SPIE (2019)
17. Shi, F., et al.: Deep learning empowered volume delineation of whole-body organs-at-risk for accelerated radiotherapy. Nat. Commun. **13**(1), 6566 (2022)
18. Thomas, S., et al.: Computer-assisted contralateral side comparison of the ankle joint using flat panel technology. Int. J. Comput. Assist. Radiol. Surg. **16**(5), 767–777 (2021). https://doi.org/10.1007/s11548-021-02329-w
19. Wang, Y., Ge, X., Ma, H., Qi, S., Zhang, G., Yao, Y.: Deep learning in medical ultrasound image analysis: a review. IEEE Access **9**, 54310–54324 (2021)
20. Wang, Z., Bovik, A.C., Sheikh, H.R., Simoncelli, E.P.: Image quality assessment: from error visibility to structural similarity. IEEE Trans. Image Process. **13**(4), 600–612 (2004)

21. Yang, X., et al.: Agent with warm start and adaptive dynamic termination for plane localization in 3D ultrasound. IEEE Trans. Med. Imaging **40**(7), 1950–1961 (2021)
22. Yang, X., et al.: Searching collaborative agents for multi-plane localization in 3D ultrasound. Med. Image Anal. **72**, 102119 (2021)
23. Yang, X., et al.: Standard plane localization in ultrasound by radial component. In: IEEE 11th International Symposium on Biomedical Imaging (ISBI), pp. 1180–1183. IEEE (2014)
24. Zhang, C., et al.: Surface extraction from neural unsigned distance fields. In: 2023 IEEE/CVF International Conference on Computer Vision (ICCV), pp. 22474–22483. IEEE (2023)
25. Zou, Y., et al.: Agent with tangent-based formulation and anatomical perception for standard plane localization in 3D ultrasound. In: Wang, L., Dou, Q., Fletcher, P.T., Speidel, S., Li, S. (eds.) MICCAI 2022. LNCS, vol. 13434. Springer, Cham (2022). https://doi.org/10.1007/978-3-031-16440-8_29

Attenuation-Resilient Alternating Optimization for Laparoscopic Liver Landmark Detection

Lanqing Liu[1(✉)], Ruize Cui[1], Jialun Pei[2(✉)], Diandian Guo[2], Tiffany Y. So[2], Pheng-Ann Heng[2], and Jing Qin[1]

[1] The Hong Kong Polytechnic University, Hong Kong, China
peijialun@gmail.com

[2] The Chinese University of Hong Kong, Hong Kong, China

Abstract. Liver surface landmark detection is a fundamental prerequisite for anatomical guidance in laparoscopic liver surgery. However, it remains unreliable in practice due to two pervasive challenges: illumination attenuation in underexposed regions and the structural mismatch between pixel-wise localization and continuous curvilinear geometry. To address these limitations, we propose A2ONet, an attenuation-resilient alternating optimization network for robust liver landmark detection. To mitigate illumination attenuation, A2ONet embraces an illumination field compensation (IFC) block that adaptively enhances dark regions while preserving structural consistency. Meanwhile, we introduce a lightweight frequencyorientation selective filter (FOSF) to suppress repetitive texture interference and preserve salient curvilinear cues. Building upon these resilient representations, we design an alternating segcurve optimization (ASCO) decoder that iteratively couples dense segmentation with explicit curve modeling, enabling mutual guidance to optimize both structural continuity and endpoint localization. Extensive evaluations on L3D-2K, L3D, and P2ILF demonstrate consistent improvements over competitive methods, establishing a more reliable foundation for intraoperative anatomy guidance. Our code is available at https://github.com/hyperiondk115/A2ONet.

Keywords: Landmark detection · Laparoscopic liver surgery · Parametric curve modeling · Low-light enhancement

1 Introduction

Laparoscopic liver surgery offers substantial benefits in reduced trauma and faster postoperative recovery [8,18]. However, the restricted field of view and absence of tactile feedback significantly complicate intraoperative anatomical orientation. To mitigate these limitations, augmented reality (AR) guidance has been increasingly explored to link intraoperative laparoscopic views with preoperative CT/MRI-derived liver models [1,13,28]. Reliable detection of anatomical

G. Yang et al. (Eds.): MICCAI 2026, LNCS 16893, pp. 54–64, 2027.
https://doi.org/10.1007/978-3-032-38236-8_6

landmarks on the liver surface, *i.e.*, ridges, falciform ligaments, and silhouette boundaries, serves as semantic anchors for establishing 2D3D correspondence and supporting accurate registration [20]. Consequently, anatomically consistent and geometrically reliable landmark detection is fundamental for robust AR-guided laparoscopic interventions.

(a) Keyframe (b) Ground Truth (c) D²GPLand+ (d) BCRNet (e) **A2ONet**

Fig. 1. Illustration of key challenges for liver landmark detection. Blue circles indicate errors caused by illumination attenuation, yellow circles denote segmentation false positives, and pink circles mark inaccurate endpoint localization. (Color figure online)

Most existing studies formulate liver landmark detection as a dense segmentation problem [1,21,24]. In real surgical scenarios, however, there exists a structural mismatch between pixel-level targets and the continuous-curve geometry of anatomical landmarks. Although mask-based segmentation methods achieve remarkable performance in pixel-level localization, they often fragment delicate curvilinear landmarks into disconnected pieces, yielding local false positives. Recent studies [6,19] leverage large vision models [12] to enhance detection robustness and combine with the depth modality to augment structural cues [7]. Despite this progress, these methods remain unable to overcome the impacts of illumination attenuation in peripheral or far-field regions on laparoscopic imaging, which result in blurred landmark boundaries and reduced contrast of surrounding tissue structures (see Fig. 1). Beyond light degradation, another challenge lies in balancing positioning accuracy with structural continuity. While incorporating curve geometry modeling enhances landmark continuity [15], it may hinder precise endpoint localization due to excessive smoothing priors. Accordingly, overcoming the "localization-continuity tradeoff" is crucial for stabilizing the consistency of predicted liver landmarks.

In this work, we present A2ONet, an Attenuation-resilient Alternating Optimization Network that unifies appearance compensation and structure-aware refinement within a unified framework. To address illumination attenuation, we introduce an *illumination field compensation* (IFC) block that adaptively restores underexposed regions while preserving structural coherence. Moreover, a lightweight *frequencyorientation selective filter* (FOSF) is embedded to suppress texture-driven ambiguities and enhance salient curvilinear structures. Building upon these attenuation-resilient representations, we further design an *alternating segcurve optimization* (ASCO) decoder that couples a segmentation branch for dense localization and a curve branch for continuous geometry. ASCO iteratively injects curve priors to regularize fragmented segmentation responses and uses refined segmentation features to guide subsequent curve updates, resulting in cascaded and mutually reinforcing optimization. The entire model is trained end-to-end with joint supervision over masks, curves, and illumination conditions. Extensive experiments on three benchmarks, L3D [19], L3D-2K [6], and P2ILF [1] demonstrate consistent improvements over state-of-the-art methods, *e.g.*, reaching 53.51% DSC and 38.32% IoU on the L3D-2K dataset, establishing a more reliable foundation for intraoperative anatomical guidance.

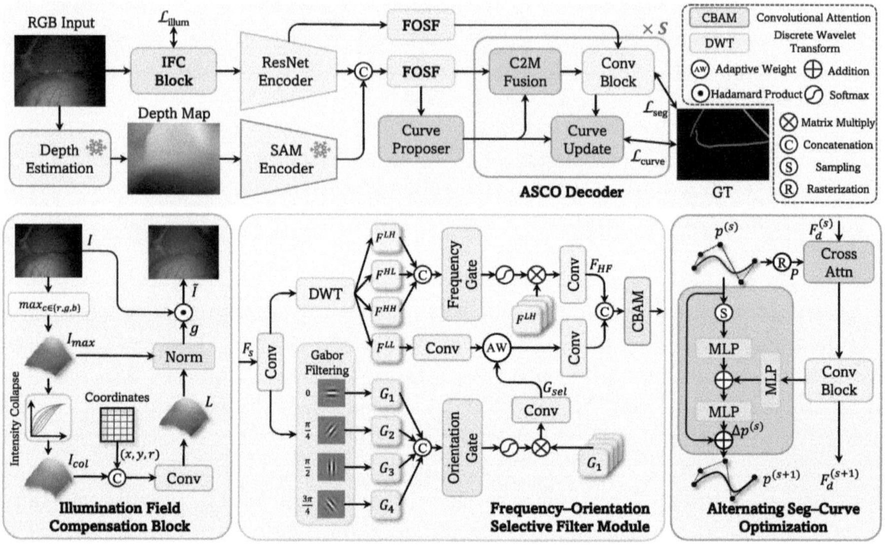

Fig. 2. Overall architecture of proposed A2ONet for liver landmark detection.

2 Methodology

As illustrated in Fig. 2, the proposed A2ONet is composed of four key components: an illumination field compensation (IFC) block, a multi-modal encoder, a lightweight frequencyorientation selective filter (FOSF), and a dual-branch alternating segcurve optimization (ASCO) decoder. Given an input RGB keyframe, A2ONet first adopts the IFC block to normalize varying illumination for mitigating peripheral attenuation and then employs a ResNet [9] to capture appearance representations from the compensated RGB image. Concurrently, following the design of D2GPLand+ [6], Depth Anything V2 [25] estimates a monocular depth map from the RGB input to supply global geometric cues complementary to visual appearance [19], followed by a frozen SAM image encoder [12] to extract depth-aware geometry features. Subsequently, we concatenate RGB-D features and utilize FOSF modules to operate on the bottleneck features, emphasizing curvilinear structures while suppressing repetitive textures. We further include a curve proposer to initialize coarse parametric curves from the deepest FOSF-enhanced feature. Building on these initial curves, the ASCO decoder integrates a segmentation branch with FOSF-based skip connections for dense localization and a curve branch for explicit landmark geometry parameterization. In successive refinement stages, injected curve priors regularize segmentation responses through curve-to-mask (C2M) fusion, and the mask features in turn guide curve updates.

2.1 Illumination Field Compensation Block

To enhance detection robustness under low-light laparoscopic environment, we design an IFC block that explicitly normalizes spatially varying illumination. Given an input RGB image $I \in \mathbb{R}^{H\times W\times 3}$, we adopt a standard reflectance-illumination decomposition assumption: $I(x) = R(x) \odot L(x)$, where $L(x)$ denotes a spatial illumination field and $R(x)$ represents illumination-invariant reflectance. Our objective is to estimate a smooth low-frequency $L(x)$ and compensate illumination while preserving structural consistency. We first derive a collapsed intensity map from channel-wise maximum: $I_{max}(x) = \max_{c\in\{r,g,b\}} I_c(x)$, followed by an adaptive intensity collapse:

$$I_{\text{col}}(x) = \left(\sin\left(\frac{\pi I_{max}(x)}{2}\right) + \epsilon\right)^{\frac{1}{k}}, k > 0, \tag{1}$$

where k is a learnable temperature parameter that modulates the dynamic-range compression intensity, enabling stable illumination estimation while maintaining details. The transformed intensity is concatenated with normalized spatial coordinates (x, y) and radial distance r to estimate $L(x)$, which is then used to normalize intensity: $I_{\text{norm}}(x) = I_{max}(x)/(L(x) + \epsilon)$. To prevent over-amplification, we derive a residual gain map: $g_{\text{raw}}(x) = I_{\text{norm}}(x)/(I_{max}(x) + \epsilon)$, and apply residual blending in the gain domain: $g(x) = 1 + \alpha\big(g_{\text{raw}}(x) - 1\big)$, where $\alpha \in [0, 1]$ controls the compensation strength. Modulating the original image produces the final illumination-compensated output: $\tilde{I}(x) = I(x) \odot g(x)$ with $g(x)$ bounded to a valid range, producing a illumination-normalized RGB image that is highly invariant to low-light degradation.

2.2 Frequency–Orientation Selective Filter

To enhance the perception of curvilinear features while suppressing texture-induced ambiguities, we design the frequency–orientation selective filter (FOSF) module to operate on bottleneck features. Given an intermediate feature $F_s \in \mathbb{R}^{H\times W\times C}$, we first construct a single-channel guidance map $x_{\text{in}} \in \mathbb{R}^{H\times W}$ for frequency-orientation analysis. Then, the Haar wavelet transform [16] is applied to obtain four frequency sub-bands $\{F^{\text{LL}}, F^{\text{LH}}, F^{\text{HL}}, F^{\text{HH}}\}$. To retain informative high-frequency components that are highly related to curvilinear features, we perform per-pixel competition among the three high-frequency sub-bands. Concretely, a lightweight gate is adopted to process $\{|F^{\text{LH}}|, |F^{\text{HL}}|, |F^{\text{HH}}|\}$ and predict normalized weights $(w_{\text{LH}}, w_{\text{HL}}, w_{\text{HH}})$ via softmax, yielding the aggregated high-frequency response:

$$F_{\text{HF}} = w_{\text{LH}}|F^{\text{LH}}| + w_{\text{HL}}|F^{\text{HL}}| + w_{\text{HH}}|F^{\text{HH}}|, \tag{2}$$

which prevents single texture-heavy band from domination. To further emphasize elongated structures possessing coherent directions, we apply T fixed-orientation Gabor filters [17] on x_{in}, producing orientation-specific responses $\{G_j\}_{j=1}^{T}$. Then, a lightweight gating network predicts pixel-wise orientation weights $\{\pi_j(x)\}_{j=1}^{T}$ from concatenated responses. The selected directional evidence is computed as

$$G_{\text{sel}}(x) = \sum_{j=1}^{T} \pi_j(x)\, G_j(x), \tag{3}$$

thereby adaptively selecting the dominant orientation at each spatial location. We then balance low-frequency context and oriented structure by predicting mixing weights (α, β) conditioned on $\{F^{\text{LL}}, G_{\text{sel}}\}$ to form an adaptive integration that jointly preserves coarse geometry continuity and directional coherence. The selected high-frequency response F_{HF} is concatenated subsequently and the fused features are finally refined by a lightweight attention block [23] and forwarded to the decoder for subsequent optimization.

2.3 Alternating Seg–Curve Optimization

To jointly model dense appearance cues and explicit curvilinear geometry, the alternating seg–curve optimization (ASCO) decoder utilizes two coupled branches to iteratively refine segmentation prediction and curve estimation. To be specific, we model each landmark as a Bezier curve C parameterized by M control points $\{p_m\}_{m=1}^{M}$, which ensures geometric continuity while enabling differentiable control-point updates. At the coarsest decoding stage, initial curve hypotheses are generated in an anchor-based manner, where each spatial location provides a normalized coordinates $a(x) \in (0,1)^2$. For each landmark class m, the proposer predicts confidence scores and regresses control-point offsets $\Delta_m(x)$ in logit space: $p_m(x) = \sigma(\text{logit}(a(x)) + \Delta_m(x))$, where $\text{logit}(x) = \log(x/(1-x))$ with x clamped to $[10^{-6}, 1-10^{-6}]$ for numerical stability, and $\sigma(\cdot)$ is the sigmoid function. The top-K sets of anchors are selected as initial geometric hypotheses, providing coarse structural initialization. To inject curve priors into dense prediction, the predicted curve is softly rasterized into a spatial prior map:

$$P(x) = \exp\left(-\frac{1}{2\sigma^2} \min_{t\in[0,1]} \|x - C(t)\|_2^2\right). \tag{4}$$

Through cross-attention, the rasterized prior constrains decoder features to align with the underlying curve geometry. Starting from the coarse proposals, the curve branch undergoes refinement using segmentation features across decoding stages. At stage s, decoder features $F_d^{(s)}$ are sampled along the current curve hypothesis $C^{(s)}$, yielding a curve embedding that predicts control-point updates:

$$p_k^{(s+1)} = p_k^{(s)} + \Delta p_k^{(s)}, \qquad \Delta p_k^{(s)} = \mathcal{R}^{(s)}\Big(\Phi\Big(F_d^{(s)}, C^{(s)}\Big)\Big), \tag{5}$$

where $\Phi(\cdot)$ denotes feature sampling and $\mathcal{R}^{(s)}(\cdot)$ is a stage-specific refinement head. Re-rasterizing the refined curve and re-injecting it into the segmentation branch forms a cascaded alternating loop executed S times.

2.4 Training Objectives

The network is trained end-to-end with a weighted multi-task objective:

$$\mathcal{L} = \mathcal{L}_{\text{seg}} + \lambda_{\text{curve}}\mathcal{L}_{\text{curve}} + \lambda_{\text{illum}}\mathcal{L}_{\text{illum}}. \tag{6}$$

The term $\mathcal{L}_{\text{seg}}$ supervises dense landmark masks using a combination of Dice and BCE losses to balance region overlap and pixel-wise classification. We further apply a modified center-line loss [7] on the curves to enforce structural continuity of elongated landmarks across refinement stages. Finally, to stabilize illumination compensation and avoid over-amplification, we regularize both the predicted illumination field and the gain map by penalizing spatial variations and excessive deviation from unity:

$$\mathcal{L}_{\text{illum}} = \|\nabla L\|_1 + \|g - \mathbf{1}\|_1. \tag{7}$$

3 Experiments

3.1 Datasets and Evaluation Metrics

We evaluate the proposed method on three public laparoscopic liver landmark benchmarks: L3D [19], L3D-2K [6], and P2ILF [1]. Specifically, L3D comprises 1,152 annotated keyframes, partitioned into 921 for training, 122 for validation, and 109 for testing. L3D-2K includes 2,000 keyframes, split into 1,532/230, and 238 images for training, validation, and testing, respectively. For P2ILF, which originally provides 183 annotated images with 167 allocated for training, the unavailability of the official testing set necessitates subdividing its training subset into 124 images for training and 43 for testing. To quantify region-level segmentation accuracy, we utilize the dice score coefficient (DSC) and intersection-over-union (IoU), alongside the average symmetric surface distance (ASSD) to evaluate the boundary localization of elongated landmarks.

3.2 Implementation Details

The RGB encoder employs a ResNet-34 backbone, while a frozen SAM-b image encoder extracts depth features. Geometrically, we use $T = 4$ Gabor filters with orientations $\{0, \frac{\pi}{4}, \frac{\pi}{2}, \frac{3\pi}{4}\}$, and each landmark curve is parameterized by $M = 5$ control points refined across $S = 4$ cascaded stages with $K = 16$ initial anchors.

For data preprocessing, input images are resized to 1024×1024 and augmented via random rotation and flipping. The framework is trained on a single NVIDIA GeForce RTX 3090 GPU with a batch size of 2 for 100 epochs. Optimization proceeds via AdamW with an initial learning rate of $1e-4$ and a weight decay of $1e-5$, guided by a cosine learning rate schedule to reach a minimum learning rate of $1e-6$. The weighting coefficients are set to $\lambda_{\text{curve}} = 0.2$ and $\lambda_{\text{illum}} = 0.1$.

Table 1. Quantitative comparison on L3D-2K, L3D and P2ILF datasets.

Methods	L3D-2K			L3D			P2ILF		
	DSC↑	IoU↑	ASSD↓	DSC↑	IoU↑	ASSD↓	DSC↑	IoU↑	ASSD↓
U-Net [21]	35.17	23.74	76.78	51.39	36.35	84.94	29.89	17.89	47.95
COSNet [14]	37.35	25.96	59.24	56.24	40.98	69.22	26.78	16.05	47.33
Res-UNet [24]	40.39	28.43	55.80	55.47	40.68	70.66	25.84	15.76	50.97
UNet++ [29]	38.70	27.26	58.70	57.09	41.92	74.31	34.96	21.57	42.39
HRNet [22]	41.19	29.36	56.40	58.36	43.50	70.02	33.64	21.31	44.16
DeepLabV3+ [4]	41.55	29.89	55.11	59.74	44.92	60.86	27.62	16.42	50.77
TransUNet [3]	37.54	25.85	46.75	56.81	41.44	76.16	25.49	15.22	52.14
CaseNet [26]	40.23	28.37	56.55	60.94	46.09	63.89	33.94	21.33	45.02
nnU-Net [11]	41.25	29.30	51.28	60.97	46.14	62.03	35.41	22.06	42.64
SAM-Adapter [5]	39.20	26.81	59.61	57.57	42.88	74.31	21.12	12.00	57.13
SAMed [27]	43.72	31.20	43.01	62.03	47.17	61.55	31.73	19.42	40.08
SAM-LST [2]	39.43	27.39	56.69	60.51	45.03	68.87	28.75	18.38	46.53
AutoSAM [10]	40.47	28.57	54.58	59.12	44.21	62.49	25.71	15.43	53.65
Double Res-UNet [1]	40.53	28.60	53.75	58.39	43.52	63.78	36.54	22.80	39.26
D^2GPLand [19]	49.31	35.76	41.34	63.52	48.68	59.38	40.55	25.87	38.73
D^2GPLand+ [6]	51.66	37.59	36.24	64.62	50.14	57.68	42.15	27.40	37.12
A2ONet	**53.51**	**38.32**	**30.97**	**65.31**	**50.87**	**49.89**	**43.02**	**27.95**	**33.47**

3.3 Comparison with State-of-the-Art

We benchmark our method against representative baselines classified into three categories: (i) general-purpose segmentation models (U-Net [21], COSNet [14], Res-UNet [24], U-Net++ [29], HRNet [22], DeepLabV3+ [4], TransUNet [3], CaseNet [26], nnU-Net [11]), (ii) foundation model-based adaptation methods (SAM-Adapter [5], SAMed [27], SAM-LST [2], AutoSAM [10]), and (iii) task-specific detection approaches (D^2GPLand [19], D^2GPLand+ [6], Double Res-UNet [1]). Direct comparison excludes curve-only methods, as their evaluation protocol, *i.e.*, expanding curves to a fixed thickness for region-based assessment,

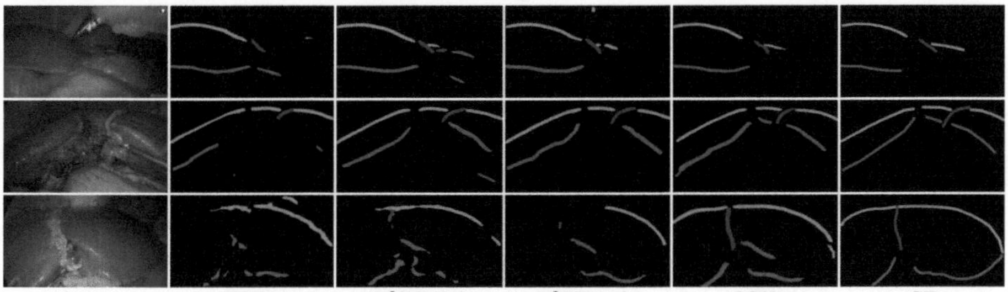

Fig. 3. Visualizations of the landmark detection results on the L3D-2K, L3D, and P2ILF datasets, arranged from top to bottom respectively.

precludes fair benchmarking against mask-based predictors, leaving curve-native comparisons for future work. Table 1 indicates that our method achieves the highest Dice and IoU across all datasets, establishing robust region-level delineation despite low-light and texture interference. Compared with D^2GPLand+, the strongest competing task-specific baseline, our framework improves DSC/IoU by 1.85%/0.73% on L3D-2K, 0.69%/0.73% on L3D, and 0.87%/0.55% on P2ILF. Notably, it also reduces ASSD by 5.27, 7.79, and 3.65 pixels on the three datasets, respectively, indicating more precise boundary alignment alongside enhanced landmark coverage. Further, paired significance tests confirm statistically significant improvements across datasets.

Qualitatively, Fig. 3 illustrates that existing baselines frequently generate fragmented predictions along thin curvilinear landmarks under low-light conditions. Conversely, our method yields continuous, geometrically consistent delineations with fewer false positives, demonstrating the advantages of explicit curve regularization and illumination stabilization (Table 2).

Table 2. Ablation study of key components on the L3D-2K dataset.

Variant	IFC	$\mathcal{L}_{illum}$	FOSF	ASCO	$\mathcal{L}_{curve}$	DSC↑	IoU↑	ASSD↓
Baseline						37.69	27.13	58.76
V1	✓					38.23	27.76	56.90
V2	✓	✓				40.45	29.04	52.36
V3			✓			39.98	28.29	53.49
V4	✓	✓	✓			42.48	31.14	47.82
V5	✓	✓	✓	✓		44.45	33.10	43.33
A2ONet	✓	✓	✓	✓	✓	**45.16**	**33.76**	**40.53**

3.4 Ablation Study

To verify the effectiveness of individual components in our framework, we conduct ablation experiments on the L3D-2K validation set. The baseline model consists of a ResNet encoder and a pretrained SAM image encoder, followed by a standard CNN decoder. Integrating the IFC block (V1) establishes consistent gains over this baseline, indicating the importance of explicitly normalizing low-light appearance. Further introducing $\mathcal{L}_{illum}$ (V2) yields a larger gain with 2.22% in DSC, 1.28% in IoU, and 4.54 pixels in ASSD, indicating that overexposure suppression stabilizes illumination compensation. Independent application of FOSF modules (V3) also improves performance, demonstrating effective suppression of texture-induced ambiguities. Combining IFC and $\mathcal{L}_{illum}$ with FOSF blocks (V4) produces the largest jump compared to previous variants, validating their strong complementarity. Building upon these feature-level enhancements, incorporating the ASCO decoder (V5) further improves overlap and boundary accuracy by 1.97% in DSC, 1.96% in IoU, and 4.49 pixels in ASSD, justifying the effectiveness of alternating optimization. Finally, applying $\mathcal{L}_{curve}$ yields the best overall configuration, confirming that explicit curve supervision provides extra geometric regularization beyond architectural coupling.

4 Conclusion

This study introduces A2ONet, an attenuation-resilient alternating optimization framework for reliable laparoscopic liver landmark detection. By jointly addressing illumination degradation and texture-induced ambiguities, A2ONet enhances representation robustness through illumination field compensation and frequency-orientation selective filtering. More importantly, the proposed alternating seg-curve optimization decoder explicitly reconciles dense pixel-wise localization with continuous curvilinear geometry, alleviating the inherent localization-continuity trade-off. Extensive experiments on L3D-2K, L3D, and P2ILF demonstrate consistent improvements over strong baselines, while comprehensive ablation studies confirm the complementary effectiveness of our core components. By yielding structurally consistent landmarks under challenging illumination, A2ONet provides a stable and robust prerequisite for AR-guided navigation.

Acknowledgments. This work was supported in part by a Shenzhen-Hong Kong-Macao Science and Technology Plan Project (Category C Project) under Shenzhen Municipal Science and Technology Innovation Commission (No. SGDX20230821092359002), in part by the Research Grants Council of the Hong Kong Special Administrative Region, China, under Project T45-401/22-N, and in part by a project under the Collaborative Research with World-leading Research Groups scheme of The Hong Kong Polytechnic University (No. G-SACF).

Disclosure of Interests. The authors have no competing interests.

References

1. Ali, S., et al.: An objective comparison of methods for augmented reality in laparoscopic liver resection by preoperative-to-intraoperative image fusion from the miccai2022 challenge. Med. Image Anal. **99**, 103371 (2025)
2. Chai, S., et al.: Ladder fine-tuning approach for sam integrating complementary network. Proc. Comput. Sci. **246**, 4951–4958 (2024)
3. Chen, J., et al.: Transunet: transformers make strong encoders for medical image segmentation. arXiv preprint arXiv:2102.04306 (2021)
4. Chen, L.C., Zhu, Y., Papandreou, G., Schroff, F., Adam, H.: Encoder-decoder with atrous separable convolution for semantic image segmentation. In: Proceedings of the European conference on computer vision (ECCV), pp. 801–818 (2018)
5. Chen, T., et al.: Sam-adapter: adapting segment anything in underperformed scenes. In: Proceedings of the IEEE/CVF International Conference on Computer Vision, pp. 3367–3375 (2023)
6. Cui, R., et al.: Depth-induced prompt learning for laparoscopic liver landmark detection. Med. Image Analy. 103940 (2026)
7. Cui, R., Zhang, J., Pei, J., Wang, K., Heng, P.A., Qin, J.: Topology-constrained learning for efficient laparoscopic liver landmark detection. In: International Conference on Medical Image Computing and Computer-Assisted Intervention, pp. 585–594. Springer (2025).https://doi.org/10.1007/978-3-032-05127-1_56
8. Guo, D., Si, W., Li, Z., Pei, J., Heng, P.A.: Surgical workflow recognition and blocking effectiveness detection in laparoscopic liver resection with pringle maneuver. In: Proceedings of the AAAI Conference on Artificial Intelligence, vol. 39, pp. 3220–3228 (2025)
9. He, K., Zhang, X., Ren, S., Sun, J.: Deep residual learning for image recognition. In: Proceedings of the IEEE Conference on Computer Vision and Pattern Recognition, pp. 770–778 (2016)
10. Hu, X., Xu, X., Shi, Y.: How to efficiently adapt large segmentation model (sam) to medical images, arXiv preprint (2023). arXiv:2306.13731
11. Isensee, F., et al.: nnu-net revisited: a call for rigorous validation in 3d medical image segmentation. In: International Conference on Medical Image Computing and Computer-Assisted Intervention, pp. 488–498. Springer (2024). https://doi.org/10.1007/978-3-031-72114-4_47
12. Kirillov, A., et al.: Segment anything. In: Proceedings of the IEEE/CVF International Conference on Computer Vision, pp. 4015–4026 (2023)
13. Koo, B., et al.: Automatic, global registration in laparoscopic liver surgery. Int. J. Comput. Assist. Radiol. Surg. **17**(1), 167–176 (2022)
14. Labrunie, M., Pizarro, D., Tilmant, C., Bartoli, A.: Automatic 3d/2d deformable registration in minimally invasive liver resection using a mesh recovery network. In: Medical imaging deep learn. (2023)
15. Li, Q., Liu, F., Yang, S., Shen, D., Jin, Y.: Bcrnet: enhancing landmark detection in laparoscopic liver surgery via bezier curve refinement. In: International Conference on Medical Image Computing and Computer-Assisted Intervention, pp. 77–87. Springer (2025), https://doi.org/10.1007/978-3-032-05127-1_8
16. Mallat, S.G.: A theory for multiresolution signal decomposition: the wavelet representation. IEEE Trans. Pattern Anal. Mach. Intell. **11**(7), 674–693 (2002)
17. Mehrotra, R., Namuduri, K.R., Ranganathan, N.: Gabor filter-based edge detection. Pattern Recogn. **25**(12), 1479–1494 (1992)

18. Nguyen, K.T., Marsh, J.W., Tsung, A., Steel, J.J.L., Gamblin, T.C., Geller, D.A.: Comparative benefits of laparoscopic vs open hepatic resection: a critical appraisal. Arch. Surg. **146**(3), 348–356 (2011)
19. Pei, J., Cui, R., Li, Y., Si, W., Qin, J., Heng, P.A.: Depth-driven geometric prompt learning for laparoscopic liver landmark detection. In: International Conference on Medical Image Computing and Computer-Assisted Intervention, pp. 154–164. Springer (2024)
20. Plantefève, R., Haouchine, N., Radoux, J.-P., Cotin, S.: Automatic alignment of pre and intraoperative data using anatomical landmarks for augmented laparoscopic liver surgery. In: Bello, F., Cotin, S. (eds.) ISBMS 2014. LNCS, vol. 8789, pp. 58–66. Springer, Cham (2014). https://doi.org/10.1007/978-3-319-12057-7_7
21. Ronneberger, O., Fischer, P., Brox, T.: U-Net: convolutional networks for biomedical image segmentation. In: Navab, N., Hornegger, J., Wells, W.M., Frangi, A.F. (eds.) MICCAI 2015. LNCS, vol. 9351, pp. 234–241. Springer, Cham (2015). https://doi.org/10.1007/978-3-319-24574-4_28
22. Wang, J., et al.: Deep high-resolution representation learning for visual recognition. IEEE Trans. Pattern Anal. Mach. Intell. **43**(10), 3349–3364 (2020)
23. Woo, S., Park, J., Lee, J.-Y., Kweon, I.S.: CBAM: convolutional block attention module. In: Ferrari, V., Hebert, M., Sminchisescu, C., Weiss, Y. (eds.) ECCV 2018. LNCS, vol. 11211, pp. 3–19. Springer, Cham (2018). https://doi.org/10.1007/978-3-030-01234-2_1
24. Xiao, X., Lian, S., Luo, Z., Li, S.: Weighted res-unet for high-quality retina vessel segmentation. In: 2018 9th International Conference on Information Technology in Medicine and Education (ITME), pp. 327–331. IEEE (2018)
25. Yang, L., et al.: Depth anything v2. Adv. Neural. Inf. Process. Syst. **37**, 21875–21911 (2024)
26. Yu, Z., Feng, C., Liu, M.Y., Ramalingam, S.: Casenet: deep category-aware semantic edge detection. In: Proceedings of the IEEE Conference on Computer Vision and Pattern Recognition, pp. 5964–5973 (2017)
27. Zhang, K., Liu, D.: Customized segment anything model for medical image segmentation, arXiv preprint arXiv:2304.13785 (2023)
28. Zhou, J., Gao, B., Wang, K., Pei, J., Heng, P.A., Qin, J.: Landmark-free preoperative-to-intraoperative registration in laparoscopic liver resection. IEEE Trans. Med. Imaging (2025)
29. Zhou, Z., Siddiquee, M.M.R., Tajbakhsh, N., Liang, J.: Unet++: redesigning skip connections to exploit multiscale features in image segmentation. IEEE Trans. Med. Imaging **39**(6), 1856–1867 (2019)

Automated Scope Pose Estimation in Real-World Robotic-Assisted Bronchoscopy with Integrated C-Arm Imaging

Dingzhong Zhang(✉), Hedyeh Rafii-Tari, and Babak Matinfar

Researchs & Development, Johnson & Johnson MedTech Surgery, Santa Clara, CA, USA
{dzhan111,hrafiita,mmatinfa}@its.jnj.com

Abstract. Robotic-assisted bronchoscopy enables physicians to access pulmonary lesions with enhanced stability and precision; however, navigation accuracy can be compromised by CT-to-body divergence due to respiratory motion, anatomical deformation during the procedure and tracking system errors. Cone-beam computed tomography (CBCT) has therefore emerged as a key intra-operative imaging modality for biopsy verification and navigation updates. A critical prerequisite for integrating CBCT into the workflow is accurate registration between the navigation system and the CBCT coordinate frame, which relies on precise bronchoscope pose estimation. Existing semi-automated solutions require manual scope tip localization and potential correction of pose parameters, introducing variability and prolonging procedure time. In this work, we propose a fully automated pipeline that estimates the bronchoscope pose directly from CBCT images, which consists of: (1) a two-stage model inferencing strategy for rapid and accurate scope tip segmentation, and (2) a context-aware robust pose estimation algorithm. Evaluated on 25 diverse real-world clinical cases, the method achieved a mean position error of 0.55 ± 0.28 mm and orientation error of $2.74 \pm 1.47°$, with an average processing time of 4.47 s, approximately 20× faster than the current approach. This combination of accuracy and efficiency enables safer and more reliable navigation updates while reducing clinician workload and minimizing user-induced errors.

Keywords: Robotic-assisted Bronchoscopy · C-Arm Integration · Bronchoscope Pose Estimation · Surgical Navigation · Image Segmentation

1 Introduction

Robotic-assisted bronchoscopy (RAB) has emerged as an effective modality for diagnosing and treating pulmonary lesions; however, navigation accuracy is often degraded by CT-to-body divergence caused by respiratory motion, anatomic

G. Yang et al. (Eds.): MICCAI 2026, LNCS 16893, pp. 65–74, 2027.
https://doi.org/10.1007/978-3-032-38236-8_7

deformation during the procedure and tracking system errors such as electromagnetic distortion [4,5,7,13]. As a result, substantial discrepancies between preoperative plans and true intra-operative lesion locations are frequently observed, leading to reduced tool-in-lesion rates and diagnostic yield if not corrected intraoperatively [4,5,14]. Cone-beam computed tomography (CBCT) has become a critical intra-operative imaging modality in RAB, providing real-time 3D volumetric information for tool-in-lesion confirmation and navigation updates [4,8,9]. Clinical studies have shown that integrating CBCT with RAB systems significantly improves navigation success and diagnostic yield [1–7,10–12]. RAB systems incorporate CBCT to update navigation by registering the CBCT coordinate frame with the tracking system. Accurate estimation of the bronchoscope pose, including both position and orientation, from CBCT images is therefore a prerequisite for computing a reliable transformation matrix. However, current semi-automated workflows require bronchoscopists to manually localize the scope tip and refine pose parameters when inaccuracies are present, a process that is time-consuming, operator-dependent, and susceptible to inter-operator variability and user-induced error [15–19].

To address these limitations, we propose a fully automated workflow for fast and accurate bronchoscope pose estimation from CBCT images. The proposed workflow comprises two key components: (1) a two-stage inferencing strategy for precise scope tip segmentation, and (2) a robust pose estimation algorithm that leverages contextual information from both the segmented scope geometry and surrounding anatomical structures. Unlike prior CBCT-guided RAB workflows that require manual or semi-automated scope pose identification, our approach eliminates manual intervention while remaining robust to metal- and motion-induced artifacts, indistinct scope boundaries, and working channel instruments. The method is validated on a diverse set of real-world RAB cases acquired during routine clinical procedures. Quantitative results demonstrate high accuracy and substantially reduced pose estimation time, thereby improving procedural reliability, efficiency, and scalability for CBCT-guided robotic bronchoscopy.

2 Methods

2.1 Scope Tip Segmentation

Segmenting the scope tip from the bronchoscopic shaft is challenging due to their continuous physical structure and shared metallic composition, which produce similarly high image intensities. This task is further complicated by artifacts, working channel instruments, and over-segmentation caused by metallic implants in real-world patient CBCT. To address these challenges, we propose a two-stage inferencing strategy, as illustrated in Fig. 1.

In the first stage, the CBCT volume is resampled to a lower resolution and processed by a coarse segmentation model to localize the scope tip. The resulting mask is used to estimate the scope tip center, which defines the center of a volume of interest (VOI). In the second stage, the original CBCT image is cropped to

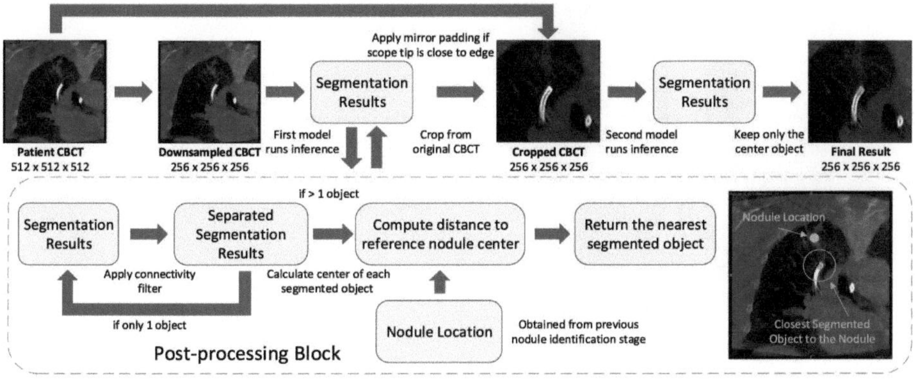

Fig. 1. Workflow of the two-stage inferencing strategy with post-processing steps.

this VOI and provided as input to a fine segmentation model for precise scope tip delineation. Mirror padding is applied to the cropped image when necessary.

The two models in the proposed inferencing strategy share the same architecture of U-Net with residual encoders [20], which has been shown to outperform Transformer-based and Mamba-based networks across a range of medical image segmentation tasks, while having relatively low GPU VRAM cost and shorter runtime compared with other CNN-based architectures [21]. While processing fewer patches on smaller volumes enables both models to effectively reduce isolated false positives due to metal implants, additional post-processing is employed to ensure clean final segmentations. Specifically, the first stage retains only the connected component nearest to the target nodule, whereas the second stage preserves only the centrally located segmented object.

2.2 Scope Pose Estimation

Scope Heading Estimation. To compute the scope heading vector, principal component analysis (PCA) is first applied to the segmented scope tip mask to extract the direction of maximum variance. The first principal component is interpreted as the principal axis of the scope tip. Since this axis is bidirectional, a context-based sampling strategy is employed to resolve the correct heading, leveraging the fact that the bronchoscope exhibits substantially higher CBCT intensity than surrounding anatomical structures. As illustrated in Fig. 2(a), two sampling spheres are placed along the principal axis. Within each sphere, a set of sampling points is generated, and the voxel intensities at these points are accumulated. The sphere with the lower total intensity is identified as containing the distal tip of the scope, thereby determining the heading direction.

While computing relative intensity differences between the two sampling regions helps reduce the impact of global intensity variations across scans, real-world CBCT images may exhibit noises, working channel instruments, metal and motion artifacts that can obscure scope boundaries and reduce inter-region

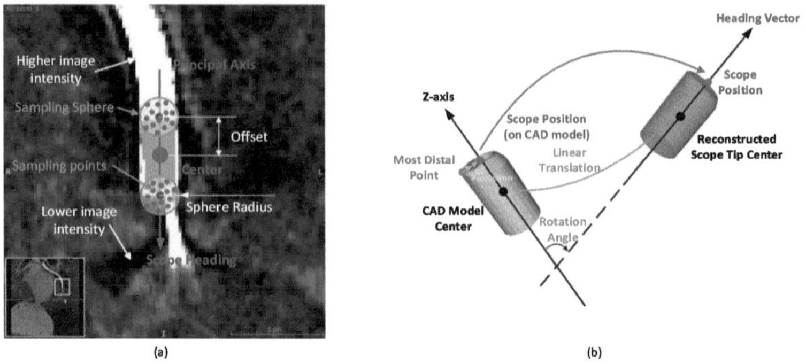

Fig. 2. Scope pose estimation. (a) Scope heading estimation using a context-based sampling method. (b) Scope position estimation using a registration-based method.

Algorithm 1. Spherical Coordinate Grid with Uniform Volume Density

Input: N (sampling points), R (sphere radius) **Definitions:** n_r (radial steps), n_θ (polar steps), n_ϕ (azimuthal steps); i (radial index), j (polar index), k (azimuthal index); r_i (radius at layer i), θ_j (polar angle), ϕ_k (azimuth angle); $p_{i,j,k} = (x, y, z)$ (Cartesian point) **Procedure:**

1. Set $n_r = \text{round}(N^{1/3})$, $n_\theta = 2n_r$, $n_\phi = 2n_r$
2. **for** $i = 1, \ldots, n_r$ **do** $r_i = R\left(\frac{i}{n_r}\right)^{1/3}$ (cube-root for uniform volume density)
3. **for** $j = 0, \ldots, n_\theta - 1$ **do** $\theta_j = \pi\frac{j+0.5}{n_\theta}$ (offset avoids pole clustering)
4. **for** $k = 0, \ldots, n_\phi - 1$ **do** $\phi_k = 2\pi\frac{k}{n_\phi}$
5. Compute $(x, y, z) = (r_i \sin\theta_j \cos\phi_k,\ r_i \sin\theta_j \sin\phi_k,\ r_i \cos\theta_j)$
6. Emit $p_{i,j,k} = (x, y, z)$
7. Return $\{p_{i,j,k}\}$

---

contrast. To enhance robustness, sampling points are generated using a spherical coordinate grid with uniform azimuthal and polar angle sampling, yielding a well-distributed point set, as shown in Algorithm 1. Sampling parameters, including sphere radius, center offset, and number of points, are derived from the bronchoscope tip CAD model and selected to maximize contrast.

Scope Position Estimation. The scope tip position is defined as the most distal point projected onto the principal axis. Directly extracting this point from the segmention mask can be challenging due to complex tip geometry and potential segmentation inaccuracies. To improve robustness, a registration-based method is employed that utilizes the known geometry of the bronchoscope tip CAD model. Specifically, the CAD model is rigidly aligned with the reconstructed scope tip by rotating its Z-axis to be parallel with the estimated heading vector and translating its center to match the center of the reconstructed scope tip. The most distal point of the aligned CAD model is then projected onto the principal axis, yielding the estimated scope tip position, as shown in Fig. 2(b).

3 Data Preparation

A total of 225 patient CBCT scans were collected during the robotic bronchoscopy procedures using MONARCH^{TM} Platform across multiple hospitals (the dataset meets HIPAA compliance). All scans were acquired using GE OCE 3D CBCT systems and reconstructed at a resolution of $512 \times 512 \times 512$. The scope tip segmentation ground truth was generated using a convex hull representation of the scope tip CAD model, as sub-surface structures cannot be captured by CBCT image. The convex hull model was aligned to the scope tip in CBCT using the semi-automated workflow from the MONARCH^{TM} Platform and then manually refined to achieve precise boundary alignment. The finalized model was converted into a binary segmentation mask. Ground truth for scope heading and position was derived from physician operation logs recorded by the intra-operative planning software, which served as the reference standard for pose estimation evaluation. All ground truth data were reviewed and validated by an experienced clinical team.

4 Experiments and Results

4.1 Scope Tip Segmentation

Among the 225 patient CBCT scans, 200 were used for training and validation and 25 for testing. For the first-stage model, CBCT volumes were resampled to $256 \times 256 \times 256$ using linear interpolation, while segmentation masks were resampled using nearest-neighbor interpolation. For the second stage, a $256 \times 256 \times 256$ VOI centered on the scope tip was cropped from the original CBCT volume, with mirror padding applied when necessary. All models were trained for 1000 epochs

Table 1. Comparison of baseline U-Net performance using different loss functions.

Loss Function	Training Dataset		Test Dataset	
	Dice Score (%)	False Positive	Dice Score (%)	False Positive
Focal	89.74	300.59	80.82	1258.48
Dice + Focal	92.15	303.12	80.13	1477.40
Focal-Tversky	91.68	408.18	80.25	1618.80
CE + Focal-Tversky	91.65	164.93	79.51	1210.88
Dice + CE	92.71	219.96	81.16	1176.04
Dice + TopK10	**93.52**	**216.57**	**83.01**	**917.68**
Dice + TopK10 + Focal	93.40	228.56	80.65	1368.76
Dice + TopK10 + CE	93.23	234.69	80.84	1335.36

Table 2. Comparison of model performance across different inferencing strategies before and after post-processing. Results are averaged over 25 real-world RAB cases.

Model	Original Results		Post-processed Results	
	Dice Score (%)	False Positive	Dice Score (%)	False Positive
First-stage	87.07	21.88	87.89	15.24
Second-stage	**86.11**	**348.16**	**89.26**	**102.12**
Single-stage	84.78	621.96	/	/
Cascaded	84.90	530.44	/	/

on dual RTX 4500 ADA GPUs (24 GB each) with data augmentation applied to improve generalization.

Loss functions were first evaluated using a baseline U-Net (Table 1). Dice+CE and Dice+TopK10 achieved higher Dice scores and lower false positives. Therefore, the first-stage model employed Dice+CE to emphasize global localization accuracy, while the second-stage model used Dice+TopK10 to specifically address challenging cases. We then compared different inferencing strategies using a large-scale U-Net with residual encoders to further enhance segmentation performance. As shown in Table 2, the proposed two-stage strategy outperformed single-stage full resolution inference, achieving the highest Dice score of 89.26% and the lowest false positive of 102.12 after post-processing. The approach also outperformed cascaded U-Net, which similarly adopt a coarse-to-fine segmentation strategy. Because in cascaded U-Net, the first-stage prediction is used directly to train the second-stage model, allowing errors to propagate and degrade the final performance. Notably, the two-stage approach achieved a higher Dice score and a lower false positive than other strategies even before post-processing due to the smaller, scope-centered input volume.

4.2 Scope Heading Identification

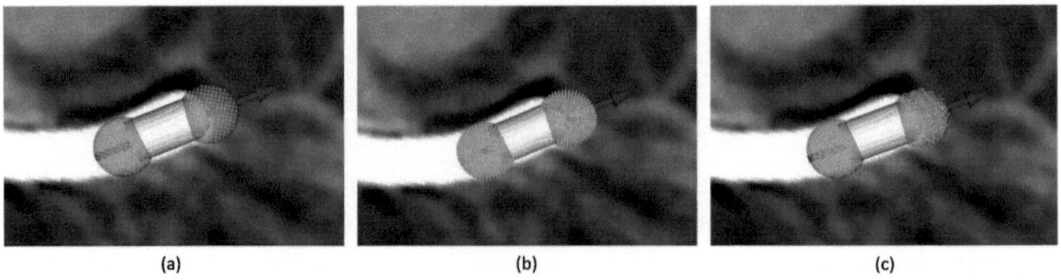

Fig. 3. Scope heading identification using context-based sampling methods. (a) Uniform Cartesian grid sampling. (b) Spherical coordinate grid sampling. (c) Spherical Fibonacci lattice sampling.

Table 3. Comparison of sampling strategies for scope heading identification. Results are averaged over 25 real-world RAB cases. High/Low denote spheres with higher/lower accumulated voxel intensity.

Sampling Method	High ($\times 10^6$)	Low ($\times 10^6$)	Diff. ($\times 10^6$)	Time (ms)
Uniform Cartesian Grid	1.02	-0.03	1.04	**0.11**
Spherical Coordinate Grid	19.12	1.42	**17.70**	1.60
Spherical Fibonacci Lattices	4.35	0.13	4.22	0.65

The proposed spherical coordinate grid sampling was compared with two alternatives: a uniform Cartesian grid and spherical Fibonacci lattices (Fig. 3). The Cartesian grid samples points uniformly along the X-, Y-, and Z-axes within the sphere, whereas the spherical Fibonacci lattice [22] uses golden-angle angular spacing with randomized radial distances to achieve quasi-uniform volumetric coverage. All methods were evaluated under identical settings: a 6.5 mm offset between the sphere and scope tip centers, a sphere radius of 3 mm, and 2000 sampling points, based on the scope tip size of approximately 7.8 mm in height and 4.4 mm in diameter. As summarized in Table 3, the spherical coordinate grid produced the largest inter-sphere intensity difference, with an average of 17.70×10^6 intensity units, substantially outperforming the Cartesian grid and

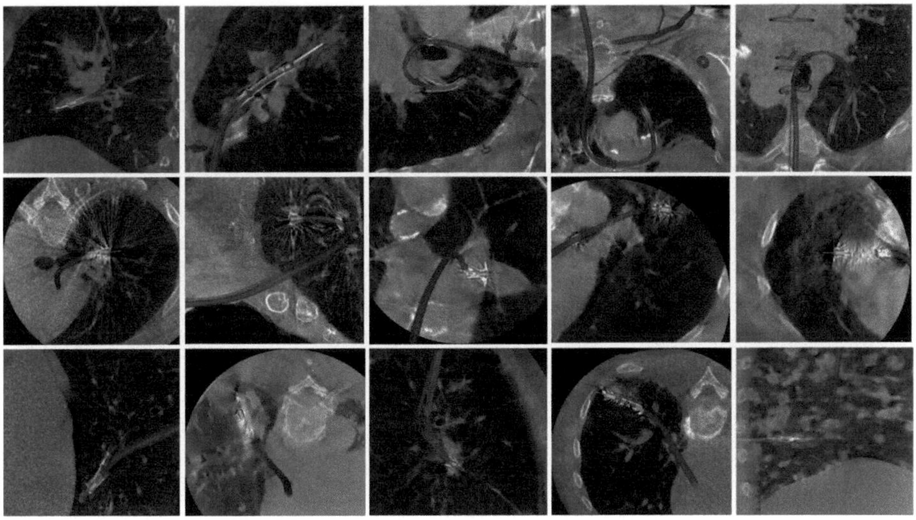

Fig. 4. Scope pose estimation results for normal cases with metal implants, working channel instruments (top row), and challenging cases with metal- and motion-induced artifacts (second and third rows). The pose is shown using the scope tip CAD model with an arrow indicating the heading; the bronchoscope is volume-rendered in blue. (Color figure online)

Fibonacci lattice methods. The larger intensity contrast enables more robust distinction between the distal and proximal ends of the scope. All sampling strategies incurred negligible computational overhead and satisfied real-time requirements.

4.3 Scope Pose Estimation

Figure 4 presents qualitative results for scope pose estimation under both normal and challenging conditions, including working channel instruments, metal implants, metal- and motion-induced artifacts, and indistinct scope boundaries. The proposed method consistently identified the correct scope position and heading across all cases, demonstrating strong robustness to perturbations commonly encountered in intra-operative CBCT.

Table 4. Comparison of scope pose estimation strategies. Results are averaged over 25 real-world RAB cases.

Strategy	Position Error (mm)	Heading Error (°)	Total Time (s)
Single-stage Inference	0.58 ± 0.31	3.12 ± 1.64	27.62
Two-stage Inference	$\mathbf{0.55 \pm 0.28}$	$\mathbf{2.74 \pm 1.47}$	**4.47** (2.26 + 2.21)

Quantitative results are summarized in Table 4. The two-stage strategy achieved a mean position error of 0.55 ± 0.28 mm and an orientation error of $2.74 \pm 1.47°$, outperforming the single-stage approach (0.58 ± 0.31 mm and $3.12 \pm 1.64°$). This improved accuracy is attributed to the higher-quality segmentation produced by the two-stage pipeline, which preserves fine scope-tip details while suppressing false positives. Additionally, both with the acceleration of NVIDIA TensorRT and parallel computation, the two-stage method reduced average processing time to 4.47 s, compared with 27.62 s for single-stage inference. When integrated into the clinical workflow, this translates to a reduction of 15% total average navigation time from previously reported 9.8 min [4] to 8.3 min, underscoring the clinical feasibility for real-time robotic bronchoscopy.

5 Conclusion and Discussion

In this work, we presented a fully automated workflow for precise and real-time bronchoscope pose estimation during robotic-assisted bronchoscopy with C-arm integration. By combining a two-stage inferencing strategy for accurate scope tip segmentation with a context-aware pose estimation algorithm, the proposed approach eliminates manual intervention for CBCT-guided navigation updates, which are time-consuming and prone to inter-operator variability. Evaluation on real-world clinical CBCT data demonstrates that the method achieves sub-millimeter position accuracy and low orientation error, while reducing total processing time to under 4.5 s, approximately 20× faster than existing semi-automated approach. The two-stage strategy achieves both high accuracy and efficiency by suppressing over-segmentations in challenging scenarios and minimizing computational cost. In addition, the proposed context-based heading determination and registration-based position estimation methods show strong robustness to metal artifacts, motion-induced distortions, and working channel instruments commonly encountered in intra-operative CBCT. While this study focuses on bronchoscope pose estimation for navigation updates, the framework is generalizable to other interventional devices and CBCT-guided procedures, enabling practical and scalable real-time C-arm-integrated navigation.

Disclosure of Interests. The authors have no competing interests to declare that are relevant to the content of this article.

References

1. Liu, Y., et al.: Intraprocedural cone-beam CT during robotic-assisted bronchoscopy improves diagnostic yield and sensitivity for malignancy. Chest **168**(4), A5926–A5927 (2025). https://doi.org/10.1016/j.chest.2025.07.3321
2. Shaller, B.D., Duong, D.K., Swenson, K.E., Free, D.R., Bedi, H.: Added value of a robotic-assisted bronchoscopy platform in cone-beam computed tomography-guided bronchoscopy for the diagnosis of pulmonary parenchymal lesions. J. Bronchol. Intervent. Pulmonol. **31**(3), e0971 (2024). https://doi.org/10.1097/LBR.0000000000000971
3. Chen, J., et al.: Diagnostic performance of Monarch robotic bronchoscopy with and without mobile cone-beam CT support. Lung Cancer **213**, 108910 (2026). https://doi.org/10.1016/j.lungcan.2026.108910
4. Cumbo-Nacheli, G., Velagapudi, R.K., Enter, M., Egan, J.P., 3rd., Conci, D.: Robotic-assisted bronchoscopy and cone-beam CT: a retrospective series. J. Bronchol. Intervent. Pulmonol. **29**(4), 303–306 (2022). https://doi.org/10.1097/LBR.0000000000000860
5. Ho, A.T.N., et al.: Virtual vs. reality in cone-beam CT-guided robotic-assisted bronchoscopy. J. Thoracic Dis. **17**(10), 9051–9062 (2025). https://doi.org/10.21037/jtd-2025-1399
6. Abdelghani, R., et al.: Cone-beam computed tomography-guided shape-sensing robotic bronchoscopy vs. electromagnetic navigation bronchoscopy for pulmonary nodules. J. Thoracic Dis. **16**(9), 5529–5538 (2024). https://doi.org/10.21037/jtd-24-178
7. Bashour, S.I., et al.: Improving shape-sensing robotic-assisted bronchoscopy outcomes with mobile cone-beam computed tomography guidance. Diagnostics **14**(17), 1955 (2024). https://doi.org/10.3390/diagnostics14171955
8. Duke, J.D., Sanborn, D., Reisenauer, J.: Enhancing nodule biopsy through technology integration. Innovations, 15569845231153640 (2023). https://doi.org/10.1177/15569845231153639
9. Ortiz-Jaimes, G., Reisenauer, J.: Real-world impact of robotic-assisted bronchoscopy on the staging and diagnosis of lung cancer: the shape of current and potential opportunities. Precis. Oncol. Rev., 75–94 (2023). https://doi.org/10.2147/POR.S395806

10. Brown, M.V., et al.: The diagnostic yield of cone beam CT combined with radial-endobronchial ultrasound for the diagnosis of peripheral pulmonary nodules: systematic review and meta-analysis. CHEST Pulmonary **2**(2), 100037 (2024). https://doi.org/10.1016/j.chpulm.2024.100037
11. Fernandez-Bussy, S., et al.: Robotic-assisted bronchoscopy: a narrative review of systems. J. Thoracic Dis. **16**(8), 5422–5434 (2024). https://doi.org/10.21037/jtd-24-456
12. Prado, R.M.G., Cicenia, J., Almeida, F.A.: Robotic-assisted bronchoscopy: a comprehensive review of system functions and analysis of outcome data. Diagnostics **14**(4), 399 (2024). https://doi.org/10.3390/diagnostics14040399
13. Chen, A.C., et al.: Accuracy of a robotic endoscopic system in cadaver models with simulated tumor targets: ACCESS study. Respiration **99**(1), 56–61 (2020). https://doi.org/10.1159/000504181
14. Pritchett, M.A., Schampaert, S., de Groot, J.A.H., Schirmer, C.C., van der Bom, I.: Cone-beam CT with augmented fluoroscopy for transbronchial biopsy. J. Bronchol. Intervent. Pulmonol. **25**(4), 274–282 (2018). https://doi.org/10.1097/LBR.0000000000000536
15. Bhadra, K., Rickman, O.B., Mahajan, A.K., Hogarth, D.K.: "Tool-in-lesion" accuracy of galaxy system—a robotic electromagnetic navigation bronchoscopy with integrated tool-in-lesion tomosynthesis technology (The MATCH Study). J. Bronchol. Intervent. Pulmonol. **31**(1), 23–29 (2024). https://doi.org/10.1097/LBR.0000000000000923
16. Aboudara, M., et al.: Improved diagnostic yield for lung nodules with digital tomosynthesis-corrected navigational bronchoscopy: initial experience with a novel adjunct. Respirology **25**(2), 206–213 (2020). https://doi.org/10.1111/resp.13609
17. Pritchett, M.A., Bhadra, K., Mattingley, J.S.: Electromagnetic navigation bronchoscopy with tomosynthesis-based visualization and positional correction: three-dimensional accuracy as confirmed by cone-beam computed tomography. J. Bronchol. Intervent. Pulmonol. **28**(1), 10–20 (2021). https://doi.org/10.1097/LBR.0000000000000687
18. Leira, O., Hofstad, E.F., Bø, L.E., Langø, T., Amundsen, T.: Navigated bronchoscopy with electromagnetic tracking—cone-beam computed tomography influence on tracking and registration accuracy. J. Bronchol. Intervent. Pulmonol. **18**(4), 329–336 (2011). https://doi.org/10.1097/LBR.0b013e318235d471
19. Bhadra, K., Setser, R.M., Condra, W., Bader, B.A., David, S.: A cone-beam CT bronchoscopy study of the ultrathin cryoprobe for biopsy of peripheral lung lesions. J. Bronchol. Intervent. Pulmonol. **31**(2), 117–125 (2024). https://doi.org/10.1097/LBR.0000000000000936
20. Isensee, F., Maier-Hein, K.: An attempt at beating the 3D U-Net. arXiv preprint arXiv:1908.02182 (2019). https://doi.org/10.48550/arXiv.1908.02182
21. Isensee, F., et al.: nnU-Net revisited: a call for rigorous validation in 3D medical image segmentation. Med. Image Comput. Comput. Assist. Intervent. **15009**, 488–498 (2024). https://doi.org/10.1007/978-3-031-72114-4_47
22. González, Á.: Measurement of areas on a sphere using Fibonacci and latitude - longitude lattices. Math. Geosci. **42**, 49–64 (2010). https://doi.org/10.1007/s11004-009-9257-x

Beyond Landmarks: Anchor-Guided Orientation Regression for Robust Spinopelvic Measurement

Yunseob Hwang[1], Youngsuk Lee[1], DaeSeok Song[1], Dong-Ho Kang[2], and Du Hyun Ro[1,3,4](✉)

[1] CONNECTEVE Co., Ltd, Seoul, Korea
duhyunro@gmail.com
[2] Department of Orthopedic Surgery, Samsung Medical Center,Seoul, Korea
[3] College of Medicine, Seoul National University, Seoul, Korea
[4] Department of Orthopedic Surgery, Seoul National University Hospital, Seoul, Korea

Abstract. Spinopelvic measurement (SPM) plays a central role in spinal deformity assessment and surgical planning. Recent AI approaches predominantly adopt multi-stage pipelines that first localize vertebral regions then detect landmarks within isolated patches. While effective and stable, such decomposition restricts models to local subtasks rather than holistic reasoning. As a single-model alternative, direct landmark detection from full radiographs encounters two fundamental challenges: independent landmark prediction suffers from anatomical ambiguity leading to vertebral swapping, and point-wise localization objectives are misaligned with angular measurement goals. We reformulate SPM by replacing point-wise landmark detection with anchor-guided orientation regression that directly models task-relevant geometric primitives. Using frozen DINOv3 vision foundation model encoders with parameter-efficient fine-tuning, we systematically compare three representation methods under controlled experimental conditions—maintaining consistent architectures, decoders, and training protocols to isolate the effect of geometric output formulation. Evaluation on 309 external validation images demonstrates that anchor-guided orientation regression improves measurement consistency (ICC from 0.932 to 0.953) and accuracy (MAE from 2.32° to 2.18°). Critically, the representation maintains ICC above 0.9 even at 256-pixel input where baseline methods degrade significantly. These improvements hold across both ViT and ConvNeXt encoders. This study demonstrates that task-aligned geometric representation—not architectural complexity—is the key determinant of robust, resolution-tolerant automated spinopelvic measurement.

Keywords: Sagittal Balance · Spinopelvic Measurement · Landmark Detection · Orientation Prediction · Vision Foundation Model

G. Yang et al. (Eds.): MICCAI 2026, LNCS 16893, pp. 75–84, 2027.
https://doi.org/10.1007/978-3-032-38236-8_8

1 Introduction

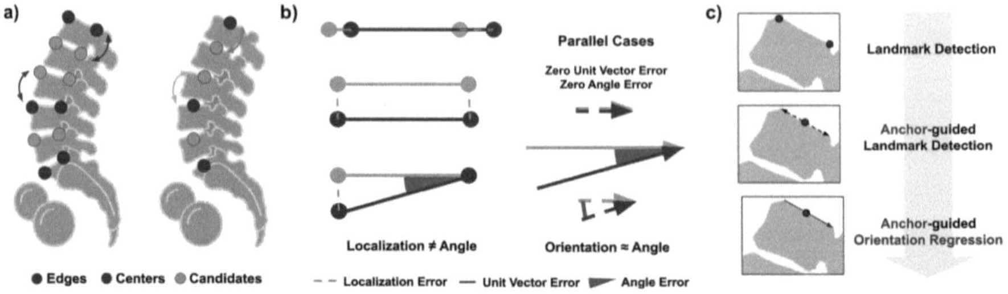

Fig. 1. Reformulating landmark detection for robust spinopelvic measurement. **(a)** Landmark prediction is reformulated in an anchor-centered reference frame to resolve anatomical ambiguity and suppress vertebral swapping. **(b)** As point-wise localization is often misaligned with clinical angular accuracy, orientation regression directly models the task-relevant geometric primitive, aligning optimization with the final measurement objective. **(c)** This progression reflects a shift from point-based landmarks to anchor-guided orientation regression (AGOR) for task-aligned geometric supervision.

Spinopelvic measurement (SPM) quantifies spinal and pelvic alignment from lateral lumbar radiographs—including lumbar lordosis (LL), L4-S1 lordosis, sacral slope (SS), pelvic incidence (PI), and pelvic tilt (PT)—and plays a critical role in orthopedic diagnosis and surgical planning [1,2,13,19]. However, manual assessment remains subject to substantial inter- and intra-observer variability [3,11,12], limiting reproducibility and motivating automated solutions.

Recent AI approaches for SPM predominantly adopt top-down pipelines that decompose the task into vertebra localization, region cropping, and landmark detection within isolated regions [5,7,9,18]. While effective in whole-spine scenarios—providing simplified context through cropping, sufficient resolution for localization, and improved overall pipeline stability—such decomposition introduces error propagation across stages and restricts models to solving local subtasks rather than reasoning over global anatomical relationships.

Direct landmark detection from the radiograph offers a single-stage alternative, yet it introduces structural ambiguity in vertebra-specific landmark detection: independently predicted vertebral edge points may be misassigned across adjacent levels, resulting in vertebral swapping (Fig. 1a). More fundamentally, conventional landmark regression trains models to improve localization accuracy, whereas SPM depends on vertebral orientation for angular computation, resulting in a misalignment between the optimization objective and the geometric primitive defining the task (Fig. 1b). While anchor-based representations have been explored for Cobb angle measurement in AP whole-spine radiographs—predicting vertebral centers with 4-corner offsets [23] or tilt angles [24]—their application to lateral lumbar SPM remains unexplored. Moreover, recent advances in vision foundation models (VFMs) such as DINOv3 [20] pretrained on 1.689 billion natural images have demonstrated remarkable performance across diverse vision tasks, including medical image analysis [14,16]. However, their application to anatomical landmark detection and angle measurement in SPM remains unexplored, requiring systematic experimental validation of VFM-based architectures for this clinical task.

To address these gaps, we investigate representation reformulation as the central design variable for SPM. In this study, we use lateral lumbar radiographs as a controlled setting to systematically compare Landmark Detection, Anchor-Guided Landmark Detection (AGLD), and Anchor-Guided Orientation Regression (AGOR). All methods are implemented under standardized model architectures comprising a DINOv3 encoder, a lightweight heatmap decoder, and task-specific geometric prediction heads, with identical training protocols across representations. This progression from point-based landmarks to anchor-centered orientation primitives is illustrated in Fig. 1c. By modifying only the geometric output formulation while keeping over 99% of the model architecture unchanged, we isolate the impact of representation choice on clinical angle measurement.

Our results demonstrate that task-aligned orientation regression improves angular accuracy and resolution robustness while simplifying pipeline design, highlighting representation alignment—not architectural complexity—as a key determinant of robust spinopelvic measurement.

2 Method

2.1 Dataset and Annotation

We curated 1,209 lateral lumbar spine X-rays from two institutions: Seoul National University Hospital (SNUH) (n = 900; 720 training, 180 validation) and Samsung Medical Center (SMC) (n = 309 external validation set). All images capture the anatomical region from lumbar vertebrae 1 (L1) through sacrum (S1) with bilateral femoral heads visible. A board-certified orthopedic surgeon with over 10 years of experience annotated 8 anatomical landmarks on each image: 6 vertebral superior endplate points (anterior and posterior for L1, L4, and S1) and 2 femoral head centers. Femoral head centers were derived through automated ellipse fitting followed by manual correction when necessary to ensure anatomical accuracy. Training and validation splits were stratified to maintain consistent parameter distributions across subsets.

2.2 Methodologies

We compare three representation methodologies (Fig. 2) that differ only in their geometric output formulation while sharing identical DINOv3 encoder architectures: Landmark Detection (8 independent landmarks), AGLD (5 centers + 12 pixel offsets encoding anterior and posterior endpoints for 3 vertebrae), and

AGOR (5 centers + 6 unit orientation vectors encoding posterior directions for 3 vertebrae).

Landmark Detection (Baseline). The baseline method predicts 8 independent heatmaps (one per landmark) using Gaussian kernels centered at ground truth coordinates. Peak locations are extracted via argmax operation, and vertebral orientation vectors are computed post-hoc by connecting anterior-posterior endplate point pairs. This independent prediction strategy provides no explicit constraints to prevent vertebral misassignment, where predicted landmarks may be incorrectly associated with adjacent vertebral levels (e.g., L1 anterior landmark assigned to thoracic vertebra T12).

Anchor-Guided Landmark Detection (AGLD). AGLD decomposes the task into anatomical grouping by predicting 5 center heatmaps (L1, L4, S1 vertebral body centers, and bilateral femoral head centers) plus 12 auxiliary offset channels. Each offset channel encodes pixel displacements ($\Delta x, \Delta y$) from vertebral centers to their corresponding anterior and posterior endplate points. Final landmark coordinates are reconstructed via:

$$\hat{P} = \hat{C}_i + \hat{\Delta}(\hat{C}_i) \tag{1}$$

where $\hat{C}_i$ is the detected center and $\hat{\Delta}(\hat{C}_i)$ is the predicted offset sampled at that center location. This anchor-guided formulation introduces structural constraints that reduce vertebral misassignment by explicitly grouping landmarks according to anatomical hierarchy.

Anchor-Guided Orientation Regression (AGOR). AGOR reformulates the representation to directly predict task-relevant geometric primitives. Instead of regressing pixel coordinates, the model predicts 5 center heatmaps plus 6 orientation channels encoding unit direction vectors from vertebral centers toward posterior endplates (a single direction suffices to define vertebral orientation). Ground truth orientation vectors are computed as:

$$\mathbf{u}_{\text{post}} = \frac{P_{\text{post}} - C_i}{\|P_{\text{post}} - C_i\|} \tag{2}$$

where P_{post} is the posterior endplate point and C_i is the vertebral center. Each orientation is encoded as a 2-channel field (u_x, u_y) representing the unit vector components. During inference, predicted orientation vectors $\hat{\mathbf{u}}_{\text{post}}$ are sampled at detected center locations $\hat{C}_i$ and used directly for angle calculation without intermediate coordinate reconstruction. This representation alignment eliminates the objective mismatch between pixel-level localization and angular measurement, enabling the model to learn vertebral orientations—the actual geometric primitive used in clinical parameter computation.

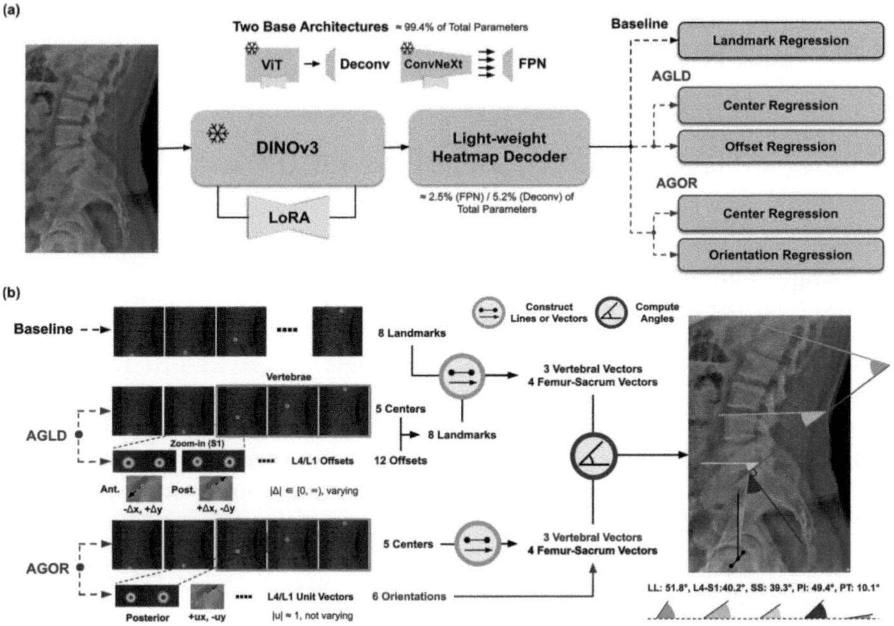

Fig. 2. Model Architecture Overview and Angle Measurement Pipeline. (a) Architecture overview: All methods share DINOv3 encoder + decoder (>99% of parameters), differing only in task-specific prediction heads (<1%). **(b)** Prediction outputs: Baseline predicts 8 landmarks; AGLD predicts 5 centers + 12 pixel offsets; AGOR predicts 5 centers + 6 unit vectors for direct angle calculation.

2.3 Model Architecture

The model employs a frozen DINOv3 encoder [20], a decoder network, and task-specific prediction heads (Fig. 2). We evaluate two encoder architectures: ViT-B/16 [4] (85.7M parameters) paired with simple deconvolution layers [22] (×4 upsampling from 1/16 resolution last layer feature), and ConvNeXt-Base [15] (87.6M parameters) with Feature Pyramid Network (FPN, multi-scale features at 1/32, 1/16, 1/8, 1/4 resolutions). During training, we apply Low-Rank Adaptation (LoRA) with rank 8 and alpha 16 for parameter-efficient fine-tuning. Both decoders produce 1/4 resolution heatmaps with 256-channel feature maps. Prediction heads vary by method, using either a single landmark head (Landmark Detection) or a dual-branch architecture with landmark and auxiliary heads (AGLD and AGOR).

2.4 Learning Objectives

Landmark Detection uses MSE loss for 8 heatmaps:

$$\mathcal{L}_{\text{heatmap}} = \frac{1}{N}\sum_{i=1}^{8} \|\mathbf{H}_i - \hat{\mathbf{H}}_i\|^2 \quad (3)$$

AGLD and AGOR use multi-task loss combining MSE for center heatmaps and Smooth L1 for offset/orientation fields:

$$\mathcal{L} = \lambda_{\text{center}}\mathcal{L}_{\text{MSE}}(\mathbf{H}) + \lambda_{\text{reg}}\mathcal{L}_{\text{SmoothL1}}(\mathbf{O}) \tag{4}$$

with $\lambda_{\text{center}} = 1.0$, $\lambda_{\text{reg}} = 0.5$ (AGLD) and 60.0 (AGOR, scaled to match offset magnitude).

2.5 Angle Calculation

All five spinopelvic parameters are derived from vertebral orientations and femoral head midpoint: LL (L1-L4 endplate angle), L4-S1 (L4-S1 lordosis), SS (S1 inclination to horizontal), PI (perpendicular to S1 endplate vs. line to femoral midpoint), PT (vertical vs. line to S1 midpoint). Landmark Detection and AGLD reconstruct angles from coordinates; AGOR directly predicts vertebral orientations, bypassing point-to-line reconstruction and mitigating error propagation in angle measurement.

3 Experiments and Results

3.1 Implementation Details

Models were implemented in PyTorch 2.0 with mixed-precision training on a single NVIDIA L40S 48GB GPU. We applied LoRA [8] (rank 8, alpha 16) to attention and feed-forward layers (ViT-B/16) or pointwise convolution layers (ConvNeXt-Base), resulting in 3.7M (4.1%) and 5.0M (5.4%) trainable parameters respectively. Ground truth heatmaps used resolution-dependent Gaussian kernels ($\sigma = 6/4.5/3/1.5$ for 1024/768/512/256px). Images were resized to target resolution preserving aspect ratio with zero-padding. Training used AdamW optimizer ($\eta = 10^{-4}$, 100 epochs, cosine annealing) with augmentation including horizontal flipping, rotation ($\pm 5°$), brightness/contrast adjustment, and noise injection. Model selection was based on best validation loss.

3.2 Evaluation Metrics

We evaluated landmark localization using Mean Radial Error (MRE, in millimeters, converted from pixels using 0.14 mm/px) and Success Detection Rate at 2mm threshold (SDR@2mm, percentage of landmarks within 2mm). Clinical angle accuracy was measured by Mean Absolute Error (MAE, in degrees) and ICC (values > 0.9 indicate excellent agreement [10]). Avg MAE and Avg ICC denote the mean across all five spinopelvic angles.

3.3 Quantitative Results

Table 1 compares three representation methods using two DINOv3 encoders on the external validation set ($n = 309$). AGOR consistently outperformed baselines, achieving ICC 0.9532 and MAE 2.18° with ConvNeXt-Base. The anchor-guided orientation formulation aligns supervision with the clinical task—learning vertebral endplate orientation rather than pixel-level landmark positions. This representation alignment improved average ICC from 0.9320 to 0.9532 (ConvNeXt-Base) and 0.9320 to 0.9444 (ViT-B/16).

Table 1. Comparison of Representation Methods and DINOv3 Encoders

Method	DINOv3 Encoder	**Landmark Localization**		**Angle Measurement**	
		MRE (mm)	SDR@2mm	Avg MAE (°)	Avg ICC
Landmark Detection	ViT-B/16	2.62	53.03	2.68	0.9320
Landmark Detection	ConvNeXt-B	2.46	61.77	2.32	0.9308
AGLD	ViT-B/16	3.12	39.52	2.61	0.9438
AGLD	ConvNeXt-B	2.48	56.11	2.33	0.9526
AGOR	ViT-B/16	2.74	45.50	2.64	0.9444
AGOR	**ConvNeXt-B**	**2.05**	**67.12**	**2.18**	**0.9532**

Comparison with Previous Works. Table 2 compares AGOR against prior automated spinopelvic measurement systems. Our single end-to-end model achieves consistently higher ICC values across all five parameters on the largest external validation set ($n = 309$), while previous approaches require 2–3 specialized models with smaller test sets (40–118 samples).

Table 2. ICC Comparison with Previous Automated Spinopelvic Measurement Systems

Study	# Models	# Test Samples	LL	L4-S1	SS	PI	PT
Orosz et al. [18]	2	100 (Pre-op)	0.92	–	0.88	0.88	0.85
Song et al. [21]	1	90	0.78	–	0.62	0.78	0.85
Löchel et al. [17]	3	118 (Pre-op)	0.81	–	0.71	0.72	0.85
Harake et al. [6]	3	40	0.94	–	0.93	0.91	0.98
Hoppe et al. [7]	2	65	0.95	–	0.93	–	–
Ours (AGOR)	**1**	**309**	**0.97**	**0.95**	**0.94**	**0.93**	**0.98**

Bland–Altman Analysis. Figure 3 presents Bland–Altman plots confirming strong AI–expert agreement for the best-performing model (AGOR, ConvNeXt-Base), with mean bias below 0.7° and limits of agreement within ±7° across all five spinopelvic parameters.

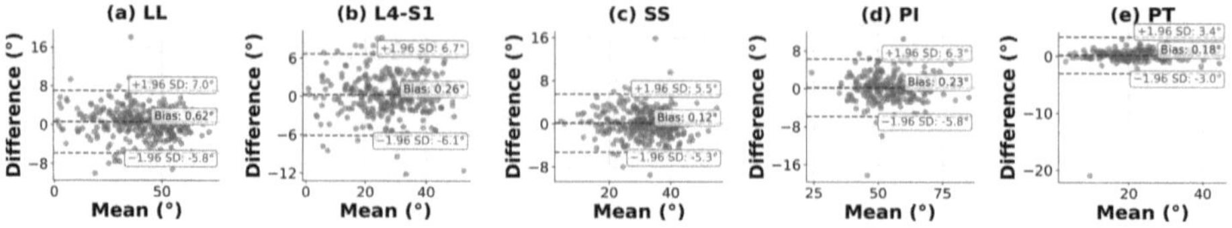

Fig. 3. Bland–Altman Analysis. AI vs. expert agreement on the external validation set.

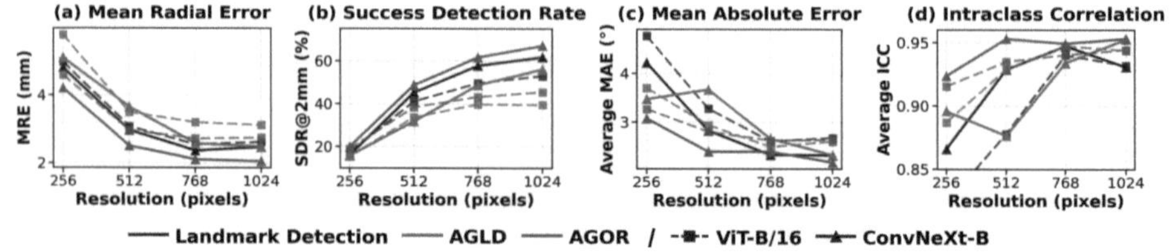

Fig. 4. Resolution Robustness. Performance at 256–1024 pixels for three methods with two backbones (ViT-B/16 dashed, ConvNeXt-Base solid). **(a)** MRE, **(b)** SDR@2mm, **(c)** MAE, **(d)** ICC. AGOR maintains superior performance across all resolutions.

Ablation Study - Resolution Robustness. Figure 4 shows performance across four resolutions. AGOR maintains ICC>0.90 even at 256px while baselines degrade below this threshold.

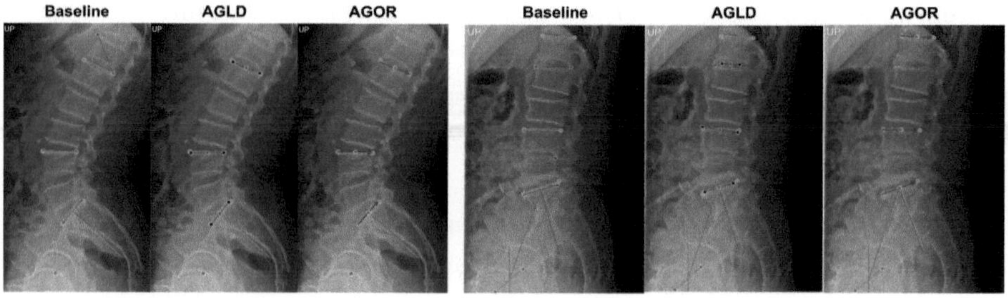

Fig. 5. Qualitative Comparison. Two representative cases comparing three methods. AGOR achieves accurate measurements while Landmark Detection (Baseline) shows vertebral swapping and AGLD exhibits localization errors propagating to angle calculation.

3.4 Qualitative Results

Figure 5 presents two representative failure cases. Landmark Detection exhibits vertebral swapping (L1 anterior misassigned to thoracic vertebra above) and both baselines mispredict L1 landmarks at L2 level, while AGOR maintains accuracy in both cases through direct orientation prediction, confirming robustness to anatomical ambiguity.

4 Conclusion

This work demonstrates that representation reformulation, rather than architectural complexity, is the key determinant of robust angle measurement in spinopelvic assessment. Comparing landmark detection, AGLD, and the proposed AGOR, we show that while anchor guidance addresses anatomical ambiguity, offset-based coordinate regression retains the mathematical mismatch between training objectives and clinical goals—which AGOR resolves by directly predicting task-relevant orientation primitives. Critically, by modifying only the task-specific prediction heads ($< 1\%$ of total parameters), AGOR improves average ICC from 0.932 to 0.953 and reduces MAE from 2.32° to 2.18° compared to the landmark detection baseline, while maintaining ICC>0.9 even at 256px where baselines degrade. These findings establish direct orientation regression as the key to accurate and robust angle measurement.

Acknowledgments. This study was approved by the Institutional Review Board of Seoul National University Hospital (IRB No. 2009–181-1161) and Samsung Medical Center (IRB No. 2024–12-119), with informed consent waived due to the retrospective nature of the study. The authors thank the clinical and annotation teams at both institutions for their contributions to data curation and quality assurance.

Disclosure of Interests. The authors have no competing interests to declare that are relevant to the content of this article.

References

1. Ames, C.P., Smith, J.S., Scheer, J.K., Bess, S., Bederman, S.S., Deviren, V., et al.: Impact of spinopelvic alignment on decision making in deformity surgery in adults: a review. J. Neurosurg. Spine **16**(6), 547–564 (2012)
2. Diebo, B.G., Varghese, J.J., Lafage, R., Schwab, F.J., Lafage, V.: Sagittal alignment of the spine: what do you need to know? Clin. Neurol. Neurosurg. **139**, 295–301 (2015)
3. Dimar, J.R., Carreon, L.Y., Labelle, H., Djurasovic, M., Weidenbaum, M., Brown, C., Roussouly, P.: Intra- and inter-observer reliability of determining radiographic sagittal parameters of the spine and pelvis using a manual and a computer-assisted methods. Eur. Spine J. **17**(10), 1373–1379 (2008)
4. Dosovitskiy, A., Beyer, L., Kolesnikov, A., Weissenborn, D., Zhai, X., Unterthiner, T.: An image is worth 16x16 words: transformers for image recognition at scale. In: International Conference on Learning Representations (ICLR) (2021)
5. Grover, P., et al.: Can artificial intelligence support or even replace physicians in measuring sagittal balance? a validation study on preoperative and postoperative full spine images of 170 patients. Eur. Spine J. **31**, 1943–1951 (2022)
6. Harake, E.S., et al.: Development and validation of an artificial intelligence model to accurately predict spinopelvic parameters. J. Neurosurg. Spine, 1–9 (2024)

7. Hoppe, B.F., Rueckel, J., Rudolph, J., Fink, N., Weidert, S., Hohlbein, W., et al.: Automated spinopelvic measurements on radiographs with artificial intelligence: a multi-reader study. Radiol. Med. (Torino) **130**(3), 359–367 (2025)
8. Hu, E.J., Shen, Y., Wallis, P., Allen-Zhu, Z., Li, Y., Wang, S.: LoRA: low-rank adaptation of large language models. In: International Conference on Learning Representations (ICLR) (2022)
9. Kang, D., et al.: Automated measurement of pelvic parameters using convolutional neural network in complex spinal deformities: Overcoming challenges in coronal deformity cases. Spine J. (2025)
10. Koo, T.K., Li, M.Y.: A guideline of selecting and reporting intraclass correlation coefficients for reliability research. J. Chiropr. Med. **15**(2), 155–163 (2016)
11. Kyrölä, K.K., Salme, J., Tuija, J., Tero, I., Eero, K., Arja, H.: Intra- and interrater reliability of sagittal spinopelvic parameters on full-spine radiographs in adults with symptomatic spinal disorders. Neurospine **15**(2), 175 (2018)
12. Lafage, R., et al.: Validation of a new computer-assisted tool to measure spino-pelvic parameters. Spine J. **15**(12), 2493–2502 (2015)
13. Le Huec, J.C., Faundez, A., Dominguez, D., Hoffmeyer, P., Aunoble, S.: Evidence showing the relationship between sagittal balance and clinical outcomes in surgical treatment of degenerative spinal diseases: a literature review. Int. Orthop. **39**(1), 87–95 (2015)
14. Li, Y., Wu, Y., Lai, Y., Hu, M., Yang, X.: MedDINOv3: how to adapt vision foundation models for medical image segmentation?. arXiv preprint arXiv:2509.02379 (2025)
15. Liu, Z., Mao, H., Wu, C.Y., Feichtenhofer, C., Darrell, T., Xie, S.: A ConvNet for the 2020s. In: IEEE/CVF Conference on Computer Vision and Pattern Recognition, pp. 11976–11986 (2022)
16. Liu, C., et al.: Does DINOv3 set a new medical vision standard? benchmarking 2D and 3D classification, segmentation, and registration. arXiv preprint arXiv:2509.06467 (2025)
17. Löchel, J., Eckstein, F., Babawale, L., Palmowski, Y., Stüber, A.T., Huppertz, A., et al.: Deep learning algorithm for fully automated measurement of sagittal balance in adult spinal deformity. Eur. Spine J. **33**(11), 4119–4124 (2024)
18. Orosz, L.D., et al.: Novel artificial intelligence algorithm: an accurate and independent measure of spinopelvic parameters. J. Neurosurg. Spine, 1–9 (2022)
19. Schwab, F., Patel, A., Ungar, B., Farcy, J.P., Lafage, V.: Adult spinal deformity–postoperative standing imbalance: how much can you tolerate? an overview of key parameters in assessing alignment and planning corrective surgery. Spine **35**(25), 2224–2231 (2010)
20. Simeoni, O., et al.: DINOv3 (2025)
21. Song, S.Y., Seo, M.S., Kim, C.W., Kim, Y.H., Yoo, B.C., Choi, H.J., et al.: AI-driven segmentation and automated analysis of the whole sagittal spine from X-ray images for spinopelvic parameter evaluation. Bioengineering **10**(10), 1229 (2023)
22. Xu, Y., Zhang, J., Zhang, Q., Tao, D.: ViTPose: simple vision transformer baselines for human pose estimation. In: Advances in Neural Information Processing Systems (NeurIPS), vol. 35, pp. 38571–38584 (2022)
23. Yi, J., Wu, P., Huang, Q., Qu, H., Metaxas, D.N.: Vertebra-focused landmark detection for scoliosis assessment. In: IEEE International Symposium on Biomedical Imaging (ISBI), pp. 736–740 (2020)
24. Zou, L., et al.: VLTENet: a deep-learning-based vertebra localization and tilt estimation network for automatic Cobb angle estimation. IEEE J. Biomed. Health Inform. **27**, 3002–3013 (2023)

Breaking Annotation Dependency in Coronary Stenosis Segmentation via Physics-Driven Sim2Real Learning

Baochang Zhang[1,2,3](✉), Fatia Kusuma Dewi[1], Shuting Liu[1](✉), Amir Yousefi[1,4], Heribert Schunkert[2,5], Reza Ghotbi[4], and Nassir Navab[1,3]

[1] Computer Aided Medical Procedures, Technical University of Munich, Munich, Germany
{shuting.liu,baochang.zhang}@tum.de
[2] German Heart Center Munich, Munich, Germany
[3] Munich Center for Machine Learning, Munich, Germany
[4] HELIOS Hospital west of Munich, Munich, Germany
[5] German Centre for Cardiovascular Research, Munich Heart Alliance, Munich, Germany

Abstract. Accurate coronary stenosis segmentation in X-ray angiography (XA) remains fundamentally limited by reliance on scarce and biased manual lesion annotations. Clinical datasets, although realistic, provide only incomplete and skewed sampling of pathological variations, constraining generalization. We address this challenge by reframing stenosis segmentation as a controllable synthetic learning problem and propose a physics-driven sim-to-real framework that eliminates dependence on real lesion labels. We generate a scalable synthetic dataset from patient-specific coronary models reconstructed from CTA, where stenosis variations with diverse severities and morphologies are deliberately designed in 3D space. A physics-based projection process produces geometry-preserving synthetic XA images with precise image-annotation alignment, enabling balanced and distribution-aware supervision beyond biased clinical sampling. A segmentation network trained on this synthetic data is subsequently adapted to real XA through uncertainty-guided self-supervised refinement. Predictive uncertainty is estimated online to select reliable pseudo-labels and drive confidence-aware consistency learning, promoting robust adaptation in ambiguous regions. On the ARCADE benchmark, our method surpasses existing self-supervised and few-shot approaches and approaches fully supervised performance without using any real stenosis annotations. These results demonstrate that physics-driven sim-to-real learning offers a principled pathway toward annotation-independent coronary lesion analysis. The code is publicly available at github.com/StenSim2realSeg.

Keywords: Stenosis Segmentation · Physics-driven Simulation · Sim-to-real Learning · Uncertainty-guided Adaptation · X-ray Angiography

G. Yang et al. (Eds.): MICCAI 2026, LNCS 16893, pp. 85–94, 2027.
https://doi.org/10.1007/978-3-032-38236-8_9

1 Introduction

Coronary artery disease remains a leading cause of mortality worldwide, and accurate assessment of coronary stenosis from X-ray angiography (XA) is critical for diagnosis and interventional planning. A rapid reduction in vessel diameter is a primary indicator of stenosis severity [2]. However, XA interpretation is challenged by vessel overlap, uneven contrast, and projection ambiguity. Manual assessment introduces inter-observer variability and limited reproducibility [5], motivating the development of automated and objective analysis systems.

Recent advances in deep learning have substantially improved automatic stenosis detection and segmentation [3,7,9]. Nevertheless, these supervised methods fundamentally rely on large-scale, high-quality lesion annotations. In practice, stenosis labeling is costly, subjective, and anatomically inconsistent. Public datasets [11] provide valuable benchmarks but reflect limited pathological diversity and protocol-specific annotation biases, which may constrain model generalization. Efforts to reduce annotation dependence include few-shot and self-supervised approaches [1,6,8,12]. Although promising for vessel segmentation, their effectiveness for subtle and highly localized stenotic patterns remains limited. Sim-to-real learning has emerged as an alternative direction. Domain adaptation techniques [10,15] and adaptive representation learning frameworks for XA [16] demonstrate that synthetic data can facilitate cross-domain generalization. However, existing approaches largely focus on vessel structures rather than controlled pathology modeling and do not explicitly address annotation independence at the lesion level.

In this work, we argue that annotation dependency represents a key bottleneck in coronary stenosis segmentation. We reformulate stenosis segmentation as a controllable synthetic learning problem. By introducing systematically designed stenosis variations into patient-specific coronary models reconstructed from CTA and projecting them through a physics-based digitally reconstructed radiograph (DRR) process, we generate scalable synthetic XA data with geometry-consistent supervision. A segmentation network trained on this data is subsequently adapted to real XA using uncertainty-guided self-supervised refinement, eliminating the need for manual lesion annotations. Our contributions are threefold: (1) We reframe coronary stenosis segmentation as a synthetic, controllable learning paradigm to break annotation dependency. (2) We develop a physics-driven sim-to-real framework that enables balanced modeling of pathological variations with precise image-annotation alignment. (3) We introduce an uncertainty-guided adaptation strategy that achieves performance comparable to fully supervised methods without real stenosis labels.

2 Method

As illustrated in Fig. 1, our framework mainly consists of two parts: controllable physics-driven stenosis modeling and uncertainty-guided self-supervised refinement in the real domain.

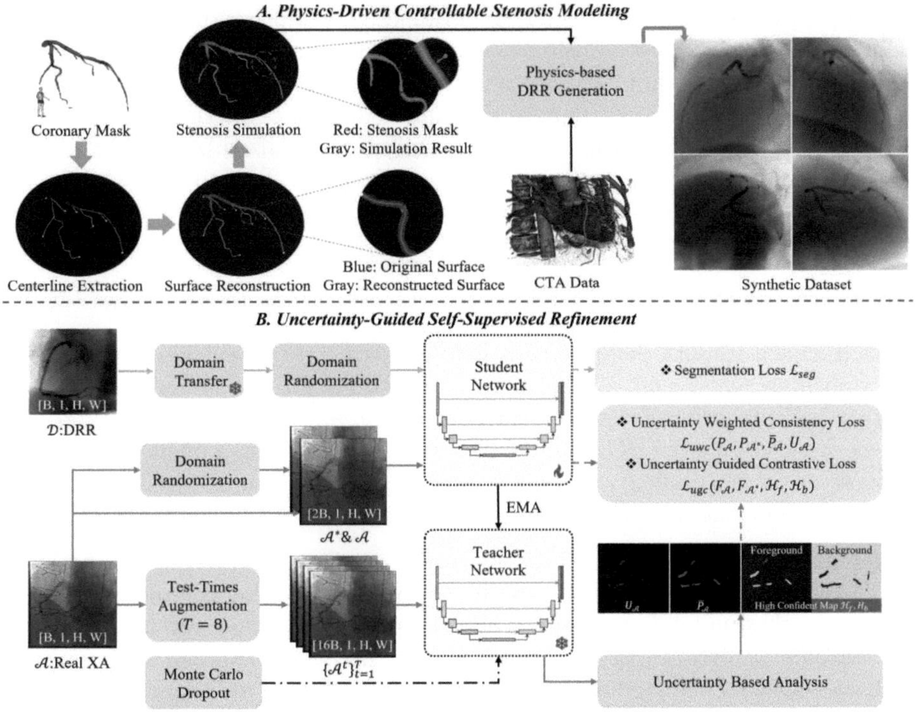

Fig. 1. Overview of the proposed framework. (A) Controllable stenosis modeling and DRR generation with precise masks. (B) Uncertainty-guided self-supervised refinement enables annotation-free stenosis segmentation on real XA.

2.1 Physics-Driven Synthetic Controllable Stenosis Modeling

Given a coronary lumen segmentation from CTA, vessel centerlines are extracted using VMTK [4]. Each branch is represented as a radius-parameterized curve $\mathcal{C} = \{\mathbf{c}(s), R(s)\}$, where $\mathbf{c}(s) \in \mathbb{R}^3$ denotes the centerline coordinate at arc-length s, and $R(s)$ the corresponding lumen radius.

Anatomically Constrained Baseline Geometry. The raw radius profile $R(s)$ may exhibit segmentation-induced oscillations that violate physiological tapering. To enforce anatomical plausibility, we construct a corrected radius field $\tilde{R}(s)$ under a proximal-to-distal tapering constraint, $d\tilde{R}(s)/ds \leq 0$. Specifically, representative control points are selected along each branch, followed by monotonic interpolation and spline-based smoothing to obtain a smooth and continuous radius profile. The refined representation $\{\mathbf{c}(s), \tilde{R}(s)\}$ is subsequently converted into a 3D baseline lumen surface $\mathcal{M} \subset \mathbb{R}^3$ via implicit sphere union modeling and isosurface extraction.

Controllable Stenosis Parameterization. For each eligible branch ($\tilde{R}(s) >$ 1 mm), a stenosis interval $\mathcal{I} = [s_0, s_1]$, its length $|\mathcal{I}|$, and severity $\alpha \in [\alpha_{\min}, \alpha_{\max}]$

are sampled within clinically meaningful ranges. A smooth radius reduction profile $g(s) \in [0, \alpha]$ is generated using Gaussian, Bzier, or spline-based functions to model diverse longitudinal narrowing patterns along the vessel centerline. Let $\mathcal{M}_\mathcal{I} = \{\mathbf{v} \in \mathcal{M} \mid s^\star(\mathbf{v}) \in \mathcal{I}\}$ denote the subset of surface vertices whose closest centerline coordinate $s^\star(\mathbf{v})$ lies within $\mathcal{I}$. Only this localized patch $\mathcal{M}_\mathcal{I}$ is modified, while the remaining surface remains unchanged. To unify concentric and eccentric lesions, a symmetry parameter $\beta \in [0, 1]$ is introduced. For a vertex $\mathbf{v} \in \mathcal{M}_\mathcal{I}$, the deformed position is defined as

$$\mathbf{v}' = \mathbf{c}(s^\star) + \beta\,\mathbf{d}(s^\star) + (1 - g(s^\star))\left[\mathbf{v} - \left(\mathbf{c}(s^\star) + \beta\,\mathbf{d}(s^\star)\right)\right], \tag{1}$$

where $\mathbf{d}(s)$ is a smooth displacement field constrained to the local normal plane and vanishing at s_0 and s_1. When $\beta = 0$, the deformation reduces to axis-symmetric contraction; for $\beta > 0$, the contraction axis is locally shifted, producing eccentric narrowing. This unified formulation enables explicit control over lesion severity, morphology, symmetry, spatial distribution, and lesion multiplicity while preserving anatomical smoothness and surface topology.

Physics-Consistent Image and Annotation Generation. Following localized deformation, the modified mesh $\mathcal{M}'$ represents the complete coronary anatomy with simulated stenoses, while the pre-deformation patch $\mathcal{M}_\mathcal{I}$ defines the anatomical territory of the lesion. Let $\mathcal{V}$ denote the original CTA volume. A physics-based DRR operator $\mathcal{P}_\theta : \mathbb{R}^3 \to \mathbb{R}^2$ is applied to generate the DRR image I_{drr} and its corresponding stenosis mask M_{sten} [14]:

$$I_{\text{drr}} = \mathcal{P}_\theta(\mathcal{V}, \mathcal{M}'), \quad M_{\text{sten}} = \mathcal{P}_\theta(\mathcal{M}_\mathcal{I}), \tag{2}$$

where θ denotes the imaging geometry parameters. Thus, the generated 2D mask is geometrically consistent with the simulated image.

2.2 Synthetic-Domain Representation Learning

Domain Transfer and Domain Randomization. To reduce the sim-to-real gap, we employ a pretrained CUT model [10,16] trained on synthetic DRRs and unlabeled XA images from the public XCAD dataset [8], independent of ARCADE, to transfer DRRs into XA style while preserving geometry and lesion structure.

To enhance robustness under real-world variability, we apply domain randomization to the synthetic XA data. In addition to general intensity and noise perturbations, we introduce X-ray-specific augmentations to better emulate clinical conditions. Specifically, random tool embedding simulates interventional devices such as catheters and wires using Bzier curve generation, and stochastic collimation simulates X-ray beam restriction by randomly reducing the effective field of view using a central rectangular aperture (80%95% of the original size).

Supervised Pre-training. Using the resulting synthetic XA data, we train a U-Net [13] segmentation network under full supervision. The segmentation objective $\mathcal{L}_{seg}$ consists of a standard combination of Dice and binary cross-entropy losses. Pre-training on large-scale, geometry-consistent synthetic data enables the model to learn anatomically grounded representations with controlled stenosis morphology and severity variations before exposure to real XA.

2.3 Uncertainty-Guided Self-Supervised Refinement

After supervised pre-training on synthetic XA, we perform real-domain adaptation via a teacher-student paradigm.

Stabilized Refinement with Synthetic Anchors. During real-domain refinement, each mini-batch jointly samples real XA and synthetic XA images. Synthetic samples continue to be optimized using the supervised segmentation objective $\mathcal{L}_{seg}$, serving as an anchor that stabilizes optimization and prevents representation drift caused by noisy pseudo supervision in the real domain.

Uncertainty-Aware Soft Pseudo Supervision. For a real XA image $\mathcal{A}$, the teacher network estimates predictive uncertainty using Monte Carlo dropout and test-time augmentation. Given T stochastic predictions $\{P_{\mathcal{A}}^t\}_{t=1}^T$, we compute the predictive mean probability map $\bar{P}_{\mathcal{A}}$ and pixel-wise epistemic uncertainty $U_{\mathcal{A}}$ as

$$\bar{P}_{\mathcal{A}} = \tfrac{1}{T}\sum_{t=1}^{T} P_{\mathcal{A}}^t, \qquad U_{\mathcal{A}} = H(\bar{P}_{\mathcal{A}}) - \tfrac{1}{T}\sum_{t=1}^{T} H(P_{\mathcal{A}}^t), \tag{3}$$

where $H(\cdot)$ denotes pixel-wise entropy. $U_{\mathcal{A}}$ is normalized to $[0, 1]$ per image for stable weighting across samples. Rather than constructing hard pseudo masks, we directly use $\bar{P}_{\mathcal{A}}$ as a soft pseudo target and use $U_{\mathcal{A}}$ to modulate student optimization in a reliability-aware manner.

Uncertainty Weighted Consistency. To enforce prediction stability under appearance perturbations, the student processes both the original image $\mathcal{A}$ and a perturbed case $\mathcal{A}^*$, producing predictions $P_{\mathcal{A}}$ and $P_{\mathcal{A}^*}$. The teacher mean prediction $\bar{P}_{\mathcal{A}}$ serves as the supervision target. We define the uncertainty-weighted consistency loss as

$$\mathcal{L}_{uwc} = \sum_{v \in \{\mathcal{A}, \mathcal{A}^*\}} \left\| (1 - U_{\mathcal{A}}) \circ \left(P_v - \bar{P}_{\mathcal{A}}\right) \right\|_2^2, \tag{4}$$

where $\circ$ denotes element-wise multiplication.

Uncertainty Guided Contrastive Learning. To enhance feature separability between stenosis and background under domain shift, we introduce a pixel-wise contrastive objective. Let $F_{\mathcal{A}}$ and $F_{\mathcal{A}^*}$ denote feature maps of $\mathcal{A}$ and $\mathcal{A}^*$ extracted from the last decoder layer of student network. High-confidence foreground $\mathcal{H}_f$ and background $\mathcal{H}_b$ regions are defined as

$$\mathcal{H}_f = \{i \mid \bar{P}_{\mathcal{A}}(i) > \tau_{fg} \wedge U_{\mathcal{A}}(i) < \tau_u\}, \tag{5}$$

$$\mathcal{H}_b = \{i \mid \bar{P}_{\mathcal{A}}(i) < \tau_{bg} \wedge U_{\mathcal{A}}(i) < \tau_u\}. \tag{6}$$

Queries $\{q_i\}_{i=1}^{n}$ are sampled from $F_{\mathcal{A}}$ at locations $i \in \mathcal{H}_f$, positives k_i^+ are taken from $F_{\mathcal{A}^*}$ at corresponding spatial locations, and negatives $\{k_j^-\}_{j=1}^{w}$ are sampled from background locations in $\mathcal{H}_b$ on the feature maps $(F_{\mathcal{A}}, F_{\mathcal{A}^*})$. The contrastive loss is defined as

$$\mathcal{L}_{ugc} = -\frac{1}{n}\sum_{i=1}^{n} \log \frac{\exp(q_i \cdot k_i^+/\tau)}{\exp(q_i \cdot k_i^+/\tau) + \sum_{j=1}^{w} \exp(q_i \cdot k_j^-/\tau)}, \tag{7}$$

where τ is a temperature parameter. Restricting sampling to low-uncertainty regions ensures semantic reliability and reduces noisy feature alignment.

The overall refinement objective for real-domain adaptation is

$$\mathcal{L}_{real} = \lambda_1 \mathcal{L}_{uwc} + \lambda_2 \mathcal{L}_{ugc}, \tag{8}$$

while synthetic samples continue to be optimized using $\mathcal{L}_{seg}$. This uncertainty-guided refinement selectively enforces reliable supervision and improves domain robustness without relying on hard pseudo labels.

2.4 Implementation Details

Stenosis length is sampled between 5 mm and 75% of the branch length, and radius reduction severity between 30% and 100%. Up to 5 stenoses are randomly simulated per coronary tree. DRR images are rendered under 11 standard angiographic projections with randomized pose perturbations. The final synthetic dataset contains 52,800 image-mask pairs at a resolution of 512×512.

For supervised pre-training on synthetic XA, the network is trained for 200 epochs with batch size 16 using Adam. The initial learning rate is 10^{-3} and decayed by a factor of 0.85 every 10 epochs. For real-domain refinement, the student network is optimized for 20 epochs with batch size 8 using Adam, with an initial learning rate of 10^{-6} decayed by 0.85 every 5 epochs. The teacher network is updated as an exponential moving average (EMA) of the student parameters with momentum 0.99.

Unless otherwise specified, we set $\tau_{fg} = 0.8$, $\tau_{bg} = 0.2$, and $\tau_u = 0.2$. In contrastive learning, the number of sampled queries is $n = 256$, the number of negatives is $w = 2048$, and the temperature parameter is $\tau = 0.1$. The loss weights are set to $\lambda_1 = \lambda_2 = 1.0$.

3 Datasets and Experimental Results

3.1 Dataset and Evaluation Metrics

We evaluate our model on the public ARCADE dataset [11], which contains 512×512 XA images with expert annotations, split into 1000 training and 300 testing samples. In ARCADE, stenosis is defined as a coronary lesion with ≥50% luminal narrowing in vessels of diameter ≥1.5 mm, and mild stenosis below this threshold is not included in the original annotations. Since our simulated stenoses

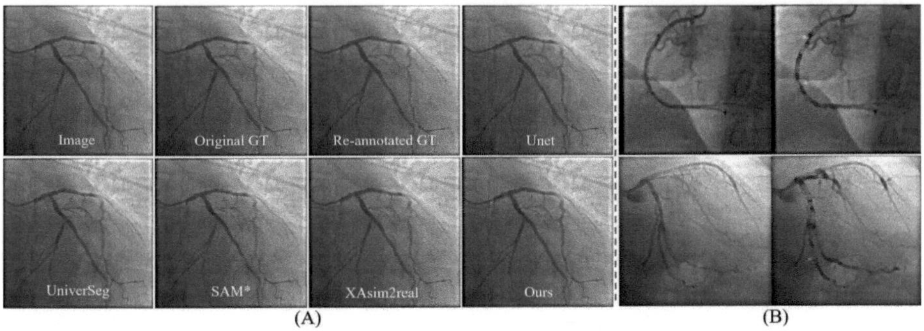

Fig. 2. (A) Qualitative comparison of stenosis segmentation on real XA images. Red regions denote predicted stenosis areas. (B) Our uncertainty map visualization on two real XA test cases. Each case shows (left) annotation and (right) XA image with uncertainty overlay. Green arrows indicate correctly detected lesions, red arrows denote additional detected constrictions, and yellow arrows indicate missed annotated regions. (Color figure online)

span 30%-100% severity, we re-annotated the testing set using 3D Slicer and reviewed it with experienced surgeons for more comprehensive evaluation. Both the original and revised masks are used for evaluation.

We assess performance using pixel-level and instance-level metrics. Pixel-wise evaluation includes Dice coefficient (Dic.) and Recall (Rec.). Since annotations are provided at the lesion level, instance-wise evaluation is performed via lesion matching: a ground-truth stenosis is counted as a true positive (TP) if at least 50% of its area is covered by a prediction; otherwise, it is treated as a false negative (FN). A predicted region is regarded as a false positive (FP) if it overlaps less than 50% with all ground-truth instances, with one-to-one matching enforced. Based on TP, FP, and FN, we report Instance-wise F1 (Ins-F1) and Instance-wise Recall (Ins-Rec.)

3.2 Quantitative Results and Ablation Study

Table 1 reports results on ARCADE. Without using any real stenosis annotations, our method approaches the fully supervised U-Net [13] trained on all 1000 labeled samples in Dice while substantially improving lesion sensitivity, with Ins-Rec. increasing from 0.658 to 0.886 under the original protocol and from 0.540 to 0.843 under the re-annotated protocol, indicating markedly fewer missed stenoses. Importantly, both our method and XAsim2real [16] are trained on the same physics-driven synthetic dataset, so the performance gain stems from the proposed uncertainty-guided refinement rather than data scale; compared with XAsim2real, Recall and Ins-Rec. are consistently higher, demonstrating more effective sim-to-real transfer. Although Dice and Ins-F1 remain comparable across methods, the slightly lower Ins-F1 under the original protocol is attributable to annotation definition (only $\geq 50\%$ stenoses labeled), whereas our

Table 1. Performance comparison under the original and re-annotated ground-truth masks. "Anno." denotes the number of annotated XA samples used for training.

Mask	Methods	Anno.	Dic.	Rec.	Ins-F1	Ins-Rec.
Original	Unet [13]	1000	0.431±0.281	0.434±0.314	**0.530**±0.394	0.658±0.451
	Universeg [1]	32	0.128±0.144	0.107±0.133	0.048±0.114	0.153±0.333
	SAM* [12]	32	0.238±0.235	0.251±0.271	0.129±0.203	0.398±0.467
	XAsim2real [16]	0	0.424±0.236	0.432±0.274	0.473±0.357	0.694±0.437
	Ours	0	**0.442**±0.192	**0.592**±0.246	0.434±0.255	**0.886**±0.302
Re-annotated	Unet [13]	1000	0.415±0.249	0.397±0.280	0.533±0.346	0.540±0.376
	Universeg [1]	32	0.118±0.128	0.095±0.117	0.066±0.120	0.133±0.243
	SAM* [12]	32	0.233±0.213	0.237±0.241	0.157±0.200	0.338±0.376
	XAsim2real [16]	0	0.486±0.237	0.457±0.267	**0.578**±0.329	0.645±0.367
	Ours	0	**0.515**±0.189	**0.635**±0.245	0.570±0.248	**0.843**±0.271

modeling spans 30%100%, leading to detection of mild stenoses that are unlabeled. Under the re-annotated protocol with more complete lesion coverage, our method achieves the best overall performance, suggesting that physics-driven sim-to-real learning improves lesion coverage without relying on manual stenosis annotations. Figure 2 shows that our method captures annotated stenoses more completely and highlights additional narrowing-like regions (red arrows) beyond the original masks, consistent with the improved Recall. The uncertainty maps exhibit higher responses around ambiguous or borderline narrowing regions, while remaining confined to the vessel lumen, indicating anatomically meaningful confidence estimation.

Table 2. Ablation study under the re-annotated protocol.

Methods	Dic.	Rec.	Ins-F1	Ins-Rec.
Ours	**0.515**±0.189	**0.635**±0.245	0.570±0.248	**0.843**±0.271
Ours w/o Ref.	0.497±0.233	0.492±0.273	**0.589**±0.321	0.671±0.361
Ours w/o $\mathcal{L}_{uwc}$	0.508±0.192	0.609±0.249	0.562±0.258	0.822±0.295
Ours w/o $\mathcal{L}_{ugc}$	0.497±0.214	0.519±0.265	0.585±0.294	0.723±0.336

Table 2 analyzes the contribution of each component under the re-annotated protocol. Removing real-domain refinement (w/o Ref.) leads to a substantial drop in Rec. (0.6350.492) and Ins-Rec. (0.8430.671), confirming that uncertainty guided adaptation is essential for transferring synthetic pathology to real XA. Although Ins-F1 slightly increases in this setting, this is mainly due to reduced lesion sensitivity, which decreases false positives at the cost of more missed detections. Removing $\mathcal{L}_{uwc}$ yields modest degradation, indicating its role in stabilizing pseudo supervision, while removing $\mathcal{L}_{ugc}$ causes broader performance drops across Dice, Recall, and Ins-Rec., highlighting the importance of uncertainty-guided feature separation for both pixel-level accuracy and lesion-level discrimination. Together, these results demonstrate that consistency and contrastive objectives provide complementary benefits for annotation-free sim-to-real learning.

4 Conclusion

In this work, we reframed coronary stenosis segmentation as a controllable synthetic learning paradigm to break dependency on manual lesion annotations. By coupling anatomically constrained stenosis modeling with physics-driven DRR projection, we enabled geometry-consistent supervision beyond biased clinical sampling. Through uncertainty-guided refinement, the learned representations are effectively transferred to real XA without requiring any lesion labels. Our results show that physics-driven sim-to-real learning can approach fully supervised performance while improving lesion sensitivity. More broadly, this study demonstrates that controllable pathology simulation offers a principled and scalable alternative to manual annotation for coronary stenosis analysis.

Acknowledgments. The project was supported by the Bavarian State Ministry of Science and Arts within the framework of the"Digitaler Herz-OP" project under the grant number 1530/891 02 and the China Scholarship Council (File No.202004910390).

Disclosure of Interests. The authors have no competing interests to declare that are relevant to the content of this article.

References

1. Butoi, V.I., Ortiz, J.J.G., Ma, T., Sabuncu, M.R., Guttag, J., Dalca, A.V.: UniverSeg: universal medical image segmentation. In: Proceedings of the IEEE/CVF International Conference on Computer Vision, pp. 21438–21451 (2023)
2. Fleming, R.M., Kirkeeide, R.L., Smalling, R.W., Gould, K.L., Stuart, Y.: Patterns in visual interpretation of coronary arteriograms as detected by quantitative coronary arteriography. J. Am. Coll. Cardiol. **18**(4), 945–951 (1991)
3. Isensee, F., Jaeger, P.F., Kohl, S.A., Petersen, J., Maier-Hein, K.H.: nnU-Net: a self-configuring method for deep learning-based biomedical image segmentation. Nat. Methods **18**(2), 203–211 (2021)
4. Izzo, R., Steinman, D., Manini, S., Antiga, L.: The vascular modeling toolkit: a python library for the analysis of tubular structures in medical images. J. Open Sour. Softw. **3**(25), 745 (2018)
5. Janssen, J.P., Rares, A., Tuinenburg, J.C., Koning, G., Lansky, A.J., Reiber, J.H.: New approaches for the assessment of vessel sizes in quantitative (cardio-) vascular x-ray analysis. Int. J. Cardiovasc. Imaging **26**, 259–271 (2010)
6. Kirillov, A., et al.: Segment anything. In: Proceedings of the IEEE/CVF international conference on computer vision, pp. 4015–4026 (2023)

7. Lin, H., Liu, T., Katsaggelos, A., Kline, A.: StenUNet: automatic stenosis detection from x-ray coronary angiography. arXiv preprint arXiv:2310.14961 (2023)
8. Ma, Y., et al.: Self-supervised vessel segmentation via adversarial learning. In: Proceedings of the IEEE/CVF International Conference on Computer Vision, pp. 7536–7545 (2021)
9. Pang, K., Ai, D., Fang, H., Fan, J., Song, H., Yang, J.: Stenosis-DetNet: sequence consistency-based stenosis detection for x-ray coronary angiography. Comput. Med. Imaging Graph. **89**, 101900 (2021)
10. Park, T., Efros, A.A., Zhang, R., Zhu, J.-Y.: Contrastive Learning for Unpaired Image-to-Image Translation. In: Vedaldi, A., Bischof, H., Brox, T., Frahm, J.-M. (eds.) ECCV 2020. LNCS, vol. 12354, pp. 319–345. Springer, Cham (2020). https://doi.org/10.1007/978-3-030-58545-7_19
11. Popov, M., et al.: Dataset for automatic region-based coronary artery disease diagnostics using x-ray angiography images. Sci. Data **11**(1), 20 (2024)
12. Qiu, Z., Hu, Y., Li, H., Liu, J.: Learnable Ophthalmology Sam. arXiv preprint arXiv:2304.13425 (2023)
13. Ronneberger, O., Fischer, P., Brox, T.: U-Net: convolutional Networks for Biomedical Image Segmentation. In: Navab, N., Hornegger, J., Wells, W.M., Frangi, A.F. (eds.) MICCAI 2015. LNCS, vol. 9351, pp. 234–241. Springer, Cham (2015). https://doi.org/10.1007/978-3-319-24574-4_28
14. Unberath, M., et al.: DeepDRR-a catalyst for machine learning in fluoroscopy-guided procedures. In: Frangi, A., Schnabel, J., Davatzikos, C., Alberola-López, C., Fichtinger, G. (eds.) International Conference on Medical Image Computing and Computer-Assisted Intervention. LNCS, pp. 98–106. Springer (2018). https://doi.org/10.1007/978-3-030-00937-3_12
15. Yang, Y., Soatto, S.: FDA: fourier domain adaptation for semantic segmentation. In: Proceedings of the IEEE/CVF Conference on Computer Vision and Pattern Recognition, pp. 4085–4095 (2020)
16. Zhang, B., Zhang, Z., Liu, S., Faghihroohi, S., Schunkert, H., Navab, N.: XA-Sim2Real: adaptive representation learning for vessel segmentation in x-ray angiography. In: International Conference on Medical Image Computing and Computer-Assisted Intervention, pp. 747–756 (2024)

Bridging the Markerless Tracking Validation Gap: Intraoperative X-Ray Workflow Integration

Connor Daly[1(✉)], Salvatore Russo[2], Jinendra Ekanayake[3], Daniel S. Elson[1], and Ferdinando Rodriguez y Baena[1]

[1] The Hamlyn Centre for Robotic Surgery, Imperial College London, London, UK
cd1723@ic.ac.uk
[2] Department of Neurosurgery, Imperial College Healthcare NHS Trust, London, UK
[3] School of Medicine, Stanford University, Stanford University, Stanford, CA, USA

Abstract. Markerless intraoperative tracking of spinal anatomy via RGB-D sensors is a promising alternative to invasive bone-anchored fiducials, yet no existing clinical dataset provides independent subsurface ground truth for validating these methods. We address this gap with a clinically viable pipeline that derives per-vertebra 6-DoF pose from routine intraoperative C-arm fluoroscopy, co-registered to the RGB-D camera frame through a multimodal fiducial array detectable in both imaging modalities. Critically, the pipeline requires no invasive instrumentation contacting the patient, no additional radiation, or deviation from standard surgical workflows, relying solely on the fluoroscopic images already acquired during routine level checks. A calibrated transform chain links the vertebral pose recovered via multi-view 2D–3D CT-to-fluoroscopy registration to the RGB-D coordinate frame, enabling direct comparison of any markerless registration estimate against a subsurface reference. Ex vivo validation against optically tracked ovine vertebrae confirms end-to-end accuracy of 2.06 ± 0.29 mm and $3.35 \pm 0.93^\circ$, sufficient to serve as independent ground truth for methods with substantially larger errors. We demonstrate the pipeline's utility by evaluating two markerless registration strategies on clinical data spanning 11 vertebrae across 1,500 frames from three surgical sequences: the first such evaluation against an independent subsurface reference in a clinical setting. The proposed framework provides reusable infrastructure for benchmarking emerging markerless tracking methods on real surgical data.

Keywords: RGB-D Tissue Tracking · Orthopedic Surgery · 2D–3D Registration

1 Introduction and Motivation

Markerless intraoperative tracking of orthopedic anatomy via RGB-D sensors is a promising emerging direction for surgical guidance [10,14]. Current surgical

G. Yang et al. (Eds.): MICCAI 2026, LNCS 16893, pp. 95–105, 2027.
https://doi.org/10.1007/978-3-032-38236-8_10

navigation systems depend on invasive bone-anchored fiducials to register (and subsequently track) preoperative imaging with the surgical scene [25,26], introducing added operative time and complication risk [7]. Markerless approaches instead extract anatomically meaningful correspondences directly from intraoperative point clouds via learned segmentation, enabling registration and tracking without physical instrumentation [10,14]. Daly *et al.* [4] advanced this direction with the first clinical markerless tracking dataset for spine surgery. However, their ground truth is inherently approximate: alignment relies on surgeon-indicated surface landmarks refined against intraoperative topology, neither of which references the pose of the subsurface anatomy. For clinical adoption, markerless systems must be validated against a gold-standard measurement offering quantifiable translational and rotational error metrics [15,21], a requirement no existing clinical dataset satisfies. Cadaveric studies have obtained accurate vertebral pose through rigidly fixed optical tracking arrays [15,16]. Liebmann *et al.* [15], for example, fixed 3D-printed constructs to vertebral bodies via K-wires, achieving sub-2 mm accuracy but requiring anterior exposure incompatible with standard posterior approaches, additional tracking hardware within the operative field, and an intraoperative CT. These requirements are not permissible within a clinical observational study, leaving a methodological gap: there is currently no clinically viable means of obtaining precise vertebral pose ground truth for evaluating markerless registration in real surgical settings. To address this, we present a pipeline that leverages routine intraoperative C-arm imaging to derive ground-truth vertebral pose within the RGB-D camera frame. Our contributions include:

1. A multimodal data capture and labelling pipeline that co-registers intraoperative RGB-D recordings with ground-truth vertebral poses derived from routine intraoperative fluoroscopy, requiring no additional radiation, no invasive instrumentation contacting the patient, or deviation from standard surgical workflows.
2. The first quantitative evaluation of markerless spine registration methods on clinical data against an independent subsurface reference, reporting per-vertebra translational and rotational error across three surgical sequences.
3. A clinically grounded evaluation framework, validated *ex vivo* to 2.06 ± 0.29 mm and $3.35 \pm 0.93°$, which can serve as reusable infrastructure for benchmarking markerless registration methods against an independent subsurface reference. CAD files for the intraoperative marker array and calibration phantom, along with the evaluation code and annotated data can be found in the accompanying repository BMTVG.

This work reports initial results from a large-scale ongoing clinical data collection study; the pipeline and evaluation framework are designed to scale as further cases are captured, enabling progressively larger-scale benchmarking of markerless methods.

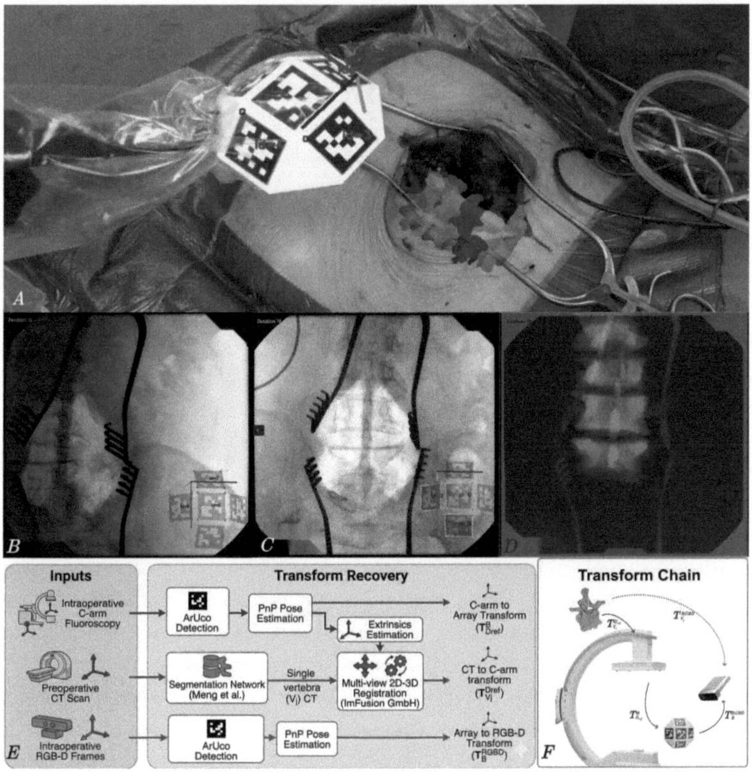

Fig. 1. **(A)** Intraoperative setup with the marker in a sterile cover, secured taut with a rubber band by the scrub nurse to maintain detectability; overlay shows automatic pose detection and projection of the preoperative CT into the scene via the transform chain in **(F)**. **(B, C)** Automatic marker pose detection in C-arm images from a fixation case, with projection errors (pixels) overlaid. **(D)** AP DRR: CT registered to C-arm images in ImFusion. **(E)** Data-processing overview: acquisition of the transforms that project preoperative CT into the RGB-D stream. **(F)** Solid lines: our full transform chain projecting vertebra j's CT into the Azure Kinect RGB-D frame.

2 Methodology

2.1 Data Capture

In contrast to the use of coarse surface features to approximate the underlying pose of the spine by Daly *et al.* [4], we integrated routine intraoperative C-arm fluoroscopy, taken alongside the RGB-D recording, to locate the patient's preoperative anatomy within the intraoperative scene. C-arm fluoroscopy is broadly accessible across clinical settings [2,18], ensuring our pipeline generalizes across institutions without requiring intraoperative CT [13]. We used established multi-view 2D–3D registration algorithms, as implemented in the ImFusion software suite (ImFusion GmbH, Germany) [11], requiring at least two fluoroscopic images from separate poses with known projection geometry. We modeled each C-arm source as a pinhole camera [9,17,22] and calibrated intrinsics using a custom multi-plane phantom [3,5] with nine radio-opaque ArUco markers [8] at known depths, estimating parameters via bundle adjustment [1,22]. Calibration images were acquired prior to surgery from AP (Anterior Posterior) and oblique angles within ±30°, reflecting the range of intraoperative C-arm positioning.

2.2 Intraoperative Capture

Ethics approval was given by the Research Ethics Committee of the Solihull Health Research Authority, Solihull, UK (IRAS 341461). Informed consent was obtained from all participants as per the study protocol. The cases we captured within our surgical study were taken from the clinical caseload of a tertiary neurosurgery department. The captured procedures are all lumbar-thoracic fixation cases. For recording RGB-D sequences, we used an Azure Kinect camera (Microsoft Corporation, USA), positioned directly over the incision using a boom arm fixed to a tripod. To co-register fluoroscopic and RGB-D coordinate frames without external tracking hardware, we designed a multimodal fiducial array, automatically detectable in both imaging modalities. Five radiopaque ArUco markers, each 30 × 30 mm, are inset on a radio-translucent PETG body. The insets were 3D-printed using PLA XRS filament (Nanovia Tech, France). The non-coplanar array layout ensured no marker overlap occurs at either AP or oblique viewing angles. The array was held on a boom arm adjacent to the exposure, beneath the C-arm detector and within the RGB-D camera field of view, and covered with an ultrasound probe cover to maintain the sterile field. An intraoperative C-arm is routinely used to provide confirmation of the vertebra level being operated on, typically from an AP view with adjacent oblique views. As the marker array was adjacent to the exposure, it is visible in the X-ray field of view during these level check shots, allowing both the determination of relative C-arm pose and the co-registration of X-ray and RGB-D coordinate frames to be performed with the same array. For each clinical case, we also collected the accompanying preoperative CT scan. We segmented the relevant bone tissue from CT using the network developed by Meng *et al.* [20].

2.3 CT Imaging to RGB-D Registration

For each C-arm shot, using the acquired intrinsic parameters from our multi-view calibration, the radiopaque ArUco markers are automatically detected within the image, and we then recovered the board-to-detector transform via PnP pose estimation [6,12]. Designating the first acquired image as the reference frame, we computed relative transforms between shots through the common marker array coordinate system, and combined these with the previously calibrated intrinsic parameters to yield projection matrices suitable for multi-view 2D–3D registration. Multi-view 2D-3D X-ray to CT registration is a well-established technique capable of achieving sub-millimeter accuracy [19]. We then performed intensity-based 2D–3D registration, optimizing over six rigid-body parameters by maximizing mutual information between digitally reconstructed radiographs

Table 1. Marker-array tracking accuracy per modality, isolated from the 2D–3D registration stage. The array was moved between four fixed positions; per transition, each modality's 6-DoF pose change is differenced against an NDI Polaris optical tracker (the reference), giving a residual against the tracker, not a modality-to-modality comparison. RGB-D uses the sterile probe cover. Transitions $1 \rightarrow 2$, $1 \rightarrow 3$ are in-plane; $1 \rightarrow 4$ is along the optical axis.

Modality	$1 \rightarrow 2$		$1 \rightarrow 3$		$1 \rightarrow 4$	
	Trans. (mm)	**Rot.** (°)	**Trans.** (mm)	**Rot.** (°)	**Trans.** (mm)	**Rot.** (°)
RGB-D tracking	0.40	0.31	0.70	0.61	0.10	1.85
X-ray tracking (AP)	0.58	0.03	1.19	0.07	0.02	0.35
X-ray tracking (oblique)	0.46	0.18	0.96	0.50	0.66	0.38

(DRRs) and the acquired fluoroscopic images, using the ImFusion software suite. This process was repeated for each segmented vertebra $\mathbf{V}_j$, yielding the transform from $\mathbf{V}_j$ to the detector coordinate frame, $\mathbf{D}_{ref}$, at the reference position. The transforms $\mathbf{T}_{\mathcal{B}}^{\mathbf{D}_{ref}}$ and $\mathbf{T}_{\mathcal{B}}^{\mathbf{RGBD}}$, locating the marker array in the reference detector frame and the RGB-D camera frame respectively, were both recovered via ArUco detection and PnP pose estimation.

Thus, we obtained the complete transform chain from the coordinate system of the vertebra $\mathbf{V}_j$ to the camera $\mathbf{C}$:

$$\mathbf{T}_{\mathbf{V}_j}^{\mathbf{RGBD}} = \mathbf{T}_{\mathcal{B}}^{\mathbf{RGBD}} \cdot \left(\mathbf{T}_{\mathcal{B}}^{\mathbf{D}_{ref}}\right)^{-1} \cdot \mathbf{T}_{\mathbf{V}_j}^{\mathbf{D}_{ref}}$$

3 Evaluation and Results

3.1 *Ex Vivo* Validation

To demonstrate the accuracy and repeatability of our data collection and labeling pipeline, we conducted several validation experiments. We first established the level of error introduced by each individual component of the transform chain. To do this, we first rigidly fixed a passive infrared tracking array to the multimodal marker array. We then directly compared how well the marker array itself could be tracked in both the C-arm imaging, as well as the Azure Kinect RGB frames, with respect to a highly accurate optical tracker (Polaris Vicra, Northern Digital Inc, Canada; 0.25 mm RMS volumetric accuracy, 0.50 mm 95% CI) [23]. For each imaging system, the marker array was moved between 4 distinct points in front of the sensor. We present the results in Table 1.

Subsequently, to validate the end-to-end accuracy of the full transform chain, we compared the difference in pose of four excised ovine vertebrae determined by our pipeline, with that found by directly tracking ArUco markers, rigidly fixed to the vertebrae. We mounted two plastic ArUco markers to each of the vertebrae with plastic screws, minimizing the markers' visibility within the C-arm

Table 2. End-to-end accuracy of the full transform chain vs. the fiducial-tracked pose of each excised ovine vertebra (the reference). Unlike Table 1 (marker tracking only), these include the 2D–3D fluoroscopy-to-CT registration stage; the increase over Table 1 ($\approx$0.9 mm, $\approx$1.5°) characterizes that stage's contribution. Combined TRE is the mean over both landmarks.

Vertebra	Combined TRE (mm)	Rotational Error (°)
T1	1.96	4.06
T2	2.32	3.40
T3	1.62	3.94
T4	2.32	1.98
Agg.	**2.06 ± 0.29**	**3.35 ± 0.93**

imaging. We then performed CT scans of each vertebra. Within the coordinate space of the generated scans, we then localized the ArUco positions, meaning then that each vertebra could be tracked directly via the RGB-D camera, bypassing the transform chain shown in Fig. 1 (F) entirely. To compute registration differences, we selected two points (the tip of the spinous process, and a point on the superior laminar margin) for establishing a Total Registration Error (TRE), with the optically tracked pose representing the target. The vertebrae and radio-opaque marker array were positioned between the source and detector of a TAU 2020 C-arm (Ziehm-Orthoscan Inc, USA), as described in Sect. 2.2. With the radio-opaque marker array visible from the RGB-D camera, we captured 2 C-arm shots with an angular disparity of 30°. This is comparable to the mean angular disparity of 25.6° seen in clinical cases we captured. Following the process described in 2.3, we projected the vertebrae from the CT coordinate space to the RGB-D camera coordinate space. We present the TRE for the point landmarks together with the rotational error in Table 2. Rotational error is the geodesic angle on SO(3), $\theta = \arccos(\frac{(\mathrm{tr}(R^\top \hat{R})-1)}{2})$, between the reference rotation R and the estimate $\hat{R}$, reported in degrees.

The independent validation of the RGB-D and X-ray pose tracking against an optical tracker reference confirms sub-millimeter translational agreement and sub-degree rotational agreement. The end-to-end pipeline, validated *ex vivo* against fiducial-tracked vertebral pose, yields a combined TRE of 2.06 ± 0.29 mm and rotational error of $3.35 \pm 0.93°$, approaching the ≤ 2 mm and $\leq 5°$ thresholds commonly cited for spinal navigation systems [21]. Critically, this level of precision is sufficient to serve as independent ground truth for evaluating markerless tracking methods, whose registration errors are substantially larger, particularly in rotation (Fig. 2).

3.2 Clinical Data Registration

With the pipeline validated in the lab, we demonstrated its utility by evaluating two markerless registration strategies on clinical data from three surgical

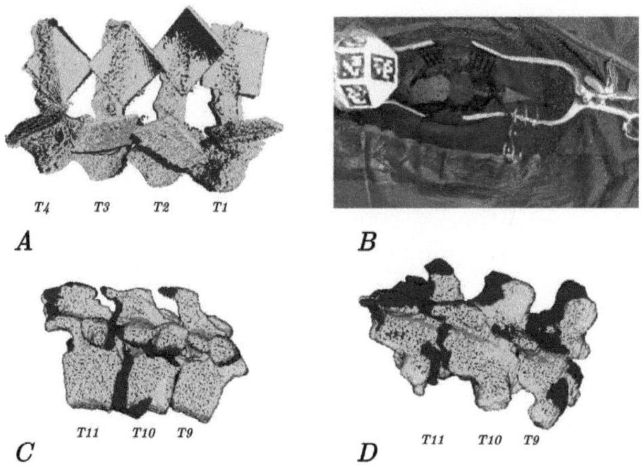

Fig. 2. **(A)** The pose of ovine CT meshes directly tracked via the Azure Kinect in blue, compared to those tracked via fluoroscopy and projected into the Kinect camera space in yellow; **(B)** Per vertebra patches predicted by the network in Sect. 3.2; **(C, D)** Intraoperative pose estimates via X-ray in yellow, through per vertebra ICP in blue.

sequences, encompassing 11 vertebrae across 1,500 frames. To our knowledge, this represents the first evaluation of markerless spine registration against an independent subsurface gold standard reference in a clinical setting. The first strategy follows [4], deforming the preoperative spine mesh via a kinematic chain model before rigidly registering it to segmented intraoperative points using ICP. This approach relies on semi-automated surface-based optimization of the kinematic chain parameters, with manual refinement, to align the deformed mesh with the intraoperative point cloud: a workflow difficult to scale to real-time intraoperative use. We therefore additionally trialed a fully automated approach inspired by [14], in which CT meshes of individual vertebrae are independently registered to per-vertebra segmentation patches. These patches were obtained via a two-stage pipeline: a PointNet++ [24] heatmap regression network, trained on manually annotated spinous process tip positions, first localizes tips within the point cloud (recall 0.95, F1 0.89, localization error 3.98 ± 1.99 mm), after which a PointNet segmentation network isolates points within 40 mm of each detection (IoU 0.71, F1 0.83). Per-vertebra segmentation labels were generated by computing mesh-to-point-cloud proximity for individual vertebral CT meshes from [4], following the same approach used therein for global spine masks. The results of both registration approaches, evaluated against our fluoroscopic pose estimates with a correspondence distance of 3 mm for both methods, are shown in Table 3, with per-vertebra and per-axis breakdowns in Table 4.

The rigid method of [4] outperforms per-vertebra ICP on rotation ($4.52° \pm 1.00°$ vs. $8.36° \pm 3.69°$) and exhibits substantially lower variance across all metrics, while mean translation errors are comparable with overlapping distributions. The per-vertebra approach, though fully automated, lacks the geometric

Table 3. Markerless registration accuracy on clinical data: per-vertebra subsurface pose error vs. the fluoroscopically-derived vertebral pose (the reference). Two strategies are compared over three 500-frame sequences: the rigid full-spine method of [4] and per-vertebra ICP. 'Exposure' is the exposed-vertebra count.

Seq.	Exposure	Subsurface Pose Error			
		Per Vertebra ICP		Rigid ICP	
		Trans. (mm)	Rot. (°)	Trans. (mm)	Rot. (°)
1	5	5.15 ± 3.65	8.21 ± 3.74	5.70 ± 1.59	4.61 ± 1.55
2	3	3.98 ± 1.81	9.10 ± 3.68	4.66 ± 0.82	3.53 ± 0.78
3	3	4.02 ± 3.10	7.86 ± 3.63	3.38 ± 0.58	5.36 ± 0.30
Overall		$\mathbf{4.52 \pm 3.00}$	$\mathbf{8.36 \pm 3.69}$	$\mathbf{4.78 \pm 1.10}$	$\mathbf{4.52 \pm 1.00}$

constraints afforded by registering the full spine as a single structure, limiting its ability to resolve orientation. While both methods achieve mean translational errors below 5 mm, neither yet meets the ≤ 2 mm and $\leq 5°$ thresholds cited for spinal navigation [21], underscoring both the value of independent pose evaluation and the headroom remaining for emerging methods.

4 Discussion

The clinical registration comparison in Table 3 demonstrates the core contribution of this work: for the first time, competing markerless registration strategies can be evaluated on real surgical data against an independent subsurface reference. Prior clinical evaluation was limited to surrogate surface metrics [4]; our pipeline provides per-vertebra 6-DoF pose estimates from routine intraoperative fluoroscopy without additional hardware or workflow disruption. Registration errors in Table 3 are measured against our fluoroscopic estimates, which carry an intrinsic uncertainty of 2.06 ± 0.29 mm and $3.35 \pm 0.93°$ (Table 2); these values thus represent upper bounds on true registration error. The rotational difference between the two methods (3.84°) exceeds our reference uncertainty, confirming that the rigid method of [4] is meaningfully more accurate in rotation. Translational errors are not statistically different. Overall, the rigid approach is clearly superior, but its reliance on manual deformation tuning remains a barrier to clinical deployment, and thus an avenue for future work. Key limitations remain. The study reports three clinical sequences and ovine *ex vivo* validation; further labeled cases, drawn from a larger ongoing clinical study, will broaden the evaluation. Accuracy is also constrained by the 2D–3D registration stage, which depends on image quality, angular separation, and the number of fluoroscopic views. Clinically, classical surface registration is intrinsically limited: the posterior vertebral surface exposed during surgery is geometrically ambiguous, leaving ICP unable to robustly resolve pose, particularly rotation. This is unlikely to improve with initialization alone. With sufficient fluoroscopic ground truth, a learned mapping from intraoperative point clouds to vertebral pose could instead leverage appearance, anatomical context, and priors beyond ICP's scope.

Table 4. Appendix. Additional breakdown of the registration errors in Table 3.

(a) Per vertebra error.

		Per Vertebra ICP		Rigid ICP [4]	
Seq.	Vert.	Trans. (mm)	Rot. (°)	Trans. (mm)	Rot. (°)
1	T7	3.97 ± 3.88	8.69 ± 3.36	4.80 ± 2.00	3.92 ± 1.56
	T8	3.33 ± 2.54	6.41 ± 3.94	4.76 ± 1.54	2.82 ± 1.27
	T9	8.89 ± 3.74	5.69 ± 3.24	6.24 ± 1.44	3.68 ± 1.44
	T10	5.42 ± 4.73	9.69 ± 4.95	6.78 ± 1.40	5.22 ± 2.05
	T11	4.15 ± 3.36	10.59 ± 3.19	5.91 ± 1.56	7.39 ± 1.41
2	T9	3.22 ± 1.47	6.62 ± 3.01	3.10 ± 0.85	4.34 ± 0.66
	T10	3.83 ± 1.84	6.73 ± 3.20	4.44 ± 0.79	3.24 ± 0.99
	T11	4.88 ± 2.11	13.95 ± 4.83	6.43 ± 0.81	3.02 ± 0.69
3	L3	2.59 ± 2.18	3.19 ± 1.79	3.07 ± 0.56	4.86 ± 0.35
	L4	4.90 ± 2.14	11.68 ± 4.85	1.87 ± 0.48	4.14 ± 0.33
	L5	4.58 ± 4.97	8.71 ± 4.26	5.21 ± 0.71	7.08 ± 0.21

(b) Rotation per axis (mean-absolute camera-frame Euler-XYZ, deg).

	Per Vertebra ICP			Rigid ICP		
Seq.	R_x	R_y	R_z	R_x	R_y	R_z
1	4.98±4.40	3.95±3.77	2.94±3.25	1.85±2.43	3.04±1.40	2.04±2.53
2	4.45±2.54	6.55±2.22	3.09±2.84	0.80±0.69	3.02±0.71	1.16±0.80
3	4.37±3.39	4.73±2.92	2.77±2.98	2.78±0.37	3.41±0.27	1.40±0.40

Acknowledgments. This work was supported by the UKRI CDT in AI for Healthcare http://ai4health.io (Grant No. EP/S023283/1) and the National Institute for Health Research (NIHR) Imperial Biomedical Research Centre (BRC).

Disclosure of Interests. The authors have no competing interests to declare.

References

1. Bradski, G., Kaehler, A.: OpenCV: open source computer vision library (2000). https://opencv.org/. Accessed 08 Feb 2026
2. Chan, Y., Banza, L., Martin, C., Jr., Harrison, W.J.: Essential fracture and orthopaedic equipment lists in low resource settings: consensus derived by survey of experts in africa. BMJ Open **8**(9), e023473 (2018)
3. Cho, Y., Moseley, D.J., Siewerdsen, J.H., Jaffray, D.A.: Accurate technique for complete geometric calibration of cone-beam computed tomography systems. Med. Phys. **32**(4), 968–983 (2005)

4. Daly, C., Marconi, E., Riva, M., Ekanayake, J., Elson, D.S., Rodriguez y Baena, F.: Towards markerless intraoperative tracking of deformable spine tissue. In: Gee, J.C., et al. International Conference on Medical Image Computing and Computer-Assisted Intervention. LNCS, pp. 627–637. Springer, Cham (2025). https://doi.org/10.1007/978-3-032-05114-1_60
5. Daly, M.J., Siewerdsen, J.H., Cho, Y.B., Jaffray, D.A., Irish, J.C.: Geometric calibration of a mobile c-arm for intraoperative cone-beam CT. Med. Phys. **35**(5), 2124–2136 (2008)
6. Fischler, M.A., Bolles, R.C.: Random sample consensus: a paradigm for model fitting with applications to image analysis and automated cartography. Commun. ACM **24**(6), 381–395 (1981)
7. Gao, Z., et al.: Mazor x robot-assisted upper and lower cervical pedicle screw fixation: a case report and literature review. BMC Geriatr. **24**(1), 916 (2024)
8. Garrido-Jurado, S., Muñoz-Salinas, R., Madrid-Cuevas, F.J., Marín-Jiménez, M.J.: Automatic generation and detection of highly reliable fiducial markers under occlusion. Pattern Recogn. **47**(6), 2280–2292 (2014)
9. Gorges, S., Kerrien, E., Berger, M.O., Trousset, Y., Pescatore, J., Anxionnat, R., Picard, L.: Model of a vascular c-arm for 3D augmented fluoroscopy in interventional radiology. In: Duncan, J.S., Gerig, G. (eds.) International Conference on Medical Image Computing and Computer-Assisted Intervention. LNCS, pp. 214–222. Springer, Berlin, Heidelberg (2005). https://doi.org/10.1007/11566489_27
10. Hu, X., Nguyen, A., Baena, F.R.y.: Occlusion-robust visual markerless bone tracking for computer-assisted orthopedic surgery. Trans. Instrum. Meas. **71**, 1–11 (2022). https://doi.org/10.1109/TIM.2021.3134764
11. ImFusion: ImFusion Suite: visual computing for medical imaging (2025). https://imfusion.com/products-overview/imfusion-suite/. Accessed 14 Nov 2025
12. Jain, A.K., Mustafa, T., Zhou, Y., Burdette, C., Chirikjian, G.S., Fichtinger, G.: Ftrac—a robust fluoroscope tracking fiducial. Med. Phys. **32**(10), 3185–3198 (2005)
13. Ji, Z.W., et al.: Enhanced safety and efficacy of o-arm navigation over c-arm guidance in percutaneous kyphoplasty for patients with osteoporotic vertebral compression fractures and spinal deformity: a comparative study. Orthop. Surg. **17**(1), 125–132 (2025)
14. Liebmann, F., et al.: Automatic registration with continuous pose updates for marker-less surgical navigation in spine surgery. Med. Image Anal. **91**, 103027 (2024)
15. Liebmann, F., et al.: SpineDepth: a multi-modal data collection approach for automatic labelling and intraoperative spinal shape reconstruction based on RGB-d data. J. Imaging **7**(9), 164 (2021)
16. Liu, H., Baena, F.R.Y.: Automatic markerless registration and tracking of the bone for computer-assisted orthopaedic surgery. IEEE Access **8**, 42010–42020 (2020)
17. Liu, W.P., et al.: 2D–3D radiograph to cone-beam computed tomography (CBCT) registration for c-arm image-guided robotic surgery. Int. J. Comput. Assist. Radiol. Surg. **10**(8), 1239–1252 (2015)
18. MacKechnie, M.C., et al.: Establishing consensus on essential resources for musculoskeletal trauma care worldwide: a modified delphi study. JBJS **106**(1), 47–55 (2024)
19. Markelj, P., Tomaževič, D., Likar, B., Pernuš, F.: A review of 3D/2D registration methods for image-guided interventions. Med. Image Anal. **16**(3), 642–661 (2012)
20. Meng, D., Boyer, E., Pujades, S.: Vertebrae localization, segmentation and identification using a graph optimization and an anatomic consistency cycle. Comput. Med. Imaging Graph. **107**, 102235 (2023)

21. Miller, C.A., Ledonio, C.G., Hunt, M.A., Siddiq, F., Polly, D.W.: Reliability of the planned pedicle screw trajectory versus the actual pedicle screw trajectory using intra-operative 3D CT and image guidance. Int. J. Spine Surg. **10** (2016)
22. Navab, N., Heining, S.M., Traub, J.: Camera augmented mobile C-arm (CAMC): calibration, accuracy study, and clinical applications. IEEE Trans. Med. Imaging **29**(7), 1412–1423 (2010)
23. Northern Digital Inc.: Polaris Vicra Technical Specifications (2018). https://www.ndigital.com/products/polaris-vicra/. p/N 10001248 (Rev 001)
24. Qi, C.R., Yi, L., Su, H., Guibas, L.J.: PointNet++: deep hierarchical feature learning on point sets in a metric space. Adv. Neural Inf. Process. Syst. **30** (2017)
25. Stealthstation s8 surgical navigation system. https://europe.medtronic.com/xd-en/healthcare-professionals/products/neurological/surgical-navigation-systems/stealthstation/stealthstation-s8.html. Accessed 26 Feb 2026
26. Wilson, J.P., Jr., Fontenot, L., Stewart, C., Kumbhare, D., Guthikonda, B., Hoang, S.: Image-guided navigation in spine surgery: from historical developments to future perspectives. J. Clin. Med. **13**(7), 2036 (2024)

CAG-WM: A Synthetic-Data-Driven Coronary World Model for Autonomous Guidewire Navigation

Yue Cao, Zhuo Zhang(✉), Xiaoshan Peng, Guipeng Lan, Shuai Xiao, and Jiachen Yang

Tianjin University, Tianjin, China
z_zhuo@tju.edu.cn

Abstract. Automated guidewire navigation in percutaneous coronary intervention can reduce radiation exposure and clinician workload. However, existing methods suffer from low sample efficiency and struggle with long-horizon guidewire navigation. World models offer a promising solution, but scarce paired angiographic-3D data leaves end-to-end world model approaches unexplored. To address these challenges, we propose CAG-WM, the first synthetic-data-driven world model for autonomous coronary guidewire navigation. Specifically, we construct dynamic synthetic coronary angiography3D data and train a world model within a SOFA-based simulation environment to learn vesselguidewire dynamics and perform internal multi-step rollouts for long-horizon navigation. CAG-WM is trained on 100 synthetic cases with full-view angiographic renderings and corresponding 3D voxelized coronary models, and evaluated on 20 multi-center clinical cases and 10 public datasets. Experimental results show that CAG-WM achieves a success rate exceeding 80% in clinical cases, significantly outperforming competing methods. Even in unsuccessful cases, the guidewire remains close to target lesion. Despite slightly longer per-step inference time, CAG-WM achieves the shortest total time (about 2 min) thanks to its higher success rate, which reduces premature termination at the maximum step limit. Code and data is available at https://github.com/CaoYue2004/CAG-WM.

Keywords: Coronary Angiography · Guidewire Navigation · World Model

1 Introduction

Autonomous guidewire navigation holds significant clinical value in percutaneous coronary intervention (PCI) [2], which analyzes real-time angiographic images to generate optimal control commands, enabling automated guidewire advancement

---

Supplementary Information The online version contains supplementary material available at https://doi.org/10.1007/978-3-032-38236-8_11.

G. Yang et al. (Eds.): MICCAI 2026, LNCS 16893, pp. 106–116, 2027.
https://doi.org/10.1007/978-3-032-38236-8_11

to stenotic lesions. It effectively reduces cumulative radiation exposure to physicians, mitigates steep learning curve of manual catheterization, and decreases inter-operator variability [15,22]. Furthermore, this task represents a compelling frontier for embodied AI, where an agent must perceive angiographic scenes, reason about vascular anatomy, and execute precise guidewire control, spurring growing interest in AI-driven endovascular intervention [17,21].

Recently, reinforcement learning-based (RL) [5,14,19,20,25] and planning-based approaches [14,20] have been explored for autonomous coronary guidewire navigation, demonstrating promising results. However, these methods lack explicit modeling of guidewire-vessel dynamics, resulting in poor sample efficiency and limited generalization across diverse coronary anatomies. Without the ability to anticipate the consequences of actions, agents cannot reason beyond immediate observations, making it difficult to plan ahead or adapt to unseen anatomical variations. World models [8] have emerged as a promising framework to tackle these limitations. By learning environment dynamics, they enable agents to plan through imagined trajectories rather than costly trial-and-error interactions.

Nevertheless, world models remain rarely underexplored in vascular domain. Robert-shaw et al. [18] introduced the first world model for autonomous guidewire navigation in aortic arch. Despite this pioneering effort, several limitations remain. The study relies on limited angiography and corresponding 3D datasets, potentially restricting its broader clinical value, and does not explicitly model vascular dynamics. Furthermore, it lacks an end-to-end mapping from angiographic images to navigation actions, and the derivation of observational states, such as guidewire position, is not clearly specified. Consequently, the development of world models for coronary intervention remains largely open.

To address these challenges, we propose **C**oronary **A**n**g**iography **W**orld **M**od-el (**CAG-WM**), the first synthetic-data-driven world model for autonomous coronary guidewire navigation. CAG-WM learns guidewire-vessel interaction dynamics from CAG observations and generates control actions to reach stenotic targets efficiently. To mitigate data scarcity, we construct a **diverse synthetic dataset** of full-view CAG paired with corresponding 3D voxelized models, incorporating dynamic vascular properties. We develop a **world model**-based framework specifically tailored for the continuous control demands of guidewire navigation, coupled with a SOFA-based [7] simulation environment that enables large-scale policy optimization and facilitates learning of environment dynamics under diverse anatomical variations. CAG-WM is trained on 100 synthetic cases and evaluated on 20 multi-center clinical cases and 10 public datasets [23]. Experimental results demonstrate a success rate exceeding 80% in real coronary navigation, significantly outperforming both RL baselines and existing world model methods. Even in unsuccessful cases, guidewire navigated by CAG-WM reaches significantly closer to target lesion compared to other methods. Although per-step inference time is slightly longer than RL methods, CAG-WM achieves the shortest total navigation time (about 2 min), owing to its higher success rate which reduces episodes terminated by reaching maximum step limit.

2 Method

We formulate coronary guidewire navigation as a sequential decision problem where the agent receives partial observations o_t (CAG images) and outputs guidewire control actions. Our objective is to learn a policy that navigates guidewire from its initial position to target while avoiding vessel wall contact and minimizing procedural time. To this end, we propose CAG-WM, a coronary world model as illustrated in Fig. 1: (1) synthetic data construction, (2) dynamic SOFA simulation, and (3) world model training for latent dynamics and optimal control inference. Each of these components is described in detail below.

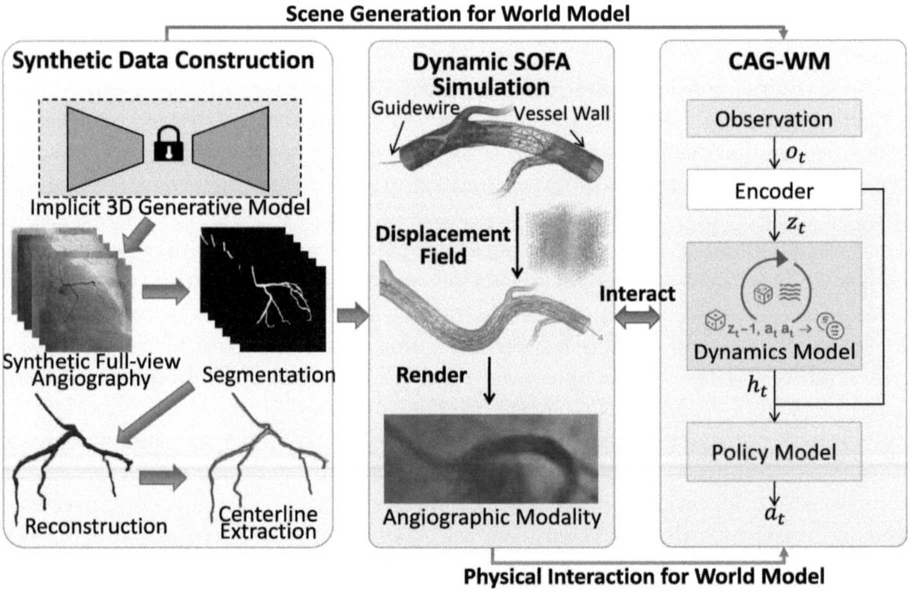

Fig. 1. Overview of the proposed CAG-WM framework.

2.1 Synthetic Data Construction

To address the scarcity of paired clinical data, we propose a synthetic framework for generating consistent coronary environments for world model training.

Given synthesized CAG images $\{I_i\}_{i=1}^N$ rendered from implicit 3D coronary models [4], we extract binary vessel masks $\{M_i\}_{i=1}^N$ via segmentation. Under known projection geometries, we apply multi-view geometric consistency constraints to reconstruct a coarse 3D voxelized volume $\mathcal{V} \subset \mathbb{R}^3$. A skeleton graph

$\mathcal{G} = (\mathcal{N}, \mathcal{E})$ is then extracted from $\mathcal{V}$ and globally connected using a minimum spanning tree. For each centerline node $n \in \mathcal{N}$, the vessel radius r_n is estimated by back-projecting n onto all views and averaging the distances to the corresponding vessel boundaries. The final 3D coronary model is defined as

$$\mathcal{M} = \bigcup_{n \in \mathcal{N}} B(n, r_n), \tag{1}$$

where $B(n, r_n)$ denotes a 3D ball centered at n with radius r_n. The resulting synthetic dataset provides full-view CAG, 3D coronary structures, and centerline representations, forming a comprehensive foundation for training CAG-WM.

2.2 Dynamic SOFA Simulation

The training environment for CAG-WM is based on a physics-driven simulation of guidewire-vessel interaction in the SOFA framework [7]. Guidewire is modeled as a deformable Timoshenko beam, while vessel wall is treated as a dynamically deforming boundary governed by a diffeomorphic displacement field that provides time-varying wall positions and velocities. The guidewire dynamics with contact constraints are solved via constraint-based formulation,

$$\begin{aligned} \left(\mathbf{M} + \Delta t\,\mathbf{D} + \Delta t^2\mathbf{K}\right)\Delta\mathbf{v} &= -\Delta t\,(\mathbf{f} + \Delta t\,\mathbf{K}\mathbf{v}) + \Delta t\,\mathbf{H}^\top\boldsymbol{\lambda}, \\ \boldsymbol{\lambda} &= \arg\min_{\lambda \geq 0} \left\| \mathbf{H}(\mathbf{v} + \Delta\mathbf{v}) + \frac{\mathbf{g}(t)}{\Delta t} - \mathbf{H}_w\mathbf{v}_w(t) \right\| \end{aligned} \tag{2}$$

where $\mathbf{M}$, $\mathbf{D}$, and $\mathbf{K}$ denote the beam mass, damping, and stiffness matrices, $\mathbf{H}$ encodes contact constraints, and $\boldsymbol{\lambda}$ are Lagrange multipliers. The bias terms $\mathbf{g}(t)$ and $\mathbf{v}_w(t)$ account for vessel wall deformation, and $\boldsymbol{\lambda}$ is solved using a Gauss–Seidel scheme for stable guidewirevessel interaction.

The 3D coronary models from Sect. 2.2 are imported into SOFA as vessel walls, with guidewire modeled using real physical parameters. CAG images with the guidewire overlaid are rendered to provide clinically realistic observations.

2.3 CAG-WM

We develop CAG-WM, a TD-MPC2-based [11] coronary world model to learn vesselguidewire dynamics for autonomous navigation. Figure 2 illustrates our framework, where observations extracted from CAG images are encoded into a latent representation and processed by the world model to generate control actions, with a reward function guiding policy optimization.

Coronary-Specific Observation Modeling. At step t, given a synthesized angiography image I_t, we randomly sample a target point $\mathbf{p}^*$ from the vessel centerline $\mathcal{C}$ [26], and obtain the guidewire position $\{\mathbf{g}_i\}_{i=1}^N$ from the SOFA simulation. The guidewire tip $\mathbf{g}_{\text{tip}}$ and its M nearest centerline points $\{\mathbf{c}_j\}_{j=1}^M$ are used to describe the local vessel structure for observation encoding.

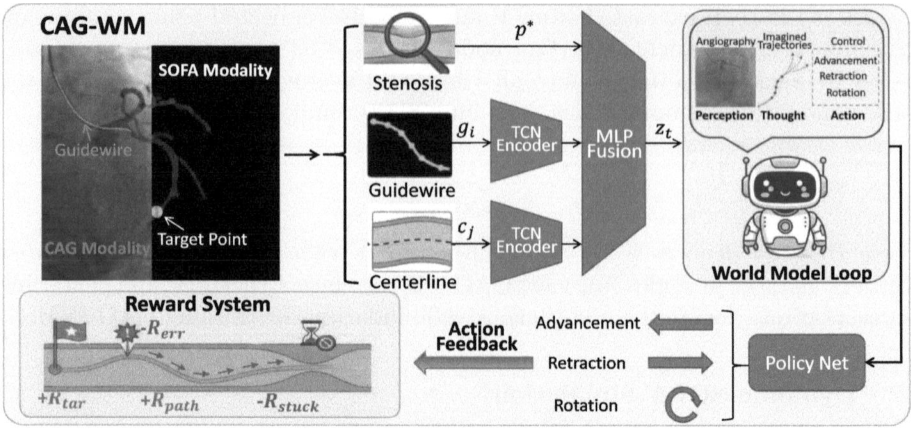

Fig. 2. Details of our CAG-WM. Observations from CAG images are encoded into a latent representation z_t via TCN, which is fed into the world model loop for imagination-based planning and action generation, guided by our reward system.

Two TCN [1] encoders are used to encode $\{\mathbf{g}_i\}_{i=1}^{N}$ and $\{\mathbf{c}_j\}_{j=1}^{M}$, capturing spatial and temporal information. The resulting features are concatenated with $\mathbf{p}^*$ and fused by an MLP to form final multimodal observation representation.

Reward Design. To promote reliable and efficient guidewire navigation, we design a task-specific reward. The reward at step t is defined as

$$R_t = \lambda_{\text{tar}} r_t^{\text{tar}} + \lambda_{\text{path}} r_t^{\text{path}} - \lambda_{\text{err}} \mathbf{1}[\text{error}_t] - \lambda_{\text{stuck}} r_t^{\text{stuck}}, \quad (3)$$

where r_t^{tar} rewards reaching the final target and intermediate waypoints along the planned path, r_t^{path} encourages forward progress by reducing the remaining path length, $\mathbf{1}[\text{error}_t]$ is an indicator of simulation failure (e.g., vessel wall damage), and r_t^{stuck} penalizes stagnation when the guidewire exhibits negligible displacement. The nonnegative weights $\lambda_{\text{tar}}, \lambda_{\text{path}}, \lambda_{\text{err}}, \lambda_{\text{stuck}}$ control the trade-off between efficiency, safety, and stability.

3 Experiments

3.1 Dataset and Metrics

Training Set. The training set consists of 100 synthetic coronary cases, comprising CAG images, 3D vessel models, and centerlines, generated using a trained implicit 3D generative model [3,4,13]. Corresponding 3D vessel models and centerlines are reconstructed following Sec 2.2. All perceptual information required by observation is pre-extracted prior to training. Dataset is available at github.

Test Set. The test set comprises 20 real clinical cases collected from five centers (InCAG) and 10 cases from public dataset, VMR [23]. For each coronary centerline, 15 target points are sampled to serve as navigation goals. For each target point, 10 repeated trials are conducted to evaluate the robustness of the methods, and the results are reported as mean ± standard deviation across trials.

Evaluation Metrics. To comprehensively evaluate the performance, efficiency, and stability of CAG-WM, we design several evaluation metrics. Success Rate (SR) is defined as the percentage of episodes that successfully reach the target. Relative Distance (RD) measures the proportion of remaining centerline distance to the target at episode termination, normalized by the total initial centerline distance from the starting point to the target, evaluated only on failed episodes. Time (T) represents the duration required to navigate from the starting point to the target. Statistical comparisons are conducted using two-tailed paired Student's t-tests, with the significance level set to $p < 0.05$.

3.2 Implementation Details

In data preparation stage, the implicit 3D generative model is trained on 30k real CAG images, achieving an FID score of 8.91. The segmentation network UNet++ [27] are trained on ARCADE [16] and achieves a Dice score of 0.761. During the training of CAG-WM, experiments are conducted on a single NVIDIA L20 GPU. Each model is trained for 10^7 steps with a learning rate of 3×10^{-4}, and the maximum number of steps per episode is set to 400. In Eq. (3), the coefficients are set as $\lambda_{\text{tar}} = 5.0$, $\lambda_{\text{path}} = 0.1$, $\lambda_{\text{err}} = 1.0$, and $\lambda_{\text{stuck}} = 0.1$.

4 Results

4.1 Comparative Experiments

To validate the superiority of CAG-WM, we conduct comprehensive comparative experiments. The baseline methods are categorized into three groups: (1) model-free RL methods, including SAC [9] and TD3 [24]; (2) planning-based methods that directly use simulator dynamics, namely CEM-MPC [6]; (3) world-model-based methods, including DreamerV3 [10], TD-MPC [12], and TD-MPC2 [11].

As shown in Table 1, CAG-WM achieves the best SR and RD on both the clinical and public datasets, reaching 84.7%/17.6% and 83.1%/18.9% respectively, significantly outperforming model-free RL methods and the planning-based CEM-MPC ($p < 0.001$). Among world model baselines, CAG-WM also demonstrates clear advantages. DreamerV3 is better suited for raw image inputs rather than extracted positional features, which limits its performance in our setting. TD-MPC struggles with continuous action spaces compared to our method. Against our backbone TD-MPC2, CAG-WM achieves approximately 10% and 8% improvements in SR and RD respectively, validating the effectiveness of our encoder modifications. Regarding the time metric, although our per-step

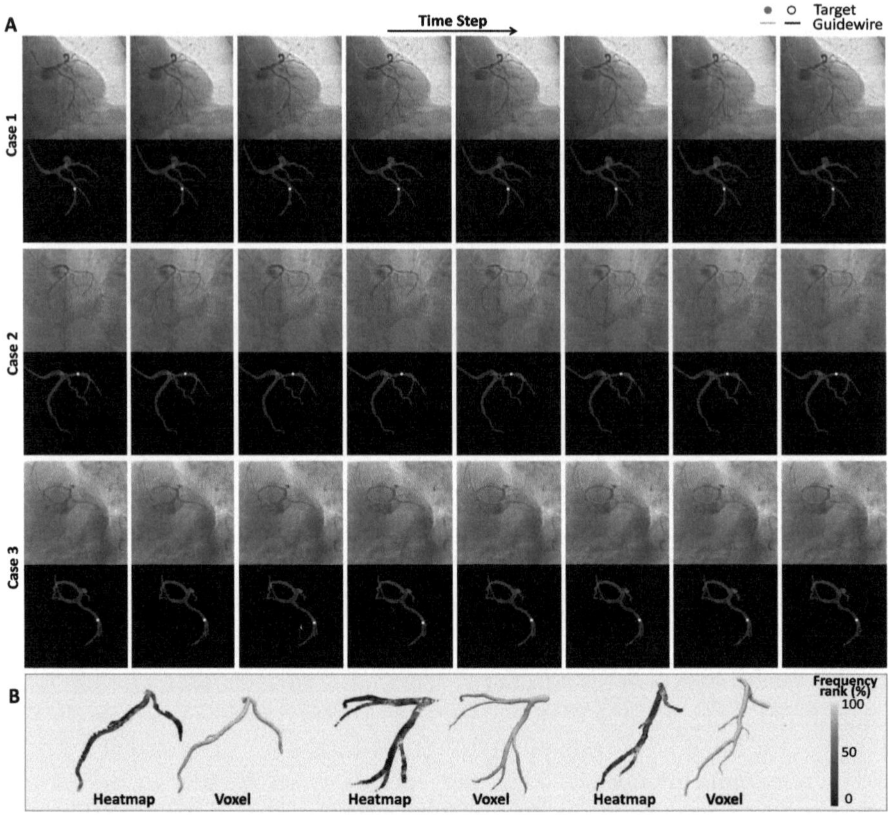

Fig. 3. A. Visualization of autonomous guidewire navigation in coronary arteries by CAG-WM. For each case, the first row shows the CAG modality (green line: guidewire; red dot: target) and the second row shows the SOFA modality (black line: guidewire; white dot: target). B. Heatmap visualization of guidewire tip positions during training and corresponding 3D coronary voxel models. (Color figure online)

inference time is slower than SAC and TD3, the higher SR reduces episodes terminated by reaching the maximum step limit, resulting in the shortest overall navigation time and highlighting the efficiency of our approach.

Figure 3.A illustrates navigation performance across three clinical casesin both CAG and SOFA modalities, where the guidewire successfully selects correct vessel branch and traverses tortuous structures, demonstrating robust comprehension of complex coronary anatomy. Figure 3.B shows guidewire tip trajectory heatmaps alongside corresponding 3D coronary voxels, revealing comprehensive exploration across entire vascular tree and confirming the guidewire's capacity to access all reachable vessel positions. More experimental videos are provided in the supplementary materials.

4.2 Ablation Study

To justify the design of our reward function, we conduct an ablation study on individual reward terms. As shown in Table 2, the full reward achieves the highest SR on both datasets, confirming that each component plays a complementary role in stabilizing learning and improving navigation performance. Without R_{s}, the guidewire frequently hesitates at vascular bifurcations due to the absence of stagnation penalty, leading to redundant movements and failed navigation. Without R_{p}, the agent lacks dense centerline guidance throughout the navigation process, and relying solely on sparse target rewards proves insufficient for effective long-horizon navigation.

Table 1. Quantitative comparison of CAG-WM with competing methods.

Method	InCAG			VMR		
	SR (%) ↑	RD (%) ↓	T (s) ↓	SR (%) ↑	RD (%) ↓	T (s) ↓
SAC [9]	$47.3_{\pm 17.1}$	$49.5_{\pm 21.9}$	$256.67_{\pm 24.34}$	$46.0_{\pm 18.3}$	$51.2_{\pm 20.4}$	$261.43_{\pm 26.17}$
TD3 [24]	$50.7_{\pm 15.4}$	$42.1_{\pm 23.8}$	$239.13_{\pm 23.48}$	$49.3_{\pm 16.2}$	$43.7_{\pm 22.5}$	$244.82_{\pm 21.93}$
CEM-MPC [6]	$52.7_{\pm 15.9}$	$40.8_{\pm 16.5}$	$279.63_{\pm 29.23}$	$52.0_{\pm 14.7}$	$41.9_{\pm 0.178}$	$283.17_{\pm 31.45}$
DreamerV3 [10]	$61.3_{\pm 12.8}$	$37.6_{\pm 17.7}$	$186.79_{\pm 20.30}$	$59.3_{\pm 13.5}$	$38.9_{\pm 16.8}$	$191.24_{\pm 22.56}$
TD-MPC [12]	$43.0_{\pm 16.4}$	$53.2_{\pm 27.1}$	$267.13_{\pm 23.10}$	$42.7_{\pm 17.1}$	$54.8_{\pm 25.9}$	$271.36_{\pm 25.83}$
TD-MPC2 [11]	$75.3_{\pm 8.3}$	$25.1_{\pm 10.4}$	$156.47_{\pm 17.66}$	$74.0_{\pm 9.1}$	$26.3_{\pm 11.2}$	$160.83_{\pm 19.24}$
CAG-WM	$\mathbf{84.7}_{\pm 7.7}$	$\mathbf{17.6}_{\pm 16.7}$	$\mathbf{127.64}_{\pm 14.34}$	$\mathbf{83.3}_{\pm 8.2}$	$\mathbf{18.9}_{\pm 15.4}$	$\mathbf{132.57}_{\pm 15.89}$

Table 2. Ablation study on reward components, where R_t: reward for reaching target point; R_p: reward for reducing centerline path distance to the target; R_e: penalty for mechanical interaction with vessel wall; R_s: penalty for guidewire being stuck.

R_t	R_p	R_e	R_s	InCAG			VMR		
				SR (%) ↑	RD (%) ↓	T (s) ↓	SR (%) ↑	RD (%) ↓	T (s) ↓
✓				$58.7_{\pm 14.2}$	$43.1_{\pm 19.8}$	$103.71_{\pm 18.23}$	$57.3_{\pm 15.6}$	$44.7_{\pm 21.1}$	$107.34_{\pm 19.87}$
✓	✓			$60.3_{\pm 13.1}$	$41.2_{\pm 18.3}$	$\mathbf{99.86}_{\pm 17.54}$	$58.7_{\pm 14.3}$	$42.8_{\pm 19.6}$	$\mathbf{103.52}_{\pm 18.63}$
✓	✓	✓		$62.9_{\pm 10.3}$	$39.6_{\pm 15.4}$	$129.33_{\pm 16.87}$	$61.3_{\pm 12.1}$	$41.5_{\pm 17.6}$	$133.17_{\pm 17.92}$
✓	✓	✓	✓	$\mathbf{84.7}_{\pm 7.7}$	$\mathbf{17.6}_{\pm 16.7}$	$127.64_{\pm 14.34}$	$\mathbf{83.3}_{\pm 0.082}$	$\mathbf{18.9}_{\pm 15.4}$	$132.57_{\pm 15.89}$

Although our full method exhibits longer navigation time, this is attributed to R_{e} enforcing mechanical constraints that prevent unrealistic vessel wall penetration, avoiding premature episode termination and ensuring physically valid trajectories that better reflect real clinical conditions.

5 Conclusion

In this study, we propose CAG-WM, the first coronary world model enabling end-to-end autonomous guidewire navigation from angiographic observations to control actions, providing a new pathway to reduce operator radiation exposure and workload. We construct a dynamic full-view coronary angiography3D synthetic dataset and integrate a world model-based framework with a SOFA-based simulation environment to model vesselguidewire interactions and optimize long-horizon decision-making. Validation on multi-center clinical cases and public datasets demonstrates that CAG-WM significantly outperforms RL and existing world model approaches in navigation success rate. Meanwhile, even in failed cases, our method achieves a closer proximity to the target point than competing methods. Furthermore, CAG-WM achieves the shortest navigation time, as its higher success rate reduces episodes terminated by the maximum step limit. This work represents the first systematic application of world modeling to dynamic coronary autonomous navigation and lays the foundation for AI-driven robotic coronary intervention. Future work will expand validation cohorts and advance evaluation on physical vascular phantoms and in vivo experiments. Beyond coronary guidewire navigation, the world model framework holds potential for broader PIC tasks, including balloon dilation and stent deployment, as well as pre-operative planning and intraoperative decision support.

Disclosure of Interests. The authors have no competing interests in the paper.

References

1. Bai, S., Kolter, J.Z., Koltun, V.: An empirical evaluation of generic convolutional and recurrent networks for sequence modeling. arXiv:1803.01271 (2018)
2. Bhatt, D.L.: Percutaneous coronary intervention in 2018. JAMA **319**(20), 2127–2128 (2018). https://doi.org/10.1001/jama.2018.5281
3. Cao, Y., et al.: Automatic translational correction of multi-view coronary angiography based on autoannotation data generation. In: Proceedings of the AAAI Conference on Artificial Intelligence Vol. 40, no. (4), pp. 2652–2660 (2026). https://doi.org/10.1609/aaai.v40i4.37253, https://ojs.aaai.org/index.php/AAAI/article/view/37253
4. Chan, E.R., et al.: Efficient geometry-aware 3D generative adversarial networks. arXiv (2021)
5. Cho, Y., Park, J.H., Choi, J., Chang, D.E.: Sim-to-real transfer of image-based autonomous guidewire navigation trained by deep deterministic policy gradient with behavior cloning for fast learning. In: 2022 IEEE/RSJ International Conference on Intelligent Robots and Systems (IROS), pp. 3468–3475 (2022)
6. Chua, K., Calandra, R., McAllister, R., Levine, S.: Deep reinforcement learning in a handful of trials using probabilistic dynamics models. In: Proceedings of the 32nd International Conference on Neural Information Processing Systems. p. 4759–4770. NIPS'18, Curran Associates Inc., Red Hook, NY, USA (2018)
7. Faure, F., et al.: SOFA: A Multi-Model Framework for Interactive Physical Simulation, pp. 283–321. Springer, Cham (2012). https://doi.org/10.1007/8415_2012_125

8. Ha, D., et al.: Recurrent world models facilitate policy evolution. In: Garnett, R. (ed.) Advances in Neural Information Processing Systems, vol. 31, Curran Associates, Inc. (2018)
9. Haarnoja, T., Zhou, A., Abbeel, P., Levine, S.: Soft Actor-Critic: Off-Policy Maximum Entropy Deep Reinforcement Learning with a Stochastic Actor. arXiv e-prints arXiv:1801.01290 (2018). https://doi.org/10.48550/arXiv.1801.01290
10. Hafner, D., Pasukonis, J., Ba, J., Lillicrap, T.: Mastering diverse control tasks through world models. Nature 1–7 (2025)
11. Hansen, N., Su, H., Wang, X.: Td-mpc2: Scalable, robust world models for continuous control (2024)
12. Hansen, N., Wang, X., Su, H.: Temporal difference learning for model predictive control (2022)
13. Li, J., et al.: Geometrically constrained stenosis editing in coronary angiography via entropic optimal transport. arXiv preprint arXiv:2605.08851 (2026)
14. Li, Z., et al.: Robust path planning via learning from demonstrations for robotic catheters in deformable environments. IEEE Trans. Biomed. Eng. **72**(1), 324–336 (2025). https://doi.org/10.1109/TBME.2024.3452034
15. Madder, R.D., et al.: Impact of robotics and a suspended lead suit on physician radiation exposure during percutaneous coronary intervention. Cardiovasc. Revasc. Med. **18**(3), 190–196 (2017). https://doi.org/10.1016/j.carrev.2016.12.011
16. Popov, M., et al.: Dataset for automatic region-based coronary artery disease diagnostics using x-ray angiography images. Sci. Data **11**(1), 20 (2024)
17. Robertshaw, H., et al.: Artificial intelligence in the autonomous navigation of endovascular interventions: a systematic review. Front. Human Neurosci. **17** (2023). https://doi.org/10.3389/fnhum.2023.1239374
18. Robertshaw, H., Wu, H.R., Granados, A., Booth, T.C.: World model for ai autonomous navigation in mechanical thrombectomy. In: Gee, J.C., et al. (eds.) Medical Image Computing and Computer Assisted Intervention - MICCAI 2025, pp. 680–690. Springer, Cham (2026)
19. Scarponi, V., Lecomte, F., Duprez, M., Nageotte, F., Cotin, S.: Autonomous guidewire navigation in dynamic environments. In: 2024 IEEE/RSJ International Conference on Intelligent Robots and Systems (IROS), pp. 6931–6938 (2024)
20. Schegg, P., et al.: Automated planning for robotic guidewire navigation in the coronary arteries. In: 2022 IEEE 5th International Conference on Soft Robotics (RoboSoft), pp. 239–246 (2022). https://doi.org/10.1109/RoboSoft54090.2022.9762096
21. Weisz, G., et al.: Safety and feasibility of robotic percutaneous coronary intervention: Precise (percutaneous robotically-enhanced coronary intervention) study. J. Am. Coll. Cardiol. **61**(15), 1596–1600 (2013). https://doi.org/10.1016/j.jacc.2012.12.045
22. Weyland, C.S., et al.: Radiation exposure per thrombectomy attempt in modern endovascular stroke treatment in the anterior circulation. Eur. Radiol. **30**(9), 5039–5047 (2020). https://doi.org/10.1007/s00330-020-06837-2
23. Wilson, N., Ortiz, A., Johnson, A.: The vascular model repository: A public resource of medical imaging data and blood flow simulation results. J. Med. Devices **7**, 0409231–409231 (2013).https://doi.org/10.1115/1.4025983
24. Wu, J., Wu, Q.M.J., Chen, S., Pourpanah, F., Huang, D.: A-td3: An adaptive asynchronous twin delayed deep deterministic for continuous action spaces. IEEE Access **10**, 128077–128089 (2022). https://doi.org/10.1109/ACCESS.2022.3226446

25. Yoo, S., Kwon, H., Choi, J., Chang, D.E.: A robust deep reinforcement learning framework for image-based autonomous guidewire navigation. In: 2025 IEEE International Conference on Robotics and Automation (ICRA), pp. 468–474 (2025). https://doi.org/10.1109/ICRA55743.2025.11127741
26. Zhao, Z., et al.: Deformcl: Learning deformable centerline representation for vessel extraction in 3d medical image. In: Proceedings of the Computer Vision and Pattern Recognition Conference, pp. 30896–30905 (2025)
27. Zhou, Z., Siddiquee, M.M.R., Tajbakhsh, N., Liang, J.: Unet++: Redesigning skip connections to exploit multiscale features in image segmentation. IEEE Trans. Med. Imaging (2019)

CoGE: Sim-to-Real Online Geometric Estimation for Monocular Colonoscopy

Liangjing Shao[1,2], Beilei Cui[1], and Hongliang Ren[1,2](✉)

[1] Department of Electronic Engineering, The Chinese University of Hong Kong, Hong Kong SAR, China
{leonking-shaw,beileicui}@link.cuhk.edu.hk, hlren@ee.cuhk.edu.hk
[2] Shenzhen Loop Area Institute, Shenzhen, China

Abstract. Geometric estimation including depth estimation and scene reconstruction is a crucial technique for colonoscopy which can provide surgeons with 3D spatial perception and navigation. However, geometric ground truth in colonoscopy is difficult to obtain due to narrow and enclosed space of the colon, while there is a large feature gap between simulated data and realistic data caused by artifacts and illumination. In this paper, we present CoGE, a novel framework for online monocular geometric estimation during colonoscopy. Firstly, we propose an illumination-aware supervision module based on the Retinex theory to address illumination diversity in different colonoscopy scenes. Moreover, a structure-aware perception module is proposed based on wavelet decomposition to extract common structural and local features of the colon. Both quantitative and qualitative results demonstrate that the proposed model solely trained on simulated data achieves state-of-the-art performance in geometric estimation for both simulated and realistic scenes.

Keywords: Depth Estimation · 3D Reconstruction · Colonoscopy

1 Introduction

Geometric estimation from monocular endoscopic videos is crucial for 3D perception, spatial navigation and path planning in colonoscopy, due to 2D vision of endoscope and long narrow closed pathway of colon.

Recently, numerous 3D reconstruction foundation models [4,8,13,14,19] have been proposed for cross-scene geometric estimation. However, existing methods usually need a large amount of realistic data with geometric ground truth including depth map, point clouds and camera parameters. Such datasets with geometric ground truth are difficult and costly to obtain in realistic colonoscopy due

Supplementary Information The online version contains supplementary material available at https://doi.org/10.1007/978-3-032-38236-8_12.

G. Yang et al. (Eds.): MICCAI 2026, LNCS 16893, pp. 117–126, 2027.
https://doi.org/10.1007/978-3-032-38236-8_12

to the narrow and closed space of colon. Thus, several self-supervised learning-based methods [6,16] have been developed for colonoscopy geometric estimation. However, the performance of self-supervised models is limited compared with supervised models. Nevertheless, geometric ground truth can be obtained by simulation software such as VR-Caps [5,11]. Therefore, sim-to-real geometric estimation has become a potential approach for 3D perception in endoscopic scenes. Currently, some existing works [9,10] have proposed sim-to-real methods for endoscopy geometric estimation. However, the proposed pipeline is evaluated after transforming the realistic data into the simulation-like data by a style translation network. Hence, the inference efficiency will be decreased due to data preprocessing, while inherent gaps between diverse realistic data and simulated data may degrade the cross-scene performance of appearance transformation models (Fig. 1).

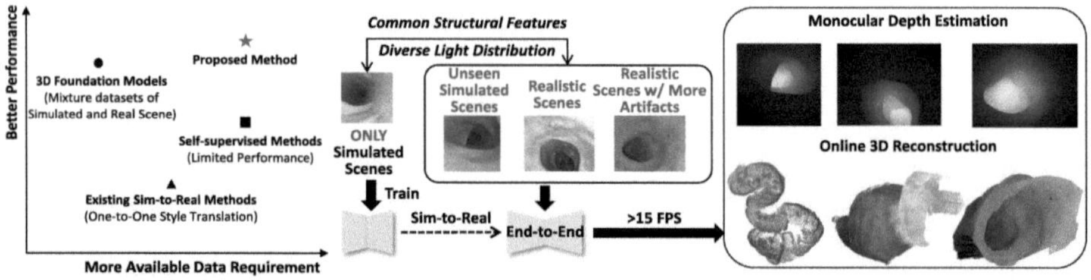

Fig. 1. Given observations from realistic and unseen scenes, our model only trained on simulated data outputs depth maps and 3D point clouds.

In this paper, we propose a feed-forward framework, **CoGE**, for sim-to-real **g**eometric **e**stimation in **co**lonoscopy. In previous work [17], wavelet decomposition has been used to perform frequency-based supervision for global tissue structure and high-frequency details. Inspired by this, a structure-aware perception module based on wavelet transformation is proposed to extract common structural features of colon from colonoscopy images. Moreover, features of colon surface are easily interfered by illumination, so a illumination-aware supervision module is proposed to control the confidence of the estimated results based on light distribution. Besides, considering long distance of colonoscopy sequence, we propose a memory forget mechanism based on attention map between feature of current frame and memory cache to prevent interference of redundant memory.

Our main contribution can be summarized as the following: **1)** A structure-aware perception block is embedded based on wavelet transformation to extract common structural features in both simulated and realistic scenes. **2)** An illumination-aware supervision module is proposed to control the confidence of the estimated results to prevent the influence of diverse illumination on colon surface. **3)** A memory forget mechanism is proposed to filter redundant irrelevant memory for current observation against interference. **4)** The proposed model only trained on simulated data achieves state-of-the-art performance for geometric estimation on both unseen simulated scenes and realistic scenes.

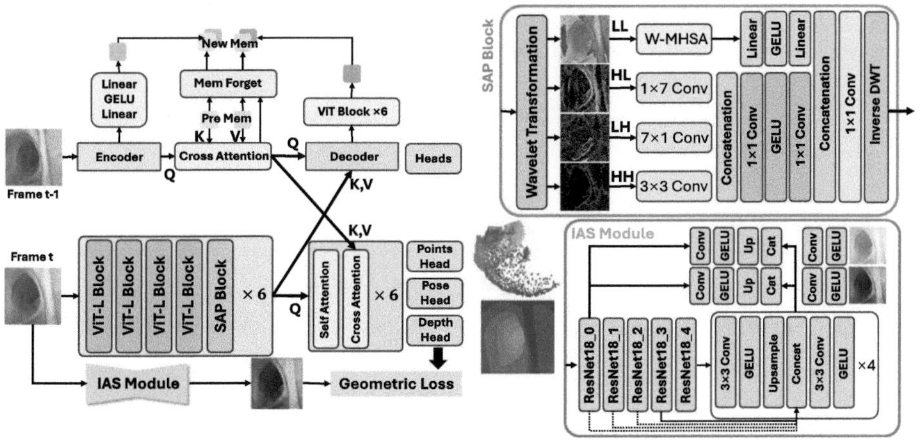

Fig. 2. The pipeline of the proposed framework.

2 Method

2.1 Overview

Given a pair of observations including cached previous observation I_{t-1} and current observation I_t, the proposed model will output the corresponding point map X_t, camera pose P_t, illumination map L_t and confidence map C_t. Meanwhile, inspired by Spann3R [13], two spatial memory caches M_k, M_v are set and they will be updated to $\hat{M}_k, \hat{M}_v$ after memory reading, memory forgetting and memory updating based on the observations. The model architecture is demonstrated in Fig. 2.

2.2 Structure-Aware Encoding

Firstly, we utilize six ViT-based modules to extract scene features from the observations $f_{t-1} = \mathcal{F}_{enc}(I_{t-1}), f_t = \mathcal{F}_{enc}(I_t)$. Each module consists of four ViT-L blocks followed by a structure-aware perception (SAP) block, which could extract common structural features from colonoscopy images. In SAP block, we firstly utilize discrete wavelet transformation to decompose the input graph into four subgraphs including low-low I_{ll} with low-frequency main approximation of the input, low-high I_{lh} with horizontal high-frequency details, high-low I_{hl} with vertical high-frequency details and high-high I_{hh} with diagonal high-frequency details. Convolution can extract high-frequency local details while attention is better for low-frequency information extraction. Thus, we utilize window-based multi-head attention (W-MHSA) to extract features f_{ll} from I_{ll}, while vertical-band convolution with 7×1 kernel, horizontal-band convolution with 1×7 kernel and diagonal convolution with 3×3 kernel are respectively utilized to extract features f_{hl}, f_{lh}, f_{hh} from I_{hl}, I_{lh} and I_{hh}. Then, features from different wavelet compositions are fused based on Eq. 1–3.

$$f_h = \mathcal{F}_{conv}^{1\times1}(\mathcal{F}_{GELU}(\mathcal{F}_{conv}^{1\times1}([f_{hl}, f_{lh}, f_{hh}]))) \tag{1}$$

$$f_l = \mathcal{F}_{lin}(\mathcal{F}_{GELU}(\mathcal{F}_{lin}(f_{ll}))) \tag{2}$$

$$f_{SAP} = \mathcal{F}_{idwt}(\mathcal{F}_{conv}^{1\times1}([f_h, f_l])) \tag{3}$$

where $\mathcal{F}_{lin}$ denotes a linear layer, $\mathcal{F}_{idwt}$ denotes inverse discrete wavelet transformation.

2.3 Memory-Related Decoding

Memory Reading. The feature from previous observation f_{t-1} is utilized to retrieve the related memory information from caches by Eq. 5.

$$W_{mem} = softmax(\frac{f_{t-1}M_k^T}{\sqrt{d}}) \tag{4}$$

$$f_{t-1}^{mem} = W_{mem}M_v + f_{t-1} \tag{5}$$

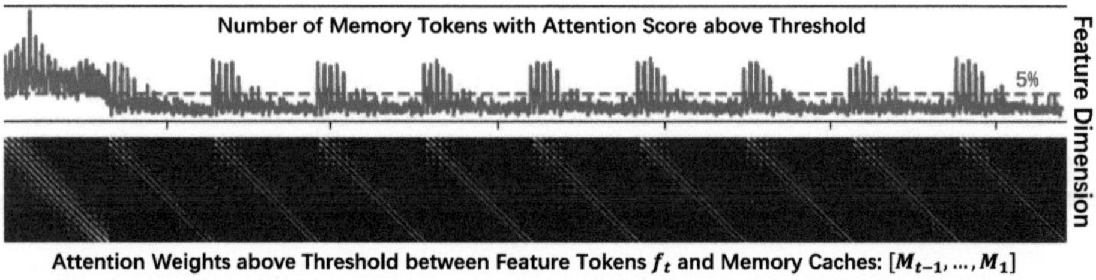

Fig. 3. Attention weights distribution between feature tokens and memory caches.

Memory Forget. For attention maps $W_{mem} \in \mathbb{R}^{d\times s}$ between feature $f_{t-1} \in \mathbb{R}^{d\times 1}$ and memory cache $M_k, M_v \in \mathbb{R}^{s\times 1}$, if there is at least 5% feature tokens $f_{t-1}(j)$ with an attention weight $W_{mem}(j,i)$ larger than 5e-4 for each memory token $M_k(i), M_v(i)$, the memory token is seemed as the relevant tokens to be retained, demonstrated as Fig. 3.

$$M_k(i), M_v(i) \rightarrow \begin{cases} retain & |\{W_{mem}(j,i) \geq \text{5e-4}\}| \geq 5\%|\{W_{mem}(\cdot,i)\}| \\ delete & \text{otherwise} \end{cases} \tag{6}$$

Decoding and Memory Updating. Given memory-related feature f_{t-1}^{mem} and current feature f_t, the output feature of current frame and previous frame can be respectively obtained by six decoding blocks, each of which consists of self-attention and cross-attention $\hat{f}_t = \mathcal{F}_{dec}(f_t, f_{t-1}^{mem}), \hat{f}_{t-1} = \mathcal{F}_{dec}(f_{t-1}^{mem}, f_t)$. The new memory of key and value are encoded from memory-related feature $\Delta M_k = \mathcal{F}_{enc}^{key}(f_{t-1}^{mem})$ and output feature of previous frame $\Delta M_v = \mathcal{F}_{enc}^{val}(\hat{f}_{t-1})$. The memory cache is updated by concatenating the new memory and filtered cached memory, $\hat{M}_k, \hat{M}_v = [M_k, \Delta M_k], [M_v, \Delta M_v]$.

Downstream Heads. Given the output feature of the current observation $\hat{f}_t$, DPT heads $\mathcal{H}_{dpt}$ are utilized to output the corresponding point map X_t, camera pose P_t and confidence map C_t, following CUT3R [14]. Furthermore, the corresponding depth map D_t can be calculated based on the point map X_t, camera parameters P_t and K:

$$X_t, P_t, C_t = \mathcal{H}_{dpt}(\hat{f}_t), D_t = \mathcal{Z}(X_t, P_t, K) \tag{7}$$

2.4 Illumination-Aware Supervision

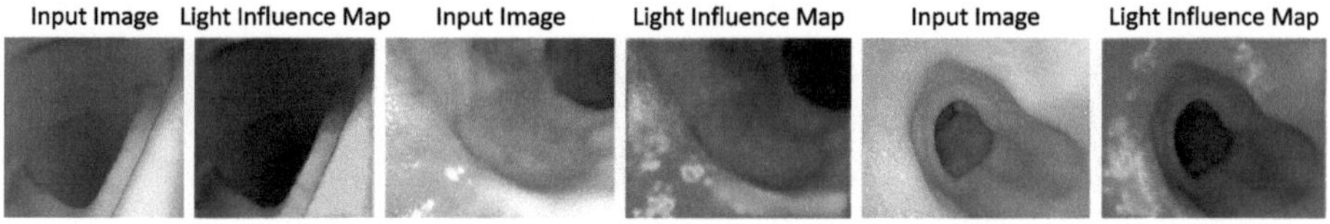

Fig. 4. Input images and corresponding light influence maps.

Considering diverse and unstable illumination in colonoscopy, we propose a self-supervised illumination-aware (IAS) module to adjust confidence map for supervision. Based on retinex theory [7], the invariance of intrinsic component A_t of image I_t to illumination condition in the gradient domain (∇) is considered to generate illumination influence distribution L_t. Given the input image I_t, the IAS module outputs the corresponding intrinsic graph A_t and light influence map L_t shown in Fig. 8. The IAS module is pretrained on the training split using the loss function Eq. 8 for 1 epoch with a batch size of 8. During the training of the whole network, L_t from the frozen IAS module is utilized to adjust confidence map C_t by Eq. 9 with a learnable weight α.

$$\mathcal{L}_{ias} = (1 - L_t) \log \nabla I_t - \log \nabla A_t \tag{8}$$

$$\hat{C}_t = \alpha C_t + (1 - \alpha) L_t \tag{9}$$

Our supervision loss is mainly based on the 3D geometric loss used in CUT3R [14], which can be formulated as Eq. 10.

$$\mathcal{L} = \mathcal{L}_{conf}(X_t, \hat{C}_t) + \mathcal{L}_{pose} + \mathcal{L}_{rgb} \tag{10}$$

3 Experiments and Results

3.1 Experiment Implementation

We use 24 simulated sequences along with corresponding camera poses and depth maps obtained by VR-Caps [5,11] for training. Simulated dataset SimCol3D [11] which includes 9 simulated scenes with 9009 frames and realistic datasets C3VD [1], C3VDv2 [3] including 11 sequences with over 3000 frames are utilized for evaluation. We also extract some in-house colonoscopy images for qualitative comparison. The evaluation splits mainly follow the setting in previous works [6,16]. The proposed model is initialized with pretrained weights from DUSt3R [15] and trained for 10 epochs with a batch size of 4 on a NVIDIA H100 GPU. All evaluations are implemented on a NVIDIA RTX 4090 GPU.

Table 1. Quantitative results of monocular depth estimation.

	Methods	Year	$Rel_{Abs}\downarrow$	$Rel_{Sq}\downarrow$	$RMSE\downarrow$	$RMSE_{log}\downarrow$	$\delta\uparrow$	FPS
SimCol	**AF-SfM [12]**	2022	0.086	0.036	0.585	0.104	0.954	193
	DepthAnything [18]	2024	0.089	0.042	0.599	0.112	0.948	89
	EndoDAC [2]	2024	0.107	0.050	0.530	0.133	0.924	53
	ColonAdapter [6]	2025	0.062	0.034	0.373	0.094	0.969	-
	MonoPCC [16]	2025	0.058	0.028	0.347	0.090	0.975	-
	Spann3R [13]	2025	0.122	0.103	0.577	0.181	0.795	30
	MonST3R [19]	2025	0.032	0.020	0.205	0.068	0.985	22
	CUT3R [14]	2025	0.036	0.032	0.231	0.070	0.985	34
	STream3R [8]	2026	0.034	0.013	0.204	0.061	0.990	35
	Ours	2026	**0.027**	**0.008**	**0.169**	**0.049**	**0.995**	19
C3VD	**AF-SfM [12]**	2022	0.117	1.324	7.520	0.171	0.882	189
	DepthAnything [18]	2024	0.121	1.155	6.239	0.165	0.874	87
	EndoDAC [2]	2024	0.103	0.652	5.306	0.147	0.890	50
	ColonAdapter [6]	2025	0.139	0.956	5.592	0.175	0.832	-
	Spann3R [13]	2025	0.090	0.523	4.152	0.132	0.891	26
	MonST3R [19]	2025	0.086	0.541	4.207	0.134	0.889	20
	CUT3R [14]	2025	0.087	0.511	4.144	0.129	0.896	29
	STream3R [8]	2026	0.085	0.493	4.105	0.130	0.900	30
	Ours	2026	**0.083**	**0.476**	**4.061**	**0.126**	**0.913**	18
C3VDv2	**Spann3R [13]**	2025	0.108	2.200	8.582	0.305	0.802	20
	MonST3R [19]	2025	0.109	2.014	8.269	0.260	0.825	26
	CUT3R [14]	2025	0.132	**1.713**	9.014	0.275	0.749	29
	STream3R [8]	2026	0.124	2.090	9.205	0.274	0.765	30
	Ours	2026	**0.098**	2.008	**7.772**	**0.250**	**0.865**	18

3.2 Results

Monocular Depth Estimation. The proposed method is compared with SOTA 3D geometric estimation methods on both simulated data and realistic data for monocular depth estimation. Following previous works [2,12], we use Abs Rel (Rel_{Abs}), Sq Rel (Rel_{Sq}), RMSE, RMSE Log ($RMSE_{log}$) and $\delta < 1.25$ (δ) as evaluation metrics. Results of MonoPCC [16] and ColonAdapter [6] are directly from public papers, while others are trained for similar time based on the same implementation by our own. Quantitative results in Table 1 and qualitative results in Fig. 5 demonstrate the outstanding performance of our model on monocular depth estimation, only with training on simulated data.

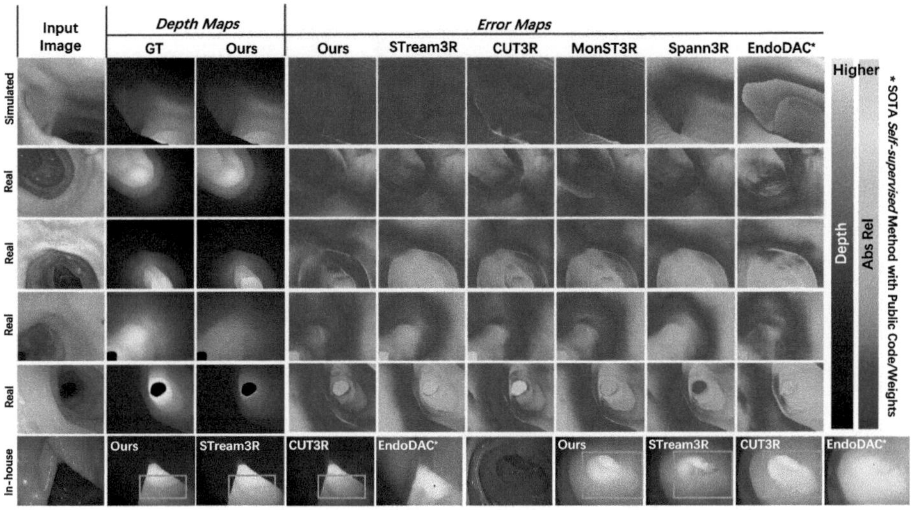

Fig. 5. Qualitative results of monocular depth estimation.

3D Reconstruction. The proposed method is also compared with several 3D foundation models for 3D reconstruction based on monocular videos. We utilize mean Euclidean Distance (mED) to the point cloud generated from ground truth and ratio of points with ED< N mm ($\delta < N$) to evaluate the reconstruction accuracy. Results in Fig. 7 demonstrate that our method provides more accurate point cloud reconstruction compared with existing reconstruction methods. Figure 6 further displays some example results from our method.

Ablation Studies. Our main contributions include memory forget gate (MemF), illumination-aware supervision module (IAS) and structure-aware perception Block (SAP) for challenges of sim-to-real geometric estimation in colonoscopy. Results shown in Table 2 and Fig. 8 demonstrate the effectiveness of each main component we propose in this paper.

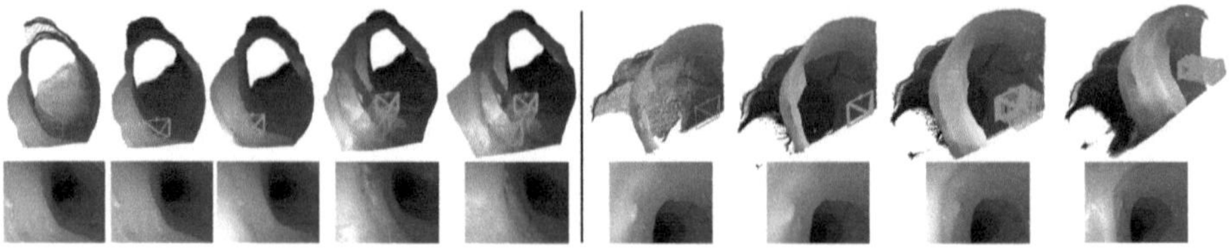

Fig. 6. Qualitative Display of Our 3D reconstruction.

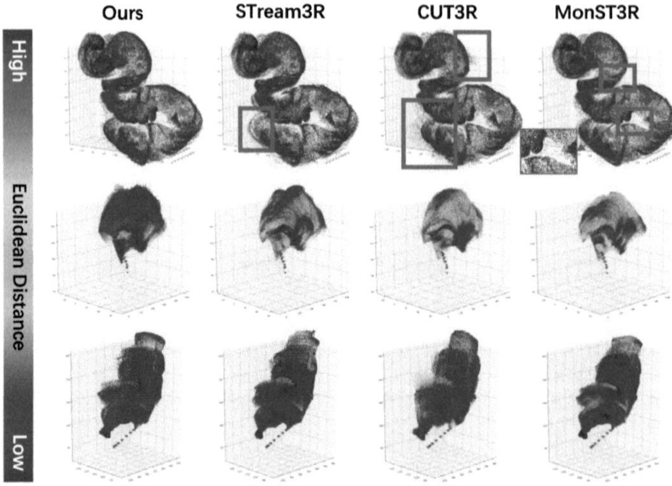

Methods	mED	δ<0.2
Ours	**0.193**	**0.656**
STream3R	0.240	0.457
CUT3R	0.221	0.417
MonST3R	0.217	0.424

Methods	mED	δ<4.0
Ours	**3.957**	**0.645**
STream3R	4.469	0.490
CUT3R	4.243	0.323
MonST3R	4.583	0.215

Methods	mED	δ<3.0
Ours	**2.805**	**0.736**
STream3R	2.952	0.531
CUT3R	3.193	0.301
MonST3R	3.087	0.264

Fig. 7. Qualitative Comparison of 3D reconstruction.

Table 2. Results of Ablation Studies

Ablations			SimCol		C3VD		C3VDv2	
MemF	IAS	SAP	Abs Rel	δ	Abs Rel	δ	Abs Rel	δ
✔	✔	✔	**0.024**	**0.994**	**0.085**	**0.913**	**0.098**	**0.865**
×	✔	✔	0.026	0.991	0.087	0.905	0.100	0.861
✔	×	✔	0.030	0.988	0.087	0.900	0.104	0.853
✔	✔	×	0.032	0.993	0.089	0.903	0.099	0.860

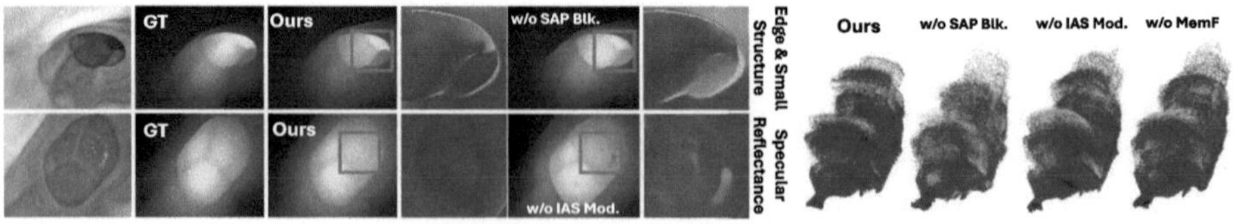

Fig. 8. Qualitative results of ablation studies.

4 Conclusion

In this paper, we propose a geometric estimation model, which is only trained on simulated data, to perform online depth estimation and 3D reconstruction in realistic colonoscopy. We focus on illumination diversity and common structure feature extraction for sim-to-real geometric estimation. Our method outperforms state-of-the-art methods based on quantitative and qualitative experimental results on realistic data, with effects of our contributions. Despite of real-time inference speed, the inference efficiency of the proposed model is still decreased due to extra structure-aware perception blocks. Moreover, the performance of the proposed model will be degraded due to motion blur, acute dynamic change and specific lesion tissue in colonoscopy.

Acknowledgments. This work was supported by Ministry of Science and Technology (MOST) of China Key Project 2025YFE0122500, Shenzhen-Hong Kong-Macau Technology Research Programme (Type C) STIC Grant SGCX20250526153900001, Hong Kong RGC CRF C4026-21G, RIF R4020-22, GRF 14211420, 14216022 & 14203323.

Disclosure of Interests. The authors have no competing interests to declare that are relevant to the content of this article.

References

1. Bobrow, T.L., Golhar, M., Vijayan, R., Akshintala, V.S., Garcia, J.R., Durr, N.J.: Colonoscopy 3d video dataset with paired depth from 2d–3d registration. Med. Image Anal. **90**, 102956 (2023)
2. Cui, B., Islam, M., Bai, L., Wang, A., Ren, H.: Endodac: Efficient adapting foundation model for self-supervised depth estimation from any endoscopic camera. In: International Conference on Medical Image Computing and Computer-Assisted Intervention, pp. 208–218. Springer, Cham (2024). https://doi.org/10.1007/978-3-031-72089-5_20
3. Golhar, M.V., Fretes, L.S.G., Ayers, L., Akshintala, V.S., Bobrow, T.L., Durr, N.J.: C3vdv2-colonoscopy 3d video dataset with enhanced realism. arXiv preprint arXiv:2506.24074 (2025)
4. Guo, J., et al.: Endo3r: Unified online reconstruction from dynamic monocular endoscopic video. In: Gee, J.C., et al. (eds.) International Conference on Medical Image Computing and Computer-Assisted Intervention, pp. 170–180. Springer, Cham (2025). https://doi.org/10.1007/978-3-032-05114-1_17
5. İncetan, K., et al.: Vr-caps: a virtual environment for capsule endoscopy. Med. Image Anal. **70**, 101990 (2021)
6. Jiang, Z., Wang, Y., Cheng, X., Ge, Z.: Colonadapter: Geometry estimation through foundation model adaptation for colonoscopy. IEEE Robot. Autom. Lett. (2025)
7. Kim, S., Park, K., Sohn, K., Lin, S.: Unified Depth Prediction and Intrinsic Image Decomposition from a Single Image via Joint Convolutional Neural Fields. In: Leibe, B., Matas, J., Sebe, N., Welling, M. (eds.) ECCV 2016. LNCS, vol. 9912, pp. 143–159. Springer, Cham (2016). https://doi.org/10.1007/978-3-319-46484-8_9

8. Lan, Y., et al.: Stream3r: Scalable sequential 3d reconstruction with causal transformer. arXiv preprint arXiv:2508.10893 (2025)
9. Mahmood, F., Chen, R., Durr, N.J.: Unsupervised reverse domain adaptation for synthetic medical images via adversarial training. IEEE Trans. Med. Imaging **37**(12), 2572–2581 (2018)
10. Mahmood, F., Durr, N.J.: Deep learning and conditional random fields-based depth estimation and topographical reconstruction from conventional endoscopy. Med. Image Anal. **48**, 230–243 (2018)
11. Rau, A., et al.: Simcol3d—3d reconstruction during colonoscopy challenge. Med. Image Anal. **96**, 103195 (2024)
12. Shao, S., et al.: Self-supervised monocular depth and ego-motion estimation in endoscopy: Appearance flow to the rescue. Med. Image Anal. **77**, 102338 (2022)
13. Wang, H., Agapito, L.: 3d reconstruction with spatial memory. In: 2025 International Conference on 3D Vision (3DV), pp. 78–89. IEEE (2025)
14. Wang, Q., Zhang, Y., Holynski, A., Efros, A.A., Kanazawa, A.: Continuous 3d perception model with persistent state. In: Proceedings of the Computer Vision and Pattern Recognition Conference, pp. 10510–10522 (2025)
15. Wang, S., Leroy, V., Cabon, Y., Chidlovskii, B., Revaud, J.: Dust3r: Geometric 3d vision made easy. In: Proceedings of the IEEE/CVF Conference on Computer Vision and Pattern Recognition, pp. 20697–20709 (2024)
16. Wang, Z., et al.: Monopcc: Photometric-invariant cycle constraint for monocular depth estimation of endoscopic images. Med. Image Anal. **102**, 103534 (2025)
17. Wu, T., et al.: Endowave: 4d gaussian splatting with rational wavelet for endoscopic reconstruction. In: 2025 IEEE International Conference on Bioinformatics and Biomedicine (BIBM), pp. 6125–6132 (2025)
18. Yang, L., Kang, B., Huang, Z., Xu, X., Feng, J., Zhao, H.: Depth anything: Unleashing the power of large-scale unlabeled data. In: Proceedings of the IEEE/CVF Conference on Computer Vision and Pattern Recognition, pp. 10371–10381 (2024)
19. Zhang, J., et al.: Monst3r: A simple approach for estimating geometry in the presence of motion. arXiv preprint arXiv:2410.03825 (2024)

Computer-Assisted Intervention in Capsule Endoscopy: A Real-Time Edge-AI Auditing System

Diego Bravo[1], Josué Ruano-Balseca[1,2], Fabio A. González[3], and Eduardo Romero[1(✉)]

[1] CIM@LAB, Universidad Nacional de Colombia, Bogotá, Colombia
edromero@unal.edu.co
[2] imec-Vision Lab, University of Antwerp, Antwerp, Belgium
[3] MindLab, Universidad Nacional de Colombia, Bogotá, Colombia

Abstract. Video capsule endoscopy (VCE) is the preferred first-line modality for visualizing the small bowel mucosa and evaluating obscure gastrointestinal bleeding. However, each examination generates over 50 thousand frames, making manual review time-consuming and prone to missed findings and inter-observer variability. Most AI systems rely on single-frame analysis, overlooking temporal dynamics and limiting their ability to distinguish anatomical transitions from transient artifacts. We propose a real-time auditing framework that jointly identifies the anatomical region along the gastrointestinal tract and detects anomalies through intrinsic temporal modeling. Consecutive frames are encoded using an endoscopy-pretrained CNN and processed by a lightweight Vision Transformer operating in a sequence-to-sequence manner, enabling frame-level predictions without post-processing. Evaluated on the multi-center Galar dataset (~3.5 million frames), the proposed system achieves a macro F1-score of 90% for anatomical classification and 67% macro recall for binary anomaly detection within a unified multi-task learning framework, outperforming prior frame-wise approaches. Deployment on a low-power edge device confirms real-time performance (30.5 ms per frame, ~33 FPS), enabling continuous monitoring of incomplete procedures, capsule retention, and persistent abnormalities. Our code is available at https://github.com/DiegoBravoH/CapsuleAudit.

Keywords: Video capsule endoscopy · Temporal modeling · Real-time

1 Introduction

Video capsule endoscopy (VCE) is a minimally invasive diagnostic modality that enables visualization of the gastrointestinal (GI) tract, particularly the small intestine, which is difficult to assess by standard gastroscopy and colonoscopy [1]. Patients swallow a pill-sized wireless camera that passively traverses the GI tract, capturing images for subsequent review. VCE is currently recommended

G. Yang et al. (Eds.): MICCAI 2026, LNCS 16893, pp. 127–137, 2027.
https://doi.org/10.1007/978-3-032-38236-8_13

as the first-line examination for obscure gastrointestinal bleeding (OGIB) and other small bowel disorders [2]. Each examination typically generates 50,000–80,000 images, requiring 40–120 min of focused interpretation [3]. Diagnostic accuracy depends heavily on sustained expert attention, and prolonged review may increase variability and the risk of missed findings, with reported detection rates of only ∼46% and moderate interobserver agreement ($\kappa \approx 0.44$) [4]. Despite technological advances in VCE [5], these limitations persist [6], underscoring the need for real-time computational support through AI-assisted procedural auditing.

Artificial intelligence (AI) is increasingly being integrated into VCE for assisted lesion detection and anatomical classification, with the potential to improve diagnostic consistency and reduce interobserver variability [7,8]. However, much of the reported performance is derived from retrospective evaluations or carefully curated datasets rather than full-length examinations under routine clinical conditions, limiting the reliability and generalizability of current systems [9]. Methodologically, most current approaches rely on single-frame classification using Convolutional Neural Networks (CNNs) to detect anatomical regions or pathological abnormalities [10–12]. Temporal consistency is typically enforced through post-processing techniques, such as Hidden Markov Models (HMMs) to constrain anatomical transitions [13,14]. Although performance improves, frame-level predictions remain unstable without post-processing, reflecting limited intrinsic temporal modeling. Furthermore, random sampling and class balancing strategies disrupt the natural temporal distribution of VCE data. Consequently, temporal coherence is imposed heuristically rather than learned directly from sequential data, limiting robust sequence-level modeling and the ability to capture long-range dependencies spanning anatomical transitions and subtle pathological evolution throughout consecutive frames in real-world VCE examinations.

This work presents a real-time computer-assisted intervention system for video capsule endoscopy (VCE) that jointly performs anatomical localization and anomaly detection. Operating at 30.5 ms/frame on an NVIDIA Jetson Nano, the system enables continuous auditing of capsule progression, examination completeness, potential capsule retention, and abnormal findings. By combining multi-task learning and temporal modeling, the proposed approach outperforms frame-wise methods without heuristic post-processing. Code, trained models, and a real-time prototype are publicly available to support reproducibility.

2 Method

Multi-frame Feature Extraction. Given a video dataset composed of clips (temporal windows), a batch of input segments is denoted as: $X \in \mathbb{R}^{B \times 3 \times F \times H \times W}$ being B the batch size, F the number of frames (tokens) per segment, and $H \times W$ the spatial resolution. Each frame is independently processed by a single pretrained ResNet-50 backbone [15]. Let $x_{i,t} \in \mathbb{R}^{3 \times H \times W}$ denote the *t-th* frame of the *i-th* segment. The CNN encoder maps each frame

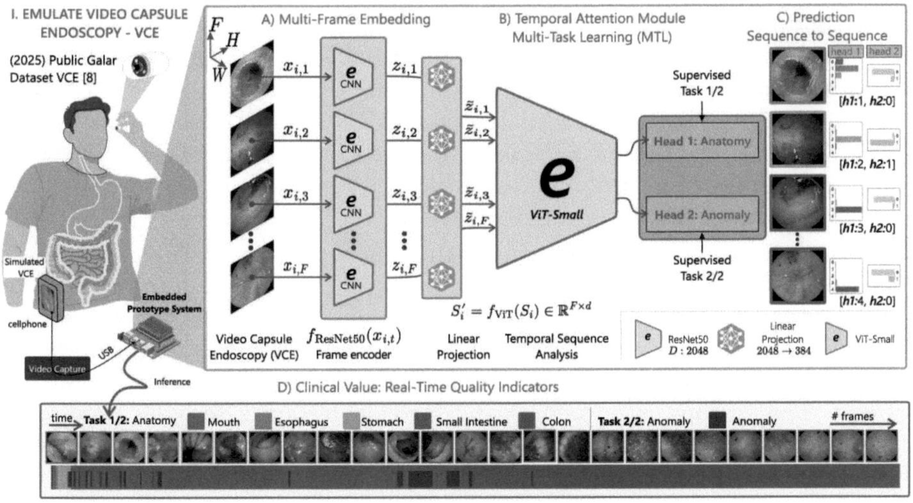

Fig. 1. Overview of the proposed multi-frame VCE auditing framework. Consecutive frames are independently encoded by a single pretrained CNN with shared weights, applied sequentially to each frame, into D-dimensional embeddings, projected and processed by a temporal Vision Transformer in a sequence-to-sequence manner. The model produces frame-wise predictions for anatomical localization and binary anomaly detection, which are aggregated to generate real-time clinical quality indicators.

into a D-dimensional embedding (with $D = 2048$): $z_{i,t} = f_{\text{ResNet50}}(x_{i,t}) \in \mathbb{R}^D$. The frame-level embeddings are stacked along the temporal dimension to form the ordered sequence: $Z_i = [z_{i,1}, z_{i,2}, \ldots, z_{i,F}] \in \mathbb{R}^{F \times D}$, which serves as input to the projection layer (see Fig. 1A).

Sequence-to-Sequence Temporal Modeling. The CNN embeddings are projected through a trainable linear layer to match the transformer embedding dimension: $\tilde{z}_{i,t} = W z_{i,t} \in \mathbb{R}^d$, $d = 384$. The projected sequence is therefore $S_i = [\tilde{z}_{i,1}, \ldots, \tilde{z}_{i,F}] \in \mathbb{R}^{F \times d}$. To capture temporal dependencies, we employ a Vision Transformer (ViT-Small [16]) operating over this sequence. Unlike standard ViT architectures that tokenize spatial patches, our model treats each projected frame embedding as a temporal token. The transformer produces a refined representation: $S'_i = f_{\text{ViT}}(S_i) \in \mathbb{R}^{F \times d}$. Temporal interactions are modeled using Multi-Head Self-Attention (MSA [17]): $\text{Attention}(Q, K, V) = \text{softmax}(QK^\top / \sqrt{d_k})V$, where Q, K, V are learned linear projections. We perform token-level prediction without using a CLS token. Each temporal token outputs a frame-level prediction rather than a single label per sequence, preserving temporal resolution and enabling real-time inference (Fig. 1B–C).

Task Definition and Report Quality Indicators. To enable automated auditing of VCE examinations, we address two tasks. Anatomical localization supports monitoring of capsule progression, detection of retrograde events, and early identification of potential capsule retention, while anomaly detection identifies clinically relevant findings during the examination. **1) Anatomical section classification:** For each frame t in segment i, the model predicts $y_{i,t}^{\text{anat}} \in \{1, \ldots, C\}$, where $C = 5$ (mouth, esophagus, stomach, small intestine, colon). **2) Binary Anomaly Detection:** The model simultaneously predicts $y_{i,t}^{\text{anom}} \in \{0, 1\}$ (see Fig. 2). Using fixed-length sliding windows (stride 1), each frame appears in multiple windows. Let $\mathbf{p}_{i,t}^{k}$ denote the predicted probability vector for frame t in window k. Final frame-level probabilities are obtained by averaging the predicted probability vectors across all windows (soft voting over probabilities). Uncertainty is estimated via Shannon entropy computed over the averaged probabilities: $H_{i,t} = -\sum_c \bar{p}_c \log(\bar{p}_c + \epsilon)$, where ϵ ensures numerical stability. The entropy is normalized by division by $\log C$ to scale it to $[0, 1]$. Higher entropy indicates temporal disagreement and supports frame-level quality assessment.

3 Experiments and Results

3.1 Experimental Setup

Datasets. Experiments were conducted on the recently released Galar video capsule endoscopy dataset [18] (2025). Galar comprises 80 fully annotated VCE studies with 3,513,539 frame-wise labeled images collected from two centers and multiple capsule systems (Olympus™ and PillCam™). In this work, we directly use the provided frame-level annotations without modification and adopt the official split of 60 studies for training/validation and 20 for testing, ensuring patient-level separation. To evaluate cross-dataset robustness, we additionally tested the trained anatomical model on the Rhode Island GI VCE dataset [19]. The official test split was used for inference without any fine-tuning, employing the anatomical model trained on Galar (Cases 1–60). As this study uses open-access human subject data released under the Creative Commons Attribution 4.0 International (CC BY 4.0) license, no additional ethical approval was required.

Implementation Details. Both the CNN and transformer backbones are initialized from GastroNet-5M foundation models [15], pretrained using self-supervised DINO learning on ¿5 million gastrointestinal endoscopy images collected from eight clinical centers [20]. The temporal encoder employs a ViT-Small backbone ($\sim 21.7M$ parameters) adapted to process variable length temporal sequences ($F \in [5, 195]$ frames). Each frame (resized to 224×224) is encoded by a ResNet50 backbone ($\sim 23.5M$ parameters), producing a 2048-dimensional embedding. These embeddings are projected via a trainable linear layer (∼0.79M parameters) into a 384-dimensional token representation before being fed into the transformer encoder. The model follows a sequence-to-sequence formulation, generating frame-wise predictions for both anatomical classification (5 classes: mouth, esophagus, stomach, small intestine, colon) and binary anomaly detection (see Fig. 1-C). The classification heads consist of two parallel MLP layers operating on the refined temporal representations. Training is performed in two phases. During a warm-up stage, only the projection and classification heads are trained for 10 epochs using a fixed learning rate of 1×10^{-3} to stabilize convergence. In the fine-tuning stage, all layers are unfrozen and optimized for up to 30 additional epochs, with early stopping based on validation macro F1-score (patience = 5 epochs). To balance the Multi-Task Learning (MTL), we employ homoscedastic uncertainty weighting [21], which learns task-specific log-variance parameters to automatically scale each loss: $\mathcal{L} = e^{-s_a}\mathcal{L}_{\text{anom}} + s_a + e^{-s_b}\mathcal{L}_{\text{anat}} + s_b$, where s_a and s_b are learnable parameters that adaptively adjust the relative contribution of each task, avoiding manual loss weighting. The model is implemented in PyTorch. Optimization is performed using Adam with a weighted Focal Loss ($\gamma = 2.0$) to mitigate class imbalance and emphasize hard-to-classify samples. The learning rate is reduced by a factor of $\gamma = 0.1$ every 3 epochs. Training was conducted on a single NVIDIA RTX 4500 GPU. The temporal transformer encoder operates on fixed temporal windows and is designed for causal inference without future frames.

Ablation Study. This study was conducted to evaluate the contribution of the temporal modeling component to both anatomical classification and binary anomaly detection. Specifically, we compared the full sequence-to-sequence model across different temporal window sizes against a frame-wise baseline (see Tables 1 and 2). We further evaluated temporal post-processing (smoothing) to assess its effect on anatomical prediction stability (see Table 1, HMM column). Importantly, post-processing was evaluated but is not considered part of the core framework, as the primary objective of this study is to preserve real-time streaming inference on an edge AI device.

3.2 Model Validation

Task 1/2 Anatomical. Table 1 summarizes the performance for anatomical classification under single-frame and multi-frame settings. In the single-frame analysis, linear probing using endoscopy-pretrained embeddings (GastroNet [15,20]) significantly outperformed ImageNet-pretrained features (macro F1: 77% vs. 51%), underscoring the importance of domain-specific pretraining. Temporal modeling significantly improved performance across all anatomical classes under both Single-Task Learning (STL) and Multi-Task Learning (MTL), compared to state-of-the-art frame-wise approaches [12,14]. Performance gains were most pronounced in mouth, followed by esophagus, stomach, colon, and small intestine (S. Bowel). Overall, these results demonstrate that intrinsic temporal modeling improves anatomical consistency over frame-wise approaches. Werner et al. [14] serves as our primary baseline, reporting single-frame MTL results with and without HMM post-processing; we compare our model against their best reported performance. In contrast, we retain all samples to preserve the intrinsic temporal structure and natural class distribution of VCE data. Clinical VCE data are inherently imbalanced, altering this distribution may limit the representativeness of real-world performance. In the STL setting, an ablation study compared CNN+GRU (Gated Recurrent Unit) and CNN+ViT (with randomly initialized ViT) models across different temporal window sizes. Macro F1-scores (%) for 5, 31, and 75 tokens were 87 vs. 89, 89 vs. 89, and 85 vs. 89, respectively.

Table 1. Performance comparison between single-frame and multi-frame approaches for anatomical classification. Models were trained/validated in 60 studies (~3.2M frames) and evaluated in 20 independent test studies (~234K frames). 95% confidence intervals were calculated using stratified bootstrapping with 1,000 resamples by case. Results are reported as class-wise F1-scores and macro F1. HMM denotes Hidden Markov Model post-processing and the column reports the resulting macro F1-score. STL: Single-Task Learning (task: anatomy) and MTL: Multi-Task Learning (tasks: anatomy, anomaly). The shaded row (MTL-75) denotes the model selected for edge deployment.

Ablation Study F1-score(%) Anatomical Task Single-frame							
Token=1	Mouth	Esophag.	Stomach	S. Bowel	Colon	Macro F1	HMM
ImageNet	10.1±5.0	26.7±15.6	61.2±11.5	90.0±3.6	68.5±12.1	51.3±6.0	88.7±6.5
GastroNet	60.9±11.3	69.0±18.4	82.4±7.5	94.0±3.5	81.0±10.4	77.5±5.8	93.3±4.4
Tokens≥5 Endoscopy-pretrained CNN+ViT (Multi-frame)							
STL 5	80.7±8.7	87.2±9.9	89.6±4.6	95.3±3.4	85.6±11.1	87.7±5.0	93.7±4.9
STL 31	**88.8±6.4**	**91.1±7.1**	**93.7±3.5**	94.5±3.6	81.8±12.0	90.0±4.6	93.9±3.9
STL 75	88.4±6.5	89.8±6.6	93.3±4.3	95.4±3.7	84.6±11.7	90.3±5.0	**93.9±3.9**
STL 195	87.4±7.2	89.3±7.8	93.3±3.7	**96.0±3.6**	**87.3±12.0**	**90.7±4.7**	93.2±4.2
MTL 5	58.7±20.2	72.8±17.5	85.6±6.5	94.5±3.5	82.8±10.6	78.9±6.5	92.4±5.1
MTL 31	70.0±19.1	89.7±7.7	93.1±3.5	94.4±3.8	81.7±11.8	85.8±6.5	93.8±4.0
MTL 75	87.0±7.6	89.5±7.7	92.1±4.7	95.9±3.5	86.9±11.2	90.3±5.3	93.0±4.2
MTL 195	22.9±12.1	67.4±18.2	92.5±4.4	95.4±3.5	85.5±11.2	72.8±6.4	92.4±4.1
Comparison with state-of-the-art single-frame approaches (same dataset)							
Token=1	Mouth	Esophag.	Stomach	S. Bowel	Colon	Macro F1	HMM
[12] 2025	42.0	65.0	78.0	93.0	75.0	71.0	-
[14] 2025	-	-	-	-	-	65.1	92.4

Similar experiments under the MTL configuration yielded macro F1-scores (%) of 73 vs. 74 (5 tokens), 89 vs. 67 (31 tokens), and 88 vs. 81 (75 tokens), showing that endoscopy-pretrained ViT initialization improved performance overall (see Table 1). Given the clinical objective of minimizing missed abnormalities, model selection prioritized sensitivity in the anomaly detection task while maintaining strong anatomical classification performance within a single multi-task framework. Based on these criteria, MTL-75 was selected as the final deployment model across all evaluated window sizes and learning settings. Although STL-195 achieved the highest anatomical macro F1-score (90.7%), MTL-75 achieved comparable anatomical classification performance (90.3%) while providing the highest anomaly macro recall (66.7%, see Table 2).

Post-processing – Hidden Markov Model. The HMM was replicated as reported in the baseline study [14], confirming performance gains in all cases, particularly for single-frame models (see Table 1, HMM column). However, it assumes a strictly forward transition sequence (Mouth → Esophagus → Stomach → Small Intestine → Colon) with a fixed initial state at the mouth. Although anatomically plausible, this constraint biases early predictions and may distort minority classes. Moreover, as a Viterbi-based post-processing step requiring full-sequence access, it is not suitable for real-time deployment. Clinically, enforcing a unidirectional structure may obscure retrograde events (e.g., gastro-esophageal or duodeno-gastric reflux, linked to Barrett's metaplasia and cancer [22]; see reflux case 28, Galar dataset), potentially masking relevant pathological findings.

Robustness. The **MTL-75** model was cross-evaluated with the Rhode Island GI VCE test set (∼1M frames) [10] without fine-tuning or post-processing. It achieved F1-scores (%) of 68 (esophagus), 91 (stomach), 94 (small intestine), and 62 (colon). As the *mouth* class is not annotated in this dataset, all predictions assigned to this category (n=347) were treated as false positives. Performance degradation in the esophagus and colon likely reflects domain shift between datasets.

Task 2/2 Anomaly. Table 2 reports binary anomaly detection performance following the state-of-the-art evaluation protocol of [14,23], using the same dataset, grouping strategy (**Normal:** Clean Mucosa; **Anomaly:** Polyp, Blood, Active Bleeding, Angiectasia, Erosion, Erythema, Ulcer), and test set (patient IDs 61–80). In clinical practice, sensitivity is critical, as missing an anomaly is more detrimental than generating a false positive alert. Under this criterion,

Table 2. Performance comparison of single-frame and multi-frame approaches for binary anomaly detection using deep learning architectures. Same data split and 95% CI estimation as in Table 1. The shaded row (MTL-75) corresponds to the final deployment model used in the edge AI prototype. **Note:** Anomaly category was extended to include inflammatory bowel disease, foreign body, hematin, cancer, and lymphangiectasis, as these findings are clinically considered abnormal.

Task 2/2 Anomaly Single-frame and Multi-frame (STL, MTL)						
Method	Micro F1	Macro F1	Macro Prec.	Macro Rec.	Model	Embedded
[14] 2025	**87.7**	54.4	54.1	54.7	ResNet50	No
[23] 2025	87.3	37.0	26.6	60.9	MobilNet-S	No
GastroNet	79.5±6.9	61.6±8.4	61.7±8.4	62.4±9.1	ResNet50	Yes
STL 75	85.7±9.3	59.7±11.1	**76.8±15.7**	58.2±7.8	CNN+ViT	Yes
MTL 75	77.0±6.2	**62.8±10.3**	61.9±9.4	**66.7±13.8**	CNN+ViT	Yes

the best-performing model was **MTL-75**, with endoscopy-pretrained initialization of both CNN and ViT backbones, achieving a macro recall of 67% and weighted recall/precision/F1 of 77%/81%/79%, respectively. This model was therefore selected for deployment on the edge AI device. In comparison, the same CNN+ViT architecture evaluated under STL/MTL settings with alternative temporal window sizes (5, 31, and 195 tokens) achieved macro F1-scores (%) of 52/59 (5 tokens), 55/62 (31 tokens), and 59/55 (195 tokens), respectively. A major challenge is frame-level label inconsistency (e.g., anomaly–normal–anomaly sequences, see Fig. 2 anomaly ground truth and entropy). Anomalies frequently occupy only a small portion of the frame, while visual artifacts such as bubbles or luminal fluids can obscure mucosal details, making consistent annotation difficult.

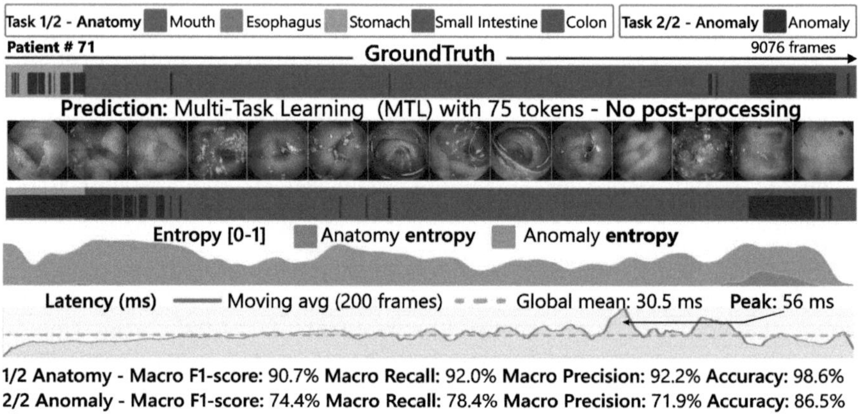

Fig. 2. Quality indicator report for Patient #71. Ground-truth and MTL-75 frame-level predictions (no post-processing) for anatomy and anomaly tasks are shown, along with entropy-based uncertainty and edge inference latency (Jetson Nano).

3.3 Real-Time Deployment on an Edge AI Device: Performance Analysis and Practical Considerations

To evaluate feasibility beyond retrospective offline benchmarking, the proposed CNN+ViT multi-task framework was deployed on a low-power NVIDIA Jetson Nano edge device (100×80 mm, 5–10 W) to assess real-time performance. The system integrates video acquisition (HDTV capture card with smartphone-based signal emulation, Fig. 1-I), feature extraction (ResNet50 backbone), temporal modeling (75-frame window), and multi-task prediction (anatomy and anomaly) within a fully parallelized pipeline. The trained PyTorch model (.pth and .ckpt) was converted to Open Neural Network eXchange (ONNX) and subsequently optimized using TensorRT. For real-time operation, temporal windows contain only past and present frames, ensuring causal online inference without future-frame access. Each frame is encoded once by the ResNet50 backbone and reused across overlapping windows (stride = 1), while the ViT-Small temporal encoder produces frame-level (token) prediction within the window. Predictions from overlapping windows are aggregated through soft voting with entropy-based uncertainty estimation (see Sect. 2). As illustrated in Fig. 2 (Patient #71), stable frame-level predictions are maintained throughout the examination (9,076 frames) with an average latency of 30.5 ms per frame (≈33 FPS), exceeding the typical 2–6 FPS acquisition rate of standard small-bowel VCE systems [24]. Importantly, deployment does not rely on post-processing (e.g., HMM smoothing), demonstrating that temporal consistency emerges directly from learned representations. These results demonstrate operational feasibility for intra-procedural, edge-based deployment, supporting on-device monitoring of examination completeness and potential capsule retention, which occur in 0.7–1.4% of examinations and contribute to incomplete visualization (∼12%) [25]. Such real-time monitoring is particularly relevant in high-risk populations, including pediatric and inflammatory bowel disease patients [7]. Further clinical and system-level validation is required prior to integration into routine practice. Code and trained models are publicly available.

4 Conclusions

We present a real-time, edge-deployable system for video capsule endoscopy that intrinsically models temporal dependencies to jointly perform anatomical localization and binary anomaly detection at the device's native acquisition rate, without heuristic post-processing. Although evaluated on a multi-center, multi-device dataset (Galar), the cohort was predominantly pathological, which may limit generalization to fully normal examinations. Further validation on larger and more diverse adult and pediatric cohorts is warranted. Future work will focus on clinical validation studies and the development of a standardized validation and alerting protocol for real-time deployment, including expert-defined thresholds for incomplete examinations, prolonged segmental transit, capsule retention, and persistent anomalies. In parallel, advances in spatiotemporal modeling, interpretability, capsule-specific foundation models for VCE, and alternative sequence architectures (e.g., state-space models such as Mamba) will be explored to improve robustness and energy-efficient deployment.

Disclosure of Interests. The authors have no competing interests to declare.

References

1. Fisher, L., et al.: The role of endoscopy in the management of obscure gi bleeding. Gastrointest. Endosc. **72**(3), 471–479 (2010)
2. Raju, G.S., Gerson, L., Das, A., Lewis, B.: American gastroenterological association (aga) institute medical position statement on obscure gastrointestinal bleeding. Gastroenterology **133**(5), 1694–1696 (2007)

3. Mishkin, D.S., et al.: Asge technology status evaluation report: wireless capsule endoscopy. Gastrointest. Endosc. **63**(4), 539–545 (2006)
4. Rondonotti, E., et al.: Can we improve the detection rate and interobserver agreement in capsule endoscopy? Dig. Liver Dis. **44**(12), 1006–1011 (2012)
5. Rahman, M., Akerman, S., DeVito, B., Miller, L., Akerman, M., Sultan, K.: Comparison of the diagnostic yield and outcomes between standard 8 h capsule endoscopy and the new 12 h capsule endoscopy for investigating small bowel pathology. World J. Gastroenterol. WJG **21**(18), 5542 (2015)
6. Wang, Y.C., et al.: Adverse events of video capsule endoscopy over the past two decades: a systematic review and proportion meta-analysis. BMC Gastroenterol. **20**(1), 364 (2020)
7. Rojas, I., Barth, B.A., Stewart, J.W.: Advances in pediatric video capsule endoscopy: current applications and future directions. Front. Pediatr. **13**, 1738998 (2026)
8. Messmann, H., et al.: Expected value of artificial intelligence in gastrointestinal endoscopy: European society of gastrointestinal endoscopy (esge) position statement. Endoscopy **54**(12), 1211–1231 (2022)
9. Piccirelli, S., et al.: Unmet needs of artificial intelligence in small bowel capsule endoscopy. Diagnostics **15**(9), 1092 (2025)
10. Charoen, A., et al.: Rhode island gastroenterology video capsule endoscopy data set. Sci. Data **9**(1), 602 (2022)
11. Smedsrud, P.H., et al.: Kvasir-capsule, a video capsule endoscopy dataset. Sci. Data **8**(1), 142 (2021)
12. Le Floch, M., et al.: Galar-a large multi-label video capsule endoscopy dataset. Sci. Data **12**(1), 828 (2025)
13. Werner, J., Gerum, C., Reiber, M., Nick, J., Bringmann, O.: Precise localization within the gi tract by combining classification of cnns and time-series analysis of hmms. In: Cao, X., Xu, X., Rekik, I., Cui, Z., Ouyang, X. (eds.) International Workshop on Machine Learning in Medical Imaging, pp. 174–183. Springer, Cham (2023). https://doi.org/10.1007/978-3-031-45676-3_18
14. Werner, J., et al.: Seeing more with less: Video capsule endoscopy with multi-task learning. In: Wu, S., Shabestari, B., Xing, L. (eds.) International Workshop on Applications of Medical AI, pp. 12–21. Springer, Cham (2025). https://doi.org/10.1007/978-3-032-09569-5_2
15. Boers, T.G., et al.: Foundation models in gastrointestinal endoscopic ai: Impact of architecture, pre-training approach and data efficiency. Med. Image Anal. **98**, 103298 (2024)
16. Dosovitskiy, A., et al.: An image is worth 16x16 words: Transformers for image recognition at scale. arXiv preprint arXiv:2010.11929 (2020)
17. Vaswani, A., et al.: Attention is all you need. Adv. Neural Inf. Process. Syst. **30** (2017)
18. Floch, M.L., et al.: Galar - a large multi-label video capsule endoscopy dataset. Figshare (2025). https://doi.org/10.25452/figshare.plus.25304616.v2
19. Charoen, A., et al.: Rhode island gastroenterology video capsule endoscopy data set (2022). https://doi.org/10.6084/m9.figshare.c.6071216.v1
20. Jong, M.R., et al.: Gastronet-5m: A multicenter dataset for developing foundation models in gastrointestinal endoscopy. Gastroenterology (2025)
21. Kendall, A., Gal, Y., Cipolla, R.: Multi-task learning using uncertainty to weigh losses for scene geometry and semantics. In: Proceedings of the IEEE Conference on Computer Vision and Pattern Recognition, pp. 7482–7491 (2018)

22. Fein, M., Maroske, J., Fuchs, K.: Importance of duodenogastric reflux in gastro-oesophageal reflux disease. J. Br. Surg. **93**(12), 1475–1482 (2006)
23. Werner, J., et al.: Enhanced anomaly detection for capsule endoscopy using ensemble learning strategies. In: 2025 47th Annual International Conference of the IEEE Engineering in Medicine and Biology Society (EMBC), pp. 1–7. IEEE (2025)
24. Melson, J., et al.: Video capsule endoscopy. Gastrointest. Endosc. **93**(4), 784–796 (2021)
25. Enns, R.A., et al.: Clinical practice guidelines for the use of video capsule endoscopy. Gastroenterology **152**(3), 497–514 (2017)

Device-Constrained Real-Time EVD Catheter Segmentation

Mustafa Seddiqi(✉), Joshua Castillo, Tiberiu Popa, and Marta Kersten-Oertel

Concordia University, Montreal, Canada
mustafa.seddiqi@concordia.ca

Abstract. Ventriculostomy, or external ventricular drain (EVD) placement, is frequently performed freehand in urgent bedside settings, resulting in high catheter misplacement rates. Portable augmented reality (AR) guidance offers a low-cost alternative to conventional navigation systems, but mobile and standalone XR hardware impose strict latency, memory, and power constraints. A key enabling component is reliable real-time segmentation of the thin, low-contrast EVD catheter in unconstrained open-field environments. To address this challenge, we propose a real-time EVD catheter segmentation framework for mobile and XR deployment that includes a structure-aware loss promoting consistency along the catheter trajectory. We construct a scene-structured bedside dataset and complement it with a 3D-driven synthetic data generation pipeline to expand geometric and viewpoint variability. Lightweight backbones are evaluated under real-only, synthetic-only, and combined supervision, with systematic cross-domain and on-device analysis of robustness and accuracylatency trade-offs under mobile/XR hardware constraints. Our results establish the feasibility of real-time catheter segmentation as a key component of future low-cost AR-guided ventriculostomy workflows. Code is available at: https://github.com/m-seddiqi/evd-catheter-segmentation.

Keywords: Ventriculostomy · Synthetic Data · Thin-Structure Segmentation · Real-Time Inference

1 Introduction

Ventriculostomy, or external ventricular drain (EVD) placement, is one of the most common neurosurgical procedures and is typically performed freehand in emergency and acute care settings [3]. Catheter misplacement remains prevalent and may require repeated insertion attempts with associated complications [11, 17]. Guidance aids, including mechanical guides, ultrasound-assisted placement, and navigation-based systems, have been investigated for EVD placement [15, 16,19]. However, conventional image-guided techniques can be time-consuming and expensive, limiting their use in urgent bedside settings [19].

G. Yang et al. (Eds.): MICCAI 2026, LNCS 16893, pp. 138–148, 2027.
https://doi.org/10.1007/978-3-032-38236-8_14

Augmented reality (AR) guidance offers a low-cost alternative by overlaying the planned catheter trajectory and ventricular anatomy directly onto the surgical field [2,4,5,12,20]. However, mobile and standalone XR hardware impose strict latency, memory, and power constraints. Unlike marker-based tracking approaches, our goal is to localize the catheter directly from RGB imagery without fiducial markers, making segmentation a key enabling component.

Achieving this is challenging. Compared with laparoscopic tool segmentation and ultrasound needle tracking [1,6,8,22], catheter segmentation targets a thin, low-contrast, elongated structure occupying a small fraction of the image which is frequently affected by motion blur, specular reflections, and occlusion. Small local segmentation errors can lead to substantial errors in the estimated catheter trajectory, making geometric continuity essential for AR guidance. While foundation models such as SAM provide strong general-purpose segmentation capabilities [7,18], their computational footprint limits practical use on embedded mobile and XR platforms. Furthermore, no publicly available dataset exists for EVD catheter segmentation, and limited real data increases the risk of overfitting under distribution shift.

To our knowledge, prior work has not examined real-time EVD catheter segmentation for mobile and XR deployment, where thin-structure segmentation must be developed and evaluated under the resource constraints of embedded platforms. In this work, we make three contributions. First, we formulate real-time EVD catheter segmentation for mobile and XR deployment and introduce a structure-aware loss that encourages catheter-axis consistency in elongated predictions. Second, we construct a scene-structured bedside dataset with strict session-level partitioning and complement it with a 3D-driven synthetic data generation pipeline to expand geometric and viewpoint variability. Third, we perform systematic cross-domain and on-device evaluation across real-only, synthetic-only, and combined supervision regimes to characterize robustness and accuracylatency trade-offs under mobile/XR hardware constraints.

2 Methods

2.1 Problem Setting and Deployment Constraints

We formulate catheter segmentation for AR-guided ventriculostomy as a fully automatic, real-time binary segmentation task under device-level constraints. Given an RGB frame $I \in \mathbb{R}^{H \times W \times 3}$ captured from a mobile or head-mounted device (HMD), the objective is to predict a dense catheter mask $M \in \{0,1\}^{H \times W}$. Beyond pixel-wise accuracy, predictions must preserve geometric continuity to ensure stable AR overlays and reliable trajectory visualization. This setting is deployment-driven rather than benchmark-driven. Inference must operate continuously at video rate on embedded mobile GPUs with limited memory, compute, and power budgets. Consequently, model evaluation jointly considers segmentation fidelity and runtime efficiency.

Although large foundation models such as SAM demonstrate strong cross-domain generalization [7,18], their computational footprint limits practical real-time XR deployment. In addition, the thin, low-contrast geometry of EVD

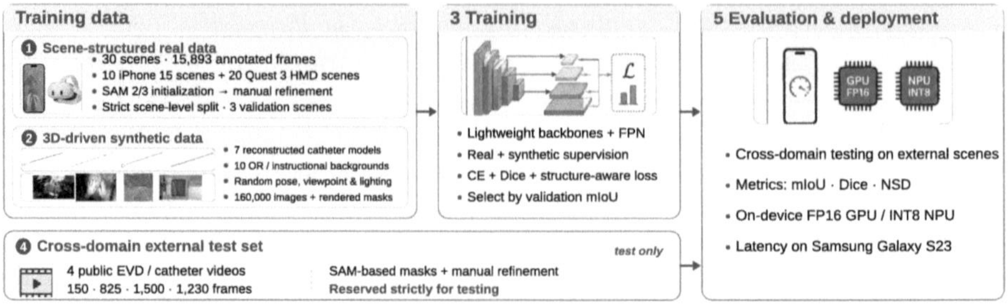

Fig. 1. Overview of real and synthetic data generation, combined-supervision training, cross-domain testing, and FP16/INT8 on-device evaluation.

catheters leads to severe class imbalance and fragmentation, motivating task-specific optimization under efficiency constraints. We therefore adopt lightweight backbones with a feature pyramid decoder to balance capacity and cost within mobile inference budgets. Figure 1 summarizes the pipeline.

2.2 Dataset Creation

To evaluate catheter segmentation under simulated bedside conditions within a controlled laboratory environment, we constructed a scene-structured dataset utilizing a handheld mobile device and a head-mounted display. Each scene captures a continuous catheter manipulation session, preserving temporal motion and viewpoint variation while preventing frame-level redundancy across dataset splits. All recordings were conducted without patient involvement and contain no protected health information.

Data collection spanned two platforms to maximize diversity. Ten scenes were recorded using an iPhone 15 under unconstrained room conditions to introduce variability in illumination and background complexity. An additional 20 scenes were captured via a Meta Quest 3 headset, providing synchronized stereo image pairs from a surgeon-centric perspective consistent with the intended AR deployment. In total, the dataset comprises 30 scenes and 15,893 annotated frames.

To prevent temporal leakage, we reserved three scenes (two stereo and one monocular) for validation and used the remaining scenes for training; external videos were strictly test-only. Ground-truth masks were initialized using SAM 2/3 and subsequently manually corrected and quality-checked, particularly in regions affected by motion blur and low contrast.

2.3 Augmentation Strategy for Domain Generalization

To improve robustness under cross-domain variation, we employ a task-aware photometric augmentation pipeline during training. All photometric transformations are applied online to the input image, while ground-truth masks remain unchanged. Standard global appearance perturbations, including Gaussian blur, color jitter, and exposure adjustments, simulate illumination variability and camera differences across recording environments. However, generic photometric augmentation is insufficient for thin-structure segmentation in open-field neurosurgical settings. The EVD catheter is particularly susceptible to motion-induced blur, specular saturation from surgical lighting, and local contrast degradation, all of which can cause spatially fragmented prediction masks.

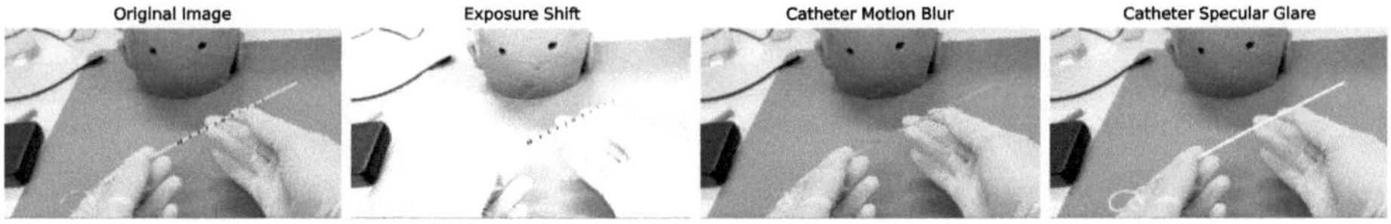

Fig. 2. Examples of the proposed photometric augmentations, including exposure variation, catheter-specific directional motion blur, and synthetic specular highlights.

To explicitly model these failure modes, we introduce catheter-aware perturbations applied selectively to the annotated catheter region. These include directional motion blur aligned with the catheter axis and synthetic specular highlights that emulate strong reflections from overhead lights. By targeting the structure of interest rather than applying image-wide perturbations, this strategy encourages robustness to artifacts that disproportionately affect slender geometries. The pipeline combines standard global photometric perturbations with catheter-aware motion blur and specular highlights to model thin-structure degradation under surgical lighting and motion while preserving mask geometry. Augmentation parameters were fixed across experiments and are released with the code. Figure 2 illustrates representative effects.

2.4 Synthetic Dataset Generation via 3D Modeling

Photometric augmentation alone does not sufficiently expand geometric diversity in viewpoint, catheter pose, and spatial context. Because thin, elongated structures are highly sensitive to pose and orientation, limited real-world data often leads to overfitting specific viewing configurations. To address this, we introduce a 3D-driven synthetic data generation pipeline inspired by recent 2D-to-3D reconstruction approaches [9]. Specifically, we constructed a library of seven 3D catheter models, reconstructed from publicly available imagery using a single-image reconstruction pipeline followed by manual refinement. These models were aligned and scale-corrected to ensure consistent physical proportions and canonical orientation. Although limited in number and containing minor reconstruction artifacts, they provide meaningful, clinically relevant variations in curvature, diameter, and tip morphology, enabling controlled sampling of pose and viewpoint.

To complement this geometric variation with environmental diversity, we curated ten background images depicting operating-room and instructional settings. Sourced from permissively licensed repositories, these backgrounds contain no identifiable patient information. Representative reconstructed catheter models and background assets are shown in Fig. 1.

Synthetic samples are generated by pairing a reconstructed catheter model with a randomly selected background, rendering it under randomized rigid transformations (rotation and translation) before compositing. To mimic continuous manipulation while preserving temporal coherence, short video sequences are produced via incremental pose perturbations across consecutive frames. Optional illumination perturbations are also applied to enhance visual realism.

In total, 160,000 synthetic images were generated across diverse catheter and background combinations. Because ground-truth masks are derived directly from rendered 3D geometry, they avoid manual annotation noise. Synthetic rendering used fixed configuration ranges for catheter pose, scale/depth, camera clipping, and tri-light illumination; complete generation settings are released with the code. This synthetic dataset supports controlled evaluation under real-only, synthetic-only, and mixed supervision paradigms, expanding both geometric and contextual diversity beyond our laboratory collection and supporting improved robustness to cross-domain shifts.

3 Experiments

3.1 Experimental Setup

Training Protocol. Main models were trained for 20 epochs using 512×512 and 384×640 crop buckets (batch size 4) and AdamW (LR 10^{-4}, 0.1× for the backbone; weight decay 10^{-4}). In the real+synthetic regime, each epoch used a synthetic shard together with a 20% subsample of the real training frames; exact shard and split manifests are released with the code. Training images were resized with aspect ratio preserved and randomly cropped to the selected bucket; validation and test frames used the closest-aspect bucket with letterbox padding. Image and mask resizing used bilinear and nearest-neighbor interpolation, respectively.

Architectures. We adopt `FastViT-T8` [21] with an FPN decoder [13] as the default backbone due to its accuracy–efficiency trade-off for mobile deployment. We also evaluate `FastViT-SA12`, `FastViT-SA36` [21], `MobileNetV3-Large` [10], and `ConvNeXt-Tiny` [14], all with the same decoder.

Loss Function. We optimize the composite objective $\mathcal{L} = \alpha\mathcal{L}_{\text{CE}} + \beta\mathcal{L}_{\text{Dice}} + \lambda\mathcal{L}_{\text{struct}}$, where the weights are set to $\alpha = 0.35$, $\beta = 0.65$, and $\lambda = 0.02$. The cross-entropy term uses a background weight of 0.5, while the Dice term provides foreground-overlap supervision. The structure-aware term complements these pixel-wise objectives by constraining the predicted response relative to the dominant catheter geometry. Given the ground-truth mask G, we estimate its principal axis through covariance analysis of the foreground coordinates and compute the absolute perpendicular distance of each pixel from this axis. Let μ_G, σ_G denote the mean and standard deviation of these distances over the

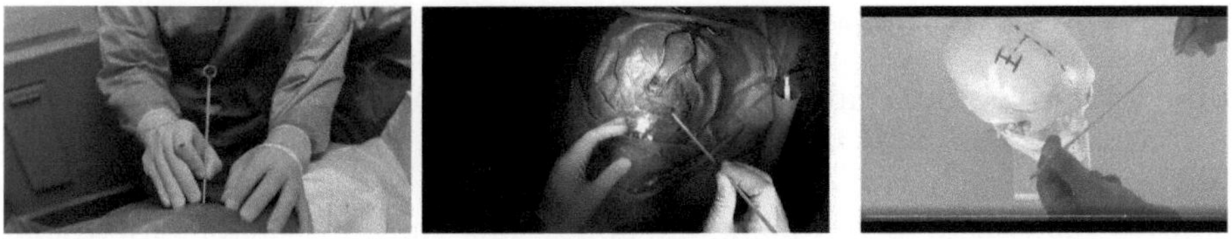

Fig. 3. Representative frames from three of the four external evaluation scenes. Scene 1: real, non-surgeon view (150 frames); Scene 2: real, surgeon-aligned view (825 frames); Scene 3: demonstration, non-surgeon view (1500 frames); Scene 4 (not shown): demonstration, non-surgeon view (1230 frames). Sequences vary substantially in viewpoint, catheter appearance, motion blur, and background relative to our data.

ground-truth foreground, and let μ_P, σ_P denote the corresponding probability-weighted statistics for the predicted foreground probabilities P. We define $\mathcal{L}_{\text{struct}} = \rho((\mu_P - \mu_G)/\max(\mu_G, 1)) + \gamma\,\rho((\sigma_P - \sigma_G)/\max(\sigma_G, 1))$, where ρ denotes the Smooth L1 penalty and $\gamma = 0.5$. Matching these statistics encourages the predicted foreground to remain concentrated around the ground-truth catheter axis, penalizing off-axis spread and fragmented responses that deviate from the dominant catheter geometry. This provides a lightweight, catheter-specific geometric regularizer that complements the cross-entropy and Dice objectives.

Metrics and Model Selection. We report mean Intersection over Union (mIoU), Dice, and Normalized Surface Dice (NSD) on the foreground class, with NSD computed using a 2-pixel surface tolerance. Models are selected by validation mIoU; Dice and NSD provide complementary overlap- and boundary-sensitive evaluation.

3.2 Cross-Domain Evaluation on External Videos

To evaluate robustness under distribution shift, we test on four publicly available videos depicting EVD placement or catheter manipulation, hereafter referred to as Scenes 14. These sequences are strictly reserved for testing and differ substantially from our collected data in viewpoint (surgeon-aligned vs. non-surgeon), catheter morphology and scale, motion blur, and background context (illustrated in Fig. 3). These external recordings are utilized solely for evaluation and are not redistributed. Furthermore, no identifiable patient information is retained in our analysis, and frames are presented strictly for illustrative purposes.

Ground-truth masks for all evaluated frames are generated using the same semi-automated annotation pipeline described in Sect. 2.2, consisting of SAM-based initialization followed by manual refinement. We report per-scene mIoU, Dice, and NSD, computing a macro-average across scenes (with equal weight per sequence) to avoid bias toward longer recordings. This protocol enables a systematic comparison of supervision strategies and backbone architectures under realistic cross-domain shift.

3.3 Training Regimes and Backbone Trade-Offs

Supervision regime. Table 1 summarizes the cross-domain comparison across supervision regimes and backbone architectures. Combined supervision yields the strongest and most consistent macro-average across metrics, indicating improved robustness to viewpoint and appearance shift. Synthetic-only training performs competitively when geometric variation is well covered, but degrades on sequences with appearance artifacts not captured by simulation. Real-only training underperforms overall, suggesting limited diversity in real data alone. These results support a complementary effect: synthetic data expands geometric coverage, while real data anchors appearance realism.

Table 1. Cross-domain performance (%) of backbone architectures across four external videos (mean ± std). Unless otherwise indicated, models are trained with combined supervision (real + synthetic). * Real-only supervision. † Synthetic-only supervision. Best macro-average per metric is highlighted in bold.

Backbone	Scene 1			Scene 2			Scene 3			Scene 4			Avg		
	mIoU ↑	Dice ↑	NSD ↑	mIoU ↑	Dice ↑	NSD ↑	mIoU ↑	Dice ↑	NSD ↑	mIoU ↑	Dice ↑	NSD ↑	mIoU ↑	Dice ↑	NSD ↑
FastViT-T8*	51.1±1.3	67.6±1.1	56.9±1.0	46.0±0.4	63.0±0.4	62.0±1.3	29.4±8.2	45.1±9.9	33.3±6.4	31.6±4.1	47.9±4.7	53.9±4.4	39.5±3.3	55.9±3.8	51.5±2.7
FastViT-T8†	70.1±4.5	82.3±3.1	71.5±2.3	55.6±0.8	71.5±0.7	73.0±0.6	22.0±6.0	35.9±8.1	27.9±5.8	29.7±6.9	45.6±8.2	44.1±11.5	44.3±0.7	58.8±0.6	54.1±1.0
FastViT-T8	68.0±3.8	80.9±2.7	70.8±3.1	67.8±1.5	80.8±1.0	82.1±1.2	31.7±4.7	48.0±5.4	36.5±3.0	44.0±1.7	61.1±1.6	68.4±0.8	52.9±1.3	67.7±1.4	64.4±1.0
FastViT-SA12	74.2±4.9	85.2±3.2	71.6±3.0	70.6±0.5	82.8±0.3	83.4±0.2	36.9±0.6	53.9±0.7	42.6±1.2	32.2±2.0	48.7±2.3	52.5±3.9	53.5±0.4	67.6±0.0	62.5±0.6
MobileNetV3-L	57.0±1.3	72.6±1.1	60.0±0.9	56.9±2.3	72.5±1.8	73.8±1.6	19.7±3.1	32.9±4.3	25.8±2.7	34.9±1.1	51.7±1.2	53.5±0.9	42.1±0.8	57.4±1.2	53.3±0.7
FastViT-SA36	73.4±5.2	84.6±3.4	72.6±4.1	63.1±5.2	77.3±3.9	79.4±3.1	51.4±5.1	67.8±4.4	60.7±4.3	40.6±0.3	57.7±0.3	68.6±1.3	57.1±1.2	71.9±0.9	70.3±1.7
ConvNeXt-T	80.0±0.2	88.9±0.2	77.4±0.2	73.6±2.3	84.8±1.5	87.0±1.1	44.0±4.0	61.1±3.8	48.2±2.3	50.1±2.3	66.7±2.0	78.3±2.4	**61.9±2.2**	**75.4±1.9**	**72.7±1.5**

Backbone Capacity. Under combined supervision, higher-capacity backbones improve cross-domain robustness, particularly in NSD, reflecting better structural continuity of the thin catheter. `ConvNeXt-Tiny` achieves the highest macro-average, with `FastViT-SA36` close behind and strong under pronounced viewpoint shifts. Lighter models (`FastViT-T8`, `MobileNetV3-Large`) show larger drops on the most shifted videos, highlighting limits in representational capacity.

Quantization and On-Device Deployment. INT8 models were calibration-quantized from ONNX and compiled through Qualcomm AI Hub at 384×640 (batch size 1) for TFLite/NPU inference. Latency was measured for model

Table 2. Accuracy (%) and on-device latency on Scene 1 under different numerical precisions. FP16 (GPU) and INT8 (NPU) models are benchmarked on Samsung Galaxy S23. Latency denotes minimum per-image inference time.

Backbone	Params (M)	FP32 (Scene 1)			FP16 GPU (Scene 1)				INT8 NPU (Scene 1)			
		mIoU ↑	Dice ↑	NSD ↑	mIoU ↑	Dice ↑	NSD ↑	Lat. (ms)	mIoU ↑	Dice ↑	NSD ↑	Lat. (ms)
FastViT-T8	8.93	65.3	79.0	68.6	61.3	76.0	65.9	21.5	37.1	54.1	50.4	5.8
MobileNetV3-L	7.98	57.9	73.4	60.6	58.0	73.4	60.6	20.5	55.2	71.1	59.2	6.3
FastViT-SA12	16.55	77.7	87.5	73.7	79.1	88.3	74.0	22.4	72.3	83.9	71.0	6.4
FastViT-SA36	36.49	69.7	82.2	69.7	74.3	85.2	72.7	29.5	69.9	82.3	71.0	10.8
ConvNeXt-T	32.91	80.2	89.0	77.5	80.1	88.9	77.1	27.0	80.2	89.0	77.0	13.5

inference only, excluding preprocessing and postprocessing, after warm-up, and the minimum per-image latency is reported. Table 2 reports Scene 1 accuracy and latency under FP32, FP16 (GPU), and INT8 (NPU). FP16 largely preserves FP32 accuracy across architectures, making it a practical reduced-precision option. INT8 substantially reduces latency, but accuracy degradation is architecture-dependent: `ConvNeXt-Tiny` remains stable, whereas `FastViT-T8` exhibits larger drops, particularly in NSD. These results support the feasibility of using the segmentation output in a future markerless mobile/XR guidance pipeline, where catheter masks could support downstream stereo trajectory reconstruction.

3.4 Ablation and Failure Analysis

Ablation on Scene 2. All configurations were trained for 10 epochs, and the checkpoint with the highest validation mIoU was selected. Using `FastViT-T8`, we progressively introduce each component and report Scene 2 test mIoU: weak augmentation (43.0) → strong augmentation (50.8) → +structure loss (56.1) → +catheter-aligned motion blur (57.7) → +random exposure (53.8). While validation mIoU increases monotonically across additions, the final configuration shows reduced performance on Scene 2. This indicates that aggressive global exposure perturbations, despite improving validation mIoU, may attenuate already low catheter contrast in real surgical footage under challenging illumination.

Structure-Aware Regularization. Smaller backbones often misclassify bright linear edges as catheter, producing spurious elongated masks when the catheter is absent or barely visible. The structure-aware term reduces these failures by matching predicted and ground-truth normal-distance statistics around the catheter axis, encouraging catheter-axis consistency and penalizing off-axis fragmented responses; larger backbones exhibit fewer such errors.

Low-Contrast Collapse. All models may fail when the catheter becomes near-transparent, occasionally collapsing to an empty mask. This reflects the inherent sensitivity of thin-structure segmentation to extreme contrast degradation.

Foundation-Model Instability Under Blur. Prompt-based foundation models may fail at initialization under strong motion blur, yielding missed or distorted masks. In the same frames, task-specific backbones, particularly larger ones, remain more stable, indicating better robustness to deployment-level blur.

4 Discussion and Conclusion

We formulated EVD catheter segmentation as a thin-structure segmentation problem under limited data and mobile deployment constraints, motivated by AR-guided ventriculostomy. Unlike conventional segmentation benchmarks, this setting requires not only high overlap accuracy but also longitudinal geometric consistency while operating within strict latency and memory budgets. We therefore evaluated segmentation performance jointly with cross-domain robustness and on-device efficiency.

Cross-domain evaluation demonstrates that thin-structure segmentation is particularly sensitive to distribution shift. While real-only training exhibited limited generalization and synthetic-only supervision lacked sufficient appearance realism, combining both sources consistently produced the strongest performance, suggesting that geometric diversity from 3D-generated data complements real-world appearance cues. Larger-capacity backbones further improved overlap and boundary stability, albeit at increased computational cost, emphasizing the importance of balancing segmentation accuracy with deployment efficiency. Finally, the proposed structure-aware loss improved segmentation performance by encouraging catheter-axis consistency, reducing off-axis fragmentation errors that could otherwise destabilize downstream AR trajectory estimation.

Our study has several limitations. The dataset is relatively small and was collected in a controlled, non-clinical environment. Moreover, we evaluated the segmentation component in isolation rather than within a complete AR guidance system. Integration with an AR platform, together with clinical and usability evaluation, remains future work.

In summary, we demonstrate that reliable real-time EVD catheter segmentation can be achieved within realistic mobile inference budgets. These results support the feasibility of deploying catheter segmentation as a core component of future low-cost AR-guided EVD systems and provide a deployment-oriented benchmark for thin-structure segmentation under resource constraints.

Acknowledgments. This work was supported by the Natural Sciences and Engineering Research Council of Canada (NSERC; RGPIN-2021-03477 and RGPIN-2017-06722).

Disclosure of Interests. The authors declare no competing interests.

References

1. Ahmed, F.A., et al.: Deep learning for surgical instrument recognition and segmentation in robotic-assisted surgeries: a systematic review. Artif. Intell. Rev. **58**, 1 (2025). https://doi.org/10.1007/s10462-024-10979-w
2. de Almeida, A.G.C., Fernandes de Oliveira Santos, B., Oliveira, J.L.M.: A neuronavigation system using a mobile augmented reality solution. World Neurosurgery **167**, e1261–e1267 (2022). https://doi.org/10.1016/j.wneu.2022.09.014
3. Amoo, M., Henry, J., Javadpour, M.: Common trajectories for freehand frontal ventriculostomy: a systematic review. World Neurosurg. **146**, 292–297 (2021). https://doi.org/10.1016/j.wneu.2020.11.065

4. Asadi, Z., Castillo, J.P., Asadi, M., Sinclair, D.S., Kersten-Oertel, M.: iSurgARy: a mobile augmented reality solution for ventriculostomy in resource-limited settings. Healthc. Technol. Lett. **12**, e12118 (2025). https://doi.org/10.1049/htl2.12118
5. Bagher Zadeh Ansari, N., Léger, É., Kersten-Oertel, M.: VentroAR: an augmented reality platform for ventriculostomy using the Microsoft HoloLens. Comput. Methods Biomech. Biomed. Eng. Imaging Visual. **11**(4), 1225–1233 (2023). https://doi.org/10.1080/21681163.2022.2156394
6. Bakiya, K., Savarimuthu, N.: Transfer learning for surgical instrument segmentation in open surgery videos: a modified u-net approach with channel amplification. SIViP **18**(11), 8061–8076 (2024). https://doi.org/10.1007/s11760-024-03451-3
7. Carion, N., et al.: SAM 3: segment anything with concepts. In: International Conference on Learning Representations (ICLR) (2026)
8. Che, H., et al.: Improving needle tip tracking and detection in ultrasound-based navigation system using deep learning-enabled approach. IEEE J. Biomed. Health Inform. **28**(5), 2930–2942 (2024). https://doi.org/10.1109/JBHI.2024.3353343
9. Chen, X., et al.: SAM 3D: 3Dfy anything in images. In: Proceedings of the IEEE/CVF Conference on Computer Vision and Pattern Recognition (CVPR), pp. 7220–7232 (2026)
10. Howard, A., et al.: Searching for MobileNetV3. In: Proceedings of the IEEE/CVF International Conference on Computer Vision (ICCV), pp. 1314–1324 (2019)
11. Hulou, M.M., Maglinger, B., McLouth, C.J., Reusche, C.M., Fraser, J.F.: Freehand frontal external ventricular drain (EVD) placement: accuracy and complications. J. Clin. Neurosci. **97**, 7–11 (2022). https://doi.org/10.1016/j.jocn.2021.12.036
12. Lin, M.A., Siu, A.F., Bae, J.H., Cutkosky, M.R., Daniel, B.L.: HoloNeedle: augmented reality guidance system for needle placement investigating the advantages of three-dimensional needle shape reconstruction. IEEE Robot. Autom. Lett. **3**(4), 4156–4162 (2018). https://doi.org/10.1109/LRA.2018.2863381
13. Lin, T.Y., Dollár, P., Girshick, R., He, K., Hariharan, B., Belongie, S.: Feature pyramid networks for object detection. In: Proceedings of the IEEE Conference on Computer Vision and Pattern Recognition (CVPR), pp. 2117–2125 (2017)
14. Liu, Z., Mao, H., Wu, C.Y., Feichtenhofer, C., Darrell, T., Xie, S.: A ConvNet for the 2020s. In: Proceedings of the IEEE/CVF Conference on Computer Vision and Pattern Recognition (CVPR), pp. 11976–11986 (2022)
15. Manfield, J.H., Yu, K.K.H.: Real-time ultrasound-guided external ventricular drain placement: technical note. Neurosurg. Focus **43**(5), E5 (2017). https://doi.org/10.3171/2017.7.FOCUS17148
16. O'Leary, S.T., Kole, M.K., Hoover, D.A., Hysell, S.E., Thomas, A., Shaffrey, C.I.: Efficacy of the Ghajar Guide revisited: a prospective study. J. Neurosurg. **92**(5), 801–803 (2000). https://doi.org/10.3171/jns.2000.92.5.0801
17. Raabe, C., Fichtner, J., Beck, J., Gralla, J., Raabe, A.: Revisiting the rules for freehand ventriculostomy: a virtual reality analysis. J. Neurosurg. **128**(4), 1250–1257 (2018). https://doi.org/10.3171/2016.11.JNS161765
18. Ravi, N., et al.: SAM 2: segment anything in images and videos. In: International Conference on Learning Representations (ICLR) (2025)
19. Sarrafzadeh, A., Smoll, N., Schaller, K.: Guided (VENTRI-GUIDE) versus freehand ventriculostomy: study protocol for a randomized controlled trial. Trials **15**, 478 (2014). https://doi.org/10.1186/1745-6215-15-478
20. Schneider, M., Kunz, C., Pal'a, A., Wirtz, C.R., Mathis-Ullrich, F., Hlaváč, M.: Augmented reality-assisted ventriculostomy. Neurosurg. Focus **50**(1), E16 (2021). https://doi.org/10.3171/2020.10.FOCUS20779

21. Vasu, P.K.A., Gabriel, J., Zhu, J., Tuzel, O., Ranjan, A.: FastViT: a fast hybrid vision transformer using structural reparameterization. In: Proceedings of the IEEE/CVF International Conference on Computer Vision (ICCV), pp. 5785–5795 (2023)
22. Yan, W., Ding, Q., Chen, J., Yan, K., Tang, R.S.Y., Cheng, S.S.: Learning-based needle tip tracking in 2D ultrasound by fusing visual tracking and motion prediction. Med. Image Anal. **88**, 102847 (2023). https://doi.org/10.1016/j.media.2023.102847

EndoDA3: Unified Depth and Pose Estimation for Endoscopic Video

Jie Tan[1], Zijun Li[1], Hongmei Tuo[2], Yunhan Fu[3], Chengyang Li[1], and Li Lu[1(✉)]

[1] College of Computer Science, Sichuan University, Chengdu, China
luli@scu.edu.cn
[2] School of Gongli Hospital Medical Technology, University of Shanghai for Science and Technology, Shanghai, China
[3] Sichuan University-Pittsburgh Institute, Chengdu, China

Abstract. Three-dimensional (3D) scene reconstruction from monocular endoscopic videos is crucial for minimally invasive surgery, yet it remains challenging due to dynamic soft-tissue deformations, textureless surfaces, and illumination variations. Although recent self-supervised learning methods and adaptations of foundation models have shown promise, they often rely on complex multi-stage pipelines and external auxiliary networks for camera parameter estimation, while predominantly performing frame-wise inference, thereby neglecting inter-frame temporal consistency. To address these limitations, we propose EndoDA3, a unified and parameter-efficient framework that leverages the robust geometric priors of Depth Anything 3 for continuous endoscopic 3D reconstruction without requiring ground-truth depth. Specifically, we introduce a novel Dual-Vector Modulated Low-Rank Adaptation (DVM-LoRA) strategy to efficiently adapt the foundation model for joint scale-consistent depth prediction and camera pose estimation within a single shared network. Furthermore, to explicitly enforce temporal continuity and mitigate the adverse effects of dynamic outliers, we design an Uncertainty-aware Projection Loss that dynamically reweights projection-based training signals and suppresses unreliable regions caused by moving instruments and non-rigid tissue deformation. Extensive experiments demonstrate that EndoDA3 achieves strong performance across two public endoscopic datasets, with improved temporal consistency and robust camera pose estimation. Code is available at EndoDA3.

Keywords: Self-supervised learning · Endoscopic surgery · Video depth estimation

---

Supplementary Information The online version contains supplementary material available at https://doi.org/10.1007/978-3-032-38236-8_15.

G. Yang et al. (Eds.): MICCAI 2026, LNCS 16893, pp. 149–159, 2027.
https://doi.org/10.1007/978-3-032-38236-8_15

1 Introduction

Three-dimensional (3D) scene reconstruction from monocular endoscopic videos plays a vital role in minimally invasive surgery (MIS). Recovering the 3D geometry of the surgical site can provide depth cues that are unavailable in standard 2D endoscopic videos. Such spatial awareness is essential for improving lesion sizing, facilitating intraoperative navigation, and enabling robotic surgical automation [5,8,25].

However, recovering scale-consistent 3D structures from endoscopic scenes remains challenging. The surgical environment is highly complex, characterized by dynamic soft-tissue deformations, textureless surfaces, and illumination variations [8]. Consequently, conventional Structure-from-Motion [14] and Simultaneous Localization and Mapping [3] methods, which heavily rely on static scene assumptions, often yield suboptimal performance and catastrophic tracking failures in deformable surgical environments.

While deep learning methods [21,22] have significantly advanced depth estimation in natural scenes, acquiring ground-truth depth in endoscopy remains intrinsically challenging. To this end, self-supervised learning (SSL) leveraging adjacent-frame geometric consistency has emerged as a prevalent paradigm [2,6]. Yet, recent SfM-like multi-stage pipelines [15,23] still suffer from error accumulation and cumbersome offline optimization. Meanwhile, foundation models such as Depth Anything [4,10,21,22] and DUSt3R series [17,18] have shown strong zero-shot generalization in general domains, but adapting them to complex endoscopic scenes entails overcoming a substantial domain gap. To bridge this gap, recent methods [6,16,24] employ Low-Rank Adaptation (LoRA) [9] to adapt these generic models to surgical videos. However, these adaptations typically rely on external auxiliary networks or explicit prior knowledge to estimate camera parameters, or they fine-tune separate, redundant encoders for depth and pose regression. More critically, most of these methods perform isolated frame-wise inference, overlooking the rich temporal continuity inherent in surgical videos.

To address these limitations, we propose **EndoDA3**, a unified and parameter-efficient framework that adapts Depth Anything 3 (DA3) to continuous endoscopic 3D reconstruction without requiring ground-truth depth or an additional pose network. Specifically, we introduce a novel parameter-efficient fine-tuning strategy named **Dual-Vector Modulated Low-Rank Adaptation (DVM-LoRA)**. By training a minimal set of parameters, EndoDA3 enables the simultaneous regression of scale-consistent depth and reliable camera poses within a single network. Furthermore, to ensure temporal continuity and mitigate the adverse effects of tissue deformation and instrument motion, we introduce an **Uncertainty-aware Projection Loss**. This objective dynamically reweights supervision signals based on prediction confidence, effectively filtering out outliers induced by dynamic instruments and deformable tissues, thereby facilitating robust learning in complex surgical environments. Our main contributions are summarized as follows.

1. We propose EndoDA3, a unified endoscopic reconstruction framework derived from Depth Anything 3. By introducing a novel Dual-Vector Modulated LoRA (DVM-LoRA) and a shared encoder backbone, we adapt the foundation model to jointly infer video depth and camera parameters with high efficiency.
2. We introduce an Uncertainty-aware Projection Loss to enforce temporal continuity and improve robustness against dynamic outliers. By weighting the reprojection depth error using confidence maps, this loss explicitly mitigates the impact of non-rigid tissue deformation and instrument motion.
3. Extensive experiments on two public endoscopic datasets demonstrate the effectiveness of EndoDA3 in improving video depth prediction, temporal consistency, and camera pose estimation.

2 Method

2.1 EndoDA3 Framework

Network Architecture. Recognizing that depth estimation and ego-motion are inherently coupled tasks rather than independent processes, we introduce a unified architecture to simultaneously predict depth and camera parameters. To establish a robust geometric representation for endoscopic reconstruction, our framework builds upon the Depth Anything 3 [10] foundation model, aiming to exploit its geometric priors for spatially consistent 3D reconstruction. As illustrated in Fig. 1, we extend the input formulation from image pairs to video sequences to better capture temporal context.

Specifically, given a video sequence of T input images $\mathcal{I} = \{I_i\}_{i=1}^{T}$, a single shared ViT encoder [10,11] employing input-adaptive "within-view" and "cross-view" attention mechanisms is utilized to extract unified features. These features are subsequently decoded by two specialized branches. In the depth estimation branch, we employ a Multi-Scale Dense Prediction Transformer (DPT) head [10,12] to capture both global contextual information and local structural details. The feature representations are progressively reassembled and fused across different resolutions to predict pixel-aligned scalar depth maps $\mathbf{D}_i \in \mathbb{R}^{H\times W\times 1}$, alongside confidence maps $\mathbf{C}_i \in \mathbb{R}^{H\times W\times 1}$ that quantify the model's pixel-wise reliability regarding the depth predictions. Concurrently, the pose branch utilizes a lightweight regression head $\mathcal{D}_C$ to estimate explicit camera parameters. These parameters are then converted into standard rotation matrices $\mathbf{R}_i$, translation vectors $\mathbf{t}_i$, and intrinsic matrices $\mathbf{K}_i$.

Self-supervised Learning Strategy. Following the self-supervised learning (SSL) paradigm [6,15], the predicted depth and camera parameters are utilized to synthesize the target frame I_t by inversely warping the adjacent source views I_s ($s \in \{t-1, t+1\}$). Accordingly, a pixel $\mathbf{p}_t = [u, v, 1]^\top$ in the target image I_t is first back-projected to a 3D point $\mathbf{P}$ in the world coordinate system using the standard pinhole camera model:

$$\mathbf{P} = \mathbf{R}_t \left(\mathbf{D}_t(u, v)\mathbf{K}_t^{-1}\mathbf{p}_t\right) + \mathbf{t}_t. \tag{1}$$

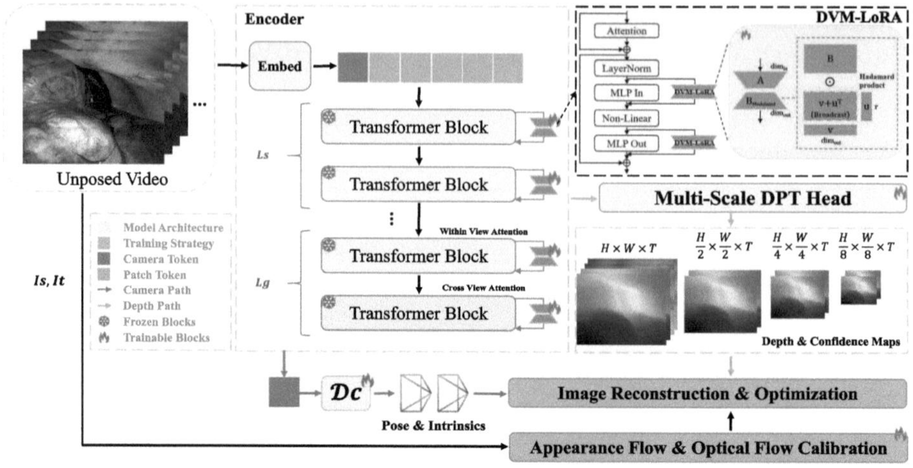

Fig. 1. Overview of the EndoDA3 self-supervised learning framework for depth and pose estimation, trained with multi-scale SSIM-based photometric reconstruction loss and the proposed uncertainty-aware projection loss.

Subsequently, these 3D coordinates are transformed into the source camera coordinate system and projected onto the source view I_s to obtain continuous 2D sampling coordinates. The synthesized target image $I_{s\to t}$ is then generated by differentiably sampling the color values from I_s at these projected coordinates via bilinear interpolation. Finally, we adopt the photometric reconstruction loss $\mathcal{L}_p$ [6] and incorporate the illumination-compensation strategy of [15] to mitigate appearance inconsistencies, thereby encouraging $I_{s\to t}$ to align as closely as possible with the original I_t.

2.2 Dual-Vector Modulated Low-Rank Adaptation

The inherent domain gap frequently leads to performance degradation in the zero-shot depth estimation of DA3 in endoscopic scenes. This gap is highly heterogeneous in endoscopic videos, where specular highlights, weak textures, occlusions, and tissue deformation affect feature representations unevenly across channels. To address this challenge, we propose Dual-Vector Modulated Low-Rank Adaptation (DVM-LoRA), an efficient fine-tuning strategy that adapts robust geometric priors while preserving the generalizable representations of the pre-trained model.

Standard LoRA [9] adapts pre-trained models by introducing trainable low-rank update matrices while keeping the original weights frozen. Let $\mathbf{W}_0 \in \mathbb{R}^{d_{out}\times d_{in}}$ be a pre-trained weight matrix and $\mathbf{x} \in \mathbb{R}^{d_{in}}$ be the input. Standard LoRA modifies the forward pass as $\mathbf{h} = \mathbf{W}_0\mathbf{x} + s\mathbf{B}\mathbf{A}\mathbf{x}$, where $\mathbf{B} \in \mathbb{R}^{d_{out}\times r}$ and $\mathbf{A} \in \mathbb{R}^{r\times d_{in}}$ are low-rank matrices ($r \ll \min(d_{in}, d_{out})$), and $s = \frac{\alpha}{r}$ serves as a constant scaling factor.

Although efficient, standard LoRA controls the magnitude of the low-rank branch using a single global scaling factor, without explicitly modeling rank-wise or output-channel-wise modulation. This may limit its flexibility when adapting to heterogeneous domain shifts in endoscopic scenes. To overcome this limitation, DVM-LoRA introduces two learnable modulation vectors at both the intermediate low-rank space and the output feature space. Specifically, we retain $\mathbf{A}$ and $\mathbf{B}$ and introduce two trainable column vectors: $\mathbf{u} \in \mathbb{R}^{r\times 1}$ and $\mathbf{v} \in \mathbb{R}^{d_{out}\times 1}$. The rank-wise vector $\mathbf{u}$ adjusts the contribution of individual low-rank components, while the output-channel-wise vector $\mathbf{v}$ provides channel-selective adaptation for the resulting feature updates. Conceptually, the weight update is modulated as follows:

$$\Delta\mathbf{W} = s\left(\mathbf{B}\mathrm{diag}(\mathbf{u})\mathbf{A} + \mathrm{diag}(\mathbf{v})\mathbf{B}\mathbf{A}\right). \tag{2}$$

In practice, to avoid the computational overhead of explicitly constructing diagonal matrices during the forward pass, we directly fuse the dual-modulation pathways within the weight space. By leveraging matrix broadcasting, the effective weight update $\Delta\mathbf{W}$ is efficiently formulated as:

$$\Delta\mathbf{W} = s\left(\mathbf{B} \odot (\mathbf{v}\mathbf{1}_r^\top + \mathbf{1}_{d_{out}}\mathbf{u}^\top)\right)\mathbf{A}, \tag{3}$$

where $\odot$ represents the Hadamard product, and $\mathbf{1}$ denotes a column vector of ones. The forward pass is then executed via a single unified matrix multiplication: $\mathbf{h} = (\mathbf{W}_0 + \Delta\mathbf{W})\mathbf{x}$. This design obviates the need to instantiate redundant activation tensors and allows for seamless zero-inference-overhead weight merging.

Regarding parameter initialization, $\mathbf{A}$, $\mathbf{u}$, and $\mathbf{v}$ are initialized using Kaiming uniform initialization, whereas $\mathbf{B}$ is strictly zero-initialized. This configuration guarantees that $\Delta\mathbf{W}$ remains zero at the onset of fine-tuning, thereby preserving the original behavior of the pre-trained model and ensuring training stability. DVM-LoRA introduces only $r + d_{out}$ additional parameters beyond standard LoRA, preserving parameter efficiency while enabling flexible adaptation to heterogeneous endoscopic domain gaps. In our architecture, DVM-LoRA is exclusively applied to the feed-forward networks (FFNs) within the Transformer blocks.

2.3 Uncertainty-Aware Projection Loss

Standard self-supervised depth estimation frameworks often lack explicit temporal constraints, leading to temporally inconsistent predictions [6,24]. To address this, we introduce a temporal depth consistency constraint [25]. Given a source frame I_s and an adjacent target frame I_t, our network predicts their corresponding depth maps $\mathbf{D}_s$ and $\mathbf{D}_t$, alongside the relative camera pose $\mathbf{T}_{t\to s}$. Using the predicted pose and camera intrinsics, we project the target depth into the source viewpoint to synthesize the warped target depth $\hat{\mathbf{D}}_{t\to s}$. The base geometric consistency is enforced by minimizing the pixel-wise depth error, defined as:

$$e_{\mathbf{p}} = |\mathbf{D}_s(\mathbf{p}) - \hat{\mathbf{D}}_{t\to s}(\mathbf{p})|. \tag{4}$$

Fig. 2. Visualization of confidence maps for an example from [19]. Brighter regions correspond to higher confidence in the depth estimation. (*a*) predicted by DA3; (*b*) predicted by EndoDA3 with LoRA.

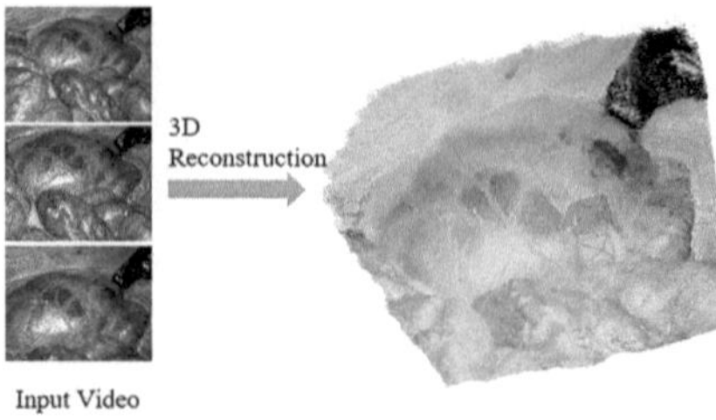

Fig. 3. Qualitative results of 3D reconstruction.

However, in endoscopic videos, the multi-view consistency assumption is frequently violated by tissue deformations and dynamic surgical instruments. Inspired by robust alignment strategies in recent reconstruction models [7], which down-weight dynamic outliers through confidence-aware filtering, we propose an uncertainty-aware projection loss tailored for surgical environments. By dynamically assigning lower confidence values to regions affected by rapid instrument motion or severe tissue deformation, we attenuate their misleading contributions to the alignment process, while concentrating higher weights on relatively static anatomical backgrounds. This loss adaptively weights the geometric depth consistency using a network-predicted confidence map **C**. The proposed uncertainty-aware projection loss is formulated as:

$$\mathcal{L}_{\text{conf}} = \frac{1}{|\Omega|} \sum_{\mathbf{p} \in \Omega} \left(\mathbf{C}_\mathbf{p} \cdot \mathcal{L}_h(e_\mathbf{p}, \delta_h) - \lambda \log(\mathbf{C}_\mathbf{p}) \right), \tag{5}$$

where Ω denotes the set of valid projected pixels, and $\mathcal{L}_h(\cdot, \delta_h)$ is the Huber loss with a threshold δ_h to further suppress extreme errors.

The first term in Eq. 5 penalizes depth inconsistencies weighted by the predicted confidence, effectively encouraging the network to assign low confidence (i.e., high uncertainty) to unreliable regions. The second regularization term, $-\lambda \log(\mathbf{C}_\mathbf{p})$, prevents the network from converging to the trivial solution of predicting minimal confidence everywhere. The overall training objective is formulated as:

$$\mathcal{L}_{\text{all}} = \mathcal{L}_{\text{EndoDAC}} + \lambda_{\text{conf}} \mathcal{L}_{\text{conf}}, \tag{6}$$

where $\mathcal{L}_{\text{EndoDAC}}$ denotes the original self-supervised training objective of EndoDAC [6], and λ_{conf} controls the contribution of the proposed uncertainty-aware projection loss. In our implementation, we empirically set $\lambda_{\text{conf}} = 0.01$ and the Huber threshold $\delta_h = 1.0$. As shown in Fig. 2, the proposed loss assigns lower confidence to regions with moving instruments and tissue deformation.

3 Experiments and Results

3.1 Datasets and Evaluation

We evaluate our proposed method on two publicly available endoscopic and laparoscopic video datasets: the SCARED dataset and the Hamlyn dataset.

SCARED Dataset. The SCARED [1] dataset provides a controlled environment for surgical data analysis. It comprises 35 endoscopic videos captured using a da Vinci Xi endoscope, yielding a total of 22,950 high-resolution frames. The dataset provides ground-truth depth maps generated via a structured light projector, alongside accurate camera poses and intrinsic parameters. Following previous work [25], the dataset is partitioned into 24 sequences for training, 3 for validation, and 8 for testing.

Hamlyn Dataset. The Hamlyn dataset offers a diverse collection of laparoscopic and endoscopic surgical videos. In our experiments, 21 selected video sequences [13] from this dataset are utilized for cross-dataset zero-shot validation.

Evaluation Metrics. Following [6,15,25], we utilize five standard metrics to assess the spatial accuracy of the depth predictions: Abs Rel, Sq Rel, RMSE, RMSE log, and $\delta < 1.25$. Furthermore, to quantitatively measure the temporal consistency of the video depth estimation, we report the Temporal Alignment Error (TAE) [20]. To evaluate the pose accuracy, we perform a 5-frame pose evaluation and adopt the Absolute Trajectory Error (ATE). Critically, for affine-invariant depth evaluation, depth predictions must be aligned to the ground truth. We perform alignment using the median and scale computed over the full video sequence [4], rather than per-frame alignment [6]. This rigorous sequence-level alignment is crucial to ensure that temporal consistency is accurately evaluated.

Table 1. Quantitative video depth comparison on SCARED and Hamlyn datasets. The best results are in bold. "Total.(M)" and "Train.(M)" refer to the total and trainable parameters utilized in the depth network. Note that since the Hamlyn dataset does not provide the camera pose annotations, we do not evaluate the TAE metric on it.

	Methods	Year	Abs Rel↓	Sq Rel↓	RMSE↓	RMSE log↓	$\delta < 1.25$ ↑	TAE↓	Total.(M)	Train.(M)	Speed (ms)
SCARED	VDA [4]	2025	0.241	7.702	18.673	0.287	0.597	1.100	113.1	-	15.9
	DA3 [10]	2025	0.110	1.699	9.169	0.139	0.858	1.305	103.8	-	19.4
	EndoDAC [6]	2024	0.146	2.389	11.863	0.178	0.790	1.843	99.0	1.6	15.0
	EndoDAV [25]	2025	0.160	2.951	12.783	0.187	0.759	0.725	113.3	0.19	16.0
	EndoDA3	-	**0.088**	**1.014**	**7.002**	**0.110**	**0.933**	**0.335**	104.5	0.78	19.5
Hamlyn	DA3 [10]	2025	0.321	12.021	22.467	0.681	0.500	-	103.8	-	19.4
	EndoDAV [25]	2025	0.223	6.277	16.329	**0.281**	0.637	-	113.3	0.19	16.0
	EndoDA3	-	**0.220**	**6.224**	**16.095**	0.328	**0.648**	-	104.5	0.78	19.5

Table 2. Comparison of Pose Estimation on the SCARED Dataset.

Methods	ATE↓
EndoDAC [6]	0.124
DA3 [10]	0.208
Endo3R [8]	0.112
EndoDA3	**0.102**

Table 3. Ablation study on SCARED dataset. The best results are in bold. Specifically, we (i) use the original LoRA [9] to replace DVM-LoRA; (ii) remove Uncertainty-aware Projection Loss.

$\mathcal{L}_{\text{conf}}$	DVM-LoRA	Abs Rel↓	Sq Rel↓	RMSE↓	RMSE log↓	$\delta < 1.25$ ↑	TAE↓
×	×	0.099	1.252	7.711	0.129	0.898	0.538
✓	×	0.095	1.212	7.518	0.120	0.908	0.376
✓	✓	**0.088**	**1.014**	**7.002**	**0.110**	**0.933**	**0.335**

3.2 Experimental Results

Implementation Details. Implemented in PyTorch on a single RTX 3090 GPU, the framework is trained for 20 epochs with a sequence length of 16. We use the AdamW optimizer (initial learning rate 1×10^{-4}) and adopt standard data augmentations [6,25]. The DVM-LoRA rank is set to $r = 4$.

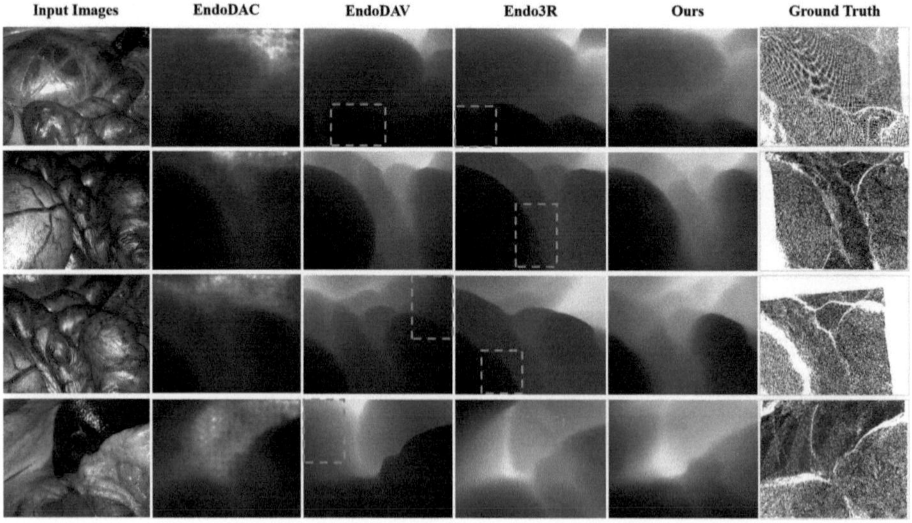

Fig. 4. Qualitative results using video sequences as input.

Quantitative Analysis. We quantitatively evaluate our proposed method on the SCARED and Hamlyn datasets against several competitive baselines. Some results are cited from the original papers. As shown in Tables 1 and 2, our approach improves both video depth and pose prediction accuracy in complex endoscopic scenes, demonstrating high spatial accuracy and robust temporal consistency. Furthermore, benefiting from a parameter-efficient design, our method achieves an inference speed comparable to the aforementioned baselines, fully supporting real-time depth estimation.

Qualitative Analysis. We present qualitative results for video depth estimation in Fig. 4, which demonstrates that EndoDA3 can generate more accurate depth maps and better relative scale. In addition, as shown in Fig. 3, our accurate depth and pose estimates enable high-quality 3D reconstruction. For more visualization results, please refer to the supplementary video.

Ablation Studies. To validate the efficacy of individual components, we conducted ablation studies on the SCARED dataset, as shown in Table 3. Experimental results demonstrate that our proposed EndoDA3 effectively enhances both depth prediction accuracy and temporal consistency across videos. Notably, the Uncertainty-aware Projection Loss improves temporal continuity, while the proposed DVM-LoRA further enhances the overall depth estimation performance.

4 Conclusion

In this paper, we proposed EndoDA3, a unified and parameter-efficient framework for continuous 3D scene reconstruction from monocular endoscopic videos. By integrating a novel Dual-Vector Modulated LoRA (DVM-LoRA) with an Uncertainty-aware Projection Loss, our approach effectively adapts foundation models to complex surgical environments while maintaining robust temporal consistency against tissue deformations and instrument motion. Extensive experiments on two public datasets demonstrate that EndoDA3 achieves superior scale-consistent depth and accurate camera pose estimation with a single shared encoder. Future work will explore real-time intraoperative optimization and downstream integration with robotic navigation systems.

Acknowledgments. This study was funded by Chengdu Science and Technology Program (2026-YF05-00762-SN).

Disclosure of Interests. The authors have no competing interests to declare that are relevant to the content of this article.

References

1. Allan, M., et al.: Stereo correspondence and reconstruction of endoscopic data challenge. arXiv preprint arXiv:2101.01133 (2021)

2. Arampatzakis, V., Pavlidis, G., Mitianoudis, N., Papamarkos, N.: Monocular depth estimation: A thorough review. IEEE Trans. Pattern Anal. Mach. Intell. **46**(04), 2396–2414 (2024)
3. Campos, C., Elvira, R., Rodríguez, J.J.G., Montiel, J.M., Tardós, J.D.: Orb-slam3: An accurate open-source library for visual, visual-inertial, and multimap slam. IEEE Trans. Rob. **37**(6), 1874–1890 (2021)
4. Chen, S., et al.: Video depth anything: Consistent depth estimation for super-long videos. In: Proceedings of the Computer Vision and Pattern Recognition Conference, pp. 22831–22840 (2025)
5. Collins, T., et al.: Augmented reality guided laparoscopic surgery of the uterus. IEEE Trans. Med. Imaging **40**(1), 371–380 (2020)
6. Cui, B., Islam, M., Bai, L., Wang, A., Ren, H.: Endodac: Efficient adapting foundation model for self-supervised depth estimation from any endoscopic camera. In: Linguraru, M.G., et al. (eds.) International Conference on Medical Image Computing and Computer-Assisted Intervention, pp. 208–218. Springer, Cham (2024). https://doi.org/10.1007/978-3-031-72089-5_20
7. Deng, K., Ti, Z., Xu, J., Yang, J., Xie, J.: Vggt-long: Chunk it, loop it, align it-pushing vggt's limits on kilometer-scale long rgb sequences. arXiv preprint arXiv:2507.16443 (2025)
8. Guo, J., et al.: Endo3r: Unified online reconstruction from dynamic monocular endoscopic video. In: Gee, J.C., et al. (eds.) International Conference on Medical Image Computing and Computer-Assisted Intervention, pp. 170–180. Springer, Cham (2025). https://doi.org/10.1007/978-3-032-05114-1_17
9. Hu, E.J., et al.: LoRA: Low-rank adaptation of large language models. In: International Conference on Learning Representations (2022)
10. Lin, H., et al.: Depth anything 3: Recovering the visual space from any views. arXiv preprint arXiv:2511.10647 (2025)
11. Oquab, M., et al.: Dinov2: Learning robust visual features without supervision. arXiv preprint arXiv:2304.07193 (2023)
12. Ranftl, R., Bochkovskiy, A., Koltun, V.: Vision transformers for dense prediction. In: Proceedings of the IEEE/CVF International Conference on Computer Vision, pp. 12179–12188 (2021)
13. Recasens, D., Lamarca, J., Fácil, J.M., Montiel, J.M., Civera, J.: Endo-depth-and-motion: Reconstruction and tracking in endoscopic videos using depth networks and photometric constraints. IEEE Robot. Autom. Lett. **6**(4), 7225–7232 (2021)
14. Schonberger, J.L., Frahm, J.M.: Structure-from-motion revisited. In: Proceedings of the IEEE Conference on Computer Vision and Pattern Recognition, pp. 4104–4113 (2016)
15. Shao, S., et al.: Self-supervised monocular depth and ego-motion estimation in endoscopy: Appearance flow to the rescue. Med. Image Anal. **77**, 102338 (2022)
16. Sheikh Zeinoddin, M., et al.: Endo-fast3r: endoscopic foundation model adaptation for structure from motion. In: Gee, J.C., et al. (eds.) International Conference on Medical Image Computing and Computer-Assisted Intervention, pp. 117–126. Springer, Cham (2025). https://doi.org/10.1007/978-3-032-05141-7_12
17. Wang, Q., Zhang, Y., Holynski, A., Efros, A.A., Kanazawa, A.: Continuous 3d perception model with persistent state. In: Proceedings of the Computer Vision and Pattern Recognition Conference, pp. 10510–10522 (2025)
18. Wang, S., Leroy, V., Cabon, Y., Chidlovskii, B., Revaud, J.: Dust3r: Geometric 3d vision made easy. In: Proceedings of the IEEE/CVF Conference on Computer Vision and Pattern Recognition, pp. 20697–20709 (2024)

19. Wang, Y., Long, Y., Fan, S.H., Dou, Q.: Neural rendering for stereo 3d reconstruction of deformable tissues in robotic surgery. In: Wang, L., Dou, Q., Fletcher, P.T., Speidel, S., Li, S. (eds.) International conference on medical image computing and computer-assisted intervention, pp. 431–441. Springer, Cham (2022). https://doi.org/10.1007/978-3-031-16449-1_41
20. Yang, H., et al.: Depth any video with scalable synthetic data. arXiv preprint arXiv:2410.10815 (2024)
21. Yang, L., Kang, B., Huang, Z., Xu, X., Feng, J., Zhao, H.: Depth anything: Unleashing the power of large-scale unlabeled data. In: Proceedings of the IEEE/CVF Conference on Computer Vision and Pattern Recognition, pp. 10371–10381 (2024)
22. Yang, L., et al.: Depth anything v2. Adv. Neural. Inf. Process. Syst. **37**, 21875–21911 (2024)
23. Yang, Z., Pan, J., Dai, J., Sun, Z., Xiao, Y.: Self-supervised lightweight depth estimation in endoscopy combining cnn and transformer. IEEE Trans. Med. Imaging **43**(5), 1934–1944 (2024)
24. Zeinoddin, M.S., et al.: Dares: Depth anything in robotic endoscopic surgery with self-supervised vector-lora of the foundation model. arXiv preprint arXiv:2408.17433 (2024)
25. Zhou, Z., Yang, C., Yang, P., Yang, X., Shen, W.: Endodav: Depth any video in endoscopy with spatiotemporal accuracy. In: Gee, J.C., et al. (eds.) International Conference on Medical Image Computing and Computer-Assisted Intervention, pp. 192–201. Springer, Cham (2025). https://doi.org/10.1007/978-3-032-05114-1_19

EndoX: A GPU-Accelerated Endoscopic Perception Simulation Framework

Kwan Tung Lam[1,2], Ping Shu Ho[1(✉)], Patt Phurtivilai[1,3], and Ka Chun Cheung[1]

[1] NVIDIA AI Technology Center, NVIDIA Corporation, Santa Clara, USA
cliffh@nvidia.com
[2] The Chinese University of Hong Kong, Hong Kong, China
[3] The University of Hong Kong, Hong Kong, China

Abstract. Endoscopic examination of gastrointestinal organs increasingly relies on 3D computer vision techniques such as depth estimation, surface reconstruction, and missing region detection. Yet rigorous method development for endoscopy remains challenging, as ground-truth data cannot be readily acquired during clinical procedures. We present *EndoX*, a GPU-accelerated synthetic data generation (SDG) framework and interactive simulator for medical endoscopy that enables efficient generation of fully annotated datasets, addressing the data scarcity gap in algorithm development. EndoX automates anatomically accurate 3D mesh generation from computed tomography (CT) data and employs physics-based rendering to produce RGB imagery together with geometric modalities: depth, surface normals, optical flow, occlusion, and camera coverage maps, with precise ground-truth geometry. For validation, we constructed organ-specific datasets by navigating a virtual capsule endoscope through anatomically accurate CT-derived organ meshes, with sensor and lighting parameters configured to approximate real capsule endoscopes. Quantitative evaluations on depth estimation, pose estimation, and 3D Gaussian Splatting demonstrate that models trained on EndoX data achieve competitive accuracy, and qualitative assessment confirms transferability to clinical endoscopy. The framework is designed for scalable deployment on GPU nodes via containerization. A sample dataset comprising three video sequences (12,000 frames) with paired ground-truth annotations and 3D models is available. The source code of the extension for NVIDIA Omniverse, documentation, and the sample dataset are available at https://beatricelam111.github.io/EndoX/.

Keywords: Endoscopy · Synthetic dataset generation · Simulated gastrointestinal tract

K. T. Lam and P. S. Ho—These authors contributed equally to this work.

Supplementary Information The online version contains supplementary material available at https://doi.org/10.1007/978-3-032-38236-8_16.

G. Yang et al. (Eds.): MICCAI 2026, LNCS 16893, pp. 160–169, 2027.
https://doi.org/10.1007/978-3-032-38236-8_16

1 Introduction

Three-dimensional (3D) computer vision techniques—including depth estimation, surface reconstruction, and coverage analysis—could transform gastrointestinal (GI) endoscopy by enabling quantitative assessment of luminal geometry and ensuring complete mucosal inspection. However, the absence of ground-truth geometric data in real procedures poses a fundamental obstacle to rigorous algorithm training, validation, and benchmarking. Unlike scenes where depth sensors or LiDAR can provide supervision, the confined intraluminal environment precludes direct geometric measurement during endoscopy, leaving algorithm development reliant on qualitative evaluation or small-scale phantom studies.

General endoscopic datasets such as Kvasir-Capsule [1] and Galar [2] support disease detection but lack spatial annotations. Specialized datasets have been introduced for depth estimation [3], visual odometry, and Simultaneous Localization and Mapping (SLAM) research [4,5]. Yet inter-patient variability, tissue deformability, inconsistent lighting across endoscopic systems, and limited anatomical coverage complicate ground-truth acquisition and algorithm robustness. Moreover, existing datasets lack the multimodality and diversity required for modern computer vision models and 3D reconstruction algorithms.

Addressing these gaps requires photorealistic imagery, spatial annotations, and 3D ground truth. **Contribution**: We propose *EndoX*, a GPU-accelerated synthetic data generation framework and high-fidelity simulator for medical endoscopy that: (i) automates anatomically accurate 3D mesh generation from CT data across diverse patient anatomies; (ii) employs real-time physically-based rendering (PBR) for optically accurate RGB imagery alongside co-registered geometric ground-truth modalities, with customizable sensor, lighting, material, and trajectory parameters; and (iii) is designed for scalable deployment for high-throughput data production with the containerized headless version.

1.1 Related Work

Endoscopic Datasets for 3D Algorithms. Existing GI endoscopic datasets provide inadequate support for the development of 3D computer vision algorithms, constrained by limited diversity. C3VD [6] and C3VDv2 [7] provide annotated imagery with 3D ground truth, but manual acquisition using colon phantoms inherently limits data diversity. The EndoSLAM dataset [4] is based on *ex-vivo* recordings in porcine organs and virtual environments using VR-Caps [8]. While providing ground-truth 3D models and camera poses, the experimental setting requires careful sample handling, precise robotic calibration, and manual tissue preparation—yielding modest data quantities insufficient to cover diverse clinical scenarios. Moreover, they lack geometric ground-truth such as depth and normal maps. The EndoNeRF dataset [9] enables evaluation of neural rendering techniques but comprises only two surgical cases without high-quality 3D geometric ground truth.

Endoscopy Simulators for Synthetic Data Generation. SDG for medical AI/ML research has emerged in response to the demand for large-scale, high-quality, privacy-preserving datasets for training and validating deep learning models. Researchers have developed endoscopy simulators to generate synthetic datasets that facilitate algorithm development for advanced medical imaging applications. Recent works such as VR-Caps [8] and SimIntestine [10] build virtual GI environments using Unity and Blender, respectively, enabling endoscopic camera navigation and data capture. However, these simulators face an inherent trade-off: VR-Caps relies on rasterization in Unity, achieving real-time performance at the cost of physically accurate rendering, while SimIntestine employs a path tracing renderer in Blender, offering photorealism but at prohibitive offline computation costs. SimuScope [11] attempts to bridge this gap by pairing Unity with Stable Diffusion v1.5 [12], fine-tuned via low-rank adaptation, for image-to-image translation with higher fidelity, yet the probabilistic nature of diffusion models limits temporal consistency across generated frames. None of these approaches efficiently delivers physically based, photorealistic imagery at scale, nor provides an automated pipeline for scalable SDG in a headless, containerized application.

2 Methods

2.1 Generation of 3D Models

EndoX automates generation of 3D GI organ meshes from clinical CT data in DICOM format (Fig. 1), supporting scalable creation of anatomical models for SDG. Clinical CT DICOM sequences are converted to volumetric NIfTI format and segmented using VISTA3D [13], producing voxel-wise binary masks that delineate organ boundaries. The masks are applied to each organ volume, followed by value-based thresholding to remove irrelevant voxels (e.g., air and imaging artifacts) and Gaussian blurring to reduce surface noise. A 3D isosurface is then extracted from each binary volume using the marching cubes algorithm [14] with the VTK package [15], retaining only the largest continuous structure.

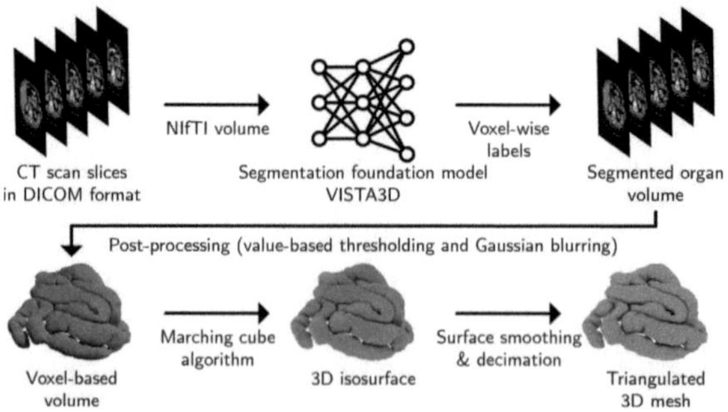

Fig. 1. CT-to-mesh reconstruction pipeline converting 2D CT slices into a 3D mesh model.

Iterative windowed-sinc smoothing and quadratic edge collapse decimation are applied to reduce mesh imperfections and decrease face count while preserving anatomical topology. The refined mesh is exported in Wavefront OBJ format.

2.2 Simulator with Physics-Based Rendering

EndoX is built on the NVIDIA Omniverse platform, using GPU-accelerated real-time ray tracing with PBR for scalable, high-fidelity image synthesis.

Environment Setup and Navigation Path. Generated 3D meshes are imported into an interactive simulation environment. Centerlines of GI tracts are automatically extracted using a Voronoi diagram-based method [16] with the VMTK package [17] to define a virtual sensor navigation path. Alternatively, user-supplied coordinate arrays in *.csv* or *.npy* format can be loaded and interpolated as custom paths.

RTX Renderer and Post-processing Stack. Leveraging the NVIDIA RTX renderer with Omniverse Replicator, EndoX employs zero-copy data extraction, directly accessing GPU memory regions without CPU-mediated transfer to enable simultaneous extraction of multiple arbitrary output variables (AOV) in a single rendering pass, with multi-GPU load balancing for near-linear scaling. Custom image modalities requiring additional array operations are accelerated using NVIDIA Warp [18], which JIT-compiles Python functions to CUDA kernels, preserving the zero-copy pipeline until the final transfer to host memory to save rendered output. The post-processing stack can be configured to simulate optical imperfections common in clinical endoscopes—tone mapping, color correction, FFT bloom, chromatic aberration, vignetting, noise and film grain, and exposure control (Fig. 2B)—and can be combined for domain randomization across synthetic frames.

Sensor Modeling and Data Acquisition. The virtual sensor is fully configurable: camera intrinsics and light source properties are exposed as adjustable parameters (Fig. 2A). As a representative use case, we model a capsule endoscope to address the scarcity of capsule endoscopy datasets. Commercial capsule endoscopes have an angle of view ranging from 140 to 174°; here we adopt a 140-degree angle of view with 512×512 image resolution. Virtual light sources are configured and attached as child objects of the capsule. The configured capsule traverses the defined navigation path, capturing RGB and geometric modalities per frame, with its world transformation matrix recorded as ground-truth pose.

Rendered Image Modalities. Surface normals are extracted per frame and encoded in two coordinate systems. In the world coordinate system, the X, Y, Z normal components are mapped to the R, G, B channels, each linearly scaled from $[-1, 1]$ to $[0, 65\,535]$ as a 16-bit color image. For the camera coordinate system, world normals $\mathbf{n}_{\text{world}}$ are transformed via the camera rotation matrix $\mathbf{R}$ as $\mathbf{n}_{\text{camera}} = \mathbf{n}_{\text{world}}\mathbf{R}^\top$ and encoded identically. *Depth* is computed per-pixel by

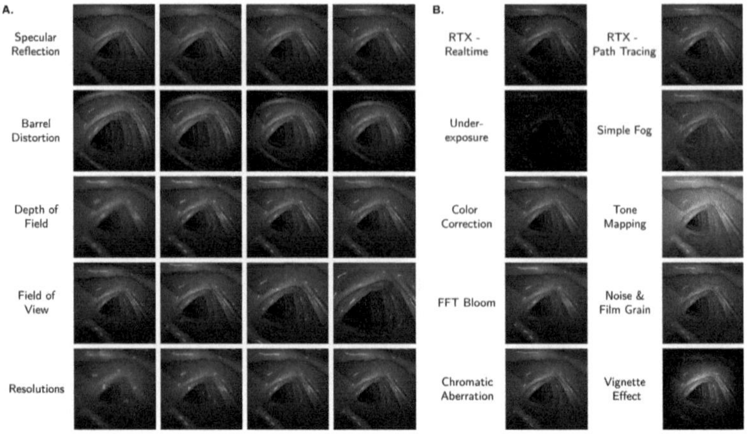

Fig. 2. A: Rendered views under varying camera intrinsics configurations using RTX Path Tracing renderer. B: Post-processing effects applied directly to the rendered views (RTX Path Tracing); RTX Real-Time mode shown for reference only.

normalizing the distance between the camera and the surface intersection point as $\text{Depth} = (d - d_{\text{near}})/(d_{\text{far}} - d_{\text{near}})$, where d is the distance from the camera to the ray–mesh intersection, and d_{near}, d_{far} are the near and far clipping planes. *Optical flow* quantifies per-pixel displacement between consecutive frames. For pixel (x, y), the motion vector is:

$$\mathbf{M}_{xy} = -\left[(\mathbf{T}_{xy,\text{curr}} + \mathbf{J}_{\text{curr}}) - (\mathbf{T}_{xy,\text{prev}} + \mathbf{J}_{\text{prev}})\right] \tag{1}$$

where $\mathbf{T}_{xy,\text{curr}}$ and $\mathbf{T}_{xy,\text{prev}}$ are screen-space pixel coordinates in the current and previous frames, and $\mathbf{J}_{\text{curr}}$, $\mathbf{J}_{\text{prev}}$ are projection jitter offsets in temporal anti-aliasing. This formulation corrects for the jitter, ensuring motion vectors reflect only actual scene and camera movement.

Computation of Occlusion Frames. Occlusion frames are computed as a custom post-processing modality to quantify scene visibility at each pixel. For each camera view, the near clipping plane is incrementally advanced from d_{near} to d_{far} in fixed steps. At each step, an 8-bit image encoding world-space positions is captured. The initial frame establishes a per-pixel reference (foreground). In subsequent frames, a pixel is considered occluded if its value differs from the reference beyond a tunable threshold ϵ and is not $(0, 0, 0)$ (background), indicating that a further mesh surface has become visible as d_{near} advances. The resulting binary occlusion map $C_{i,j}$, formalized as:

$$C_{i,j} = \begin{cases} 1 & \text{if } \exists\, k \in \{1, \ldots, N\} : \|\mathbf{p}_{k,i,j} - \mathbf{p}_{0,i,j}\| > \epsilon \text{ and } \mathbf{p}_{k,i,j} \neq \mathbf{0} \\ 0 & \text{otherwise} \end{cases} \tag{2}$$

where $\mathbf{p}_{k,i,j}$ is the world position at step k and pixel (i, j), $\mathbf{p}_{0,i,j}$ is the reference value, and N is the total number of near-plane advancements.

Table 1. Performance of depth estimation models trained with synthetic datasets.

	Metric3D v2			Monodepth2			EndoDAC		
	ES-U	SI	EndoX	ES-U	SI	EndoX	ES-U	SI	EndoX
RMSE ↓	**0.0082**	0.0798	0.0108	**0.0506**	0.1947	0.0539	**0.0477**	0.1247	0.0897
RMSLE ↓	0.0953	0.1992	**0.0680**	0.5405	0.7182	**0.3018**	0.5122	0.4129	**0.3238**
Abs. Rel. ↓	0.0682	0.1616	**0.0530**	0.5334	0.5375	**0.2611**	0.5066	0.3509	**0.2996**
Sq. Rel. ↓	**0.0007**	0.0122	0.0007	0.0324	0.0805	**0.0180**	**0.0285**	0.0347	0.0420
a1 ↑	0.9742	0.7347	**0.9875**	0.3262	0.2635	**0.5191**	0.3375	0.4926	**0.6051**
a2 ↑	0.9940	0.9772	**0.9999**	0.5891	0.5343	**0.8572**	0.6183	0.7820	**0.8436**
a3 ↑	0.9977	0.9941	**0.9999**	0.7765	0.7083	**0.9796**	0.8022	0.8916	**0.9352**

Computation of Coverage Maps. The coverage map records whether each mesh vertex is visible from the camera during traversal, computed via view–projection transforms and Z-buffer visibility testing. Each world-space vertex $\mathbf{v}_w = \begin{bmatrix} x\ y\ z\ 1 \end{bmatrix}$ is projected to normalized device coordinates (NDC) by $\mathbf{v}_{\text{NDC}} = \begin{bmatrix} x'\ y'\ z' \end{bmatrix}/w'$, where $\begin{bmatrix} x'\ y'\ z'\ w' \end{bmatrix} = \mathbf{v}_w VP$ with view matrix V and projection matrix P (row-vector convention), then mapped to screen space as $\mathbf{v}_{\text{screen}} = [\frac{W}{2}(x_{\text{ndc}} + 1),\ \frac{H}{2}(1 - y_{\text{ndc}})]$, where W and H are image dimensions in pixels. Mesh faces are rasterized via barycentric interpolation, and a Z-buffer $\mathcal{Z}$ (initialized to $+\infty$) is updated at each pixel (p_x, p_y) with the smallest encountered z. For each vertex v_i with projected depth z_i and screen position $(p_{x,i}, p_{y,i})$, the visibility boolean is defined with floating-point tolerance $\tau = 1 \times 10^{-8}$ as:

$$\gamma_i = \begin{cases} 1 & \text{if } |z_i - \mathcal{Z}(p_{x,i}, p_{y,i})| < \tau \\ 0 & \text{otherwise} \end{cases} \tag{3}$$

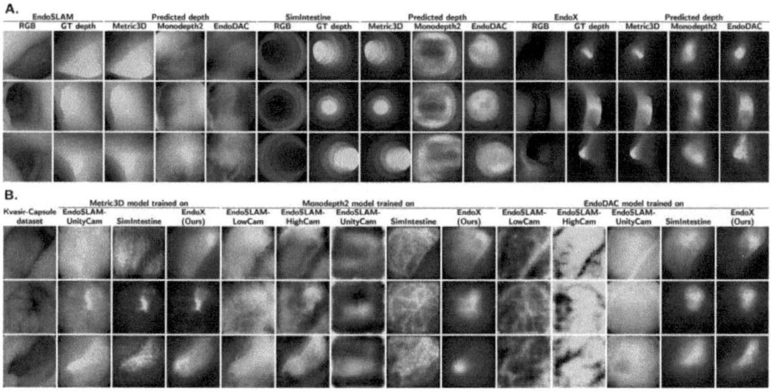

Fig. 3. A. Ground-truth and predicted depth maps of synthetically trained models evaluated on synthetic frames. B. Predicted depth maps of the models tested on clinical Kvasir-Capsule images.

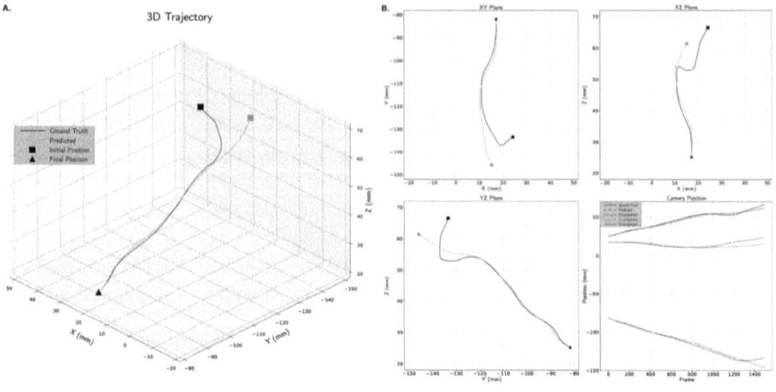

Fig. 4. Pose estimation results using Monodepth2 trained on EndoX small intestine data. A. 3D trajectories. B. 2D plane projections of trajectories and per-axis component comparison between ground-truth and predicted trajectories.

3 Evaluated Tasks and Results

Evaluation with Depth Estimation Models. Metric3D v2 [19], Monodepth2 [20], and EndoDAC [21] were each independently trained and evaluated on the small intestine frames from three synthetic datasets: EndoSLAM-UnityCam (ES-U), SimIntestine (SI), and EndoX. For each dataset, data were split 7:2 for training and testing, with a further 9:1 training/validation split; each model was trained on the training split of a given dataset and evaluated against the ground-truth depth maps of the corresponding test split. Performance is reported in Table 1 using standard error metrics and threshold accuracy a_i, defined as the percentage of pixels satisfying $\max(d_{\text{pred}}/d_{\text{gt}},\ d_{\text{gt}}/d_{\text{pred}}) < 1.25^i$ for $i \in \{1, 2, 3\}$.

Results confirm that EndoX synthetic data effectively supports depth estimation model training across both supervised and self-supervised paradigms. For Metric3D v2, EndoX achieves the lowest Abs. Rel. (0.053) and near-perfect a_1 (0.987). For Monodepth2 and EndoDAC, EndoX-trained models consistently yield the best threshold accuracies and relative errors, while ES-U retains marginal RMSE advantages. Across all architectures, EndoX performs strongly on relative and ratio-based metrics, suggesting that EndoX produces well-calibrated RGB–depth pairs suitable for depth learning. Predictions on synthetic frames compared against the ground truth are shown in Fig. 3A. Since ground-truth depth is unavailable for clinical capsule endoscopy, the trained models were qualitatively evaluated on the Kvasir-Capsule dataset [1] (Fig. 3B). The models trained on EndoX data produce smoother, higher-contrast depth maps with better structural detail preservation compared to those trained on EndoSLAM or SimIntestine data, indicating that EndoX closely approximates the visual characteristics of real endoscopic imagery.

Evaluation with Pose Estimation Model. Pose estimation was evaluated using Monodepth2 [20] trained on a 7,000-frame sequence from the EndoX small intestine dataset and tested on a separate 1,000-frame sequence. The predicted trajectory is compared against the ground-truth path in Fig. 4, showing both 3D and per-axis component decomposition. The predicted trajectory follows the ground truth, with an absolute trajectory error (ATE) of 3.92 mm. The per-component plots confirm that the model captures the dominant motion trends along each axis, though minor drift accumulates over the sequence. These results validate that EndoX synthetic data, with accurate camera pose annotations, provides a suitable training signal for self-supervised visual odometry in endoscopy.

Evaluation with 3D Reconstruction Technique. We evaluated 3D reconstruction on the EndoX small intestine dataset by projecting each pixel into 3D point clouds via Open3D using ground-truth depth and training a vanilla 3D Gaussian Splatting (3DGS) model. Novel views were rendered from held-out test poses and quantitatively compared against ground-truth frames. The model achieves a PSNR of 40.27 dB, SSIM of 0.978, and LPIPS of 0.231, confirming high photometric fidelity of the reconstructed scene. Representative novel-view rendering and per-pixel MAE loss map are shown in Fig. 5, with values in [0, 0.24] and an average MAE of 0.007 across test views. A video showing the rendered 3DGS is provided in the supplementary materials.

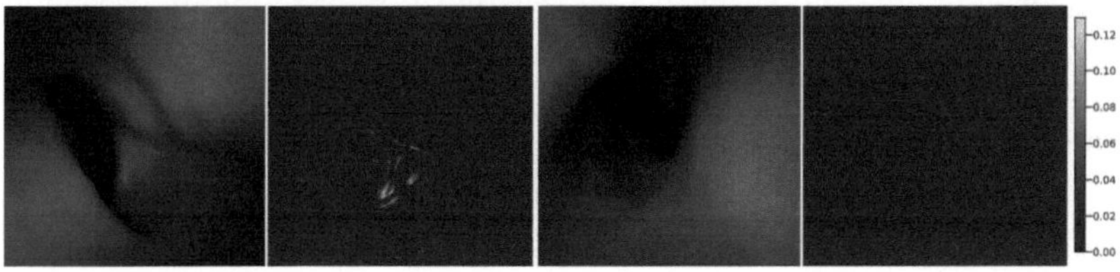

Fig. 5. Representative novel views by 3DGS models and corresponding loss maps.

Conclusion. We introduced EndoX, a framework integrating automated anatomical mesh reconstruction with a GPU-accelerated data processing pipeline to generate annotated endoscopic imagery. Evaluations on depth estimation, pose estimation, and 3DGS show that models trained on EndoX data achieve competitive accuracy and generalize to clinical capsule endoscopy.

4 Datasets and Distribution

The example scene in the sample dataset was reconstructed from CT colonography data (CC BY 3.0) [22], with the mesh surface texture adopted from VR-Caps [8]. For each video sequence, we provide: (i) a triangulated *3D mesh* reconstructed from CT data (Wavefront OBJ), and (ii) a vertex-wise *coverage map* in vertex indices array in .npz format; a video visualizing the coverage map is included in the supplementary materials. For every frame, we provide the annotations: *Depth*—distance from the camera plane to the surface, clamped to the near/far clipping planes (0.1–100 mm), linearly normalized, and encoded as a 16-bit grayscale image; *Surface normals*—reported in world and camera coordinates, with the X, Y, Z components stored in the R, G, B channels, each linearly mapped from $[-1, 1]$ to $[0, 65\,535]$ as a 16-bit color image; *Optical flow*—per-pixel displacement between consecutive frames, where the R and G channels encode X- and Y-direction motion (± 512 px), each linearly mapped to $[0, 65\,535]$ as a 16-bit color image (the first frame carries no flow value); *Occlusion*—an 8-bit binary mask within the 1–100 mm clipping range, with pixels occluding other mesh faces set to 255 and all others to 0; and *Camera pose*—per-frame world-space translation and rotation stored as `tx, ty, tz, qx, qy, qz, qw` (unit quaternion) in a text file.

Limitations. Quantitative evaluation of sim-to-real transfer on clinical capsule endoscopy was not performed, owing to the absence of suitable real-world datasets with ground-truth geometry. The sample datasets cover only the colon and small bowel as demo cases, though the framework supports any GI organ that can be reconstructed from CT. Pathology-bearing CT inputs are supported for generating imagery with clinical abnormalities; however, physical artifacts such as debris, blood, and surgical tools currently require manual scene authoring.

Disclosure of Interests. Kwan Tung Lam is an intern at NVIDIA Corporation. Ping Shu Ho and Ka Chun Cheung are employees of NVIDIA Corporation. The remaining author has no competing interests to declare that are relevant to the content of this article.

References

1. Smedsrud, P.H., et al.: Kvasir-Capsule, a video capsule endoscopy dataset. Sci. Data **8**, 142 (2021)
2. Le Floch, M., et al.: Galar - a large multi-label video capsule endoscopy dataset. Sci. Data **12**, 828 (2025)
3. Allan, M., et al.: Stereo correspondence and reconstruction of endoscopic data challenge. arXiv preprint arXiv:2101.01133 (2021)
4. Ozyoruk, K.B., et al.: EndoSLAM dataset and an unsupervised monocular visual odometry and depth estimation approach for endoscopic videos. Med. Image Anal. **71**, 102058 (2021)
5. Azagra, P., et al.: Endomapper dataset of complete calibrated endoscopy procedures. Sci. Data **10**, 671 (2023)
6. Bobrow, T.L., Golhar, M., Vijayan, R., Akshintala, V.S., Garcia, J.R., Durr, N.J.: Colonoscopy 3D video dataset with paired depth from 2D–3D registration. Med. Image Anal. **90**, 102956 (2023)
7. Golhar, M.V., Galeano Fretes, L.S., Ayers, L., Akshintala, V.S., Bobrow, T.L., Durr, N.J.: C3VDv2 - Colonoscopy 3D video dataset with enhanced realism. arXiv preprint arXiv:2506.24074 (2026)

8. İncetan, K., et al.: VR-Caps: a virtual environment for capsule endoscopy. Med. Image Anal. **70**, 101990 (2021)
9. Wang, Y., Long, Y., Fan, S.H., Dou, Q.: Neural rendering for stereo 3D reconstruction of deformable tissues in robotic surgery. In: International Conference on Medical Image Computing and Computer-Assisted Intervention (MICCAI) 2022. LNCS, vol. 13437, pp. 431–441. Springer, Cham (2022)
10. Singh, S., Bhaumik, B., Chatterjee, S.: SimIntestine: a synthetic dataset from virtual capsule endoscope. Med. Image Anal. **105**, 103706 (2025)
11. Martyniak, S., Kaleta, J., Dall'Alba, D., Naskret, M., Płotka, S., Korzeniowski, P.: SimuScope: realistic endoscopic synthetic dataset generation through surgical simulation and diffusion models. In: IEEE/CVF Winter Conference on Applications of Computer Vision (WACV) 2025, pp. 4268–4278. IEEE Press, New York (2025)
12. Rombach, R., Blattmann, A., Lorenz, D., Esser, P., Ommer, B.: High-resolution image synthesis with latent diffusion models. In: IEEE/CVF Conference on Computer Vision and Pattern Recognition (CVPR) 2022, pp. 10684–10695. IEEE Press, New York (2022)
13. He, Y., et al.: VISTA3D: a unified segmentation foundation model for 3D medical imaging. In: IEEE/CVF Conference on Computer Vision and Pattern Recognition (CVPR) 2025, pp. 20863–20873. IEEE Press, New York (2025)
14. Lorensen, W.E., Cline, H.E.: Marching cubes: a high resolution 3D surface construction algorithm. In: 14th Annual Conference on Computer Graphics and Interactive Techniques (SIGGRAPH 1987), pp. 163–169. ACM, New York (1987)
15. Schroeder, W., Martin, K., Lorensen, B.: The Visualization Toolkit, 4th edn. Kitware, New York (2006)
16. Antiga, L., Ene-Iordache, B., Remuzzi, A.: Centerline computation and geometric analysis of branching tubular surfaces with application to blood vessel modeling. In: 11th International Conference in Central Europe on Computer Graphics, Visualization and Computer Vision (WSCG), University of West Bohemia, Plzen (2003)
17. Izzo, R., Steinman, D., Manini, S., Antiga, L.: The vascular modeling toolkit: a python library for the analysis of tubular structures in medical images. J. Open Source Softw. **3**(25), 745 (2018)
18. Macklin, M.: Warp: a high-performance Python framework for GPU simulation and graphics. In: NVIDIA GPU Technology Conference (GTC) (2022)
19. Hu, M., et al.: Metric3Dv2: a versatile monocular geometric foundation model for zero-shot metric depth and surface normal estimation. IEEE Trans. Pattern Anal. Mach. Intell. **46**(12), 10579–10596 (2024)
20. Godard, C., Mac Aodha, O., Firman, M., Brostow, G.: Digging into self-supervised monocular depth estimation. In: IEEE/CVF International Conference on Computer Vision (ICCV) 2019, pp. 3827–3837. IEEE Press, New York (2019)
21. Cui, B., Islam, M., Bai, L., Wang, A., Ren, H.: EndoDAC: efficient adapting foundation model for self-supervised depth estimation from any endoscopic camera. In: International Conference on Medical Image Computing and Computer-Assisted Intervention (MICCAI) 2024. LNCS, vol. 15006, pp. 208–218. Springer, Cham (2024)
22. Smith, K., et al.: Data from CT colonography. The Cancer Imaging Archive (2015)

Fast Few-Shot Embolization Simulations in Ischemic Stroke Using Equivariant Neural Fields

Thijs P. Kuipers[1,2,3](✉), Mahsa Mojtahedi[3], Emiel D. den Haan[3], Praneeta R. Konduri[4], Henk A. Marquering[1,2], and Erik J. Bekkers[5]

[1] Department of Biomedical Engineering and Physics, Amsterdam UMC, Amsterdam, The Netherlands
t.p.kuipers@amsterdamumc.nl
[2] Department of Radiology and Nuclear Medicine, Amsterdam UMC, Amsterdam, The Netherlands
[3] inSteps B.V., Amsterdam, The Netherlands
[4] Stanford University, Stanford, USA
[5] Informatics Institute, University of Amsterdam, Amsterdam, The Netherlands

Abstract. Ischemic stroke is a leading cause of death and disability, in which rapid restoration of blood flow is critical to patient outcome. During embolization, the lodging location of the occluding clot within the cerebral vasculature strongly influences treatment difficulty, as clot stiffness, deformability, and vessel anatomy determine the clot retrievability during endovascular thrombectomy. High-fidelity finite-element method (FEM) simulations can simulate embolization, but their computational cost makes them impractical for real-time clinical use. We propose a fast and data-efficient meshless neural surrogate for simulating Lagrangian embolization dynamics. Our model predicts particle acceleration updates using SE(3)-equivariant neural fields, allowing training from sparsely sampled high-resolution simulations while supporting inference at full spatial resolution. By combining neural dynamics with rotation and translation equivariance, the surrogate generalizes across patient-specific vascular geometries using only 20 training simulations. On held-out test simulations, our approach achieves stable rollouts with a median error of 1.76 mm (Q1–Q3: 0.93–2.82), a median lodging error of 1.27 mm (0.77–1.42), corresponding to a median relative localization error of 1.8%, and a 200–400× speedup over FEM simulations, demonstrating both the accuracy and efficiency of our approach.

Keywords: neural dynamics · finite element method · implicit neural representation · digital twin · ischemic stroke

---

Supplementary Information The online version contains supplementary material available at https://doi.org/10.1007/978-3-032-38236-8_17.

G. Yang et al. (Eds.): MICCAI 2026, LNCS 16893, pp. 170–179, 2027.
https://doi.org/10.1007/978-3-032-38236-8_17

1 Introduction

Treating acute ischemic stroke (AIS) is a race against time: the brain loses an estimated 1.9 million neurons for every minute of untreated ischemia [19]. AIS occurs when a blood clot occludes an artery in the brain, preventing blood flow. In large-vessel occlusions, endovascular thrombectomy (EVT), in which the occluding clot is mechanically removed, is the standard of care. Clinical outcome is strongly time dependent, with the best recovery when the clot is removed in a single pass [8,23]. In addition, embolization, where the clot enters and subsequently lodges in the cerebral vasculature, plays an important role in determining downstream treatment difficulty and outcome. This phase determines factors including the clot's location, geometry, and mechanical state, all of which influence retrievability during EVT [7,16,22]. These factors vary substantially between patients, which has motivated the development of digital twins for patient-specific, in-silico modeling of endovascular treatment strategies and stroke progression [2,5,9]. Accurately capturing embolization, therefore, provides meaningful, patient-specific insight and establishes realistic initial conditions for subsequent EVT treatment simulations.

High-fidelity finite-element modeling (FEM) is capable of simulating EVT, including embolization, and can provide informative visualizations to support treatment planning [11,14]. However, the computational cost of FEM simulations makes them impractical for time-critical clinical use. Neural surrogate models offer a potential alternative by learning system dynamics directly from simulation data. Eulerian formulations, where physical quantities evolve on a fixed spatial mesh, have previously been used to model artery wall shear stress prediction [21] and cardiovascular flow simulations [17]. However, embolization is inherently a Lagrangian process, characterized by particles moving through space. Lagrangian neural models have been explored for particle and mesh-based dynamics [1,18], but these methods typically require large numbers of high-fidelity training simulations.

Embolization dynamics are equivariant to rigid body transformations, as rotating or translating the system does not alter clot–vessel interactions. We therefore propose a fast, meshless neural surrogate based on SE(3)-equivariant neural field representations, allowing for learning from sparsely sampled high-resolution simulations while supporting full-resolution inference. Our approach achieves strong generalization, outperforming state-of-the-art neural physics solvers X-MeshGraphNet [15] and Transolver++ [12], across patient-specific vascular geometries while being trained on only 20 reference simulations. Code is available.[1]

2 Method

The equivariant neural dynamics model follows an encoder-decoder design built from a single shared equivariant cross-attention block: the encoder maps the

[1] https://github.com/ThijsKuipers1995/neural_clot_sim.

particle state to a compact latent representation, and the decoder queries this latent state to compute clot accelerations. An overview is shown in Fig. 1.

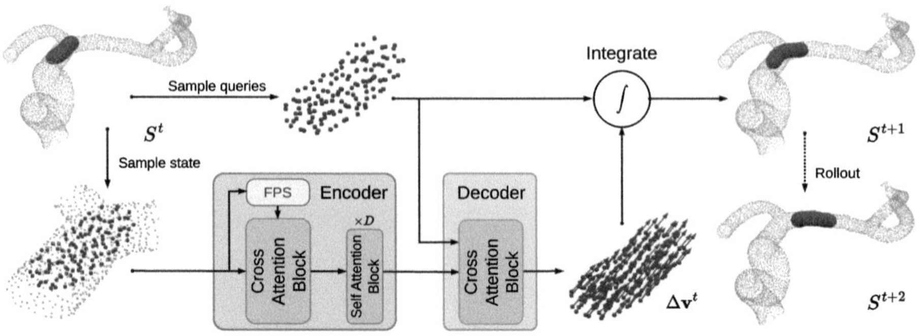

Fig. 1. Given the full system state S^t, we first perform spatial subsampling and discard vessel nodes located more than 2 mm away from the clot. The reduced state is encoded via cross-attention and farthest point sampling (FPS) to obtain a latent state. Subsequently, a decoder predicts velocity increments $\Delta\mathbf{v}^t$ for query points sampled on the clot volume and integrates them to advance the system to the next state S^{t+1}.

2.1 Problem Formulation

We consider a discrete-time Lagrangian particle system for simulating clot dynamics within a blood vessel. At each time step t, the system state is represented as a point cloud:

$$\mathcal{S}^t = \{(\mathbf{x}_i^t, \mathbf{v}_i^t, \mathbf{u}_i^t))\}_{i=1}^N, \tag{1}$$

where $\mathbf{x}_i^t \in \mathbb{R}^3$ and $\mathbf{v}_i^t \in \mathbb{R}^3$ are the particle positions and velocities, and $\mathbf{u}_i^t = P(\mathbf{x}_i^t)$ is a precomputed pressure-driven flow field. Particles are divided into static nodes and dynamic nodes that evolve. The system evolves with a fixed timestep ($\Delta t = 1$). Our objective is to learn a function:

$$f_\theta : S_t \mapsto \{\Delta\mathbf{v}_i^t\}_{i=1}^N, \tag{2}$$

that predicts per-particle velocity increments given the current state. State updates are performed using a first-order Euler integration scheme:

$$\mathbf{v}^{t+1} = \mathbf{v}^t + \Delta\mathbf{v}^t \quad \text{and} \quad \mathbf{x}^{t+1} = \mathbf{x}^t + \mathbf{v}^{t+1}. \tag{3}$$

2.2 Embolization Simulations

We construct two embolization simulation datasets: a high-fidelity dataset with complex vascular geometries, and a simplified dataset with tapering tube geometries featuring a single 180-degree bend.

Complex Vessel Dataset. We performed high-fidelity FEM simulations in Abaqus (SIMULIA, Providence, RI) of large vessel occlusion with varying cerebral vessel geometries. A 10 mm clot enters the internal carotid artery (ICA) and lodges in the proximal or distal segment of the first branch of the middle cerebral artery (MCA-M1). Clots are modeled using a Hyperfoam material formulation with parameters selected following prior computational thrombectomy studies [4,13]. Clot entry and lodging are driven by a constant pressure load of 0.002 MPa. Vessel geometries are rigid and generated as described in [10]. Each simulation consists of 195 states and approximately 27000 nodes, and requires 30–60 min on an AMD Ryzen 9 9950X3D 16-core CPU.

Simple Bent Tube Dataset. We additionally construct a simplified tube dataset consisting of 20 simulations of a bent cylindrical vessel in which the clot lodges at a single curvature. Each simulation contains 80 timesteps and 1000 nodes. This controlled setting serves as a sanity check to verify baseline behavior. It is not used for model selection or tuning.

2.3 SE(3)-Equivariant Neural Dynamics

The core of the proposed model is a G-equivariant kernelized cross-attention operator, which we adapt from [6]. For G, we consider the platonic subgroups of SO(3). For an input sequence of length N and feature dimension d, feature ($\mathbf{H}$) and coordinate ($\mathbf{X}$) tensors are defined over the group:

$$\mathbf{H} \in \mathbb{R}^{|G|\times N\times d}, \quad \mathbf{X} \in \mathbb{R}^{|G|\times N\times 3}. \tag{4}$$

Given query and context tensors $(\mathbf{H}_q, \mathbf{X}_q)$ and $(\mathbf{H}_c, \mathbf{X}_c)$, cross-attention is computed independently for each group element $g \in G$ in parallel using kernelized attention [3], which makes computation time scale linearly with the context length:

$$\text{Attn}(\mathbf{H}_q, \mathbf{X}_q; \mathbf{H}_c, \mathbf{X}_c) = \frac{1}{N_c} \bigoplus_{g\in G} \mathbf{Q}^g((\mathbf{K}^g)^\top V^g), \tag{5}$$

where $\bigoplus$ denotes concatenation along the group dimension and $(\cdot)^g \in \mathbb{R}^{N\times d}$ denotes tensors in the reference frame corresponding to group element g. The query, key, and value tensors are defined as:

$$\mathbf{Q}^g = \text{RoPE}(\phi_q(\mathbf{H}_q)^g, \mathbf{X}_q^g), \quad \mathbf{K}^g = \text{RoPE}(\mathbf{1}, \mathbf{X}_c^g), \quad \mathbf{V}^g = \phi_c(\mathbf{H}_c)^g. \tag{6}$$

Here, ϕ_q and ϕ_c are learnable equivariant linear projections and $\mathbf{1}$ denotes a tensor of ones. Rotary positional embeddings (RoPE) [20] inject relative geometric information, ensuring translation equivariance. Because the keys depend only on coordinates, information propagation is guided by the system's geometry.

Importantly, the attention operator retains the original kernelized attention form. Equivariance is induced by evaluating shared embeddings across transformed group elements. This weight-sharing constrains the operator to be G-equivariant, preserving the original computation graph, and inducing equivariance without additional computational overhead. When $q = c$, Eq. 5 reduces to the self-attention. We construct attention blocks containing one equivariant attention layer followed by an equivariant two-layer MLP with GeLU activation using pre-layer normalization.

Encoder. At time t, the input state $\mathcal{S}^t$ consists of a sequence of N node coordinates ($\mathbf{x}_i^t$), scalar features (one-hot encoded node types distinguishing clot and vessel nodes), and vector features (velocity $\mathbf{v}_i^t$, flow $\mathbf{u}_i^t$, and zero-mean mesh-space coordinates $\mathbf{x}_i^{t=0}$). Vector features transform under rotations, whereas scalars remain invariant. Coordinates and vector features are lifted by rotating them for each $g \in G$. Scalars are copied across G. The input state is first downsampled to $M < N$ latent points using farthest point sampling, ensuring uniform geometric coverage. The latent state is obtained using a single cross-attention block (Eq. 5) with the downsampled points as queries and the full-resolution state as context. The latent state is then updated using a sequence of D self-attention blocks.

Decoder and Neural Field Dynamics. To predict per-particle velocity increments $\Delta\mathbf{v}^t$, query points are sampled from the clot domain at time t. Query features consist of the same scalar and vector quantities as in the encoder and are lifted to G accordingly. A single cross-attention block updates these queries using the latent dynamics state as context, defining a neural field representation of the system dynamics. The resulting equivariant features are projected back to $\mathbb{R}^3$ to obtain $\Delta\mathbf{v}^t$, which are integrated using Eq. 3.

2.4 Implementation and Training Details

The model uses the tetrahedral subgroup of SO(3) with $|G| = 12$ rotations and two attention heads per group element. We use 768 channels (32 channels per head). The encoder consists of $D = 1$ equivariant self-attention blocks. Input states are first sampled from the full simulation state by uniformly sampling 512 vessel nodes and 1536 clot nodes. Latent states consist of $M = 512$ points. During training, 2048 query points are sampled to predict velocity increments. Clot-vessel interactions are restricted to vessel nodes within radius $r = 2$ mm of clot nodes to introduce locality and improve computational efficiency. During training, both input states and queries are augmented with Gaussian noise with a standard deviation of 1×10^{-4}. The data is augmented with random rotations during training for all models, including baselines. Models are trained for 1000 epochs with batch size 8 using AdamW, an initial learning rate of 5×10^{-6}, cosine decay to 1×10^{-6}, and linear warmup during the first 10 epochs. We use mean squared error loss. Input features are scaled by a factor of 0.5. The 30 vessel simulations are split into 20 development cases and 10 held-out test cases. Five-fold cross-validation is performed on the development set using a 16/4 train/validation split. The final model is trained on all 20 development simulations and evaluated on the test set. The simple tube dataset uses a 13/1/6 train/val/test split. Models are trained on an NVIDIA RTX 5070 GPU.

3 Experiments and Results

We evaluate the predictive accuracy, rollout stability, computational efficiency, and generalization across vessel geometries. Model selection is performed via five-fold cross-validation, followed by comparison to established neural physics solver baselines on a held-out test set and additional analyses of robustness and out-of-domain behavior. During inference, rollouts stop when the clot's 10-step average velocity falls below 0.05 mm/Δt, indicating that it has lodged.

Model Validation: 5-Fold Cross-Validation. We assess the effect of rotational equivariance by comparing the proposed SE(3)-equivariant model to a translation-equivariant variant. Performance is evaluated using three metrics on the vessel dataset. The per-step root mean squared error (RMSE) measures one-step prediction accuracy by comparing predictions computed from the reference state at each timestep of the simulation. The rollout RMSE quantifies error accumulation when the model is iteratively applied to generate the full trajectory and assesses simulation stability. Lodging error is the Euclidean distance between the final predicted and reference clot positions. RMSEs are averaged over three seeds per trajectory and across trajectories within each fold.

The final results are reported as median (Q1–Q3) across folds in Table 1. Both models achieve comparable per-step RMSE, while the SE(3)-equivariant model yields substantially lower rollout and lodging errors, indicating improved rollout stability. Our model achieves a full-resolution rollout in approximately 8 s, corresponding to a 200–400× speedup when compared to the high-fidelity FEM simulations.

Table 1. Cross-validation results comparing SE(3)-equivariant and translation-equivariant models. Values are median (Q1-Q3) in mm across five folds, with RMSEs averaged over three seeds per trajectory. Best results in **bold**.

Equivariance	Per-step RMSE	Rollout RMSE	Lodging Error
Translation	**0.12** (0.11–0.13)	3.39 (3.18–4.29)	6.70 (3.05–7.32)
SE(3)	0.14 (0.12–0.14)	**2.33** (2.11–2.36)	**3.69** (2.35–5.45)

Test-Set Comparison to Baselines. We evaluate on held-out simulations from both the simple tube and complex vessel datasets. We compare against two state-of-the-art neural physics solvers: X-MeshGraphNet [15] (MGN) and Transolver++ [12]. Baselines and training details are adapted from their original implementations and tuned on the validation sets. MGN uses a single scale 5-nearest-neighbor graph augmented with explicit clot-vessel interaction edges, 12 message-passing layers with 128 channels. Transolver++ uses 5 attention blocks with 8 heads with 256 channels.

Table 2. Comparison of baseline models on the test set. We report the median as well as the interquartile range (Q1-Q3) in mm calculated over all test trajectories and three different seeds. Best results in **bold**. (MGN: X-MeshGraphNet).

Dataset	Model	Per-step RMSE	Rollout RMSE	Lodging Error
Tube	MGN	0.12 (0.11–0.14)	**0.24** (0.23–0.25)	0.40 (0.35–0.45)
	Transolver++	**0.05** (0.05–0.07)	0.44 (0.41–0.45)	0.48 (0.26–0.61)
	Ours	0.24 (0.24–0.25)	1.09 (1.09–1.10)	**0.39** (0.35–0.45)
Vessel	MGN	0.10 (0.08–0.13)	5.12 (3.87–5.65)	18.0 (16.5–23.8)
	Transolver++	**0.07** (0.06–0.9)	3.34 (2.59–5.15)	17.7 (11.7–23.1)
	Ours	0.14 (0.13–0.16)	**1.76** (0.93–2.82)	**1.27** (0.77–1.42)

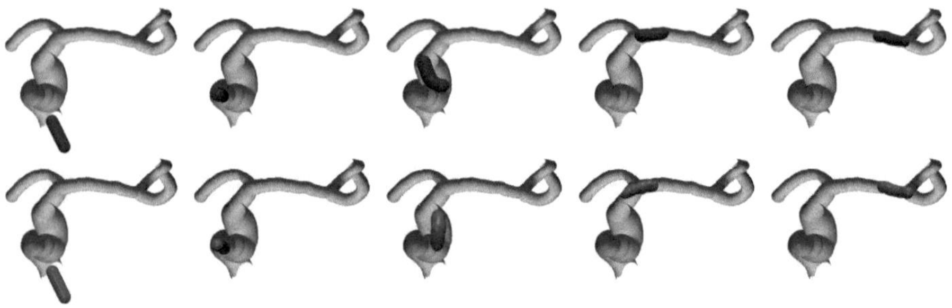

Fig. 2. Rollout trajectory of the clot (length: 10 mm) within the vessel. The predicted rollout is shown in red, while the reference (ground truth) trajectory is shown in green.

We report our results in Table 2, with a representative rollout shown in Fig. 2. On the tube dataset, all methods perform well. On the vessel dataset, Transolver++ maintains the lowest per-step error, while our method achieves substantially lower rollout and lodging errors than both baselines. The median lodging error of 1.27 mm corresponds to approximately 1.8% of the total clot trajectory length. We note that the baseline models exhibit instabilities during all rollouts on the vessel dataset, including clipping through the vessel wall and partial clot fragmentation. In contrast, these instabilities are absent in our model, although one out of the ten trajectories showed consistent early lodging. Because the model depends on stochastic input states, we assess stability across three seeds using the mean pairwise Euclidean distance. Rollouts with different seeds differ on average by 1.02 mm (SD 1.14 mm).

Out-of-Domain Geometries. We assess generalization to unseen vessel geometries using three out-of-domain tubes: short (20 mm), sine (200 mm), and straight (160 mm). The short and sine tubes taper from 2.5 mm to 0.2 mm, while the straight tube maintains a constant radius of 2.5 mm. We evaluate whether the model lodges the clot earlier, later, or not at all, and whether lodging is driven by geometric narrowing rather than implicit velocity thresholds.

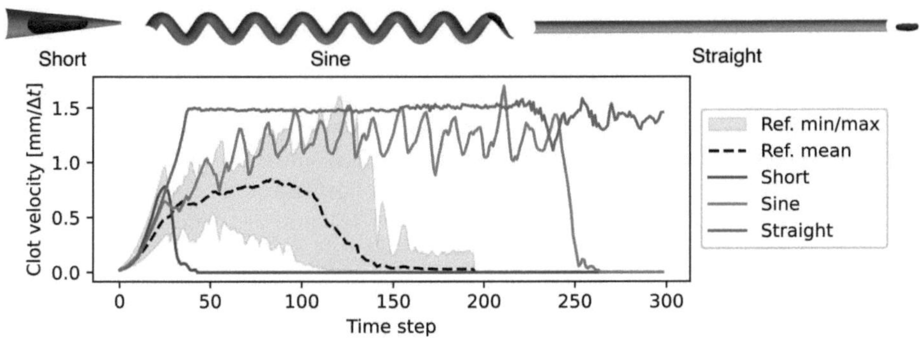

Fig. 3. Out-of-domain geometries (short, sine, and straight) with predicted clot rollouts that induce significantly different velocity profiles than seen in the training set.

Results are shown in Fig. 3. In the short and sine tubes, the model successfully lodges the clot (velocity goes to zero), occurring notably earlier and later than in the training set. No lodging occurs in the straight tube, as expected. Notably, for the sine tube, the number of velocity oscillations matches the number of geometric extrema, indicating a direct coupling between vessel curvature and clot dynamics. The sine and straight tubes require substantially longer rollouts (250–300 steps) than the reference simulations (130–160 steps), demonstrating stable long-horizon behavior, as well as generalization to out-of-domain geometries.

4 Discussion and Conclusion

We have presented a data-efficient, meshless neural surrogate for simulating Lagrangian dynamics of embolization in ischemic stroke. Our validation experiments demonstrate that explicitly incorporating SE(3) equivariance substantially improves long-horizon stability. While per-step errors are similar to a translation-equivariant variant, the equivariant model better captures the coupled interactions between clot and vessel, which are highly sensitive to small perturbations in position and velocity. By enforcing rotational and translational symmetry, the model generalizes across different orientations and positions of the system, resulting in more robust rollouts and more accurate clot lodging even with only 20 training simulations.

Comparisons to state-of-the-art neural physics solvers further highlight the importance of equivariance for long-horizon stability in a few-shot setting. Both MGN and Transolver++ achieved low per-step errors on both datasets. Despite successfully simulating the simple dataset, the baselines do not reliably lodge the clot on the complex vessel dataset. It seems that their lack of explicit constraints on rotational symmetry prevents these models from accurately capturing the intricate interactions between the clot and vessel. This leads to error accumulation over time and unstable rollouts. In contrast, our model demonstrates physically plausible behavior across diverse and out-of-distribution vessel geometries, including long trajectories and correct clot lodging driven by geometric constraints rather than implicit velocity thresholds.

While our approach demonstrates strong performance in a few-shot regime, we do not assess how well it scales with larger training datasets. Additionally, although the model can perform rollouts at full resolution, it still relies on a fixed-resolution encoding of the input state. The current simulation setup uses a single set of clot mechanical parameters and a constant, clot-independent pressure field. Addressing these limitations and extending our model to include additional stages of the EVT treatment are important next steps toward full in-silico treatment simulation.

Overall, our results indicate that meshless, SE(3)-equivariant neural field dynamics can efficiently capture the complex clot–vessel interactions that determine lodging and trajectory, providing accurate, robust predictions in a few-shot regime. Our approach enables fast, patient-specific simulations of embolization in ischemic stroke and lays the groundwork for future extensions to full neural treatment modeling.

Acknowledgments. This project has received funding from the European Union's Horizon Europe research and innovation programme under grant agreement No 101136438 (GEMINI project). This publication reflects only the author's view and the European Commission is not responsible for any use that may be made of the information it contains.

Disclosure of Interests. Authors Thijs P. Kuipers, Mahsa Mojtahedi, and Emiel D. den Haan were employed by inSteps B.V. during the conduct of this work. Henk A. Marquering owns stock in inSteps B.V. and Nicolab B.V. Praneeta R. Konduri owns stock in inSteps B.V.

References

1. Alkin, B., Fürst, A., Schmid, S., Gruber, L., Holzleitner, M., Brandstetter, J.: Universal physics transformers: a framework for efficiently scaling neural operators. Adv. Neural. Inf. Process. Syst. **37**, 25152–25194 (2024)
2. Chaparro-Cárdenas, S.L., et al.: A technological review of digital twins and artificial intelligence for personalized and predictive healthcare. In: Healthcare, vol. 13, p. 1763. MDPI (2025)
3. Choromanski, K., et al.: Rethinking attention with performers. arXiv preprint arXiv:2009.14794 (2020)
4. Fregona, V., et al.: Impact of thrombus composition on virtual thrombectomy procedures using human clot analogues mechanical data. J. Mech. Behav. Biomed. Mater. **163**, 106886 (2025)
5. Hoekstra, A.G., Marquering, H., GEMINI consortium https://dth-gemini.eu/team/: Towards a generation of digital twins in healthcare of ischaemic and haemorrhagic stroke. In: International Conference on Computational Science, pp. 239–245. Springer (2024)
6. Islam, M.M., et al.: Platonic transformers: a solid choice for equivariance. arXiv preprint arXiv:2510.03511 (2025)

7. Johnson, S., et al.: Mechanical behavior of in vitro blood clots and the implications for acute ischemic stroke treatment. J. Neurointerv. Surg. **12**(9), 853–857 (2020)
8. Kang, D.H., et al.: Effects of first pass recanalization on outcomes of contact aspiration thrombectomy. J. NeuroInterv. Surg. **12**(5), 466–470 (2020)
9. Katsoulakis, E., et al.: Digital twins for health: a scoping review. NPJ Digit. Med. **7**(1), 77 (2024)
10. Kuipers, T.P., Konduri, P.R., Marquering, H., Bekkers, E.J.: Generating cerebral vessel trees of acute ischemic stroke patients using conditional set-diffusion. In: Medical Imaging with Deep Learning (2024)
11. Liu, R., Jin, C., Wang, L., Yang, Y., Fan, Y., Wang, W.: Simulation of stent retriever thrombectomy in acute ischemic stroke by finite element analysis. Comput. Methods Biomech. Biomed. Engin. **25**(7), 740–749 (2022)
12. Luo, H., et al.: Transolver++: an accurate neural solver for PDEs on million-scale geometries. arXiv preprint arXiv:2502.02414 (2025)
13. Luraghi, G., et al.: Combined stent-retriever and aspiration intra-arterial thrombectomy performance for fragmentable blood clots: a proof-of-concept computational study. J. Mech. Behav. Biomed. Mater. **135**, 105462 (2022)
14. Luraghi, G., et al.: The first virtual patient-specific thrombectomy procedure. J. Biomech. **126**, 110622 (2021)
15. Nabian, M.A., Liu, C., Ranade, R., Choudhry, S.: X-meshgraphnet: scalable multi-scale graph neural networks for physics simulation. arXiv preprint arXiv:2411.17164 (2024)
16. Patki, P., Simon, S., Manning, K.B., Costanzo, F.: Computational analysis of effects of clot length on acute ischemic stroke recanalization under different cyclic aspiration loading conditions. Int. J. Numer. Methods Biomed. Eng. **39**(2), e3667 (2023)
17. Pegolotti, L., et al.: Learning reduced-order models for cardiovascular simulations with graph neural networks. Comput. Biol. Med. **168**, 107676 (2024)
18. Pfaff, T., Fortunato, M., Sanchez-Gonzalez, A., Battaglia, P.: Learning mesh-based simulation with graph networks. In: International Conference on Learning Representations (2020)
19. Saver, J.L.: Time is brain—quantified. Stroke **37**(1), 263–266 (2006)
20. Su, J., Ahmed, M., Lu, Y., Pan, S., Bo, W., Liu, Y.: Roformer: enhanced transformer with rotary position embedding. Neurocomputing **568**, 127063 (2024)
21. Suk, J., de Haan, P., Lippe, P., Brune, C., Wolterink, J.M.: Mesh neural networks for se (3)-equivariant hemodynamics estimation on the artery wall. Comput. Biol. Med. **173**, 108328 (2024)
22. Vandelanotte, S., et al.: Association between thrombus composition and first-pass recanalization after thrombectomy in acute ischemic stroke. J. Thromb. Haemost. **22**(9), 2555–2561 (2024)
23. Zaidat, O.O., et al.: First pass effect: a new measure for stroke thrombectomy devices. Stroke **49**(3), 660–666 (2018)

Fine-Grained Cerebrovascular Parsing in DSA via Structurally-Grounded Semantic Disentanglement

Kai Zhu[1,2], Le Cao[3], Li Chen[1], Jun Cheng[4], Lei Mou[2(✉)], and Yitian Zhao[2(✉)]

[1] Wuhan University of Science and Technology, Wuhan, China
[2] Laboratory of Advanced Theranostic Materials and Technology, Ningbo Institute of Materials Technology and Engineering, Chinese Academy of Sciences, Ningbo, China
{moulei,yitian.zhao}@nimte.ac.cn
[3] West China Hospital of Sichuan University, Chengdu, China
[4] Institute for Infocomm Research (I2R), Agency for Science, Technology and Research (A*STAR), Singapore, Singapore

Abstract. Accurate quantitative cerebrovascular assessment and clinical intervention rely fundamentally on vessel parsing in Digital Subtraction Angiography (DSA) to segment and distinctly label the vascular tree. However, the intricate vascular topology, pronounced vessel overlap, and inconsistent contrast enhancement inherent in DSA present formidable obstacles; consequently, most existing works have been limited to binary vessel segmentation, overlooking the fine-grained anatomical categorization required for detailed clinical analysis. To address this, we propose AngioParse, a multi-encoder collaborative framework explicitly designed for fine-grained vascular parsing. AngioParse ensures parsing precision through three key mechanisms: (1) a dual-stream encoder synergy module that improves localization accuracy by fusing a high-recall global binary prior with fine-grained anatomical features from heterogeneous encoders; (2) a self-consistent structural grounding mechanism that regularizes fine-grained parsing with a high-recall binary vascular prior by constraining the union of anatomical-wise predictions to lie within the vessel support, improving connectivity and topological validity; and (3) a decoupled orthogonal prediction module that enhances class discrimination by separating multi-target learning into parallel branches to minimize feature confusion. Experiments on a public DSA dataset demonstrate that AngioParse not only achieves state-of-the-art segmentation performance but also exhibits superior capability in accurately parsing and differentiating six distinct vascular categories. The code is available at https://github.com/kylechuuuuu/AngioParse.git.

Keywords: DSA · Vascular Parsing · Multi-Encoder Fusion

G. Yang et al. (Eds.): MICCAI 2026, LNCS 16893, pp. 180–189, 2027.
https://doi.org/10.1007/978-3-032-38236-8_18

1 Introduction

Digital Subtraction Angiography (DSA) stands as the clinical gold standard for visualizing cerebrovascular architecture, offering the high-fidelity spatial resolution essential for the diagnosis and management of neurovascular disorders [6]. Beyond mere visualization, as shown in Fig. 1(a-b), the clinical utility of DSA relies on the anatomical categorization of the vascular tree into several distinct functional segments, including the carotid artery (CA), vertebral artery (VA), anterior cerebral artery (ACA), middle cerebral artery (MCA), posterior cerebral artery (PCA), and others, as depicted in Fig. 1(c). This fine-grained parcellation is clinically pivotal, as specific vascular segments dictate disparate therapeutic protocols and prognostic outcomes.

Despite the clinical necessity of semantic parsing, current automated analysis of DSA images has remained predominantly focused on binary vascular segmentation. These approaches aim to extract the geometric structure of the vessel tree from complex background, with state-of-the-art models [1,5,9,11,20] achieving high fidelity in pixel-wise extraction. However, these methods typically stop at the structural level, restricted to coarse categorizations such as distinguishing major arteries from peripheral branches [16,19] or binary artery-vein separation [14]. Consequently, there remains a significant semantic gap between these binary vascular maps and the comprehensive anatomical parsing required for advanced clinical workflows.

The tendency of existing research to prioritize segmentation over parsing is largely driven by the inherent complexity of the cerebrovascular hierarchy and the formidable challenges of resolving it in 2D space. The projective superposition of 3D vascular hierarchies onto 2D planes creates a profound disconnect between local visual morphology and global anatomical identity. Tortuous branching patterns and pronounced overlaps obscure clear delineation, creating ambiguities where segments share similar local textures but possess distinct anatomical identities. Current models, lacking the global topological constraints required to resolve these conflicts, fail to distinguish these overlapping structures. As a result, the labor-intensive and subjective manual identification of these segments remains the bottleneck, underscoring the urgent demand for automated parsing solutions capable of overcoming these projective ambiguities.

To address the limitations of existing binary segmentation methods in meeting clinical diagnostic needs, we propose AngioParse, a novel framework that redefines cerebrovascular parsing as a task of structure-aware semantic disentanglement. By reconciling the discord between 2D visual morphology and 3D anatomical identity, AngioParse directly addresses the bottlenecks of projective overlap and vessel fragmentation that hinder automated clinical workflows. The main contributions of this work are summarized as follows:

- We propose AngioParse, the first framework dedicated to closing the semantic gap between binary vessel extraction and fine-grained anatomical parsing. By synergizing global morphological cues with local anatomical signatures, it enables the precise categorization of the cerebrovascular tree into six clinically distinct functional segments.

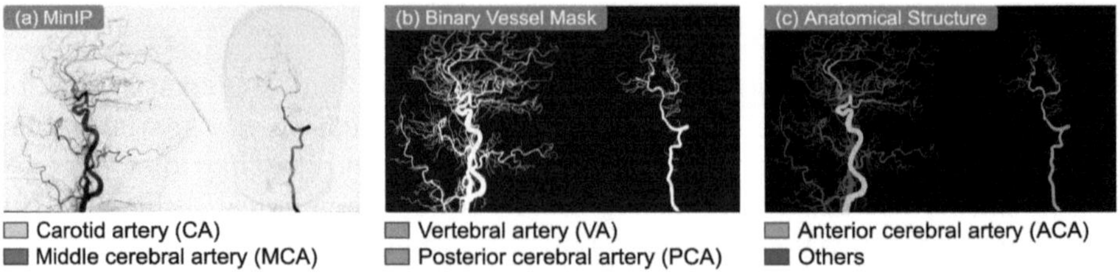

Fig. 1. Visualization of cerebrovascular complexities and vasculature parsing: (a) Minimum intensity projection (MinIP) of a DSA sequence; (b) the corresponding binary vessel mask; and (c) vasculature parsing into distinct anatomical structures.

- We introduce a self-consistent structural grounding strategy to maintain the topological continuity of individual arterial segments. By enforcing prior-guided consistency between the global vascular tree and local anatomical predictions, it mitigates vessel fragmentation, ensuring that parsed segments remain topologically valid for downstream clinical quantification.
- We propose an orthogonal semantic disentanglement module to resolve the projective ambiguity inherent in 2D DSA. By enforcing feature orthogonality in the latent space, it minimizes semantic confusion at vessel crossovers, effectively disentangling overlapping arteries to ensure high-fidelity anatomical labeling.

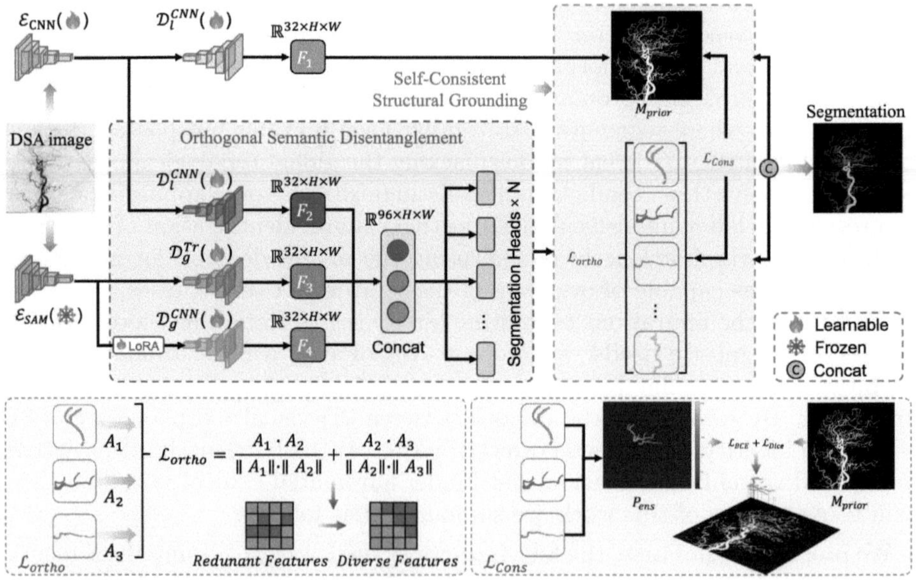

Fig. 2. Architecture of the proposed AngioParse.

2 Method

The proposed AngioParse is a structure-aware framework that reconciles morphological anchors with anatomical signatures through a dual-pathway architecture. It primarily consists of two core components: self-consistent structural grounding (SCSG) and orthogonal semantic disentanglement (OSD). The overall pipeline is illustrated in Fig. 2.

2.1 Self-Consistent Structural Grounding

The SCSG structure enforces self-consistency between the decoupled anatomical predictions and a global binary vascular prior. This coupling improves anatomical parsing in two aspects: it strengthens the spatial localization of each label and preserves topological agreement with the overall vessel tree. In DSA parsing, a common failure mode is spatial confusion, where pixels of one anatomical segment can be spuriously activated at distant locations due to projective overlap and morphological similarity. We specifically design the binary stream to favor high recall, ensuring it captures the complete vascular topology to serve as a reliable anchor for the subsequent parsing branches.

To handle the diverse shapes and scales of vascular structures, we employ a hybrid multi-encoder stream that integrates complementary architectural priors. Given an input DSA image X, a CNN-based encoder ($\mathcal{E}_{CNN}$) leverages local inductive biases to extract fine-grained feature representations F_{local}. Simultaneously, we utilize a SAM2 [12] encoder to capture long-range structural dependencies. By injecting LoRA [7] into the frozen SAM2 encoder, we generate a domain-aligned global representation F_{global}. The feature extraction process is formulated as:

$$F_{local} = \mathcal{E}_{CNN}(X), \quad F_{global} = \mathcal{E}_{SAM}(X; \theta_{lora}), \tag{1}$$

where θ_{lora} denotes the trainable adapter parameters. F_{local} preserves high-resolution edge details essential for boundary delineation, while F_{global} encapsulates the high-level topology of the cerebrovascular tree.

These heterogeneous representations are subsequently processed through distinct decoding pathways. The local features F_{local} are decoded by a binary decoder $\mathcal{D}_{CNN}$ into a holistic vessel prior M_{prior}, which serves as a structural anchor delineating the valid vascular support:

$$M_{prior} = \sigma(\mathcal{D}_{CNN}(F_{local})), \tag{2}$$

where σ denotes the sigmoid activation. Conversely, the global features F_{global} guide the OSD module to generate decoupled anatomical-wise probability maps $\{A_i\}_{i=1}^{N}$ for the N anatomical structures.

Finally, to enforce coherence between the binary prior and anatomical-wise predictions, we introduce a self-consistent grounding constraint requiring the union of anatomical-wise probabilities to agree with the vessel support indicated by M_{prior}. Since OSD outputs N parallel sigmoid maps, we aggregate them into an ensemble probability P_{ens}. Under the mild assumption that different anatomy heads are approximately decorrelated (encouraged by Orthogonality Loss in Sec. 2.2), we use a probabilistic noisy-OR to approximate the union:

$$P_{ens} = 1 - \prod_{i=1}^{N}(1 - A_i). \quad (3)$$

We constrain P_{ens} to match the high-recall vessel prior via a consistency loss:

$$\mathcal{L}_{Cons} = \mathcal{L}_{BCE}(P_{ens}, M_{prior}) + \mathcal{L}_{Dice}(P_{ens}, M_{prior}). \quad (4)$$

This alignment suppresses anatomy predictions outside the vascular support and stabilizes fine-grained parsing to remain structurally consistent.

2.2 Orthogonal Semantic Disentanglement

The OSD module is designed to alleviate semantic ambiguity induced by 2D projective overlaps by disentangling anatomical structures in a decoupled latent space. Given the local encoder feature F_{local} and the global grounding feature F_{global}, OSD first performs multi-branch decoding to obtain complementary, spatially aligned representations. Specifically, we employ three parallel decoders: a local CNN decoder ($\mathcal{D}_l^{CNN}$) and two global decoders, one CNN-based ($\mathcal{D}_g^{CNN}$) and one Transformer-based ($\mathcal{D}_g^{Tr}$), to capture both fine boundary details and long-range topology cues. Each decoder projects features to a common dimension $\mathbb{R}^{32\times H\times W}$. The three decoded features are then concatenated to form a diverse fused representation $P \in \mathbb{R}^{96\times H\times W}$:

$$P = \text{Concat}\big(\mathcal{D}_l^{CNN}(F_{local}),\ \mathcal{D}_g^{CNN}(F_{global}),\ \mathcal{D}_g^{Tr}(F_{global})\big). \quad (5)$$

This design preserves high-frequency vessel boundaries from the local stream while injecting global, topology-aware context from the grounding stream, which is crucial for resolving overlaps and mitigating fragmentation in low-contrast DSA images.

Standard multi-class segmentation models typically rely on a single competitive layer, which often leads to feature suppression, where the dominant signal of a major vessel interferes with the identification of overlapping or adjacent peripheral structures. To resolve this, OSD decomposes the multi-target parsing task into N parallel binary heads, treating each anatomical structure as an independent task within its own feature subspace. Given the fused feature P, the i-th head produces an anatomy-specific probability map A_i:

$$A_i = \sigma\big(\Phi_i(P)\big), \quad i = 1, \ldots, N, \quad (6)$$

where Φ_i denotes the i-th prediction branch consisting of a 3×3 convolution, ReLU activation, and a 1×1 convolution, and σ is the sigmoid function. This parallel design avoids mutual suppression inherent in traditional output layers.

To further promote feature diversity and minimize cross-branch redundancy, we introduce an Orthogonality Loss $\mathcal{L}_{ortho}$:

$$\mathcal{L}_{ortho} = \sum_{1 \leq j < k \leq N} \left(\frac{A_j \cdot A_k}{\|A_j\| \|A_k\|} \right)^2, \tag{7}$$

where A_j and A_k are the flattened probability vectors. This constraint forces each branch to capture unique anatomical characteristics, effectively disentangling the intertwined vascular hierarchies.

2.3 Loss Function

We optimize AngioParse via a multi-task objective supervising both the global vessel prior and N anatomical predictions. Given the ground-truth binary mask Y_{bin} and structure-wise masks $Y_i \in \{0,1\}^{H \times W}$, the total loss is:

$$\mathcal{L}_{total} = \mathcal{L}_{seg}(M_{prior}, Y_{bin}) + \sum_{i=1}^{N} \mathcal{L}_{seg}(A_i, Y_i) + \alpha \mathcal{L}_{ortho} + \beta \mathcal{L}_{Cons}, \tag{8}$$

where $\mathcal{L}_{seg}(P,Y) = \mathcal{L}_{BCE}(P,Y) + \mathcal{L}_{Dice}(P,Y)$ combines pixel-wise binary cross-entropy and soft Dice loss. $\mathcal{L}_{Cons}$ and $\mathcal{L}_{ortho}$ (Sec. 2.1–2.2) enforce structural grounding and semantic disentanglement, respectively, with weighting hyperparameters α and β.

3 Experiments

3.1 Dataset and Implementation Details

To validate the parsing capabilities of AngioParse, we established a new semantic annotation standard based on the DSCA benchmark [19]. While the original benchmark focused on binary segmentation, this extended dataset features high-fidelity, pixel-level annotations performed by senior interventional neuroradiologists. The annotations classify the cerebrovascular architecture into six distinct anatomical segments: CA, VA, ACA, MCA, PCA, and others. The dataset consists of high-resolution DSA MinIP images, stratified into a training set of 175 images and a test set of 45 images. Figure 1 illustrates the label distribution and color coding used throughout this study.

Implemented in PyTorch, the framework was trained on an NVIDIA RTX 5090 for 350 epochs using a batch size of 1. We employed the AdamW optimizer (initial $LR = 1 \times 10^{-4}$) with a cosine annealing scheduler and standard data augmentations. For fair comparison, all baselines were evaluated under identical settings. For SAM-based methods (SAM-Adapter), we adopt the ViT-L pretrained weight. For SAM2-based approaches (SAM2-Unet and our SAM2 encoder backbone), we utilize the SAM 2.1 Hiera Large pretrained weights. Performance was measured via Dice and IoU for overlap accuracy, and clDice for topological connectivity.

3.2 Comparison with State-of-the-Art Methods

We compare AngioParse against representative state-of-the-art methods, including CNN-based (U-Net [13], CS^{2}Net [10], nnU-Net [8], BCU-Net [18]), Transformer-based (Swin-unet [2], TransUNet [3], Segformer [15]), and foundation model-based architectures (SAM-Adapter [4], SAM2-Unet [17]).

As shown in Table 1, CNN-based architectures such as nnU-Net and BCU-Net perform robustly on this structured task. In contrast, pure Transformer and foundation model-based approaches, including Swin-Unet and SAM2-Unet, struggle significantly with fine-grained multi-target labels. AngioParse achieves state-of-the-art results across nearly all metrics. Notably, AngioParse excels in segmenting delicate structures, reaching 86.82% Dice for Others and 94.03% for cervical vessels. Furthermore, its high clDice scores across most categories demonstrate a superior ability to preserve vascular connectivity, outperforming the runner-up by a significant margin in anatomical classification.

The qualitative results across three representative scenarios are visualized in Fig. 3. In case (a), the magnified regions demonstrate that AngioParse successfully identifies distal vascular branches (highlighted in green), which are frequently omitted or misclassified by baseline models. In case (b), our approach exhibits superior precision at complex bifurcation points, maintaining accurate category assignment and eliminating the inter-class leakage prevalent in competing methods. For case (c), AngioParse yields the most robust anatomical parsing by effectively mitigating both false positives (leakage) and false negatives (missing segments). These visual results confirm that the synergy of complementary multi-encoder features and structural priors enables AngioParse to produce more reliable, topologically consistent vascular maps compared to existing state-of-the-art frameworks.

Table 1. Performance comparison on the DSCA dataset (%). "Cervic. V." refers to cervical vessels (CA and VA segments).

Methods	Mean			Cervic. V.			ACA			MCA			PCA			Others		
	Dice	IoU	clD.	Dice	IoU	clD.	Dice	IoU	clD.	Dice	IoU	clD.	Dice	IoU	clD.	Dice	IoU	clD.
U-Net [13]	44.79	32.45	23.89	65.81	49.04	24.81	9.84	5.18	8.70	43.48	27.78	17.86	21.63	12.13	10.38	80.23	66.99	63.04
CS^{2}Net [10]	50.66	37.77	30.78	72.22	56.51	34.82	5.73	2.95	6.20	40.39	25.31	19.36	36.02	21.97	20.81	78.88	65.12	62.13
nnU-Net [8]	<u>75.48</u>	<u>62.33</u>	<u>51.51</u>	<u>89.88</u>	<u>81.62</u>	<u>59.62</u>	<u>66.23</u>	<u>49.51</u>	**44.57**	<u>64.25</u>	<u>47.33</u>	<u>39.26</u>	58.84	41.68	36.76	83.39	71.51	65.44
BCU-Net [18]	72.88	59.09	48.02	86.32	75.93	53.54	58.81	41.65	34.26	60.91	43.79	35.05	<u>59.13</u>	<u>41.98</u>	<u>38.72</u>	<u>84.82</u>	<u>73.64</u>	<u>67.70</u>
Swin-unet [2]	19.97	12.39	4.42	31.16	18.46	4.88	4.38	2.24	1.23	0.83	0.051	0.05	0.34	0.03	0.03	51.97	35.10	15.45
TransUNet [3]	28.84	19.43	7.97	52.90	35.96	14.66	3.34	2.12	1.12	7.50	3.90	0.67	0.70	0.04	0.004	55.70	38.60	16.72
Segformer [15]	47.10	32.62	22.97	66.80	50.15	29.05	23.06	13.03	12.12	36.53	22.35	16.75	29.38	17.22	14.26	62.17	45.11	32.48
SAM-Adapter [4]	64.79	50.16	32.25	84.34	72.92	42.48	48.71	32.20	25.11	50.09	33.42	18.99	48.63	32.12	23.78	71.49	55.63	37.54
SAM2-Unet [17]	60.94	47.13	19.92	87.64	78.01	37.49	47.54	31.18	11.51	50.56	33.84	12.43	42.25	26.78	10.64	47.99	31.57	7.87
AngioParse	**78.51**	**67.79**	**53.70**	**94.03**	**88.74**	**63.14**	**68.75**	**52.38**	<u>44.11</u>	**67.74**	**51.22**	**42.77**	**65.71**	**48.93**	**41.22**	**86.82**	**76.70**	**67.83**

3.3 Ablation Study

We validated the effectiveness of each component through a stepwise ablation study (Table 2). Starting with the baseline, the integration of the SCSG module yielded a substantial gain (+12.23% Dice), underscoring the critical role of

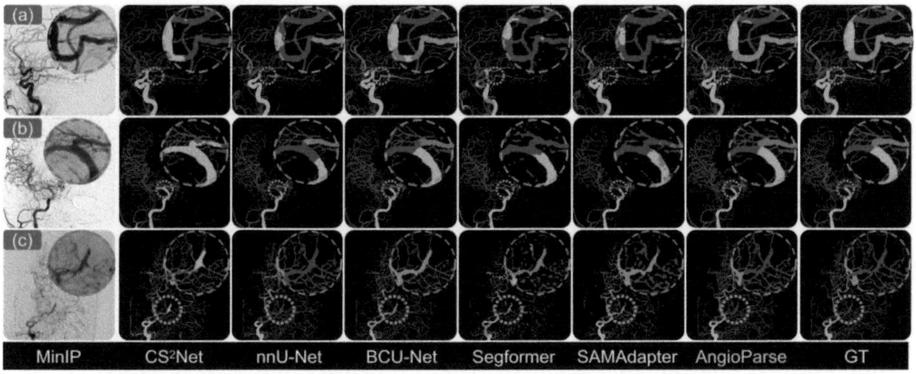

Fig. 3. Qualitative comparison of anatomical parsing results on DSCA dataset.

Table 2. Ablation of components.

SCSG	OSD	Dice	mIoU	clD.
✗	✗	65.81	54.58	45.86
✓	✗	78.04	65.40	51.72
✗	✓	75.10	63.90	49.60
✓	✓	**78.51**	**67.79**	**53.70**

Table 3. Ablation of decoders.

$\mathcal{D}_l^{CNN}$	$\mathcal{D}_g^{Tr}$	$\mathcal{D}_g^{CNN}$	Dice	mIoU	clD.
✓	✗	✗	77.35	64.15	51.62
✓	✓	✗	77.62	64.48	51.65
✓	✓	✓	**78.51**	**67.79**	**53.70**

global binary priors in anchoring fine-grained parsing. The OSD module also provided significant improvement (+9.29% Dice) by effectively mitigating inter-class feature redundancy. The synergic integration of both modules yielded the best overall performance, specifically boosting topological continuity as evidenced by the high clDice and mIoU scores. Hyperparameter sensitivity analysis (Fig. 4) identified an optimal performance peak (78.51% mean Dice) at $\alpha = 0.6$ and $\beta = 0.1$, striking an effective balance between structural consistency and semantic orthogonality.

A granular analysis of the multi-source decoders (Table 3) reveals the additive benefit of our decoding architecture. The sequential incorporation of the local CNN decoder ($\mathcal{D}_l^{CNN}$), global Transformer decoder ($\mathcal{D}_g^{Tr}$), and global CNN decoder ($\mathcal{D}_g^{CNN}$) results in progressive performance gains. This confirms that combining local high-frequency details with global topological context is essential for resolving complex vascular hierarchies. Qualitative visualizations in Fig. 5 further corroborate these findings, distinguishing the specific contributions of each decoder branch in capturing sharp gradients versus semantic continuity.

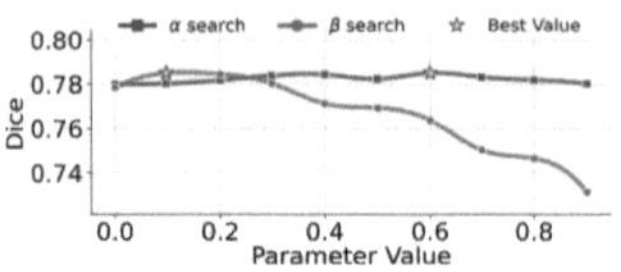

Fig. 4. Analysis of α and β.

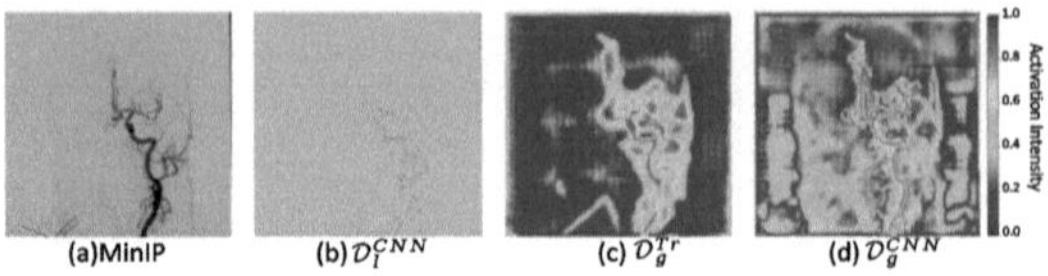

Fig. 5. Visualization of decoder activations.

4 Conclusions

In this study, we presented AngioParse, a novel framework specifically designed for fine-grained anatomical parsing of the cerebrovascular tree in DSA. By synergizing local CNN encoders with global foundation model priors, our approach successfully bridges the semantic gap between binary vessel extraction and detailed anatomical categorization. The proposed mechanisms, including SCSG and OSD, effectively address the challenges of topological connectivity and projective ambiguity inherent in 2D imaging. Experimental results on the DSCA dataset demonstrate that AngioParse achieves state-of-the-art performance, accurately differentiating six vascular categories while maintaining structural integrity. Despite these advancements, the computational complexity inherent in the multi-encoder architecture and the requirement for high-quality pixel-level annotations represent practical constraints. Future work will focus on optimizing architectural efficiency and exploring semi-supervised learning strategies to reduce the reliance on manual annotation.

Acknowledgments. This work is supported by the National Science Foundation Program of China (62422122, 62272444, 62271359), the Key Research and Development Program of Zhejiang Province (2024C03281), the Ningbo 'KeChuang Yongjiang 2035' Key R&D Program (2024Z230), and the Agency for Science, Technology and Research (A*STAR) under its MTC Programmatic Funds (Grant No. M23L7b0021).

Disclosure of Interests. The authors have no competing interests to declare that are relevant to the content of this article.

References

1. Ahmed, R.M., et al.: Msa-unet3+: multi-scale attention unet3+ with new supervised prototypical contrastive loss for coronary DSA image segmentation. Biomed. Signal Process. Control **123**, 110539 (2026)
2. Cao, H., et al.: Swin-unet: Unet-like pure transformer for medical image segmentation. In: European Conference on Computer Vision, pp. 205–218. Springer (2022)
3. Chen, J., et al.: Transunet: rethinking the u-net architecture design for medical image segmentation through the lens of transformers. Med. Image Anal. 103280 (2024)
4. Chen, T., et al.: Sam-adapter: adapting segment anything in underperformed scenes. In: Proceedings of the IEEE/CVF International Conference on Computer Vision, pp. 3367–3375 (2023)

5. Deng, H., Liu, X., et al.: DFA-Net: dual multi-scale feature aggregation network for vessel segmentation in X-ray digital subtraction angiography. J. Big Data **11**(1), 57 (2024)
6. Goyal, M., et al.: Endovascular treatment of stroke due to medium-vessel occlusion. N. Engl. J. Med. **392**(14), 1385–1395 (2025)
7. Hu, E.J., et al.: LoRA: low-rank adaptation of large language models. In: International Conference on Learning Representations (2022)
8. Isensee, F., Jaeger, P.F., Kohl, S.A., Petersen, J., Maier-Hein, K.H.: nnu-net: a self-configuring method for deep learning-based biomedical image segmentation. Nat. Methods **18**(2), 203–211 (2021)
9. Luo, Y., Sun, L.: Digital subtraction angiography image segmentation based on multiscale hessian matrix applied to medical diagnosis and clinical nursing of coronary stenting patients. J. Radiat. Res. Appl. Sci. **16**(2), 100603 (2023)
10. Mou, L., et al.: CS2-Net: deep learning segmentation of curvilinear structures in medical imaging. Med. Image Anal. **67**, 101874 (2021)
11. Qin, J., Luo, H., et al.: DSA-former: a network of hybrid variable structures for liver and liver tumour segmentation. Int. J. Med. Robot. Comput. Assist. Surg. (2024)
12. Ravi, N., et al.: Sam 2: segment anything in images and videos. In: International Conference on Learning Representations, vol. 2025, pp. 28085–28128 (2025)
13. Ronneberger, O., Fischer, P., Brox, T.: U-Net: convolutional networks for biomedical image segmentation. In: Navab, N., Hornegger, J., Wells, W.M., Frangi, A.F. (eds.) MICCAI 2015. LNCS, vol. 9351, pp. 234–241. Springer, Cham (2015). https://doi.org/10.1007/978-3-319-24574-4_28
14. Su, R., van der Sluijs, P.M., et al.: Cave: cerebral artery-vein segmentation in digital subtraction angiography. Comput. Med. Imaging Graph. **115**, 102392 (2024)
15. Xie, E., Wang, W., Yu, Z., Anandkumar, A., Alvarez, J.M., Luo, P.: Segformer: simple and efficient design for semantic segmentation with transformers. In: Neural Information Processing Systems (NeurIPS) (2021)
16. Xie, Q., Zhang, D.: Dsnet: a spatio-temporal consistency network for cerebrovascular segmentation in digital subtraction angiography sequences. In: International Conference on Medical Image Computing and Computer-Assisted Intervention (MICCAI) (2023)
17. Xiong, X., et al.: Sam2-unet: segment anything 2 makes strong encoder for natural and medical image segmentation. Vis. Intell. **4**(1), 2 (2026)
18. Zhang, H., et al.: BCU-Net: bridging convnext and U-net for medical image segmentation. Comput. Biol. Med. **159**, 106960 (2023)
19. Zhang, J., Xie, Q., et al.: DSCA: a digital subtraction angiography sequence dataset and spatio-temporal model for cerebral artery segmentation. IEEE Trans. Med. Imaging **44**(6), 2515–2527 (2025)
20. Zhang, L., Jiang, X.: Temsam: temporal-aware segment anything model for cerebrovascular segmentation in digital subtraction angiography sequences. In: International Conference on Medical Image Computing and Computer-Assisted Intervention (MICCAI) (2024)

FOCUS: Towards Fetal Obstetric Corrective UltraSound Guidance

Hala Lamdouar[1(✉)], Angela Feixue Wang[1], Xiaoqing Guo[2], Qianhui Men[3], Jayne Lander[4], Aris T. Papageorghiou[4], and J. Alison Noble[1]

[1] Institute of Biomedical Engineering, University of Oxford, Oxford, UK
hala.lamdouar@eng.ox.ac.uk

[2] Department of Computer Science, Hong Kong Baptist University, Hong Kong SAR, China

[3] School of Engineering Mathematics and Technology, University of Bristol, Bristol, UK

[4] Nuffield Department of Womens and Reproductive Health, University of Oxford, Oxford, UK

Abstract. Guidance is essential in teaching the required skills for performing highly technical obstetric ultrasound examination. These skills include selecting the appropriate control panel functions, making correct image adjustments, and positioning the probe effectively to acquire high quality anatomical views. Existing work mainly focused on assessing image quality, without identifying where errors occur during ultrasound scanning or how a trainee should correct them. We introduce FOCUS, the Fetal Obstetric Corrective UltraSound instructor, a new multimodal framework designed to learn and deliver corrective guidance for trainee sonographers using both video and text. FOCUS analyses ultrasound video sequences and provides corrective feedback indicating specific actions needed to improve technical performance. To develop this framework, we collect obstetric ultrasound data captured by trainees, annotated with corrective instruction labels, anatomical labels, and accompanying expert textual feedback. Our experiments demonstrate that FOCUS effectively learns to recognise suboptimal image patterns and generate targeted corrective feedback. We provide the code at https://github.com/hlamdouar/focus-ultrasound-guidance.

Keywords: Fetal Ultrasound · Generated feedback · Corrective instruction · Human AI collaboration

1 Introduction

Obstetric ultrasound examination is a highly complex task that involves the detection and recognition of key structures, the capture of specific anatomical views, and the measurement of biometry to assess the progress of the pregnancy and its associated care plan. Typically, during the examination, the operator aims to maintain the target fetal or maternal anatomical area in the centre of the

G. Yang et al. (Eds.): MICCAI 2026, LNCS 16893, pp. 190–199, 2027.
https://doi.org/10.1007/978-3-032-38236-8_19

screen, and to maximise image quality. To this end, the operator proceeds with a sequence of actions: *(i)* manipulating the transducer, *i.e.* through movements of rotation, translation, and inclination; and *(ii)* selecting optimal parameters on the control panel, *i.e.* depth, sector width, focal zones, magnification *etc.*. In addition to the complexity of actions, sonographers have to react to other factors that may occur during the scan that increase the difficulty *e.g.*, fetal movements, acoustic shadow. Learning to scan well can take years of practice to achieve the very high levels of proficiency needed for tasks such as fetal echocardiography. Even for basic skills such as fetal biometry, there is a worldwide lack of qualified sonographers, and a scarcity of training resources, particularly in resource-constrained environments where demand is high [20].

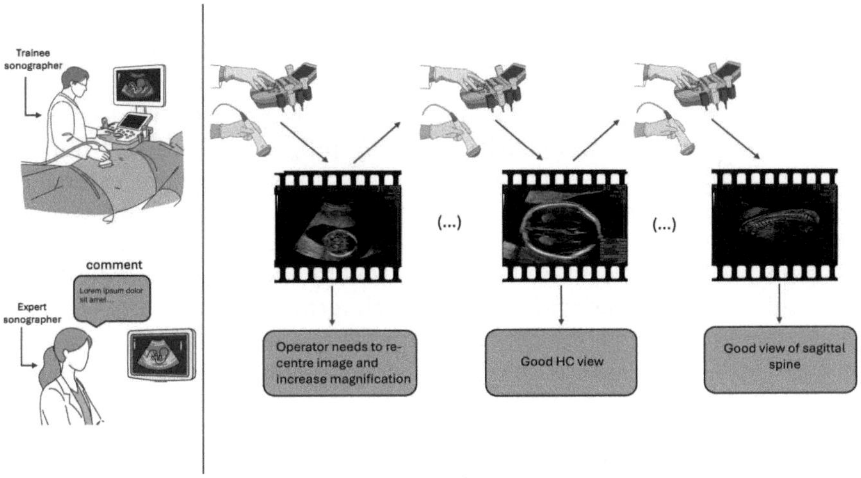

Fig. 1. Obstetric Ultrasound Trainee dataset: In our setting, a trainee ultrasound operator examines different fetal and maternal anatomies by performing a sequence of probe motions and keyboard actions. Retrospectively, an expert sonographer observes the ultrasound video and comments on the subsequences.

Current advances in Artificial Intelligence (AI) offer a great foundation for developing tools to support trainee sonographers and to help with their learning process. This capability is also relevant to non-ultrasound specialists who want to develop basic ultrasound skills for simple tasks on an occasional basis (such as a General Practitioner in a community or rural settings). Previous works have tackled ultrasound image quality problems, such as acoustic shadow estimation [10,12,13,21], and more recently Point-of-Care Ultrasound (POCUS), as acquired by non-experts, it suffers from noisy suboptimal views. Recent work has explored language-based approaches for ultrasound captioning [1], and multimodal frameworks, including large language models, for report generation, visual grounding, and summarisation [7,9,14,18]. More recently, research has shifted towards human–AI collaboration [8], with interactive systems providing real-time feedback and guidance to sonographers during acquisition [4,15].

In this work, we reframe ultrasound guidance around the concept of sonographer learners. Rather than treating guidance as static-image interpretation, we model it as training an AI instructor that behaves like an expert standing over a trainee's shoulder. The system evaluates live scanning behavior and issues corrective feedback when needed—e.g., "structures are unclear; increase magnification and re-centre the view" or "adjust the probe to eliminate shadowing from ...". To support this vision, we construct a dedicated dataset of trainee scanning sessions paired with retrospective expert commentary, and propose a multimodal framework FOCUS that generates temporally grounded, actionable feedback, shifting ultrasound AI guidance from static image analysis towards interaction-based, context-aware instruction that mirrors real-world teaching.

We make the following contributions: *(i)* We introduce CorLM, a lightweight transformer-based language module explicitly conditioned on anatomy, corrective instruction, and visual embeddings. Unlike generic captioning systems, CorLM generates clinically meaningful, anatomy-aware corrective feedback tailored to obstetric ultrasound training. *(ii)* We propose a dual-head framework that disentangles anatomical context from prescriptive guidance via dedicated decoders, producing semantic embeddings that consistently ground the language generator. This design enables fine-grained visual understanding and improves the reliability of downstream feedback. *(iii)* Finally, we describe a dataset framework of trainee sonographer videos paired with retrospective expert commentary and introduce an embedding-based semantic detection metric to assess whether generated comments capture the intended anatomical or corrective concept. While the dataset is private, we provide a transparent construction protocol.

2 Method

Motivation. Consider a dataset $\{\mathcal{V}_i, t_i\}$, comprising video sequences acquired during obstetric examinations, here performed by trainee sonographers, paired with corresponding retrospective expert commentary providing corrective feedback. We argue that each corrective instruction (e.g., increasing gain, adjusting magnification) is intrinsically tied to the specific anatomy, fetal or maternal, being examined. As anatomical structures differ in appearance, echotexture, depth, and acoustic context, the visual manifestation of a required correction varies accordingly across views. To capture these dependencies, we adopt a conditioned language module whose generative output is grounded in learned semantic representations associated with both the corrective instruction and the underlying anatomy. This conditioning ensures that generated feedback is context-aware, anatomically appropriate, and aligned with expert guidance.

Visual Stream. The goal of this component is to provide the downstream language module with stable anatomical and contextual cues necessary for grounded corrective feedback. To extract semantically meaningful representations from ultrasound video sequences, we adopt a pretrained vision transformer

(ViT)style [5] encoder with frozen backbone weights. Formally, given an ultrasound frame $\mathcal{V}_i^{(t)}$, the encoder produces a d-dimensional representation

$$f_{\mathcal{V}}^{(t)} = \mathrm{ViT}(\mathcal{V}_i^{(t)}) \in \mathbb{R}^d, \tag{1}$$

These embeddings are aggregated in a temporal fusion using a lightweight pooling operator:

$$f_{\mathcal{V}} = \mathrm{Pool}\Big(f_{\mathcal{V}}^{(1)}, \ldots, f_{\mathcal{V}}^{(T)}\Big), \tag{2}$$

which captures anatomical appearance and overall image appearance (Fig. 2).

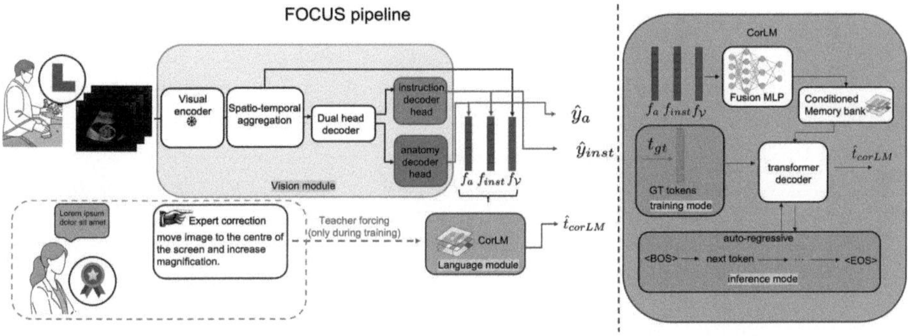

Fig. 2. FOCUS pipeline. We leverage retrospective expert commentary to train CorLM, a conditioned language module that generates corrective feedback for trainee sonographers. CorLM distills rich semantic information by attending to anatomy embeddings f_a, instruction embeddings f_{inst}, and vision embeddings $f_{\mathcal{V}}$. Conditioned on these complementary signals, the model produces detailed, context-aware instructive feedback to guide skill acquisition.

Dual Decoder Head. On top of the shared visual encoder, we employ a dual–decoder design consisting of (i) an *anatomy decoder* and (ii) an *instruction decoder*. Each decoder receives the clip-level visual representation $f_{\mathcal{V}} \in \mathbb{R}^D$ and produces a semantically meaningful embedding aligned to its respective prediction task. The anatomy decoder maps the visual features to an embedding $f_a = \mathrm{MLP}_a(f_{\mathcal{V}})$, which is subsequently classified into one of the annotated fetal or maternal anatomical structures via a softmax operator. Similarly, the instruction decoder forms an embedding $f_{\mathrm{inst}} = \mathrm{MLP}_{\mathrm{inst}}(f_{\mathcal{V}})$, which is used to classify the corrective action appropriate for the given view (e.g., adjust gain, magnify, or re-centre the structure). This dual-headed design encourages the encoder to learn disentangled representations of anatomy and corrective instruction, providing richer supervision and improving the grounding of generated feedback.

Conditioned Language Module. To generate anatomically grounded and contextually appropriate corrective feedback, we incorporate a conditioned language module that leverages the semantic signals extracted by the dual decoders and the visual encoder. Let f_a and f_{inst} denote the anatomy and instruction embeddings, respectively, and let $f_{\mathcal{V}}$ denote the visual embedding produced by the backbone. These components are fused by a lightweight multilayer perceptron:

$$f_{\text{cond}} = \text{MLP}_{\text{fusion}}([\, f_{\mathcal{V}},\, f_a,\, f_{\text{inst}}\,])\,, \tag{3}$$

which yields a compact conditioning vector that summarises the anatomical context, the intended corrective action, and the visual characteristics of the ultrasound clip.

This fused vector is inserted into the transformer language decoder as a *conditioning memory token.* Formally, we treat $M = f_{\text{cond}} \in \mathbb{R}^{1\times d}$ as the key–value memory for all cross-attention layers within the decoder. During training, the decoder operates in a teacher-forcing regime; it receives the ground-truth token sequence, attends to the conditioning memory M, and predicts next-token logits which are optimised with a cross-entropy loss. At inference time, the decoder generates text autoregressively, producing one token at a time while continually attending to the same conditioning vector M.

By integrating both explicit semantic embeddings and trainable memory slots, the conditioned language module produces text that is structurally coherent and semantically grounded in the underlying anatomy, the corrective instruction, and the visual appearance of the ultrasound clip.

Training Objective: We adopt the cross entropy loss to train the visual module. Given logits $\hat{\mathbf{y}}_{inst}$ and $\hat{\mathbf{y}}_a$ for corrective instruction and anatomy respectively:

$$\mathcal{L}_{\text{inst}} = \mathcal{L}_{\text{CE}}(\mathbf{y}^{\text{gt}}_{inst}, \hat{\mathbf{y}}_{inst}), \qquad \mathcal{L}_{\text{a}} = \mathcal{L}_{\text{CE}}(\mathbf{y}^{\text{gt}}_{a}, \hat{\mathbf{y}}_{a}), \tag{4}$$

For training the corrective feedback module, we adopt a masked language loss where the ground-truth tokens are shifted by one position to define next-token targets, and padding tokens are masked:

$$\mathcal{L}_{\text{corLM}} = -\frac{1}{|\mathcal{M}|} \sum_{(i,t)\in\mathcal{M}} \sum_{v} q_{i,t}(v)\, \log p_{i,t}(v), \tag{5}$$

where $\mathcal{M}$ is the set of non-<**pad**> positions, $q_{i,t}$ is the smoothed target distribution, and $p_{i,t}$ the probability distribution over the vocabulary at timestep t.

The total objective is:

$$\mathcal{L}_{\text{total}} = \lambda_{\text{inst}}\mathcal{L}_{\text{inst}} + \lambda_{\text{a}}\mathcal{L}_{\text{a}} + \lambda_{\text{corLM}}\mathcal{L}_{\text{corLM}}. \tag{6}$$

3 Experiments

3.1 Obstetric Ultrasound Skill Dataset

We collected and annotated 7 s trimester obstetrics ultrasound examination videos with expert audio commentary. Video durations range from 20 min to 31 min, totalling 2 h 53 min 32 s, with more than 260K frames at an imaging frame rate of 25fps. These videos were extracted from the PULSE project [6] with ethic approval and written consent from the participants.

Expert audio commentary was provided by an experienced sonographer trainer for each video, addressing their suggested corrections as well as the fetal anatomies observed, as presented in Fig. 1. The audio was processed in two stages. First, WhisperX [2] was used to transcribe the audio into text with sentence-level timestamps. Next, video clips corresponding to correction and anatomy commentary were extracted by a trained researcher, with manual validation of transcripts and clip boundaries. This produced a dataset of 324 clips, ranging from 0.042 s to 60.665 s, with a variety of examined anatomies and expert suggested corrections, as visualised in a mosaic plot in Fig. 3. The dataset is split into 70% for training, 10% for validation, and 20% for testing, ensuring that all correction categories are present in the validation and test sets for unbiased model evaluation and avoiding data leakage.

The eight expert-suggested correction categories identified from the extracted clips are described below, with explanations detailing actions that the trainee could take to improve the quality of the image:

- "good view": when a standard plane was obtained according to guidelines.
- "poor view: deep focal depth": indicates that the trainee should decrease focal depth.
- "poor view: high gain": indicates that the trainee should decrease the gain.
- "poor view: high magnification": indicates that the trainee should decrease magnification.
- "poor view: low gain": indicates that the trainee should increase the gain.
- "poor view: low magnification": indicates that the trainee should increase the magnification.
- "poor view: not center": indicates that the trainee should adjust the probe so that the anatomy of interest moves to the center of the screen.
- "poor view: shadow": indicates presence of acoustic shadowing over the anatomy of interest, either from fetal or maternal anatomy. The trainee should avoid these.

3.2 Implementation Details

Models were trained with a batch size of 8 on ultrasound clips of 8 frames, sampled at one frame every five time steps. Each frame was resized to 448×448 and normalised using the pretrained backbone statistics and encoded into embeddings of dimension $d = 512$. We train all components end-to-end with the Adam optimizer and an initial learning rate of 10^{-4}. We use $\lambda_{\text{inst}} = \lambda_{\text{corLM}} = 1.0$ and $\lambda_{\text{a}} = 0.5$. All experiments are conducted on a single NVIDIA Quadro RTX 5000 GPU. Text is tokenized with a custom 230-word vocabulary extracted from the expert commentary. We use <bos>, <eos>, and <pad> special tokens. During training, teacher forcing was applied for sequence generation.

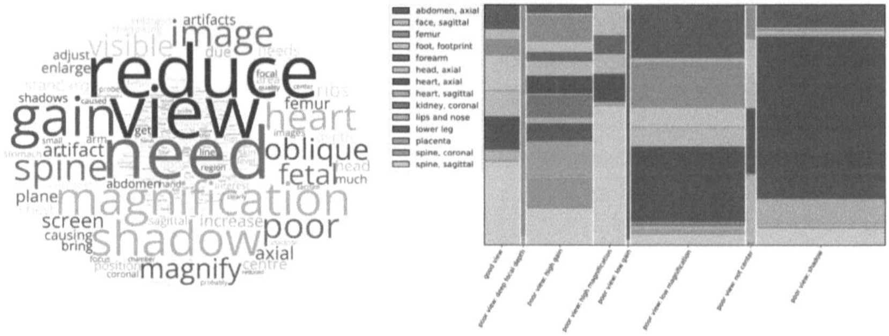

(a) Word Cloud (b) Mosaic plot

Fig. 3. Distribution of dataset across instructions and fetal anatomies

Table 1. Comparison on US instruction and fetal anatomy classification, and commentary generation metrics ($Rouge_L$ [16], Bleu [19] and METEOR [3]).

Model	Instruction				Anatomy				Commentary		
	Acc	**P**	**R**	**F1**	**Acc**	**P**	**R**	**F1**	**B**	**R-L**	**M**
Ours-w/o dual	65.4	64.9	65.5	64.7	63.7	64.1	63.8	61.1	8.4	27.6	21.8
Ours-ResNet50	**68.4**	**68.9**	**68.4**	**68.2**	64.8	67.2	64.8	61.7	**13.4**	**31.9**	**28.4**
Ours-SwinT	64.7	67.6	61.8	63.3	**74.5**	**74.1**	**71.4**	**70.3**	10.2	28.3	24.4

3.3 Quantitative Results

Table 1 summarizes performance across three dimensions: (i) anatomy recognition, (ii) corrective instruction classification, and (iii) the semantic quality of generated feedback. We evaluate our architecture with two visual backbones: ResNet50 [11] and Swin-T [17]. Interestingly, the model that achieves the strongest performance on corrective instruction prediction (the ResNet50-based variant) and delivers superior results on the corrective comment generation task, outperforming its Swin-T counterpart. This suggests that accurate instruction grounding directly benefits downstream language generation quality. In addition, we train an ablated model in which the language decoder is deprived of instructionanatomy conditioning: "ours-w/o dual". This results in a significant decrease in performance showing the effectiveness of our conditioning design. A per-class analysis of the results in Table 1 reveals performance discrepancies, likely due to class imbalance. For instance, Ours w/o dual achieves 62.5% on Good View, 33.3% on High Gain, 22.2% on High Magnification, 81.2% on Low Magnification, and 66.3% on Shadow.

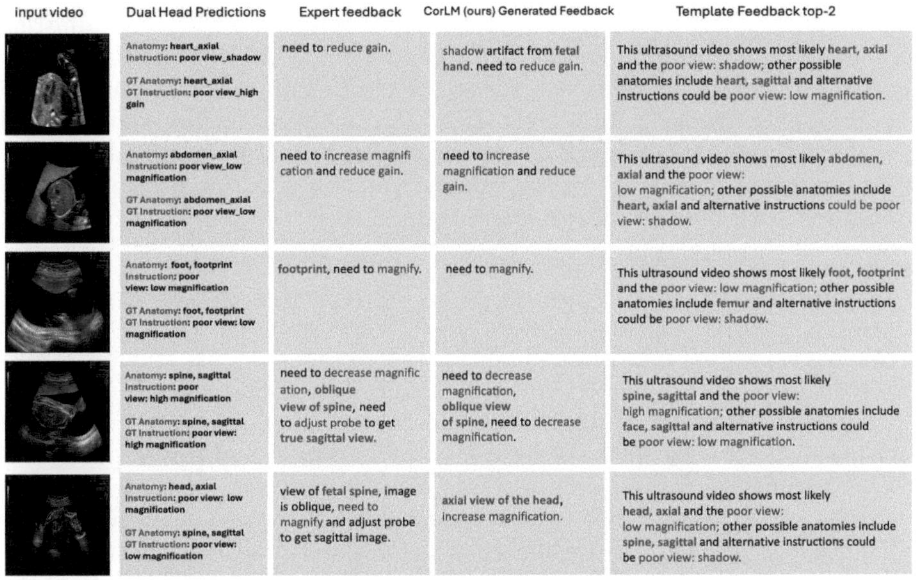

Fig. 4. Qualitative Results. From left to right: image from ultrasound video sequence, Dual head predictions and ground truth, Ground truth expert feedback, our generated corrective feedback and a template generated feedback.

3.4 Qualitative Results

We present qualitative test examples from our dataset in Fig. 4. The model consistently produces rich, context-aware feedback, in some cases offering observations that go beyond the original expert commentary. For instance, while the ground-truth instruction in the first example was simply to reduce the gain, the model also identifies the presence of acoustic shadowing and, given that the scanned structure is a fetal heart, correctly attributes it to a plausible cause ("shadow artifact from fetal hand"). In some instances, the generated feedback omits explicit reference to the underlying anatomy, as illustrated in the second and third examples. This reflects the nature of the training annotations, where the expert did not always include anatomical descriptions when they were not considered clinically relevant for the clip. We also observe failure modes for severely degraded inputs. In the final example, the model incorrectly predicts an axial head view, whereas the correct anatomy is the sagittal spine. Notably, the correct label appears among the model's top-2 predictions (cf. template).

3.5 Limitations

Our dataset is annotated by an expert sonographer instructor, following standard guidelines for obstetric ultrasound examinations. However, the subjective nature of human judgment means that the expert commentary may reflect a degree of subjectivity. For example, one expert might consider an anatomical view good, while another expert would continue to change acquisition setting, *e.g.* adjusting the gain and magnification in search of a more optimal view. While we carefully curated our dataset to capture a variety of challenging subtasks encountered by sonographer trainees, its current scale and imbalance reflect the practical challenges of obtaining expert annotations in obstetric ultrasound. Larger-scale validation remains necessary for clinical deployment, and future work will extend this dataset with broader expert annotations.

4 Conclusion

In this paper, we present a framework for the automated generation of corrective feedback for ultrasound trainee performance during obstetric examinations. Our approach leverages a conditioned multimodal language model to produce anatomically grounded feedback from visual anatomical and instructional context. Experimental results demonstrate that the proposed method generates feedback closely aligned with expert commentary while remaining lightweight and efficient. These findings highlight the potential of compact multimodal language models to provide efficient, data-driven guidance for trainee sonographers, supporting more effective and scalable ultrasound training.

Acknowledgement. This research is funded by the EPSRC Turing AI Fellowship: Ultra Sound Multi-modal video-based human-machine collaboration EP/X040186/1.

Disclosure of Interests. The authors have no financial conflicts of interest to disclose related to this work.

References

1. Alsharid, M., Sharma, H., Drukker, L., Chatelain, P., Papageorghiou, A.T., Noble, J.A.: Captioning ultrasound images automatically. In: International Conference on Medical Image Computing and Computer-Assisted Intervention, pp. 338–346. Springer (2019)
2. Bain, M., Huh, J., Han, T., Zisserman, A.: Whisperx: time-accurate speech transcription of long-form audio. In: INTERSPEECH 2023 (2023)
3. Banerjee, S., Lavie, A.: Meteor: an automatic metric for mt evaluation with improved correlation with human judgments. In: Proceedings of the ACL Workshop on Intrinsic and Extrinsic Evaluation Measures for Machine Translation and/or Summarization, pp. 65–72 (2005)
4. Bashir, Z., et al.: Clinical validation of explainable ai for fetal growth scans through multi-level, cross-institutional prospective end-user evaluation. Sci. Rep. **15**(1), 2074 (2025)
5. Dosovitskiy, A., et al.: An image is worth 16x16 words: transformers for image recognition at scale. In: International Conference on Learning Representations (2020)
6. Drukker, L., et al.: Transforming obstetric ultrasound into data science using eye tracking, voice recording, transducer motion and ultrasound video. Sci. Rep. **11**(1), 14109 (2021)

7. Guo, X., et al.: A visually grounded language model for fetal ultrasound understanding. Nat. Biomed. Eng. 1–17 (2026)
8. Guo, X., et al.: Human-AI Collaboration: First International Workshop, HAIC 2025, Held in Conjunction with MICCAI 2025, Daejeon, South Korea, 27 September 2025, Proceedings. Springer (2026)
9. Guo, X., Men, Q., Noble, J.A.: Mmsummary: multimodal summary generation for fetal ultrasound video. In: International Conference on Medical Image Computing and Computer-Assisted Intervention, pp. 678–688. Springer (2024)
10. Hacihaliloglu, I.: Enhancement of bone shadow region using local phase-based ultrasound transmission maps. Int. J. Comput. Assist. Radiol. Surg. **12**(6), 951–960 (2017). https://doi.org/10.1007/s11548-017-1556-y
11. He, K., Zhang, X., Ren, S., Sun, J.: Deep residual learning for image recognition. In: Proceedings of the IEEE Conference on Computer Vision and Pattern Recognition, pp. 770–778 (2016)
12. Hellier, P., Coupé, P., Morandi, X., Collins, D.L.: An automatic geometrical and statistical method to detect acoustic shadows in intraoperative ultrasound brain images. Med. Image Anal. **14**(2), 195–204 (2010)
13. Hu, R., Singla, R., Deeba, F., Rohling, R.N.: Acoustic shadow detection: study and statistics of b-mode and radiofrequency data. Ultrasound Med. Biol. **45**(8), 2248–2257 (2019)
14. Li, J., et al.: Ultrasound report generation with cross-modality feature alignment via unsupervised guidance. IEEE Trans. Med. Imaging **44**(1), 19–30 (2024)
15. Li, X., Huang, D., Zhang, Y., Navab, N., Jiang, Z.: Semantic scene graph for ultrasound image explanation and scanning guidance. In: International Conference on Medical Image Computing and Computer-Assisted Intervention, pp. 500–510. Springer (2025)
16. Lin, C.Y.: Rouge: a package for automatic evaluation of summaries. In: Text Summarization Branches Out, pp. 74–81 (2004)
17. Liu, Z., et al.: Swin transformer: hierarchical vision transformer using shifted windows. In: Proceedings of the IEEE/CVF International Conference on Computer Vision, pp. 10012–10022 (2021)
18. Maani, F., et al.: Fetalclip: a visual-language foundation model for fetal ultrasound image analysis. NPJ Digit. Med. (2026)
19. Papineni, K., Roukos, S., Ward, T., Zhu, W.J.: Bleu: a method for automatic evaluation of machine translation. In: Proceedings of the 40th Annual Meeting of the Association for Computational Linguistics, pp. 311–318 (2002)
20. Stewart, K.A., et al.: Trends in ultrasound use in low and middle income countries: a systematic review. Int. J. Matern. Child Health AIDS **9**(1), 103 (2020)
21. Yasutomi, S., et al.: Shadow estimation for ultrasound images using auto-encoding structures and synthetic shadows. Appl. Sci. **11**(3), 1127 (2021)

From Geometry to Clinic: A Physics-Aware Evaluation Framework and Benchmark for Automated Dental Crown Design

Jiamin Wu[1,2], Wendong Huang[3], Jiaying Gu[4,5], Jing Hao[1], Yuanfei Fu[4,5], Yilei Wang[3], Peichao Lai[6], and James Kit Hon Tsoi[1(✉)]

[1] Faculty of Dentistry, The University of Hong Kong, Hong Kong, China
jkhtsoi@hku.hk
[2] Forma AI Ltd., Hong Kong, China
[3] College of Computer and Data Science, Fuzhou University, Fujian, China
[4] Shanghai Ninth People's Hospital, Shanghai Jiao Tong University, Shanghai, China
[5] National Center for Stomatology & National Clinical Research Center for Oral Diseases & Shanghai Key Laboratory of Stomatology & Shanghai Research Institute of Stomatology, Shanghai, China
[6] School of Computer Science, Peking University, Beijing, China
lpc@pku.edu.cn

Abstract. Recent advances in deep learning have demonstrated remarkable potential in automating dental crown design. However, existing evaluation protocols predominantly rely on geometric similarity metrics (e.g., Chamfer Distance), which are clinically agnostic and fail to capture functional failures such as occlusal interference or open contacts. To bridge this gap, we present CrownBench, a physics-aware evaluation framework and benchmark that shifts the paradigm from geometric approximation to clinical validity. We propose a set of clinically-interpretable digital metrics, mathematically formulating implicit clinical experiences into explicit constraints: Feasibility Metrics (e.g., Occlusal/Proximal Feasibility Rates) for survival validation, and Quality Metrics (e.g., Occlusal Contact Distribution) for personalized quality assessment. Benchmarking state-of-the-art methods on CrownBench reveals a severe "Geometric Trap," where geometrically accurate models still suffer from low clinical success rates. Furthermore, a rigorous blind user study confirms that our framework aligns significantly better with human expert judgments than traditional metrics. Our code and dataset are released at https://github.com/JiaminWoo/CrownBench.

Keywords: Digital Dentistry · Dental Restoration · Benchmark

J. Wu and W. Huang—Contributed equally.

G. Yang et al. (Eds.): MICCAI 2026, LNCS 16893, pp. 200–209, 2027.
https://doi.org/10.1007/978-3-032-38236-8_20

1 Introduction

Digital dentistry has witnessed a paradigm shift from manual wax-up procedures to Computer-Aided Design and Manufacturing (CAD/CAM) [4]. While traditional CAD software streamlines the workflow, it still heavily relies on the manual manipulation of complex parameters by experienced technicians, which is labor-intensive and subject to inter-operator variability. Recently, deep learning methods [2,6,11,14,15] have shown meaningful promise in digital dentistry. In automated crown design, the data-driven approaches [5,8,10,12,16] aim to generate patient-specific restorations that satisfy complicated clinical criteria.

Despite these algorithmic advances, a critical gap remains between geometric plausibility and clinical applicability. Current State-of-the-Art (SOTA) methods predominately rely on geometric similarity metrics, such as Chamfer Distance (CD) and Hausdorff Distance (HD), to evaluate generation quality. While effective for general 3D shape reconstruction, these metrics are clinically agnostic. A generated crown can achieve a low CD score by visually resembling a generic tooth, yet fail catastrophically in a clinical setting due to functional violations, such as occlusal interferences (penetration into opposing teeth), open proximal contacts (food impaction risks), or poor marginal adaptation (secondary caries risks) [7]. Consequently, the community faces a "geometric trap": models are optimized for shape similarity rather than functional survival, and evaluations often revert to non-scalable subjective visual inspections by clinicians.

To deploy AI agents in real-world clinical workflows, evaluation protocols must evolve from measuring "how much it looks like a tooth" to "how well it functions as a restoration." This requires translating implicit clinical experiences—such as the delicate balance of occlusal forces and the precision of proximal contacts—into explicit, computable, and physics-aware mathematical formulations. However, establishing such a unified benchmark is challenging due to the complex, multi-dimensional constraints involved in the stomatognathic system, where tolerance is measured in microns and constraints vary between "hard" survival limits and "soft" functional harmonies.

To bridge this chasm, we present CrownBench, a novel physics-aware evaluation framework and benchmark designed to standardize the assessment of automated dental crown design. Unlike previous works that treat crown generation as a pure shape completion task, CrownBench reformulates evaluation through the lens of clinical physics. We define a comprehensive set of digital clinical metrics, categorizing constraints into Feasibility Metrics for safety validation and Functional Metrics for personalized quality assessment. By grounding evaluation in the physical interactions between the restoration and its biological environment (opposing and adjacent dentition), our framework provides a rigorous "stress test" for generative models. Our main contributions are three-fold:

- A Paradigm-Shifting Evaluation Framework: We propose the first clinically-quantifiable evaluation framework that maps implicit clinical criteria (occlusion, proximal contact, margin) into explicit, physics-aware metrics, distinguishing between hard survival constraints and soft quality harmonies.

- The CrownBench Benchmark: We establish a comprehensive benchmark comparing SOTA crown generation methods. Our extensive experiments reveal a significant disconnect between geometric similarity metrics (CD/HD) and clinical success rates, highlighting the necessity of our proposed metrics.
- Human-AI Alignment Validation: We conduct a rigorous user study with experienced dentists, demonstrating that CrownBench rankings align significantly better with human expert judgments than traditional geometric metrics, validating its potential as a trusted standard for future research.

2 Method

We propose a comprehensive evaluation framework that transcends traditional geometric similarity metrics (e.g., Chamfer Distance). We formulate clinical experience into rigorous mathematical definitions, categorized into Feasibility Metrics (Hard Constraints) for safety validation and personalized functional quality (Soft Constraints) for personalized functional assessment.

2.1 Preliminary: Region-Aware Semantic Parsing

Given a generated dental crown mesh $\mathcal{M}_{gen}$ and the opposing dentition $\mathcal{M}_{opp}$, adjacent teeth $\mathcal{M}_{adj}$, and the preparation margin line $\mathcal{C}_{margin}$. We first compute the Signed Distance Fields (SDF) of the environmental scans: $\Phi_{opp}(\cdot)$ and $\Phi_{adj}(\cdot)$. To evaluate specific functional areas, we extract Regions of Interest (ROI) by querying the SDF values of the crown's surface points:

(1) Occlusal Surface (Ω_{occ}): Vertices on the crown top that are within a functional interaction range.
(2) Proximal Surface (Ω_{prox}): Vertices on the mesial/distal sides facing adjacent teeth.
(3) Finish Line ($\mathcal{C}_{GT}$): Critical curve that shall align with the boundary of crown.

2.2 Clinical Feasibility Assessment

These metrics determine whether a generated crown is clinically "safe" to fit without causing irreversible failure (e.g., open contacts or severe penetration). We simulate standard physical inspection tools used by dentists to define binary Pass/Fail indicators.

Occlusal Feasibility Rate (OFR). In clinical practice, dentists use articulating paper to check for high spots (interference). Inspired by this, we propose a Virtual Articulating Paper algorithm. We treat the Signed Distance Field (SDF) of the opposing teeth as the "ink thickness." We define a Valid Occlusal Interval $\mathcal{I}_{occ} = [-0.2\,\text{mm}, 0.5\,\text{mm}]$. The lower bound ($-0.2\,\text{mm}$) tolerates slight penetration (simulating periodontal elasticity), while the upper bound ($0.5\,\text{mm}$) allows for functional clearance but prevents open bite (simulating "no ink mark" on the paper). For a generated crown, we calculate the minimum distance (worst-case deviation) to the opposing teeth:

$$d_{occ}^{min} = \min_{p \in \Omega_{occ}} \Phi_{opp}(p) \tag{1}$$

The crown is classified as "Clinically Acceptable" if $d_{occ}^{min} \in \mathcal{I}_{occ}$. Otherwise, it is classified as Over-Penetration ($d < -0.2$) or Occlusal Loss ($d > 0.5$). The OFR is the percentage of successful cases in the test set.

Proximal Feasibility Rate (PFR). Proximal tightness is clinically verified using dental floss. The contact must be tight enough to snap the floss (preventing food impaction) but passable. For digital evaluation, excessive contact is adjustable (grindable), but open contact is irreversible. Hence, we mimic this Digital Dental Floss by defining an asymmetric Valid Proximal Interval $\mathcal{I}_{prox} = [-0.3\,\text{mm}, 0\,\text{mm}]$. The lower bound ($-0.3\,\text{mm}$) tolerates slight penetration, while the upper bound ($0\,\text{mm}$) simulates the floss passes without resistance.

We evaluate the closest point on the proximal surface:

$$d_{prox}^{min} = \min_{p \in \Omega_{prox}} \Phi_{adj}(p) \tag{2}$$

A case passes if $d_{prox}^{min} \in \mathcal{I}_{prox}$. This asymmetric threshold explicitly reflects the clinical preference for "tight contact" over "open gaps."

Marginal Seal Integrity (MSI). The crown margin must perfectly align with the preparation finish line to prevent secondary caries. We compute the one-sided Hausdorff Distance from the crown boundary $\partial\mathcal{M}_{gen}$ to the ground truth margin curve $\mathcal{C}_{GT}$:

$$HD_{margin} = \max_{p \in \partial\mathcal{M}_{gen}} \min_{q \in \mathcal{C}_{GT}} \|p - q\|_2 \tag{3}$$

A strictly low HD_{margin} is required for clinical acceptance.

2.3 Personalized Functional Quality

Beyond binary survival, a high-quality crown must adapt to the personalized oral environment. We propose physics-aware metrics to quantify the digital design quality.

Contextual Occlusal Consistency (COC). Occlusal contact area varies among patients (e.g., wear facets in elders vs. sharp cusps in youth). We propose a Reference-Based Evaluation using the adjacent tooth as a reference context. We define the Functional Contact Ratio (FCR) which represents the effective "ink mark area" left by our Virtual Articulating Paper:

$$FCR(\mathcal{M}) = \frac{\text{Count}(\{p \in \mathcal{M} \mid \Phi_{opp}(p) \le \tau_{contact}\})}{\text{Count}(\{p \in \mathcal{M} \mid \Phi_{opp}(p) \le \tau_{area}\})} \tag{4}$$

The COC measures the consistency between the generated crown's FCR and the neighbor's FCR using a negative exponential decay function:

$$COC_{\mathcal{M}} = \exp\left(-|FCR(\mathcal{M}_{gen}) - FCR(\mathcal{M}_{neighbor})|\right) \tag{5}$$

A higher $COC_{\mathcal{M}}$ indicates that the AI model has successfully learned the personalized occlusal pattern.

Occlusal Contact Distribution (OCD). Effective occlusion relies not only on the total contact area but also on the spatial distribution of forces. A stable restoration requires widely distributed contact points (e.g., tripodism) rather than a single concentrated stress point, which risks porcelain fracture or instability. We formulate this as a Density-Based Clustering problem on the manifold. Let $\mathcal{P}_{contact} = \{p \in \Omega_{occ} \mid \Phi_{opp}(p) \leq \tau_{cluster}\}$ be the set of effective contact vertices. We apply the DBSCAN algorithm (Density-Based Spatial Clustering of Applications with Noise) to partition $\mathcal{P}_{contact}$ into disjoint topological clusters $\{C_1, C_2, \ldots, C_k\}$:

$$\mathcal{C} = \text{DBSCAN}(\mathcal{P}_{contact}, \epsilon, MinPts) \tag{6}$$

where ϵ is the spatial neighborhood radius and $MinPts$ is the density threshold. The metric is defined as the Number of Valid Clusters ($N_{clusters} = |\mathcal{C}|$). A higher $N_{clusters}$ (typically aiming for ≥ 3 for molars) indicates a mechanically stable, multi-point contact distribution.

Anatomical Detail Fidelity (ADF). To evaluate whether the generated surface preserves functional features (cusps and grooves) or is over-smoothed, we evaluate the Normal Consistency Score. Specifically, we first sample N points $\{p_i\}_{i=1}^{N}$ on the generated mesh surface $\mathcal{S}_{gen}$, and find their nearest corresponding points $\{q_i\}_{i=1}^{N}$ on the ground truth surface $\mathcal{S}_{GT}$. Then we compute the average cosine similarity of their normals:

$$S_{ADF} = \frac{1}{N}\sum_{i=1}^{N}\langle \mathbf{n}_{gen}(p_i), \mathbf{n}_{GT}(q_i)\rangle \tag{7}$$

where $\mathbf{n}(\cdot)$ denotes the normalized surface normal vector, and $\langle\cdot,\cdot\rangle$ is the dot product. A score closer to 1.0 indicates high fidelity in preserving anatomical morphology.

3 Experiments

3.1 Experimental Settings

Dataset Construction. To rigorously benchmark the clinical applicability of automated dental restoration, we constructed a real-world restoration dataset, comprising 500 paired molar crown cases collected from partner clinical institutions. Each case consists of dental model scans of the preparation jaw, the opposing jaw, and the corresponding Ground Truth (GT) crown designed by senior dental technicians using commercial CAD software. We randomly partitioned the dataset into training, validation, and test sets with a ratio of 8:1:1. Note that the test set is exclusively reserved as our proposed CrownBench, which was not seen during the training of any baseline models and test through our evaluation framework.

Data Preprocessing and Standardization. To ensure a fair and standardized comparison across different generative architectures, we implemented a unified data processing pipeline: We first employed a state-of-the-art dental segmentation network, 3DTeethSeg [3], to semantically parse the raw scans into individual components (preparation tooth, adjacent teeth, and antagonists). To eliminate algorithmic errors, the segmentation results underwent a rigorous Human-in-the-Loop verification process, where two dentists reviewed and refined the masks, particularly at the contact regions. The preparation margin lines were explicitly extracted from the GT designs to serve as boundary constraints.

Furthermore, to facilitate generative modeling, all mesh data were spatially normalized. We established a local canonical coordinate system for each case based on the GT crown's PCA axes [1], ensuring the insertion axis aligns with the Y-axis. All meshes were centered to the origin. This standardization ensures that performance differences arise solely from the generative models' capabilities rather than data inconsistencies.

Implementation Details. We benchmarked SOTA crown generation methods, including Dental-GAN, DCPR-GAN, 3D-Dental-GAN, PoinTr, DMC, VBCD, 3DShape2Vecset. All baseline models were retrained on the *CrownBench* training split until convergence, strictly following their official hyperparameter settings. The evaluation experiments were conducted on a RTX 4090 GPU using PyTorch framework. We set the SDF threshold of occlusal surface as 1.5mm to the opposing teeth. All hyperparameters can be adjusted to satisfy different manufacturing standards.

3.2 Experimental Results

Comprehensive Benchmarking on CrownBench. Table 1 presents the quantitative comparison across 50 test cases. While recent methods like 3Dshape2Vecset [18] and VBCD [13] achieve remarkable geometric accuracy ($CD \approx 0.25 - 0.40\,\text{mm}$), a significant gap remains in clinical feasibility. Specifically, although VBCD reduces the CD to 0.251 mm, its Occlusal Feasibility Rate (OFR) is only 82.0%, implying that nearly 1 in 5 "geometrically precise" crowns still suffer from functional failures (penetration or open bite). Furthermore, regarding Functional Quality, most methods struggle to reproduce the complex occlusal topography found in human designs (GT), as evidenced by lower OCD scores (< 2.0) compared to GT (3.12). This quantitative benchmark exposes the limitation of current SOTA methods: they master the overall shape distribution but often miss the fine-grained physical constraints essential for clinical survival.

Table 1. Quantitative benchmarking on CrownBench. Note the discrepancy between geometric metrics (CD/HD) and clinical metrics (Feasibility/Quality).

Method	Geometric		Clinical Feasibility			Functional Quality		
	CD(↓)	HD(↓)	OFR(↑)	PFR(↑)	MSI(↓)	COC(↑)	ADF(↑)	OCD
Dental-GAN[10]	1.641	4.951	0.58	0.08	5.05	0.71	0.83	1.91
DCPR-GAN[12]	0.976	1.459	0.62	0.20	0.36	0.73	0.27	1.84
3D-Dental-GAN[5]	0.839	2.233	0.32	0.14	1.80	0.79	0.48	1.54
PoinTr[17]	0.958	2.366	0.46	0.20	1.36	0.79	0.49	1.81
DMC[9]	0.489	1.130	0.52	0.16	0.83	0.80	0.87	1.96
3Dshape2Vecset[18]	0.397	1.149	0.78	0.62	0.62	0.81	0.95	2.59
VBCD[13]	0.251	1.122	0.82	0.76	0.63	0.82	0.95	3.96
Human Design (Ref)	0.000	0.000	0.92	0.90	0.00	0.83	1.00	3.12

Threshold Robustness. We performed a sensitivity analysis around the feasibility intervals by perturbing the OFR lower/upper bounds and the PFR lower bound by ±0.05 mm. Absolute pass rates changed with tolerance strictness, but method rankings remained unchanged, indicating that the main trend in Table 1 is not an artifact of one empirical threshold.

The "Geometric Trap" in High-Fidelity Generation. To validate the necessity of physics-aware evaluation, we investigated whether geometric metrics remain reliable when the generation quality is already high. We curated a subset of 50 high-fidelity cases from the top-performing models (VBCD and 3Dshape2Vecset), both of which exhibit low Chamfer Distances ($CD < 0.5$ mm). Figure 1(a) visualizes the correlation analysis. Despite the low geometric error, we observe a distinct **"Geometric Trap"**: the CD shows negligible or even counter-intuitive correlation with clinical precision (Occlusal Precision $\rho = -0.137, P = 0.344$; Proximal Precision $\rho = 0.268, P = 0.09$). This confirms that in the high-precision regime, geometric similarity decouples from clinical utility.

As shown in Fig. 1(b), we visualize two representative "Trap Cases" with minimal geometric errors. Although visually plausible, the heatmaps reveal critical failures: one exhibits deep occlusal penetration (−0.4 mm), and the other shows severe proximal interference. These defects render the crowns clinically unusable despite their "perfect" CD scores.

Human-AI Alignment Validation. To verify that *CrownBench* serves as a reliable surrogate for expert judgment, we conducted a blind user study on the same subset of 50 high-fidelity cases. Three senior dentists (experience > 5 years) rated each case on a Likert scale (1–5) across four dimensions: *Occlusion*, *Proximal Contact*, *Marginal Adaptation*, and *Overall Acceptability*. Dentists reviewed anonymized 3D visualizations with method identity hidden and sample order randomized; mean ratings served as human references for Spearman analysis,

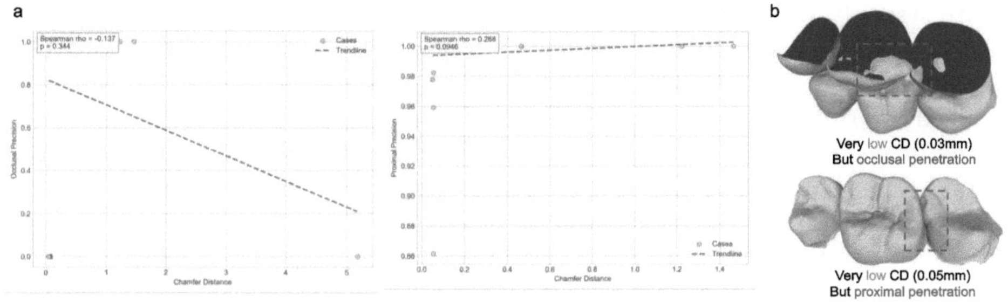

Fig. 1. Analysis of the "Geometric Trap". (a) Scatter plots showing no significant correlation between Chamfer Distance (CD) and clinical precision (Occlusal/Proximal) on 50 high-fidelity samples. (b) Visualization of two "Trap Cases": crowns with extremely low CD scores that nevertheless fail due to occlusal penetration (left) or proximal interference (right). Red regions indicate clinically unacceptable penetration.

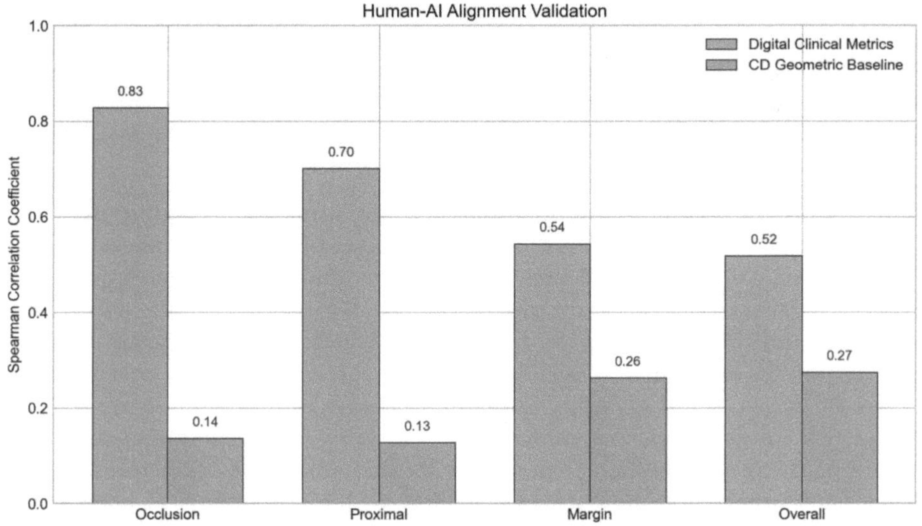

Fig. 2. Human-AI Alignment Study. Spearman correlation coefficients between automated metrics (Blue: Our DCMs; Red: Chamfer Distance) and human expert ratings across four clinical dimensions. Our framework demonstrates significantly higher alignment with dentists' judgments, particularly in functional dimensions (Occlusion/Proximal), validating its reliability as a clinical benchmark.

with high inter-rater agreement (ICC = 0.868, 0.874, 0.884, and 0.844 for occlusion, proximal, margin and overall acceptability).

Figure 2 reports the Spearman correlation coefficients (ρ) between automated metrics and human scores. Our proposed Digital Clinical Metrics (DCMs) demonstrate superior alignment with human perception compared to CD. For *Occlusion* and *Proximal* dimensions, our physics-aware metrics (OFR/PFR) correlate strongly with dentist ratings ($\rho > 0.8$), whereas CD shows weak correlation ($\rho < 0.3$). This indicates that dentists prioritize functional safety over global shape similarity. For *Overall Acceptability*, dimension-specific metrics were normalized to $[0, 1]$ and averaged with equal weights. Our comprehensive framework aligns much better with expert decisions. In clinical deployment, CrownBench can be used as an interpretable report card where OFR/PFR/MSI serve as safety gates before COC/OCD/ADF evaluate personalized quality.

4 Discussion and Conclusion

Limitations. Despite the promising results, CrownBench has several limitations. First, it focuses on relatively structured posterior molar cases with available opposing dentition, mesial/distal adjacent teeth, and a clear preparation margin. Corner cases such as missing adjacent teeth, pathological wear, or unusual occlusal schemes may require upstream screening and condition-specific thresholds. Second, extending the framework to anterior teeth would require incorporating aesthetic metrics such as symmetry and smile line alignment. Finally, although we formulate differentiable metrics, this study focuses on evaluation. Integrating these physics-aware constraints directly into the training loop (e.g., via Reinforcement Learning) to explicitly optimize for clinical feasibility is a promising avenue for future work.

Conclusion. In this paper, we identified and quantified the "Geometric Trap" in automated dental restoration: the disconnect between geometric similarity and clinical utility. To address this, we introduced CrownBench, the first clinically-quantifiable evaluation framework that digitizes implicit expert knowledge into clinically-interpretable, physics-aware metrics. Our extensive benchmarking reveals that current SOTA methods, while geometrically precise, often fail to meet basic clinical safety standards. Moreover, our user study demonstrates that these metrics, spanning hard feasibility constraints and soft functional quality, serve as reliable surrogates for human expert evaluation. CrownBench thus provides a standardized benchmark for developing AI agents that restore function rather than only reconstruct shape.

Acknowledgments. This research study is supported by General Research Fund from the Research Grants Council, Hong Kong (GRF 17126724).

Disclosure of Interests. The authors have no competing interests to declare that are relevant to the content of this article.

References

1. Abdi, H., Williams, L.J.: Principal component analysis. Wiley Interdisc. Rev. Comput. Stat. **2**(4), 433–459 (2010)
2. Bao, N., Luo, Q., Wu, J., Cui, Z., Zhao, Y.: Toothaxis: generalizable tooth axis estimation network from CBCT or IoS models. IEEE J. Biomed. Health Inform. (2025)

3. Ben-Hamadou, A., et al.: 3dteethseg'22: 3D teeth scan segmentation and labeling challenge. arXiv preprint arXiv:2305.18277 (2023)
4. Bohner, L.O.L., Neto, P.T., Ahmed, A.S., Mori, M., Laganá, D.C., Sesma, N.: CEREC chairside system to register and design the occlusion in restorative dentistry: a systematic literature review. J. Esthet. Restor. Dent. **28**(4), 208–220 (2016)
5. Ding, H., et al.: Morphology and mechanical performance of dental crown designed by 3D-DCGAN. Dental Mater. **39**(3), 320–332 (2023)
6. Ding, H., Wu, J., Zhao, W., Matinlinna, J.P., Burrow, M.F., Tsoi, J.K.: Artificial intelligence in dentistry—a review. Front. Dental Med. **4**, 1085251 (2023)
7. Hickel, R., et al.: FDI world dental federation: clinical criteria for the evaluation of direct and indirect restorations—update and clinical examples. Clin. Oral Invest. **14**, 349–366 (2010)
8. Hosseinimanesh, G., Alsheghri, A., Keren, J., Cheriet, F., Guibault, F.: Personalized dental crown design: a point-to-mesh completion network. Med. Image Anal. **101**, 103439 (2025)
9. Hosseinimanesh, G., Ghadiri, F., Guibault, F., Cheriet, F., Keren, J.: From mesh completion to ai designed crown. In: International Conference on Medical Image Computing and Computer-Assisted Intervention, pp. 555–565. Springer (2023)
10. Hwang, J.J., Azernikov, S., Efros, A.A., Yu, S.X.: Learning beyond human expertise with generative models for dental restorations. arXiv preprint arXiv:1804.00064 (2018)
11. Li, M.X., et al.: Metadent: labeling clinical images for vision-language models in dentistry. J. Dental Res. 00220345261424242 (2026)
12. Tian, S., et al.: DCPR-GAN: dental crown prosthesis restoration using two-stage generative adversarial networks. IEEE J. Biomed. Health Inform. **26**(1), 151–160 (2021)
13. Wei, L., Liu, C., Zhang, W., Zhang, Z., Zhang, S., Li, H.: VBCD: a voxel-based framework for personalized dental crown design. In: International Conference on Medical Image Computing and Computer-Assisted Intervention, pp. 627–636. Springer (2025)
14. Wu, J., Tsoi, J.K.H.: AI-powered digital probing improves periodontal disease diagnosis. Cell Rep. Med. **6**(6) (2025)
15. Wu, J., Yuen, K.H., Lee, Y.H., Liu, Y., Tsoi, J.K.H., Lam, W.Y.H.: The use of artificial intelligence in predicting maximal intercuspal position: a feasibility study. J. Prosthodont. Res. **69**(3), 389–393 (2025)
16. Yang, S., et al.: Dcrownformer: morphology-aware point-to-mesh generation transformer for dental crown prosthesis from 3D scan data of antagonist and preparation teeth. In: International Conference on Medical Image Computing and Computer-Assisted Intervention, pp. 109–119. Springer (2024)
17. Yu, X., Rao, Y., Wang, Z., Liu, Z., Lu, J., Zhou, J.: Pointr: diverse point cloud completion with geometry-aware transformers. In: Proceedings of the IEEE/CVF International Conference on Computer Vision, pp. 12498–12507 (2021)
18. Zhang, B., Tang, J., Niessner, M., Wonka, P.: 3dshape2vecset: a 3D shape representation for neural fields and generative diffusion models. ACM Trans. Graph. (TOG) **42**(4), 1–16 (2023)

From Scanning Guidelines to Action: A Robotic Ultrasound Agent with LLM-Based Reasoning

Yuan Bi[1,2](✉), Yiping Zhou[1], Pei Liu[1], Feng Li[1,2], Zhongliang Jiang[3], and Nassir Navab[1]

[1] Chair for Computer-Aided Medical Procedures and Augmented Reality, Technical University of Munich, Munich, Germany

[2] Munich Center for Machine Learning, Munich, Germany

yuan.bi@tum.com

[3] Medical Intelligence and Robotic Cognition Lab, The University of Hong Kong, Hong Kong, China

Abstract. Robotic ultrasound offers advantages over free-hand scanning, including improved reproducibility and reduced operator dependency. In clinical practice, US acquisition relies heavily on the sonographer's experience and situational judgment. When transferring this process to robotic systems, such expertise is often encoded explicitly through fixed procedures and task-specific models, yielding pipelines that can be difficult to adapt to new scanning tasks. In this work, we propose a unified framework for autonomous robotic US scanning that leverages a large language model (LLM)-based agent to interpret US scanning guidelines and execute scans by dynamically invoking a set of provided software tools. Instead of encoding fixed scanning procedures, the LLM agent retrieves and reasons over guideline steps from scanning handbooks and adapts its planning decisions based on observations and the current scanning state. This enables the system to handle variable and decision-dependent workflows, such as adjusting scanning strategies, repeating steps, or selecting the appropriate next tool call in response to image quality or anatomical findings. Because the reasoning underlying tool selection is also critical for transparent and trustworthy planning, we further fine tune the LLM agent using a RL based strategy to improve both its reasoning quality and the correctness of tool selection and parameterization, while maintaining robust generalization to unseen guidelines and related tasks. We first validate the approach via verbal execution on 10 ultrasound scanning guidelines, assessing reasoning as well as tool selection and parameterization, and showing the benefit of RL fine tuning. We then demonstrate real world feasibility on robotic scanning of the gallbladder, spine, and kidney. Overall, the framework follows diverse guidelines and enables reliable autonomous scanning across multiple anatomical targets within a unified system. Code: https://github.com/yuan-12138/RUSSAgent; Video: https://youtu.be/pfMOc4e2IGA.

Y. Bi and Y. Zhou—These authors contributed equally to this work.

G. Yang et al. (Eds.): MICCAI 2026, LNCS 16893, pp. 210–220, 2027.
https://doi.org/10.1007/978-3-032-38236-8_21

Keywords: robotic ultrasound · embodied AI · LLM

1 Introduction

Ultrasound (US) is widely used in clinical practice due to its real-time feedback, portability, and lack of ionizing radiation. However, free-hand scanning is highly operator dependent, with image quality varying with the sonographer's expertise, which limits standardization across operators and sites and can lead to fatigue and work-related musculoskeletal injuries. Robotic US offers a promising alternative by providing precise and repeatable motion for more standardized and reproducible scanning, while integrated force sensing and control can regulate probe–tissue contact to improve safety and support consistent image quality [1,15].

Most prior approaches toward autonomous US scanning follow a rule-based design. These systems typically use an external RGB-D camera to reconstruct the patient surface and a robotic arm to manipulate the US probe. Scanning is then guided by anatomy-specific, hand-crafted protocols, often coupled with dedicated US segmentation models. Most prior approaches to autonomous US scanning are rule based. They typically use an external RGBD camera to reconstruct the patient surface [21] and a robotic arm to manipulate the probe, with scanning guided by anatomy-specific hand-crafted protocols, often combined with dedicated segmentation models. Representative systems include robotic spine US [32], autonomous carotid scanning with tailored protocols [13], and breathing compensation for aortic US [30], as well as additional components such as force-based vertebral localization [29] and pulsation-informed artery segmentation [12]. While effective, these rule-based designs are often task-specific and transfer poorly to new anatomies and scanning objectives.

Beyond hand-crafted rule-based designs, robot learning methods have been explored to acquire scanning behaviors from interaction [3] or expert demonstrations. Early work often trained reinforcement learning (RL) agents in simulation, such as RL navigation toward standard spine planes [19] and VesNetRL for carotid standard views [2]. More recent studies increasingly learn from expert demonstrations to mitigate sim-to-real gaps, including inverse RL to learn the "language of sonography" [14] and Diffusion Policy for robotic carotid scanning [7]. While effective in targeted scenarios, achieving flexible behavior and robust generalization across diverse scanning tasks remains challenging.

Large language models (LLMs) have demonstrated strong general-purpose capabilities and can benefit robotics by enabling flexible task understanding and high-level decision making [23]. In navigation and manipulation, LLMs are often integrated in a zero-shot manner as high-level planners for tool selection and long-horizon reasoning, while low-level controllers and perception modules execute the actions [22,25–27]. However, this transfer is less direct in the medical domain, where general-purpose LLMs may lack domain-specific knowledge. As a result, early attempts to integrate LLMs into robotic US have incorporated clinical scanning guidelines to appropriately constrain the planning process and improve reliability [31]. Chen *et al.* [6] proposed USPilot, an LLM-based framework for robotic US scanning across multiple organs. However, the reasoning capability of the LLM agent is often not explicitly modeled or evaluated in prior work. As a result, existing systems typically emphasize guideline execution and tool use, while offering less insight into the agent's intermediate reasoning that underlies its planning and tool selection decisions.

In this work, we propose a unified agentic framework for autonomous robotic US, in which an LLM interprets scanning guidelines and translates them into actions by dynamically selecting from a set of perception and control tools. By retrieving protocol steps from handbooks and reasoning over the current scanning state and observations, the agent can execute variable, decision-dependent workflows (e.g., repeating steps, adapting strategies, or adjusting force based on image quality) rather than following a fixed sequence. To strengthen reasoning over planning decisions, we further introduce a RL strategy to fine-tune the LLM agent for more reliable reasoning and tool-calling behavior. We evaluate the proposed framework through verbal interaction experiments on unseen US scanning protocols, and we further demonstrate end-to-end feasibility in real-world robotic experiments on human volunteers across three representative examinations: gallbladder, spine, and kidney (Fig. 1).

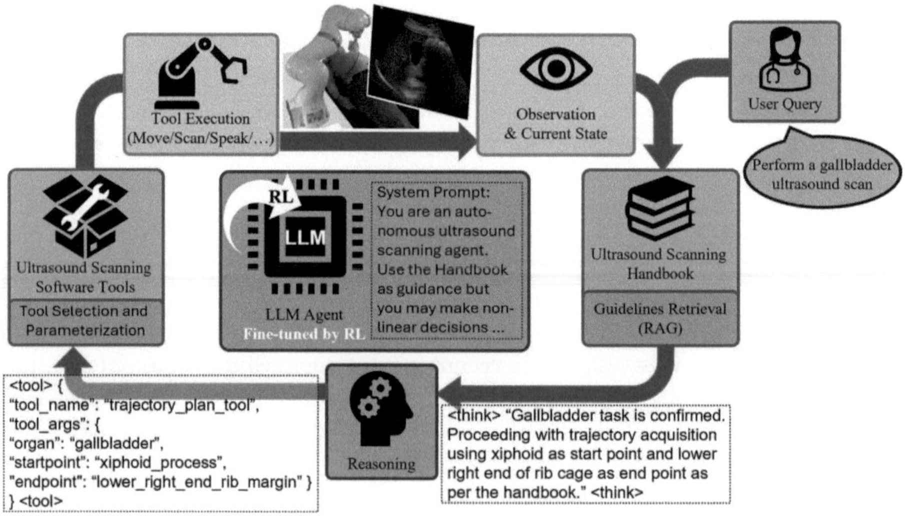

Fig. 1. Overview of the proposed guideline-driven agentic robotic US system. An RL fine tuned LLM retrieves guideline steps from the scanning handbook, reasons over the current state and observations, and generates structured tool calls with parameters. Executed tools update the state, enabling closed loop, non linear scanning workflows.

2 Methods

LLMs have strong reasoning and decision-making capabilities. We leverage an LLM as a high-level agent for autonomous US scanning by equipping it with software tools for image processing, perception, and robot control, and by providing access to a database of scanning guidelines to supply domain knowledge. Conditioned on the user query and current observations, the agent retrieves guideline steps, selects and parameterizes tools, and executes the requested scanning task. We further apply RL-based fine tuning to adapt a small LLM to robotic US, improving planning-oriented reasoning and tool calling while still generalizing robustly to unseen guidelines and producing plausible reasoning traces to support transparency and clinician inspection.

2.1 Agentic LLM for Robotic US

Our proposed framework follows an agentic paradigm similar to [8,9,24], but targets autonomous robotic US scanning through guideline-driven planning and tool use rather than verbal or image analysis tasks. It consists of three components: (1) robotic and perception tools for path generation, patient-robot interaction, etc.; (2) a guideline database containing US workflow steps; and (3) an LLM that serves as the high-level planner. At initialization, a prefix prompt defines the LLM role for sequential problem solving and tool-based response generation. Given a user query, the system retrieves relevant guideline instructions via retrieval-augmented generation [18] and the agent selects and parameterizes tools accordingly. At each step, the agent reasons over the current observations and outputs a <think> reasoning trace followed by a <tool> token with a structured JSON tool call. Tool outputs are appended to the history to guide subsequent decisions, enabling variable, decision-dependent workflows such as repeating steps, adapting scanning strategies, and adjusting trajectory or force based on US observations until the guideline objectives are met.

2.2 Tools Design

In order to give the LLM the ability to perform automatic US scanning and analyses the scanning status, specific tools are designed for imaging processing and robot execution.

Trajectory Planning Tool is designed to generate an initial US scanning trajectory based on the input query. As shown in Fig. 2, first, the RGBD camera mounted on the robot end effector is used to capture the patient body surface. Due to the limited field of view of the RGBD camera, multiple views are acquired and fused to reconstruct a whole body surface representation of the patient. A skeletal atlas is then registered to the patient using an open-source model [17,20], which enables the detection of anatomical landmarks for trajectory planning. Based on LLM-provided inputs specifying the target organ and the start and end points of the scan defined with respect to anatomical landmarks, the tool determines a scanning path and projects it into 3D space using the patient point

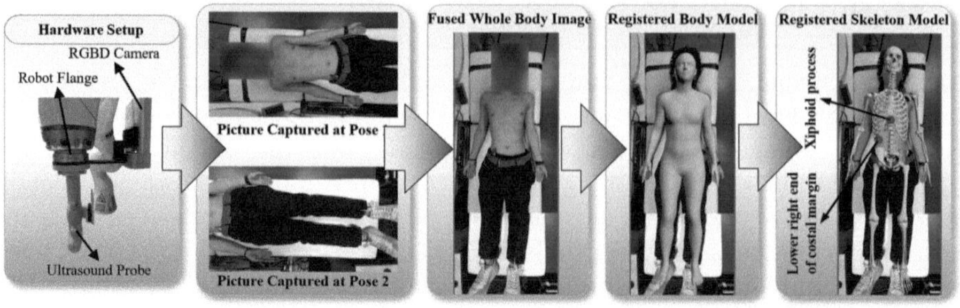

Fig. 2. Trajectory planning pipeline for initial scan generation.

cloud. In summary, the inputs to the tool include the target organ and landmark-referenced start and end points of the scanning trajectory, and the output is a 3D US scanning trajectory.

Robot Execution Tool receives either a scanning trajectory or a target pose as input, together with the execution speed. It then executes the corresponding motion command to move the robot to the specified pose or along the specified trajectory for US scanning or RGBD image acquisition.

Contact Adjustment Tool evaluates US image quality and probe contact quality based on the US confidence map [16], and then adjusts the robot pose to establish proper contact with the patient surface [4,5]. The input to this tool is the US image, and the output is adjusted robot pose or trajectory.

Voice Guidance Tool generates the verbal instructions needed to guide the patient during scanning. These instructions include breath-hold cues and body pose adjustment guidance. US scanning is a highly interactive procedure, and effective communication with the patient is essential for adjusting body posture and obtaining an appropriate acoustic window. For example, such guidance is particularly important for gallbladder scanning, because without proper instructions, such as a deep-inhalation breath hold, it is often difficult to visualize the gallbladder beneath the rib cage and avoid acoustic shadowing caused by bone. The input to the tool is the message that needs to be conveyed to the patient.

Trajectory Refinement Tool evaluates the results of the initial scan and refines the trajectory when necessary. Since the initial scan is planned only based on the registered skeletal atlas and anatomical priors, the target organ may not appear in the center of the US image. Therefore, after the initial scan, a target-organ-specific segmentation model is applied to localize the organ in 3D space, and the scanning trajectory is then replanned to enable a refined scan. If the organ is already sufficiently centered and well visualized in the initial scan, no refinement is performed. The input to the tool is the tracked US data from the initial scan, and the output is a replanned trajectory when it is necessary.

2.3 RL-Based Fine-Tuning

Given the response time constraints in robotic applications, using a very large LLM is often impractical. Although the proposed framework is not a vision language action model that requires a response frequency above 20 Hz, an agentic system for robotic US still benefits from sufficiently fast response time on accessible GPU hardware. Therefore, fine tuning a smaller model is necessary to obtain reliable reasoning and tool calling behavior, since smaller models typically have more limited capacity and generalization than larger models. At the same time, the fine tuned model should still robustly generalize to other guidelines and related tasks.

To this end, we construct a guideline driven tool use dataset by collecting stepwise agent traces from a set of training US scanning guidelines. For each guideline step, a larger LLM is used to generate a reference response consisting of <think> reasoning and a <tool> JSON command with the correct tool and parameters. We first perform supervised fine tuning (SFT) on these reference traces to teach the small model the structured output format and basic tool use behavior. We then apply RL, which is increasingly used to improve reasoning behavior and response correctness in LLMs [10]. Specifically, we adopt Proximal Policy Optimization to further optimize the agent. We define a dense reward for each predicted tool call by comparing the structured output $\hat{y} = \{\hat{t}, \hat{\mathbf{a}}\}$ to a reference tool call $y = \{t, \mathbf{a}\}$, where t and $\hat{t}$ are tool names and $\mathbf{a}, \hat{\mathbf{a}}$ are JSON argument dictionaries. Let $\mathcal{A}$ and $\hat{\mathcal{A}}$ denote the sets of argument keys in $\mathbf{a}$ and $\hat{\mathbf{a}}$, and let $\mathcal{K} \subseteq \mathcal{A}$ be the set of scored keys with tool-specific weights w_k.

$$r(\hat{y}, y) = \begin{cases} -0.5, & \hat{t} \neq t \\ \mathrm{clip}_{[0,1]}(0.1 + 0.9\, s_{\mathrm{args}}), & \hat{t} = t \end{cases} \tag{1}$$

This equation assigns negative reward if the predicted tool name is incorrect, and otherwise combines a small base reward with a dense argument score.

$$s_{\mathrm{args}} = \mathrm{clip}_{[0,1]}(0.5\, s_{\mathrm{pres}} + 0.5\, s_{\mathrm{corr}} - 0.1\, s_{\mathrm{extra}}) \tag{2}$$

This equation defines the dense argument score as a mixture of key presence and value correctness, with a penalty for spurious extra arguments.

$$s_{\mathrm{pres}} = \frac{\sum_{k \in \mathcal{K}} w_k\, \mathbf{1}\left[k \in \hat{\mathcal{A}}\right]}{\sum_{k \in \mathcal{K}} w_k}, \qquad s_{\mathrm{corr}} = \frac{\sum_{k \in \mathcal{K}} w_k\, \mathbf{1}[\hat{a}_k \approx a_k]}{\sum_{k \in \mathcal{K}} w_k} \tag{3}$$

Here, s_{pres} rewards including the required argument keys, while s_{corr} rewards correct argument values, using exact matching for discrete fields and tolerance-based matching for selected numeric fields in the relation $\hat{a}_k \approx a_k$.

$$s_{\mathrm{extra}} = \frac{\left|\hat{\mathcal{A}} \setminus \mathcal{A}\right|}{\max\left\{1,\ |\hat{\mathcal{A}}|\right\}}. \tag{4}$$

This term penalizes extra argument keys that are not expected by the reference tool call, encouraging concise and executable tool commands. The reward is defined based on tool calling correctness with respect to the reference tool calling JSON, assigning higher reward to outputs that select the correct tool and provide valid arguments, and penalizing incorrect tool selection, malformed JSON, or incorrect argument values. The model is fine tuned with LoRA [11] using a rank of 16 for SFT and a rank of 8 for RL.

3 Experiments and Results

Verbal Interaction Experiments. We create 20 US scanning guidelines and split them into 10 training guidelines and 10 held-out testing guidelines, with no overlap in guideline content. The tool set remains identical across training and testing. To obtain reference outputs, we use Qwen3-30B-A3B-Instruct-2507 [28] to generate guideline-conditioned agent traces consisting of `<think>` reasoning and `<tool>` JSON commands. We fine-tune Qwen3-4B-Instruct-2507 [28] on the training guidelines and evaluate on the held-out guidelines to assess robustness to unseen guideline instructions, measuring tool selection and parameterization accuracy together with structured output validity.

We then compare the base model and the RL fine tuned model under identical guideline and tool settings. Specifically, we report the overall scanning task success rate, defined as successful completion of the guideline specified scan. In addition, we evaluate step-level tool use by measuring, at each guideline step, whether the agent selects the correct tool and provides correct tool arguments. The results are shown in Tab. 1. Overall, RL fine tuning leads to a clear improvement across both task success and step-level tool calling accuracy.

Table 1. Performance comparison before and after fine-tuning.

	Base Model	After Fine Tuning
Step-wise Accuracy	0.6512	0.8973
Overall Success Rate	0.5384	0.9230

We also include qualitative examples comparing tool calls generated by the base model and the RL fine tuned model (Fig. 3), illustrating differences in tool parameterization and reasoning at representative guideline step. Qualitatively, the base model often produces minimal or uninformative reasoning traces, whereas the RL fine tuned model generates more coherent and task-relevant rationales alongside its tool calls.

Real-world Robotic Experiments. We further validate the proposed system in real-world robotic US experiments on three human volunteers, demonstrating autonomous scanning of the gallbladder, spine, and kidney, with each organ scanned twice per volunteer. Ethical approval was obtained from the institutional

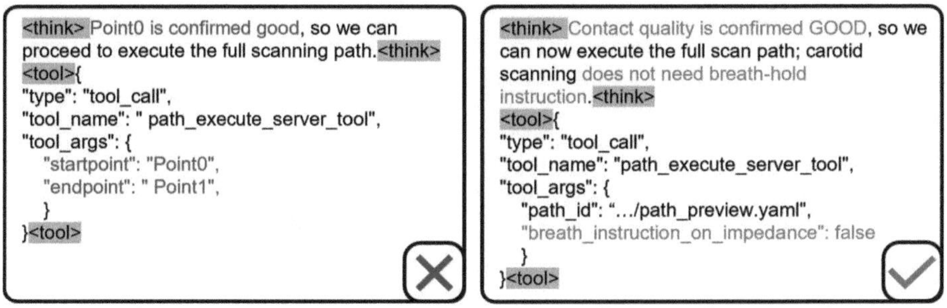

(a) Impropriate Reasoning and Parameterization Before Fine Tuning

(b) Accurate Reasoning and Parameterization After Fine Tuning

Fig. 3. Verbal Experiments Examples.

review board of the Technical University of Munich, and all participants provided written informed consent. The scanning setup is shown in Fig. 2. We use a KUKA LBR iiwa robot equipped with a Siemens ACUSON Juniper US system and a 5C1 probe mounted via a 3D printed holder, with US images acquired through an Epiphan frame grabber. An RGBD camera, Azure Kinect by Microsoft, is mounted on the robot end effector to capture the 3D surface of the scanning target. We evaluate task success based on whether the system can correctly visualize the target organ in the US image. One exemplary scanning scenario is shown in Fig. 4. All spine and kidney experiments were successful, resulting in 100% success rate. For gallbladder scanning, one case failed, resulting in a success rate of 83.3%. This is mainly due to the higher procedural complexity, as breathing-induced organ motion can shift the gallbladder out of the acoustic window, making the scan highly dependent on accurate breath-hold instructions and close patient–robot coordination.

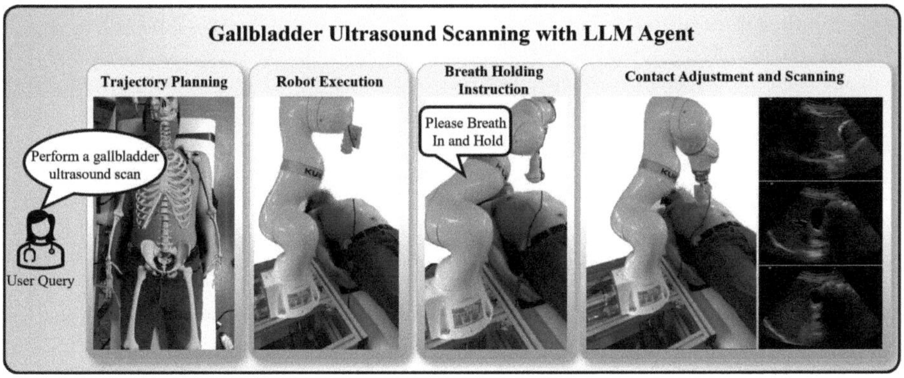

Fig. 4. Real Scenario Experiments Examples.

4 Conclusion

In this work, we presented a guideline-driven agentic framework for autonomous robotic ultrasound that uses an RL fine tuned LLM to retrieve scanning guidelines, reason over the current scanning state, and generate structured tool calls for execution. Experiments on held-out guidelines and real-world volunteer studies across gallbladder, spine, and kidney scanning demonstrate that the proposed system can robustly follow diverse guidelines and achieve reliable autonomous scanning within a unified pipeline.

Acknowledgement. This work was supported in part by the Multi-Scale Medical Robotics Center, AIR@InnoHK, Hong Kong.

Disclosure of Interests. The authors have no competing interests to declare that are relevant to the content of this article.

Informed consent. Informed consent was obtained from all individual participants included in the study.

References

1. Bi, Y., Jiang, Z., Duelmer, F., Huang, D., Navab, N.: Machine learning in robotic ultrasound imaging: challenges and perspectives. Robot. Auton. Syst. **7** (2024). Annual Review of Control
2. Bi, Y., Jiang, Z., Gao, Y., Wendler, T., Karlas, A., Navab, N.: VesNet-RL: simulation-based reinforcement learning for real-world us probe navigation. IEEE Robot. Autom. Lett. **7**(3), 6638–6645 (2022)
3. Bi, Y., Qian, C., Zhang, Z., Navab, N., Jiang, Z.: Autonomous path planning for intercostal robotic ultrasound imaging using reinforcement learning. Sci. Rep. **16**(1), 6356 (2026)
4. Bi, Y., Su, Y., Navab, N., Jiang, Z.: Gaze-guided robotic vascular ultrasound leveraging human intention estimation. IEEE Robot. Autom. Lett. (2025)
5. Chatelain, P., Krupa, A., Navab, N.: Confidence-driven control of an ultrasound probe. IEEE Trans. Rob. **33**(6), 1410–1424 (2017)
6. Chen, M., Fan, S., Cao, G., Liu, Y.h., Liu, H.: USPilot: an embodied robotic assistant ultrasound system with large language model enhanced graph planner. arXiv preprint arXiv:2502.12498 (2025)
7. Chen, R., Yan, X., Lv, K., Huang, G., Li, Z., Li, X.: UltraDP: generalizable carotid ultrasound scanning with force-aware diffusion policy. In: 2025 IEEE/RSJ International Conference on Intelligent Robots and Systems (IROS), pp. 20074–20080. IEEE (2025)
8. Daghyani, M., et al.: EchoAgent: guideline-centric reasoning agent for echocardiography measurement and interpretation. arXiv preprint arXiv:2511.13948 (2025)
9. Fallahpour, A., Ma, J., Munim, A., Lyu, H., Wang, B.: MedRAX: medical reasoning agent for chest X-ray (2025). arXiv:2502.02673 arXiv preprint
10. Guo, D., et al.: DeepSeek-R1: incentivizing reasoning capability in LLMs via reinforcement learning. arXiv preprint arXiv:2501.12948 (2025)

11. Hu, E.J., et al.: LoRA: low-rank adaptation of large language models. ICLR **1**(2), 3 (2022)
12. Huang, D., Bi, Y., Navab, N., Jiang, Z.: Motion magnification in robotic sonography: enabling pulsation-aware artery segmentation. In: 2023 IEEE/RSJ International Conference on Intelligent Robots and Systems (IROS), pp. 6565–6570. IEEE (2023)
13. Huang, Q., Gao, B., Wang, M.: Robot-assisted autonomous ultrasound imaging for carotid artery. IEEE Trans. Instrum. Meas. **73**, 1–9 (2024)
14. Jiang, Z., Bi, Y., Zhou, M., Hu, Y., Burke, M., Navab, N.: Intelligent robotic sonographer: mutual information-based disentangled reward learning from few demonstrations. Int. J. Robot. Res. **43**(7), 981–1002 (2024)
15. Jiang, Z., Salcudean, S.E., Navab, N.: Robotic ultrasound imaging: state-of-the-art and future perspectives. Med. Image Anal. **89**, 102878 (2023)
16. Karamalis, A., Wein, W., Klein, T., Navab, N.: Ultrasound confidence maps using random walks. Med. Image Anal. **16**(6), 1101–1112 (2012)
17. Keller, M., et al.: From skin to skeleton: towards biomechanically accurate 3d digital humans. ACM Trans. Graph. (TOG) **42**(6), 1–12 (2023)
18. Lewis, P., et al.: Retrieval-augmented generation for knowledge-intensive NLP tasks. Adv. Neural. Inf. Process. Syst. **33**, 9459–9474 (2020)
19. Li, K., et al.: Autonomous navigation of an ultrasound probe towards standard scan planes with deep reinforcement learning. In: 2021 IEEE International Conference on Robotics and Automation (ICRA), pp. 8302–8308. IEEE (2021)
20. Li, Z., Liu, J., Zhang, Z., Xu, S., Yan, Y.: CLIFF: carrying location information in full frames into human pose and shape estimation. In: European Conference on Computer Vision (ECCV), pp. 590–606. Springer, Cham (2022)
21. Nardi, D., Lamon, E., Fontanelli, D., Saveriano, M., Palopoli, L.: An anatomy-aware shared control approach for assisted teleoperation of lung ultrasound examinations. IEEE Robot. Autom. Lett. **11**(3), 2570–2577 (2026)
22. Rana, K., Haviland, J., Garg, S., Abou-Chakra, J., Reid, I., Suenderhauf, N.: Say-Plan: grounding large language models using 3D scene graphs for scalable robot task planning (2023). arXiv:2307.06135 arXiv preprint
23. Raptis, E.K., Kapoutsis, A.C., Kosmatopoulos, E.B.: Agentic LLM-based robotic systems for real-world applications: a review on their agenticness and ethics. Front. Robot. AI **12**, 1605405 (2025)
24. Schick, T., et al.: ToolFormer: language models can teach themselves to use tools. Adv. Neural. Inf. Process. Syst. **36**, 68539–68551 (2023)
25. Shah, D., Osiński, B., Levine, S.: LM-Nav: robotic navigation with large pre-trained models of language, vision, and action. In: Conference on Robot Learning, pp. 492–504 (2023). PMLR
26. Singh, H., Das, R.J., Han, M., Nakov, P., Laptev, I.: MalMM: multi-agent large language models for zero-shot robotic manipulation. In: 2025 IEEE/RSJ International Conference on Intelligent Robots and Systems (IROS), pp. 20386–20393. IEEE (2025)
27. Stone, A., et al.: Open-world object manipulation using pre-trained vision-language models (2023). arXiv:2303.00905 arXiv preprint
28. Team, Q.: Qwen3 technical report (2025). https://arxiv.org/abs/2505.09388
29. Tirindelli, M., et al.: Force-ultrasound fusion: bringing spine robotic-us to the next "level." IEEE Robot. Autom. Lett. **5**(4), 5661–5668 (2020)

30. Velikova, Y., Azampour, M.F., Simson, W., Esposito, M., Navab, N.: Implicit neural representations for breathing-compensated volume reconstruction in robotic ultrasound. In: 2024 IEEE International Conference on Robotics and Automation (ICRA), pp. 1316–1322. IEEE (2024)
31. Xu, H., Wu, J., Cao, G., Chen, Z., Lei, Z., Liu, H.: Transforming surgical interventions with embodied intelligence for ultrasound robotics. In: International Conference on Medical Image Computing and Computer-Assisted Intervention, pp. 703–713. Springer (2024)
32. Yang, C., Jiang, M., Chen, M., Fu, M., Li, J., Huang, Q.: Automatic 3-D imaging and measurement of human spines with a robotic ultrasound system. IEEE Trans. Instrum. Meas. **70**, 1–13 (2021)

GCM-Net: Anatomy-Aware Gaussian-Contrastive Multi-layer Fusion Network for Abdominal Ultrasound Standard Plane Classification

Anqi Wang[1], Zihan Li[1], Lei Zhang[2], Xinye Zhang[1], Yingni Wang[1], Xinshan Yang[1], Mingxuan Liu[1], Xiuming Wang[2], Hongen Liao[1], and Guochen Ning[1(✉)]

[1] School of Biomedical Engineering, Tsinghua University, Beijing, P.R. China
ningguochen@tsinghua.edu.cn

[2] School of Clinical Medicine (Beijing Tsinghua Changgung Hospital), Tsinghua University, Beijing, P.R. China

Abstract. Reliable classification of standard abdominal ultrasound planes is essential for sonography and autonomous diagnosis. However, this task remains challenging due to the inherent low contrast and speckle noise in ultrasound imaging, further compounded by subtle inter-plane differences within subjects and substantial anatomical variations across the population. Here, we propose the Gaussian-contrastive multi-layer fusion network (GCM-Net), which comprises a learnable multi-layer feature fusion (LMFF) module to synergistically integrate hierarchical spatial details with high-level semantics, an adaptive anisotropic Gaussian refinement (AAGR) module to spatially focus on critical anatomical structures, and a supervised contrastive learning branch to enhance feature discriminability. Systematic evaluation on the publicly available FPUS23 dataset for fetal ultrasound and the private AbdoSP-9 dataset for abdominal ultrasound demonstrates that GCM-Net outperformed existing methods across key classification metrics. Additionally, GCM-Net demonstrated robust performance in real-time causal processing of clinical ultrasound videos, achieving an expert-validated accuracy of 81.25% through the temporal confidence refinement (TCR) framework. These results underscore GCM-Net's potential not only to streamline routine clinical diagnosis but also to serve as a high-level controller for autonomous robotic ultrasound. Code: https://github.com/diligentwaq-spec/GCM-Net.

Keywords: Ultrasound Imaging · Standard Plane Classification · Feature Fusion · Contrastive Learning

A. Wang and Z. Li—Equal contribution.

G. Yang et al. (Eds.): MICCAI 2026, LNCS 16893, pp. 221–231, 2027.
https://doi.org/10.1007/978-3-032-38236-8_22

1 Introduction

Abdominal ultrasound is pivotal for clinical diagnosis due to its real-time, non-invasive nature [1,2]. Its diagnostic validity relies on acquiring and interpreting standard planes (SPs), which are anatomical sections rich in morphological and pathological information. These SPs underpin biometrics and disease assessment [3] and serve as critical visual landmarks for autonomous robotic navigation and standardized image acquisition [4–7]. However, recognizing SPs from continuous scanning sequences remains challenging due to low contrast, speckle noise, substantial anatomical variations across the population, and subtle differences between adjacent planes [8], leading to high operator dependency [9]. A robust, structured visual representation framework is therefore essential for reliable SP recognition, a critical step toward standardized clinical diagnosis and autonomous robotic ultrasound.

Deep learning has significantly advanced SP recognition. Early approaches relied on convolutional neural networks (CNNs) such as ResNet and VGG to extract localized structural features [10,11], later improved by lightweight pyramid convolution (LPC) modules [12], yet remained constrained by limited receptive fields. To address this, Transformer-based architectures and hybrid frameworks integrating state-space models (SSMs) were introduced to leverage self-attention for modeling long-range dependencies [13–15].

Despite these architectural improvements, imaging artifacts and anatomical variations still induce severe visual ambiguity in SP recognition [16]. Moreover, most existing studies remain limited to single-organ settings and a few highly distinguishable planes, failing to meet the comprehensive screening requirements of clinical practice [17]. Consequently, the high intra-class variability and subtle inter-class differences of ultrasound images still cause elevated false-positive rates when distinguishing morphologically similar planes [18].

Effective visual representations are pivotal for accurate SP classification. Recent visual foundation models, especially those pre-trained on large-scale ultrasound datasets, demonstrate strong feature extraction capability [19,20]. However, adapting these models directly to SP recognition remains challenging. Their generic representations often lack the task-specific granularity needed to distinguish subtle inter-plane differences, which are critical for clinical reliability.

To address this gap, we propose GCM-Net (Gaussian-Contrastive Multi-layer Fusion Network), a new anatomy-aware network that integrates cross-layer feature fusion with anatomical geometric constraints. The network leverages a pre-trained foundation model for strong general representation capacity and introduces a learnable multi-layer feature fusion (LMFF) module to adaptively aggregate multi-scale information. An adaptive anisotropic Gaussian refinement (AAGR) module further improves interpretability by generating spatial weight maps for focused enhancement in key regions. In addition, a memory-bank-based supervised contrastive learning strategy strengthens feature discriminability under low-contrast and highly similar imaging conditions.

We evaluated our method on a self-constructed abdominal ultrasound dataset containing nine categories of SPs, as well as on one public FPUS23 [21] dataset.

The results demonstrate that GCM-Net outperforms existing methods across multiple metrics. Crucially, experimental validation in ultrasound video streams proves that GCM-Net achieves stable and high-confidence automated assessment, indicating strong potential for clinical application.

2 Methodology

GCM-Net achieves precise classification of SPs in continuous scanning videos by utilizing three key innovations (Fig. 1): (a) adaptation of a medical foundation model for robust feature representation, (b) multi-scale feature fusion and spatial refinement module for enhanced discrimination, and (c) dual-head optimization strategy employing memory-bank-augmented contrastive loss to enhance anatomical distinctiveness.

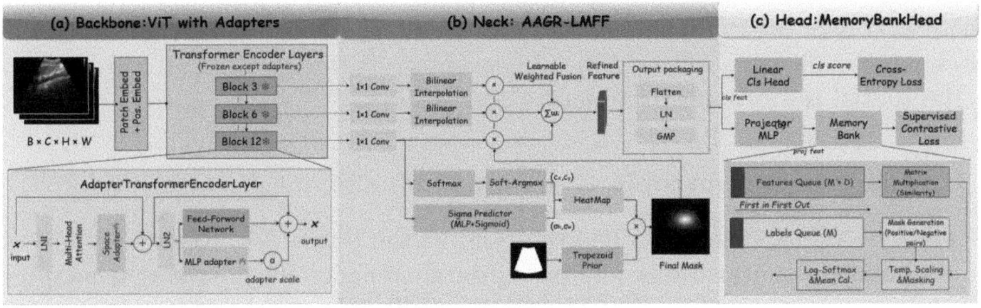

Fig. 1. Architecture of proposed GCM-Net. (a) Backbone: Vision Transformer (ViT) with adapters for parameter-efficient fine-tuning. (b) Neck: adaptive anisotropic Gaussian refinement (AAGR) and learnable multi-layer feature fusion (LMFF). (c) Head: dual-branch head consisting of a linear head for class-score prediction and a projection head for contrastive representation learning.

2.1 Feature Extraction via MED-SA

GCM-Net adopts the MED-SA backbone [22] with Parameter-Efficient Fine-Tuning (PEFT) for robust and efficient image representations from ultrasound images. Specifically, the pre-trained ViT [19] is frozen with lightweight adapters inserted. For the l-th layer, let z_l denote the input feature representation. The intermediate state z'_l and the subsequent output z_{l+1} are formulated as:

$$z'_l = \text{Adap}_s(\text{MSA}(\text{LN}(z_l)))+z_l,\; z_{l+1} = \text{FFN}(\text{LN}(z'_l))+z'_l+s\cdot\text{Adap}_m(\text{LN}(z'_l)) \quad (1)$$

where s denotes the scaling factor for the residual adaptation, LN represents Layer Normalization, and MSA is Multi-head Self-Attention. Here, Adap_s and Adap_m represent the spatial and MLP adapters respectively. The multi-scale feature pyramid $F = \{F_3, F_6, F_{12}\}$ is constructed by extracting and reshaping the outputs from specific layers, utilizing F_{12} as the primary semantic anchor.

2.2 Learnable Multi-scale Feature Fusion (LMFF)

To effectively aggregate local textural details and global semantic contexts from the learned representations, we propose the learnable multi-scale feature fusion (LMFF) module. Unlike static summation or concatenation, LMFF introduces a set of learnable scalar weights $\alpha = \{\alpha_3, \alpha_6, \alpha_{12}\}$ to dynamically re-weight features based on their contribution to the recognition task. The weights are normalized via *Softmax*. By weighted summation of spatially aligned maps, the fused feature F_{fuse} is obtained:

$$\omega_l = \frac{\exp(\alpha_l)}{\sum_{k\in\{3,6,12\}} \exp(\alpha_k)}, \quad l \in \{3, 6, 12\} \tag{2}$$

$$F_{\text{fuse}} = \sum_{l\in\{3,6,12\}} \omega_l \cdot \psi(F_l) \tag{3}$$

where $\psi(\cdot)$ denotes the transformation consisting of a 1×1 lateral convolution for channel unification followed by bilinear interpolation to align all feature maps to the spatial resolution of the master feature F_{12}.

2.3 Adaptive Anisotropic Gaussian Refinement (AAGR)

To effectively focus the model's attention on the diagnostic Region of Interest amidst inherent speckle noise and background artifacts, we propose the adaptive anisotropic Gaussian refinement (AAGR) module. This module processes semantic features F_{12} through anatomical centroid regression and anisotropic Gaussian modeling, thereby integrating semantic attention with geometric constraints. It should be noted that no manual landmark annotation was provided for centroid supervision in our setting; the anatomical relevance of the attention focus is instead an emergent property of the classification objective, as qualitatively demonstrated in Fig. 2(e).

Anatomical Centroid Regression. Standard coordinate extraction methods (e.g., *Argmax*) are non-differentiable and suffer from quantization errors. To overcome this and enable end-to-end training, we employ the *Soft-argmax* operator [23]. This mechanism differentiably regresses the sub-pixel centroid coordinates (c_x, c_y) directly from the deepest feature map F_{12}, ensuring that the attention center aligns robustly with the semantic core of the target organ.

Anisotropic Gaussian Modeling. Instead of rigid bounding boxes, we model the region of interest as a probabilistic field using an anisotropic Gaussian distribution to accommodate irregular or elongated anatomy. The model predicts independent vertical and horizontal standard deviations (σ_w, σ_h) from the network outputs, allowing the attention window to adapt its aspect ratio to organ shape. The resulting Gaussian spatial attention map M_{gauss} models the decay of certainty from the anatomical center to the periphery:

$$M_{gauss}(x, y) = \exp\left(-\frac{(x - c_x)^2}{2\sigma_w^2} - \frac{(y - c_y)^2}{2\sigma_h^2}\right) \quad (4)$$

Finally, to confine the analysis to the valid scanning sector, we impose a physical constraint using a pre-defined Trapezoidal Mask (M_{trap}) based on the probe's geometry. The final spatial attention map is derived via the element-wise product $M_{total} = M_{gauss} \odot M_{trap}$. This operation effectively confines the feature response within the intersection of the anatomically probable region and the physically valid imaging area, filtering out irrelevant background noise with minimal parameter overhead.

2.4 Dual-Head Objective Function

To enhance the discriminative power of the learned representations, particularly for visually similar SPs, we employ a dual optimization framework with a classification head and a contrastive projection head. The classification head optimizes the standard cross-entropy loss $\mathcal{L}_{ce}$. Meanwhile, the contrastive projection head employs a supervised contrastive loss ($\mathcal{L}_{supcon}$) to increase the similarity of embeddings from the same class while pushing apart those from different classes. To further mitigate the impact of small batch sizes on contrastive learning, a first-in-first-out memory bank $\mathcal{M}$ is integrated to store historical projection embeddings [24]. By retrieving negative samples from $\mathcal{M}$, the model accesses a significantly larger distribution of negative pairs, facilitating a more compact and distinct feature space. The supervised contrastive loss is formulated as:

$$\mathcal{L}_{supcon} = -\sum_{i \in I} \frac{1}{|\mathcal{P}(i)|} \sum_{p \in \mathcal{P}(i)} \log \frac{\exp(z_i \cdot z_p / \tau)}{\sum_{\substack{k \in [A(i) \cup \mathcal{M}] \\ k \neq i}} \exp(z_i \cdot z_k / \tau)} \quad (5)$$

where $i \in I$ is the index of the anchor sample, τ is the temperature parameter, and $A(i)$ represents the current mini-batch. The terms z_i, z_p, and z_k represent the L_2-normalized projection embeddings. The set $\mathcal{P}(i)$ defines the indices of all positive samples in the combined set $\{A(i) \cup \mathcal{M}\}$ with respect to the anchor, with its cardinality $|\mathcal{P}(i)|$ serving as a normalization factor. The model is optimized by minimizing the total joint loss:

$$\mathcal{L}_{total} = \mathcal{L}_{ce} + \lambda \mathcal{L}_{supcon} \quad (6)$$

where λ is a balancing hyperparameter.

3 Experiments

3.1 Experimental Setup

Datasets and Evaluation Metrics. We utilized an abdominal ultrasound dataset consisting of nine categories, hereafter referred to as AbdoSP-9, curated by chief physicians from a hospital in accordance with routine clinical examination protocols, with written informed consent obtained from all participants. Annotation reliability was verified by independent re-labelling of 30 subjects by one chief physician and two attending physicians, with discrepancies resolved by consensus, yielding Fleiss' κ=0.7114. The dataset encompasses eight clinically significant standard planes (SPs), including the Abdominal Aorta (AA), Caudate Lobe (CL), Inferior Vena Cava (IVC), Left Portal Vein (LPV), Three Hepatic Veins (THV), IVC with Gallbladder (IVC-GB), Pancreatic Body (PB), and Pancreatic Tail (PT), all of which serve as essential landmarks for liver and pancreatic assessment. Additionally, a Non-SP (NSP) category comprising transitional frames and motion blur was incorporated to enhance the model's robustness against background noise and indistinct structures frequently encountered in dynamic scanning sequences.

To assess generalization and real-world stability, we evaluated on the public FPUS23 dataset [21] for fetal growth monitoring, including Abdominal Circumference (AC), Femur Length (FL), Biparietal Diameter (BPD), and Background (No Plane), and collected six additional continuous-scanning video sequences to measure inference speed and frame-to-frame consistency in dynamic scenarios. Comprehensive comparison used accuracy, precision, recall, and F1-score, while dynamic performance on empirical scans was assessed by success rate, mean absolute error (MAE), and temporal localization bias (Table 1).

Table 1. Distribution of samples across the AbdoSP-9 dataset

SPs	AA	CL	IVC	LPV	THV	IVC-GB	PB	PT	NSP
Number	326	380	328	544	264	391	191	369	222

Implementation Details. GCM-Net was implemented in PyTorch and trained on four NVIDIA RTX 4080 GPUs. Inputs were resized to 1024 $\times$ 1024 and augmented with random resizing, horizontal flipping, and color jittering. We used Adam with a learning rate of 10^{-4} and AMP. The mini-batch size was 2 with gradient accumulation of 4, and the supervised-contrastive weight was set to $\lambda = 0.6$ based on extensive experiments. The memory bank size is set to $M = 512$, and the model is trained for 10000 iterations. Inference latency on an NVIDIA RTX 4080 with FP16/TF32 mixed precision is 65.25 ms/frame, encompassing pre-processing (1024$\times$1024 resizing and normalization), model inference, and post-processing, satisfying the real-time requirement for clinical deployment.

3.2 Quantitative Comparison

We evaluated our GCM-Net against a diverse set of benchmark methodologies, including the ultrasound-specific classification model SonoNet64 [10], leading vision foundation models such as DINOv3 [25], and cutting-edge medical-task-specific models like MedViTV2 [13].

As summarized in Table 2, GCM-Net achieved state-of-the-art performance across both datasets, reaching 99.53% accuracy on FPUS23 and 81.37% on the more complex AbdoSP-9 dataset. These results represented significant improvements, specifically outperforming DINOv3 by 3.89% on FPUS23 and surpassing the second-best MedViTV2-small by 7.93% on the AbdoSP-9 task. Furthermore, GCM-Net outperformed established benchmarks such as SonoNet-64 and DINOv3. This demonstrated superior discriminative power and robustness in capturing subtle anatomical features within complex clinical scenarios.

3.3 Ablation Study

To quantitatively evaluate the contribution of each proposed module to the model performance, we conducted a systematic ablation study on AbdoSP-9 dataset. The evaluation compared the baseline backbone with several variants produced by individually removing the LMFF module, the AAGR module, and the contrastive learning branch. Table 3 summarizes the experimental results.

Table 2. Quantitative comparisons of different models

Method	FPUS23				AbdoSP-9			
	Acc(%)	Prec(%)	Rec(%)	F1(%)	Acc(%)	Prec(%)	Rec(%)	F1(%)
SonoNet64 [10]	94.22	94.50	94.24	94.02	58.78	53.54	54.63	53.42
DINOv3 [25]	95.64	96.00	95.75	95.75	57.25	58.67	54.75	55.56
MedViTV2-small [13]	97.91	97.92	97.91	97.90	73.44	78.79	73.44	74.31
GCM-Net(Ours)	**99.53**	**99.53**	**99.53**	**99.52**	**81.37**	**83.85**	**79.14**	**78.80**

Table 3. Ablation study on the AbdoSP-9 dataset

Setting	LMFF	AAGR	SupCon	Acc(%)	Prec(%)	Rec(%)	F1(%)
Only Backbone				72.37	69.41	68.72	66.78
w/o LMFF		✓	✓	80.61	81.94	78.87	78.27
w/o AAGR	✓		✓	78.63	81.01	73.90	72.55
w/o SupCon	✓	✓		75.88	77.34	72.45	70.19
Full Model	✓	✓	✓	**81.37**	**83.85**	**79.14**	**78.80**

Ablation results demonstrated that GCM-Net significantly outperformed the baseline, yielding improvements of 9.00% in accuracy and 12.02% in F1-score. These findings validated the synergy of the integrated modules. Contrastive learning proved to be the most critical component and its removal resulted in a 5.49% accuracy drop, indicating its essential role in enhancing feature discriminability. Furthermore, the AAGR module was vital for anatomical capture, as evidenced by a 5.24% recall decrease upon its removal. Finally, the LMFF module contributed a 1.91% precision gain through granular feature fusion.

We ablate τ and λ on AbdoSP-9. Low τ=0.1 achieves peak accuracy (81.37%) by sharpening the contrastive distribution for hard negative mining. Higher values over-smooth it (e.g., 76.03% at τ=0.5). For loss weight, λ=0.6 (81.37%) balances contrastive regularization with classification, with under-weighting (λ=0.2, 76.49%) and over-weighting (λ=1.0, 78.47%) degrading performance.

3.4 Robustness Analysis in Real-World Scenarios

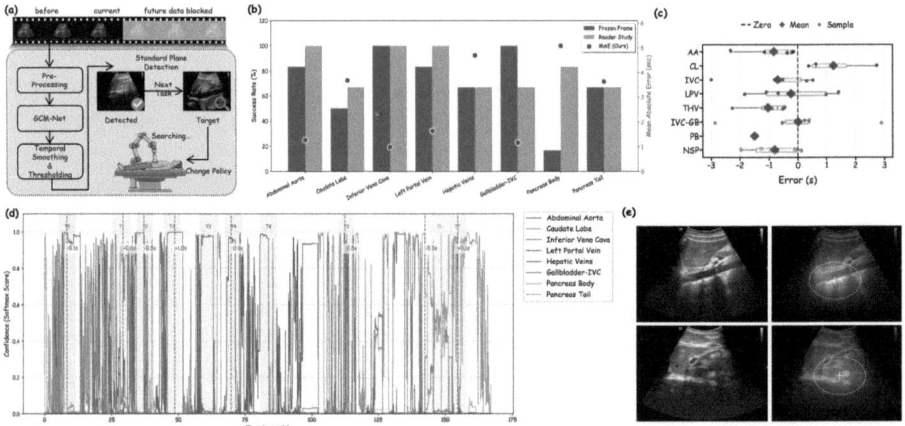

Fig. 2. Evaluation of GCM-Net for real-time causal processing of in vivo ultrasound scans. (a) Causal inference pipeline and conceptual framework for robotic ultrasound guidance. (b) Success rates and mean absolute error (MAE) of temporal localization across all anatomical planes. (c) Error distribution for successful detections shown as boxplots. (d) Temporal confidence refinement (TCR) results. (e) Representative AAGR Gaussian attention maps overlaid on ultrasound frames.

Figure 2(a) illustrates the causal inference pipeline for real-time ultrasound processing using GCM-Net. GCM-Net processes each frame at 30 fps, maintaining a W_s=30-frame moving-average confidence $\bar{c}_t^{(k)}$ per class k. After a 3.0 s warm-up, the system enters peak-tracking mode once $\bar{c}_t^{(k)}$ exceeds a validation-derived threshold θ_k, continuously updating the candidate peak t^*. Detection locks when no improvement is observed within a W_p=60-frame patience window:

$$t^* = \arg\max_{t \geq t_{\text{warm}}} \bar{c}_t^{(k)}, \quad s_{n,k} = \mathbf{1}[\text{TCR fires}] \cdot \mathbf{1}[|t^*_{n,k} - t^{\text{GT}}_{n,k}| \leq \delta], \tag{7}$$

where a detection is counted successful if TCR fires and the temporal error falls within δ=3.0 s.

Figure 2(d) presents the temporal confidence refinement (TCR) result on a representative clinical scan, where temporally correlated detection peaks suppress single-frame false positives while preserving the stability needed for robust scanning guidance. Quantitatively (green bars, Fig. 2(b)), GCM-Net performs robustly across all tasks, achieving a 70.83% overall success rate and a low temporal MAE of 1.06 s among successful detections. To assess clinical utility, a reader study had a chief physician review the frames selected by GCM-Net, yielding a clinical accuracy of 81.25% (39/48 tasks, light green bars) that surpasses the mathematical metric. This discrepancy is evident in challenging tasks such as pancreatic body classification, where clinicians often rewind the video to retrospectively select an optimal frame, causing the ground-truth timestamp (defined at the freeze-frame) to lag behind the model's real-time detection. Overall, GCM-Net's real-time causal inference shows significant potential as a high-level controller for autonomous robotic ultrasound (Fig. 2(a)) and an intelligent assistant for manual scanning.

4 Conclusion

We propose GCM-Net, an anatomy-aware framework for robust standard plane classification in abdominal ultrasound. By integrating differentiable spatial gating with foundation model adaptation and a memory-bank-based dual-head objective, GCM-Net effectively enhances feature discriminability while suppressing noise and artifacts. Evaluations on abdominal and fetal datasets demonstrate superior accuracy and robust causal video inference, establishing a scalable pathway toward standardized diagnosis and autonomous robotic ultrasound.

Acknowledgments. This work was supported by the National Key Research and Development Program of China (2025YFC2425700, 2022YFC2405200), National Natural Science Foundation of China (82472115), Beijing Natural Science Foundation (L252049, L252007) and Tsinghua University Dushi Program.

Disclosure of Interests. The authors have no competing interests to declare that are relevant to the content of this article.

References

1. Leigh, N., Hammill, C.W.: Liver ultrasound: normal anatomy and pathologic findings. Surgery Open Sci. **19**, 178–198 (2024)
2. Zhang, T., et al.: Application of ultrasound localization microscopy in evaluating the type 2 diabetes progression. Cyborg Bionic Syst. **6**, 0117 (2025)
3. Kamaya, A., Fetzer, D.T., Seow, J.H., et al.: LI-RADS US surveillance version 2024 for surveillance of hepatocellular carcinoma: an update to the American college of radiology US LI-RADS. Radiology **313**, e240169 (2024)

4. Li, Z., et al: Beyond hospital reach: autonomous lightweight ultrasound robot for liver sonography. arXiv preprint arXiv:2510.08106 (2025)
5. Liang, H., Zhang, S., Ning, G., Luo, J., Liao, H.: Quasi-static elastography-driven automated robotic ultrasound screening and localization. IEEE Trans. Biomed. Eng., 1–14 (2025)
6. Han, T., et al.: Toward clinical applications of intelligent robotic ultrasound systems. IEEE Rev. Biomed. Eng. **19**, 227–247 (2026)
7. Wu, Z., Wang, X., Cao, Y., Zhang, W., Xu, Q.: Robotic ultrasound scanning end-effector with adjustable constant contact force. Cyborg Bionic Syst. **6**, 0251 (2025)
8. Chen, H., et al.: Automatic fetal ultrasound standard plane detection using knowledge transferred recurrent neural networks. In: Medical Image Computing and Computer-Assisted Intervention – MICCAI 2015, pp. 507–514. Springer International Publishing (2015)
9. Maraci, M.A., Napolitano, R., Papageorghiou, A., Noble, J.A.: Searching for structures of interest in an ultrasound video sequence. In: Machine Learning in Medical Imaging, pp. 133–140. Springer International Publishing (2014)
10. Baumgartner, C.F., et al.: SonoNet: real-time detection and localisation of fetal standard scan planes in freehand ultrasound. IEEE Trans. Med. Imag. **36**, 2204–2215 (2017)
11. Lawley, A., Hampson, R., Worrall, K., Dobie, G.: Analysis of neural networks for routine classification of sixteen ultrasound upper abdominal cross sections. Abdom. Radiol. **49**, 651–661 (2024)
12. Yu, T., Tsui, P.H., Leonov, D., Wu, S., Bin, G., Zhou, Z.: LPC-SonoNet: a lightweight network based on sononet and light pyramid convolution for. fetal ultrasound standard plane detection. Sensors (Basel) **24** (2024)
13. Nejati Manzari, O., Asgariandehkordi, H., Koleilat, T., Xiao, Y., Rivaz, H.: Medical image classification with KAN-integrated transformers and dilated neighborhood attention. Appl. Soft Comput. **186**, 114045 (2026)
14. Tehsin, S., Alshaya, H., Bouchelligua, W., Nasir, I.M.: Hybrid state-space and vision transformer framework for fetal ultrasound plane classification in prenatal diagnostics. Diagnostics (Basel) **15** (2025)
15. Chowdary, G.J., Yin, Z.: Med-Former: a transformer based architecture for medical image classification. In: International Conference on Medical Image Computing and Computer-assisted Intervention, pp. 448–457. Springer (2024)
16. Fiorentino, M.C., Villani, F.P., Di Cosmo, M., Frontoni, E., Moccia, S.: A review on deep-learning algorithms for fetal ultrasound-image analysis. Med. Image Anal. **83**, 102629 (2023)
17. Cohen, H.L., et al.: AIUM practice guideline for the performance of an ultrasound examination of the abdomen and/or retroperitoneum. J. Ultrasound Med. **27**, 319–326 (2008)
18. Conti, E., Rosati, R., Federici, L., Mancini, A., Fiorentin, M.C.: Challenging DINOv3 foundation model under low inter-class variability: a case study on fetal brain ultrasound (2025). arXiv:2511.01915 arXiv preprint
19. Meyer, A., Murali, A., Zarin, F., Mutter, D., Padoy, N.: UltraSam: a foundation model for ultrasound using large open-access segmentation datasets. Int. J. Comput. Assist. Radiol. Surg. (2025)
20. Jiao, J., et al.: USFM: a universal ultrasound foundation model generalized to tasks and organs towards label efficient image analysis. Med. Image Anal. **96**, 103202 (2024)

21. Prabakaran, B.S., Hamelmann, P., Ostrowski, E., Shafique, M.: FPUS23: an ultrasound fetus phantom dataset with deep neural network evaluations for fetus orientations, fetal planes, and anatomical features. IEEE Access **11**, 58308–58317 (2023)
22. Wu, J., et al.: Medical SAM adapter: adapting segment anything model for medical image segmentation. Med. Image Anal. **102**, 103547 (2025)
23. Nibali, A., He, Z., Morgan, S., Prendergast, L.: Numerical coordinate regression with convolutional neural networks (2018). arXiv:1801.07372 arXiv preprint
24. Wu, Z., Xiong, Y., Yu, S.X., Lin, D.: Unsupervised feature learning via non-parametric instance discrimination. In: IEEE/CVF Conference on Computer Vision and Pattern Recognition, pp. 3733–3742 (2018)
25. Siméoni, O., et al.: Dinov3. arXiv preprint arXiv:2508.10104 (2025)

Interactive MWA Planning via Probabilistic Inverse Inference

Francesco Dettori(✉), Ilias Nahmed, Michel Duprez, Pablo Alvarez, and Stéphane Cotin

ICube, Université de Strasbourg, CNRS, Inria, Strasbourg 67000, France
francesco.dettori@inria.fr

Abstract. Microwave ablation (MWA) is a well-established curative treatment for unresectable tumors. However, current clinical planning strategies rely predominantly on geometric heuristics that neglect patient-specific physiology, often resulting in incomplete tumor ablation or unintended damage to healthy tissues. While physics-based bioheat finite element simulations can model the underlying electromagnetic and thermal interactions, their computational cost renders them impractical for interactive clinical planning. We propose a novel, human-in-the-loop computational framework for interactive, patient-specific preoperative MWA planning. At its core there is a deep learning inverse model that directly infers clinically actionable ablation parameters (generator power, ablation duration, and axial depth) given a target tumor mask. The model assesses with sub-second latency the feasibility of insertion paths proposed by the clinician. When viable, it predicts optimal settings to maximize tumor coverage while minimizing collateral damage. Our framework also supports multi-antenna strategies via a sequential optimization scheme. It has been validated against *in vivo* porcine experiments and tested on patient data. Our solution achieved an overall Technical Success Rate of 97% across 116 clinical cases and generated viable multi-antenna treatment plans with sub-second latency (~300 ms per antenna). This interactive framework bridges the gap between high-fidelity bioheat modeling and interactive clinical decision-making, enabling safe, efficient, and personalized MWA strategies.

Keywords: Thermal ablation · Planning · Deep Learning

1 Introduction

For cancer patients ineligible for surgical resection, minimally invasive thermal ablation represents the preferred curative alternative. While Radiofrequency Ablation (RFA) has historically been the clinical standard, Microwave Ablation (MWA) is now a preferred option as it permits obtaining larger and more uniform

---

Supplementary Information The online version contains supplementary material available at https://doi.org/10.1007/978-3-032-38236-8_23.

G. Yang et al. (Eds.): MICCAI 2026, LNCS 16893, pp. 232–241, 2027.
https://doi.org/10.1007/978-3-032-38236-8_23

ablation zones in shorter times [1,12,13]. Performing MWA procedures, however, is challenging, and planning is key to achieving optimal results. Currently, this planning relies essentially on manufacturer charts linking power and duration to expected lesion sizes. Such geometric heuristics neglect patient-specific physiology, particularly the heat-sink effect caused by perfused tissue and adjacent vasculature, leading to systematic errors in tumor coverage or unnecessary damage to healthy parenchyma [2,4].

Unlike RFA, where treatment control is primarily temporal, MWA is governed by a sophisticated interplay between tissue dielectric properties, electromagnetic propagation, and heat diffusion. Optimizing MWA, therefore, requires the simultaneous coordination of multiple coupled parameters - generator power, exposure time, and antenna pose - under anatomical and physiological constraints. Due to this complexity, no existing work provides a simulation-based framework for MWA planning. The few efforts toward automated ablation planning primarily target RFA. Some rely entirely on geometric heuristics, assuming predefined ablation shapes while neglecting the underlying physics [8]. Conversely, recent learning-based studies for RFA focus on accelerating forward simulations [9,10,15]. While some of these frameworks demonstrate planning as a downstream application, they rely on iterative optimization loops to exhaustively search for a solution, such as incrementally adjusting ablation diameters, rather than performing direct parameter inference [10]. While such iterative approaches are feasible for RFA, where the parameter space is relatively small, they do not scale to MWA planning. Introducing generator power as an additional coupled parameter expands the search space. Consequently, achieving interactive MWA planning requires a shift toward a direct inverse-parameter inference approach.

To develop an interactive planning solution for MWA, a computational framework capable of simulating outcomes in real time is essential. Solving the coupled electromagnetic-thermal equations (Maxwell and Pennes equations) remains numerically challenging and computationally prohibitive [3,4,14]. Keshavamurthy *et al.* proposed a deep learning solution requiring a large database of CT ablation images for training and limited to low-perfusion tissues [7], making it unsuitable for capturing complex heat-sink effects.

We introduce a novel inverse model that directly infers optimal treatment parameters, specifically, generator power, ablation duration, and axial depth adjustment along a user-defined trajectory from a target tumor mask, a patient-specific perfusion map, and a clinician-proposed initial trajectory. The system instantly evaluates the safety of the proposed trajectory, identifying the plan as infeasible if it intersects critical anatomical structures or if a complete ablation is impossible with realistic parameters. For viable initializations, it instantly fine-tunes depth and energy delivery to balance tumor coverage with healthy tissue preservation. To enable both the training and instantaneous evaluation of this inverse planner, we simultaneously introduce a forward surrogate model. Trained on high-fidelity synthetic FEM-generated data, this surrogate takes as input a 3D map of the patient's blood perfusion together with the antenna position, power, and duration, to predict ablation outcomes in real time. Integrated into an interactive interface, these components enable the immediate, safety-aware exploration of multi-antenna strategies. We validate lesion prediction on *in vivo* porcine liver ablations and evaluate preoperative planning on a clinical dataset of hepatic tumors.

2 Methods

2.1 FEM Simulation Framework

Heat transfer during MWA was modeled using coupled electromagnetic and thermal equations (Maxwell and Pennes equations). The resulting multiphysics problem was discretized and solved using the finite element method framework described in [5].

Tissue temperature evolution follows the classical Pennes bioheat equation [11], with microwave power deposition derived from a frequency-domain electromagnetic solve at 2.45 GHz under standard boundary conditions, and the resulting thermal damage was quantified using an Arrhenius model. As demonstrated in [5], these biophysical simulations are exceptionally sensitive to the blood perfusion parameter, which dictates the magnitude of the local heat-sink effect. Therefore, rather than assuming constant tissue properties, blood perfusion was explicitly modeled as a spatially heterogeneous field $\omega_b(\mathbf{x})$ distinguishing between liver parenchyma, macroscopic blood vessels, and tumor tissue.

2.2 Forward Surrogate Model

To enable rapid plan evaluation and provide differentiable supervision for the inverse planner, we developed a forward surrogate model. This model predicts the 3D ablation zone from a patient-specific perfusion map and three procedural parameters: generator power P, ablation duration t, and the axial insertion depth d along the planned trajectory. To reduce the spatial variance the network must learn, inputs are mapped into an antenna-centric space. Specifically, the perfusion volume is resampled so that the clinician-defined insertion trajectory aligns precisely with the longitudinal Z-axis, ensuring the position of the microwave antenna is fully defined by the axial depth d.

The surrogate architecture is based on a conditioned 3D U-Net. To inject strong spatial priors, the scalar depth d is converted into a 3D Gaussian distance heatmap H along the canonical Z-axis, explicitly modeling the active antenna tip. This heatmap H is concatenated with the perfusion volume, forming a two-channel, 5D tensor $[B, C, X, Y, Z]$ that is passed to the model alongside a spatial coordinate vector, where B is the batch size. The global conditions P and t are concatenated, linearly projected to match the bottleneck channel dimension, and fused with the encoded features at the deepest U-Net level. The decoder then reconstructs these features to output a voxel-wise probability map $\hat{M}$, supervised end-to-end by the FEM-derived necrosis mask M. To ensure smooth gradients and handle spatial class imbalance, we minimize a Soft Dice loss over all N voxels i:

$$\mathcal{L}_{\text{fwd}} = 1 - \left(2\sum_{i=1}^{N} M_i\hat{M}_i + \epsilon\right) / \left(\sum_{i=1}^{N} M_i + \sum_{i=1}^{N} \hat{M}_i + \epsilon\right), \tag{1}$$

where ϵ ensures numerical stability. Once trained, this fully differentiable surrogate cuts plan evaluation time from several minutes to a fraction of a second. The architecture is detailed in Fig. 1b.

2.3 Probabilistic Inverse Planning Model

The core of our framework is a deep learning inverse model that directly predicts the optimal ablation strategy from a clinician-proposed trajectory. The input volume is rotated to align the trajectory with the canonical Z-axis. The model processes a two-channel 3D tensor comprising the perfusion map $\mathbf{V}_{\text{perf}}$ and the target tumor mask $\mathbf{T}$.

A 3D CNN encoder extracts latent spatial features, which are fed into a Probabilistic Mixture Density Network (MDN) regression head. Because inverse thermodynamic problems are ill-posed (multiple parameter combinations can yield similar ablations), the MDN predicts the parameters of a Gaussian mixture model ($K = 5$). This approach provides multiple plausible treatment strategies, each with associated confidence scores, thereby intrinsically supporting our safety-aware framework. The network outputs three clinically actionable parameters: axial depth adjustment $\hat{d}$, generator power $\hat{P}$, and ablation duration $\hat{t}$.

Directly supervising this model via parameter-space distances (*e.g.* Mean Squared Error) is suboptimal, as it ignores the non-linear thermodynamic consequences of parameter deviations. Instead, we optimize the inverse model end-to-end via a forward-in-the-loop strategy (Fig. 1a). The predicted parameter set $\hat{\phi} = (\hat{d}, \hat{P}, \hat{t})$ and $\mathbf{V}_{\text{perf}}$ are passed through the pre-trained, frozen forward surrogate to generate the predicted ablation zone $\hat{\mathbf{M}}$. The inverse model is then penalized based directly on the clinical quality of $\hat{\mathbf{M}}$ relative to $\mathbf{T}$.

The objective function mirrors clinical priorities: ensuring complete tumor destruction before minimizing collateral damage. The total loss is defined as:

$$\mathcal{L}_{\text{total}} = \alpha\mathcal{L}_{\text{c}} + \Gamma(C)\left(\lambda_{\text{s}}(1 - \text{AE}) + \lambda_{\text{e}}\mathcal{L}_{\text{energy}}\right) + \lambda_{\text{b}}\mathcal{L}_{\text{bounds}}. \tag{2}$$

The components evaluate specific clinical metrics: **Coverage** ($\mathcal{L}_{\text{c}} = 1 - C$) ensures total tumor ablation, where $C = (\sum \mathbf{T}\hat{\mathbf{M}} + \epsilon)/(\sum \mathbf{T} + \epsilon)$. **Tissue Sparing** $(1 - \text{AE})$ penalizes ablation in healthy parenchyma, where Ablation Efficiency (AE) is computed as $(\sum \mathbf{T}\hat{\mathbf{M}} + \epsilon)/(\sum \hat{\mathbf{M}} + \epsilon)$. **Energy Regularization** ($\mathcal{L}_{\text{energy}} = \frac{1}{2}(\hat{P}^2 + \hat{t}^2)$) prevents excessive heating. Note that $\hat{P}$ and $\hat{t}$ are min-max normalized to $[0, 1]$. **Parameter Bounds** ($\mathcal{L}_{\text{bounds}}$) penalizes predictions that fall outside the physical operating limits of the MWA generator (*i.e.* power outside 30–130 W or duration outside 180–500 s). The sparing and energy penalties are modulated by a dynamic coverage gate $\Gamma(C) = \sigma(k(C - 1.0))$. This smooth step-function ensures the network focuses entirely on destroying the tumor

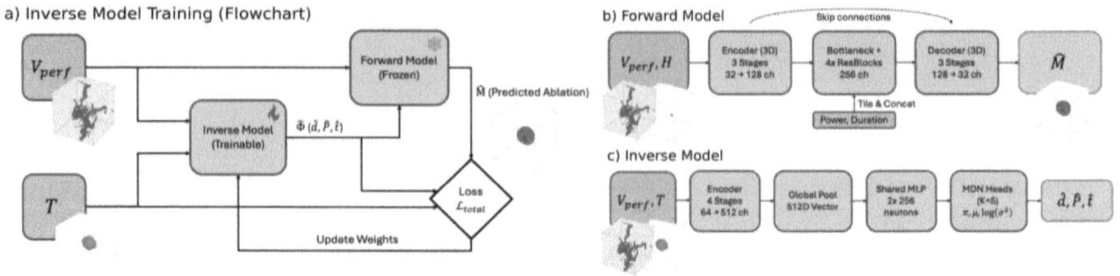

Fig. 1. (a) Training flowchart: the inverse model predicts parameters $\hat{\phi} = (\hat{d}, \hat{P}, \hat{t})$, which are passed to the frozen forward surrogate to optimize the network directly on the expected clinical outcome. (b) Forward model: a 3D U-Net mapping a tensor $[B, C, X, Y, Z]$ (perfusion V_{perf}; antenna tip Gaussian heatmap H) and a coordinate vector to a predicted necrosis mask $\hat{M}$. (c) Inverse model: a 3D CNN with a Mixture Density Network (MDN) head (K=5) inferring multiple plausible treatment strategies.

until complete ablation ($C_{\text{target}} = 1.0$) is achieved, safely refining parameters only after satisfying this primary clinical endpoint. The weighting coefficients $(\alpha, \lambda_{\text{s}}, \lambda_{\text{e}}, \lambda_{\text{b}})$ were empirically fine-tuned to balance coverage maximization and tissue preservation objectives. Figure 1a depicts a flowchart of the inverse model training, while Fig. 1c details its architecture.

2.4 Synthetic Dataset Generation

To train the proposed forward and inverse models, while ensuring they learn generalized electromagnetic and bioheat physics rather than memorizing static patient anatomies, we generated a fully synthetic dataset of 2400 procedurally perfused parenchymal volumes using the aforementioned FEM pipeline. Each training sample contains the exact inputs and targets required by our framework: (i) a heterogeneous perfusion map $\mathbf{V}_{\text{perf}}$; (ii) the procedural parameters (axial insertion depth d, generator power P, and ablation duration t); and (iii) the resultant necrosis mask M obtained from FEM simulation.

For each synthetic case, we initialize a label map as background tissue and procedurally generate vascular trees. A tumor, modeled as an irregular ellipsoidal mask with random morphological perturbations, is then inserted and spatially carved against the vessels to ensure anatomical realism. For every accepted anatomy-tumor configuration, treatment parameters are uniformly sampled, with generator power ranging from 30 to 130 W, and ablation duration from 180 to 500 s. Finally, heterogeneous perfusion values are assigned: background perfusion is randomly sampled from 4 discrete levels within $[0.015, 0.075]$ s^{-1}; vessel perfusion is scaled according to the vessel radius [5]; and tumor perfusion is fixed at 1.5 times the surrounding parenchymal rate [18].

2.5 Multi-antenna Sequential Planning

Complete ablation of large or irregular tumors typically requires multiple ablations, performed either simultaneously or, more commonly, sequentially [6]. For the first antenna, the clinician specifies an insertion trajectory. The system immediately verifies its safety by tracing the shaft within the global volume, and any intersection with critical anatomy (*e.g.* major vessels, ribs) triggers an instant collision warning, prompting path correction. Once a viable trajectory is confirmed, the inverse model processes the antenna-centered perfusion volume to infer the optimal parameters $\hat{\phi}_1 = (\hat{d}_1, \hat{P}_1, \hat{t}_1)$. The forward surrogate then evaluates these parameters to predict the initial ablation zone. For each subsequent antenna k, the target is dynamically updated by subtracting the cumulative ablation mask $\mathbf{U}_{k-1}$, yielding a residual tumor mask $\mathbf{M}_{\text{res},k} = \mathbf{T} \setminus \mathbf{U}_{k-1}$. If $\mathbf{M}_{\text{res},k} = \emptyset$, full coverage is achieved; Otherwise, the clinician proposes a new trajectory targeting the remaining tumoral tissue and the inverse model infers $\hat{\phi}_k$ for the updated spatial crop. This loop enables clinicians to rapidly and safely iterate complex multi-antenna strategies within seconds.

2.6 Experimental Setup and Evaluation Metrics

The model was trained and evaluated across three data domains. The synthetic dataset ($n = 2400$) was divided into 2100 training and 300 validation cases to optimize the core networks. Physical accuracy of the forward surrogate was validated on an *in vivo* porcine liver dataset ($n = 6$ procedures, ethics committee approved). Finally, the clinical viability of the inverse planner was evaluated on the public 3D-IRCADb-01 dataset (20 patients, 116 hepatic tumors) [16]. 12 tumors were excluded from the evaluation: 5 were located outside the liver parenchyma (patients 7, 12, 14), and 7 exceeded the maximum treatable volume for MWA, as attempting complete coverage for targets of this size is generally contraindicated and would require a clinically impractical number of antennas. Forward predictions were compared with ground-truth macroscopic necrosis using the Dice Similarity Coefficient (DSC) and the 95th percentile Hausdorff Distance (HD95). Inverse model clinical efficacy was measured via the Technical Success Rate (TSR), defined as the percentage of plans achieving a Tumor Coverage (C) = 100%. Healthy parenchyma preservation was quantified using Ablation Efficiency (AE), defined as the ratio of the ablated target volume to the total ablation volume, using a clinically suggested 5 mm margin-expanded target, rather than the raw tumor. This isolates true algorithmic over-treatment from necessary oncological safety margins [17]. Computational performance was assessed by recording the inference time for sequential multi-antenna planning against traditional iterative FEM solvers. Both the forward and inverse models were trained using an Adam optimizer (learning rate 10^{-4}, batch size 4) over 250 epochs.

3 Results

3.1 *In Vivo* validation of the forward surrogate

To ensure optimization against a physically accurate baseline, we evaluated the forward surrogate on the *in vivo* porcine dataset. The surrogate achieved a mean

DSC of 0.82 ± 0.04 and an HD95 of 2.0 ± 0.4 mm against ground-truth necrosis, outperforming the manufacturer's standard charts (DSC: 0.59 ± 0.12). Furthermore, the surrogate demonstrated high fidelity to the FEM solver, achieving a DSC of 0.90 ± 0.00 for *in vivo* ablations and 0.94 ± 0.01 across 300 synthetic samples. Figure 2a displays a CT scan from ablation session 5, where the model prediction (red) is overlaid with the ground-truth necrosis segmentation (blue). The FEM solver required ∼3 min per antenna, whereas our surrogate model needed only 4 ms on an NVIDIA GeForce RTX 5070 GPU.

3.2 Clinical Efficacy of the Inverse Planner

On the clinical IRCAD dataset, trajectories were initialized by an expert clinician. The framework achieved an overall TSR of 97% over the $n = 116$ tumors (Table 1). For the 38 tumors out of 116 requiring multi-antenna configurations, defined by a maximum diameter > 3 cm, the sequential strategy maintained a mean coverage of 99.3% with an Ablation Efficiency of 0.71. Our overall AE of 0.52 compares favorably to the work of Meister et al. [10], which used an identical 5 mm margin expansion and reported an AE between 24% and 50%. This comparison highlights our network's success in balancing the tissue-sparing penalty (1 − AE) against the geometric requirements for total margin-inclusive tumor destruction. Lower AE values were primarily observed in single-antenna treatments for sub-centimeter tumors (n = 23; maximum diameter < 10 mm), reflecting the fact that even the lowest MWA settings generate a minimum lesion of approximately 20 mm in diameter, rather than an optimization failure. The complete inverse planning loop, including spatial crop extraction, parameter inference ($\hat{\phi}$), and safety-aware forward verification, averaged 0.3 s per antenna. This sub-second latency enables a truly interactive, clinician-in-the-loop workflow. Figure 2b illustrates the graphical user interface (GUI) used for interactive treatment planning.

Table 1. Clinical evaluation on the 3D-IRCADb-01 dataset ($n = 116$).

Metric	Single-Antenna	Multi-Antenna	Overall
TSR ($C = 100\%$)	100%	89%	97%
Tumor Coverage (C)	$100\% \pm 0\%$	$99.3\% \pm 1.2\%$	$99.8\% \pm 0.8\%$
Ablation Efficiency (AE)	0.44 ± 0.21	0.71 ± 0.12	0.52 ± 0.23

4 Discussion and Conclusion

We presented a clinician-in-the-loop framework for interactive, patient-specific MWA planning. Unlike prior RFA and MWA methods that rely on accelerated forward simulations [9,10,15] or geometric heuristics [8], our approach learns

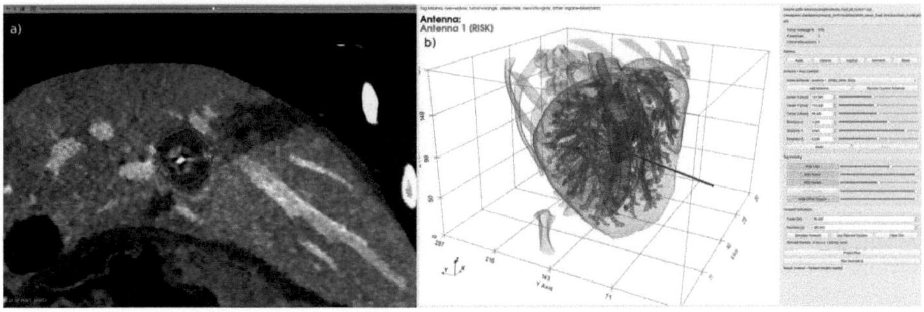

Fig. 2. ***In Vivo* validation and Planning interface.** (a) Comparison between predicted ablation zone (red) and *in vivo* macroscopic necrosis (blue) in porcine liver. (b) Interactive GUI showcasing the features of the implemented framework.

the inverse mapping from target outcomes to procedural parameters, enabling instant inference without iterative search. By adopting a probabilistic MDN-based formulation, the model captures multiple feasible strategies consistent with biophysical constraints. We demonstrated a DSC of 0.82 during *in vivo* porcine studies, providing a rare evaluation against macroscopic necrosis that successfully accounts for active heat-sink effects, unlike previous studies that used *ex vivo* ablations. Despite challenges like tissue contraction and dynamic perfusion, this spatial overlap confirms the forward surrogate provides realistic physical constraints for the inverse planner. On the 3D-IRCADb-01 dataset, the model successfully generalized from synthetic training to complex human anatomies. A 97% TSR across single- and multi-antenna treatments demonstrates that the loss function prioritizes tumor destruction, while Ablation Efficiency indicates that the MDN effectively refined power and duration to spare healthy tissue. A key advantage is seamless clinical integration: radiologists retain trajectory autonomy while the planner replaces static vendor charts with physiology-aware thermodynamic parameters. Reducing computation time from minutes to milliseconds enables interactive planning with automated safety checks. Because training relies on procedurally generated anatomies, the surrogate learns the underlying physics rather than memorizing cases, ensuring robustness.

Despite this potential, limitations exist. First, "optimality" is difficult to validate *in vivo* as ablations cannot be repeated on the same tumor. Consequently, validation is restricted to comparing the forward surrogate against observed necrosis, while clinical efficacy is demonstrated retrospectively. Second, the framework assumes unchanged anatomy during antenna insertion, neglecting possible deformation and target displacement. Third, our sequential multi-antenna strategy is greedy and keeps pre-treatment tissue properties after each virtual ablation, which may limit global optimality. Future work will focus on the *in vivo* validation of the inverse planner's generated treatment plans on porcine models to assess actual clinical efficacy. Furthermore, we plan to investigate joint multi-antenna optimization architectures to improve global thermodynamic outcomes compared to the current sequential strategy.

Acknowledgments. This work was funded by the MEDITWIN Bpifrance i-Demo project as part of the France 2030 program. The authors thank Dr. Juan Verde and the *Institut Hospitalo-Universitaire (IHU) de Strasbourg* for their support.

Disclosure of Interests. The authors have no competing interests to declare that are relevant to the content of this article.

References

1. Ahmed, M., Brace, C.L., Lee, F.T., Goldberg, S.N.: Principles of and advances in percutaneous ablation. Radiology **258**(2), 351–369 (2011). https://doi.org/10.1148/radiol.10081634
2. Audigier, C., et al.: Efficient lattice Boltzmann solver for patient-specific radiofrequency ablation of hepatic tumors. IEEE Trans. Med. Imag. **34**(7), 1576–1589 (2015). https://doi.org/10.1109/TMI.2015.2406575
3. Boregowda, G., Mariappan, P.: Effect of high blood flow on heat distribution and ablation zone during microwave ablation-numerical approach. Int. J. Num. Meth. Biomed. Eng. **40**(8), e3835 (2024). https://doi.org/10.1002/cnm.3835
4. Chiang, J., Wang, P., Brace, C.L.: Computational modelling of microwave Tumour ablations. Int. J. Hyperth. **29**(4), 308–317 (2013). https://doi.org/10.3109/02656736.2013.799295
5. Dettori, F., Nahmed, I., Duprez, M., Verde, J., Alvarez, P., Cotin, S.: Personalization of liver microwave ablation simulation. Int. J. Comput. Assist. Radiol. Surg. (2026). https://doi.org/10.1007/s11548-026-03712-1
6. Lee, M., et al.: Microwave Ablation: comparison of simultaneous and sequential activation of multiple antennas in liver model systems. Radiology **278**(1), 95–103 (2016). https://doi.org/10.1148/radiol.2015142151
7. Keshavamurthy, K.N., Eickhoff, C., Ziv, E.: Preoperative lung ablation prediction using deep learning. Eur. Radiol. **34**(11), 7161–7172 (2024). https://doi.org/10.1007/s00330-024-10767-8
8. Lukes, A., Bale, R., Freysinger, W.: Automatic trajectory planning for stereotactic radiofrequency ablation in non-discrete search space. Int. J. Comput. Assis. Radiol. Surg., 1349–1360 (2025). https://doi.org/10.1007/s11548-025-03386-1
9. Mehtali, J., Verde, J.M., Essert, C.: C-NCA: chained neural cellular automata for fast and accurate thermal ablation estimation. In: Medical Image Computing and Computer Assisted Intervention – MICCAI 2025, pp. 67–77. Springer Nature Switzerland, Cham (2026). https://doi.org/10.1007/978-3-032-04965-0_7
10. Meister, F., et al.: Fast automatic liver tumor radiofrequency ablation planning via learned physics model. In: Wang, L., Dou, Q., Fletcher, P.T., Speidel, S., Li, S. (eds.) Medical Image Computing and Computer Assisted Intervention – MICCAI 2022, pp. 167–176. Springer Nature Switzerland (2022). https://doi.org/10.1007/978-3-031-16449-1_17
11. Pennes, H.H.: Analysis of tissue and arterial blood temperatures in the resting human forearm. J. Appl. Physiol. **1**(2), 93–122 (1948). https://doi.org/10.1152/jappl.1948.1.2.93

12. Philips, C.A., Rajesh, S., Nair, D.C., Ahamed, R., Abduljaleel, J.K., Augustine, P.: Hepatocellular carcinoma in 2021: an exhaustive update. Cureus **13**(11), e19274 (2021). https://doi.org/10.7759/cureus.19274
13. Poggi, G., et al.: Microwave ablation of hepatocellular carcinoma using a new percutaneous device: preliminary results. Anticancer Res. **33**(3), 1221–1227 (2013). publisher: International Institute of Anticancer Research Section: Clinical Studies
14. Radmilović-Radjenović, M., Bošković, N., Radjenović, B.: Computational modeling of microwave tumor ablation. Bioengineering **9**(11), 656 (2022). https://doi.org/10.3390/bioengineering9110656
15. Shin, M., et al.: PhysRFANet: physics-guided neural network for real-time prediction of thermal effect during radiofrequency ablation treatment. Eng. Appl. Artif. Intell. **138**, 109349 (2024). https://doi.org/10.1016/j.engappai.2024.109349
16. Soler, L., et al.: 3D image reconstruction for comparison of algorithm database: a patient specific anatomical and medical image database. Technical report, IRCAD, Strasbourg, France (2010)
17. Vogl, T.J., Nour-Eldin, N.E.A., Hammerstingl, R.M., Panahi, B., Naguib, N.N.N.: Microwave ablation (MWA): basics, technique and results in primary and metastatic liver neoplasms - review article. RoFo: Fortschritte Auf Dem Gebiete Der Rontgenstrahlen Und Der Nuklearmedizin **189**(11), 1055–1066 (2017). https://doi.org/10.1055/s-0043-117410
18. Wang, Y., Hobbs, B.P., Ng, C.S.: CT perfusion characteristics identify metastatic sites in liver. Biomed. Res. Int. **2015**(1), 120749 (2015). https://doi.org/10.1155/2015/120749

Landmark-Free Assessment of Lower-Limb Alignment with Implicit Neural Shape Functions from Knee Radiographs

Zhisen Hu[1](✉), Antti Kemppainen[2,3], David Johnson[4,5,6], Egor Panfilov[2], Huy Hoang Nguyen[2], Timothy Cootes[1], Claudia Lindner[1], and Aleksei Tiulpin[7]

[1] Division of Informatics, Imaging and Data Sciences, The University of Manchester, Manchester, UK
zhisen.hu@postgrad.manchester.ac.uk
[2] Research Unit of Health Sciences and Technology, University of Oulu, Oulu, Finland
[3] Medical Research Center Oulu, University of Oulu and Oulu University Hospital, Oulu, Finland
[4] Department of Trauma and Orthopaedics, Stockport NHS Foundation Trust, Stepping Hill Hospital, Stockport, UK
[5] School of Health and Society, University of Salford, Salford, UK
[6] School of Biological Sciences, The University of Manchester, Manchester, UK
[7] Weill Cornell Medicine, Cornell University, New York, USA

Abstract. Radiographic assessment of lower-limb alignment (LLA) is important for predicting joint health and surgical outcomes in total knee arthroplasty. Traditional measurement methods are manual and time-consuming, while recent machine learning approaches typically rely on locating a fixed set of anatomical landmarks. This dependence limits flexibility and may require re-annotation when clinical definitions change. To address this, we propose an automated workflow using Implicit Neural Shape Functions (INSF). Rather than relying on explicit landmark coordinates, we encode the anatomy into a compact latent space and regress clinical alignment measurements directly from these latent codes. This architecture allows for rapid extendability to new tasks without altering the backbone representation. We trained our method on an internal dataset of 566 knee radiographs, each annotated with the outline of the femur and tibia. We evaluated it on both an internal test dataset of 50 patients and a separate external set of 402 preoperative cases from the MRKR dataset. Performance was comparable to state-of-the-art landmark-based methods and manual agreement, while offering a flexible shape representation that can be extended to additional measurement tasks. The MRKR measurement data is available at https://huggingface.co/datasets/imedslab/mrkr-knee-alignment.

Keywords: Lower-limb Alignment · Shape Model · Deep Learning

G. Yang et al. (Eds.): MICCAI 2026, LNCS 16893, pp. 242–252, 2027.
https://doi.org/10.1007/978-3-032-38236-8_24

1 Introduction

Knee osteoarthritis (OA) is a common and significant health issue that heavily burdens healthcare systems [1]. Total knee replacement (TKR) may be offered as treatment for end-stage knee OA. Nevertheless, TKR is invasive, involving prosthesis implantation at the knee joint, and around 10% of patients are dissatisfied following TKR [2,3]. Pre-operative and post-operative lower-limb alignment (LLA) affects the outcomes following TKR, with radiographs revealing anomalies such as deformities of the femur and tibia, as well as incorrect positioning of the implants [4,5]. Accurate assessment of LLA in radiographs is important for successful treatment outcomes and long-term joint health. Traditional LLA measurement methods are manual and time-consuming. Machine learning-based automated techniques have now been widely used in the medical imaging area [6,7], including orthopaedics [8,9]. Such automated methods for measuring LLA in knee radiographs are potentially clinically valuable for reducing costs and improving the efficiency of the knee OA treatment pathway.

Recent machine learning approaches [10–12] for measuring LLA primarily rely on point-based models to predict a predefined set of anatomical landmarks [8,13], from which the angles representing LLA are subsequently computed. These landmarks must be densely and consistently annotated across images, which is both time-consuming and costly to perform. An example of generating angles such as anatomical tibio-femoral angle (aTFA), anatomical medial proximal angle (aMPTA), and joint line convergence angle (JLCA) from landmark positions is shown in Fig. 1a. While this strategy enables direct computation of established clinical metrics, it inherently constrains the model to a discrete and predefined geometric representation of anatomy.

Deep implicit shape representations [14] have been introduced to model shapes using a compact latent space and a signed distance function (SDF) auto-decoder. DISSM developed by Raju *et al.* [15] adopts this auto-decoder idea and proposes a complete workflow for modelling 3D liver and larynx shapes from CT images. In the orthopaedic field, for example, Pai *et al.* [16] employed neural shape models to quantify bone shape parameters from knee MRI.

In this study, we leverage Implicit Neural Shape Functions (INSF) to model bone morphology from X-ray images using a SIREN-based auto-decoder framework [17]. Instead of relying on explicit anatomical landmarks, the proposed method encodes bone geometry into a compact latent space and directly regresses LLA measurements from these learned representations using a multilayer perceptron (MLP). This continuous shape representation captures global anatomical structure and enables flexible adaptation to new clinical tasks without requiring predefined landmark definitions. To model multiple anatomical structures, the implicit representation is structured with one output channel per bone, allowing independent yet coordinated encoding of femoral and tibial geometry. The method was validated on both internal and external datasets (Fig. 1b). To our knowledge, this is the first application of INSF to knee radiographs and the first use of implicit neural representations for automated LLA assessment.

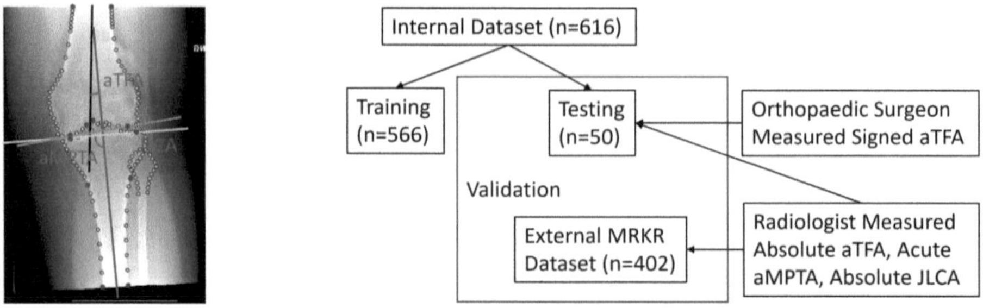

(a) (b)

Fig. 1. (a) Angles derived from landmarks. In landmark-based approaches, landmark positions (purple points) are used to fit several lines which form the angles. Black: anatomical femoral axis; Red: anatomical tibial axis; Blue: femoral joint line; Yellow: tibial joint line. aTFA is formed by the anatomical axes of femur (black) and tibia (red). aMPTA is formed by the anatomical tibial axis (red) and the tibial joint line (yellow), usually measured on the medial side. JLCA is formed by the femoral (blue) and tibial (yellow) joint lines. (b) Our study design. We trained our model with the internal training set and validated it using both internal and external testing sets. (Color figure online)

2 Methodology

2.1 Overview

The overall inference workflow of our automated LLA assessment framework is illustrated in Fig. 2. ① We first align all the shapes using two reference points at the corners of the tibial plateau. ② Then, we predict the SDFs from the aligned images. The predicted SDF contains two channels, with separate signed distance maps for the outlines of femur and tibia. ③ Each testing sample is then directly fitted to the learned latent shape space via test-time optimisation. ④ Finally, we directly regress the angular measurements with a compact 4-layer neural network (MLP).

2.2 Data

Image Data. Our internal image data consists of anonymised standard antero-posterior (AP) unilateral knee radiographs from patients undergoing TKR. To standardise anatomical orientation, all right knee images were horizontally flipped to appear as left knees. The radiographs were retrospectively collected from Stockport NHS Foundation Trust (approved by the Health Research Authority, IRAS 244130). This internal dataset includes 566 pre-operative images for training and 50 patients for testing.

Our external dataset includes 402 knees, comprising both bilateral and unilateral images randomly selected from the Emory Knee Radiograph (MRKR) Dataset [18]. To ensure consistency with the internal data, bilateral images were split, and all right knee radiographs were flipped to maintain uniform orientation.

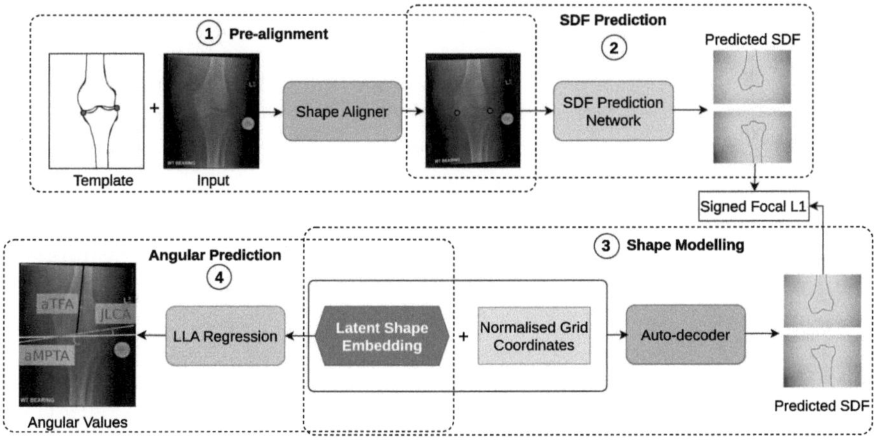

Fig. 2. Overview of test-time shape embedding optimisation and LLA regression.

LLA Angular Data. For training, ground-truth angles were derived from manually annotated landmarks. For internal testing, aTFA was independently measured by an orthopaedic surgeon and a radiologist. Each clinician performed two measurements 7–10 d apart, with the second blinded to the first; the mean of the two measurements was used as the final ground truth. The external evaluation included 402 cases from the Emory Knee Radiograph (MRKR) Dataset [18]. Ground-truth measurements were obtained by the same radiologist. The radiologist recorded absolute aTFA and JLCA and measured the acute aMPTA.

2.3 CNN-Based SDF Prediction

Following [11,12], we first trained an Hourglass-based [13,19] CNN to detect two reference points from the image for aligning all images into the canonical space. Subsequently, a U-Net [20] was trained to predict the canonical SDFs from the aligned knee images.

As our dataset consists of knee radiographs centered on the knee joint, portions of the femoral or tibial shafts are occasionally truncated before reaching the image boundaries. It has been shown that incorporating a greater extent of shaft anatomy in the model improves the accuracy of aTFA measurements [10]. To preserve anatomically consistent bone geometry and incorporate more shaft anatomy during training, we manually extended truncated shaft contours toward the image margins along estimated shaft tangents. This preprocessing step for the training data enables the U-Net model to learn consistent shaft geometry and to infer anatomically plausible shaft extensions toward the image boundaries at test time.

2.4 Implicit Shape Representation Learning

We adopt SIREN [17] as an auto-decoder to learn compact latent shape representations and to model bone geometries using SDFs, which output the distance from a queried spatial coordinate to the shape surface:

$$f_\theta(x, z) = d : x \in \mathbb{R}^2,\ d \in [-1, 1] \tag{1}$$

where θ is the network weights, z is the latent shape code, x is the input 2D normalised coordinates, the signed distance value d is negative inside the shape and positive outside, with the surface defined by the zero level set ($d = 0$).

Following the auto-decoder paradigm in [14,15], we construct K aligned canonical SDF training samples, $\{\mathcal{X}_k\}_{k=1}^K$, and associate each sample with a corresponding latent vector, $\{z_k\}_{k=1}^K$. The MLP decoder takes both spatial coordinates and the latent vector as input. During training, the network parameters and the latent shape embedding are optimised jointly. To better capture high-frequency geometric details, such as highly curved surface, we employ the Signed Focal L1 loss proposed in [21]. The overall optimisation objective is:

$$\arg\min_{\theta,z} \sum_{k=1}^{K} \left(\sum_{i=1}^{|\mathcal{X}_k|} \frac{1}{|\Omega|} \sum_{i\in\Omega} |S_i - P_{i,k}| \frac{|S_i - P_{i,k}|^\gamma\ \mathbb{I}(S_i P_{i,k} \geq 0)}{\max(|S_i|, |P_{i,k}|) + \epsilon} \right) \tag{2}$$

where $P_{i,k}$ includes the use of the tanh function to convert the network output into the range $[-1, 1]$ ($P_{i,k} = \tanh\big(f_\theta(x_i, z_k)\big)$), S is the ground-truth SDF value, ϵ is a positive constant to avoid numerical issues, Ω denotes the set of spatial coordinates sampled in the image domain for SDF supervision, γ is a positive hyperparameter, and $\mathbb{I}(\cdot)$ is the indicator function. The summations are nested: outer over training samples k, inner averaging focal-L1 loss over sampled coordinates.

2.5 Test-Time Optimisation and LLA Regression

Prior work typically fits each sample to the implicit shape model by training an additional network to predict the latent code [15]. We use a simpler approach. We use a U-Net to predict the SDF for each image. We then perform an optimisation to find the latent vector, z, which minimises the focal loss between the generated SDF and that from the U-Net.

Unlike traditional methods for LLA assessment, which explicitly compute geometric measurements from localised anatomical landmarks, we directly regress the angular values that quantify LLA using a simple MLP. The MLP takes the latent shape codes as input and outputs the corresponding angle measurements.

3 Results

Shape Modelling. We constructed a latent shape space represented by 128-dimensional vectors. To investigate the relationship between each latent dimension and LLA, we computed the Pearson correlation coefficient ($|r|$) between the latent codes and the angular values in the training set. The dimensions were then ranked according to their absolute correlation coefficients. All three angles exhibited at least moderate correlations ($|r| > 0.6$) with their respective most strongly associated latent dimensions. Notably, signed aTFA and JLCA demonstrated strong correlations ($|r| \approx 0.8$) with their most correlated latent dimensions (Fig. 3a and 3c). Latent dimension 116 exhibited the strongest correlation with both aTFA and JLCA, whereas latent dimension 112 was most strongly associated with aMPTA. The latent dimensions are learned in an unsupervised manner and are not explicitly constrained to correspond to predefined anatomical variables. Consequently, the numerical indices (e.g., 116 and 112) have no inherent meaning and are not fixed: the identity and ordering of the dimensions can change across training runs. A given dimension becomes interpretable only through its observed statistical association with the angular measurements.

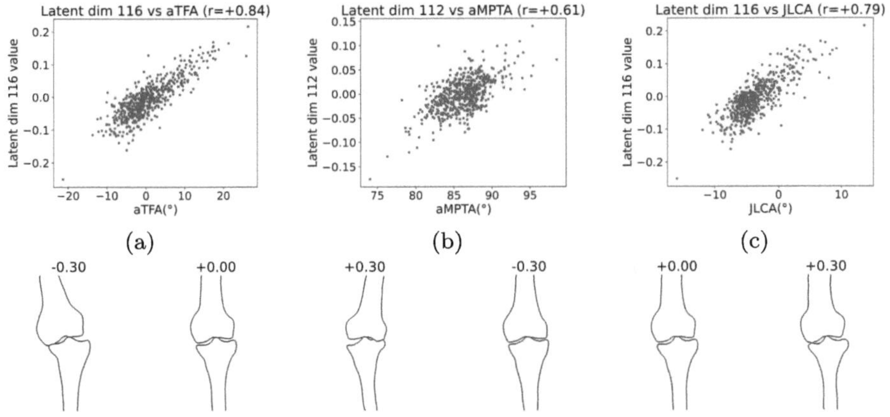

(d) Shape Variation on Latent Dimension 116 (e) Shape Variation on Latent Dimension 112

Fig. 3. (a-c) Correlation analysis between selected latent dimensions and angles, and (d-e) visualisation of shape variation on the most correlated dimensions.

We further analysed how variations on the most strongly correlated dimension of each angle (116, 112) affected the shape contours, similar to visualisations in point-based shape models [22,23]. We visualised the mean shape and systematically varied the corresponding latent parameter from 0.3 to 0.3 while keeping all other dimensions fixed (Fig. 3d and 3e). For latent dimension 116, increasing the parameter produced progressive rightward shifts of the femoral and tibial shafts, indicating that the learned shape model automatically captures pose-related information that influences aTFA and JLCA, thereby affecting LLA.

LLA Assessment. Intraclass correlation coefficient (ICC) and mean absolute difference (MAD) were used to evaluate the agreement between the measurements assessed in various ways. We first compared our approach with the methods proposed in [10,12], where the anatomical landmark positions of the knee joint are predicted first and angular measurements are subsequently derived from selected landmark subsets. We also compared our method against intra- and inter-rater agreements, using the aTFA measurements obtained by both clinicians on the internal dataset ($n = 50$). When comparing automated methods with the ground-truth aTFA values measured by the orthopaedic surgeon, our method achieved comparable results ($MAD = 1.2°$; $ICC = 0.97$) with both [10] ($MAD = 1.2°$; $ICC = 0.97$) and [12] ($MAD = 1.1°$; $ICC = 0.97$). However, all automated methods performed marginally worse than the intra-rater agreement. For comparison with ground-truth aTFA values measured by the radiologist, automated methods were comparable to intra- or inter-rater agreements ($MAD \approx 1.0°$; $ICC \approx 0.95$).

When stratified by shaft length, our autoshaft extension approach outperformed the same method without shaft extension for aTFA measurement. Specifically, when compared with the orthopaedic surgeon's measurements, the MAD decreased from 1.8° to 1.2°, and the ICC improved from 0.94 to 0.97. Similarly, when compared with the radiologist's measurements, the MAD decreased from 1.6° to 1.0°, and the ICC increased from 0.87 to 0.94. These findings demonstrate that incorporating shaft extension enhances both measurement accuracy and agreement with expert assessments.

We additionally evaluated our method on a subset ($n = 402$) of the external MRKR dataset [18], comparing it with the approach in [12] and manual intra-rater agreement. In addition to aTFA, we included aMPTA and JLCA in the generalisation experiment to assess extendability. On this dataset, our method achieved performance comparable to [12] for aTFA, with no statistically significant difference observed. For the other angles, our method showed marginally lower numerical performance. Both automated approaches underperformed relative to manual intra-rater agreement.

The comparison of our method, [12], along with the intra-rater agreement, is presented in Table 1. Statistical testing was performed to determine whether the MAD exceeded $\pm 1°$, using a two one-sided tests scheme with BonferroniHolm adjustment. All p-values were < 0.0001 and are therefore not reported. Overall, the statistical analysis indicates that the evaluated methods perform equivalently within a $\pm 1°$ difference threshold.

Table 1. Agreement analysis: mean absolute difference (MAD; °) and intraclass correlation coefficient (ICC) for internal and external datasets. Statistical testing was done to verify if the MAD exceeds ±1°. All p-values were < 0.0001. Here, OS indicates orthopaedic surgeon and RA indicates board-certified radiologist.

Dataset	#	Angle	Method	MAD (°)	ICC
Internal	50	aTFA	Ours vs. OS	1.19 (0.92, 1.54)	0.97 (0.94, 0.98)
			Hu *et al.* [12] vs. OS	1.09 (0.84, 1.40)	0.97 (0.95, 0.98)
			Ours vs. RA	1.03 (0.80, 1.32)	0.94 (0.90, 0.96)
			Hu *et al.* [12] vs. RA	0.95 (0.74, 1.22)	0.96 (0.92, 0.97)
			OS (intra-rater)	0.89 (0.69, 1.14)	0.99 (0.98, 0.99)
			RA (intra-rater)	0.94 (0.73, 1.20)	0.95 (0.92, 0.97)
			OS vs. RA (inter-rater)	0.97 (0.75, 1.26)	0.95 (0.90, 0.97)
External	402	aTFA	Ours	1.08 (0.98, 1.19)	0.84 (0.81, 0.87)
			Hu *et al.* [12]	0.91 (0.83, 1.01)	0.87 (0.85, 0.90)
			RA (intra-rater)	0.65 (0.59, 0.72)	0.93 (0.92, 0.94)
		aMPTA	Ours	1.29 (1.17, 1.42)	0.58 (0.30, 0.74)
			Hu *et al.* [12]	0.88 (0.80, 0.97)	0.72 (0.64, 0.78)
			RA (intra-rater)	0.77 (0.70, 0.85)	0.79 (0.76, 0.83)
		JLCA	Ours	0.94 (0.85, 1.03)	0.67 (0.61, 0.72)
			Hu *et al.* [12]	0.75 (0.68, 0.83)	0.80 (0.72, 0.86)
			RA (intra-rater)	0.49 (0.45, 0.54)	0.89 (0.86, 0.91)

4 Discussions and Conclusions

In this paper, we have shown that implicit neural representations capture variations associated with LLA. The proposed LLA assessment workflow achieved performance comparable to landmark-based methods and to manual intra- or inter-rater agreement on the internal dataset, but declined slightly on the external dataset, where it was slightly inferior to the landmark-based method and manual agreement. This reduction in generalisability may reflect population differences. The internal dataset predominantly comprised White patients, whereas the external MRKR dataset [18] included approximately 40% White and 40% African American patients. In addition, the mean age of the internal dataset was approximately ten years higher than that of the MRKR cohort. These findings suggest that further refinement may improve robustness across diverse populations.

Performance differences were generally small between methods, and variability in clinician annotations and measurement protocols may have influenced the results. We observed no significant differences between automated approaches, as performance is inherently dependent on the underlying clinical annotations. Despite minor performance discrepancies, none of the observed effects was statistically or clinically significant. The methods were found equivalent to the ground truth measurements, as well as to each other ($p < 0.0001$).

When it comes to the interpretability of the latent space, its correlations with aTFA or JLCA were strong, whereas the association with aMPTA was comparatively weaker. This may reflect the model's more accurate representation of relative bone positioning rather than displacement of individual bones.

A key limitation of this study is that we utilised the pre-processing step from [11,13] for shape pre-alignment out of convenience. This, however, can easily be incorporated within one UNet model. In general, our training targets were derived from landmark-based annotations, which may inherently favor landmark-driven approaches and constrain the evaluation of the full advantages offered by a landmark-free representation. Future work should focus on directly regressing measurements that cannot be readily derived from landmark positions. This would enable a more comprehensive assessment of the proposed approach and more convincingly demonstrate its extendability.

Nevertheless, our framework offers important advantages. By encoding global anatomical shape information into latent representations, it learns LLA-related features without predefined landmarks. This enables compact shape representation in latent vectors and facilitates extension to new clinical tasks. Such flexibility is particularly valuable when landmarks are difficult to detect or inconsistently defined, making the framework well suited to evolving clinical definitions where traditional point-based models are impractical.

Acknowledgments. ZH is funded by European Laboratory for Learning and Intelligent Systems (ELLIS) Unit Manchester. CL is funded by a Sir Henry Dale Fellowship jointly funded by the Wellcome Trust and the Royal Society (223267/Z/21/Z). This work was supported by the European Union's Horizon Programme under projects STAGE (grant 101137146; HHN) and UltraSense (grant 101130192; EP and HHN), as well as by the Research Council of Finland (project 336449; EP and AT).

Disclosure of Interests. The authors have no competing interests to declare.

References

1. Steinmetz, J.D., et al.: Global, regional, and national burden of osteoarthritis, 1990–2020 and projections to 2050: a systematic analysis for the Global Burden of Disease Study 2021. Lancet Rheumat. **5**(9), e508–e522 (2023)
2. Özden, V.E., Osman, W.S., Morii, T., Pastor, J.C.M., Abdelaal, A.M., Younis, A.S.: What percentage of patients are dissatisfied post-primary total hip and total knee arthroplasty? J. Arthroplasty **40**(2), S55–S56 (2025)
3. DeFrance, M.J., Scuderi, G.R.: Are 20% of patients actually dissatisfied following total knee arthroplasty? A systematic review of the literature. J. Arthroplasty **38**(3), 594–599 (2023)
4. Ritter, M.A., Davis, K.E., Meding, J.B., Pierson, J.L., Berend, M.E., Malinzak, R.A.: The effect of alignment and BMI on failure of total knee replacement. JBJS **93**(17), 1588–1596 (2011)

5. Ritter, M.A., et al.: Preoperative malalignment increases risk of failure after total knee arthroplasty. JBJS **95**(2), 126–131 (2013)
6. Zhang, Z., et al: Large-scale multi-center CT and MRI segmentation of pancreas with deep learning. Med. Image Anal. **99**, 103328 (2025)
7. Lin, Y., et al.: Vascular graph network for ovarian lesion classification using optical-resolution photoacoustic microscopy. Photoacoustics, 100794 (2025)
8. Lindner, C., Thiagarajah, S., Wilkinson, J.M., arcOGEN Consortium, Wallis, G.A. and Cootes, T.F.: Accurate bone segmentation in 2D radiographs using fully automatic shape model matching based on regression-voting. In Medical Image Computing and Computer-Assisted Intervention, pp. 181–189. Springer Berlin Heidelberg (2013)
9. Tiulpin, A., Thevenot, J., Rahtu, E., Lehenkari, P., Saarakkala, S.: Automatic knee osteoarthritis diagnosis from plain radiographs: a deep learning-based approach. Sci. Rep. **8**(1), 1727 (2018)
10. Cullen, D., Thompson, P., Johnson, D., Lindner, C.: An AI-based system for fully automated knee alignment assessment in standard knee AP radiographs. Knee **54**, 99–110 (2025)
11. Hu, Z., et al.: Automated measurements of knee alignment with deep learning: accuracy and reliability. Osteoarthr. Cartil. **33**, S100–S101 (2025)
12. Hu, Z., et al.: Deep learning-based alignment measurement in knee radiographs. In International Conference on Medical Image Computing and Computer-Assisted Intervention, pp. 121–130. Cham: Springer Nature Switzerland (2025)
13. Tiulpin, A., Melekhov, I., Saarakkala, S.: KNEEL: knee anatomical landmark localization using hourglass networks. In: 2019 IEEE/CVF International Conference on Computer Vision Workshop (ICCVW), pp. 352–361. IEEE (2019)
14. Park, J.J., Florence, P., Straub, J., Newcombe, R., Lovegrove, S.: DeepSDF: learning continuous signed distance functions for shape representation. In: Proceedings of the IEEE/CVF Conference on Computer Vision and Pattern Recognition, pp. 165–174 (2019)
15. Raju, A., Miao, S., Jin, D., Lu, L., Huang, J., Harrison, A.P.: Deep implicit statistical shape models for 3D medical image delineation. In Proceedings of the AAAI Conference on Artificial Intelligence, vol. 36, no. 2, pp. 2135–2143 (2022)
16. Pai, S.A., et al.: Neural shape model quantifies early and progressive bone shape changes after ACLR. Osteoarth. Imag. **5**, 100342 (2025)
17. Sitzmann, V., Martel, J., Bergman, A., Lindell, D., Wetzstein, G.: Implicit neural representations with periodic activation functions. Adv. Neural. Inf. Process. Syst. **33**, 7462–7473 (2020)
18. Price, B., et al.: Emory Knee Radiograph (2024). arXiv:2411.00866 MRKR) Dataset. arXiv preprint
19. Newell, A., Yang, K., Deng, J.: Stacked hourglass networks for human pose estimation (2016). arXiv:1603.06937 arXiv preprint
20. Ronneberger, O., Fischer, P., Brox, T.: U-Net: convolutional networks for biomedical image segmentation (2015). arXiv:1505.04597 arXiv preprint
21. Dang, T., Nguyen, H.H., Tiulpin, A.: SingR: brain tumor segmentation via signed normalized geodesic transform regression. In: International Conference on Medical Image Computing and Computer-Assisted Intervention, pp. 593–603. Springer Nature Switzerland, Cham (2024)

22. Cootes, T.F., Taylor, C.J., Cooper, D.H., Graham, J.: Active shape models-their training and application. Comput. Vis. Image Underst. **61**(1), 38–59 (1995)
23. Cootes, T.F., Ionita, M.C., Lindner, C., Sauer, P.: Robust and accurate shape model fitting using random forest regression voting. In European Conference on Computer Vision, pp. 278–291. Springer Berlin Heidelberg (2012)

LOT-Bridge: A Latent Optimal Transport Bridge Based on Signed Distance Fields for Automatic Skull Defect Reconstruction

Yanghui Yan[1], Xingce Wang[1(✉)], Zhongke Wu[1], Xiaodong Ju[2(✉)], Jingyi Liu[3], Changkai Ji[4], Yicheng Zhu[5], and Wuyang Shui[6]

[1] School of Artificial Intelligence, Beijing Normal University, Beijing, China
wangxingce@bnu.edu.cn
[2] Institute of Sports Medicine, Peking University Third Hospital, Beijing, China
juxiaodong@puh3.net.cn
[3] Department of Radiology, Peking Union Medical College Hospital, Beijing, China
[4] School of Automation and Intelligent Sensing, Shanghai Jiao Tong University, Shanghai, China
[5] Department of Neurology, Peking Union Medical College Hospital, Beijing, China
[6] Alder Hey Children's Hospital, Liverpool, UK

Abstract. Due to the reliance on manually designed implants, traditional skull defect reconstruction is time-consuming. Although latent diffusion models based on Signed Distance Fields (SDFs) accelerate the implant design, Gaussian noise initialization and stochastic differential equations lead to many iterations and may introduce incorrect geometric details. Moreover, separately training the decoder and latent-space network can accumulate errors across stages. To address these limitations, a Latent Optimal Transport Bridge (LOT-Bridge) based on SDFs is proposed. We model automatic skull reconstruction as an Optimal Transport (OT) problem in the latent and data spaces, and design an efficient training strategy to achieve accurate generation with fewer iterations. Firstly, to accelerate inference and improve the determinism of generation, we introduce a latent bridge model, where the reverse sampling begins from the defective data and follows an ordinary differential equation. Secondly, a joint training strategy performs OT-based optimization in the latent and data spaces while ensuring high-quality implant SDF prediction. Finally, the adaptive morphological block refines SDF features through dilation and erosion, enhancing surface reconstruction. Extensive experiments on three datasets demonstrate that LOT-Bridge generates more accurate implants with faster inference than existing methods. Code: https://github.com/yanaynghui1998/LOT-Bridge.

Keywords: Automatic Skull Defect Reconstruction · Generative Model · Signed Distance Fields · Optimal Transport

G. Yang et al. (Eds.): MICCAI 2026, LNCS 16893, pp. 253–263, 2027.
https://doi.org/10.1007/978-3-032-38236-8_25

1 Introduction

The automatic skull defect reconstruction is crucial for patients with accidental injuries or brain surgery. However, due to the significant heterogeneity between cranial defects, personalized implant design is necessary [8]. This process is generally performed manually by software, which is costly and time-consuming [18].

To accelerate the implant design, Deep Learning (DL) methods represent shapes as binary volumes [13,24,26] or point clouds [9,25] and train a 3D network [16,20] for end-to-end shape completion. Recently, several studies [3,4] combine Signed Distance Fields (SDFs) with diffusion models for shape completion. SDFs provide richer surface descriptions than other representations and can be directly converted into meshes [1,27]. Diffusion models avoid overfitting and yield more accurate shapes than end-to-end DL models [4,19]. Latent Diffusion Models (LDMs) [2,21] perform reverse sampling in the latent space, reducing the high memory cost caused by voxelized SDFs and enabling fast generation. However, due to Gaussian noise initialization, LDMs still require lengthy iterations to fit the high-quality complete skull. Moreover, stochastic differential equations make LDMs less deterministic [5,15], which may produce distorted geometric details. Finally, most LDMs directly adopt the decoder pre-trained at the first stage to achieve the final reconstruction. This accumulates approximation errors from different training stages, resulting in suboptimal completion performance.

To address these problems, we propose a Latent Optimal Transport Bridge (LOT-Bridge) based on SDFs for automatic skull defect reconstruction. Our core idea is to model skull reconstruction as an Optimal Transport (OT) problem in both latent and data spaces and solve it with an effective model and training strategy. Main contributions are as follows: (1) Based on an Ordinary Differential Equation (ODE) derived from the dynamic OT problem, we introduce a bridge model in the latent space. The bridge model learns the optimal vector field and builds OT paths between defective and complete samples, achieving fast and deterministic inference. (2) A joint training strategy is designed to simultaneously optimize the bridge model and the decoder. Specifically, the adversarial and reconstruction losses enforce OT between the reconstructed and complete skulls in data space. The implant loss enhances implant SDF prediction. Combining them with the latent-space loss, LOT-Bridge captures a high-quality generative ability. (3) The Adaptive Morphological Block (AMB) is proposed and is incorporated into the decoder. AMB can adaptively perform erosion and dilation at different upsampling stages, improving the final surface reconstruction.

2 Methodology

2.1 Problem Formulation

Given paired complete and defective SDF volumes $x_0 \sim \mathcal{P}_0$ and $x_1 \sim \mathcal{P}_1(\cdot|x_0)$, and their latent codes $z_0 \sim \mathcal{Q}_0(\cdot|x_0)$ and $z_1 \sim \mathcal{Q}_1(\cdot|x_1)$, our goal is to solve the following OT problem:

$$\inf_{\{T_t(z_0)\}_{t\in[0,1]}} \frac{1}{2}\int_0^1 \left\| \frac{d}{dt}T_t(z_0)\right\|_2^2 dt + \inf_{\Gamma\in\Pi} \int_{\mathcal{X}\times\mathcal{X}} \|x_0 - x_{0|1}\|_2^2 \, d\Gamma(x_0, x_{0|1}) \quad (1)$$

The first term represents the dynamic OT problem in the latent space and is constrained by $T_0(z_0) = z_0$ and $T_1(z_0) = z_1$, where $\{T_t(z_0)\}_{t\in[0,1]}$ is the OT path from z_0 to z_1, and $dT_t(z_0)/dt$ is the optimal vector field. We consider this OT problem only with fixed endpoints. The second term is the OT problem in the data space $\mathcal{X}$, where $x_{0|1} \sim \mathcal{P}_{0|1}(\cdot \mid z_{0|1})$ is the final reconstructed SDF volume, $z_{0|1}$ is the complete latent code generated by the latent-space model, and Π is the set of all joint probability distributions with marginals $\mathcal{P}_0$ and $\mathcal{P}_{0|1}$. We refer to $z_{0|1}$ and $x_{0|1}$ as the fake complete latent code and SDF volume.

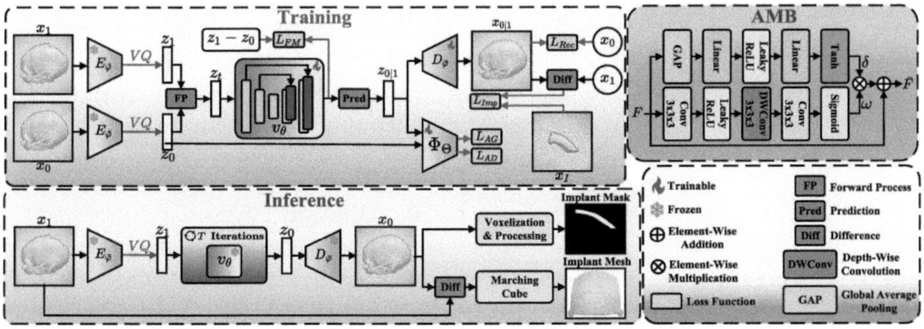

Fig. 1. Overview of LOT-Bridge and AMB. $\tilde{\varphi}$, $\bar{\varphi}$, θ and Θ are network parameters

2.2 Latent Optimal Transport Bridge

The overview of LOT-Bridge is shown in Fig. 1. **During training**, the encoder $E_{\tilde{\varphi}}$, the quantizer VQ, and the decoder $D_{\bar{\varphi}}$ are initialized from a pre-trained Vector Quantized Variational Autoencoder (VQ-VAE). The complete and defective SDF volumes x_0 and x_1 are encoded and quantized into latent codes z_0 and z_1. The 3D U-Net v_θ receives the forward result z_t (Sect. 2.2.2) and approximates $z_1 - z_0$ with the flow matching loss L_{FM} (3). v_θ predicts the fake complete latent code $z_{0|1}$ (Sect. 2.2.3), which is decoded to the fake complete SDF volume $x_{0|1}$ for computing the reconstruction loss L_{Rec} (4). By the difference operation, the implant SDF is obtained and is enforced to match the ground-truth implant x_I using the implant loss L_{Imp} (7). Finally, z_0 and $z_{0|1}$ are fed into the discriminator Φ_Θ to calculate the adversarial losses L_{AG} (5) and L_{AD} (6). L_{FM}, L_{Rec}, L_{AG}, and L_{Imp} jointly optimize v_θ and $D_{\bar{\varphi}}$. Subsequently, L_{AD} updates Φ_Θ.

During inference, the trained v_θ transforms z_1 to z_0 over T iterations, and the trained $D_{\bar{\varphi}}$ upsamples z_0 to x_0. Through voxelization and post-processing, the binary implant mask is produced. Specifically, x_0 is first voxelized into a binary mask by setting SDF values > 0 to 0 and ≤ 0 to 1. The Boolean difference operation is then performed between this mask and the defective mask to obtain the implant mask. Finally, the opening operation and the connected component analysis remove noise and retain the largest connected component. Moreover, the implant SDF can be computed directly by the difference operation (7) between x_0 and x_1, from which the implant mesh is extracted using the marching cube.

VQ-VAE with Adoptive Morphological Block. A variant of VQ-VAE is designed, where the encoder and the quantizer follow [2]. For the decoder, we add AMB after each upsampling layer to enhances the final surface reconstruction. As shown in Fig. 1, AMB consists of two branches. The upper branch selects erosion or dilation, while the lower branch controls the intensity. Given an upsampled feature $F \in \mathbb{R}^{B\times C\times D\times H\times W}$, the upper branch compresses F into a factor $\delta \in \mathbb{R}^{B\times 1\times 1\times 1\times 1}$, which is constrained within $[-1, 1]$ by a Tanh activation. As δ changes, the boundary of the SDF features shrinks or expands, performing erosion or dilation. The lower branch reduces the channel number of F to 1 and employs a Sigmoid activation to obtain a positive scaling map $\omega \in \mathbb{R}^{B\times 1\times D\times H\times W}$. The morphological operation of AMB can be defined as:

$$\bar{F} = F + \delta\omega \quad \delta \begin{cases} > 0 & \text{Erosion} \\ < 0 & \text{Dilation} \end{cases} \tag{2}$$

where $\bar{F}$ is the output of AMB. Following [2], we train VQ-VAE only on complete SDF volumes with the reconstruction (L_2), commitment, and VQ losses.

Bridge Model in the Latent Space. To achieve fast and deterministic generation, we introduce an ODE-based bridge model. Firstly, we define the forward process, which can transport the complete sample z_0 to the defective sample z_1 along the optimal vector field $dT_t(z_0)/dt$ in (1). According to the Euler–Lagrange equations [11], the constrained first term of (1) leads to an ODE: $dT_t(z_0)/dt = (z_1 - z_0)$, where $t \in [0, 1]$. The solution to the ODE is $T_t(z_0) = z_t = tz_1 + (1-t)z_0$, which is the forward process (**FP** in Fig. 1). A U-Net v_θ learns the optimal vector field with fixed direction $(z_1 - z_0)$ using L_{FM}:

$$L_{FM} = \mathbb{E}_{t\sim\mathcal{U}([0,1]),z_0\sim\mathcal{Q}_0,z_1\sim\mathcal{Q}_1}\left[\|(z_1 - z_0) - v_\theta(z_t, t)\|_2^2\right] \tag{3}$$

Finally, the deterministic DDPM posterior [14] enables the reverse sampling, which is: $z_s = \frac{s}{t}z_t + (1 - \frac{s}{t})z_0$, where s and t are two consecutive time steps $(s < t)$. Since v_θ learns the instantaneous velocity, there is a direct estimation from z_t to z_0: $z_{0,t} = z_t - t\,v_\theta(z_t, t)$. By replacing z_0 with $z_{0,t}$ and sampling time steps at equal intervals between $[0, 1]$, the reverse sampling starts from z_1 and progressively generates z_0 in the latent space (**Inference** in Fig. 1).

Joint Training Strategy. A joint training strategy is designed to enhance the generative ability of LOT-Bridge (**Training** in Fig. 1). We first realize OT in the data space by solving the second term of (1). Generating the fake complete latent code $z_{0|1}$ (Sect. 2.1) via reverse sampling leads to a lengthy training time. Therefore, based on (3), we propose a one-step prediction from z_1 to z_0 (**Pred** in Fig. 1) : $z_{0|1} = z_1 - v_\theta(z_t, t)$. Since $z_0 \sim \mathcal{Q}_0(\cdot \mid x_0)$ and $z_1 \sim \mathcal{Q}_1(\cdot \mid x_1)$, $z_{0|1}$

follows the conditional distribution $\mathcal{Q}_{0|1}(\cdot \mid x_1, x_0, t; \theta)$. According to [22], instead of optimizing over couplings Γ in (1), we minimize the transport cost between the real complete skull $x_0 \sim \mathcal{P}_0$ and the fake complete skull $x_{0|1} \sim \mathcal{P}_{0|1}(\cdot \mid z_{0|1}; \bar{\varphi})$ in the data space via L_{Rec}, while enforcing $\mathcal{Q}_{0|1}(\cdot \mid x_0, x_1, t; \theta)$ to match $\mathcal{Q}_0(\cdot \mid x_0)$ in the latent space using L_{AG} and L_{AD}. These losses are defined as follows:

$$L_{Rec} = \mathbb{E}_{x_0 \sim \mathcal{P}_0, x_{0|1} \sim \mathcal{P}_{0|1}} \left[\|x_0 - x_{0|1}\|_2^2 \right] \tag{4}$$

$$L_{\mathrm{AG}} = -\mathbb{E}_{z_{0|1} \sim \mathcal{Q}_{0|1}} \left[\log \Phi_\Theta(z_{0|1}) \right] \tag{5}$$

$$L_{AD} = \mathbb{E}_{z_0 \sim \mathcal{Q}_0} \left[\log \Phi_\Theta(z_0) \right] + \mathbb{E}_{z_{0|1} \sim \mathcal{Q}_{0|1}} \left[\log(1 - \Phi_\Theta(z_{0|1})) \right] \tag{6}$$

where $x_{0|1} = D_{\bar{\varphi}}(z_{0|1})$. LOT-Bridge cannot directly produce the implant SDF. Therefore, we apply a difference operation (**Diff** in Fig. 1) [17] to extract a pseudo implant x_{PI}, where $x_{PI} = max(x_{0|1}, -x_1)$, and max compares the SDF voxels in $x_{0|1}$ and $-x_1$ and retains the larger value. Then, L_{Imp} reduces the difference between $x_{PI} \sim \mathcal{P}_{PI}(\cdot \mid x_{0|1}, x_1)$ and the reference implant $x_I \sim \mathcal{P}_I$:

$$L_{Imp} = \mathbb{E}_{x_I \sim \mathcal{P}_I, x_{PI} \sim \mathcal{P}_{PI}} \left[\|x_I - x_{PI}\|_2^2 \right] \tag{7}$$

The total loss function L_{Total} for joint training v_θ and $D_{\bar{\varphi}}$ is defined as follows:

$$L_{Total} = L_{FM} + L_{Rec} + L_{AG} + \lambda L_{Imp} \tag{8}$$

where λ is a hyperparameter. After each update of v_θ and $D_{\bar{\varphi}}$, L_{AD} optimizes Φ_Θ. Note that all loss functions are computed using the same $t \sim \mathcal{U}([0,1])$.

3 Experiments

Datasets and Implementation Details. LOT-Bridge is evaluated on the SkullBreak, SkullFix [10], and MUG500 datasets [12]. The SkullBreak and SkullFix datasets contain paired 3D complete and defective binary masks. The SkullBreak dataset is downsampled to $256 \times 256 \times 256$ with a voxel size of $0.8 \times 0.8 \times 0.8\text{mm}^3$ and is split into 430 training and 140 testing masks. The SkullFix dataset is resampled, downsampled, and zero-padded to $256 \times 256 \times 256$ with a voxel size of $0.9 \times 0.9 \times 0.9\text{mm}^3$, and is divided into 75 training and 25 testing masks. The MUG500 dataset provides the paired defective and implant meshes. which are merged and converted to $256 \times 256 \times 256$ binary masks with a voxel size of $1.0 \times 1.0 \times 1.0\text{mm}^3$ using trimesh. The MUG500 dataset is split into 19 training and 10 testing masks. Data augmentation in [7] expands the training samples to 1290 for SkullBreak, 825 for SkullFix, and 265 for MUG500. The SDF volumes with the same size are extracted from binary masks using SimpleITK [28] and are scaled to fit $[-1, 1]^3$, and then clipped to the truncated range $[-0.3, 0.3]$.

We adopt 3D VQ-VAE in [2], the discriminator Φ_Θ in [6], and the 3D U-Net v_θ in [14]. VQ-VAE is pre-trained for 500 epochs with a learning rate of 4×10^{-6} and batch size of 4. During training, the learning rate of v_θ and the decoder $D_{\bar{\varphi}}$

is 5×10^{-8}, the learning rate of Φ_Θ is 5×10^{-6}. The batch size is 4, the training epoch is 800, and $\lambda = 0.5$ in (8). During inference, we set $T = 5$ in Fig. 1. Experiments are conducted on an NVIDIA A800 80 GB GPU with the Adam optimizer. We chose the Dice Score (DSC), the Boundary Dice score (BDSC), the 95th percentile Hausdorff Distance (HD95), and the Mean Surface Distance (MSD) as quantitative metrics. Higher DSC and BDSC, along with lower HD95 and MSD, indicate better quality of the generated implant mask.

Table 1. Quantitative comparison on the SkullBreak, SkullFix and MUG500 datasets. **Bold** and Underlined values indicate the best and second-best results. All metrics are reported as mean values.

Method	SkullBreak				SkullFix				MUG500			
	DSC↑	BDSC↑	HD95↓	MSD↓	DSC↑	BDSC↑	HD95↓	MSD↓	DSC↑	BDSC↑	HD95↓	MSD↓
PBT	0.856	0.899	2.597	0.806	0.884	0.912	2.321	0.788	0.841	0.857	1.253	0.350
SegRegNet	0.928	0.936	1.412	0.483	0.936	0.945	1.331	0.453	0.920	0.934	0.974	0.193
PCTrans	0.887	0.912	1.858	0.656	0.902	0.927	1.650	0.569	0.916	0.940	0.983	0.201
PCDiff	0.912	0.914	1.768	0.615	0.917	0.927	1.618	0.552	0.923	0.942	0.924	0.185
SDFusion	0.917	0.930	1.528	0.515	0.921	0.931	1.524	0.507	0.935	0.939	0.941	0.188
OctGPT	0.920	0.935	1.468	0.493	0.934	0.944	1.374	0.463	0.941	0.945	0.911	0.174
LOT-Bridge	**0.938**	**0.945**	**1.358**	**0.459**	**0.948**	**0.960**	**1.313**	**0.414**	**0.949**	**0.955**	**0.813**	**0.144**

3.1 Results and Discussion

Comparison Experiments. LOT-Bridge is compared with six methods: two binary volume-based skull reconstruction methods: a patch-based training method (PBT [13]) and a residual UNet with symmetry networks (SegRegNet [24]), two point cloud-based skull reconstruction methods: a transformer-based method (PCTrans [25]) and a diffusion-based method (PCDiff [9]), two SDF-based shape completion and generation methods: a LDM-based method (SDFusion [2]) and an autoregressive method for latent-space generation (OctGPT [23]).

The quantitative results are shown in Table 1. LOT-Bridge obtains the best metrics on all datasets. Moreover, SDF-based methods exhibit better performance than point cloud-based methods and PBT, highlighting the superiority of the SDF representation. Due to the SDE framework and the separate training of the latent-space network and decoder, SDFusion typically underperforms SegRegNet. Compared with SegRegNet, LOT-Bridge improves BDSC by 0.015 and reduces HD95 by 0.018 mm on the SkullFix dataset. This benefits from the ODE framework, the joint training strategy, and AMB. The complexity comparisons are reported in Table 2, where Time denotes the inference time, and Param denotes the number of trainable parameters. Due to operating on volumetric data, binary volume-based and SDF-based methods generally maintain a large number of network parameters. Meanwhile, data-space methods show

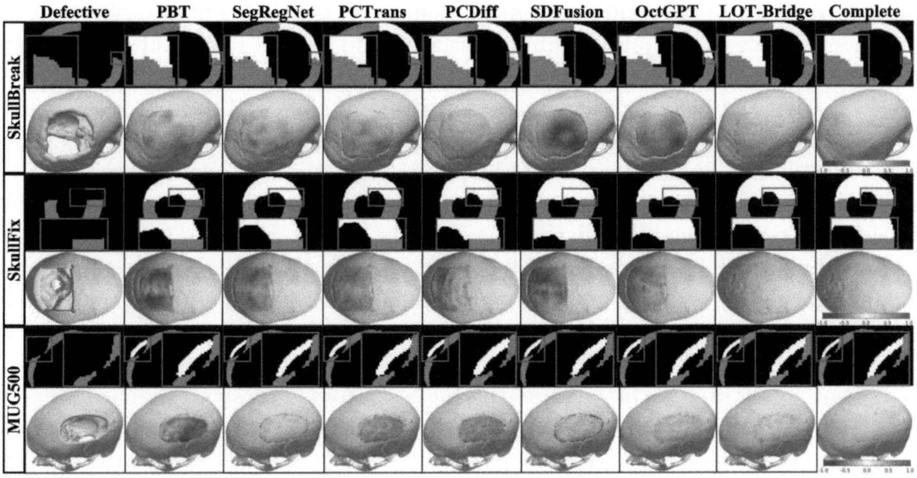

Fig. 2. Qualitative comparison on the SkullBreak, SkullFix, and MUG500 datasets. Rows 1, 3, and 5 are binary masks in the sagittal, axial, and coronal views. Rows 2, 4, and 6 are meshes. Surface distances between the predicted and ground-truth implants are shown by a blue–white–red colormap centered at zero. Please zoom in for details. (Color figure online)

Table 2. Complexity comparison on the SkullFix datasets. All methods are tested on an NVIDIA A800 GPU. (Number) denotes the number of sampling steps, s denotes seconds, M denotes million, and T denotes Tera, where 1Tera = 1000Giga.

Method	Time(s)	Param(M)	MACs(T)
PBT	15.195	**22.863**	10.791
SegRegNet	10.720	140.354	11.350
PCTrans	10.613	57.296	**3.121**
PCDiff(1000)	1096.647	50.508	250.095
SDFusion(100)	10.125	552.115	131.577
OctGPT	7.364	417.196	17.065
LOT-Bridge(5)	**1.812**	539.081	10.353

Table 3. Ablation study of the joint training strategy and AMB on the SkullFix dataset.

Method	DSC↑	BDSC↑	HD95↓	MSD↓
Base	0.931	0.940	1.502	0.529
w AMB	0.937	0.946	1.430	0.497
w L_{Adv}	0.933	0.942	1.476	0.519
w L_{Rec}	0.935	0.944	1.453	0.513
w L_{Imp}	0.934	0.944	1.457	0.515
w/o AMB	0.942	0.950	1.408	0.448
w/o L_{Adv}	0.943	0.952	1.354	0.430
w/o L_{Rec}	0.941	0.948	1.374	0.437
w/o L_{Imp}	0.944	0.953	1.333	0.424
Our	**0.948**	**0.960**	**1.313**	**0.414**

a slower reconstruction speed than latent-space methods. Among latent-space models, LOT-Bridge achieves the fastest inference and relatively low MACs.

We present the qualitative results in Fig. 2. For implant mask prediction, the other methods suffer from overly thick boundaries, non-smooth curvatures, and poor connectivity with the defective skull. In comparison, LOT-Bridge reconstructs implant masks closely matching the ground truth and enables an accurate transition from the implant to the defect boundary. Similarly, LOT-Bridge generates implant meshes with the smallest surface errors among all methods.

Ablation Study. We conduct ablation studies on the SkullFix dataset to verify the effectiveness of the joint training strategy and AMB. The results are shown in Table 3, where Base indicates directly combining the pre-trained original VQ-VAE [2] with the bridge model trained using only L_{FM} (3), Our indicates the full method, w indicates adding the key component into Base, w/o indicates removing the key component from Our, and L_{Adv} indicates using both L_{AG} (5) and L_{AD} (6). Note that Base, w AMB, and w L_{Adv} all use the separate training for the bridge model and the decoder. As shown in Table 3 and Fig. 3(a), AMB enhances the performance of LOT-Bridge and contributes to generating the implant masks and meshes with accurate boundaries and surfaces. Moreover, w/o AMB boosts the generative ability of Base, validating the effectiveness of the joint training strategy. Due to the powerful synergy between AMB and the joint training strategy, Our attains the highest scores across all metrics.

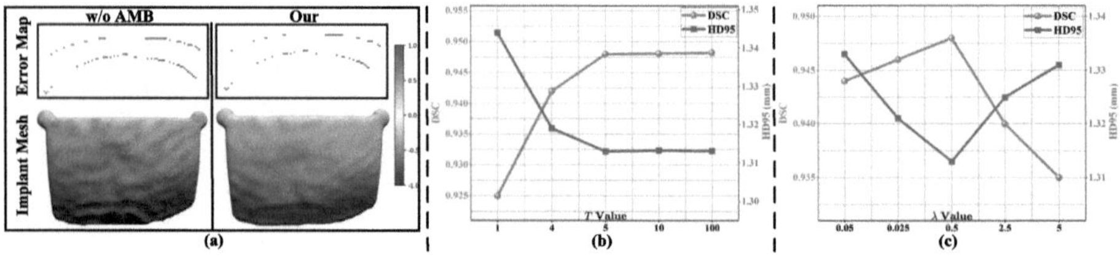

Fig. 3. (**a**) Row 1 shows the error maps between the predicted implant masks and the ground truth, and Row 2 presents the surface distances between the predicted implant meshes and the ground truth. (**b**) and (**c**) report DSC and HD95 values on the SkullFix dataset under different numbers of iterations (T) and hyperparameter settings (λ). In other experiments, we set $T = 5$ and $\lambda = 0.5$ by default. Please zoom in for details.

To assess the effect of the number of iterations, the reverse sampling is performed with iterations $T = [1, 4, 5, 10, 100]$. As shown in Fig. 3(b), LOT-Bridge reaches a performance bottleneck at $T = 5$. Therefore, by combining the bridge model, the joint training strategy, and AMB, LOT-Bridge yields high-quality skull reconstructions with fewer sampling steps. To explore the impact of the hyperparameter in (8), we set $\lambda = [0.05, 0.025, 0.5, 2.5, 5]$. As shown in Fig. 3(c), once λ exceeds 0.5, the generation accuracy of LOT-Bridge drops markedly. This suggests that L_{Imp} provides more valuable supervision when $\lambda = 0.5$.

4 Conclusion

We propose LOT-Bridge based on SDFs for automatic skull defect reconstruction. In the latent space, an ODE-based bridge model transports defective data to complete data along the deterministic OT path with fewer iterations. Meanwhile, a joint training strategy enables OT in the latent and data spaces, as well as the direct acquisition of the reliable implant SDF. To improve the surface, AMB adaptively applies erosion and dilation during upsampling, generating more accurate details on the final implants. Compared with other encoder-decoder generative models, our method is based on the OT framework. Extensive experiments have demonstrated that LOT-Bridge surpasses other methods in both reconstruction quality and inference speed, highlighting its potential for clinical implant design. Moreover, LOT-Bridge is highly scalable and can be applied to general shape completion and transformation tasks.

Acknowledgments. This work was funded in part by the National Natural Science Foundation of China (No. 62072045), in part by the Beijing Municipal Science and Technology Commission, and the Zhongguancun Science Park Management Committee (No. Z221100002722020), and in part by the Natural Science Foundation of Beijing (No. 7242167).

Disclosure of Interests. The authors have no competing interests to declare that are relevant to the content of this article.

References

1. Chen, Z., et al.: 3DTopia-XL: scaling high-quality 3D asset generation via primitive diffusion. In: Proceedings of the IEEE/CVF Conference on Computer Vision and Pattern Recognition, pp. 26576–26586 (2025)
2. Cheng, Y.C., Lee, H.Y., Tulyakov, S., Schwing, A.G., Gui, L.Y.: SDFusion: multimodal 3D shape completion, reconstruction, and generation. In: Proceedings of the IEEE/CVF Conference on Computer Vision and Pattern Recognition, pp. 4456–4465 (2023)
3. Chou, G., Bahat, Y., Heide, F.: Diffusion-sdf: conditional generative modeling of signed distance functions. In: Proceedings of the IEEE/CVF International Conference on Computer Vision, pp. 2262–2272.(2023)
4. Chu, R., et al.: Diffcomplete: diffusion-based generative 3D shape completion. In: Advances in Neural Information Processing Systems, vol. 36, pp. 75951–75966 (2023)
5. Chung, H., Kim, J., Ye, J.C.: Direct diffusion bridge using data consistency for inverse problems. In: Advances in Neural Information Processing Systems, vol. 36, pp. 7158–7169 (2023)
6. Corona-Figueroa, A., et al.: Unaligned 2D to 3D translation with conditional vector-quantized code diffusion using transformers. In: Proceedings of the IEEE/CVF International Conference on Computer Vision, pp. 14585–14594 (2023)
7. Ellis, D.G., Aizenberg, M.R.: Deep Learning Using Augmentation via Registration: 1st Place Solution to the AutoImplant 2020 Challenge. In: Li, J., Egger, J. (eds.) AutoImplant 2020. LNCS, vol. 12439, pp. 47–55. Springer, Cham (2020). https://doi.org/10.1007/978-3-030-64327-0_6

8. Fishman, Z., Mainprize, J.G., Edwards, G., Antonyshyn, O., Hardisty, M., Whyne, C.M.: Thickness and design features of clinical cranial implants–what should automated methods strive to replicate? Int. J. Comput. Assist. Radiol. Surg. **19**(4), 747–756 (2024)
9. Friedrich, P., Wolleb, J., Bieder, F., Thieringer, F.M., Cattin, P.C.: Point cloud diffusion models for automatic implant generation. In: International Conference on Medical Image Computing and Computer-Assisted Intervention, pp. 112–122. Springer (2023). https://doi.org/10.1007/978-3-031-43996-4_11
10. Kodym, O., et al.: SkullBreak/SkullFix-dataset for automatic cranial implant design and a benchmark for volumetric shape learning tasks. Data Brief **35**, 106902 (2021)
11. Kornilov, N., Mokrov, P., Gasnikov, A., Korotin, A.: Optimal flow matching: Learning straight trajectories in just one step. In: Advances in Neural Information Processing Systems, vol. 37, pp. 104180–104204 (2024)
12. Li, J., et al.: Mug500+: database of 500 high-resolution healthy human skulls and 29 craniotomy skulls and implants. Data Brief **39**, 107524 (2021)
13. Li, J., et al.: Automatic skull defect restoration and cranial implant generation for cranioplasty. Med. Image Anal. **73**, 102171 (2021)
14. Liu, G.H., Vahdat, A., Huang, D.A., Theodorou, E., Nie, W., Anandkumar, A.: I2SB: image-to-Image Schrödinger Bridge. In: International Conference on Machine Learning, pp. 22042–22062 (2023)
15. Liu, X., Gong, C.: Flow straight and fast: learning to generate and transfer data with rectified flow. In: International Conference on Learning Representations, pp. 23666–23698 (2023)
16. Mahdi, H., et al.: A U-Net based system for cranial implant design with preprocessing and learned implant filtering. In: Li, J., Egger, J. (eds.) AutoImplant 2021. LNCS, vol. 13123, pp. 63–79. Springer, Cham (2021). https://doi.org/10.1007/978-3-030-92652-6_6
17. Marschner, Z., Sellán, S., Liu, H.T.D., Jacobson, A.: Constructive solid geometry on neural signed distance fields. In: ACM SIGGRAPH Conference and Exhibition on Computer Graphics and Interactive Techniques in Asia, pp. 1–12 (2023)
18. Memon, A.R., Shi, H., Memon, T.R., Egger, J., Chen, X.: Deep learning-based automatic cranial implant design through direct defect shape prediction and its comparison study. Med. Biol. Eng. Comput. **63**(9), 2815–2826 (2025)
19. Nunes, L., Marcuzzi, R., Mersch, B., Behley, J., Stachniss, C.: Scaling diffusion models to real-world 3D lidar scene completion. In: Proceedings of the IEEE/CVF Conference on Computer Vision and Pattern Recognition, pp. 14770–14780 (2024)
20. Pathak, S., Sindhura, C., Gorthi, R.K.S.S., Kiran, D.V., Gorthi, S.: Cranial implant design using v-net based region of interest reconstruction. In: Li, J., Egger, J. (eds.) AutoImplant 2021. LNCS, vol. 13123, pp. 116–128. Springer, Cham (2021). https://doi.org/10.1007/978-3-030-92652-6_10
21. Rombach, R., Blattmann, A., Lorenz, D., Esser, P., Ommer, B.: High-resolution image synthesis with latent diffusion models. In: Proceedings of the IEEE/CVF Conference on Computer Vision and Pattern Recognition, pp. 10684–10695. (2022)
22. Tolstikhin, I., Bousquet, O., Gelly, S., Schölkopf, B.: Wasserstein Auto-Encoders. In: International Conference on Learning Representations, pp. 197–212 (2018)
23. Wei, S.T., Wang, R.H., Zhou, C.Z., Chen, B., Wang, P.S.: Octgpt: octree-based multiscale autoregressive models for 3D shape generation. In: Proceedings of the Special Interest Group on Computer Graphics and Interactive Techniques Conference Conference Papers, pp. 1–11 (2025)

24. Wodzinski, M., Daniol, M., Hemmerling, D.: Automatic skull reconstruction by deep learnable symmetry enforcement. Comput. Methods Programs Biomed. **263**, 108670 (2025)
25. Wodzinski, M., Daniol, M., Hemmerling, D., Socha, M.: High-resolution cranial defect reconstruction by iterative, low-resolution, point cloud completion transformers. In: International Conference on Medical Image Computing and Computer-Assisted Intervention, pp. 333–343. Springer (2023). https://doi.org/10.1007/978-3-031-43996-4_32
26. Wodzinski, M., Kwarciak, K., Daniol, M., Hemmerling, D.: Improving deep learning-based automatic cranial defect reconstruction by heavy data augmentation: from image registration to latent diffusion models. Comput. Biol. Med. **182**, 109129 (2024)
27. Xiang, H., et al.: Gaussianroom: improving 3D gaussian splatting with sdf guidance and monocular cues for indoor scene reconstruction. In: 2025 IEEE International Conference on Robotics and Automation, pp. 2686–2693. IEEE (2025)
28. Yaniv, Z., Lowekamp, B.C., Johnson, H.J., Beare, R.: Simpleitk image-analysis notebooks: a collaborative environment for education and reproducible research. J. Digit. Imaging **31**(3), 290–303 (2018)

Multi-camera AR Guidance System for Surgical Instrument Handling and Assembly: Investigating Workload and Efficiency

Shiyu Li[1,2,3](✉), Julian Kreimeier[1,2,3,4], Hannah Schieber[1,2,3,4], Dirk Müller[2], Bernhard Kainz[4,5], Rüdiger von Eisenhart-Rothe[2,3], and Daniel Roth[1,2,3]

[1] Technical University of Munich, Human-Centered-Computing and Extended Reality Lab, Munich, Germany
{shiyu.li,julian.kreimeier,daniel.roth}@tum.de
[2] TUM University Hospital, Orthopedics and Sports Orthopedics, Munich, Germany
[3] Munich Institute of Robotics and Machine Intelligence (MIRMI), Munich, Germany
[4] FAU Erlangen-Nürnberg, Erlangen, Germany
[5] Department of Computing, Imperial College London, London, UK

Abstract. The handling and assembly of instruments during surgery impose high cognitive demands on scrub nurses, particularly when instruments are unfamiliar. We present a supporting guidance system for surgical instrumentation combining multi-camera marker-free 6D pose estimation with augmented reality (AR) in-situ visualization on a head-mounted display. Pose estimation and consecutive camera calibration are achieved through known objects. Our 6D pose estimation is purely trained on synthetic data, aiming for better generalizability and real-world applicability. The AR guidance displays tooltip localization cues and step-wise assembly animations. Via gaze-based selection and a foot pedal, users can switch assembly steps in intraoperative use.

In a technical evaluation, we outperform state-of-the-art 6D pose estimation. A user study with 29 scrub nurses conducted in a surgical simulation of knee arthroplasty compares our system against a paper manual. Our AR system significantly reduced the perceived workload. Objectively, AR guidance reduced task completion time by 21.3% (4.76 minutes). Specifically, less-experienced scrub nurses benefited from our approach. Error frequencies were comparable between conditions. Qualitative feedback highlighted improved process clarity, reduced information overload, and perceived independence. To summarize, our marker-free multi-camera AR guidance approach for surgical instruments can, subjectively and objectively, improve intraoperative instrumentation performance, particularly for untrained scrub nurses.

Keywords: Augmented Reality · Pose Estimation · Guidance

S. Li and J. Kreimeier—equal contribution.

G. Yang et al. (Eds.): MICCAI 2026, LNCS 16893, pp. 264–274, 2027.
https://doi.org/10.1007/978-3-032-38236-8_26

1 Introduction and Related Work

In the Operating Room (OR), scrub nurses sterilely support surgeons in a sensitive environment under time pressure. Endoprosthetic instruments, as a typical example, which are used for replacing damaged or diseased joints with artificial implants, have become very complex and manufacturer-dependent. Due to this and a general workforce shortage, inexperienced staff may need to handle unfamiliar instruments [5]. Yet flawless handling remains essential for efficiency and patient safety, as pauses during surgery pose unnecessary risks.

The WHO's Patient Health and Safety plan [27] requires operating manuals and safety instructions to be available at the point of use. Currently, when problems occur, PDF or paper manuals are requested, often from outside of the OR, and reviewed, commonly by additional personnel. This results in longer interruptions [10]. Linear digital manuals or tools for assembly guidance provided by different manufacturers are not broadly embedded, nor are they context dependent. Augmented Reality (AR) guidance with in-situ instrument detection could serve as a solution to fulfill the WHO criteria.

Augmented Reality Guidance recently focuses on surgeons' real-time navigation and visualization [1], instrumentation [23], and registration with deformable tissue [29]. Also, marker-free situs registration is being extensively researched [20]. However, prior to the surgeons' activities, handling and assembly of the instruments by the scrub nurse has not been extensively investigated, though this process is often a pain point for inexperienced staff and promising to support by AR guidance [16]. Using relevant objects' pose information, an AR system can show in-situ tooltips ("pick those") and assembly animations ("assemble them like this"), providing step-by-step guidance [15], reducing cognitive load, errors, and task completion time [3].

Surgical Instrument Detection is predominantly studied in endoscopic videos [6]. Extending detection to 6D pose estimation often relies on fiducial markers [12,22] or is limited to two surgical tools [2,11]. Given this context, a recent approach introduced nine surgical tools being used to perform static and dynamic camera calibration on-the-fly without a calibration board [19]. Also, the potential of synthetically-trained deep learning–based approaches is not fully leveraged [17,25]. It remains unclear how multi-camera, entirely marker-free pose estimation performs in a full-fidelity surgical simulation to inform an AR guidance system for inexperienced scrub nurses. To address these gaps, we contribute:

- An AR guidance system for surgical instrument handling assembly connected to deep learning-based 6D pose estimation.
- A multi-camera pose estimation method trained on synthetic data, overcoming challenges in data annotation, allowing for generalization to manifold instrument sets.
- A technical evaluation of the system's performance.
- An expert user study with scrub nurses comparing paper-based manuals and our AR guidance system in a simulated AR scenario.

Our work is the first to benchmark multi-camera AR assembly guidance in an AR scenario. We focus on adapting and extending pose estimation methods for AR-guided surgical workflow support. Our guided AR system improved overall user experience and reduced task completion time by 21.3% or 4.76 minutes, respectively, in a sample of scrub nurses with different levels of experience.

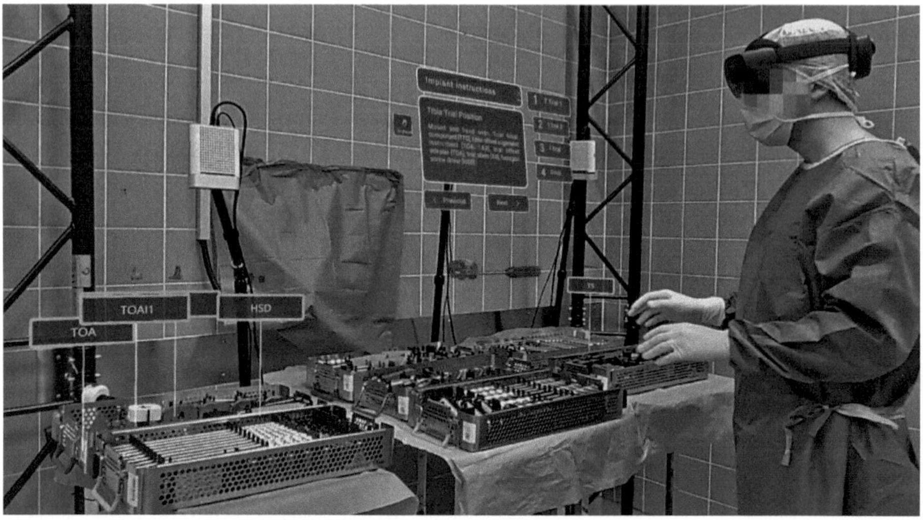

Fig. 1. Informed by marker-free multi-camera pose estimation, our AR guidance system visualizes tooltips and an assembly animation for knee arthroplasty.

2 Method

We propose an end-to-end approach for multi-object, multi-camera 6D pose estimation connected to an in-situ AR application building upon user requirements [5], allowing users to assemble challenging medical instruments. Our guidance system, purely trained on synthetic data, estimates poses of a) surgical trays and instruments on the assembly table, and b) provides visual guidance by means of AR in-situ tool tips and assembly visualizations. The backend extends [19] to a hierarchical marker-free multi-camera pose estimation to comply with sterility and space constraints in the OR. We leverage object pose estimation to calibrate the head-mounted display (HMD) with non-overlapping static cameras for maximum coverage. The HMD runs a Unity application (MRTK2) highlighting the object locations detected by our pose estimator.

2.1 Synthetic Data Generation

We scan each component[1] with a Shining EinScann-SP 3D Scanner with up to 0.05 mm accuracy in a scanning volume of $1200 \times 1200 \times 1200\, mm^3$. We mitigate texture artifacts via MeshLab raster layers. The post-processed scans are used in BlenderProc [7], adding domain randomization (varying backgrounds, lighting, camera poses, distractor objects [24]) to generate randomized and realistic training data, which helps to overcome the sim-to-real gap.

2.2 Hierarchical Multi-camera Pose Estimation

Model Configuration. Our pose detection model integrates a real-time capable object detector and pose estimator to balance speed and accuracy. We use object and keypoint detection modules within the YOLOX architecture [9]. We integrate DCC from RTMO [21] to increase keypoint accuracy from regressed bounding boxes (bbox). Object poses are recovered via RANSAC-based Perspectiven-Point (PnP) from predicted bbox and keypoints [18,25].

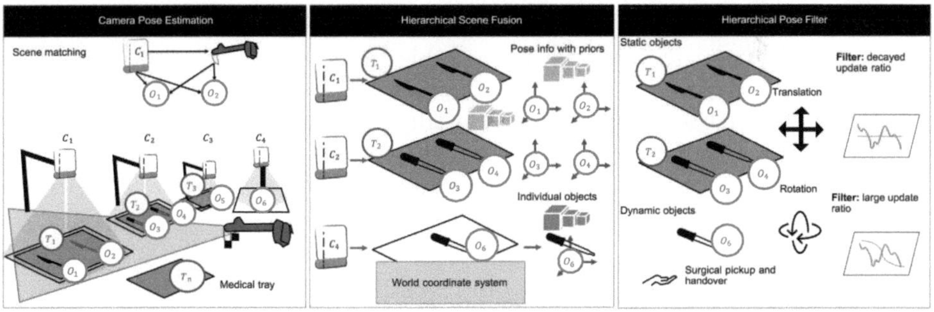

Fig. 2. System overview: Four static top-down cameras observe the surgical trays and deposit table (left), with RGB data fused and processed on a server for marker-free pose estimation and camera calibration (center, right).

Training. We exclusively use synthetic images (Sect. 2.1). To optimize the convolutional neural network (CNN), we use the 2D MLE, 3D keypoint [13] and proxy loss following MultiCam [19]. Hyperparameter selection follows RTMO [21].

Inference. We use the same configuration as during training, but extend the model with filtering, optimizing robustness for real-world OR conditions, and reducing pose misalignment [14]. We combine individual instrument pose estimation and surgical instrument trays via the HMD camera and Kinect cameras [19]. Instrument poses are first estimated on the instrument table; if unsuccessful, the instrument is assumed to remain in its tray. Since relative poses within trays are predefined, the world pose of an instrument can be approximated.

[1] DePuy Synthes TFN-ADVANCED^{TM} Proximal Femoral Nailing System and Implantcast GenuX MK implant.

Hierarchical Scene Fusion. We calculate each camera pose using spatiotemporal overlapping object candidates following [17,19]. Then, we define our hierarchical scene structure with camera and object nodes. Given each camera pose, we fuse the object poses from trays and individual objects in each camera view.

Hierarchical Pose Filter All pose estimates are processed by a two-stage filter: First, a plausibility check rejects physically implausible poses (e.g., excessive distance, camera proximity, or inverted trays). Second, valid poses are smoothed using an exponential moving average, with linear filtering for translations and spherical linear interpolation for rotations as follows:

$$\mathbf{t}_{\text{smooth}} = \alpha \mathbf{t}_{\text{curr}} + (1 - \alpha)\mathbf{t}_{\text{prev}}, \quad \mathbf{q}_{\text{smooth}} = \text{slerp}(\mathbf{q}_{\text{prev}}, \mathbf{q}_{\text{curr}}, \alpha) \tag{1}$$

where $\mathbf{t}_{\text{curr}} \in \mathbf{R}^3$ and $\mathbf{q}_{\text{curr}}$ are the current translation and rotation, $\mathbf{t}_{\text{prev}}$ and $\mathbf{q}_{\text{prev}}$ are the previous ones, and $\alpha \in [0, 1]$ is the filter coefficient.

Considering static and dynamic objects in the scene, we apply a hierarchical pose filter using different filter coefficients, i.e., a fixed coefficient $\alpha = 0.2$ for individual dynamic instruments and an exponentially decayed coefficient $\alpha = e^{\frac{-i}{300}}$ for static trays to converge to a stable pose, where i is the number of frames. We assume static cameras and trays for the technical evaluation and the user study. To enable the use of moving trays and cameras, static constraints can be disabled. Given top-down cameras, these filters also make pose data more robust in terms of occlusions by hands picking objects from the trays.

2.3 System Architecture

We use RGB feeds from four Azure Kinect cameras and a Microsoft HoloLens 2 HMD (Fig. 2). We use the HoloLens because it is an optical-see-through HMD, which is good for the medical environment, as video-see-through can fail. Our C++ server builds upon OpenMMLab [4,21], achieving an average runtime around 200 ms per frame on a workstation with an RTX 4080 GPU (16 GB VRAM) and an AMD Ryzen 9 9900X CPU with 64 GB RAM. The HMD sends video streams to the workstation, and after the multi-camera, multi-object 6D pose estimation, the workstation sends pose information back using WiFi via TCP [8]. The measured end-to-end latency for data streaming from the workstation to the HMD is approx. 60 ms. The server analyzes the video streams from four static and one dynamic camera, each with 15 frames per second (tradeoff between computation speed and precision). Our HMD visualization pose refreshment rate is 3 s to account for battery life and system heating.

3 Technical Evaluation

To technically evaluate our system, we calculate runtime and pose estimation accuracy in ADD(-S) using 3785 frames of images in 720P resolution from one

HMD (HoloLens 2) and four static external RGB cameras (Azure Kinect). Our ground truth data is annotated by the Optitrack motion capture system with Motive 3.1.4 and six infrared Primex 13 cameras. Furthermore, to assess the quality of the multi-view multi-object evaluation, we compare our method to CosyPose [17], as shown in Table 1. Our method shows overall better accuracy with $ADD(-S)AUC$ 44.34 for trays and 31.73 for instruments due to improved scene matching and pose filter. The average camera pose error is less than 70 mm and rotation error less than 6°C, see Fig. 3 for qualitative results.

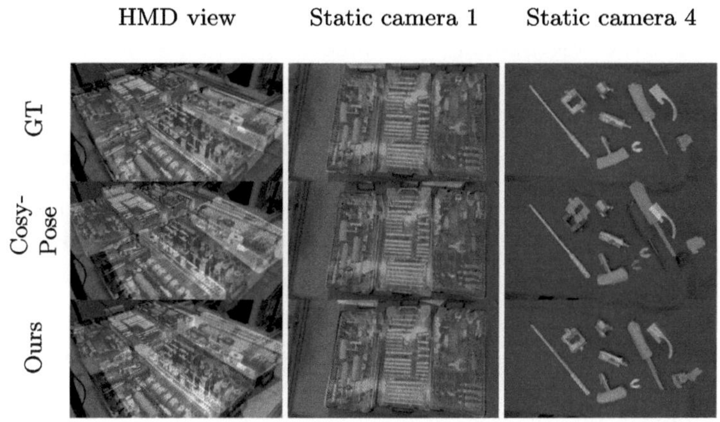

Fig. 3. Visualization of pose estimation for surgical trays and instruments (real data). Our approach shows less visualization error compared to CosyPose [17].

Table 1. Camera and object pose evaluation on our real test data.

Assets	Methods	Condition pose filter	Object pose $ADD(-S)AUC \uparrow$	Camera pose $e_{trans} \downarrow$	$e_{rot} \downarrow$	Overall runtime ms
Entire trays	CosyPose [17]	✗	38.26	84.46	9.79	**183.47**
	Ours	✗	21.80	73.81	7.12	186.92
		✓	**44.34**	**66.95**	**5.20**	184.95
Instruments in trays	CosyPose [17]	✗	16.94	94.14	8.37	167.37
	Ours	✗	24.24	72.56	6.13	**111.59**
		✓	**31.73**	**69.66**	**5.79**	118.08

$ADD(-S)AUC$ = average distance metric under the accuracy-threshold curve [28], e_{trans} = translation error in mm, e_{rot} = rotation error in degree

4 User Study

Our system was compared to a paper manual (current standard) in a within-subjects study using a simulated surgical scenario, see Fig. 1. We measured assembly time, error rate, and workload (raw NASA TLX) [26]. Ethical approval was obtained from the ethics board of the Technical University of Munich (approval 2025–106-S-NP), following the declaration of Helsinki.

Sample, Procedure, and Task. We recruited 29 scrub nurses (25 female, 4 male; 30.9 ± 10.9 years; OR experience from 0.5 to 32 years). 22 used the tested Implantcast GenuX MK implant ≤ 3 times (Fig. 4 mid shows the distribution of experience). Having obtained informed consent, participants first completed an AR tutorial using a subset of the TFNA instruments for familiarization. Second, they assisted two parts of a simulated knee arthroplasty surgery (tibia and femur preparation, each 25–30 parts and 15–40 min), comparing paper manuals and our AR system. Counterbalancing was complete for 28 participants. An additional participant introduces only a negligible imbalance without biasing condition comparisons.

Quantitative Results. Our system significantly outperformed the paper manual in time to completion ($F(1) = 12.036, p = .001, \eta_p^2 = .108$), see Fig. 4. We found main effects for the type of bone ($F(1) = 16.989, p < .001, \eta_p^2 = .167$) and experience with the instruments ($F(3) = 5.455, p = .003, \eta_p^2 = .160$). This underlines that specifically less experienced staff benefit from the AR guidance, whereas a turning point can be identified between 4 and 6 previous uses. With AR, the timing differences between the femur and tibia in terms of complexity become clearer than with paper. No significant differences were observed in the error rates. Our system further resulted in a significantly lower perceived workload (mental, temporal, performance, effort, and frustration; see Table 2).

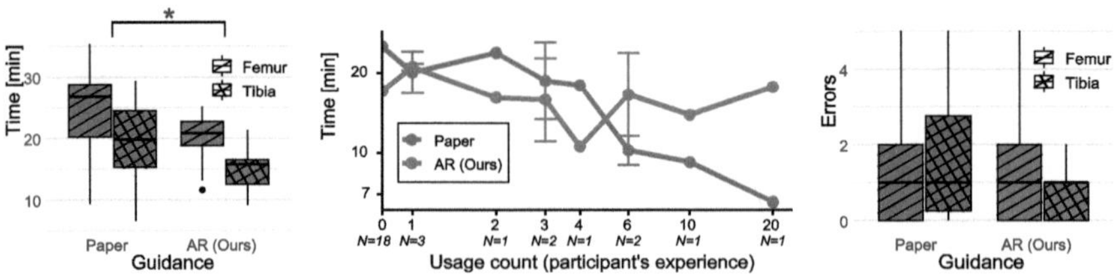

Fig. 4. Simulated surgery times for each guidance and surgery type (left), participants' experience (middle), and errors (right). The results show that our system benefits practitioners with up to four prior OR experiences with the sets.

Table 2. Subjective results for paper and AR condition.

Raw NASA-TLX	P_M	P_{SD}	AR_M	AR_{SD}	$p \leq$	Effect
Mental	75.86	17.88	43.28	26.33	**.001**	$r = 0.84$
Physical	35.35	27.61	27.24	23.78	.266	$r = 0.21$
Temporal	73.28	20.63	33.45	24.28	**.001**	$r = 0.96$
Performance	53.45	24.39	30.17	18.54	**.001**	$d = 1.07$
Effort	63.45	22.96	32.07	15.15	**.001**	$d = 1.59$
Frustration	68.28	20.37	33.97	23.16	**.001**	$d = 1.57$

P = paper manual, AR = AR guidance, M = mean, SD = standard deviation

Qualitative Results. The participants expressed an overall positive attitude toward our approach due to the step-wise instructions, clear menu structure, and the combination of assembly animations with tooltips on parts to pick. In contrast to the paper manual, selective AR information presentation was associated with effective visualization and reduced information overload. The system was described as particularly suitable for training and supporting users with limited prior experience. Both gaze and hand-based interaction (moveable user interface) were described as supportive of system use.

5 Discussion

We introduce an AR guidance system driven by real-time 6D pose estimation trained on synthetic data. We outperform CosyPose [17] in evaluation metrics. Given manufacturers' CAD models, our approach could be scaled to manifold instrument sets. We support a flexible, multi-component instrument setup without the need of camera calibration. Our non-overlapping multi-camera setup is used for field of view (FoV) extension, rather than a multi-view pose accuracy improvement [2,11,17]. Our approach is leveraging known object knowledge [19] and combines hierarchical fusion and dynamic filtering. To our knowledge, this is the first AR system for pick, assemble, and handover tasks for scrub nurses, rather than surgeons' tasks [1,29].

The present system was validated by scrub nurses in a simulated surgery, demonstrating a clear advantage over traditional paper-based instructions for instrumentation. As intended, our system is especially beneficial for novices and inexperienced scrub nurses with a turnover point between 4 and 6 previous uses (Fig. 4, middle). Error frequencies remained similar. Time differences for femur and tibia preparation become more apparent as the guided handling of more complex parts scales. Overall, handling our AR system was perceived as positive throughout.

Limitations noted by participants included ergonomic constraints, limited field of view, sterility concerns, and acclimatization requirements (learning curve). Technical challenges included rare gaze calibration problems, delayed feedback, and tooltip inaccuracies. The fact that guidance text instructions have to be implemented manually represents a remaining challenge for the future.

Future Work will focus on improving pose estimation accuracy, generalization, incorporating new instruments, adaptive and context-aware visualization, and validation under real OR conditions across additional instrument sets. Overall, we established a baseline for integrating AR guidance into routine surgical practice, potentially expanding to monitoring systems for experienced users.

6 Conclusion

We present a multi-view pose-estimation-driven AR guidance system for surgical instrumentation. Our approach demonstrates measurable improvements in task performance and usability, particularly for inexperienced scrub nurses. Our combination of marker-free pose estimation and spatially registered visualization provides context-aware, situated guidance that supports efficiency, reduces uncertainty, and enhances procedural confidence in surgical workflows. Our findings indicate that the system itself is technically robust and clinically promising.

Acknowledgments. This work was funded by the German Federal Ministry of Education and Research (BMBF) in the grant program "AI-based assistance systems for in-process health applications", grant number 16SV8973. Shiyu Li acknowledges the financial support from the China Scholarship Council. This work was partially supported by the TU Munich, through its MIRMI Seed Fund program, and by the Robotics Institute Germany (RIG) under grant 16ME0997K. The authors thank implantcast GmbH for lending the surgical equipment. We acknowledge HPC resources (NHR@FAU b143dc, b180dc), funded by federal and Bavarian state authorities, and Gerhard Wellein's HPC approach. NHR@FAU hardware is partially funded by DFG 440719683. Additional support by ERC projects MIA-NORMAL 101083647, DFG 513220538 and 512819079, and the state of Bavaria (HTA and the Bavarian Foundation Model Initiative).

Disclosure of Interests. The authors have no relevant competing interests.

References

1. Acar, A., et al.: NAVIUS: navigated augmented reality visualization for ureteroscopic surgery. In: Gee, J.C., et al. International Conference on Medical Image Computing and Computer-Assisted Intervention. LNCS, vol. 15970, pp. 433–443. Springer, Cham (2025). https://doi.org/10.1007/978-3-032-05141-7_42
2. Agethen, N., Rosskamp, J., Koller, T.L., Klein, J., Zachmann, G.: Recurrent multi-view 6dof pose estimation for marker-less surgical tool tracking. Int. J. Comput. Assist. Radiol. Surg., 1–11 (2025)
3. Blattgerste, J., Renner, P., Strenge, B., Pfeiffer, T.: In-situ instructions exceed side-by-side instructions in augmented reality assisted assembly. In: Proceedings of the 11th PErvasive Technologies Related to Assistive Environments Conference, pp. 133–140. ACM, Corfu Greece (2018)
4. Contributors, M.: Openmmlab pose estimation toolbox and benchmark (2020). https://github.com/open-mmlab/mmpose
5. Cramer, E., et al: Requirement analysis for an AI-based AR assistance system for surgical tools in the operating room: stakeholder requirements and technical perspectives. Int. J. Comput. Assist. Radiol. Surg., pp. 1–10 (2024)

6. Demir, K.C., et al.: Deep learning in surgical workflow analysis: a review of phase and step recognition. IEEE J. Biomed. Health Inform. **27**(11), 5405–5417 (2023)
7. Denninger, M., et al.: BlenderProc: reducing the Reality Gap with Photorealistic Rendering (2020)
8. Dibene, J.C., Dunn, E.: Hololens 2 sensor streaming. arXiv preprint arXiv:2211.02648 (2022)
9. Ge, Z., Liu, S., Wang, F., Li, Z., Sun, J.: YOLOX: exceeding yolo series in 2021. arXiv preprint arXiv:2107.08430 (2021)
10. Göras, C., et al.: Tasks, multitasking and interruptions among the surgical team in an operating room: a prospective observational study. BMJ Open **9**(5), e026410 (2019)
11. Hein, J., et al.: Next-generation surgical navigation: marker-less multi-view 6dof pose estimation of surgical instruments. Med. Image Anal. **103**, 103613 (2025)
12. Hogenkamp, M., Stauffer, T., Lohmeyer, Q., Meboldt, M.: 6D object pose tracking for orthopedic surgical training using visual-inertial sensor fusion. In: Gee, J.C., et al. International Conference on Medical Image Computing and Computer-Assisted Intervention. LNCS, vol. 15968, pp. 13–23. Springer, Cham (2025). https://doi.org/10.1007/978-3-032-05114-1_2
13. Hu, Y., Speierer, S., Jakob, W., Fua, P., Salzmann, M.: Wide-depth-range 6D object pose estimation in space. In: Proceedings of the IEEE/CVF Conference on Computer Vision and Pattern Recognition, pp. 15870–15879 (2021)
14. Khuong, B.M., Kiyokawa, K., Miller, A., La Viola, J.J., Mashita, T., Takemura, H.: The effectiveness of an AR-based context-aware assembly support system in object assembly: 21st IEEE Virtual Reality Conference, VR 2014. 2014 IEEE Virtual Reality, VR 2014 - Proceedings, pp. 57–62. publisher: IEEE Computer Society (2014)
15. Kleinbeck, C., Schieber, H., Andress, S., Krautz, C., Roth, D.: ARTFM: augmented Reality Visualization of Tool Functionality Manuals in Operating Rooms. In: 2022 IEEE Conference on Virtual Reality and 3D User Interfaces Abstracts and Workshops (VRW), pp. 736–737 (2022)
16. Kreimeier, J., Schieber, H., Li, S., Martin-Gomez, A., Roth, D.: Visual Guidance for Assembly Processes. In: 2024 IEEE International Symposium on Mixed and Augmented Reality Adjunct (ISMAR-Adjunct), pp. 652–653 (2024). iSSN: 2771-1110
17. Labbé, Y., Carpentier, J., Aubry, M., Sivic, J.: CosyPose: Consistent Multi-view Multi-object 6D Pose Estimation. In: Vedaldi, A., Bischof, H., Brox, T., Frahm, J.-M. (eds.) ECCV 2020. LNCS, vol. 12362, pp. 574–591. Springer, Cham (2020). https://doi.org/10.1007/978-3-030-58520-4_34
18. Li, S., Schieber, H., Corell, N., Egger, B., Kreimeier, J., Roth, D.: GBOT: graph-Based 3D object tracking for augmented reality-assisted assembly guidance. In: 2024 IEEE Conference Virtual Reality and 3D User Interfaces (VR), pp. 513–523 (2024). iSSN: 2642-5254
19. Li, S., Schieber, H., Waldow, K., Busam, B., Kreimeier, J., Roth, D.: MultiCam: on-the-fly multi-camera pose estimation using spatiotemporal overlaps of known objects. IEEE Trans. Visual Comput. Graph. (2026)
20. Liebmann, F., et al.: Automatic registration with continuous pose updates for marker-less surgical navigation in spine surgery. Med. Image Anal. **91**, 103027 (2024)
21. Lu, P., Jiang, T., Li, Y., Li, X., Chen, K., Yang, W.: RTMO: towards high-performance one-stage real-time multi-person pose estimation (2023)

22. Martin-Gomez, A., et al.: STTAR: surgical tool tracking using off-the-shelf augmented reality head-mounted displays. IEEE Trans. Visual Comput. Graph. **30**(7), 3578–3593 (2023)
23. Müller, F., Roner, S., Liebmann, F., Spirig, J.M., Fürnstahl, P., Farshad, M.: Augmented reality navigation for spinal pedicle screw instrumentation using intraoperative 3D imaging. Spine J. **20**(4), 621–628 (2020)
24. Schieber, H., Demir, K.C., Kleinbeck, C., Yang, S.H., Roth, D.: Indoor synthetic data generation: a systematic review. Comput. Vis. Image Underst., 103907 (2024)
25. Schieber, H., Li, S., Corell, N., Beckerle, P., Kreimeier, J., Roth, D.: ASDF: assembly state detection utilizing late fusion by integrating 6D pose estimation. In: 2024 IEEE International Symposium on Mixed and Augmented Reality (ISMAR), pp. 190–199 (2024). iSSN: 2473-0726
26. Tubbs-Cooley, H.L., Mara, C.A., Carle, A.C., Gurses, A.P.: The NASA Task Load Index as a measure of overall workload among neonatal, paediatric and adult intensive care nurses. Intensive Crit. Care Nurs. **46**, 64–69 (2018)
27. (WHO), W.H.O.: Global Patient Safety Action Plan 2021-2030. https://www.who.int/teams/integrated-health-services/patient-safety/policy/global-patient-safety-action-plan
28. Xiang, Y., Schmidt, T., Narayanan, V., Fox, D.: PoseCNN: a convolutional neural network for 6D object pose estimation in cluttered scenes. arXiv preprint arXiv:1711.00199 (2017)
29. Yang, Q.,et al.: Augmented reality-based guidance with deformable registration in head and neck tumor resection. In: Gee, J.C., et al. International Conference on Medical Image Computing and Computer-Assisted Intervention. LNCS, vol. 15968, pp. 45–54. Springer, Cham (2025). https://doi.org/10.1007/978-3-032-05114-1_5

Non-linear INR-Based Motion Modeling for 4D Radiotherapy

Johannes B. Gebauer[1,2(✉)], Laura E. Büttgen[1,3], Thilo Sentker[1,2], and René Werner[1,2]

[1] Institute for Applied Medical Informatics, University Medical Center Hamburg-Eppendorf, Hamburg, Germany
{j.gebauer,l.buettgen,t.sentker,r.werner}@uke.de
[2] Institute of Computational Neuroscience, University Medical Center Hamburg-Eppendorf, Hamburg, Germany
[3] Department of Radiotherapy and Radiation Oncology, University Medical Center Hamburg-Eppendorf, Hamburg, Germany

Abstract. Accurate motion management via patient-specific motion models is critical for motion compensation and tumor tracking in 4D radiotherapy. Existing approaches typically rely on a two-step pipeline combining deformable image registration (DIR) and linear surrogate-based regression, limiting their ability to capture complex, nonlinear surrogate-to-motion relationships. We propose a novel implicit neural representation (INR) motion model that jointly optimizes DIR and surrogate regression, directly predicting continuous deformation vector fields from arbitrary surrogate states. The framework simultaneously learns forward and backward motion models with enforced cyclic consistency, and adapts the SIREN architecture with anisotropic frequency scaling to account for the differing spatial and temporal dynamics of the input. Evaluated on the DIR-Lab 4DCT dataset, our method achieves a mean TRE of 1.08 mm and DSC of 0.625, outperforming classical and INR-based two-step baselines while yielding strictly zero folding across all cases. Source code is available at https://github.com/IPMI-ICNS-UKE/INR-Motion-Modeling.

Keywords: Motion Modelling · Image Registration · Implicit Neural Representation

1 Introduction

Respiratory-induced motion makes the treatment of lung and liver tumors clinically challenging [9]. Precise motion management of the patient is therefore crucial for accurately calculating the delivered dose to the tumor and organs at risk (OAR) [20]. Specifically, this requires patient-specific motion modeling: establishing a mathematical relationship between an external surrogate signal,

T. Sentker and R. Werner—These authors contributed equally as last authors.

G. Yang et al. (Eds.): MICCAI 2026, LNCS 16893, pp. 275–284, 2027.
https://doi.org/10.1007/978-3-032-38236-8_27

acquired during treatment, and the internal motion of the region of interest, typically represented as a dense deformation vector field (DVF). Common surrogate signals include optical tracking of a marker block placed on the thorax and real-time imaging [2]. Accurate motion modeling can furthermore benefit the reconstruction of the treatment-day 4D cone-beam CT (4DCBCT) by enabling prior-guided, motion-compensated reconstruction methods [13].

Patient-specific motion models are typically derived from the patient's planning 4DCT, which commonly comprises 10 phase volumes paired with their respective surrogate signals over a median respiratory cycle. The objective of such a motion model is to predict a DVF that maps a reference anatomical state to any target respiratory state guided by the surrogate signal [10]. Constructing such a model first requires pair-wise registration between the reference phase and all other phases. Subsequently, standard modeling approaches assume a linear relationship between the surrogates and the DVFs, and solve for a system matrix via linear regression [17]. Recent works have extended this classic linear model by optimizing the surrogate and allowing it to vary in the superior-inferior (SI) direction [8]. While providing a multi-dimensional surrogate allows linear models to approximate hysteresis, they remain restricted to a simple linear combination of these global inputs. Consequently, they inherently struggle to accurately capture highly complex, non-linear surrogate-motion interactions, such as localized variations in hysteresis or spatially heterogeneous tissue deformations.

A complementary line of work has focused on improving the spatial representation of deformation fields themselves. In this context, implicit neural representations (INRs) have emerged as a flexible and expressive framework for deformable image registration (DIR) [5,15,18]. INRs represent dense DVFs as continuous functions rather than relying on discrete 3D voxel grids. In particular, models using sinusoidal representation networks (SIREN) [14] have demonstrated high efficacy for such spatial transformations. Furthermore, INRs have been adapted to model dynamic scenes [12], including applications as internal motion models for 4DCBCT motion-compensated reconstruction [19] and group image reconstruction in cardiac MRI [6]. However, such internal models rely exclusively on the intrinsic ordering of the phase images and do not explicitly incorporate an external surrogate signal to control motion.

Building upon these advancements, we propose a SIREN-based patient-specific motion model capable of predicting continuous DVFs inside the lung with respect to a reference state, conditioned on an external surrogate signal. In contrast to classical sequential pipelines, our approach eliminates the need for prior pairwise registrations. Instead, it represents respiratory motion as a continuous implicit function jointly parameterized by spatial location and the surrogate signal.

In summary, our main contributions are threefold: **1** we introduce a novel patient-specific respiratory motion model based on the SIREN framework that predicts continuous, high-resolution DVFs directly from a patient-specific surrogate; **2** we enforce cyclic consistency by simultaneously learning forward and backward transformations and introduce an anisotropic frequency scaling in the

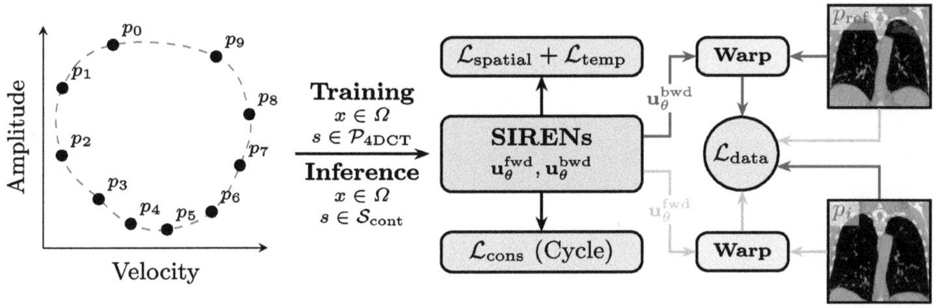

Fig. 1. Overview of the proposed continuous motion modeling framework. Left: The 2D surrogate space, illustrating the discrete 4DCT phases ($\mathcal{P}_{\text{4DCT}}$) used for training and the continuous domain ($\mathcal{S}_{\text{cont}}$) available for inference. Right: Forward ($\mathbf{u}^{\text{fwd}}$) and backward ($\mathbf{u}^{\text{bwd}}$) deformation fields are predicted by individual SIRENs from spatial coordinates $\mathbf{x}$ and surrogate states $\mathbf{s}$. A data loss ($\mathcal{L}_{\text{data}}$) drives the optimization by matching the reference (p_{ref}) and target (p_i) images via forward (light arrows) and backward (dark arrows) warping. Training is further regularized by cycle consistency ($\mathcal{L}_{\text{cons}}$) and spatio-temporal smoothness ($\mathcal{L}_{\text{spatial}}, \mathcal{L}_{\text{temp}}$).

first SIREN layer to accommodate the spatial and temporal differences; and **3** we demonstrate the efficacy of our proposed framework through a comprehensive evaluation on the publicly available DIR-Lab 4DCT dataset [3].

2 Methods

2.1 Problem Formulation and Classical Modeling

A patient-specific respiratory motion model aims to predict the transformation $\mathbf{\Phi}$ from a reference phase to an arbitrary respiratory state parameterized by an external surrogate signal. In this work, we choose the end-exhale (EE) phase (typically corresponding to the 50% phase in a 4DCT) as the reference, as it represents the most reproducible anatomical state. We further represent $\mathbf{\Phi}$ via the displacement field $\mathbf{u}$:

$$\mathbf{\Phi}(\mathbf{x}) = \mathbf{x} + \mathbf{u}(\mathbf{x}), \tag{1}$$

where $\mathbf{x}$ is a coordinate in the image domain Ω. In the following, we use the terms DVF and $\mathbf{u}$ interchangeably.

Motion models can be formulated in two directional variants. In the forward-warping formulation, the DVF maps the reference to the surrogate-driven target state, enabling the tracking of anatomical landmarks. In the backward-warping formulation, the DVF maps the target state back to the reference, allowing images or segmentation masks defined in the reference to be propagated to arbitrary respiratory states, which is essential for dose accumulation.

Commonly, classical motion models are constructed in a sequential two-step process. First, ground-truth DVFs, denoted as $U \in \mathbb{R}^{m \times n_{\text{ph}}}$, are calculated between the reference phase and all other n_{ph} phases via DIR, where $m = 3N_{\text{vox}}$ represents the number of image voxels multiplied by the spatial dimensions. Each column of U corresponds to a flattened DVF for one respiratory phase. Subsequently, a linear relationship between the DVFs and the corresponding surrogate signal $S \in \mathbb{R}^{n_{\text{ind}} \times n_{\text{ph}}}$ (with n_{ind} being the dimensionality of the surrogate) is assumed:

$$U = BS, \tag{2}$$

where $B \in \mathbb{R}^{m \times n_{\text{ind}}}$ is the desired system matrix. Equation 2 can be solved in a least-squares sense via multivariate linear regression, as described by Wilms et al. [17].

2.2 Implicit Motion Model

We model respiratory motion as a continuous displacement field

$$\mathbf{u}(\mathbf{x}, \mathbf{s}) \in \mathbb{R}^3, \tag{3}$$

where $\mathbf{x} \in [-1, 1]^3$ denotes the normalized spatial position and $\mathbf{s} \in [-1, 1]^{n_{\text{ind}}}$ represents the respiratory surrogate signal. Specifically, we implement $\mathbf{u}$ as a SIREN [14]

$$\mathbf{u}_{\text{non-linear}}(\mathbf{x}, \mathbf{s}) = f_\theta([\mathbf{x}, \mathbf{s}]), \tag{4}$$

with $f_\theta : \mathbb{R}^{3+n_{\text{ind}}} \rightarrow \mathbb{R}^3$, and θ being the model parameters optimized during training. The full model framework is illustrated in Fig. 1.

An important hyperparameter of SIRENs is their frequency scaling parameter ω_0 in their activations $\sin(\omega_0 \cdot \mathbf{W}\mathbf{x} + \mathbf{b})$ [14]. It is commonly set to a large value (e.g., $\omega_0 = 30$), to enable the network to represent high-frequency components across the input domain $[-1, 1]$. Acknowledging the anisotropy of our input, i.e. high-frequency components in space and smooth variations in the surrogate, we set ω_0 individually per input channel. Specifically, we use $\omega_{0,\mathbf{x}} = 30$ for spatial and $\omega_{0,\mathbf{s}} = \pi/2$ for surrogate inputs. The latter ensures that the surrogate inputs only span half a period over the input domain.

Ablation Models. We train the following ablation models to disentangle the effect of joint spatio-temporal optimization, the nature of the surrogate relationship and the impact of INR-based DIR. First, we train a (temporal)-linear SIREN:

$$\mathbf{u}_{\text{linear}}(\mathbf{x}, \mathbf{s}) = b_\theta(\mathbf{x})\mathbf{s}, \tag{5}$$

where $b_\theta : \mathbb{R}^3 \rightarrow \mathbb{R}^{3 \times n_{\text{ind}}}$ represents a spatially continuous analogue of the system matrix B in Eq. 2, enforcing a strictly linear relationship with respect to the surrogate signal.

We then build two variants of the two-step procedure as described in Eq. 2. The required pair-wise DVFs are, for the first model, acquired via classical variational registration (VarReg) [4], and for the second with DIR-SIRENs as proposed in [18]. The latter is then sampled on a regular grid before the second step.

2.3 Training Objective

The network parameters are optimized by minimizing a joint training objective, defined as a weighted sum of four loss components:

$$\mathcal{L} = \mathcal{L}_{\text{data}} + \lambda_{\text{spatial}}\mathcal{L}_{\text{spatial}} + \lambda_{\text{temp}}\mathcal{L}_{\text{temp}} + \lambda_{\text{cons}}\mathcal{L}_{\text{cons}}, \tag{6}$$

where λ_{spatial}, λ_{temp}, and λ_{cons} are hyperparameters controlling the relative influence of each regularization term. The individual terms are defined as follows:
(1) Data term ($\mathcal{L}_{\text{data}}$): We utilize the masked normalized cross-correlation (NCC) to evaluate the similarity between the deformed reference and the target phase images strictly within the lung regions.
(2) Spatial regularization ($\mathcal{L}_{\text{spatial}}$): To ensure biologically plausible deformations, we penalize local folding and enforce spatial smoothness using a Jacobian determinant penalty and a Laplacian penalty, respectively:

$$\mathcal{L}_{\text{spatial}} = \|\det(I + \nabla \mathbf{u}) - 1\|_2^2 + \lambda_{\text{Lap}} \|\Delta \mathbf{u}\|_2^2 . \tag{7}$$

(3) Temporal regularization ($\mathcal{L}_{\text{temp}}$): To encourage smooth motion trajectories over time, we apply a Laplacian smoothness penalty with respect to the surrogate inputs for the non-linear model. For the linear baseline model, we penalize the L_2-norm of the first derivatives with respect to the surrogates.
(4) Consistency term ($\mathcal{L}_{\text{cons}}$): As demonstrated by van Harten et al. [15], training of the DIR-SIRENs can be stabilized by enforcing forward-backward cycle consistency. We adopt these findings and simultaneously train both directions and formulate the following L_2 penalty on the residual displacement:

$$\mathcal{L}_{\text{cons}} = \left\|\mathbf{u}^{\text{fwd}}(\mathbf{x}, \mathbf{s}) + \mathbf{u}^{\text{bwd}}\big(\mathbf{x} + \mathbf{u}^{\text{fwd}}(\mathbf{x}, \mathbf{s}), \mathbf{s}\big)\right\|_2^2 . \tag{8}$$

2.4 Implementation Details

Our framework is implemented in PyTorch [11], utilizing its autograd functionality to analytically compute all spatial and temporal gradients required for the training objective. During each training step, we randomly sample 1,000 continuous spatial coordinates per phase from the union of the phase-specific lung masks. We apply intra-voxel jitter to these coordinates to fully leverage the continuous spatial domain of the INRs. For the data loss computation, image intensities at these continuous coordinates are obtained via trilinear interpolation from the discrete voxel grids. We set individual weights in Eq. 6 to $\lambda_{\text{spatial}} = 0.01$, $\lambda_{\text{temp}} = 0.1$ and $\lambda_{\text{cons}} = 0.1$.

The network parameters are optimized using the AdamW optimizer with an initial learning rate of 10^{-4}. The learning rate is modulated by a cosine annealing schedule following a 20-step linear warmup. Each model is trained for a total of 10,000 iterations, requiring approximately 15 min of training. However, since we observed earlier convergence in many cases, this duration could be reduced by introducing early stopping criteria. All SIRENs are configured with 3 hidden layers, each having a width of 256. We set $\omega_0 = 30$, excluding the anisotropic scaling described in Sect. 2.2.

2.5 Dataset and Surrogate Extraction

We evaluate our proposed method on the publicly available DIR-Lab 4DCT dataset [3], which consists of 10 patient cases. Each case comprises 10 distinct 3D respiratory phase images covering a full breathing cycle. In this dataset, phase 0 represents the maximum/end-inhale (EI) state, and phase 5 represents the maximum/end-exhale (EE) state. Consequently, phases 1 through 4 capture the exhalation, while phases 6 through 9 capture the inhalation.

We aim to evaluate our model on a 2D surrogate $\mathbf{s} \in \mathbb{R}^2$, often given by the displacement amplitude and its temporal derivative of an external marker block, allowing for the differentiation between inhalation and exhalation. Because the original DIR-Lab surrogate traces are unavailable, we derive an internal signal as a replacement. Specifically, we extract the phase-wise lung volumes from automatically predicted lung masks and use these as the signal amplitudes. We then assume an equal phase-spacing of the images, allowing us to extract the derivative.

2.6 Evaluation Metrics

Registration accuracy is commonly assessed via the target registration error (TRE) computed on paired ground-truth landmarks. The DIR-Lab dataset provides 300 expert-annotated landmarks per case, available only at the extreme respiratory states. For intermediate phases, only automatically propagated landmarks are available and exclusively for the exhalation, precluding a balanced evaluation across the full respiratory cycle. We therefore adopt lung vessel maps as a dense anatomical proxy, with vessel probability maps extracted automatically using TotalSegmentator [16].

To avoid interpolation artifacts, we apply the predicted DVFs directly to continuous vessel probability maps via trilinear interpolation before binarizing at a 0.5 threshold. We report DSC and Average Symmetric Surface Distance (ASSD), the latter being more robust than DSC for thin tubular structures, as well as TRE evaluated on the 300 extreme-phase landmarks. To assess spatial regularity, we compute the Jacobian determinant $|J|$ of each transformation, reporting the fraction of voxels with $|J| \leq 0$ as an indicator of non-physiological folding and $\text{std}(|J|)$ as a measure of transformation smoothness.

3 Results

For clarity, we restrict the evaluation to the backward models, as we observed similar trends for both directions. Quantitative results are shown in Table 1. Our proposed full implicit SIREN outperforms all ablation models across all registration accuracy metrics. Regarding topological plausibility, it is the only model to achieve strictly zero folding, while all other models exhibit near-zero but non-zero rates (order 10^{-6}). DVF smoothness as measured by std($|J|$) is consistent across all SIREN-based methods.

Figure 2 provides a per-case, per-phase breakdown of DSC. As expected, all models perform best for small respiratory motion, evident in higher DSC values for phases adjacent to the reference (p_5) and for cases with limited overall motion (e.g., cases 1 and 2). The most performance gains occur at two transitions: first, from classical to INR-based DIR, and second, moving from the temporal-linear assumption to our fully joint SIREN approach.

Finally, Fig. 3 visualizes the behavior of the SIREN motion models in the surrogate phase space. The linear SIREN produces a globally uniform displacement field, paired with a steady increase of spatial irregularity. Standard (isotropic) SIREN (FULL (ISO.)) exhibits temporal overfitting, leading to deviations outside the physiological breathing cycle. Introducing our proposed anisotropic frequency scaling (FULL (ANISO.)) suppresses these artifacts, yielding a smooth temporal motion model.

Table 1. Quantitative comparison of motion models evaluated on lung vessel maps and landmarks. DSC↑, ASSD↓ [mm], TRE↓ [mm], % of $|J|_{\leq 0}$ ↓ and std($|J|$) ↓.

Model		DSC ↑	ASSD ↓	TRE ↓	% of $\|J\|_{\leq 0}$ ↓	$std(\|J\|)$ ↓
2-Step Seq.	CLASSICAL	0.562	0.816	1.521	6.0e−7	0.127
	INR	0.571	0.786	1.341	3.5e−6	**0.072**
Joint SIREN	LINEAR	0.573	0.785	1.404	2.4e−6	**0.072**
	FULL	**0.625**	**0.682**	**1.084**	**0.0**	0.080

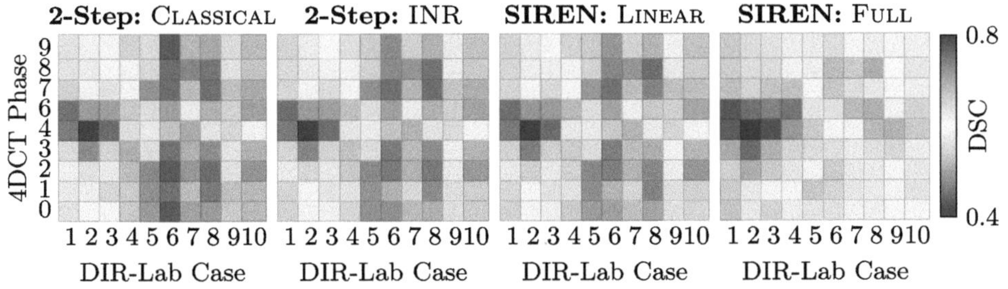

Fig. 2. Phase-wise DSC for all cases and models. Phase 5 serves as the fixed reference and is thus omitted. Our proposed approach (FULL) mitigates the performance drops observed in challenging cases across all baseline models.

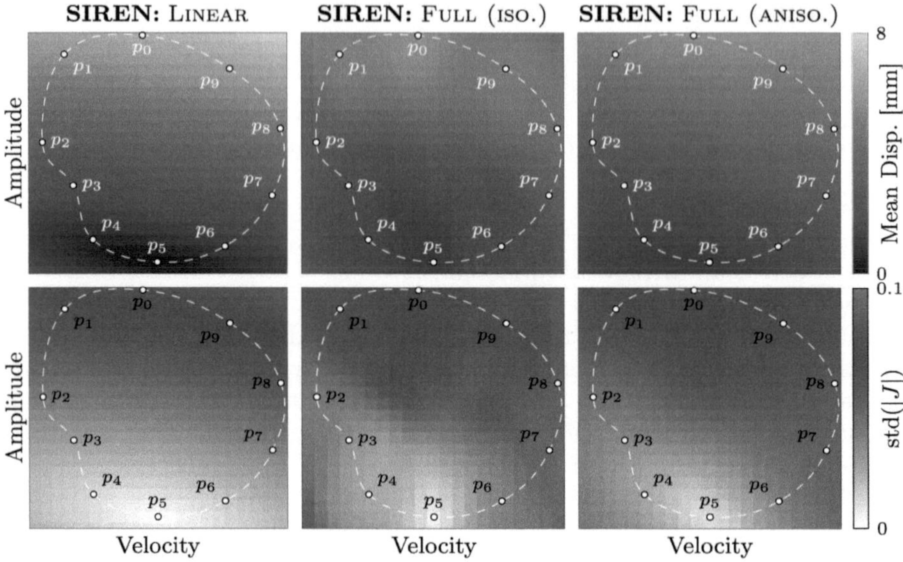

Fig. 3. Continuous motion model behavior in the surrogate phase space. Top row: Mean displacement [mm]. Bottom row: DVF regularity (std($|J|$)). The dashed line represents the respiratory trajectory with discrete 4DCT phases (p_0–p_9) for case 9 and reference phase 5. High-frequency artifacts both inside and outside the observed breathing cycle are effectively suppressed by our proposed anisotropic frequency scaling.

4 Discussion

In this work, we proposed an INR-based motion model for the lung, predicting dense deformation vector fields conditioned on a 2D surrogate signal. Case-specific models were trained and evaluated on the 10 open-access DIR-Lab 4DCTs. INR-based DIR yields a modest improvement over classical registration, while joint spatio-temporal optimization alone does not surpass the two-step pipeline. The largest performance gain arises when joint optimization is combined with a nonlinear surrogate-to-motion relationship, as in the full implicit SIREN. The strictly zero folding and generally smooth deformations of our model further highlight the efficacy of SIREN-based registration with continuous regularization, consistent with prior work [5,15,18]. Our proposed anisotropic frequency scaling further ensures smoothness in the surrogate space.

Several aspects remain to be addressed before clinical deployment. First, this work relied on an internal lung-volume signal as a surrogate substitute, since the original DIR-Lab traces are unavailable. Translating the method to a true external signal is therefore an important next step. We expect the model to generalize well here, as its nonlinear formulation is not constrained to the linear manifold of a potentially sub-optimal external signal. Second, the stability of the model when transferred from the planning 4DCT to the treatment day remains an open question, given known instability issues for classical baselines [1]. Here, fine-tuning on a pre-treatment cone-beam CT is a possible mitigation strategy. Finally, extension to higher-dimensional surrogates, such as real-time imaging during treatment [7], represents a promising direction toward fully online adaptive radiotherapy workflows.

Disclosure of Interests. R.W. receives a research grant from Siemens Healthineers.

References

1. Büttgen, L.E., Werner, R., Gauer, T.: Stability analysis of patient-specific 4DCT- and 4DCBCT-based correspondence models. Med. Phys. **51**(9), 5890–5900 (2024). https://doi.org/10.1002/mp.17304
2. Caillet, V., Booth, J.T., Keall, P.: IGRT and motion management during lung SBRT delivery. Physica Med. **44**, 113–122 (2017). https://doi.org/10.1016/j.ejmp.2017.06.006
3. Castillo, R., et al.: A framework for evaluation of deformable image registration spatial accuracy using large landmark point sets. Phys. Med. Biol. **54**(7), 1849 (2009). https://doi.org/10.1088/0031-9155/54/7/001
4. Ehrhardt, J., Schmidt-Richberg, A., Werner, R., Handels, H.: Variational Registration. In: Handels, H., Deserno, T.M., Meinzer, H.P., Tolxdorff, T. (eds.) Bildverarbeitung Für Die Medizin 2015, pp. 209–214. Springer, Berlin, Heidelberg (2015). https://doi.org/10.1007/978-3-662-46224-9_37
5. Fischer, B., Modersitzki, J.: Curvature based image registration. J. Math. Imaging Vis. **18**(1), 81–85 (2003). https://doi.org/10.1023/A:1021897212261
6. Garzia, S., Rygiel, P., Dummer, S., Cademartiri, F., Celi, S., Wolterink, J.M.: Neural fields for continuous periodic motion estimation in 4D cardiovascular imaging. In: Camara, O., et al. (eds.) Statistical Atlases and Computational Models of the Heart. Workshop, CMRxRecon and MBAS Challenge Papers, pp. 378–389. Springer Nature Switzerland, Cham (2025). https://doi.org/10.1007/978-3-031-87756-8_37
7. Hindley, N., Keall, P.J.: An open-source deep learning framework for respiratory motion monitoring and volumetric imaging during radiation therapy. Med. Phys. **52**(7), e18015 (2025). https://doi.org/10.1002/mp.18015
8. Huang, Y., Eiben, B., Thielemans, K., McClelland, J.R.: Resolving variable respiratory motion from unsorted 4D computed tomography. In: Linguraru, M.G., et al. (eds.) Medical Image Computing and Computer Assisted Intervention – MICCAI 2024. MICCAI 2024. LNCS, vol. 15001, pp. 588–597. Springer, Cham (2024). https://doi.org/10.1007/978-3-031-72378-0_55
9. Keall, P.J., et al.: The management of respiratory motion in radiation oncology report of AAPM Task Group 76a). Med. Phys. **33**(10), 3874–3900 (2006). https://doi.org/10.1118/1.2349696
10. McClelland, J.R., Hawkes, D.J., Schaeffter, T., King, A.P.: Respiratory motion models: a review. Med. Image Anal. **17**(1), 19–42 (2013). https://doi.org/10.1016/j.media.2012.09.005
11. Paszke, A., et al.: PyTorch: an imperative style, high-performance deep learning library, pp. 8026–8037. No. 721, Curran Associates Inc., Red Hook, NY, USA (2019)

12. Pumarola, A., Corona, E., Pons-Moll, G., Moreno-Noguer, F.: D-NeRF: Neural Radiance Fields for dynamic scenes (2020). https://doi.org/10.48550/arXiv.2011.13961
13. Rit, S., Wolthaus, J.W.H., van Herk, M., Sonke, J.J.: On-the-fly motion-compensated cone-beam CT using an a priori model of the respiratory motion. Med. Phys. **36**(6Part1), 2283–2296 (2009). https://doi.org/10.1118/1.3115691
14. Sitzmann, V., Martel, J.N.P., Bergman, A.W., Lindell, D.B., Wetzstein, G.: Implicit neural representations with periodic activation functions (2020). https://doi.org/10.48550/arXiv.2006.09661
15. van Harten, L.D., Stoker, J., Išgum, I.: Robust deformable image registration using cycle-consistent implicit representations. IEEE Trans. Med. Imaging **43**(2), 784–793 (2024). https://doi.org/10.1109/TMI.2023.3321425
16. Wasserthal, J., et al.: TotalSegmentator: robust segmentation of 104 anatomic structures in CT images. Radiol. Artif. Intell. **5**(5), e230024 (2023). https://doi.org/10.1148/ryai.230024
17. Wilms, M., Werner, R., Ehrhardt, J., Schmidt-Richberg, A., Schlemmer, H.P., Handels, H.: Multivariate regression approaches for surrogate-based diffeomorphic estimation of respiratory motion in radiation therapy. Phys. Med. Biol. **59**(5), 1147 (2014). https://doi.org/10.1088/0031-9155/59/5/1147
18. Wolterink, J.M., Zwienenberg, J.C., Brune, C.: Implicit neural representations for deformable image registration. In: Proceedings of The 5th International Conference on Medical Imaging with Deep Learning, pp. 1349–1359. PMLR (2022)
19. Long, Y., Lyu, T., Rao, F., Yuan, P., Chen, Y., Zhu, W.: D-NAF: dynamic neural attenuation fields for 4D CBCT reconstruction in pulmonary imaging. In: 2024 IEEE International Conference on Bioinformatics and Biomedicine (BIBM), pp. 3549–3554 (2024). https://doi.org/10.1109/BIBM62325.2024.10822834
20. Zhang, Q., et al.: A patient-specific respiratory model of anatomical motion for radiation treatment planning. Med. Phys. **34**(12), 4772–4781 (2007). https://doi.org/10.1118/1.2804576

OpenRC: An Open-Source Robotic Colonoscopy Framework for Multimodal Data Acquisition and Autonomy Research

Siddhartha Kapuria[1(✉)], Mohammad Rafiee Javazm[1], Naruhiko Ikoma[2], Joga Ivatury[3], Mohammad Ali Nasseri[4], Nassir Navab[4], and Farshid Alambeigi[1]

[1] Walker Department of Mechanical Engineering, The University of Texas at Austin, Austin, TX 78712, USA
skapuria@utexas.edu, {farshid.alambeigi}@austin.utexas.edu
[2] Department of Surgical Oncology, Division of Surgery, The University of Texas MD Anderson Cancer Center, Houston, TX 77030, USA
[3] Department of Surgery & Perioperative Care, Dell Medical School, The University of Texas at Austin, Austin, TX 78712, USA
[4] School of Medicine and Health, Technical University of Munich, Munich, Germany

Abstract. Colorectal cancer screening critically depends on colonoscopy, yet existing platforms offer limited support for systematically studying the coupled dynamics of operator control, instrument motion, and visual feedback. This gap restricts reproducible closed-loop research in robotic colonoscopy, medical imaging, and emerging vision-language-action (VLA) learning paradigms. To address this challenge, we present OpenRC, an open-source modular robotic colonoscopy framework that retrofits conventional scopes while preserving clinical workflow. The framework supports simultaneous recording of video, operator commands, actuation state, and distal tip pose. We experimentally validated motion consistency and quantified cross-modal latency across sensing streams. Using this platform, we collected a multimodal dataset comprising 1,894 teleoperated episodes (∼19 h) across 10 structured task variations of routine navigation, failure events, and recovery behaviors. By unifying open hardware and an aligned multimodal dataset, OpenRC provides a reproducible foundation for research in multimodal robotic colonoscopy and surgical autonomy. Both the hardware design and dataset are available at https://github.com/artslab2019/openrc-robotic-colonoscopy. The dataset has been contributed to the Open-H-Embodiment Initiative by NVIDIA.

Keywords: Robotic Colonoscopy · Multimodal Dataset · Surgical Robotics

---

Supplementary Information The online version contains supplementary material available at https://doi.org/10.1007/978-3-032-38236-8_28.

G. Yang et al. (Eds.): MICCAI 2026, LNCS 16893, pp. 285–295, 2027.
https://doi.org/10.1007/978-3-032-38236-8_28

Table 1. Comparison of colonoscopy datasets and resources by available modalities

Dataset	Video	Operator Actions	Actuation State	6DoF Pose	Cross-Modal Alignment	Open Hardware
Clinical image/video datasets [4–6,12]	✓	✗	✗	✗	✗	✗
SimCol / SimCol3D [23,24]	✓	✗	✗	✓ (synthetic)	✓	✗
EndoSLAM [22]	✓	✗	✗	✓	✓	✗
EndoMapper [2]	✓	✗	✗	✓ (simulated subset)	✓	✗
C3VDv2 [10]	✓	✗	✗	✓	✓	Phantom STL/CAD
Copenhagen Colonoscopy Coordinate DB [9]	✗	✗	✗	✓	Single-modality	✗
OpenRC (Ours)	✓	✓	✓	✓	✓	✓

1 Introduction

Colorectal cancer (CRC) is a major global health burden, ranking as the third most common cancer worldwide, with 1.9 million new cases and 935,000 deaths in 2020 [25,28]. Early detection is critical, as survival strongly depends on stage of cancer. Although colonoscopy is the gold standard and reduces mortality through removal of precancerous lesions [11], it still has adenoma miss rates of up to 34% [29]. These limitations arise from optical challenges (e.g., occlusion, blur), operator variability, and device ergonomics [15].

Investigating the literature, prior efforts in addressing colonoscopy challenges can broadly be categorized into two largely independent directions. The first emphasizes robotic and hardware innovation, including robotic platforms and motorized retrofits designed to improve dexterity, stability, and ergonomics (e.g., [3,7,16,17]). The second group focuses on AI-driven assistance through perception, classification, and SLAM, solely relying on colonoscopic video feed without considering instrument kinematics and control (e.g., [19,22,26]). Consequently, perception and control in these groups of efforts are typically studied in isolation.

Emerging autonomy-driven frameworks, particularly Vision-Language-Action (VLA) systems, require joint access to observations, actions, and system state. While such multimodal datasets are standard in broader robotics domains [21,27], comparable resources remain limited in colonoscopy. Existing open-source datasets predominantly provide video data and, in some cases, distal pose measurements, but rarely capture synchronized operator actions or internal actuation state (Table 1). Furthermore, there is currently no unified open-source hardware and software platform enabling reproducible closed-loop experimentation in colonoscopy. This lack of integrated platforms and datasets presents a fundamental barrier to reproducible research in robotic assistance and autonomy.

To address these challenges, we introduce *OpenRC, an open-source robotic colonoscopy research framework* for reproducible closed-loop experimentation and unified multimodal data collection. This low-cost platform retrofits conventional colonoscopes with modular actuation while preserving clinical workflow and synchronizes operator commands, actuation state, electromagnetic (EM) - tracked distal tip pose, and video. Unlike existing systems that are proprietary,

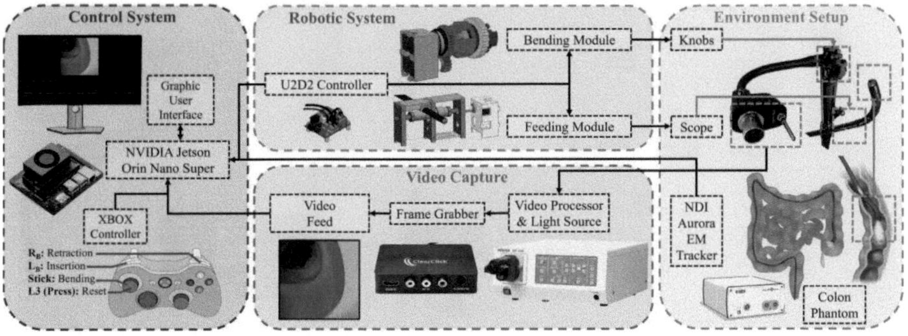

Fig. 1. Overview of the proposed OpenRC framework, including hardware interfaces, actuation, data acquisition, and sensing via EM tracking.

expensive, or require specialized equipment (e.g. [16,17]), OpenRC provides an accessible, validated, and easy-to-adopt platform designed to interface with existing clinical hardware, rather than rebuilding the robotic platform from scratch. Using this system, we conducted comprehensive hardware and data acquisition validation studies, and collected a multimodal dataset comprising 1,894 teleoperated episodes (∼19 h) spanning navigation and failure-recovery scenarios. The hardware design and dataset are made available at https://github.com/artslab2019/openrc-robotic-colonoscopy to support research in surgical autonomy, control-aware perception, and multimodal learning.

2 Methods

As shown in Fig. 1, to support research in computer vision, surgical autonomy, control-aware perception, and multimodal learning for colonoscopy procedures, the proposed open-source platform comprises four main modules: (1) a retrofitted robotic actuation unit for conventional colonoscopes; (2) integrated sensing and synchronized data logging; (3) configurable phantom testbeds; and (4) a ROS-based software architecture with a unified user interface. The entire framework (excluding the EM tracker) can be assembled for under $5,000 USD, promoting accessibility and reproducibility. The following sections will describe these modules in detail.

2.1 Robotic Platform for Colonoscopy

The OpenRC system is designed to retrofit conventional commercially available colonoscopes, allowing for the development of a low-cost robotic system with repeated actuation and synchronized sensing without modifying the original device. In particular, it targets the three clinically relevant degrees-of-freedom (DoFs): insertion/retraction and distal-tip bending in the lateral and vertical directions. Without loss of generality, for this study, we use a PENTAX

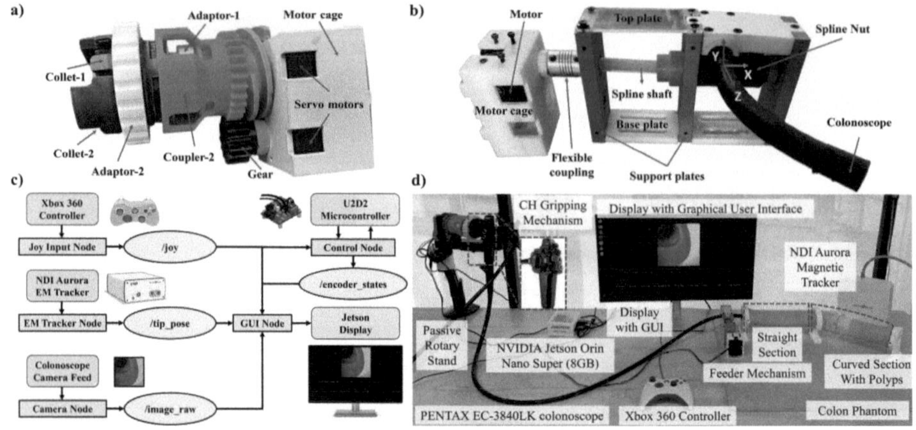

Fig. 2. OpenRC components: (a) bending module, (b) feeding module, (c) ROS 2 graph showing data streams, and (d) experimental setup for data collection.

EC-3840LK colonoscope (Pentax Medical, Japan) as a representative model, although the system is designed to be compatible with other colonoscopes.

Bending Module. As shown in Fig. 2(a), the bending DoFs are motorized using two nested 3D-printed collets that transmit torque directly to the existing control-handle (CH) knobs without modifying the colonoscope. Inspired by a drill collet, the concentric multi-jaw design enables secure gripping and rapid attachment/detachment. Two DYNAMIXEL `XM540-W270-R` servos (1:270 gearbox, 12-bit absolute encoder; 0.088° output resolution) provide actuation, delivering integrated sensing and sufficient holding torque, eliminating the need for the native lock. An additional 1:2 reduction in the outer collet improves command resolution. Components are fabricated from nylon-carbon fiber composite and ABS plastic to balance strength and manufacturability.

Feeding Module. As shown in Fig. 2(b), the feeding module uses a compact friction-based drive for insertion and retraction of the scope. A motor-driven urethane-sleeved feeder roller is used to provide traction, while a low-friction idler-ball guide applies an adjustable normal force via preload screws, ensuring consistent and controllable grip. The applied pressure can be tuned to accommodate different colonoscope diameters and to balance reliable advancement with safe force application. Any slippage at the roller interface remains observable and correctable in real time. The roller is actuated using a DYNAMIXEL `XM430-W350-R` servo (1:350 gearbox, 12-bit absolute encoder; 0.088° resolution). The feeding unit is mechanically independent of the bending module.

2.2 Software Architecture and Control Interface

As shown in Fig. 2(c), the system is built on a compact ROS 2 (Humble) stack running on an embedded NVIDIA Jetson Orin Nano Super (8 GB). Commands for bending and insertion actuation are issued to the DYNAMIXEL servos over an RS-485 daisy chain (ROBOTIS, South Korea) via a U2D2 interface and power hub board. Operator inputs are provided through an Xbox 360 controller and mapped to an action vector (`bend_x`, `bend_y`, `insertion`, `home`) normalized to $[-1, 1]$, enabling simultaneous 3-DoF control and a reset-to-home command. The modular ROS 2 design enables straightforward integration of additional sensing modalities or autonomous control policies. Teleoperation and `rosbag` logging execute in parallel to preserve control timing and ensure lossless recording.

2.3 Sensing and Logged Modalities

Through the ROS-based architecture described in Sect. 2.2, the OpenRC platform records multiple sensing modalities during colonoscope navigation via `rosbag`, timestamped using a shared system clock. The following streams can be recorded:

Colonoscope Video. Video is captured at 30 frames per second at 383×396 pixels (native resolution) using the inbuilt camera at the distal tip of the colonoscope. As shown in Fig. 1, this feed is streamed via a Video to USB 1080P Capture device (ClearClick, USA) connected to a Video Processor and Light Source EPM 3300 (Pentax Medical, Japan) attached to the colonoscope.

Operator Commands. Operator intent is recorded as a four-dimensional action vector as described in Sect. 2.2, at a rate of 50 Hz. The normalized inputs provide a compact, abstracted representation of high-level operator commands independent of controller button mappings.

Robot State. In addition to operator commands, the joint-space actuation states are recorded at 50 Hz from the motor controllers. These signals comprise encoder-derived measurements for dual-axis distal bending and longitudinal translation, normalized to output shaft degrees-of-rotation to decouple encoder resolution from physical actuation. Importantly, due to the device's inherent flexibility and environmental coupling, this joint-space representation does not uniquely map to the task-space distal tip pose.

Distal Tip Pose. Distal tip pose is measured at 6-DoF using an EM tracking system (NDI Aurora; Northern Digital Inc., Canada), represented as Cartesian position (m) and quaternion orientation. Since the colonoscope's inherent flexibility and environmental interaction preclude a fixed spatial calibration, pose data are reported directly in the tracker's coordinate frame.

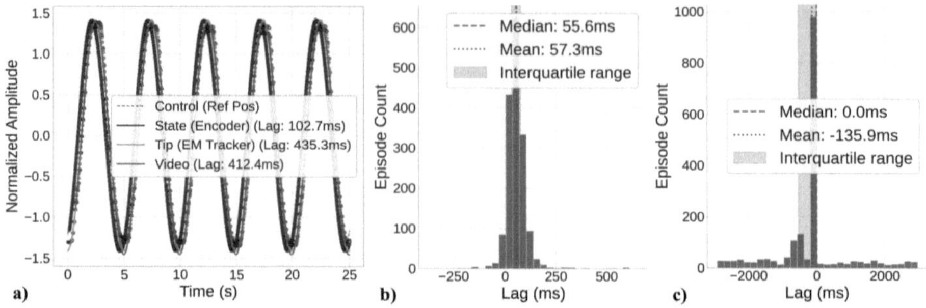

Fig. 3. Results for characterization and synchronization showing: (a) sinusoidal system response characterization, and histograms of estimated residual lag distributions for (b) Operator Action vs State, and (c) State vs Tip Position.

2.4 Phantom Testbeds

We used two flexible colon phantoms: (i) a custom-built silicone phantom with embedded polyps and (ii) a commercially available training phantom. Importantly, the phantom-based setting enables acquisition of precise 6-DoF ground truth, which is not always feasible in clinical practice. Using both phantoms increases variation in geometry, surface appearance, and deformation characteristics without changing the robotic actuation and logging stack, improving the diversity of the resulting multimodal dataset.

Custom Polyp Phantom. Our custom phantom was designed to support both navigation and lesion-observation studies by permanently embedding realistic silicone polyps along the lumen. In brief, polyps were designed following the Paris classification [13,14], cast in silicone using 3D-printed molds, and integrated into a modular silicone colon segment during fabrication. The phantom diameter was selected based on reported average human colon dimensions [1]. Multiple segments can be joined to adjust overall length and curvature.

Commercial Flexible Phantom. We also collected data in a commercially available flexible colonoscopy training phantom (Kyoto Kagaku, Japan).

3 System Characterization

As described in Sect. 2.3, OpenRC integrates operator input, joint-space motor states, EM-based distal tip tracking, and colonoscope video, which operate through independent acquisition pipelines. These readings are not inherently time-synchronized. Therefore, to assess hardware motion consistency and quantify cross-modal latency, we performed controlled excitation experiments. Specifically, we applied a low-frequency sinusoidal bending command (0.2 Hz) along the

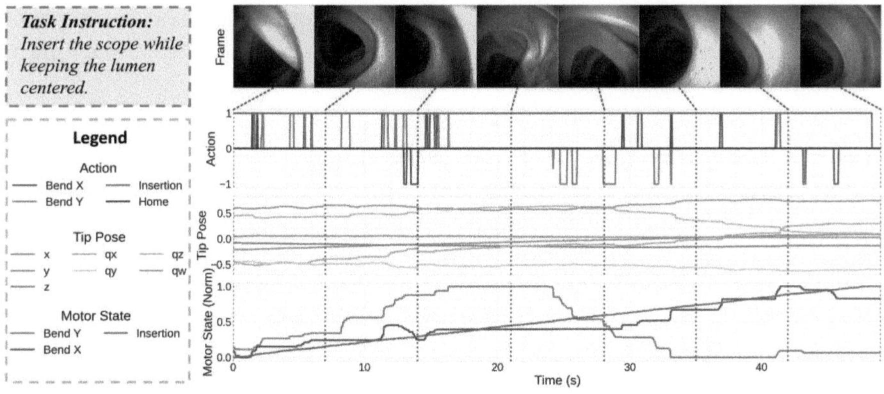

Fig. 4. Example episode with synchronized multimodal recordings from the robotic colonoscopy dataset. From top to bottom: colonoscope video snapshots sampled from the same time axis as data streams; operator control actions; distal tip pose; robot state (normalized to $[-1, 1]$ per axis for ease of visualization).

X axis in the feeding module frame (Fig. 2(b)). This excitation produced smooth, periodic motion observable across control commands, motor encoder measurements, distal tip position reported by the EM tracker, and motion estimates derived from optical flow (computed via the Lucas-Kanade method [18] and averaged across 5 manually selected representative keypoints in the video frame). For each modality, a sinusoidal model was fitted to the measured response, and relative phase differences were computed via least-squares regression. As shown in Fig. 3(a), the measured responses closely follow the commanded input, indicating consistent actuation. The estimated temporal offsets relative to the control action are approximately 102 ms for motor encoder state, 435 ms for EM tracking, and 412 ms for optical-flow-derived motion. These differences in offsets are consistent with the external data acquisition pipelines for each modality.

4 Multimodal Robotic Colonoscopy Dataset

Using the OpenRC framework, we collected a comprehensive multimodal dataset that captures data streams across the modalities described in Sect. 2.3. This section outlines the dataset structure, key features, technical validation, and potential applications in advancing robotic colonoscopy and autonomy research. To ensure accessibility, the dataset is saved in the LeRobot 2.1 format [8].

Episode Definition. The dataset is organized into episodes, where each episode corresponds to a single continuous teleoperated navigation trial performed within a colon phantom. Episodes include active manipulation, pauses, and adjustments, with durations varying by operator behavior and phantom geometry. For each episode, a short natural language instruction describing the intended task or navigation objective is recorded as metadata. Figure 4 illustrates a representative teleoperated episode from the dataset for the insertion task, showing the temporal evolution across modalities.

Dataset Characteristics. The dataset comprises 1,894 episodes spanning ~19 h of teleoperated navigation across 10 task variations focused on insertion-retraction and structured wall-scanning behaviors. Specifically, tasks 0–4 correspond to `insertion` with structured scanning objectives: `bottom wall` (0), `left wall` (1), `right wall` (2), `top wall` (3), and `lumen-centered navigation` (4). Tasks 5–9 mirror these objectives during `retraction`. As shown in Fig. 5(c), lumen-centered insertion and retraction tasks (tasks 4 and 9) predominate, reflecting their central role in scope manipulation, while wall-scanning tasks (tasks 0–3 and 5–8) are less frequent due to increased steering complexity. The dataset also includes 142 `failure` and 141 `recovery` episodes capturing common challenges such as lumen loss, wall contact, and fold engagement, along with corrective maneuvers. This enables structured study of error recovery in colonoscopic navigation. Episode-level statistics in Fig. 5(a–b) show a clear separation between routine navigation and failure/recovery segments. Navigation episodes are substantially longer and involve greater trajectory lengths, whereas failure and recovery segments are shorter and more localized in motion.

Data Synchronization. To ensure accurate cross-modal analysis and support typical VLA learning pipelines, all data streams are resampled to 30 Hz and calibrated using the offsets from Sect. 3, with the video feed as reference. To validate post-alignment stability, we estimated the residual temporal lag τ^* between modality pairs (x, y), namely, operator action vs. actuation state, and actuation state vs. EM tip pose. To reduce sensitivity to absolute offsets, we extracted normalized, velocity-like representations. For a given signal x (and identically for y), we computed the finite difference Euclidean norm $v_t^x = \|x_t - x_{t-1}\|_2$, and applied min-max normalization as $\hat{v}^x = (v^x - \min(v^x))/(\max(v^x) - \min(v^x))$. The residual offset was defined as the lag that maximizes the Pearson correlation coefficient ρ over a bounded symmetric window $[-\tau_{\max}, \tau_{\max}]$, formulated as $\tau^* = \arg\max_\tau \rho(\hat{v}_t^x, \hat{v}_{t+\tau}^y)$, where ρ was computed over the valid temporal overlap of the two signals. As shown in Fig. 3(b-c), residual lag distributions show temporal stability across modalities. Action vs. state (Fig. 3(b)) shows a tightly clustered median offset of 55.6 ms (~1.6 frames), well within acceptable limits for downstream policy learning. State vs. distal tip positions (Fig. 3(c)) center at 0.0 ms, validating the baseline controller-to-tracker alignment. The wider variance and fat tails in this case can be attributed to the continuum dynamics of the deformable environment, which can decouple distal motion from actuation.

5 Discussion and Conclusion

In this work, we introduced OpenRC, a low-cost ($< \$5,000$ USD) open-source robotic colonoscopy framework designed to retrofit conventional colonoscopes

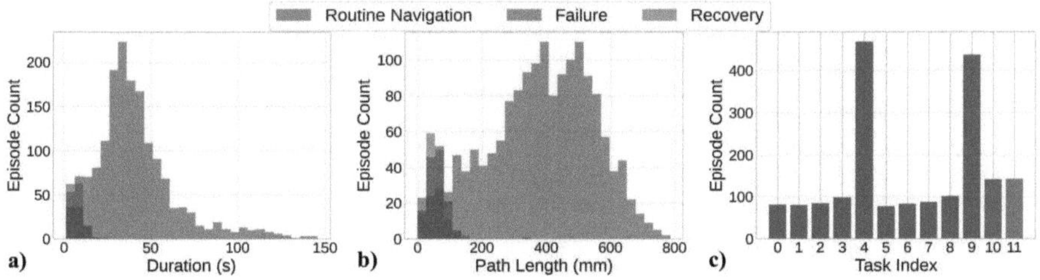

Fig. 5. Episode-level characteristics of the OpenRC Dataset showing distributions of (a) episode duration, (b) trajectory length, and (c) recorded task. Detailed task descriptions will be provided in the dataset repository.

for reproducible closed-loop experimentation and unified multimodal data collection. The platform provides modular actuation of the clinically relevant DoFs, integrated multimodal sensing, and a ROS 2-based teleoperation and logging framework. Furthermore, we release a temporally synchronized multimodal dataset (in LeRobot 2.1 format) collected using this platform, comprising 1,894 episodes (∼19 h) of teleoperated procedures, including insertion, retraction, structured wall-scanning, and failure/recovery scenarios. Experimental validation confirmed reliable system actuation and yielded a stable post-alignment median residual lag of 55.6 ms between operator actions and actuation states, and 0.0 ms between motor states and EM-tracked distal tip poses. The collected synchronized action-state-pose-video trajectories provide a reproducible foundation for advancing research in surgical autonomy, control-aware perception, and multimodal learning in colonoscopy procedures. This dataset has been contributed to the Open-H-Embodiment Initiative by NVIDIA [20].

We acknowledge that the scope of our platform and dataset is currently limited by the controlled phantom environment used for data collection. Specifically, these *in vitro* setups do not comprehensively capture patient-specific anatomical variability and dynamic physiological motion. Despite this limitation, since the platform is modular and the dataset follows a standardized format, other researchers can collect compatible multimodal data using their own colonoscopes and phantoms, enabling community-driven expansion of this resource. In the future, we plan to test the system on more realistic colon phantoms and animal models. We will also leverage this platform and dataset to train and evaluate robust VLA models for autonomous colonoscopic navigation and error recovery.

Acknowledgments. This work was supported by the National Cancer Institute of the National Institutes of Health under Award Number R21CA280747, the IC^2 Institute, and Texas Robotics Seed Collaborative Funding at the University of Texas at Austin.

Disclosure of Interests. The authors have no competing interests to declare that are relevant to the content of this article.

References

1. Alazmani, A., Hood, A., Jayne, D.G., Neville, A., Culmer, P.: Quantitative assessment of colorectal morphology: implications for robotic colonoscopy. Med. Eng. Phys. **38**(2), 148–54 (2016)
2. Azagra, P., et al.: Endomapper dataset of complete calibrated endoscopy procedures. Sci. Data **10** (2022)
3. Basha, S., et al.: A generic scope actuation system for flexible endoscopes. Surg. Endosc. **38**, 1096–1105 (2023)
4. Bernal, J., Sánchez, F.J., Fernández-Esparrach, G., Gil, D., Rodríguez, C., Vilariño, F.: WM-DOVA maps for accurate polyp highlighting in colonoscopy: Validation vs. saliency maps from physicians. Comput. Med. Imaging Graph. **43**, 99–111 (2015)
5. Biffi, C., et al.: REAL-Colon: a dataset for developing real-world AI applications in colonoscopy. Sci. Data **11** (2024)
6. Borgli, H., et al.: HyperKvasir, a comprehensive multi-class image and video dataset for gastrointestinal endoscopy. Sci. Data **7**(1), 283 (2020)
7. Boškoski, I., et al.: Robotics and artificial intelligence in gastrointestinal endoscopy: updated review of the literature and state of the art. Curr. Robot. Rep. **2**(1), 43–54 (2021)
8. Cadene, R., et al.: LeRobot: state-of-the-art machine learning for real-world robotics in PyTorch (2024). https://github.com/huggingface/lerobot
9. Cold, K.M., et al.: Mapping the colon through the colonoscope's coordinates - the copenhagen colonoscopy coordinate database. Sci. Data **12** (2025)
10. Golhar, M.V., Fretes, L.S.G., Ayers, L., Akshintala, V.S., Bobrow, T.L., Durr, N.J.: C3VDv2-Colonoscopy 3D video dataset with enhanced realism. arXiv preprint arXiv:2506.24074 (2025)
11. Jemal, A., Thomas, A., Murray, T., Thun, M.J.: Cancer statistics, 2002. CA: Cancer J. Clin. **52** (2002)
12. Jha, D., et al.: Kvasir-SEG: a segmented polyp dataset. In: Ro, Y.M., et al. (eds.) MMM 2020. LNCS, vol. 11962, pp. 451–462. Springer, Cham (2020). https://doi.org/10.1007/978-3-030-37734-2_37
13. Kaltenbach, T., et al.: Endoscopic removal of colorectal lesions-recommendations by the us multi-society task force on colorectal cancer. Gastroenterology (2020)
14. Kara, O.C., Venkatayogi, N., Ikoma, N., Alambeigi, F.: A reliable and sensitive framework for simultaneous type and stage detection of colorectal cancer polyps. Ann. Biomed. Eng. **51**, 1499–1512 (2023)
15. Ko, C.W., Dominitz, J.A.: Complications of colonoscopy: magnitude and management. Gastrointest. Endosc. Clin. N. Am. **20**(4), 659–71 (2010)
16. Kume, K., Sakai, N., Goto, T.: Development of a novel endoscopic manipulation system: the endoscopic operation robot ver.3. Endoscopy **47**, 815–819 (2015)
17. Lee, D.H., Cheon, B., Kim, J., Kwon, D.S.: EasyEndo robotic endoscopy system: development and usability test in a randomized controlled trial with novices and physicians. Int. J. Med. Robot. Comput. Assist. Surg. **17**(3), e2168 (2020)
18. Lucas, B.D., Kanade, T.: An iterative image registration technique with an application to stereo vision. In: Proceedings of the 7th international joint conference on Artificial intelligence-Volume 2. pp. 674–679. Morgan Kaufmann Publishers Inc (1981)
19. Nie, Z., Xu, M., Wang, Z., Lu, X., Song, W.: A review of application of deep learning in endoscopic image processing. J. Imaging **10**(11), 275 (2024)

20. Open-H-Embodiment Consortium: Open-H-Embodiment: a large-scale dataset for enabling foundation models in medical robotics (2026). https://arxiv.org/abs/2604.21017
21. Open X-Embodiment Collaboration: Open X-Embodiment: Robotic learning datasets and RT-X models (2023). https://arxiv.org/abs/2310.08864
22. Ozyoruk, K.B., et al.: EndoSLAM dataset and an unsupervised monocular visual odometry and depth estimation approach for endoscopic videos. Med. Image Anal. **71**, 102058 (2021)
23. Rau, A., et al.: SimCol3D-3D reconstruction during colonoscopy challenge. Med. Image Anal. **96**, 103195 (2024)
24. Rau, A., Bhattarai, B., Agapito, L., Stoyanov, D.: Bimodal camera pose prediction for endoscopy. IEEE Trans. Med. Robot. Bionics **5**(4), 978–989 (2023)
25. Sung, H., et al.: Global cancer statistics 2020: globocan estimates of incidence and mortality worldwide for 36 cancers in 185 countries. CA Cancer J. Clin. **71**, 209–249 (2021)
26. Tham, S., et al.: The imitation game: a review of the use of artificial intelligence in colonoscopy, and endoscopists' perceptions thereof. Ann. Coloproctol. **39**(5), 385 (2023)
27. Walke, H., et al.: BridgeData V2: a dataset for robot learning at scale. In: Conference on Robot Learning (CoRL) (2023)
28. Xi, Y., Xu, P.: Global colorectal cancer burden in 2020 and projections to 2040. Transl. Oncol. **14**(10), 101174 (2021)
29. Zhao, S.B., et al.: Magnitude, risk factors, and factors associated with adenoma miss rate of tandem colonoscopy: A systematic review and meta-analysis. Gastroenterology **156**(6), 1661-1674.e11 (2019)

OT-Coupled Flow: Towards Realistic TEE Simulation via Unpaired Cross-Modality Translation with Anatomical Consistency

Yunhao Li[1], Yidan Feng[1(✉)], Ho-On Alston Conrad Chiu[2], Simon Cheung-Chi Lam[2], Yan Pang[3], Qiong Wang[3], Chun-Ka Wong[2], and Jing Qin[1,4,5]

[1] The Center for Smart Health, School of Nursing, The Hong Kong Polytechnic University, Hong Kong, China
yunhaol.li@connect.polyu.hk, {yidan2.feng,harry.qin}@polyu.edu.hk

[2] Queen Mary Hospital, LKS Faculty of Medicine, The University of Hong Kong, Hong Kong, China
wongeck@hku.hk

[3] Shenzhen Institute of Advanced Technology, Chinese Academy of Sciences, Shenzhen, China
{yan.pang,wangqiong}@siat.ac.cn

[4] CAS SIAT-PolyU Multi-modal Medical Molecular Imaging Joint Laboratory, The Hong Kong Polytechnic University, Hong Kong, China

[5] PolyU-Qianhai Technology and Innovation Research Centre, The Hong Kong Polytechnic University, Hong Kong, China

Abstract. CT-based transesophageal echocardiography (TEE) simulation provides a vital environment for procedural training and autonomous robotic navigation. While recent advances approach realistic simulation via conditional generative models, they typically require strictly paired cross-modal data or costly expert annotations. Acquiring such supervision is practically infeasible due to the intrinsic mismatch between static 3D CT and dynamic operator-dependent 2D TEE, compounded by disparate imaging physics and non-rigid tissue deformations. To address this, we present the first generative TEE simulation engine capable of synthesizing high-fidelity TEE images directly from local CT slices without paired supervision. Our framework operates in a latent space constrained by an adversarial VQ-VAE, pre-trained on a large-scale TEE database to capture the modality-consistent prior. To tackle the central challenge of unpaired translation, we introduce Optimal Transport Coupled Flow Matching (OTC-Flow) as our core technical design, which establishes reliable pseudo-correspondences between CT-conditioned features and target TEE latents, enabling robust flow matching regression. Furthermore, as an indispensable complement, we integrate a pseudo-supervised anatomical consistency loop that leverages robust CT geometry to enforce strict spatial alignment in a completely label-free manner. Extensive experiments demonstrate that our framework significantly outperforms representative unpaired translation models in both fidelity and anatomical consistency. Code, preprocessing scripts, and split details are available at yunhaoli24/OTC-Flow.

G. Yang et al. (Eds.): MICCAI 2026, LNCS 16893, pp. 296–306, 2027.
https://doi.org/10.1007/978-3-032-38236-8_29

Keywords: Transesophageal Echocardiograph · Cross-Modality Translation · Optimal Transport · Conditional Flow Matching

1 Introduction

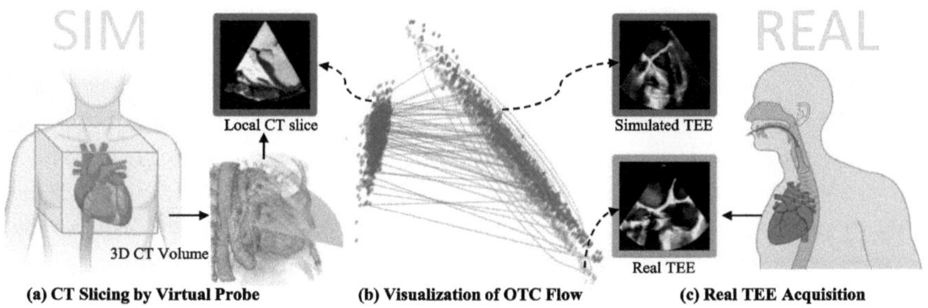

Fig. 1. Illustration of our realistic TEE simulation system. OTC Flow utilizes abundant unpaired real TEE data and guarantees the simulated TEE within the real domain.

While transthoracic echocardiography (TTE) remains the primary cardiovascular screening tool, it is frequently compromised by limited acoustic windows and signal attenuation through the chest wall [12]. In contrast, Transesophageal echocardiography (TEE) is performed from within the esophagus, directly adjacent to the heart, providing high-fidelity visualization of posterior cardiac structures. This anatomical advantage drives its rapidly expanding role in modern cardiology, especially as an indispensable guide for complex, minimally invasive catheter procedures [15,22]. However, blind navigation, complex probe steering, and the risk of esophageal injury makes TEE acquisition technically demanding, creating a critical global shortage of proficient operators [15]. Patient-specific TEE simulation derived from CT has emerged as a scalable solution to this critical bottleneck. Unlike generic phantoms, CT-based simulation provides a diverse, risk-free anatomical environment for procedural planning and operator training [23]. Furthermore, realistic TEE simulation serves as a foundational platform for developing autonomous robotic navigation systems [2,3,14], and bridges the data gap by enabling the transfer of abundant anatomical annotations from CT to the label-scarce TEE domain. Current TEE simulators typically render ultrasound by ray-casting over segmented anatomical labels rather than leveraging the fine-grained tissue textures in the original CT volumes [1,24]. As a result, the simulated images lack the characteristic acoustic texture and visual complexity of real TEE, leading to a domain mismatch with real clinical data that degrades the transfer of downstream models [2,14]. Recent work [3] introduced CycleGAN as a data engine for robotic ultrasound simulation, attempting to bridge the domain gap by training on unpaired real ultrasound data. However, CycleGAN is known to suffer from mode collapse, anatomical hallucinations, and distribution shifts [4]. These limitations have been substantially alleviated by the rapid progress of deep generative modeling, with diffusion probabilistic models [11,26] and flow matching [6,16,17] emerging as the state-of-the-art for high-fidelity synthesis. These advanced architectures have been adapted for conditional ultrasound generation, employing techniques such as ControlNet [7] or conditional flow matching [25] to guide synthesis. Crucially, however, these methods rely on paired masks as condition for real ultrasound frames to explicitly model the joint distribution. This strict supervised requirement poses a severe limitation for CT-based TEE simulation, as expert annotations are exceptionally scarce. More importantly, we aim to leverage the rich anatomical details from CT, yet acquiring perfectly paired CT-TEE data is practically infeasible. As illustrated in Fig. 1, the intrinsic disparity between a one-time 3D CT scan and a dynamic, operator-dependent 2D TEE process, compounded by disparate imaging physics and complex intraoperative deformations, severely hinders accurate cross-modal alignment.

In this paper, we present the first generative TEE simulation engine that produces realistic TEE images directly from local CT slices. We first pre-train an adversarial vector-quantized variational autoencoder (aVQ-VAE) on over 81,510 unlabeled clinical TEE frames to learn a modality-consistent latent prior. Building on this latent representation, we tackle the central challenge of unpaired CT-conditioned synthesis: the model must preserve CT-consistent anatomy while avoiding artefacts from CT-specific structures unobservable in ultrasound, entirely without paired data or TEE masks. We address this with a novel translation framework driven by Optimal Transport Coupled Flow Matching (OTC-Flow). As our core technical contribution, OTC-Flow leverages a global optimal transport coupling to provide pseudo-correspondences between CT-conditioned features and real TEE latent codes. This enables robust conditional flow matching in an unpaired setting, ensuring the generated distribution faithfully matches the real TEE manifold. Building upon this generative foundation, we further introduce a pseudo-supervised anatomical consistency loop as a supplementary structural constraint. Leveraging mature CT analysis tools, this mechanism forces the generated TEE to align with the robustly segmented structures of the source CT, fully utilizing CT's inherent structural information for precise, label-free alignment. Finally, extensive experiments demonstrate that our framework achieves superior fidelity in anatomical consistency and TEE realism compared to representative unpaired translation alternatives, supported by in-depth ablations validating our key design choices.

2 Method

2.1 Framework Overview

As illustrated in Fig. 2, our framework consists of two stages. Stage I pre-trains an adversarial VQ-VAE on unlabeled TEE frames and freezes it to provide a modality-consistent latent prior. Stage II tackles the unpaired cross-modality translation from the CT to the TEE domain. To achieve this, we introduce

Optimal Transport Coupled Flow Matching (OTC-Flow) as our key technical design to synthesize realistic TEE images from unaligned CT fan slices. During synthesis, a structural encoder E_{ct} extracts a semantic condition $\mathbf{x}_c$ from an input CT fan slice x_{fan}^{CT}. To overcome the challenge of unpaired training, our OTC-Flow mechanism maintains a cross-iteration latent bank storing unpaired real TEE encodings. By employing a global optimal transport coupling, OTC-Flow establishes a pseudo-correspondence between the CT condition $\mathbf{x}_c$ and a target TEE latent code $\mathbf{y}_{\text{coupled}}$. This dynamically matched endpoint guides a time-dependent vector field $v_\theta(\cdot, t, \mathbf{x}_c)$, transporting sampled noise $\mathbf{z}_0 \sim \mathcal{N}(0, \mathbf{I})$ along a trajectory over $t \in [0, 1]$. The terminal latent state $\mathbf{z}_{t=1}$ is quantized and decoded by the frozen aVQ-VAE to yield the synthesized image $\tilde{x}^{TEE}$. To enforce strict spatial alignment alongside this generation process, the framework incorporates a pseudo-supervised anatomical consistency loop. Specifically, an auxiliary segmentation network S processes the synthesized output $\tilde{x}^{TEE}$ to predict semantic anatomical maps $\hat{y}^{TEE}$. These predictions are explicitly supervised by structural pseudo-labels derived directly from the corresponding CT. By providing this explicit anatomical feedback, the consistency loop imposes a strong low-frequency geometric constraint, ensuring that the synthesized TEE strictly preserves subject-specific cardiac shapes without requiring manual ultrasound annotations.

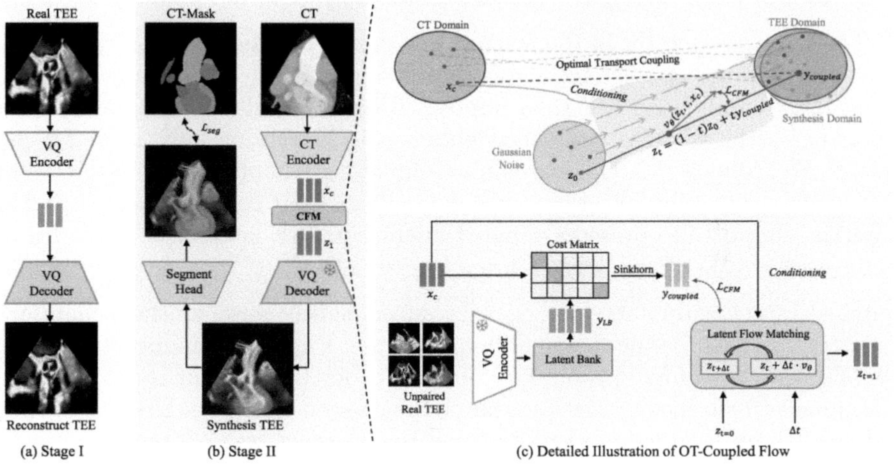

Fig. 2. Framework overview. Stage I: Pre-training of aVQ-VAE. Stage II: Unpaired cross-modality translation with a pseudo-supervised anatomical consistency loop.

2.2 Optimal Transport Coupling

Standard conditional flow matching learns a time-dependent velocity field by regressing toward targets specified by paired endpoints. However, in unpaired

CT-to-TEE synthesis, stochastic endpoint pairing would induce semantically inconsistent targets and inevitably increase the variance of velocity regression. We address this challenge by computing a global optimal transport plan to dynamically assign each CT condition a semantically consistent pseudo-correspondence. Specifically, our method maintains a latent bank (LB) that aggregates empirical TEE latent representations across training iterations. Let $\{\mathbf{x}_c^{(i)}\}_{i=1}^B$ and $\{\mathbf{y}_{\text{LB}}^{(j)}\}_{j=1}^Q$ denote the condition embeddings extracted from the CT inputs for the current mini-batch and the candidate latent embeddings of TEE retrieved from the LB, respectively. An optimal transport cost matrix $C \in \mathbb{R}^{B\times Q}$ quantifies the pairwise distances between features, establishing a reliable metric for the semantic alignment between these cross-modal representations:

$$C_{ij} = \left\|\mathbf{x}_c^{(i)} - \mathbf{y}_{\text{LB}}^{(j)}\right\|_2^2. \tag{1}$$

Given the cost matrix, the assignment across the mini-batch is determined by an entropic optimal transport plan that minimizes the aggregated semantic discrepancy. Specifically, the optimal assignment is determined by the entropic optimal transport plan $P^\star \in \mathbb{R}_+^{B\times Q}$, obtained by solving the following objective under uniform marginal constraints $a = \frac{1}{B}\mathbf{1}_B$ and $b = \frac{1}{Q}\mathbf{1}_Q$:

$$P^\star = \arg \min_{P\mathbf{1}_Q=a,\ P^\top\mathbf{1}_B=b} \langle P, C\rangle - \epsilon \sum_{i,j} P_{ij}\left(\log P_{ij} - 1\right). \tag{2}$$

The L2 cost operates in the learned latent space rather than on raw images, providing a target preference between CT-conditioned embeddings and TEE latent-bank candidates. OT then imposes a balanced global assignment across the mini-batch, whereas nearest-neighbor pairing retains only local L2 preference. We solve Eq. 2 via log-domain Sinkhorn-Knopp iterations [5]. While barycentric projection provides a soft interpolation, it can map samples off the empirical support. To preserve support fidelity of TEE latents, we extract a discrete pairing from $P^\star$ by $j^\star(i) = \arg\max_j P^\star_{ij}$ and set $\mathbf{y}_{\text{coupled}}^{(i)} = \mathbf{y}_{\text{LB}}^{(j^\star(i))}$. These matched target endpoints $\{\mathbf{y}_{\text{coupled}}^{(i)}\}_{i=1}^B$ subsequently serve as the semantically consistent targets for the flow matching process. Finally, to maintain a continuous and diverse supply of candidate representations, the latent codes of the real TEE images from the current mini-batch are enqueued into the LB. OT coupling and the LB are used only during training to construct stable latent supervision. At inference, synthesis requires the CT encoder, the learned latent transport, and the frozen VQ-VAE decoder.

2.3 Conditional Latent Flow Matching

Driven by the optimal transport coupling, the flow matching component of OTC-Flow provides a deterministic generative path learning a continuous mapping from a simple prior to a target distribution. Unlike diffusion models relying on a stochastic reverse process, Flow Matching directly trains a neural network to approximate a velocity field defining an interpolation path.

Let $\mathbf{y}_{\text{coupled}}$ denote the target endpoint established via our OT pseudo-correspondence, and $\mathbf{x}_c$ the CT-derived condition embedding. With Gaussian noise $\mathbf{z}_0 \sim \mathcal{N}(0, \mathbf{I})$, we define a probability path where $t = 0$ represents the noise state and $t = 1$ the target data. The conditional linear interpolation path:

$$\mathbf{z}_t = (1-t)\mathbf{z}_0 + t\mathbf{y}_{\text{coupled}},$$
$$u_t(\mathbf{z}_0, \mathbf{y}_{\text{coupled}}) = \frac{d\mathbf{z}_t}{dt} = \mathbf{y}_{\text{coupled}} - \mathbf{z}_0, \tag{3}$$

where $u_t(\mathbf{z}_0, \mathbf{y}_{\text{coupled}})$ represents the instantaneous ground-truth velocity vector that drives the interpolation from the noise $\mathbf{z}_0$ to the paired sample $\mathbf{y}_{\text{coupled}}$. Training involves learning a time-dependent conditional vector field $v_\theta(\mathbf{z}_t, t, \mathbf{x}_c)$ by minimizing the flow matching regression loss:

$$\mathcal{L}_{\text{CFM}}(\theta) = \mathbb{E}_{t,\mathbf{z}_0,\mathbf{y}_{\text{coupled}},\mathbf{x}_c}\left[\left|v_\theta(\mathbf{z}_t, t, \mathbf{x}_c) - (\mathbf{y}_{\text{coupled}} - \mathbf{z}_0)\right|^2\right]. \tag{4}$$

During inference, given a sampled noise $\mathbf{z}_0 \sim \mathcal{N}(0, \mathbf{I})$ and a condition $\mathbf{x}_c$, the target sample is generated by solving the ordinary differential equation:

$$\frac{d\mathbf{z}}{dt} = v_\theta(\mathbf{z}, t, \mathbf{x}_c), \quad \text{with } \mathbf{z}(0) = \mathbf{z}_0, \tag{5}$$

over the interval $t \in [0, 1]$. We employ an Euler solver to discretize $[0, 1]$ into N steps with step size $\Delta t = 1/N$, updating the state as follows:

$$\mathbf{z}_{t+\Delta t} = \mathbf{z}_t + \Delta t \cdot v_\theta(\mathbf{z}_t, t, \mathbf{x}_c). \tag{6}$$

After N steps, the final output $\mathbf{z}_{t=1}$ is obtained as the approximation of $\mathbf{y}_{\text{coupled}}$, guaranteeing that generated features lie robustly on the real TEE manifold.

2.4 Training Objective

The overall loss function involves a composite of $\mathcal{L}_{seg}$ and $\mathcal{L}_{CFM}$ alongside auxiliary regularizers to stabilize synthesis and enhance visual quality. Specifically, $\mathcal{L}_{seg}$ explicitly drives the pseudo-supervised anatomical consistency loop by supervising the anatomical prediction $\hat{y}^{TEE} = S(\tilde{x}^{TEE})$ against the condition-projected pseudo label $\tilde{y}^{TEE}$ via a Dice objective. While the OTC-Flow targets the realistic texture distribution of $\mathbf{y}_{\text{coupled}}$, $\mathcal{L}_{seg}$ imposes a critical geometric constraint. This ensures the synthesized anatomy remains faithful to the CT condition $\mathbf{x}_c$. The conditional flow matching loss $\mathcal{L}_{CFM}$ is computed using endpoints $(\mathbf{z}_0, \mathbf{y}_{\text{coupled}})$ and condition $\mathbf{x}_c$. To mitigate quantization drift and enforce consistency, we employ a latent consistency loss penalizing the discrepancy between the transported latent vector $\mathbf{z}_{t=1}$ and its re-encoded representation $\hat{\mathbf{z}}_{t=1} = E_{vq}(\tilde{x}^{TEE})$ from the VQ encoder. Furthermore, a radial power spectral density loss aligns texture statistics by matching frequency-domain profiles of real and synthesized TEE. Finally, a lightweight path-space discriminator provides an adversarial signal to enhance perceptual realism.

Table 1. Quantitative comparison results with unpaired image translation methods.

Method	Generative Metrics			Perceptual & Anatomical Metrics		
	KID↓	FID↓	FRD↓	LPIPS↓	NIQE↓	Dice↑
CycleGAN [29]	10.74 (+2.35)	110.50 (+31.22)	86.82 (+59.49)	43.65 (+6.18)	10.57 (+3.05)	91.20 (-6.80)
CUT [21]	9.82 (+1.43)	102.99 (+23.71)	52.13 (+24.80)	47.87 (+10.40)	8.19 (+0.67)	93.10 (-4.90)
OTCS [9]	10.43 (+2.04)	93.11 (+13.83)	43.38 (+16.05)	40.12 (+2.65)	8.65 (+1.13)	95.30 (-2.70)
SynDiff [20]	10.55 (+2.16)	93.84 (+14.56)	38.90 (+11.57)	41.23 (+3.76)	7.88 (+0.36)	96.15 (-1.85)
UNSB [27]	8.66 (+0.27)	88.03 (+8.75)	47.28 (+19.95)	39.21 (+1.74)	8.42 (+0.90)	96.50 (-1.50)
OTC-Flow	**8.39**	**79.28**	**27.33**	**37.47**	**7.52**	**98.00**

3 Experiments

3.1 Datasets

We utilized the Multi-Modality Whole Heart Segmentation (MMWHS) dataset [30] as the source domain, using 20 CT volumes with seven key anatomical labels (LV, LABC, LVBC, RABC, RVBC, AO, and PA) to supervise anatomical consistency. For the target domain, we collected 81,510 real TEE images from 377 patients undergoing LAA closure or MitraClip procedures at two hospitals, acquired via a Philips EPIQ CVx system with an X8-2t probe. These frames were extracted from complete intraoperative videos after de-identification, with long-dwell repeated frames removed. To simulate TEE views, we segmented the esophagus from CT volumes to constrain the probe action space. We then sampled virtual probe poses and depths to extract 60,000 corresponding fan-shaped 2D CT slices. All comparisons and ablations used the same data construction procedure and an 8:2 train/validation split.

3.2 Implementation Details and Evaluation Metrics

Our method is implemented in PyTorch Lightning on two NVIDIA 3090 GPUs using AdamW [18] with an initial learning rate of 1×10^{-4}. Training 20 epochs with a batch size of 32. The CT encoder and segment head use a UNet backbone. The latent velocity network for flow matching comprises CNN blocks, four time-step integration steps, and a 0.1 output scale. For optimal transport, we maintained a 4096-size queue; the Sinkhorn plan was computed over 50 iterations with 0.1 adaptive epsilon scaling. The VQ-VAE encoder used 16,384 codebook embeddings of dimension 8. For assessment, we employ generative metrics to measure the distance between the synthesized and real TEE data distributions. Specifically, we utilize FID [10] to evaluate global realism, KID [8] as an unbiased estimator, and FRD [13] for robust feature-level comparison. Complementarily, LPIPS [28] and NIQE [19] are used to assess perceptual fidelity. Dice evaluates CT-conditioned anatomical consistency: CT labels are projected through the same fan grid into pseudo-TEE labels, and segmentations predicted from synthesized TEE images are compared with the projected CT labels.

3.3 Comparison Study

We compared OTC-Flow against representative SOTA conditional generation models capable of unpaired modality translation. Table 1 reports quantitative results for TEE synthesis. OTC-Flow achieves top performance across distributional, perceptual and anatomical metrics, substantially better than the strongest baseline UNSB based on Schrödinger Bridge. This validates the effectiveness of our design in achieving robust domain matching and anatomical consistency. This is further supported by visual comparison results Fig. 3. Our method preserves coherent cardiac structures and generates modality-consistent ultrasound textures. Conversely, existing baselines frequently exhibit over-smoothed textures, structural distortions, or inconsistent appearances.

Table 2. Ablation results. NN: Nearest-neighbor. ADM: Adversarial domain matching.

Variant	Latent alignment				Supervision	Metrics					
	FM	OT	NN	ADM	Seg	KID↓	FID↓	FRD↓	LPIPS↓	NIQE↓	Dice↑
OTC-Flow	✓	✓	×	×	✓	8.39	79.28	27.33	37.47	7.52	98.00
w/o OT	✓	×	×	×	✓	11.25	105.62	41.50	45.10	8.35	88.42
NN pair	✓	×	✓	×	✓	9.35	88.90	33.65	40.12	7.81	93.50
ADM	×	—	—	✓	✓	13.40	118.33	45.80	48.90	8.65	82.19
w/o FM	×	—	—	×	✓	9.88	92.15	35.40	42.30	8.05	94.15
w/o Seg	✓	✓	×	×	×	9.10	86.45	48.22	46.55	7.89	-

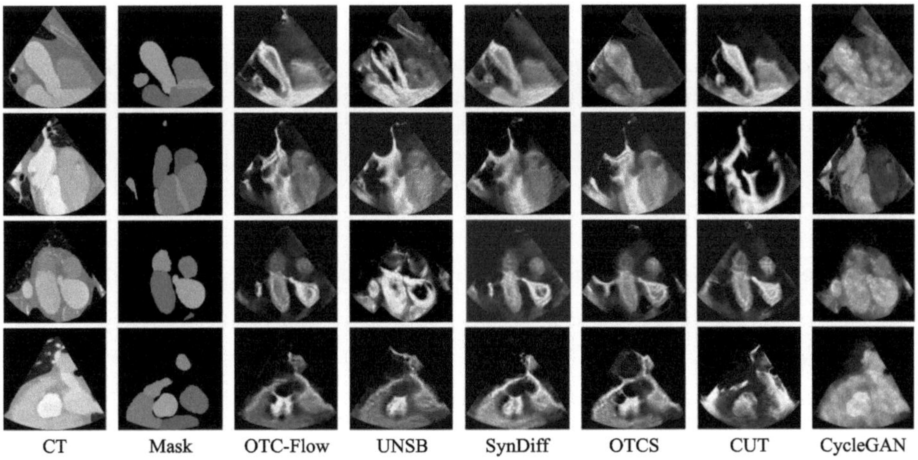

Fig. 3. Qualitative comparison with generative alternatives.

3.4 Ablation Study

Results in Table 2 validate our design in two key aspects: 1) Latent distribution alignment: Our OT-based coupling (OTC-Flow) significantly outperforms both nearest-neighbor (NN pair) and random pairing (w/o OT) within the flow matching framework. Random pairing removes cost-aware target selection, whereas NN pair preserves local L2 preference without the global marginal constraints of OT; their inferior FRD values support the complementary roles of latent-space target preference and balanced OT assignment. Notably, ineffective latent matching strategies (random pairing or adversarial domain matching at latent space (ADM)) prove detrimental, yielding results inferior to the baseline without flow matching (w/o FM). 2) Anatomical consistency: Removing the segmentation supervision causes a marked degradation in FRD and LPIPS. Since FRD quantifies radiomic discrepancies in texture and morphology, this drop confirms that our pseudo-supervised loop is vital for synthesizing realistic, ultrasound-specific anatomy, while the LPIPS results highlight its role in suppressing generative artifacts.

4 Conclusion

We presented OTC-Flow, the first generative engine for unpaired CT-to-TEE simulation. By integrating optimal transport coupling into flow matching, our framework establishes robust cross-modal correspondences to overcome intrinsic CT-TEE misalignment. Complemented by a pseudo-supervised anatomical consistency loop, it ensures strict structural fidelity leveraging CT geometry. Experiments confirm that OTC-Flow synthesizes realistic ultrasound textures with high anatomical precision, offering a scalable, risk-free platform for procedural training and autonomous robotic navigation.

Acknowledgements. This work was supported by a grant under the Hong Kong RGC Collaborative Research Fund (project no. C5055-24G), the Natural Science Foundation of China under Grant U23A20391 & 62576335, in part by the Guangdong Natural Science Foundation under Grant 2025A1515010276, and in part by the Shenzhen Science and Technology Program under Grant JCYJ20241202152803005 & KJZD20240903102717023.

Disclosure of Interests. The authors have no competing interests to declare.

References

1. Amadou, A.A., et al.: Cardiac ultrasound simulation for autonomous ultrasound navigation. Front. Cardiovasc. Med. **11**, 1384421 (2024)
2. Amadou, A.A., et al.: Goal-conditioned reinforcement learning for ultrasound navigation guidance. In: Linguraru, M.G., et al. (eds.) International Conference on Medical Image Computing and Computer-Assisted Intervention, pp. 319–329. Springer (2024). https://doi.org/10.1007/978-3-031-72120-5_30

3. Ao, Y., et al.: SonoGYM: high performance simulation for challenging surgical tasks with robotic ultrasound. In: Advances in Neural Information Processing Systems (2025)
4. Cohen, J.P., Luck, M., Honari, S.: Distribution matching losses can hallucinate features in medical image translation. In: Frangi, A., Schnabel, J., Davatzikos, C., Alberola-López, C., Fichtinger, G. (eds.) International Conference on Medical Image Computing and Computer-Assisted Intervention, pp. 529–536. Springer (2018). https://doi.org/10.1007/978-3-030-00928-1_60
5. Cuturi, M.: Sinkhorn distances: lightspeed computation of optimal transport. Adv. Neural. Inf. Process. Syst. **26** (2013)
6. Dao, Q., Phung, H., Nguyen, B., Tran, A.: Flow matching in latent space. arXiv preprint arXiv:2307.08698t (2023)
7. Freiche, B., et al.: Ultrasound image generation using latent diffusion models. In: Medical Imaging 2025: Ultrasonic Imaging and Tomography, vol. 13412, pp. 287–292. SPIE (2025)
8. Gretton, A., Borgwardt, K.M., Rasch, M.J., Schölkopf, B., Smola, A.: A kernel two-sample test. J. Mach. Learn. Res. **13**(1), 723–773 (2012)
9. Gu, X., Yang, L., Sun, J., Xu, Z.: Optimal transport-guided conditional score-based diffusion model. Adv. Neural. Inf. Process. Syst. **36**, 36540–36552 (2023)
10. Heusel, M., Ramsauer, H., Unterthiner, T., Nessler, B., Hochreiter, S.: GANs trained by a two time-scale update rule converge to a local NASH equilibrium. In: Advances in Neural Information Processing Systems, p. 30 (2017)
11. Ho, J., Jain, A., Abbeel, P.: Denoising diffusion probabilistic models. Adv. Neural. Inf. Process. Syst. **33**, 6840–6851 (2020)
12. Huang, S.J., McLean, A.S.: Appreciating the strengths and weaknesses of transthoracic echocardiography in hemodynamic assessments. Cardiol. Res. Pract. **2012**(1), 894308 (2012)
13. Konz, N., et al.: Fréchet Radiomic Distance (FRD): a versatile metric for comparing medical imaging datasets. Med. Image Anal., 103943 (2026)
14. Li, K., Li, A., Xu, Y., Xiong, H., Meng, M.Q.H.: RL-TEE: autonomous probe guidance for transesophageal echocardiography based on attention-augmented deep reinforcement learning. IEEE Trans. Autom. Sci. Eng. **21**(2), 1526–1538 (2023)
15. Liang, J., Ma, X., Liang, G.: Transesophageal echocardiography: revolutionizing perioperative cardiac care. Biomol. Biomed. **25**(2), 314 (2024)
16. Lipman, Y., Chen, R.T., Ben-Hamu, H., Nickel, M., Le, M.: Flow matching for generative modeling. In: The Eleventh International Conference on Learning Representations (2022)
17. Liu, X., Gong, C.: Flow straight and fast: Learning to generate and transfer data with rectified flow. In: The Eleventh International Conference on Learning Representations (2022)
18. Loshchilov, I., Hutter, F.: Decoupled weight decay regularization. In: International Conference on Learning Representations
19. Mittal, A., Soundararajan, R., Bovik, A.C.: Making a "completely blind" image quality analyzer. IEEE Signal Process. Lett. **20**(3), 209–212 (2012)
20. Özbey, M., et al.: Unsupervised medical image translation with adversarial diffusion models. IEEE Trans. Med. Imaging **42**(12), 3524–3539 (2023)
21. Park, T., Efros, A.A., Zhang, R., Zhu, J.Y.: Contrastive learning for unpaired image-to-image translation. In: Vedaldi, A., Bischof, H., Brox, T., Frahm, JM. (eds.) European Conference on Computer Vision, pp. 319–345. Springer (2020). https://doi.org/10.1007/978-3-030-58545-7_19

22. Perk, G., et al.: Use of real time three-dimensional transesophageal echocardiography in intracardiac catheter based interventions. J. Am. Soc. Echocardiogr. **22**(8), 865–882 (2009)
23. Pezel, T., et al.: Effectiveness of simulation-based training on transesophageal echocardiography learning: the simulator randomized clinical trial. JAMA Cardiol. **8**(3), 248–256 (2023)
24. Piórkowski, A., Kempny, A.: The transesophageal echocardiography simulator based on computed tomography images. IEEE Trans. Biomed. Eng. **60**(2), 292–299 (2012)
25. Reynaud, H., Gomez, A., Leeson, P., Meng, Q., Kainz, B.: EchoFlow: a foundation model for cardiac ultrasound image and video generation. arXiv preprint arXiv:2503.22357 (2025)
26. Rombach, R., Blattmann, A., Lorenz, D., Esser, P., Ommer, B.: High-resolution image synthesis with latent diffusion models. In: Proceedings of the IEEE/CVF Conference on Computer Vision and Pattern Recognition, pp. 10684–10695 (2022)
27. Ye, J.C., Kim, B., Kwon, G., et al.: Unpaired image-to-image translation via neural schrödinger bridge. In: The Twelfth International Conference on Learning Representations, ICLR 2024. International Conference on Learning Representations (2024)
28. Zhang, R., Isola, P., Efros, A.A., Shechtman, E., Wang, O.: The unreasonable effectiveness of deep features as a perceptual metric. In: Proceedings of the IEEE Conference on Computer Vision and Pattern Recognition, pp. 586–595 (2018)
29. Zhu, J.Y., Park, T., Isola, P., Efros, A.A.: Unpaired image-to-image translation using cycle-consistent adversarial networks. In: Proceedings of the IEEE International Conference on Computer Vision, pp. 2223–2232 (2017)
30. Zhuang, X., et al.: Evaluation of algorithms for multi-modality whole heart segmentation: an open-access grand challenge. Med. Image Anal. **58**, 101537 (2019)

Percept-Aware Surgical Planning for Visual Cortical Prostheses with Vascular Avoidance

Galen Pogoncheff[1], Alvin Wang[1,2], Jacob Granley[1], and Michael Beyeler[1,3](✉)

[1] Department of Computer Science, University of California, Santa Barbara, USA
[2] School of Computer Science, Carnegie Mellon University, Pittsburgh, USA
[3] Department of Psychological and Brain Sciences, University of California, Santa Barbara, USA

mbeleyer@ucsb.edu

Abstract. Cortical visual prostheses aim to restore sight by electrically stimulating early visual cortex (V1). As high-density and flexible neural interfaces emerge, electrode placement within folded cortex becomes a critical surgical planning problem. Existing strategies emphasize visual-field coverage and anatomical heuristics, but do not directly optimize predicted perceptual outcomes under safety constraints. We present a percept-aware framework that formulates cortical electrode placement as constrained optimization in anatomical space. Electrode coordinates are treated as learnable parameters and optimized end-to-end using a differentiable model of prosthetic vision. The objective minimizes task-level perceptual error while incorporating vascular avoidance and gray matter feasibility. Using realistic folded cortical geometry (FreeSurfer *fsaverage*), we evaluate the method on simulated reading and natural-image tasks. Percept-aware optimization improves reconstruction fidelity relative to visual-field tiling and improves or matches coverage-based placement depending on task structure. Vascular constraints eliminate safety-margin violations with only modest effects on perceptual performance, and the framework supports co-optimization of multi-electrode thread configurations under fixed insertion budgets. These results show how differentiable percept models can support anatomically grounded, safety-aware planning for cortical visual prostheses.

Keywords: Visual Prostheses · Surgical Planning · Neural Interfaces

1 Introduction

Cortical visual neuroprostheses aim to restore sight by electrically stimulating early visual cortex, eliciting visual percepts known as phosphenes [10]. With the emergence of high-density and flexible neural interfaces [20,21], surgeons face a critical planning question: where should electrodes be placed to maximize functional visual benefit?

G. Yang et al. (Eds.): MICCAI 2026, LNCS 16893, pp. 307–316, 2027.
https://doi.org/10.1007/978-3-032-38236-8_30

Large-scale stimulation of primary visual cortex (V1) has demonstrated phosphene-based pattern vision in non-human primates [8], but translation to humans is complicated by cortical folding and inter-individual variability [2]. The functional organization of early visual cortex is nevertheless largely predictable from cortical anatomy [1], which is especially important in blind patients where visually driven fMRI mapping is often infeasible [24]. Electrode placement and cortical geometry therefore jointly shape the resulting phosphene map.

Current placement strategies rely on anatomical landmarks and retinotopic maps [11], targeting foveal representation while avoiding vasculature. Although safety-aware, these approaches remain geometric and coverage-driven rather than optimized for predicted perceptual fidelity. Prior work has optimized stimulation for fixed implants or arranged electrodes to maximize visual-field coverage [7,17], but perceptual objectives and surgical constraints have not been jointly optimized within a unified planning framework.

Computational modeling has shown that stimulation parameters and electrode location shape phosphene structure [4,12,15]. These models suggest that placement should be evaluated not only by anatomical access or visual-field coverage, but also by the percepts expected from the resulting electrode map.

We introduce a model-driven approach for pre-operative planning that directly optimizes cortical electrode placement for perceptual fidelity under anatomical constraints. Electrode coordinates are treated as learnable parameters and optimized end-to-end using differentiable percept models. The framework incorporates retinotopic mapping and vascular avoidance, enabling percept-aware optimization on realistic folded cortex. We demonstrate the method on the FreeSurfer *fsaverage* cortical template, providing a consistent anatomical reference space for optimization.

The main contributions of our work include (1) a percept-aware optimization framework for three-dimensional cortical electrode placement that directly minimizes predicted task relevant perceptual error, (2) explicit integration of vascular avoidance and anatomical feasibility constraints into the placement optimization, and (3) demonstration that optimized configurations can reduce cortical insertions while preserving functional performance.

2 Related Work

Visual neuroprosthesis optimization has largely followed two lines: optimizing stimulation for fixed implants and optimizing implant placement for visual-field coverage. Our work connects these lines by optimizing cortical electrode placement using a perceptual objective under anatomical constraints.

Prior work on fixed implants has optimized current amplitudes and electrode combinations [6,22], calibrated electrode sensitivity profiles [13], and learned image-to-stimulation encoding strategies [14,23]. These approaches improve predicted perceptual outcomes but assume fixed implant geometry and therefore do not address surgical placement.

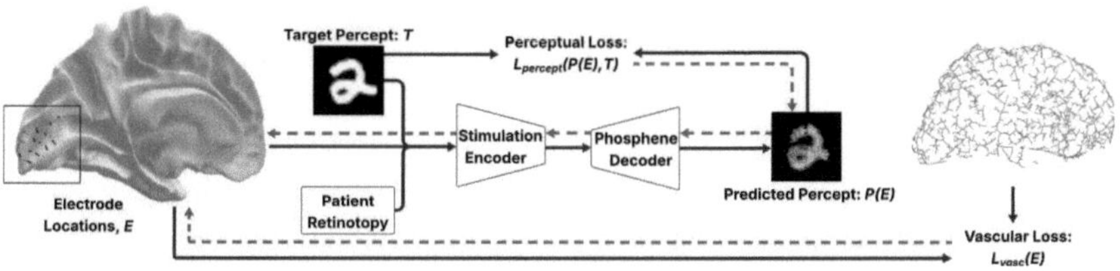

Fig. 1. Percept-aware optimization framework. Electrode coordinates on FreeSurfer *fsaverage* anatomy are mapped through retinotopy and a differentiable prosthetic vision model to predict elicited percepts, then updated to minimize perceptual error under vascular safety constraints. Solid arrows indicate forward simulation; dashed arrows indicate gradient-based coordinate updates.

A complementary line of work examines how implant location affects perceptual structure. In retinal implants, electrode position shapes phosphene geometry through axonal organization [4], motivating model-based selection of implant configurations [3] and visual-field tiling strategies [7]. In cortex, retinotopic maps have been used to position electrodes to maximize projected visual-field coverage [17]. These methods optimize geometric coverage rather than task-level perceptual fidelity and generally do not integrate surgical constraints.

Literature Gap: Existing work either optimizes stimulation for fixed implants or optimizes placement using coverage-based objectives. Perceptual fidelity, task-relevant utility, and surgical constraints have not been jointly optimized within a planning framework. In contrast, we formulate cortical electrode placement as a percept-aware optimization problem in 3D brain space, integrating retinotopy and vascular constraints to support pre-operative surgical planning.

3 Methods

3.1 Surgical Planning Formulation

We formulate cortical electrode placement as a constrained optimization in three-dimensional anatomical space. Let $\Omega \subset \mathbb{R}^3$ denote the feasible gray matter region in early visual cortex. Electrode locations are parameterized as $E = \{\mathbf{p}_e\}_{e=1}^N$, where $\mathbf{p}_e = (x_e, y_e, z_e) \in \Omega$ represents the cortical coordinate of electrode e, and N is the fixed number of stimulation sites determined by device design.

Given a retinotopic map, a vascular map, and task-relevant target percepts $T \sim \mathcal{D}$, the goal is to optimize electrode locations for predicted perceptual fidelity while satisfying anatomical safety constraints (Fig. 1). A differentiable forward model maps electrode coordinates to predicted percepts, enabling gradient-based optimization directly in anatomical space.

We solve for optimal placement via the following multi-objective formulation: $E^* = \arg\min_{E \subset \Omega} \mathbb{E}_{T \sim \mathcal{D}} [\mathcal{L}_{\text{percept}}(P(E),\ \text{T})] + \lambda_{\text{vasc}} \mathcal{L}_{\text{vasc}}(E) + \lambda_{\text{cortex}} \mathcal{L}_{\text{cortex}}(E)$, where $\mathcal{L}_{\text{percept}}$ measures task-level perceptual error, $\mathcal{L}_{\text{vasc}}$ penalizes vascular safety-margin violations, and $\mathcal{L}_{\text{cortex}}$ enforces anatomical feasibility.

3.2 Anatomical Representation

Electrode placement was performed on the FreeSurfer *fsaverage* cortical template. The template provides a folded gray matter surface mesh and volumetric representation, enabling optimization directly within realistic cortical geometry.

The feasible region Ω was defined as cortical gray matter within early visual cortex. Gray matter localization was obtained from the template segmentation and used to constrain electrode coordinates to anatomically plausible locations. Although laminar boundaries were not explicitly modeled, confinement to gray matter serves as a proxy for targeting layer 4, the typical stimulation depth for intracortical visual prostheses.

Retinotopic mappings were obtained from the Benson et al. [1] Bayesian retinotopy prior defined in *fsaverage* surface space. The cerebrovascular atlas [18] was registered to the same coordinate system, enabling direct computation of electrode-to-vessel distances. All anatomical constraints and percept simulations were therefore evaluated in a common neuroanatomical reference frame.

3.3 Perceptual Forward Model

We define a differentiable forward model that maps cortical electrode coordinates to predicted visual percepts. The model consists of two stages: (i) a retinotopic mapping from cortical space to visual field coordinates, and (ii) a phosphene generation model that predicts the elicited percept.

Retinotopic Mapping: For an electrode at cortical location $\mathbf{p}_e$, its visual field coordinate $\mathbf{s}_e$ is estimated by distance-weighted interpolation over the k nearest retinotopic sites, $\mathcal{N}_k(\mathbf{p}_e)$, each with cortical coordinate $\mathbf{c}_j$ and mapped visual field location $\mathbf{v}_j$:

$$\mathbf{s}_e = \frac{\sum_{j\in\mathcal{N}_k(\mathbf{p}_e)} w_{ej}\mathbf{v}_j}{\sum_{j\in\mathcal{N}_k(\mathbf{p}_e)} w_{ej}}, \qquad w_{ej} = \frac{1}{\|\mathbf{p}_e - \mathbf{c}_j\|_2}. \tag{1}$$

Phosphene Generation: Stimulation amplitude a_e is sampled from the target at $\mathbf{s}_e$, and the percept is modeled as a sum of isotropic Gaussians with spread ρ: $P(x,y) = \sum_{e=1}^{N} a_e \exp\left(-\frac{(x-\mathbf{s}_{e,x})^2+(y-\mathbf{s}_{e,y})^2}{2\rho^2}\right)$.

This formulation provides a differentiable mapping from cortical electrode coordinates to image-space percepts, enabling gradient-based optimization in anatomical space. While Gaussian phosphenes with linear superposition provide a tractable approximation consistent with prior modeling work [11,15], the framework readily generalizes to alternative, differentiable percept models.

Perceptual Objective: Perceptual fidelity is measured using a foveally weighted mean squared error: $\mathcal{L}_{\text{percept}}(P,T) = \sum_{(x,y)} w(x,y)\,(P(x,y) - T(x,y))^2$, where $w(x,y)$ increases toward the fovea to reflect the higher functional importance of central vision in many tasks.

3.4 Anatomical and Safety Constraints

Electrode placement is subject to anatomical feasibility and vascular safety constraints. These are incorporated as differentiable penalty terms within the optimization objective.

Avoidance of cortical vasculature is a primary safety consideration in intracortical implantation. Prior studies report vascular disruption extending up to 300 µm from insertion sites [5], motivating an explicit safety margin. Let $\mathcal{V}$ denote the vasculature and $d(\mathbf{p}_e, \mathcal{V})$ the nearest vessel distance. Vascular avoidance was penalized as

$$\mathcal{L}_{\text{vasc}}(E) = \frac{1}{|E|} \sum_{e \in E} \left[\max\left(0, \tau - d(\mathbf{p}_e, \mathcal{V})\right)\right]^2, \tag{2}$$

with safety margin $\tau = 300\,\mu\text{m}$.

Intracortical stimulation targets neurons within cortical gray matter. To ensure anatomically plausible placements, we penalize electrode coordinates outside the gray matter mask. Let $d_{\text{gm}}(\mathbf{p}_e)$ denote the signed distance to gray matter. We define $\mathcal{L}_{\text{cortex}}(E) = \frac{1}{|E|} \sum_{e \in E} d_{\text{gm}}(\mathbf{p}_e)^2$.

Together, these terms embed surgical feasibility directly into the differentiable planning framework, enabling trade-offs between functional performance and safety to be explored continuously during optimization.

3.5 Optimization Procedure

Optimization was performed using gradient-based updates in anatomical space. Because the forward percept model and constraint terms are differentiable w.r.t. electrode coordinates, gradients were computed via automatic differentiation. During optimization, vascular and gray matter penalties were jointly applied with perceptual loss, allowing electrode locations to be continuously adjusted to balance functional performance and surgical safety.

Electrode coordinates were initialized uniformly within the feasible cortical region Ω. We used the Adam optimizer with fixed learning rate and optimized electrode positions until convergence of the objective on training data. Experiments were performed in Python using TensorFlow. Optimization for a single configuration required less than 10 min. on a NVIDIA RTX 3090 GPU.

3.6 Experimental Protocol

Datasets: We evaluated placement strategies using two image datasets representing distinct functional goals of visual prostheses: handwritten digits from MNIST [9], approximating structured symbol recognition (e.g., reading), and natural images from CIFAR-10 [19], representing more complex visual scenes.

Experimental Configurations: Experiments were conducted across electrode counts, $N \in \{64 - 1024\}$, and phosphene spreads, $\rho \in \{500 - 1500\}$ µm. For each configuration, optimization was performed over 3 random initializations.

For device-architecture experiments, we also considered threaded arrays inspired by flexible multi-electrode shanks [21], where multiple stimulation contacts share a common cortical insertion trajectory. These experiments fixed the number of cortical insertions at $N_{\text{insert}} = 128$ and optimized both entry location and trajectory.

Baselines: We compared the proposed percept-aware optimization against two placement strategies: (i) *Visual Field Tiling*, which uniformly tiles the visual field, and (ii) *Visual Field Coverage*, which optimizes electrode positions to maximize coverage of the visual field represented in the training images [17].

Evaluation Metrics: Perceptual fidelity was quantified using structural similarity index measure (SSIM) and mean squared error (MSE) between target images and simulated percepts, along with downstream classification accuracy. Learned perceptual metrics were not used because prosthetic percepts deviate from natural-image statistics, particularly at low electrode counts [14]. Classification accuracy was used only as a task proxy: we trained ResNet-50 classifiers [16] on target images and evaluated whether simulated phosphenes preserved information needed for symbol and object identification [13].

Statistical Analysis: Results were aggregated across experimental configurations and random initializations. Statistical comparisons between methods were performed using Wilcoxon signed-rank tests with significance threshold $p \leq 0.01$.

4 Results

4.1 Percept-Aware Optimization Improves Functional Fidelity

We first evaluated placement optimization without anatomical constraints to isolate functional performance. Across electrode counts and phosphene spread parameters, percept-aware optimization consistently reduced reconstruction error relative to both Visual Field Tiling and Visual Field Coverage.

On MNIST, percept-aware optimization reduced median MSE by up to 67.7% relative to tiling and 33.4% relative to coverage, increased downstream classification accuracy by 62.6% and 22.4%, respectively, and yielded corresponding improvements in SSIM (Table 1). On CIFAR-10, percept-aware placement substantially outperformed tiling and achieved performance comparable to

Table 1. Relative change in MSE, SSIM, and downstream classification accuracy (Acc.) of the proposed method versus baselines. Values are median percent difference [IQR] across electrode counts and phosphene spreads (ρ). * indicates $p \leq 0.01$.

Baseline	Dataset	Δ MSE (%) ↓	Δ SSIM (%) ↑	Δ Acc. (%) ↑
VF Tiling	MNIST	−67.7* [−73.6, −47.2]	11.1* [7.8, 16.7]	62.6* [28.9, 119.9]
VF Coverage		−33.4* [−42.0, −16.3]	4.7* [3.1, 7.3]	22.4* [7.8, 34.7]
VF Tiling	CIFAR-10	−58.4* [−87.4, −24.1]	57.4* [35.3, 102.2]	10.2* [5.5, 29.2]
VF Coverage		16.0 [−25.2, 39.1]	−10.6 [−24.7, 0.2]	−2.2 [−9.1, 6.25]

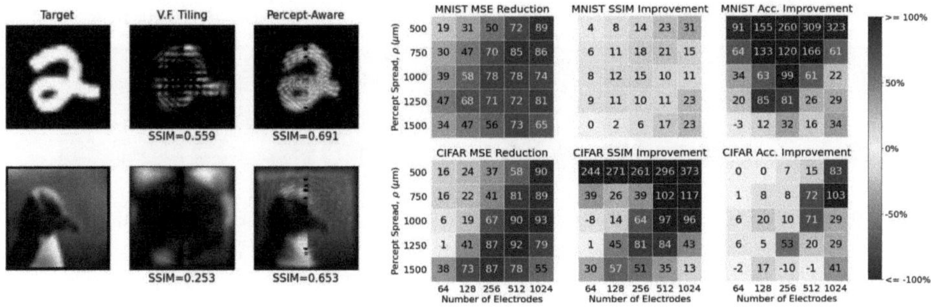

Fig. 2. Comparing percept-aware electrode optimization and Visual Field Tiling. *Left*: Simulated phosphenes for reading (MNIST) and natural image (CIFAR-10) tasks. *Right*: Relative changes in perceptual fidelity across experimental configurations; lower MSE and higher SSIM indicate better reconstruction.

coverage-based optimization. The latter is expected because CIFAR-10 images typically occupy the full visual field, aligning coverage objectives with reconstruction fidelity. Qualitative examples (Fig. 2) show clearer symbol structure and improved spatial coherence under percept-aware placement.

4.2 Safety-Aware Optimization Preserves Perceptual Performance

We next incorporated vascular avoidance into the optimization objective. Without safety constraints, a large fraction of electrodes violated the 300 μm safety margin. Incorporating the vascular penalty eliminated all margin violations.

Perceptual quality changed only modestly in these simulations. Across configurations, SSIM decreased by only 1.7% on MNIST and 4.4% on CIFAR-10 relative to unconstrained optimization (Fig. 3), suggesting that functional performance can be largely maintained while satisfying clinically-motivated vascular safety constraints.

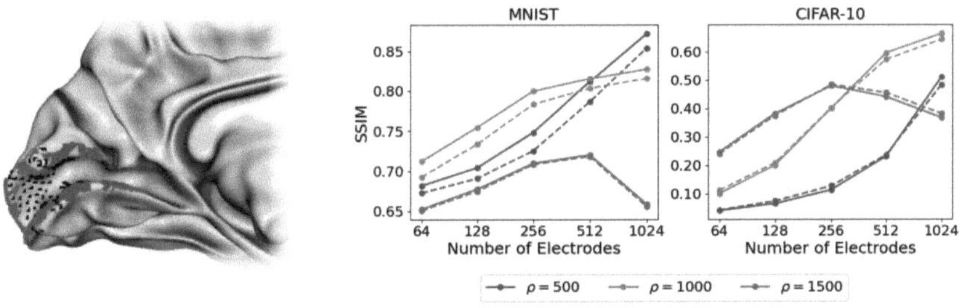

Fig. 3. Safety-aware electrode optimization with vascular constraints. *Left*: Cortical surface (*fsaverage* left occipital) with high-resolution vascular map (red, displayed in V1 only) and optimized electrode locations (black). *Right*: Percept SSIM scores without (solid lines) and with (dashed lines) vascular avoidance.

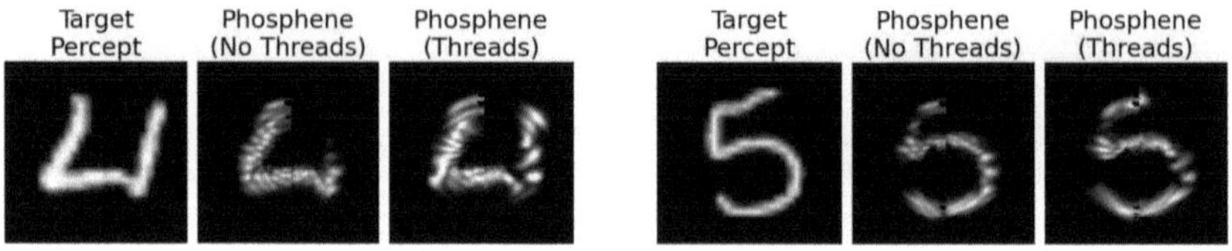

Fig. 4. Simulated phosphenes using percept-aware optimization with and without multi-electrode threads under a fixed number of cortical insertions (128). Threaded designs improve percept quality without increasing number of cortical insertions.

4.3 Device Architecture Co-optimization with Threaded Arrays

We extended the framework to optimize threaded arrays, where multiple electrode contacts share a single cortical insertion trajectory. Under the fixed insertion budget defined above, threaded configurations improved perceptual fidelity relative to single-electrode placements (Fig. 4).

5 Discussion

We present a percept-aware surgical planning framework for cortical visual prostheses that directly optimizes electrode placement in three-dimensional brain space under anatomical constraints. By integrating differentiable percept modeling with realistic cortical geometry and vascular avoidance, the proposed approach aligns surgical decision-making with predicted functional outcomes.

Across simulated reading and natural image tasks, percept-aware placement improved reconstruction fidelity relative to visual-field tiling and provided task-dependent benefits relative to coverage-based strategies. Improvements were strongest for symbol-like images, whereas performance on CIFAR-10 was comparable to coverage-based placement, likely because natural images occupied much of the visual field and therefore aligned well with the coverage objective.

Several limitations remain. First, experiments were conducted on the widely used *fsaverage* template rather than subject-specific anatomy. However, the framework is fully compatible with patient-specific cortical reconstructions, retinotopic mapping (e.g., fMRI), and angiographic data. Second, the perceptual forward model uses simplified Gaussian phosphenes and linear superposition. Future work will incorporate more detailed biophysical models. Third, the present study evaluates the planning objective rather than a complete surgical workflow. In practice, optimized coordinates would need to be transformed into patient-specific stereotactic space and integrated with neuronavigation, trajectory planning, and intraoperative constraints. Thus, the current framework should be viewed as a pre-operative decision-support tool for comparing candidate implant configurations, not as a stand-alone intraoperative guidance system.

Overall, this work introduces perceptual objectives into computer-assisted planning for cortical neural interfaces and establishes a framework for anatomically grounded, safety-aware optimization of next-generation visual prostheses.

Acknowledgments. Supported by the National Library of Medicine of the National Institutes of Health (NIH) under Award Number DP2-LM014268. The content is solely the responsibility of the authors and does not necessarily represent the official views of the NIH.

Disclosure of Interests. The authors declare no competing interests.

References

1. Benson, N.C., Winawer, J.: Bayesian analysis of retinotopic maps. Elife **7**, e40224 (2018)
2. Benson, N.C., Yoon, J.M.D., Forenzo, D., Engel, S.A., Kay, K.N., Winawer, J.: Variability of the surface area of the V1, V2, and V3 maps in a large sample of human observers. J. Neurosci. **42**(46), 8629–8646 (2022). https://doi.org/10.1523/JNEUROSCI.0690-21.2022
3. Beyeler, M., Boynton, G.M., Fine, I., Rokem, A.: Model-based recommendations for optimal surgical placement of epiretinal implants. In: Shen, D., et al. (eds.) MICCAI 2019. LNCS, vol. 11768, pp. 394–402. Springer, Cham (2019). https://doi.org/10.1007/978-3-030-32254-0_44
4. Beyeler, M., Nanduri, D., Weiland, J.D., Rokem, A., Boynton, G.M., Fine, I.: A model of ganglion axon pathways accounts for percepts elicited by retinal implants. Sci. Rep. **9**(1), 1–16 (2019). https://doi.org/10.1038/s41598-019-45416-4
5. Bjornsson, C., et al.: Effects of insertion conditions on tissue strain and vascular damage during neuroprosthetic device insertion. J. Neural Eng. **3**(3), 196 (2006)
6. Bratu, E., Dwyer, R., Noble, J.: A graph-based method for optimal active electrode selection in cochlear implants. In: Martel, A.L., Abolmaesumi, P., Stoyanov, D., Mateus, D., Zuluaga, M.A., Zhou, S.K., Racoceanu, D., Joskowicz, L. (eds.) Medical Image Computing and Computer Assisted Intervention – MICCAI 2020, pp. 34–43. LNCS, Springer International Publishing, Cham (2020). https://doi.org/10.1007/978-3-030-59716-0_4
7. Bruce, A., Beyeler, M.: Greedy optimization of electrode arrangement for epiretinal prostheses. In: Medical Image Computing and Computer Assisted Intervention – MICCAI 2022. Springer International Publishing (2022). https://doi.org/10.1007/978-3-031-16449-1_57
8. Chen, X., Wang, F., Fernandez, E., Roelfsema, P.R.: Shape perception via a high-channel-count neuroprosthesis in monkey visual cortex. Science **370**(6521), 1191–1196 (2020). https://doi.org/10.1126/science.abd7435
9. Deng, L.: The MNIST database of handwritten digit images for machine learning research [best of the web]. IEEE Signal Process. Mag. **29**(6), 141–142 (2012)
10. Fernandez, E.: Development of visual Neuroprostheses: trends and challenges. Bioelectron. Med. **4**(1), 12 (2018). https://doi.org/10.1186/s42234-018-0013-8
11. Fernández, E., et al.: Visual percepts evoked with an intracortical 96-channel microelectrode array inserted in human occipital cortex. J. Clin. Investig. **131**(23) (2021)
12. Fine, I., Boynton, G.M.: A virtual patient simulation modeling the neural and perceptual effects of human visual cortical stimulation, from pulse trains to percepts. Sci. Rep. **14**(1), 17400 (2024). https://doi.org/10.1038/s41598-024-65337-1
13. Granley, J., Fauvel, T., Chalk, M., Beyeler, M.: Human-in-the-loop optimization for deep stimulus encoding in visual prostheses. In: Thirty-seventh Conference on Neural Information Processing Systems (2023)

14. Granley, J., Relic, L., Beyeler, M.: Hybrid neural autoencoders for stimulus encoding in visual and other sensory neuroprostheses. In: Advances in Neural Information Processing Systems, vol. 35, pp. 22671–22685 (2022)
15. van der Grinten, M.L., et al.: Towards biologically plausible phosphene simulation for the differentiable optimization of visual cortical prostheses (2024). https://doi.org/10.7554/eLife.85812
16. He, K., Zhang, X., Ren, S., Sun, J.: Deep residual learning for image recognition. In: Proceedings of the IEEE Conference on Computer Vision and Pattern Recognition, pp. 770–778 (2016)
17. van Hoof, R., Lozano, A., Wang, F., Klink, P.C., Roelfsema, P.R., Goebel, R.: Optimal placement of high-channel visual prostheses in human retinotopic visual cortex (2025). https://doi.org/10.1088/1741-2552/adaeef
18. Ii, S., Kitade, H., Ishida, S., Imai, Y., Watanabe, Y., Wada, S.: Multiscale modeling of human cerebrovasculature: a hybrid approach using image-based geometry and a mathematical algorithm. PLoS Comput. Biol. **16**(6), e1007943 (2020)
19. Krizhevsky, A., Hinton, G.: Learning multiple layers of features from tiny images (2009)
20. Merken, L., Schelles, M., Ceyssens, F., Kraft, M., Janssen, P.: Thin flexible arrays for long-term multi-electrode recordings in macaque primary visual cortex. J. Neural Eng. **19**(6), 066039 (2022). https://doi.org/10.1088/1741-2552/ac98e2
21. Musk, E.: Neuralink: an integrated brain-machine interface platform with thousands of channels. J. Med. Internet Res. **21**(10), e16194 (2019). https://doi.org/10.2196/16194
22. Shah, N.P., et al.: Optimization of electrical stimulation for a high-fidelity artificial retina. In: 2019 9th International IEEE/EMBS Conference on Neural Engineering (NER), pp. 714–718 (2019). https://doi.org/10.1109/NER.2019.8716987
23. de Ruyter van Steveninck, J., Güçlü, U., van Wezel, R., van Gerven, M.: End-to-end optimization of prosthetic vision. J. Vis. **22**(2), 20 (2022). https://doi.org/10.1167/jov.22.2.20
24. Striem-Amit, E., Ovadia-Caro, S., Caramazza, A., Margulies, D.S., Villringer, A., Amedi, A.: Functional connectivity of visual cortex in the blind follows retinotopic organization principles. Brain: J. Neurol. **138**(Pt 6), 1679–1695 (2015). https://doi.org/10.1093/brain/awv083

Physics-Based iOCT Sonification for Real-Time Interaction Awareness in Subretinal Injection

Luis D. Reyes Vargas[1,5(✉)], Veronica Ruozzi[1,5], Andrea K. M. Ross[2], Shervin Dehghani[1,5], Michael Sommersperger[1,5], Koorosh Faridpooya[3], Mohammad Ali Nasseri[2], Merle Fairhurst[4,6], Nassir Navab[1,5], and Sasan Matinfar[1,5,6]

[1] Computer Aided Medical Procedures, Technische Universität München, Munich, Germany
luis.reyes@tum.de
[2] TUM Klinikum Rechts der Isar, Technische Universität München, Munich, Germany
[3] Rotterdam Eye Hospital, Rotterdam, The Netherlands
[4] Centre for Tactile Internet with Human-in-the-Loop, Technische Universität Dresden, Dresden, Germany
[5] Munich Center for Machine Learning, Munich, Germany
[6] Chair for Social Affective Touch, Technische Universität Dresden, Dresden, Germany

Abstract. Subretinal injection is a delicate vitreoretinal procedure requiring precise needle placement within the subretinal space while avoiding perforation of the retinal pigment epithelium (RPE), a layer directly beneath the target with extremely limited regenerative capacity. To enhance depth perception during cannula advancement, intraoperative optical coherence tomography (iOCT) offers high-resolution cross-sectional visualization of needle–tissue interaction; however, interpreting these images requires sustained visual attention alongside the en face microscope view, thereby increasing cognitive load during critical phases and placing additional demands on the surgeon's proprioceptive control. In this paper, we propose a structured, real-time sonification framework designed for extensible mapping of iOCT-derived anatomical features into perceptual auditory feedback. The method employs a physics-inspired acoustic model driven by segmented retinal layers from a stream of iOCT B-scans, with needle motion and injection-induced retinal layer displacements serving as excitation inputs to the sound model, enabling perception of tool position and retinal deformation. In a controlled user study (n = 34), the proposed sonification achieved high retinal layer identification accuracy and robust detection of retinal deformation–related

L. D. Reyes Vargas and V. Ruozzi—These authors contributed equally to this work.

Supplementary Information The online version contains supplementary material available at https://doi.org/10.1007/978-3-032-38236-8_31.

G. Yang et al. (Eds.): MICCAI 2026, LNCS 16893, pp. 317–328, 2027.
https://doi.org/10.1007/978-3-032-38236-8_31

events, significantly outperforming a state-of-the-art baseline in overall event identification (83.4% vs. 60.6%, $p < 0.001$), with gains driven primarily by enhanced detection of injection-induced retinal deformation. Participants also reported higher confidence with the proposed method correlating with correctness, indicating the auditory mapping was perceptually interpretable. Evaluation by experts ($n = 4$) confirmed the clinical relevance and potential intraoperative applicability of the method. These results establish structured iOCT sonification as a viable complementary modality for real-time surgical guidance in subretinal injection.

Keywords: Surgical Sonification · Subretinal Injection · Optical Coherence Tomography (OCT) · Auditory Feedback · Microsurgical Guidance

1 Introduction

Subretinal injection is a delicate vitreoretinal procedure in which a microsurgical cannula is advanced through the neurosensory retina to deliver therapeutics into the subretinal space. This approach demonstrates significant potential for application in cell- and gene-based therapies [13,15]. The cannula must first penetrate the Inner Limiting Membrane (ILM) before advancing within the subsequent layers for injection, which in the macular region measures only approximately 250 μm in thickness on average [14]. Immediately beneath the target lies the retinal pigment epithelium (RPE), a layer with very limited regenerative capacity where even minimal overshoot may cause irreversible damage [8,27]. Because penetration forces are extremely small and masked by friction along the instrument shaft, tactile cues are largely imperceptible, forcing surgeons to rely almost exclusively on visual feedback during insertion [9].

In clinical practice, the en face surgical microscope view serves as the primary guidance modality; however, it provides mainly surface-level information and lacks direct visualization of needle penetration depth relative to the RPE. To address this limitation, intraoperative OCT (iOCT) provides high-resolution cross-sectional views of retinal layers and tool position that are directly relevant for depth control in subretinal injection. In current workflows, iOCT is typically displayed as an overlay on the primary microscope image, requiring simultaneous interpretation of both visual streams. Large prospective studies report that iOCT influences intraoperative decision-making in only a minority of posterior-segment cases ($\approx 30\%$) [6], suggesting that cross-sectional information may not be optimally integrated into routine surgical practice despite its clinical relevance. The addition of this secondary high-bandwidth visual stream may increase cognitive load and promote attentional tunneling during critical phases such as needle insertion [12,23], when precise depth estimation is essential.

Prior work on OCT-based sonification has focused on epiretinal membrane (ERM) peeling [17]. However, its auditory guidance is designed to support positioning before direct tool–tissue interaction and does not account for needle penetration or dynamic tissue deformation. Beyond localizing the needle, subretinal injection requires monitoring interaction-induced structural changes. In particular, successful fluid delivery produces a localized retinal detachment, commonly referred to as a subretinal bleb, whose formation and expansion must be monitored.

To address this gap, we introduce a real-time, deformation-aware sonification framework for subretinal injection. Unlike prior work relying on simulation of preoperative imaging dynamics [22] or focusing on pre-interaction auditory mappings [17], the proposed method encodes interaction-driven retinal deformation directly from intraoperative OCT using a physics-inspired acoustic model anchored to anatomical segmentations. This structured auditory representation enables unified encoding of needle depth, safety boundaries, and fluid-induced tissue deformation within a single extensible framework. In the context of subretinal injection, we focus on signals corresponding to ILM penetration marking retinal entry, proximity to the RPE as a critical safety boundary, and formation of the subretinal bleb confirming successful delivery. The system operates in real time and is compatible with interactive surgical workflows. Code is available at https://github.com/luisdavid64/ioct-subretinal-sonification.

We evaluate the proposed framework across simulated and ex vivo porcine iOCT sequences and assess its clinical relevance through expert feedback. In a controlled user study with 30 novices and 4 expert participants, the proposed sonification significantly improved identification of ILM penetration, RPE contact, and subretinal bleb formation compared to a parameter-mapping baseline. The largest gains were observed in detecting deformation associated with bleb formation, supporting the framework's ability to convey dynamic interaction cues through audio alone and suggesting its potential to preserve visual focus during critical insertion phases.

2 Related Work

Medical Sonification. Medical sonification has demonstrated great promise in augmenting clinical procedures through auditory displays [3,19]. Early work applied to vitreoretinal surgery discretized the anatomical workspace into zones and used musical cues to convey tool-tip position and procedural state [18]. Subsequent approaches moved beyond musical or simple parameter mappings, introducing model-based sound synthesis frameworks that map imaging-derived signals to parameters of a physics-inspired acoustic model, thereby generating structured auditory feedback [16]. However, these methods typically rely on preoperative imaging and therefore cannot accurately reflect dynamic intraoperative anatomical changes.

A more recent study has explored sonification of tissue deformation signals rather than tool localization alone [22], aiming to provide richer insight into anatomical interaction. However, these approaches rely on simulated deformation derived from preoperative imaging, limiting their ability to reflect patient-specific and interaction-driven dynamics encountered intraoperatively.

OCT-specific sonification has been proposed for ERM peeling, mapping A-scans to a physics-inspired acoustic model to provide structural auditory feedback for identifying gaps between the ERM and ILM during membrane localization and peeling initiation [17]. The auditory feedback primarily supports structural assessment prior to direct tool–tissue interaction and does not encode interaction-driven deformation dynamics relevant to subretinal injection.

iOCT Processing for Subretinal Injection. In parallel, robotic and computer-assisted subretinal injection has emerged as an active research area, driven by physiological limitations such as hand tremor and the difficulty of processing iOCT data in real time [1]. This work has enabled key components for iOCT-guided insertion, including tool localization, real-time segmentation of retinal layers and instrument position, and extraction of tool-aligned B-scans from volumetric OCT data [1,2,5,28]. Although these methods improve geometric estimation and visualization, effective intraoperative communication of this information remains challenging.

3 Method

Let $I_t \in \mathbb{R}^{H \times W}$ denote the incoming iOCT B-scan at frame t. Our goal is to map the image stream to a continuous audio signal $y(\tau)$ that reflects subretinal injection dynamics. The framework consists of (i) an initialization phase at $t = 0$, in which a physics-inspired sound model is instantiated and aligned with the segmented retinal anatomy, and (ii) a real-time update and audio rendering loop for $t > 0$.

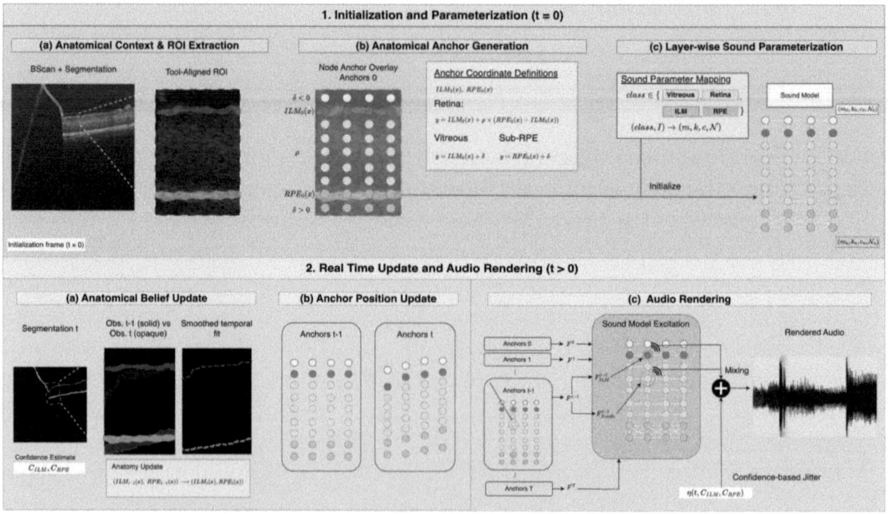

Fig. 1. iOCT Sonification framework.

3.1 Initialization and Parameterization

The underlying sound model is formulated as a two-dimensional mass–spring–damper system that produces audible resonances under external excitation [26], following prior work in medical sonification [17,22]. The system consists of interconnected masses whose vibrational dynamics are governed by stiffness and damping parameters. During initialization, both the spatial configuration and physical properties are derived from geometric and semantic information extracted from the first segmented B-scan, thereby anchoring the model to the retinal anatomy. These parameters shape the spectral and resonant characteristics of the synthesized sound when nodes are excited, enabling contrastive feedback across tissue layers, implicitly encoding tool–tissue proximity, and intuitively reflecting deformations such as bleb formation.

Anatomical Context and Tool-Aligned ROI Extraction. We process an initialization frame I_0 acquired during setup, where the needle shaft is visible in iOCT. A coarse segmentation S_0 of the ILM, RPE, and needle is obtained using a pre-trained U-Net, with low-confidence predictions suppressed as in [5]. From S_0, we estimate the dominant retinal orientation and compute a rotation matrix R to align the tissue horizontally. The needle shaft is modeled by fitting a line ℓ to the segmented needle pixels using a robust Huber regressor [5,11]. After applying R, a rotated rectangular region of interest (ROI) is extracted around the intersection of ℓ with the anatomical layers and extended to include the vitreous region above the ILM. If direct overlap is not detected (e.g., due to shadowing), the ROI is estimated from a local neighborhood search or from the needle trajectory alone.

Anatomical Node Generation. As shown in Fig. 1b, a uniform grid is overlaid on the ROI to define sound model nodes. Each node is assigned an anatomical class (vitreous, ILM, retina, RPE) via majority voting within its support, with ILM and RPE up-weighted to account for their thin structure.

Node positions are parameterized relative to the segmented ILM_0 and RPE_0 to ensure deformation-consistent alignment. For retinal nodes, axial position is defined by a normalized depth parameter $\rho \in [0, 1]$:

$$y = \mathrm{ILM}_0(x) + \rho\big(\mathrm{RPE}_0(x) - \mathrm{ILM}_0(x)\big). \tag{1}$$

Nodes outside the retina are defined by offsets δ to the nearest boundary, enabling runtime updates that preserve anatomical consistency of the anchors under deformation.

Layer-Wise Sound Parameterization. Our $m \times n$ anchor grid defines the masses of a physics-based sound model. To complete the mass–spring–damper system, we assign node-specific physical parameters and define the connectivity between neighboring masses to instantiate spring–damper elements.

Based on anatomical class labels and local intensity statistics within the ROI, we define a hand-crafted mapping

$$\mathbf{M} : (\text{class}, I) \rightarrow (m, k, d, \mathcal{N}), \tag{2}$$

which assigns mass m, stiffness k, and damping d to each node.

Nodes are connected in a regular lattice defined by a neighborhood order $\mathcal{N} \in \{1, 2\}$, indicating first- or second-order ordinal proximity. First-order connectivity links each node to its immediate neighbors along the Cartesian axes, i.e., $(i \pm 1, j)$ and $(i, j \pm 1)$. Second-order connectivity extends coupling to the diagonal neighbors $(i \pm 1, j \pm 1)$.

For each neighboring pair $(i, j) \in \mathcal{N}$, spring stiffness and damping are defined symmetrically as

$$k_{ij} = \tfrac{1}{2}(k_i + k_j), \qquad d_{ij} = \tfrac{1}{2}(d_i + d_j). \tag{3}$$

3.2 Real-Time Anatomical Update (t>0)

Following initialization, the sound model is updated online using the incoming iOCT B-scan stream. At fixed temporal intervals, each frame is segmented to obtain updated ILM_t, RPE_t, and needle estimates with associated confidence measures. To ensure robustness under partial occlusion and shadowing, ILM and RPE trajectories are modeled using cubic spline fitting with confidence-weighted regularization [4,25] applied along the lateral axis. This lightweight temporal modeling enables smooth extrapolation across missing or low-confidence regions while remaining compatible with real-time processing constraints.

The updated anatomical estimates are then used to recompute node positions according to the relative parameterization introduced in the previous section. In particular, each node preserves its relative depth parameters (ρ, δ), while its absolute position is updated based on the current $ILM_t(x)$ and $RPE_t(x)$ geometry. This allows the anchors to follow tissue deformation over time.

3.3 Excitation Protocol and Audio Rendering

The sound model is driven by a set of excitation mechanisms designed to reflect both tool–tissue position and ongoing anatomical changes, while also conveying the reliability of the underlying visual estimates.

Tool-Driven Excitation. Excitations are derived from the estimated needle tip position. As the needle advances or interacts with tissue, forces are applied to the nearest node and propagated through the spring–damper lattice. Excitation magnitude is scaled by local stiffness [22], ensuring anatomically consistent response across tissue types. This produces auditory events reflecting needle proximity and contact.

Anatomy-Driven Excitation. Surgical events such as tissue penetration or fluid injection induce localized deformation of the retinal layers, which manifests as differential axial motion between the ILM and RPE. Rather than directly measuring deformations in noisy iOCT scans, we estimate a coarse deformation by comparing temporal changes in the positions of these anatomical layers in the vicinity of the needle tip.

At each time step t, we define a lateral window $\mathcal{W}(x_t)$ centered at the current injection site (approximated by the needle tip position x_t). This focuses the analysis on tool–tissue and fluid injection–related interaction regions rather than global anatomical drift. Within this window, we compute the local ILM–RPE separation from the segmentations.

$$d_t(x) = RPE_t(x) - ILM_t(x), \quad x \in \mathcal{W}(x_t). \tag{4}$$

The robust temporal change in separation is then defined as

$$\Delta d_t = \mathrm{P}_{95}(d_t(x) - d_{t-1}(x)), \quad x \in \mathcal{W}(x_t), \tag{5}$$

where $\mathrm{P}_{95}(\cdot)$ denotes the 95th percentile, used to suppress outliers due to segmentation noise. Finally, we define the deformation-driven excitation proxy

$$f_{ILM} = \min\big(2,\ \max(0,\ \Delta d_t)\big), \tag{6}$$

which retains responsiveness to positive separation increases corresponding to injection-induced retinal elevation while suppressing compression. The resulting signal is used to modulate excitation strength in the acoustic model. To prevent excessive excitation, f_{ILM} is bounded to a predefined range.

Confidence-Modulated Rendering. Confidence estimates are used to modulate a stochastic post-processing component in the sound synthesis $\eta(t, C_{ILM}, C_{RPE})$, such that lower confidence results in increased temporal jitter.

4 Experiments and Result

The sound model was implemented using the miPhysics library[1], and the physical parameter mapping M was designed based on psychoacoustic principles [24].

Qualitative Results. We qualitatively evaluate the method on a publicly available porcine insertion [20] and a representative synthetic sequence exhibiting bleb formation (Fig. 2). We provide corresponding supplementary videos for these two cases (S01 and S02). In both cases, detected events align closely with annotated ground truth, indicating accurate temporal localization. We additionally provide an example with vivid confidence modulation (S03).

[1] https://github.com/mi-creative/miPhysics_Processing.

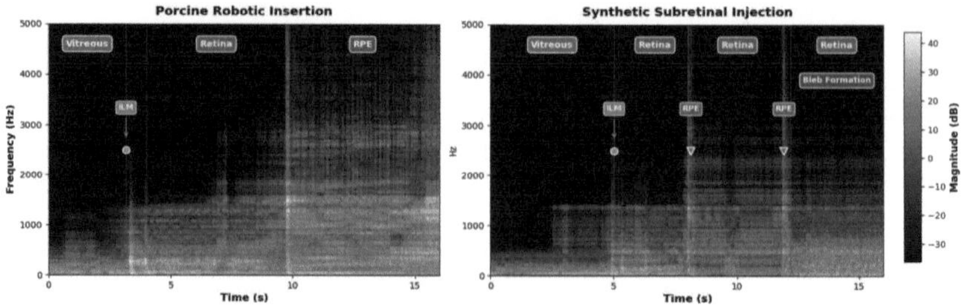

Fig. 2. Spectrograms of sonified iOCT signals from (left) ex vivo porcine robotic insertion and (right) a synthetic subretinal injection sequence. In the synthetic example, bleb formation is characterized by a broadband increase in spectral energy.

Real-Time System Runtime Performance. We demonstrate the full system operates in real time within an interactive simulated subretinal injection environment (supplementary video S04). We evaluate runtime on a CPU-bound system across 10 insertion sequences at 512 $\times$ 512 resolution. The full pipeline requires 27.8 ± 1.5 ms per frame (mean $\pm$ SD), corresponding to approximately 36 FPS. Segmentation and spline fitting dominated computation time, while all other components required <1 ms per frame.

User Study. We conducted a controlled within-subject study comparing the proposed sonification with a parameter-mapping baseline on realistic simulated subretinal injection sequences. Thirty-five participants were recruited; one was excluded (<25% accuracy in both methods), resulting in 34 analyzed participants, from which 30 are novices and 4 are clinical experts. Each completed 20 trials (10 per method), identifying ILM contact, RPE contact, and bleb onset while rating confidence (1–5). Trials included single- and multi-event scenarios requiring correct temporal ordering. Method order was randomized, and trials were stratified by difficulty and randomized within strata. Differences (Δ) are reported as proposed minus baseline and tested using the Wilcoxon signed-rank test. **The baseline** builds on pitch-based anatomical encoding strategies from prior surgical sonification frameworks [18,21], where static pitch represents anatomical zones and pulse-rate modulation proportional to ILM–RPE distance provides proximity feedback [19]. Parameterization follows established psychoacoustic principles [7], and prior work has demonstrated its effectiveness in supporting perceptual discrimination of anatomical regions. Bleb formation is conveyed indirectly through distance-dependent modulation rather than explicit deformation encoding.

User Study Results. The proposed sonification significantly improved overall event identification accuracy compared to the baseline (83.4% vs. 60.6%; $\Delta =$ 22.8 percentage points, 95% CI [15.7, 30.1], $p < 0.001$). Component-wise analysis showed that gains were primarily driven by improved bleb identification (63.6%

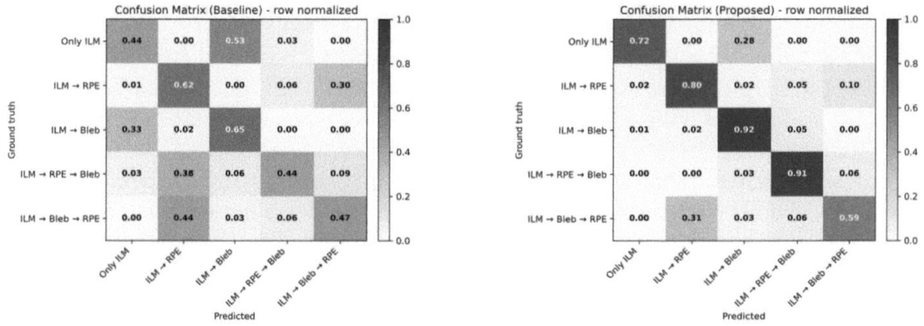

(a) Baseline method (b) Proposed method

Fig. 3. Row-normalized confusion matrices (n = 34). The baseline shows entanglement between contact-only and deformation states, while the proposed method improves separation of bleb-related events, reflected by stronger diagonal concentration.

vs. 85.5%; $\Delta = 21.8$ percentage points, $p < 0.001$), while ILM exhibited a minor numerical increase (+0.9%) and RPE a small decrease (−1.6%), neither statistically significant. As illustrated in Fig. 3, the proposed method reduces structured confusions between contact-only and deformation states related to bleb formation. Participants reported significantly higher confidence on average under the proposed sonification (4.20 vs. 3.73; $\Delta = +0.47$, 95% CI $[0.23, 0.71]$, $p < 0.001$), with the median confidence increasing from 4 to 5. Confidence was positively correlated with correctness in both conditions (Spearman $\rho = 0.27$ for both methods; both $p < 0.001$), indicating that subjective certainty reflected actual performance.

Expert Feedback. Two vitreoretinal surgeons and two residents (n = 4) from the main cohort provided additional interview feedback. In this group, recognition accuracy increased descriptively from 65% (baseline) to 75% (proposed), with comparable gains in bleb detection. Experts highlighted the method's clinical relevance and its potential to reduce reliance on visual iOCT interpretation in favor of the optical microscope, potentially alleviating visual load [23].

5 Discussion and Conclusion

We presented a real-time sonification framework for subretinal injection that converts iOCT B-scans into structured auditory feedback. Anchored in segmented retinal anatomy, a physics-inspired sound model encodes interaction-driven cues directly from intraoperative imaging rather than static proximity mappings. The user study demonstrated significantly improved identification of clinically relevant events, with the largest gains in bleb detection. These gains likely stem from the model's physical formulation, which integrates deformation signals observable in iOCT, whereas the baseline relies on rigid parameterizations that do not accommodate such interaction cues. The framework supports real-time workflows and is extensible to additional interaction structures. Reported sound roughness by a few participants motivates future work in auditory and perceptual refinement [10] to further enhance usability.

Acknowledgments. This work was primarily supported by the German Research Foundation (DFG) under Project No. 560596849. Further support was provided by the German Research Foundation (DFG) under Germany's Excellence Strategy – EXC 2050/2 – Project No. 390696704 – Cluster of Excellence "Centre for Tactile Internet with Human-in-the-Loop" (CeTI) at Technische Universität Dresden. The authors would like to thank SynthesEyes for supporting this work through data provision and technical collaboration. Shervin Dehghani and Michael Sommersperger were partially supported by the Bavarian Research Foundation (BFS) under Grant No. AZ-1569-22.

Disclosure of Interests. The authors have no competing interests to declare that are relevant to the content of this article.

References

1. Arikan, D., et al.: Real-time deformation-aware control for autonomous robotic subretinal injection under IOCT guidance. In: 2025 IEEE International Conference on Robotics and Automation (ICRA), pp. 10531–10537 (2024). https://api.semanticscholar.org/CorpusID:273963767
2. Arikan, D., et al.: Towards motion compensation in autonomous robotic subretinal injections. In: 2025 International Symposium on Medical Robotics (ISMR), pp. 66–72 (2024). https://api.semanticscholar.org/CorpusID:274306241
3. Black, D., Hansen, C., Nabavi, A., Kikinis, R., Hahn, H.K.: A survey of auditory display in image-guided interventions. Int. J. Comput. Assist. Radiol. Surg. **12**, 1665–1676 (2017). https://api.semanticscholar.org/CorpusID:11833443
4. de Boor, C.: A practical guide to splines. Appl. Math. Sci. (1978). https://api.semanticscholar.org/CorpusID:122101452
5. Dehghani, S., et al.: Robotic navigation autonomy for subretinal injection via intelligent real-time virtual IOCT volume slicing. In: 2023 IEEE International Conference on Robotics and Automation (ICRA), pp. 4724–4731 (2023). https://api.semanticscholar.org/CorpusID:255998244
6. Ehlers, J.P., et al.: The discover study 3-year results: feasibility and usefulness of microscope-integrated intraoperative oct during ophthalmic surgery. Ophthalmology **1257**, 1014–1027 (2018). https://api.semanticscholar.org/CorpusID:3781305
7. Fastl, H., Zwicker, E.: Psychoacoustics: Facts and models (1990). https://api.semanticscholar.org/CorpusID:144689350
8. George, S.M., Lu, F., Rao, M., Leach, L.L., Gross, J.M.: The retinal pigment epithelium: development, injury responses, and regenerative potential in mammalian and non-mammalian systems. Progress Retinal Eye Res. **85** (2021). https://api.semanticscholar.org/CorpusID:233354736
9. Gupta, P.K., Jensen, P.S., de Juan, E.: Surgical forces and tactile perception during retinal microsurgery. In: International Conference on Medical Image Computing and Computer-Assisted Intervention (1999). https://api.semanticscholar.org/CorpusID:12455806

10. Hermann, T., Weger, M.: Data-driven auditory contrast enhancement for everyday sounds and sonifications. In: Proceedings of the 25th International Conference on Auditory Display (ICAD 2019) (2019). https://api.semanticscholar.org/CorpusID:197859996
11. Huber, P.J.: Robust methods of estimation of regression coefficients. Statistics (Berlin, DDR) **8**(1), 41–53 (1977). https://doi.org/10.1080/02331887708801356
12. Hughes-Hallett, A., et al.: Inattention blindness in surgery. Surg. Endosc. **29**(11), 3184–3189 (2015). https://doi.org/10.1007/s00464-014-4051-3
13. Irigoyen, C., et al.: Subretinal injection techniques for retinal disease: a review. J. Clin. Med. **11**(16), 4717 (2022). https://doi.org/10.3390/jcm11164717, https://www.mdpi.com/2077-0383/11/16/4717
14. Jo, Y.J., Heo, D.W., Shin, Y.I., Kim, J.Y.: Diurnal variation of retina thickness measured with time domain and spectral domain optical coherence tomography in healthy subjects. Investigat. Ophthalmol. Vis. Sci. **52**(9), 6497–6500 (2011). https://doi.org/10.1167/iovs.11-7403
15. Ling, S., et al.: Lentiviral delivery of co-packaged CAS9 MRNA AND a VEGFA-targeting guide RNA prevents wet age-related macular degeneration in mice. Nat. Biomed. Eng. **5**, 1–13 (2021). https://doi.org/10.1038/s41551-020-00656-y
16. Matinfar, S., et al.: From tissue to sound: a new paradigm for medical sonic interaction design. Med. Image Anal. **103**, 103571 (2025)
17. Matinfar, S., Dehghani, S., Sommersperger, M., Faridpooya, K., Fairhurst, M., Navab, N.: Ocular stethoscope: auditory support for retinal membrane peeling. In: International Conference on Medical Image Computing and Computer-Assisted Intervention (2024). https://api.semanticscholar.org/CorpusID:273232345
18. Matinfar, S., et al.: Surgical soundtracks: automatic acoustic augmentation of surgical procedures. Int. J. Comput. Assist. Radiol. Surg. **13**(9), 1345–1355 (2018). https://doi.org/10.1007/s11548-018-1827-2
19. Matinfar, S., et al.: Sonification as a reliable alternative to conventional visual surgical navigation. Sci. Rep. **13** (2022). https://api.semanticscholar.org/CorpusID:250144608
20. Pannek, S., et al.: Exploring the needle tip interaction force with retinal tissue deformation in vitreoretinal surgery. In: 2024 IEEE International Conference on Robotics and Automation (ICRA), pp. 16999–17005 (2024). https://api.semanticscholar.org/CorpusID:271798975
21. Roodaki, H., Navab, N., Eslami, A., Stapleton, C., Navab, N.: Sonifeye: sonification of visual information using physical modeling sound synthesis. IEEE Trans. Visual Comput. Graphics **23**(11), 2366–2371 (2017). https://doi.org/10.1109/TVCG.2017.2734327
22. Ruozzi, V., et al.: BIOSONIX: can physics-based sonification perceptualize tissue deformations from tool interactions? In: Oguz, I., Zhang, S., Metaxas, D.N. (eds.) Information Processing in Medical Imaging (IPMI 2025). LNCS, vol. 15830, pp. 19–33. Springer Nature Switzerland, Cham (2025). https://doi.org/10.1007/978-3-031-96625-5_2
23. Schütz, L., Dehghani, S., Sommersperger, M., Faridpooya, K., Navab, N.: The impact of intraoperative optical coherence tomography on cognitive load in virtual reality vitreoretinal surgery training. Sci. Rep. **15**(1) (2025). https://doi.org/10.1038/s41598-025-07670-7
24. Serafin, S., Franinović, K., Hermann, T., Lemaitre, G., Rinott, M., Rocchesso, D.: The sonification handbook (2011). https://api.semanticscholar.org/CorpusID:31502560

25. Unser, M.A.: Splines: a perfect fit for signal and image processing. IEEE Signal Process. Mag. **16**, 22–38 (1999). https://api.semanticscholar.org/CorpusID:62688047
26. Villeneuve, J., Leonard, J.: Mass-interaction physical models for sound ANS multisensory creation: starting anew (2019). https://api.semanticscholar.org/CorpusID:204780346
27. ping Zhao, C., et al.: Development of a refined protocol for trans-scleral subretinal transplantation of human retinal pigment epithelial cells into rat eyes. J. Visual. Exp. JoVE **126** (2017). https://api.semanticscholar.org/CorpusID:13764597
28. Zhou, M., et al.: Needle detection and localisation for robot-assisted subretinal injection using deep learning. CAAI Trans. Intell. Technol. **10**, 703–715 (2025). https://api.semanticscholar.org/CorpusID:280322493

Physio-Anatomical Prior-Guided Probabilistic Field Learning for Ultrasound-Based Neuro-Fascial Interface Landmark Localization

Guowei Dai[1], Duwei Dai[2], Yi Zhang[3], Yulong Ji[4(✉)], and Hu Chen[1(✉)]

[1] College of Computer Science, Sichuan University, Chengdu, China
huchen@scu.edu.cn
[2] Second Affiliated Hospital of Xi'an Jiaotong University, Xi'an, China
[3] School of Cyber Science and Engineering, Sichuan University, Chengdu, China
[4] School of Aeronautics and Astronautics, Sichuan University, Chengdu, China
jyl@scu.edu.cn

Abstract. Accurate localization of acupoints in ultrasound imaging is critical for safe and effective acupuncture, yet remains challenging due to low tissue contrast, speckle noise, and significant inter-subject anatomical variability. Existing methods often rely on implicit texture learning or rigid landmark detection, failing to account for the depth-dependent physiological nature of the Deqi response. To address these limitations, we propose the Physio-Anatomical Probability Field Network (PAPF-Net), a novel framework that shifts from deterministic point regression to uncertainty-aware distribution modeling. The core technical contribution lies in synergizing two complementary mechanisms. To address anatomical heterogeneity, the Category-Conditional Anatomical Prototype (CCAP) module explicitly incorporates site-specific priors by deforming learnable templates to conform to individual anatomical geometries. Concurrently, to mitigate acoustic ambiguity, the Uncertainty-Aware Decoder transitions from deterministic regression to probabilistic modeling, capturing signal attenuation in deep tissues through distribution-aware Sinkhorn supervision. Validated across a large multi-center cohort, our approach surpasses current standards in both accuracy and robustness. Its focus on neuro-fascial interfaces ensures physiological plausibility, offering an interpretable, standardized basis for ultrasound-guided acupuncture.

Keywords: Ultrasound Navigation · Landmark Detection · Anatomical Priors · Uncertainty Estimation · Deqi Localization

1 Introduction

Acupuncture has demonstrated notable bio-regulatory effects in the rehabilitation of neurological disorders, the management of chronic pain, and the treatment

G. Yang et al. (Eds.): MICCAI 2026, LNCS 16893, pp. 329–339, 2027.
https://doi.org/10.1007/978-3-032-38236-8_32

of functional illnesses [6,19]. The therapeutic efficacy of acupuncture is closely linked to inducing the Deqi state, a key determinant of treatment success [12,19]. Physiologically, Deqi manifests as a composite sensation, subjectively perceived by the patient as soreness, numbness, distension, or heaviness, and objectively felt by the practitioner as a needle grasp from the surrounding tissue [15,18]. Modern anatomical and interventional ultrasound studies have shown that this phenomenon arises from the mechanical interaction between the needle tip and deep anatomical structures, particularly the neuro-fascial interfaces, including deep fascia, neurovascular bundles, and intermuscular septa.

Automating this localization process is critical for standardizing acupuncture therapy but presents unique computer vision challenges [7,9,18]. Unlike typical landmark detection tasks (e.g., facial keypoints or anatomical landmarks) where targets are visually distinct [3,13], the Deqi response zone is functionally defined and visually ambiguous, often lacking clear boundaries in ultrasound images. The anatomical structures surrounding acupoints (e.g., the metacarpal spacing for Hegu versus the forearm muscles for Shousanli) exhibit significant morphological heterogeneity across subjects and sites, rendering standard template matching ineffective [4,5,8]. The Deqi sensation is inherently probabilistic; the optimal stimulation point is not a Dirac delta function but a spatial field whose spread correlates with tissue depth and patient sensitivity [20]. Deterministic regression models fail to capture this aleatoric uncertainty, leading to overconfident but physiologically implausible predictions.

To address these challenges, we propose the Physio-Anatomical Probability Field Network (PAPF-Net), which reformulates acupoint localization from deterministic coordinate regression to uncertainty-aware probability field learning. Targeting the morphological heterogeneity of musculoskeletal structures, we introduce a Category-Conditional Anatomical Prototype (CCAP) module. This component retrieves site-specific structural priors and dynamically registers them to the input via deformable alignment, explicitly injecting geometric constraints to robustify feature learning against speckle noise. Simultaneously, to capture the aleatoric uncertainty arising from acoustic attenuation, we design a Dual-Head Uncertainty Decoder. By modeling the output as a heteroscedastic Gaussian distribution, the network provides depth-adaptive confidence maps that align with the physical reality of ultrasound propagation. We validate our method on Deqi-US-1k, a curated multi-center dataset of 1,000 subjects with labels verified by patient feedback during needle insertion. The dataset provides functional Deqi response annotations for deep ultrasound analysis. Our main contributions are summarized as follows:

- We propose PAPF-Net, a deep learning framework dedicated to localizing functional Deqi response zones in ultrasound, bridging the gap between traditional medicine and modern computer vision.
- We introduce the CCAP module, which leverages deformable alignment to inject site-specific structural priors, effectively handling anatomical heterogeneity.

– We formulate a depth-adaptive uncertainty learning mechanism that models the Deqi response as a probabilistic field, offering physiologically interpretable confidence maps.

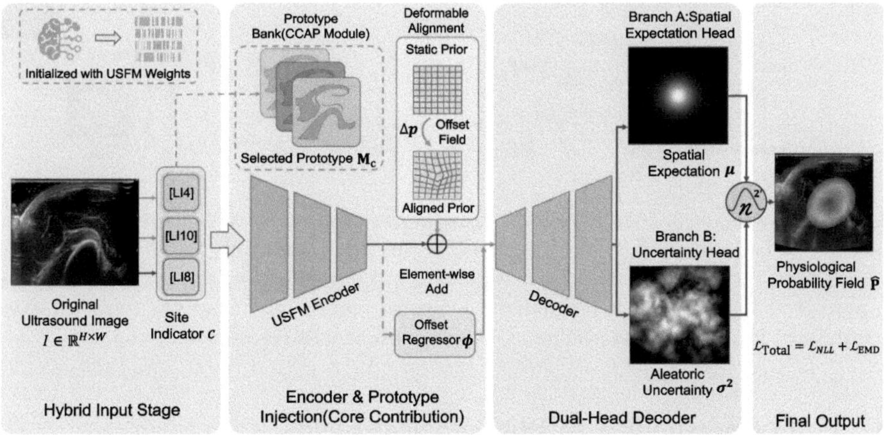

Fig. 1. Overview of PAPF-Net. Given input (I, c), where c is the site indicator, CCAP selects the corresponding learnable prototype $\mathbf{M}_c$ from a bank of K site-specific prototypes and aligns it with offsets $\Delta\mathbf{p}$. A dual-head decoder then regresses $(\boldsymbol{\mu}, \boldsymbol{\sigma}^2)$ to generate the final *Deqi* probability field $\hat{\mathbf{P}}$.

2 Method

We propose the Physio-Anatomical Probability Field Network (PAPF-Net) to localize functional Deqi response zones as probabilistic fields rather than deterministic coordinates. As shown in Fig. 1, the architecture synergizes deep acoustic features with explicit anatomical priors through a U-shaped design operating on B-mode images I and a site indicator $c \in \{1, \ldots, K\}$, where K is the number of anatomical categories. To tackle significant morphological heterogeneity across anatomical sites, the bottleneck incorporates a CCAP module. This mechanism retrieves a learnable, site-specific structural template and dynamically aligns it to the input via deformable registration, thereby injecting geometric constraints such as bone curvature and fascial depth into the latent representation. Complementing this structural guidance, a Dual-Head Uncertainty Decoder models observation-dependent aleatoric uncertainty induced by ultrasound attenuation. By jointly regressing a spatial expectation $\boldsymbol{\mu}$ and a depth-adaptive variance map $\boldsymbol{\sigma}^2$, the network constructs a heteroscedastic Gaussian field, ensuring uncertainty-aware predictions in visually ambiguous deep tissue regions.

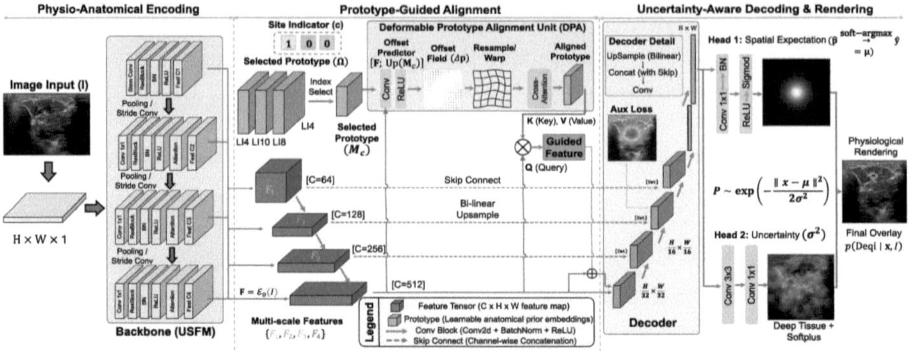

Fig. 2. Mechanisms of PAPF-Net. (a) Prototype alignment to features $\mathbf{F}$ via offsets $\Delta\mathbf{p}$, where $\mathbf{M}_c$ is selected by the site indicator c. (b) Uncertainty: shallow (low σ^2) vs. deep (high σ^2) regions. (c) Sinkhorn supervision minimizes the transport cost between the predicted field $\hat{\mathbf{P}}$ and a normalized Gaussian target heatmap $\mathbf{Q}_i$ centered at $\mathbf{y}_i$; the auxiliary branch applies the same supervision at 1/4 resolution.

2.1 From Coordinates to Physiological Fields

Let $\mathcal{D} = \{(I_i, \mathbf{y}_i, c_i)\}_{i=1}^N$ denote the dataset, where I_i is the ultrasound image, c_i represents the anatomical site, and $\mathbf{y}_i$ is the ground-truth coordinate verified by functional *Deqi* feedback (Fig. 2). Unlike conventional methods that model landmarks as deterministic Dirac deltas, we postulate the *Deqi* response as a continuous probability density function governed by neuro-fascial mechanics. Our goal is to learn a mapping $\mathcal{F}_\Theta : (I, c) \mapsto \hat{\mathbf{P}}$ that quantifies this physiological field.

We employ a U-shaped architecture where the encoder $\mathcal{E}_\theta$ extracts hierarchical features $\{\mathbf{F}_\ell\}_{\ell=1}^4$. The bottleneck $\mathbf{F}_4$ is processed by the prototype module (Sect. 2.2), and the decoder $\mathcal{D}_\psi$ progressively aggregates features via skip connections. Crucially, to capture observation-dependent aleatoric uncertainty arising from acoustic attenuation, the decoder terminates in two coupled heads: (1) an *Expectation Head* producing the normalized field $\hat{\mathbf{P}}$, from which the spatial mean is derived via differentiable soft-argmax as $\hat{\mathbf{y}} = \sum_{\mathbf{x}} \mathbf{x}\,\hat{\mathbf{P}}(\mathbf{x})$; and (2) an *Uncertainty Head* predicting a pixel-wise variance map $\hat{\sigma}^2(\mathbf{x})$ via softplus activation. The uncertainty head does not estimate epistemic uncertainty over model weights; instead, it models image-dependent ambiguity caused by attenuation and shadowing, and we use the variance at the predicted location, $\hat{\sigma}_i^2 = \hat{\sigma}^2(\hat{\mathbf{y}}_i)$, in Eq. 1.

$$p(\mathbf{y}_i \mid I_i) = \mathcal{N}\big(\mathbf{y}_i;\, \hat{\mathbf{y}}_i,\, \hat{\sigma}_i^2\big)\,, \tag{1}$$

where $\hat{\sigma}_i^2$ is the sample-wise variance predicted by the uncertainty head. This formulation allows the network to adaptively relax localization precision in regions with high anatomical complexity or shadowing, transforming rigid regression into uncertainty-aware estimation.

2.2 Category-Conditional Anatomical Prototype Injection

Anatomical contexts vary drastically across acupoints (e.g., metacarpal LI4 versus radial-ulnar LI10), rendering single global priors ill-posed. To capture this heterogeneity, we propose a CCAP mechanism.

Learnable Prototype Bank. We construct a bank $\mathcal{M} = \{\mathbf{M}_k\}_{k=1}^{K}$ where K is the number of site categories and each prototype $\mathbf{M}_k$ encodes a site-specific latent structural template (Fig. 2). The site label $c \in \{1, \ldots, K\}$ is represented as a one-hot indicator in implementation, and the corresponding prototype $\mathbf{M}_c$ is selected for each sample. In our implementation, each prototype is a randomly initialized learnable tensor with the same shape as the bottleneck feature map and is optimized end-to-end with the network. To ensure distinctiveness and prevent mode collapse, we enforce an orthogonality regularization on the prototype embeddings:

$$\mathcal{L}_{\text{ortho}} = \sum_{k \neq k'} \langle \text{vec}(\mathbf{M}_k), \text{vec}(\mathbf{M}_{k'}) \rangle^2 . \tag{2}$$

Deformable Alignment and Injection. Direct fusion of canonical prototypes with instance features $\mathbf{F}$ is suboptimal due to variations in patient pose and probe orientation. We address this via a Deformable Prototype Alignment (DPA) module. A lightweight network $\mathcal{G}_\phi$ first estimates a dense offset field $\Delta\mathbf{p}$ based on the correlation between the feature map and the upsampled prototype:

$$\Delta\mathbf{p} = \mathcal{G}_\phi([\mathbf{F};\ \text{Up}(\mathbf{M}_c)]). \tag{3}$$

The prototype is then spatially warped to match the instance anatomy via a differentiable sampling operation $\mathcal{W}$, yielding $\widetilde{\mathbf{M}}_c = \mathcal{W}(\mathbf{M}_c, \Delta\mathbf{p})$. Finally, to rigorously constrain the feature learning, the aligned prototype is injected into the visual stream via a gated cross-attention mechanism:

$$\mathbf{F}_{\text{guided}} = \mathbf{F} + \alpha \cdot \text{CrossAttn}(\mathbf{F}, \widetilde{\mathbf{M}}_c, \widetilde{\mathbf{M}}_c), \tag{4}$$

where α is a zero-initialized learnable scalar. This design allows the network to selectively attend to relevant structural priors (e.g., bone boundaries) while gradually adapting to patient-specific morphology during training.

2.3 Training Objective and Notation

The full training objective is written explicitly to avoid ambiguity. For each sample, the landmark coordinate $\mathbf{y}_i$ is converted into a normalized Gaussian target heatmap $\mathbf{Q}_i$ at the supervision resolution:

$$\mathbf{Q}_i(\mathbf{x}) = \frac{\exp\left(-\|\mathbf{x} - \mathbf{y}_i\|_2^2 / 2\tau^2\right)}{\sum_{\mathbf{x}'} \exp(-\|\mathbf{x}' - \mathbf{y}_i\|_2^2 / 2\tau^2)}. \tag{5}$$

The Sinkhorn term is computed between the predicted probability field and $\mathbf{Q}_i$, and the auxiliary branch applies the same supervision at $1/4$ resolution:

$$\mathcal{L}_{\text{Sinkhorn}} = \text{Sinkhorn}(\hat{\mathbf{P}}_i, \mathbf{Q}_i) + \text{Sinkhorn}(\hat{\mathbf{P}}_i^{1/4}, \mathbf{Q}_i^{1/4}). \tag{6}$$

The heteroscedastic Gaussian negative log-likelihood is applied to the coordinate prediction:

$$\mathcal{L}_{\text{NLL}} = -\log \mathcal{N}(\mathbf{y}_i; \hat{\mathbf{y}}_i, \hat{\sigma}_i^2), \tag{7}$$

where $\hat{\mathbf{y}}_i = \sum_{\mathbf{x}} \mathbf{x} \hat{\mathbf{P}}_i(\mathbf{x})$. The final objective is

$$\mathcal{L}_{\text{total}} = \lambda_{\text{nll}} \mathcal{L}_{\text{NLL}} + \lambda_{\text{sink}} \mathcal{L}_{\text{Sinkhorn}} + \lambda_{\text{reg}} \mathcal{L}_{\text{ortho}}. \tag{8}$$

Here, λ_{nll}, λ_{sink}, and λ_{reg} are the only optimization weights reported in the implementation details; the auxiliary branch is included inside $\mathcal{L}_{\text{Sinkhorn}}$ rather than treated as an additional independent term.

3 Experiments

3.1 Experimental Setup

Dataset and Protocols. We validate our method on Deqi-US-1k, a large-scale ultrasound dataset from a multi-center randomized controlled trial coordinated by a collaborating hospital. The cohort comprises 1,000 subjects with peripheral facial paralysis. High-resolution B-mode sequences were acquired using Mindray Resona 7/9 systems. The dataset targets three acupoints with distinct anatomical contexts: *Hegu* (LI4, $N = 330$), *Shousanli* (LI10, $N = 330$), and *Xialian* (LI8, $N = 340$). A rigorous function-driven protocol was enforced: ground truth coordinates $\mathbf{y}_i$ were annotated at the needle tip position only upon patient confirmation of the Deqi sensation, ensuring labels reflect physiological response zones rather than surface approximations.

Implementation Details. The proposed framework is implemented in PyTorch and trained on 4× NVIDIA A100 GPUs (80GB). We use the AdamW optimizer with a base learning rate of 5×10^{-4} and weight decay of 1×10^{-4}. The learning rate follows a cosine annealing schedule with 5 warm-up epochs. Input images are resized to 384×384. Data augmentation includes random rotation ($\pm 15°$), scaling ($0.8 - 1.2\times$), and intensity jittering. Loss weights are set to $\lambda_{nll} = 1.0$, $\lambda_{sink} = 0.5$, and $\lambda_{reg} = 0.1$; the auxiliary 1/4-resolution branch uses the same Sinkhorn supervision and is absorbed into λ_{sink}. The prototype bank contains one randomly initialized tensor per site, and the backbone is initialized with pre-trained weights from the Universal Ultrasound Foundation Model (USFM) [10]. Training takes approximately 4 h for 100 epochs with a total batch size of 32.

Evaluation Metrics. We employ standard Mean Radial Error (MRE) and Successful Detection Rate (SDR) with thresholds $\delta \in \{0.5, 1.0, 1.5\}$ mm to evaluate geometric accuracy. To rigorously validate physiological plausibility, we propose the Anatomical Layer Hit Rate (ALHR). Unlike geometric distance, ALHR measures whether the predicted peak $\hat{\mathbf{y}}_i$ falls within the correct neuro-fascial tissue layer (e.g., deep fascia) defined by expert-annotated masks $\mathcal{S}_i$. It is a task-specific layer-consistency metric rather than a generic segmentation precision score. It is formulated as:

$$\text{ALHR} = \frac{1}{N}\sum_{i=1}^{N} \mathbb{I}\left(\hat{\mathbf{y}}_i \in \mathcal{S}_i\right) \times 100\% \tag{9}$$

where N is the number of test samples and $\mathbb{I}(\cdot)$ is the indicator function returning 1 if the condition holds, and 0 otherwise.

Table 1. Performance comparison of different landmark localization methods. Lower MRE is better, while higher SDR and ALHR are better. The best results are highlighted in **bold**, and the second-best results are underlined. The reported values represent the mean ± standard deviation across a 5-fold cross-validation scheme.

Method	MRE (mm) ↓		SDR (%) ↑			ALHR (%) ↑
	L_1	L_2	0.5 mm	1.0 mm	1.5 mm	
U-Net [11]	0.51 ± 0.034	0.68 ± 0.052	64.80 ± 2.81	92.17 ± 0.72	97.40 ± 1.37	60.5
DM-ResNet [16]	0.47 ± 0.031	0.62 ± 0.045	71.25 ± 2.14	94.30 ± 0.65	98.12 ± 0.98	66.8
HRNet [14]	0.45 ± 0.028	0.59 ± 0.041	74.60 ± 1.95	95.55 ± 0.58	98.80 ± 0.82	69.4
TransUNet [2]	0.44 ± 0.026	0.57 ± 0.038	76.12 ± 1.88	96.02 ± 0.51	99.05 ± 0.65	71.2
FARNet [1]	0.43 ± 0.024	0.56 ± 0.033	78.35 ± 1.76	96.88 ± 0.45	99.20 ± 0.55	73.5
TGCN-ICF [7]	0.41 ± 0.021	0.53 ± 0.029	81.50 ± 1.62	97.45 ± 0.40	99.45 ± 0.42	76.8
EDA [17]	0.40 ± 0.019	0.52 ± 0.027	82.85 ± 1.55	97.90 ± 0.38	99.60 ± 0.35	78.1
IT-UNet [8]	0.39 ± 0.017	0.49 ± 0.022	84.15 ± 1.48	98.10 ± 0.35	99.68 ± 0.31	79.8
CalibratedSL [3]	0.38 ± 0.013	0.50 ± 0.025	84.90 ± 1.50	98.80 ± 0.32	99.75 ± 0.28	80.5
DGMLD [4]	0.39 ± 0.015	0.51 ± 0.024	85.60 ± 1.40	98.65 ± 0.28	99.80 ± 0.22	81.2
PAPF-Net (Ours)	**0.36 ± 0.011**	**0.46 ± 0.018**	**88.45 ± 1.25**	**99.15 ± 0.20**	**99.92 ± 0.10**	**83.6**

3.2 Comparison with State-of-the-Art

Table 1 compares our PAPF-Net against ten leading methods, spanning generic medical segmentation and specialized landmark detection. Our method consistently achieves the best performance across all metrics. Specifically, it reduces the Mean Radial Error (L_2) to 0.46 mm, outperforming the second-best DGMLD by a significant margin of 9.8%. For the strict 0.5 mm threshold, PAPF-Net attains an SDR of 88.45%, demonstrating superior fine-grained localization in speckle-heavy ultrasound images. Notably, while generic CNNs struggle with low-contrast fascial interfaces (MRE > 0.6 mm), specialized models like HRNet improve geometric consistency but lack explicit structural guidance. The gains of PAPF-Net mainly come from CCAP and uncertainty-aware modeling. The 83.6% ALHR surpasses the nearest competitor by 2.4%. This metric indicates that our probabilistic field approach is not only geometrically precise but also physiologically plausible, correctly targeting the deep neuro-fascial response zones rather than superficial tissues.

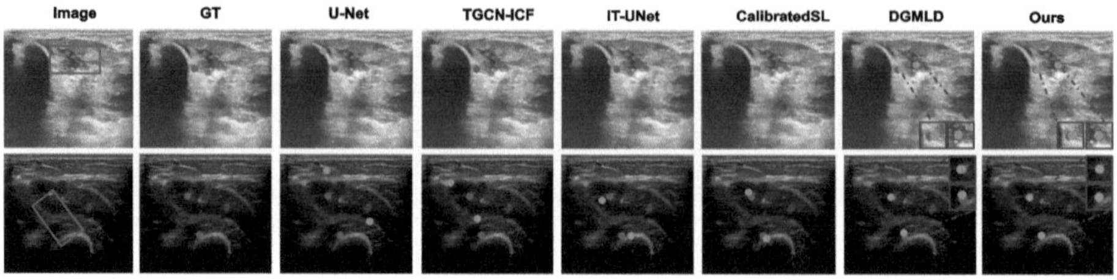

Fig. 3. Qualitative comparison showing PAPF-Net robust localization of neuro-fascial interfaces under severe acoustic shadowing and ambiguous multi-layer textures, surpassing competing methods limited by local speckle noise.

3.3 Qualitative Analysis

Figure 3 visualizes the localization performance on challenging samples characterized by severe acoustic shadowing and ambiguous multi-layer fascial textures. Generic methods (e.g., U-Net, TGCN-ICF) exhibit significant spatial deviations, often gravitating towards high-contrast bone surfaces or incorrect muscle layers due to their reliance on local texture features, which are easily corrupted by speckle noise. Even specialized baselines like DGMLD show minor misalignments in layer selection. PAPF-Net aligns more closely with the ground truth in the zoomed-in regions. The CCAP module imposes global structural constraints that reduce local anatomical ambiguity, and the uncertainty-aware mechanism suppresses false positives in noisy regions. As a result, the predictions target the physiologically correct neuro-fascial interface rather than merely salient image features.

Table 2. Component-wise ablation study on the Deqi-US-1k dataset. **Proto**: Static Anatomical Prototype Injection; **DPA**: Deformable Prototype Alignment; **Uncert**: Uncertainty-Aware Head; **EMD**: Sinkhorn supervision between the predicted field and the normalized Gaussian target heatmap.

Model ID	Components				MRE	SDR (%) ↑			ALHR
	Proto	DPA	Uncert	EMD	(mm) ↓	0.5 mm	1.0 mm	1.5 mm	(%) ↑
Baseline	–	–	–	–	0.58 ± 0.04	64.2	92.5	97.1	68.4
Static	✓	–	–	–	0.52 ± 0.03	71.8	94.8	98.2	74.2
Deform	✓	✓	–	–	0.45 ± 0.02	79.5	97.2	99.0	79.6
Prob.	✓	✓	✓	–	0.40 ± 0.02	84.1	98.4	99.5	81.8
PAPF-Net	✓	✓	✓	✓	**0.36 ± 0.01**	**88.5**	**99.2**	**99.9**	**83.6**

3.4 Ablation Study

Table 2 dissects the contribution of each proposed module. The Baseline model, relying solely on visual features, yields a suboptimal MRE of 0.58 mm and a low ALHR of 68.4%, indicating that implicit texture learning is insufficient to overcome the inherent speckle noise and low contrast of fascial interfaces. Injecting a Static Prototype provides global anatomical guidance, reducing the MRE to 0.52 mm. However, the most significant performance leap occurs with the DPA, which boosts the SDR@0.5mm by 7.7% and ALHR by 5.4%. This confirms that rigid priors are inadequate for handling inter-subject morphological heterogeneity. The DPA module effectively warps the canonical template to match patient-specific bone curvature, ensuring the features are strictly constrained within the valid anatomical manifold. Incorporating the Uncertainty-Aware Head further reduces the MRE to 0.40 mm. By modeling observation-dependent aleatoric uncertainty, the network learns to distrust ambiguous signals in deep tissues and to focus on high-confidence structural landmarks. Finally, introducing the EMD achieves the best overall performance. Unlike pixel-wise regression, which penalizes local coordinate shifts rigidly, EMD optimizes the global geometry of the predicted probability field against the Gaussian target heatmap, ensuring that the Deqi response distribution aligns with the ground-truth neuro-fascial pathway.

4 Conclusion

In this paper, we present PAPF-Net, a novel framework that redefines ultrasound acupoint localization by integrating explicit anatomical priors with uncertainty-aware modeling. Unlike conventional regression methods limited by speckle noise, our approach leverages deformable prototypes to disentangle complex inter-subject anatomical variations and utilizes depth-adaptive probability fields to capture the physiological nature of the Deqi response. Extensive validation on a multi-center dataset demonstrates that PAPF-Net achieves superior geometric accuracy and robustly targets the correct neuro-fascial interfaces. By bridging the gap between data-driven vision and physiological reality, this work provides a reliable, interpretable foundation for safe ultrasound-guided automated acupuncture. The current evaluation covers three clinically distinct acupoint categories; broader anatomical coverage and prospective external validation remain future work.

Acknowledgments. This work was supported in part by the Sichuan Natural Science Foundation under Grant 2024NSFSC0725.

Disclosure of Interests. The authors have no competing interests to declare that are relevant to the content of this article.

References

1. Ao, Y., Wu, H.: Feature aggregation and refinement network for 2D anatomical landmark detection. J. Digit. Imaging **36**(2), 547–561 (2022)
2. Chen, J.: TransUNet: transformers make strong encoders for medical image segmentation. In: Proceedings of the International Conference on Machine Learning Workshop on Interpretable Machine Learning in Healthcare, pp. 1–13 (2021)
3. Feng, Y., Yang, J., Tang, L.: Uncertainty quantification and quality control for heatmap-based landmark detection models. IEEE Trans. Med. Imaging **44**(8), 3451–3463 (2025)
4. Gong, H., Lu, Y., Wan, X.: Domain generalized medical landmark detection via robust boundary-aware pre-training. In: Proceedings of the AAAI Conference on Artificial Intelligence, vol. 39, no. 3, pp. 3140–3148 (2025)
5. Gong, H., Wan, B., Kang, L.: Boundary as the bridge: toward heterogeneous partially-labeled medical image segmentation and landmark detection. IEEE Trans. Med. Imaging **44**(7), 2747–2756 (2025)
6. Han, R., Hu, J.: Acupuncture: an overview on its functions, meridian pathways and molecular mechanisms. Am. J. Chin. Med. **52**(05), 1215–1244 (2024)
7. Huang, T., et al.: Topological GCN for improving detection of hip landmarks from B-mode ultrasound images. In: Linguraru, M.G., Dou, Q., Feragen, A. (eds.) Medical Image Computing and Computer Assisted Intervention – MICCAI 2024, vol. 15005, pp. 692–701. Springer Nature Switzerland, Cham (2024). https://doi.org/10.1007/978-3-031-72086-4_65
8. Huang, T., Shi, J., Li, J.: Involution transformer based U-Net for landmark detection in ultrasound images for diagnosis of infantile DDH. IEEE J. Biomed. Health Informat. **28**(8), 4797–4809 (2024)
9. Kim, J.H., Noh, Y., Lee, H.: Toward automated detection of microbleeds with anatomical scale localization using deep learning. Medical Image Anal. **101**, 103415 (2025)
10. Ma, C., et al.: TinyUSFM: towards compact and efficient ultrasound foundation models. IEEE J. Biomed. Health Informat. (2026)
11. Ronneberger, O., Fischer, P., Brox, T.: U-Net: convolutional networks for biomedical image segmentation. In: Navab, N., Hornegger, J., Wells, W.M. (eds.) Medical Image Computing and Computer-Assisted Intervention – MICCAI 2015, vol. 9351, pp. 234–241. Springer International Publishing, Cham (2015)
12. Sun, W.Z., Chen, C.C., Lin, J.G.: When SNG meets acupuncture - a paradigm-shift biomarker for translational research. J. Tradit. Complement. Med. **15**(1), 1–5 (2025)
13. Wang, A., Elbatel, M., Liu, K.: Geometric-guided few-shot dental landmark detection with human-centric foundation model. In: Linguraru, M.G., et al. (eds.) Medical Image Computing and Computer Assisted Intervention – MICCAI 2025, vol. 15964, pp. 197–207. Springer Nature Switzerland, Cham (2026). https://doi.org/10.1007/978-3-031-72120-5_30
14. Wang, J., Sun, K., Cheng, T.: Deep high-resolution representation learning for visual recognition. IEEE Trans. Pattern Anal. Mach. Intell. **43**(10), 3349–3364 (2021)
15. Wu, J., Zhang, J., Gao, B.: Temporal characteristics of microstate changes representing the neuromodulation effect of acupuncture at PC6 with twirling manipulation. IEEE Trans. Comput. Soc. Syst., 1–13 (2025)

16. Xu, J., Xie, H., Liu, C.: Hip landmark detection with dependency mining in ultrasound image. IEEE Trans. Med. Imaging **40**(12), 3762–3774 (2021)
17. Yang, F., Zhou, S.K.: EDA: Enhanced Domain-Adversarial training for anatomical landmark detection. In: 2025 IEEE 22nd International Symposium on Biomedical Imaging (ISBI), pp. 1–5. IEEE, Houston, TX, USA (2025)
18. Yang, S., Li, Y., Zou, H.: Exploring an innovative deep learning solution for acupuncture point localization on the weak feature body surface of the human back. IEEE J. Biomed. Health Informat. **29**(7), 4599–4611 (2025)
19. Yu, H., Lin, Z., Li, F.: Spatiospectral representation and neural decoding of somatic perception of acupuncture stimulations. IEEE J. Biomed. Health Informat., 1–14 (2025)
20. Zhong, Z., Yao, L., Liu, Y.Z., et al.: Objectivization study of acupuncture DEQI and brain modulation mechanisms: a review. Front. Neurosci. **18**, 1386108 (2024)

PICA: Physics-Guided Implicit Neural Fields with Boundary Conditioning for Intracranial Aneurysm Hemodynamics

Mengfan Hu, Siyu Li, and Zeng Zhang(✉)

School of Biomedical Engineering and State Key Laboratory of Advanced Medical Materials and Devices, ShanghaiTech University, Shanghai 201210, China
zhangzeng@shanghaitech.edu.cn

Abstract. Patient-specific hemodynamic assessment is critical for intracranial aneurysm rupture risk stratification, yet standard computational fluid dynamics (CFD) pipelines are too time-consuming for routine clinical use. Existing learning-based surrogates enable fast inference but often produce over-smoothed velocity fields, obscuring near-wall gradients and fine-scale vortical structures that are important for clinically relevant biomarkers. We propose PICA, a boundary-conditioned implicit neural field for continuous 3D hemodynamic prediction directly from voxelized aneurysm geometries. PICA encodes signed distance field (SDF)-augmented inputs with a multi-scale backbone and conditions the representation on patient-specific inlet parameters via feature-wise modulation, enabling robust adaptation across flow regimes. An implicit coordinate-based decoder queries the learned representation at arbitrary 3D locations to generate dense velocity fields without meshing or geometric reconstruction. To improve physical fidelity, we incorporate physics-guided regularization that enforces incompressibility and steady-state Navier–Stokes consistency, together with a progressive two-stage training curriculum to enhance cross-anatomy generalization. On the Aneumo benchmark, PICA achieves sub-second inference and reduces Mean Normalised Absolute Error by 25.4% compared to DeepONet-SwinT, while better recovering complex intra-saccular vortices and near-wall flow patterns.

Keywords: Intracranial Aneurysm · Hemodynamics · Implicit Neural Representations · Physics-Guided Deep Learning

1 Introduction

Intracranial aneurysms (IAs) affect 3 to 5% of the adult population and are a leading cause of aneurysmal subarachnoid hemorrhage, carrying high early mortality and severe neurological sequelae in survivors [4,19]. Key hemodynamic parameters, such as wall shear stress (WSS), oscillatory shear index (OSI), and intra-saccular flow complexity, directly drive endothelial mechanobiology and

G. Yang et al. (Eds.): MICCAI 2026, LNCS 16893, pp. 340–350, 2027.
https://doi.org/10.1007/978-3-032-38236-8_33

progressive sac growth [6]. This interplay between biomechanical forces and wall degeneration makes patient-specific hemodynamic evaluation highly discriminative for rupture risk stratification [18,19,21]. Although computational fluid dynamics (CFD) is the gold standard for quantifying these forces, its conventional pipeline (vascular segmentation, mesh generation, and iterative Navier-Stokes solving) demands expert intervention and hours of computation per case [1,8]. Consequently, CFD remains impractical for emergency triage, population screening, and intraoperative planning.

To address these computational bottlenecks, deep learning surrogates have emerged to approximate 3D blood flow fields at a fraction of the CFD cost [7,16]. However, voxel-based CNNs are limited by fixed spatial resolutions and poor near-wall flow fidelity. Operator-learning methods like Deep Operator Networks (DeepONets) [3,11] and Fourier Neural Operators (FNOs) [5,9] offer mesh-free inference but suffer from systematic over-smoothing. This artifact suppresses crucial vortical structures and near-wall low-WSS gradients, which are precisely the features correlated with pathological wall degradation and imminent rupture [19]. Implicit neural representations (INRs) [12,13] excel in coordinate-based continuous signal encoding yet remain largely unexplored for aneurysm flow modeling. The recent Aneumo benchmark [8] highlights these inherent limitations in existing DeepONet and Swin Transformer baselines, underscoring the urgent need for a framework that ensures physical consistency, boundary condition coupling, and high-fidelity local flow resolution.

To bridge this gap, we propose **PICA** (**P**hysics-guided **I**mplicit **C**onditional **A**neurysm hemodynamics network). PICA recasts 3D hemodynamic prediction as learning a boundary condition-guided implicit neural field over an SDF-enriched voxel representation [14]. A multi-scale 3D U-Net encoder [2] extracts hierarchical geometric features, while Feature-wise Linear Modulation (FiLM) [15] explicitly conditions these features on patient-specific boundary parameters (inlet centroid position, surface normal direction, and volumetric flow rate Q). A coordinate-aware implicit decoder with Fourier positional encoding [20] then generates continuous velocity predictions at arbitrary 3D coordinates. To guarantee physical fidelity without requiring extra labeled data, dual physics-guided regularization terms enforce divergence-free and momentum-conserving outputs [17].

In summary, our main contributions are:

- We introduce PICA, an INR-based surrogate integrating SDF-enriched geometry, hierarchical FiLM boundary conditioning, and physics-guided regularization for mesh-free 3D aneurysm hemodynamic prediction.
- By enforcing divergence-free and vorticity transport constraints, PICA substantially improves the near-wall velocity field and recovers fine-grained vortical structures suppressed by existing operator-learning surrogates.
- PICA reduces MNAE by 25.4% over DeepONet-SwinT while maintaining sub-second inference, establishing state-of-the-art performance on the Aneumo benchmark.

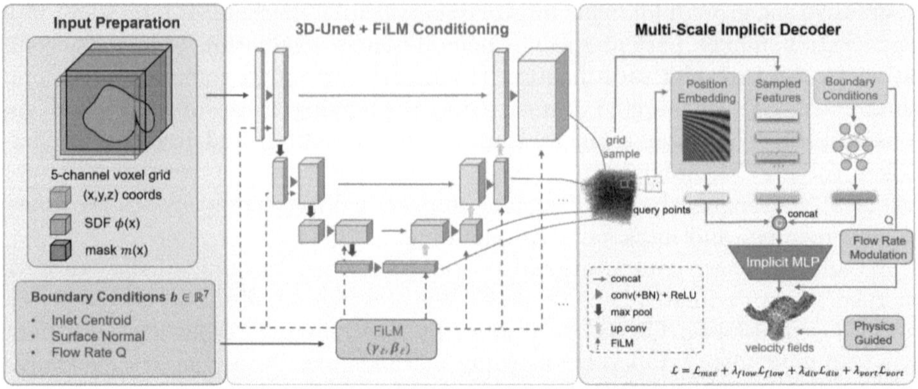

Fig. 1. Overview of the proposed PICA framework. **Left:** The input preparation module ingests a 5-channel voxel grid (3D spatial coordinates, SDF $\phi(\mathbf{x})$, and binary mask $m(\mathbf{x})$) alongside patient-specific boundary conditions $\mathbf{b} \in \mathbb{R}^7$. **Middle:** A 3D U-Net extracts multi-scale geometric features, while FiLM layers dynamically inject boundary parameters (inlet centroid, surface normal, and flow rate Q) across the feature hierarchy. **Right:** The Multi-Scale Implicit Decoder queries features at arbitrary 3D coordinates via trilinear interpolation, concatenates Fourier positional embeddings and boundary conditions, and predicts continuous 3D velocity fields supervised by a composite loss ($\mathcal{L}_{\text{mse}}$, $\mathcal{L}_{\text{div}}$, $\mathcal{L}_{\text{vort}}$) enforcing physical consistency.

2 Method

PICA maps a five-channel voxelized geometric representation $\mathcal{V} \in \mathbb{R}^{5\times 128^3}$ and patient-specific inlet boundary conditions $\mathbf{b} \in \mathbb{R}^7$ (centroid, normal direction, and flow rate Q) to a continuous 3D velocity field $\hat{\mathbf{u}}(\mathbf{x}) \in \mathbb{R}^3$ at arbitrary query coordinates $\mathbf{x}$. As illustrated in Fig. 1, the framework comprises an SDF-augmented encoder with FiLM conditioning, a multi-scale implicit decoder, and physics-guided regularization.

2.1 Geometric Encoding and FiLM Conditioning

Input Representation. While the binary lumen mask $m(\mathbf{x})$ delineates the fluid domain, the additional explicit spatial coordinates (x, y, z) and SDF $\phi(\mathbf{x})$ provide absolute positional context and continuous wall-proximity awareness. This enriched representation is critical for resolving steep near-wall velocity gradients that a mask-only input cannot capture, as confirmed by our ablation study (Table 2).

Boundary Vector Construction. For each case, the boundary vector is defined as $\mathbf{b} = [c_x, c_y, c_z, n_x, n_y, n_z, Q] \in \mathbb{R}^7$, where $\mathbf{c}$ is the inlet centroid, $\mathbf{n}$ is the unit inlet normal, and Q is the prescribed volumetric flow rate. The centroid and normal are computed automatically from the inlet boundary surface during preprocessing, without using the target CFD velocity or pressure fields; Q is taken from the simulation boundary-condition metadata and normalized using training-set statistics.

Boundary Conditioning via FiLM. $\mathcal{V}$ is processed by a symmetric 3D U-Net backbone. To adapt geometric features to patient-specific hemodynamics, boundary conditions $\mathbf{b}$ are injected across all encoder and decoder levels using Feature-wise Linear Modulation (FiLM) [15]. At each network stage ℓ, an MLP maps $\mathbf{b}$ into affine parameters $(\boldsymbol{\gamma}_\ell, \boldsymbol{\beta}_\ell)$, modulating the intermediate feature maps as $\widetilde{F}_\ell = \boldsymbol{\gamma}_\ell(\mathbf{b}) \odot F_\ell + \boldsymbol{\beta}_\ell(\mathbf{b})$. This mechanism effectively couples the static geometry with dynamic flow regimes throughout the feature hierarchy.

2.2 Coordinate-Aware Implicit Decoding

To predict continuous velocity fields without mesh generation, features are queried at arbitrary continuous coordinates $\mathbf{x}$. First, $\mathbf{x}$ is mapped to 63-dimensional high-frequency components via Fourier positional encoding [12] to capture fine-grained flow details. Concurrently, multi-resolution geometric features $\mathbf{f}(\mathbf{x})$ are sampled from four U-Net decoder stages via trilinear interpolation and fused using a learned weighted sum.

The implicit decoder, modeled as a 12-layer MLP, concatenates the Fourier-encoded coordinates, the aggregated geometric features $\mathbf{f}(\mathbf{x})$, and the re-encoded boundary conditions to predict base velocities $\hat{\mathbf{u}}_0 = [\hat{u}_0, \hat{v}_0, \hat{w}_0]^\top$. Finally, an auxiliary MLP branch predicts component-wise scaling factors $s_\eta(Q) \in \mathbb{R}^3_+$ derived from the inlet flow rate Q. The final physical velocity field is obtained via multiplicative modulation:

$$\hat{\mathbf{u}}(\mathbf{x}) = \big(s_\eta(Q) + \mathbf{1}\big) \odot \hat{\mathbf{u}}_0, \tag{1}$$

where $\mathbf{1} \in \mathbb{R}^3$ denotes the all-ones vector, whose inclusion as a learnable bias initializes the scale factors near unity to stabilize early training dynamics.

2.3 Physics-Guided Training Objective

PICA is supervised by a composite loss $\mathcal{L}$ evaluated over a set of query points $\mathcal{P}$, which combines data-driven fidelity with physics-guided regularization:

$$\mathcal{L} = \mathcal{L}_{\text{mse}} + \lambda_{\text{flow}}\mathcal{L}_{\text{flow}} + \lambda_{\text{div}}\mathcal{L}_{\text{div}} + \lambda_{\text{vort}}\mathcal{L}_{\text{vort}}. \tag{2}$$

To balance the dimensionally heterogeneous loss terms, we adopt an uncertainty-based adaptive weighting strategy. Each auxiliary objective is associated with a learnable log-variance parameter, allowing the model to automatically adjust the relative contribution of data fidelity, flow-rate consistency, incompressibility, and vorticity transport constraints during training. We initialize the auxiliary terms with scale factors $\lambda_{\text{flow}} = 10^{-6}$, $\lambda_{\text{div}} = 10^{-3}$, and

$\lambda_{\text{vort}} = 10^{-4}$ for numerical stability, while the final effective weights are learned jointly with the network parameters.

Fidelity and Scaling. The primary data-driven objective is the mean squared error (MSE) between the predicted velocity $\hat{\mathbf{u}}$ and the CFD ground-truth $\mathbf{u}^*$:

$$\mathcal{L}_{\text{mse}} = \frac{1}{|\mathcal{P}|} \sum_{\mathbf{x} \in \mathcal{P}} \left\| \hat{\mathbf{u}}(\mathbf{x}) - \mathbf{u}^*(\mathbf{x}) \right\|^2. \tag{3}$$

Additionally, assuming velocity scales linearly with the inlet flow rate Q under steady viscous conditions, we apply a soft regularization prior that penalizes inconsistencies in flow-rate-normalized mean velocity magnitudes:

$$\mathcal{L}_{\text{flow}} = \left(\frac{1}{|\mathcal{P}|} \sum_{\mathbf{x} \in \mathcal{P}} \frac{\|\hat{\mathbf{u}}(\mathbf{x})\|}{Q} - \frac{1}{|\mathcal{P}|} \sum_{\mathbf{x} \in \mathcal{P}} \frac{\|\mathbf{u}^*(\mathbf{x})\|}{Q} \right)^2, \tag{4}$$

where the summations are taken over all query points $\mathbf{x} \in \mathcal{P}$ sampled within the lumen.

Incompressibility Loss. To enforce mass conservation for incompressible blood flow, we impose a soft divergence-free constraint. Spatial partial derivatives are computed analytically via automatic differentiation, penalizing the divergence residual:

$$\mathcal{L}_{\text{div}} = \frac{1}{|\mathcal{P}|} \sum_{\mathbf{x} \in \mathcal{P}} (\nabla \cdot \hat{\mathbf{u}})^2. \tag{5}$$

Vorticity Transport Loss. Addressing the over-smoothing artifacts typical of deep learning surrogates requires explicit supervision of local flow rotational structures. Under steady-state assumptions, the vorticity $\boldsymbol{\omega} = \nabla \times \hat{\mathbf{u}}$ must satisfy the steady vorticity transport equation, derived by taking the curl of the Navier-Stokes momentum equation. We penalize this residual at each query point:

$$\mathcal{L}_{\text{vort}} = \frac{1}{|\mathcal{P}|} \sum_{\mathbf{x} \in \mathcal{P}} \left\| (\hat{\mathbf{u}} \cdot \nabla)\boldsymbol{\omega} - (\boldsymbol{\omega} \cdot \nabla)\hat{\mathbf{u}} - \nu \nabla^2 \boldsymbol{\omega} \right\|^2, \tag{6}$$

where ν denotes kinematic viscosity. This formulation explicitly models the material advection of vorticity against vortex stretching $(\boldsymbol{\omega} \cdot \nabla)\hat{\mathbf{u}}$ and viscous diffusion $\nu \nabla^2 \boldsymbol{\omega}$, effectively steering the network toward physically admissible, fine-grained solutions without requiring extra labeled data.

2.4 Two-Stage Progressive Training

To improve convergence and cross-anatomy generalization, we adopt a two-stage curriculum using identical training data for both stages.

Stage 1 (End-to-End Pretraining): The entire network is trained to establish stable, geometry-aware feature hierarchies that capture global vessel topology and local wall proximity.

Stage 2 (Decoder-Focused Fine-Tuning): The U-Net encoder weights are frozen, and only the FiLM generators and implicit decoder MLP are updated. Concentrating gradient updates on boundary-condition adaptation and local coordinate decoding prevents the degradation of generalized geometric features and mitigates overfitting.

3 Experiments and Results

3.1 Experimental Settings

Dataset. We evaluate PICA on the publicly available Aneumo benchmark [8], a large-scale repository of steady-state Navier-Stokes CFD simulations for patient-specific intracranial aneurysms. To ensure geometric independence and prevent shape leakage, the selection of the training and testing sets strictly follows the standard benchmark split established in the original paper. From the raw simulation data, we extract dense pointwise velocity ground-truth within the lumen, and construct a 5-channel voxel grid $\mathcal{V} \in \mathbb{R}^{5\times128^3}$ alongside a boundary vector $\mathbf{b} \in \mathbb{R}^7$ as our model inputs.

Implementation Details. Voxel grids are generated at an isotropic 128^3 resolution. During training, $M = 4,096$ query points are uniformly sampled within the lumen per forward pass. The PICA model ($\sim$5M parameters) is optimized using AdamW (learning rate 10^{-4}, weight decay 10^{-5}). Stage 1 pretrains all parameters end-to-end for 5000 epochs (batch size 4). Stage 2 freezes the encoder, fine-tuning only the FiLM layers and implicit decoder for an additional 1000 epochs. Models were trained on two NVIDIA RTX 6000 Ada GPUs via DistributedDataParallel.

Baselines and Metrics. We compare PICA against two representative neural operators from the Aneumo benchmark [8]: **DeepONet** [11], a branch-trunk architecture lacking explicit voxel geometry encoding; and **DeepONet-SwinT** [8], an enhanced variant using a Swin Transformer [10] branch to capture volumetric features. Both baselines were trained from scratch using the identical data split. We focus on these directly comparable benchmark baselines because they share the same data split, input-output setting, and evaluation protocol; broader comparisons with graph-based or continuous-field CFD surrogates are left for future work. We report the component-wise relative ℓ_2 errors (e_u, e_v, e_w), Mean Normalised Absolute Error (MNAE $= \frac{1}{N}\sum_{i=1}^{N}|y_i - \hat{y}_i|/(\max(\mathbf{y}) - \min(\mathbf{y}))$), and per-case inference time.

3.2 Experimental Results

Quantitative Performance. Table 1 presents the predictive performance on the test set. PICA achieves the lowest errors across all metrics. Compared to the strongest baseline, DeepONet-SwinT, PICA reduces the MNAE by 25.4% while maintaining comparable sub-second inference speeds. The significant improvement over plain DeepONet highlights that point-cloud or mesh queries alone are insufficient; integrating SDF-enriched voxel features with hierarchical FiLM conditioning is crucial for resolving complex near-wall gradients under limited training data.

Qualitative Analysis. Figure 2 visualizes cross-sectional velocity magnitude contours alongside absolute error distributions. DeepONet broadly overestimates intra-saccular velocities due to its lack of spatial context. DeepONet-SwinT captures the general topology but distorts the central high-velocity jet. In contrast, PICA recovers sharp boundary transitions and accurately delineates primary flow structures. The error maps (bottom row) confirm that PICA's residuals are sparse and low-magnitude, outperforming the baselines.

Table 1. Quantitative comparison on the Aneumo test set. e_u, e_v, e_w: component-wise relative ℓ_2 error (%). MNAE: Mean Normalised Absolute Error. Best results are highlighted in **bold**.

Method	e_u (↓)	e_v (↓)	e_w (↓)	MNAE (↓)	Time (s) (↓)
DeepONet [11]	0.5044	0.4930	0.4651	0.0635	**0.0020**
DeepONet-SwinT [8]	0.4480	0.4306	0.3990	0.0512	0.0100
PICA (Ours)	**0.3531**	**0.3770**	**0.3466**	**0.0382**	0.0083

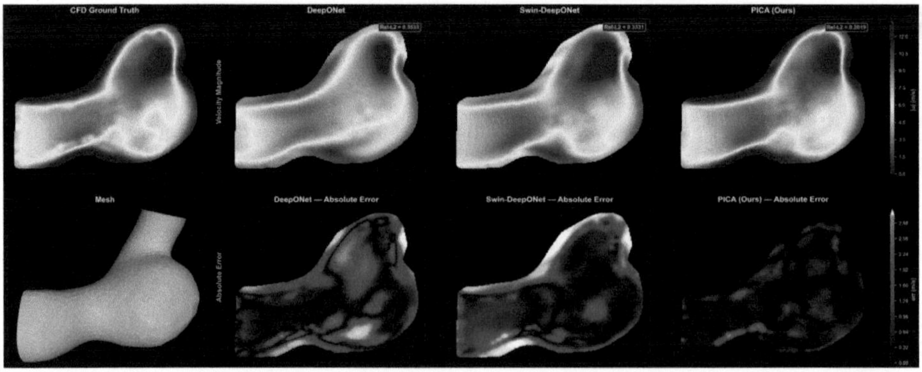

Fig. 2. Qualitative comparison of velocity magnitudes on a representative test geometry (Case 191). Top: Cross-sectional contour maps of CFD ground-truth and surrogate predictions, annotated with relative ℓ_2 errors. **Bottom:** 3D geometric mesh and corresponding absolute error maps. PICA significantly reduces local residuals, especially near the high-velocity jet and the vessel wall.

Further 3D flow evaluations are presented in Fig. 3. Streamline visualizations (Fig. 3a) reveal that both baselines suffer from severe over-smoothing, failing to reconstruct the complex swirling vortex within the aneurysm sac. PICA, guided by its vorticity transport loss, faithfully reproduces these fine-grained vortical structures, achieving an ℓ_2 error of 0.347. Furthermore, near-wall flow distributions (Fig. 3b) show that PICA accurately maps the high- and low-flow spatial regimes, effectively overcoming the systematic over-smoothing limitations of existing models.

3.3 Ablation Studies

Table 2 quantifies the contribution of PICA's core components using the test-set MNAE. Replacing the 5-channel input with a mask-only representation causes the largest performance drop (+52.1%), indicating that explicit spatial coordinates and SDF are the most critical cues for near-wall velocity resolution.

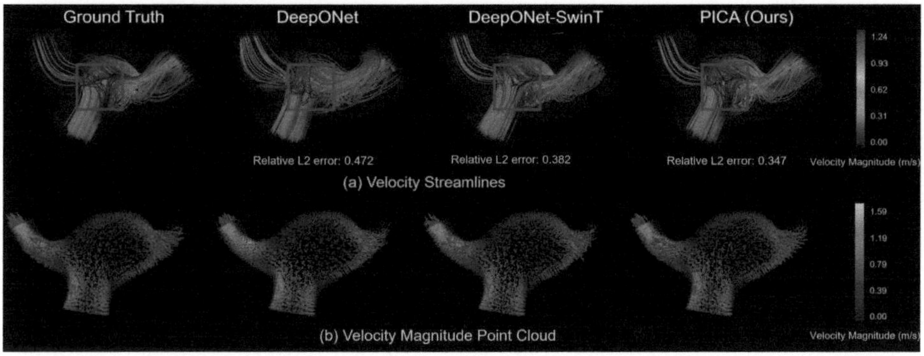

Fig. 3. 3D hemodynamic flow reconstruction. (a) Velocity streamlines highlighting complex intra-saccular recirculation (red boxes). PICA effectively mitigates the over-smoothing seen in baselines. **(b)** Cross-sectional velocity magnitude point clouds demonstrating PICA's superior fidelity in capturing near-wall gradients.

Table 2. Ablation study on the Aneumo test set. MNAE is averaged across all velocity components. Δ denotes the relative error increase compared to the full model (↑ indicates a performance drop when the component is removed). Best result is in **bold**.

Configuration	**MNAE** (↓)	Δ
w/o Geometric Encoding (Mask only)	0.0581	+52.1% (↑)
w/o Hierarchical FiLM (Late fusion)	0.0493	+29.0% (↑)
w/o Multi-scale Querying	0.0452	+18.3% (↑)
w/o Physics Constraints ($\mathcal{L}_{\text{flow,div,vort}}$)	0.0438	+14.6% (↑)
w/o Two-stage Training (Single-stage)	0.0415	+8.6% (↑)
PICA (Full Model)	**0.0382**	–

Reducing the 9-stage hierarchical FiLM to a single late-fusion concatenation raises errors by 29.0%, confirming the necessity of deep boundary-condition adaptation. Removing the multi-scale decoder feature sampling degrades accuracy by 18.3%, validating the importance of coarse-to-fine aggregation. Omitting the physics constraints ($\mathcal{L}_{\text{flow,div,vort}}$) impairs performance by 14.6%, specifically harming the prediction of high-velocity jets and vortical flows. Finally, reverting to single-stage training (without encoder freezing) increases errors by 8.6%, proving that our progressive curriculum actively mitigates overfitting and enhances geometric feature generalization without requiring additional data.

4 Discussion and Conclusion

In this work, we propose PICA, a physics-guided implicit neural framework that recasts 3D intracranial aneurysm hemodynamic prediction as a boundary-conditioned continuous field learning problem. By synergistically integrating SDF-enriched geometric encoding with hierarchical FiLM-based boundary conditioning, PICA circumvents the severe over-smoothing artifacts pervasive in existing operator-learning surrogates. Evaluated on the Aneumo benchmark, our method significantly outperforms state-of-the-art DeepONet baselines, recovering fine-grained near-wall gradients and complex vortical structures while maintaining sub-second inference speeds. Furthermore, our two-stage progressive training curriculum establishes highly robust geometric representations, ensuring strong cross-anatomy generalization under limited training data.

Despite these advances, PICA currently focuses on steady-state velocity predictions within synthetic geometries. This setting enables efficient reconstruction of patient-specific velocity fields and serves as a foundation for future extensions toward richer hemodynamic analyses. Temporal indices such as OSI and pressure-related analyses require time-resolved pulsatile modeling, and will therefore be explored in future extensions. Future work will further extend the implicit formulation to capture pulsatile flow dynamics and intravascular pressure variations, compare with broader surrogate families, and validate the framework on in-vivo, patient-specific clinical data.

Acknowledgments. This work is supported by ShanghaiTech AI4S Initiative SHTAI4S202404.

Disclosure of Interests. The authors have no competing interests to declare that are relevant to the content of this article.

References

1. Cebral, J.R., Mut, F., Weir, J., Putman, C.M.: Association of hemodynamic characteristics and cerebral aneurysm rupture. Am. J. Neuroradiol. **32**(2), 264–270 (2011)

2. Çiçek, Ö., Abdulkadir, A., Lienkamp, S.S., Brox, T., Ronneberger, O.: 3D U-Net: learning dense volumetric segmentation from sparse annotation. In: International Conference on Medical Image Computing and Computer-Assisted Intervention, pp. 424–432. Springer (2016)
3. Cruz-González, O.L., Deplano, V., Ghattas, B.: Enhanced vascular flow simulations in aortic aneurysm via physics-informed neural networks and deep operator networks. Mech. Res. Commun. **153**, 104642 (2026)
4. Etminan, N., Rinkel, G.J.: Unruptured intracranial aneurysms: development, rupture and preventive management. Nat. Rev. Neurol. **12**(12), 699–713 (2016)
5. Flouris, K., et al.: Localized FNO for spatiotemporal hemodynamic upsampling in aneurysm MRI. In: International Workshop on Reconstruction and Imaging Motion Estimation, pp. 65–75. Springer (2025)
6. Kadem, M., Garber, L., Abdelkhalek, M., Al-Khazraji, B.K., Keshavarz-Motamed, Z.: Hemodynamic modeling, medical imaging, and machine learning and their applications to cardiovascular interventions. IEEE Rev. Biomed. Eng. **16**, 403–423 (2022)
7. Kochkov, D., Smith, J.A., Alieva, A., Wang, Q., Brenner, M.P., Hoyer, S.: Machine learning-accelerated computational fluid dynamics. Proc. Natl. Acad. Sci. **118**(21), e2101784118 (2021)
8. Li, X., et al.: Aneumo: A large-scale comprehensive synthetic dataset of aneurysm hemodynamics. arXiv preprint arXiv:2501.09980 (2025)
9. Li, Z., et al.: Fourier neural operator for parametric partial differential equations. arXiv preprint arXiv:2010.08895 (2020)
10. Liu, Z., et al.: Swin transformer: hierarchical vision transformer using shifted windows. In: Proceedings of the IEEE/CVF International Conference on Computer Vision, pp. 10012–10022 (2021)
11. Lu, L., Jin, P., Pang, G., Zhang, Z., Karniadakis, G.E.: Learning nonlinear operators via DeepONet based on the universal approximation theorem of operators. Nat. Mach. Intell. **3**(3), 218–229 (2021)
12. Mildenhall, B., Srinivasan, P.P., Tancik, M., Barron, J.T., Ramamoorthi, R., Ng, R.: NeRF: representing scenes as neural radiance fields for view synthesis. Commun. ACM **65**(1), 99–106 (2021)
13. Molaei, A., et al.: Implicit neural representation in medical imaging: a comparative survey. In: Proceedings of the IEEE/CVF International Conference on Computer Vision, pp. 2381–2391 (2023)
14. Park, J.J., Florence, P., Straub, J., Newcombe, R., Lovegrove, S.: DeepSDF: learning continuous signed distance functions for shape representation. In: Proceedings of the IEEE/CVF Conference on Computer Vision and Pattern Recognition, pp. 165–174 (2019)
15. Perez, E., Strub, F., De Vries, H., Dumoulin, V., Courville, A.: FiLM: visual reasoning with a general conditioning layer. In: Proceedings of the AAAI Conference on Artificial Intelligence, vol. 32 (2018)
16. Pfaff, T., Fortunato, M., Sanchez-Gonzalez, A., Battaglia, P.: Learning mesh-based simulation with graph networks. In: International Conference on Learning Representations (2020)
17. Raissi, M., Perdikaris, P., Karniadakis, G.E.: Physics-informed neural networks: a deep learning framework for solving forward and inverse problems involving nonlinear partial differential equations. J. Comput. Phys. **378**, 686–707 (2019)
18. Sforza, D.M., Putman, C.M., Cebral, J.R.: Hemodynamics of cerebral aneurysms. Annu. Rev. Fluid Mech. **41**(1), 91–107 (2009)

19. Soldozy, S., et al.: The biophysical role of hemodynamics in the pathogenesis of cerebral aneurysm formation and rupture. Neurosurg. Focus **47**(1), E11 (2019)
20. Tancik, M., et al.: Fourier features let networks learn high frequency functions in low dimensional domains. Adv. Neural. Inf. Process. Syst. **33**, 7537–7547 (2020)
21. Turjman, A.S., Turjman, F., Edelman, E.R.: Role of fluid dynamics and inflammation in intracranial aneurysm formation. Circulation **129**(3), 373–382 (2014)

PINNOCHIO: Physics-Informed Neural Network for Coupled Hyperelastic Interface-Volume Simulation in Orthognathic Surgery

Jungwook Lee[1], Daeseung Kim[2], Kevin Gu[2], Zhangfeng Hu[1], Tianshu Kuang[2], Finn Hopeman[1], Michael A. K. Liebschner[3], Jaime Gateno[2], and Pingkun Yan[1](✉)

[1] Department of Biomedical Engineering and Center for Biotechnology and Interdisciplinary Studies, Rensselaer Polytechnic Institute, Troy, NY 12180, USA
yanp2@rpi.edu

[2] Department of Oral and Maxillofacial Surgery, Houston Methodist Research Institute, Houston, TX 77030, USA

[3] Department of Neurosurgery, Baylor College of Medicine, Houston, TX 77030, USA

Abstract. Predicting patient-specific facial soft-tissue deformation is critical for iterative orthognathic surgery planning. However, current computational methods face a strict accuracy-efficiency trade-off: high-fidelity Finite Element Methods (FEM) are computationally prohibitive, whereas pure deep learning models often produce biomechanically inconsistent results. While Physics-Informed Neural Networks (PINNs) offer a promising avenue, learning the complex heterogeneous mechanics of bone–soft-tissue interactions with only partial clinical supervision (i.e., outer facial surfaces) remains highly unstable. To overcome these challenges, we present PINNOCHIO, a novel physics-informed framework for facial soft-tissue simulation. PINNOCHIO introduces a hybrid sequential decomposition that explicitly decouples discontinuous bone–soft-tissue interface movements from continuous volumetric hyperelastic deformation. This structural separation enables stable training and facilitates a physics-enabled sim-to-real adaptation strategy, ensuring internal biomechanical consistency without requiring volumetric ground truth. Evaluated on a 40-patient clinical cohort, PINNOCHIO outperforms existing baselines in both surface accuracy and physical validity. Furthermore, it achieves a substantial speedup over FEM, successfully resolving the accuracy-efficiency trade-off to provide a highly reliable and practical tool for interactive surgical planning. Source code is available at https://github.com/RPIDIAL/PINNOCHIO.

Keywords: Orthognathic Surgery · Physics-Informed Neural Networks · Facial Soft-tissue Simulation · Biomechanics

G. Yang et al. (Eds.): MICCAI 2026, LNCS 16893, pp. 351–361, 2027.
https://doi.org/10.1007/978-3-032-38236-8_34

1 Introduction

Orthognathic surgery aims to correct dentofacial deformities by repositioning the jawbones to restore facial harmony. To achieve optimal outcomes, surgeons must iteratively evaluate multiple candidate plans by simulating the corresponding soft-tissue responses [5,19,22]. However, this task is fundamentally challenging due to the highly non-linear mechanical relationship between the rigid bone and the surrounding soft tissues [7,15]. Consequently, there is a pressing clinical need for simulation tools that balance biomechanical rigor with computational efficiency, enabling interactive planning while reducing manual trial-and-error [1,15,16,25]. Current computational methods face a fundamental trade-off between accuracy and efficiency [1]. High-fidelity patient-specific finite element methods (FEM) provide biomechanical rigor but are computationally prohibitive and require extensive subject-specific parameter tuning, limiting their practicality for iterative planning [1,15,20]. Conversely, pure data-driven deep learning models [3,6] offer rapid inference speeds but remain physics-agnostic. Lacking physical constraints, these approaches may produce geometrically plausible surfaces, yet they often yield biomechanically inconsistent internal behaviors, such as volumetric distortion or element inversion [10,21].

Physics-Informed Neural Networks (PINNs) [12,23,24] offer a promising avenue to reconcile this trade-off by incorporating governing physical equations directly into the loss function. However, applying a unified PINN framework to real-world orthognathic planning is hindered by two fundamental barriers. First, surgical deformation exhibits heterogeneous mechanics: discontinuous sliding at the bone–soft-tissue interface and large, continuous hyperelastic deformation within the tissue volume [13]. Jointly optimizing these mechanically distinct regimes within a single PINN often results in unstable training dynamics and degraded convergence [14]. Second, clinical supervision is inherently limited; while post-operative volumetric imaging (e.g., CT/CBCT) is available, internal tissue motion lacks dense correspondence [18]. This confines supervision primarily to the outer facial surface [2,8], where purely data-driven learning cannot guarantee physically consistent internal fields. Crucially, internal tissue behavior is itself clinically relevant: surgeons assess how muscle and fat redistribute to judge whether a candidate bone plan is plausible, so a simulation matching the outer surface yet producing invalid internal deformation cannot support this reasoning. Together, these challenges motivate a structured, sequential architecture that (i) predicts interface displacements and (ii) propagates them through the volume with physical constraints, allowing for end-to-end fine-tuning under surface-only clinical supervision.

To address these challenges, we propose **PINNOCHIO** (Physics-Informed Neural Network for Coupled Hyperelastic Interface-Volume Simulation in Orthognathic Surgery), a framework for simulating soft-tissue deformation driven by skeletal repositioning that integrates data-driven efficiency with physics-based regularization. Our main contributions are summarized as follows:

- **Resolving Accuracy-Efficiency Trade-off**: We present a fast, physics-consistent simulator that bridges the accuracy gap to high-fidelity FEM simulations, enabling rapid and biomechanically valid iterative planning.
- **Hybrid Sequential Decomposition**: We propose a sequential decomposition to handle heterogeneous surgical mechanics by explicitly decoupling discontinuous interface motion from continuous volumetric hyperelastic deformation, improving training stability and convergence on complex anatomies.
- **Physics-Enabled Sim-to-Real Adaptation**: We introduce an adaptation strategy that bridges synthetic FEM supervision and clinical data by fine-tuning with postoperative outer facial surface supervision only, encouraging internal physical consistency without requiring volumetric ground truth.

Quantitative validation on a 40-patient clinical cohort demonstrates that PINNOCHIO outperforms representative baselines in both surface accuracy and physical validity, supporting its clinical viability for real-world surgical planning.

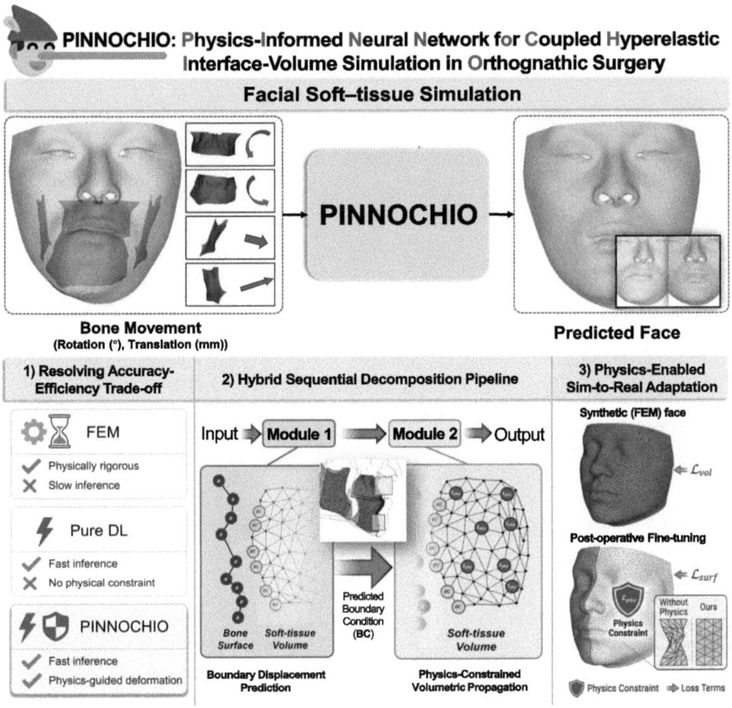

Fig. 1. PINNOCHIO for facial soft-tissue simulation. **1)** Accuracy-efficiency trade-off in existing FEM and physics-agnostic deep learning. **2)** Proposed sequential decomposition: interface prediction followed by physics-constrained volumetric propagation. **3)** Physics-guided sim-to-real adaptation using surface-only clinical supervision.

2 Problem Setup

Let $\Omega_0 \subset \mathbb{R}^3$ denote the patient's preoperative soft-tissue volume (muscle, fat, and skin). Our goal is to estimate a 3D displacement field u mapping Ω_0 to its postoperative configuration (Fig. 1). We focus on two clinically meaningful boundary subsets $\partial\Omega_0$: (i) the bone–soft-tissue interface Γ_{bnd}, where soft-tissue contacts the repositioned bony segments, and (ii) the facial outer surface Γ_{face}, corresponding to the visible external skin surface.

To characterize surgical contact behavior, we partition the Γ_{bnd} nodes into three subsets: *fixed* regions that remain fixed during surgery, *moving* regions that are strictly following the prescribed rigid bone movement, and *sliding* regions where non-rigid interface movement may occur. Let V denote the set of all discretized nodes in Ω_0, which we partition into the interface node set V_{bnd} and the remaining free node $V_{\text{free}} := V \setminus V_{\text{bnd}}$, where mechanical equilibrium is enforced. The input is a bone plan $\mathcal{P} = \{(R_k, t_k)\}_{k=1}^{K}$, representing the rigid transformations (rotation R_k, translation t_k) for K bone segments.

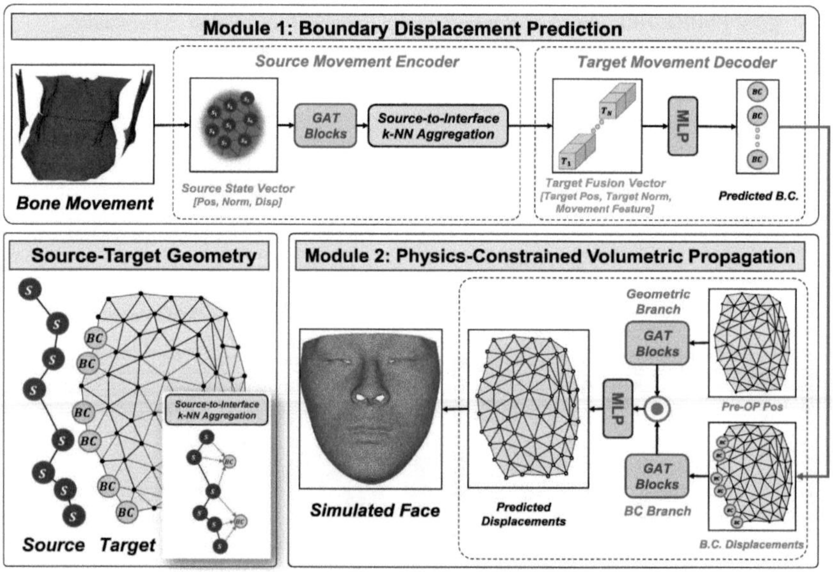

Fig. 2. PINNOCHIO architecture. The boundary displacement prediction module estimates interface displacements from bone movements, and the volumetric propagation module propagates these displacements throughout the volume.

3 PINNOCHIO Framework

3.1 Overview of the PINNOCHIO Framework

To address the heterogeneous biomechanics of facial soft tissue, where discontinuous sliding at contact interfaces coexists with continuous hyperelastic deformation within the volume, PINNOCHIO adopts a hybrid sequential inference pipeline (Fig. 2). The framework consists of two coupled modules: **(1) Boundary Displacement Prediction**, which estimates non-rigid displacements on the bone–soft-tissue interface, and **(2) Physics-Constrained Volumetric Propagation**, which treats these predictions as boundary conditions to propagate deformation throughout the volume under physics-based constraints. To reflect heterogeneous tissue properties, we partition the preoperative volume Ω_0 into two distinct anatomical layers: a deep muscular layer Ω_{mus} (contractile tissues), and a superficial layer Ω_{sup} (fat and skin).

3.2 Network Modules

Boundary Displacement Prediction. To predict boundary displacements u_{bnd} on the interface node set V_{bnd}, we implement the predictor P_{bnd} as an encoder–decoder that maps a source-structure graph (bone or muscle) to interface-vertex displacements (Fig. 2). Because different interfaces are driven by different anatomical structures (e.g., bone–muscle, bone–superficial, and muscle–superficial), we adopt a flexible source–target design. First, a Source Encoder processes the relevant source structure using a Graph Attention Network (GAT) [4] to capture local geometry and varying kinematic patterns. Next, through Source-to-Interface k-NN Aggregation, we collect and apply max-pooling features from k nearby source nodes to form a local context vector for each interface vertex. Finally, an MLP Decoder predicts the final boundary displacement by combining the aggregated features with a reference movement cue c_{ref}. This cue embeds known surgical priors: zero for *fixed* regions and rigid bone movement for *moving* regions. Crucially, a binary reliability mask indicates where this cue is valid, guiding the network to focus entirely on learning the unknown, non-trivial *sliding* regions.

Volumetric Propagation. The Volumetric Propagator P_{vol} propagates the predicted boundary displacement u_{bnd} throughout the soft-tissue domain to estimate a nodal displacement field u over the entire volumetric mesh, including free nodes V_{free}. We implement P_{vol} as a Dual-Branch GNN that fuses mesh geometry with boundary displacement cues. The Geometric Branch encodes the preoperative coordinates of the mesh, while the Boundary Condition (BC) Branch encodes the sparse boundary signal u_{sparse} (where $u_{\text{sparse}} = u_{\text{bnd}}$ on V_{bnd} and zero elsewhere) alongside a mask m indicating nodes with prescribed boundary displacements. Both branches utilize GAT blocks to aggregate local neighborhood information. The resulting embeddings are concatenated and passed through an MLP decoder to predict the final dense volumetric displacement field u.

3.3 Physics-Constrained Training of PINNOCHIO

Physics Loss. To encourage biomechanical validity without internal ground truth, we model facial soft tissue as a Neo-Hookean hyperelastic material [26]. For each tetrahedral element with volume V_e, the deformation gradient is defined as $F_e = I + \nabla u$, where ∇u is the element-wise displacement gradient. The strain energy density is defined as:

$$\Psi(F_e) = \frac{\mu}{2}(\mathrm{tr}(F_e^\top F_e) - 3) - \mu \ln J_e + \frac{\lambda}{2}(\ln J_e)^2, \quad (1)$$

where $J_e = \det(F_e)$, and the Lamé parameters μ and λ are spatially assigned to reflect heterogeneous tissue stiffness. We derive the first Piola–Kirchhoff stress $P_e = \frac{\partial \Psi}{\partial F_e}$ [9] to compute nodal internal forces $f_{\mathrm{int}}(v_i)$ using standard finite-element shape-function gradients. We enforce quasi-static equilibrium on free interior nodes V_{free} by penalizing the internal force residual:

$$\mathcal{L}_{\mathrm{phy}} = \frac{1}{|V_{\mathrm{free}}|} \sum_{v_i \in V_{\mathrm{free}}} \|f_{\mathrm{int}}(v_i)\|_2^2. \quad (2)$$

Outer-Surface Loss. Since dense point-to-point correspondence is unavailable for the clinically observed postoperative outer surface Γ_{face}, we enforce surface agreement using the symmetric Chamfer Distance between the predicted surface (S_{pred}) and post-operative surface (S_{post}):

$$\mathcal{L}_{\mathrm{surf}} = \mathcal{L}_{\mathrm{CD}}(S_{\mathrm{pred}}, S_{\mathrm{post}}) \quad (3)$$

Boundary Consistency Loss. Since the boundary displacement u_{bnd} is provided as a boundary displacement input to the volumetric propagator, we encourage the predicted displacement field u to remain consistent with u_{int} on the boundary nodes V_{bnd}, enforcing soft consistency rather than hard constraints:

$$\mathcal{L}_{\mathrm{bnd}} = \frac{1}{|V_{\mathrm{bnd}}|} \sum_{v_i \in V_{\mathrm{bnd}}} \|u(v_i) - u_{\mathrm{bnd}}(v_i)\|_2^2. \quad (4)$$

Overall Training Objective. The total loss balances these objectives with weighting coefficients (λ_{phy}, λ_{surf}, and λ_{bnd}) that balance physical consistency, clinical surface agreement, and interface boundary consistency:

$$\mathcal{L}_{\mathrm{total}} = \lambda_{\mathrm{phy}} \mathcal{L}_{\mathrm{phy}} + \lambda_{\mathrm{surf}} \mathcal{L}_{\mathrm{surf}} + \lambda_{\mathrm{bnd}} \mathcal{L}_{\mathrm{bnd}}, \quad (5)$$

Physics-Enabled Sim-to-Real Adaptation. To stabilize optimization, we first pretrain PINNOCHIO on FEM-simulated data, replacing the outer-surface loss with a volumetric mean-squared error (MSE) against ground-truth displacements. We then fine-tune end-to-end on real postoperative cases using the overall objective ($\mathcal{L}_{\mathrm{total}}$), relying on the outer-surface loss ($\mathcal{L}_{\mathrm{surf}}$) alongside the physics and boundary constraints. PINNOCHIO is trained in a population-wise manner; once trained, it is applied to new cases without per-case re-training.

4 Experiments and Results

4.1 Experimental Setup

We evaluated PINNOCHIO on 40 clinical orthognathic surgery cases (IRB: MOD00005116) using five-fold cross-validation. Each case includes a planned rigid movement of four bone segments (LeFort I, mandibular distal, and bilateral distal segments). From pre-operative CT scans, we obtained anatomical segmentations (bone, muscle, and superficial tissue) using Skull-Engine [17], and further refined to reflect the surgical movements. The bone was represented as a triangular surface mesh, while muscle and superficial tissue were tetrahedral volumetric meshes. Post-operative outer facial surfaces were extracted from 3dMD scans for supervision. For sim-to-real pre-training, FEM-simulated data were generated using FEM-RLSE [13], the same simulator as our FEM baseline. Pre-training and clinical fine-tuning were conducted under the same five-fold split with strict patient-level separation, ensuring no data leakage between the two stages.

We compared PINNOCHIO against a high-fidelity FEM simulator (FEM-RLSE [13]) and representative deep learning baselines (ACMT-Net [6], DGCFP [11]). Surface accuracy was evaluated using Chamfer Distance (CD) and Hausdorff Distance (HD), and Patient-level Within-threshold Rate (PWR, %), defined as the percentage of the facial surface area where the prediction error falls below a predefined clinical threshold (e.g., 2 mm), averaged across all patients. Mesh validity was assessed using the minimum Jacobian determinant (J) for element inversion, and Equilibrium Residual (EqRes) for physical consistency. Statistical significance was evaluated using the Wilcoxon signed-rank test [27]. Loss weights ($\lambda_{\text{phy}}, \lambda_{\text{surf}}, \lambda_{\text{bnd}}$) were empirically set to $(1.0, 2.0, 1.0)$. Hyperelastic parameters were set per tissue type, with Young's modulus $E = 6$ kPa and Poisson's ratio $\nu = 0.49$ for muscle, and $E = 4$ kPa, $\nu = 0.49$ for the superficial layer. To stabilize optimization, each module is trained separately and then combined for end-to-end fine-tuning, avoiding joint-optimization instability; FEM pre-training further provides a physics-consistent initialization. Training takes approximately 4 h for pre-training and 2 h for fine-tuning, and inference time was measured on a NVIDIA DGX-1 server with V100 GPUs.

Table 1. Quantitative comparison on whole-face surface accuracy and inference time. ↑/↓: higher/lower is better. Best results are in bold.

Method	CD(mm)↓	HD(mm)↓	PWR@1mm(%)↑	PWR@2mm(%)↑	Time(s)↓
ACMT-Net [6]	2.19±0.79*	5.56±2.35*	36.04±12.98*	63.59±14.97*	**0.10**
DGCFP [11]	1.71±0.62*	4.94±2.03*	47.28±12.36*	72.43±12.18*	0.54
FEM-RLSE [13]	1.30±0.29*	3.16±0.80*	50.83±10.97*	80.90±10.12*	1.26×10^4
PINNOCHIO	**1.12±0.26**	**2.73±0.69**	**58.36±12.60**	**86.55±8.42**	3.24

Table 2. Incremental ablation of decomposition and physics regularization. Lower is better for CD and EqRes, while higher is better for PWR and J.

Decomposition	Physics Loss	Surface Distance		Mesh Validity	
		CD(mm)↓	PWR@1mm(%)↑	EqRes↓	J↑
	✓	1.04±0.27*	62.35±11.74*	0.25±0.34	0.86±0.04
✓		1.02±0.24*	64.10±12.63	1.73±1.14*	0.68±0.14*
✓	✓	**0.98±0.22**	**64.88±11.58**	**0.20±0.34**	**0.87±0.05**

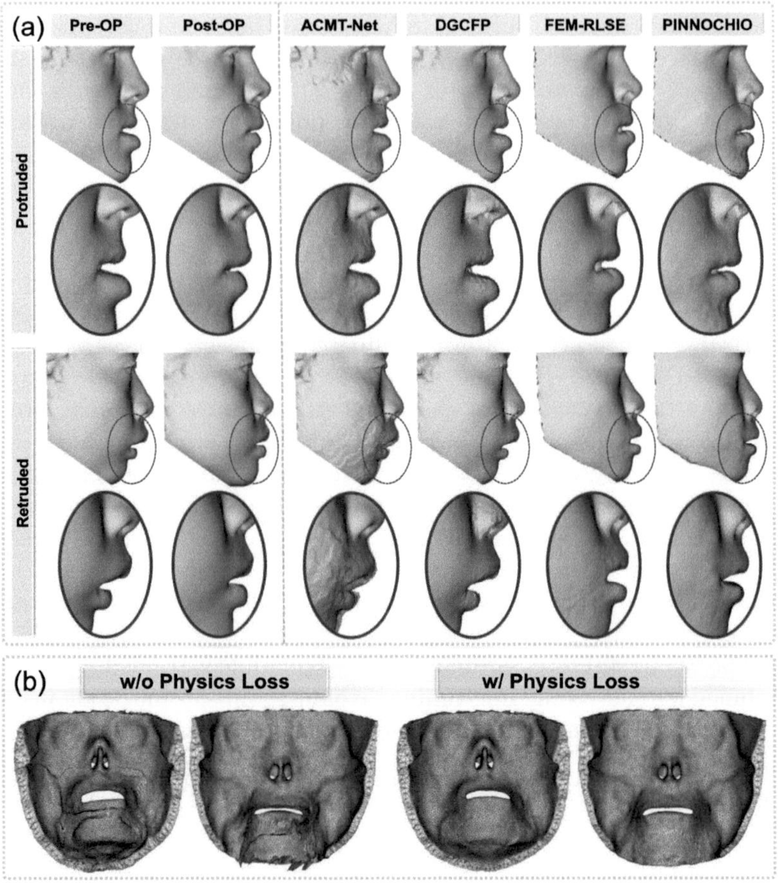

Fig. 3. Qualitative results. **(a)** Predicted results compared with baselines and ground truth on representative cases. **(b)** Impact of physics-based regularization ($\mathcal{L}_{\text{phy}}$). Posterior views show how physics constraints suppress element inversion and artifacts.

4.2 Results

Table 1 compares PINNOCHIO with FEM (FEM-RLSE) and deep learning baselines (ACMT-Net, DGCFP). Our method achieved the lowest surface error (CD: 1.12 mm, HD: 2.73 mm) and highest PWR@2mm (86.55%). Furthermore, PIN-

NOCHIO required only 3.24 seconds per case, compared to 3.5 hours (1.26×10^4 s) for FEM-RLSE, achieving a substantial speedup while maintaining superior accuracy. Qualitatively (Fig. **3(a)**), PINNOCHIO's predictions closely resemble the post-operative ground truth on par with FEM-RLSE across both protruded and retruded patient profiles, accurately capturing complex soft-tissue deformations where deep learning baselines fail.

Table 2 ablates the sequential decomposition against a unified PINN structure that jointly models the interface and volumetric domains. This decomposition yielded meaningful improvements in surface accuracy and physical equilibrium (EqRes), demonstrating that decoupling heterogeneous mechanics facilitates more effective learning. Additionally, removing the physics loss increased surface errors and degraded volumetric mesh validity (J), indicating reduced biomechanical consistency. As shown in Fig. **3(b)**, relying solely on outer-surface supervision produced geometrically unstable internal deformations, whereas the physics term ensured smooth, physically coherent volumes.

5 Conclusions

We presented PINNOCHIO, a physics-informed framework for facial soft-tissue simulation in orthognathic surgery. By sequentially decomposing interface prediction and volumetric propagation, our approach enables stable learning under surface-only supervision. Achieving competitive accuracy and a substantial speedup over FEM, it facilitates real-time iterative planning. Future work will incorporate broader surgical variations (e.g., genioplasty) and integrating patient-specific material estimation (e.g., via ultrasound) to further enhance biomechanical fidelity. Overall, PINNOCHIO provides a practical and extensible basis for clinically deployable surgical planning.

Acknowledgments. This work was supported by the National Institutes of Health (NIH) under awards R01DE027251 and R01DE021863.

Disclosure of Interests. No competing interests declared.

References

1. Alcañiz, P., et al.: Soft-tissue simulation for computational planning of orthognathic surgery. J. Personalized Med. **11**(10), 982 (2021)
2. Awad, D., Reinert, S., Kluba, S.: Accuracy of three-dimensional soft-tissue prediction considering the facial aesthetic units using a virtual planning system in orthognathic surgery. J. Personalized Med. **12**(9), 1379 (2022)
3. Berends, B., et al.: Soft-tissue prediction based on 3D photographs for virtual surgery planning of orthognathic surgery. Comput. Biol. Med. **194**, 110529 (2025)
4. Brody, S., Alon, U., Yahav, E.: How attentive are graph attention networks?. arXiv preprint arXiv:2105.14491 (2021)
5. Dall'Magro, A.K., Dogenski, L.C., Dall'Magro, E., Figur, N.S., Trentin, M.S., De Carli, J.P.: Orthognathic surgery and orthodontics associated with orofacial harmonization: case report. Int. J. Surg. Case Rep. **83**, 106013 (2021)

6. Fang, X., et al.: Correspondence attention for facial appearance simulation. Med. Image Anal. **93**, 103094 (2024)
7. Flynn, C., Taberner, A.J., Nielsen, P.M., Fels, S.: Simulating the three-dimensional deformation of in vivo facial skin. J. Mech. Behav. Biomed. Mater. **28**, 484–494 (2013)
8. Franco, A.A., et al.: Three-dimensional long-term assessment of soft tissue stability after orthognathic mandibular advancement for class II malocclusion correction. Clin. Oral Invest. **29**(3), 167 (2025)
9. Holzapfel, G.A.: Nonlinear solid mechanics: a continuum approach for engineering science (2002)
10. Hu, S., Chen, X.: Preventing self-intersection with cycle regularization in neural networks for mesh reconstruction from a single RGB image. Comput. Aided Geom. Des. **72**, 84–97 (2019)
11. Huang, X., He, D., Li, Z., Zhang, X., Wang, X.: Maxillofacial bone movements-aware dual graph convolution approach for postoperative facial appearance prediction. Med. Image Anal. **99**, 103350 (2025)
12. Karniadakis, G.E., Kevrekidis, I.G., Lu, L., Perdikaris, P., Wang, S., Yang, L.: Physics-informed machine learning. Nat. Rev. Phys. **3**(6), 422–440 (2021)
13. Kim, D., Kuang, T., Rodrigues, Y.L., Gateno, J., Shen, S.G., Wang, X., Stein, K., Deng, H.H., Liebschner, M.A., Xia, J.J.: A novel incremental simulation of facial changes following orthognathic surgery using fem with realistic lip sliding effect. Med. Image Anal. **72**, 102095 (2021)
14. Krishnapriyan, A., Gholami, A., Zhe, S., Kirby, R., Mahoney, M.W.: Characterizing possible failure modes in physics-informed neural networks. Adv. Neural. Inf. Process. Syst. **34**, 26548–26560 (2021)
15. Lampen, N., et al.: Deep learning for biomechanical modeling of facial tissue deformation in orthognathic surgical planning. Int. J. Comput. Assist. Radiol. Surg. **17**(5), 945–952 (2022)
16. Lampen, N., et al.: Spatiotemporal incremental mechanics modeling of facial tissue change. In: International Conference on Medical Image Computing and Computer-Assisted Intervention. LNCS, vol. 14228, pp. 566–575. Springer, Cham (2023). https://doi.org/10.1007/978-3-031-43996-4_54
17. Liu, Q., Deng, H., Lian, C., Chen, X., Xiao, D., Ma, L., Chen, X., Kuang, T., Gateno, J., Yap, P.-T., Xia, J.J.: SkullEngine: A Multi-stage CNN Framework for Collaborative CBCT Image Segmentation and Landmark Detection. In: Lian, C., Cao, X., Rekik, I., Xu, X., Yan, P. (eds.) MLMI 2021. LNCS, vol. 12966, pp. 606–614. Springer, Cham (2021). https://doi.org/10.1007/978-3-030-87589-3_62
18. Mollemans, W., Schutyser, F., Nadjmi, N., Maes, F., Suetens, P.: Predicting soft tissue deformations for a maxillofacial surgery planning system: from computational strategies to a complete clinical validation. Med. Image Anal. **11**(3), 282–301 (2007)
19. Naini, F.B.: Facial aesthetics: concepts and clinical diagnosis. John Wiley & Sons (2025)
20. Otamendi, G.S.V.: Designing deformable models of soft tissue for virtual surgery planning and simulation using the mass-spring model. University of Navarra, Spain (2011)
21. Pal, S., Tennant, M., Ray, N.: Towards positive jacobian: learn to postprocess for diffeomorphic image registration with matrix exponential. In: 2022 26th International Conference on Pattern Recognition (ICPR), pp. 3391–3398. IEEE (2022)
22. Proffit, W.R., Fields, H., Larson, B., Sarver, D.M.: Contemporary orthodontics-E-book: contemporary orthodontics-E-book. Elsevier Health Sciences (2018)

23. Raissi, M., Perdikaris, P., Karniadakis, G.E.: Physics-informed neural networks: a deep learning framework for solving forward and inverse problems involving nonlinear partial differential equations. J. Comput. Phys. **378**, 686–707 (2019)
24. Raissi, M., Perdikaris, P., Karniadakis, G.E.: Physics informed deep learning (part I): data-driven solutions of nonlinear partial differential equations. arXiv preprint arXiv:1711.10561 (2017)
25. Ruggiero, F., et al.: Soft tissue prediction in orthognathic surgery: improving accuracy by means of anatomical details. PLoS ONE **18**(11), e0294640 (2023)
26. Simo, J.C., Taylor, R.L.: Quasi-incompressible finite elasticity in principal stretches. continuum basis and numerical algorithms. Comput. Methods Appl. Mech. Eng. **85**(3), 273–310 (1991)
27. Wilcoxon, F.: Individual comparisons by ranking methods. In: Kotz, S., Johnson, N.L. (eds.) Breakthroughs in statistics: methodology and distribution, pp. 196–202. Springer, New York, NY (1992). https://doi.org/10.1007/978-1-4612-4380-9_16

Planning the Perfect Burn: Multi-objective PSO for Multi-needle Thermal Ablation

Jonas Mehtali[1(✉)], Juan Manuel Verde[1,2,3], and Caroline Essert[1]

[1] ICube, University of Strasbourg, CNRS, Strasbourg, France
j.mehtali@unistra.fr
[2] IHU Strasbourg - Institute of Image-Guided Surgery, Strasbourg, France
[3] INRIA, Strasbourg, France

Abstract. Percutaneous thermal ablation is a localized treatment for hepatic tumors for which multi-needle planning remains mostly manual, while the difficulty grows sharply with the number of needles and the complexity of the targets. We present a GPU-accelerated pipeline that jointly optimizes all needle placements and ablation parameters in a single run, to aim for a perfect burn. Our pipeline uses a decomposition-based multi-objective particle swarm optimizer, with four clinical objectives (coverage, efficiency, safety, insertion depth), per-needle activation variables to optimize needle count, a CUDA-based fitness evaluation, and Vulkan-rendered safety maps. Tested on 94 tumors, the method achieves better coverage, larger distance to critical structures, and less collateral damage than the expert plan, in less than 6 s. An expert rated 88% of auto-plannings as clinically acceptable as is ($\geq$4/5) and 99% as requiring only minor adjustments ($\geq$3/5), with 97% judged equivalent or superior to manual plans (87% preferred, 10% equivalent).

Keywords: Thermal ablation · Treatment planning · Multi-objective optimization · GPU acceleration · Particle swarm optimization

1 Introduction

Percutaneous thermal ablation (PTA) is a first-line treatment for hepatic tumors [6,9] in which a needle-like applicator delivers thermal energy at its tip to induce localized tumor necrosis. Tumor recurrence depends critically on the *minimal ablation margin* (MAM), a 5–10 mm layer of destroyed tissue surrounding the tumor. Insufficient MAM is an independent predictor of recurrence [11]. For large or irregular tumors, multiple impacts, either through the same (pullback) or different applicators, may be needed to fully cover the margin. This complex combinatorial problem involves a dozen decision variables per needle, and the clinician must balance four conflicting objectives simultaneously. In practice, this time-consuming task is performed mentally with limited 3D spatial reasoning.

For more than two decades, the literature has addressed mostly parts of this problem. *Trajectory-only* methods [2,3,17,22] optimize single-needle insertion

G. Yang et al. (Eds.): MICCAI 2026, LNCS 16893, pp. 362–372, 2027.
https://doi.org/10.1007/978-3-032-38236-8_35

but ignore needle count, ablation parameters, and composite multi-needle coverage. *Sequential multi-needle* methods [14,16,21] place needles in stages, preventing revision of earlier decisions and potentially leading to suboptimal composite plans. In the most recent study, Pan et al. [21] achieved automatic planning in 22 s using whale optimization with extensive clinical constraints, but predefined needle targets and ablation dimensions. Lukes et al. [17] jointly optimized multiple trajectories with adaptive needle count but fixed ablation geometry and relied on weighted-sum scalarization, which may overlook portions of the Pareto front [10]. *Simulation-based* methods [15] improve accuracy via thermal modeling but incur prohibitive computational cost ($\sim$480 s on CPU [15]), precluding intra-operative replanning. *Learning-based* approaches [4,20] offer fast inference but remain limited to single needles or single targets. Recent surveys [8,23,27] confirmed that no existing method simultaneously provides: (a) joint optimization of all needles, (b) true multi-objective Pareto optimization across coverage, efficiency, safety, and depth, (c) adaptive needle count including pullback ablations, (d) safety-aware trajectory selection inside the optimization loop, and (e) speed compatible with intra-operative use.

We address these gaps with the following contributions:

1. GPU-accelerated 4-objective pipeline that **jointly** optimizes multi-needle trajectories, ablation parameters, and safety.
2. **MOEA/D–PSO formulation** yielding a clinically meaningful Pareto front.
3. **Per-needle activation encoding with efficiency-driven parsimony**, determining needle count within a single run.
4. Native support for **pullback ablations**, enabling multiple ablations at different depths along a single insertion via controlled retraction.
5. **Evaluation on 50 clinical hepatic cases** (94 targets, 3 difficulty tiers), combining quantitative metrics with expert review.

2 Method

2.1 Problem Formulation

Given T target tumor meshes $\{\mathcal{M}_t\}_{t=1}^{T}$, K obstacle meshes $\{\mathcal{O}_k\}_{k=1}^{K}$, and a skin surface $\mathcal{S}$, we seek a plan $\mathbf{P}$ optimizing four objectives f_1 to f_4. $\mathbf{P}$ contains an optimal number of needles N, and for each needle $i = 1, \ldots, N$, a tip position $\mathbf{p}_i \in \mathbb{R}^3$, an orientation (θ_i, ϕ_i) in spherical coordinates, and an ablation preset a_i. Each target is optimized independently and combined into a unified plan.

The four objectives reflect the placement criteria most commonly adopted in PTA decision-making:

$$f_1(\mathbf{P}) = \frac{n_{\text{TP}}}{n_{\text{TP}} + n_{\text{FN}}} \qquad \text{(Coverage } \textit{or Sensitivity}\text{)} \tag{1}$$

$$f_2(\mathbf{P}) = \frac{n_{\text{TP}}}{n_{\text{TP}} + n_{\text{FP}}} \qquad \text{(Efficiency } \textit{or Precision}\text{)} \tag{2}$$

$$f_3(\mathbf{P}) = \frac{\sum_i s_i \, e^{-ks_i}}{\sum_i e^{-ks_i}} \qquad \text{(Safety)} \tag{3}$$

$$f_4(\mathbf{P}) = 1 - \frac{1}{N} \sum_{i=1}^{N} \hat{d}_i^2 \qquad \text{(Depth)} \tag{4}$$

where $n_{\text{TP}}/n_{\text{FP}}/n_{\text{FN}}$ are respectively the true positive, false positive, and false negative voxel counts sampled on a grid over the ablation and margin volumes, $s_i \in [0, 1]$ a per-trajectory safety, N the active needle count, and $\hat{d}_i$ the insertion depth, clamped to $[40, 200]$ mm and normalized to $[0, 1]$. Safety (3) uses a Boltzmann softmin ($k=5$), ensuring the optimizer cannot hide one dangerous trajectory behind several safe ones. Needle parsimony is implicitly included in efficiency (2): in general additional needles add false positives (collateral damage), lowering this score. Coverage is evaluated against the MAM during optimization.

Our approach models this multi-needle planning problem as a *joint* multi-objective search, in which all needles associated with a given tumor are optimized simultaneously, rather than placed sequentially. To achieve this, we propose a pipeline in three stages (Fig. 1): (1) safety-map generation via Vulkan GPU fisheye rendering, (2) MOEA/D–PSO optimization with CUDA fitness evaluation, and (3) metrics computation.

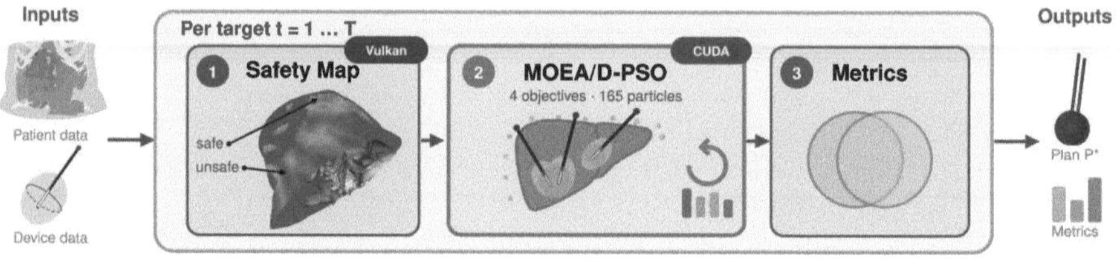

Fig. 1. Three-stage pipeline overview: (1) safety-map generation, (2) MOEA/D–PSO optimization, and (3) metrics computation against tumor and margin.

2.2 Safety Map Generation

Safety is integrated in the optimization objective by pre-computing a dense safety map as a texture via GPU fisheye rendering (Fig. 2). Directions are sampled on a 256×128 sphere texture. For each direction, a camera is placed on the skin

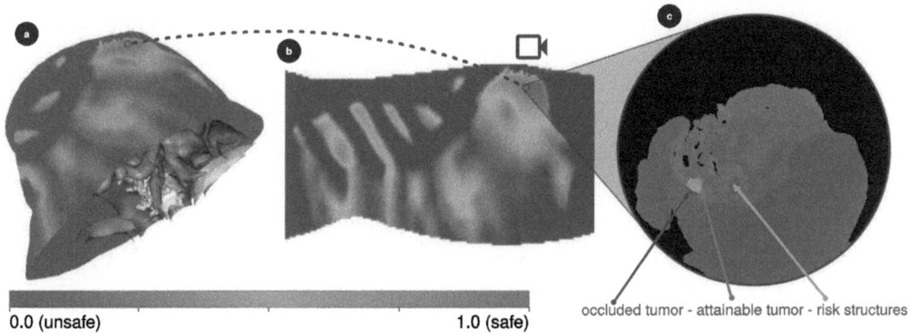

Fig. 2. **(a)** Safety map texture applied on the 3D mesh of the skin (color range from green = safe to red = unsafe). **(b)** Sphere safety map as a texture. **(c)** Occlusion rendering of anatomy and tumor from one specific entry point. (Color figure online)

surface looking inside the body and renders a 256^2 fisheye depth map in two passes: (1) obstacle MIN-blend and *back-face* target MAX-blend, yielding safety as the unoccluded target ratio; (2) liver-margin clearance (<10 mm discarded). Validated points are indexed in a 32×16-bin spherical grid for $O(1)$ lookup. The map is computed once per case before optimization and remains static throughout the search, with needle safety queried per-particle by a single texture fetch during GPU fitness evaluation.

2.3 MOEA/D–PSO Optimization

With four competing objectives, dominance-based algorithms such as NSGA-II suffer from weak selection pressure in high-dimensional objective spaces [29]. We adopted a Multiobjective Evolutionary Algorithm based on Decomposition (MOEA/D) [29] with Particle Swarm Optimization (PSO) as the search operator. While decomposition-based multi-objective PSO has been explored previously in other contexts [1,28], our contributions lie in the clinical planning formulation and domain-specific operators described below.

PSO is a population-based search method in which candidate solutions ("particles") iteratively move through the decision space by combining their own momentum with attraction toward known good positions. Rather than comparing solutions via dominance, MOEA/D decomposes the 4-objective problem into N_w scalar sub-problems, each defined by a *weight vector* $\boldsymbol{\lambda} = (\lambda_1, \ldots, \lambda_4)$ that assigns a different relative priority to the four objectives ($\lambda_i \geq 0$, $\sum_i \lambda_i = 1$). Das–Dennis vectors [7] distribute these weights uniformly on the 4-simplex by discretizing each component into multiples of $1/H$; with granularity $H = 8$ this yields $N_w = \binom{4+H-1}{H} = 165$ vectors, each defining one sub-problem optimized by a dedicated particle. Boundary vectors are added to better cover extreme Pareto regions (e.g. pure coverage or pure safety).

Each sub-problem converts its 4-objective evaluation into a single scalar via Penalty-based Boundary Intersection (PBI) scalarization [29]: $g^{\mathrm{PBI}} = d_1 + \vartheta \cdot d_2$, where d_1 is the projection of the objective vector onto the weight direction (measuring *convergence* toward the ideal point $\mathbf{z}^*$) and d_2 is the perpendicular distance from that direction (penalizing deviation from the assigned trade-off). The ideal point $\mathbf{z}^* = (z_1^*, \ldots, z_4^*)$ tracks the best value found so far and is updated every iteration. We set $\vartheta = 5.0$, providing strong diversity pressure to prevent sub-problems from collapsing on the same region of the Pareto front [29]. Particle velocity is updated via the Clerc–Kennedy constriction rule [5]: $\mathbf{v}_{t+1} = \chi(\mathbf{v}_t + c_1 r_1(\mathbf{p}_{\text{best}} - \mathbf{x}_t) + c_2 r_2(\mathbf{g}_{\text{best}} - \mathbf{x}_t))$, with $c_1 = c_2 = 2.05$ and $\chi \approx 0.7298$, ensuring stable convergence without inertia tuning.

Each particle encodes a plan as a vector with 12 variables per needle: direction (θ, ϕ) in spherical coordinates, tip position (p^x, p^y, p^z), primary burn size scalar $s \in [0, 1]$ (mapped to ellipsoid dimensions via manufacturer-calibrated profiles), number of burns $n \in 1, 2, 3$ along the direction of the needles to allow for pullback ablation strategies, pullback spacings δ^j, per-burn sizes s^j, and activation a (≥ 0.5: active, otherwise suppressed). Total dimensionality is $N_{\text{max}} \times 12$, with N_{max} the maximum number of needles allowed. The *needle tip* is the decision variable anchor; the ablation epicenter is derived as $\mathbf{e} = \mathbf{p} - \hat{\mathbf{d}} \cdot \delta_{\text{offset}}$, and pullback burns are positioned along the shaft at $\mathbf{c}_j = \mathbf{e} + \hat{\mathbf{d}} \cdot \sum_{k=1}^{j} \delta^k$.

Each particle maintains $T_n = 20$ weight-vector neighbors; $\mathbf{g}_{\text{best}}$ is the best-PBI particle among the T_n neighbors, with $n_r = 2$ replacements per iteration. Domain-aware continuous mutations (direction rotation up to π rad, position $\pm 15\%$, size $\pm 20\%$; probability 0.1 per needle) and needle-level crossover (every 7 iterations) preserve geometric structure. Discrete structural mutations (add/remove/replace, every 13 iterations) enable variable needle count. Optimization terminates via multi-criteria early stopping: all four objectives must individually stagnate (<0.1% improvement over 100 iterations) after a 25% grace period, confirmed over 5 consecutive checks.

2.4 GPU Fitness Evaluation

The evaluation of N_w candidate plans per iteration, each requiring volumetric coverage assessment, constitutes a computational bottleneck. We accelerated this with CUDA, using a signed distance field (SDF) at $\sim$2 mm resolution uploaded as a 3D texture for mesh-accurate containment queries via trilinear interpolation. A single kernel evaluates all particles in parallel: needle ellipsoids are decoded into shared memory, the tight union bounding box is sampled on an adaptive grid and each point is tested for ellipsoid and target membership. To avoid local recurrence, full coverage of a MAM of at least $+\delta = 5$ mm from the tumor surface is mandatory [11,25]. However, in practice, the multi-objective optimization tends to produce ablations that conform too tightly to the MAM surface, occasionally leaving irregular parts of the margin under-covered. To guarantee full margin coverage, we chose to inflate δ by an additional 3 mm during optimization. Values for $n_{\text{TP}}/n_{\text{FP}}/n_{\text{FN}}$ are accumulated via shared-memory reduction. Safety is evaluated by associating each needle's position and direction to the corresponding insertion point on the safety map.

Prior methods fixed needle count *a priori* or estimated it from volumetric ratios before optimization [13,14,16], committing structural decisions before the full plan is known. In our approach, all $N_{\max}$ needles are encoded in every particle; the activation variable determines which are active ($a_i \geq 0.5$). The optimizer selects the appropriate count: adding a superfluous needle increases false positives, lowering efficiency (2), while discrete mutations (add/remove/replace) explore different counts across the Pareto front.

3 Dataset and Metrics

The dataset used in this study was built from the Colorectal-Liver-Metastases (CRLM) database of pre-segmented images [26]. Filters were used to select cases as per the COLLISION classification of ablability [12]: Tier 1 has single tumors with simple access and lowest risk ; Tier 2 includes intermediate cases with either multiple lesions or bilobar distribution ; Tier 3 contains multi-lesion and bilobar tumors, with the highest planning complexity . A total of 50 cases, comprising 94 individual tumors, was selected by an expert clinician among cases with no extrahepatic disease and maximal tumor diameter $\leq$ 4.3 cm, with the following distribution: Tier 1: 25 cases (50%), Tier 2: 15 cases (30%), Tier 3: 10 cases (20%). Mean tumor diameter was 12.0 ± 6.6 mm. The average distance to the closest critical structure across tumors was 4.8 ± 4.4 mm, hepatic vessels (hepatic veins, portal vein, inferior vena cava) being the nearest obstacle in 64% of cases. In 59% of cases, the tumor was located < 5 mm from the liver surface, requiring angled insertions through parenchyma before reaching the tumor. Mean distance to the skin surface was 54.3 ± 25.3 mm, reflecting the range of insertion depths encountered in clinical practice.

For each case, all segmented structures (liver, tumors, vasculature, skin, and 15 organs) were reconstructed as 3D surface meshes. A manual plan was created by a hepato-biliary surgeon under clinical routine conditions, placing needles interactively on 2D slices using Medtronic Emprint microwave presets identical to those available to the auto-planner. The full dataset has been made publicly available at: https://figshare.com/s/13c01677c744eb1625c6.

Because our optimizer aims to cover the MAM, we computed metrics mostly against the margin. Coverage, efficiency, and Dice similarity coefficient (DSC) quantify the voxel overlap between the ablation zone and the margin volume. All overlap metrics were computed at 0.5 mm isotropic resolution. The 95th-percentile Hausdorff distance (HD95), less sensitive to outliers than the full Hausdorff distance, measures boundary agreement. We additionally computed the distance from needle to closest critical structure (DTC, in mm), a standard safety metric [13,24] and the average needle insertion depth (mm). Finally, Cohen's d and q-value were computed to evaluate significance of the results.

To complement quantitative metrics, the same surgeon-scientist independently reviewed all 94 auto-planner targets and assessed: (1) *Acceptability* on a 5-point Likert scale (1=unacceptable, 2=major changes needed, 3=minor changes needed, 4=minor optional, 5=fully acceptable), and (2) *Preference*, indicating which plan they would follow clinically (Auto-planner, Expert or Either). Free-text comments were collected to identify recurring clinical concerns and planning biases.

4 Experiments and Results

All experiments were run on a dedicated workstation equipped with an Intel Core i9 processor, 32.0 GiB of RAM, and an NVIDIA RTX 4080 SUPER graphics processing unit. Median per-target optimization time was 5.2 s (mean 5.4 s), with a one-time safety map pre-computation of 2.8 s per case.

Table 1. Per-case comparison between automatic and expert planning averaged over 94 targets from 50 cases: Average (SD) are reported with difference (Δ) and statistical significance (Wilcoxon signed-rank test, Benjamini–Hochberg FDR correction).

Structure	Metric	Auto	Expert	Δ	Cohen's d	q-value
Margin	Coverage	**1.000** (0.000)	0.939 (0.100)	+0.061	0.61	<0.001
	Efficiency	**0.829** (0.067)	0.394 (0.159)	+0.435	3.00	<0.001
	DSC	**0.892** (0.040)	0.525 (0.145)	+0.366	2.75	<0.001
	DTC (mm)	**6.0** (3.1)	4.4 (2.8)	+1.6	0.51	<0.001
	Depth (mm)	102.5 (23.3)	**98.0** (20.5)	+4.5	0.20	0.214
	HD95 (mm)	**5.9** (1.0)	9.1 (2.6)	−3.2	−1.23	<0.001

Table 1 shows paired results. The auto-planner achieved full MAM coverage in 100% of cases, significantly improving DSC (0.892 vs. 0.525), and maintaining wider safety margins (DTC 6.0 vs. 4.4 mm) (Fig. 3B). Efficiency shows that expert plans caused ~61% collateral damage on healthy tissue vs. ~17% for the auto-planner. Both methods provided comparable insertion depth (102.5 vs. 98.0 mm, q=0.214), indicating equivalent complexity of execution.

The difference between methods increased with case difficulty (Fig. 3A). Expert DSC dropped from 0.578 on Tier 1 to 0.450–0.464 in Tiers 2–3, while the auto-planner maintained DSC at 0.899, 0.875, and 0.898. Expert efficiency declined from 0.445 (Tier 1) to 0.314–0.336 in complex cases (Fig. 4), whereas the auto-planner maintained conformal plans regardless of target count. The auto-planner achieved consistently lower HD95 (Fig. 3C) suggesting better centering of ablations and less over-treatment. Figure 4 shows representative plans across tiers. Auto-planned ablation zones conform more closely to the margin boundary while expert plans show over-ablation, particularly in multi-target cases.

The expert clinical review yielded a mean acceptability of 4.4 ± 0.8 across all 94 targets: 88% scored ≥ 4 (acceptable with at most minor optional improvements) and 99% scored ≥ 3 (minor changes at most). The auto-planner was preferred in 87% of targets, while 10% were rated as equivalent, the expert plan being preferred in only 3%. Acceptability remained stable across tiers (Tier 1:

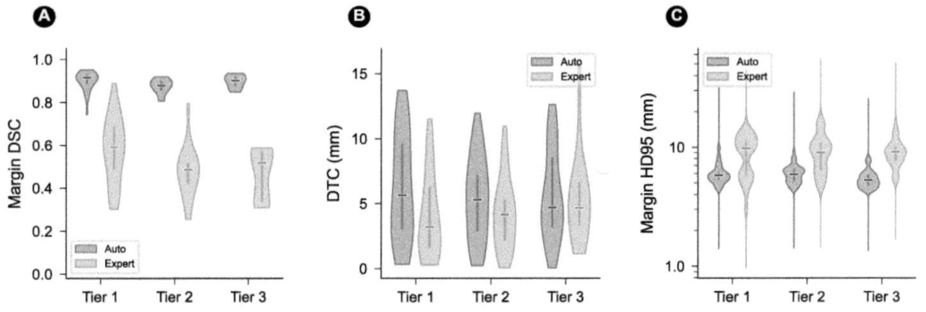

Fig. 3. Quantitative results per tier: **(A)** Margin DSC, **(B)** DTC, **(C)** Margin HD95.

4.4 ± 0.9, Tier 2: 4.5 ± 0.7, Tier 3: 4.5 ± 0.7), confirming that clinical quality did not degrade with case complexity. The most frequent reason for preferring the auto-planner was inadequate coverage of the margin in the expert plan, explicitly noted in 40% of targets, underlining both the difficulty of planning manually from 2D slices and the importance of a full MAM coverage.

Recurrent concerns included trajectories leaving the liver (10%), superfluous applicators (13%), and overly tangential approaches (7%), suggesting future constraints on intrahepatic path length and entry angle. The reviewer also noted cognitive biases in manual plans (*in-plane trajectory bias*, *landmark bias*), highlighting the value of automated planning.

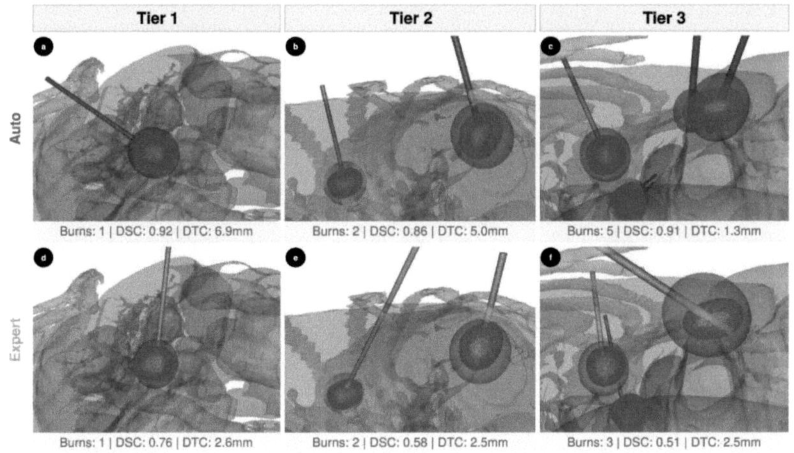

Fig. 4. Qualitative comparison across tiers. Top: auto-planner; bottom: expert. Tumors and margins (green), ablation zones and needles (blue/yellow), translucent organs. (Color figure online)

5 Conclusion

We presented a GPU-accelerated pipeline that jointly optimizes multi-needle placement, ablation parameters, and trajectory safety for percutaneous thermal ablation. A 4-objective MOEA/D–PSO formulation with per-needle activation encoding determines needle configurations and count in a median of 5.2 s per target without sequential commitment of individual needles.

On 50 paired clinical hepatic cases, the auto-planner improves on almost all metrics compared to the expert. Multi-target planning, where clinicians must mentally coordinate high-dimensional trade-offs, is where the method offers the largest measured improvement. An expert review confirmed clinical acceptability with minor or no adjustments in 99% of cases (single-reviewer assessment; multi-reader validation remains future work). A few outliers remain, indicating potential gains from added constraints suggested through the questionnaire, or multi-run selection. To get even closer to the perfect burn, in future work we intend to integrate our fast physics-based ablation zone simulations [18,19], that account for multi-needle thermal interaction effects where overlapping zones are not simply additive.

Acknowledgments. This work of the Interdisciplinary Thematic Institute HealthTech, as part of the ITI 2021–2028 program of the University of Strasbourg, CNRS and Inserm, was supported by IdEx Unistra (ANR-10-IDEX-0002) and SFRI (STRAT'US project, ANR-20-SFRI-0012) under the framework of the French Investments for the Future Program. It has been partially funded under the framework of the French Investments for the Future Program, by French state funds managed within the "Plan Investissements d'Avenir", by the ANR (reference ANR-10-IAHU-02).

Disclosure of Interests. The authors have no conflict of interest to declare.

References

1. Al Moubayed, N., Petrovski, A., McCall, J.: D2MOPSO: MOPSO based on decomposition and dominance with archiving using crowding distance in objective and solution spaces. Evol. Comput. **22**(1), 47–77 (2014). https://doi.org/10.1162/EVCO_a_00104
2. Baegert, C., Villard, C., Schreck, P., Soler, L., Gangi, A.: Trajectory optimization for the planning of percutaneous radiofrequency ablation of hepatic tumors. Comput. Aided Surg. **12**(2), 82–90 (2007). https://doi.org/10.3109/10929080701312000
3. Butz, T., et al.: Pre- and intra-operative planning and simulation of percutaneous tumor ablation. In: Proceedings of MICCAI 2000. LNCS, vol. 1935, pp. 317–326. Springer (2000). https://doi.org/10.1007/978-3-540-40899-4_32
4. Chaitanya, K., Audigier, C., Balascuta, L.E., Mansi, T.: Automatic planning of liver tumor thermal ablation using deep reinforcement learning. In: Proceedings of MIDL 2022. PMLR, vol. 172, pp. 219–230 (2022)
5. Clerc, M., Kennedy, J.: The particle swarm - explosion, stability, and convergence in a multidimensional complex space. IEEE Trans. Evol. Comput. **6**(1), 58–73 (2002). https://doi.org/10.1109/4235.985692

6. Crocetti, L., de Baére, T., Pereira, P.L., Tarantino, F.P.: CIRSE standards of practice on thermal ablation of liver tumours. Cardiovasc. Intervent. Radiol. **43**(7), 951–962 (2020). https://doi.org/10.1007/s00270-020-02471-z
7. Das, I., Dennis, J.E.: Normal-boundary intersection: a new method for generating the Pareto surface in nonlinear multicriteria optimization problems. SIAM J. Optim. **8**(3), 631–657 (1998). https://doi.org/10.1137/S1052623496307510
8. Ding, F., Wu, W., Jiang, W., Zhou, Z., Wu, S.: Computer-assisted treatment planning and mathematical modeling for percutaneous liver tumor ablation: an updated survey. Ann. Biomed. Eng. (2025). https://doi.org/10.1007/s10439-025-03850-8
9. Galle, P.R., et al.: EASL clinical practice guidelines: management of hepatocellular carcinoma. J. Hepatol. **69**(1), 182–236 (2018). https://doi.org/10.1016/j.jhep.2018.03.019
10. Hamzé, N., et al.: Pareto front vs. weighted sum for automatic trajectory planning of deep brain stimulation. In: Ourselin, S., Joskowicz, L., Sabuncu, M.R., Unal, G., Wells, W. (eds.) MICCAI 2016. LNCS, vol. 9900, pp. 534–541. Springer, Cham (2016). https://doi.org/10.1007/978-3-319-46720-7_62
11. Laimer, G., et al.: Minimal ablative margin (MAM) assessment with image fusion: an independent predictor for local tumor progression in hepatocellular carcinoma after stereotactic radiofrequency ablation. Eur. Radiol. **30**(5), 2463–2472 (2019). https://doi.org/10.1007/s00330-019-06609-7
12. Lei, S.v.d., Puijk, R.S., et al.: Thermal ablation versus surgical resection of small-size colorectal liver metastases (COLLISION): an international, randomised, controlled, phase 3 non-inferiority trial. Lancet Oncol. **26**(2), 187–199 (2025). https://doi.org/10.1016/S1470-2045(24)00660-0
13. Li, J., Xu, Y., Shen, N., Feng, L., Ran, Z., Deng, Z.: A practical pretreatment planning method of multiple puncturing for thermal ablation surgery. Biocybern. Biomed. Eng. **40**(4), 1469–1485 (2020). https://doi.org/10.1016/j.bbe.2020.08.004
14. Li, S., et al.: Multi-stage automatic and rapid ablation and needle trajectory planning method for CT-guided percutaneous liver tumor ablation. Med. Phys. **52**(1), 113–130 (2025). https://doi.org/10.1002/mp.17450
15. Liang, L., Cool, D., Kakani, N., Wang, G., Ding, H., Fenster, A.: Automatic radiofrequency ablation planning for liver tumors with multiple constraints based on set covering. IEEE Trans. Med. Imaging **39**(5), 1459–1471 (2020). https://doi.org/10.1109/TMI.2019.2950947
16. Liu, S., et al.: Automatic multiple-needle surgical planning of robotic-assisted microwave coagulation in large liver tumor therapy. PLoS ONE **11**(3), e0149482 (2016). https://doi.org/10.1371/journal.pone.0149482
17. Lukes, A., Bale, R., Freysinger, W.: Automatic trajectory planning for stereotactic radiofrequency ablation in non-discrete search space. IJCARS **20**, 1349–1360 (2025). https://doi.org/10.1007/s11548-025-03386-1
18. Mehtali, J., Verde, J.M., Essert, C.: C-NCA: chained neural cellular automata for fast and accurate thermal ablation estimation. In: Proceedings of MICCAI 2025, pp. 67–77. LNCS, Springer (2025). https://doi.org/10.1007/978-3-032-04965-0_7
19. Mehtali, J., Verde, J.M., Essert, C.: HEAT: high-efficiency simulation for thermal ablation therapy. Int. J. Comput. Assist. Radiol. Surg. **20**(6), 1135–1143 (2025). https://doi.org/10.1007/s11548-025-03350-z
20. Meister, F., et al.: Fast automatic liver tumor radiofrequency ablation planning via learned physics model. In: Proceedings of MICCAI 2022. LNCS, vol. 13437, pp. 167–176. Springer (2022). https://doi.org/10.1007/978-3-031-16449-1_17

21. Pan, K., Qin, J., Qin, G.: A rapid path planning approach for liver tumor ablation with comprehensive constraints. BMC Med. Imaging **26**, 73 (2026). https://doi.org/10.1186/s12880-025-02120-2
22. Schumann, C., et al.: Interactive multi-criteria planning for radiofrequency ablation. IJCARS **10**(6), 879–889 (2015). https://doi.org/10.1007/s11548-015-1201-6
23. Scorza, D., et al.: Surgical planning assistance in keyhole and percutaneous surgery: a systematic review. Med. Image Anal. **67**, 101820 (2021). https://doi.org/10.1016/j.media.2020.101820
24. Seitel, A., Engel, M., Sommer, C.M., Radeleff, B.A., Essert-Villard, C., et al.: Computer-assisted trajectory planning for percutaneous needle insertions. Med. Phys. **38**(6), 3246–3259 (2011). https://doi.org/10.1118/1.3590374
25. Shady, W., Petre, E.N., Gonen, M., Erinjeri, J.P., Brown, K.T., et al.: Percutaneous radiofrequency ablation of colorectal cancer liver metastases: Factors affecting outcomes–a 10-year experience at a single center. Radiology **278**(2), 601–611 (2016). https://doi.org/10.1148/radiol.2015142489
26. Simpson, A.L., Peoples, J., Creasy, J.M., Fichtinger, G., et al.: Preoperative CT and survival data for patients undergoing resection of colorectal liver metastases. Sci. Data **11**(1), 172 (2024). https://doi.org/10.1038/s41597-024-02981-2
27. Westby, K., Westby, D., McKevitt, K., Moloney, B.M.: Artificial intelligence in thermal ablation: current applications and future directions in microwave technologies. Biomimetics **10**(12), 818 (2025). https://doi.org/10.3390/biomimetics10120818
28. Zapotecas Martínez, S., Coello Coello, C.A.: A multi-objective particle swarm optimizer based on decomposition. In: Proceedings of GECCO 2011, pp. 69–76. ACM (2011). https://doi.org/10.1145/2001576.2001587
29. Zhang, Q., Li, H.: MOEA/D: a multiobjective evolutionary algorithm based on decomposition. IEEE Trans. Evol. Comput. **11**(6), 712–731 (2007). https://doi.org/10.1109/TEVC.2007.892759

Preoperative Simulation of Personalized Breast Reconstruction via Implant Prior Controllable Diffusion

Yizhi Wang[1,2], Tianze Yu[3], Hengjie Yu[2], Maoling Liu[5], Wenxuan Pan[2], Zhongxiang Ding[6], Peifen Fu[4(✉)], and Yaochu Jin[2(✉)]

[1] Zhejiang University, Hangzhou 310003, China
[2] School of Engineering, Westlake University, Hangzhou Zhejiang 310030, China
jinyaochu@westlake.edu.cn
[3] School of Medicine, Zhejiang University, Hangzhou 310003, China
[4] Department of Breast Surgery, The First Affiliated Hospital, School of Medicine, Zhejiang University, Hangzhou 310003, China
fupeifen@zju.edu.cn
[5] Hangzhou Medical College, Hangzhou Zhejiang 310013, China
[6] Department of Radiology, Affiliated Hangzhou First People's Hospital, Westlake University School of Medicine, Hangzhou 310006, China

Abstract. Breast reconstruction plays a crucial role in restoring body image and psychosocial well-being after mastectomy, yet preoperative planning relies heavily on surgeons' experience and lacks practical planning tools. In this work, we present a controllable generative framework to simulate postoperative breast reconstruction outcomes from preoperative chest CT. Our pipeline comprises three components: (1) a conditional 3D latent diffusion model with an inpainting scheme that enables high-fidelity synthesis within the surgical region; (2) an implant canonical template library and anatomy-aware alignment method to construct a physiologically plausible implant spatial prior for guiding the generation; (3) a dedicated control branch that injects the implant prior into the diffusion process to enforce the implant and breast geometry changes. Experiments show that our framework can generate realistic postoperative volumes, and spatial prior injection substantially improves the geometry accuracy, leading to superior performance over competing baselines in both fidelity and controllability. We further demonstrate that simulated outcomes vary coherently with the user-defined implant configurations. Overall, our work enables preoperative visualization under diverse surgical configurations and supports decision-making with a flexible, patient-specific planning tool for breast reconstruction. The source code is available at https://github.com/wangyz0915/DiffuBreast.

Keywords: Breast Reconstruction · Simulation and Visualization · Latent Diffusion Models · Controllable Generation

Y. Wang and T. Yu—Contributed equally to this work.

G. Yang et al. (Eds.): MICCAI 2026, LNCS 16893, pp. 373–382, 2027.
https://doi.org/10.1007/978-3-032-38236-8_36

1 Introduction

According to the global cancer statistics, breast cancer ranked as the second most frequently diagnosed cancer and the fourth leading cause of cancer-related mortality [1]. For many patients, mastectomy remains the primary surgical option [2]. To improve women's quality of life and reduce the psychological distress from mastectomy, an increasing number of breast reconstructions have been performed worldwide [3]. To restore the breast appearance disrupted by mastectomy, breast reconstruction is commonly performed to recreate a natural breast mound and match the contralateral breast [4]. In clinical practice, selection and placement of implants often rely on preoperative coarse measurement and intraoperative repeated adjustments, an experience-driven process that is procedure-intensive, lacks standardized criteria, and may prolong operative time and increase complication risk [5, 6]. Moreover, appropriate implant sizing and accurate placement are critical for achieving optimal postoperative breast morphology. However, constrained by the manufacturers' discrete, predefined shapes and volumes, available implants may not fit patient's breast geometry. Consequently, postoperative asymmetry and suboptimal aesthetic outcomes remain common, highlighting the need for accurate preoperative simulation and decision support to enable patient-specific planning and expectation management.

Recent advances in AI methods have driven broader clinical applications, with growing interest in AI-assisted surgical planning [7, 8] and operative outcome simulation [9, 10]. However, methods for breast reconstruction remain limited. Existing studies provide cosmetic assessment of breast reconstruction outcomes using postoperative photographs [11–13] or CT scans [14], with limited utility for preoperative planning. Specifically, Chartier et al. proposed BreastGAN [15], and Zeng et al. trained a Stable Diffusion model to simulate breast augmentation outcomes from photographs [16], where the model is not readily shareable due to privacy concerns. More importantly, they generate outcomes without modeling key surgical variables (e.g., clinical attributes and implant parameters). In parallel, existing commercial platforms provide 3D body rendering of breast augmentation results for manufacturer-defined implant models, yet they prioritize visual plausibility over anatomical and morphological fidelity. Notably, unlike the bilateral enlargement, reconstruction aims to restore the mastectomy side to a natural appearance and achieve symmetry with the contralateral breast, making augmentation-oriented simulation methods less applicable to reconstruction. These gaps motivate the development of open, patient-specific tools that can accurately simulate reconstruction outcomes across diverse, user-defined surgical configurations, going beyond qualitative visualization toward reliable preoperative planning.

2 Methodology

2.1 Problem Formulation

Given a patient's preoperative chest CT volume $\mathbf{x}^{pre}$ and a binary mask $\mathbf{m}$ delineating the surgical breast region of interest (ROI), our goal is to synthesize the postoperative volume $\hat{\mathbf{x}}^{post}$ based on the clinical attributes $\mathbf{c}_c$ and implant configuration $\mathbf{c}_i$. The synthesized result should (i) be consistent with the anatomy outside the ROI, and (ii) realistically capture implant-induced changes in breast appearance within the ROI, approximating the true postoperative volume $\mathbf{x}^{post}$ (Fig. 1).

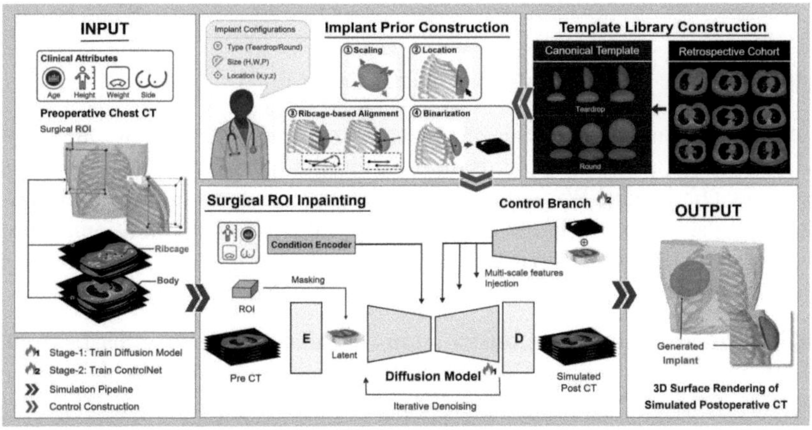

Fig. 1. Overview of the proposed breast reconstruction simulation framework. Inputs are the preoperative chest CT, ROI mask, and clinical attributes $\mathbf{c}_c$. Given an intended implant configuration, the corresponding implant template is retrieved from the library, then 1) scaled, 2) placed, and 3) reoriented to 4) form the implant mask. A diffusion inpainting model iteratively denoises in the latent space and generates the outcome within the ROI. The implant prior mask is injected via control branch, whose multi-scale features are added to the diffusion UNet decoder to enforce implant geometry during denoising. The output is a simulated postoperative CT with faithful anatomy and morphology, visualized via 3D surface rendering

2.2 Latent Diffusion Inpainting for Breast ROI Generation

Diffusion models generate samples through progressive denoising from Gaussian noise, enabling high-fidelity and diverse synthesis [17]. In this study, we adopt the conditional Latent Diffusion Model (LDM) with the inpainting scheme to reduce the computational cost for 3D synthesis, while restricting generation within the surgical ROI [18]. Let $\mathbf{z}_0 = E(\mathbf{x}^{post})$ denote the encoded latent of the postoperative volume, and the ROI $\mathbf{m}$ be downsampled to the latent resolution. At diffusion timestep t, the ROI with surgical outcomes is perturbed, while context outside the ROI is unchanged, yielding the partially noised latent:

$$\mathbf{z}_t = \left(\sqrt{\bar{\alpha}_t}\,\mathbf{z}_0 + \sqrt{1-\bar{\alpha}_t}\,\boldsymbol{\epsilon}\right) \odot \mathbf{m} + \mathbf{z}_0 \odot (1-\mathbf{m}) \tag{1}$$

where $\boldsymbol{\epsilon} \sim \mathcal{N}(0, \mathbf{I})$ is Gaussian noise, and $\bar{\alpha}_t$ controls the noise level. The denoising UNet $\boldsymbol{\epsilon}_\theta$ is trained with a region-restricted noise-prediction loss to predicts the injected noised within the ROI for every step t:

$$\mathcal{L}_{\text{Breast}} = \mathbb{E}_{\boldsymbol{\epsilon}}\left[\frac{1}{|\,\mathbf{m}\,|}\|(\boldsymbol{\epsilon} - \boldsymbol{\epsilon}_\theta(\mathbf{z}_t, t, \mathbf{m}, \mathbf{c}_c)) \odot \mathbf{m}\|_2^2\right] \tag{2}$$

During inference, we encode the preoperative volume $\mathbf{x}^{pre}$ and mask the planned surgical region with ϵ. The model then iteratively denoises within the ROI conditioned on the clinical attribute $\mathbf{c}_c$ while preserving the contralateral breast outside $\mathbf{m}$. The final latent is decoded to obtain the simulated postoperative volume $\hat{\mathbf{x}}^{post} = D(\hat{\mathbf{z}}_0)$.

2.3 Implant Prior Construction for Spatial Control

In our cohort, implant is parameterized by type and mass: type follows manufacturer-defined families (e.g., teardrop vs. round), while the mass corresponds to geometric specifications (H: height, W: width, P: projection; cm). We initially condition these attributes together with $\mathbf{c}_c$ via cross-attention, yet this implicit conditioning provides only weak geometric supervision. We therefore model the implant configuration as the explicit 3D spatial prior, providing stronger guidance during synthesis.

Canonical Implant Template Construction. We annotate implant masks from post-operative CTs to build a template library for each type-mass configuration. To overcome the variability from soft tissue confinement and implant rotation, we center each implant at its centroid and align the orientation by rotating PCA axes into a shared canonical coordinate frame. The aligned masks of the same type–mass are voxel-wise averaged to obtain the canonical implant template. Notably, we enable anisotropic scaling of the canonical template to continuously adjust (H, W, P), allowing synthesis beyond manufacturer catalog entries and facilitating flexible preoperative planning.

Patient-Specific Implant Prior Construction. Given a preoperative CT, with the specifies the implant type, size and placement center (x, y, z), we retrieve the corresponding template and estimate the in-vivo implant orientation from the PCA axes of ribcage mask of local placement region. We rotate the implant to align its projection axis (the PCA axis with the smallest eigenvalue) with the corresponding ribcage principal direction, while preserving axes orthogonality, yielding an anatomically plausible pose that conforms implant base to the chest wall. Accordingly, the implicit configuration $\mathbf{c}_i$ is converted into a spatial implant prior $\mathbf{I}_p$, providing control for synthesis.

2.4 Spatial Implant Controllable Generation

Building on the inpainting LDM (Sec. 2.2), we enforce the specific implant configuration by injecting the implant prior $\mathbf{I}_p$ via ControlNet [19, 20]. A trainable control branch g_ϕ (initialized from the UNet encoder) encodes $\mathbf{I}_p$ into multi-scale features that are added to the UNet mid and up blocks. The resulting noise predictor is:

$$\epsilon_{\theta,\phi} = \epsilon_\theta\left(\mathbf{z}_t, t, \mathbf{m}, \mathbf{c}_c, g_\phi(\mathbf{I}_p)\right) \tag{3}$$

Training follows the same region-restricted denoising objective (Eq. (2)), replacing ϵ_θ by $\epsilon_{\theta,\phi}$. We freeze the pretrained backbone ϵ_θ and optimize only g_ϕ. To sharpen implant boundaries and reduce edge jitter, we additionally fine-tune the g_ϕ with implant consistency feedback. For early diffusion steps ($t \leq 500$), where denoising predominantly recovers low-level structural details, we use an intermediate denoised postoperative estimation and decode it into the image space:

$$\hat{\mathbf{x}}_{0,t}^{post} = D\left(\frac{\mathbf{z}_t - \sqrt{1-\bar{\alpha}_t}\,\boldsymbol{\epsilon}_{\theta,\phi})}{\sqrt{\bar{\alpha}_t}} \odot \mathbf{m} + \mathbf{z}_0 \odot (1-\mathbf{m})\right) \tag{4}$$

where $D(\cdot)$ denotes the VAE decoder. We feed $\hat{\mathbf{x}}_{0,t}^{post}$ into the frozen implant segmentation network, and minimize the Dice loss [21] between the predicted implant mask and the prior I_p, encouraging stable, accurate implant contours in the synthesized ROI.

3 Experiments

3.1 Experiments Settings

Dataset. We retrospectively collected chest CT scans of patients undergoing mastectomy with immediate breast reconstruction at The First Affiliated Hospital, Zhejiang University School of Medicine, for training and validation. To evaluate preoperative applicability and cross-institutional generalization, we additionally curated paired pre/postoperative CT cases from Hangzhou First People's Hospital, Affiliated Hospital of Westlake University School of Medicine, as an external test set. For each patient, we recorded clinical attributes (age, height, weight, surgical side) and implant configurations (type, mass). After excluding cases with severe implant deformation and displacement, 470/107/87 subjects were used for training/validation/testing with patient-level splits.

Preprocessing and Implementation Details. We annotate implant masks from CT scans, and train SwinUNETR [22] for automatic implant segmentation. Ribcage and body masks are obtained using TotalSegmentator [23]. For the LDM, we adopt a 3D UNet [24] with attention module at the deepest layer. CT volumes are resampled to $256 \times 256 \times 160$ and encoded using MedVAE [25]. Models are trained using AdamW with learning rate 2×10^{-6} scaled by batch size. We use a cosine noise schedule with 1000 timesteps and perform inference with DDIM [26] sampling using 200 steps.

Competing Methods and Protocols. We compare against a conditional LDM baseline that conditions on clinical attributes and implant-configuration via cross-attention, using either (i) BiomedCLIP [27] encoded text prompts or (ii) MLP encoded numeric attributes. We further benchmark representative spatially controllable diffusion variants: (iii) GLIGEN [28], (iv) Simple-ControlNet [29]; and (v) T2I-Adapter [30]. For fair comparison, the controllable baselines are adapted by replacing the 2D convolutional modules with 3D counterparts and flattening volumetric tokens for the attention modules, while sharing the same 3D LDM backbone, training data, with only their control branches fine-tuned. We report SSIM, PSNR, MAE, LPIPS, GMSD, and additionally assess controllability by implant Dice/IoU between real and synthesized CT volumes.

Table 1. Quantitative comparison of synthesis quality across competing methods. Best results are highlighted in bold

Model	LPIPS↓	SSIM↑	PSNR↑	MAE↓	GMSD↓
Text-encoded	0.088	0.904	28.382	0.028	0.144
Num-encoded	0.089	0.904	27.590	0.030	0.146
GLIGEN	0.086	0.91	28.646	0.027	0.141
Simple-ControlNet	0.088	0.908	28.480	0.028	0.142
T2I-Adapter	0.082	0.911	28.772	0.027	0.140
Ours	**0.080**	**0.912**	**29.046**	**0.025**	**0.137**

3.2 Results

Generative Quality. As shown in Table 1, our method achieves the best synthesis quality across all metrics. Compared with implicit cross-attention conditioning (Text-/Num-encoded), methods with spatial control consistently improve fidelity, yielding lower perceptual/pixel-wise errors (LPIPS, MAE) and higher structural similarity (SSIM), even when only the control branch is fine-tuned. Since the dominant appearance changes in the ROI are driven by implant placement and geometry, the spatial prior provides the model with geometric guidance, yielding more consistent outputs. In particular, the lower GMSD indicates better agreement of the implant and breast contour boundaries within the ROI.

Table 2. Quantitative comparison of implant mask agreement between synthesized and reference postoperative CT volumes

Model	Dice↑	IoU↑
Text-encoded	0.599	0.449
Num-encoded	0.544	0.395
GLIGEN	0.613	0.456
Simple-ControlNet	0.606	0.452
T2I-Adapter	0.722	0.600
Ours	**0.750**	**0.627**

Segmentation Results. Table 2 reports implant Dice/IoU between the synthesized and reference postoperative CTs. The Text-/Num-encoded baselines inject implant configuration solely through cross-attention. Although visually plausible, the condition is weakly coupled to the generated implant geometry, resulting in low Dice and IoU. This limitation is particularly evident in challenging scenarios (e.g., the second case in Fig. 2, where the implant within the ROI is larger than the native breast), where strong preoperative context in the inpainting can bias the generated ROI toward the unmasked context and follow the contralateral breast shape rather than the intended condition. These observations highlight the need for explicit, spatially grounded control.

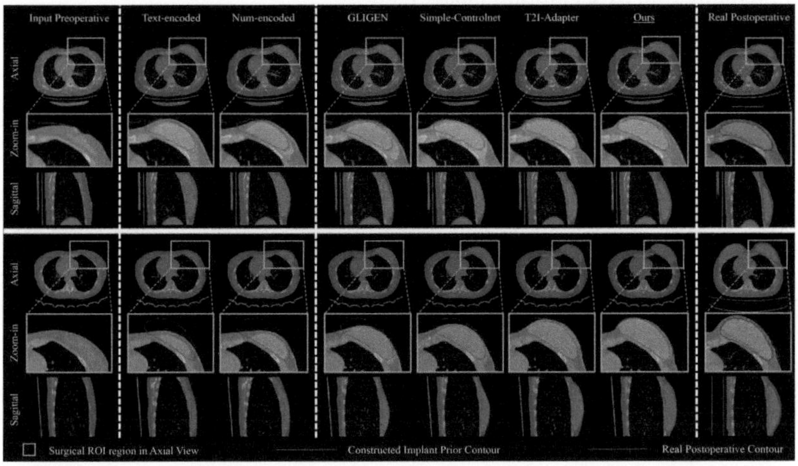

Fig. 2. Qualitative comparison of synthesis. Axial (top) and sagittal (bottom) views are shown for two patients: (a) unilateral reconstruction with an implant size close to the native breast; (b) bilateral reconstruction with larger implants. The postoperative implant contour is outlined in blue, and the implant spatial prior used for spatial control is outlined in red. (Color figure online)

With the proposed spatial control signal, close agreement between the injected control (red) and the reference postoperative implant contour (blue) in Fig. 2 suggests that this prior provides a reliable geometric cue. It substantially improves implant accuracy across controllable variants, with T2I-Adapter and our method achieving the best overlap. We attribute the inferior performance of GLIGEN and Simple-ControlNet to attention-based control injection, which is applied at the lowest resolution of UNet in our implementation for memory constraints and may be attenuated during decoding. In contrast, T2I-Adapter and our approach inject control features into convolutional feature maps across scales, enabling stronger enforcement of geometric constraints. Finally, with the segmentation-consistency fine-tuning, our method produces sharper implant boundaries and attains the highest Dice/IoU in Table 2.

Simulation Results. Figure 3 visualizes controllable simulations generated from preoperative volumes. Row 1 shows the unilateral reconstruction case. Under the ground truth implant configuration (middle column), the synthesis closely matches the real postoperative implant contour and skin-surface profile. By iteratively reducing P and increasing H, our edited configuration (H : 13.3, W : 13, P : 3.3) produces a plausible alternative with a smoother breast contour transition and improved symmetry compared with the real postoperative outcome.

Row 2 shows a bilateral reconstruction case, where we vary implant mass from small to large. We simulate bilateral reconstruction by sequentially synthesizing the ROI of each breast. Consistent with prior findings, the injected spatial implant prior reduces over-reliance on the contralateral breast, enforces the specified configuration, and produces the expected change in breast prominence. Overall, our framework supports patient-specific preoperative simulation under user-defined implant configurations, facilitating surgical planning and expectation management.

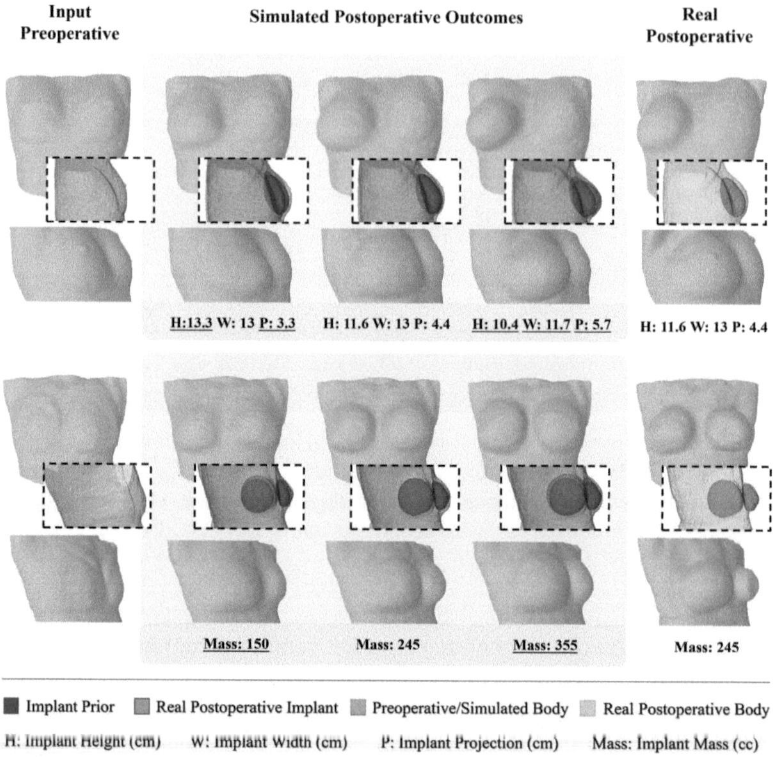

Fig. 3. Qualitative demonstration of controllable simulation using our framework (skin surface renderings derived from CT). Starting from the same preoperative input (left), we generate multiple postoperative simulations by editing the implant configuration. Insets show the injected implant prior (red) and the postoperative implant contour (blue). Row 1 presents a unilateral reconstruction case with varying implant size parameters (H, W, P), and Row 2 presents a bilateral reconstruction case with varying implant mass (corresponds to fixed H W P combinations defined by manufacturer). For each case, the result under the real surgical configuration is shown in the **middle simulated column**; edited configuration variables for the synthesized results are underlined. (Color figure online)

4 Conclusion

In this study, we presented a controllable generative framework for patient-specific simulation of postmastectomy breast reconstruction outcomes from preoperative chest CT. By integrating latent diffusion based inpainting with an explicit, editable 3D implant spatial prior injected through a dedicated control branch, our method enables anatomically consistent synthesis while providing fine-grained control over implant geometry and placement. Our model consistently improves both fidelity and implant segmentation accuracy over competing baselines and generalizes robustly in cross-institution evaluation. A limitation is that the simulation remains most reliable when the postoperative implants do not deform much, and the pretrained rib segmentation model works accurately. Future work will try to model biomechanically implant–tissue interaction and deformation, explore parametric controls that map implant configurations directly to simulation outcomes to reduce reliance on spatial priors. Overall, the proposed framework offers a practical route to preoperative visualization and decision support for breast reconstruction planning.

Acknowledgments. We thank the clinician Minya Yao from the Department of Breast Surgery, The First Affiliated Hospital, School of Medicine, Zhejiang University, for her valuable assistance in reconstructive surgery. We also thank Kun Shu from Affiliated Hangzhou First People's Hospital, Westlake University School of Medicine, for facilitating communication and helpful discussions. This work is funded in part by an International Collaboration Fund for Creative Research of National Natural Science Foundation of China (NSFC ICFCRT) under the Grant no. W2441019.

Disclosure of Interests. The authors have no competing interests to declare that are relevant to the content of this article.

References

1. Bray, F., et al.: Global cancer statistics 2022: GLOBOCAN estimates of incidence and mortality worldwide for 36 cancers in 185 countries. CA Cancer J. Clin. **74**, 229–263 (2024)
2. Rocco, N., et al.: Implants versus autologous tissue flaps for breast reconstruction following mastectomy. Cochrane Database Syst. Rev. **10**, CD013821 (2024)
3. Bolliger, M., Gambone, L., Haeusler, T., Mikula, F., Kampf, S., Fitzal, F.: Patient satisfaction, esthetic outcome, and quality of life in Oncoplastic and reconstructive breast surgery: a single center experience. Breast Care (Basel). **19**, 215–222 (2024)
4. Gilmour, A., et al.: Oncoplastic breast surgery: a guide to good practice. Eur. J. Surg. Oncol. **47**, 2272–2285 (2021)
5. Puckett, Y., Schaffner, A.D.: Implant-based breast reconstruction. In: StatPearls. StatPearls Publishing, Treasure Island (FL) (2025)
6. Zhong, T., et al.: Postmastectomy breast reconstruction in patients with non-metastatic breast cancer: a systematic review. Curr. Oncol. **32**, 231 (2025)
7. Xu, J., Wei, Y., Jiang, S., Zhou, H., Li, Y., Chen, X.: Intelligent surgical planning for automatic reconstruction of orbital blowout fracture using a prior adversarial generative network. Med. Image Anal. **99**, 103332 (2025)
8. Lee, J., et al.: Facial Appearance Prediction with Conditional Multi-scale Autoregressive Modeling for Orthognathic Surgical Planning
9. Ji, Z., Li, N., Xue, P., Dong, Y., Ma, L.: 3D Dynamic Prediction of Missing Teeth in Diverse Patterns via Centroid-prompted Diffusion Model
10. Kawata, N., et al.: Generation of short-term follow-up chest CT images using a latent diffusion model in COVID-19. Jpn. J. Radiol. **43**, 622–633 (2025)
11. Park, S., et al.: Objective and interpretable breast cosmesis evaluation with attention guided denoising diffusion anomaly detection model (2024). http://arxiv.org/abs/2402.18362

12. Park, J.K., Baek, S., Heo, C.Y., Jeong, J.H., Myung, Y.: A novel, deep learning-based, automatic photometric analysis software for breast aesthetic scoring. Arch. Plast. Surg. **51**, 30–35 (2024)
13. Guo, C., et al.: A fully automatic framework for evaluating cosmetic results of breast conserving therapy. Mach. Learn. Appl. **10**, 100430 (2022)
14. Kim, D.-Y., et al.: Feasibility of anomaly score detected with deep learning in irradiated breast cancer patients with reconstruction. NPJ Digit. Med. **5**, 1–7 (2022)
15. Chartier, C., Watt, A., Lin, O., Chandawarkar, A., Lee, J., Hall-Findlay, E.: BreastGAN: artificial intelligence-enabled breast augmentation simulation. Aesthetic Surg. J. Open Forum. **4**, ojab052 (2022)
16. Zeng, W., Schroeder, A., Moyer, K., Thompson, J.: Augmentation AI: use of a novel deep learning-based generative artificial intelligence system as a tool for breast augmentation simulation. Aesthetic Surg. J. Open Forum. **7**, ojaf018.019 (2025)
17. Ho, J., Jain, A., Abbeel, P.: Denoising diffusion probabilistic models (2020). http://arxiv.org/abs/2006.11239
18. Lugmayr, A., Danelljan, M., Romero, A., Yu, F., Timofte, R., Gool, L.V.: RePaint: inpainting using denoising diffusion probabilistic models (2022). http://arxiv.org/abs/2201.09865
19. Zhang, L., Rao, A., Agrawala, M.: Adding conditional control to text-to-image diffusion models. In: Presented at the Proceedings of the IEEE/CVF International Conference on Computer Vision (2023)
20. Li, M., et al.: ControlNet++: Improving conditional controls with efficient consistency feedback (2024). http://arxiv.org/abs/2404.07987
21. Milletari, F., Navab, N., Ahmadi, S.-A.: V-Net: fully convolutional neural networks for volumetric medical image segmentation (2016). http://arxiv.org/abs/1606.04797
22. Hatamizadeh, A., Nath, V., Tang, Y., Yang, D., Roth, H., Xu, D.: Swin UNETR: swin transformers for semantic segmentation of brain tumors in MRI images (2022). http://arxiv.org/abs/2201.01266
23. Wasserthal, J., et al.: TotalSegmentator: robust segmentation of 104 anatomical structures in CT images. Radiol. Artif. Intell. **5**, e230024 (2023)
24. Ronneberger, O., Fischer, P., Brox, T.: U-Net: convolutional networks for biomedical image segmentation (2015). http://arxiv.org/abs/1505.04597
25. Varma, M., et al.: MedVAE: efficient automated interpretation of medical images with large-scale generalizable autoencoders (2025). http://arxiv.org/abs/2502.14753
26. Song, J., Meng, C., Ermon, S.: Denoising diffusion implicit models (2022). http://arxiv.org/abs/2010.02502
27. Zhang, S., et al.: BiomedCLIP: a multimodal biomedical foundation model pretrained from fifteen million scientific image-text pairs (2025).. http://arxiv.org/abs/2303.00915
28. Li, Y., et al.: GLIGEN: open-set grounded text-to-image generation (2023). http://arxiv.org/abs/2301.07093
29. Feng, Z., Chen, L., Sun, Y., Liu, J., Feng, S.: Simplifying control mechanism in text-to-image diffusion models. In: Proceedings of the AAAI Conference on Artificial Intelligence., vol. 39, pp. 3013–3021 (2025)
30. Mou, C., et al.: T2I-adapter: learning adapters to dig out more controllable ability for text-to-image diffusion models. In: Proceedings of the AAAI Conference on Artificial Intelligence., vol. 38, pp. 4296–4304 (2024)

RaD-Seg: Region-Aware Disentangled Learning for Plan-Guided Longitudinal Tumor Segmentation in Head-and-Neck Adaptive Radiotherapy

Hee Guan Khor[1], Fang Chen[2], Yingni Wang[1], Longfei Ma[1], and Hongen Liao[1,2](✉)

[1] School of Biomedical Engineering, Tsinghua Medicine, Tsinghua University, Beijing, China
liao@tsinghua.edu.cn

[2] School of Biomedical Engineering and the Institute of Medical Robotics, Shanghai Jiao Tong University, Shanghai, China

Abstract. Adaptive radiotherapy (ART) for head-and-neck (H&N) cancer requires reliable longitudinal delineation of primary and nodal gross tumor volumes (GTVp/GTVn) to update treatment plans under evolving anatomy. Clinically, mid-treatment (midRT) contouring anchors to stable anatomical landmarks while interpreting deviations in tumor-bearing regions as treatment response; however, many learning-based methods either decouple pre-treatment (preRT) from midRT or impose overly global temporal consistency, thereby under-modeling the heterogeneous, target-dependent evolution of GTVp/GTVn. We propose **RaD-Seg**, a clinically grounded framework that mirrors the plan–verify–adapt workflow via three modules: (i) **Region-Aware Dual-Stream Contrastive Learning** uses region prototypes to disentangle stable anatomical anchors from response-sensitive features, maintaining spatial reliability and sensitivity to regression; (ii) **Temporal-Difference Response Encoding** encodes cumulative radiation effects as an explicit preRT–midRT residual code to modulate midRT representations, rather than conflating response with incidental appearance variation; and (iii) **Plan-Guided Asymmetric Regularization** anchors midRT semantics to the preRT planning definition in anatomically stable regions while permitting clinically plausible target evolution. Patient-level cross-validation on HNTS-MRG 2024 shows significant gains in midRT GTVp/GTVn delineation over strong baselines.

Keywords: Adaptive Radiotherapy · Longitudinal Segmentation · Disentangled Representation · Head and Neck Cancer · Contrastive Learning

1 Introduction

Head-and-neck (H&N) adaptive radiotherapy (ART) follows a clinically structured plan–verify–adapt workflow, in which target volumes delineated on the

G. Yang et al. (Eds.): MICCAI 2026, LNCS 16893, pp. 383–392, 2027.
https://doi.org/10.1007/978-3-032-38236-8_37

pre-treatment (preRT) planning scan must be re-assessed and re-delineated on the mid-treatment (midRT) verification scan to reflect interval anatomical deformation and therapy-induced response. In this setting, accurate longitudinal segmentation of the primary and nodal gross tumor volumes (GTVp/GTVn) is critical, as even small contour deviations may propagate into clinically meaningful target undercoverage or unnecessary irradiation of surrounding organs-at-risk, ultimately compromising dose conformity and adaptive decision-making. Importantly, this problem is inherently heterogeneous and asymmetric across tumor subregions: GTVp often undergoes substantial regression, shape deformation, and boundary migration during treatment, whereas GTVn typically exhibits more subtle changes and is confounded by radiation-induced edema, inflammation, and local tissue distortion. In routine practice, clinicians address this complexity by anchoring contour updates to relatively stable anatomical landmarks while interpreting localized deviations within tumor-bearing regions as treatment-response signals. However, this anatomy-guided yet response-aware reasoning process is only weakly captured by existing learning-based methods, which often emphasize global feature consistency but insufficiently model longitudinal response patterns and meaningful anchor-to-change relationships.

Recent deep models for ART segmentation are promising [1,5–9,11,12,14], yet many either treat preRT and midRT as separate domains or enforce global alignment/consistency that ignores the inherent asymmetry between stable anatomy and regressing targets [4,10,15]. While DIR supports contour propagation, correspondence can fail in regions with regression or appearance shifts, causing biased transfers [2]. Indiscriminate temporal invariance may suppress GTVp regression, whereas weak modeling of subtle GTVn evolution can lead to over-smoothing and missed contours [13]. Naive multi-timepoint fusion may further entangle treatment-induced appearance changes with true anatomical evolution, reducing interpretability [3,10,15]. These issues motivate preserving stable preRT plan semantics while enabling target-specific temporal adaptation.

In this work, we present **RaD-Seg**, a clinically motivated framework for longitudinal H&N target delineation that explicitly aligns with the ART plan–verify–adapt workflow. We first introduce **Region-Aware Dual-Stream Contrastive Learning** (RDC), which leverages region prototypes to disentangle time-invariant anatomical anchors from response-sensitive target representations, preserving stability in anatomically reliable regions while remaining responsive to expected regression. We then propose **Temporal-Difference Response Encoding** (TDRE), modeling cumulative radiation effects as an explicit residual shift between preRT and midRT feature states, rather than as incidental appearance variation. Finally, we propose **Plan-Guided Asymmetric Regularization** (PGAR) to anchor midRT semantics to the preRT planning definition under deformation, while allowing clinically plausible target evolution. We evaluate RaD-Seg on the HNTS-MRG 2024 cohort[1] for midRT GTVp/GTVn segmentation, achieving significant gains over SOTA baselines by

[1] https://hntsmrg24.grand-challenge.org/overview/.

modeling region-dependent temporal evolution and plan-guided asymmetry in ART.

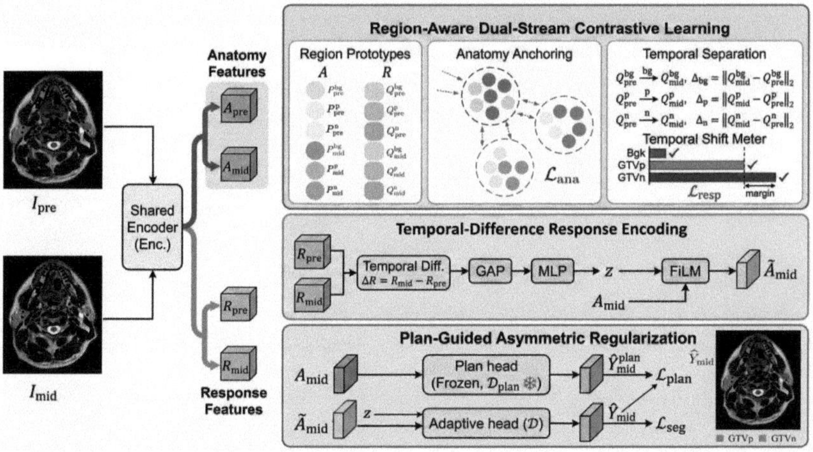

Fig. 1. Overview of RaD-Seg. Given paired preRT–midRT scans, RaD-Seg explicitly disentangles stable anatomical anchors from treatment-response representations, encodes longitudinal temporal residuals into a compact response code, and leverages plan-guided asymmetric regularization to model the distinct evolution patterns of GTVp and GTVn, thereby enabling clinically consistent midRT segmentation.

2 Methodology

2.1 Overview of RaD-Seg

In H&N ART, clinicians delineate planning targets on preRT and re-contour on midRT to account for regression and heterogeneous response; we formalize this as paired samples $\{(I^{(i)}_{\text{pre}}, I^{(i)}_{\text{mid}}, Y^{(i)}_{\text{pre}}, Y^{(i)}_{\text{mid}})\}_{i=1}^{N}$ with $Y_{\text{pre}}, Y_{\text{mid}} \in \{0,1\}^{K\times H\times W\times D}$ for $K{=}3$ classes (background, GTVp, GTVn), and predict $\widehat{Y}_{\text{mid}}$ from $(I_{\text{pre}}, I_{\text{mid}})$ while preserving stable anatomy and modeling target-dependent temporal dynamics consistent with the preRT plan. RaD-Seg integrates three components (Fig. 1): RDC (region-level disentanglement of anatomical anchors vs. response-sensitive features), TDRE (compact encoding of preRT–midRT response residuals), and PGAR (plan-guided asymmetric anchoring in reliable regions with flexibility for plausible target evolution). A shared encoder E extracts $F_t{=}E(I_t)$ for $t \in \{\text{pre}, \text{mid}\}$, projection heads produce $(A_t, R_t){=}(g_{\text{ana}}(F_t),\, g_{\text{resp}}(F_t))$, TDRE derives a response code Z from $(R_{\text{mid}}{-}R_{\text{pre}})$ and modulates midRT anatomy to $\widetilde{A}_{\text{mid}}$, and the decoder outputs $\widehat{Y}_{\text{mid}}{=}D(\widetilde{A}_{\text{mid}}, Z)$; supervision is used only during training, while inference requires only $(I_{\text{pre}}, I_{\text{mid}})$.

2.2 Region-Aware Dual-Stream Contrastive Learning

Clinicians interpret longitudinal change by anchoring edits to stable anatomy while allowing target regions to evolve under treatment. To formulate this region-dependent asymmetry, we aggregate voxel-wise features into class-specific region prototypes for both the anatomical stream A_t and the response stream R_t. For each class $c \in \mathcal{C} = \{\mathrm{bg}, \mathrm{p}, \mathrm{n}\}$ (background, GTVp, GTVn) and time $t \in \{\mathrm{pre}, \mathrm{mid}\}$, we compute mask-weighted average:

$$P_t^c = \frac{\sum_x M_t^c(x)\, A_t(x)}{\sum_x M_t^c(x) + \epsilon}, \qquad Q_t^c = \frac{\sum_x M_t^c(x)\, R_t(x)}{\sum_x M_t^c(x) + \epsilon}, \tag{1}$$

where x indexes voxels, M_t^c is the binary mask of class c at time t, and ϵ avoids division by zero. Importantly, these masks are used only during training to form region prototypes; no annotations are required at inference.

Stable anatomical structures serve as the reference for interpreting tumor evolution. We therefore enforce temporal consistency of background prototypes in the anatomical stream using an InfoNCE loss with in-batch negatives:

$$\mathcal{L}_{\mathrm{ana}} = -\log \frac{\exp\Big(\mathrm{sim}(\bar{P}_{\mathrm{pre}}^{\mathrm{bg}}, \bar{P}_{\mathrm{mid}}^{\mathrm{bg}})/\tau\Big)}{\sum_{j=1}^{B} \exp\Big(\mathrm{sim}(\bar{P}_{\mathrm{pre}}^{\mathrm{bg}}, \bar{P}_{\mathrm{mid}}^{\mathrm{bg},(j)})/\tau\Big)}, \tag{2}$$

where $\bar{P}$ denotes ℓ_2-normalized prototypes, $\mathrm{sim}(\cdot,\cdot)$ is cosine similarity, τ is a temperature parameter, B is the mini-batch size, and negatives are background prototypes from other patients within the batch. This objective promotes a time-invariant anatomical embedding in A_{pre} and A_{mid}, reflecting clinical anchoring to stable anatomy. Since GTVp often regresses markedly while GTVn changes more subtly under edema/inflammation, the response stream should remain stable on anatomical anchors yet preserve non-trivial temporal variation within tumor regions; we therefore measure prototype residual magnitudes:

$$\Delta_{\mathrm{bg}} = \left\|\bar{Q}_{\mathrm{mid}}^{\mathrm{bg}} - \bar{Q}_{\mathrm{pre}}^{\mathrm{bg}}\right\|_2, \Delta_{\mathrm{p}} = \left\|\bar{Q}_{\mathrm{mid}}^{\mathrm{p}} - \bar{Q}_{\mathrm{pre}}^{\mathrm{p}}\right\|_2, \Delta_{\mathrm{n}} = \left\|\bar{Q}_{\mathrm{mid}}^{\mathrm{n}} - \bar{Q}_{\mathrm{pre}}^{\mathrm{n}}\right\|_2, \tag{3}$$

and impose a margin that encourages (i) low temporal drift for background anchors and (ii) non-trivial temporal signatures for both targets:

$$\mathcal{L}_{\mathrm{resp}} = \Delta_{\mathrm{bg}} + \frac{1}{2}\Big(\max(0, m - \Delta_{\mathrm{p}}) + \max(0, m - \Delta_{\mathrm{n}})\Big), \tag{4}$$

where $m > 0$ is a margin. Together, Eq. (2)–(4) realize region-aware disentanglement: the anatomical stream is anchored to stable background, while the response stream preserves learnable temporal change in target regions, aligning with the asymmetric nature of ART contour refinement.

2.3 Temporal-Difference Response Encoding

Clinicians attribute midRT deviations from the preRT plan to cumulative treatment effects; accordingly, we encode radiation response as a temporal residual in the response stream to calibrate midRT anatomical representations, computing a residual feature volume:

$$\Delta R = R_{\text{mid}} - R_{\text{pre}}, \tag{5}$$

and summarize it into a compact treatment-state representations:

$$Z = h(\text{GAP}(\Delta R)), \tag{6}$$

where $\text{GAP}(\cdot)$ is global average pooling and $h(\cdot)$ is a lightweight multilayer perceptron (MLP); despite ΔR being spatially distributed, the global code Z summarizes patient-level response context while preserving spatial structure in the anatomical stream. We inject Z via Feature-wise Linear Modulation (FiLM) by applying channel-wise affine modulation to the midRT anatomical features:

$$\widetilde{A}_{\text{mid}} = \gamma(Z) \odot A_{\text{mid}} + \beta(Z), \tag{7}$$

where $\gamma(\cdot)$ and $\beta(\cdot)$ are learned linear maps producing per-channel scale and shift, and $\odot$ denotes the Hadamard product. TDRE thus disentangles longitudinal cues into (i) a spatially structured anatomical baseline A_{mid} and (ii) a compact response code Z summarizing systematic treatment effects, enabling the decoder to interpret midRT appearance changes in a plan-consistent coordinate system.

2.4 Plan-Guided Asymmetric Regularization

In ART, the preRT plan provides canonical target semantics that midRT adaptation should respect despite deformation and appearance shifts; thus, we train a plan-optimized teacher on the anatomical stream and impose an asymmetric (plan→adapt) constraint on midRT predictions, first learning a planning decoder D_{plan} from A_{pre}:

$$\widehat{Y}_{\text{pre}}^{\text{plan}} = D_{\text{plan}}(A_{\text{pre}}), \qquad \mathcal{L}_{\text{pre}} = \mathcal{L}_{\text{seg}}(\widehat{Y}_{\text{pre}}^{\text{plan}}, Y_{\text{pre}}), \tag{8}$$

and then freeze D_{plan} to serve as a fixed semantic reference. During joint optimization, the teacher produces a plan-consistent midRT distribution from the midRT anatomical stream:

$$\widehat{Y}_{\text{mid}}^{\text{plan}} = D_{\text{plan}}(A_{\text{mid}}). \tag{9}$$

The plan constraint should act strongly in regions whose semantics are expected to remain invariant (stable anatomy), while relaxing in tumor-bearing regions where genuine regression/migration is expected. To avoid using midRT labels to define this weighting, we derive an anchor mask from the preRT plan:

$$\Omega_{\text{anc}} = \{x \in \Omega \mid x \notin \text{Dilate}(\Omega_{\text{tum}}^{\text{pre}}, r)\}, \quad \Omega_{\text{tum}}^{\text{pre}} = \{x \in \Omega \mid Y_{\text{pre}}(x) \neq \text{bg}\}, \tag{10}$$

where Ω is the voxel grid and $\mathrm{Dilate}(\cdot, r)$ denotes morphological dilation with fixed radius r; thus, Ω_{anc} preserves reliable background while excluding a conservative margin around preRT targets to allow plausible evolution. We then regularize the student $\widehat{Y}_{\mathrm{mid}} = D(\widetilde{A}_{\mathrm{mid}}, Z)$ toward the frozen plan teacher only within Ω_{anc}:

$$\mathcal{L}_{\mathrm{plan}} = \sum_{x \in \Omega} w(x)\, \mathrm{KL}\Big(\widehat{Y}^{\mathrm{plan}}_{\mathrm{mid}}(x) \parallel \widehat{Y}_{\mathrm{mid}}(x)\Big), \qquad w(x) = \mathbf{1}[x \in \Omega_{\mathrm{anc}}], \tag{11}$$

where $\mathrm{KL}(\cdot \| \cdot)$ denotes the Kullback–Leibler divergence. The PGAR constraint is designed to be asymmetric, anchoring midRT predictions to plan-derived semantics within stable anatomical regions without requiring preRT features to explain treatment-induced midRT variations, thereby allowing target regions to evolve during therapy. Importantly, PGAR is used only during training. The anchor region Ω_{anc} is derived from the preRT planning label to regularize reliable non-target areas, while $Y_{\mathrm{pre}}, Y_{\mathrm{mid}}, \Omega_{\mathrm{anc}}$, and the frozen plan teacher are not required at inference. After training, the student directly predicts $\widehat{Y}_{\mathrm{mid}}$ from $(I_{\mathrm{pre}}, I_{\mathrm{mid}})$, indicating that the plan prior is distilled into the learned representation and decoder while maintaining label-free deployment.

2.5 Segmentation Objective

We supervise midRT prediction using a standard composite segmentation loss:

$$\mathcal{L}_{\mathrm{seg}} = \mathrm{CE}(\widehat{Y}_{\mathrm{mid}}, Y_{\mathrm{mid}}) + \mathrm{Dice}(\widehat{Y}_{\mathrm{mid}}, Y_{\mathrm{mid}}), \tag{12}$$

where $\mathrm{CE}(\cdot, \cdot)$ is voxel-wise cross-entropy and $\mathrm{Dice}(\cdot, \cdot)$ is the soft Dice loss over K classes. The full objective combines segmentation supervision with the proposed regularizers:

$$\mathcal{L} = \lambda_{\mathrm{seg}} \mathcal{L}_{\mathrm{seg}} + \lambda_{\mathrm{ana}} \mathcal{L}_{\mathrm{ana}} + \lambda_{\mathrm{resp}} \mathcal{L}_{\mathrm{resp}} + \lambda_{\mathrm{plan}} \mathcal{L}_{\mathrm{plan}}. \tag{13}$$

Across all experiments, the four loss terms used equal weights ($\lambda_{\mathrm{seg}} = \lambda_{\mathrm{ana}} = \lambda_{\mathrm{resp}} = \lambda_{\mathrm{plan}} = 1.0$). We set $\tau = 0.1$ in Eq. (2), $m = 1.0$ in Eq. (4), and $r = 5$ voxels in Eq. (10) after resampling to 1-mm isotropic spacing. All hyperparameters were fixed across folds, ablations, and comparisons without test-set tuning.

3 Experiments

3.1 Experimental Setup

We evaluate RaD-Seg on the public HNTS-MRG 2024 longitudinal H&N MRI cohort[2] (N=150 paired preRT/midRT T2w scans with expert GTVp/GTVn labels) using patient-level K-fold cross-validation (default K=5) with fixed folds for fair comparison and paired testing. Volumes are resampled to 1 mm isotropic

[2] https://hntsmrg24.grand-challenge.org/overview/.

spacing and min–max normalized, without additional DIR beyond the provided pairs. We train on an RTX A6000 (48 GB) with AdamW (learning rate 2×10^{-4}, weight decay 1×10^{-5}), and cosine annealing for 500 epochs, following a two-stage schedule: pretrain D_{plan} on preRT with $\mathcal{L}_{\text{seg}}$, then freeze it and optimize the full model on midRT; PGAR uses Ω_{anc} derived from the preRT plan (Eq. (10)), and inference requires only $(I_{\text{pre}}, I_{\text{mid}})$. All baselines share the same folds and inputs, and we report Dice similarity coefficient (DSC, %) and 95th percentile Hausdorff distance (HD_{95}, mm) for GTVp/GTVn with two-sided Wilcoxon signed-rank tests on paired per-patient scores ($p < 0.05$). Results are reported as mean±std (median) across patients and then averaged over cross-validation folds.

Table 1. Ablation study. † indicates that RaD-Seg significantly outperforms the corresponding variant ($p < 0.05$). The best results are highlighted in **bold**.

Method Variant	**GTVp**		**GTVn**	
	DSC (%) ↑	**HD_{95} (mm) ↓**	**DSC (%) ↑**	**HD_{95} (mm) ↓**
Baseline (concat. preRT+midRT)	74.43 ± 12.53 $(74.17)^\dagger$	7.99 ± 5.31 $(7.27)^\dagger$	66.12 ± 15.47 $(68.78)^\dagger$	11.52 ± 6.73 $(10.57)^\dagger$
+ RDC (anatomy anchoring)	76.13 ± 12.87 $(77.52)^\dagger$	6.14 ± 3.56 $(5.23)^\dagger$	67.12 ± 17.58 $(69.84)^\dagger$	10.15 ± 5.42 $(8.97)^\dagger$
+ TDRE (response residual)	74.82 ± 13.91 $(76.53)^\dagger$	7.23 ± 3.94 $(6.42)^\dagger$	68.23 ± 16.82 $(70.14)^\dagger$	9.21 ± 4.83 $(8.12)^\dagger$
+ PGAR (plan semantics)	75.46 ± 13.14 $(76.92)^\dagger$	6.93 ± 3.82 $(6.15)^\dagger$	67.51 ± 17.06 $(69.57)^\dagger$	9.82 ± 5.14 $(8.63)^\dagger$
TDRE + PGAR	75.92 ± 12.54 $(77.26)^\dagger$	6.53 ± 3.31 $(5.82)^\dagger$	69.13 ± 14.82 $(70.83)^\dagger$	8.05 ± 4.12 $(7.14)^\dagger$
RDC + TDRE	76.84 ± 11.23 $(77.93)^\dagger$	5.26 ± 2.94 $(4.52)^\dagger$	68.91 ± 15.12 $(70.52)^\dagger$	8.13 ± 4.24 $(7.23)^\dagger$
RDC + PGAR	77.12 ± 10.57 $(78.24)^\dagger$	4.82 ± 2.64 $(4.13)^\dagger$	67.92 ± 16.23 $(69.91)^\dagger$	9.15 ± 4.63 $(8.24)^\dagger$
RaD-Seg (Ours)	**77.35 ± 9.81 (78.43)**	**4.25 ± 2.12 (3.51)**	**69.48 ± 13.20 (71.13)**	**7.55 ± 3.50 (6.20)**

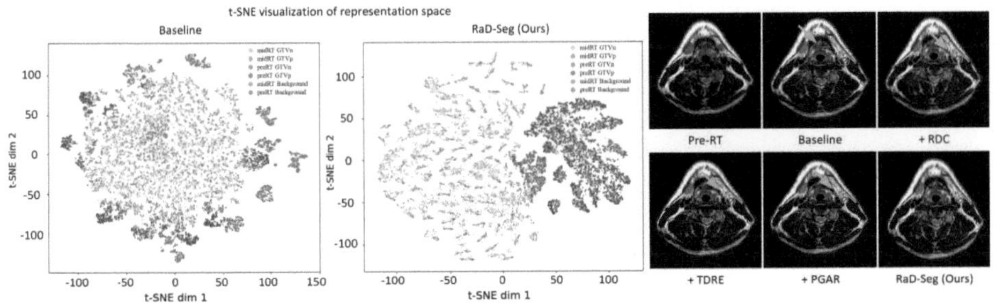

Fig. 2. Ablation analysis of RaD-Seg. Left: t-SNE on the test set shows improved feature disentanglement, with clearer separation of anatomy-anchored and response-sensitive embeddings. **Right:** MidRT GTVp/GTVn ablations show progressive contour refinement from RDC, TDRE, and PGAR. Arrows highlight reduced boundary leakage and false positives, yielding more clinically plausible delineation under deformation and edema-related shifts (GT GTVp: red; GT GTVn: purple; predicted GTVn: green). (Color figure online)

4 Results

4.1 Ablation Study

Table 1 and Fig. 2 show that RDC, TDRE, and PGAR provide complementary gains. Using the same 3D ResNet encoder–decoder with concatenated preRT–midRT inputs and only $\mathcal{L}_{\text{seg}}$, the ablation baseline isolates module effects without changing capacity. RDC mainly improves geometric accuracy through anatomy anchoring (GTVp HD_{95}: 7.99 → 6.14 mm; GTVn: 11.52 → 10.15 mm), whereas TDRE enhances temporal response modeling and nodal delineation under edema-confounded changes (GTVn DSC: 66.12 → 68.23%; HD_{95}: 11.52 → 9.21 mm). PGAR further stabilizes midRT predictions by preserving reliable plan semantics while allowing plausible target evolution. Among two-module variants, TDRE + PGAR gives the best nodal results, while RDC+PGAR achieves the best primary-target geometry. The full RaD-Seg produces more structured embeddings, tighter contours, and significantly outperforms all ablated variants (paired Wilcoxon, $p < 0.05$).

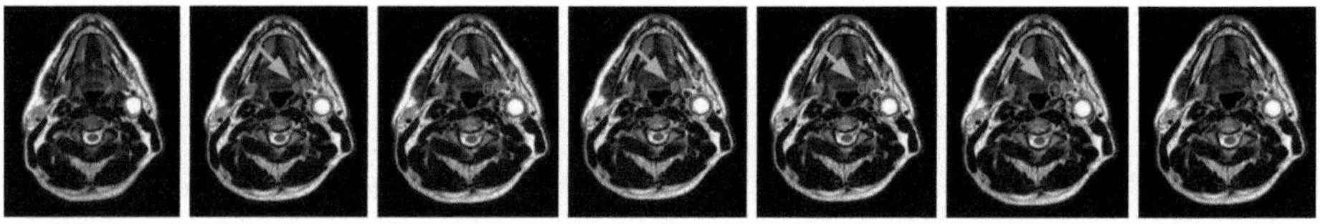

Fig. 3. Qualitative midRT segmentation comparison. SOTA methods show over-delineation in arrow-marked regions, whereas RaD-Seg yields more clinically plausible contours by modeling treatment response and enforcing plan-guided asymmetry. PreRT images are shown only as longitudinal references; all predictions are evaluated on midRT segmentation (GT GTVp: red; GT GTVn: purple; predicted GTVn: green). (Color figure online)

Table 2. Quantitative comparison with SOTA methods. † indicates that RaD-Seg significantly outperforms the corresponding method ($p < 0.05$).

Method	GTVp		GTVn	
	DSC (%) ↑	HD_{95} (mm) ↓	DSC (%) ↑	HD_{95} (mm) ↓
VoxelMorph [2]	76.54 ± 12.30 (78.13)†	6.82 ± 3.15 (5.98)†	67.20 ± 15.40 (69.54)†	10.45 ± 5.20 (9.11)†
nnU-Net [3]	73.12 ± 14.84 (75.25)†	8.15 ± 4.52 (7.21)†	64.89 ± 17.11 (66.49)†	12.30 ± 6.14 (10.87)†
LongiSeg [4]	75.43 ± 13.10 (77.05)†	7.17 ± 3.81 (6.41)†	66.56 ± 16.20 (68.15)†	11.05 ± 5.50 (9.84)†
Dual Flow UNet [15]	77.15 ± 11.52 (78.35)†	6.45 ± 2.91 (5.57)†	68.17 ± 14.80 (70.21)†	9.81 ± 4.85 (8.53)†
UMambaAdj [10]	74.21 ± 14.51 (76.12)†	7.81 ± 4.22 (6.91)†	66.54 ± 18.20 (69.36)†	10.97 ± 5.97 (9.54)†
RaD-Seg (Ours)	**77.35 ± 9.81 (78.43)**	**4.25 ± 2.12 (3.51)**	**69.48 ± 13.20 (71.13)**	**7.55 ± 3.50 (6.20)**

4.2 Comparison to State-of-the-Art

We compare RaD-Seg with representative ART/longitudinal baselines, including VoxelMorph [2], nnU-Net [3], LongiSeg [4], Dual Flow UNet [15], and UMambaAdj [10]. VoxelMorph is used for registration-based contour propagation by warping preRT images and GTVp/GTVn labels to midRT space. As shown in Table 2, RaD-Seg achieves the best overall performance, with the highest DSC and lowest HD_{95} for both GTVp (77.35%/4.25 mm) and GTVn (69.48%/7.55 mm). Compared with the strongest baseline, Dual Flow UNet, RaD-Seg improves both overlap and boundary accuracy, reflecting its anatomy anchoring and response-aware modeling. Figure 3 shows reduced drift and leakage with more plausible contours. All improvements are significant (paired Wilcoxon, $p < 0.05$).

5 Conclusion

Overall, RaD-Seg follows the plan–verify–adapt paradigm by integrating stable anatomy anchoring, explicit response modeling, and plan-guided asymmetric regularization to stabilize midRT segmentation while preserving plausible target evolution. Experiments on HNTS-MRG 2024 show statistically significant SOTA performance for both GTVp and GTVn, with ablations confirming each module's contribution. Future work will extend RaD-Seg toward uncertainty-aware clinician-in-the-loop adaptation and robust multi-sequence, multi-center deployment.

Acknowledgments. This study was funded by National Key Research and Development Program of China (2022YFC2405200), National Natural Science Foundation of China (U22A2051, 62271246), and Natural Science Foundation of Beijing Municipality (L252201, L252126).

Disclosure of Interests. The authors have no competing interests to declare that are relevant to the content of this article.

References

1. Andrearczyk, V., et al.: Overview of the HECKTOR challenge at MICCAI 2021: automatic head and neck tumor segmentation and outcome prediction in PET/CT images. In: 3D Head and Neck Tumor Segmentation in PET/CT Challenge, pp. 1–37. Springer (2021)
2. Balakrishnan, G., Zhao, A., Sabuncu, M.R., Guttag, J., Dalca, A.V.: VoxelMorph: a learning framework for deformable medical image registration. IEEE Trans. Med. Imaging **38**(8), 1788–1800 (2019)
3. Isensee, F., Jaeger, P.F., Kohl, S.A., Petersen, J., Maier-Hein, K.H.: nnU-Net: a self-configuring method for deep learning-based biomedical image segmentation. Nat. Methods **18**(2), 203–211 (2021)

4. Kächele, J., Zenk, M., Rokuss, M., Ulrich, C., Wald, T., Maier-Hein, K.H.: Enhanced nnU-Net architectures for automated MRI segmentation of head and neck tumors in adaptive radiation therapy. In: Challenge on Head and Neck Tumor Segmentation for MRI-Guided Applications, pp. 50–64. Springer (2024)
5. Khor, H.G., Chen, F., Liao, H.: CFM-SAM2: CNN-prompt-guided segment anything 2 with cross-modal fusion and contextual feature assimilation for gross target volume segmentation in nasopharyngeal carcinoma. In: Proceedings of the 2025 2nd International Conference on Smart Healthcare and Wearable Intelligent Devices, pp. 149–154 (2025)
6. Khor, H.G., et al.: RT-SAM: visual-prompt fusion and uncertainty enhancement for nasopharyngeal carcinoma radiotherapy target delineation. IEEE J. Biomed. Health Inform. **30**(9), 7586–7599 (2026). https://doi.org/10.1109/JBHI.2026.3669979
7. Khor, H.G., et al.: Unified prompt-visual interactive segmentation of clinical target volume in CT for nasopharyngeal carcinoma with prior anatomical information. In: International Conference on Medical Image Computing and Computer-Assisted Intervention, pp. 659–669. Springer (2024)
8. Li, Z., et al.: Patient-specific daily updated deep learning auto-segmentation for MRI-guided adaptive radiotherapy. Radiother. Oncol. **177**, 222–230 (2022)
9. McDonald, B.A., et al.: Investigation of autosegmentation techniques on T2-weighted MRI for off-line dose reconstruction in MR-linac workflow for head and neck cancers. Med. Phys. **51**(1), 278–291 (2024)
10. Ren, J., Hochreuter, K., Kallehauge, J.F., Korreman, S.S.: UMamba adjustment: advancing GTV segmentation for head and neck cancer in MRI-guided RT with UMamba and nnU-Net ResEnc planner. In: Challenge on Head and Neck Tumor Segmentation for MRI-Guided Applications, pp. 123–135. Springer (2024)
11. Ren, J., Hochreuter, K., Rasmussen, M.E., Kallehauge, J.F., Korreman, S.S.: Gradient map-assisted head and neck tumor segmentation: a Pre-RT to Mid-RT approach in MRI-guided radiotherapy. In: Challenge on Head and Neck Tumor Segmentation for MRI-Guided Applications, pp. 36–49. Springer (2024)
12. Tie, X., Chen, W., Huemann, Z., Schott, B., Liu, N., Bradshaw, T.J.: Deep learning for longitudinal gross tumor volume segmentation in MRI-guided adaptive radiotherapy for head and neck cancer. In: Challenge on Head and Neck Tumor Segmentation for MRI-Guided Applications, pp. 99–111. Springer (2024)
13. Vizitiu, A., Mohaiu, A.T., Popdan, I.M., Balachandran, A., Ghesu, F.C., Comaniciu, D.: Multi-scale self-supervised learning for longitudinal lesion tracking with optional supervision. In: International Conference on Medical Image Computing and Computer-Assisted Intervention, pp. 573–582. Springer (2023)
14. Wahid, K.A., et al.: Overview of the head and neck tumor segmentation for magnetic resonance guided applications (HNTS-MRG) 2024 challenge. In: Challenge on Head and Neck Tumor Segmentation for MRI-Guided Applications, pp. 1–35. Springer (2024)
15. Wang, L., Liao, W., Zhang, S., Wang, G.: Head and neck tumor segmentation of MRI from pre-and mid-radiotherapy with pre-training, data augmentation and dual flow UNet. In: Challenge on Head and Neck Tumor Segmentation for MRI-Guided Applications, pp. 75–86. Springer (2024)

Real-Time 6D Ultrasound Probe Pose Tracking in Freehand Scanning

Jungjae Son[1], Guil Jung[1], Seok-Hwan Oh[2], Hyeonjik Lee[1], Young-Min Kim[2], Sang-Yun Kim[1], Myeong-Gee Kim[2], HyukSool Kwon[3], and Hyeon-Min Bae[1(✉)]

[1] Korea Advanced Institute of Science and Technology (KAIST), Daejeon, South Korea
{jjson0509,hmbae}@kaist.ac.kr

[2] Barreleye Inc., Seoul, South Korea

[3] Seoul National University Bundang Hospital (SNUBH), Seongnam, South Korea

Abstract. The quality of ultrasound images strongly depends on the operator's experience and expertise. To mitigate this operator dependence, recent studies have investigated methods to support sonographer training, skill assessment, and probe guidance systems. These applications require accurate and robust estimation of the 6D ultrasound probe pose during freehand scanning. In this study, we propose a real-time 6D ultrasound probe pose tracking framework using a single RGB-D camera. This framework is designed to operate under real-world scanning conditions, where hand-induced occlusion and dynamic motion frequently occur. The proposed framework consists of two stages: probe keypoint detection and keypoint-guided pose estimation. The probe keypoint detection is introduced to enhance tracking robustness even under hand occlusion and rapid motion. Guided by the detected keypoints, the pose estimation finally determines the 6D pose of the probe. Furthermore, we develop an automated self-training strategy which significantly reduces manual annotation effort utilizing a pose estimation foundation model. As a result, the proposed framework achieves state-of-the-art pose accuracy and tracking robustness simultaneously compared to existing methods, while maintaining real-time performance above 25 fps.

Keywords: Ultrasound probe pose estimation · Real-time ultrasound probe pose tracking · Probe localization

1 Introduction

Ultrasound imaging is widely used due to its real-time capability, cost-effectiveness, and non-invasive nature. However, the ultrasound scanning process is highly dependent on operator, requiring substantial training to ensure diagnostic-quality imaging. Consequently, recent studies have explored sonographer training, skill assessment, and probe guidance systems to mitigate the operator dependence and improve scan quality [26].

G. Yang et al. (Eds.): MICCAI 2026, LNCS 16893, pp. 393–403, 2027.
https://doi.org/10.1007/978-3-032-38236-8_38

Accurate 6D pose estimation of the ultrasound probe is fundamental to these systems. Traditional approaches rely on external devices such as electromagnetic (EM), optical, or inertial measurement unit (IMU)-based tracking systems [2,11,13,15,16]. Although these devices provide high accuracy, they increase system cost and hardware complexity and limit clinical usability. Therefore, there remains a need for trackerless and markerless approaches to improve usability and enable unconstrained freehand scanning.

Object 6D pose estimation has been extensively studied in generic object settings [5,7,10,21–23]. Notably, pose estimation foundation models such as FoundationPose [23] demonstrates that real-time pose tracking of a novel object can be achieved using only appearance cues. However, in ultrasound probe scanning scenarios, additional challenges arise due to frequent hand occlusion and dynamic motion, which cause tracking instability and limit the direct use of existing methods. Although recent studies have investigated probe pose estimation in hand–object interaction scenarios [1], the validation has been confined to controlled settings, with limited evaluation under real-world conditions.

In this paper, we propose a real-time 6D ultrasound probe pose tracking framework, UPTrack (Ultrasound Probe Tracking), using a single RGB-D camera. Our markerless and trackerless approach is specifically designed to handle realistic scanning scenarios involving severe hand occlusion and dynamic motion. The framework leverages a pose estimation foundation model integrated with novel keypoint-based guidance to enhance tracking robustness. Furthermore, we introduce an automated training pipeline for the keypoint detection network, enabling self-training without manual annotation. As a result, the proposed framework achieves state-of-the-art tracking accuracy and robustness while maintaining real-time performance.

Our contributions can be summarized as follows:

- A real-time 6D ultrasound probe pose tracking framework for freehand scanning using a single RGB-D camera
- A novel keypoint-guided tracking architecture that achieves robust performance under hand occlusion and dynamic probe motion
- An automated self-training pipeline for probe keypoint detection that significantly reduces manual annotation effort
- Comprehensive validation demonstrating state-of-the-art accuracy and real-time stability under realistic freehand scanning conditions

2 Methods

UPTrack, the proposed framework, performs real-time tracking of the 6D ultrasound probe pose from an RGB-D input sequence as shown in Fig. 1. The tracking pipeline consists of two processes: Initial Frame Pose Registration which estimates the initial pose by selecting the pose candidate that best explains the observed frame among multiple hypotheses, and Next Frame Pose Tracking which updates the current pose by comparing the rendered frame from the

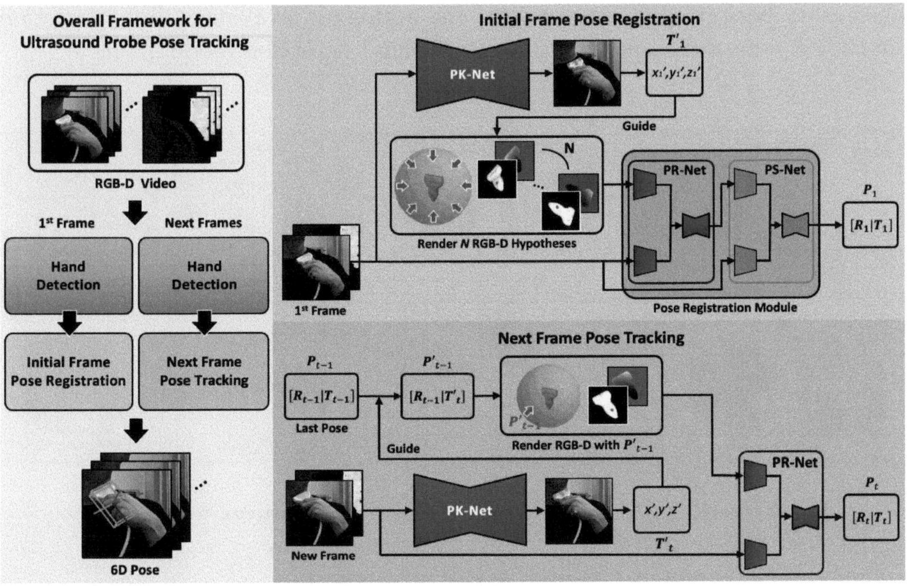

Fig. 1. Overview of the real-time 6D ultrasound probe pose tracking framework.

previous pose with the observed frame. Both processes share two core stages: Probe Keypoint Detection (Sect. 2.1) and Keypoint-Guided Probe Pose Estimation (Sect. 2.2).

2.1 Probe Keypoint Detection

A Probe Keypoint Net (PK-Net) is designed to predict a predefined set of landmarks on the ultrasound probe from a single RGB image. The five landmarks are selected from regions with distinctive structural and textural features to ensure stable detection. Specifically, they include: (1,2) the two side endpoints of the transducer, (3) the center of the transducer, (4) the top-center of the probe body, and (5) the tail of the probe.

PK-Net is designed as a lightweight architecture consisting of a ResNeXt-based encoder [25] and a deconvolutional decoder [24]. This design enables real-time performance within the overall framework. The network outputs five probability heatmaps corresponding to predefined probe keypoints, from which 2D keypoint locations are obtained via peak extraction during inference. During training, instead of directly regressing keypoint coordinates, PK-Net is supervised to predict a probability heatmap for each keypoint. Each heatmap is generated as a 2D Gaussian centered at the annotated keypoint location. This supervision mitigates label noise and stabilizes learning, particularly for occluded keypoints whose precise locations are difficult to annotate.

To reduce computational cost, keypoint detection is performed only within a region of interest (ROI) around the hand holding the probe. This strategy avoids unnecessary background computation and stabilizes probe keypoint prediction. The ROI is determined using a pretrained hand detection model [27].

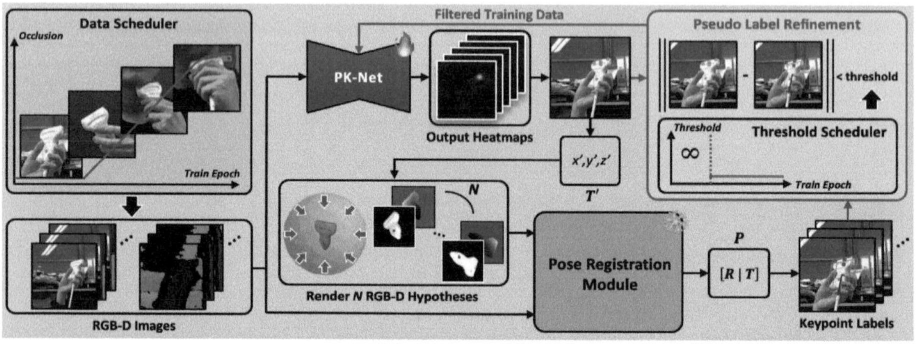

Fig. 2. Overview of the automated self-training strategy for PK-Net.

Automated Self-training Strategy. To achieve robust performance across diverse operators and probe grasping styles, training PK-Net on large-scale data collected under varied conditions is essential. However, manual annotation of dataset of this scale requires substantial effort. To address this challenge, we propose an automated training pipeline as illustrated in Fig. 2.

With this training strategy, PK-Net progressively improves its robustness to occlusion via self-training without manual annotation. We utilize a Pose Registration Module composed of the pretrained Pose Refinement Network (PR-Net) and Pose Selection Network (PS-Net) from FoundationPose [23]. This module selects and outputs the pose that best matches the current frame among N pose hypotheses. As the probe is a rigid object, keypoint pseudo labels can be automatically generated from the estimated pose based on its geometric dimensions.

However, without a sufficiently trained PK-Net, the Pose Registration Module is vulnerable to occlusion. Therefore, we adopt a data scheduler that structures the training data from minimally occluded samples to increasingly occluded samples as PK-Net learns. Furthermore, a refinement step is applied before they are fed to PK-Net for training since incorrect pose estimation can generate noisy pseudo labels. Samples are filtered out if the average pixel L2 distance between pseudo keypoints and PK-Net predictions exceeds a threshold, which is set to infinity for the first 10 epochs and limited to 6 pixels from epochs 10 to 25.

2.2 Keypoint-Guided Probe Pose Estimation

In this stage, the final 6D pose of the ultrasound probe is determined based on the keypoints obtained from the PK-Net. For a given RGB-D video sequence, the first frame undergoes Initial Frame Pose Registration, while all subsequent frames are sequentially processed via Next Frame Pose Tracking.

In Initial Frame Pose Registration, pose prediction is performed using keypoint-based guidance together with PR-Net and PS-Net. In Next Frame Pose Tracking, keypoint-based guidance and PR-Net are used to perform pose updates.

Keypoint-Based Guidance. After probe keypoint detection, the 2D coordinates of the five predefined keypoints are obtained. The 2D probe center (u_0, v_0) is approximated as the midpoint between the transducer center keypoint and the probe tail keypoint. The probe depth is estimated from the detected keypoints and the corresponding depth map captured by the RGB-D camera.

Given the 2D pixel coordinates (u, v) and the corresponding depth value d, the 3D coordinates of each keypoint in the camera coordinate system are computed as:

$$\mathbf{X}_{cam} = d\,\mathbf{K}^{-1}\tilde{\mathbf{u}}, \quad \tilde{\mathbf{u}} = \begin{bmatrix} u \; v \; 1 \end{bmatrix}^{\top}, \tag{1}$$

where $\mathbf{X}_{cam} = [x, y, z]^{\top}$ denotes the 3D coordinates in the camera coordinate system, and $\mathbf{K}$ is the camera intrinsic matrix. Using (u_0, v_0) and Eq. (1), an estimated translation of the 3D probe center $\mathbf{T}' = [x', y', z']^{\top}$ is obtained. This is used to guide the translation component of the 6D pose $\mathbf{P} = [\mathbf{R} \mid \mathbf{T}]$, where $\mathbf{R} \in SO(3)$ denotes rotation and $\mathbf{T} \in \mathbf{R}^3$ denotes translation.

Initial Frame Pose Registration. Through keypoint-based guidance, a coarse translation of the probe in the initial frame is obtained as $\mathbf{T}'_1 = [x'_1, y'_1, z'_1]^{\top}$. Subsequently, N rotation hypotheses are generated, producing multiple pose candidates. Specifically, we sampled 42 viewpoints on a sphere using an icosphere-based sampling and applied 6 in-plane rotations per viewpoint, yielding $N = 252$ pose hypotheses. For each pose candidate, a rendered RGB-D result is obtained.

PR-Net takes two inputs: the rendered RGB-D frame corresponding to a pose hypothesis and the actual RGB-D frame. It predicts the relative pose offsets, $\Delta\mathbf{R}$ and $\Delta\mathbf{T}$, required to better align the rendered object with the observed appearance in the captured real RGB-D frame. By updating each pose hypothesis with the predicted pose offset, all pose candidates are refined toward the true pose. Given the relative pose offsets $\Delta\mathbf{R}$ and $\Delta\mathbf{T}$ predicted by PR-Net, the pose is updated as

$$\mathbf{R}_{new} = \Delta\mathbf{R}\mathbf{R}_{old}, \quad \mathbf{T}_{new} = \mathbf{T}_{old} + \Delta\mathbf{T}. \tag{2}$$

After PR-Net refines the pose candidates, PS-Net takes the rendered RGB-D image of each refined candidate and the actual RGB-D frame as input. It outputs the scores indicating how well each candidate explains the observed appearance, and the highest-scoring candidate is selected as the final pose.

Next Frame Pose Tracking. In the Next Frame Pose Tracking process, the pose from the previous frame $\mathbf{P}_{t-1} = [\mathbf{R}_{t-1} \mid \mathbf{T}_{t-1}]$ is updated to obtain the current pose $\mathbf{P}_t = [\mathbf{R}_t \mid \mathbf{T}_t]$. This process consists of two sequential updates: first through keypoint-based guidance and second through PR-Net.

First, the keypoint-based guided translation $\mathbf{T}' = [x', y', z']^\top$ estimated from the detected keypoints replaces the translation component of $\mathbf{P}_{t-1}$, yielding $\mathbf{P}'_{t-1} = [\mathbf{R}_{t-1} \mid \mathbf{T}']$. Second, a rendered RGB-D frame based on $\mathbf{P}'_{t-1}$ and the captured RGB-D frame at time t are fed into PR-Net. PR-Net predicts $\Delta\mathbf{R}$ and $\Delta\mathbf{T}$, and the pose is updated according to Eq. (2) to obtain $\mathbf{P}_t$.

Table 1. Keypoint localization accuracy of the proposed PK-Net.

Keypoint	Mean L2 [px]	PCK @2px	PCK @4px	PCK @8px
Transducer Sides	2.251	0.458	0.857	0.998
Transducer Center	1.954	0.511	0.918	1.000
Probe Top-Center	1.782	0.546	0.953	1.000
Probe Tail	4.973	0.145	0.413	0.829
Total	2.698	0.425	0.786	0.959

3 Experiments

To validate the proposed framework under real-world scanning conditions, we conducted three experiments: (1) keypoint detection accuracy, (2) pose tracking accuracy, and (3) pose estimation robustness through an ablation study.

Data were acquired using an Intel RealSense D455 camera [4,18,19] at a resolution of 1280×720 for RGB-D capture and GE Linear Probe L3-12. Ground truth poses were acquired using an NDI Polaris Vega optical tracker [6,8,9, 14], which provides sub-millimeter volumetric accuracy (IQR < 0.1 mm) [3]. All experiments were performed on a system with an NVIDIA RTX 4090 GPU.

Probe scanning was conducted at distances of 0.5–1.5 m from the RGB-D camera. This range was chosen considering the depth reliability of the RealSense D455 and realistic clinical scanning environments.

For quantitative pose evaluation, the optical tracker marker was attached to the probe via a long, thin, and rigid 3D-printed bridge structure. This setup prevented the marker from interfering with natural probe grasping and minimized its influence on vision-based inference. For the qualitative results in Fig. 3, we used a marker-free setup to demonstrate pose inference under practical real-world conditions without markers.

3.1 Keypoint Detection Accuracy

We evaluated the proposed PK-Net by comparing the predicted 2D keypoint locations with ground truth. Localization accuracy was measured using mean L2 error (in pixel, px) and Percentage of Correct Keypoints (PCK).

Table 1 provides the results. The network achieved an overall mean L2 error of 2.698 pixels. For the transducer side keypoints, symmetry was considered during evaluation. The probe tail showed larger error due to frequent hand occlusion.

3.2 Pose Tracking Accuracy

We evaluated the 6D probe pose tracking accuracy on 35 RGB-D test videos using Absolute Trajectory Error (ATE) and Relative Pose Error (RPE) [12, 20]. The test videos were captured under unconstrained freehand scanning by multiple subjects. To exclude sequences in which all methods completely fail tracking, severe occlusion and rapid motion were not included. For methods that use segmentation masks, probe masks were generated using SAM2 [17].

Table 2. Quantitative evaluation of the proposed framework, including comparisons with existing 6D pose estimation methods in probe pose accuracy (ATE/RPE: t = translation [mm], r = rotation [°]) and runtime performance (FPS). Runtime denotes end-to-end pose tracking speed, excluding GUI rendering overhead.

Method	Seg. Mask	Occlusion	ATE_t mae ↓	ATE_t rmse ↓	RPE_t mae ↓	RPE_t rmse ↓	RPE_r mae ↓	RPE_r rmse ↓	FPS ↑
Any6D	SAM2	No-occ	27.72	30.42	24.38	51.14	63.47	88.63	<1
		Hand-occ	41.23	46.02	40.62	32.00	77.20	93.20	
SAM6D	SAM2	No-occ	10.99	17.40	12.58	23.82	9.16	15.02	13.70
		Hand-occ	34.50	50.00	35.09	60.41	18.00	25.54	
BundleSDF	SAM2	No-occ	2.42	2.67	1.86	2.11	3.17	3.62	13.33
		Hand-occ	17.46	19.11	7.59	8.35	6.41	7.13	
Ours	Not required	No-occ	**2.17**	**2.44**	**1.77**	**2.01**	**2.73**	**3.09**	**25.62**
		Hand-occ	**13.04**	**15.00**	**7.50**	**8.31**	**4.95**	**5.58**	

Table 2 shows quantitative tracking accuracy results and presents a comparative study against representative pose estimation models [7,10,22]. Overall, the proposed framework achieved the highest tracking accuracy and FPS among the compared methods, while operating without requiring a precomputed segmentation mask.

3.3 Ablation Study on Pose Estimation Robustness

We conducted an ablation study on the proposed keypoint-based guidance using PK-Net to analyze its contribution to tracking robustness. Robustness is evaluated separately for initial frame pose registration and next frame pose tracking. The evaluation is performed on RGB-D videos and quantified by the success rate, defined as the absence of pose registration failure or pose tracking failure within each sequence. A total of 110 test videos were collected from multiple subjects under diverse real-world environments, including severe hand occlusion and dynamic motion. The subjects were instructed to grasp the probe in the manner typically used by sonographers during freehand scanning. Tracking failure is defined with respect to optical ground truth, and a frame is considered failed if the translation error exceeds 20 mm or the rotation error exceeds 20°.

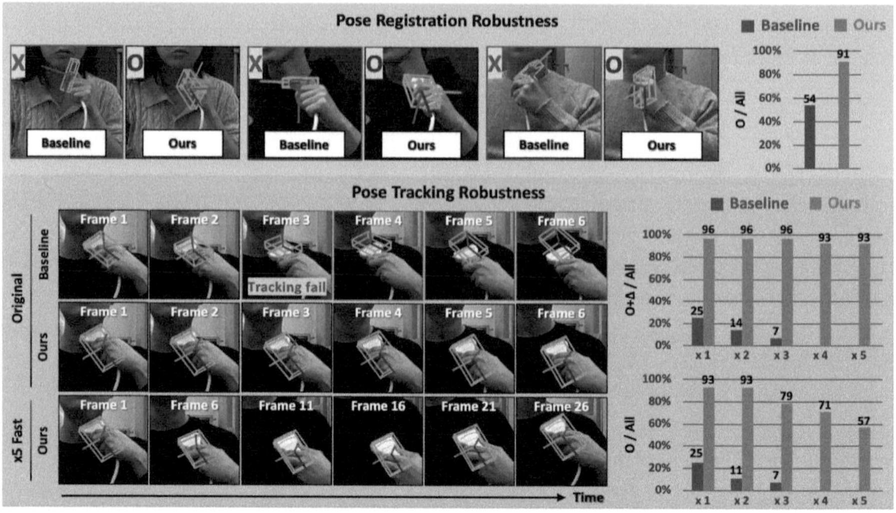

Fig. 3. (Top) Pose Registration Robustness: qualitative results and pose estimation success rate comparison. (Bottom) Pose Tracking Robustness: qualitative results and tracking success rate comparison under varying motion speeds.

Initial Frame Pose Registration. As shown in Fig. 3 (Top), the pose estimation success rate on the first frame of each test video is evaluated. Under severe hand occlusion, the baseline achieves a success rate of 54%, whereas the proposed framework achieves 91%. The segmentation-based baseline more frequently fails to estimate probe translation, leading to registration errors. In contrast, the proposed keypoint-guided approach successfully localizes probe keypoints, including those in occluded regions, resulting in more robust pose registration.

Next Frame Pose Tracking. Tracking robustness is presented in Fig. 3 (Bottom). A sequence is considered strictly successful (O) if no tracking failure occurs throughout the sequence. Under the relaxed criterion (△), a sequence is also considered successful provided that tracking failures do not occur for three or more consecutive frames.

Furthermore, to evaluate robustness under dynamic motion, frame dropping is applied to emulate fast scanning motion, where 0 drop denotes the original video and 1–4 drops correspond to ×2–×5 motion speeds, respectively. The baseline achieves 25% robustness on the original videos and fails on all sequences at ×4 speed. In contrast, the proposed framework achieves 93% robustness (O) and 96% robustness (O+△) on the original videos, and maintains stable tracking even at ×5 motion speed, achieving 57% (O) and 93% (O+△). Additionally, Fig. 4 visualizes representative trajectory comparisons between the baseline and the proposed method, where the baseline fails to maintain tracking while the proposed method remains stable.

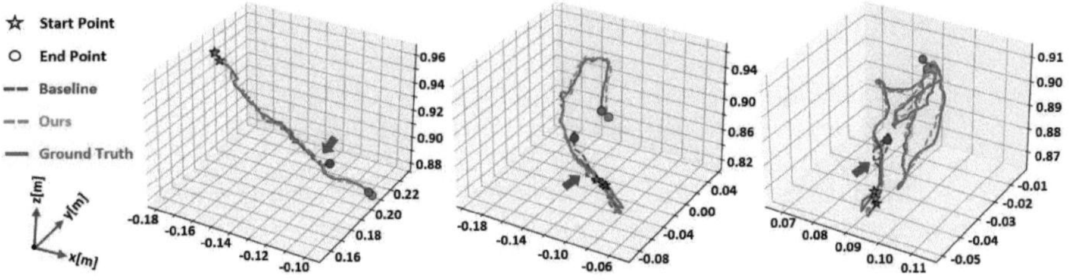

Fig. 4. Trajectory comparison of the proposed method and baseline, with red arrows indicating baseline tracking failure points. (Color figure online)

4 Conclusion

We propose UPTrack, a real-time 6D ultrasound probe pose tracking framework for freehand scanning using a single RGB-D camera, eliminating the need for markers or external tracking devices. By integrating probe keypoint detection with keypoint-guided pose estimation, the framework achieves robust performance under hand occlusion and dynamic probe motion. Additionally, by leveraging a pose estimation foundation model with automated self-training, it enables adaptation with minimal annotation effort. Experiments demonstrate state-of-the-art accuracy and tracking robustness compared to existing pose estimation methods. The proposed framework can be further extended to downstream applications, such as sonographer training, skill assessment, and probe guidance systems, for validation in practical clinical scenarios.

Disclosure of Interests. The authors have no competing interests to declare that are relevant to the content of this article.

References

1. Birlo, M., Caramalau, R., Edwards, P.J., Dromey, B., Clarkson, M.J., Stoyanov, D.: HUP-3D: a 3D multi-view synthetic dataset for assisted-egocentric hand-ultrasound-probe pose estimation. In: proceedings of Medical Image Computing and Computer Assisted Intervention - MICCAI 2024. LNCS, vol. 15001, Springer Nature, Switzerland (2024)
2. Cai, Q., Peng, C., Prieto, J.C., Rosenbaum, A.J., Stringer, J.S., Jiang, X.: A low-cost camera-based ultrasound probe tracking system: design and prototype. In: IEEE International Ultrasonics Symposium (IUS), pp. 997–999. IEEE (2019)
3. Fattori, G., Lomax, A.J., Weber, D.C., Safai, S.: Technical assessment of the NDI Polaris Vega optical tracking system. Radiat. Oncol. **16**(1), 87 (2021)
4. Intel Corporation (2025), includes specifications for RealSense D455. In: Intel Corporation: Intel RealSense D400 Series Datasheet (2025). Revision 022
5. Labbé, Y., et al.: MegaPose: 6D pose estimation of novel objects via render & compare. arXiv preprint arXiv:2212.06870 (2022)
6. Lee, S., et al.: Enhancing free-hand 3D photoacoustic and ultrasound reconstruction using deep learning. IEEE Transactions on Medical Imaging (2025)

7. Lee, T., Wen, B., Kang, M., Kang, G., Kweon, I.S., Yoon, K.J.: Any6D: model-free 6D pose estimation of novel objects. In: Proceedings of the Computer Vision and Pattern Recognition Conference, pp. 11633–11643 (2025)
8. Li, Q., et al.: Long-term dependency for 3D reconstruction of freehand ultrasound without external tracker. IEEE Trans. Biomed. Eng. **71**(3), 1033–1042 (2023)
9. Li, Q., et al.: Nonrigid Reconstruction of Freehand Ultrasound without a Tracker. In: Proceedings of Medical Image Computing and Computer Assisted Intervention - MICCAI 2024. LNCS, vol. 15004, Springer Nature, Switzerland (2024)
10. Lin, J., Liu, L., Lu, D., Jia, K.: SAM-6D: segment anything model meets zero-shot 6D object pose estimation. In: Proceedings of the IEEE/CVF Conference on Computer Vision and Pattern Recognition (CVPR), pp. 27906–27916 (2024)
11. Luo, M., et al.: Multi-IMU with online self-consistency for freehand 3D ultrasound reconstruction. In: International Conference on Medical Image Computing and Computer-Assisted Intervention, pp. 342–351. Springer (2023)
12. Meng, X., et al.: DynOPETs: a versatile benchmark for dynamic object pose estimation and tracking in moving camera scenarios. IEEE Robotics and Automation Letters (2025)
13. Mozaffari, M.H., Lee, W.S.: Freehand 3-D ultrasound imaging: a systematic review. Ultrasound Med. Biol. **43**(10), 2099–2124 (2017)
14. Naheem, M., Shyam, A., Dumpuri, P., Lakshmanan, M., Sivaprakasam, M.: Optical tracker assessment for image guided surgical interventions. In: 2022 IEEE International Symposium on Medical Measurements and Applications (MeMeA), pp. 1–6. IEEE (2022)
15. Paralikar, A., Mantripragada, P., Nguyen, T., Arjoune, Y., Shekhar, R., Monfaredi, R.: Robot-assisted ultrasound probe calibration for image-guided interventions. Int. J. Comput. Assist. Radiol. Surg. **20**(5), 859–868 (2025)
16. Peng, C., Cai, Q., Chen, M., Jiang, X.: Recent advances in tracking devices for biomedical ultrasound imaging applications. Micromachines **13**(11), 1855 (2022)
17. Ravi, N., et al.: SAM 2: segment anything in images and videos. In: The Thirteenth International Conference on Learning Representations (2025). https://openreview.net/forum?id=Ha6RTeWMd0
18. Servi, M., et al.: Metrological characterization and comparison of D415, D455, L515 RealSense devices in the close range. Sensors **21**(22), 7770 (2021)
19. Servi, M., Profili, A., Furferi, R., Volpe, Y.: Comparative evaluation of intel RealSense D415, D435I, D455 and Microsoft azure Kinect DK sensors for 3D vision applications. IEEE Access (2024)
20. Sturm, J., Engelhard, N., Endres, F., Burgard, W., Cremers, D.: A benchmark for the evaluation of RGB-D SLAM systems. In: 2012 IEEE/RSJ International Conference on Intelligent Robots and Systems, pp. 573–580. IEEE (2012)
21. Wen, B., Bekris, K.: BundleTrack: 6D pose tracking for novel objects without instance or category-level 3D models. In: 2021 IEEE/RSJ International Conference on Intelligent Robots and Systems (IROS), pp. 8067–8074. IEEE (2021)
22. Wen, B., et al.: BundleSDF: neural 6-DoF tracking and 3D reconstruction of unknown objects. In: Proceedings of the IEEE/CVF Conference on Computer Vision and Pattern Recognition, pp. 606–617 (2023)
23. Wen, B., Yang, W., Kautz, J., Birchfield, S.: FoundationPose: unified 6d pose estimation and tracking of novel objects. In: Proceedings of the IEEE/CVF Conference on Computer Vision and Pattern Recognition, pp. 17868–17879 (2024)
24. Xiao, B., Wu, H., Wei, Y.: Simple baselines for human pose estimation and tracking. In: Proceedings of the European Conference on Computer Vision (ECCV), pp. 466–481 (2018)

25. Xie, S., Girshick, R., Dollár, P., Tu, Z., He, K.: Aggregated residual transformations for deep neural networks. In: Proceedings of the IEEE Conference on Computer Vision and Pattern Recognition, pp. 1492–1500 (2017)
26. Yeo, L., Romero, R.: Optical ultrasound simulation-based training in obstetric sonography. J. Matern. Fetal Neonatal Med. **35**(13), 2469–2484 (2022)
27. Zhang, F., et al.: MediaPipe hands: On-device real-time hand tracking. arXiv preprint arXiv:2006.10214 (2020)

Real-Time Hardware-Free HIFU Interference Suppression via Teacher-Student Diffusion Framework

Dejia Cai[1], Ali Abdollahi[1], Xi Wang[1], Kun Yang[2], Zhaohui Guo[3], Xiaowei Zhou[2(✉)], and Hao Chen[1,4,5,6,7(✉)]

[1] Department of Computer Science and Engineering, The Hong Kong University of Science and Technology, New Territories, Hong Kong SAR, China
jhc@cse.ust.hk

[2] State Key Laboratory of Ultrasound Engineering in Medicine, Chongqing Medical University, Chongqing 400016, China
zhou.xiaowei@cqmu.edu.cn

[3] School of Microelectronics, Tianjin University, Tianjin 300072, China

[4] Department of Chemical and Biological Engineering, The Hong Kong University of Science and Technology, New Territories, Hong Kong SAR, China

[5] Division of Life Science, The Hong Kong University of Science and Technology, New Territories, Hong Kong SAR, China

[6] HKUST Shenzhen-Hong Kong Collaborative Innovation Research Institute, The Hong Kong University of Science and Technology, Futian, Shenzhen, China

[7] State Key Laboratory of Nervous System Disorders, The Hong Kong University of Science and Technology, New Territories, Hong Kong SAR, China

Abstract. High-Intensity Focused Ultrasound (HIFU) is a non-invasive therapy, yet its safety is often degraded by severe acoustic interference during continuous ultrasound guidance. Existing suppression methods heavily rely on proprietary raw Radio-Frequency (RF) data or hardware synchronization, limiting their clinical utility and preventing real-time implementation. We propose Manifold-Constrained Hyper-Connections Diffusion (mHC-Diff), an image-domain diffusion framework for real-time interference suppression without specialized hardware synchronization, disentangling complex interference from anatomical structures while ensuring high reconstruction fidelity. To achieve clinical real-time application, mHC-Diff first learns an anatomy-aware prior with a high-fidelity multi-step diffusion Teacher, then distills it into a one-step Student. On a clinically representative dataset spanning diverse therapeutic scenarios, mHC-Diff achieves 26.65 dB PSNR and real-time inference (∼20 FPS) on a single NVIDIA RTX 4090, a ∼6.8× speedup over iterative diffusion baselines such as HIFU-Diff. These results suggest a practical route to deployable, hardware-free interference suppression for ultrasound-guided HIFU interventions. Code is available at https://github.com/caidejia/HIFU-mHC-Diff.

D. Cai and A. Abdollahi—Equal Contribution.

G. Yang et al. (Eds.): MICCAI 2026, LNCS 16893, pp. 404–414, 2027.
https://doi.org/10.1007/978-3-032-38236-8_39

Keywords: HIFU · Interference Suppression · Diffusion Models · Manifold Learning · Model Distillation · Real-time Imaging

1 Introduction

High-Intensity Focused Ultrasound (HIFU) has emerged as a widely adopted non-invasive therapeutic modality [1,6,11], used to treat various pathologies, including uterine fibroids [8], breast fibroadenomas [12], and adenomyosis [15]. Although HIFU surpasses conventional surgical interventions in patient recovery and tissue preservation, its clinical success depends fundamentally on high-precision, real-time monitoring. Ultrasound imaging provides cost-effective, dynamic intra-operative guidance. However, the intense acoustic waves emitted by the therapeutic HIFU transducer interfere with the imaging pulses, degrading the signal-to-noise ratio of the acquired images. To mitigate this, current protocols rely on a "stop-and-shoot" approach, pausing sonication during imaging. This compromise can prolong procedure times, reduce treatment efficacy, and increase clinical risks associated with unguided sonication [12].

To enable concurrent ultrasound monitoring during continuous sonication, various signal processing and deep learning algorithms have been propose [2,14,17,19–21,23,24]. Traditional methods, like FRPCA [24] or encoded excitations [19–21], often lack clinical generalization or impose high computational overhead. Recently, deep learning architectures, ranging from FUS-Net [14] to diffusion-based HIFU-Diff [3], have emerged as powerful alternatives for robust interference suppression. However, these methods share a major bottleneck: they predominantly rely on accessing raw Radio-Frequency (RF) data or demand complex hardware synchronization. In clinical practice, raw RF data is typically proprietary and restricted on commercial scanners. Furthermore, processing raw RF signals is computationally demanding, complicating real-time deployment and limiting clinical versatility.

Consequently, there is an urgent need for a hardware-free, image-domain solution operating on standard B-mode images. We conceptualize the restoration of corrupted images as mapping contaminated observations back into the clean anatomical domain. While diffusion models [7,9,10,26] effectively capture such complex manifolds [16,18], translating them to real-time HIFU guidance is challenged by slow iterative sampling and the limited capacity of existing U-Nets under extreme interference. To bridge this gap, we propose mHC-Diff, an image-domain diffusion framework that enables high-fidelity prior learning and facilitates knowledge distillation for single-step, real-time acceleration. Specifically, our framework leverages the mHC-UNet architecture, which incorporates manifold-constrained Hyper-Connections (mHC) to expand model capacity via multi-stream residual pathways with minimal computational overhead. By enforcing manifold constraints inspired by [22], this design stably disentangles intense acoustic artifacts from anatomical structures, ensuring high structural fidelity without destructive signal loss. Our primary contributions are:

- We introduce mHC-Diff, an image-domain diffusion framework for HIFU interference suppression operating on standard B-mode inputs, obviating proprietary raw RF access and specialized hardware synchronization.
- We propose the mHC-UNet architecture and a two-stage knowledge distillation strategy that disentangles interference from anatomy. This approach achieves superior restoration (26.65 dB PSNR), while accelerating inference to real-time clinical standards (~20 FPS).
- We constructed a large-scale clinical equivalent HIFU interference suppression dataset comprising 17,464 image pairs from ex vivo and in vivo tissues, covering three typical imaging modes and four HIFU irradiation intensities to support the development of HIFU interference suppression methods.

2 Methods

mHC-Diff is a framework for real-time restoration of ultrasound images corrupted by high-intensity focused ultrasound (HIFU) interference, as show in Fig. 1. It operates in two stages: (i) manifold prior acquisition, where a conditional diffusion Teacher is trained to capture anatomy-consistent clean anatomical distributions; and (ii) where the learned prior is distilled into a single-step Student for real-time inference. Both stages utilize mHC-UNet (Sect. 2.1) to disentangle acoustic interference from anatomical structures.

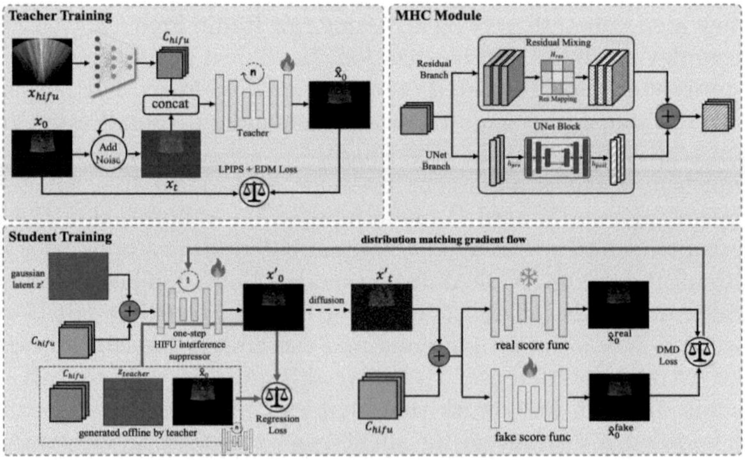

Fig. 1. The mHC-Diff framework. A two-stage pipeline for real-time interference suppression: (i) prior learning via a diffusion-based Teacher, and (ii) knowledge distillation into a single-step Student for real-time inference.

2.1 Network Architecture: Concat-Conditioned mHC-UNet

We propose a shared denoiser backbone for the Teacher, Student, and critic: an mHC-UNet augmented by manifold constraints inspired by [22].

Conditioning and Network Input. Given a corrupted frame x_{hifu} and a noisy target x, We extract spatial conditioning features $C_{\text{hifu}} = E_{\psi}(x_{\text{hifu}})$, where E_{ψ} denotes the HIFU-aware conditioning encoder. We concatenate them as $u = [x, C_{\text{hifu}}]$ and feed u into the U-Net stem, where the initial feature map is explicitly broadcast into $n = 4$ parallel latent streams. The noise level σ is injected into all blocks as a global conditional signal, and the n streams are aggregated via feature averaging prior to the final prediction layer.

Multi-stream Residual Pathways with mHC Routing. Following the paradigm in [22], our architecture maintains $n = 4$ parallel streams exclusively along the residual pathways throughout the UNet structure, applying shared-weight projections per stream to improve parameter efficiency.

Cross-stream interaction and integration with standard U-Net blocks are achieved via the adopted mHC module. Because the core U-Net operator $\mathcal{F}(\cdot, \sigma)$ requires a single unified input, the module predicts non-negative read and write gates, $h_{\text{pre}}(p), h_{\text{post}}(p) \in \mathbb{R}^n_+$, alongside a residual stream-mixing matrix $H_{\text{res}}(p) \in \mathbb{R}^{n \times n}$. At spatial location p, the read gates aggregate the n residual streams $x_k(p)$ into a unified representation $r(p)$ for the U-Net block. The write gates then distribute the resulting update $u(p)$ back to the individual streams, which are concurrently mixed by H_{res}:

$$\begin{aligned} r(p) &= \textstyle\sum_{k=1}^{n} h_{\text{pre},k}(p)\, x_k(p), \qquad u(p) = \mathcal{F}(r(p), \sigma)\,, \\ x_i^{\text{out}}(p) &= \textstyle\sum_{j=1}^{n} H_{\text{res},ij}(p)\, x_j(p) \;+\; h_{\text{post},i}(p)\, u(p), \qquad \forall i \in \{1, \dots, n\}. \end{aligned} \tag{1}$$

To ensure stability and identity mapping, we enforce manifold constraints: H_{res} is Sinkhorn-normalized to the Birkhoff polytope to conserve feature magnitude, while sigmoid-activated gates prevent destructive signal cancellation.

2.2 Teacher Prior Learning and Single-Step Distillation

To balance restoration fidelity and real-time efficiency, we propose a two-stage strategy: first, capturing an anatomy-aware prior via an Elucidated Diffusion Model (EDM) [13], and then accelerating inference through Distribution Matching Distillation (DMD) [25].

Stage I: Teacher Optimization via Elucidated Diffusion Model. We first train a Teacher μ_{Teacher} to capture the clean anatomical manifold. Following EDM, we corrupt the clean target x_0 with noise level $\hat{\sigma}$ to obtain $x_t = x_0 + \hat{\sigma}\epsilon$. To preserve fine acoustic textures, the Teacher is optimized to reconstruct x_0 conditioned on frozen C_{hifu} via a perceptual-augmented loss:

$$\mathcal{L}_{\text{Teacher}} = \mathbb{E}_{\hat{\sigma}} \left[\hat{\sigma}^{-2} \, \|\hat{x}_0 - x_0\|_2^2 + \lambda_{\text{perc}} \, \text{LPIPS}(\hat{x}_0, x_0) \right], \tag{2}$$

where $\hat{x}_0 = \mu_{\text{Teacher}}([x_t, C_{\text{hifu}}], \hat{\sigma})$ is the reconstructed image, $\hat{\sigma}$ is the standard deviation of injected noise. Once fully trained, the Teacher is frozen as a reference denoiser μ_{real} for the subsequent phase.

Stage II: One-Step Distillation and Denoising Field Matching. We distill μ_{real} into a one-step Student generator G_ϕ via DMD, involving the Student G_ϕ, the frozen Teacher μ_{real}, and a trainable critic μ_{fake} sharing the mHC-UNet backbone. The Student generates $x'_0 = G_\phi([\sigma_g z', C_{\text{hifu}}], \sigma_g)$ where $z' \sim \mathcal{N}(0, I)$ and σ_g is the generation noise scale and we align the Student's denoising field with the Teacher's prior. For a noisy state $x'_t = x'_0 + \sigma_t \epsilon$ perturbed at a sampled noise level σ_t within the EDM distribution, both denoisers are evaluated:

$$\hat{x}_0^{\text{real}} = \mu_{\text{real}}([x'_t, C_{\text{hifu}}], \sigma_t), \qquad \hat{x}_0^{\text{fake}} = \mu_{\text{fake}}([x'_t, C_{\text{hifu}}], \sigma_t). \tag{3}$$

The update direction g is computed as:

$$w = \text{mean}_{c,p}\left[\,\left|x'_0 - \hat{x}_0^{\text{real}}\right|\,\right], \qquad g = \frac{\hat{x}_0^{\text{fake}} - \hat{x}_0^{\text{real}}}{w + \epsilon}. \tag{4}$$

where $\epsilon = 10^{-6}$ is a small constant for numerical stability. To ensure stability, the Student and critic are optimized via decoupled gradient flows:

$$\begin{aligned} \mathcal{L}_{\text{DMD}} &= \frac{1}{2}\left\|x'_0 - \text{sg}(x'_0 - g)\right\|_2^2, \\ \mathcal{L}_{\text{critic}} &= \mathbb{E}_t\left[\left(\frac{1}{\sigma_t^2} + \frac{1}{\sigma_{\text{data}}^2}\right)\left\|\mu_{\text{fake}}([x'_t, C_{\text{hifu}}], \sigma_t) - x'_0\right\|_2^2\right], \end{aligned} \tag{5}$$

where $\text{sg}(\cdot)$ denotes the stop-gradient operation. To prevent mode collapse in distillation procedure, we apply a supervised anchor $\mathcal{L}_{\text{reg}} = \text{LPIPS}(\hat{x}_0, x'_0)$ on a reference generation, and the final Student objective is $\mathcal{L}_G = \mathcal{L}_{\text{DMD}} + \lambda_{\text{reg}} \mathcal{L}_{\text{reg}}$.

3 Experiments

3.1 Datasets and Implementation

To evaluate the proposed framework, we constructed a large-scale dataset using a clinically equivalent HIFU therapy system (Focused Ultrasound Tumor Therapeutic System, JC200, Chongqing Haifu Medical Technology Co., Ltd.) integrated with a Verasonics Vantage 256 ultrasound research platform (Verasonics Inc., USA). The HIFU waveform was generated by a PC-controlled RIGOL DG4202 signal generator as a continuous 0.97 MHz signal, amplified, and delivered through an electrical matching box to the HIFU transducer. As illustrated in Fig. 2, the HIFU transducer (0.97 MHz) was configured coaxially with an imaging probe to ensure aligned visualization and consistent monitoring of the focal region. The therapeutic transducer had a 0.97 MHz central frequency, 220 mm outer diameter, and 80 mm inner diameter, enabling coaxial placement of the imaging transducer.

Data Acquisition and Protocol. A consistent imaging depth of 135–140 mm was maintained across all imaging techniques. We implemented three clinically established beamforming strategies, i.e., Diverging Wave, Wide Beam, and Line Scan imaging, across four power levels (123 W–277 W). Paired corrupted and

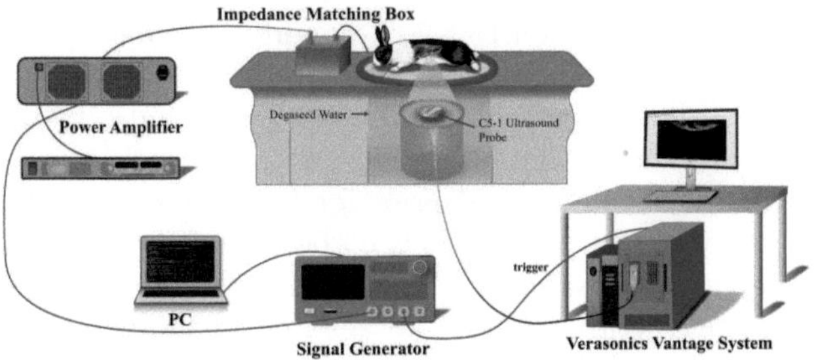

Fig. 2. Schematic illustration of the experimental setup. A clinical-grade HIFU therapy system is integrated with a 256-channel ultrasound research platform.

clean frames were acquired using a pulse-width modulation protocol (200 ms cycles), yielding 50 labeled paired samples per session. The final dataset comprises 17,464 image pairs, acquired at 512×512 and spatially resized to 256×256 for training, from ex vivo bovine and porcine tissues and in vivo rabbit models. To ensure independence, data were split at the subject/session level (7:1:2), yielding 12,225 training, 1,746 validation, and 3,493 test pairs. No session contributed frames to more than one split.

Architecture and Training Details. Both teacher and student models utilize an mHC-UNet backbone (128 channels, $n = 4$, multipliers: $[2, 2, 2]$) coupled with an interference-aware encoder featuring five NAF blocks [5]. We adopt a two-stage training strategy: the encoder is jointly pre-trained alongside the teacher and then frozen during distillation to provide stable feature guidance. EDM parameters are set as $\sigma_{min} = 0.002, \sigma_{max} = 80, \sigma_{data} = 0.5$. The teacher underwent 200 epochs of training (batch size 16, LR 1×10^{-4}), and the student used the same teacher configuration to ensure manifold consistency for DMD. The implementation was executed using PyTorch mixed precision on an NVIDIA H100, requiring ∼24 h for end-to-end training. For fair comparison, all learning-based baselines followed the same preprocessing pipeline and subject/session-level splits, and supervised baselines were trained with identical restoration losses.

3.2 Performance Evaluation and Comparison

We compare mHC-Diff against SOTA baselines, including signal processing methods (FRPCA) operating on raw RF signal, and deep learning architectures (FUS-Net, SwinUnet, and HIFU-Diff) in the image domain. We evaluate restoration quality using PSNR and SSIM (reported as mean with 95% bootstrap confidence intervals).

Quantitative Evaluation. As shown in Table 1, mHC-Diff consistently outperforms all baselines across all beamforming modes. Specifically, in line-scan imaging, it yields a 27.29 dB PSNR, surpassing the strongest baseline (SwinUnet) by 2.05 dB. This superiority persists in more challenging wide-beam and diverging-wave scenarios, with narrow 95% confidence intervals (via 1,000 bootstrap resamples) confirming its statistical stability. While FUS-Net and SwinUnet show moderate suppression, their lower SSIM indicates an inability to fully preserve fine anatomical details. SwinUnet benefits from global attention, but lacks an interference-conditioned prior for lesion fidelity. Notably, standard HIFU-Diff fails in the image domain as the absence of RF phase information in B-mode data creates nonlinear coupling between artifacts and anatomy, necessitating the robust priors of mHC-Diff for reliable disentanglement.

Table 1. Quantitative comparison of different methods across three imaging modalities: Line Scan, Wide Beam, and Diverging Wave. Results are presented as Mean (95% CI). Best results are highlighted in bold.

Method	Line Scan		Wide Beam		Diverging Wave	
	PSNR ↑	SSIM ↑	PSNR ↑	SSIM ↑	PSNR ↑	SSIM ↑
FUS-Net [14]	23.83 (23.66–24.00)	0.812 (0.809–0.814)	23.82 (23.68–23.96)	0.809 (0.806–0.812)	22.82 (22.63–22.99)	0.805 (0.802–0.808)
HIFU-Diff [3]	8.84 (8.50–9.16)	0.587 (0.576–0.598)	7.31 (7.02–7.58)	0.535 (0.524–0.545)	7.65 (7.35–7.96)	0.537 (0.528–0.548)
SwinUnet [4]	25.24 (25.08–25.41)	0.838 (0.835–0.841)	25.02 (24.88–25.17)	0.838 (0.835–0.841)	25.01 (24.83–25.20)	0.836 (0.833–0.840)
FRPCA [24]	15.59 (15.33–15.81)	0.740 (0.732–0.747)	10.77 (10.56–10.99)	0.522 (0.515–0.529)	13.44 (13.28–13.60)	0.585 (0.581–0.589)
Ours (mHC-Diff)	**27.29 (27.14–27.44)**	**0.858 (0.856–0.861)**	**26.20 (26.05–26.35)**	**0.858 (0.855–0.861)**	**25.49 (25.29–25.66)**	**0.850 (0.846–0.853)**

Qualitative Analysis. As shown in Fig. 3, mHC-Diff achieves robust interference suppression while preserving anatomical structures across both ex vivo and in vivo settings. Conventional methods such as FRPCA and FUS-Net either fail to remove dense vertical streaks or suppress them at the cost of noticeable signal loss and contrast degradation. In contrast, mHC-Diff restores more natural speckle patterns and tissue contrast, even at the maximum power level (277 W). Crucially, HIFU-induced lesions (red arrows) are reconstructed with sharp edges and clear hyperechoic contrast, whereas baseline results are often blurred and partially merge lesion regions with background textures. With real-time inference at ~20 FPS on a single NVIDIA RTX 4090, our framework provides reliable visual feedback for continuous ultrasound-guided HIFU procedures.

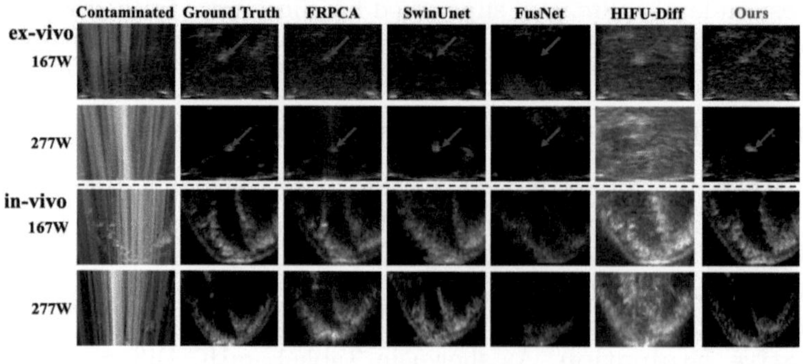

Fig. 3. Qualitative comparison across ex-vivo (top) and in-vivo (bottom) scenarios under varying power levels. **Red arrows** indicate critical HIFU-induced lesions.

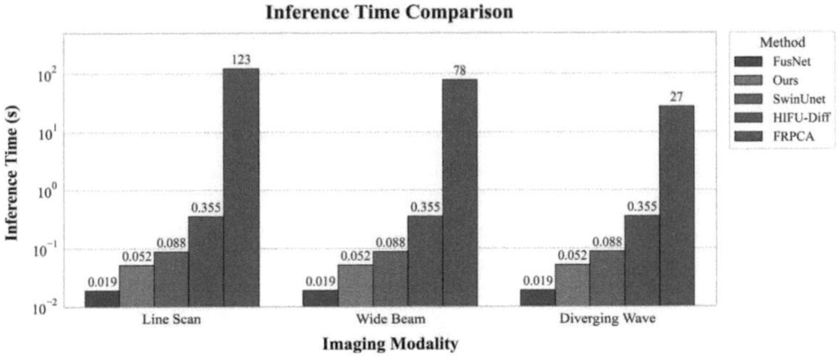

Fig. 4. Inference latency comparison. Our mHC-Diff maintains real-time throughput ($\approx$0.05 s) across modalities, significantly faster than HIFU-Diff and FRPCA baselines.

3.3 Inference Efficiency

Figure 4 compares computational efficiency across all modalities to assess intra-operative suitability. Traditional FRPCA exhibits prohibitive latency (e.g., 123 s/frame in line-scan mode), rendering it clinically incompatible. The standard HIFU-Diff requires 0.355 s/frame due to iterative sampling, creating a severe temporal bottleneck. Conversely, our one-step Student achieves a consistent 0.052 s/frame ($\sim$20 FPS) across all modalities. Although FUS-Net is the fastest (0.019 s/frame), its failure to preserve therapeutic features (Sect. 3.2) renders it clinically unreliable. SwinUnet (0.088 s/frame) remains significantly slower than our approach. By bypassing iterative sampling, our framework strikes an optimal balance between manifold integrity and real-time throughput. This enables seamless clinical integration for high-fidelity, low-latency visual feedback during active treatment.

3.4 Ablation Study

Table 2 quantifies the individual and synergistic contributions of the manifold-constrained Hyper-Connections (mHC) and Single-step Distillation (SD).

Impact of Single-Step Distillation. The standard iterative baseline (EDM teacher without mHC) achieves strong restoration (26.52 dB) but incurs high latency (499.0 ms). Distilling this teacher into a one-step student (Baseline+Distill) substantially reduces latency to 38.5 ms, at the cost of a PSNR drop to 25.39 dB. Despite this trade-off, the distilled model still outperforms supervised baselines such as SwinUnet (24.59 dB) and FUS-Net (23.50 dB). The teacher therefore serves as a training-time prior, not a deployed module. In contrast, directly applying HIFU-Diff to B-mode data yields very low PSNR (7.93 dB), suggesting that a dedicated image-domain prior is crucial for stable interference suppression.

Synergy of mHC Routing and Distillation. Integrating mHC to the iterative baseline improves the upper-bound restoration quality, where the mHC-equipped teacher achieves 27.35 dB PSNR and 0.0018 MSE. After distillation,

Table 2. Performance comparison and ablation study. The **Baseline** denotes the iterative EDM model without mHC or distillation, while **mHC-Diff** integrates both components. Best results are in **bold**.

Method	PSNR ↑	SSIM ↑	MSE ↓	MS-SSIM ↑	LPIPS ↓	Time (ms) ↓
FUS-Net [14]	23.50	0.809	0.0054	0.6988	0.2068	**19.0**
HIFU-Diff [3]	7.93	0.553	0.2540	0.3779	0.2761	355.0
SwinUnet [4]	24.59	0.828	0.0040	0.8561	0.1539	88.0
FRPCA [24]	14.33	0.648	0.0474	0.5930	0.1671	7.6×10^4
Baseline	26.52	0.843	0.0022	0.8697	0.1431	499.0
Baseline + mHC	**27.35**	0.851	**0.0018**	**0.8892**	0.1426	592.5
Baseline + Distill	25.39	0.839	0.0029	0.8658	0.1499	38.5
mHC-Diff (Ours)	26.65	**0.856**	0.0022	0.8875	**0.1402**	52.0

our full model mHC-Diff recovers much of the fidelity typically lost in the one-step setting. Compared to Baseline+Distill (25.39 dB), mHC-Diff reaches 26.65 dB with the best structural and perceptual quality (0.856 SSIM; 0.1402 LPIPS). These results indicate that mHC routing effectively compensates for information loss introduced by distillation, yielding a favorable trade-off between image quality and real-time throughput for ultrasound-guided HIFU procedures.

4 Conclusion

We presented mHC-Diff, a two-stage framework for real-time HIFU interference suppression. By coupling manifold-constrained Hyper-Connections (mHC) with a one-step distillation paradigm, our approach effectively disentangles acoustic artifacts from anatomy, achieving 20 FPS inference. Extensive evaluations on a physically-consistent and clinically-representative corpus demonstrate superior reconstruction accuracy and structural fidelity over state-of-the-art benchmarks. The high-fidelity visualization of lesion boundaries in clinical scenarios underscores its potential for precise intraoperative guidance. Future work will focus on clinical hardware integration and broader cross-domain validation to further establish its robustness and therapeutic efficacy.

Acknowledgements. This work was supported by the National Natural Science Foundation of China under grants 12304508 and 62402458, HKUST Research Project (Project No. 24251460C049), Hong Kong Innovation and Technology Commission (Project No. MHP/002/22), and Shenzhen Science and Technology Innovation Committee Fund (Project No. KCXFZ20230731094059008).

Disclosure of Interests. The authors have no competing interests to declare.

References

1. Bond, A.E., et al.: Safety and efficacy of focused ultrasound thalamotomy for patients with medication-refractory, tremor-dominant parkinson disease: a randomized clinical trial. JAMA Neurol. **74**(12), 1412–1418 (2017)

2. Cai, D., et al.: A novel diffusion-based deep learning model to suppress acoustic interference for real-time monitoring in ultrasound-guided HIFU surgery. In: IEEE Ultrasonics, Ferroelectrics, and Frequency Control Joint Symposium (UFFC-JS), pp. 1–4. IEEE (2024). https://doi.org/10.1109/UFFC-JS60046.2024.10793861
3. Cai, D., et al.: Suppressing the HIFU interference in ultrasound guiding images with a diffusion-based deep learning model. Comput. Methods Programs Biomed. **254**, 108304 (2024)
4. Cao, H., et al.: Swin-UNet: UNet-like pure transformer for medical image segmentation. In: Karlinsky, L., Michaeli, T., Nishino, K. (eds.) ECCV 2022. LNCS, vol. 13803, pp. 205–218. Springer, Cham (2022). https://doi.org/10.1007/978-3-031-25066-8_9
5. Chen, L., Chu, X., Zhang, X., Sun, J.: Simple baselines for image restoration. In: Avidan, S., Brostow, G., Cissé, M., Farinella, G.M., Hassner, T. (eds.) ECCV 2022. LNCS, vol. 13667, pp. 17–33. Springer, Cham (2022). https://doi.org/10.1007/978-3-031-20071-7_2
6. Chen, Z., Cheng, L., Zhang, W., He, W.: Ultrasound-guided thermal ablation for hyperparathyroidism: current status and prospects. Int. J. Hyperth. **39**(1), 466–474 (2022)
7. Dhariwal, P., Nichol, A.: Diffusion models beat GANs on image synthesis. Adv. Neural. Inf. Process. Syst. **34**, 8780–8794 (2021)
8. Dou, Y., Zhang, L., Liu, Y., He, M., Wang, Y., Wang, Z.: Long-term outcome and risk factors of reintervention after high intensity focused ultrasound ablation for uterine fibroids: a systematic review and meta-analysis. Int. J. Hyperth. **41**(1), 2299479 (2024)
9. Esser, P., Rombach, R., Ommer, B.: Taming transformers for high-resolution image synthesis. In: Proceedings of the IEEE/CVF Conference on Computer Vision and Pattern Recognition, pp. 12873–12883 (2021)
10. Ho, J., Jain, A., Abbeel, P.: Denoising diffusion probabilistic models. Adv. Neural. Inf. Process. Syst. **33**, 6840–6851 (2020)
11. Hynynen, K., Darkazanli, A., Unger, E., Schenck, J.F.: MRI-guided noninvasive ultrasound surgery. Med. Phys. **20**(1), 107–115 (1993)
12. Imankulov, S., Tuganbekov, T., Razbadauskas, A., Seidagaliyeva, Z.: HIFU treatment for fibroadenoma-a clinical study at national scientific research Centre, Astana, Kazakhstan. J Pak Med Assoc **68**(9), 1378–80 (2018)
13. Karras, T., Aittala, M., Aila, T., Laine, S.: Elucidating the design space of diffusion-based generative models. arXiv preprint arXiv:2206.00364 (2022). https://doi.org/10.48550/arXiv.2206.00364
14. Lee, S.A., Konofagou, E.E.: FUS-Net: U-Net-based FUS interference filtering. IEEE Trans. Med. Imaging **41**(4), 915–924 (2021)
15. Liu, Z., Liu, Z., Wang, Y., Wan, X., Huang, X.: Machine learning-based predictive analysis of energy efficiency factors necessary for the HIFU treatment of adenomyosis. Front. Physiol. **16**, 1602866 (2025). https://doi.org/10.3389/fphys.2025.1602866
16. Niu, A., et al.: ACDMSR: accelerated conditional diffusion models for single image super-resolution. IEEE Trans. Broadcast. **70**(2), 492–504 (2024)
17. Payen, T., et al.: Passive Elastography for clinical HIFU lesion detection. IEEE Trans. Med. Imaging **43**(4), 1594–1604 (2023)
18. Saharia, C., Ho, J., Chan, W., Salimans, T., Fleet, D.J., Norouzi, M.: Image super-resolution via iterative refinement. IEEE Trans. Pattern Anal. Mach. Intell. **45**(4), 4713–4726 (2022)

19. Shen, C.C., Lin, R.C., Wu, N.H.: Golay-encoded ultrasound monitoring of simultaneous high-intensity focused ultrasound treatment: a phantom study. IEEE Trans. Ultrason. Ferroelectr. Freq. Control **69**(4), 1370–1381 (2022)
20. Shen, C.C., Wu, N.H.: Ultrasound monitoring of simultaneous high-intensity focused ultrasound (HIFU) therapy using minimum-peak-sidelobe coded excitation. Ultrasonics **138**, 107224 (2024)
21. Song, J.H., Chang, J.H.: Correspondence-an effective pulse sequence for simultaneous HIFU Insonation and monitoring. IEEE Trans. Ultrason. Ferroelectr. Freq. Control **61**(9), 1580–1587 (2014)
22. Xie, Z., et al.: MHC: manifold-constrained hyper-connections. arXiv preprint arXiv:2512.24880 (2025)
23. Yang, K., et al.: Suppressing HIFU interference in ultrasound images using 1D U-Net-based neural networks. Phys. Med. Biol. **69**(7), 075006 (2024)
24. Yang, K., et al.: Frequency-domain robust PCA for real-time monitoring of HIFU treatment. IEEE Trans. Med. Imaging **43**(8), 3001–3012 (2024)
25. Yin, T., et al.: One-step diffusion with distribution matching distillation. arXiv preprint arXiv:2311.18828. https://doi.org/10.48550/arXiv.2311.18828 (2024)
26. Zhang, K., Liang, J., Van Gool, L., Timofte, R.: Designing a practical degradation model for deep blind image super-resolution. In: Proceedings of the IEEE/CVF International Conference on Computer Vision, pp. 4791–4800 (2021)

Reasoning Text-to-Video Retrieval for Operating Room Clips via Action-Driven Digital Twins

Yiqing Shen, Hao Ding, and Mathias Unberath(✉)

Johns Hopkins University, Baltimore, MD, USA
{yshen92,unberath}@jhu.edu

Abstract. Text-to-video retrieval in operating rooms (OR) is an enabling technology for OR safety, as it allows stakeholders to retrieve and inspect recordings of specific events. However, because the most safety critical events may not follow the common structure, to unlock its full potential text-to-video retrieval must be able to handle implicit queries that require reasoning to identify the right videos (*e.g.*, "*the step right before clipping*"). However, existing methods rely on global embeddings that cannot reason over such queries. We propose OR^3, a text-to-video retrieval method that converts clips into action-driven digital twins (ActDTs), grouping concurrent subject-action-object triplets under non-overlapping temporal intervals. Moreover, rather than cross-modal matching through paired encoders, OR^3 performs imagination-based retrieval where an LLM generates hypothetical ActDTs from queries. This enables intra-modal matching via a single encoder trained with ActDT-tailored hard negatives. Finally, evidence-grounded refinement revises imagined ActDTs based on discrepancies with top candidates to capture procedure-specific patterns. We construct a benchmark from MM-OR with 276 implicit queries across four reasoning categories over 386 clips from robotic knee procedures. OR^3 achieves 57.6% R@1 and 77.3% R@5, outperforming the strongest baseline. These results demonstrate that OR^3 enables fine-grained discrimination between visually similar OR video clips through temporal action reasoning.

Keywords: Text-to-Video Retrieval · Reasoning Retrieval · Digital Twin · Operating Room Analysis · Large Language Models

1 Introduction

Operating rooms (ORs) can produce thousands of hours of video from room-mounted cameras, yet users typically need only short clips that last seconds to minutes [10,16]. For example, surgical trainees may search for a specific dissection technique [9,26], while quality teams may need to locate moments of miscommunication [8,22]. Because entire OR videos typically span multiple hours, clip-level text-to-video retrieval is a natural formulation where the OR videos

G. Yang et al. (Eds.): MICCAI 2026, LNCS 16893, pp. 415–424, 2027.
https://doi.org/10.1007/978-3-032-38236-8_40

are first segmented by surgical phase and steps [27]. Unlike conventional text-to-video retrieval where queries explicitly describe visual content, OR retrieval must handle implicit queries demanding reasoning (*e.g.*, "*the step right before clipping*" or "*the action that caused bleeding*") [21,22]. Moreover, the OR video retrieval demands fine-grained discrimination because these clips from the same procedure appear visually near-identical, differing only in actions performed and entity interactions [18].

Existing text-to-video retrieval methods learn aligned text and video embeddings based on global similarity, but offer no mechanism to reason over implicit queries [24,28]. Recent work on reasoning text-to-video retrieval addresses this by converting videos into digital twins (DTs) over which large language models (LLMs) can reason during retrieval [20,22]. However, its object-centric DTs focus on per-frame entities and their visual attributes, which fail to discriminate between consecutive OR clips that share identical objects, but differ in actions and state transitions [20]. Moreover, its cross-modal matching between DT representation and query through paired encoders struggles to bridge the semantic gap between abstract implicit queries and concrete DT representation in OR contexts [3].

We propose OR^3 (operating room reasoning retrieval), a reasoning retrieval method for OR clips. OR^3 represents each clip as an action-driven digital twin (ActDT), a two-level structure that groups concurrent object interactions under non-overlapping temporal intervals. This action-centric representation captures state transitions and their dynamics, enabling discrimination between visually near-identical clips. Rather than matching queries against ActDTs through cross-modal paired encoders, OR^3 performs imagination-based retrieval by generating a hypothetical ActDT from the query itself. This casts retrieval as intra-modal matching and eliminates the semantic gap between abstract implicit queries and concrete ActDTs. When discrepancies emerge between imagined and actual ActDTs, evidence-grounded refinement revises the imagined ActDT to reflect procedure-specific patterns.

The contributions of this paper are three-fold. First, we introduce text-to-video reasoning retrieval for OR clips, a task requiring fine-grained discrimination between visually near-identical clips through implicit queries that demand reasoning. Correspondingly, we propose OR^3, which introduces ActDTs to encode temporal object interaction dynamics for OR clip retrieval. Second, we introduce imagination-based retrieval to eliminate cross-modal semantic gaps, and evidence-grounded refinement to adapt query interpretation to procedure-specific patterns. Third, we construct a benchmark for OR text-to-video reasoning retrieval.

2 Methods

Overview. Consider an OR video segmented into an ordered clip sequence $\mathcal{C} = \{C_1, C_2, \ldots, C_M\}$ based on surgical phases and steps [5,16]. Given an

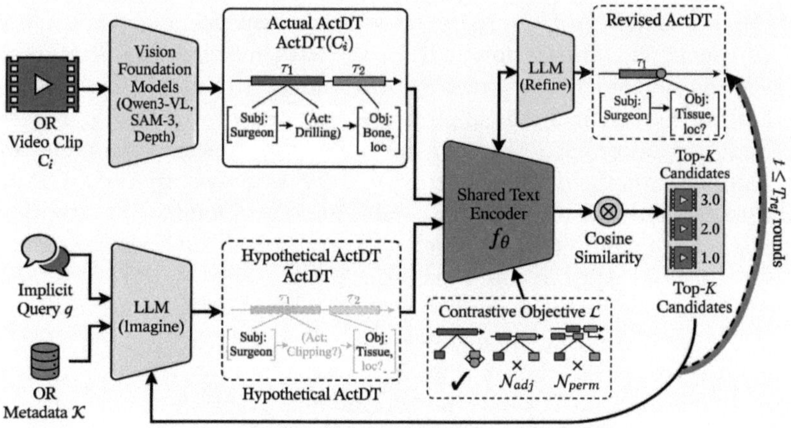

Fig. 1. Overview of OR[3]. Each OR video clip C_i is converted into an actual ActDT through vision foundation models (Qwen3-VL, SAM-3, DepthAnythingV3), encoding subject-action-object triplets within non-overlapping temporal intervals. Given an implicit query q and OR metadata $\mathcal{K}$, an LLM imagines a hypothetical ActDT $\widehat{\text{ActDT}}_q$ that predicts the action primitives the target clip would contain. A shared text encoder f_θ, trained with a contrastive objective over adjacent-clip ($\mathcal{N}_{\text{adj}}$) and temporal-permutation ($\mathcal{N}_{\text{perm}}$) hard negatives [17], encodes both representations and ranks clips by cosine similarity. The top-K candidates are then passed to an LLM that performs evidence-grounded refinement, revising the hypothetical ActDT across up to T_{ref} rounds to align with procedure-specific patterns observed in the retrieved candidates.

implicit text query q that requires reasoning, our goal is to retrieve a ranked list of clips $\{(C_i, r_i)\}_{i=1}^{K}$, where $C_i \in \mathcal{C}$, $r_i \in [0,1]$ denotes the relevance score, and K is the number of clips returned [20]. To address this, OR[3] (shown in Fig. 1) first converts each clip into an action-driven digital twin (ActDT) that encodes concurrent object interactions as temporally structured action primitives [6] serialized in JSON. Imagination-based retrieval then employs an LLM to generate a hypothetical ActDT from the query itself, and matches this imagined representation against actual clip ActDTs using a single text encoder. Evidence-grounded refinement further revises the imagined ActDT based on discrepancies with top-ranked candidates, adapting to procedure-specific patterns. The refined ActDT is re-encoded and matched against clip ActDTs to produce the final ranked results.

Action-Driven Digital Twin. We represent each clip C_i as an action-driven digital twin (ActDT), a sequence of action primitives that encode the object and their interactions. Each ActDT is serialized as structured JSON text so that LLMs can process it directly without visual token compression of the raw video clips [19,21,22]. Formally, ActDT can be defined as $\text{ActDT}(C_i) = [\{\texttt{interval}: \tau_k,\ \texttt{actions}: [\{\texttt{subj}: \mathtt{s}_{k,n},\ \texttt{act}: v_{k,n},\ \texttt{obj}: \mathbf{o}_{k,n}\}]_{n=1}^{N_k}\}]_{k=1}^{T_i}$, where $T_i \in$

$\mathbb{N}^+$ denotes the number of temporal intervals in clip C_i, and $N_k \in \mathbb{N}^+$ is the number of concurrent interactions within the k-th interval. Each interval $\tau_k = [t_k^{\mathrm{s}}, t_k^{\mathrm{e}}] \in \mathbb{R}^2$ is defined by its start t_k^{s} and end t_k^{e} timestamps, with intervals not overlapping and their union spanning the entire duration of C_i. The subject $\mathbf{s}_{k,n} = \{\texttt{cat}: c,\ \texttt{attr}: d,\ \texttt{loc}: \ell\}$ and object $\mathbf{o}_{k,n}$ share the same format, each containing three fields. The category $c \in \mathcal{E}$ is drawn from an OR-specific vocabulary $\mathcal{E}$ of surgical roles, instruments, and equipment. The attribute d is a natural-language summary of properties such as posture or instrument state, generated by a VLM [1] from the RGB frames of C_i. The location $\ell \in \mathbb{R}^5$ encodes the bounding-box coordinates derived from the SAM-3 [2] segmentation masks and the depth prediction in the object centroids of DepthAnythingV3 [12]. The action $v_{k,n} \in \mathcal{V}$ records the interaction linking $\mathbf{s}_{k,n}$ to $\mathbf{o}_{k,n}$, also produced by the VLM and drawn from an OR-specific action vocabulary $\mathcal{V}$.

Imagination-Based Retrieval. OR^3 reformulates retrieval as intra-modal matching rather than cross-modal alignment. Given a query q, an LLM generates a hypothetical ActDT $\widehat{\mathrm{ActDT}}_q = \mathrm{LLM}_{\mathrm{imagine}}(q, \mathcal{K})$, where $\mathcal{K}$ is procedural information drawn from OR video metadata. The LLM does not rephrase q but instead predicts the action primitives the target clip would contain. The hypothetical ActDT shares the same interval-action structure as actual ActDTs but omits ℓ and replaces VLM-generated attributes d with procedure-informed properties predicted by the LLM, as no visual frames are available at query time. Because both hypothetical and actual ActDTs are serialized as JSON text, we encode them with a single text encoder f_θ and compute

$$r_i = \mathrm{sim}\Big(f_\theta(\widehat{\mathrm{ActDT}}_q),\ f_\theta(\mathrm{ActDT}(C_i))\Big), \tag{1}$$

where $\mathrm{sim}(\cdot,\cdot)$ denotes cosine similarity and r_i is the relevance score for clip C_i. We train f_θ with a contrastive objective combining two types of hard negatives tailored to ActDT. The first type is temporally adjacent clips, which share nearly identical entities but differ in actions, forcing the encoder to attend to action-level distinctions. The second type is temporal-permutation negatives, where a random permutation σ reorders the intervals of each ActDT to produce $\mathrm{ActDT}^\sigma(C_i) = [\mathrm{ActDT}(C_i)_{\sigma(k)}]_{k=1}^{T_i}$, preserving action primitives while disrupting their temporal arrangement. To bridge the structural gap between hypothetical and actual ActDTs, we apply field-dropout augmentation, independently masking each field with probability p_{drop} to produce $\widetilde{\mathrm{ActDT}}(C_i) = \mathcal{M}(\mathrm{ActDT}(C_i), p_{\mathrm{drop}})$, where $\mathcal{M}$ replaces selected fields with a null token. This makes f_θ tolerant to the absence of the field in hypothetical ActDTs. The training loss [4,15] over the positive pair (q, C^+) where C^+ is the ground-truth clip for q, adjacent negatives $\mathcal{N}_{\mathrm{adj}}(C^+)$ drawn from temporally neighboring clips, and permutation negatives $\mathcal{N}_{\mathrm{perm}}(C^+)$ constructed by interval reordering is

$$\mathcal{L} = -\sum_{(q,C^+)} \log \frac{\exp(r^+/\gamma)}{\exp(r^+/\gamma) + \sum_{C^- \in \mathcal{N}_{\mathrm{adj}} \cup \mathcal{N}_{\mathrm{perm}}} \exp(r^-/\gamma)}, \tag{2}$$

where
γ is a temperature parameter, and $r^+ = \mathrm{sim}(f_\theta(\widehat{\mathrm{ActDT}}_q), f_\theta(\widetilde{\mathrm{ActDT}}(C^+)))$, $r^- = \mathrm{sim}(f_\theta(\widehat{\mathrm{ActDT}}_q), f_\theta(\widetilde{\mathrm{ActDT}}(C^-)))$. The top-$K$ candidates ranked by r_i proceed to evidence-grounded refinement.

Evidence-Grounded Refinement. The initial hypothetical ActDT relies on the LLM's generic knowledge, which may not capture the conventions of a specific procedure [19,20]. OR^3 revises the imagined ActDT itself based on evidence from retrieved candidates. After the initial ranking produces the top candidates K with actual ActDTs $\{\mathrm{ActDT}(C_{i_k})\}_{k=1}^{K}$, the LLM receives the original query q, the current hypothetical $\widehat{\mathrm{ActDT}}_q$, and the candidate ActDTs, then identifies discrepancies between the imagined and observed action primitives. Afterwards, the LLM generates a revised hypothetical, namely $\widehat{\mathrm{ActDT}}_q^{(t+1)} = \mathrm{LLM}_{\mathrm{refine}}\left(q, \widehat{\mathrm{ActDT}}_q^{(t)}, \{\mathrm{ActDT}(C_{i_k})\}_{k=1}^{K}\right)$, where t indexes the refinement round and $\widehat{\mathrm{ActDT}}_q^{(0)} = \widehat{\mathrm{ActDT}}_q$ is the initial imagined ActDT. The revised hypothetical ActDT is re-encoded by f_θ, and relevance scores r_i are recomputed over $\mathcal{C}$ to produce an updated ranking. This process iterates for at most T_{ref} rounds or terminates early when the top-ranked clip remains unchanged.

Benchmark. We construct an OR reasoning retrieval benchmark from the MM-OR dataset [16] to evaluate clip-level retrieval under implicit queries. Each of the 17 full-length recordings is segmented into non-overlapping clips according to the annotated surgical phases and procedural steps, yielding 386 clips with durations ranging from 20 s to 10 min. Two annotators with surgical domain knowledge independently come up implicit queries in four reasoning categories: temporal (*e.g.*, "*the step right before bone sawing*"), causal (*e.g.*, "*the action that triggered a sterility breach*"), procedural (*e.g.*, "*the first use of the drill after robot calibration*"), and role-based (*e.g.*, "*what the nurse prepared while the surgeon was sawing*"). Each query is mapped to one or more ground-truth clips and cross-verified by the other annotator, with disagreements resolved through discussion to ensure unambiguous correspondence. The final benchmark contains 276 implicit queries over 386 clips, split into training (162 queries, 218 clips), validation (48 queries, 72 clips), and test (66 queries, 96 clips) following the original MM-OR data partitions.

3 Experiments

Implementation Details. We construct ActDTs using Qwen3-VL-8B [1] as the VLM for generating action descriptions and entity attributes, SAM-3 [2] for instance segmentation masks, and DepthAnythingV3 [12] for depth estimation at object centroids. For imagination-based retrieval and evidence-grounded refinement, we employ Gemini-3-Pro as the LLM backbone, with top-$K = 10$ candidates forwarded to refinement and a maximum of $T_{\mathrm{ref}} = 3$ refinement rounds.

The text encoder f_θ is initialized from the BERT-base model [7] and trained with AdamW and learning rate 2×10^{-5}, weight decay 0.01 for 80 epochs on a 8 NVIDIA GeForce RTX 4090 GPUs, with temperature $\gamma = 0.07$, field-dropout probability $p_{\text{drop}} = 0.3$, and two temporally adjacent clips on each side as hard negatives. We report Recall at rank K (R@K) for $K \in \{1, 5, 10\}$, measuring the fraction of queries for which at least one ground-truth clip appears within the top-K results. All metrics are averaged over five runs with different random seeds, and we report mean ± standard deviation.

Table 1. Retrieval performance on the OR reasoning retrieval benchmark. Methods are grouped into embedding-based retrieval, LLM approaches, reasoning retrieval, and our OR^3. Bold and underline mark the best and second-best results.

Method	Temporal			Causal			Procedural			Role-based			Overall		
	R@1	R@5	R@10	R@1	R@5	R@10	R@1	R@5	R@10	R@1	R@5	R@10	R@1	R@5	R@10
CLIP4Clip [13]	$10.5_{\pm2.4}$	$26.3_{\pm3.4}$	$36.8_{\pm3.8}$	$5.3_{\pm1.9}$	$15.8_{\pm3.1}$	$23.7_{\pm3.6}$	$8.8_{\pm2.1}$	$20.6_{\pm3.0}$	$29.4_{\pm3.4}$	$11.8_{\pm2.6}$	$26.5_{\pm3.6}$	$38.2_{\pm3.9}$	$9.1_{\pm1.8}$	$22.7_{\pm2.7}$	$31.8_{\pm3.0}$
X-CLIP [14]	$14.2_{\pm2.7}$	$31.6_{\pm3.6}$	$42.1_{\pm3.8}$	$7.9_{\pm2.3}$	$18.4_{\pm3.3}$	$28.9_{\pm3.8}$	$11.8_{\pm2.4}$	$23.5_{\pm3.2}$	$32.4_{\pm3.5}$	$14.7_{\pm2.9}$	$32.4_{\pm3.8}$	$44.1_{\pm4.0}$	$12.1_{\pm2.1}$	$25.8_{\pm2.8}$	$36.4_{\pm3.1}$
InternVideo2 [25]	$17.6_{\pm3.0}$	$36.8_{\pm3.8}$	$47.4_{\pm3.9}$	$10.5_{\pm2.6}$	$23.7_{\pm3.6}$	$34.2_{\pm4.0}$	$14.7_{\pm2.6}$	$32.4_{\pm3.5}$	$41.2_{\pm3.7}$	$17.6_{\pm3.1}$	$38.2_{\pm3.9}$	$52.9_{\pm4.0}$	$15.2_{\pm2.3}$	$33.3_{\pm3.0}$	$43.9_{\pm3.2}$
TeachCLIP [23]	$12.3_{\pm2.5}$	$28.1_{\pm3.5}$	$40.4_{\pm3.8}$	$5.3_{\pm1.9}$	$15.8_{\pm3.1}$	$26.3_{\pm3.7}$	$11.8_{\pm2.4}$	$23.5_{\pm3.2}$	$32.4_{\pm3.5}$	$12.9_{\pm2.7}$	$29.4_{\pm3.7}$	$41.2_{\pm4.0}$	$10.6_{\pm2.0}$	$24.2_{\pm2.7}$	$34.8_{\pm3.1}$
Qwen3-VL-8B [1]	$21.1_{\pm3.2}$	$42.1_{\pm3.8}$	$52.6_{\pm3.9}$	$15.8_{\pm3.1}$	$28.9_{\pm3.8}$	$39.5_{\pm4.1}$	$17.6_{\pm2.8}$	$35.3_{\pm3.6}$	$47.1_{\pm3.7}$	$23.5_{\pm3.4}$	$44.1_{\pm4.0}$	$55.9_{\pm4.0}$	$19.7_{\pm2.5}$	$37.9_{\pm3.1}$	$48.5_{\pm3.2}$
Gemini3	$15.8_{\pm2.8}$	$33.3_{\pm3.7}$	$45.6_{\pm3.9}$	$10.5_{\pm2.6}$	$21.1_{\pm3.5}$	$31.6_{\pm3.9}$	$11.8_{\pm2.4}$	$29.4_{\pm3.4}$	$38.2_{\pm3.7}$	$17.6_{\pm3.1}$	$35.3_{\pm3.9}$	$47.1_{\pm4.0}$	$13.6_{\pm2.2}$	$30.3_{\pm2.9}$	$40.9_{\pm3.2}$
ReasonT2V [20]	$\underline{26.3}_{\pm3.4}$	$\underline{47.4}_{\pm3.9}$	$\underline{57.9}_{\pm3.8}$	$\underline{15.8}_{\pm3.1}$	$\underline{31.6}_{\pm3.9}$	$\underline{42.1}_{\pm4.2}$	$\underline{23.5}_{\pm3.2}$	$\underline{41.2}_{\pm3.7}$	$\underline{50.0}_{\pm3.7}$	$\underline{29.4}_{\pm3.7}$	$\underline{47.1}_{\pm4.0}$	$\underline{61.8}_{\pm3.9}$	$\underline{24.2}_{\pm2.8}$	$\underline{42.4}_{\pm3.2}$	$\underline{53.0}_{\pm3.2}$
OR^3 (Ours)	$\mathbf{63.2}_{\pm3.8}$	$\mathbf{82.5}_{\pm3.0}$	$\mathbf{89.5}_{\pm2.4}$	$\mathbf{42.1}_{\pm4.2}$	$\mathbf{63.2}_{\pm4.1}$	$\mathbf{73.7}_{\pm3.7}$	$\mathbf{58.8}_{\pm3.7}$	$\mathbf{76.5}_{\pm3.2}$	$\mathbf{85.3}_{\pm2.6}$	$\mathbf{67.6}_{\pm3.8}$	$\mathbf{85.3}_{\pm2.9}$	$\mathbf{91.2}_{\pm2.3}$	$\mathbf{57.6}_{\pm3.2}$	$\mathbf{77.3}_{\pm2.7}$	$\mathbf{84.8}_{\pm2.3}$

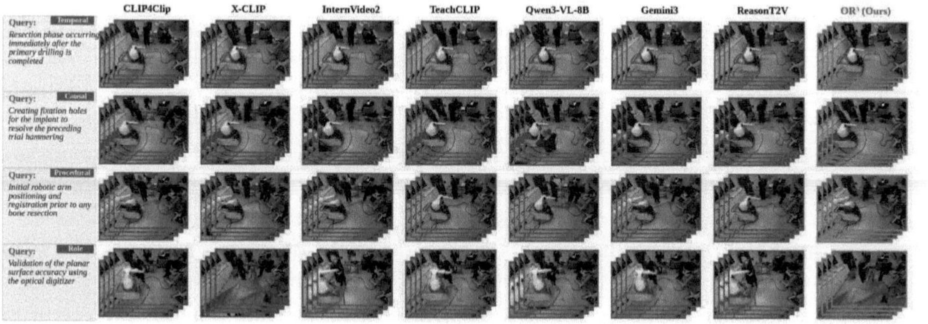

Fig. 2. Qualitative comparison on the OR reasoning retrieval benchmark across four query categories. Red borders indicate incorrect retrievals where methods return clips that do not match the query, while green borders denote correct retrievals by OR^3 (Color figure online).

Retrieval Performance. Table 1 compares OR^3 with embedding-based retrieval [13,14,23], LLM-based approaches [1,25], and ReasonT2V [20] on our OR reasoning retrieval benchmark. OR^3 achieves 57.6% R@1, outperforming ReasonT2V [20] by 33.4 percentage points and confirming that ActDT captures action-level differences while imagination-based retrieval bridges the semantic gap between abstract implicit queries and digital twin representations. Embedding-based methods [13,14,23] remain below 16% R@1, as global similarity matching cannot reason over implicit queries nor discriminate between visually near-identical OR clips differing only in actions. LLM-based approaches improve through partial language reasoning, yet visual token compression [11,20] discards fine-grained action and temporal structure needed for OR clip retrieval. ReasonT2V [20] reaches 24.2% R@1 through digital twin representations, but its object-centric design fails to capture action-level state transitions distinguishing consecutive surgical clips. Across query categories, causal queries show most challenging, with OR^3 achieving 42.1% versus 15.8% for ReasonT2V, as resolving cause-effect chains requires both temporal ordering and action-level reasoning. Temporal and procedural queries show the largest absolute gains of 36.9 and 35.3 R@1 points over ReasonT2V, reflecting ActDT's interval-structured action primitives for queries referencing sequential ordering or workflow position. Role-based queries yield the highest performance at 67.6% R@1, since identifying agent-action pairs aligns naturally with the subject-action-object triplets in each ActDT interval.

Table 2. Ablation study on the OR reasoning retrieval benchmark (R@1). ActDT: action-driven digital twin (replaced by object-centric digital twin of ReasonT2V when absent). Imag.: imagination-based retrieval (replaced by cross-modal paired-encoder matching when absent). Ref.: evidence-grounded refinement. Adj.: adjacent-clip hard negatives. Perm.: temporal-permutation negatives. FD: field-dropout augmentation.

ActDT	Imag.	Ref.	Adj.	Perm.	FD	Temp.	Caus.	Proc.	Role	Overall
✗	✓	✓	✓	✓	✓	$47.4_{\pm 3.9}$	$28.9_{\pm 3.8}$	$41.2_{\pm 3.7}$	$52.9_{\pm 4.0}$	$42.4_{\pm 3.2}$
✓	✗	✓	✓	✓	✓	$50.9_{\pm 3.9}$	$31.6_{\pm 3.9}$	$44.1_{\pm 3.7}$	$55.9_{\pm 4.0}$	$45.5_{\pm 3.2}$
✓	✓	✗	✓	✓	✓	$54.4_{\pm 3.9}$	$34.2_{\pm 4.0}$	$50.0_{\pm 3.7}$	$61.8_{\pm 3.9}$	$50.0_{\pm 3.2}$
✓	✓	✓	✗	✓	✓	$57.9_{\pm 3.9}$	$36.8_{\pm 4.1}$	$50.0_{\pm 3.7}$	$61.8_{\pm 3.9}$	$51.5_{\pm 3.1}$
✓	✓	✓	✓	✗	✓	$59.6_{\pm 3.8}$	$39.5_{\pm 4.1}$	$55.9_{\pm 3.7}$	$58.8_{\pm 3.9}$	$53.0_{\pm 3.1}$
✓	✓	✓	✓	✓	✗	$56.1_{\pm 3.9}$	$36.8_{\pm 4.1}$	$55.9_{\pm 3.7}$	$61.8_{\pm 3.9}$	$52.3_{\pm 3.2}$
✓	✓	✓	✓	✓	✓	$\mathbf{63.2}_{\pm 3.8}$	$\mathbf{42.1}_{\pm 4.2}$	$\mathbf{58.8}_{\pm 3.7}$	$\mathbf{67.6}_{\pm 3.8}$	$\mathbf{57.6}_{\pm 3.2}$

Figure 2 shows qualitative results in all four query categories. Embedding-based methods [13,14,23] and video-LLMs consistently retrieve visually similar but incorrect clips, as consecutive OR phases share nearly identical room layouts and personnel configurations. ReasonT2V [20] narrows the gap through digital twin reasoning yet still confuses clips whose objects overlap but whose actions differ. OR^3 retrieves the correct clip in each case, confirming that action-driven digital twins and imagination-based matching together resolve the fine-grained distinctions that other approaches miss.

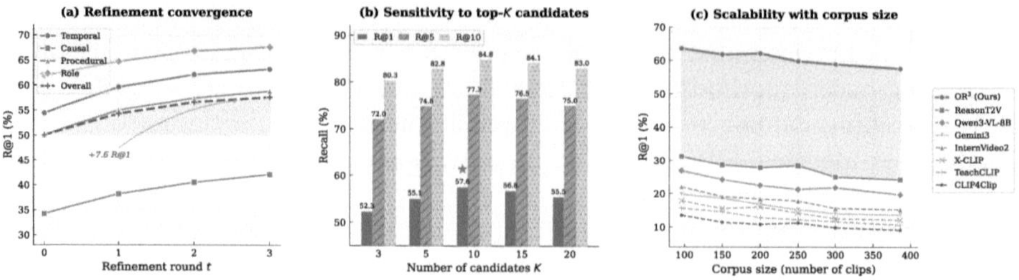

Fig. 3. Additional analyses of OR^3. (a) R@1 per query category as a function of evidence-grounded refinement round t, where $t = 0$ corresponds to the initial imagined ActDT before any refinement. (b) Sensitivity to the number of top-K candidates forwarded from imagination-based retrieval to refinement, with the star marking the selected operating point ($K = 10$). (c) R@1 of all compared methods as the retrieval corpus grows from 96 to 386 clips; the shaded region indicates the margin of OR^3 over the strongest baseline.

Ablation Study. Table 2 isolates each component by removing one at a time and reporting R@1 across query categories. Replacing ActDT with ReasonT2V's object-centric digital twin representation [20] causes the largest drop of 15.2% overall, with procedural queries falling 17.6% and temporal queries 15.8%, confirming that interval-structured action primitives drive fine-grained clip discrimination. This aligns with the large performance gap in Table 1 between OR^3 and ReasonT2V [20] on temporal and procedural queries, where sequential action ordering determines relevance. Eliminating imagination-based retrieval reduces overall R@1 by 12.1%, validating that matching of the same-space eliminates the semantic gap between abstract queries and concrete ActDT representations. Without evidence-grounded refinement, overall R@1 drops 7.6%, with causal queries declining 7.9%, as procedure-specific conventions matter most for resolving cause-effect chains. Among training strategies, adjacent-clip hard negatives contribute 6.1% by forcing the encoder to distinguish action-level differences between temporally neighboring clips. Field-dropout augmentation adds 5.3% by tolerating missing visual attributes in hypothetical ActDTs, while temporal-permutation negatives yield 4.6% by preserving interval ordering. All components produce additive gains exceeding their individual contributions, indicating mutual reinforcement. Figure 3 presents additional analyses of refinement convergence, candidate pool sensitivity, and corpus scalability. Evidence-grounded refinement yields monotonic R@1 gains across all query categories, with causal queries benefiting the most (34.2% → 42.1% over three rounds) and diminishing returns after $t = 2$ supporting the early-stopping criterion. Performance peaks at $K = 10$ candidates, as smaller pools risk excluding the ground-truth clip while larger pools dilute the evidence set presented to the LLM. As the corpus grows from 96 to 386 clips, OR^3 loses only 6.0 R@1 points compared to 7.0 for ReasonT2V and up to half the initial accuracy for embedding-based methods, confirming that ActDT-based discrimination scales more gracefully with increasing visual ambiguity.

4 Conclusion

We present OR^3, a reasoning retrieval method that addresses the gap between how users search for OR clips and how the existing text-to-video retrieval method operates. By shifting from object-centric to action-driven digital twins, our approach captures the temporal dynamics and state transitions that distinguish visually similar OR clips. Imagination-based retrieval further reframes cross-modal matching as an intra-modal problem, while evidence-grounded refinement adapts query interpretation to the conventions of individual procedures. Future work can explore evaluation of other procedure types and larger clip collections. Extending the framework to support multi-turn queries and real-time retrieval during live procedures can be another promising future direction.

Acknowledgments. Y. Shen was supported in part by the JHU Amazon Initiative for Artificial Intelligence (AI2AI) fellowship program.

Disclosure of Interests. The authors have no competing interests in the paper.

References

1. Bai, S., et al.: Qwen3-vl technical report. arXiv preprint arXiv:2511.21631 (2025)
2. Carion, N., et al.: Sam 3: Segment anything with concepts. arXiv preprint arXiv:2511.16719 (2025)
3. Che, Z., Guo, H.: Cross-modal video retrieval model based on video-text dual alignment. Int. J. Adv. Comput. Sci. Appl. **15**(2) (2024)
4. Chen, T., Kornblith, S., Norouzi, M., Hinton, G.: A simple framework for contrastive learning of visual representations. In: International Conference on Machine Learning, pp. 1597–1607. PmLR (2020)
5. Czempiel, T., et al.: TeCNO: surgical phase recognition with multi-stage temporal convolutional networks. In: Martel, A.L., et al. (eds.) MICCAI 2020. LNCS, vol. 12263, pp. 343–352. Springer, Cham (2020). https://doi.org/10.1007/978-3-030-59716-0_33
6. Dessalene, E., Maynord, M., Fermüller, C., Aloimonos, Y.: Therbligs in action: video understanding through motion primitives. In: Proceedings of the IEEE/CVF Conference on Computer Vision and Pattern Recognition, pp. 10618–10626 (2023)
7. Devlin, J., et al.: Bert: pre-training of deep bidirectional transformers for language understanding. In: Proceedings of the 2019 Conference of the North American Chapter of the Association for Computational Linguistics: Human Language Technologies, volume 1 (Long and Short Papers), pp. 4171–4186 (2019)
8. Grüter, A.A.J., et al.: Video-based tools for surgical quality assessment of technical skills in laparoscopic procedures: a systematic review. Surg. Endosc. **37**(6), 4279–4297 (2023)
9. Grant, M., et al.: Henning: a step toward modernization of urologic training: incorporation of a novel surgical intelligence platform for robotic prostatectomy video review. J. Endourol. **39**(11), 1204–1210 (2025)

10. Levin, M., et al.: Surgical data recording in the operating room: a systematic review of modalities and metrics. Br. J. Surg. **108**(6), 613–621 (2021)
11. Li, J.: Fcot-vl: Advancing text-oriented large vision-language models with efficient visual token compression. arXiv preprint arXiv:2502.18512 (2025)
12. Lin, H., et al.: Depth anything 3: recovering the visual space from any views. arXiv preprint arXiv:2511.10647 (2025)
13. Luo, H., et al.: Clip4clip: an empirical study of clip for end to end video clip retrieval. arXiv preprint arXiv:2104.08860 (2021)
14. Ma, Y., et al.: X-clip: end-to-end multi-grained contrastive learning for video-text retrieval. In: Proceedings of the 30th ACM International Conference on Multimedia, pp. 638–647 (2022)
15. van den Oord, A., Li, Y., Vinyals, O.: Representation learning with contrastive predictive coding. arXiv preprint arXiv:1807.03748 (2018)
16. Özsoy, E., et al.: MM-OR: a large multimodal operating room dataset for semantic understanding of high-intensity surgical environments. In: Proceedings of the Computer Vision and Pattern Recognition Conference, pp. 19378–19389 (2025)
17. Robinson, J., Chuang, C.-Y., Sra, S., Jegelka, S.: Contrastive learning with hard negative samples. arXiv preprint arXiv:2010.04592 (2020)
18. Sharma, S., et al.: Fine-clip: enhancing zero-shot fine-grained surgical action recognition with vision-language models. arXiv preprint arXiv:2503.19670 (2025)
19. Shen, Y., et al.: Online reasoning video segmentation with just-in-time digital twins. In: Proceedings of the IEEE/CVF International Conference on Computer Vision, pp. 24698–24706 (2025)
20. Shen, Y., et al.: Reasoning text-to-video retrieval via digital twin video representations and large language models. arXiv preprint arXiv:2511.12371 (2025)
21. Shen, Y., et al.: Temporally-constrained video reasoning segmentation and automated benchmark construction. In: Jeong, WK., Kim, H.J., Deng, Z., Shen, Y., Aviles-Rivero, A.I., Zhang, S. (eds.) MedAGI 2025. LNCS, vol. 16112, pp. 150–158. Springer, Cham (2025). https://doi.org/10.1007/978-3-032-07845-2_15
22. Shen, Y., Li, C., Liu, B., Li, C.-Y., Porras, T., Unberath, M.: Operating room workflow analysis via reasoning segmentation over digital twins. In: Gee, J.C., et al. (eds.) MICCAI 2025. LNCS, vol. 15968, 415–424. Springer, Cham (2025). https://doi.org/10.1007/978-3-032-05114-1_40
23. Tian, K., et al.: Teachclip: multi-grained teaching for efficient text-to-video retrieval. arXiv preprint arXiv:2308.01217 (2023)
24. Wang, X., et al.: T2vlad: global-local sequence alignment for text-video retrieval. In: Proceedings of the IEEE/CVF Conference on Computer Vision and Pattern Recognition, pp. 5079–5088 (2021)
25. Wang, Y., et al.: Internvideo2: scaling foundation models for multimodal video understanding. In: Leonardis, A., Ricci, E., Roth, S., Russakovsky, O., Sattler, T., Varol, G. (eds.) ECCV 2024. LNCS, vol. 15143, pp. 396–416. Springer, Cham (2024). https://doi.org/10.1007/978-3-031-73013-9_23
26. Samy Cheikh, Y., et al.: Learning surgical skills through video-based education: a systematic review. Surgical Innovation **30**(2), 220–238 (2023)
27. Tong, Y., et al.: Live laparoscopic video retrieval with compressed uncertainty. Med. Image Anal. **88**, 102866 (2023)
28. Zhang, H., et al.: Text-video retrieval with global-local semantic consistent learning. In: IEEE Transactions on Image Processing (2025)

RefTr: Recurrent Refinement of Confluent Trajectories for 3D Tubular Tree Centerlines

Roman Naeem(✉), David Hagerman, Jennifer Alvén, and Fredrik Kahl

Chalmers University of Technology, 412 96 Gothenburg, Sweden
{nroman,david.hagerman,alven,fredrik.kahl}@chalmers.se

Abstract. Tubular tree structures such as blood vessels and lung airways are central to many clinical tasks, including diagnosis, treatment planning, and surgical navigation. Accurate centerline extraction with correct topology is essential, as missing small branches can lead to incomplete assessments or overlooked abnormalities. We propose RefTr, a 3D image-to-graph framework that generates tubular tree centerlines via recurrent refinement of confluent trajectories. RefTr adopts a Transformer-based Producer–Refiner architecture in which the Producer predicts candidate trajectories and a shared Refiner iteratively aligns with target branches. The confluent trajectory representation enables whole-branch refinement while explicitly enforcing valid topology. This recurrent scheme improves precision and reduces decoder parameters by 2.4× compared to the state-of-the-art. We further introduce an efficient non-maximum suppression algorithm for spatial tree graphs to merge duplicate branches and extend evaluation metrics to be radius-aware for robust comparison. Experiments on multiple public datasets demonstrate higher recall and precision, faster inference, and substantially fewer parameters, highlighting the effectiveness of RefTr for 3D tubular tree analysis. Code is available at https://github.com/RomStriker/RefTr.

Keywords: Image-to-graph · Centerline Extraction · Tree Topology

1 Introduction

Tubular trees such as blood vessels and lung airways are essential for material transport in the human body, and abnormalities in these networks are linked to many diseases. Accurate, topologically correct centerline extraction is essential for diagnosis and treatment planning [8,11], surgical navigation [5], hemodynamic analysis [10], and vascular morphometry [3,6]. Missing small branches can lead to incomplete assessments and clinical risk, making high recall crucial. Centerline graphs provide a compact, interpretable representation, easier to annotate than dense masks and amenable to enforcing valid tree topology.

Segmentation-based methods, including topology-preserving and skeletonization losses [16,19,20,22], require costly voxel-level labels and post-processing,

G. Yang et al. (Eds.): MICCAI 2026, LNCS 16893, pp. 425–434, 2027.
https://doi.org/10.1007/978-3-032-38236-8_41

and lack end-to-end graph prediction, addressing a different problem setting than ours. Graph-based methods [15,18] predict nodes and edges but do not guarantee valid tree topology and scale poorly. Sequential tracking methods [13,14] iteratively generate centerlines but suffer from low recall due to imbalanced bifurcation/termination classification and cannot correct early errors. Classical multiple-hypothesis tracking [17] retains several candidate trees during reconstruction but ultimately prunes all but one, discarding potentially useful structures.

To address these limitations, we propose RefTr, a parameter-efficient Transformer based [1,21] 3D image-to-graph model that generates centerline trees via recurrent refinement of confluent trajectories. Prior work [24] defines confluence as a geometric property of overlapping oriented smooth curves and enforces it to reconstruct vessel trees in an unsupervised setting; we instead learn a discrete confluent trajectory representation in which trajectories share a prefix and split at a divergence index, as illustrated in Fig. 1a. A Producer predicts multiple trajectory candidates rooted at the patch center and a shared Refiner recurrently aligns them with the target, reducing decoder parameters by 2.4× versus the state-of-the-art Trexplorer Super [13].

To maximize recall, RefTr predicts multiple candidates per target via many-to-one matching, creating an ensembling effect. The resulting duplicate trajectories are suppressed at the patch level using pairwise divergence positions (duplicates do not diverge), and globally via Tree Non-Maximum Suppression (TNMS), a novel, efficient algorithm that merges overlapping branches while preserving topology. For robust comparison, we extend the Trexplorer Super [13] evaluation framework with radius-aware thresholds that scale with local branch radius.

Our contributions include: (1) RefTr, a parameter-efficient 3D image-to-graph framework predicting confluent trajectories with the highest recall and precision among compared methods; (2) Tree Non-Maximum Suppression, an efficient algorithm for removing duplicate branches while preserving tree topology; and (3) radius-aware evaluation metrics for robust comparison across datasets with varying branch radii.

2 Method

RefTr generates centerline graphs of tubular trees from CT volumes using a Transformer-based Producer–Refiner architecture and a confluent trajectory representation. The model architecture is shown in Fig. 1.

Problem Formulation and Inference. The goal is to infer a centerline tree graph $G = (V, E)$ from a 3D image patch. Each node $\mathbf{v} \in V$ represents a spatial position and the branch radius at that position. RefTr represents the tree as a set of confluent trajectories $\mathcal{T} = \{T_i\}_{i=1}^{n}$, as shown in Fig. 1a. Each trajectory $T_i = (\mathbf{v}_{i,1}, \ldots, \mathbf{v}_{i,L})$ is a node sequence rooted at the patch center. The set is confluent in that any pair T_i, T_j shares an identical prefix and separates only at a predicted pairwise divergence index d_{ij}, i.e. $\mathbf{v}_{i,k} = \mathbf{v}_{j,k}$ for $k \leq d_{ij}$.

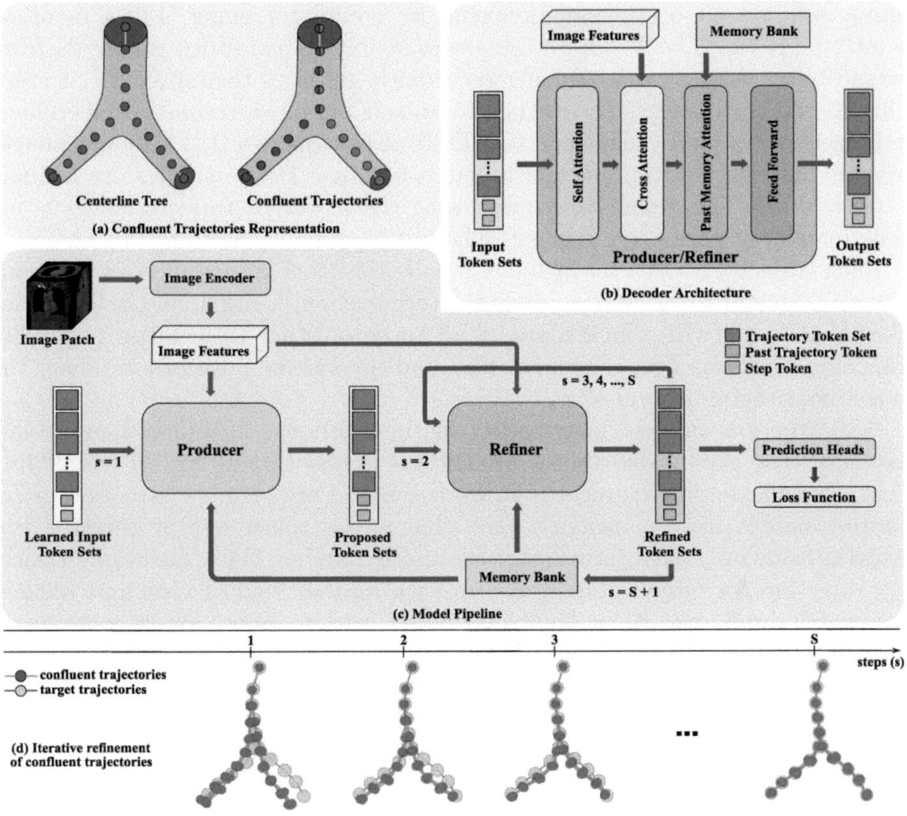

Fig. 1. Overview of the RefTr architecture. **(a)** A tubular tree centerline graph with corresponding confluent trajectories and divergence position at the fifth node. **(b)** Producer/Refiner architecture with Self-, Cross-, and Past-Memory attention. **(c)** Model pipeline including Image Encoder, Producer, Refiner, and prediction heads. The Producer uses learned token sets and image features to propose multiple trajectory embeddings, which the Refiner iteratively refines over S steps. Loss is computed at every step, including the Producer step (omitted for clarity). One refined token set per continuing branch is stored in the Memory Bank for the next patch. **(d)** Recurrent refinement of multiple confluent trajectories toward two target trajectories over S steps.

Unlike per node tracking, this representation refines whole branches jointly and maps to a tree by construction: shared prefixes become shared paths, divergence indices become bifurcations, and predicted end positions become terminations. Topology is therefore valid independently of TNMS, which only merges duplicate branches. During inference, branches extending beyond trajectory length are explored recursively using new patches.

RefTr Architecture. RefTr consists of an image encoder and a customized Transformer decoder with two modules, a Producer and a Refiner. For a fair comparison, we adopt the same encoder as Trexplorer Super [13], a modified SwinUNETR [4]. The Producer generates n initial trajectory proposals from learned token sets, and the Refiner recurrently updates them over $S-1$ steps using shared parameters. The learned token sets are fixed, trainable embeddings optimized end-to-end (analogous to DETR object queries [1]); they are image-agnostic until cross-attention injects patch features. Both modules use a single decoder block. This refines alignment with the m target trajectories ($n > m$) while remaining parameter-efficient. The full pipeline is shown in Fig. 1c.

Each trajectory token set includes L node tokens that predict node positions and radii, an end token that predicts the termination position, and a divergence token that is pairwise concatenated with those of other trajectories to predict branching positions between them. End and divergence positions lie along the trajectory, ranging from 0 to L.

Self-attention models inter-trajectory interactions, enabling many-to-one matching that evenly distributes predictions across targets for an ensembling effect. Cross-attention aggregates image features. Past-Memory attention incorporates context from a memory bank that stores token sets of ancestor trajectories from up to five previously processed patches. This maintains trajectory direction for large-radius branches with limited field of view and reduces cross-patch duplicates. As in Trexplorer Super, each training sample contains six patches along a single trajectory, so the memory bank holds up to five ancestor token sets. The detailed decoder architecture is shown in Fig. 1b.

We further use a past trajectory token encoding up to the last ten positions and radii from the patch center, helping determine centerline direction, especially when the memory bank is empty. We also include a step token that indicates the current refinement step and regulates the Refiner's update magnitude.

Matching and Loss. Predicted trajectories are matched to targets using a combined L1 (Manhattan) cost over position and radius differences. To allow multiple predictions per branch, we employ many-to-one matching by replicating targets and solving a bipartite assignment with the Hungarian algorithm [7]. Unlike one-to-many DETR variants [2,25] that discard surplus predictions at inference, RefTr keeps and merges them, yielding an inference-time ensemble.

All components use L1 loss. The total loss aggregates position and radius errors across steps, with end and divergence position losses at the final step, where trajectories are most refined:

$$\mathcal{L} = \sum_{s} (\alpha_{\text{pos}} \mathcal{L}_{\text{pos}}^{(s)} + \alpha_{\text{rad}} \mathcal{L}_{\text{rad}}^{(s)}) + \alpha_{\text{end}} \mathcal{L}_{\text{end}} + \alpha_{\text{div}} \mathcal{L}_{\text{div}}. \tag{1}$$

To ensure consistent supervision, the matching is computed only once using the predictions from the first step and reused for the remaining $S-1$ steps. We set $\alpha_{\text{pos}} = 4.2$, $\alpha_{\text{rad}} = 1.2$, $\alpha_{\text{end}} = 0.9$, $\alpha_{\text{div}} = 0.3$, tuned on the validation split. Re-matching at every step destabilizes training, as reassignment disrupts the progressive alignment of each trajectory with its target.

Tree Non-Maximum Suppression. Many-to-one matching yields an ensembling effect at the cost of duplicate trajectories, which are first filtered at the patch level using the pairwise divergence position. To remove residual duplicates globally, we introduce Tree Non-Maximum Suppression (TNMS), an efficient algorithm that merges overlapping branches while preserving tree topology.

Given a predicted tree with N nodes, TNMS performs a pre-order traversal and flags duplicate nodes using a radius-adaptive spatial threshold $\tau = \max(\tau_{\min}, \tau_{\text{pos}} \cdot r)$, with $\tau_{\text{pos}} = 0.3$ and $\tau_{\min} = 2.0$. Branches whose duplicate fraction exceeds $\rho = 0.2$ are merged, and any cycles are resolved by retaining edges closest to the root. Using KD-tree queries, the algorithm runs in $\mathcal{O}(N \log N)$ time, processing graphs with thousands of nodes in under one second on a CPU.

3 Experiments and Results

Datasets. We evaluate on the benchmark centerline datasets [12,13]: a synthetic dataset, the ATM'22 airway dataset [23], and the Parse 2022 pulmonary artery dataset [9].

Evaluation Metrics. Following Trexplorer Super [13], we report metrics at the node, branch, and graph levels. To enable a more robust evaluation, we introduce radius-aware matching thresholds that scale with the ground truth branch radius. A predicted node is considered a true positive if it lies within $\max(1.5, \tau^{\text{rad}} \cdot r)$ of a previously unmatched target node. Duplicate predictions are treated as false positives. At the node-level, we report radius-aware Average Precision (rAP), Average Recall (rAR), and Average F1-score (rF1), averaged over $\tau^{\text{rad}} = 0.25{:}0.05{:}0.75$ to reduce threshold sensitivity. For matched node pairs, we additionally report the mean absolute difference between predicted and ground truth radii.

For branch-level evaluation, a predicted branch is counted as a true positive if it overlaps with at least a fraction τ^{match} of nodes from an unmatched target branch. We report branch-level counterparts rBAP, rBAR, and rBF1, averaged over $\tau^{\text{match}} = 0.4{:}0.05{:}0.8$, with τ^{rad} fixed at 0.5. For graph-level evaluation, we report topological metrics, specifically the mean absolute error of Betti-0 (connected components) and Betti-1 (cycles), following Trexplorer Super. We retain the same dataset splits and protocol as prior work, upgrading only the matching thresholds; conclusions are unchanged under the legacy fixed-threshold metrics.

Implementation Details. Experiments were conducted on a single node with four NVIDIA A100 GPUs using mixed precision. RefTr was trained for 1.9 million iterations with $S = 8$ refinement steps, trajectory length $L = 10$, and $n = 20$ predicted branches. To ensure fair comparison with Trexplorer and Trexplorer Super [13,14], we used the same dataset and train–test split, adopting the authors' reported hyperparameters (26 tokens per bifurcation node, maximum 196 tokens) and trained for 2 million iterations. For Vesselformer [15], we report the best performance obtained using the published hyperparameters, with 80 object tokens and 12 million training iterations. All models were trained from scratch under identical data splits.

Table 1. Comparison of various models using point-level metrics.

Model	Point-level@ τ^{rad} = [0.25:0.05:0.75]			
	rAP(%)↑	rAR(%)↑	rF1(%)↑	Radius (MAE)↓
Synthetic Dataset				
Vesselformer	48.53 ± 10.35	70.05 ± 2.76	53.15 ± 8.19	0.43 ± 0.011
Trexplorer	31.10 ± 9.52	78.64 ± 4.10	39.64 ± 8.68	0.23 ± 0.032
Trexplorer Super	92.10 ± 3.29	70.58 ± 3.03	77.98 ± 1.90	**0.10 ± 0.006**
RefTr (ours)	**94.88 ± 0.77**	**79.39 ± 1.03**	**85.69 ± 1.30**	0.45 ± 0.093
ATM'22 Dataset				
Vesselformer	24.85 ± 1.47	38.48 ± 1.00	29.84 ± 1.37	0.79 ± 0.020
Trexplorer	4.54 ± 1.44	5.90 ± 0.70	4.49 ± 0.29	0.98 ± 0.086
Trexplorer Super	71.32 ± 1.22	60.84 ± 3.38	61.45 ± 1.23	**0.40 ± 0.021**
RefTr (ours)	**74.92 ± 1.17**	**66.73 ± 1.48**	**68.15 ± 0.59**	0.60 ± 0.036
Parse 2022 Dataset				
Vesselformer	21.93 ± 2.06	18.21 ± 1.00	19.54 ± 2.69	1.11 ± 0.027
Trexplorer	11.37 ± 3.73	13.42 ± 7.80	11.36 ± 5.17	1.22 ± 0.304
Trexplorer Super	53.65 ± 5.91	35.91 ± 3.22	40.01 ± 3.86	**0.58 ± 0.025**
RefTr (ours)	**53.68 ± 1.09**	**36.69 ± 1.12**	**42.37 ± 1.13**	0.75 ± 0.054

Results. Tables 1 and 2 report mean and standard deviation over five runs across point-, branch-, and graph-level metrics. At the point level, RefTr achieves the highest recall and precision across all datasets. On Parse 2022, improvements are smaller due to missing small branches in the ground truth, which RefTr correctly predicts (as verified by a radiologist review) but is penalized for, and encoder limitations from limited training data (72 training examples). RefTr's radius MAE, while higher than Trexplorer Super's, stays sub-voxel and has limited practical impact.

RefTr achieves superior branch-level metrics on the Synthetic and ATM'22 datasets. On Parse 2022, performance is comparable; here the missing small branches in the ground truth have a larger impact, since branches are weighted equally regardless of size. Graph-level metrics confirm topologically correct trees.

Table 3 shows RefTr reduces decoder parameters by 2.4× versus Trexplorer Super, with faster inference and substantially less training time and memory.

Figure 2 provides a qualitative comparison for one example from each dataset. Compared to the previous state-of-the-art Trexplorer Super, RefTr shows visibly higher recall, capturing branches that Trexplorer Super misses.

Table 2. Comparison of various models using branch-level and graph-level metrics.

Model	Branch-level@ $\tau^{\text{match}} = [0.4{:}0.05{:}0.8]$			Graph-level (MAE)	
	rBAP(%)↑	rBAR(%)↑	rBF1(%)↑	Betti-0↓	Betti-1↓
Synthetic Dataset					
Vesselformer	20.43 ± 4.22	43.63 ± 4.72	25.43 ± 3.75	81.7 ± 16.8	653.5 ± 138.7
Trexplorer	30.58 ± 8.66	77.47 ± 4.11	39.40 ± 7.82	**0.00 ± 0.0**	**0.00 ± 0.0**
Trexplorer Super	92.35 ± 3.54	70.82 ± 3.06	78.22 ± 1.78	**0.00 ± 0.0**	**0.00 ± 0.0**
RefTr (ours)	**96.75 ± 0.72**	**79.96 ± 1.15**	**86.76 ± 1.38**	**0.00 ± 0.0**	**0.00 ± 0.0**
ATM'22 Dataset					
Vesselformer	11.70 ± 0.73	16.77 ± 1.07	13.46 ± 0.81	312.5 ± 25.1	180.4 ± 35.9
Trexplorer	4.02 ± 1.71	2.06 ± 0.46	2.33 ± 0.31	**0.00 ± 0.0**	**0.00 ± 0.0**
Trexplorer Super	68.25 ± 1.75	60.91 ± 3.64	59.87 ± 1.39	**0.00 ± 0.0**	**0.00 ± 0.0**
RefTr (ours)	**68.40 ± 1.97**	**66.41 ± 1.53**	**64.23 ± 0.89**	**0.00 ± 0.0**	**0.00 ± 0.0**
Parse 2022 Dataset					
Vesselformer	9.23 ± 0.80	6.31 ± 0.85	7.30 ± 0.45	410.1 ± 23.9	246.7 ± 78.1
Trexplorer	11.32 ± 3.56	11.77 ± 7.22	10.45 ± 4.98	**0.00 ± 0.0**	**0.00 ± 0.0**
Trexplorer Super	**51.42 ± 5.58**	**34.41 ± 1.09**	**38.17 ± 3.63**	**0.00 ± 0.0**	**0.00 ± 0.0**
RefTr (ours)	47.17 ± 1.19	32.31 ± 1.13	37.09 ± 1.16	**0.00 ± 0.0**	**0.00 ± 0.0**

Table 3. Number of parameters, runtime, training time, and memory usage for the compared models. Note: Vesselformer has a much higher effective runtime due to a multi-hour post-processing. Experiments conducted on four Nvidia A100 80GB GPUs.

Model	Parameters (M)			Runtime	Training	GPU Mem.
	Encoder	Decoder	Total	(ms/patch)	(hrs)	(GBs)
Vesselformer	82.83	13.59	98.73	23*	37.4	**13.8**
Trexplorer	23.31	25.22	55.46	222	18.6	51.34
Trexplorer Super	23.12	25.22	55.27	189	37.2	73.9
RefTr (ours)	**23.12**	**10.50**	**42.32**	**156**	**18.2**	39.5

Ablation Study. Table 4 presents an extensive ablation study of our method's key components, including Recurrent Refinement, Many-to-One matching, Tree Non-Maximum Suppression (TNMS), Past-Attention, and Producer/Refiner design choices. We report the mean and standard deviation over three runs.

The study shows that Recurrent Refinement, Many-to-One matching, and Past-Memory attention are essential for achieving high recall. Removing TNMS instead leaves recall essentially unchanged but sharply lowers precision (Table 4), confirming that the core generation mechanism recovers the structures, while TNMS only reclaims precision lost to residual cross-patch duplicates.

Sharing one decoder block between Producer and Refiner is suboptimal, as it must process two input types: learned and already refined token sets. Increasing the number of Producer blocks makes the initial proposals overly rigid, which limits the Refiner's ability to correct early errors. Conversely, adding Refiner

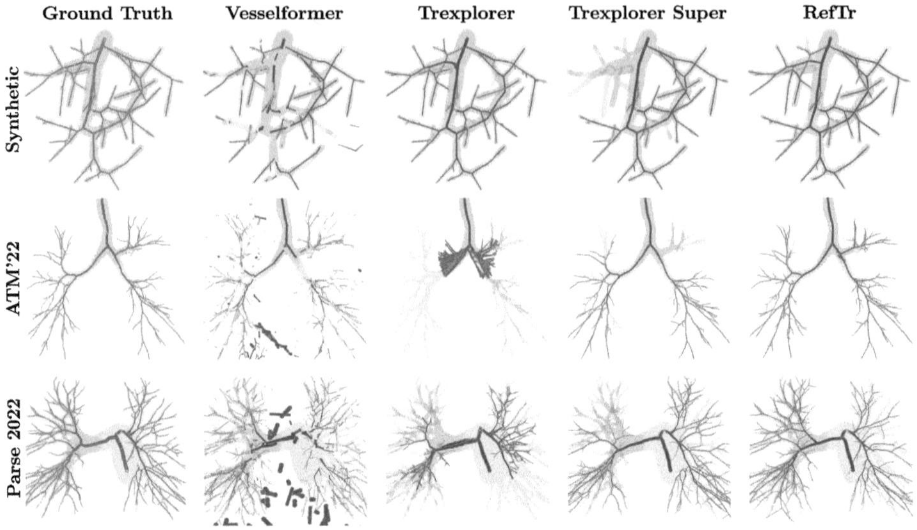

Fig. 2. Visual comparison of ground truth and predictions from RefTr and baseline methods on one sample per dataset. Marker sizes are proportional to local branch radii at node positions. The tubular structure mask (green) is for visualization only and not used during training or evaluation. (Color figure online)

Table 4. Ablation study evaluating the impact of the key components and design choices for the RefTr model on the ATM'22 dataset.

Description	Point-level@ τ^{rad} = [0.25:0.05:0.75]		
	rAP(%)↑	rAR(%)↑	rF1(%)↑
Key High-level Components			
No Recurrent Refinement ($S = 2$)	61.96 ± 2.17	58.08 ± 1.17	56.70 ± 1.66
No Many-to-one Matching	66.70 ± 1.27	63.25 ± 3.49	61.34 ± 1.68
No Tree Non-Max Suppression	37.98 ± 2.42	**69.96 ± 1.12**	37.98 ± 3.87
Recurrent Refinement Steps			
Refinement Steps: $S = 4$	65.10 ± 6.32	55.72 ± 2.83	58.17 ± 3.42
Refinement Steps: $S = 6$	64.39 ± 5.17	60.93 ± 2.57	59.42 ± 3.19
Refinement Steps: $S = 10$	71.43 ± 3.12	65.16 ± 1.58	65.60 ± 1.91
Past Trajectory and Memory Attention			
No Past Trajectory Token	**78.85 ± 3.24**	37.07 ± 1.21	48.34 ± 2.78
No Past-Memory Attention	61.27 ± 2.12	66.38 ± 1.87	60.46 ± 2.24
Producer and Refiner Design Configurations			
Shared Producer and Refiner	65.18 ± 1.44	61.76 ± 1.32	60.27 ± 1.78
Increase Producer Blocks: 2	68.80 ± 2.24	62.88 ± 1.11	63.19 ± 1.83
Increase Refiner Blocks: 2	71.81 ± 2.07	64.67 ± 1.57	64.46 ± 1.98
Proposed Model	74.16 ± 1.45	67.72 ± 1.49	**68.35 ± 1.27**

blocks makes each step apply larger updates that can push predictions off track and hinder recovery. Overall, the best performance is achieved with separate Producer and Refiner modules, each using a single decoder block and $S = 8$ refinement steps.

4 Conclusion

We present RefTr, a parameter-efficient framework for generating topologically accurate centerline graphs of tubular trees from 3D medical images. By predicting confluent trajectories and refining them recurrently, RefTr delivers state-of-the-art performance with substantially improved efficiency across multiple datasets, showing strong potential for clinical analysis. Future work will focus on improving the image encoder to further enhance feature quality and performance on challenging cases.

Acknowledgments. Compute and storage resources were provided by NAISS (grant 2022-06725, Swedish Research Council) and the Berzelius system at the National Supercomputer Centre, funded by the Knut and Alice Wallenberg Foundation.

Disclosure of Interests. The authors have no competing interests to declare that are relevant to the content of this article.

References

1. Carion, N., Massa, F., Synnaeve, G., Usunier, N., Kirillov, A., Zagoruyko, S.: End-to-end object detection with transformers. In: Vedaldi, A., Bischof, H., Brox, T., Frahm, J.-M. (eds.) ECCV 2020. LNCS, vol. 12346, pp. 213–229. Springer, Cham (2020). https://doi.org/10.1007/978-3-030-58452-8_13
2. Chen, Q., et al.: Group DETR: fast DETR training with group-wise one-to-many assignment. In: Proceedings of the IEEE/CVF International Conference on Computer Vision, pp. 6633–6642 (2023)
3. Choi, A.D., et al.: CT evaluation by artificial intelligence for atherosclerosis, stenosis and vascular morphology (CLARIFY): a multi-center, international study. J. Cardiovasc. Comput. Tomogr. **15**(6), 470–476 (2021)
4. Hatamizadeh, A., Nath, V., Tang, Y., Yang, D., Roth, H.R., Xu, D.: Swin UNETR: Swin Transformers for semantic segmentation of brain tumors in MRI images. In: Crimi, A., Bakas, S. (eds.) BrainLes 2021. LNCS, vol 12962, pp. 272–284. Springer, Cham (2021). https://doi.org/10.1007/978-3-031-08999-2_22
5. Huang, D., Tang, W., Ding, Y., Wan, T., Chen, Y.: An interactive 3D preoperative planning and training system for minimally invasive vascular surgery. In: 12th International Conference on Computer-Aided Design and Computer Graphics, pp. 443–449. IEEE (2011)
6. Khan, Z., et al.: Three-dimensional morphometric analysis of the renal vasculature. Am. J. Physiol.-Renal Physiol. **314**(5), F715–F725 (2018)
7. Kuhn, H.W.: The Hungarian method for the assignment problem. Naval Res. Logist. Quart. **2**(1–2), 83–97 (1955)

8. Li, H., Tang, Z., Nan, Y., Yang, G.: Human treelike tubular structure segmentation: a comprehensive review and future perspectives. Comput. Biol. Med. **151**, 106241 (2022)
9. Luo, G., et al.: Efficient automatic segmentation for multi-level pulmonary arteries: the PARSE challenge. arXiv preprint arXiv:2304.03708 (2023)
10. Miraucourt, O., Salmon, S., Szopos, M., Thiriet, M.: Blood flow in the cerebral venous system: modeling and simulation. Comput. Methods Biomech. Biomed. Engin. **20**(5), 471–482 (2017)
11. Moccia, S., De Momi, E., El Hadji, S., Mattos, L.S.: Blood vessel segmentation algorithms-review of methods, datasets and evaluation metrics. Comput. Methods Programs Biomed. **158**, 71–91 (2018)
12. Naeem, R.: Trexplorer Super datasets (1.0) (2025). https://doi.org/10.5281/zenodo.15888958
13. Naeem, R., Hagerman, D., Alvén, J., Svensson, L., Kahl, F.: Trexplorer Super: topologically correct centerline tree tracking of tubular objects in CT volumes. In: Gee, J.C., et al. (eds.) MICCAI 2025. LNCS, vol. 15967, pp. 595–605. Springer, Cham (2025). https://doi.org/10.1007/978-3-032-04984-1_57
14. Naeem, R., Hagerman, D., Svensson, L., Kahl, F.: Trexplorer: recurrent DETR for topologically correct tree centerline tracking. In: Linguraru, M.G., et al. (eds.) MICCAI 2024. LNCS, vol. 15011, pp. 744–754. Springer, Cham (2024). https://doi.org/10.1007/978-3-031-72120-5_69
15. Prabhakar, C., et al.: Vesselformer: towards complete 3D vessel graph generation from images. In: Medical Imaging with Deep Learning, pp. 320–331. PMLR (2024)
16. Qiu, Y., et al.: A topology-preserving three-stage framework for fully-connected coronary artery extraction. Med. Image Anal. **103**, 103578 (2025)
17. Selvan, R., Petersen, J., Pedersen, J.H., de Bruijne, M.: Extracting tree structures in CT data by tracking multiple statistically ranked hypotheses. Med. Phys. **46**(10), 4431–4440 (2019)
18. Shit, S., et al.: Relationformer: a unified framework for image-to-graph generation. In: Avidan, S., Brostow, G., Cissé, M., Farinella, G.M., Hassner, T. (eds.) ECCV 2022. LNCS, vol. 13697, pp. 422–439. Springer, Cham (2022). https://doi.org/10.1007/978-3-031-19836-6_24
19. Shit, S., et al.: clDice—a novel topology-preserving loss function for tubular structure segmentation. In: Proceedings of the IEEE/CVF Conference on Computer Vision and Pattern Recognition, pp. 16560–16569 (2021)
20. Tetteh, G., et al.: DeepVesselNet: vessel segmentation, centerline prediction, and bifurcation detection in 3-D angiographic volumes. Front. Neurosci. **14**, 1285 (2020)
21. Vaswani, A., et al.: Attention is all you need. In: Advances in Neural Information Processing Systems **30** (2017)
22. Wittmann, B., Wattenberg, Y., Amiranashvili, T., Shit, S., Menze, B.: vesselFM: a foundation model for universal 3D blood vessel segmentation. In: Proceedings of the IEEE/CVF Conference on Computer Vision and Pattern Recognition, pp. 20874–20884 (2025)
23. Zhang, M., et al.: Multi-site, multi-domain airway tree modeling. Med. Image Anal. **90**, 102957 (2023)
24. Zhang, Z., Marin, D., Drangova, M., Boykov, Y.: Confluent vessel trees with accurate bifurcations. In: Proceedings of the IEEE/CVF Conference on Computer Vision and Pattern Recognition, pp. 9573–9582 (2021)
25. Zong, Z., Song, G., Liu, Y.: DETRs with collaborative hybrid assignments training. In: Proceedings of the IEEE/CVF International Conference on Computer Vision, pp. 6748–6758 (2023)

Robotic Ultrasound Makes CBCT Alive

Feng Li[1,2(✉)], Ziyuan Li[1], Zhongliang Jiang[3], Nassir Navab[1,2], and Yuan Bi[1,2]

[1] Chair for Computer-Aided Medical Procedures and Augmented Reality, Technical University of Munich, Munich, Germany
feng.li@tum.de
[2] Munich Center for Machine Learning, Munich, Germany
[3] The University of Hong Kong, Hong Kong, China

Abstract. Intraoperative Cone Beam Computed Tomography (CBCT) provides a reliable 3D anatomical context for interventional planning. However, its static nature fails to provide continuous monitoring of soft-tissue deformations induced by respiration, probe pressure, and surgical manipulation, leading to navigation discrepancies. We propose a deformation-aware CBCT updating framework that leverages robotic ultrasound as a dynamic proxy to infer tissue motion and update static CBCT slices in real time. Starting from calibration-initialized alignment with linear correlation of linear combination (LC2)-based rigid refinement, our method establishes multimodal correspondence. To capture intraoperative dynamics, we introduce the ultrasound correlation UNet (USCorUNet), a lightweight network trained with optical flow-guided supervision to learn deformation-aware correlation representations, enabling accurate, real-time dense deformation field estimation from ultrasound streams. The inferred deformation is spatially regularized and transferred to the CBCT reference to produce deformation-consistent visualizations without repeated radiation exposure. We validate the approach through deformation estimation and ultrasound-guided CBCT updating experiments. Results demonstrate real-time end-to-end CBCT slice updating and physically plausible deformation estimation, enabling dynamic refinement of static CBCT guidance during robotic ultrasound-assisted interventions. The source code is publicly available at https://github.com/ziyuan-li/robotic-us-cbct-updating.

Keywords: Robotic ultrasound · CBCT · Deformation

1 Introduction

In recent years, robotic ultrasound has emerged as a promising paradigm for autonomous and reproducible intraoperative imaging, offering real-time visual-

F. Li and Z. Li—These authors contributed equally to this work.

Supplementary Information The online version contains supplementary material available at https://doi.org/10.1007/978-3-032-38236-8_42.

G. Yang et al. (Eds.): MICCAI 2026, LNCS 16893, pp. 436–446, 2027.
https://doi.org/10.1007/978-3-032-38236-8_42

ization with high soft-tissue contrast and vascular sensitivity [2,3]. Robotic control enables precise probe positioning, regulation of contact force, and automated scanning [4,10,21], supporting applications such as 3D compounding, motion-aware imaging, deformation recovery, and elastography [11]. However, its limited acoustic window restricts imaging to local soft tissues, which remain prone to artifacts and occlusions. Ultrasound captures only deformation-dependent observations without a consistent global reference, providing dynamic tissue information but not comprehensive anatomical context.

Cone beam computed tomography (CBCT) provides high-resolution volumetric imaging and has become an important intraoperative modality due to its compact design, lower radiation dose, and flexible integration into the operating room. Commercial systems such as C-armbased platforms [23] and Loop-X devices [15] offer on-demand 3D imaging with a large field of view, supporting surgical navigation and serving as detailed volumetric priors. However, CBCT captures only a static snapshot [22], while anatomy evolves during procedures due to respiration, patient movement, or probe interaction. Repeated CBCT is limited by radiation and workflow constraints, motivating integration with real-time ultrasound. Prior work using electromagnetic [19] and optical tracking [17] has enabled rigid CBCTultrasound alignment, but deformation-aware multimodal updating remains a key challenge for accurate intraoperative guidance.

In CBCTultrasound integration, deformation poses a fundamental challenge [12]. Ultrasound sequences encode rich temporal information, with adjacent frames reflecting tissue motion from respiration and probe interaction. Classical methods such as speckle tracking [6] and optical flow [18] have been explored for motion estimation, but modern speckle suppression reduces tracking reliability, and large probe-induced deformations remain difficult to capture. Deep learningbased optical flow models, like recurrent all-pairs field transforms (RAFT) [24], improve robustness to large displacements, yet ultrasound artifacts and depth-dependent distortions violate standard assumptions. Purely data-driven approaches also lack physical constraints, potentially producing biomechanically implausible deformation fields. These limitations motivate dedicated deformation modeling for CBCTultrasound integration.

To address these challenges, we propose a robotic-ultrasound-driven framework for deformation-aware CBCT updating in image-guided intervention. Our main contributions are: (1) a workflow-compatible robotic US-CBCT pipeline that integrates calibration, LC2-based refinement, ultrasound deformation estimation, and ultrasound-informed CBCT slice updating; (2) USCorUNet, a lightweight bidirectional correlation-enhanced network for real-time ultrasound-to-ultrasound deformation estimation with optical-flow-guided supervision; (3) real-time CBCT slice updating for probe- and externally induced deformations; and (4) multi-dataset in vivo and phantom validation, showing a favorable accuracy-efficiency trade-off against RAFT-based and classical baselines.

2 Methods

Our system has four modules (Fig. 1). Calibration-based rigid initialization establishes the CBCTultrasound spatial relationship (Fig. 1(a)), refined by LC2 to correct residual alignment errors (Fig. 1(b)). Non-rigid deformation between consecutive ultrasound frames is estimated with USCorUNet using pedagogical supervision (Fig. 1(c)). The resulting deformation is applied to update the corresponding CBCT slice, producing a dynamically deformed CBCT for visualization and guidance (Fig. 1(d)).

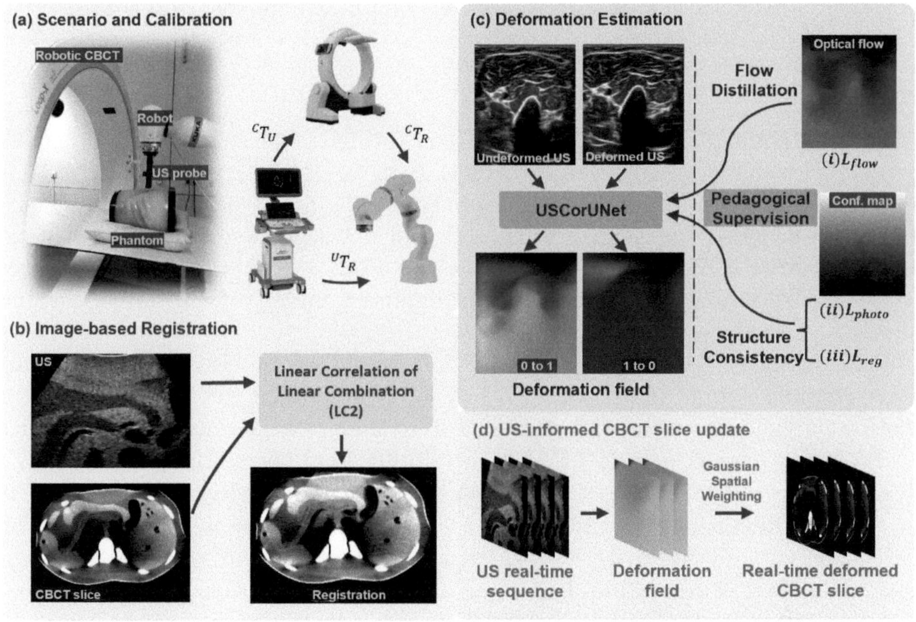

Fig. 1. System overview. (a) Rigid calibration between robotic ultrasound and CBCT. (b) Image-based registration refinement. (c) Deformation estimation with USCorUNet. (d) Deformation transfer for CBCT slice updating. Ultrasound examples from the in vivo arm dataset (c) and the CT-mapped phantom dataset (b,d) illustrate cross-domain applicability. Conf. map is confidence map.

2.1 Calibration and Registration

For spatial calibration, we adopted the hand-eye calibration framework proposed in [17]. Ultrasound (US) images can be projected into the CBCT volume via the spatial relationships among the CBCT, robot, and probe. The rigid transformation between a US image and CBCT slice, ${}^{C}\mathbf{T}_U$, is computed as ${}^{C}\mathbf{T}_U = {}^{C}\mathbf{T}_R({}^{U}\mathbf{T}_R)^{-1}$, where ${}^{C}\mathbf{T}_R$ and ${}^{U}\mathbf{T}_R$ map the CBCT and US image to the robot base frame.

Although calibration achieves a mean alignment error of approximately 1–2 mm, residual misalignment persists without image-based refinement, which can be clinically significant in precision-sensitive procedures such as needle insertion. To improve accuracy, we incorporate multimodal rigid registration using the LC2 similarity metric [26], which models the relationship between CBCT intensities and ultrasound appearance via a local linear approximation: $f(x_i) = \alpha \mathbf{p_i} + \beta \mathbf{g_i} + \gamma$, where p_i and g_i denote CBCT intensity and gradient magnitude, and α, β, γ estimate the local cross-modal relationship. Initialized by calibration, LC2 searches only in-plane translations within ± 10 CBCT pixels around the projected US position, while the slice and orientation are fixed by the calibrated geometry. This constrained search reduces computational cost and runtime.

2.2 Deformation Field Acquisition

Building on the rigid alignment, USCorUNet estimates dense bidirectional deformation fields between ultrasound frames $I_0, I_1 \in \mathbb{R}^{H \times W}$, yielding $F_{01}, F_{10} \in \mathbb{R}^{H \times W \times 2}$. We distill pseudo-labels from RAFT [24]. For each pair, we generate a direct RAFT candidate on (I_0, I_1) and a bisect candidate via an intermediate frame, composed as $(F \oplus G)(\mathbf{x}) = F(\mathbf{x}) + G(\mathbf{x} + F(\mathbf{x}))$, and select the candidate with lower post-warp misalignment under differentiable warping $\mathcal{W}(I, F)(\mathbf{x}) = I(\mathbf{x} + F(\mathbf{x}))$.

Figure 2 shows the architecture of USCorUNet. A preprocessing module forms a five-channel input $\left[I_0, I_1, (I_1 - I_0), |\nabla I_0|, |\nabla I_1|\right]$. The network combines a ResUNet-style context encoder-decoder with a shared-weight correlation encoder g_ϕ. From features $f_i = g_\phi([I_i, |\nabla I_i|])$, we build local correlation volumes, e.g., $CV_{01}(\mathbf{x}, \Delta) = \frac{1}{\sqrt{C}} \langle f_0(\mathbf{x}), f_1(\mathbf{x} + \Delta) \rangle$, and define CV_{10} analogously, where C is the feature dimension and Δ indexes a local displacement neighborhood. The correlation volumes are fused with same-scale context features and decoded into dense fields at 1/8 resolution, balancing efficiency and reliable matching.

Since appearance-driven pseudo-labels do not explicitly enforce physical plausibility [8], we train USCorUNet with a bidirectional objective that combines optical flow distillation $\mathcal{L}_{\text{flow}}$, confidence-weighted photometric consistency $\mathcal{L}_{\text{photo}}$, and regularization $\mathcal{L}_{\text{reg}}$. Specifically, $\mathcal{L}_{\text{flow}}$ is an ℓ_1 loss to the optical flows, $\mathcal{L}_{\text{photo}}$ is a confidence-weighted Charbonnier penalty [5] on post-warp intensity residuals using random-walk confidence maps [14], and $\mathcal{L}_{\text{reg}}$ combines edge-aware smoothness [9] and a Jacobian-based folding penalty [20]. The final objective is $\mathcal{L} = \lambda_{\text{flow}} \mathcal{L}_{\text{flow}} + \lambda_{\text{photo}} \mathcal{L}_{\text{photo}} + \lambda_{\text{reg}} \mathcal{L}_{\text{reg}}$, with $\lambda_{\text{flow}} = 1$, $\lambda_{\text{photo}} = 0.2$, and $\lambda_{\text{reg}} = 0.05$, chosen to prioritize flow distillation while using photometric consistency as a complementary cue and regularization as a mild physical prior.

2.3 Ultrasound Guided CBCT Updating

The estimated deformation field updates the CBCT slice in real time, accounting for probe and external motion. Specifically for probe-induced motion, we correct non-uniform convex compression using a Gaussian profile $P(x) = d_{\text{robot}} \cdot$

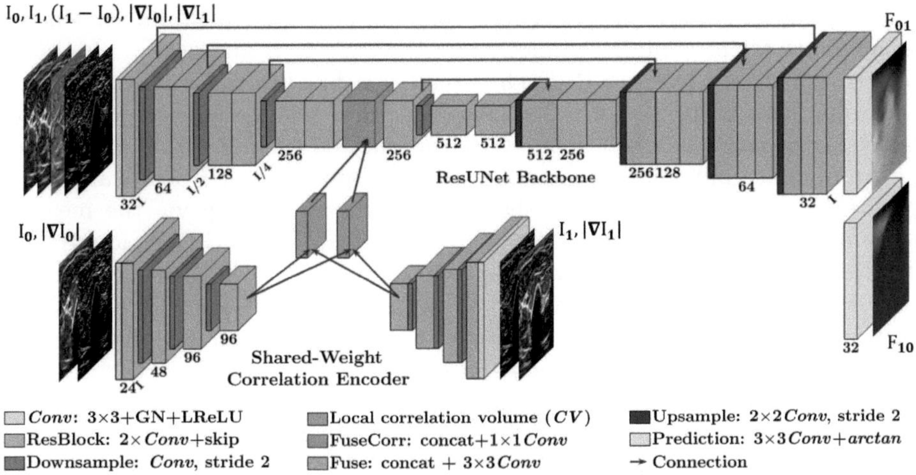

Fig. 2. Architecture of USCorUNet.

$\exp(-(x-c_x)^2/2\sigma_{\text{probe}}^2)$, where d_{robot} denotes the probe displacement magnitude, c_x the lateral midpoint, and σ_{probe} the curvature. This profile corrects the vertical deformation component: $\mathbf{D}\text{geo}^y = \mathbf{D}\text{raw}^y - P(x)$.

To align the local ultrasound field with the larger CBCT ROI, we use Euclidean Distance Transform (EDT)-based spatial weighting. The corrected field is padded to $\mathbf{D}$pad and scaled by $W(x,y) = \exp(-\mathcal{D}(x,y)/\sigma\text{smooth})$, where $\mathcal{D} = \text{EDT}(1-M)$ denotes the distance to the ultrasound boundary. The final field $\mathbf{D}\text{final} = \mathbf{D}\text{pad} \odot W$ enforces smooth decay of deformation from the probe contact region across the CBCT slice.

3 Experiments and Results

3.1 Experimental Protocol

The experimental setup integrates a KUKA LBR iiwa 14 R820 robot and Siemens ACUSON Juniper ultrasound (5C1 probe) via a 3D-printed holder, with images acquired through an Epiphan frame grabber. A Loop-X Imaging Ring provided CBCT data.

Experiments were conducted on four datasets: (A) in vivo forearm/upper-arm ultrasound from DefCor-Net [13], collected under IRB approval No. 2022-87-S-KK; (B) a pork-tissue gel phantom; (C) a chicken/pork gel phantom; and (D) an abdominal phantom (Kyoto Kagaku US-22). Datasets B–D are phantom datasets used for controlled probe-induced deformation experiments, with Dataset B additionally including finger-press compression to simulate externally induced deformation.

USCorUNet was trained on Dataset A (8:1:1 split) as a base model using (I_0, I_1) pairs and AdamW for 50 epochs (batch size 4, learning rate 2×10^{-4}, weight decay 10^{-4}, mixed precision). From the base model, we fine-tuned two variants: one for probe-induced motion on Datasets B–D and one for externally induced motion on Dataset B. Each variant was fine-tuned for 20 epochs with a learning rate of 10^{-4}, with the split and other settings unchanged. Across datasets, validation and test splits were held out and excluded from fine-tuning.

We evaluate bidirectional deformation estimates using (i) post-warp alignment (MAE, NCC), (ii) forward–backward (FB) consistency via the mean ℓ_2 norm of $r_{01} = F_{01} \oplus F_{10}$ and $r_{10} = F_{10} \oplus F_{01}$ (mean FB residual) [25], and (iii) physical plausibility via the folding ratio, i.e., the fraction of pixels with $\det(I + \nabla F) < 0$. On Dataset A, we additionally report Dice on SAM-segmented [16] bone masks after nearest-neighbor warping. For deformation-warped CT volumes, we report bone-mask Dice and SSIM.

As the primary baseline, we evaluate the selected optical flow under the same metrics as a reference for USCorUNet. We further conduct Dataset A ablations by (i) removing the correlation branch (w/o Corr.), (ii) disabling confidence-map weighting (w/o Conf.), and (iii) simplifying the training objective to $\mathcal{L}$flow + $\mathcal{L}$photo or $\mathcal{L}$flow + $\mathcal{L}$reg.

3.2 Results of Deformation Field Acquisition

Base Model. Table 1 shows that USCorUNet matches the optical flow in photometric alignment, slightly improves bone-mask Dice, and markedly improves deformation quality, reducing the mean FB residual by around 53% and lowering the folding ratio. Ablations further show that removing the correlation branch causes the largest drop in photometric alignment with only a mild Dice decrease, suggesting its primary benefit is improved correspondence in non-bone texture regions. Disabling confidence weighting or removing $\mathcal{L}_{\text{reg}}$ mainly worsens FB consistency and increases foldings, whereas removing $\mathcal{L}_{\text{photo}}$ yields the largest Dice drop, indicating that photometric supervision is important for anatomically faithful deformations.

Table 1. Test-set performance of the base model on Dataset A, averaged over both directions ($I_0 \rightarrow I_1$, $I_1 \rightarrow I_0$) and reported as mean ± standard deviation.

	Method	MAE ↓	NCC ↑	FB ↓	Fold(%) ↓	Dice(%) ↑
Baseline	RAFT	**0.05 ± 0.02**	**0.85 ± 0.10**	1.81 ± 1.22	0.24 ± 0.14	90.31 ± 4.14
Ours	USCorUNet	**0.05 ± 0.02**	**0.85 ± 0.09**	**0.85 ± 0.57**	**0.13 ± 0.10**	**90.62 ± 3.76**
Ablation Study	w/o Corr.	0.08 ± 0.03	0.61 ± 0.18	1.32 ± 3.14	0.56 ± 0.51	89.10 ± 3.33
	w/o Conf.	0.06 ± 0.06	0.74 ± 0.16	1.55 ± 1.20	0.17 ± 0.11	87.03 ± 6.17
	w/o $\mathcal{L}_{\text{reg}}$	0.06 ± 0.02	0.79 ± 0.12	1.21 ± 0.92	0.41 ± 0.22	89.30 ± 4.23
	w/o $\mathcal{L}_{\text{photo}}$	0.07 ± 0.03	0.72 ± 0.17	1.38 ± 1.03	0.19 ± 0.19	85.45 ± 6.28

Table 2 compares USCorUNet with DefCor-Net [13] on the same in-vivo ultrasound dataset (Dataset A) under their force-stratified evaluation protocol. In this protocol, the contact force between the robot and the probe is synchronized with B-mode frames and grouped into 1–6 N force levels. Improvements are more pronounced at higher forces, which correspond to larger and more challenging compressions.

Table 2. Bone-mask Dice under the force-stratified protocol of DefCor-Net [13] on Dataset A. Dice is reported for the $I_1 \rightarrow I_0$ direction.

Method	1 N	2 N	3 N	4 N	5 N	6 N
DefCor-Net	**95.9 ± 3.3**	92.4 ± 4.8	91.1 ± 7.5	87.8 ± 7.1	87.8 ± 12.2	82.6 ± 12.1
USCorUNet	95.4 ± 2.6	**94.1 ± 2.4**	**94.0 ± 3.6**	**93.2 ± 1.8**	**89.8 ± 1.5**	**87.5 ± 1.2**

Fine-Tuned Models. Table 3 shows that regime-specific fine-tuning improves performance, especially FB consistency and physical plausibility. For probe-induced motion, fine-tuning reduces mean FB residuals and folding ratios while preserving alignment. For externally induced motion, it mitigates the domain shift of the base model and restores alignment. Overall, the base checkpoint provides a robust, transferable initialization across interaction patterns. Visual results are shown in Fig. 3.

Table 3. Test-set performance of fine-tuned models on Datasets B–D (probe-induced) and Dataset B (externally induced), averaged over both directions.

Motion	Method	MAE ↓	NCC ↑	FB ↓	Fold(%) ↓
Probe- induced	RAFT	**0.03 ± 0.01**	**0.94 ± 0.03**	1.03 ± 2.27	0.23 ± 0.14
	Base model	0.04 ± 0.01	0.84 ± 0.08	0.84 ± 0.65	0.15 ± 0.11
	Probe-adapted	**0.03 ± 0.01**	0.93 ± 0.03	**0.33 ± 0.28**	**0.09 ± 0.10**
Externally induced	RAFT	**0.03 ± 0.01**	**0.93 ± 0.05**	0.91 ± 1.35	0.14 ± 0.13
	Base model	0.05 ± 0.02	0.71 ± 0.17	1.28 ± 1.95	0.45 ± 0.55
	External-adapted	**0.03 ± 0.01**	0.92 ± 0.05	**0.23 ± 0.24**	**0.07 ± 0.07**

3.3 Results of Ultrasound Guided CBCT Updating

Table 4 compares our method with RAFT-based and classical LC2-FFD [7] baselines. Our approach achieves the best qualityefficiency trade-off, slightly outperforming RAFT while reducing runtime by 5×. In addition, RAFT can exhibit tearing artifacts. Although LC2-FFD shows comparable MAE and SSIM, it introduces geometric distortions and is 512× slower. As absolute metrics are affected by robotic artifacts, this serves as a controlled relative comparison. Visual results are shown in Fig. 4.

Table 4. CBCT updating results on Dataset D using ultrasound-based deformation. Methods share identical conditions; runtime is end-to-end.

Model	MAE ↓	SSIM ↑	Dice (%) ↑	Timing (ms) ↓
USCorUNet	**0.33 ± 0.04**	**0.22 ± 0.02**	**82.22 ± 10.54**	**11.25 ± 0.44**
RAFT	0.34 ± 0.04	0.21 ± 0.03	79.86 ± 12.31	56.24 ± 1.78
LC2-FFD	**0.33 ± 0.05**	**0.22 ± 0.03**	58.91 ± 8.77	5764.26 ± 510.63

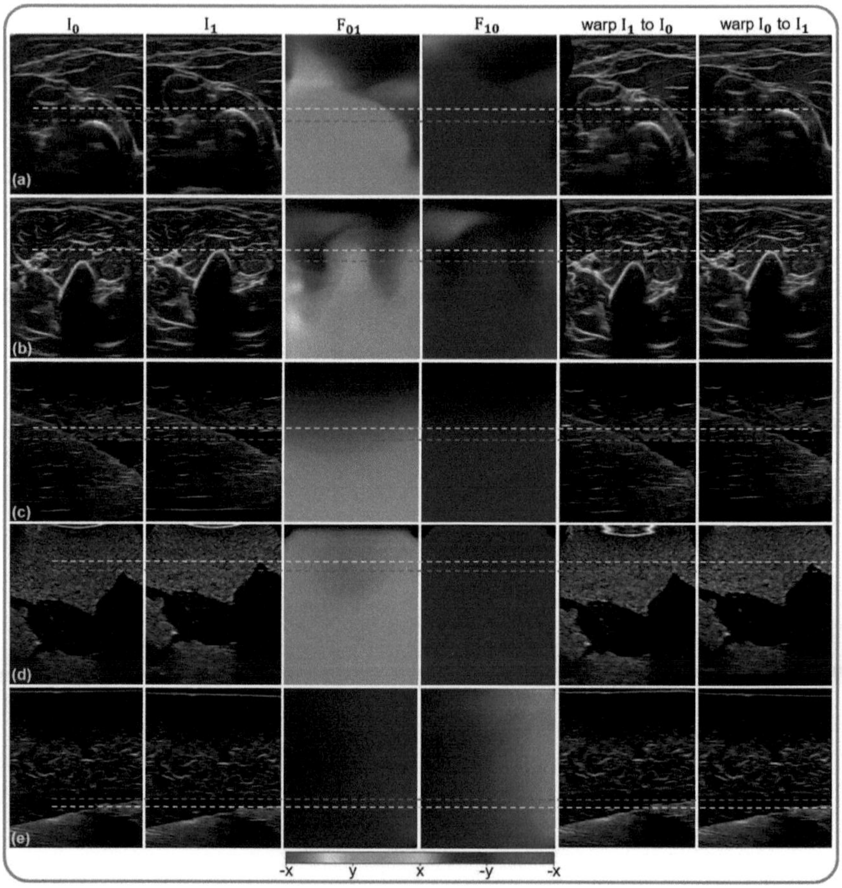

Fig. 3. Bidirectional deformation estimation results. (a,b) In vivo arm examples (Dataset A); (c,d) probe-induced motion (Datasets B and D); (e) externally induced motion (Dataset B). Orange/yellow dashed lines indicate visual alignment guides for I_0, I_1. The color bar indicates flow direction (x/y). (Color figure online)

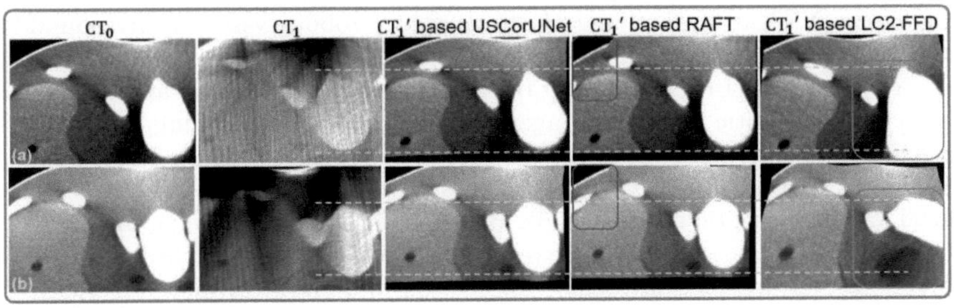

Fig. 4. CT_1' update results on two representative abdominal phantom cases (Dataset D) using USCorUNet, RAFT, and LC2-FFD (CT_0: source; CT_1: target). Red/orange boxes indicate structural artifacts/severe deformation regions. (Color figure online)

4 Discussion and Conclusion

In this paper, we introduced a deformation-aware CBCT updating framework that integrates rigid calibration, registration, and deformation field estimation for real-time end-to-end CBCT slice updating and enhanced intraoperative visualization. The proposed USCorUNet efficiently estimates deformation fields from adjacent ultrasound frames while preserving structural consistency.

Compared to RAFT and LC2-FFD baselines, our method achieves a superior trade-off between registration accuracy and computational efficiency. Future work will extend the current slice-level CBCT updating framework toward multi-plane or volumetric ultrasound guidance, and may further incorporate semantic segmentation [1] into the registration pipeline. While the current approach relies on intensity and structural features, integrating semantic information could further refine deformation details in complex anatomical regions, ultimately paving the way for more reliable intraoperative guidance.

Acknowledgments. This work was supported in part by the Multi-Scale Medical Robotics Center, AIR@InnoHK, Hong Kong; in part by the NVIDIA Academic Grant Program.

Disclosure of Interests. The authors have no competing interests to declare that are relevant to the content of this article.

References

1. Bi, Y., Jiang, Z., Clarenbach, R., Ghotbi, R., Karlas, A., Navab, N.: MI-SegNet: mutual information-based us segmentation for unseen domain generalization. In: Greenspan, H., et al. (eds.) MICCAI 2023. LNCS, vol. 14223, pp. 130–140. Springer, Cham (2023)
2. Bi, Y., Jiang, Z., Duelmer, F., Huang, D., Navab, N.: Machine learning in robotic ultrasound imaging: challenges and perspectives. Ann. Rev. Control Robot. Auton. Syst. **7** (2024)

3. Bi, Y., Su, Y., Navab, N., Jiang, Z.: Gaze-guided robotic vascular ultrasound leveraging human intention estimation. IEEE Robot. Autom. Lett. (2025)
4. Bi, Y., Zhou, Y., Liu, P., Li, F., Jiang, Z., Navab, N.: From scanning guidelines to action: a robotic ultrasound agent with LLM-based reasoning. arXiv preprint arXiv:2603.14393 (2026)
5. Bruhn, A., Weickert, J., Schnörr, C.: Lucas/kanade meets horn/schunck: combining local and global optic flow methods. Int. J. Comput. Vision **61**(3), 211–231 (2005)
6. Curiale, A.H., Vegas-Sánchez-Ferrero, G., Aja-Fernández, S.: Influence of ultrasound speckle tracking strategies for motion and strain estimation. Med. Image Anal. **32**, 184–200 (2016)
7. Fuerst, B., Wein, W., Müller, M., Navab, N.: Automatic ultrasound-MRI registration for neurosurgery using the 2D and 3D LC2 metric. Med. Image Anal. **18**(8), 1312–1319 (2014)
8. Greer, H., Kwitt, R., Vialard, F.X., Niethammer, M.: Icon: learning regular maps through inverse consistency. In: Proceedings of the IEEE/CVF International Conference on Computer Vision, pp. 3396–3405 (2021)
9. Janai, J., Güney, F., Ranjan, A., Black, M., Geiger, A.: Unsupervised learning of multi-frame optical flow with occlusions. In: Ferrari, V., Hebert, M., Sminchisescu, C., Weiss, Y. (eds.) ECCV 2018. LNCS, vol. 11220, pp. 713–731. Springer, Cham (2018). https://doi.org/10.1007/978-3-030-01270-0_42
10. Jiang, Z., Bi, Y., Zhou, M., Hu, Y., Burke, M., Navab, N.: Intelligent robotic sonographer: mutual information-based disentangled reward learning from few demonstrations. Int. J. Robot. Res. **43**(7), 981–1002 (2024)
11. Jiang, Z., Salcudean, S.E., Navab, N.: Robotic ultrasound imaging: state-of-the-art and future perspectives. Med. Image Anal. **89**, 102878 (2023)
12. Jiang, Z., Zhou, Y., Bi, Y., Zhou, M., Wendler, T., Navab, N.: Deformation-aware robotic 3D ultrasound. IEEE Robot. Autom. Lett. **6**(4), 7675–7682 (2021)
13. Jiang, Z., Zhou, Y., Cao, D., Navab, N.: Defcor-net: physics-aware ultrasound deformation correction. Med. Image Anal. **90**, 102923 (2023)
14. Karamalis, A., Wein, W., Klein, T., Navab, N.: Ultrasound confidence maps using random walks. Med. Image Anal. **16**(6), 1101–1112 (2012)
15. Karius, A., Leifeld, L.M., Strnad, V., Fietkau, R., Bert, C.: First implementation of an innovative infra-red camera system integrated into a mobile CBCT scanner for applicator tracking in brachytherapy–initial performance characterization. J. Appl. Clin. Med. Phys., e14364 (2024)
16. Kirillov, A., et al.: Segment anything. In: Proceedings of the IEEE/CVF International Conference on Computer Vision, pp. 4015–4026 (2023)
17. Li, F., Bi, Y., Huang, D., Jiang, Z., Navab, N.: Robotic CBCT meets robotic ultrasound. Int. J. Comput. Assist. Radiol. Surg., 1–9 (2025)
18. Li, F., Bi, Y., Song, T., Jiang, Z., Navab, N.: Ultrasound-guided real-time spinal motion visualization for spinal instability assessment. arXiv preprint arXiv:2602.12917 (2026)
19. Monfardini, L., et al.: Real-time us/cone-beam CT fusion imaging for percutaneous ablation of small renal Tumours: a technical note. Eur. Radiol. **31**(10), 7523–7528 (2021)
20. Shen, Z., Han, X., Xu, Z., Niethammer, M.: Networks for joint affine and non-parametric image registration. In: Proceedings of the IEEE/CVF Conference on Computer Vision and Pattern Recognition, pp. 4224–4233 (2019)
21. Song, T., et al.: Intelligent virtual sonographer (IVS): enhancing physician-robot-patient communication. In: Gee, J.C., et al. (eds.) MICCAI 2025. LNCS, vol.

15969, pp. 287–297. Springer, Cham (2025). https://doi.org/10.1007/978-3-032-05127-1_28
22. Song, T., et al.: Comparative study of ultrasound shape completion and CBCT-based AR workflows for spinal needle interventions. Int. J. Comput. Assist. Radiol. Surg., 1–9 (2026)
23. Tanaka, M.: Low radiation protocol for intraoperative robotic c-arm can enhance adolescent idiopathic scoliosis deformity correction accuracy and safety. Global Spine J. **14**(5), 1504–1514 (2024)
24. Teed, Z., Deng, J.: RAFT: recurrent all-pairs field transforms for optical flow. In: Vedaldi, A., Bischof, H., Brox, T., Frahm, J.-M. (eds.) ECCV 2020. LNCS, vol. 12347, pp. 402–419. Springer, Cham (2020). https://doi.org/10.1007/978-3-030-58536-5_24
25. Varadhan, R., Karangelis, G., Krishnan, K., Hui, S.: A framework for deformable image registration validation in radiotherapy clinical applications. J. Appl. Clin. Med. Phys. **14**(1), 192–213 (2013)
26. Wein, W., Ladikos, A., Fuerst, B., Shah, A., Sharma, K., Navab, N.: Global registration of ultrasound to MRI using the LC^2 metric for enabling neurosurgical guidance. In: Mori, K., Sakuma, I., Sato, Y., Barillot, C., Navab, N. (eds.) MICCAI 2013. LNCS, vol. 8149, pp. 34–41. Springer, Heidelberg (2013). https://doi.org/10.1007/978-3-642-40811-3_5

SAW: Toward a Surgical Action World Model via Controllable and Scalable Video Generation

Sampath Rapuri[1], Lalithkumar Seenivasan[1], Dominik Schneider[1], Roger Soberanis-Mukul[1], Yufan He[2], Hao Ding[1], Jiru Xu[1], Chenhao Yu[1], Chenyan Jing[1], Pengfei Guo[2], Daguang Xu[2], and Mathias Unberath[1(✉)]

[1] Johns Hopkins University, Baltimore, MD, USA
Mathias@jhu.edu
[2] NVIDIA, Santa Clara, CA, USA

Abstract. A surgical world model capable of generating realistic surgical action videos with precise control over tool-tissue interactions can address fundamental challenges in surgical AI and simulation – from data scarcity and rare event synthesis to bridging the sim-to-real gap for surgical automation. However, current video generation methods, the core of such surgical world models, require expensive annotations or complex structured intermediates as conditioning signals at inference, limiting their scalability. Other approaches exhibit limited temporal consistency across complex laparoscopic scenes and do not possess sufficient realism. We propose Surgical Action World (SAW) – a step toward surgical action world modeling through video diffusion conditioned on four lightweight signals: language prompts encoding tool-action context, a reference surgical scene, tissue affordance mask, and 2D tool-tip trajectories. We design a conditional video diffusion approach that reformulates video-to-video diffusion into trajectory-conditioned surgical action synthesis. The backbone diffusion model is fine-tuned on a custom-curated dataset of 12,044 laparoscopic clips with lightweight spatiotemporal conditioning signals, leveraging a depth consistency loss to enforce geometric plausibility without requiring depth at inference. SAW achieves state-of-the-art temporal consistency (CD-FVD: 199.19 vs. 546.82) and strong visual quality on held-out test data. Furthermore, we demonstrate its downstream utility for (a) surgical AI, where augmenting rare actions with SAW-generated videos improves action recognition (clipping F1-score: 20.93% to 43.14%; cutting: 0.00% to 8.33%) on real test data, and (b) surgical simulation, where rendering tool-tissue interaction videos from simulator-derived trajectory points toward a visually faithful simulation engine.

S. Rapuri and L. Seenivasan—Equal contribution.

Supplementary Information The online version contains supplementary material available at https://doi.org/10.1007/978-3-032-38236-8_43.

G. Yang et al. (Eds.): MICCAI 2026, LNCS 16893, pp. 447–457, 2027.
https://doi.org/10.1007/978-3-032-38236-8_43

Keywords: Surgical World Model · Surgical Video Generation · Deep Learning · Action Recognition · Surgical Simulator

1 Introduction

A surgical world model that enables controllable, scalable video synthesis of surgical actions with realistic tool-tissue interaction has the potential to transform both surgical AI and the next generation of high-fidelity surgical simulators. For surgical AI, it offers a path to overcome the fundamental data scarcity that is a bottleneck for developing perception models, and enables targeted synthesis of rare but clinically critical events without costly setups or tissue use [20,24,26,33]. For simulation, such a generative world model can bridge the persistent sim-to-real gap by enabling visually realistic closed-loop environments where instrument motion drives controllable tool-tissue interactions. This supports both accelerated curation of paired kinematics-video data necessary for automating surgical actions and the development of digital twins for surgical safety evaluation through the forward simulation of tool actions [10,19,22,30]. Realizing such world models hinges on advances in controllable and realistic video generation. While recent surgical video generation methods [2,6,21] have demonstrated potential in producing visually plausible outputs, they remain limited in inference-time controllability and scalability: HieraSurg relies on expensive dense annotations such as per-frame segmentation masks [2]; SG2VID depends on structured intermediates (spatio-temporal scene graphs) that are difficult to obtain or manipulate at inference [21]; SurgVisionWM does not allow for interpretable, user-defined action conditioning signals [13]; and SurgSora, which employs flexible trajectory-conditioning, is constrained by limited inference windows ($W = 21$) and struggle to maintain temporal consistency [6]. Reinforcement Learning-based surgical world models that learn dynamics in low-dimensional state spaces have also been explored [8], but differ fundamentally from generative world models that treat video as state and condition on user-defined actions.

To this end, we propose Surgical Action World (SAW), a step toward a surgical action world model aligned with the modern generative formulation [3,4]. SAW enables controllable and scalable video diffusion conditioned on four lightweight signals: (i) structured language prompts encoding instrument and action context, (ii) a reference first frame anchoring scene appearance, (iii) tissue affordance masks specifying interaction regions, and (iv) 2D tool-tip trajectory across the surgical scene. **Our key contributions are**: (1) a curated dataset of 12,044 laparoscopic video clips with spatiotemporal annotations including video-level tool-action labels and tissue affordance along with frame-level tool-tip trajectories; (2) a video diffusion approach that reformulates video-to-video generation for scalable, highly controllable surgical action synthesis without relying on expensive inference-time conditioning signals, and incorporates a novel depth consistency loss enforcing geometric plausibility without requiring depth at inference; and (3) demonstration of two downstream applications – augmentation of rare surgical actions to improve action recognition on real test data, and rendering realistic tool-tissue interactions from simulator-derived tool trajectories to drive visually faithful surgical simulation.

2 Surgical Action World (SAW) Model

To advance surgical world modeling, we propose Surgical Action World (SAW), which reformulates video-to-video diffusion for controllable surgical action synthesis. By conditioning on instrument trajectories and tissue affordance alongside standard text and image inputs, SAW models tool-tissue interaction dynamics for scalable and realistic video generation (Fig. 1). The diffusion process is defined as $z_{i-1} = \mathcal{D}(z_i, t_i, \mathbf{z^a}, \mathbf{z^f}, \mathbf{z^p}, \mathbf{z}^\gamma)$, where z_i is the latent embedding from the previous denoising stage, t_i the denoising iteration with $i = 1, \ldots, N = 50$, and $z_0 = x_0$ the clean video. Generation is conditioned on four lightweight signals: a language prompt $\mathbf{z^a}$ encoding tool-action context, a reference frame $\mathbf{z^f}$ anchoring scene appearance, an instrument trajectory $\mathbf{z^p}$ controlling tool-tip motion, and a tissue affordance map $\mathbf{z}^\gamma$ specifying interaction regions, each of which can be provided independently or in combination at inference.

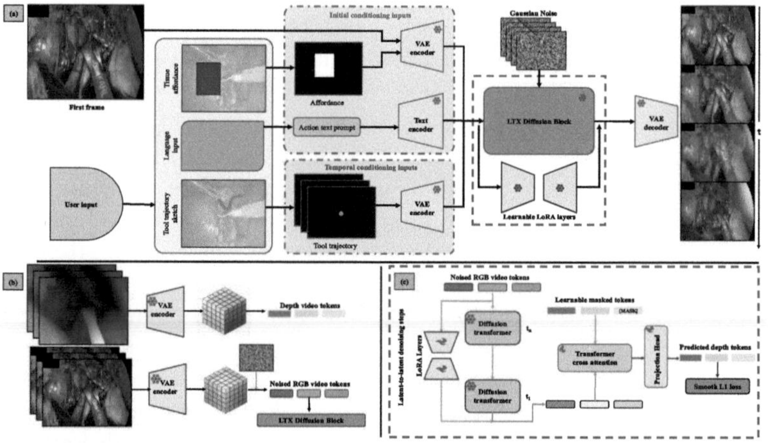

Fig. 1. a) At inference, SAW leverages a user-inputted 2D tool trajectory, language prompt, tissue affordance, and a background surgical scene, enabling realistic and controllable video diffusion.**b)** During training, normalized depth and RGB videos are encoded using a frozen VAE, while the RGB video embedding is then flattened and noised into a sequence of noisy tokens. The LoRA layers within the diffusion transformer are updated.**c)** During training, we compute a depth consistency loss ($\mathcal{L}_{\text{DC}}$) as a Smooth L1 loss between predicted masked depth video tokens and pseudo-ground-truth depth tokens derived solely from the denoised RGB video tokens.

2.1 Video Diffusion Model

We adopt LTX-Video [11] as the backbone for SAW, a transformer-based latent diffusion model that natively supports multi-modal conditioning (text, video, image). LTX performs diffusion in latent space using a variational autoencoder (VAE) for spatiotemporal downsampling, with denoising via a diffusion transformer trained using flow-matching [15]. We fine-tune LTX using In-Context Low Rank Adaptation (IC-LoRA) [12], a parameter-efficient fine-tuning strategy to fine-tune the model via learnable low-rank weight adaptations, for surgical action synthesis with four conditioning embeddings: a reference frame $\mathbf{z^f}$, language prompt $\mathbf{z^a}$, tissue affordance map $\mathbf{z}^\gamma$, and temporal tool-tip trajectory $\mathbf{z^p}$, enabling the model to generate temporally coherent surgical action videos with realistic tool-tissue interactions (Fig. 1a).

2.2 Lightweight Conditioning Signals

Language Prompting ($\mathbf{z^a}$): To incorporate tool-action context, we condition on language prompts via LTX's text mechanism, following the template: "A robotic da Vinci {tool} performs {action} during a cholecystectomy. The laparoscopic camera view shows the {tool} within the abdominal cavity. The {tool} moves precisely as it executes the {action} motion." Affordance Conditioning ($\mathbf{z}^\gamma$): To guide where tool-tissue interaction occurs, we condition the model on a 2D binary affordance map I_a defined with respect to the reference frame I_f. The affordance embedding $\mathbf{z}^\gamma$ is extracted via a VAE encoder. Tool Trajectory ($\mathbf{z^p}$): To precisely control instrument tip motion and tool-tissue interaction, we encode the tool trajectory as a temporal sequence of 2D maps $I_p^i \in \mathbb{R}^{h \times w \times 3}$, $i \in [0, k]$, where k is the sequence length. A trajectory point at time i is represented as a fixed-radius circle centered at the tool-tip (x, y) in I_p^i, with instrument class encoded through the R and G channels. Encoding the tool tip and its class directly in the RGB channels lets us reformulate our task as video-to-video diffusion without requiring major architectural changes. The embedding $\mathbf{z^p}$ is obtained by passing the sequence through a VAE encoder.

2.3 Depth Consistency Loss

In the presented formulation, all spatial conditioning signals are expressed as 2D inputs, with control in the Z-dimension learned implicitly by LTX during training. However, due to the presence of vital anatomy in the surgical scene, omitting depth guidance may result in inaccurate movements that violate critical safety constraints. This motivates the introduction of depth control during training, leading us to develop a novel loss for depth consistency ($\mathcal{L}_{\mathrm{DC}}$). We first generate corresponding depth-mask videos for all RGB videos in our training dataset using Depth Anything V2 [29]. After encoding these depth videos into the latent space (Fig. 1b), we introduced a cross-attention layer and a projection head that learns to reconstruct masked depth latents. This reconstruction uses the denoised RGB latent tokens created after a forward pass of the diffusion transformer. The depth consistency loss (Fig. 1c), $\mathcal{L}_{DC}$, is then computed using a Smooth ℓ_1 loss, which follows an ℓ_2 loss for small errors and an ℓ_1 loss for large ones, providing robustness to outlier depth token predictions. Through this loss, we enforce geometric consistency in the Z-dimension without requiring explicit depth inputs at inference time. Unlike GeoVideo [1], which regularizes geometry using reprojected 3D depths, SAW uses a local Smooth-L1 loss on depth reconstructed from RGB video tokens, requiring no depth at inference.

3 Experiment and Results

3.1 Experimental Setup

Dataset: We custom-curate a dataset of 12,044 video clips from 101 surgical videos sourced from 21 Youtube videos (2,760 video clips) and 80 videos (12,878 video clips) taken from four publicly available datasets: 10 videos from HeiChole (1,794 video clips) [26], 30 videos from Cholec80 (6,042 video clips) [24], 32 videos from SurgVU (4,278 video clips) [33], and 8 videos from CRCD (764 video clips) [17]. Each video clip was segmented to capture a *single surgical action* and was manually annotated for *video-level action* (clipping, grasping, cutting, or dissecting) and *active tool usage* (grasper, hook, clipper, or scissors) as well as *tissue affordance*, which indicates the tissue region undergoing tool-tissue interaction. Frame-wise annotations are provided for *tool-tip positions* p = (x, y) in pixel coordinates. All video clips are preprocessed to remove black borders, letterboxing, and text overlay. We standardized all video clips to 81 frames at 25 fps, truncating longer videos and padding shorter ones by repeating the final frame. All videos were then processed at a resolution of 1024x576. The dataset is partitioned based on the 101 source videos, with the train set containing 11,502 video clips (clipping = 443, grasping = 1,964, cutting = 273, dissecting = 8,822), and the test set comprising 542 video clips (clipping = 29, grasping = 126, cutting = 20, dissecting = 367).
Training and Inference. All our experiments are conducted using a single NVIDIA A100. We fine-tuned LTX using IC-LoRA for 7,500 steps, with $\alpha = 128$, lr $= 2 \times 10^{-4}$, AdamW optimizer, and bfloat16 mixed precision training. To improve alignment with groundtruth videos and enhance generation diversity, we employ classifier-free guidance with first-frame conditioning in 20% of cases. During inference, we use 50 denoising steps with a guidance scale = 3.5. All generated videos are 81 frames.
Evaluation Metrics. We evaluate the visual quality of generated video using FVD [25], CD-FVD [9], SSIM [28], PSNR, and LPIPS [32] metrics. FVD assesses visual realism at the video level. Since frame-level perceptual metrics cannot directly assess the accuracy of tool-tissue interactions, we rely on CD-FVD, which is sensitive to temporal inconsistencies [9], to implicitly capture irregular tool-tissue motion. We further report SSIM, PSNR, and LPIPS to quantify frame-wise structural and perceptual image quality.

Table 1. Quantitative evaluation of our model performance in video generation against state-of-the-art models on a held-out test set. WAN [27] and LTX_b [11] are used off-the-shelf whereas SurgSora [6] is fine-tuned on our training dataset.

Model	FVD ↓	CD-FVD ↓	SSIM ↑	PSNR ↑	LPIPS ↓
WAN [27]	439.60	429.67	0.5750	15.82	0.4480
LTX_b [11]	319.37	504.31	0.5630	15.07	0.4920
SurgSora [6]	541.61	546.82	0.4163	17.10	**0.3825**
Ours (SAW)	**224.28**	**199.19**	**0.5948**	**17.36**	0.4100

3.2 Results and Ablation Studies

Baseline Comparison: Table 1 highlights the performance of our model compared to existing generative models. SAW achieves the lowest FVD at 224.28. Moreover, it excels at generating temporally consistent videos, demonstrated through a CD-FVD of 199.19, outperforming the 546.82 of the also trajectory-conditioned surgical generative model SurgSora. For non-trajectory-conditioned models, the closest CD-FVD belongs to WAN with 429.67, suggesting the benefit of incorporating a large pretraining dataset for video generation. On frame-level content and structural metrics, SAW also outperforms all baselines with an SSIM of 0.5948 and PSNR of 17.36. SAW also demonstrated competitive frame-wise perceptual similarity with a LPIPS of 0.41. Figure 2 illustrates the quality of the generated videos across two separate actions. Even in the presence of endoscopic artifacts, our model can produce a coherent video that reflects the underlying action, demonstrating its controllability, robustness, and realism.

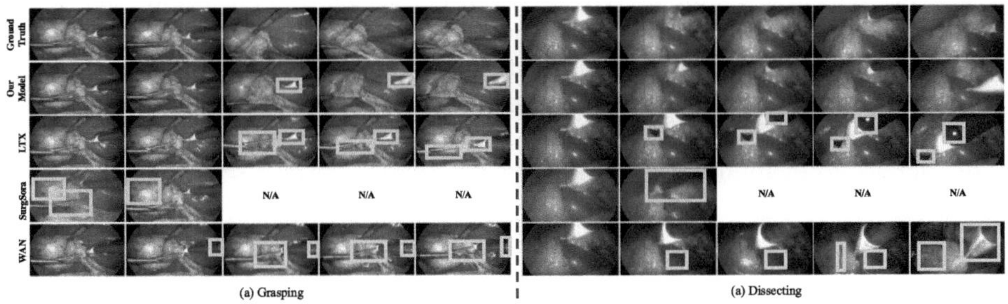

Fig. 2. Qualitative examples of generated surgical videos for **(a)** grasping and **(b)** dissecting actions. Red overlays indicate where a generated video lacks realism or becomes visually distorted in comparison to the ground truth video at the corresponding frame.

Ablation Studies: We assess the impact of our design choices and conditioning strategies in Table 2. Removing trajectory conditioning significantly impacts performance, as indicated by a consistent decrease in all the evaluation metrics. Removing first-frame conditioning reduces visual quality, as indicated by drop

Table 2. Ablation study across conditioning modalities and loss components. Each row removes a single conditioning signal or loss term from the full model. Best results per metric are in **bold**.

Ablated Component	FVD ↓	CD-FVD ↓	LPIPS ↓	SSIM ↑	PSNR ↑
SAW	224.28	**199.19**	0.4100	0.5948	17.36
Ablation on Conditioning signals					
w/o Affordance	223.78	200.10	0.4101	0.5945	17.33
w/o First Frame	1096.21	338.75	0.6217	0.4848	12.50
w/o Language	219.23	204.89	0.4052	**0.5977**	**17.47**
w/o Trajectory	278.26	344.79	0.4325	0.5818	16.45
Model trained without depth consistency loss					
w/o $\mathcal{L}_{\text{DC}}$	**188.34**	207.59	**0.4017**	0.5922	17.37

Table 3. Per-class action recognition F1 score before and after video augmentation. Best results per action label are in **bold**.

Actions	Spatiotemporal CNN [23]		ViT [7]	
	w/o Aug	with Aug	w/o Aug	with Aug
Clipping	20.93	**43.14**	**84.62**	83.64
Cutting	0.00	**8.33**	30.77	**47.06**
Grasping	**58.52**	55.87	**74.19**	73.80
Dissection	83.87	**84.25**	86.27	**88.26**

performance in FVD, LPIPS, and SSIM. Furthermore, temporal consistency is affected as reflected by an increased CD-FVD to 338.75. Disabling the depth consistency loss, $\mathcal{L}_{\text{DC}}$, primarily increases CD-FVD, suggesting a reduction in temporal consistency of tool and tissue movements. A paired bootstrap test on the test set confirms this improvement is significant (CD-FVD: 199.19 vs. 207.59, $p < 0.05$). Overall, SAW with all design choices is the most balanced model across all evaluation metrics.

4 Downstream Applications

We also demonstrate two downstream applications of our SAW model: (a) synthesizing rare surgical action videos to address class imbalance and enhance model performance on a real test set, and (b) exploring its potential to serve as a simulation engine for generating realistic tool–tissue interactions from surgical scenes and simulator-derived instrument trajectories.

4.1 Synthetic Video Generation for Action Recognition

With action recognition being a major research topic in surgical AI [14,20], we design and conduct an experiment to demonstrate our framework's potential in augmenting rare action videos to improve model performance. Our train set exhibits a long-tail distribution, with cutting (273 clips) and clipping (443 clips) actions significantly underrepresented compared to dissecting (8, 822 clips) and grasping (1, 964 clips). Generating Synthetic Videos of Rare Events: Leveraging our controllable video generation framework, we generated synthetic videos of rare actions (cutting and clipping) to augment the training set. As Fig. 3b describes, we overlay segmented surgical tools using SAM3 [5] onto diverse background surgical scenes, and leverage the tissue affordance and tool trajectory extracted from the source background video –substituted with the target tool class – to condition generation of the augmented video. Superimposed surgical tools, which are acquired from existing training video clips, are blended into the background scene using Poisson image blending [18] to increase realism of the starting scene used to guide the diffusion process. While background scenes were diverse, we ensured relevance to each action – for example, clipping actions were paired with scenes containing blood vessels, increasing the diversity of tool – anatomy pairings. In total, we generated 287 synthetic videos: 110 clipping and 177 cutting. Experimental Setup: We train two AI models – a spatiotemporal CNN [23] and a vision transformer (ViT) model [7] – for video action recognition. Consistent with state-of-the-art approaches in surgical action prediction [20], both models take as input 16-frame segments from each video to predict the action. To evaluate our framework's utility in enhancing model performance through data augmentation, we train each model under two settings: (i) using video clips only from the original training set, and (ii) augmenting the training set with synthetically generated video clips of rare actions. Results and Discussion: Table 3 summarizes the performance of both models trained with and without synthetic rare action videos and evaluated on a held-out real test set. For both models, we observe that augmentation with synthetic videos can improve recognition of underrepresented actions (clipping and cutting) on real test videos, validating our framework's utility in generating realistic and effective training data. Since augmentation targets only the underrepresented classes, improvements are visible in these actions, while grasping and dissection remain largely unchanged.

4.2 Realistic Tool Tissue Interaction Engine for Surgical Simulation

While physics-based surgical simulators have made significant progress, they struggle to accurately model complex tissue-tool interactions and tissue deformation in real time [31]. Towards addressing this challenge, we explore our controllable surgical action video generation framework as a potential engine to model realistic tool-tissue interaction and tissue deformation in near real-time. Qualitative Experimental Setup: As shown in Fig. 3, we build a surgical simulator using Isaac lab [16], encompassing surgical tools in an empty background. Given a set of simulator-derived data (instrument segmentation, their corresponding tool tip trajectories, and tissue affordance), we demonstrate our framework's flexibility and controllability in generating surgical action videos – modeling tool-tissue interaction with realistic tissue deformations – with any

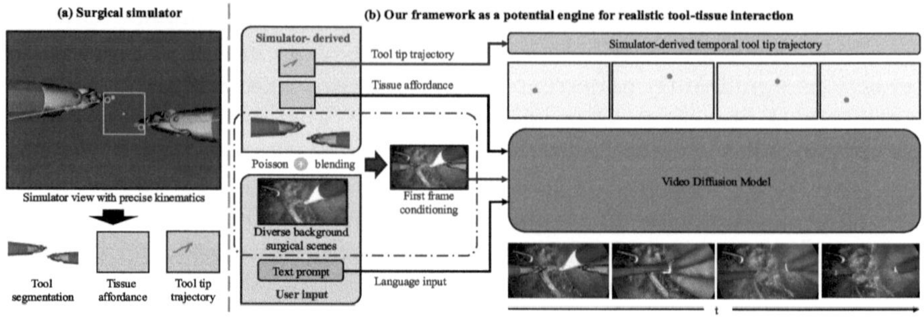

Fig. 3. a) Simulator-derived tool segmentations, tissue affordance, tool tip trajectory. **b)** Simulator-derived tools are overlayed on a background surgical scene and used as conditional inputs to our video diffusion model, allowing us to model both tool kinematics and background tissue deformation.

given background surgical scene. However, this represents an initial proof-of-concept. Future work will address enforcing instrument joint kinematics, supporting more instruments and scenes, expert ratings of generated videos, and real-time inference.

5 Conclusion

We present Surgical Action World (SAW) – a step toward surgical action world modeling through controllable and scalable video diffusion. By conditioning on four lightweight signals (language prompts, reference frame, tissue affordance mask, and tool-tip trajectories), SAW achieves state-of-the-art temporal consistency and visual quality while enabling scalable inference without expensive annotations. A depth consistency loss further encourages geometric coherence in tool motion, promoting plausible tool-tissue interactions that extend beyond purely 2D trajectory conditioning. We demonstrate the downstream utility of SAW for surgical AI through rare action augmentation that improves action recognition on real data, and for simulation through rendering tool-tissue interactions from simulator-derived trajectories. Future work will focus on improving the integration of affordance and language cues for richer scene understanding, extending to longer video generation, incorporating additional instruments and anatomical scenes, and achieving real-time inference for closed-loop simulation.

Acknowledgments. This work was in part supported by the Johns Hopkins University SURPASS Grant, Malone Center Seed Grant, and Johns Hopkins University internal funds.

Disclosure of Interests. The authors have no competing interests.

References

1. Bai, Y., Fang, S., Yu, C., Wang, F., Huang, Q.: GeoVideo: introducing geometric regularization into video generation model. Adv. Neural. Inf. Process. Syst. **38**, 57602–57622 (2026)
2. Biagini, D., Navab, N., Farshad, A.: HieraSurg: hierarchy-aware diffusion model for surgical video generation. In: International Conference on Medical Image Computing and Computer-Assisted Intervention, pp. 310–319. Springer (2025)
3. Brooks, T., et al.: Video generation models as world simulators. OpenAI Blog **1**(8), 1 (2024)
4. Bruce, J., et al.: Genie: generative interactive environments. In: Forty-first International Conference on Machine Learning (2024)
5. Carion, N., et al.: SAM 3: segment anything with concepts. arXiv preprint arXiv:2511.16719 (2025)
6. Chen, T., Yang, S., Wang, J., Bai, L., Ren, H., Zhou, L.: SurgSora: object-aware diffusion model for controllable surgical video generation. In: International Conference on Medical Image Computing and Computer-Assisted Intervention, pp. 521–531. Springer (2025)
7. Dosovitskiy, A., et al.: An image is worth 16×16 words: transformers for image recognition at scale (2020). arXiv:2010.11929 arXiv preprint
8. Fazzari, E., Stefanini, C.: Deep reinforcement learning for surgical robotics with state and image information: a survey (2026)
9. Ge, S., Mahapatra, A., Parmar, G., Zhu, J.Y., Huang, J.B.: On the content bias in fréchet video distance. In: Proceedings of the IEEE/CVF Conference on Computer Vision and Pattern Recognition, pp. 7277–7288 (2024)
10. Ha, D., Schmidhuber, J.: World models. arXiv preprint arXiv:1803.10122 **2**(3), 440 (2018)
11. HaCohen, Y., et al.: LTX-Video: realtime video latent diffusion. arXiv preprint arXiv:2501.00103 (2024)
12. Huang, L., et al.: In-context LoRA for diffusion transformers (2024). arXiv:2410.23775 arXiv preprint
13. Koju, S., et al.: Surgical vision world model. In: MICCAI Workshop on Data Engineering in Medical Imaging, pp. 1–10. Springer (2025)
14. Liao, W., et al.: Artificial intelligence-assisted phase recognition and skill assessment in laparoscopic surgery: a systematic review. Front. Surg. **12**, 1551838 (2025)
15. Lipman, Y., Chen, R.T., Ben-Hamu, H., Nickel, M., Le, M.: Flow matching for generative modeling (2022). arXiv:2210.02747 arXiv preprint
16. Mittal, M., et al.: Isaac Lab: a GPU-accelerated simulation framework for multimodal robot learning (2025). arXiv:2511.04831 arXiv preprint
17. Oh, K.H., et al.: Expanded comprehensive robotic cholecystectomy dataset (CRCD) (2024). arXiv:2412.12238 arXiv preprint
18. Pérez, P., Gangnet, M., Blake, A.: Poisson image editing. In: Seminal Graphics Papers: pushing the boundaries, vol. 2, pp. 577–582 (2023)
19. Scheikl, P.M., et al.: Sim-to-real transfer for visual reinforcement learning of deformable object manipulation for robot-assisted surgery. IEEE Robot. Autom. Lett. **8**(2), 560–567 (2022)
20. Sharma, S., Nwoye, C.I., Mutter, D., Padoy, N.: Rendezvous in time: an attention-based temporal fusion approach for surgical triplet recognition. Int. J. Comput. Assist. Radiol. Surg. **18**(6), 1053–1059 (2023)

21. Sivakumar, S.K., Frisch, Y., Ghazaei, G., Mukhopadhyay, A.: SG2Vid: scene graphs enable fine-grained control for video synthesis. In: International Conference on Medical Image Computing and Computer-Assisted Intervention, pp. 511–521. Springer (2025)
22. Tagliabue, E., Pore, A., Dall'Alba, D., Magnabosco, E., Piccinelli, M., Fiorini, P.: Soft tissue simulation environment to learn manipulation tasks in autonomous robotic surgery. In: 2020 IEEE/RSJ International Conference on Intelligent Robots and Systems (IROS), pp. 3261–3266. IEEE (2020)
23. Tran, D., Wang, H., Torresani, L., Ray, J., LeCun, Y., Paluri, M.: A closer look at spatiotemporal convolutions for action recognition. In: Proceedings of the IEEE Conference on Computer Vision and Pattern Recognition, pp. 6450–6459 (2018)
24. Twinanda, A.P., Shehata, S., Mutter, D., Marescaux, J., De Mathelin, M., Padoy, N.: EndoNet: a deep architecture for recognition tasks on laparoscopic videos. IEEE Trans. Med. Imag. **36**(1), 86–97 (2016)
25. Unterthiner, T., Van Steenkiste, S., Kurach, K., Marinier, R., Michalski, M., Gelly, S.: Towards accurate generative models of video: a new metric & challenges. arXiv preprint arXiv:1812.01717 (2018)
26. Wagner, M., Müller-Stich, B.P., Kisilenko, A., Tran, D., Heger, P., Mündermann, L., Lubotsky, D.M., Müller, B., Davitashvili, T., Capek, M., et al.: Comparative validation of machine learning algorithms for surgical workflow and skill analysis with the heichole benchmark. Med. Image Anal. **86**, 102770 (2023)
27. Wang, A., et al.: WAN: open and advanced large-scale video generative models. arXiv preprint arXiv:2503.20314 **3**(4), 6 (2025)
28. Wang, Z., Bovik, A.C., Sheikh, H.R., Simoncelli, E.P.: Image quality assessment: from error visibility to structural similarity. IEEE Trans. Image Process. **13**(4), 600–612 (2004)
29. Yang, L., et al.: Depth anything V2. Adv. Neural. Inf. Process. Syst. **37**, 21875–21911 (2024)
30. Yang, M., Du, Y., Ghasemipour, K., Tompson, J., Schuurmans, D., Abbeel, P.: Learning interactive real-world simulators. arXiv preprint arXiv:2310.06114 **1**(2), 6 (2023)
31. Zhang, J., Zhong, Y., Gu, C.: Deformable models for surgical simulation: a survey. IEEE Rev. Biomed. Eng. **11**, 143–164 (2017)
32. Zhang, R., Isola, P., Efros, A.A., Shechtman, E., Wang, O.: The unreasonable effectiveness of deep features as a perceptual metric. In: Proceedings of the IEEE Conference on Computer Vision and Pattern Recognition, pp. 586–595 (2018)
33. Zia, A., et al.: Surgical visual understanding (SurgVU) dataset (2025). arXiv:2501.09209 arXiv preprint

SeedPro: Place Brachytherapy Seeds Like Expert Clinicians via Hierarchical Reinforcement Agents

Haitao Li[1], Jiaxuan Liu[1], Wei Huang[2], Zhongmin Wang[2], and Xiaojun Chen[1](✉)

[1] Shanghai Jiao Tong University, Shanghai 200240, China
xiaojunchen@sjtu.edu.cn

[2] Ruijin Hospital Shanghai Jiao Tong University School of Medicine, Shanghai, China

Abstract. Brachytherapy is an evidence-based, well-established treatment for intracorporeal tumors. A high-quality preoperative planning scheme is critical to ensuring optimal intraoperative efficacy. However, existing preoperative planning approaches often suffer from poor reproducibility, suboptimal dose distributions, and labor-intensive workflows. To address these limitations, we propose *SeedPro*, an automatic and fine-grained preoperative planning framework for brachytherapy that efficiently produces expert-level treatment plans with reduced computational costs, driven by hierarchical reinforcement learning agents. Experiments show that *SeedPro* achieves 1220% reduction in OAR exposure and reduces puncture numbers by 25% compared to SOTA on both internal and external datasets. This work establishes a practical paradigm for intelligent and precision-oriented brachytherapy. The source code is available at https://github.com/Haitao-Lee/SeedPro.

Keywords: Brachytherapy · Reinforcement learning · Surgical planning

1 Introduction

Brachytherapy is an evidence-based, well-established treatment for intracorporeal tumors [1]. By directly placing radioactive seeds intratumourally, it delivers a potent radiation dose that effectively kills cells nearby [4], as shown in Fig. 1. Compared with external beam radiotherapy, brachytherapy provides highly precise radiation with a prolonged therapeutic effect and minimal impact on healthy tissues, making it increasingly important for tumor suppression [6].

Accurate preoperative planning plays a pivotal role in brachytherapy, as it determines the dosimetric quality and therapeutic efficacy [7]. The core task is to devise a precise seed placement strategy that defines the number of radioactive seeds, their injection trajectories, and the spatial position and orientation of each seed. The conventional planning process typically begins with segmentation of

G. Yang et al. (Eds.): MICCAI 2026, LNCS 16893, pp. 458–468, 2027.
https://doi.org/10.1007/978-3-032-38236-8_44

the clinical target volume (CTV) and organs at risk (OARs) from preoperative images. Subsequently, clinicians manually review image slices to iteratively add or refine seed placements based on their clinical expertise and feedback from dose-calculation results generated by the treatment planning system (TPS) [9]. Throughout this process, dosimetric performance metrics, such as dose-volume histograms (DVH) [28], are continuously evaluated to iteratively refine the seed placement strategy until the prescribed treatment objectives are achieved. Intraoperatively, for each trajectory, a puncture needle is injected into the lesion to the predefined depth guided by surgical navigation or patient-specific templates [24], and as it is gradually withdrawn, radioactive seeds are deposited at specific intervals–an approach reminiscent of "laying eggs" along the trajectory [25].

However, the aforementioned planning approach exhibits significant limitations, including poor reproducibility, limited planning granularity, suboptimal dose distribution, and labor-intensive, time-consuming procedures [8]. Rapid advances in AI have enabled fast and precise 3D dose calculation in brachytherapy based on imaging data and the spatial distribution of seeds [11]. Compared with conventional Monte Carlo simulations [15] in the mainstream TPSs, the computation time for a single seed has been reduced to the millisecond scale, enabling the computationally intensive inverse seed placement planning to be performed efficiently, thereby potentially addressing the aforementioned limitations.

Several pioneering studies have explored related strategies. The current SOTA solution is *BrachyPlan* [14], which still relies on rule-based searching, and may perform suboptimally when dealing with irregularly shaped tumors. [16] introduced BRIGHT, an AI-driven framework capable of generating multiple near-optimal plans, while clinical evaluation [17] showed limited performance and a time-intensive workflow. [18] presented a knowledge-based approach for cervical brachytherapy, enhancing plan consistency and treatment outcomes. [26] applied reinforcement learning to brachytherapy, producing plans of comparable or higher quality with fewer needles. Other relevant efforts include [19,22,23]. The above studies indicate that deep reinforcement learning has emerged as a valuable tool for brachytherapy planning. Nevertheless, these methods share a common limitation: they predominantly focus on optimizing dose distribution, often yielding plans with excellent dosimetric performance but mechanically rigid seed arrangements that lack clinical practicality. One manifestation of this issue is that, in pursuit of dosimetric metrics, the resulting plans may involve an excessive number of punctures, sometimes requiring a separate puncture for a single seed [17]. In contrast, expert manual planning also places particular emphasis on surgical complexity and intraoperative implantation efficiency [33]. Therefore, it is significant to develop a planning system that places brachytherapy seeds like expert clinicians while ensuring reproducibility, efficacy, and efficiency.

2 Methods

Against the above background, we propose *SeedPro*, a fine-grained brachytherapy planning framework that enables efficient and expert-like seed placement

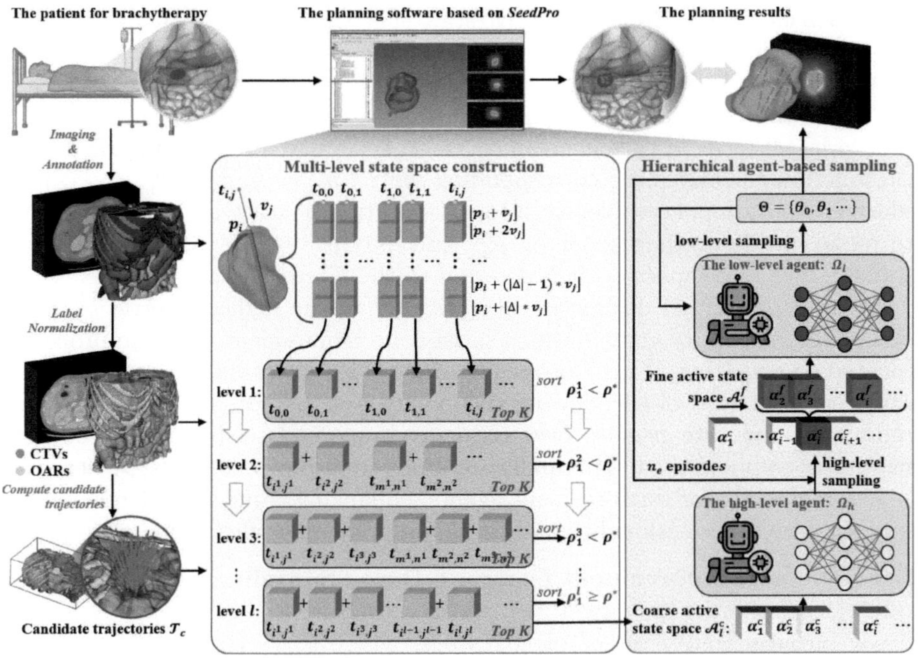

Fig. 1. The workflow of the *SeedPro*.

through hierarchical reinforcement agents, as shown in Fig. 1. The main contributions are: 1) A multi-level state space generation algorithm that emulates clinical decision-making patterns, enabling global fine-grained optimization; 2) A coarse-to-fine hierarchical reinforcement agents-based sampling strategy; 3) A segmented adaptive objective function ensuring compliance with CTV dosimetric endpoints while minimizing OARs exposure.

Expert-Like Multi-Level State Space Construction: The inputs are preoperative images $\mathcal{I}_o \in \mathbb{R}^{D \times H \times W}$ and segmented masks $\mathcal{I}_s$ (with CTV, OARs, and background assigned values of ϵ_c, ϵ_o, and 0, respectively). From $\mathcal{I}_s$, the 3D coordinates of all CTV voxels are extracted to form a point cloud $\mathcal{P}_c = \{p_i\}_{i=1}^{|\mathcal{P}_c|}$. Following [14], the candidate trajectory set is constructed as $\tilde{\mathcal{T}}_c = \{t_{i,j} = \{\langle p_i, v_j \rangle, \Delta\}\}$, where p_i is the entry point, v_j is the direction, and Δ defines the permissible step sizes within $\mathcal{P}_c$. To avoid geometric interference, each trajectory $t_{i,j} \in \tilde{\mathcal{T}}_c$ is densely populated with seeds $S_{i,j}$, yielding the lowest-level active state space $\mathcal{A}_1 = \{\{\langle t_{i,j}, S_{i,j} \rangle\}, \cdots\}$. For higher levels $l = 2, 3, \ldots$, the corresponding active state space is recursively constructed as:

$$
\begin{aligned}
&\mathcal{A}_l = \{\{\langle t_{i_1,j_1}, S_{i_1,j_1} \rangle, \cdots, \langle t_{i_l,j_l}, S_{i_l,j_l} \rangle\}, \cdots\} \\
&s.t. \quad \{\langle t_{i_1,j_1}, S_{i_1,j_1} \rangle, \cdots, \langle t_{i_{l-1},j_{l-1}}, S_{i_{l-1},j_{l-1}} \rangle\} \in \mathcal{A}_{l-1}, \\
&\qquad \min_{n=1,\cdots,l-1} \|S_{i_l,j_l}, S_{i_n,j_n}\|_2 > 2r_s, \quad \{\langle t_{i_l,j_l}, S_{i_l,j_l} \rangle\} \in \mathcal{A}_1
\end{aligned}
\tag{1}
$$

where each element in the l-level active state space $\mathcal{A}_l$ consists of l non-interfering seed-filled trajectories, $\|\cdot\|_2$ represents the minimum Euclidean distance between seeds, and r_s is the seed radius.

During the construction of $\mathcal{A}_l$, the cumulative dose field $\Psi_m^l \in \mathbb{R}^{D\times H\times W}$ induced by all seeds in each element $\pi_m^l \in \mathcal{A}_l$ is computed. A dosimetric evaluation function calculates the corresponding metric $\rho_m^l = f_{\text{eval}}(\mathcal{I}_s, \Psi_m^l, \epsilon_c, \cdots)$. To reduce computational complexity, a top-K selection strategy is applied: elements are ranked in descending order by ρ_m^l, and only the top K configurations are retained. The state space is then updated to the filtered set $\mathcal{A}_l = \{\pi_1^l, \cdots, \pi_k^l\}$.

Given a prescribed dosimetric objective ρ^*, if the highest metric $\rho_1^l < \rho^*$, none of the trajectory combinations satisfy the requirement, and the process is repeated to construct $\mathcal{A}_{l+1}$. Conversely, if $\rho_1^l \geq \rho^*$, a feasible trajectory combination emerges at level l. Following the expert-style paradigm–which prioritizes minimizing puncture needles over reducing implanted seeds–subsequent optimization is confined to $\mathcal{A}_l$. Hierarchically built from previous levels, $\mathcal{A}_l$ serves as the active domain for reinforcement agents, enhancing clinical consistency while reducing search dimensionality and improving planning efficiency.

Hierarchical Reinforcement Learning-Based Sampling: For $\pi_k^l \in \mathcal{A}_l$, each available position in its trajectories serves as a potential state. Let $\Theta = \{\theta_i\}$ be the initially empty set of placed seeds, where $\theta_i = \{\langle p_i, v_i\rangle, \delta_i\}$ indicates placement at $\lfloor p_i + \delta_i v_i \rfloor$ with orientation v_i. Using a distance map $\mathcal{I}_d$ of the CTV, feasible positions for new seeds along each trajectory in $\mathcal{A}_l$ are calculated:

$$\alpha_k^l = \{\delta \mid \forall\delta \in \Delta, \forall\langle t_{i,j} = \{\langle p_i, v_j\rangle, \Delta\}, S_{i,j}\rangle \in \pi_k^l\}$$
$$s.t. \quad \min_{\forall\theta_m\in\Theta} \|(\delta v_j - \delta_m v_m)v_j\|_2 > l_s \vee v_m \neq v_j \vee p_m \neq p_j, \; \mathcal{I}_d[\lfloor p_i + \delta v_j \rfloor] \geq \frac{l_s}{2} \tag{2}$$

where $\lfloor\cdot\rfloor$ is the floor function and l_s is the seed length. The flattened, coarse active state space is defined as $\mathcal{A}_l^c = \bigcup_{k=1}^{|\mathcal{A}_l|} \alpha_k^l = \{\alpha_1^c, \alpha_2^c, \ldots\}$, where α_i^c is a candidate action.

A hierarchical policy on $\mathcal{A}_l^c$ efficiently identifies optimal plans. The high-level agent Ω_h coarsely selects needle trajectory combinations from $\mathcal{A}_l$, while the low-level agent Ω_l determines the optimal positions of individual seeds along each selected trajectory until dosimetric objectives are met. Both use lightweight MLPs: Ω_h outputs $(b, |\mathcal{A}_l^c|)$ logits, and Ω_l adapts its output dimension dynamically. Initialized at state $\omega_c = 0$, Ω_h generates $z_h \in \mathbb{R}^{b\times|\mathcal{A}_l^c|}$ to sample a high-level action $\delta_h \sim p(\alpha_i^c \mid \omega_c) = \frac{\exp(z_{h,i})}{\sum_j \exp(z_{h,j})}$. Using δ_h's index i_h, the trajectory and subset indices (n^*, k^*) are determined by $\sum_{n=1}^{k-1}|\alpha_n^l| + \sum_{m=1}^{n-1}|\Delta_m| \leq i_h < \sum_{n=1}^{k-1}|\alpha_n^l| + \sum_{m=1}^{n}|\Delta_m|$ for $\pi_k^l \in \mathcal{A}_l$. The trajectory for the first seed is $t_{i_{n^*}, j_{n^*}} \in \pi_{k^*}^l$. We add $\theta_0 = \{\langle p_{i_{n^*}}, v_{j_{n^*}}\rangle, \delta_h\}$ to Θ, construct the fine active state space $\mathcal{A}_l^f = \alpha_{k^*}^f$, and generate an availability mask $\mathcal{M}$ to prevent interference:

$$\begin{aligned} &\mathcal{M} = \{m_1, m_2, \cdots, m_{|\mathcal{A}_l^f|}\} \\ s.t. \quad &m_i = \mathbb{I}\left(\min_{\forall \theta_j \in \Theta} \|(\alpha_i^f v_{i_h} - \delta_j v_j)v_i\|_2 > l_s \vee v_{i_h} \neq v_j \vee p_{i_h} \neq p_j\right) \\ &\text{for } \textstyle\sum_{m=1}^{h-1} |\Delta_m| \leq i < \sum_{m=1}^{h} |\Delta_m|, \;\; h = 1, 2, \cdots, l \end{aligned} \tag{3}$$

where $\mathbb{I}(\cdot)$ is the indicator function ($m_i = 1$ if feasible, 0 otherwise). Resetting $\omega_c = 0$, Ω_l produces a sampling vector $z_l \in \mathbb{R}^{b \times |\mathcal{A}_l^f|}$, converted to a masked probability $p(\alpha_i^f \mid \omega_c, \mathcal{M}) = \frac{\exp(z_{l,i})}{\sum_j \exp(z_{l,j})} \times m_i$. The next action $\delta_{l,1}$ is sampled, and $\theta_1 = \{\langle p_{l,1}, v_{l,1}\rangle, \delta_{l,1}\}$ is appended to Θ. This iteratively generates $\theta_2, \theta_3, \ldots$ until reaching the dosimetric endpoint or $\sum m_i = 0$, forming a complete solution.

This procedure runs per episode, with Ω_h constructing a dedicated policy network for Ω_l. Only Ω_h updates via backpropagation to approximate expert decisions, while Ω_l reinitializes. A two-stage learning strategy is employed: during the first $n_e/2$ episodes, agents explore global configurations. Addressing "trajectory under-saturation", the second stage refines the best scheme Θ^* and its fine state space $\mathcal{A}_l^{f,*}$. For the remaining $n_e/2$ episodes, Θ^* is cleared, and placement proceeds within $\mathcal{A}_l^{f,*}$ until targets are met, continuously updating Ω_l via backpropagation. Finally, the highest-performing trajectory from $\mathcal{A}_l$ serves as a reference to evaluate the final plan.

Segmented Adaptive Objective Function: For the currently placed seeds $\Theta_c = \{\theta_0, \theta_1, \ldots, \theta_{n_c}\}$, where n_c denotes the number of seeds, the cumulative dose distribution Ψ_c is computed via the dose calculator. A predefined D_X threshold μ_X is specified, where X represents the percentage of the CTV volume required to receive at least μ_X Gy. Notably, the objective function is compatible with standard clinical metrics, including V_x, D_{2cc}, D_{1cc}, $D_{0.5cc}$, D_{mean}, or any institution-specific criterion, without requiring architectural modifications. Given these parameters, the objective function is formulated as follows:

$$\begin{aligned} &r_{n_c} = f_{eval}(\Theta_c, \mathcal{I}_o, \mathcal{I}_s, \mu_X, X) = \rho_{n_c} + \mathbb{I}(\rho_{n_c} \geq X)\,\tfrac{D_c}{D_o}, \\ &\text{s.t.} \begin{cases} \Psi_c = f_{dose}(\Theta_c, \mathcal{I}_o) \\ D_c = \displaystyle\sum_{p \in \mathcal{I}_s,\, \mathcal{I}_s[p] = \epsilon_c} \Psi_c[p], \\ D_o = \displaystyle\sum_{p \in \mathcal{I}_s,\, \mathcal{I}_s[p] = \epsilon_o} \Psi_c[p], \\ \rho_{n_c} = \dfrac{\sum_{p \in \mathcal{I}_s} \mathbb{I}((\mathcal{I}_s[p] = \epsilon_c) \wedge (\Psi_c[p] \geq \mu_X))}{\sum_{p \in \mathcal{I}_s} \mathbb{I}(\mathcal{I}_s[p] = \epsilon_c)} \times 100. \end{cases} \end{aligned} \tag{4}$$

where f_{dose} denotes the dose calculation function based on the dose calculator; $\mathbb{I}(a)$ denotes the indicator function, which returns 1 when the condition a is satisfied and 0 otherwise; $\wedge$ represents the logical AND operation, indicating the conjunction of multiple conditions in formal logic; $A[b]$ denotes the value of matrix A at coordinate b; r_{n_c} represents the reward obtained after placing the n_c^{th} seed θ_{n_c}, and the corresponding reward set is denoted as $R_c = \{r_0, r_1, \cdots, r_{n_c}\}$.

3 Experiments and Discussion

3.1 Dataset and Experimental Setting

To evaluate the proposed *SeedPro* system, we constructed an in-house clinical dataset of 17 patients from The Ruijin Hospital Affiliated to Shanghai Jiao Tong University School of Medicine, including cases of pancreatic, head and neck, and other tumor types, alongside 282 pancreatic cancer cases from the open-source external Medical Segmentation Decathlon (MSD) dataset [36]. All patients in our in-house dataset underwent ^{125}I seed brachytherapy, with each seed measuring 0.4 mm in radius and 4.5 mm in length. Prescribed CTV dosimetric objectives were set as $D_{90} \geq 120$ Gy and $V_{100} \geq 90\%$, following the OpenKBP standard [35]. CT scans were acquired with 5 mm slice thickness and 1 mm in-plane resolution, comprising 12–90 slices per volume depending on lesion size. CTVs and OARs were manually delineated by experienced interventional radiologists. Experiments were performed on a workstation with dual NVIDIA RTX 3090 GPUs, and the policy network was optimized with a learning rate of 10^{-3}. It is worth noting that sensitivity and ablation studies as well as robustness evaluations were conducted exclusively on the in-house dataset. The external dataset was specifically utilized in the comparative study to rigorously assess the generalizability of our method across a large cohort. Importantly, *SeedPro*, developed and validated on this small-scale in-house cohort, achieves superior performance on a substantially larger independent external dataset without any targeted tuning, directly demonstrating the robustness and reliability of the proposed framework.

3.2 Sensitivity Study

Evaluation of K: In state space construction, a top-K selection strategy is introduced to reduce computational overhead in constructing the expert-inspired multi-level active state space. To evaluate its effect, K was set to 10, 50, 100, 200, and 400 to generate $\mathcal{A}_l$ according to Eq. (1), and the $\langle \pi^l_m, \Psi^l_m, \rho^l_m \rangle$ with the highest D_{90} was selected for evaluation. While exceeding the prescribed dosimetric targets does not imply better clinical quality, larger D_{90} and V_{100} here indicate greater optimization potential and higher-quality $\mathcal{A}_l$. The construction time for $\mathcal{A}_l$ was also recorded to quantify computational cost. Results are summarized in Fig. 2a, with SR denoting the success rate of meeting the prescribed V_{100} and D_{90}.

Evaluation of n_e: In the proposed coarse-to-fine two-stage learning strategy, the total number of episodes is defined as n_e. To assess the sensitivity of *SeedPro*'s performance with respect to different n_e settings, n_e was set to 50, 100, 200, 400, and 800 for comparative evaluation. To clearly demonstrate the direct influence of n_e on the reinforcement agents Ω_h and Ω_l, we did not employ the baseline mechanism introduced in Sect. 2; instead, the final results were generated solely by the reinforcement agents. We calculated the success rate (SR), V_{100}, D_{90}, and computation time for each configuration, as shown in Fig. 2b.

K	SR (%, ↑)	V_{100} (%, ≥90)	D_{90} (Gy, ≥120)	Times (s, ↓)
10	70.59	91.19±6.71	122.72±31.08	0.80±0.82
50	88.24	93.48±3.88	133.06±17.49	0.82±0.82
100	94.12	93.92±3.55	135.17±15.73	0.91±0.86
200	100.00	94.27±3.23	135.90±13.49	1.06±0.92
400	100.00	94.46±3.40	135.36±14.58	1.39±1.07

(a) Evaluation of K

n_e	SR (%, ↑)	V_{100} (%, ≥90)	D_{90} (Gy, ≥120)	Times (s, ↓)
50	64.71	89.84 ± 1.50	119.59±3.17	6.06±3.40
100	76.47	89.98 ± 1.55	119.45±3.38	10.70±6.26
200	76.47	90.01 ± 1.48	119.69±3.54	19.93±12.12
400	82.35	90.12 ± 1.32	120.17±3.48	37.30±21.46
800	82.35	90.29 ± 1.20	120.61±2.83	73.50±44.78

(b) Evaluation of n_e

Fig. 2. (a) Evaluation of K (b) Evaluation of n_e

Table 1. Ablation study

Configuration	SR $(\%,\uparrow)_{V_{100}(\%,\geq 90),D_{90}(Gy,\geq 120)}$	$\tilde{V}_{150}(\%,\downarrow)$	$\tilde{V}_{100}(\%,\downarrow)$	$\tilde{V}_{50}(\%,\downarrow)$	Times (s, ↓)
Baseline	$100.00_{94.90\pm2.94,137.04\pm12.20}$	45.99 ± 31.44	150.10 ± 86.42	650.37 ± 303.48	**34.98 ± 19.92**
+ segmented adaptive objective function	$100.00_{90.76\pm0.80,121.81\pm1.82}$	28.30 ± 25.89	85.37 ± 54.87	502.90 ± 227.75	40.52±24.03
+ two stage learning strategy	$100.00_{90.53\pm0.48,121.40\pm1.24}$	**27.78 ± 24.66**	**84.77 ± 53.97**	**502.85 ± 223.50**	37.30±21.46

3.3 Ablation Study

We conducted an ablation study to evaluate the core modules of *SeedPro*. Setting the optimal trajectory combination from the multi-level state space as the baseline, we incrementally integrated the segmented adaptive objective function and the coarse-to-fine two-stage optimization strategy. Table 1 reports the success rate (SR), time cost, and $\tilde{V}_x$ (the fraction of OAR volume receiving $\geq x\% \times D_{90}$, where lower indicates better OAR sparing). Both modules progressively enhanced OAR protection while maintaining target coverage.

3.4 Comparison Study

To evaluate the superiority and generalizability of *SeedPro* on both in-house and external datasets, we selected the recent SOTA method, *BrachyPlan* [14], as our baseline. As *SeedPro* represents a direct methodological advancement over *BrachyPlan*–which has been rigorously validated to achieve clinical equivalence compared to expert manual plans–this comparison provides a stringent and representative evaluation of our method's clinical potential.

The evaluation metrics included the success rate (SR), dosimetric indices $\tilde{V}_x$, the number of puncture needles (n_p), and the number of implanted seeds (n_s). Here, n_p reflects procedural complexity–fewer punctures indicate greater intraoperative convenience–while n_s represents the precision of dose field control, as

Table 2. Quantitative comparison of different methods under the dosimetric requirement of μ_{90} = 120 Gy, evaluated on both the internal (17 cases) and external (282 cases) datasets.

Dataset	Methods	SR $(\%,\uparrow)_{V_{100}(\%,\geq 90),D_{90}(Gy,\geq \mu_{90})}$	$\tilde{V}_{150}$ (%, ↓)	$\tilde{V}_{100}$ (%, ↓)	$\tilde{V}_{50}$ (%, ↓)	n_p ↓	n_s ↓
Internal	BrachyPlan	$100.00_{91.54\pm1.32,124.78\pm4.44}$	39.83 ± 24.27	130.80 ± 67.22	674.43 ± 351.97	8.06 ± 3.98	35.06 ± 19.72
	SeedPro (ours)	$100.00_{90.53\pm0.48,121.40\pm1.24}$	**27.78 ± 24.66**	**84.77 ± 53.97**	**502.85 ± 223.50**	**6.06 ± 3.02**	**30.59 ± 18.59**
External	BrachyPlan	$81.91_{93.20\pm5.15,141.22\pm22.71}$	69.67 ± 90.55	163.22 ± 370.01	670.07 ± 767.45	2.85 ± 1.01	8.62 ± 7.05
	SeedPro (ours)	$\mathbf{88.65}_{91.25\pm4.33,125.51\pm13.86}$	**30.28 ± 92.24**	**86.18 ± 370.46**	**356.10 ± 755.19**	**2.45 ± 0.80**	**6.99 ± 6.89**

Table 3. Robustness study under $\mu_{90} = 100$ Gy and 140 Gy to simulate varying clinical scenarios.

Methods		SR (%, ↑)$_{V_{100}(\%,\geq 90), D_{90}(Gy,\geq \mu_{90})}$	$\tilde{V}_{150}$ (%, ↓)	$\tilde{V}_{100}$ (%, ↓)	$\tilde{V}_{50}$ (%, ↓)	n_p ↓	n_s ↓
$\mu_{90} = 100$ Gy	BrachyPlan	100.00$_{92.26\pm1.90,106.55\pm5.81}$	73.17 ± 42.21	215.11 ± 104.48	804.30 ± 390.26	6.29 ± 3.34	31.94 ± 18.34
	SeedPro (ours)	100.00$_{90.91\pm0.78,101.75\pm1.60}$	**32.95 ± 27.43**	**98.72 ± 58.94**	**573.66 ± 280.05**	**5.35 ± 2.81**	**26.12 ± 15.53**
$\mu_{90} = 140$ Gy	BrachyPlan	94.12$_{91.45\pm1.12,145.12\pm3.67}$	53.91 ± 28.19	152.11 ± 60.42	690.40 ± 309.06	8.50 ± 4.08	40.65 ± 24.03
	SeedPro (ours)	**100.00**$_{90.37\pm0.36,141.25\pm1.36}$	**27.31 ± 22.77**	**82.13 ± 52.26**	**475.26 ± 206.53**	**6.82 ± 3.50**	**34.76 ± 21.18**

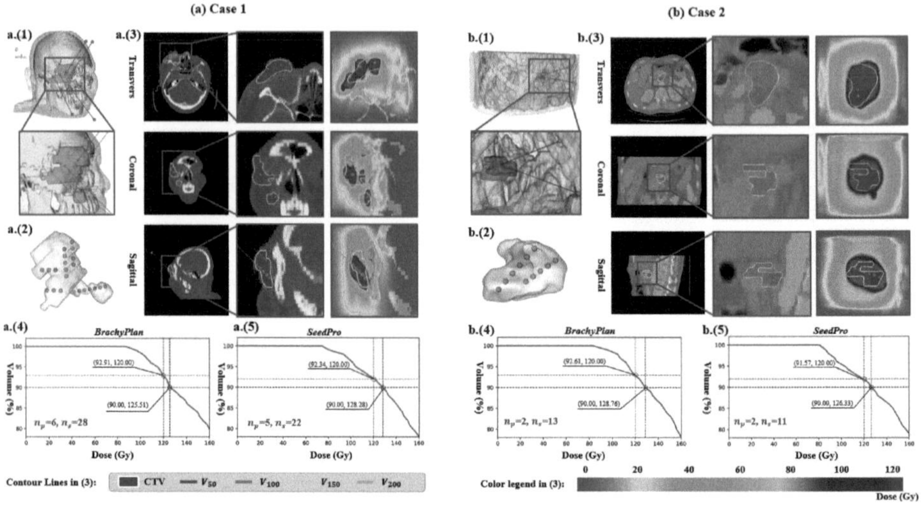

Fig. 3. The planning results of two randomly selected cases by *SeedPro*: (1-2) 3D visualization results; (3) dose distribution results with 2D CTV contour lines; (4-5) corresponding DVH curves.

achieving comparable dosimetric outcomes with fewer seeds implies a more fine-grained and efficient planning strategy. The quantitative results are summarized in Table 2 and visually illustrated in Fig. 3. *SeedPro* consistently outperformed *BrachyPlan* across both datasets, particularly demonstrating superior OAR protection and a notable reduction in surgical complexity.

3.5 Robustness Study

To further assess robustness and confirm safety under extreme or diverse prescription contexts, *SeedPro* was evaluated under varying dosimetric requirements. Specifically, we simulated clinical scenarios with different tumor malignancy grades by setting target doses of $D_{90} = 100$ Gy and 140 Gy. All comparative results against the baseline are summarized in Table 3. *SeedPro* maintained exceptional consistency and robustness, achieving a 100% success rate across the diverse target doses while continuing to guarantee optimal tissue protection and high needle efficiency.

4 Conclusion

In this work, we propose *SeedPro*, a novel framework for expert-like brachytherapy planning, and demonstrate its superiority through comprehensive experiments. Future work will focus on incorporating larger-scale and multi-center clinical datasets to further enhance robustness and generalizability, and on validating *SeedPro* across additional anatomical sites, including prostate.

Disclosure of Interests. The authors have no competing interests to declare that are relevant to the content of this article.

References

1. Chargari, C., Deutsch, E., Blanchard, P.: Brachytherapy: An overview for clinicians. CA Cancer J. Clin. **69**(5), 386–401 (2019)
2. Lim, Y.K., Kim, D.: Brachytherapy: a comprehensive review. Progress Med. Phys. **32**(2), 25–39 (2021)
3. Ragde, H., Grado, G.L., Nadir, B., et al.: Modern prostate brachytherapy. CA: A Cancer J. Clin. **50**(6), 380–393 (2000)
4. Pathak, P., Thomas, J.J., Baghwala, A., et al.: Personalized brachytherapy: applications and future directions. Cancers **16**(19), 3424 (2024)
5. Pötter, R., Tanderup, K., Schmid, M.P., et al.: MRI-guided adaptive brachytherapy in locally advanced cervical cancer (EMBRACE-I): a multicentre prospective cohort study. Lancet Oncol. **22**(4), 538–547 (2021)
6. Serre, R., Gabro, A., Andraud, M.: Brachytherapy: Perspectives for combined treatments with immunotherapy. Clin. Transl. Radiation Oncol. 100924 (2025)
7. Blasko, J.C.: Low-dose-rate brachytherapy for prostate cancer: Preplanning vs. intraoperative planning-Preplanning is best. Brachytherapy **5**(3), 139–142 (2006)
8. Matzkin, H., Chen, J., German, L., et al.: Comparison between preoperative and real-time intraoperative planning 125I permanent prostate brachytherapy: Long-term clinical biochemical outcome. Radiat. Oncol. **8**(1), 288 (2013)
9. Berger, D., Van Dyk, S., Beaulieu, L., et al.: Modern tools for modern brachytherapy. Clin. Oncol. **35**(8), e453–e468 (2023)
10. Liu, T., Wen, S., Wang, S., et al.: Artificial intelligence in brachytherapy. J. Radiat. Res. Appl. Sci. **17**(2), 100925 (2024)
11. Chen, J., Qiu, R.L.J., Wang, T., et al.: A review of artificial intelligence in brachytherapy. J. Appl. Clin. Med. Phys. e70034 (2025)
12. Gautam, S., Osman, A.F.I., Richeson, D., et al.: Attention 3D U-NET for dose distribution prediction of high-dose-rate brachytherapy of cervical cancer: direction modulated brachytherapy tandem applicator. Med. Phys. **51**(8), 5593–5603 (2024)
13. Quetin, S., Bahoric, B., Maleki, F., et al.: Deep learning for high-resolution dose prediction in high dose rate brachytherapy for breast cancer treatment. Phys. Med. Biol. **69**(10), 105011 (2024)
14. Liu, J., Li, H., Shi, H.: BrachyPlan: a fine-grained efficient dose-guided inverse planning strategy for low-dose-rate brachytherapy. Med. Image Anal., 103852 (2025)
15. Bonenfant, É., Magnoux, V., Hissoiny, S., et al.: Fast GPU-based Monte Carlo simulations for LDR prostate brachytherapy. Phys. Med. Biol. **60**(13), 4973 (2015)

16. Dickhoff, L.R.M., Scholman, R.J., Barten, D.L.J., et al.: Keeping your best options open with AI-based treatment planning in prostate and cervix brachytherapy. Brachytherapy **23**(2), 188–198 (2024)
17. Barten, D.L.J., Pieters, B.R., Bouter, A., et al.: Towards artificial intelligence-based automated treatment planning in clinical practice: a prospective study of the first clinical experiences in high-dose-rate prostate brachytherapy. Brachytherapy **22**(2), 279–289 (2023)
18. Gautam, S., Flower, E., Richeson, D., et al.: Improving plan quality in cervical cancer brachytherapy using knowledge-based planning for direction modulated brachytherapy tandem applicator. Brachytherapy **24**(1), 144–153 (2025)
19. Jiang, H., Li, A., Ke, K., et al.: Three-dimensional treatment-planning-based prediction of seed migration to chest after 125I seed brachytherapy for hepatic malignancy. Brachytherapy **23**(4), 478–488 (2024)
20. Pu, G., Jiang, S., Yang, Z., et al.: Deep reinforcement learning for treatment planning in high-dose-rate cervical brachytherapy. Phys. Med. **94**, 1–7 (2022)
21. Kallis, K., Moore, L.C., Cortes, K.G., et al.: Automated treatment planning framework for brachytherapy of cervical cancer using 3D dose predictions. Phys. Med. Biol. **68**(8), 085011 (2023)
22. Xiao, Z., Xiong, T., Geng, L., et al.: Automatic planning for head and neck seed implant brachytherapy based on deep convolutional neural network dose engine. Med. Phys. **51**(2), 1460–1473 (2024)
23. Aumüller, P.: An Inverse Treatment Planning System for Robotic Seed Brachytherapy (2024). PhD thesis
24. Li, Y., Jiang, J., Jiang, Q., et al.: Advanced navigation technology enables endobronchial brachytherapy for peripheral lung cancer: an old technique plays a new role. Brachytherapy **23**(2), 199–206 (2024)
25. Hu, P., Huang, J., Zhang, Y., et al.: Iodine-125 seed implantation in the treatment of malignant tumors. J. Intervent. Med. **6**(3), 111–115 (2023)
26. Wang, T., Feng, Y., Yang, X.: Automatic Treatment Planning using Reinforcement Learning for High-dose-rate Prostate Brachytherapy. arXiv preprint arXiv:2506.09805 (2025)
27. Qian, Y., Washington, P., Podder, T.K., et al.: A linear programming and deep reinforcement learning framework to choose dwell positions and dwell time in high-dose-rate prostate brachytherapy using curvilinear catheters. In: ASME International Mechanical Engineering Congress and Exposition, vol. 88629, pp. V004T06A030. ASME (2024)
28. Kirisits, C., Siebert, F.A., Baltas, D., et al.: Accuracy of volume and DVH parameters determined with different brachytherapy treatment planning systems. Radiother. Oncol. **84**(3), 290–297 (2007)
29. Lindegaard, J.C., Tanderup, K., Nielsen, S.K.: MRI-guided 3D optimization significantly improves DVH parameters of pulsed-dose-rate brachytherapy in locally advanced cervical cancer. Int. J. Radiat. Oncol.*Biol.*Phys. **71**, 756–764 (2008)
30. Merrick, G.S., Butler, W.M., Dorsey, A.T., et al.: Potential role of various dosimetric quality indicators in prostate brachytherapy. Int. J. Radiat. Oncol. Biol. Phys. **44**(3), 717–724 (1999)
31. Shi, J., Chen, J., He, G., et al.: Artificial intelligence in high-dose-rate brachytherapy treatment planning for cervical cancer: a review. Front. Oncol. **15**, 1507592 (2025)
32. Rossi, L., Bijman, R., Chopra, S.: Rule-based AI automated adaptive treatment planning for image guided cervical cancer brachytherapy. Brachytherapy (2025)

33. Li, M., Li, X., Qiu, B., et al.: Experts consensus on 3D-printing template-assisted CT-guided radioactive iodine-125 seed implantation for recurrent soft tissue carcinoma in China. Clin. Exp. Med. **25**(1), 52 (2025)
34. Chitmanee, P., Sampaongen, T., Klomjit, N.: Factors affecting D90 high-risk clinical target volumes (HR-CTV dose) of intracavitary and interstitial brachytherapy in locally advanced cervical cancer. Clin. Oncol. **37**, 103701 (2025)
35. Babier, A., Zhang, B., Mahmood, R., et al.: OpenKBP: the open-access knowledge-based planning grand challenge and dataset. Med. Phys. **48**(9), 5549–5561 (2021)
36. Antonelli, M., Reinke, A., Bakas, S., et al.: The medical segmentation decathlon. Nat. Commun. **13**, 4128 (2022)

SHINE: An Entropy-Guided Digital Twin Framework for 3D Myocardial Scar Reconstruction from Sparse CMR

Dexiang Zong[1], Shuang Leng[1], Xiaodan Zhao[1], Ru-San Tan[1], Lei Chen[4], Jun Cheng[5], Xulei Yang[5], Ching-Hui Sia[6], Mark Chan[6], Derek Hausenloy[1], and Liang Zhong[1,2,3](✉)

[1] National Heart Centre Singapore, Singapore, Singapore
zhong.liang@nhcs.com.sg
[2] Duke-NUS Medical School, Singapore, Singapore
[3] Department of Biomedical Engineering, National University of Singapore, Singapore, Singapore
[4] Tongji University, Shanghai, China
[5] Agency for Science, Technology and Research (A*STAR), Singapore, Singapore
[6] National University Health System, Singapore, Singapore

Abstract. Accurate reconstruction of the arrhythmogenic myocardial substrate—specifically the conducting isthmuses essential for ventricular tachycardia (VT) ablation—depends on capturing fine-scale scar topology from sparse, anisotropic Late Gadolinium Enhancement (LGE) MRI. Given the pronounced anisotropy (e.g., $1.2 \times 1.2 \times 8.0$ mm) and limited slice sampling, volumetric reconstruction constitutes a highly ill-posed inverse problem, often leading to aliasing artifacts and discontinuous "staircase" geometries under discrete interpolation schemes. To address this challenge, we propose substrate reconstruction as a continuous function learning task defined on a patient-specific anatomical manifold. We introduce SHINE (Scar Heterogeneity via Implicit Neural Encoding), a framework that constructs a mathematically consistent "Digital Twin" of the diseased myocardium. The pipeline integrates automated biventricular segmentation with a Statistical Shape Model (SSM) to establish a continuous anatomical prior. To reconstruct detailed scar morphology, we employ a Bayesian SIREN architecture with sinusoidal activation functions, enabling the representation of high-frequency geometric structures and mitigating the spectral bias persistent in conventional Neural Fields. Importantly, we introduce an Entropy-Weighted Dirichlet Energy loss, which uses epistemic uncertainty to adaptively enforce smoothness in data-sparse regions while preserving high-fidelity details in data-rich regions. Evaluated on a clinical VT cohort of 40 patients, SHINE significantly outperformed discrete interpolation and weakly supervised benchmarks, achieving a Dice Similarity Coefficient of 0.93 and a volumetric error of 3.1%. Notably, our method effectively addresses the Nyquist sampling gap, enabling recovery of sub-voxel conducting channels within a unified, topology-preserving 3D framework to support precision electrophysiology planning.

G. Yang et al. (Eds.): MICCAI 2026, LNCS 16893, pp. 469–478, 2027.
https://doi.org/10.1007/978-3-032-38236-8_45

Keywords: Myocardial Scar Reconstruction · Physics-Informed Neural Fields · Entropy-Guided Regularization · Anatomical Digital Twin · Sparse-to-Dense · Uncertainty Quantification

1 Introduction

Sudden Cardiac Death (SCD) secondary to ventricular tachyarrhythmias remains a leading cause of mortality. While the field of medical electronics has evolved significantly since its infancy [1], and quantitative image analysis has become a cornerstone of clinical practice [2], identifying the specific arrhythmogenic substrate remains challenging. This substrate is predominantly characterized by the Heterogeneous Zone (HZ), where dense scar interdigitates with viable myocytes to form complex conducting pathways. Identifying narrow "conducting isthmuses" within this substrate is paramount, as these channels sustain reentrant circuits and constitute critical targets for catheter ablation [3].

While Late Gadolinium Enhancement (LGE) MRI offers a unique non-invasive method to assess myocardial fibrosis, its clinical utility is severely impeded by acquisition constraints. To balance breath-hold duration and signal-to-noise ratio (SNR), clinical protocols typically adopt highly anisotropic voxel dimensions (e.g., 1.2 × 1.2 × 8.0 mm). This sparse through-plane resolution leaves approximately 80% of the myocardial volume unobserved [4], rendering the reconstruction of a continuous, topology-preserving 3D structure a mathematically ill-posed inverse problem. Traditional interpolation methods fail to address this fundamental limitation; for instance, Log-Odds interpolation [5] assumes local linearity, resulting in "staircase artifacts" that artificially sever the subtle conducting pathways required for reentry. Similarly, standard deep learning approaches [6,7] utilizing Convolutional Neural Networks (CNNs) suffer from spectral bias [8]. These networks preferentially learn low-frequency components, effectively smoothing out the sharp, high-frequency details of narrow isthmuses. Recent advances in Implicit Neural Representations (INRs), popularized by Neural Radiance Fields [9], have shown promise in medical imaging [10,11], yet applying them to sparse LGE-MRI requires careful regularization to avoid hallucinations. Crucially, existing deterministic models lack the capacity to quantify predictive reliability in unobserved gaps. Without uncertainty quantification, these "black-box" models risk synthesizing unrealistic anatomical structures in "blind zones," rendering the reconstruction clinically unsafe for precision ablation planning [16].

To resolve these challenges, we propose SHINE (Scar Heterogeneity via Implicit Neural Encoding), an Entropy-Guided Digital Twin framework. Unlike standard Implicit Neural Representations (Vanilla INRs) that act as deterministic 'black boxes' and are prone to generating non-physical 'hallucinations' in unobserved regions, SHINE introduces a fundamentally robust algorithmic paradigm. By seamlessly integrating patient-specific physical constraints (via anatomical manifolds) with a novel uncertainty-aware loss function, our framework inherently quantifies epistemic uncertainty. This enables the model to adaptively enforce topological continuity in data-sparse 'blind zones' while rigorously preserving high-frequency substrate details where observations are available. We reformulate substrate reconstruction not as discrete voxel in-painting, but as a continuous function learning problem on a patient-specific anatomical manifold. Transcending discrete grids, SHINE constructs a mathematically consistent Digital Twin of the pathological myocardium that is resolution-independent and topologically accurate [12]. Recent studies have further demonstrated the clinical prognostic value of such digital twin models in complex cardiovascular conditions [13]. Our specific contributions are threefold:

1. **Entropy-Guided Physics-Informed Neural Field:** We introduce a reconstruction paradigm that integrates anatomical priors with INRs [14]. By treating the myocardium as a continuous manifold, our method recovers sub-voxel conducting channels, effectively bridging the Nyquist sampling gap.
2. **Bayesian SIREN Backbone:** We employ a Bayesian SIREN architecture [15]. By leveraging periodic activations within a variational framework [16], we enable the representation of high-frequency geometric structures to overcome spectral bias while providing a rigorous measure of predictive uncertainty.
3. **Entropy-Weighted Dirichlet Energy Loss:** We propose a novel regularization mechanism that leverages the model's epistemic uncertainty. This loss function adaptively enforces physical smoothness (Dirichlet energy) in high-uncertainty gaps while preserving high-fidelity topological details in data-rich regions.

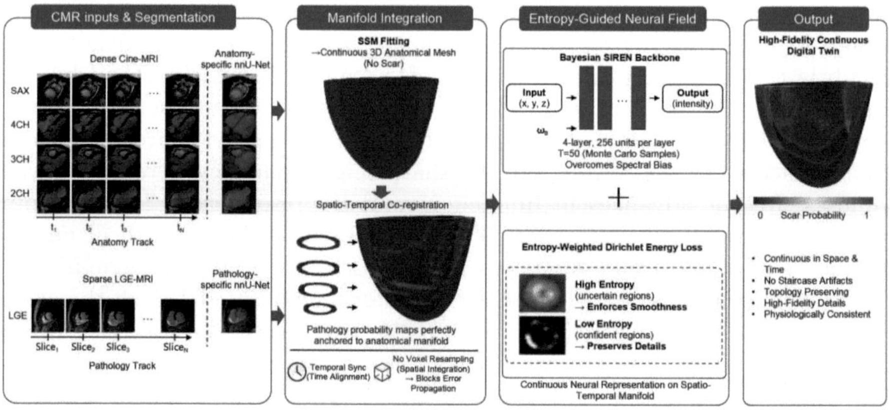

Fig. 1. Overview of SHINE, which integrates Cine-derived anatomical manifolds, sparse LGE pathology, co-registration, and entropy-guided Bayesian SIREN reconstruction into a resolution-independent cardiac digital twin.

2 Methodology

We formulate 3D myocardial substrate reconstruction as a Bayesian inverse problem on a patient-specific Riemannian manifold. The proposed framework,

SHINE, decouples the geometric reconstruction (Anatomical Digital Twin) from the pathological function learning (Entropy-Guided Neural Field) (Fig. 1).

2.1 Problem Formulation

Let $\Omega \subset \mathbb{R}^3$ denote the volumetric domain of the left ventricle (LV). We model the myocardial substrate as a continuous scalar field $f : \Omega \to [0, 1]$, where $f(x)$ represents the latent scar probability at a spatial coordinate $x \in \Omega$. Clinical LGE-MRI provides a set of sparse, anisotropic observations $D_{obs} = \{(x_i, y_i)\}_{i=1}^{N}$ sampled exclusively on imaging planes $P_{slices} \subset \Omega$. Our objective is to estimate the posterior distribution $p(f|D_{obs})$.

2.2 The Anatomical Digital Twin: Geometric Prior Construction

To constrain the ill-posed nature of reconstructing f, we impose a patient-specific geometric prior by constructing an anatomical manifold M.

Geometric Manifold Fitting. Let $I = \{I_{sax}, I_{2ch}, I_{3ch}, I_{4ch}\}$ denote multi-view Cine MRI sequences. We utilize a pre-trained nnU-Net [17] to generate dense 2D segmentations. To achieve a continuous representation, we fit a Statistical Shape Model (SSM) [18] to these contours: $S = \bar{S} + \sum_{k=1}^{K} \alpha_k p_k$, where $\bar{S}$ is the population mean shape and p_k are principal modes. Coefficients are optimized via Chamfer distance minimization.

Spatio-Temporal Co-registration. Consistency is maintained via rigorous alignment and multi-view integration [19]:

- Temporal Synchronization: Cardiac phases are synchronized using DICOM metadata.
- Spatial Integration: Physical coordinates rigidly map sparse LGE slices into the 3D Cine-derived manifold without voxel resampling.

2.3 Bayesian SIREN for Pathological Substrate Representation

We represent the scar probability field f as an Implicit Neural Representation (INR) parameterized by weights θ. Unlike discrete voxel arrays, this continuous formulation enables resolution-independent reconstruction on the anatomical manifold.

Input Standardization. To mitigate variability, we utilize softmax probability maps generated by a pathology-specific nnU-Net [17] as input $y_i \in [0, 1]$.

Bayesian SIREN Backbone. To overcome spectral bias, we employ a Bayesian SIREN backbone [15]. The activation for the l-th layer is: $h^{(l)}(x) = \sin(\omega_0(W^{(l)}x + b^{(l)}))$. To quantify predictive reliability, we treat θ as random variables with a variational posterior $q_\phi(\theta)$ approximated via MC Dropout [16]. Predictive mean $\hat{y}(x)$, predictive entropy $H(x)$, and normalized entropy $\tilde{H}(x)$ are estimated through T stochastic forward passes.

2.4 Entropy-Weighted Dirichlet Energy Loss

To prevent non-physical "hallucinations" in unobserved gaps, we introduce an adaptive objective function that leverages predictive uncertainty:

$$L_{total} = L_{BCE}(\hat{y}, y_{obs}) + \lambda \cdot L_{entropy\_reg} \tag{1}$$

where

$$L_{entropy\_reg} = \int_{\Omega_{myo}} \tilde{H}(x) \cdot \|\nabla_x \hat{y}(x)\|_2^2 \, dx \tag{2}$$

Theoretical Mechanism: In data-rich regions ($\tilde{H} \to 0$), the regularization vanishes. In sparse gaps ($\tilde{H} \to 1$), the loss enforces a harmonic constraint ($\Delta f = 0$), forcing smooth transitions.

2.5 Implementation Details

To ensure reproducibility, our framework utilizes a 4-layer Bayesian SIREN backbone with 256 hidden units per layer. The predictive mean and epistemic uncertainty are estimated through $T = 50$ stochastic forward passes. The entropy regularization weight is set to $\lambda = 5 \times 10^{-4}$. The source code and pre-trained models are publicly available at https://github.com/FluxVisionAI/SHINE.

3 Results and Discussion

3.1 Comparative Analysis and the Fidelity Paradox

We evaluated SHINE on a clinical cohort of 40 patients originating from two centers with different MRI scanners (1.5T Siemens Avanto vs. 3.0T Biograph mMR), providing evidence of robustness across acquisition settings. All acquisitions were analyzed at a nominal 1.2 × 1.2 × 8.0 mm sparse LGE resolution. We employed a dual-track validation protocol: (i) a Geometric Track using high-resolution Cine-MRI as an anatomical reference, and (ii) a Pathological Track via Leave-One-Slice-Out (LOSO) cross-validation. Specifically, the LOSO protocol evaluated SHINE against 455 physical slices covering extreme infarct sizes (4.7%–56.1%), validating the framework's reliability across diverse pathological conditions. Although absolute 3D ground truth data, such as 3D single-breath-hold LGE-CMR, are not available in the current study, our data provides relatively dense spatial sampling (8-16 slices/patient). To address this limitation, we utilize the LOSO cross-validation protocol as a rigorous surrogate ground truth. By withholding true physical LGE slices (completely isolated from optimization), we establish a reliable baseline. Evaluated against these hidden slices, SHINE achieves high spatial overlap (DSC 0.93) and strong intensity fidelity (MSE 4×10^{-5}), supporting the anatomical plausibility of the reconstructed fine-scale structures rather than non-physical hallucinations. As shown in Table 1, SHINE significantly outperforms baselines, achieving a DSC of 0.93

and an intensity fidelity (MSE) of 4×10^{-5}—three orders of magnitude superior to Log-Odds interpolation. This performance substantiates our validation: the negligible MSE reflects high pathological fidelity (Track 2), while the 3.1% volumetric error confirms precise anatomical anchoring (Track 1). Qualitative results (Fig. 2, 3) further demonstrate that SHINE maintains topological continuity across 8.0 mm gaps, resolving the 'Fidelity Paradox' where Vanilla INRs exhibit high DSC but catastrophic 15.2% volumetric errors due to fragmented hallucinations.

Table 1. Performance benchmark against state-of-the-art reconstruction methods.

Method	Dice Score (DSC) ↑	MSE (Fidelity) ↓	Vol. Error ↓
Log-Odds [5]	0.71	8.2×10^{-2}	23.5%
SR-CNN [7]	0.88	4.5×10^{-2}	10.8%
Weakly Supervised DL [6]	0.91	1.9×10^{-2}	7.1%
Vanilla INR [15]	0.91	2.0×10^{-3}	15.2%
SHINE (Proposed)	**0.93**	$\mathbf{4.0 \times 10^{-5}}$	**3.1%**

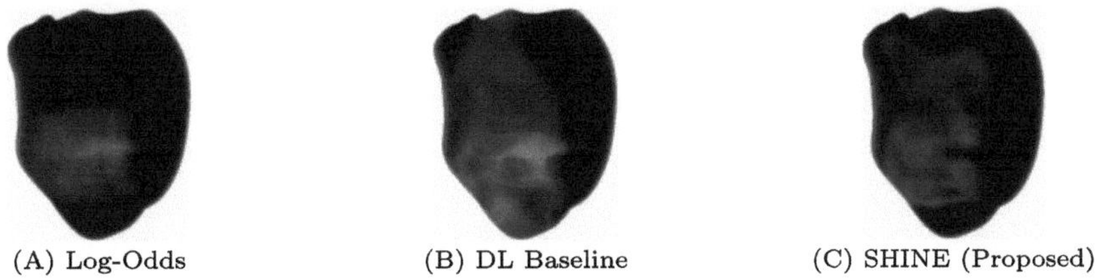

Fig. 2. Qualitative 3D reconstruction benchmarking. SHINE recovers sub-voxel topological continuity, whereas Log-Odds and DL baselines show staircase artifacts or blurred channels.

SHINE (Proposed) achieves near-perfect intensity fidelity ($\text{MSE} = 4 \times 10^{-5}$), which is vital for clinical simulations where small errors in scar border can significantly impact reentry prediction. This confirms that standard INRs lack the necessary constraints to maintain physical consistency, leading to significant overestimation of scar burden.

The volumetric error paradox in Table 2 further highlights the need for topology-aware evaluation. Although removing entropy regularization yields a lower volumetric error (1.4%), its high hidden-slice MSE (1.9×10^{-3}) and Fig. 4A indicate fragmented salt-and-pepper artifacts caused by cancellation between over- and under-estimation. SHINE instead prioritizes topological fidelity, achieving low MSE (4×10^{-5}) and reliable conducting-channel continuity despite a 3.1% volumetric error.

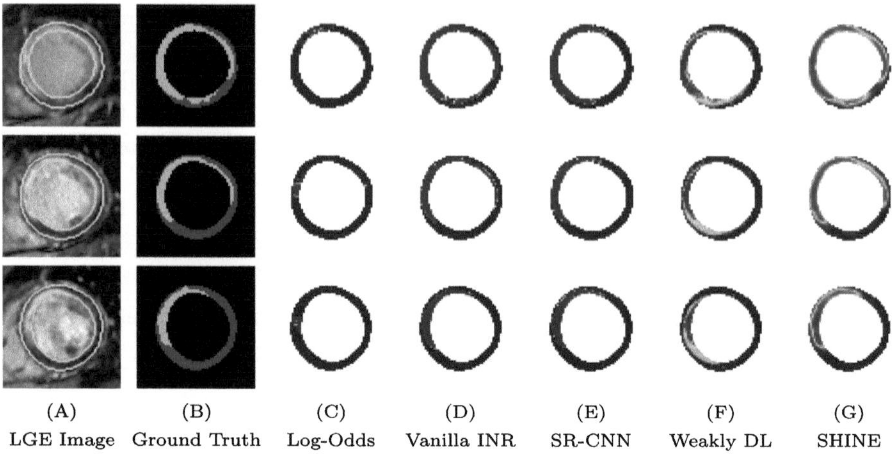

Fig. 3. Qualitative slice-wise benchmarking. Compared with Log-Odds [5], Vanilla INR [15], SR-CNN [7], and Weakly Supervised DL [6], SHINE best preserves sharp boundaries and sub-voxel conducting-channel continuity.

To address potential upstream error propagation [21,22], we analyzed the relationship between segmentation/SSM geometric deviations and downstream reconstruction errors. No significant correlation was observed ($r=0.20$, $p=0.34$; mean deviation 1.59 ± 0.22 mm), indicating that SHINE's manifold alignment decouples anatomical geometry from pathological texture learning and mitigates propagation of geometric noise into scar topology.

3.2 Ablation Study and Spectral Bias Resolution

We conducted a systematic ablation study to isolate the contribution of each core component. Quantitative results are summarized in Table 2, revealing a critical "Performance Inversion" between Variants (c) and (d). Visual evidence in Fig. 4 corroborates the findings.

Table 2. Architectural ablation study and component-wise performance analysis.

Method	Backbone	Align.	Ent-Reg.	Dice Score (DSC) ↑	MSE ↓	Vol. Error ↓
SHINE (Proposed)	SIREN	✓	✓	0.93	4.0×10^{-5}	3.1%
(a) w/o Entropy-Reg	SIREN	✓	×	0.92	1.9×10^{-3}	1.4%
(b) w/o Alignment	SIREN	×	✓	0.89	0.6×10^{-3}	2.6%
(c) w/o SIREN	ReLU+PE	✓	✓	0.74	0.6×10^{-3}	14.0%
(d) Naive Baseline	ReLU+PE	×	×	0.86	4.6×10^{-3}	5.4%
(e) Vanilla INR	SIREN	×	×	0.91	2.0×10^{-3}	15.2%

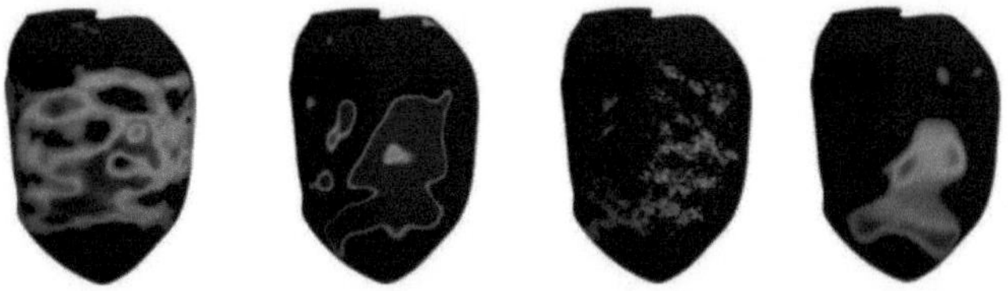

(A) w/o Ent-Reg (B) w/o Align (C) w/o SIREN (D) SHINE

Fig. 4. Qualitative analysis of ablation variants. Removing entropy regularization, alignment, or SIREN introduces hallucinations, geometric distortion, or spectral-bias-induced blurring, respectively.

Architectural Synergy and Spectral Bias. The results substantiate that the SIREN backbone is the most critical architectural element. Comparing Vanilla INR (0.91) with the Naive Baseline (0.86) reveals a significant performance leap provided by sinusoidal activations. Interestingly, replacing SIREN with a ReLU+PE MLP (Variant c) [8] leads to a substantial collapse in DSC to 0.74, which is notably lower than the Naive Baseline. This performance inversion between (c) and (d) identifies a conflict where low-capacity ReLU kernels struggle to satisfy strict manifold constraints, indicating that SIREN provides a critical inductive bias for this task. Furthermore, the excessive Volumetric Error in Variant (e) (15.2%) substantiates the critical role of entropy-guided regularization. Without this adaptive mechanism, the neural field is prone to non-physical oscillations and "hallucinations" in unobserved regions.

3.3 Clinical Safety Maps and Computational Efficiency

Beyond numerical accuracy, SHINE provides essential uncertainty-aware clinical safety maps (Fig. 5). High entropy alerts clinicians to unobserved inter-slice gaps, while low entropy correlates with verified LGE findings. Regarding computational complexity, the patient-specific manifold fitting requires approximately 7.5 min per case. Crucially, this is strictly a pre-operative process, which seam-

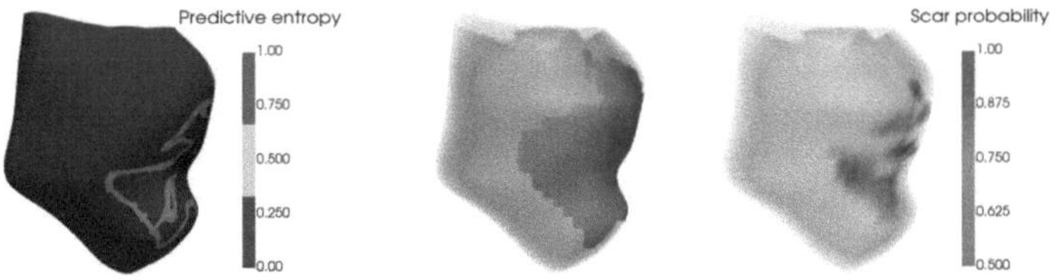

(A) Predictive Uncertainty (B) Blind Zones (C) Clinical Safety Map

Fig. 5. Uncertainty-aware clinical safety maps. High-entropy regions indicate unobserved inter-slice gaps, whereas low-entropy regions correspond to verified LGE findings.

lessly enables highly efficient, real-time intraoperative inference taking only 0.54 s per patient on an NVIDIA RTX 4090 GPU.

4 Conclusion

This paper introduced SHINE, an entropy-guided Bayesian neural field for 3D myocardial scar reconstruction from sparse clinical CMR. By learning a continuous scar probability function on patient-specific anatomical manifolds, SHINE mitigates discretization artifacts and spectral bias while quantifying epistemic uncertainty. In a 40-patient VT cohort evaluated with leave-one-slice-out validation, SHINE achieved a DSC of 0.93, a volumetric error of 3.1%, and real-time inference in 0.54 s per case. Future work will validate the framework on a multi-center cohort of over 500 cases across three institutions [20].

Acknowledgments. This study is supported by the National Health Innovation Centre (NHIC-I2D-2502365), the National Medical Research Council Open Fund Individual Research Grant (MOH-001903-01), the SingHealth Duke-NUS AMC–A*STAR Healthcare Translation Partnership (07 FY2023 HTP P2 15-A2), and the SingHealth Duke-NUS Academic Medicine Research Grants AM/TP098/2025 and AM/TP032/2020. L. Zhong is supported by the National Medical Research Council Clinician Innovator Award (MOH-001647-00).

Disclosure of Interests. The authors have no competing interests to declare that are relevant to the content of this article.

References

1. Lusted, L.B.: Medical electronics. New Engl. J. Med. **252**(14), 580–585 (1955)
2. Giger, M.L., Chan, H.P., Boone, J.: Anniversary paper: history and status of CAD and quantitative image analysis: the role of medical physics and AAPM. Med. Phys. **35**(11), 5799–5820 (2008)
3. Perez-David, E., Arenal, A., Rubio-Guivernau, J.L., et al.: Noninvasive identification of ventricular tachycardia-related conducting channels using contrast-enhanced magnetic resonance imaging in patients with chronic myocardial infarction. J. Am. Coll. Cardiol. **57**(2), 184–194 (2011)
4. Lustig, M., Donoho, D., Pauly, J.M.: Sparse MRI: The application of compressed sensing for rapid MR imaging. Magn. Reson. Med. **58**(6), 1182–1195 (2007)
5. Ukwatta, E.: Image-based reconstruction of three-dimensional myocardial infarct geometry for patient-specific modeling of cardiac electrophysiology. Med. Phys. **42**(8), 4579–4590 (2015)
6. Sen, A., Rohrer, U., Bhagirath, P., et al.: Weakly supervised learning for scar reconstruction in personalized cardiac models: integrating 2D MRI to 3D anatomical models. Comput. Biol. Med. **198**, 111219 (2025)
7. Schlemper, J., Caballero, J., Hajnal, J.V., et al.: A deep cascade of convolutional neural networks for dynamic MR image reconstruction. IEEE Trans. Med. Imaging **37**(2), 491–503 (2018)

8. Rahaman, N., Baratin, A., Arpit, D.: On the spectral bias of neural networks. In: Proceedings of the ICML, vol. 97, pp. 5301–5310 (2019)
9. Mildenhall, B., Srinivasan, P.P., Tancik, M.: NeRF: Representing scenes as neural radiance fields for view synthesis. In: Proceedings of the ECCV, pp. 405–421 (2020)
10. Zhu, Y., Liu, Y., Zhang, Y., Liang, D.: Implicit neural representation for medical image reconstruction. Phys. Med. Biol. **70**(12) (2025)
11. Shen, C., Zhu, H., Zhou, Y., et al.: Continuous 3D myocardial motion tracking via echocardiography. IEEE Trans. Med. Imaging **43**(12), 4236–4252 (2024)
12. Corral-Acero, J., Mezger, F., Jagoda, P., et al.: The 'digital twin' to enable the vision of precision cardiology. Eur. Heart J. **41**(48), 4556–4564 (2020)
13. Leng, S., Guo, J., Alabed, S., et al.: Digital twin model predicts prognosis in pulmonary arterial hypertension. JACC Cardiovasc. Imaging **19**(4), 565–567 (2026)
14. Raissi, M., Perdikaris, P., Karniadakis, G.E.: Physics-informed neural networks: a deep learning framework for solving forward and inverse problems involving nonlinear partial differential equations. J. Comput. Phys. **378**, 686–707 (2019)
15. Sitzmann, V., Martel, J., Bergman, A.: Implicit neural representations with periodic activation functions. In: Proceedings of the NeurIPS, vol. 33, pp. 7462–7473 (2020)
16. Gal, Y., Ghahramani, Z.: Dropout as a Bayesian approximation: representing model uncertainty in deep learning. In: Proceedings of the ICML, pp. 1050–1059 (2016)
17. Isensee, F., Jaeger, P.F., Kohl, S.A.A., et al.: nnU-Net: a self-configuring method for deep learning-based biomedical image segmentation. Nat. Methods **18**(2), 203–211 (2021)
18. Mauger, C.A., Gilbert, K., Lee, A.M., et al.: Right ventricular shape and function: cardiovascular magnetic resonance reference morphology and biventricular risk factor morphometrics in UK Biobank. J. Cardiovasc. Magn. Reson. **21**, 41 (2019)
19. Sun, A., Chen, X., Wan, X., et al.: Deep learning reconstruction enhanced myocardial scar detection on late gadolinium enhancement MRI in patients with ventricular arrhythmias. Meta-Radiol. **4**(2), 100204 (2026)
20. Yang, P., Leng, S., Zong, D., et al.: Prognostic value of end-to-end deep learning assessment of myocardial scar and microvascular obstruction on late gadolinium enhancement cardiovascular magnetic resonance. J. Cardiovasc. Magn. Reson. **28**(1), 102712 (2026)
21. Li, L., Camps, J., Wang, Z.J., et al.: Toward enabling cardiac digital twins of myocardial infarction using deep computational models for inverse inference. IEEE Trans. Med. Imaging **43**(7), 2466–2478 (2024)
22. Zou, R.: ScarElastic: continuous elasticity field modeling for myocardial scar delineation in LGE-CMR. NPJ Digit. Med. **9**(1), 3 (2025)

SMART-KNEE: Sparse-Morphology Based Anatomical Reconstruction Using Topology-Aware Networks for Imageless Total Knee Arthroplasty

Durga Rajasekar[1,2], S. Swetha Lakshmi[1,2], M. R. Vishnu[2], Vivek Maik[2](✉), Manojkumar Lakshmanan[2], and Mohanasankar Sivaprakasam[1]

[1] Department of Electrical Engineering, Indian Institute of Technology Madras, Chennai, India
mohan@ee.iitm.ac.in

[2] Healthcare Technology Innovation Centre (HTIC), IIT Madras, Chennai, India
maik.vivek@htic.iitm.ac.in

Abstract. Imageless Total Knee Arthroplasty (ITKA) requires real-time acquisition of patient-specific anatomical landmarks without preoperative CT or MRI, posing a significant challenge for intraoperative planning. Despite utilising 3D knee reconstruction algorithms, modern ITKA systems continue to struggle with accurate knee shape estimation and the anatomical axis alignment - both prerequisites for reliable ITKA planning. We present SMART-KNEE, a cascaded anatomy-aware reconstruction framework that generates patient-specific Femoral (F) and Tibial(T) bone morphology from a minimal set of intraoperatively collected anatomical landmarks, without preoperative imaging. In the first stage, a Topology-Aware Equivariant Graph Neural Network (EGNN) predicts the complete anatomical landmark set from four intraoperative anchor landmarks, enforcing topological consistency and anatomical plausibility under E(3)-equivariance (invariance to 3D euclidean transformations). In the second stage, an Anatomy-Aware GAN reconstructs complete patient-specific bone surfaces by fusing the EGNN-predicted landmarks with partial intraoperative surface point clouds. SMART-KNEE achieves precise landmark localization error (F: 2.28 mm ± 1.68 mm; T: 1.65 mm ± 0.83 mm). Test cohort surface reconstruction yields Dice F-87%, T-92.477%, Hausdorff Distance F-5, T-4.3 mm and ground truth - generated knee distances of 1.89 mm (F) and 2.87 mm (T), enabling accurate patient-specific morphology retrieval for intraoperative ITKA planning.Git-Hub

Keywords: Imageless total knee arthroplasty · Topology-aware EGNN · Anatomy-aware GAN · landmark prediction · patient-specific bone reconstruction · intraoperative navigation

---

D. Rajasekar and S. Lakshmi S—Equal contribution.

Supplementary Information The online version contains supplementary material available at https://doi.org/10.1007/978-3-032-38236-8_46.

G. Yang et al. (Eds.): MICCAI 2026, LNCS 16893, pp. 479–488, 2027.
https://doi.org/10.1007/978-3-032-38236-8_46

1 Introduction

ITKA achieves accurate implant positioning while reducing radiation exposure and cost compared to image-based and conventional systems [12,14,17]. It relies on real-time intraoperative data from an optical tracking system, where reference markers on the femur (F) and tibia (T) digitize anatomical landmarks in 3D via a calibrated probe [5], from which a patient-specific knee model is reconstructed to support surgical planning [2,3]. However, sparse landmark-based reconstruction relies on shape assumptions and parametric models [7], often causing inaccurate anatomical axis reconstruction, suboptimal implant sizing, and soft-tissue imbalance [3,4], thereby undermining ITKA relative to imaging-based TKA [10].

Related Works: 3D reconstruction of patient-specific bone morphology from sparse data remains a core challenge in computational orthopaedics. Reconstructing the complete F surface and mechanical axis from sparse landmarks via a Statistical Shape Model (SSM) [8], achieving mechanical axis deviation below 3.5°; however, the fixed low-dimensional shape space limits patient-specific detail. Extended this by morphing SSMs from digitised landmarks for both F and T [13], outperforming linear scaling yet remaining bound to statistical priors. [1] formulated a probabilistic SSM as a Gaussian Mixture Model for surface reconstruction from sparse point clouds, improving robustness, but unable to recover morphological detail beyond the encoded prior. Generative methods using globallocal context discriminators have improved region-of-interest fidelity in medical reconstruction [11], motivating context-aware anatomical conditioning. In parallel, E(3)-equivariant graph neural networks have demonstrated substantially improved performance over standard GNNs for 3D biological structure tasks by preserving geometric consistency under arbitrary rotations and translations [15,16]. Existing methods remain constrained by population subspaces and preoperative imaging, leaving a clear gap for a unified imageless framework capable of joint landmark completion and full knee surface reconstruction from sparse intraoperative data.

Contributions: We present SMART-KNEE, a framework combining a Topology-Aware EGNN and an Anatomy-Aware GAN [9] to reconstruct patient-specific F and T morphology from sparse intraoperative data, achieving clinically acceptable accuracy within 3 mm [19]. We further release a publicly available dataset of 361 annotated F and T models with anatomical landmarks and critical distal and proximal surface regions.

2 Methodology

Dataset: The dataset comprises patient-specific F and T bone models from a publicly available repository [6], each annotated with 12 F and 11 T landmarks (Table 1), of which 4 anchors per bone serve as known intraoperative inputs, and the remainder are predicted by the EGNN. Beyond the joint-line ROI, the predicted landmark set includes the hip centre (FHC) and ankle centre (AC),

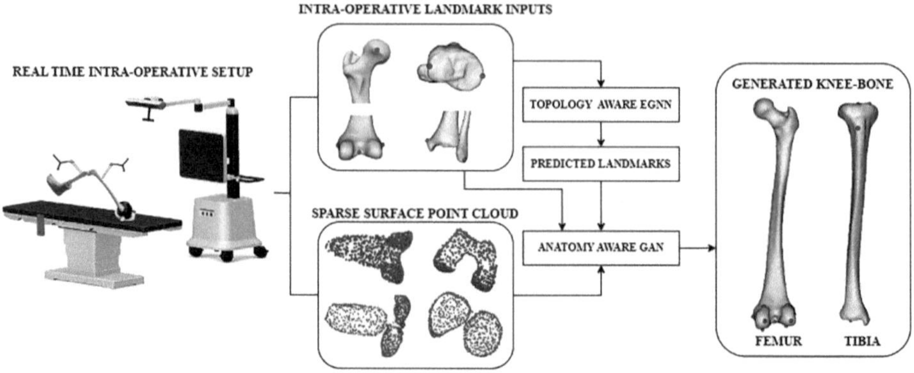

Fig. 1. SMART-KNEE framework: Intraoperative anchor landmarks are processed by the Topology-Aware EGNN to complete the landmark set, which the Anatomy-Aware GAN fuses with the partial point cloud to reconstruct complete patient-specific F and T bone surfaces for ITKA planning.

Table 1. Anatomical landmarks annotated per bone in the SMART-KNEE dataset.(F – Femur, T – Tibia, Med. – Medial, Lat. – Lateral, Ant. – Anterior, Post. – Posterior, Cond. – Condyle, Prox. – Proximal, Lig. – Ligament.)

Femur		
ID	**Acro.**	**Landmark**
0	FHC	Hip Center
1	FKC	Knee Center
2	FME	Medial Epicondyle
3	FLE	Lateral Epicondyle
4	FMDC	Medial Distal Condyle
5	FLDC	Lateral Distal Condyle
6	FMPC	Medial Post. Condyle
7	FLPC	Lateral Post. Condyle
8	FMAC	Medial Ant. Cortex
9	FLAC	Lateral Ant. Cortex
10	FMCPP	Med. Cond. Prox. Post.
11	FLCPP	Lat. Cond. Prox. Post.

Tibia		
ID	**Acro.**	**Landmark**
0	TKC	Knee Center
1	TMP	Medial Plateau
2	TLP	Lateral Plateau
3	TMC	Medial Condyle
4	TLC	Lateral Condyle
5	TT	Tuberosity
6	TPCL	Post. Cruciate Lig.
7	TACL	Ant. Cruciate Lig.
8	MM	Medial Malleolus
9	LM	Lateral Malleolus
10	AC	Ankle Center

enabling mechanical-axis alignment computation, a core requirement for TKA planning. Sparse point clouds sampled from the F anterior cortex, distal and posterior condyles, and proximal T plateaus and tuberosity simulate intraoperative probe acquisition, and together with the predicted landmarks from the two conditioning inputs to the Anatomy-Aware GAN (Fig. 1).

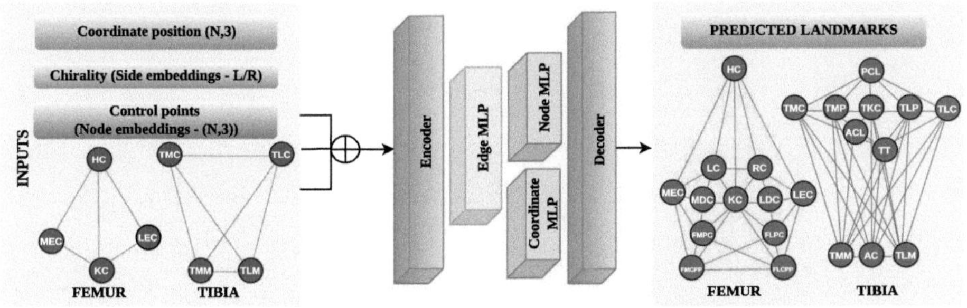

Fig. 2. Topology-Aware EGNN for intraoperative landmark prediction, mapping sparse known anchor nodes (red) from F and T graphs to a complete set of predicted anatomical landmarks (green) via equivariant message passing over geometric and chirality-conditioned node embeddings. (Color figure online)

Algorithm 1. Topology-Aware EGNN for Landmark Completion

Require: $A_{m \times n}$ (Initial Positions), b_m (Target Positions), $\bar{n}_p$ (Mean Shape Template), $\mathcal{E}$ (Graph Edges), $w_{\text{position}}, w_{\text{edge}}$ (Loss Weights)
Ensure: Predicted coordinates n_i^{final}, nodes weights x_w
  Initialisation: $n_i^{(0)} \leftarrow s^* R^* \bar{n}_p + t^*$ via Kabsch–Umeyama
  Node Encoding: $h_i^{(0)} \leftarrow \text{MLP}_{\text{enc}}(e_{\text{side}} \oplus e_{\text{known}} \oplus n_i^{(0)} \oplus g_i)$
  for $l = 0$ to $L - 1$ **do**
    $m_{ij}^{(l)} = \text{MLP}_{\text{edge}}(h_i^{(l)}, h_j^{(l)}, \|n_i^{(l)} - n_j^{(l)}\|^2)$
    $h_i^{(l+1)} = \text{MLP}_{\text{node}}(h_i^{(l)}, \sum m_{ij}^{(l)})$
  end for
  Decoding: $n_i^{\text{final}} \leftarrow n_i^{(0)} + \text{clip}(\text{MLP}_{\text{dec}}(h_i^{(L)}), -0.5, 0.5) + \bar{c}_k$
  Loss: $\mathcal{L} = w_{\text{pos}} \sum \|n_i^{\text{final}} - n_i^{\text{target}}\|_1 + w_{\text{edge}} \sum \big| \|n_i^{\text{final}} - n_j^{\text{final}}\|_2 - d_{ij}^{\text{target}} \big|$
  if $A_{ij} x_w = b_{j_{\min}}$ **then** $x_w \leftarrow I$
  else $x_w \leftarrow (A_{ij}^T A_{ij})^{-1} A_{ij}^T b_{j_{\min}}$
  end if

Topology-Aware EGNN-Based Landmark Completion: Knee anatomy is modelled as a graph where landmarks are nodes and spatial interactions are edges, partitioned into $K = 4$ known anchors and $|\mathcal{U}| = N - K$ unknown targets-8 F and 7 T. The Kabsch–Umeyama transform aligns the mean canonical shape to the known anchors, providing anatomically plausible initial coordinates [18]. Each node encodes its known/unknown status, knee chirality, and geometric descriptors; over $L = 4$ equivariant message-passing layers, landmarks iteratively refine both feature states and 3D positions via learnt gated aggregation. A decoder MLP then applies a clipped coordinate correction, denormalized to millimeter space. Training minimises a composite loss penalising positional error, inter-landmark distance deviation, and ensuring anatomical fidelity across all predicted landmarks (Fig. 2) (Algorithm 1).

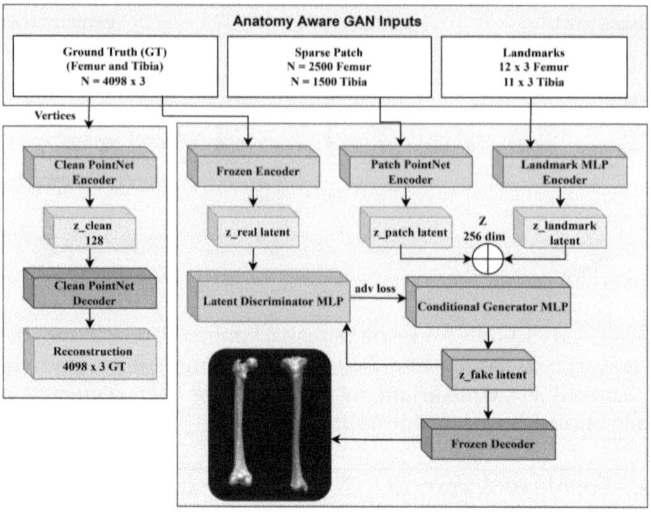

Fig. 3. Anatomy-Aware GAN architecture for patient-specific knee (F&T) surface reconstruction.

Algorithm 2. Anatomy-Aware GAN for 3D Bone Surface Reconstruction

---

Require: P (partial surface), S (complete bone), L (landmarks), $d = 128$, $N = 4096$
Ensure: Watertight mesh $\mathcal{M}$

Phase 1: $z_{\text{clean}} \leftarrow \text{PointNetEnc}(S)$; $\hat{S} \leftarrow \text{PointNetDec}(z_{\text{clean}})$; freeze weights after minimising:

$$\mathcal{L}_{\text{CD}}(S, \hat{S}) = \frac{1}{|S|} \sum_{x \in S} \min_{y \in \hat{S}} \|x - y\|_2 + \frac{1}{|\hat{S}|} \sum_{y \in \hat{S}} \min_{x \in S} \|x - y\|_2$$

Phase 2: $z_{\text{gen}} \leftarrow \text{Gen}([\text{PatchEnc}(P) \| \text{LmkEnc}(L)])$; $\hat{S}_{\text{gen}} \leftarrow \text{FrozenDec}(z_{\text{gen}})$

$$\mathcal{L}_D = \tfrac{1}{2}\mathbb{E}[(D(z_{\text{clean}}) - 1)^2] + \tfrac{1}{2}\mathbb{E}[(D(z_{\text{gen}}))^2]$$

$$\mathcal{L}_{\text{Total}} = \alpha \, \mathcal{L}_{G_{\text{adv}}} + \beta \max_{p \in P} \min_{q \in \hat{S}_{\text{gen}}} \|p - q\|_2 + \gamma \frac{1}{N_L} \sum_{l \in L} \min_{q \in \hat{S}_{\text{gen}}} \|l - q\|_2^2$$

Phase 3: $\hat{S}_{\text{patient}} \leftarrow (\hat{S}_{\text{gen}} \cdot \mathbf{V}^\top) \cdot \text{scale} + \text{centroid}$; Poisson $\rightarrow \mathcal{M}$
if left-sided **then** $\hat{S}_{\text{patient}} \leftarrow \hat{S}_{\text{patient}} \cdot \text{diag}(-1, 1, 1)$
end if

Anatomy-Aware GAN-Based Bone Surface Reconstruction: The framework reconstructs complete 3D knee surfaces from partial intraoperative point clouds conditioned on EGNN-predicted landmarks, trained in two phases: autoencoder training followed by conditional adversarial training (Algorithm 2).

A PointNet autoencoder is trained on complete knee surfaces to establish a structured latent geometry manifold (Fig. 3), optimised via the symmetric Chamfer Distance $\mathcal{L}_{\text{CD}}$. Once trained, all weights are frozen and reused in Phase 2. The generator encodes the patch encoder, and a landmark encoder captures local surface topology and patient-specific proportions, respectively. It fuses both into a single latent code z_{gen}, rendered into a complete point cloud by the Frozen Decoder, supervised jointly by adversarial realism $\mathcal{L}_{G_{\text{adv}}}$, patch surface coverage $\mathcal{L}_{\text{Patch}}$, and landmark fidelity $\mathcal{L}_{\text{Lmk}}$ losses.

The discriminator utilizes a lightweight MLP to discriminate in the latent space between the frozen encoder's ground-truth code z_{clean} and the generator's code z_{gen} under the LS-GAN objective, driving the generator onto the pretrained geometry manifold. At inference, the output point cloud is unscaled to millimeter space and converted to a watertight mesh via Poisson surface reconstruction.

3 Results and Discussion

The dataset of 361 annotated F and T pairs was divided into 70% training, 15% validation, and 15% testing, with stratified splits to ensure balanced representation of left- and right-sided bones. The 4 known anchor points for each bone were provided intraoperatively, whereas the remaining 8 unknown landmarks for the F and 7 for the T were predicted. Performance was assessed by measuring the per- node landmark Euclidean distance (mm) between predicted and ground-truth coordinates for all unknown nodes.

Table 2. Per-node landmark localisation error (mm, mean) comparing SMART-KNEE against VN-EGNN [16] and E(3) [15]. Nodes 0–3 (Femur) and 3, 4, 9, 10 (Tibia) are known anchors (error = 0).

Femur				Tibia			
ID	VN-EGNN	E(3)	Ours	ID	VN-EGNN	E(3)	Ours
0	0.00	0.00	0.00	0	8.37	12.72	**2.01**
1	0.00	0.00	0.00	1	8.00	12.29	**1.15**
2	0.00	0.00	0.00	2	8.37	12.47	**1.62**
3	0.00	0.00	0.00	3	0.00	0.00	0.00
4	6.88	9.29	**2.90**	4	0.00	0.00	0.00
5	5.71	9.05	**2.71**	5	6.08	10.16	**1.75**
6	7.60	8.36	**3.06**	6	7.40	11.94	**1.29**
7	7.20	8.45	**2.69**	7	8.37	12.84	**0.45**
8	8.05	7.84	**2.41**	8	8.08	12.39	**3.58**
9	9.71	7.94	**2.76**	9	0.00	0.00	0.00
10	7.22	6.18	**1.61**	10	0.00	0.00	0.00
11	6.75	6.17	**1.45**				
Mean	7.50	7.91	**1.25**	**Mean**	7.81	12.12	**1.69**

The EGNN achieved a mean localisation error of 2.28 ± 1.68 mm for the F and 1.65 ± 0.83 mm for the T. The T yields lower localisation error due to its compact and symmetric proximal geometry, which imposes tighter geometric constraints during equivariant message passing. By contrast, the F's posterior condyle and anterior cortical markers (FMCPP, FLCPP, FMAC, FLAC) lie farther from the four anchor nodes and exhibit greater inter-patient morphological variability. Condylar and plateaus landmarks (FMDC, FLDC, TMP, TLP) consistently achieved errors below 1.5 mm, while proximal-posterior cortex landmarks relied more heavily on global geometric context propagated through the four message-passing layers, with worst-case predictions approaching 3–4 mm.
The flagged anchor geometric diversity drives localisation accuracy: clustering anchors distally (e.g., {3,4,5,6}) yields F errors up to 10.00 mm, while optimal configurations {0,1,2,3} and {3,4,9,10} achieve 2.28 ± 1.68 mm and 1.65 ± 0.83 mm for F and T respectively (4.4× and 4.7× improvements), both within the 3 mm ITKA threshold [19]As shown in Table 2, SMART-KNEE outperforms VN-EGNN [16] and EquiPPIS [15] by up to 6× on F(1.25 ± 0.75 mm vs. 7.50 mm and 7.91 mm) and T(1.69 ± 0.09 mm vs. 7.81 mm and 12.12 mm), with the greatest gains at geometrically remote nodes where topology-aware equivariant message passing most effectively propagates anchor constraints.
The Anatomy-Aware GAN was evaluated on the 39 held-out test subjects by measuring surface reconstruction quality across four standard volumetric and geometric metrics, as illustrated in Fig. 4.

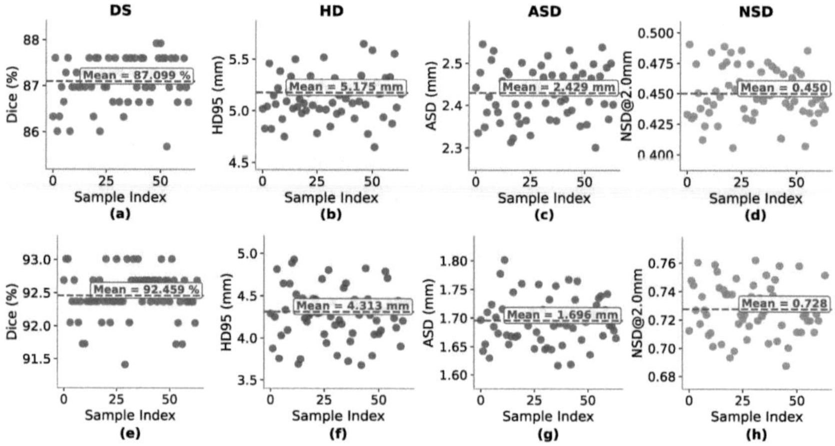

Fig. 4. Assessment of test set using (a,e) Dice Score, (b,f) HD, (c,g) ASD and (d,h) NSD for F (a,b,c,d) and T (e,f,g,h)

The reconstructed bone surfaces achieved a mean Dice score (DS) of F-87%, T-92.477%, Hausdorff Distance (HD95) of F-5.1, T-4.3 mm, Average Surface Distance (ASD) of F-2.4, T-1.6 mm, Normal Surface Distance (NSD) of F-0.45, T-0.7 at a 2.0 mm tolerance, confirming strong volumetric overlap and clinically

acceptable surface proximity to ground truth [19]. Per-bone surface distances ground truth to the generated Knee of 2.87 mm for the T and 1.97 mm for the F. reflect the greater morphological complexity of the distal F, particularly the posterior condylar regions, where sparse intraoperative point cloud coverage requires the generator to extrapolate beyond directly sampled geometry.
Maintaining consistent reconstruction quality across diverse morphologies required a dual-conditioning architecture that combined local surface topology from the Patch Encoder with patient-specific anatomical proportions from the Landmark Encoder. Wider articular higher HD95 values, indicating that reconstruction quality is limited by intraoperative surface acquisition, not generative architecture. The Anatomy-Aware GAN delivers patient-specific bone morphology with adequate geometric fidelity for intraoperative implant planning without preoperative CT or MRI, as the mean ASD of 1.694 mm falls within the accuracy criterion for ITKA [19].

Clinical Evaluation. To validate the end-to-end SMART-KNEE pipeline under realistic intraoperative conditions, a clinical evaluation was conducted on a held-out set of subjects. As illustrated in Fig. 5, the integrated system achieved a Landmark RMSE of 0.25 mm and 0.36 mm for the F and T, respectively, confirming that the predicted landmarks align closely with ground-truth positions after registration. The GAN-reconstructed bone surfaces yielded Surface Distances of 0.38 mm (F) and 0.26 mm (T) against the ground-truth CT-derived meshes, demonstrating that the reconstructed morphology faithfully captures true bone geometry.Both metrics fall substantially within the 3 mm ITKA accuracy threshold [19], confirming that the full landmark prediction and surface reconstruction pipeline meets clinical accuracy requirements without preoperative imaging.

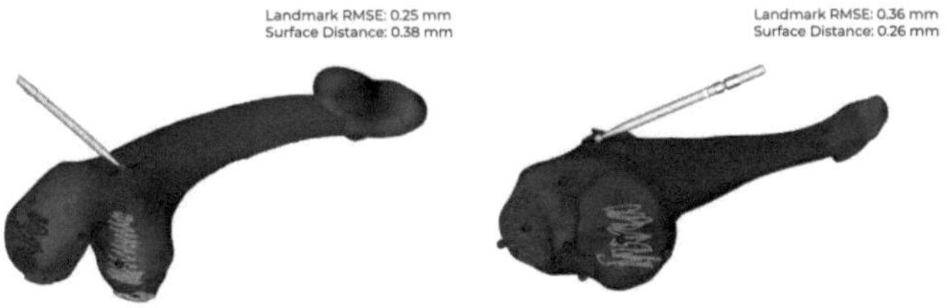

Fig. 5. SMART-KNEE clinical evaluation on a physical phantom: F (left) and T (right) showing predicted landmarks (blue) and acquired surface point clouds (coloured regions) with registration errors. (Color figure online)

4 Conclusion

SMART-KNEE presents a two-stage cascaded framework for knee reconstruction in ITKA. A Topology-Aware EGNN first completes the full anatomical landmark set from four sparse intraoperative anchors, where graph-centrality-based anchor selection proves critical to localisation accuracy. An Anatomy-Aware GAN then fuses the predicted landmarks with a sparse surface point cloud to reconstruct complete, patient-specific F and T morphology. All surface errors fall below the clinical threshold for ITKA on both the held-out test cohort and a 3D-printed, CT-derived phantom under optical tracking, demonstrating that the pipeline achieves the geometric accuracy required for imageless implant planning and sizing. These phantom-based results motivate extending validation to cadaveric specimens and real intraoperative, patient-specific TKA settings in future work.

Disclosure of Interests. The authors have no competing interests to declare that are relevant to the content of this article.

References

1. Bernard, F., et al.: Shape-aware surface reconstruction from sparse 3d point-clouds. Med. Image Anal. **38**, 77–89 (May 2017). https://doi.org/10.1016/j.media.2017.02.005
2. Bollars, P., et al.: Imageless handheld robotic-assisted total knee arthroplasty showed better clinical outcomes than conventional total knee arthroplasty: A randomized controlled trial with preliminary results at 1-year follow up. The Knee **56**, 232–240 (Oct 2025). https://doi.org/10.1016/j.knee.2025.05.028
3. Bosco, F., et al.: Accuracy and learning curve of imageless robotic-assisted total knee arthroplasty. J. Orthop. **66**, 77–83 (2025). https://doi.org/10.1016/j.jor.2024.12.029
4. Cochrane, N.H., et al.: Revision total knee arthroplasty with an imageless, second-generation robotic system. J. Arthroplasty **39**(8), S280–S284 (Aug 2024). https://doi.org/10.1016/j.arth.2024.02.018
5. Edelstein, A.I., Orsi, A.D., Plaskos, C., Coffey, S., Suleiman, L.I.: Imageless robotic total knee arthroplasty determines similar coronal plane alignment of the knee (cpak) parameters to long leg radiographs. Arthroplasty **6**(1), (2024). https://doi.org/10.1186/s42836-024-00231-9
6. Fischer, M.C.M.: Database of segmentations and surface models of bones of the entire lower body created from cadaver CT scans. Scientific Data **10**(1), (2023). https://doi.org/10.1038/s41597-023-02669-z
7. Hirschmann, M.T., Avram, G., Graichen, H., Tandogan, R.N., Mengis, N., Zaffagnini, S.: Same same but different-image-based versus imageless robotic-assisted total knee arthroplasty. J. Experimental Orthopaedics **11**(4) (2024). https://doi.org/10.1002/jeo2.70062
8. Kompella, G., et al.: Segmentation of femoral cartilage from knee ultrasound images using mask R-CNN. In: 2019 41st Annual International Conference of the IEEE Engineering in Medicine and Biology Society (EMBC). IEEE (July 2019). https://doi.org/10.1109/embc.2019.8857645
9. Lambrechts, A., Wirix-Speetjens, R., Maes, F., Van Huffel, S.: Artificial intelligence based patient-specific preoperative planning algorithm for total knee arthroplasty. Front. Robot. AI **9** (Mar 2022).https://doi.org/10.3389/frobt.2022.840282

10. Li, S., Liu, X., Chen, X., Xu, H., Zhang, Y., Qian, W.: Development and validation of an artificial intelligence preoperative planning and patient-specific instrumentation system for total knee arthroplasty. Bioengineering **10**(12), 1417 (Dec 2023). https://doi.org/10.3390/bioengineering10121417
11. Murugesan, B., Vijaya Raghavan, S., Sarveswaran, K., Ram, K., Sivaprakasam, M.: Recon-GLGAN: a global-local context based generative adversarial network for MRI reconstruction. In: Knoll, F., Maier, A., Rueckert, D., Ye, J.C. (eds.) MLMIR 2019. LNCS, vol. 11905, pp. 3–15. Springer, Cham (2019). https://doi.org/10.1007/978-3-030-33843-5_1
12. Narkbunnam, R., Chorunchan, Y., Chareancholvanich, K., Achawakulthep, C., Awirotananon, K., Pornrattanamaneewong, C.: Imageless and imagebased roboticassisted total knee arthroplasty achieve equivalent radiographic accuracy: A randomised controlled trial. Knee Surgery, Sports Traumatology, Arthroscopy (Oct 2025). https://doi.org/10.1002/ksa.70123
13. Nolte, D., Ko, S.T., Bull, A.M., Kedgley, A.E.: Reconstruction of the lower limb bones from digitised anatomical landmarks using statistical shape modelling. Gait & Posture **77**, 269–275 (Mar 2020). https://doi.org/10.1016/j.gaitpost.2020.02.010
14. Rajasekaran, S., et al.: Comparison of imageless robotic assisted total knee arthroplasty and conventional total knee arthroplasty: early clinical and radiological outcomes of 200 knees. J. Robot. Surg. **18**(1) (Apr 2024). https://doi.org/10.1007/s11701-024-01905-x
15. Roche, R., Moussad, B., Shuvo, M.H., Bhattacharya, D.: E(3) equivariant graph neural networks for robust and accurate protein-protein interaction site prediction. PLOS Comput. Biol. **19**(8), e1011435 (Aug 2023). https://doi.org/10.1371/journal.pcbi.1011435
16. Sestak, F., Schneckenreiter, L., Brandstetter, J., Hochreiter, S., Mayr, A., Klambauer, G.: Vn-egnn: E(3)-equivariant graph neural networks with virtual nodes enhance protein binding site identification (2024). https://doi.org/10.48550/ARXIV.2404.07194
17. Tran, J.Y.S., et al.: Handheld imageless robotic total knee arthroplasty improves accuracy and early clinical outcomes when compared with navigation. Arthroplasty **7**(1) (Apr 2025). https://doi.org/10.1186/s42836-025-00303-4
18. Umeyama, S.: Least-squares estimation of transformation parameters between two point patterns. IEEE Trans. Pattern Anal. Mach. Intell. **13**(4), 376–380 (1991). https://doi.org/10.1109/34.88573
19. Wakelin, E.A., et al.: Accurate determination of post-operative 3D component positioning in total knee arthroplasty: the aurora protocol. J. Orthopaedic Surg. Res. **13**(1) (Oct 2018).https://doi.org/10.1186/s13018-018-0957-0

SurfMark3D: Surface-Based Graph Convolution Framework for Distal Femoral Landmark Localisation in Total Knee Arthroplasty

B. Dharshan[1], Pranav Hyagreev[1], Vivek Maik[1(✉)], Suhail Ansari T. A.[1], Manojkumar Lakshmanan[1], and Mohanasankar Sivaprakasam[2]

[1] Healthcare Technology Innovation Centre, IIT Madras, Chennai, India
maik.vivek@htic.iitm.ac.in
[2] Indian Institute of Technology (IIT) Madras, Chennai, India

Abstract. Accurate localisation of anatomical landmarks on distal femur is a critical prerequisite for surgical planning in image-based Total Knee Arthroplasty (TKA). Manual annotation is time-consuming and prone to variability, which can lead to inconsistent implant sizing. Existing classical and deep learning methods remain limited by latency, computational cost, and modality dependence. To address these issues, we operate on segmented 3D surface point clouds and formulate distal femoral landmark localisation as a heatmap regression task that predicts dense probability fields. Ground-truth heatmaps are constructed as Euclidean Gaussians on the femoral surface using learnable landmark-specific sigmas. We introduce a hybrid graph-convolution backbone that combines Low-Rank Adaptive Graph Convolution (LR-AGConv) for local feature extraction and Bi-level Routing Point Attention (BRPA) for efficient global semantic modelling. The network is trained using Adaptive Wing (AWing) loss and PointSTAR, a novel point-cloud adaptation of Self-adaptive Ambiguity Reduction (STAR) loss, with uncertainty-based multi-task weighting. We curate and release a clinically validated dataset of 550 distal femurs derived from the ShapeMed Knee study with expert landmark annotations. Experimental results demonstrate that the proposed method consistently outperforms state-of-the-art baselines, achieving a Mean Euclidean Error (MEE) of 1.24 ± 0.84 mm across all 11 anatomical landmarks. Code and dataset are available at https://github.com/IGRS-Imaging/SurfMark3D.

Keywords: Total Knee Arthroplasty · Landmark Localisation · Graph Convolution

B. Dharshan, P. Hyagreev—Equal contribution.

Supplementary Information The online version contains supplementary material available at https://doi.org/10.1007/978-3-032-38236-8_47.

G. Yang et al. (Eds.): MICCAI 2026, LNCS 16893, pp. 489–499, 2027.
https://doi.org/10.1007/978-3-032-38236-8_47

1 Introduction

TKA success relies on accurate implant placement governed by morphometric measurements of distal femur and proximal tibia landmarks [6]. Manual annotation is labor-intensive and suffers from high inter- and intra-observer variability. Classical automated approaches (e.g., statistical shape models, atlas-based registration [1,8]) report 2–6 mm errors but are sensitive to initialization and anatomical variance. Hybrid elastic template methods [5] improve accuracy at the cost of high latency. Recent volumetric [2] and multi-view 2D deep learning methods [15] reduce errors to 2–3 mm but remain computationally expensive and modality-dependent.

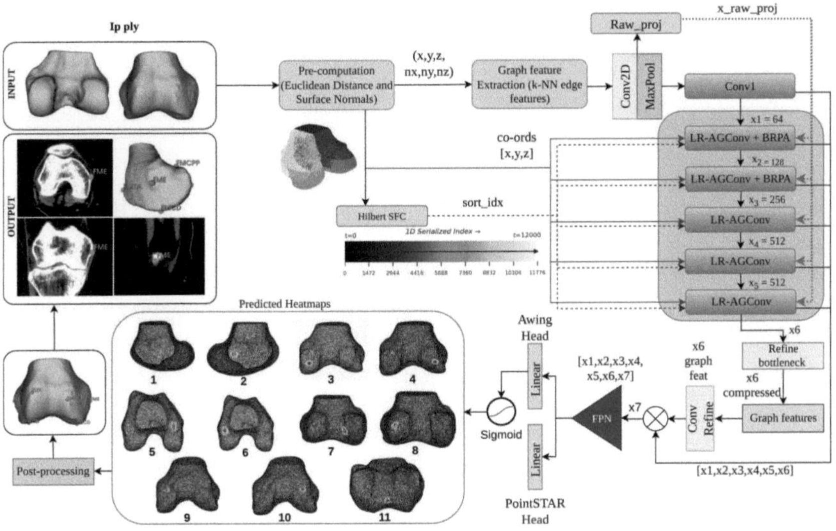

Fig. 1. Overall architecture of the proposed framework.

To be modality-agnostic, anatomical landmark localisation is increasingly performed directly on segmented 3D point clouds [10,20]. Earlier methods relied on coordinate regression for landmark localisation. However, predicting a single coordinate is noisy and discards structural context. Probabilistic heatmap regression better models spatial context but typically relies on fixed isotropic Gaussian spreads that fail to capture the inherent distinctiveness of individual landmarks [20]. Furthermore, standard regression losses do not explicitly handle semantic ambiguity caused by irregular annotations and localisation uncertainty [26]. For instance, landmarks like FLTA (Table 1) form a highly anisotropic distribution along the trochlear ridge rather than a tight, isotropic peak.

Extracting local features with convolutional kernels involves a strict performance efficiency trade-off. Many kernels [17,21,24] either lack the adaptivity required for complex bone geometries or rely on complex parameter-heavy kernel constructions. Attention mechanisms are increasingly used to capture global context in point clouds. However, standard self-attention incurs prohibitive quadratic memory costs [18] and even efficient variants [22,23] lack the selective regional filtering crucial for efficiently capturing long-range dependencies.

Table 1. Annotated distal femur landmarks. The prefix 'F' denotes 'Femoral'.

#	Abbr.	Name	#	Abbr.	Name
1	FME	Medial Epicondyle	7	FMTA	Medial Trochlea Anterior
2	FLE	Lateral Epicondyle	8	FLTA	Lateral Trochlea Anterior
3	FMCP	Medial Condyle Posterior	9	FMCPP	Medial Condyle Post. Prox.
4	FLCP	Lateral Condyle Posterior	10	FLCPP	Lateral Condyle Post. Prox.
5	FMCD	Medial Condyle Distal	11	Notch	Notch
6	FLCD	Lateral Condyle Distal			

We formulate our task as probabilistic surface heatmap regression with dynamic, learnable landmark-specific Gaussian sigmas [16]. We propose a hybrid architecture featuring Low-Rank Adaptive Graph Convolution (LR-AGConv) [25] for efficient local expressivity, complemented by Bi-Level Routing Point Attention (BRPA), a novel adaptation of Bi-Level Routing Attention [27] for point clouds to selectively route queries to informative regions (Fig. 1). The network is optimized via Adaptive Wing loss [19] and PointSTAR, a novel 3D reformulation of STAR Loss [26] that resolves semantic ambiguity arising from surface anisotropy. Although open benchmarks (e.g., Teeth3DS+) have accelerated landmark localisation in other anatomies, orthopedics remains bottlenecked by a lack of public data. To advance research, we release a clinically validated benchmark dataset for distal femur landmark localisation.

In summary, our main contributions are: **(1)** A modality agnostic framework operating on 3D point clouds with dynamic heatmap spreads to model landmark-specific uncertainty; **(2)** A highly efficient hybrid backbone comprising LR-AGConv and BRPA; **(3)** A dynamic loss objective integrating AWing and PointSTAR loss; and **(4)** The release of a robust clinical benchmark of 550 expert-annotated distal femur meshes for landmark localisation.

2 Methods

2.1 Dataset and Annotation

We establish a novel clinical benchmark using distal femur meshes from ShapeMed Knee [4] (Baseline OAI 3D DESS MRIs), which reports expert-level segmentation quality (femoral DSC 0.99, ASSD 0.08–0.15 mm). Our dataset features 11 surgeon-validated manually annotated landmarks. Note that while the landmark framework itself is modality-agnostic, the pipeline requires an upstream segmentation step to generate meshes, which remains modality-dependent. We filter the cohort to non-osteophytic subjects (KL ≤ 1), consistent with [2,5,8], as degenerative morphological changes substantially increase landmarking errors [8], making reliable annotation infeasible on advanced OA surfaces. To ensure robust generalization, meshes undergo randomized Laplacian smoothing (15–25 iterations) and subjects are stratified across OAI demographic metadata (age, sex, race, ethnicity, BMI).

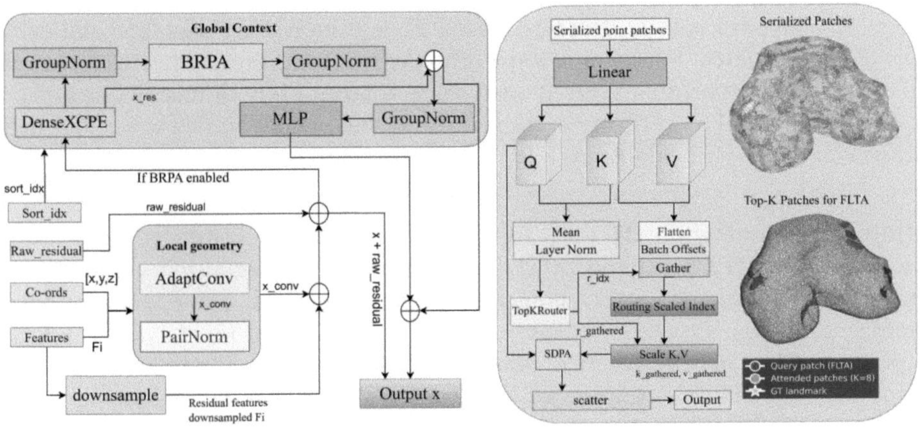

(a) Hybrid block (b) BRPA block

Fig. 2. Architectural components of the proposed framework.

2.2 Architecture

Input Representation. The distal femur is processed as a point cloud ($N = 12000$ via FPS) with 6D features (spatial coordinates and normals). To preserve spatial locality efficiently for the attention mechanism, the cloud is serialized into a 1D sequence via a Hilbert space-filling curve, while maintaining the topology of the point cloud [22].

Hybrid Backbone. Our 6-layer backbone maintains full spatial resolution N for vertex-level precision. Inspired by DeepGCN [11], we utilize dilated k-NN graphs, PairNorm and input residuals across all layers. The architecture (Fig. 1) operates in two phases: Stages 1–3 (Fig. 2a) combine LR-AGConv and BRPA (Fig. 2b) to jointly model local geometry and long-range semantics. Jointly leveraging global and local context has likewise proven effective in other medical imaging tasks [13]. Stages $4-6$ employ LR-AGConv only, isolating local surface details critical for precise localisation.

Low-Rank Adaptive Graph Convolution (LR-AGConv). To mitigate AGConv memory overhead, we propose a low-rank kernel decomposition. Input features of dimension C are compressed to $f'_i \in \mathbb{R}^{C_b}$ via a linear bottleneck, where C_b is the reduced channel size. Dynamic basis weights are synthesized from the feature graph. For point i and neighbor j, the convolution is:

$$A_{ij} = \mathrm{MLP}\big([f'_i,\ f'_j - f'_i]\big); \quad \tilde{f}_i = W_{\mathrm{out}}\left(\max_{j\in\mathcal{N}(i)} \sum_{t=1}^{T} A_{ij}^{(t)}\, s_{ij}^{(t)}\right) \tag{1}$$

where, $A_{ij} \in \mathbb{R}^{R\times T}$ denotes low-rank adaptive kernels (rank R), $s_{ij} = [p_i, p_j - p_i] \in \mathbb{R}^T$ encodes spatial geometry, with $T = 6$ capturing absolute and relative 3D coordinates. Performing sequential aggregation directly in this low-rank space without generating large intermediate tensors reduces memory complexity to $\mathcal{O}(kC_bT)$. The projection W_{out} restores the output dimension, efficiently preserving geometric adaptivity.

Global Context with BRPA. To capture long-range dependencies efficiently, we integrate BRPA. Inspired by [22], the N points are serialized via a Hilbert curve and partitioned into G non-overlapping regions of size P_s. Region-level queries and keys $(\bar{Q}_r, \bar{K}_r)$ are computed from token-level inputs (Q, K, V) via average-pooling and Layer Normalization (LN). A routing mechanism (TopkRouter) restricts fine-grained self-attention to top-k relevant regions:

$$\begin{aligned}\bar{Q}_r, \bar{K}_r &= \mathrm{LN}(\mathrm{Avg}_{i\in r}\{Q_i, K_i\}), \quad W_r, I_r = \mathrm{TopkRouter}\left(\frac{\bar{Q}_r\bar{K}^\top}{\sqrt{d}}\right)\\ \{K_r^g, V_r^g\} &= \mathrm{Gather}(K, V, I_r)\odot W_r, \quad \mathrm{Attn}(Q_r) = \mathrm{softmax}\left(\frac{Q_r(K_r^g)^\top}{\sqrt{d}}\right)V_r^g\end{aligned} \tag{2}$$

The gathered keys and values (K_r^g, V_r^g) are explicitly scaled by routing weights W_r before the token-level dot product (d is head dimension). Restricting computation to these top-k regions reduces quadratic complexity to $\mathcal{O}(N \cdot k \cdot P_s)$.

Multi-scale Fusion and Prediction. Multi-scale backbone features are projected to a uniform FPN dimension, concatenated, and enriched with globally pooled context. A shared MLP processes these features before branching into a primary AWing head and an auxiliary PointSTAR head (which acts as a training regularizer and is discarded during inference). During post-processing, the predicted landmark is computed as the weighted center-of-mass of the top-K points in the predicted heatmap response ($K = 10$).

2.3 Loss Functions

Adaptive Wing Loss. We use AWing Loss to perform heatmap regression. For a ground truth y and prediction $\hat{y}$ at a given point, the loss is defined as:

$$\mathcal{L}_{AWing}(y,\hat{y}) = \begin{cases} \omega \ln\left(1 + \left|\frac{y-\hat{y}}{\epsilon}\right|^{\alpha-y}\right), & |y-\hat{y}| < \theta, \\ A|y-\hat{y}| - C, & \text{otherwise.} \end{cases} \tag{3}$$

where $(\alpha, \omega, \epsilon, \theta)$ are curvature hyperparameters, and A and C are the linear extension slope and intercept, respectively [19], ensuring continuity at the piecewise boundary. This base loss is subsequently integrated into our uncertainty formulation (Eq. 5).

PointSTAR Loss. Unlike 2D STAR loss [26], PointSTAR respects the surface manifold by decoupling normal and tangential uncertainties. Given a predicted local covariance Σ and surface normal n, we project Σ onto the tangent plane via $P = (I - nn^\top)$, yielding $\Sigma_{\text{proj}} = P\Sigma P^\top$. Its eigen-decomposition produces eigenvalues $(\lambda_0 \leq \lambda_1 \leq \lambda_2)$ and eigenvectors e_m. The smallest eigenvalue (λ_0) aligns with the normal, while λ_1, λ_2 span the tangent plane, capturing semantic ambiguity. Projecting the coordinate error $\Delta p = p - \hat{p}$ onto these axes, we apply normal (w_n) and tangential (w_t) weights to enforce strict surface-perpendicular localisation while tolerating manifold ambiguity:

$$\mathcal{L}_{\text{anis}} = w_n \frac{\mathcal{D}(\langle \Delta p, e_0 \rangle)}{\sqrt{\lambda_0}} + w_t \sum_{m=1}^{2} \frac{\mathcal{D}(\langle \Delta p, e_m \rangle)}{\sqrt{\lambda_m}} \tag{4}$$

where $\mathcal{D}(\cdot)$ is the Smooth L_1 distance. To prevent variance explosion and the consequent collapse of the distance penalty, we regularize $\mathcal{L}_{\text{var}} = \sum_{m=0}^{2} |\lambda_m|$. The final objective, $\mathcal{L}_{\text{PointSTAR}} = \mathcal{L}_{\text{anis}} + \beta\mathcal{L}_{\text{var}}$, projects the anisotropic penalty onto the manifold, ensuring strict convergence along the normal.

2.4 Hierarchical Uncertainty and Multi-Task Optimization

We propose a two-level homoscedastic uncertainty framework [3] to dynamically balance landmark-specific heatmap spreads and global multi-task objectives. At the landmark level, the spread σ_l of each landmark l is a learnable parameter. To stabilize training, $\mathcal{L}_{\text{AWing}}^{(l)}$ is scaled by a constant γ and weighted by σ_l. At the task level, we introduce homoscedastic uncertainties σ_{aw} and $\sigma_{\text{PointSTAR}}$ to automatically balance $\mathcal{L}_{\text{AWing}}^{(l)}$ and $\mathcal{L}_{\text{PointSTAR}}$ objectives. The joint optimization is formulated as:

$$\begin{aligned} \mathcal{L}_{\text{Reg}}^{(l)} &= \frac{\gamma}{2\sigma_l^2}\mathcal{L}_{\text{AWing}}^{(l)} + \log(\sigma_l), \\ \mathcal{L}_{\text{Total}} &= \frac{1}{2\sigma_{\text{aw}}^2}\left(\frac{1}{L}\sum_{l=1}^{L}\mathcal{L}_{\text{Reg}}^{(l)}\right) + \frac{\mathcal{L}_{\text{PointSTAR}}}{2\sigma_{\text{PointSTAR}}^2} + \log(\sigma_{\text{aw}}\sigma_{\text{PointSTAR}}) \end{aligned} \tag{5}$$

where L is the total number of landmarks. This hierarchical decoupling guarantees that landmark spreads modeled by σ_l do not interfere with the global balancing of multi-task gradients managed by σ_{aw} and $\sigma_{\text{PointSTAR}}$.

3 Experiments and Results

Implementation and Evaluation Details. The dataset was partitioned into 440/55/55 samples (train/val/test), evaluated against a 50-case clinical baseline with inter- and intra-annotator variabilities of 1.24±1.05 mm and 1.18±0.90 mm. Models were trained for > 100 epochs using AdamW (LR=10^{-4}) on an NVIDIA A100. Key hyperparameters: LR-AGConv ($k = 60$, $C_b = 128$, $R = 32$); BRPA (8 heads, patch size 32, top-$k = 8$); and learnable sigmas initialized at 0.075 (clamped ≥ 0.03). We dynamically balanced Weighted AWing and PointSTAR loss ($k = 64$, ramped over epochs 10–20) via homoscedastic uncertainty. Results are averaged over three runs across MEE, SD (Standard Deviation), Median, and Success Detection Rate (SDR) at 1, 1.5, 2, and 4 mm thresholds. For clinical deployment, our full model requires only 1 GB VRAM with a median total inference latency of 1.7 s (0.3–0.5 s forward pass).

Comparative Analysis. We evaluate architectural variants on the test set using our exact heatmap, loss formulations to isolate backbone impact (Table 2).

Backbone Comparison: PointNet++ [14], PointMLP [12] rely on hierarchical aggregation with global pooling and PtV3 uses an encoder-decoder architecture with serialized attentions. However, these are suboptimal (Table 2) for capturing both femoral global geometry and fine-grained local structure. Our hybrid architecture better balances local surface detail with global context.

GCN Operators: LR-AGConv generates dynamic kernels tailored to local anatomy, outperforming both DeltaConv and PAConv. Crucially, our low-rank formulation reduces peak training memory by 43.1% (40.4 GB → 23.0 GB) versus standard dense AGConv without degrading accuracy.

Attention Mechanisms: Standard MSA (Multi-Head Self Attention) is computationally prohibitive for training (65.5 GB VRAM, 1.18 s/scan). BRPA reduces this training memory to ~27.5 GB. Although PTv3 is marginally faster, BRPA incurs negligible latency overhead while yielding better SDR (+4%).

Ablation Studies Table 2 also details our component-wise ablation. The base model (LR-AGConv + AWing) establishes a strong baseline. Integrating BRPA efficiently injects global semantic context; notably, it also stabilizes the convergence of the PointSTAR loss significantly smoother in V4 compared to V3 (Fig. 4). Adding PointSTAR loss explicitly addresses anisotropic ambiguity, notably reducing MEE for geometrically ambiguous landmarks like the FLTA (1.64 → 1.41 mm) and FMCD (1.86 → 1.60 mm). Furthermore, the addition of PointSTAR (V3, V4) accelerates overall training convergence to just 60 epochs with better performance, whereas models without it (V1, V2) require > 100 epochs (Fig. 4). Finally, learnable sigmas outperform fixed variants by adapting to the distinctive learning dynamics of each landmark (Fig. 3).

Table 2. Performance evaluation on the test set. Top: Inter-architecture comparison against baselines. Bottom: Component-wise ablation study. MEE, SD, and Med. are in mm. SDR is in %. All models are trained with learnable sigmas, "Ours" refers to Base model trained with BRPA and PointSTAR.

Model	MEE±SD	Med.	SDR@t			
			1.0	1.5	2.0	4.0
Inter-architecture comparison						
PointNet++	1.39±0.93	1.16	40.6	63.6	78.4	98.1
PointMLP	1.38±1.13	1.12	42.1	68.3	82.3	97.2
PTv3	1.48±1.01	1.23	37.0	60.2	76.6	97.4
DeltaConv	1.54±1.04	1.30	36.0	58.1	74.2	96.3
PAConv	1.30±0.95	1.10	45.0	69.3	84.3	97.1
Self Attn	1.29±1.00	1.03	48.7	71.8	84.3	97.6
PTv2 Attn	1.43±1.32	1.10	44.2	68.5	81.5	95.3
PTv3 Attn	1.32±0.99	1.08	43.0	68.7	82.8	98.2
Intra-ablation study						
Base (LR-AGConv)	1.28±0.90	1.06	46.9	69.5	83.6	98.0
Base + BRPA	1.27±0.89	1.08	47.5	71.8	85.7	**98.7**
Base + PointSTAR	1.26±0.84	1.07	46.8	71.8	**86.3**	98.5
Ours w/o Learnable σ	1.28±0.92	1.08	46.8	70.3	84.0	97.9
Ours	**1.24±0.84**	**1.05**	**48.9**	**72.5**	85.6	**98.7**

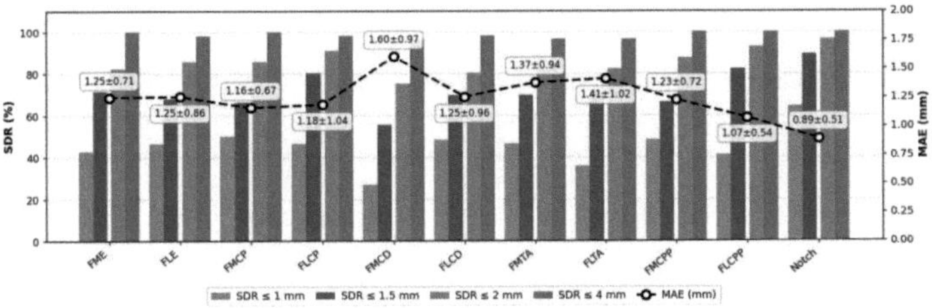

Fig. 3. Landmark-wise SDR and MAE ± SD for our model.

Clinical Generalizability and Cross-Modality Validation Our model demonstrates robust zero-shot transferability, achieving a 1.5±0.9 mm error on 56 CT-derived VSD point clouds despite the MRI-to-CT modality shift [9]. Adapting our architecture to geodesic heatmaps yielded a 1.8±1.35 mm error on a complex scapula dataset [7], proving broad anatomical generalizability.

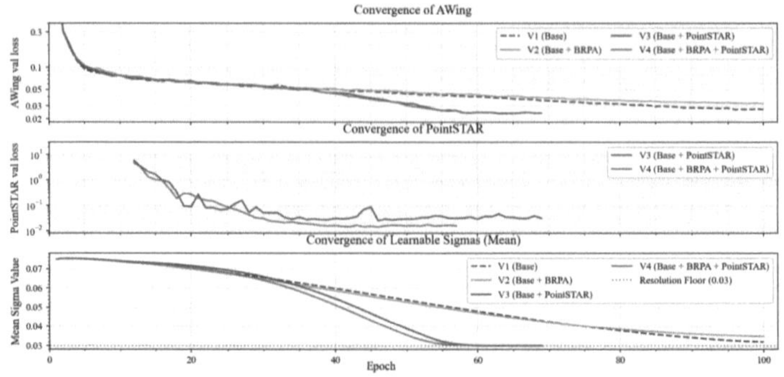

Fig. 4. Loss and sigma convergence.

4 Conclusion and Future Work

We present a modality-agnostic framework achieving state-of-the-art distal femur landmark localisation. Integrating LR-AGConv with BRPA captures rich local-to-global context while optimizing memory costs. Additionally, our novel PointSTAR loss explicitly resolves the geometric ambiguity of anisotropic surfaces to mitigate annotator variability. To advance research, we release an open, expert-annotated clinical benchmark dataset. Future work will extend this framework to explore downstream planning measurements from predicted landmarks, prediction robustness on osteophytic cases as well as tibial landmarks for comprehensive, fully automated TKA preoperative planning.

Disclosure of Interests. The authors have no competing interests.

References

1. Baek, S.Y., Wang, J.H., Song, I., Lee, K., Lee, J., Koo, S.: Automated bone landmarks prediction on the femur using anatomical deformation technique. Comput. Aided Des. **45**(2), 505–510 (2013). https://doi.org/10.1016/j.cad.2012.10.033
2. Berger, L., Bröẞner, P., Ehreiser, S., Tokunaga, K., Okamoto, M., Radermacher, K.: Validation and comparison of three different methods for automated identification of distal femoral landmarks in 3D. Biomed. Eng./Biomedizinische Technik **70**(5), 425–431 (2025). https://doi.org/10.1515/bmt-2025-0026
3. Cipolla, R., Gal, Y., Kendall, A.: Multi-task learning using uncertainty to weigh losses for scene geometry and semantics. In: 2018 IEEE/CVF Conference on Computer Vision and Pattern Recognition. pp. 7482—-7491 (2018). https://doi.org/10.1109/cvpr.2018.00781
4. Gatti, A.A., et al.: ShapeMed-Knee: a dataset and neural shape model benchmark for modeling 3D femurs (2024). https://doi.org/10.1101/2024.05.06.24306965
5. Grammens, J., Van Haver, A., Lumban-Gaol, I., Danckaers, F., Verdonk, P., Sijbers, J.: Automated landmark annotation for morphometric analysis of distal femur and proximal tibia. J. Imaging **10**(4), 90 (2024). https://doi.org/10.3390/jimaging10040090

6. Gromov, K., Korchi, M., Thomsen, M.G., Husted, H., Troelsen, A.: What is the optimal alignment of the tibial and femoral components in knee arthroplasty?: an overview of the literature. Acta Orthop. **85**(5), 480–487 (2014). https://doi.org/10.3109/17453674.2014.940573
7. Henninger, H.B.: 3D models of the human scapula and humerus with defined anatomic landmarks (2025). https://doi.org/10.5281/ZENODO.14590062
8. Horteur, C., et al.: Accuracy evaluation of an automatic landmarking method based on 3D segmented CT scans of full lower limbs with knee osteoarthritis. Eur. J. Radiol. **191**, 112292 (2025). https://doi.org/10.1016/j.ejrad.2025.112292
9. Kistler, M., Bonaretti, S., Pfahrer, M., Niklaus, R., Büchler, P.: The virtual skeleton database: an open access repository for biomedical research and collaboration. J. Med. Internet Res. **15**(11), e245 (2013). https://doi.org/10.2196/jmir.2930
10. Kompella, G., et al.: Segmentation of femoral cartilage from knee ultrasound images using mask R-CNN. In: 2019 41st Annual International Conference of the IEEE Engineering in Medicine and Biology Society (EMBC) (2019). https://doi.org/10.1109/embc.2019.8857645
11. Li, G., Müller, M., Thabet, A., Ghanem, B.: DeepGCNs: can GCNs go as deep as CNNs? (2019). https://doi.org/10.48550/ARXIV.1904.03751
12. Ma, X., Qin, C., You, H., Ran, H., Fu, Y.: Rethinking network design and local geometry in point cloud: a simple residual MLP framework. In: Proceedings of the International Conference on Learning Representations (ICLR) (2022). https://doi.org/10.48550/arXiv.2202.07123
13. Murugesan, B., Vijaya Raghavan, S., Sarveswaran, K., Ram, K., Sivaprakasam, M.: Recon-GLGAN: a global-local context based generative adversarial network for MRI reconstruction. pp. 3—-15 (2019). https://doi.org/10.1007/978-3-030-33843-5_1
14. Qi, C.R., Yi, L., Su, H., Guibas, L.J.: Pointnet++: deep hierarchical feature learning on point sets in a metric space. In: Advances in Neural Information Processing Systems (NeurIPS), pp. 5099–5108 (2017). https://doi.org/10.48550/arXiv.1612.00593
15. Rostamian, R., Shariat Panahi, M., Karimpour, M., Kashani, H.G., Abi, A.: A deep learning-based multi-view approach to automatic 3D landmarking and deformity assessment of lower limb. Sci. Rep. **15**(1) (Jan 2025). https://doi.org/10.1038/s41598-024-84387-z
16. Thaler, F., Payer, C., Urschler, M., Stern, D.: Modeling annotation uncertainty with gaussian heatmaps in landmark localization (2021). https://doi.org/10.48550/ARXIV.2109.09533
17. Thomas, H., Qi, C.R., Deschaud, J.E., Marcotegui, B., Goulette, F., Guibas, L.J.: KPConv: flexible and deformable convolution for point clouds (2019). https://doi.org/10.48550/ARXIV.1904.08889
18. Vaswani, A., et al.: attention is all you need (2017). https://doi.org/10.48550/ARXIV.1706.03762
19. Wang, X., Bo, L., Fuxin, L.: Adaptive wing loss for robust face alignment via heatmap regression (2019). https://doi.org/10.48550/ARXIV.1904.07399
20. Wang, Y., Cao, M., Fan, Z., Peng, S.: Learning to detect 3D facial landmarks via heatmap regression with graph convolutional network. In: Proceedings of the AAAI Conference on Artificial Intelligence, vol. 36, pp. 2595–2603 (2022). https://doi.org/10.1609/aaai.v36i3.20161
21. Wiersma, R., Nasikun, A., Eisemann, E., Hildebrandt, K.: DeltaConv: anisotropic operators for geometric deep learning on point cloud. https://doi.org/10.48550/ARXIV.2111.08799 (2021)

22. Wu, X., et al.: Point transformer V3: simpler, faster, stronger (2023). https://doi.org/10.48550/ARXIV.2312.10035
23. Wu, X., Lao, Y., Jiang, L., Liu, X., Zhao, H.: Point transformer V2: grouped vector attention and partition-based pooling (2022). https://doi.org/10.48550/ARXIV.2210.05666
24. Xu, M., Ding, R., Zhao, H., Qi, X.: PaConv: position adaptive convolution with dynamic kernel assembling on point clouds. In: 2021 IEEE/CVF Conference on Computer Vision and Pattern Recognition (CVPR), pp. 3172—-3181 (2021). https://doi.org/10.1109/cvpr46437.2021.00319
25. Zhou, H., Feng, Y., Fang, M., Wei, M., Qin, J., Lu, T.: Adaptive graph convolution for point cloud analysis (2021). https://doi.org/10.48550/ARXIV.2108.08035
26. Zhou, Z., Li, H., Liu, H., Wang, N., Yu, G., Ji, R.: Star loss: reducing semantic ambiguity in facial landmark detection (2023). https://doi.org/10.48550/ARXIV.2306.02763
27. Zhu, L., Wang, X., Ke, Z., Zhang, W., Lau, R.: BiFormer: vision transformer with bi-level routing attention (2023). https://doi.org/10.48550/ARXIV.2303.08810

SurgRFO: Foundation Model Based Compositional Synthesis of Critical Retained Foreign Objects in Intraoperative Chest X-Rays

Yuanyun Hu[1,2,3], Yuli Wang[2,3], Noemi Acevedo Rodriguez[2], Ronald Yang[2], Wen-Chi Hsu[4], Siwei Luo[5], Zihao Bai[1], Jing Wu[6], Yuwei Dai[2], Shaoju Wu[2], Jonathon Lindquist[2], Justin Honce[2], Premal Trivedi[2], Zhicheng Jiao[7], Ihab Kamel[2], Elliott Haut[3], Pamela Johnson[3], John Eng[3], Cheng Ting Lin[3], Nan Su[1], Bo Chen[8(✉)], Sun Yu[9], and Harrison Bai[2(✉)]

[1] Department of Electronic Engineering, Tsinghua University, Beijing, China
[2] Department of Radiology, University of Colorado Denver Anschutz Medical Campus, Denver, USA
harrison.bai@cuanschutz.edu
[3] Department of Radiology and Radiological Science, Johns Hopkins University School of Medicine, Baltimore, USA
[4] Department of Medical Imaging and Intervention, Chang Gung Memorial Hospital at Linkou, Taoyuan, Taiwan
[5] Department of Electronic Engineering, Southwest University of Science and Technology, Mianyang, China
[6] Department of Radiology, Second Xiangya Hospital, Central South University, Changsha, Hunan, China
[7] Department of Diagnostic Imaging, Brown University Health, Providence, USA
[8] School of Clinical Medicine, Tsinghua University, Beijing, China
cba04570@btch.edu.cn
[9] Department of Electrical and Computer Engineering, Johns Hopkins University, Baltimore, USA

Abstract. Critical retained foreign objects (RFOs) on intraoperative chest radiographs are rare but high-risk events. Their scarcity limits robust automated detection model training and generalization. We introduce **SurgRFO**, a two-stage synthesis framework for generating realistic RFO-present intraoperative chest X-rays. In **Stage 1**, a Roentgen chest X-ray foundation model is fine-tuned on surgical-domain images to generate realistic RFO-free backgrounds that preserve anatomy, indwelling lines and tubes, and intraoperative imaging characteristics. In **Stage 2**, a lightweight generator trained on localized RFO patches from limited positive cases synthesizes diverse RFO instances, which are composited onto generated backgrounds using conditional Poisson fusion to improve photometric consistency. We evaluate SurgRFO through (i) a blinded clinician study assessing realism and clinical plausibility, and (ii) downstream detection experiments in which synthesized data are used to aug-

Y. Hu and Y. Wang—These authors contributed equally to this work.

G. Yang et al. (Eds.): MICCAI 2026, LNCS 16893, pp. 500–510, 2027.
https://doi.org/10.1007/978-3-032-38236-8_48

ment Faster R-CNN, YOLOv8, and RetinaNet. SurgRFO consistently improves sensitivity at low false-positive-per-image (FPPI) operating points on internal and external test sets. Clinician ratings indicate that the synthesized images achieve realism comparable to real intraoperative images. Ablation analyses further examine fusion strategies and synthesis scale. Ethical safeguards for synthetic surgical data are also discussed. The code is publicly available on GitHub at https://github.com/Yuanyun936/SurgRFO.

Keywords: Image Synthesis · Critical Retained Foreign Objects · Data Augmentation · Surgical X-rays

1 Introduction

Critical retained foreign objects (RFOs), such as surgical sponges and needle fragments, are rare but high-impact patient safety events. Unlike non-critical, intentionally placed objects, critical RFOs are unintended remnants that may cause severe complications, re-operations, and substantial medico-legal and financial burden. [8,13,16–18,22,23]. Clinically, intraoperative imaging aims to rule out RFOs before procedure completion, where missed detections can have serious consequences. However, work explicitly targeting critical RFOs remains limited. Most prior studies focus on standardized chest X-rays (CXRs) and predominantly address *non-critical* objects [10,21,24,30]. Robust detection of critical RFOs in real-world intraoperative X-rays, therefore, remains an open and clinically significant challenge.

Critical RFO detection relies on intraoperative radiographs acquired under far less controlled conditions than standard CXRs, with cluttered scenes, overlapping instruments, variable anatomy exposure, and heterogeneous imaging settings. Two major challenges arise. First, visual cues are often subtle and confounded by surgical context. Sponges or needle fragments may be blood-soaked, partially occluded, or blended with surrounding tissue, producing weak signals that are difficult to recognize, even for experienced clinicians. [11,14]. False negatives are therefore not uncommon, and prior studies suggest that intraoperative imaging may fail to detect a substantial fraction of RFO cases [2]. Second, positive cases are extremely rare and difficult to scale. Even at a large hospital, only low hundreds of cases may accumulate over decades, and to our knowledge, no public dataset of intraoperative radiographs dedicated to critical RFO detection exists. Together, these constraints create a fundamental limitation: accurate detection requires sensitivity to subtle local patterns, yet available data provide limited exposure to such events, challenging conventional supervised learning approaches.

Synthetic data augmentation is a natural strategy to mitigate data scarcity. Physics-based RFO synthesis, such as CT-projection pipelines with rendered 3D objects [31], provides controllable images with precise annotations. However, these approaches typically insert object models into relatively clean CT volumes

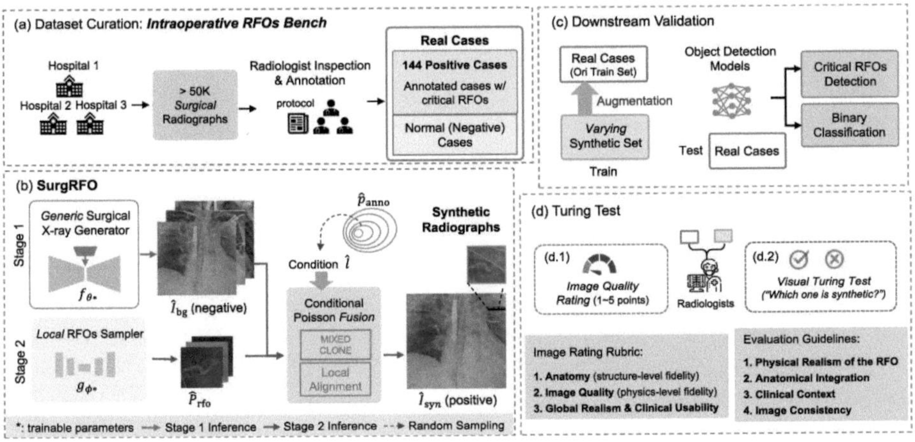

Fig. 1. Overview of the **Intraoperative RFO Bench** and **SurgRFO** pipeline. (a) Multi-institutional intraoperative radiographs are curated and expert-annotated as real positive (critical RFO) and negative cases. (b) SurgRFO applies a two-stage synthesis framework, combining surgical X-ray background generation with localized RFO sampling and fusion to create annotated synthetic images. (c) Synthetic data are used for training augmentation and evaluated on held-out real cases for critical RFO detection and classification. (d) A radiologist-led Turing test assesses visual realism through confidence-based quality ratings and image discrimination tasks.

and project them to X-ray images, leaving a substantial domain gap to real intraoperative radiographs acquired in cluttered surgical workflows. Recent advances in diffusion models (DMs), which generate images through iterative denoising of a learned reverse process [5], have enabled high-fidelity and diverse X-ray synthesis [1,25,27,29,31], supporting augmentation for imbalanced medical imaging tasks [6,7,9,12,15,28]. However, fully end-to-end generation of critical RFO radiographs remains unreliable. The same rarity and subtle visual signatures that hinder detection also limit generative fidelity: standard pipelines struggle to simultaneously preserve complex surgical context and localized RFO cues, often leading to visually implausible samples for training detectors (see comparisons in Sect. 3). To address this gap, we propose **SurgRFO**, a two-stage synthesis framework for generating surgical radiographs with critical RFOs. Stage 1 learns a strong prior over cluttered surgical radiographs by training a latent diffusion model (LDM) as a generic surgical X-ray generator. Stage 2 trains a lightweight U-Net to model local critical RFO appearance, then conditionally fuses the sampled RFO content into Stage 1 backgrounds via a Poisson-based blending mechanism guided by a prior over plausible RFO locations and sizes.

We also release **Intraoperative RFO Bench**, to our knowledge the first publicly available real de-identified intraoperative chest radiograph dataset dedicated to *critical* RFOs, comprising 144 expert-annotated positive cases curated from 18 years of surgical radiographs from two health systems (Johns Hopkins Hospital (JHH) and University of Colorado (CU)). Augmenting training with

SurgRFO yields consistent improvements across multiple detector families. In a radiologist-led Turing-style evaluation, synthetic images are frequently indistinguishable from real cases. Together, these results demonstrate the value of releasing this benchmark and the effectiveness of the proposed framework for advancing critical RFO detection.

2 Method

2.1 Dataset Curation

Under institutional review board approval, we retrospectively curated surgical chest radiographs from the JHH, comprising 144 *critical* RFO-positive cases and 944 negative cases with no RFOs. An additional 20 *critical* RFO-positive cases were collected from CU for external evaluation. Positives were identified via structured report search and expert verification using radiology reports and operative notes. All images were de-identified and annotated by trained radiologists under a standardized protocol, including image-level labels and object-level annotations (bounding boxes or polygons), with each foreign object categorized as critical or non-critical. Patient-level splits into training, validation, and test sets were applied consistently across cohorts to prevent information leakage. Training images were preprocessed with center cropping, resolution normalization, and artifact filtering.

2.2 SurgRFO

Let $\Omega \subset \mathbb{R}^2$ denote the image lattice, and let $I \in \mathbb{R}^{H \times W}$ denote a radiograph defined on Ω. Two datasets are considered, $\mathcal{D}_{\text{bg}} = \{I_i\}_{i=1}^{N_{\text{bg}}}$ and $\mathcal{D}_{\text{rfo}} = \{(I_j, M_j, y_j)\}_{j=1}^{N_{\text{rfo}}}$. The set $\mathcal{D}_{\text{bg}}$ contains surgical-domain negative radiographs that provide RFO-free backgrounds. The set $\mathcal{D}_{\text{rfo}}$ contains radiographs with annotated critical RFOs. The mask $M_j \subset \Omega$ specifies the RFO support, and the label $y_j \in \mathcal{Y}$ specifies the semantic type.

SurgRFO is a two-stage synthesis framework that decouples global background modeling from local critical RFO modeling. Stage 1 learns a generic prior over surgical radiograph backgrounds. Stage 2 learns a local sampler for critical RFO appearance and composes sampled RFO evidence onto Stage 1 backgrounds through a controlled fusion mechanism.

Stage 1: Generic Surgical Radiograph Generator. A background generator is defined as a conditional LDM f_θ parameterized by θ. Background sampling is written as

$$\hat{I}_{\text{bg}} \sim p_\theta(I \mid t, z_1), \qquad z_1 \sim \mathcal{N}(0, I), \tag{1}$$

where $\hat{I}_{\text{bg}}$ denotes an RFO-free surgical background, t denotes a domain anchor text token, and z_1 denotes the diffusion noise seed. Stage 1 is designed for domain-level background modeling rather than instance-specific textual control. A fixed domain anchor prompt is therefore used, and diversity is induced primarily by the stochasticity of z_1. In implementation, we adapt RoentGen [1], an advanced CXRs LDM, to surgical X-ray domain leveraging $\mathcal{D}_{\text{bg}}$.

Stage 2: Local RFO Sampler and Conditional Fusion. A local RFO sampler is defined by a compact generator g_ϕ that models patch-level RFO appearance. For each annotated sample $(I, M, y) \in \mathcal{D}_{\mathrm{rfo}}$, an RFO-centered canonical patch is extracted by a mask-driven cropping operator $\mathcal{C}_M$,

$$P = \mathcal{C}_M(I). \tag{2}$$

A plausible RFO patch is sampled from a noise seed z_2 as

$$\hat{P}_{\mathrm{rfo}} \sim p_\phi(P \mid z_2), \qquad z_2 \sim \mathcal{N}(0, I), \tag{3}$$

where p_ϕ denotes the implicit patch distribution defined by g_ϕ.

An anatomically plausible placement is specified by a location-scale variable $\ell = (x, y, s)$, where (x, y) denotes the insertion center on the background canvas and s denotes the insertion scale. An empirical placement prior $\hat{p}_{\mathrm{anno}}(\ell)$ is estimated from annotation statistics, and a concrete placement parameter is drawn as $\hat{\ell} \sim \hat{p}_{\mathrm{anno}}(\ell)$. A placement operator $\mathcal{T}_{\hat{\ell}}$ maps both the sampled patch and its support to the full image grid,

$$\hat{P}_{\hat{\ell}} = \mathcal{T}_{\hat{\ell}}(\hat{P}_{\mathrm{rfo}}), \qquad M_{\hat{\ell}} = \mathcal{T}_{\hat{\ell}}(S(\hat{P}_{\mathrm{rfo}})), \tag{4}$$

where $S(\cdot)$ produces a coarse support mask in patch coordinates and $M_{\hat{\ell}}$ denotes the corresponding insertion support on the $H \times W$ canvas.

The final composite image I_{syn} is defined by an aligned mixed-cloning objective over the insertion region $\Omega_{\hat{\ell}} = \{\mathbf{u} \in \Omega : M_{\hat{\ell}}(\mathbf{u}) = 1\}$,

$$I_{\mathrm{syn}} = \arg\min_{I} \sum_{\mathbf{u} \in \Omega_{\hat{\ell}}} \left\| \nabla I(\mathbf{u}) - \Big(\beta \nabla \mathcal{A}_\alpha(\hat{P}_{\hat{\ell}})(\mathbf{u}) + (1-\beta) \nabla \hat{I}_{\mathrm{bg}}(\mathbf{u})\Big) \right\|_2^2, \tag{5}$$

where ∇ denotes the spatial gradient operator. The parameter $\beta \in [0, 1]$ controls the strength of mixed cloning by balancing patch-driven gradients and background-driven gradients. The operator $\mathcal{A}_\alpha$ performs local intensity alignment of the placed patch to the background within $M_{\hat{\ell}}$. The parameter $\alpha \in [0, 1]$ controls the degree of alignment by interpolating between the raw patch intensity and an intensity level matched to the local background statistics.

3 Experiments and Results

Experimental Setup. SurgRFO is evaluated on the Intraoperative RFOs Bench, which is split into training, validation, and test sets with a 6:1:3 patient-level ratio. In Stage 1, we instantiate the generator from RoentGen under the Stable Diffusion (SD) latent diffusion formulation [19], and adapt it to the surgical background cohort using a fixed domain prompt and varying noise seeds for diversity. Stage 2 trains a compact U-Net diffusion sampler [3] on RFO-centered crops from the positive cohort and synthesizes RFO-positive composites via conditional fusion. We evaluate SurgRFO from: (i) synthesis quality, and (ii) the impact of synthetic augmentation on downstream critical RFO detection. We

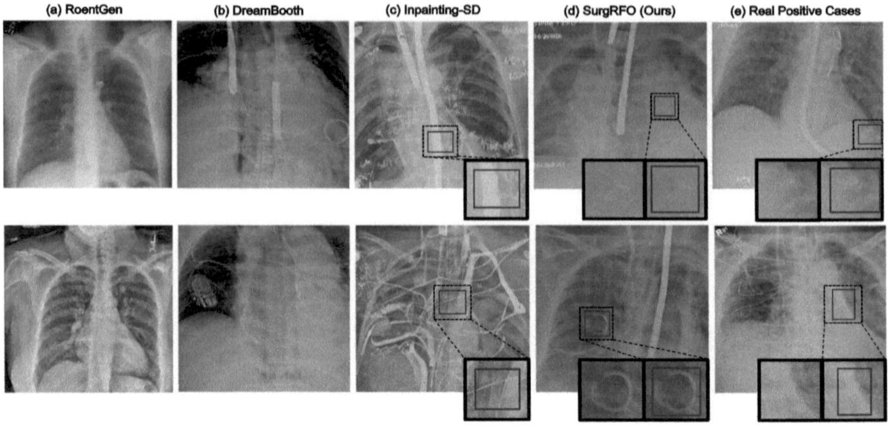

Fig. 2. Visualization of synthesis results. Each row shows one representative case. Columns (a-b) show Stage-1 RFO-negative background generation using the original RoentGen and DreamBooth fine-tuning. Columns (c–d) compare Stage-2 RFO-positive synthesis using inpainting Stable Diffusion versus the proposed SurgRFO framework, with real positive cases shown in (e) for reference. Black insets provide zoomed views; red boxes mark target regions, and turquoise overlays indicate critical RFOs. SurgRFO maintains surgical radiograph fidelity while generating clinically plausible critical RFO appearances.

use FID [4] and MS-SSIM [26] for qualifying synthesis quality. Baselines include DreamBooth fine-tuning [20], and an inpainting SD [19]. RoentGen serves as the common initialization for both the baselines and SurgRFO. Downstream performance is evaluated on held-out real radiographs using detection metrics, including mean average precision (mAP), false negative rate (FNR), false omission rate (FOR), free-response receiver operating characteristic (FROC), and binary classification accuracy (ACC) for positive versus negative prediction.

3.1 Synthesis Quality

Table 1 evaluates Stage-1 RFO-negative synthesis on 5k images. Compared with the original RoentGen SD and a DreamBooth-adapted baseline, SurgRFO achieves consistently lower FID across checkpoints, with the best fidelity at 2k steps (FID 43.675). While DreamBooth improves domain alignment compared to the original RoentGen Model, it remains inferior to SurgRFO. Diversity improves with training and is best at 4k steps (lowest MS-SSIM), suggesting that Stage 1 captures surgical radiograph appearance with a selectable fidelity–diversity trade-off along training. Table 2 assesses final RFO-positive composites after Stage 2. SurgRFO improves fidelity over both the original RoentGen and inpainting baselines. Because Stage 2 edits only localized regions, MS-SSIM is dominated by preserved backgrounds and is reported as a secondary diagnostic, while FID remains the primary criterion for comparison. Visual comparisons (Fig. 2) further demonstrate that end-to-end baselines struggle to maintain

Table 1. Quantitative assessment of image fidelity and diversity for Stage-1 RFO-negative synthesis. FID and MS-SSIM for surgical background generation. **Bold** indicates the best, and underlined indicates the second best among adapted models across training steps.

Method	Steps	FID ↓	MS-SSIM ↓
Original RoentGen SD (no fine-tuning)	–	175.167	0.262 ± 0.130
DreamBooth SD (few-shot fine-tuning)	–	80.963	0.424 ± 0.085
Ours	1k	48.568	0.406 ± 0.071
	2k	**43.675**	0.474 ± 0.079
	3k	46.100	0.460 ± 0.052
	4k	57.896	**0.362 ± 0.054**
	5k	47.948	0.393 ± 0.059

radiographic realism and render subtle RFO cues under limited positive data. In contrast, SurgRFO preserves global surgical fidelity and produces coherent, clinically plausible critical RFO appearances, as evidenced by the zoomed-in insets.

Table 2. Quantitative assessment for Stage-2 RFO-positive synthesis.Bold indicates the best FID among compared methods.

Method	FID ↓	MS-SSIM ↓
Original RoentGen SD	197.837	0.262 ± 0.130
Inpainting SD	154.523	0.118 ± 0.045
Ours	**69.178**	0.480 ± 0.064

3.2 Downstream Detection with SurgRFO Augmentation

Internal Evaluation. The downstream evaluation assesses whether SurgRFO improves critical RFO detection on real radiographs. As shown in Table 3, augmenting training with synthetic positives yields consistent gains across three detector families, suggesting that synthetic samples broaden effective training coverage rather than favoring a specific detector. Faster R-CNN demonstrates marked performance improvement with a substantial reduction in missed positive cases. RetinaNet shows monotonic gains as more synthetic samples are added. YOLOv8l performs poorly when trained on the base regime alone but achieves meaningful detection once synthetic samples are introduced, indicating particular benefit under limited positive supervision.

External Evaluation. Generalization is further evaluated on an external real-world cohort from the CU. After SurgRFO-based augmentation, all models demonstrate clear improvement, with consistent reductions in false negatives and gains in overall accuracy. RetinaNet shows the largest benefit, with mAP@0.3 improving by +0.260, FNR decreasing by -0.750, FOR decreasing by -0.321, FROC increasing by +0.083, and ACC improving by +0.428, transitioning to meaningful retrieval performance. Faster R-CNN and YOLOv8l also exhibit reduced FNR (-0.250 each) and improved accuracy (+0.142 each), with YOLOv8l achieving a notable FROC gain (+0.250). These findings indicate that synthesized positives provide effective supervision beyond the development cohort and enhance robustness under dataset shift.

Table 3. Downstream critical RFO detection with synthetic augmentation. Detectors are trained on the base real set with additional SurgRFO-generated positive samples at varying amounts. **Bold** marks the best result and underlined marks the second best within each detector block.

Model	Training Set	**mAP@0.3** ↑	FNR ↓	FOR ↓	FROC ↑	ACC ↑
Faster R-CNN	Base	0.184	78.79%	8.72%	0.242	0.672
	Base+500	0.304	66.67%	7.48%	0.424	0.928
	Base+1000	0.390	60.61%	6.87%	0.455	0.931
	Base+2000	**0.510**	**33.33%**	**3.93%**	**0.636**	**0.954**
RetinaNet	Base	0.099	72.73%	8.11%	0.455	0.921
	Base+500	0.364	63.64%	7.17%	0.485	0.931
	Base+1000	0.455	54.55%	6.23%	0.667	0.938
	Base+2000	**0.564**	**36.36%**	**4.26%**	**0.727**	**0.954**
YOLOv8l	Base	0.000	100.00%	10.82%	–	0.892
	Base+500	0.290	69.70%	7.85%	0.303	0.918
	Base+1000	**0.357**	**60.61%**	**6.87%**	0.394	**0.931**
	Base+2000	0.355	63.64%	7.24%	**0.394**	0.921

4 Radiologist-Driven Turing Test

To assess clinical plausibility beyond automated metrics, we conducted a blinded radiologist evaluation using a Turing-style protocol (Fig. 1 d) comprising two tasks: (1) blinded image quality rating without disclosure of provenance, and (2) explicit discriminability between real and synthetic images.

Turing Test 1: Blinded Image Quality Rating. Radiologists independently scored randomized radiographs using a five-point Likert rubric. As shown in Table 4 (a), synthetic images received quality ratings not significantly different from real images under Welch's test, indicating the synthetic cohort preserves clinically plausible radiographic appearance under blinded assessment.

Table 4. Radiologist-driven Turing tests for clinical realism.

(a) **Blinded image-quality ratings on a 1–5 Likert scale.** Values are mean±standard deviation. Welch's test compares real and synthetic images per rater.

	Real	Synthetic	Welch p
Rater 1	2.86±1.11	2.47±1.02	0.166
Rater 2	2.64±1.22	2.31±0.74	0.220

(b) **Discrimination between real and synthetic images.** Metrics include accuracy, F1 score, the fraction of synthetic images labeled as real, and confidence–accuracy AUC.

	Acc	F1	Syn→Real	ConfAUC
Rater 1	0.750	0.762	0.30	0.558
Rater 2	0.750	0.750	0.25	0.495

Turing Test 2: Real Versus Synthetic Discrimination with Confidence. Radiologists classified each image as real or synthetic and assigned a five-point confidence score. As shown in Table 4 (b), both raters achieved moderate discrimination, indicating that some synthetic cues remain detectable. However, a substantial fraction of synthetic images were labeled as real, supporting their visual plausibility. Confidence was only weakly correlated with correctness, suggesting limited calibration in this setting.

5 Conclusion

Critical RFO detection represents a clinically important yet data-scarce regime, where positive samples are rare and diagnostic cues are subtle and highly localized, challenging both conventional supervised learning and end-to-end synthesis. We introduced SurgRFO, a two-stage synthesis framework that separates surgical background modeling from localized RFO evidence generation. By combining a background diffusion generator with a lightweight local sampler through controlled fusion, SurgRFO produces high-quality RFO-positive radiographs for augmentation. We also released the Intraoperative RFO Bench, the first public benchmark dedicated to critical RFOs with expert annotations. On this benchmark, SurgRFO-augmented training yielded consistent improvements across multiple detector families, including under cross-institutional evaluation. A blinded radiologist study further supported the clinical plausibility of synthetic images, with comparable quality ratings to real radiographs and only moderate discriminability. These results demonstrate that structured synthesis can expand exposure to rare critical events and enhance detection sensitivity, while emphasizing the need for continued clinician-centered and workflow-aware validation prior to deployment.

Acknowledgments. No funding was received for this work.

Disclosure of Interests. The authors have no competing interests to declare that are relevant to the content of this article.

References

1. Bluethgen, C.: A vision-language foundation model for the generation of realistic chest X-ray images. Nat. Biomed. Eng. **9**(4), 494–506 (2025)
2. Cima, R.R., Kollengode, A., Garnatz, J., Storsveen, A., Weisbrod, C., Deschamps, C.: Incidence and characteristics of potential and actual retained foreign object events in surgical patients. J. Am. Coll. Surg. **207**(1), 80–87 (2008)
3. Dhariwal, P., Nichol, A.: Diffusion models beat GANs on image synthesis. Adv. Neural. Inf. Process. Syst. **34**, 8780–8794 (2021)
4. Heusel, M., Ramsauer, H., Unterthiner, T., Nessler, B., Hochreiter, S.: GANs trained by a two time-scale update rule converge to a local nash equilibrium. Adv. Neural Inf. Proces. Syst. **30** (2017)
5. Ho, J., Jain, A., Abbeel, P.: Denoising diffusion probabilistic models. Adv. Neural. Inf. Process. Syst. **33**, 6840–6851 (2020)
6. Hsu, W.C., et al.: MRI-based ovarian lesion classification via a foundation segmentation model and multimodal analysis: a multicenter study. Radiology **316**(2), e243412 (2025)
7. Huijben, E.M., Pluim, J.P., van Eijnatten, M.A.: Denoising diffusion probabilistic models for addressing data limitations in chest X-ray classification. Inform. Med. Unlocked **50**, 101575 (2024)
8. Kawakubo, M., et al.: A deep learning model based on fusion images of chest radiography and X-ray sponge images supports human visual characteristics of retained surgical items detection. Int. J. Comput. Assist. Radiol. Surg. **18**(8), 1459–1467 (2023)
9. Khosravi, B., et al.: Synthetically enhanced: unveiling synthetic data's potential in medical imaging research. EBioMedicine **104** (2024)
10. Kufel, J.: Chest X-ray foreign objects detection using artificial intelligence. J. Clin. Med. **12**(18), 5841 (2023)
11. Kumar, G.S., Ramani, S., Mahajan, A., Jain, N., Sequeira, R., Thakur, M.: Imaging of retained surgical items: a pictorial review including new innovations. Indian J. Radiol. Imaging **27**(03), 354–361 (2017)
12. Mahaulpatha, P., Abeywardane, T., George, T.: DDPM based X-ray image synthesizer. arXiv:preprintarXiv:2401.01539 (2024)
13. Moffatt-Bruce, S.D., Cook, C.H., Steinberg, S.M., Stawicki, S.P.: Risk factors for retained surgical items: a meta-analysis and proposed risk stratification system. J. Surgical Res. **190**(2), 429–436 (2014)
14. O'Connor, A.R., Coakley, F.V., Meng, M.V., Eberhardt, S.: Imaging of retained surgical sponges in the abdomen and pelvis. Am. J. Roentgenol. **180**(2), 481–489 (2003)
15. Prakash, E., et al.: Evaluating and improving the effectiveness of synthetic chest x-rays for medical image analysis. In: Proceedings of the IEEE/CVF International Conference on Computer Vision, pp. 4413–4421 (2025)
16. Rajagopal, A., Martin, J.: Gossypiboma–"a surgeon's legacy" report of a case and review of the literature. Dis. Colon Rectum **45**(1), 119–120 (2002)
17. Regenbogen, S.E., et al.: Prevention of retained surgical sponges: a decision-analytic model predicting relative cost-effectiveness. Surgery **145**(5), 527–535 (2009)
18. Rigamonti, D., Rigamonti, K.H., Rigamonti, A.S.: Retained foreign object signals a dangerous atmosphere in the operating room. Cureus **17**(3) (2025)

19. Rombach, R., Blattmann, A., Lorenz, D., Esser, P., Ommer, B.: High-resolution image synthesis with latent diffusion models. In: Proceedings of the IEEE/CVF Conference on Computer Vision and Pattern Recognition, pp. 10684–10695 (2022)
20. Ruiz, N., Li, Y., Jampani, V., Pritch, Y., Rubinstein, M., Aberman, K.: DreamBooth: fine tuning text-to-image diffusion models for subject-driven generation. In: Proceedings of the IEEE/CVF Conference on Computer Vision and Pattern Recognition, pp. 22500–22510 (2023)
21. Santosh, K., Roy, S., Allu, S.: Generic foreign object detection in chest X-rays. In: International Conference on Recent Trends in Image Processing and Pattern Recognition, pp. 93–104. Springer (2021)
22. Stawicki, S.P.: Retained surgical foreign bodies: a comprehensive review of risks and preventive strategies. Scand. J. Surg. **98**(1), 8–17 (2009)
23. Sun, H.S., Chen, S.L., Kuo, C.C., Wang, S.C., Kao, Y.L.: Gossypiboma–retained surgical sponge. J. Chin. Med. Assoc. **70**(11), 511–513 (2007)
24. Viola, P., Jones, M.: Rapid object detection using a boosted cascade of simple features. In: Proceedings of the 2001 IEEE Computer Society Conference on Computer Vision and Pattern Recognition, CVPR 2001, vol. 1, IEEE (2001)
25. Wang, Y., et al.: Dataset and benchmark for enhancing critical retained foreign object detection. arXiv preprint arXiv:2507.06937 (2025)
26. Wang, Z., Simoncelli, E.P., Bovik, A.C.: Multiscale structural similarity for image quality assessment. In: The Thrity-Seventh asilomar Conference on Signals, Systems & Computers, 2003, vol. 2, pp. 1398–1402. IEEE (2003)
27. Weber, T., Ingrisch, M., Bischl, B., Rügamer, D.: Cascaded latent diffusion models for high-resolution chest X-ray synthesis. In: Pacific-Asia Conference on Knowledge Discovery and Data Mining, pp. 180–191. Springer (2023)
28. Wu, J., et al.: Vision-language foundation model for 3D medical imaging. NPJ Artif. Intell. **1**(1), 17 (2025)
29. Xie, C., Yoshii, Y., Kitahara, I.: SV-DRR: high-fidelity novel view X-ray synthesis using diffusion model. In: International Conference on Medical Image Computing and Computer-Assisted Intervention, pp. 572–582. Springer (2025)
30. Xue, Z., et al.: Foreign object detection in chest X-rays. In: 2015 IEEE International Conference on Bioinformatics and Biomedicine (BIBM), pp. 956–961. IEEE (2015)
31. Zhou, L., et al.: A dataset and benchmark for enhancing retained foreign object detection through physics-based image synthesis. MICCAI Workshop on Data Engineering in Medical Imaging, 147–156. Springer (2025)

SutureFormer: Learning Surgical Trajectories via Goal-Conditioned Offline RL in Pixel Space

Huanrong Liu[1,2], Chunlin Tian[1], Tongyu Jia[3], Tailai Zhou[3], Qin Liu[1], Yu Gao[3], Yutong Ban[7], Yun Gu[5,6], Guy Rosman[4(✉)], Xin Ma[3(✉)], and Qingbiao Li[1,2(✉)]

[1] Faculty of Science and Technology, University of Macau, Macau, China
qingbiaoli@um.edu.mo
[2] University of Macau Advanced Research Institute in Hengqin, Zhuhai, China
[3] Senior Department of Urology, The Chinese PLA General Hospital, Beijing, China
[4] School of Medicine, Duke University, Durham, NC, USA
[5] Shanghai Key Laboratory of Flexible Medical Robotics, Tongren Hospital, Institute of Medical Robotics, Shanghai Jiao Tong University, Shanghai, China
[6] School of Automation and Intelligent Sensing, Shanghai Jiao Tong University, Shanghai, China
[7] Global College, Shanghai Jiao Tong University, Shanghai, China

Abstract. Predicting surgical needle trajectories from endoscopic video is critical for robot-assisted suturing, enabling anticipatory planning, real-time guidance, and safer motion execution. However, most surgical recordings lack synchronized robot kinematics, and dense frame-level annotations are prohibitively expensive to obtain from clinical experts. To address these challenges, we propose SutureFormer, a goal-conditioned offline reinforcement learning framework that reformulates trajectory prediction as visual navigation in pixel space. SutureFormer operates solely on raw image sequences under sparse supervision, eliminating the need for kinematic signals or dense annotations. It encodes variable-length video observations using a Spatial CNN and Transformer architecture to capture both local spatial cues and long-range temporal dependencies. It then autoregressively predicts future waypoints within an action space comprising discrete directions and continuous magnitudes. A guidance channel constructed from nine sparse keyframe waypoints provides goal conditioning. To enable stable offline training from expert demonstrations, we adopt Conservative Q-Learning with confidence-weighted rewards and behavioral cloning regularization. We evaluate SutureFormer on a new kidney wound suturing dataset comprising 1,158 trajectories from 50 patients, where it reduces Average Displacement Error by 56.8% compared to the strongest baseline, demon-

H. Liu, C. Tian, T. Jia and T. Zhou—Equal contribution.

Supplementary Information The online version contains supplementary material available at https://doi.org/10.1007/978-3-032-38236-8_49.

G. Yang et al. (Eds.): MICCAI 2026, LNCS 16893, pp. 511–520, 2027.
https://doi.org/10.1007/978-3-032-38236-8_49

strating the effectiveness of pixel-level sequential action modeling and the offline RL formulation for surgical trajectory prediction. The code will be available in https://github.com/HaroldHuanrongLIU/MICCAI2026_SutureFormer.

Keywords: Surgical Trajectory Prediction · Offline Reinforcement Learning · Robot-Assisted Surgery · Endoscopic Video Analysis

1 Introduction

Robot-assisted surgery is evolving from tele-operation toward task-level autonomy, where intelligent systems anticipate surgical intent and provide proactive assistance [1,21]. Within this paradigm, the capacity to predict instrument trajectories, particularly during suturing, one of the most technically demanding and outcome-sensitive maneuvers in minimally invasive procedures.

From the perspective of bounded rationality [18], surgeons operate under inherent cognitive constraints: limited attention span, finite working memory, and time pressure collectively bound the optimality of intraoperative decisions. A learning-based trajectory prediction system that distills expert demonstrations into anticipatory guidance can therefore serve as a decision-support mechanism, helping less experienced surgeons approximate expert-level performance and ultimately improving access to high-quality surgical care.

Despite growing interest in deep learning for surgical scene analysis [12], including workflow recognition [9] and scene understanding [13], research on precise procedural assistance for trajectory prediction remains nascent. Current methods face two critical practical barriers. First, most approaches depend on robot kinematic signals, including joint angles, end-effector poses, and gripper states [15,17,20]. Such data are available only on platforms with accessible kinematic interfaces (e.g., the da Vinci Research Kit) and often require direct collaboration with device manufacturers. This dependency fundamentally limits transferability: a policy trained on one robotic platform cannot generalize to another, let alone to the vast archive of conventional laparoscopic video where no kinematic readout exists. In addition, many methods require dense temporal annotations, which are prohibitively expensive to obtain.

Learning control from pixels is a challenging but transformative idea, one that has seen remarkable success in adjacent fields. For instance, purely vision-based imitation learning agents have mastered complex control tasks like driving, learning to navigate and plan by directly mapping image inputs to steering commands [3,14]. Cai et al. [4] demonstrated that cost functions for reinforcement learning (RL) can be learned directly from images, bypassing the need for explicit state estimation. Similarly, Tamar et al. proposed Value Iteration Networks (VIN) [19] that a neural network can learn to perform goal-directed reasoning, generalizing its policy to novel environments by embedding a computational process akin to planning within its architecture. These insights suggest that the "kinematic bottleneck" in surgical trajectory prediction is not a technological inevitability, but a design choice.

To address these limitations, we propose SutureFormer, which reformulates surgical trajectory prediction as goal-conditioned visual navigation in pixel space using offline expert demonstrations. A goal-conditioned policy iteratively predicts future needle waypoints based solely on local visual context and sparse keyframe guidance. The observation encoder combines a Spatial CNN and Transformer to capture spatial cues and long-range temporal dependencies. A discrete-action Conservative Q-Learning (CQL) agent then autoregressively generates trajectory waypoints using a 9 direction action space with continuous step magnitudes, conditioned on keyframe goals during training and polynomial extrapolation at inference. In practice, SutureFormer requires only endoscopic video frames and 9 sparse keyframes annotations per trajectory. To our knowledge, this is the first framework to formulate surgical trajectory prediction as visual navigation task with offline RL in pixel space. Our method outperforms current state-of-the-art methods, demonstrating the viability of offline RL for surgical trajectory prediction.

2 Methods

Problem Statement. Given a variable-length observed video sequence $V_{0:T_P} = \{I_t\}_{t=0}^{T_P}$ with corresponding needle tip coordinates $\{(x_t, y_t)\}_{t=0}^{T_P}$, our goal is to predict the remaining trajectory $\{(\hat{x}_t, \hat{y}_t)\}_{t=T_P+1}^{T_P+T_F}$, where T_P and T_F denote the number of observed and predicted frames, respectively. We formulate this task as a goal-conditioned Markov Decision Process and solve it using offline CQL. Figure 1 illustrates the overall architecture, which employs an encoder-decoder framework where the decoder functions as a pixel-space reinforcement learning trajectory generator conditioned on the past frames.

2.1 Observation Encoder

Each frame is represented by a 128×128 local crop extracted from the full image and centered at the needle tip. The crop is augmented with a guidance channel, a single-channel heatmap encoding the trajectory path confidence at each pixel, and concatenated with the RGB data to form a 4-channel input. The observation encoder comprises: (i) a SpatialCNN extracts features from all observed input frames $\{I_t\}_{t=0}^{T_P}$; (ii) a sinusoidal coordinate encoder that maps all 2D coordinate $\{(x_t, y_t)\}_{t=0}^{T_P}$, normalized to the range $[0, 1]$, then subsequently transformed by a two-layer MLP; and (iii) a Transformer that aggregates the variable-length observation sequence.

Specifically, for each trajectory, an image feature $\mathbf{f}^{\text{img}}$ and a coordinate feature $\mathbf{f}^{\text{coord}}$ are extracted from historical observation, concatenated, and projected into the Transformer dimension of d_{model}. The Transformer employs a causal attention mask and a padding mask to support variable observation lengths T_{obs}. Finally, LayerNorm is applied to the last valid output token to yield the contextual representation $\mathbf{z}_c$.

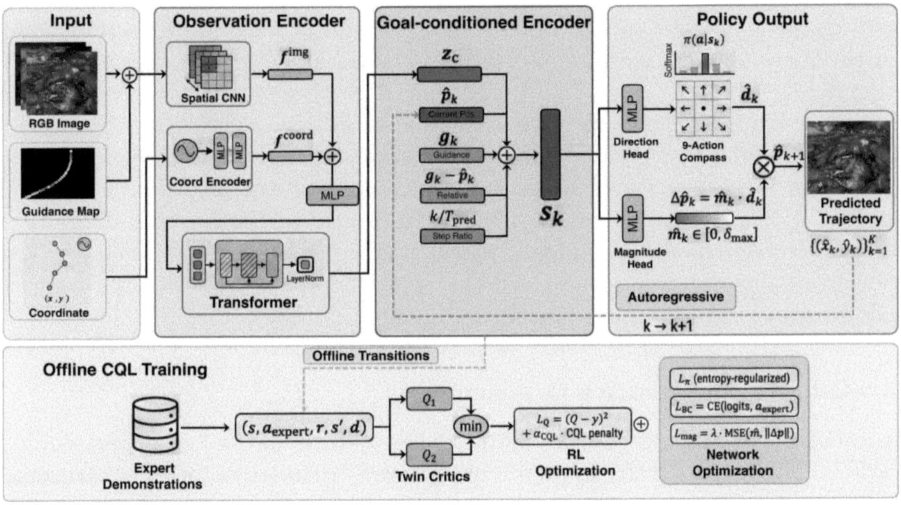

Fig. 1. Overview of the proposed framework. The Observation Encoder fuses visual and coordinate features and aggregates them via a Transformer to produce $\mathbf{z}_c$. The Goal-conditioned Encoder combines $\mathbf{z}_c$ with the current position, guidance target, relative displacement, and step ratio into a unified state $\mathbf{s}_k$. The Policy Output predicts direction and magnitude to autoregressively generate the trajectory. The model is trained entirely offline via Conservative Q-Learning with twin critics and supplementary behavior cloning and magnitude supervision losses.

2.2 Goal-Conditioned Encoder

At each prediction step k, a state representation is constructed by combining the observation context with the current navigation state:

$$\mathbf{s}_k = \phi\big(\mathbf{z}_c,\ \hat{\mathbf{p}}_k,\ \mathbf{g}_k,\ \mathbf{g}_k - \hat{\mathbf{p}}_k,\ k/T_{\text{pred}}\big) \tag{1}$$

where $\mathbf{g}_k$ denotes the guidance coordinate at step k. Three independent sinusoidal coordinate encoders are utilized to map the current position $\hat{\mathbf{p}}_k$, the guidance target $\mathbf{g}_k$, and the relative displacement $\mathbf{g}_k - \hat{\mathbf{p}}_k$. Additionally, a linear layer maps the scalar step ratio k/T_{pred} to a feature space. The concatenation ϕ of these encoded features with the contextual representation $\mathbf{z}_c$ yields the final state vector $\mathbf{s}_k$.

The proposed method employs a discrete 9-direction action space. A direction head outputs the logits over these 9 actions, whereas a magnitude head predicts a continuous scalar step magnitude $\hat{m}_k \in [0, \delta_{\text{max}}]$. During inference, the predicted displacement is formulated as:

$$\hat{\mathbf{d}}_k = \sum_{a=1}^{9} \pi(a|\mathbf{s}_k)\,\mathbf{u}_a \Delta\hat{\mathbf{p}}_k = \hat{m}_k\,\hat{\mathbf{d}}_k, \qquad \hat{\mathbf{p}}_{k+1} = \text{clip}(\hat{\mathbf{p}}_k + \Delta\hat{\mathbf{p}}_k, 0, 1) \tag{2}$$

where $\hat{\mathbf{d}}_k = \sum_{a=1}^{9} \pi(a|\mathbf{s}_k)\,\mathbf{u}_a$ represents the softmax-weighted direction vector that produces smooth motion, and $\mathbf{u}_a$ denotes the unit vector corresponding to action a.

During training, the guidance coordinates $\mathbf{g}_k$ are constructed by placing confidence-weighted annotated trajectory points within the 128×128 crop, applying dilation via a 3×3 max filter, and concatenating the result with the RGB data to form a 4-channel input. During testing, due to the unavailability of future trajectory points, pseudo-guidance is generated via polynomial extrapolation from the observed points. All the positions are clamped to the range of $[0, 1]^2$ to avoid exceeding the normalized image boundary.

2.3 Offline Conservative Q-Learning

SutureFormer is trained entirely offline using a static dataset of expert demonstrations. During the training phase, the ground-truth trajectories are traversed to extract expert transitions. At each step k, the spatial displacement $\mathbf{p}_{k+1} - \mathbf{p}_k$ is discretized into the nearest compass direction via cosine similarity (assigned an idle action if $\|\mathbf{p}_{k+1} - \mathbf{p}_k\| < 10^{-6}$), and the corresponding expert magnitude is defined as $m_k^* = \|\mathbf{p}_{k+1} - \mathbf{p}_k\|_2$.

The proposed framework adopts Conservative Q-Learning (CQL) [10], which incorporates a penalty into the standard Bellman backup to mitigate the over-estimation of the Q-function for out-of-distribution actions. By penalizing the Q-values associated with unobserved actions, this approach ensures that the learned policy remains proximate to the demonstrated expert behavior. The critic loss for a given transition $(\mathbf{s}, a_{\text{expert}}, r, \mathbf{s}', d)$ is formulated as

$$\mathcal{L}_Q = (Q(\mathbf{s}, a_{\text{expert}}) - y)^2 + \alpha_{\text{CQL}} \cdot \left(\log \sum_{a'} \exp Q(\mathbf{s}, a') - Q(\mathbf{s}, a_{\text{expert}}) \right) \quad (3)$$

where $y = r + \gamma^n (1 - d) \cdot V(\mathbf{s}')$ represents the n-step target with a discount factor $\gamma = 0.95$, whereas the parameter $\alpha_{\text{CQL}} = 0.01$ controls the strength of the conservative regularization. The maximum-entropy soft value target $V(\mathbf{s}')$ is computed as:

$$V(\mathbf{s}') = \sum_{a'} \pi(a'|\mathbf{s}') \left[\min(Q_1^{\text{tgt}}(\mathbf{s}', a'), Q_2^{\text{tgt}}(\mathbf{s}', a')) - \alpha \log \pi(a'|\mathbf{s}') \right] \quad (4)$$

where $\alpha = 0.2$ denotes a fixed entropy temperature. Furthermore, the actor is optimized via an entropy-regularized objective function utilizing the estimated Q-values:

$$\mathcal{L}_\pi = \mathbb{E}_{\mathbf{s}} \left[\sum_a \pi(a \mid \mathbf{s}) \left(\alpha \log \pi(a \mid \mathbf{s}) - \min(Q_1(\mathbf{s}, a), Q_2(\mathbf{s}, a)) \right) \right] \quad (5)$$

This objective is supplemented by a behavior cloning loss $\mathcal{L}_{\text{BC}} = \text{CE}(\text{logits}, a_{\text{expert}})$ with a weighting coefficient $\lambda_{\text{BC}} = 1.0$, and a supervised magnitude loss $\mathcal{L}_{\text{mag}} = \lambda_{\text{mag}} \cdot \text{MSE}(\hat{m}, \|\mathbf{p}_{\text{target}} - \mathbf{p}_{\text{current}}\|_2)$ with $\lambda_{\text{mag}} = 100$.

We note a critical design choice of separating gradient flows. Specifically, the Q-networks receive states with detached gradients to prevent the propagation of gradients into the observation encoder. Conversely, the losses associated with the actor and the step magnitude allow gradients to propagate through the state encoder and into the contextual representation $\mathbf{z}_c$. This configuration ensures that the objectives of trajectory prediction, rather than those of value estimation, dictate the formation of the visual representations.

2.4 Reward Design with Sparse Keyframe Supervision

At each prediction step k, the reward comprises three components: a constant time penalty $r_{\text{time}} = -0.01$ encouraging efficient trajectories, a confidence-weighted proximity reward based on the distance d_k to the ground truth, and an exponential terminal bonus at the final step. The proximity reward is positive (up to $r_{\text{prox,max}} = 0.5$) when d_k falls within a threshold of 0.02 in normalized coordinates, and negative otherwise. Since clinical experts annotate only 9 keyframes per trajectory while intermediate positions are obtained via temporal interpolation, we apply confidence-based weighting: keyframe steps receive full weight ($w = 1.0$), whereas interpolated steps are down-weighted proportionally ($w = 0.5 + 0.5 \cdot confidence$, see detail in Sect. 3), providing dense training signals while reflecting the lower certainty of non-keyframe positions. To handle variable-length observation and prediction sequences, we employ masked attention within the Transformer encoder to selectively attend to valid time steps while ignoring padded positions. Furthermore, we use bucketed batch sampling, which groups sequences of similar lengths into the same batch, thereby minimizing padding overhead and improving training efficiency.

3 Experiments

Datasets. We evaluate SutureFormer on real clinical dataset of robotic-assisted laparoscopic kidney wound suturing operated by expert surgeon. The dataset comprises surgical videos from 50 patients and contains a total of 1,158 trajectories, where clinical experts annotate 9 keyframes within each trajectory. The dataset is partitioned at the patient level into training, validation, and test sets, consisting of 35, 8, and 7 patients (corresponding to 861, 151, and 146 trajectories), respectively.

Interpolated Annotation. To obtain dense per-frame annotations, we independently apply cubic spline interpolation [5] to the x and y coordinate sequences as functions of the frame index. Given the 9 keyframe positions, we fit two natural cubic spline functions, $S_x(t)$ and $S_y(t)$, evaluating them at every intermediate frame within the temporal range. The interpolated coordinates are rounded to the nearest integer to yield valid pixel locations, without extrapolation beyond the first and last keyframes. Each interpolated frame receives a confidence score from 0.45 to 0.9 based on its temporal proximity to the nearest keyframe, assigning higher scores to closer frames. The expert annotated keyframes retain a confidence score of 1.0.

Implementation Details. The model is trained for 100 epochs with batch size 8 on an NVIDIA RTX 5090 GPU. We use four Adam optimizers with cosine annealing decaying to 1% of the initial learning rates: 1×10^{-4} for the observation encoder and 3×10^{-4} for the actor, critic, and magnitude heads. CQL hyperparameters are $\alpha_{\text{CQL}} = 0.01$, $\gamma = 0.95$, and $n =$ 3-step returns, with soft target updates $\tau = 0.005$. Policy and magnitude updates subsample up to 2,048 transitions per batch.
Evaluation Metrics. All metrics are computed in pixel space by rescaling normalized coordinates to the original 1264×902 resolution. We report Average Displacement Error (ADE), the mean Euclidean distance across all prediction steps; Final Displacement Error (FDE), the Euclidean distance at the last step; and discrete Fréchet Distance (FD), measuring global trajectory shape similarity. Lower values indicate better performance for all three metrics.

Table 1. Quantitative comparison on the test set under two setting (Obs = 6, Pred = 3 and Obs = 3, Pred = 6). Specifically, Obs = 6 denotes an observed surgical trajectory comprising 6 annotated keyframes, whereas Pred = 3 represents the prediction of the future trajectory containing 3 keyframes. All metrics are evaluated in pixel space (lower is better), with the best results highlighted in **bold** and second best in **underline**.

Method	Obs = 6, Pred = 3			Obs = 3, Pred = 6		
	ADE (↓)	FDE (↓)	FD (↓)	ADE (↓)	FDE (↓)	FD (↓)
BC [2]	<u>128.15</u>	<u>146.24</u>	<u>156.83</u>	<u>137.06</u>	<u>184.69</u>	<u>195.13</u>
GAIL [8]	269.79	282.99	305.86	249.19	254.41	318.82
IBC [6]	243.97	262.12	285.60	225.74	260.49	296.82
iDiff-IL [11]	187.38	207.32	220.21	223.75	259.90	296.62
CondDiff [11]	165.20	189.47	200.31	184.15	236.84	255.62
MID [7]	151.23	165.24	192.79	172.67	229.83	246.65
Ours	**55.29**	**84.23**	**86.00**	**94.85**	**154.68**	**158.46**

4 Results

4.1 Comparison with Baselines

We compare SutureFormer against following baselines: (1) Behavioral Cloning (BC) [2], which encodes stacked frames via a U-Net [16] and regresses future coordinates with an MLP; (2) Generative Adversarial Imitation Learning (GAIL) [8], which generates trajectories conditioned on a random latent vector with a discriminator distinguishing real from generated pairs; (3) Implicit Behavioral Cloning (IBC) [6], an energy based model trained with InfoNCE loss and sampled via Langevin MCMC at inference; (4) Implicit Diffusion Policy (iDiff-IL) [11], a joint image trajectory diffusion method using a dual-head UNet to denoise

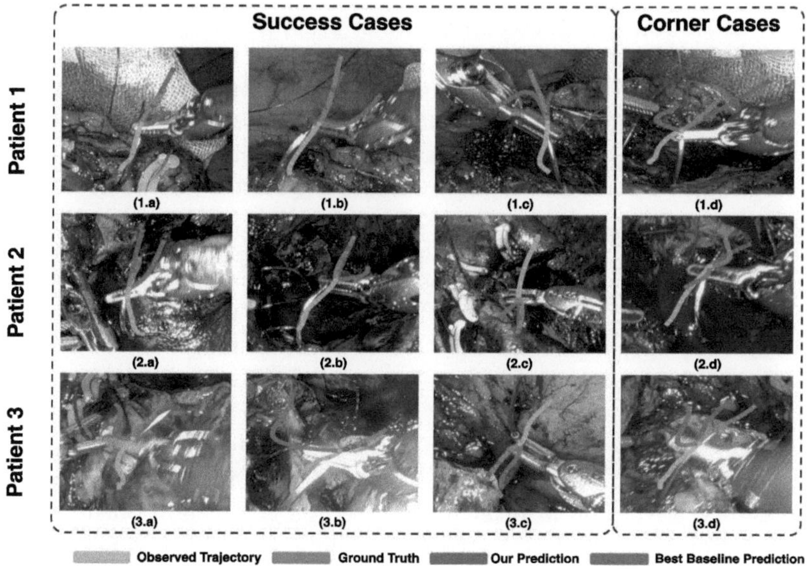

Fig. 2. Qualitative comparison of predicted trajectories on the testset. The **yellow** curve denotes the observed trajectory, the **green** curve represents the ground truth future trajectory, the **red** curve shows the prediction from our SutureFormer and the **blue** curve indicates the best baseline prediction. (Color figure online)

both spaces simultaneously; (5) Conditional Diffusion Policy (CondDiff) [11], a variant applying DDPM denoising in trajectory space only, conditioned on the image; and (6) Motion Indeterminacy Diffusion (MID) [7], a latent-space diffusion method that encodes frames into a context vector and applies a Transformer-based DDPM denoiser for trajectory generation.

Quantitative Results. Table 1 reports results under two experimental settings. SutureFormer consistently outperforms all baselines across all metrics. With Obs = 6, Pred = 3, SutureFormer achieves an ADE of 55.29 (56.8% reduction over BC at 128.15) and FD of 84.23 (vs. 146.24 for BC), indicating substantially better trajectory shape fidelity. Under the more challenging Obs = 3, Pred = 6 setting, all methods degrade as historical observational information decreases, yet ours remains the best, achieving ADE 94.85, FDE 154.68 and FD 158.46. SutureFormer maintains clear advantages in ADE (30.7% reduction over BC), FDE (16.2% reduction) and FD (18.7% reduction), demonstrating that the CQL-based policy produces more accurate trajectories with better shape consistency even under sparse observations. The goal-conditioned navigation formulation proves particularly beneficial when visual context is limited, as explicit target guidance compensates for reduced observational evidence. To further isolate the contribution of conservative offline reinforcement learning, we remove CQL from the training objective and observe 23.5%, 18.6%, and 18.1% degradation in ADE, FDE, and FD, respectively. This indicates that the performance gain is not merely attributable to the architecture or preprocessing, but is substantially supported by conservative offline RL.

Qualitative Results. Figure 2 illustrates representative predicted trajectories overlaid on surgical images, alongside the corresponding ground-truth paths and prediction results from selected state-of-art baseline method. As observed across diverse suturing scenarios from multiple patients, the baseline method frequently struggles to capture the complex spatial dynamics of the surgical instruments, resulting in predicted trajectories that significantly deviate from the true paths. In contrast, our proposed approach consistently maintains high fidelity to the ground truth. The proposed model generates smooth trajectories that conform to the general curvature of the suturing path.

5 Conclusion

This paper introduces SutureFormer, a novel framework that reformulates surgical trajectory prediction in pixel space based on goal-conditioned offline reinforcement learning using Conservative Q-Learning. By requiring only 9 keyframe annotations per trajectory and operating without robot kinematics, the framework demonstrates broad applicability to existing clinical video archives. Experimental results on 1,158 trajectories demonstrate that SutureFormer significantly outperforms best diffusion and imitation learning baselines, achieving up to a 56.8% reduction in ADE. Future work will extend SutureFormer to broader laparoscopic procedures and validate its performance through ex-vivo porcine experiments on robotic platforms, facilitating its transition toward precise, advancing its translation toward real-world cognitive surgical assistance.

Acknowledgments. This work was supported by the University of Macau under Grants SRG2024-00056-FST, 0078/2024/RIB2, and FST/SP01/2024, the Dr. Stanley Ho Medical Development Foundation under Grant SHMDF-AI/2026/002, the Natural Science Foundation of China under Grant 62373243, the Shanghai Municipal Health Commission Smart Healthcare Project under Grant 2025ZHYL021, and the Shanghai Tongren Hospital Medical-Engineering Collaboration Project under Grant lhyjzx2024-xm03. The surgical records of robot-assisted partial nephrectomy used in this work were collected by the Chinese PLA General Hospital and annotated by two expert surgeons.

Disclosure of Interests. The authors have no competing interests.

References

1. Attanasio, A., Scaglioni, B., De Momi, E., Fiorini, P., Valdastri, P.: Autonomy in surgical robotics. Ann. Rev. Control Rob. Auton. Syst. **4**, 651–679 (2021). https://doi.org/10.1146/annurev-control-062420-090543. https://www.annualreviews.org/content/journals/10.1146/annurev-control-062420-090543
2. Bain, M., Sammut, C.: A framework for behavioural cloning. In: Machine Intelligence 15, Intelligent Agents [St. Catherine's College, Oxford, July 1995], pp. 103–129. Oxford University, GBR (1999)

3. Bojarski, M., et al.: End to end learning for self-driving cars (2016). arXiv preprint arXiv:1604.07316
4. Cai, P., Wang, H., Huang, H., Liu, Y., Liu, M.: Vision-based autonomous car racing using deep imitative reinforcement learning. IEEE Rob. Autom. Lett. **6**(4), 7262–7269 (2021)
5. De Boor, C., De Boor, C.: A Practical Guide to Splines, vol. 27. springer, New York (1978)
6. Florence, P., et al.: Implicit behavioral cloning. In: Faust, A., Hsu, D., Neumann, G. (eds.) Proceedings of the 5th Conference on Robot Learning. PMLR, vol. 164, pp. 158–168. PMLR (2022). https://proceedings.mlr.press/v164/florence22a.html
7. Gu, T., et al.: Stochastic trajectory prediction via motion indeterminacy diffusion. In: 2022 IEEE/CVF Conference on Computer Vision and Pattern Recognition (CVPR), pp. 17092–17101 (2022). https://doi.org/10.1109/CVPR52688.2022.01660
8. Ho, J., Ermon, S.: Generative adversarial imitation learning. In: NIPS, pp. 4572–4580. Curran Associates Inc., Red Hook, NY, USA (2016)
9. Jin, Y., Long, Y., Gao, X., Stoyanov, D., Dou, Q., Heng, P.A.: Trans-SVNet: hybrid embedding aggregation transformer for surgical workflow analysis. Int. J. Comput. Assist. Radiol. Surg. **17**(12), 2193–2202 (2022)
10. Kumar, A., Zhou, A., Tucker, G., Levine, S.: Conservative Q-learning for offline reinforcement learning. In: NeurIPS. Curran Associates Inc., Red Hook, NY, USA (2020)
11. Li, J., et al.: Imitation learning from expert video data for dissection trajectory prediction in endoscopic surgical procedure. In: MICCAI, pp. 494–504. Springer-Verlag, Heidelberg (2023). https://doi.org/10.1007/978-3-031-43996-4_47
12. Maier-Hein, L., et al.: Surgical data science for next-generation interventions. Nat. Biomed. Eng. **1**(9), 691–696 (2017)
13. Nwoye, C.I., et al.: Rendezvous: attention mechanisms for the recognition of surgical action triplets in endoscopic videos. Med. Image Anal. **78**, 102433 (2022)
14. Pomerleau, D.A.: ALVINN: an autonomous land vehicle in a neural network. In: NIPS 1988, pp. 305–313. MIT Press, Cambridge, MA, USA (1988)
15. Qin, Y., Feyzabadi, S., Allan, M., Burdick, J.W., Azizian, M.: daVinciNet: joint prediction of motion and surgical state in robot-assisted surgery. In: IROS, pp. 2921–2928 (2020). https://doi.org/10.1109/IROS45743.2020.9340723
16. Ronneberger, O., Fischer, P., Brox, T.: U-Net: convolutional networks for biomedical image segmentation. In: MICCAI, pp. 234–241. Springer (2015)
17. Shi, C., Zheng, Y., Fey, A.M.: Recognition and prediction of surgical gestures and trajectories using transformer models in robot-assisted surgery. In: IROS, pp. 8017–8024 (2022). https://doi.org/10.1109/IROS47612.2022.9981611
18. Simon, H.A., et al.: Theories of bounded rationality. Decis. Organization **1**(1), 161–176 (1972)
19. Tamar, A., Wu, Y., Thomas, G., Levine, S., Abbeel, P.: Value iteration networks. In: Advances in Neural Information Processing Systems, vol. 29 (2016)
20. Weerasinghe, K., Reza Roodabeh, S.H., Hutchinson, K., Alemzadeh, H.: Multimodal transformers for real-time surgical activity prediction. In: ICRA, pp. 13323–13330 (2024). https://doi.org/10.1109/ICRA57147.2024.10611048
21. Yang, G.Z., et al.: Medical robotics—regulatory, ethical, and legal considerations for increasing levels of autonomy (2017)

SWoMo: Neuro-Symbolic World Model for Cataract Surgery Simulation

Ssharvien Kumar Sivakumar[1,2](✉), Akwele Johnson[1], Anirudh Dhingra[1], Yannik Frisch[1,3], Ghazal Ghazaei[2], and Anirban Mukhopadhyay[1]

[1] Technical University Darmstadt, Darmstadt, Germany
[2] Carl Zeiss AG, Munich, Germany
ssharvien_kumar.sivakumar@tu-darmstadt.de
[3] AICM, Medical Faculty of Heidelberg University, Heidelberg University, Heidelberg, Germany

Abstract. Realistic surgical simulation plays a crucial role in training novice surgeons and in the development of autonomous agents. World models can scale such simulation environments to realistic and diverse procedures by predicting future patient states conditioned on current observations and surgical actions. However, current state-of-the-art approaches often fail to satisfy key criteria required for clinical applicability, including visual realism, physically grounded interactions, and the ability to simulate scenarios beyond the training distribution. Hence, we introduce SWoMo, a neuro-symbolic world model for cataract surgery simulation that decouples motion generation from visual realism. The symbolic component, consisting of a rule-based simulator and scene graph representations, models motion dynamics and tool-tissue interactions, while a diffusion model produces realistic visual appearance, including textures and tissue deformations. We propose an inverse pairing strategy that reconstructs real surgical videos in the simulator to obtain paired simulated and real videos, which are then used to train our video diffusion model for the reverse objective of sim-to-real translation. Our experiments show both qualitative and quantitative improvements over prior work. We demonstrate that our simulator further satisfies the key criteria, including generalisation to unseen interaction geometries, improvements in downstream phase detection, and unsupervised video style transfer. The code, data, and model weights are available at: https://ssharvienkumar.github.io/SWoMo/.

Keywords: World Model · Video Generation · Interactive Simulation

1 Introduction

Surgery demands high precision, where irreversible actions must be carefully coordinated through structured spatial reasoning and causal understanding [6].

Supplementary Information The online version contains supplementary material available at https://doi.org/10.1007/978-3-032-38236-8_50.

G. Yang et al. (Eds.): MICCAI 2026, LNCS 16893, pp. 521–531, 2027.
https://doi.org/10.1007/978-3-032-38236-8_50

Simulated environments provide a safe and controllable setting in which such dependencies can be explored [8], enabling applications ranging from risk-free, immersive surgical skills training for novice surgeons to the development of autonomous surgical robotic agents that can reason and plan interactively [23,25]. However, scaling such environments to realistic and diverse procedures requires models that integrate continuous perception with explicit representations of the geometry and dynamics of the surgical scene [3]. Surgical world models address this need by enabling *interactive simulation* and *predictive modelling* of future patient states conditioned on current observations and actions [11,20], thereby *unifying perception, dynamics, and action* within a single framework [3].

However, the clinical applicability of a surgical world model hinges on satisfying three key criteria: **(I)** The simulated environment must achieve **high visual realism** to minimise the sim-to-real gap, as low fidelity limits policy transfer [18]. Yet this remains a major challenge for traditional simulators, particularly in modelling complex instrument-tissue interactions [20,28]. **(II)** Equally important is ensuring **physically grounded interactions**, so that both learning agents and human trainees acquire behaviours that transfer reliably to real high-stakes surgical settings [34]. **(III)** The **dynamic representation of the world model must go beyond the training distribution**, enabling the generation of plausible outcomes under unseen tool geometries, insertion angles, and novel surgical workflows.

Unfortunately, state-of-the-art research typically excels on one criterion while failing to satisfy others. Methods that attempt to control video generative models via various conditioning signals [2,12,26,28] fall short of interactive surgical simulation due to the lack of step-wise action conditioning. As a result, they provide limited fine-grained control for agent or trainee intervention and cannot be considered true world models. Their behaviour is also tightly coupled to the training distribution, degrading significantly under out-of-distribution (OOD) conditions [6]. World-model based approaches, such as SurgWM [20], inspired by Genie [4], learn interactive environments from unstructured surgical videos, but limit interaction to latent action codes rather than direct tool control. DreamGen [17] and SurgWorld [13] generate paired video-action data using inverse dynamics, improving policy learning, yet they lack physical grounding. Unpaired image translation methods [24,32] have also been explored to address the sim-to-real gap, but remain insufficient for modelling complex spatiotemporal tool-tissue interactions.

Hence, we introduce SWoMo, an interactive neuro-symbolic world model for cataract surgery, as shown in Fig. 1, in which **symbolic scene graphs and a rule-based physics simulator** explicitly encode structure and constraints, while a **diffusion model** provides high-fidelity visual synthesis. Our proposed method *explicitly decouples the modelling of surgical motion and interaction dynamics from visual appearance.* This allows precise tool and anatomical motions to be preserved through physically grounded simulation while enabling the generation of entirely novel scenarios beyond the training distribution. Visual

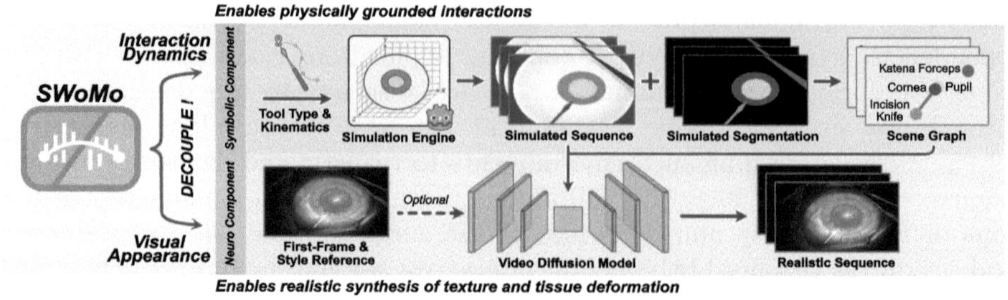

Fig. 1. Neuro-symbolic World Model for interactive cataract surgery simulation that decouples surgical interaction dynamics from visual appearance.

realism, such as texture and tissue deformation, is learned through data-driven synthesis using a diffusion model. To achieve this, we introduce **inverse pairing strategy** in which tool and anatomical motions are extracted from real surgical videos and replayed in the simulator, producing large-scale paired simulated and real videos. These pairs are then used to train a video-to-video diffusion model that translates simulated renderings back into realistic surgical videos. The simulator also produces corresponding segmentations, which are used to construct scene graphs that efficiently encode the scene and object relationships in a structured graphical format. We show that conditioning the diffusion model on scene graphs is crucial for mitigating issues caused by residual misalignment between simulated and real videos. Optional initial frame or style reference conditioning is added for subject-specific surgical simulation. We further demonstrate generalisation to unseen surgical interactions, notable improvements in downstream phase detection, and unsupervised video style transfer across datasets.

2 Method

Our surgical world model decouples motion generation from visual realism. Motion and interaction dynamics are governed by symbolic components comprising of scene graphs $\mathcal{G}$ and a rule-based simulator $T(\cdot)$, while visual appearance is generated by a denoising diffusion model, employing a neural network $\epsilon_\theta(\cdot)$. We begin by extracting the anatomical configuration k_t^{anat} and tool kinematics k_t^{tool} from real surgical video $x_{1:T}$, and use them to construct a digital twin of the eye and replay these signals in this simulator. At time step t, we define the simulator state as $\bar{x}_t = \{k_t^{\text{anat}}, k_t^{\text{tool}}\}$. Actions correspond to explicit surgical tool motions, $a_t = \Delta k_t^{\text{tool}}$. State transitions are governed by $T(\cdot)$ such that $(\bar{x}_{t+1}, \bar{m}_{t+1}) = T(\bar{x}_t, a_t)$, where $\bar{x}_{t+1}$ denotes the next state along with its rendered simulated frame, and $\bar{m}_{t+1}$ is the corresponding segmentation. From each simulator state, a scene graph is generated, $\mathcal{G}_t = S(\bar{x}_t, \bar{m}_t)$, encoding object geometry and relational structure. Final observations are then generated according to $p_\theta(x_{t:t+n} \mid \bar{x}_{t:t+n}, \mathcal{G}_{t:t+n})$, parameterized by the diffusion model, which translates simulated sequence $\bar{x}_{t:t+n}$ into realistic sequence $x_{t:t+n}$.

Here, n denotes the number of consecutive simulated frames jointly provided as conditioning to the diffusion model.

Inverse Pairing: In this section, we describe the extraction of k_t^{anat} and k_t^{tool} from real surgical video $x_{1:T}$. We start by segmenting pupil and iris employing nnU-Net [16], and corresponding segmentations are fitted with ellipses to obtain compact geometric parameters k_t^{iris} and k_t^{pupil} encoding centroid, orientation, and axis lengths. Motion of the eye globe decomposes into global and local components. *Global motion*, arising from camera or patient movement, is estimated by annotating skin landmarks in the first frame x_1 and tracking them over time using pre-trained CoTracker [19]. The resulting trajectories define a global transformation g_t used to estimate the displacement of the eye globe centroid. *Local motion* corresponds to rotational movement of the eye globe and is derived from the centroid trajectory of the pupil mask, yielding rotational parameters r_t. Formally, the globe motion is represented as $k_t^{\text{globe}} = \{g_t, r_t\}$. The anatomical configuration is thus defined as $k_t^{\text{anat}} = \{k_t^{\text{globe}}, k_t^{\text{iris}}, k_t^{\text{pupil}}\}$. Tool kinematics are recovered from tool masks generated using SASVi [29] and SAM2-based [27] manual interactive annotation tool. From these masks, we extract geometric parameters $k_t^{\text{tool}} = \{c_t, \theta_t, \beta_t\}$ where c_t denotes tool tip position, θ_t orientation, and β_t articulation parameters such as bending angle and opening angle.

Rule-Based Simulator: The recovered anatomical and tool parameters $\{k_t^{\text{anat}}, k_t^{\text{tool}}\}$ are used to drive a rule-based simulator $T(\cdot)$ on Godot game engine [10]. The simulator instantiates a parameterised eye globe and surgical tools, whose mesh transformations are directly controlled by these parameters. The global translation g_t is mapped from image coordinates to simulator space through normalisation and fixed scaling, defining the eye globe position, while rotational parameters r_t control eye globe orientation via yaw and pitch. Anatomical meshes are updated using k_t^{iris} and k_t^{pupil}. Iris and pupil geometry are scaled according to their estimated axis lengths, enabling subject-specific variation.

Tool meshes are controlled by $k_t^{\text{tool}} = \{c_t, \theta_t, \beta_t\}$. Tool tip positions c_t are mapped to simulator space using the same normalisation as global globe motion, while orientations θ_t directly determine tool rotation. For articulated instruments such as forceps, articulation parameters β_t control relative mesh rotations to reproduce opening motions, while for angled tools they adjust the shaft bend to maintain geometric consistency. Final tool positions are defined relative to the eye globe surface with an offset scaled by the globe's anatomical scaling factor, ensuring consistent placement in the simulated video $\bar{x}_{1:T}$. We present a real video and its simulated pair, along with segmentations, in Supplementary E.

Symbolic Scene Graph: We form scene graphs $\mathcal{G}_{1:n}$ from $\bar{x}_{1:n}$ and its segmentation $\bar{m}_{1:n}$ and subsequently encode $\mathcal{G}_{1:n}$ following a strategy inspired by SG2VID [28]. Each node in $\mathcal{G}_{1:n}$ represents a connected component from $\bar{m}_{1:n}$ and stores high-level component attributes, including centroid, spatial spreading, and average optical flow within the corresponding region. We pre-trained two separate graph encoders, global encoder $E_{\mathcal{G}}^{glob}$ and local encoder $E_{\mathcal{G}}^{loc}$. The $E_{\mathcal{G}}^{glob}$

learns high-level structural relationships via contrastive learning between $\mathcal{G}_{1:n}$ and $\bar{m}_{1:n}$. In contrast, $E_{\mathcal{G}}^{loc}$ focuses on appearance cues by learning to reconstruct masked regions in the real sequence $x_{1:n}$ using information from $\mathcal{G}_{1:n}$. We find the additional $\mathcal{G}_{1:n}$ conditioning to be important for visual fidelity and conditional adherence, as also highlighted by the ablation study in Table 1. It contributes in two main ways: *first*, $\mathcal{G}_{1:n}$ provides explicit class-level information that is not available from the $\bar{x}_{1:n}$ alone, helping the model distinguish object identities. *Second*, we observe regions near component boundaries, especially near tool-tissue interaction, often suffer from degraded synthesis due to misalignments between $\bar{x}_{1:n}$ used for video conditioning and $x_{1:n}$, which introduce conflicting training signals. When such inconsistencies occur repeatedly, the model tends to average visual features across boundaries, causing smoothing artifacts. Incorporating $\mathcal{G}_{1:n}$ alleviates this by abstracting local pixel-level misalignments, as the node's component-level attributes remain relatively stable under small boundary shifts. Moreover, $\mathcal{G}_{1:n}$ provides only higher-level structural guidance, allowing generator to infer realistic visual boundaries by itself from the learned appearance priors rather than strictly following misaligned $\bar{x}_{1:n}$ conditioning.

Video Diffusion Model with Graph-Image-Video Conditioning: Our diffusion model for translating simulated sequence $\bar{x}_{t:t+n}$ into realistic sequence $x_{t:t+n}$ is trained in two stages, as illustrated in Fig. 2: *first*, learning image and graph to video generation, and *subsequently* incorporating video-level conditioning through ControlNet [35] training. Diffusion models [14] rely on a parameterised network ϵ_θ that is trained to reverse the gradual noise injection process $p(x_{t,\tau-1} \mid x_{t,\tau}, c)$, where τ denotes the diffusion timestep. Training is performed by minimizing a mean squared error objective between the true noise and the noise predicted by ϵ_θ: $\min_\theta \mathbb{E}_{\tau,x_{t,0},\epsilon}\left[\|\epsilon - \epsilon_\theta(x_{t,\tau}, \tau, c)\|^2\right]$. To extend diffusion models to video generation [15], the model is augmented with temporal layers. Specifically, temporal convolution and attention layers are interleaved with spatial layers, enabling the model to capture temporal dependencies and motion dynamics across frames. In the first stage, the conditioning signal c consists of the first-frame x_1 and the sequence scene graphs $\mathcal{G}_{1:n}$. For first-frame conditioning, the noise term ϵ_1 is replaced with the actual first-frame x_1. The resulting model input is therefore constructed as $\hat{\epsilon} = \{x_1, \epsilon_2, \epsilon_3, \ldots, \epsilon_n\}$. For graph conditioning, we concatenate the outputs of $E_{\mathcal{G}}^{glob}$ and $E_{\mathcal{G}}^{loc}$ and further concatenate the result with the timestep embedding before passing it to ϵ_θ.

In the *second stage*, we enable conditioning on the simulated sequence $\bar{x}_{1:n}$. For that, we freeze the parameters θ of the pre-trained diffusion backbone ϵ_θ from the previous stage and create a separate, trainable copy of its encoder with parameters θ_c. The frozen backbone ϵ_θ and the trainable encoder are connected through zero-initialised convolutional layers at multiple resolutions [35], allowing the conditioning simulated sequence $\bar{x}_{1:n}$ to modulate intermediate feature representations without disrupting the pretrained generative prior of ϵ_θ and preserving its visual quality. The $\bar{x}_{1:n}$ is encoded through this control branch, and the resulting features are injected into the corresponding layers of ϵ_θ.

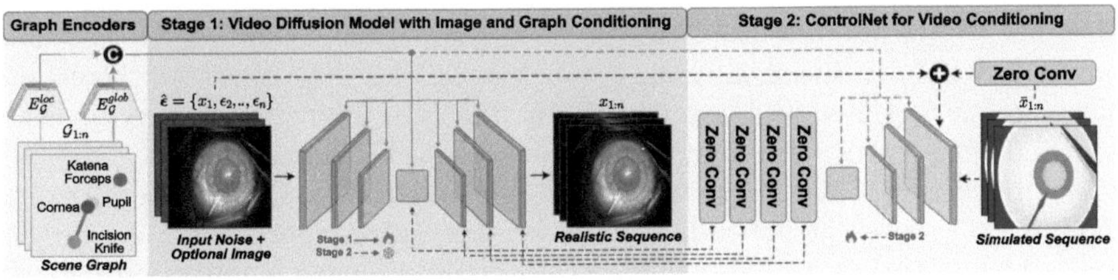

Fig. 2. Overview of SWoMo's two-stage video diffusion training.

3 Experiments and Results

We evaluate our method on two publicly available cataract surgery datasets: CATARACTS [1] and Cataract-1k [9]. To limit the need for extensive frame-level annotations, we restrict our modelling to safety-critical phases, which together account for around half of the video: *Idle, Incision, Viscoelastic, Capsulorhexis, Hydrodissection*, and *Phacoemulsification*. After this filtering, the datasets contain 868 videos from Cataract-1k and 50 videos from CATARACTS, with a mean duration of just over three minutes. For training, videos are temporally sampled at 4 frames per second into sequences of 16 frames and spatially resized to 128×128. Data splits are created at the video level, using a 50/6/44 ratio for CATARACTS and 80/10/10 for Cataract-1k. The training of the diffusion model is distributed across four NVIDIA A40 GPUs.

Table 1. Quantitative Comparisons of Synthesis Quality and Conditioning Adherence.

	CATARACTS [1]					**Cataract-1k** [9]				
Method	FVD↓	FID↓	LPIPS↑	BB IoU↑	F1↑	FVD↓	FID↓	LPIPS↑	BB IoU↑	F1↑
StyleGAN-V [30]	581.5	107.2	0.379	–	–	501.2	116.4	0.286	–	–
Endora [21]	436.8	58.4	0.456	–	–	258.7	40.0	0.379	–	–
MedSora [33]	1243.3	127.6	0.403	–	–	809.9	147.6	0.324	–	–
LVDM [12]	1604.6	131.0	0.557	0.228	0.154	1469.6	176.6	0.519	0.213	0.188
MOFA [26]	993.4	105.6	0.446	0.432	0.282	716.7	94.6	0.358	0.418	0.404
SG2VID [28]	363.8	47.3	0.436	0.497	0.391	73.0	14.9	0.392	0.607	0.623
SWoMo	265.4	40.8	0.450	0.522	0.412	123.0	20.1	0.388	0.645	0.656
SWoMo-✗IMG	329.3	42.3	0.451	0.514	0.406	134.3	20.2	0.389	0.622	0.642
SWoMo-✗SG	390.7	52.1	0.463	0.377	0.296	283.6	35.5	0.434	0.529	0.554

Quantitative Comparison and Ablation: We evaluate the quality and diversity of synthesised videos using FID, FVD [31], and the LPIPS diversity score [36], as shown in Table 1. For conditional methods, we additionally measure adherence to conditioning using detection-based metrics, including F1 score and bounding box IoU. Specifically, we train Mask2Former [7] to detect tools and anatomical structures, and compare bounding box predictions across synthesised and real videos. Our method is benchmarked against multiple baselines with publicly available implementations. StyleGAN-V [30], Endora [21], and MedSora [33] represent unconditional video generation approaches. We further modify LVDM [12] to enable text-based conditioning using scene graph triplets, whereas SG2VID [28] directly conditions on scene graphs. MOFA [26] conditions generation on both the initial frame and motion trajectory derived from sparse optical flow. SWoMo outperforms most baselines in terms of visual fidelity and achieves substantial improvements over all baselines in terms of conditioning adherence. In Table 1, we also provide ablations without scene graph conditioning (SWoMo-✗SG) and without image conditioning (SWoMo-✗IMG) to illustrate the contribution of each conditioning component.

Qualitative Assessment: We present SWoMo's qualitative results in Fig. 3, with additional samples in Supplementary A and a qualitative comparison in Supplementary B. SWoMo leverages both the simulated video and an initial frame for video synthesis, whereas SWoMo-✗IMG relies solely on the simulated video. These results highlight how SWoMo's sim-to-real transfer task reduces major implementation effort on the simulator, for example, by eliminating the need to explicitly model textures and deformation, while still accurately following tool movements and anatomical configurations from the simulated video.

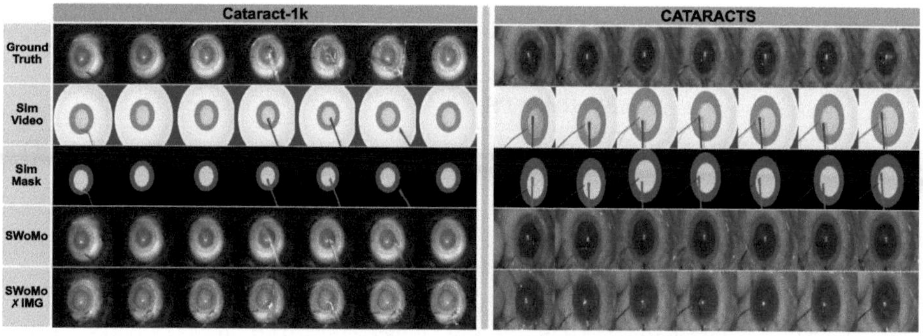

Fig. 3. Qualitative Results of Sim-to-Real Video Transfer.

Unsupervised Video Style Transfer: SWoMo enables unsupervised style transfer between the CATARACTS and Cataract-1k domains without training on paired sequences. This is achieved through a shared intermediate representation of the simulated sequence that is used across both datasets. Specifically, we utilise the simulated sequence from the source domain with the initial-frame conditioning from the target domain to synthesise videos in the target style. Because the intermediate representation encodes geometry and motion independently of appearance, the model preserves interaction dynamics while adopting the visual characteristics of the target domain. The style transfer results are shown in Fig. 4 (top) for both datasets, with full videos provided in Supplementary C.

Improved Generalisation to Novel Tool Motions: Generative models are fundamentally constrained by their training distributions and often degrade on sequences far outside these distributions. By introducing an intermediate simulated sequence representation that provides explicit structural and motion guidance, we further push the boundaries of what the model can handle. Using the simulator, we generate difficult cases, including tools with novel entry directions and tool combinations that never co-occur in the training data. Visual results are shown in Fig. 4 (bottom), with additional examples provided in Supplementary D, demonstrating that the intermediate representation substantially improves generalisation under OOD conditions.

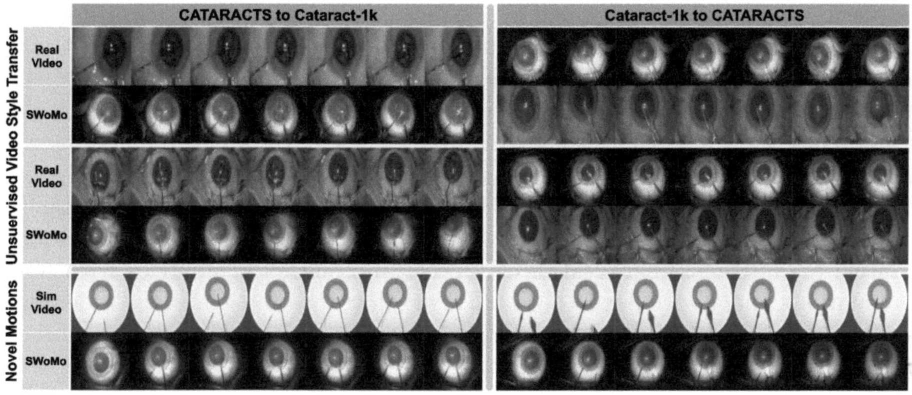

Fig. 4. Unsupervised Video Style Transfer and Generalisation to Novel Tool Motion.

Downstream Evaluation on Phase Recognition: We use synthesised videos to augment the training data of a downstream model for phase recognition during cataract surgery. The phase recognition is performed using MS-TCN++ [22] trained on DINO features [5]. To generate a synthesised video, two real videos are randomly selected from the training set. The visual style is taken from the first video, while the tool and anatomical motion patterns are taken from the second. Phase annotations are inherited from the second video, since the underlying surgical actions remain unchanged, making this process a form of generative data augmentation. To generate full-length surgical videos, sequences are synthesised autoregressively by first generating a sequence and then using its last frame as the first-frame conditioning input for the subsequent sequence. Using this strategy, we effectively double the number of training videos. Table 2 presents the results, demonstrating improvements over training on real data alone and also over generative augmentation with other methods.

Table 2. Performance on Downstream Phase Recognition.

	CATARACTS [1]		Cataract-1k [9]	
Training data	Accuracy↑	F1-Score↑	Accuracy↑	F1-Score↑
Real Only	79.4	79.3	93.7	94.9
Real + LVDM [12]	63.6 (-15.8)	65.3 (-14.0)	71.3 (-22.4)	72.4 (−22.5)
Real + SG2VID [28]	80.5 (+1.1)	81.6 (+2.3)	94.0 (+0.3)	95.3 (+0.4)
Real + SWoMo (Ours)	82.5 (+3.1)	83.0 (+3.7)	94.2 (+0.5)	95.2 (+0.3)

4 Conclusion

We present SWoMo, a neuro-symbolic world model for cataract surgery in which tool kinematics are fed into a rule-based simulator, whose outputs are then converted into realistic videos, effectively combining the strengths of physical simulation and generative modelling. SWoMo fulfils the role of a world model; given the current simulation state and action input, it predicts the next state and generates the corresponding future video frame. Unlike world models that rely primarily on implicit or latent representations, SWoMo explicitly models scene dynamics, which is particularly important for physically grounded interactions and improved generalisation beyond the training distribution, where purely implicit world models may struggle. We demonstrate several unique capabilities of SWoMo, including precise unsupervised video style transfer without additional training and strong generalisation to unseen interaction geometries with novel tool motions and co-occurrences. Finally, we show that the generated videos can effectively augment existing datasets and improve performance on downstream tasks such as surgical phase recognition.

Acknowledgments. The work is partially funded by the German Federal Ministry of Education and Research as part of the Software Campus (research grant 01|S23067).

Disclosure of Interests. The authors have no competing interests to declare that are relevant to the content of this article.

References

1. Al Hajj, H., et al.: Cataracts: challenge on automatic tool annotation for cataract surgery. Media **52**, 24–41 (2019)
2. Biagini, D., Navab, N., Farshad, A.: HieraSurg: hierarchy-aware diffusion model for surgical video generation. In: MICCAI, pp. 310–319. Springer (2025)
3. Boels, M., Robertshaw, H., Booth, T.C., Granados, A., Dasgupta, P., Ourselin, S.: Surgical robot learning: from demonstration and simulation to world models-a review. Authorea Preprints (2025)
4. Bruce, J., et al.: Genie: generative interactive environments. In: ICML (2024)
5. Caron, M., Touvron, H., Misra, I., Jégou, H., Mairal, J., Bojanowski, P., Joulin, A.: Emerging properties in self-supervised vision transformers. In: ICCV, pp. 9650–9660 (2021)

6. Chen, Z., et al.: How far are surgeons from surgical world models? A pilot study on zero-shot surgical video generation with expert assessment (2025). arXiv:2511.01775
7. Cheng, B., Misra, I., Schwing, A.G., Kirillov, A., Girdhar, R.: Masked-attention mask transformer for universal image segmentation. In: CVPR, pp. 1280–1289 (2021)
8. Frisch, Y., et al.: SurGrID: controllable surgical simulation via scene graph to image diffusion. Int. J. CARS **20**(7), 1421–1429 (2025)
9. Ghamsarian, N., et al.: Cataract-1K: cataract surgery dataset for scene segmentation, phase recognition, and irregularity detection (2023). arXiv:2312.06295
10. Godot Engine Contributors: Godot engine (2024). https://godotengine.org, free and open-source 2D and 3D game engine
11. Ha, D., Schmidhuber, J.: World models. arXiv:1803.10122 **2**(3) (2018)
12. He, Y., Yang, T., Zhang, Y., Shan, Y., Chen, Q.: Latent video diffusion models for high-fidelity long video generation (2022). arXiv:2211.13221
13. He, Y., G et al.: SurgWorld: learning surgical robot policies from videos via world modeling. arXiv:2512.23162 (2025)
14. Ho, J., Jain, A., Abbeel, P.: Denoising diffusion probabilistic models. NeurIPS **33**, 6840–6851 (2020)
15. Ho, J., Salimans, T., Gritsenko, A., Chan, W., Norouzi, M., Fleet, D.J.: Video diffusion models. NeurIPS **35**, 8633–8646 (2022)
16. Isensee, F., Jaeger, P.F., Kohl, S.A., Petersen, J., Maier-Hein, K.H.: NNU-Net: a self-configuring method for deep learning-based biomedical image segmentation. Nat. Meth. **18**(2), 203–211 (2021)
17. Jang, J., Y et al.: DreamGen: unlocking generalization in robot learning through video world models. arXiv:2505.12705 (2025)
18. Kadian, A., et al.: Sim2Real Predictivity: does evaluation in simulation predict real-world performance? IEEE Robot. Autom. Let. **5**(4), 6670–6677 (2020)
19. Karaev, N., Rocco, I., Graham, B., Neverova, N., Vedaldi, A., Rupprecht, C.: Cotracker: it is 472 better to track together, vol. 473 (2023). arXiv:2307.07635
20. Koju, S., et al.: Surgical vision world model. In: MICCAI Workshop on Data Engineering in Medical Imaging, pp. 1–10. Springer (2025)
21. Li, C., et al.: Endora: video generation models as endoscopy simulators. In: MICCAI, pp. 230–240. Springer (2024)
22. Li, S., Farha, Y.A., Liu, Y., Cheng, M.M., Gall, J.: MS-TCN++: multi-stage temporal convolutional network for action segmentation. IEEE TPAMI **45**(6) (2020)
23. Lin, H., Li, B., Au, K.W.S.: Visuomotor grasping with world models for surgical robots (2025). arXiv:2508.11200
24. Martyniak, S., Kaleta, J., Dall'Alba, D., Naskręt, M., Płotka, S., Korzeniowski, P.: SimuScope: realistic endoscopic synthetic dataset generation through surgical simulation and diffusion models. In: WACV, pp. 4268–4278. IEEE (2025)
25. Nair, A.G., et al.: Effectiveness of simulation-based training for manual small incision cataract surgery among novice surgeons: a randomized controlled trial. Sci. Rep. **11**(1), 10945 (2021)
26. Niu, M., Cun, X., Wang, X., Zhang, Y., Shan, Y., Zheng, Y.: MOFA-Video: controllable image animation via generative motion field adaptions in frozen image-to-video diffusion model. In: ECCV, pp. 111–128. Springer (2024)
27. Ravi, N., et al.: SAM 2: segment anything in images and videos. arXiv:2408.00714 (2024)

28. Sivakumar, S.K., Frisch, Y., Ghazaei, G., Mukhopadhyay, A.: SG2VID: scene graphs enable fine-grained control for video synthesis. In: MICCAI, pp. 511–521. Springer (2025)
29. Sivakumar, S.K., Frisch, Y., Ranem, A., Mukhopadhyay, A.: SASVI: segment any surgical video. Int. J. CARS **20**(7), 1409–1419 (2025)
30. Skorokhodov, I., Tulyakov, S., Elhoseiny, M.: StyleGAN-V: a continuous video generator with the price, image quality and perks of styleGAN2. In: CVPR, pp. 3626–3636 (2022)
31. Unterthiner, T., Van Steenkiste, S., Kurach, K., Marinier, R., Michalski, M., Gelly, S.: Towards accurate generative models of video: a new metric & challenges. arXiv:1812.01717 (2018)
32. Venkatesh, D.K., Rivoir, D., Pfeiffer, M., Speidel, S.: Surgical-CD: generating surgical images via unpaired image translation with latent consistency diffusion models. In: European Conference on Computer Vision, pp. 218–235. Springer (2024)
33. Wang, Z., Zhang, L., Wang, L., Zhu, M., Zhang, Z.: Optical flow representation alignment mamba diffusion model for medical video generation. arXiv:2411.01647 (2024)
34. Yang, Y., Zhang, Z., Zhang, X., Zeng, Y., Li, H., Zuo, W.: PhysWorld: from real videos to world models of deformable objects via physics-aware demonstration synthesis. arXiv:2510.21447 (2025)
35. Zhang, L., Rao, A., Agrawala, M.: Adding conditional control to text-to-image diffusion models. In: ICCV, pp. 3836–3847 (2023)
36. Zhang, R., Isola, P., Efros, A.A., Shechtman, E., Wang, O.: The unreasonable effectiveness of deep features as a perceptual metric. In: CVPR, pp. 586–595 (2018)

Towards Versatile and Safe Multi-electrode Path Planning for SEEG Implantation

Ziqiao Qu[1,2], Yangyang Shi[5], Yuanqing Wang[3], Linxia Xiao[4(✉)], and Weixin Si[2(✉)]

[1] Southern University of Science and Technology, Shenzhen, China
[2] Shenzhen University of Advanced Technology, Shenzhen, China
siweixin@suat-sz.edu.cn
[3] The Second People's Hospital of Shenzhen, Shenzhen, China
[4] Shenzhen Institutes of Advanced Technology, Chinese Academy of Sciences, Shenzhen, China
lx.xiao@siat.ac.cn
[5] School of Computer Science and Engineering, Central South University, Changsha, China

Abstract. Stereo-electroencephalography (SEEG) enables minimally invasive recording from deep and sulcal brain regions to localize epileptogenic networks for epilepsy surgery. However, traditional multiple SEEG electrodes planning remains largely manual, requiring experts to iteratively pick targets and search safe implantation paths while avoiding vessels, sulci, and other critical structures. To tackle this issue, we propose a coverage-aware planning method that integrates joint target localization and cooperative multi-electrode trajectory optimization into a unified reinforcement learning framework. Specifically, we introduce a capsule-based coverage model that represents functional recording sensitivity as a continuous region around each trajectory and maximizes overall region-of-interest (ROI) coverage through one-shot decision making. To ensure safety, we incorporate multi-layer constraints and inter-electrode spacing into deterministic projection with fixed constraint checking, enabling constraint-satisfying planning without manual penalty tuning. To validate the proposed method, we conducted planning on 8 retrospective temporal lobe epilepsy cases (84 electrodes) with CT/MRI-derived anatomical segmentations, achieving an 82% improvement in mean ROI coverage and an 88% increase in minimum inter-electrode spacing compared with existing methods while maintaining an 88% collision-free rate, supporting a versatile and safe planning framework that can adapt to diverse epilepsy treatment requirements and facilitate clinical deployment. Code is available at https://github.com/Joe-Galaxy/safe-seeg-multielectrode-planning.

Keywords: Multi-electrode planning · Trajectory optimization · Reinforcement learning · Coverage-aware planning

Z. Qu and Y. Shi—Equal contribution.

G. Yang et al. (Eds.): MICCAI 2026, LNCS 16893, pp. 532–541, 2027.
https://doi.org/10.1007/978-3-032-38236-8_51

1 Introduction

Drug-resistant focal epilepsy affects a substantial fraction of patients with epilepsy and is associated with increased morbidity and mortality [1]. For selected candidates, epilepsy surgery can improve seizure control and quality of life, but requires precise localization of epileptogenic networks [2]. Stereo-electroencephalography (SEEG) supports this presurgical evaluation by implanting multiple depth electrodes to sample deep and sulcal structures [3], with complementary roles compared to subdural grids and strips [4]. Despite its clinical value, SEEG planning remains challenging because teams must jointly determine targets and safe paths that avoid critical anatomy [5] while maintaining operating-room accuracy [6,7].

Recent computer-assisted planning (CAP) tools aim to reduce the manual workload and standardize trajectory design. Dasgupta *et al.* [8] enhance CAP with center-specific spatial priors to improve safety and reduce manual adjustments, while immersive visualization systems such as PreVISE provide virtual-reality support for interactive SEEG planning [9]. Beyond geometric safety, Dessert *et al.* [10] optimize patient-specific recording sensitivity as an objective for SEEG implantation. In parallel, personalized network modeling continues to improve hypothesis-driven targeting and interpretation [11]. However, existing approaches typically address target selection and trajectory optimization in separate stages or rely on soft penalties that may leave constraint violations when planning multiple electrodes simultaneously.

We formulate SEEG planning as sequential patient-level decision making with a one-shot action for each rigid electrode. Given patient-specific meshes and region-of-interest (ROI) candidates, the policy proposes a target refinement and insertion direction at each step, followed by deterministic projection and fixed checking under anatomical and inter-electrode constraints. Clinically, this action corresponds to the two decisions required for one rigid SEEG electrode: where the contact-bearing segment should sample the ROI and which insertion direction should connect it to a skull entry point. Accepted trajectories then become spacing and collision constraints for later electrodes, making the problem a coupled patient-level plan rather than a collection of independent trajectory regressions. This coupling is important because a target-direction pair that is acceptable in isolation may become undesirable after other electrodes have occupied nearby corridors.

The main contributions of this work are as follows.

- We formulate multi-electrode SEEG planning as reinforcement learning over patient-specific 3D meshes, jointly optimizing target locations and insertion trajectories.
- We introduce capsule-based coverage to refine candidate targets toward high-sensitivity regions while selecting straight insertion directions through per-electrode one-shot actions.
- We combine deterministic projection with fixed anatomical/inter-electrode constraint checking, and validate against CAP and sensitivity-based methods on retrospective temporal lobe epilepsy cases.

2 Related Work

Target Localization and Coverage Modeling. Target selection in SEEG is driven by clinical hypotheses about the epileptogenic network, and recent quantitative pipelines aim to strengthen this process with data-driven evidence. For example, Wang *et al.* [11] propose a personalized modeling workflow to delineate epileptogenic networks from multimodal data. From the planning perspective, Dessert *et al.* [10] explicitly optimize patient-specific recording sensitivity to prioritize trajectories that better sample the intended regions. Multi-center studies further highlight that targeting conventions and implantation strategies vary substantially across institutions [12]. In practice, multi-electrode SEEG planning revolves around two key aspects: target localization and multi-electrode trajectory planning.

Multi-electrode Trajectory Planning Under Safety Constraints. CAP systems compute collision-free trajectories by incorporating anatomical constraints and clinician-defined preferences, and can be enhanced with priors learned from historical implantations [8]. Spiegler *et al.* [9] introduce PreVISE to support interactive, immersive multi-trajectory planning in virtual reality. Optimization-based methods have also been explored for multi-electrode planning, including case-based formulations [13] and temporal lobe implantation strategies [14]. Beyond SEEG, multi-constrained trajectory planning has been studied in related interventions such as multi-needle thermal ablation [15], and safe reinforcement learning has been used to enforce hard constraints in screw trajectory planning [16]. Nevertheless, existing SEEG planners often decouple target selection from trajectory optimization and may not provide a unified mechanism to enforce inter-electrode constraints while optimizing coverage-driven objectives for all electrodes.

3 Method

3.1 Data Processing and Anatomical Modeling

We retrospectively collected CT (post-implant) and MRI (pre-implant) volumes from 8 temporal lobe epilepsy cases. Each case was segmented into (i) gray matter and cortex surface, (ii) skull, (iii) vasculature, and (iv) deep structures (e.g., ventricles and brainstem). Vessels were segmented from available vascular imaging (e.g., MR angiography/venography or CT angiography) and converted into 3D meshes [5]. All structures were represented as triangle meshes, downsampled to 10k points, and converted to signed distance fields (SDFs) for vessel, deep-structure, cortex, and skull distance queries. For each electrode k, Ω_k denotes the segmented ROI mesh points, and a cone corridor from the ROI center constrains candidate entry locations. The SDF representation converts patient-specific vessel, deep-structure, skull, and cortex boundaries into fast geometric margin queries, while the cone corridor encodes clinically preferred burr-hole directions without replacing surgeon-defined hypotheses. Non-entry intersections with cortex/skull are treated as forbidden events, whereas the selected skull entry is evaluated with the local skull normal for entry-angle checking.

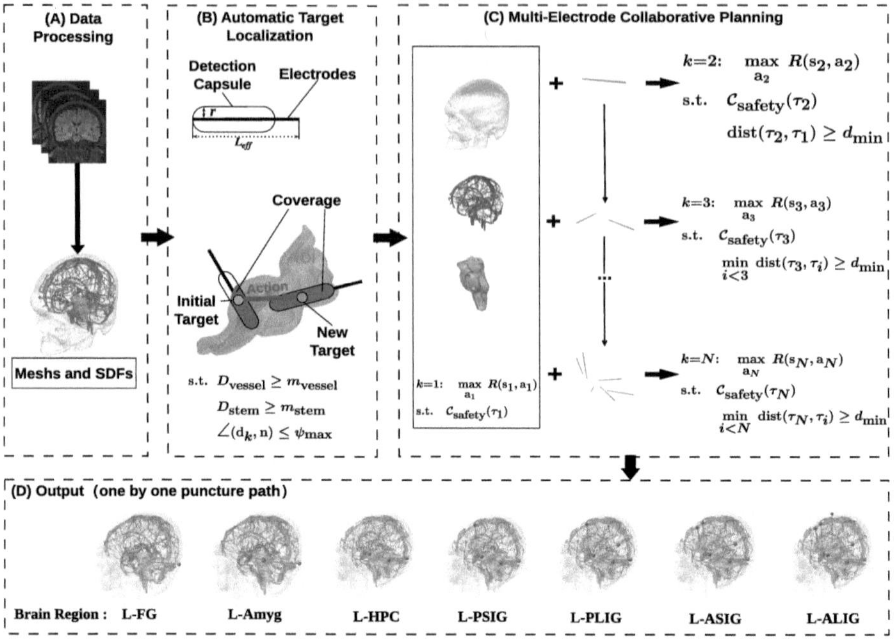

Fig. 1. Overview. (A) Patient-specific meshes are converted to signed distance fields (SDFs). (B) Capsule coverage refines ROI targets. (C) A one-shot RL policy proposes target offsets and directions; deterministic projection obtains candidate skull entries, and fixed checking validates anatomical and inter-electrode constraints. (D) The output is a checked multi-electrode trajectory set. R denotes the checked reward.

3.2 MDP-Guided One-Shot Multi-electrode Implantation Planning

We plan a set of electrodes indexed by $k = 1, \ldots, K$ (Fig. 1), where each electrode must (i) cover its ROI and (ii) satisfy strict anatomical safety constraints. We formulate patient-level planning as $M = (S, A, T, R, \gamma)$ with horizon K and $\gamma = 1$. At step k, the state contains anatomy, ROI/corridor, target-reference geometry, SDF distances, and accepted trajectories; the 5D action proposes one rigid electrode; the transition constructs/checks its straight trajectory and appends accepted paths as later spacing/collision constraints. Thus, "one-shot" means one electrode proposal, while the patient plan is produced by the sequential K-step process. This formulation follows the clinical workflow more closely than treating each implanted electrode as an independent sample. The policy observes previously accepted trajectories so that later proposals can account for inter-electrode spacing and collision rules, and the checked reward couples ROI coverage with path preferences after geometric validation. PPO is used because no ground-truth target-direction labels are available for these coupled decisions.
Action and Trajectory Construction. As illustrated in Fig. 1(B), the policy outputs a 5D action $\mathbf{a}_k = (\Delta\mathbf{t}_k, \theta_k, \phi_k)$, where $\Delta\mathbf{t}_k \in \mathbb{R}^3$ refines the candidate

target and (θ_k, ϕ_k) parameterize the insertion direction. We set $\mathbf{t}_k = \mathbf{t}_k^{(0)} + \Delta\mathbf{t}_k$ and convert angles to a unit direction $\mathbf{d}_k$. Ray-casting from $\mathbf{t}_k$ along $-\mathbf{d}_k$ gives the skull entry $\mathbf{e}_k$ and straight trajectory τ_k, matching the clinical output of target, burr-hole entry, and rigid shaft with workflow preferences encoded geometrically.

Capsule-Based Target Localization via Coverage. We model the recording sensitivity of a straight trajectory as a capsule of radius r (Fig. 1(B)), abstracting the contact-bearing shaft's effective sampling range; r follows electrode specifications or clinician-defined range and does not replace patient-specific biophysical models. As illustrated in Fig. 1(B), we define the capsule coverage of ROI mesh Ω_k as

$$c_k(\tau_k) = \frac{1}{|\Omega_k|} \sum_{\mathbf{v} \in \Omega_k} 1[d(\mathbf{v}, \tau_k) \leq r], \tag{1}$$

where $d(\mathbf{v}, \tau_k)$ is the Euclidean distance from point $\mathbf{v}$ to the line segment of τ_k. Maximizing c_k encourages the target refinement $\Delta\mathbf{t}_k$ to move toward regions that are better covered by the trajectory, thereby achieving coverage-aware target localization.

Deterministic Projection with Multi-constraint Checking. The RL policy selects ROI subregions, searches the 5D target-direction space, and learns geometry preferences from distance features, accepted trajectories, and checked rewards. Projection $\Pi(\cdot)$ only extends the proposed shaft to the skull entry and performs fixed accept/reject checking before reward evaluation; it is not a shortest-path planner and does not optimize capsule coverage. Given the policy proposal, checking validates vessel/deep-structure distance, forbidden non-entry cortex/skull intersections, path length, entry angle, corridor membership, and spacing to previously accepted electrodes. Only accepted trajectories are appended to the patient state and used as constraints for subsequent electrodes. Vessel, non-entry cortex/skull, and deep-structure distances use precomputed SDFs [18]. For an accepted electrode k, the checked trajectory $\hat{\tau}_k = \Pi(\tau_k)$ must satisfy:

$$\begin{aligned} &d(\hat{\tau}_k, \mathcal{V}) \geq \varepsilon_{\text{vessel}}, \quad d(\hat{\tau}_k, \mathcal{C}_{\text{non}}) \geq \varepsilon_{\text{cortex}}, \quad d(\hat{\tau}_k, \mathcal{B}) \geq \varepsilon_{\text{deep}}, \\ &L(\hat{\tau}_k) \leq L_{\max}, \quad \angle(\hat{\tau}_k, \mathbf{n}_{\text{skull}}) \leq \alpha_{\max}, \quad d(\hat{\tau}_k, \hat{\tau}_j) \geq \varepsilon_{\text{IE}}, \ \forall j < k, \end{aligned} \tag{2}$$

Here $\mathcal{V}$, $\mathcal{C}_{\text{non}}$, and $\mathcal{B}$ denote vessels, forbidden non-entry cortex/skull intersections, and deep structures; $\mathbf{n}_{\text{skull}}$ is the outward skull normal at entry, and ε_{IE} enforces inter-electrode spacing.

Training Objective. Because Eq. (2) is checked before reward evaluation, the reward focuses on coverage and mild secondary preferences among accepted trajectories: $R_k = c_k(\hat{\tau}_k) - \lambda_L \frac{L(\hat{\tau}_k)}{L_{\max}}$. We train π_θ with a PPO-style actor–critic objective [17,19], since ground-truth target-direction labels are unavailable for the joint coverage-and-constraint objective.

4 Experiments

4.1 Dataset and Setup

We evaluated on 8 retrospective temporal lobe epilepsy cases (84 electrodes) with CT/MRI-derived segmentations. Training/testing used patient-level 4/4 splits, so electrodes from the same patient were never used as independent train/test subjects; the 84 electrodes are implantation instances nested within patient maps. Although the number of patients is pilot-scale, each case requires detailed vascular/skull reconstruction and a faithful patient-specific planning environment. Each electrode first interacts with its own target and anatomical corridor, and then affects the full plan because accepted trajectories constrain later electrodes through spacing and collision rules. This makes the 84 electrode-implantation instances meaningful for evaluating the planner while preserving the patient-level split. ROIs included clinically common temporal targets such as left fusiform gyrus (L-FG), left inferior occipital gyrus (L-IOG), left hippocampus head (L-HPC-H), and right amygdala (R-Amyg). We compared against (i) manual plans from an experienced neurosurgeon (Doctor), (ii) CAP augmented with spatial priors (CAP+Priors) [8], and (iii) a recording-sensitivity optimizer (RS-Opt) [10]. All methods were evaluated under the same hard constraints in Eq. (2); our goal is plan quality under comparable time rather than runtime advantage. Implementation code will be released upon publication.

4.2 Evaluation Metrics

We report capsule coverage c_k in Eq. (1), where higher coverage means more hypothesized epileptogenic gray matter lies within the electrode's effective sensing range. To quantify multi-electrode coordination, we measure the minimum inter-electrode spacing, defined as the minimum distance between any pair of planned trajectories in the same patient. Safety-related metrics include mean margins to vessels/deep structures, a CAP-style vessel-risk score, and the collision-free rate under Eq. (2). The margin summarizes SDF-based clearance to critical structures, while the risk score penalizes vessel-proximal paths; together with collision-free rate, these metrics assess evaluated safety under the same anatomical thresholds. We also report path length and average runtime per plan.

Table 1. Quantitative comparison on 8 retrospective cases (84 electrodes). CAP (spatial priors) and RS-Opt are re-implemented baselines [8,10]. Values are averaged over electrodes; spacing is plan-level min/avg (mm), time is minutes/case, and Collision-Free counts electrodes satisfying Eq. (2). Best values are bold.

Method	ROI Cov.↑	Safety Margin↑	Risk Score↓	Path Length↓	Coll.- Free↑	Spacing↑ (min/avg)	Time (min)↓
Clinical (Expert)	5.6%	1.08	1.055	74.3	**76/84 (90.5%)**	**10.2**/12.7	90
CAP (spatial priors) [8]	7.0%	1.00	1.024	54.4	50/84 (59.5%)	4.9/8.0	15
RS-Opt [10]	6.7%	1.20	1.107	60.5	55/84 (65.5%)	6.8/**13.6**	**14**
Proposed	**10.2%**	**1.88**	**0.917**	**52.2**	74/84 (88.1%)	9.2/10.9	28

4.3 Results

Table 1 reports quantitative results on 8 retrospective cases (84 electrodes) under identical anatomical inputs and evaluation thresholds. The proposed method achieves the best ROI coverage rate (10.2%). Higher coverage means that more gray matter inside the hypothesized epileptogenic ROI falls within the electrode's effective sensing range, increasing the chance of capturing early ictal activity. It also yields the largest SDF-based margin (1.88 mm) and the lowest risk score (0.917). Compared with the clinical plan, ROI coverage increases from 5.6% to 10.2% while the margin improves from 1.08 mm to 1.88 mm, indicating stronger functional coverage with preserved evaluated safety margins. The planned paths are also shorter on average (52.2 mm vs. 74.3 mm for the clinical plan), which is clinically desirable because shorter intracerebral trajectories reduce the amount of tissue traversed and can simplify implantation while still reaching the intended ROI.

Although the proposed method does not attain the highest collision-free rate (74/84, 88.1%), it is close to the clinical plan (76/84, 90.5%), with only two fewer electrodes satisfying all constraints, and outperforms CAP and RS-Opt (59.5% and 65.5%). The minimum inter-electrode spacing is likewise comparable to the clinical plan (9.2 mm vs. 10.2 mm), supporting coordination under the spacing constraint in Sect. 3.2. The method reduces planning time from 90 to 28 min per case; although slower than automated baselines (14–15 min), it provides stronger overall plan quality under the same protocol.

Target Localization Results. Figure 2 visualizes capsule-to-ROI overlap for a representative electrode targeting the left fusiform gyrus. Under identical trajectory constraints, the proposed method refines the centroid initialization to better align the electrode capsule with the ROI, achieving 7.0% coverage vs. 3.5% for the clinical plan and 0.8%/5.8% for CAP+Priors/RS-Opt [8, 10].

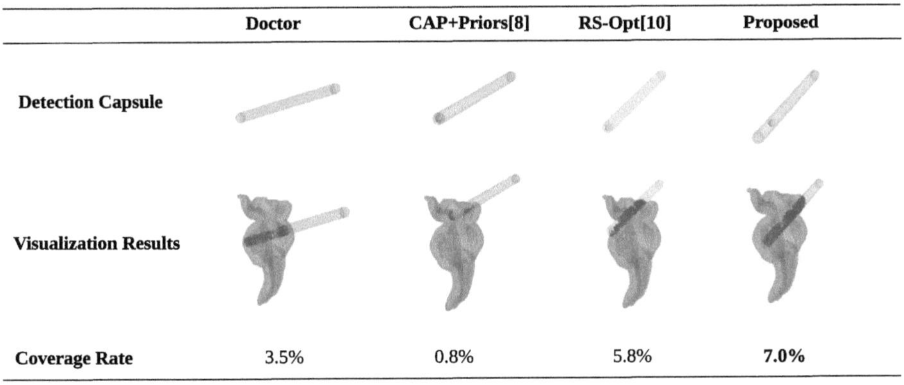

Fig. 2. Capsule-to-ROI overlap on the left fusiform gyrus. The proposed method achieves higher ROI coverage (7.0%) than the clinical plan (3.5%) and CAP/RS-Opt (0.8%, 5.8%) [8, 10].

Multi-electrode Cooperative Planning and Constraint Satisfaction. Figure 3 compares full bundles in a representative 11-electrode case.

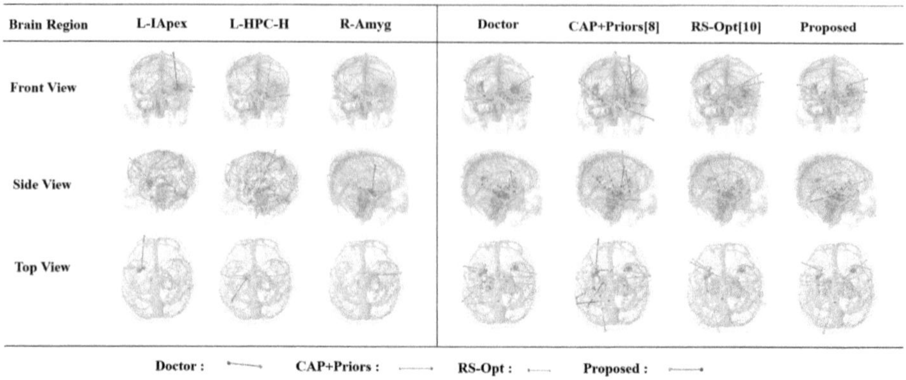

Fig. 3. Qualitative trajectory comparison. Left: three representative target regions (L-IApex, L-HPC-H, and R-Amyg) highlighting common failure modes. Right: a representative 11-electrode case comparing Doctor, CAP+Priors [8], RS-Opt [10], and the proposed method. CAP+Priors may produce unnecessarily long implantation paths, while RS-Opt can yield clinically implausible entry locations or hemisphere-crossing trajectories. The proposed method produces shorter, clinically plausible, and spatially coordinated trajectories under the same evaluation protocol.

CAP+Priors [8] often produces unnecessarily long paths (L-IApex, R-Amyg). RS-Opt [10] may generate clinically implausible entries, e.g., a contralateral trajectory to the left L-HPC-H target and an occipital entry for R-Amyg, increasing collision risk. Our method yields ipsilateral bundles with reasonable entry sites while satisfying the spacing constraint (Sect. 3.2).

5 Conclusion

We present a reinforcement-learning-based framework for multi-electrode SEEG planning that jointly localizes targets and generates straight-line trajectories under predefined anatomical and geometric constraints. By modeling an electrode's effective sensing range as a capsule, the proposed method directly optimizes ROI coverage during target localization, mitigating the decoupling between target selection and trajectory search common in prior pipelines. Deterministic projection and SDF-based constraint checking support fixed validation and cooperative multi-electrode planning via explicit inter-electrode spacing constraints. Experiments on 8 retrospective epilepsy cases (84 electrodes) support the promise of the coverage-aware planning approach, especially for improving ROI coverage while maintaining evaluated safety margins and coordinated inter-electrode spacing.

However, our work has several limitations, including the pilot-scale dataset, reliance on pre-segmented anatomical structures, and the use of straight-line trajectories, which may not fully reflect clinical preferences in highly constrained scenarios. Larger multi-center validation is needed to test robustness across heterogeneous implantation conventions, imaging protocols, and target hypotheses. In future work, we will investigate uncertainty-aware anatomical segmentation and explicit vascular modeling to improve robustness, and incorporate clinical priors and clinician-in-the-loop refinement to enhance routine clinical usability.

Acknowledgments. This work was supported in part by the National Natural Science Foundation of China (Nos. 62372441, 62303442), the Guangdong Basic and Applied Basic Research Foundation (Nos. 2026B1515020093, 2025A1515010423, 2024A1515140078), the Shenzhen Science and Technology Program (Grant No. RCYX20231211090127030), and the Research Program of the Department of Education of Guangdong Province (Grant No. 2025ZDZX3027).

Disclosure of Interests. The authors declare no competing interests.

References

1. Perucca, E., Perucca, P., White, H.S., Wirrell, E.C.: Drug resistance in epilepsy. Lancet Neurol. **22**(8), 723–734 (2023)
2. Duncan, J.S., Taylor, P.N.: Optimising epilepsy surgery. Lancet Neurol. **22**(5), 373–374 (2023)
3. Delgado-Garcia, G., Frauscher, B.: Future of neurology & technology: stereoelectroencephalography in presurgical epilepsy evaluation. Neurology **98**(4), e437–e440 (2022)
4. Wu, S., Issa, N.P., Rose, S.L., et al.: Depth versus surface: a critical review of subdural and depth electrodes in intracranial electroencephalographic studies. Epilepsia **65**(7), 1868–1878 (2024)
5. Szmidel, M., Hunn, M., Neal, A., et al.: Vascular imaging for stereoelectroencephalography: a safety and planning study. J. Clin. Neurosci. **127**, 110762 (2024)
6. Liakina, T., Bartley, A., Carstam, L., Rydenhag, B., Nilsson, D.: Stereoelectroencephalography for drug resistant epilepsy: precision and complications in stepwise improvement of frameless implantation. Acta Neurochir. **167**(1), 75 (2025)
7. Girgis, F., Royz, E., Kennedy, J., Seyal, M., Shahlaie, K., Saez, I.: Superior accuracy and precision of SEEG electrode insertion with frame-based vs. Frameless Stereotaxy methods. Acta Neurochir. **162**(10), 2527–2532 (2020)
8. Dasgupta, D., Elliott, C.A., O'Keeffe, A.G., et al.: Computer-assisted stereoelectroencephalography planning: center-specific priors enhance planning. Front. Neurol. **16**, 1514442 (2025)
9. Spiegler, P., Abdelsalam, H., Hellum, O., Hadjinicolaou, A., Weil, A.G., Xiao, Y.: PreVISE: an efficient virtual reality system for SEEG surgical planning. Virtual Real. **29**(1), 13 (2025)
10. Dessert, G.E., Thio, B.J., Grill, W.M.: Optimization of patient-specific stereo-EEG recording sensitivity. Brain Commun. **5**(6), fcad304 (2023)
11. Wang, H.E., Woodman, M., Triebkorn, P., et al.: Delineating epileptogenic networks using brain imaging data and personalized modeling in drug-resistant epilepsy. Sci. Transl. Med. **15**, eabp8982 (2023)

12. Thomas, J., Abdallah, C., Cai, Z., et al.: Investigating current clinical opinions in stereoelectroencephalography-informed epilepsy surgery. Epilepsia **65**(9), 2662–2672 (2024)
13. Chen, Y.W., et al.: Computer-assisted surgery in medical and dental applications. Expert Rev. Med. Devices **18**(7), 669–696 (2021)
14. Sparks, R., Zombori, G., Rodionov, R., et al.: Automated multiple trajectory planning algorithm for the placement of stereo-electroencephalography (SEEG) electrodes in epilepsy treatment. Int. J. Comput. Assist. Radiol. Surg. **12**(1), 123–136 (2017)
15. Li, R., Shi, Y., Si, W., et al.: Versatile multi-constrained planning for thermal ablation of large liver tumors. Comput. Med. Imaging Graph. **94**, 101993 (2021)
16. Ao, Y., Esfandiari, H., Carrillo, F., et al.: SafeRPlan: safe deep reinforcement learning for intraoperative planning of pedicle screw placement. Med. Image Anal. **99**, 103345 (2025)
17. Amadou, A.A., Singh, V., Ghesu, F.C.: Goal-conditioned reinforcement learning for ultrasound navigation guidance. In: Medical Image Computing and Computer Assisted Intervention - MICCAI 2024. Springer Nature, Switzerland (2024)
18. Johari, M.M., Carta, C., Fleuret, F.: ESLAM: efficient dense SLAM system based on hybrid representation of signed distance fields. In: Proceedings IEEE/CVF Conference Comput. Vis. Pattern Recognit. (CVPR), pp. 17408–17419 (2023)
19. Son, S., Zheng, L., Sullivan, R., Qiao, Y.-L., Lin, M.: Gradient informed proximal policy optimization. In: Advances in Neural Information Processing Systems, vol. 36, Curran Associates, Inc. (2023)

Track2Map: Online Deformable SLAM with Motion-Aware Pose Optimization in Robotic Surgery

Tianyi Song[1(✉)], Sierra Bonilla[1], Xinwei Ju[1], Evangelos Mazomenos[1], Danail Stoyanov[1], Adam Schmidt[2], Omid Mohareri[2], Sophia Bano[1], and Francisco Vasconcelos[1]

[1] Department of Computer Science and UCL Hawkes Institute, University College London, London WC1E 6BT, UK
{tianyi.song.24,sierra.bonilla.21}@ucl.ac.uk
[2] Intuitive Surgical, Inc., Sunnyvale, CA 94086, USA

Abstract. Gaussian splatting is the current state-of-the-art for dense, deformable 3D anatomy reconstruction in robot-assisted minimally invasive surgery (RAMIS); however, most pipelines are offline and depend on accurate camera trajectory priors (often from robotic kinematics), limiting applicability when priors are missing or noisy. To address these limitations, we propose **Track2Map**, an online 3D Gaussian Splatting pipeline that jointly optimizes camera trajectory and 3D deformable scene representation directly from surgical video. Track2Map is therefore capable of robust 3D reconstructions when camera trajectory priors are either absent or noisy, and due to its online nature it effectively works as a Simultaneous Localisation and Mapping (SLAM) method. To stabilize optimization in the presence of tissue motion and ambiguous visual cues, we introduce a track-anchored deformation initialization using dense 2D point tracks. Track statistics are further utilized to disentangle camera motion from scene deformation by detecting static camera periods and reducing drift during incremental mapping. Experiments on StereoMIS show improved reconstruction quality and camera trajectory against competing SLAM methods, as well as compared to non-SLAM methods that utilize camera trajectory priors. The code is available at https://track2map.github.io/.

Keywords: Robot-assisted surgery · Stereo endoscopy · Online 3D reconstruction · Camera pose optimization

T. Song and S. Bonilla—These authors contributed equally.

Supplementary Information The online version contains supplementary material available at https://doi.org/10.1007/978-3-032-38236-8_52.

G. Yang et al. (Eds.): MICCAI 2026, LNCS 16893, pp. 542–552, 2027.
https://doi.org/10.1007/978-3-032-38236-8_52

1 Introduction

Online 3D reconstruction of deformable tissue is a key prerequisite for developing a range of computer guidance techniques in RAMIS, including characterisation of instrument-tissue interactions, autonomous manipulation, and stable augmented reality overlays. However, achieving metric, stable reconstruction in RAMIS remains difficult because the scene is non-rigid, frequently occluded by instruments, and captured with limited viewpoint variation.

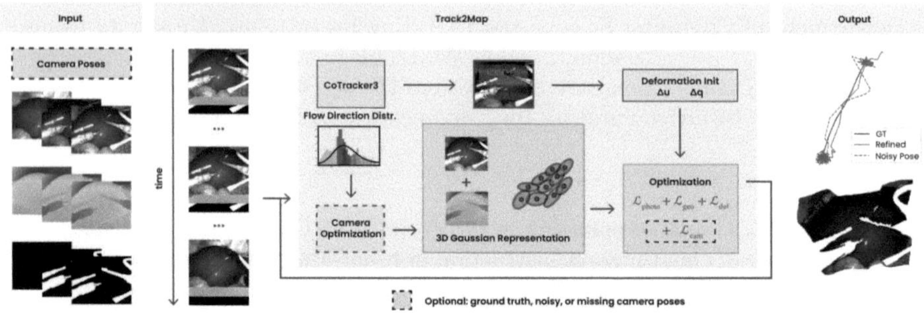

Fig. 1. Given stereo RGB frames, depth maps, and *optional* (clean/noisy) pose extrinsics/intrinsics and tool masks, Track2Map jointly performs 2D tracking and online deformable 3D reconstruction. [12] provides 2D correspondences that are lifted to 3D and used to estimate/refine camera motion via motion-gated pose optimization and initialize sparse anchor-based deformation. A Gaussian representation like [8] is updated online. The system outputs refined poses and metric reconstruction; 2D/3D tracks are available as by-products of the correspondence module and 3D lifting.

3D reconstruction methods have progressed from classical SfM [19] to neural radiance fields [15] and 3D Gaussian Splatting (3DGS) [14] representations tailored to endoscopy [4,21,25]. However, extending these representations to deformable surgical scenes introduces a fundamental coupling problem: camera pose, non-rigid deformation, and appearance/geometry estimation must be estimated jointly, but supervision and priors are often unreliable. Most surgical neural/3DGS methods either assume static or known camera motion, or depend on relatively clean pose inputs to prevent drift in deformable sequences [8,10]. In RAMIS, camera pose is often calculated from robot joint kinematics, which can be inaccurate due to calibration errors and measurement noise, and may also not always be available in a clinical setting. Therefore, camera motion availability and quality varies widely across available surgical datasets; some provide accurate trajectories [7], others provide noisy priors [3], and many tracking benchmarks provide none [5,18]. This motivates deformable reconstruction systems that can exploit pose priors when available, remain stable when priors are corrupted, and can initialize and operate when pose is absent.

Joint estimation of camera motion and deformable structure has a long history in NRSfM and non-rigid SLAM, including locally NRSfM [22], sequential physical-prior NRSfM [2], online self-calibrating NRSfM [1], and deformable SLAM [28]. These works establish the broader paradigm of coupling camera motion with non-rigid scene structure, while our setting targets online dense 3DGS reconstruction from surgical stereo video with optional or noisy pose priors. In surgical neural/3DGS mapping, recent systems have begun to jointly optimize camera motion and deformable scene structure [24,27]. However, a key failure mode persists in RAMIS: endoscope motion is often intermittent, so long segments have a nearly static camera while tools deform tissue. In these intervals, image motion is dominated by local deformation and instrument motion, and indiscriminate pose optimization can incorrectly attribute tissue dynamics to camera motion, causing trajectory drift and destabilizing reconstruction. Our work addresses these issues by introducing two key additions. First, rather than completely eliminating pose priors, we use them as initial estimates whenever available, making our system flexible enough to operate both as a SLAM system and as an online 3D reconstruction pipeline that can handle noisy camera priors. Second, we use dense 2D point tracking to disentangle camera motion from tissue deformation. This allows us to detect when the camera view is static and dynamically introduce camera pose constraints that improve 3D reconstruction quality and reduce camera trajectory drift. Modern methods for dense 2D point tracking build on deep optical flow [23] and sequence models [12,16]. Surgical extensions improve robustness and efficiency [13,18,20]; in this work, we use CoTracker3 [12] as our 2D tracking initialization for Gaussian Splatting after empirically verifying its state-of-the-art performance on the STIR2024 benchmark [18].

Experiments on StereoMIS [7] demonstrate Track2Map's improved camera tracking and scene reconstruction over baselines including [12,16], and robustness under pose corruption and absence. Our core contributions are as follows:

- An online stereo 3D Gaussian reconstruction pipeline in which dense 2D correspondences are lifted to 3D anchors to initialize and constrain deformation.
- A pose update strategy that prevents drift during camera-static periods and enables joint optimization of pose and deformation when motion is detected.
- A unified system that operates with *clean*, *noisy*, or *absent* pose priors without retuning, including a vision-only initialization via robust 3D alignment of tracked anchor points when priors are unavailable.
- Improved reconstruction quality and robust pose recovery compared to prior deformable 3DGS pipelines.

2 Method

Figure 1 summarizes Track2Map's online inference loop. The central technical challenge is disentangling camera motion from non-rigid tissue motion under limited viewpoint change: inverse rendering on essentially one viewpoint (two short-baseline stereo images) provides weak constraints on pose when the scene itself also deforms, and unconstrained pose updates can easily absorb tissue deformation or tool motion, leading to significant errors. Track2Map therefore injects two procedure-driven priors into the optimization: (i) stereo depth provides metric 3D support for lifting correspondences, and (ii) endoscope motion is typically intermittent. Within RAMIS, the endoscope arm is often stationary while surgical tools operate on the scene. Therefore, pose should be updated conservatively and only when the observed motion is consistent with camera motion rather than local deformation or tool interaction.

Following [8], we represent the scene as 3D Gaussians [14] coupled with a sparse set of deformation control points. We use the tracked correspondences from [12] as the primary coupling signal between tracking and mapping in three stages: (1) compute a robust per-frame motion score from track displacements and use this score to gate pose updates to occur only when global motion is detected (Sect. 2.1); (2) lift the same correspondences to 3D and use their displacements to initialize a sparse anchor deformation prior, interpolated to the full set of Gaussians (Sect. 2.2); and (3) jointly refine scene parameters (and pose when enabled) using photometric and geometric rendering losses, deformation regularization, and 2D reprojection consistency of anchors (Sect. 2.3).

2.1 Motion-Aware Camera Update

At frame t, the tracker [12] works on a sliding window and provides 2D correspondences $\{(\mathbf{q}_k^{t-1}, \mathbf{q}_k^t)\}_{k\in\mathcal{K}_t}$ with flow $\mathbf{f}_k^t = \mathbf{q}_k^t - \mathbf{q}_k^{t-1}$. We use these tracks to decide when pose refinement is warranted. When the camera moves, tracked points exhibit a coherent global displacement field; when the camera is stationary, observed motion is dominated by heterogeneous tissue deformation and tool interaction. So we gate pose refinement using a simple statistic of the optical-flow direction distribution. We compute the flow direction, $\theta_k^t = \operatorname{atan2}(f_{k,y}^t, f_{k,x}^t)$. Empirically, camera motion produces a narrow, unimodal distribution of $\{\theta_k^t\}$ (low dispersion), whereas camera-static periods produce a broad distribution (high dispersion) due to local tissue deformation, tool motion, and physiological effects (distribution visualizations are provided in the supplementary material). We quantify dispersion using the (circular) standard deviation of flow directions. Let

$$\bar{c}_t = \frac{1}{|\mathcal{K}_t|}\sum_{k\in\mathcal{K}_t}\cos\theta_k^t, \qquad \bar{s}_t = \frac{1}{|\mathcal{K}_t|}\sum_{k\in\mathcal{K}_t}\sin\theta_k^t, \qquad R_t = \sqrt{\bar{c}_t^2 + \bar{s}_t^2} \tag{1}$$

We then compute the circular standard deviation $\sigma_{\theta,t} = \sqrt{-2\ln(R_t)}$. Low $\sigma_{\theta,t}$ indicates camera-dominant motion, while high $\sigma_{\theta,t}$ indicates scene motion. The motion gate is $g_t = \mathbb{I}[\sigma_{\theta,t} \le \tau]$ where τ is set empirically.

When no pose prior is available, we initialize the relative motion $\Delta\mathbf{T}_t$ by aligning 3D anchor positions across frames where anchors are initialized once by sparsely subsampling gaussian centers similarly to [8]. Each tracked 2D point

$\mathbf{q}_k^t$ is lifted to 3D using stereo depth and intrinsics, yielding $\mathbf{P}_k^{t-1}$ and $\mathbf{P}_k^t$. We estimate $\Delta\mathbf{T}_t \in SE(3)$ via robust weighted alignment:

$$\Delta\mathbf{T}_t = \arg\min_{\Delta\mathbf{T}\in SE(3)} \sum_{k\in\mathcal{K}_t} \omega_k\, \rho\big(\|\mathbf{P}_k^t - \Delta\mathbf{T}\,\mathbf{P}_k^{t-1}\|_2^2\big) \tag{2}$$

where ω_k is the tracker confidence and $\rho(\cdot)$ is a robust kernel. We set $\mathbf{T}_t^{\text{init}} = \Delta\mathbf{T}_t\,\mathbf{T}_{t-1}$. If $g_t = 0$, we freeze the pose to avoid absorbing non-rigid motion into the camera trajectory. If $g_t = 1$, we refine pose with a small 6D increment $\delta\boldsymbol{\xi} \in \mathbb{R}^6$ (3D translation + 3D rotation in $\mathfrak{se}(3)$), optimized with the scene (Sect. 2.3) where $\exp(\cdot^\wedge)$ projects the vector on to a valid transformation matrix:

$$\mathbf{T}_t = \exp\big(\delta\boldsymbol{\xi}^\wedge\big)\ \mathbf{T}_t^{\text{init}} \tag{3}$$

2.2 Tracker-Guided Deformation Initialization

We represent tissue deformation using the same sparse anchor set $\mathcal{K}$ used for pose estimation (Eq. 2). Unlike prior work [8], which treats control-point offsets as free variables optimized per frame, we explicitly drive the deformation field using tracked anchor motion. For each anchor $k \in \mathcal{K}$, its 3D displacement between consecutive frames is:

$$\Delta\mathbf{P}_k = \mathbf{P}_k^t - \mathbf{P}_k^{t-1}, \tag{4}$$

where $\mathbf{P}_k^t$ is obtained by lifting the tracked 2D correspondence $\mathbf{q}_k^t$ using stereo depth and the current camera pose $\mathbf{T}_t$. The initial deformation offset $\Delta\mathbf{x}_i^{(0)}$ for each Gaussian center $\mathbf{x}_i$ is then interpolated over its N nearest anchors:

$$\Delta\mathbf{x}_i^{(0)} = \sum_{k\in\mathcal{N}_i} w_{ik}\,\Delta\mathbf{P}_k, \qquad w_{ik} \propto \exp\big(-\alpha\,\|\mathbf{x}_i - \mathbf{P}_k^{t-1}\|_2\big) \tag{5}$$

2.3 Joint Online Optimization

Given the deformation initialization from Sect. 2.2 and the pose initialization from Sect. 2.1, we jointly refine the 3D scene and camera pose. The scene loss is:

$$\mathcal{L}_{\text{scene}} = w_{\text{photo}}\mathcal{L}_{\text{photo}} + w_{\text{geo}}\mathcal{L}_{\text{geo}} + w_{\text{def}}\mathcal{L}_{\text{def}} \tag{6}$$

where $\mathcal{L}_{\text{photo}}$ and $\mathcal{L}_{\text{geo}}$ are masked photometric and geometric rendering losses, and $\mathcal{L}_{\text{def}}$ regularizes the deformation field, as in [8]. The photometric and geometric losses are defined as the average distance between the rendered $(\hat{I}, \hat{D})$ and input (I, D) color and depth maps over valid pixels Ω_t and the deformation loss is defined by $\mathcal{L}_{\text{def}} = \sum_k \lambda_k \mathcal{L}_k$, incorporating local rigidity, isometry, and rotation consistency losses as in [8]. When the camera is static ($g_t = 0$), only $\mathcal{L}_{\text{scene}}$ is minimized. If $g_t = 1$, we additionally optimize an incremental pose update $\delta\boldsymbol{\xi} \in SE(3)$ via:

$$\mathcal{L}_{\text{joint}} = \mathcal{L}_{\text{scene}} + w_{\text{trk}}\,\mathcal{L}_{\text{trk}} + w_{\text{reg}}\|\delta\boldsymbol{\xi}\|^2, \tag{7}$$

where the $\mathcal{L}_{\text{trk}}$ loss enforces 2D reprojection consistency of the tracked anchors under the estimated camera motion:

$$\mathcal{L}_{\text{trk}} = \frac{1}{|\mathcal{K}_t|} \sum_{k \in \mathcal{K}_t} \left\| \mathbf{q}_k^t - \text{proj}\big(\mathbf{T}_t \, \mathbf{P}_k^{t-1}\big) \right\|_1 \tag{8}$$

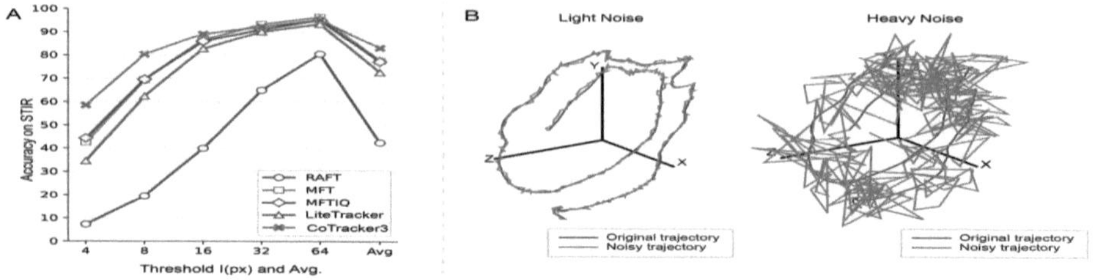

Fig. 2. Illustrating method and experimental design choices. A) 2D tracker selection showing SOTA tracking accuracy across pixel thresholds and average on STIR [17], attributed to [12]. B) Pose noise perturbation strategy applied to sequence P2_1 from [7]. Light noise: $\sigma_t = 6 \times 10^{-4}$, $\sigma_r = 0.6°$. Heavy noise: $\sigma_t = 6 \times 10^{-3}$, $\sigma_r = 0.6°$.

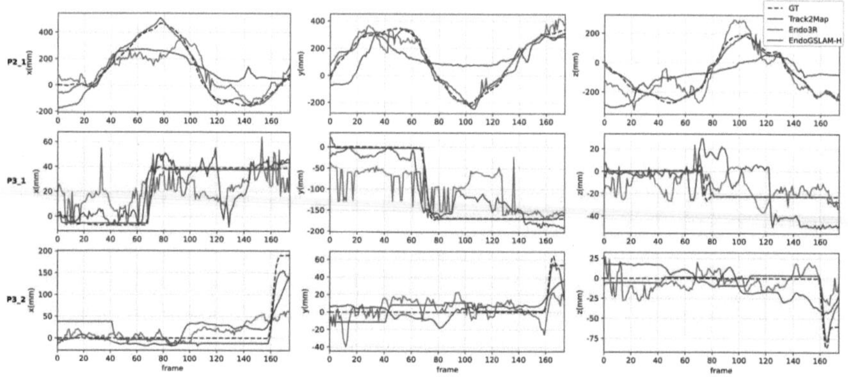

Fig. 3. Comparison of estimation of pose on three StereoMIS [7] sequences compared to a direct pose estimation network [6] and SLAM method [25].

3 Experimental Setup and Results

3.1 Experimental Setup

We benchmark 2D point tracker accuracy on STIRC2024 [18] to select CoTracker3 as the correspondence module used by Track2Map (Fig. 2A). In

Table 1. 3D reconstruction performance on StereoMIS grouped by pose initialization regime. Online-endo-track [8] is evaluated only when poses are available. Track2Map (Monocular) uses left RGB with Depth Anything V2 [29]; Track2Map (Stereo) is the main setting.

Pose Init	Method	PSNR↑	SSIM↑	LPIPS↓
None	Endo-2DTAM [9]	15.15	0.35	0.55
	EndoGSLAM-H [25]	16.67	0.52	0.45
	ESLAM [11]	18.70	0.54	0.57
	EndoSD-SLAM [24]	19.56	0.65	0.31
	EndoFlow-SLAM [27]	21.96	0.59	**0.27**
	Track2Map (Monocular)	26.70	0.70	0.31
	Track2Map (Stereo)	**27.58**	**0.745**	0.274
Noisy	Online-endo-track(light noise) [8]	27.31	0.727	0.349
	Online-endo-track(heavy noise) [8]	24.78	0.661	0.452
	Track2Map (Stereo)(light noise)	**27.68**	**0.747**	**0.276**
	Track2Map (Stereo)(heavy noise)	**27.56**	**0.742**	**0.302**
Clean	Online-endo-track [8]	27.58	0.744	0.235
	Track2Map (Stereo)	**27.83**	**0.750**	**0.201**

Table 2. Pose estimation on StereoMIS. ATE and consecutive-motion RPE are reported.

Method	ATE(m) ↓	RPE_r (deg) ↓	RPE_t(m) ↓
EndoGSLAM-H [25]	0.1077	2.4840	0.0131
Endo3R [6]	0.0897	3.4796	0.0354
Track2Map	**0.0285**	**0.2903**	**0.0061**

Table 1 we evaluate the scene reconstruction quality of Track2Map. Without pose priors, we compare it against SLAM baselines, and with pose priors (clean and noisy) we compare it against [8]. The noise magnitudes injected to pose priors in this experiment can be visualised in Fig. 2B. In Table 2 and Fig. 3 we evaluate camera pose estimation against a direct pose regression model [6] and a SLAM baseline [25]. We perform an ablation in Table 3 to quantify the effect of pose optimisation, static camera gating, and deformation in our method.

We use public CoTracker3 online weights [12] with an 8-frame sliding window, stereo depth from [26], a conservative motion-gating threshold of 0.38 (Sect. 2.1), and PyTorch on an NVIDIA Tesla V100. Key loss weights are set as: $w_{\text{depth}} = 10$, $w_{\text{color}} = 5$, $w_{\text{pose\_prior}} = 0.25$.

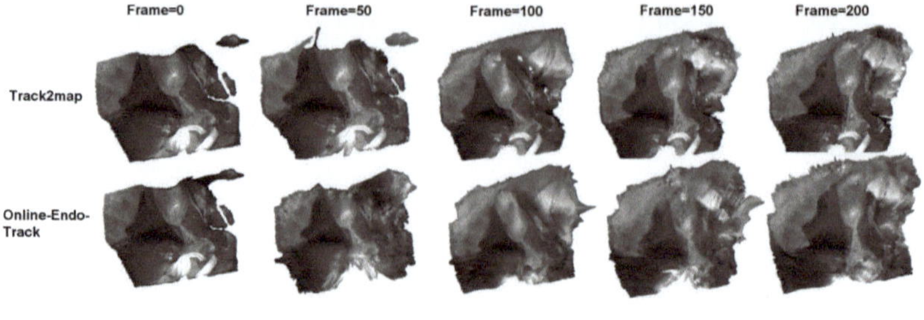

Fig. 4. Comparison of reconstruction under heavy noise poses.

Table 3. Reconstruction ablations on StereoMIS under noisy pose priors.

Method Variant	Heavy noise			Light noise		
	PSNR↑	SSIM↑	LPIPS↓	PSNR↑	SSIM↑	LPIPS↓
w/o Pose Opt.	25.42	0.676	0.359	27.54	0.744	0.244
w/o Gating	24.41	0.632	0.410	26.43	0.675	0.263
w/o Deformation	20.64	0.602	0.451	23.25	0.638	0.330
Full Track2Map	**27.56**	**0.742**	**0.302**	**27.68**	**0.747**	**0.276**

3.2 Results and Discussion

Table 1 summarizes reconstruction on StereoMIS under absent, noisy, and clean pose initialization. In the no-pose regime, Track2Map substantially improves PSNR and SSIM over prior endoscopic SLAM and neural mapping baselines, and achieves the strongest overall reconstruction when run in stereo. This improvement is likely driven by two factors: stereo input grounds the reconstruction in a consistent metric scale, and the coupling of online mapping with motion-aware pose updates prevents pose drift during camera-static intervals, stabilizing the incremental mapping process under deformable motion. These components allow the system to recover coherent geometry without relying on robot kinematics or precomputed trajectories. When noisy pose priors are provided, Track2Map has nearly the same reconstruction results as compared to the clean setting. In contrast, methods that depend more directly on the accuracy of pose initialization, such as [8], exhibit larger performance drops under heavy corruption. The qualitative comparison in Fig. 4 further illustrates this robustness under heavy pose noise: Track2Map maintains more coherent anatomy and fewer visible geometric distortions than the pose-prior baseline, consistent with the quantitative gains in Table 1. For pose estimation, Track2Map achieves lower ATE and RPE than both Endo3R [6] and EndoGSLAM [25] (Table 2), with trajectories visually improved in Fig. 3.

Table 3 isolates each component under noisy pose priors. Removing deformation causes the largest drop, confirming that deformation priors are critical for stable reconstruction from limited viewpoints. Disabling motion gating also degrades performance, especially under heavy noise, as local tissue motion can be absorbed into the camera trajectory. Removing pose optimization further reduces quality when pose noise is large. Overall, the full model performs best, showing that deformation modeling, motion-aware gating, and pose refinement are complementary.

Limitations and Assumptions. The current implementation of Track2Map is not real time, running at 6 s per frame, so we recommend keyframe processing. The motion gate assumes that coherent global flow is more likely to indicate camera motion, whereas heterogeneous or local flow is more likely to indicate tissue/tool deformation. This assumption may fail under optical-axis motion in tubular structures, large coherent tissue motion, tracker failure, substantial tool occlusion, or weakly textured tissue. Finally, evaluation is mainly performed on StereoMIS, so broader generalization should be validated on additional datasets and surgical scenarios.

4 Conclusion

We presented Track2Map, an online deformable reconstruction system for surgical video that remains stable when camera pose priors are missing or corrupted. Across StereoMIS, it improves reconstruction quality under clean, noisy, and no-pose settings, and yields more accurate camera trajectories. Robust deformable mapping in RAMIS can therefore be achieved without precise kinematics by leveraging constraints from stereo depth, consistent 2D correspondences, and assumptions about typical endoscopic motion during surgical procedures.

Acknowledgments. This work was supported in whole, or in part, by the Wellcome/EPSRC Centre for Interventional and Surgical Sciences (WEISS) [203145/Z/16/Z], EPSRC Optical and Acoustic Imaging for Surgical and Interventional Sciences (OASIS) [UKRI145], the Department of Science, Innovation and Technology (DSIT) and the Royal Academy of Engineering under the Chair in Emerging Technologies programme, EPSRC [EP/W00805X/1, EP/Y01958X/1], the EPSRC HuMIRoS grant [EP/Z534754/1], and the UCL Centre for Digital Innovation (CDI) Scholarship.

Disclosure of Interests. Some authors have current or prior affiliations with an industry partner involved in robotic surgery. The authors declare no other competing interests relevant to the content of this work.

References

1. Agudo, A.: Total estimation from rgb video: on-line camera self-calibration, non-rigid shape and motion. In: 2020 25th International Conference on Pattern Recognition (ICPR), pp. 8140–8147. IEEE (2021)

2. Agudo, A., Moreno-Noguer, F., Calvo, B., Montiel, J.M.M.: Sequential non-rigid structure from motion using physical priors. IEEE Trans. Pattern Anal. Mach. Intell. **38**(5), 979–994 (2015)
3. Bobrow, T.L., Golhar, M., Vijayan, R., Akshintala, V.S., Garcia, J.R., Durr, N.J.: Colonoscopy 3d video dataset with paired depth from 2d–3d registration. Med. Image Anal. **90**, 102956 (2023)
4. Bonilla, S., Zhang, S., Psychogyios, D., Stoyanov, D., Vasconcelos, F., Bano, S.: Gaussian pancakes: geometrically-regularized 3d gaussian splatting for realistic endoscopic reconstruction. In: International Conference on Medical Image Computing and Computer-Assisted Intervention, pp. 274–283. Springer (2024)
5. Cartucho, J., et al.: Surgt challenge: benchmark of soft-tissue trackers for robotic surgery. Med. Image Anal. **91**, 102985 (2024)
6. Guo, J., et al.: Endo3r: unified online reconstruction from dynamic monocular endoscopic video. In: International Conference on Medical Image Computing and Computer-Assisted Intervention, pp. 170–180. Springer (2025)
7. Hayoz, M., et al.: Learning how to robustly estimate camera pose in endoscopic videos. Int. J. Comput. Assist. Radiol. Surg. (2023)
8. Hayoz, M., et al.: Online 3d reconstruction and dense tracking in endoscopic videos. In: International Conference on Medical Image Computing and Computer-Assisted Intervention, pp. 444–454. Springer (2024)
9. Huang, Y., et al.: Advancing dense endoscopic reconstruction with gaussian splatting-driven surface normal-aware tracking and mapping. In: 2025 IEEE International Conference on Robotics and Automation (ICRA), pp. 4084–4091. IEEE (2025)
10. Huang, Y., et al.: Endo-4dgs: endoscopic monocular scene reconstruction with 4d gaussian splatting. In: International Conference on Medical Image Computing and Computer-Assisted Intervention, pp. 197–207. Springer (2024)
11. Johari, M.M., Carta, C., Fleuret, F.: Eslam: efficient dense slam system based on hybrid representation of signed distance fields. In: Proceedings of the IEEE/CVF Conference on Computer Vision and Pattern Recognition, pp. 17408–17419 (2023)
12. Karaev, N., Makarov, Y., Wang, J., Neverova, N., Vedaldi, A., Rupprecht, C.: Cotracker3: simpler and better point tracking by pseudo-labelling real videos. In: Proceedings of the IEEE/CVF International Conference on Computer Vision, pp. 6013–6022 (2025)
13. Karaoglu, M.A., Ji, W., Abbas, A., Navab, N., Busam, B., Ladikos, A.: Litetracker: leveraging temporal causality for accurate low-latency tissue tracking. In: International Conference on Medical Image Computing and Computer-Assisted Intervention, pp. 308–317. Springer (2025)
14. Kerbl, B., Kopanas, G., Leimkühler, T., Drettakis, G., et al.: 3d gaussian splatting for real-time radiance field rendering. ACM Trans. Graph. **42**(4), 139–1 (2023)
15. Mildenhall, B., Srinivasan, P.P., Tancik, M., Barron, J.T., Ramamoorthi, R., Ng, R.: Nerf: representing scenes as neural radiance fields for view synthesis. Commun. ACM **65**(1), 99–106 (2021)
16. Neoral, M., Šerỳch, J., Matas, J.: Mft: long-term tracking of every pixel. In: Proceedings of the IEEE/CVF Winter Conference on Applications of Computer Vision, pp. 6837–6847 (2024)
17. Schmidt, A., et al.: Point tracking in surgery-the 2024 surgical tattoos in infrared (stir) challenge. arXiv preprint arXiv:2503.24306 (2025)
18. Schmidt, A., Mohareri, O., DiMaio, S., Yip, M.C., Salcudean, S.E.: Tracking and mapping in medical computer vision: a review. medical image analysis (2024)

19. Schonberger, J.L., Frahm, J.M.: Structure-from-motion revisited. In: IEEE Conference on Computer Vision and Pattern Recognition, pp. 4104–4113 (2016)
20. Seenivasan, L., et al.: Endotracker: robustly tracking any point in endoscopic surgical scene. In: International Workshop on Foundation Models for General Medical AI, pp. 140–149. Springer (2025)
21. Song, T., Stoyanov, D., Mazomenos, E., Vasconcelos, F.: Diff2DGS: reliable reconstruction of occluded surgical scenes via 2D gaussian splatting. IEEE Robot. Autom. Lett. **11**(10), 11251–11258 (2026). https://doi.org/10.1109/LRA.2026.3723286
22. Taylor, J., Jepson, A.D., Kutulakos, K.N.: Non-rigid structure from locally-rigid motion. In: IEEE Computer Society Conference on Computer Vision and Pattern Recognition, pp. 2761–2768. IEEE (2010)
23. Teed, Z., Deng, J.: Raft: Recurrent all-pairs field transforms for optical flow. In: European Conference on Computer Vision (ECCV), pp. 402–419. Springer (2020)
24. Wang, K., Yang, C., Lin, R., Yang, X., Shen, W.: Endosd-slam: real-time deformable endoscopic slam via sparse-dense hybrid representation. In: 2025 IEEE International Conference on Bioinformatics and Biomedicine (BIBM), pp. 4214–4219. IEEE (2025)
25. Wang, K., et al.: Endogslam: real-time dense reconstruction and tracking in endoscopic surgeries using gaussian splatting. In: International Conference on Medical Image Computing and Computer-Assisted Intervention, pp. 219–229. Springer (2024)
26. Wen, B., Trepte, M., Aribido, J., Kautz, J., Gallo, O., Birchfield, S.: Foundationstereo: zero-shot stereo matching. In: Proceedings of the IEEE/CVF Conference on Computer Vision and Pattern Recognition (CVPR), pp. 5249–5260 (2025)
27. Wu, T., et al.: Endoflow-slam: real-time endoscopic slam with flow-constrained gaussian splatting. In: International Conference on Medical Image Computing and Computer-Assisted Intervention, pp. 202–212. Springer (2025)
28. Xu, M., Zhao, L., Huang, S., Hao, Q.: Active slam in 3d deformable environments. In: 2022 IEEE/RSJ International Conference on Intelligent Robots and Systems (IROS), pp. 7952–7958. IEEE (2022)
29. Yang, L., et al.: Depth anything v2. Adv. Neural. Inf. Process. Syst. **37**, 21875–21911 (2024)

Trackerless Ultrasound Pose Estimation via Correspondence-Aware Tokenization and Flow-Matching Transformers

Sang-yun Kim[1], Seok-Hwan Oh[2], Myeong-Gee Kim[2], Young-Min Kim[2], Guil Jung[1], Hyeonjik Lee[1], Jungjae Son[1], Hyuk-Sool Kwon[3], and Hyeon-Min Bae[1(✉)]

[1] Electrical Engineering Department, KAIST, Daejeon 34141, South Korea
hmbae@kaist.ac.kr
[2] Barreleye Inc., Seoul 06211, South Korea
[3] Department of Emergency Medicine, SNUBH, Seong-nam 13620, South Korea

Abstract. Trackerless freehand 3D ultrasound reconstructs volumes from 2D B-mode sequences by estimating probe motion without external tracking. In B-mode ultrasound, accurate motion estimation hinges on recognizing subtle inter-frame appearance changes, yet repetitive speckle and weak visual anchors make correspondences ambiguous and drift accumulates when composing relative transforms. We propose a correspondence-amplifying conditioning pipeline with a flow-matching transformer for pose-delta sequence generation. For each adjacent frame pair, we build a bidirectionally supported token correspondence distribution from ViT features, use it to align current-frame evidence onto the previous token grid, and derive a correspondence-induced lattice displacement cue. We further apply entropy-based confidence weighting to suppress ambiguous regions and aggregate high-dimensional correspondence-aware tokens into compact context tokens via a Q-Former. Conditioned on this context, a flow-matching DiT generates coherent pose-delta sequences through ODE sampling. Experiments on tracked freehand ultrasound sequences show improved step accuracy and substantially reduced long-horizon drift.

Keywords: Trackerless ultrasound · Freehand 3D ultrasound · Flow matching · Diffusion Transformer

1 Introduction

Three-dimensional ultrasound (3D-US) is increasingly used for image-guided diagnosis and intervention because it provides a volumetric context that is difficult to infer from isolated 2D B-mode frames. In routine practice, however, reliable 3D-US acquisition remains challenging, since dedicated 3D probes and external tracking systems are cost-prohibitive and constrain standard scanning workflows. These limitations have motivated learning-based trackerless freehand 3D-US, where probe motion is inferred directly from the ultrasound image stream.

G. Yang et al. (Eds.): MICCAI 2026, LNCS 16893, pp. 553–562, 2027.
https://doi.org/10.1007/978-3-032-38236-8_53

A key challenge is that B-mode ultrasound image provides ambiguous motion signals at the frame-to-frame level. Due to speckle patterns, shadowing, and the limited stable visual anchors, it is difficult to capture reliable inter-frame feature changes. Consequently, inferring accurate inter-frame pose deltas is challenging. As a result, the estimation is prone to small per-step pose errors, which can accumulate into substantial drift when composing relative transforms for 3D reconstruction.

Prior trackerless freehand 3D-US methods have demonstrated deep contextual learning for inter-frame transformation prediction, often augmented with attention mechanisms, correlation-style objectives [3,4,14,16], and sequence modeling [9,10] to better exploit temporal structure. Nevertheless, the correspondence signal in ultrasound is often implicit. Previous pipelines rely on a network to internally discover subtle patch-level alignments from nearly repetitive appearance, which can lead to spurious associations and systematic biases that compound over time.

In this work, we address this challenge by explicitly constructing and amplifying inter-frame correspondences before pose estimation. We introduce a correspondence-aware tokenization that forms a mutual correspondence distribution between patch tokens extracted through ViT [1] and aligns current-frame evidence onto the previous token grid, revealing subtle matched appearance changes together with a correspondence-induced displacement cue. We further apply entropy-based confidence weighting to suppress ambiguous speckle regions, and distill patch-level correspondence evidence into compact conditioning tokens via a Q-Former [7]. Finally, a context-conditioned Transformer [15] trained with flow matching [12] generates pose-delta sequences through ODE sampling, improving stability and reducing long-horizon drift.

2 Method

2.1 Pose-Delta Labels and Representation

Given N ultrasound frames $\{I_0, \dots, I_{N-1}\}$, we supervise the model with relative probe motion between consecutive calibrated ultrasound image planes. Let $T_k \in SE(3)$ denote the calibrated image-plane pose in the tracker coordinate system at frame k. We define

$$\Delta T_k = T_{k-1}^{-1} T_k, \quad k = 1, \dots, N-1, \qquad \Delta T_0 = \mathbf{I}_4, \tag{1}$$

Thus, each pose delta is a relative rigid transform, and the target sequence has length N with a pivot at $k = 0$. Each ΔT_k is represented as a 9D vector

$$y_k = [r_k^{(6)}; t_k] \in \mathbb{R}^9, \tag{2}$$

where $r_k^{(6)}$ is the 6D continuous rotation representation proposed in [17] and $t_k \in \mathbb{R}^3$.

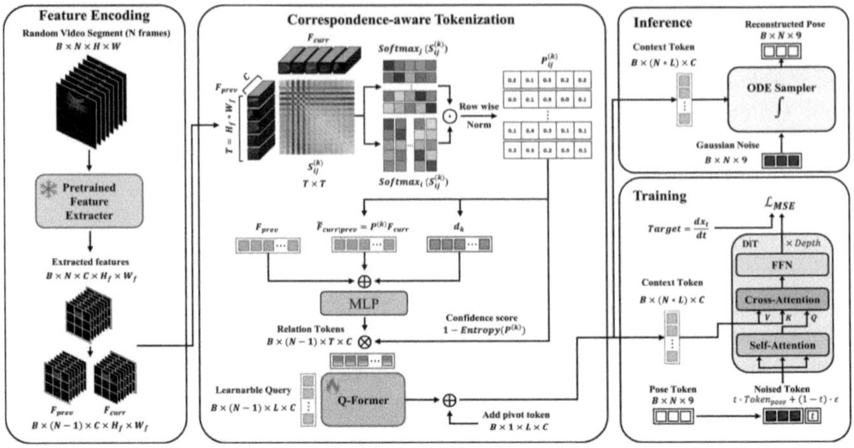

Fig. 1. Overview of the proposed framework. A frozen ultrasound-pretrained ViT encodes B-mode frames into token grids. CAT builds confidence-weighted correspondence-aware tokens from adjacent frames. A Q-Former compresses these tokens, and a flow-matching DiT generates pose deltas through ODE sampling.

2.2 Correspondence-Amplifying Conditioning

Figure 1 introduces the overview of the proposed framework. The key idea is to make motion evidence explicit before pose generation by constructing correspondence-aware tokens from consecutive frames.

To effectively capture ultrasound-specific appearance cues, we leverage a large-scale ultrasound-pretrained feature encoder. Specifically, we used a frozen ViT-B [1] backbone pretrained on B-mode images via masked autoencoding (MAE) [5]. Given an input frame I_k, the encoder extracts a patch-token grid $F_k = [f_{k,1}; \dots; f_{k,T}] \in \mathbb{R}^{T \times C}$, where H_f and W_f denote the token-grid height and width, and $T = H_f W_f$. We form $(N-1)$ adjacent frame pairs $(k-1, k)$ for $k = 1, \dots, N-1$. For the k-th pair, we denote $F_{\text{prev}}^{(k)} = F_{k-1}$ and $F_{\text{curr}}^{(k)} = F_k$ for notational convenience.

Next, we construct inter-frame token correspondences by computing a cosine similarity between ℓ_2-normalized tokens:

$$S_{ij}^{(k)} = \langle \hat{f}_{k-1,i}, \hat{f}_{k,j} \rangle, \tag{3}$$

where $S_{ij}^{(k)}$ is a similarity score between token i in frame $(k-1)$ and token j in frame k.

In ultrasound, repetitive speckle can make many locations appear similarly plausible, producing asymmetric matches where a token strongly prefers a candidate in one direction, but the reverse association is weak. To suppress such asymmetric correspondences, we compute matching distributions in both directions:

$$A_{ij}^{(k)} = \text{softmax}_j(S_{ij}^{(k)}), \qquad B_{ij}^{(k)} = \text{softmax}_i(S_{ij}^{(k)}), \tag{4}$$

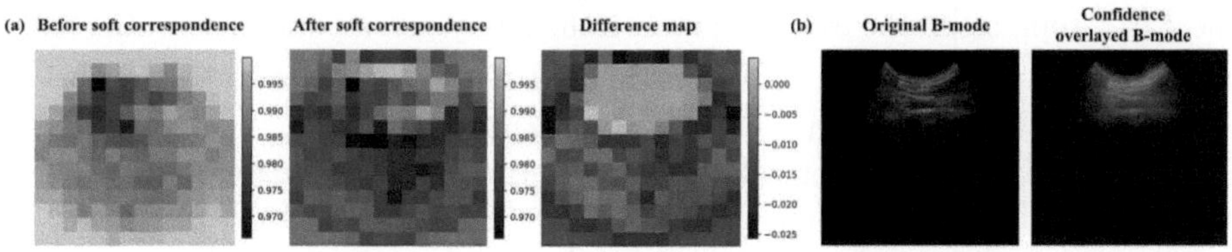

Fig. 2. Visual intuition for correspondence-aware tokenization. (a) Soft matching aligns current evidence to the previous token grid, revealing localized changes that are obscured without explicit correspondence alignment. (b) Entropy-based confidence weighting emphasizes matchable anatomy and suppresses ambiguous speckle/background regions.

and keep only mutually supported matches via the elementwise product

$$M_{ij}^{(k)} = A_{ij}^{(k)} B_{ij}^{(k)}. \tag{5}$$

We finally normalize each row of $M^{(k)}$ to obtain a row-stochastic correspondence distribution:

$$P_{ij}^{(k)} = \frac{M_{ij}^{(k)}}{\sum_{j'} M_{ij'}^{(k)} + \epsilon}, \qquad \sum_{j} P_{ij}^{(k)} = 1. \tag{6}$$

Each row $P_{i\cdot}$ can be interpreted as a probability distribution over candidate locations in the current frame for token i in the previous frame: it becomes peaked when a clear match exists, and remains spread when several candidates are similarly plausible.

Figure 2(a) illustrates why explicit correspondence is helpful. In B-mode image sequences, many regions exhibit similar speckle statistics and lack distinctive visual anchors, so multiple candidate locations can obtain comparable similarity scores. As a result, the similarity landscape can be low-contrast and motion cues remain implicit. By constructing $P^{(k)}$, we explicitly re-weight current-frame evidence for each previous-frame token, making subtle motion-related changes easier to expose after alignment:

$$\tilde{f}_{k|k-1,i} = \sum_{j=1}^{T} P_{ij}^{(k)} f_{k,j} \in \mathbb{R}^{C}. \tag{7}$$

This alignment is crucial because $f_{k,j}$ and $\tilde{f}_{k|k-1,i}$ now refer to the corresponding locations in expectation, so direct comparisons become meaningful descriptors of motion-induced change rather than artifacts of fixed indexing.

We also encode $P^{(k)}$ as a compact geometric cue on the token lattice. Let $p_i \in [-1, 1]^2$ denote the fixed coordinate of the token i on the $H_f \times W_f$ grid. We compute the expected matched coordinate and its displacement:

$$\tilde{p}_i^{(k)} = \sum_{j=1}^{T} P_{ij}^{(k)} p_j, \qquad d_i^{(k)} = \tilde{p}_i^{(k)} - p_i \in \mathbb{R}^2. \tag{8}$$

where $d_i^{(k)}$ represents the expected shift induced by correspondence on the token grid: it is stable when $P_{i\cdot}^{(k)}$ is confident and naturally degenerates toward an uninformative average when $P_{i\cdot}^{(k)}$ is less concentrated.

We construct a compact relation descriptor from the aligned feature pair and an explicit correspondence shift. Since the alignment in Eq. (7) already brings current evidence to the previous token grid, motion signals can be read directly from the pair $(f_{k-1,i}, \tilde{f}_{k|k-1,i})$. We also add a geometric cue via the correspondence-induced displacement in Eq. (8). Specifically, we embed the displacement with the MLP $\psi(\cdot)$ and concatenate

$$u_i^{(k)} = \left[f_{k-1,i},\ \tilde{f}_{k|k-1,i},\ \psi(d_i^{(k)})\right], \qquad r_i^{(k)} = \phi(u_i^{(k)}) \in \mathbb{R}^C. \tag{9}$$

followed by a projection head $\phi(\cdot)$ to obtain the relation token $r_i^{(k)} = \phi(u_i^{(k)}) \in \mathbb{R}^C$. The aligned feature pair encodes the degree of appearance consistency at the matched location, while $\psi(d_i)$ encodes how the correspondence shifts on the grid, helping to disambiguate repetitive speckle.

In homogeneous speckle or low-texture regions, $P_{i\cdot}$ tends to spread out and the soft alignment in Eq. (7) becomes less informative. We address this by encoding uncertainty with the entropy of each assignment row:

$$H_i^{(k)} = -\sum_{j=1}^{T} P_{ij}^{(k)} \log\left(P_{ij}^{(k)} + \epsilon\right), \qquad c_i^{(k)} = 1 - \frac{H_i^{(k)}}{\log T}, \tag{10}$$

and weight correspondence-aware tokens as $\bar{r}_i^{(k)} = c_i^{(k)} r_i^{(k)}$. Here, $c_i^{(k)}$ is close to 1 when $P_{i\cdot}^{(k)}$ is confident and approaches 0 when the match is ambiguous. As visualized in Fig. 2(b), high-confidence regions concentrate on stable anatomical structures, while background and repetitive speckle are downweighted. This prevents unreliable correspondences from dominating the conditioning signal, improving robustness of per-step motion estimation, and reducing long-horizon drift when composing pose deltas.

Q-Former Context Compression. Correspondence-aware tokens are high-dimensional ($T = H_f W_f$), so directly conditioning the pose generator on all tokens is costly. We adopt a Q-Former [7] as a learnable query bottleneck, where a small set of queries cross-attends to the full 2D token grid and adaptively aggregates salient spatial evidence into a fixed-length context. We compress confidence-weighted tokens $\bar{R}_k \in \mathbb{R}^{T\times C}$ for each pair $(k-1, k)$ into L learned queries:

$$Z_k = \mathrm{QFormer}(Q, \bar{R}_k) \in \mathbb{R}^{L\times C}, \qquad k = 1, \ldots, N-1, \tag{11}$$

where $Q \in \mathbb{R}^{L\times C}$ are learnable query tokens. We set the pivot context to zeros ($Z_0 = \mathbf{0}$), yielding $Z \in \mathbb{R}^{N\times L\times C}$, which is flattened into $B \times (NL) \times C$ context tokens for cross-attention.

2.3 Flow-Matching DiT for Pose-Delta Generation

To obtain accurate and stable pose-delta sequence prediction, we formulate pose generation as conditional flow matching and learn a velocity field that maps Gaussian noise to the target pose-delta sequence. Given ground truth $y \in \mathbb{R}^{N\times 9}$ and noise $\epsilon \sim \mathcal{N}(0, \sigma^2 I)$, we sample $t \in [0,1]$ and define

$$x_t = (1-t)\epsilon + ty, \qquad v^\star = \frac{dx_t}{dt} = y - \epsilon. \tag{12}$$

A context-conditioned DiT [15] predicts $v_\theta(x_t, t\,;\, Z) \in \mathbb{R}^{N\times 9}$ using self-attention to pose tokens and cross-attention to context tokens. We train with a flow-matching [12] objective:

$$\mathcal{L}_{\mathrm{FM}} = \mathbb{E}\big[\|v_\theta(x_t, t\,;\, Z) - v^\star\|_2^2\big]. \tag{13}$$

2.4 ODE Sampling and Trajectory Composition

At inference, we sample $z_0 \sim \mathcal{N}(0, \sigma^2 I)$ and solve the ordinary differential equation (ODE):

$$\frac{dz_t}{dt} = v_\theta(z_t, t\,;\, Z), \quad t \in [0,1], \tag{14}$$

with an Euler solver for 50 steps, yielding predicted deltas $\hat{y} = z_1$. Anchored poses for reconstruction are obtained by composing $\widehat{\Delta T}_k$:

$$\widehat{T}_0 = \mathbf{I}_4, \qquad \widehat{T}_k = \widehat{T}_{k-1}\widehat{\Delta T}_k. \tag{15}$$

3 Experiments

3.1 Dataset and Splits

We evaluated on the public TUS-REC challenge dataset [8], which contains 1,272 tracked freehand 2D B-mode forearm ultrasound scans from 53 volunteers across diverse probe orientations, scan directions, and L-, C-, and S-shaped trajectories. We follow the public subject-disjoint protocol of the challenge, using 1,080 scans from 45 subjects for training, 120 scans from 5 subjects for model selection, and 72 scans from 3 subjects for the final validation in Table 1. These 72 scans are the official public validation split and are never used for training.

3.2 Implementation Details

All frames are resized to 224×224 and normalized to $[0,1]$. During training, we sample subsequences of length $N = 32$. We used a frozen ViT-B [1] encoder pretrained with masked autoencoding (MAE) to extract dense features ($C = 768$, $H_f \times W_f = 14 \times 14$, $T = 196$ tokens per frame). For each adjacent pair, we compute a mutual, row-stochastic correspondence matrix P to align current-frame features with the previous frame features and estimate a correspondence-induced displacement on the token lattice. Correspondence-aware tokens are confidence-weighted using row-wise entropy. We compress dense tokens into $L = 16$ query tokens per timestep using a Q-Former [7], and the resulting context tokens condition a flow-matching DiT [12,15] (hidden size 768, 8 blocks, 12 heads). We train with Adam (lr 10^{-4}, batch size 32) and exponential moving average (EMA). At inference, pose deltas are generated via Euler ODE sampling with 50 steps.

3.3 Qualitative Assessment

We qualitatively assess reconstruction fidelity by overlaying the composed probe trajectory with the ground-truth trajectory on representative scan patterns, as shown in Fig. 3.

Baseline conditions the model using simple feature concatenation from two adjacent frames, followed by a linear layer that compresses the concatenated features into a fixed-size conditioning vector. **Baseline + CAT** replaces this naive concatenation with our correspondence-aware tokenization (CAT). **Proposed** method further applies Q-Former (QF) compression, distilling dense correspondence-aware tokens into a compact set of query tokens per timestep.

Across all scan shapes in Fig. 3, the Baseline trajectory exhibits noticeable drift and shape distortion. Adding CAT improves alignment to the ground truth by making subtle inter-frame motion evidence more explicit, reducing accumulated deviation along the trajectory. The proposed method achieves the closest agreement with the ground truth, with visibly reduced long-horizon drift and a more stable reconstruction of the overall scan geometry.

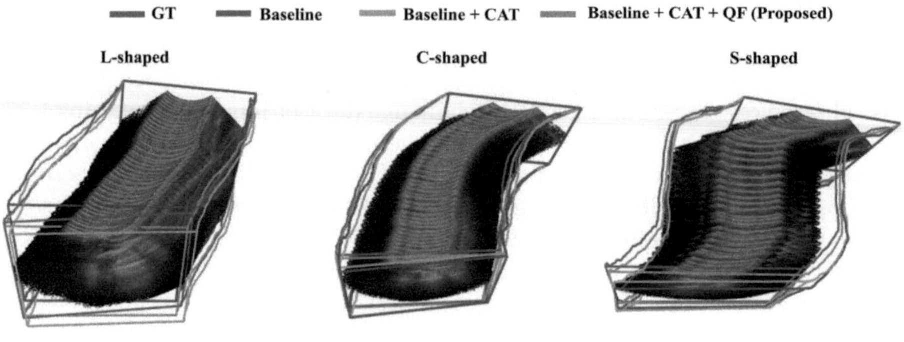

Fig. 3. Qualitative trajectory overlays for representative scan shapes. The proposed correspondence-aware tokenization with Q-Former conditioning more closely matches the ground-truth trajectory and reduces long-horizon drift compared to feature concatenation and linear-only conditioning.

Table 1. Quantitative comparison on the official public TUS-REC evaluation split.

Method	GPE (mm)↓	LPE (mm)↓	FDR (%)↓
DCL-Net [4]	11.77	0.134	17.68
PLPPI [2]	9.80	0.133	13.24
NR-Rec-FUS [11]	9.12	0.128	12.11
MoGLo [6]	8.09	0.124	10.45
Baseline	12.58	0.145	17.89
Baseline + CAT	5.84	0.123	9.91
Baseline + CAT + QF (Proposed)	**5.31**	**0.121**	**8.56**

3.4 Quantitative Assessment

We evaluate pose accuracy using the point-wise distance error introduced in [8] with four image-corner points, and report the mean Euclidean distance for both the local and global reconstructions.

Local point error (LPE) reflects single-step motion accuracy, while the use of composed transforms anchored at the first frame yields the **global point error (GPE)**, which captures long-horizon drift accumulation. In addition, we report the **final drift rate (FDR)** introduced in [13], which measures endpoint drift normalized by the accumulated scan length. We compare against reproducible methods reported in [8] benchmark and recent trackerless networks that operate in an offline, feed-forward manner without external tracking hardware. Table 1 summarizes the results.

Table 1 shows that the Baseline suffers from severe drift, as it conditions the pose generator using unaligned features from two adjacent frames and compresses them with a single linear projection, leaving the model to infer inter-frame correspondences implicitly. Replacing this step with CAT yields a large improvement in both local and global accuracy which indicates that explicitly forming correspondence-aware relation tokens provides a substantially more reliable conditioning signal in the presence of repetitive speckle and weak anchors. Replacing the simple linear projection with Q-Former yields further consistent improvements, suggesting that query-based attention pooling better preserves task-relevant correspondence cues for conditioning than a single linear compression.

4 Conclusion

We proposed a correspondence-amplifying conditioning framework for trackerless freehand 3D ultrasound, targeting the core difficulty of B-mode imaging where inter-frame motion cues are subtle and correspondences are often ambiguous due to repetitive speckle and weak visual anchors. Our key idea is to explicitly construct a token-level correspondence distribution and use it to align current-frame evidence onto the previous token grid, exposing matched appearance changes together with an expected lattice-displacement cue. We further incorporate entropy-based confidence weighting to suppress unreliable regions and adopt a Q-Former to distill patch-level correspondence evidence into compact context tokens for efficient conditioning. Conditioned on this context, a flow-matching DiT generates coherent pose-delta sequences via ODE sampling, improving robustness to accumulated drift. Experiments on the TUS-REC dataset demonstrate consistent gains in step accuracy and substantial reductions in long-horizon drift over feature-concatenation baselines and competitive trackerless methods, leading to precise trajectory reconstruction across diverse scan patterns.

Acknowledgments. This work was supported by Institute of Information communications Technology Planning Evaluation(IITP) grant funded by the Korean government (MSIT) (No. RS-2024-00444862), the National Research Foundation of Korea (NRF) grant funded by the Korean government (MSIT) (No. RS-2024-00349441), and BK21 FOUR (Connected AI Education & Research Program for Industry and Society Innovation, KAIST EE, No. 4120200113769).

Disclosure of Interests. S-Y. Kim, Y-M. Kim, G. Jung and H. Lee are under contracts with Ministry of Korea National Defense. S-Y. Kim and H. Lee are under scholarship from the Korea Government Scholarship Program.

References

1. Dosovitskiy, A., et al.: An image is worth 16x16 words: transformers for image recognition at scale. arXiv preprint arXiv:2010.11929 (2020)
2. Dou, Y., Mu, F., Li, Y., Varghese, T.: Sensorless end-to-end freehand 3-d ultrasound reconstruction with physics-guided deep learning. IEEE Trans. Ultrason. Ferroelectr. Freq. Control **71**(11), 1514–1525 (2024)
3. Guo, H., Chao, H., Xu, S., Wood, B.J., Wang, J., Yan, P.: Ultrasound volume reconstruction from freehand scans without tracking. IEEE Trans. Biomed. Eng. **70**(3), 970–979 (2022)
4. Guo, H., Xu, S., Wood, B., Yan, P.: Sensorless freehand 3d ultrasound reconstruction via deep contextual learning. In: International Conference on Medical Image Computing and Computer-Assisted Intervention, pp. 463–472. Springer (2020)
5. He, K., Chen, X., Xie, S., Li, Y., Dollár, P., Girshick, R.: Masked autoencoders are scalable vision learners. In: Proceedings of the IEEE/CVF Conference on Computer Vision and Pattern Recognition, pp. 16000–16009 (2022)
6. Lee, S., et al.: Enhancing free-hand 3d photoacoustic and ultrasound reconstruction using deep learning. IEEE Trans. Med. Imaging (2025)
7. Li, J., Li, D., Savarese, S., Hoi, S.: Blip-2: bootstrapping language-image pre-training with frozen image encoders and large language models. In: International Conference on Machine Learning, pp. 19730–19742. PMLR (2023)
8. Li, Q., et al.: Tus-rec2024: a challenge to reconstruct 3d freehand ultrasound without external tracker. arXiv preprint arXiv:2506.21765 (2025)
9. Li, Q., et al.: Long-term dependency for 3d reconstruction of freehand ultrasound without external tracker. IEEE Trans. Biomed. Eng. **71**(3), 1033–1042 (2023)

10. Li, Q., et al.: Trackerless freehand ultrasound with sequence modelling and auxiliary transformation over past and future frames. In: 2023 IEEE 20th International Symposium on Biomedical Imaging (ISBI), pp. 1–5. IEEE (2023)
11. Li, Q., et al.: Nonrigid reconstruction of freehand ultrasound without a tracker. In: International Conference on Medical Image Computing and Computer-Assisted Intervention, pp. 689–699. Springer (2024)
12. Lipman, Y., Chen, R.T., Ben-Hamu, H., Nickel, M., Le, M.: Flow matching for generative modeling. arXiv preprint arXiv:2210.02747 (2022)
13. Luo, M., et al.: Self context and shape prior for sensorless freehand 3d ultrasound reconstruction. In: International Conference on Medical Image Computing and Computer-Assisted Intervention, pp. 201–210. Springer (2021)
14. Luo, M., Yang, X., Wang, H., Du, L., Ni, D.: Deep motion network for freehand 3d ultrasound reconstruction. In: International Conference on Medical Image Computing and Computer-Assisted Intervention, pp. 290–299. Springer (2022)
15. Peebles, W., Xie, S.: Scalable diffusion models with transformers. In: Proceedings of the IEEE/CVF International Conference on Computer Vision, pp. 4195–4205 (2023)
16. Prevost, R., et al.: Deep learning-based 3d freehand ultrasound reconstruction with inertial measurement units (2018)
17. Zhou, Y., Barnes, C., Lu, J., Yang, J., Li, H.: On the continuity of rotation representations in neural networks. In: Proceedings of the IEEE/CVF Conference on Computer Vision and Pattern Recognition, pp. 5745–5753 (2019)

UltraStar: Semantic-Aware Star Graph Modeling for Echocardiography Navigation

Teng Wang[1], Haojun Jiang[1], Chenxi Li[1], Diwen Wang[2], Yihang Tang[2], Zhenguo Sun[3], Yujiao Deng[4], Shiji Song[1], and Gao Huang[1(✉)]

[1] Department of Automation, BNRist, Tsinghua University, Beijing, China
{t-wang25,jhj20}@mails.tsinghua.edu.cn, gaohuang@tsinghua.edu.cn
[2] School of Automation, Beijing Institute of Technology, Beijing, China
[3] Beijing Academy of Artificial Intelligence, Beijing, China
[4] Chinese PLA General Hospital, Beijing, China

Abstract. Echocardiography is critical for diagnosing cardiovascular diseases, yet the shortage of skilled sonographers hinders timely patient care, due to high operational difficulties. Consequently, research on automated probe navigation has significant clinical potential. To achieve robust navigation, it is essential to leverage historical scanning information, mimicking how experts rely on past feedback to adjust subsequent maneuvers. Practical scanning is an exploratory trial-and-error process that inherently generates noisy trajectories. However, existing methods typically model this history as a sequential chain, forcing models to overfit these noisy paths, leading to performance degradation on long sequences. In this paper, we propose UltraStar, which reformulates probe navigation from path regression to anchor-based global localization. By establishing a Star Graph, UltraStar treats historical keyframes as spatial anchors connected directly to the current view, explicitly modeling geometric constraints for precise positioning. We further enhance the Star Graph with a semantic-aware sampling strategy that actively selects the representative landmarks from massive history logs, reducing redundancy for accurate anchoring. Extensive experiments on a dataset with over 1.31 million samples demonstrate that UltraStar outperforms baselines and scales better with longer input lengths, revealing a more effective topology for history modeling under noisy exploration. Code is available at https://github.com/LeapLabTHU/UltraStar.

Keywords: Echocardiography · Star Graph Modeling · Semantic-aware Sampling · Probe Navigation

1 Introduction

Cardiovascular diseases are the leading cause of death [19]. To assess cardiovascular health, echocardiography is an effective method [17], being both non-invasive

T. Wang, H. Jiang—Equal Contribution.
H. Jiang—Guided this work.

G. Yang et al. (Eds.): MICCAI 2026, LNCS 16893, pp. 563–573, 2027.
https://doi.org/10.1007/978-3-032-38236-8_54

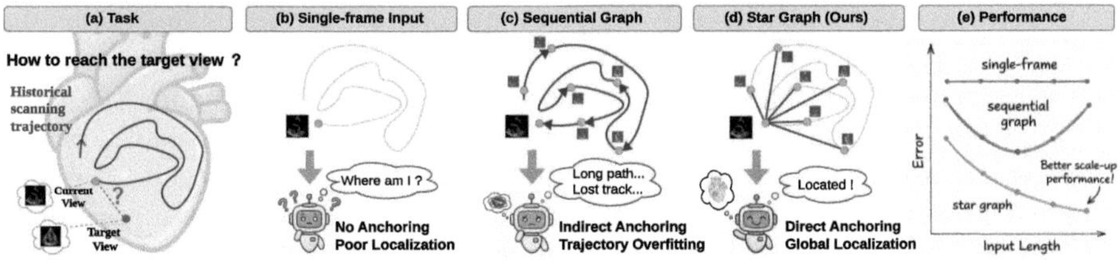

Fig. 1. Comparison of modeling paradigms. (a) The echocardiography navigation task. (b) Single-frame methods struggle with localization due to limited context. (c) Sequential Graph methods model history as a chain, forcing the model to overfit noisy exploration trajectories and degrading localization accuracy. (d) Our Star Graph breaks the chain, treating historical keyframes as global anchors and learning direct geometric constraints for precise localization. (e) Our method achieves lower error and scales better.

and free from radiation. In practice, sonographers need to manually adjust and explore the probe between the ribs, continuously optimizing the angle based on previous exploration trajectory to approach the target view. This demanding process requires strong anatomical knowledge and proficient skills, contributing to the scarcity of trained professionals [21].

To address this issue, with the rapid adoption of AI techniques in medical imaging [6,15,16,23,24], researchers have begun leveraging AI to empower ultrasound probe navigation systems [2,4,8,13,14,18,22], aimed at achieving precise probe navigation to assist sonographers or drive autonomous robotic ultrasound systems. Several previous studies have demonstrated the potential of AI-driven guidance. For example, Narang et al. [18] proposed a commercial CNN-based echocardiography navigation system to guide nurses in acquiring standard views, but it is closed-source, limiting broader development. Bao et al. [2] proposed a convolutional model for rotational suggestions, but it is limited to A4C and A2C views, reducing its clinical scope. Droste et al. [8] introduced US-GuideNet, which uses a GRU to model historical image-motion sequences for fetal plane scanning. Jiang et al. [13] proposed UltraSeP, which leverages a sequence-aware pre-training paradigm to learn personalized cardiac structures. Wang et al. [20] developed UltraHiT, employing a hierarchical transformer to model history scanning sequences for autonomous internal carotid artery scanning. Additionally, Yue et al. [22] proposed EchoWorld, a motion-aware world modeling framework that pre-trains a cardiac world model to improve probe guidance.

As mentioned earlier, cardiac ultrasound scanning is typically a process of exploration followed by gradual convergence, where sonographers rely on prior exploration to guide subsequent maneuvers. Therefore, leveraging historical scanning data is indispensable for robust probe navigation, as single-frame input methods [11,12] lack sufficient context to resolve the ambiguity of the complex cardiac anatomy. While recent works adopt sequence modeling to capture this context, limitations still remain in the utilization of historical information. As illustrated in Fig. 1, cardiac ultrasound scanning is a complex trial-and-error exploration process. Consequently, the raw history contains substantial redundant or noisy motions that do not directly aid target acquisition. However, most existing sequential methods [8,13,20] model the history as a chain (Fig. 1(c)). This paradigm forces the model to overfit the noisy exploration path, paying excessive attention to step-by-step wandering motions. As a result, the geometric constraints needed for navigation are weakened, and performance often degrades as the sequence length grows. A key insight of our work is that the main value of history lies not in reconstructing the trajectory, but in global localization—helping the agent understand its current position relative to the anatomy. To this end, we propose UltraStar, a simple yet effective framework that shifts from chain-based modeling to a Star Graph topology (Fig. 1(d)). By treating historical keyframes as spatial anchors and directly connecting them to the current view, UltraStar learns the geometric constraints between the current state and historical landmarks, enabling robust localization and superior scalability. Furthermore, raw scanning history can be excessively long and sparse, making full-trajectory processing computationally infeasible. We therefore propose a semantic-aware sampling strategy that selects keyframe landmarks with high semantic divergence, constructing a compact yet informative map for the Star Graph. We validate our method on a large-scale dataset of 1.31 million samples, where UltraStar outperforms baselines and demonstrates superior scalability.

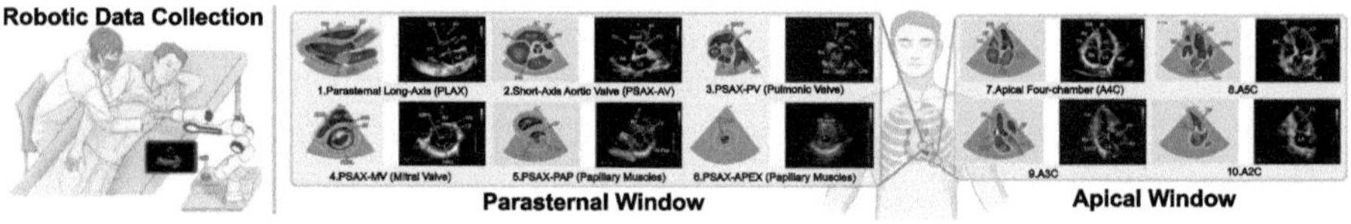

Fig. 2. Illustration of the dataset. The view images are sourced from [17].

2 Dataset and Method

In this section, we first describe the echocardiography scanning dataset to provide a background about our task. Next, we introduce the Star Graph modeling paradigm. Lastly, we introduce the semantic-aware sampling strategy.

2.1 Echocardiography Scanning Dataset

In this work, we focus on six imaging planes in the parasternal window and four imaging planes in the apical window (Fig. 2 right). To support model training, we built a robotic acquisition system in which a sonographer operates a probe mounted on a robotic arm (Fig. 2 left), while the probe captures images and the system records its 6-DOF pose. The pose is represented by position (x, y, z) and orientation (Euler angles about x, y, z). Each scan yields a sequence $\{(\mathbf{I}_t, \mathbf{p}_t)\}_{t=1}^{T}$, where $\mathbf{I}_t$ is the image and $\mathbf{p}_t$ is the pose at time t, and the relative action $\mathbf{a}_{i\to j}$ between two poses $\mathbf{p}_i$ and $\mathbf{p}_j$ can be computed. During each scan, sonographers annotate timestamps $\{t_i\}_{i=1}^{10}$ corresponding to the ten standard planes, from which the target poses $\mathbf{p}_{t_i}$ are obtained. For any other frame $(\mathbf{I}_{t_j}, \mathbf{p}_{t_j})$ with $j \neq i$, we compute the action $\mathbf{a}_{t_j \to t_i}$ to the target plane as supervision for training. Our dataset was collected by two expert sonographers from 178 adult patients, resulting in 356 scanning trajectories and 1.31M samples in total.

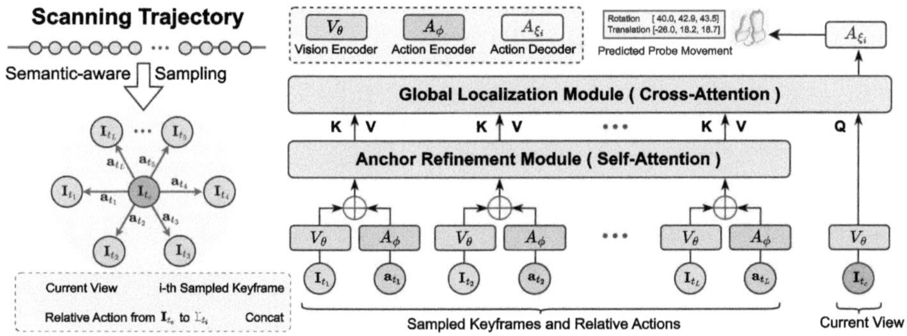

Fig. 3. Illustration of the Star Graph modeling paradigm.

2.2 Star Graph Modeling Paradigm

The core motivation of our method is to utilize historical data for global localization rather than trajectory reconstruction. By explicitly modeling the geometric relationship between the current view and historical landmarks, the model can determine its precise location in the cardiac anatomy. In the following sections, we provide a detailed explanation of our approach, as shown in Fig. 3.

Input. Given the current image $\mathbf{I}_{t_c}$ from a scan, we first sample $L-1$ historical keyframes $\{\mathbf{I}_{t_1}, \ldots, \mathbf{I}_{t_{L-1}}\}$ using the strategy described in Sect. 2.3. Unlike sequential methods that model the path between adjacent historical frames, we construct a Star Graph topology. We compute the relative actions $\mathbf{a}_{t_c \to t_i} \in \mathbb{R}^6$ from the current view $\mathbf{I}_{t_c}$ to each sampled keyframe $\mathbf{I}_{t_i}$. This forms a set of spatial anchors, where each anchor consists of a visual appearance and its geometric position relative to the current view:

$$\mathcal{S} = \{(\mathbf{I}_{t_i}, \mathbf{a}_{t_c \to t_i}) \mid i = 1, \ldots, L-1\}. \tag{1}$$

Feature Encoding. We utilize a shared vision encoder V_θ (ViT [7]) to extract visual features. The current view $\mathbf{I}_{t_c}$ is encoded into a query feature $\mathbf{f}_c^v \in \mathbb{R}^C$. Similarly, each historical keyframe $\mathbf{I}_{t_i}$ is encoded into a visual feature $\mathbf{f}_i^v \in \mathbb{R}^C$.

Simultaneously, the relative 6-DOF actions are processed by an action encoder A_ϕ to map the geometric constraints into the same feature space:

$$\mathbf{f}_c^v = V_\theta(\mathbf{I}_{t_c}), \quad \mathbf{f}_i^v = V_\theta(\mathbf{I}_{t_i}), \quad \mathbf{f}_i^a = A_\phi(\mathbf{a}_{t_c \to t_i}), \quad \mathbf{f} \in \mathbb{R}^C. \tag{2}$$

Star Graph Reasoning. The reasoning process consists of two stages: Anchor Refinement and Global Localization. First, to construct robust multimodal anchors, we concatenate the visual and action features for each sampled keyframe. These raw anchors are then fed into an Anchor Refinement Module (implemented as a two-layer Self-Attention block) to model the correlations among historical landmarks and filter noise:

$$\mathbf{h}_i = \mathrm{Concat}(\mathbf{f}_i^v, \mathbf{f}_i^a) \in \mathbb{R}^{2C}, \tag{3}$$

$$[\hat{\mathbf{h}}_1, \ldots, \hat{\mathbf{h}}_{L-1}] = \mathrm{SelfAttn}([\mathbf{h}_1, \ldots, \mathbf{h}_{L-1}]). \tag{4}$$

Next, we employ a Global Localization Module. We project the refined anchors $\hat{\mathbf{h}}$ to dimension C as the Key and Value, and use the current view feature $\mathbf{f}_c^v$ as the Query for the Cross-Attention mechanism. This operation aggregates geometric evidence from the map to localize the current state:

$$\mathbf{m} = \mathrm{CrossAttn}(Q = \mathbf{f}_c^v, K = \hat{\mathbf{h}}, V = \hat{\mathbf{h}}). \tag{5}$$

Prediction and Loss. Finally, the localized feature $\mathbf{m}$ is passed to task-specific action decoders A_{ξ_k} to predict the relative action $\mathbf{a}_{t_c \to \mathbf{target}_k}$ required to reach the k-th standard plane. We adopt millimeters for translation and degrees for rotation. This unit choice brings both components to the same order of magnitude, allowing us to assign equal weights to translation and rotation errors during optimization. The model is trained using the Smooth L1 Loss:

$$\mathbf{a}' = A_{\xi_k}(\mathbf{m}), \quad \mathcal{L} = \mathcal{L}_{\mathrm{SmoothL1}}(\mathbf{a}_{\mathrm{gt}}, \mathbf{a}'). \tag{6}$$

2.3 Semantic-Aware Sampling Strategy

The efficacy of our UltraStar framework relies on the quality of the spatial anchors used for map construction. To achieve precise global localization, the constructed Star Graph must be informationally dense: a set of redundant anchors provides weak geometric constraints, whereas a diverse map facilitates robust triangulation. Let L denote the number of nodes in the input graph. Our goal is to select $L-1$ informative historical anchors from the raw scanning history.

Segmental Sampling. As a representative baseline, segmental sampling divides the historical trajectory into $L-1$ equal temporal segments and randomly selects one point from each segment (see Fig. 4(a)). This strategy improves temporal coverage compared with unconstrained sampling by encouraging anchors to

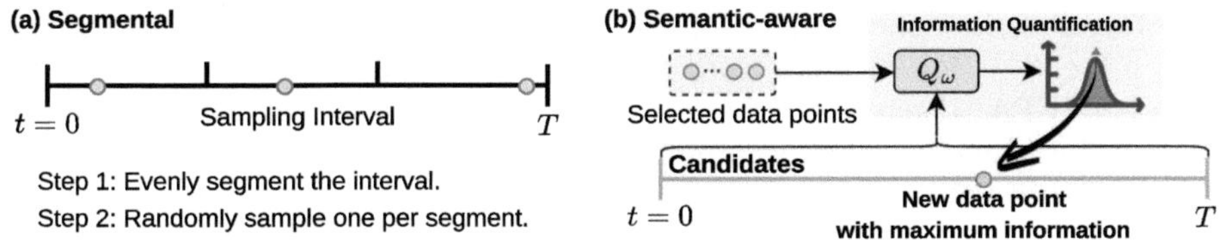

Fig. 4. Diagram of segmental sampling and idea of semantic-aware sampling.

be distributed across the full exploration process. However, it remains content-agnostic and does not consider the actual visual information, often resulting in homogeneous anchors that fail to represent the global anatomy effectively.

Semantic-Aware Strategy. To construct an informationally rich map for the Star Graph, we propose a semantic-aware strategy that enhances basic sampling by maximizing the semantic diversity of the anchors (see Fig. 4(b)). Specifically, we train a view classification model Q_ω to quantify the semantic content of each frame. For an image $\mathbf{I}$, Q_ω outputs a probability distribution $\mathbf{z} \in \mathbb{R}^{10}$ over 10 standard views. The sampling process is designed to minimize redundancy. When selecting a new anchor, we compute its semantic similarity against the current view $\mathbf{I}_t$ and all previously sampled anchors using cosine similarity on their distribution vectors $\mathbf{z}$. We sum these similarity scores to measure the redundancy of a candidate frame relative to the existing graph nodes. To ensure diversity while maintaining randomness, we identify the K candidates with the lowest total similarity (i.e., the most distinct frames) and randomly select one as the new anchor. This iterative process ensures that the resulting Star Graph covers the widest possible semantic range within the cardiac anatomy.

3 Experiments

3.1 Implementation Details

Dataset. The dataset was collected using a GE machine (*General Electric*) equipped with a M5S probe. We use 284 scans for training and 72 scans for validation, with a strict patient-level split. The validation set comprises individuals not encountered during training. The vision encoder V_θ and view classification model Q_ω were trained only on training scans to prevent data leakage. The data collection was approved by the University Medical Ethics Committee.

Model Architecture. We use a ViT-Small/16 model as the default vision encoder. The action encoder is a linear layer that maps the original 6-DOF actions to a 192-dimensional action space to match the vision feature dimension. The Anchor Refinement Module is implemented as a two-layer Self-Attention block with 4 attention heads. The Global Localization Module consists of a single Cross-Attention layer with 4 attention heads. The action decoder is a two-layer MLP with a GELU function in between. For the view classification model Q_ω, we adopt a ResNet-34 [10] trained on 123K annotated samples.

Training Details. The model is optimized with AdamW (batch size 128, learning rate 1×10^{-4}) for 5 epochs using a cosine decay schedule. The vision encoder V_θ loads I-JEPA [1] parameters pre-trained on our dataset and is frozen during training. For semantic-aware sampling, the candidate selection hyperparameter K is set to 128. All experiments are performed on 8 H20 GPUs.

Evaluation Metric. The metric used is the Mean Absolute Error (MAE) between the predicted probe movement action $\mathbf{a}'$ and the ground truth $\mathbf{a_{gt}}$.

Table 1. Comparison with baselines using MAE for **translation (mm)** and **rotation** (°). We report the average MAE over six standard views from Parasternal Window, four standard views from Apical Window (Fig. 2), and the overall average across all views.

Type	Method	**Parasternal**		**Apical**		**Average**	
		Trans.	Rot.	Trans.	Rot.	Trans.	Rot.
Single-frame	BioMedCLIP [24]	8.24	8.55	8.75	9.76	8.44	9.03
	LVM-Med [16]	8.35	8.46	8.86	9.56	8.56	8.90
	US-MoCo [5]	8.37	8.44	8.74	9.60	8.51	8.90
	US-IJEPA [1]	8.13	8.20	8.67	9.38	8.35	8.67
	US-MAE [9]	8.13	8.19	8.46	9.36	8.26	8.66
	USFM [15]	8.12	8.19	8.36	9.27	8.21	8.62
	EchoCLIP [6]	8.14	8.16	8.33	9.05	8.21	8.52
Sequential Graph	GRU (from US-GuideNet [8])	6.97	7.20	5.09	8.26	6.22	7.62
	Causal self-attn (from Decision-T [3])	7.04	7.00	4.80	8.18	6.14	7.53
	Non-causal self-attn (from UltraSeP [13])	6.45	6.70	4.39	7.78	5.63	7.13
FC Graph	Motion-aware attn (from EchoWorld [22])	5.60	6.09	4.00	7.83	4.96	6.79
Star Graph	**UltraStar (Ours)**	**5.30**	**5.67**	**3.60**	**7.50**	**4.62** (↓7%)	**6.40** (↓6%)

*

3.2 Results and Analysis

Comparison with Baseline. Table 1 presents the quantitative comparison with an input graph size of $L = 8$. To isolate the impact of modeling paradigms, all non-single-frame methods share the same frozen vision encoder. To ensure a rigorous evaluation, we explicitly exclude frames in the scanning trajectory that are visually similar to the target view from the candidate pool, preventing potential data leakage. As observed, UltraStar achieves state-of-the-art performance across all metrics. Sequential Graph methods lag behind because the chain structure encourages overfitting to noisy exploration trajectories. The Fully Connected Graph also underperforms compared to our method; its dense connectivity introduces excessive noisy edges irrelevant to the current decision, thereby confusing the model. In contrast, Star Graph establishes direct geometric links between historical anchors and the current view, enabling precise localization. Furthermore, we analyze the impact of input length in Fig. 5 (left). As the input graph size increases, UltraStar demonstrates superior scalability, with a consistent reduction in navigation errors. This indicates that our method effectively leverages extended historical information to refine localization, whereas baselines saturate or degrade due to the noise introduced by longer trajectories. We further conduct an ablation study on sampling strategies, as shown in Fig. 5 (right). Our semantic-aware sampling strategy consistently yields the lowest errors across all modeling paradigms, confirming its universality and effectiveness in selecting high-quality keyframes.

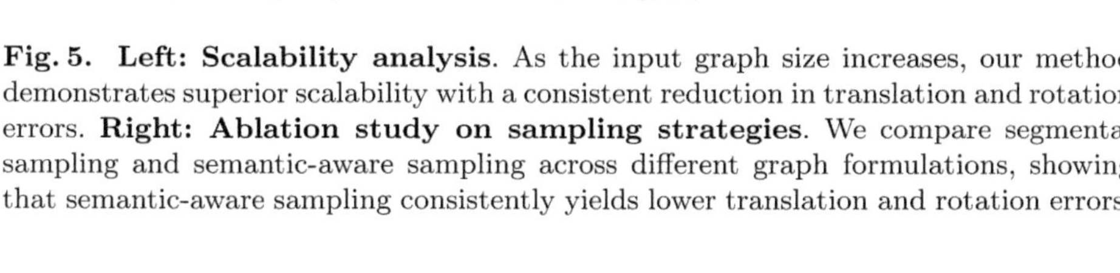

Fig. 5. Left: Scalability analysis. As the input graph size increases, our method demonstrates superior scalability with a consistent reduction in translation and rotation errors. **Right: Ablation study on sampling strategies.** We compare segmental sampling and semantic-aware sampling across different graph formulations, showing that semantic-aware sampling consistently yields lower translation and rotation errors.

Visualization. First, with the input graph size set to 6, Fig. 6(a) illustrates the outcomes of different sampling strategies. Segmental sampling exhibits distinct semantic redundancy, where multiple sampled keyframes convey repetitive visual information. In contrast, our semantic-aware strategy selects diverse landmarks, effectively maximizing the information entropy of the Star Graph. Second, to intuitively demonstrate the model's output, we calculate the final view pose based on the current view's pose and predicted probe movement action. Using

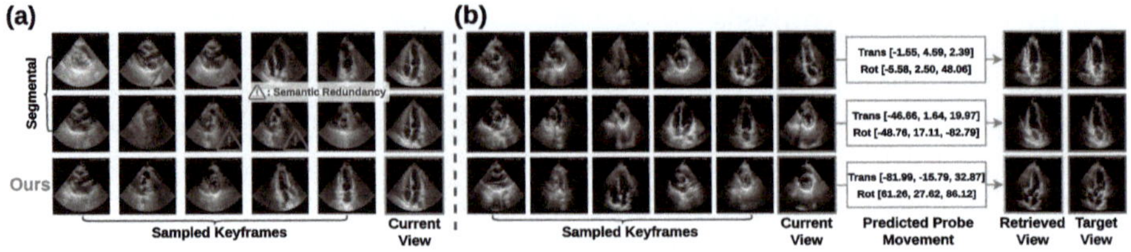

Fig. 6. (a) Visualization of the outcome of sampling strategies. (b) Visualization of the model prediction. Inputs include sampled keyframes, the current view, and the relative probe motions from the current view to each sampled keyframe.

this pose, we perform the nearest-neighbor retrieval from the same scan. We can observe from Fig. 6(b) that our model can output correct probe movement actions, bringing the probe closer to target views.

4 Conclusion

In this paper, we presented UltraStar, a framework that reformulates echocardiography probe navigation from path modeling to anchor-based global localization. By replacing the sequential chain with a Star Graph topology, UltraStar leverages historical frames as spatial anchors for geometric reasoning, establishing direct spatial constraints that ensure precise global localization. We further introduce a semantic-aware sampling strategy to select representative landmarks, constructing a compact yet informative map from massive scanning logs. Experiments on a large-scale dataset show that UltraStar achieves state-of-the-art performance and scales better with longer history lengths, enabling precise and scalable ultrasound probe navigation. Beyond echocardiography, UltraStar offers a general anchor-based perspective for history modeling under noisy exploration. Future work could further explore the deployment of UltraStar on a robotic ultrasound platform to evaluate its closed-loop performance in real-world settings.

Acknowledgments. This work is supported in part by the National Key Research and Development Program of China under Grant 2024YFB4708200, and the Scientific Research Innovation Capability Support Project for Young Faculty under Grant ZYGXQNJSKYCXNLZCXM-I20, and the National Natural Science Foundation of China under Grant 62461160307.

Disclosure of Interests. The authors have no competing interests to declare that are relevant to the content of this article.

References

1. Assran, M., et al.: Self-supervised learning from images with a joint-embedding predictive architecture. In: Proceedings of the IEEE/CVF Conference on Computer Vision and Pattern Recognition, pp. 15619–15629 (2023)

2. Bao, M., et al.: Real-world visual navigation for cardiac ultrasound view planning. In: International Conference on Medical Image Computing and Computer-Assisted Intervention, pp. 317–326. Springer (2024)
3. Chen, L., et al.: Decision transformer: reinforcement learning via sequence modeling. Adv. Neural. Inf. Process. Syst. **34**, 15084–15097 (2021)
4. Chen, R., Yan, X., Lv, K., Huang, G., Li, Z., Li, X.: Ultradp: generalizable carotid ultrasound scanning with force-aware diffusion policy. In: 2025 IEEE/RSJ International Conference on Intelligent Robots and Systems (IROS), pp. 20074–20080 (2025)
5. Chen, X., Xie, S., He, K.: An empirical study of training self-supervised vision transformers. In: Proceedings of the IEEE/CVF International Conference on Computer Vision, pp. 9640–9649 (2021)
6. Christensen, M., Vukadinovic, M., Yuan, N., Ouyang, D.: Vision-language foundation model for echocardiogram interpretation. Nat. Med. 1–8 (2024)
7. Dosovitskiy, A., et al.: An image is worth 16x16 words: transformers for image recognition at scale. arXiv preprint arXiv:2010.11929 (2020)
8. Droste, R., Drukker, L., Papageorghiou, A.T., Noble, J.A.: Automatic probe movement guidance for freehand obstetric ultrasound. In: Martel, A.L., et al. (eds.) MICCAI 2020. LNCS, vol. 12263, pp. 583–592. Springer, Cham (2020). https://doi.org/10.1007/978-3-030-59716-0_56
9. He, K., Chen, X., Xie, S., Li, Y., Dollár, P., Girshick, R.: Masked autoencoders are scalable vision learners. In: Proceedings of the IEEE/CVF Conference on Computer Vision and Pattern Recognition, pp. 16000–16009 (2022)
10. He, K., Zhang, X., Ren, S., Sun, J.: Deep residual learning for image recognition. In: Proceedings of the IEEE Conference on Computer Vision and Pattern Recognition, pp. 770–778 (2016)
11. Jiang, H., et al.: Structure-aware world model for probe guidance via large-scale self-supervised pre-train. In: International Workshop on Advances in Simplifying Medical Ultrasound, pp. 58–67 (2024)
12. Jiang, H., et al.: Cardiac copilot: automatic probe guidance for echocardiography with world model. In: International Conference on Medical Image Computing and Computer-Assisted Intervention, pp. 190–199 (2024)
13. Jiang, H., et al.: Ultrasep: sequence-aware pre-training for echocardiography probe movement guidance. Pattern Recogn. 112600 (2025)
14. Jiang, H., et al.: Towards expert-level autonomous carotid ultrasonography with large-scale learning-based robotic system. Nat. Commun. **16**(1), 7893 (2025)
15. Jiao, J., et al.: Usfm: a universal ultrasound foundation model generalized to tasks and organs towards label efficient image analysis. Med. Image Anal. **96**, 103202 (2024)
16. MH Nguyen, D., et al.: Lvm-med: learning large-scale self-supervised vision models for medical imaging via second-order graph matching. In: Advances in Neural Information Processing Systems, vol. 36 (2024)
17. Mitchell, C., et al.: Guidelines for performing a comprehensive transthoracic echocardiographic examination in adults: recommendations from the american society of echocardiography. J. Am. Soc. Echocardiogr. **32**(1), 1–64 (2019)
18. Narang, A., et al.: Utility of a deep-learning algorithm to guide novices to acquire echocardiograms for limited diagnostic use. JAMA Cardiol. **6**(6), 624–632 (2021)
19. Roth, G.A., et al.: Global, regional, and national burden of cardiovascular diseases for 10 causes, 1990 to 2015. J. Am. Coll. Cardiol. **70**(1), 1–25 (2017)

20. Wang, T., et al.: Ultrahit: a hierarchical transformer architecture for generalizable internal carotid artery robotic ultrasonography. arXiv preprint arXiv:2509.13832 (2025)
21. Won, D., Walker, J., Horowitz, R., Bharadwaj, S., Carlton, E., Gabriel, H.: Sound the alarm: the sonographer shortage is echoing across healthcare. J. Ultrasound Med. (2024)
22. Yue, Y., Wang, Y., Jiang, H., Liu, P., Song, S., Huang, G.: Echoworld: learning motion-aware world models for echocardiography probe guidance. In: Proceedings of the Computer Vision and Pattern Recognition Conference, pp. 25993–26003 (2025)
23. Yue, Y., Wang, Y., Tao, C., Liu, P., Song, S., Huang, G.: Chexworld: exploring image world modeling for radiograph representation learning. In: Proceedings of the Computer Vision and Pattern Recognition Conference, pp. 20778–20788 (2025)
24. Zhang, S., et al.: Biomedclip: a multimodal biomedical foundation model pretrained from fifteen million scientific image-text pairs. arXiv preprint arXiv:2303.00915 (2023)

VA-Adapter: Adapting Ultrasound Foundation Model to Echocardiography Probe Guidance

Teng Wang[1], Haojun Jiang[1], Yuxuan Wang[2], Zhenguo Sun[3], Yujiao Deng[4], Shiji Song[1], and Gao Huang[1(✉)]

[1] Department of Automation, BNRist, Tsinghua University, Beijing, China
{t-wang25,jhj20}@mails.tsinghua.edu.cn, gaohuang@tsinghua.edu.cn
[2] School of Computer Science and Technology, Xidian University, Xi'an, China
[3] Beijing Academy of Artificial Intelligence, Beijing, China
[4] Chinese PLA General Hospital, Beijing, China

Abstract. Echocardiography is a critical tool for detecting heart diseases, yet its steep operational difficulty causes a shortage of skilled personnel. Probe guidance systems, which assist in acquiring high-quality images, offer a promising solution to lower this operational barrier. However, robust probe guidance remains challenging due to significant individual variability. This variability manifests as differences in low-level features within two-dimensional (2D) images, which complicates image feature understanding, and differences in individual three-dimensional (3D) structures, which poses challenges for precise navigation. To address these challenges, we first propose leveraging the robust image representations learned by ultrasound foundation models from vast datasets. Yet, applying these models to probe navigation is non-trivial due to their lack of understanding of individual 3D structures. To this end, we meticulously design a Vision-Action Adapter (VA-Adapter) to online inject the capability of understanding individual 3D structures. Specifically, by embedding the VA-Adapter into the foundation model's image encoder, the model can infer cardiac anatomy from historical vision-action sequences, mimicking the cognitive process of a sonographer. Extensive experiments on a dataset with over 1.31M samples demonstrate that the VA-Adapter outperforms strong probe guidance models while requiring approximately 33 times fewer trained parameters. Code is available at https://github.com/LeapLabTHU/VA-Adapter.

Keywords: Echocardiography · Adapter · Probe Guidance · Foundation Model · Sequence Modeling

1 Introduction

Cardiovascular diseases have become a significant factor affecting human lifespan [22]. Echocardiography is a commonly used imaging technique for diagnos-

T. Wang and H. Jiang—Equal contribution.

H. Jiang—Guided this work.

G. Yang et al. (Eds.): MICCAI 2026, LNCS 16893, pp. 574–584, 2027.
https://doi.org/10.1007/978-3-032-38236-8_55

ing cardiovascular diseases, allowing the observation of the health conditions of heart chambers, valves, and blood vessels [18]. With technological advancements, AI-driven echocardiography diagnostic models [5,7,21] have demonstrated remarkable capabilities. As shown in Fig. 1(a), representative models include EchoCLIP [5], pre-trained on over one million paired cardiac ultrasound videos and expert reports; USFM [14], pre-trained on over two million ultrasound images across 12 organs; and BiomedCLIP [28], pre-trained on 15.3 million image-text pairs from 4.4 million PubMed articles. All three models demonstrate strong capabilities in interpreting cardiac ultrasound images.

Undoubtedly, the prerequisite for these powerful diagnostic models to function effectively is the availability of high-quality ultrasound images. However, due to the inherently high operational difficulty of cardiac ultrasound, it takes years of training for a beginner to master the technique, resulting in a scarcity of skilled professionals. Therefore, leveraging AI technology to assist in cardiac ultrasound scanning is a crucial research direction.

In recent years, researchers [2,6,10–13,15,19,25,27] have developed AI-driven probe guidance systems to acquire higher-quality ultrasound images. Droste et al. [6] proposed US-GuideNet for fetal plane scanning. Narang et al. [19] collected large-scale echocardiography scanning data and trained a CNN-based guidance system from scratch, but it is commercial and closed-source. Li et al. [15] used cardiac CT as a simulation environment and applied reinforcement learning to learn guidance policies. Despite progress, these works study probe guidance separately from diagnosis and do not leverage advances in diagnostic foundation models [5,14,28] (e.g., EchoCLIP). Since both scanning and diagnosis require understanding cardiac ultrasound structures and making decisions, we hypothesize that diagnostic-model advances can also improve probe guidance.

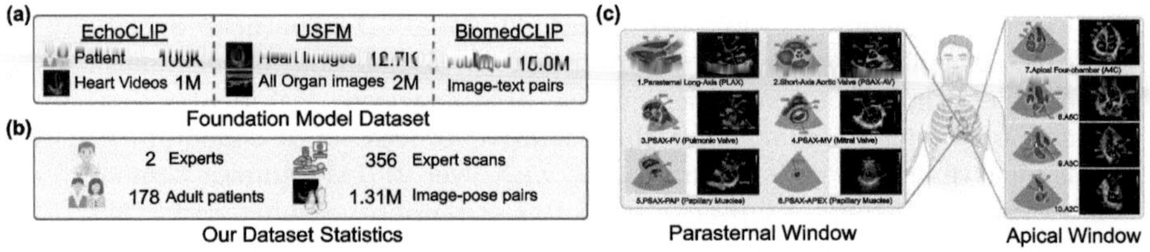

Fig. 1. Illustration of the dataset. (a) Large-scale diagnostic foundation model dataset. (b) Our dataset statistic. (c) Standard planes (images from [18]).

In this paper, we aim to build upon the ultrasound foundation model's ability to interpret cardiac ultrasound images by equipping it with the capability to understand three-dimensional (3D) cardiac structures and reason about probe adjustment actions. First, to preserve the basic capabilities learned by foundation model from large-scale data as much as possible, we employ a parameter-efficient fine-tuning strategy called Adapter, which freezes the foundation model's image encoder and only optimizes the parameters within the adapter. Further, to better exploit individual 3D anatomy, we propose a Vision-Action Adapter (VA-Adapter) that encodes vision-action sequences and learns individual-specific cardiac structure from them. Specifically, VA-Adapters are inserted into deeper encoder layers of foundation model, where features are more task-relevant [26]. Finally, extensive experiments show that the VA-Adapter equips diagnostic foundation models with better probe guidance capability at a low training cost.

2 Method

In this section, We first describe the cardiac ultrasound scanning dataset, then introduce our Vision-Action Adapter.

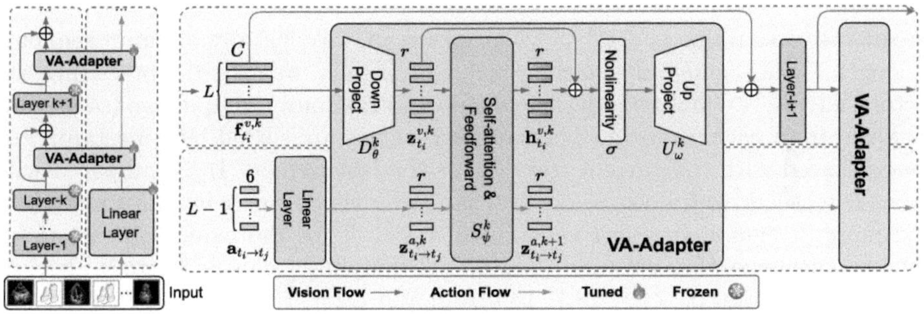

Fig. 2. Illustration of the architecture of the VA-Adapter. The left side shows that we insert VA-Adapter into the deep layers of foundation models, and the right side shows the internal structure of VA-Adapter.

2.1 Dataset Acquisition

The dataset used in our work was collected from 178 adult subjects and includes 356 expert scanning trajectories, totaling 1.31 million image-action pairs. The data was gathered by two senior sonographers with over 10 years of experience. They performed continuous scans of 10 standard echocardiographic planes (Fig. 1(c)) using an ultrasound probe attached to the end of a robotic arm. The data collection system recorded real-time images acquired by the probe and the corresponding probe pose data. This created a scanning sequence $\{(\mathbf{I}_t, \mathbf{p}_t)\}_{t=1}^{T}$, where $\mathbf{I}_t \in \mathbb{R}^{3\times H\times W}$ is the ultrasound image at time t, and $\mathbf{p}_t \in \mathbb{SE}(3)$ is the corresponding probe's 6D pose (3D position $\mathbf{P} \in \mathbb{R}^3$ and 3D orientation $\mathbf{R} \in \mathbb{SO}(3)$). During the scan, the sonographer marked the standard views. Then we can calculate the relative motion of any image $\mathbf{I}_i$ to the standard view $\mathbf{I}_j$: $\mathbf{a}_{i\to j} = \mathbf{T}_{p_i}^{-1}\mathbf{T}_{p_j}$, where $\mathbf{T}_{p_i}$ and $\mathbf{T}_{p_j}$ represent the transformation matrices corresponding to the probe poses $\mathbf{p}_i$ and $\mathbf{p}_j$. Then we use this motion value as the supervisory signal for the ultrasound probe guidance task. Notably, sonographers sometimes pause at a probe position to observe cardiac dynamics. As a result, the dataset includes many images from the same probe position but different cardiac phases. These frames share the same motion label, providing implicit supervision that encourages robustness to cardiac-cycle variation.

2.2 Vision-Action Adapter

Echocardiography probe guidance is an emerging area, but progress is limited by data-collection challenges. In contrast, ultrasound image understanding and diagnosis have advanced rapidly, with recent foundation models achieving strong baseline performance. Since probe guidance also requires understanding ultrasound structures, we propose the Vision-Action Adapter to leverage these foundation models for probe guidance. Next, we detail our approach in Fig. 2.

Input. Given a frame $\mathbf{I}_t \in \mathbb{R}^{3\times H\times W}$ from a scan, we construct an input sequence of length L via segmental sampling [24]. Specifically, we split the preceding trajectory into $L-1$ equal temporal segments and randomly sample one frame (and its pose) from each segment. The sampled frames are sorted by timestamp and concatenated with the current frame $\mathbf{I}_t$ as the last element $\mathbf{I}_{t_L}$. Compared with using L consecutive frames, segmental sampling yields larger inter-frame motion and more diverse anatomical viewpoints, which helps the model capture richer 3D structural cues. For reference, segmental sampling yields an average absolute inter-frame motion of [21.8, 18.7, 14.0] mm and [12.6, 23.3, 40.9]° between adjacent frames, indicating substantial variation in both position and orientation. We then compute relative actions $\mathbf{a}_{t_i\to t_j} \in \mathbb{R}^6$ from the corresponding poses, forming the input trajectory: $[\mathbf{I}_{t_1}, \mathbf{a}_{t_1\to t_2}, \cdots, \mathbf{I}_{t_{L-1}}, \mathbf{a}_{t_{L-1}\to t_L}, \mathbf{I}_{t_L}]$.

Forward Propagation. We insert VA-Adapters into the latter part of the foundation model's vision encoder, where features are more task-relevant [26]. For CNN encoders (e.g., EchoCLIP), VA-Adapters are placed between late-stage blocks; for Transformer encoders (e.g., USFM, BiomedCLIP), two VA-Adapters are inserted in each selected block (after attention and after MLP). During training, only VA-Adapters are updated while the backbone remains frozen to preserve its learned knowledge. Given an image $\mathbf{I}_{t_i}$, after the first k vision layers we obtain $\mathbf{f}_{t_i}^{v,k} \in \mathbb{R}^C$ (for CNNs, global average pooling is applied). We project visual features and actions to the bottleneck space and add timestep embeddings:

$$\mathbf{z}_{t_i}^{v,k} = D_\theta^k(\mathbf{f}_{t_i}^{v,k}) + \mathbf{T}_i, \quad \mathbf{z}_{t_i\to t_j}^{a,k} = A_\phi^k(\mathbf{a}_{t_i\to t_j}) + \mathbf{T}_i, \quad \mathbf{z}_{t_i}^{v,k}, \mathbf{z}_{t_i\to t_j}^{a,k} \in \mathbb{R}^r, \tag{1}$$

where $\mathbf{T} \in \mathbb{R}^{L\times r}$ is timestep embedding, and r is the bottleneck dimension. The interleaved vision–action tokens are then processed by a vision–action interaction module S_ψ^k, designed to extract underlying cardiac structure information:

$$[\mathbf{h}_{t_1}^{v,k}, \mathbf{z}_{t_1\to t_2}^{a,k+1}, \cdots, \mathbf{h}_{t_L}^{v,k}] = S_\psi^k([\mathbf{z}_{t_1}^{v,k}, \mathbf{z}_{t_1\to t_2}^{a,k}, \cdots, \mathbf{z}_{t_{L-1}}^{v,k}, \mathbf{z}_{t_{L-1}\to t_L}^{a,k}, \mathbf{z}_{t_L}^{v,k}]). \tag{2}$$

The action tokens are forwarded to the next adapter layer, while visual tokens are mapped back to the backbone feature space with a residual connection:

$$\mathbf{z}_{t_i}^{v,k+1} = U_\omega^k\left(\sigma(\mathbf{h}_{t_i}^{v,k} + \mathbf{z}_{t_i}^{v,k})\right) + \mathbf{f}_{t_i}^{v,k}. \tag{3}$$

2.3 Task Prediction Head

After passing through all layers (assuming the network has M layers in total), we obtain the final interleaved sequence features:

$$\mathbf{Z}^M = [\mathbf{z}_{t_1}^{v,M}, \mathbf{z}_{t_1 \to t_2}^{a,M}, \cdots, \mathbf{z}_{t_{L-1}}^{v,M}, \mathbf{z}_{t_{L-1} \to t_L}^{a,M}, \mathbf{z}_{t_L}^{v,M}]. \tag{4}$$

We then apply a GRU-based sequence encoder E_ρ to further aggregate sequential information, and use ten prediction heads $\{H_{\xi_i}\}_{i=1}^{10}$ to predict the action toward each standard plane:

$$\mathbf{V} = E_\rho(\mathbf{Z}^M), \quad \mathbf{a}'_{t_L \to t_i} = H_{\xi_i}(\mathbf{v}_{t_L}), \tag{5}$$

where $\mathbf{V} = [\mathbf{v}_{t_1}, \ldots, \mathbf{v}_{t_L}]$ denotes the GRU outputs, and $\mathbf{v}_{t_L}$ corresponds to the current frame $\mathbf{I}_{t_L}$. Finally, the loss is calculated using the Smooth L1 Loss between the predicted action and the target $\mathbf{a}_{t_L \to t_{i\text{-th standard plane}}}$ as follows:

$$\mathcal{L} = \mathcal{L}_{\text{SmoothL1}}(\mathbf{a}_{t_L \to t_{i\text{-th standard plane}}}, \mathbf{a}'_{t_L \to t_{i\text{-th standard plane}}}). \tag{6}$$

In (6), translation and rotation are equally weighted; we normalize units in preprocessing (mm for translation, degrees for rotation) to match magnitudes.

3 Experiments

3.1 Datasets and Implementation Details

Datasets. Data were collected with a GE machine (*General Electric, USA*) equipped with a M5S probe (Sect. 2.1) under approval and supervision of the University Medical Ethics Committee. We use 284 scans for training and 72 for validation, with data from different subjects in each set.

Model Architecture. By default, the input sequence length is L=4 and the adapter bottleneck dimension (adapter dimension) is r=64, with ReLU activation. The core vision–action interaction module S_ψ is a Transformer block with 4 attention heads and an MLP ratio of 2, using 1D sincos positional encoding. We initialize linear/conv weights with truncated normal (σ=0.02) and set biases to 0; LayerNorm weights are initialized to 1 and biases to 0. After the image encoder, image and action features are each projected to 128-d and concatenated as input to the GRU sequence encoder E_ρ (input 256, hidden 128). Each prediction head H_{ξ_i} is a two-layer MLP with GELU in between.

Training Strategy. We train with Adam (batch size 256) for 5 epochs, using a cosine-decayed learning rate from 1×10^{-4} to 1×10^{-6}, and all experiments are performed on four A100 GPUs.

Evaluation Metric. We report trainable parameters and the Mean Absolute Error (MAE) between predicted $\mathbf{a}'$ and ground-truth $\mathbf{a}$, computed separately for translation and rotation:

$$\text{MAE of Trans.} = \frac{1}{3}\sum_{i=1}^{3} |\mathbf{a}_i - \mathbf{a}_i^{'}|, \quad \text{MAE of Rot.} = \frac{1}{3}\sum_{i=4}^{6} |\mathbf{a}_i - \mathbf{a}_i^{'}|. \tag{7}$$

Table 1. Comparison with baseline methods in terms of translation and rotation dimensions. Results include the number of trained parameters and the corresponding errors. "Avg." denotes the average Mean Absolute Error computed across ten standard planes.†indicates that these methods use the pre-trained encoder from DeiT.

Setting	Method	Trained Params	Translation Avg. (mm)	Rotation Avg. (°)
Single-frame, ImageNet-pretrained	DeiT [23]	22.60M	8.43	8.84
	DINOv2 [20]	90.28M	8.22	8.72
Single-frame, Pre-trained on ultrasound data	BiomedCLIP [28]	89.50M	8.44	9.03
	LVM-Med [17]	89.44M	8.56	8.90
	US-MoCo [4]	22.60M	8.51	8.80
	US-IJEPA [1]	22.59M	8.35	8.67
	US-MAE [8]	22.00M	8.26	8.66
	USFM [14]	92.94M	8.26	8.62
	EchoCLIP [5]	89.74M	8.21	8.52
Sequential, ImageNet-pretrained	US-GuideNet† [6]	22.05M	7.53	7.83
	Decision-T† [3]	22.27M	7.38	7.88
Sequential, Pre-trained on ultrasound data	BiomedCLIP	86.15M	7.29	7.80
	BiomedCLIP+Ours	**3.94M**	**5.55**	**6.69**
	USFM	87.04M	7.15	7.81
	USFM+Ours	**3.97M**	**5.35**	**6.71**
	EchoCLIP	88.41M	6.56	7.66
	EchoCLIP+Ours	**2.61M**	**5.40**	**6.74**

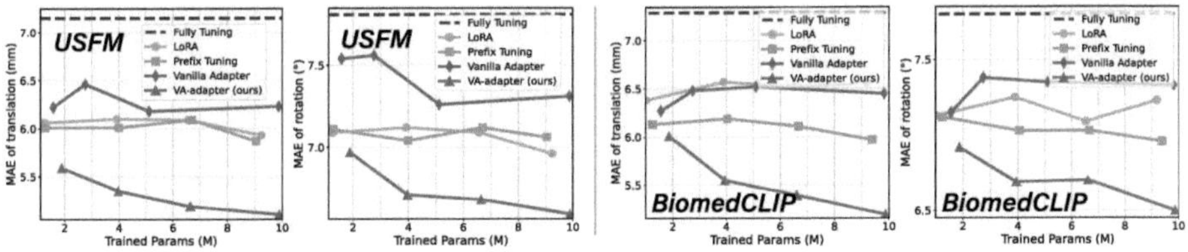

Fig. 3. Performance comparison of PEFT methods on USFM and BiomedCLIP.

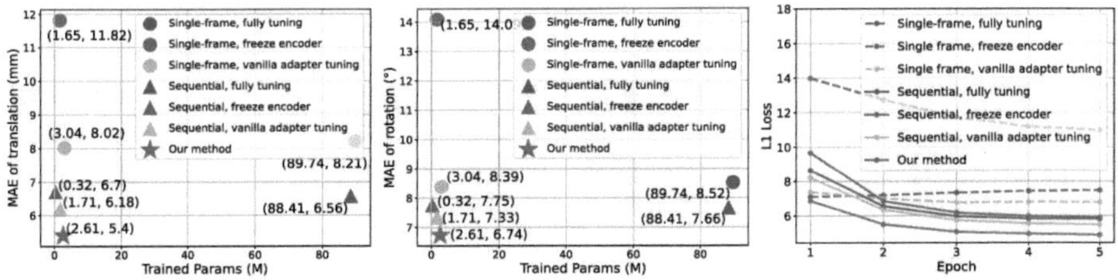

Fig. 4. Ablation on vision-action interaction module of the EchoCLIP model.

3.2 Comparison with Baselines

We evaluated our method on ten standard views, as shown in Table 1. Our method outperforms baselines in both MAE and parameter efficiency. Although only averaged errors are reported, this improvement is consistent across all ten standard views. Single-frame models rely only on the current image and cannot capture structural variation, leading to poor performance. Baseline sequential models [3,6] typically fuse image and action features only in the prediction head, underusing structural cues in the sequence, and require full fine-tuning with high training cost. In contrast, our lightweight VA-Adapter is inserted into the image encoder, enabling progressive structure learning during feature extraction while improving both efficiency and accuracy.

We also compare with other common PEFT methods, including LoRA [9] and Prefix Tuning [16]. Since they are designed for transformer-based backbones, we evaluate them only on USFM and BiomedCLIP. As shown in Fig. 3, VA-Adapter performs best. This is likely because VA-Adapter explicitly models vision–action interactions to capture cardiac structure, whereas other PEFT methods mainly improve efficiency without enhancing structural understanding.

3.3 Ablation Study

Vision-Action Interaction Module. We compare seven training baselines for EchoCLIP in Fig. 4. The vanilla adapter removes the vision–action interaction module while keeping other settings unchanged. With 2.61M trainable parameters, our method achieves the lowest MAE and the best parameter–accuracy trade-off. Compared with the vanilla adapter of similar scale, it reduces MAE by 12.6% / 8.0% (Trans./Rot.) with only 0.9M extra parameters, demonstrating

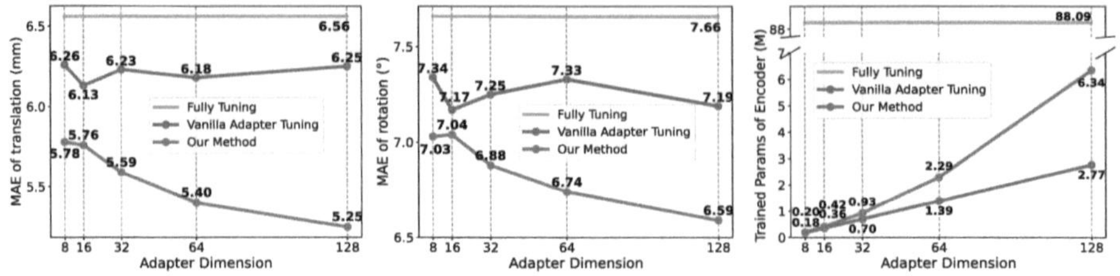

Fig. 5. Ablation study on adapter dimension of the EchoCLIP model.

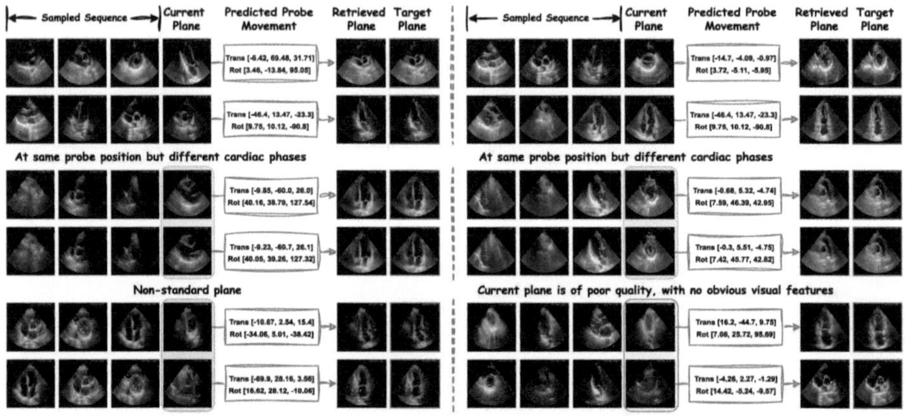

Fig. 6. Visualization of the model's prediction.

that the performance gains from the vision-action interaction mechanism outweigh the marginal cost of extra parameters. Furthermore, it also demonstrates faster convergence, outperforming other methods after the first epoch.

Adapter Dimension. We study the effect of adapter dimension on performance (Fig. 5). With dimension $r=8$, our method introduces only 0.2M parameters (0.23% of full fine-tuning) yet reduces MAE by 11.9% / 8.2% (Trans./Rot.), whereas the vanilla Adapter with similar size achieves only 4.6% / 4.2%. This indicates that our VA-Adapter captures cardiac structural cues more effectively under tight parameter budgets. As r increases from 8 to 128, our parameters grow by 31.7× while MAE further drops by 9.2% / 6.3%. In contrast, the vanilla adapter grows by 15.4× with only 0.2% / 2.0% additional MAE reduction, indicating that our interaction module uses added parameters more efficiently.

3.4 Visualization

We visualize the model outputs in Fig. 6. We apply the predicted action to obtain the resulting pose, then perform nearest-neighbor retrieval in the scan sequence and compare the retrieved plane with the target. Results show that the model guides the probe toward the target plane. The outputs are consistent across frames from the same probe position but different cardiac phases, indicating robustness to the cardiac cycle. Moreover, for non-standard or low-quality planes with weak visual cues, the sequence model can still infer correct actions from vision-action relationships, which single-frame models cannot.

3.5 Inference Real-Time Analysis

We benchmark inference on RTX 3090. Across all backbones, a single sequence takes ~10.0–11.1 ms without VA-Adapter and ~10.5–11.8 ms with VA-Adapter, satisfying real-time requirements. The added latency is marginal, indicating VA-Adapter preserves deployment efficiency in time-sensitive ultrasound guidance.

4 Conclusion

In this paper, we propose VA-Adapter, a lightweight module that empowers ultrasound foundation models with probe guidance capability by modeling vision-action interactions during feature encoding. By combining basic knowledge from the foundation model with personalized 3D cardiac structures learned from the VA-Adapter, our method updates 95.4%-97.0% fewer parameters and reduces guidance error by 12.0%-25.2%, with extensive experiments validating superior efficiency and performance over state-of-the-art baselines. This superior performance supports practical clinical scenarios, such as offering real-time assistance to junior sonographers and serving as the decision-making core for fully autonomous robotic ultrasound systems.

Acknowledgments. This work is supported in part by the National Key Research and Development Program of China under Grant 2024YFB4708200, and the Scientific Research Innovation Capability Support Project for Young Faculty under Grant ZYGXQNJSKYCXNLZCXM-I20, and the National Natural Science Foundation of China under Grant 62461160307.

Disclosure of Interests. The authors have no competing interests to declare that are relevant to the content of this article.

References

1. Assran, M., et al.: Self-supervised learning from images with a joint-embedding predictive architecture. In: Proceedings of the IEEE/CVF Conference on Computer Vision and Pattern Recognition, pp. 15619–15629 (2023)
2. Bao, M., et al.: Real-world visual navigation for cardiac ultrasound view planning. In: International Conference on Medical Image Computing and Computer-Assisted Intervention, pp. 317–326. Springer (2024)
3. Chen, L., et al.: Decision transformer: reinforcement learning via sequence modeling. Adv. Neural. Inf. Process. Syst. **34**, 15084–15097 (2021)

4. Chen, X., Xie, S., He, K.: An empirical study of training self-supervised vision transformers. In: Proceedings of the IEEE/CVF International Conference on Computer Vision, pp. 9640–9649 (2021)
5. Christensen, M., Vukadinovic, M., Yuan, N., Ouyang, D.: Vision-language foundation model for echocardiogram interpretation. Nat. Med., 1–8 (2024)
6. Droste, R., Drukker, L., Papageorghiou, A.T., Noble, J.A.: Automatic Probe Movement Guidance for Freehand Obstetric Ultrasound. In: Martel, A.L., Abolmaesumi, P., Stoyanov, D., Mateus, D., Zuluaga, M.A., Zhou, S.K., Racoceanu, D., Joskowicz, L. (eds.) MICCAI 2020. LNCS, vol. 12263, pp. 583–592. Springer, Cham (2020). https://doi.org/10.1007/978-3-030-59716-0_56
7. Ghorbani, A., et al.: Deep learning interpretation of echocardiograms. NPJ Digit. Med. **3**(1), 10 (2020)
8. He, K., Chen, X., Xie, S., Li, Y., Dollár, P., Girshick, R.: Masked autoencoders are scalable vision learners. In: Proceedings of the IEEE/CVF Conference on Computer Vision and Pattern Recognition, pp. 16000–16009 (2022)
9. Hu, E.J., et al.: LoRA: low-rank adaptation of large language models. CORR arxiv:abs/2106.09685 (2021)
10. Jiang, H., et al.: Structure-aware world model for probe guidance via large-scale self-supervised pre-train. arXiv preprint arXiv:2406.19756 (2024)
11. Jiang, H., et al.: Cardiac Copilot: automatic probe guidance for echocardiography with world model. arXiv preprint arXiv:2406.13165 (2024)
12. Jiang, H., et al.: UltraSep: sequence-aware pre-training for echocardiography probe movement guidance. Pattern Recogn. 112600 (2025)
13. Jiang, H., et al.: Towards expert-level autonomous carotid ultrasonography with large-scale learning-based robotic system. Nat. Commun. **16**(1), 7893 (2025)
14. Jiao, J., et al.: USFM: a universal ultrasound foundation model generalized to tasks and organs towards label efficient image analysis. Med. Image Anal. **96**, 103202 (2024)
15. Li, K., Li, A., Xu, Y., Xiong, H., Meng, M.Q.H.: RL-TEE: autonomous probe guidance for transesophageal echocardiography based on attention-augmented deep reinforcement learning. IEEE Trans. Autom. Sci. Eng. **21**(2), 1526–1538 (2023)
16. Li, X.L., Liang, P.: Prefix-Tuning: optimizing continuous prompts for generation. In: Proceedings of the 59th Annual Meeting of the Association for Computational Linguistics and the 11th International Joint Conference on Natural Language Processing (Volume 1: Long Papers) (2021)
17. MH Nguyen, D., et al.: LVM-MED: learning large-scale self-supervised vision models for medical imaging via second-order graph matching. Adv. Neural Inf. Proces. Syst. **36** (2024)
18. Mitchell, C., et al.: Guidelines for performing a comprehensive transthoracic echocardiographic examination in adults: recommendations from the American society of echocardiography. J. Am. Soc. Echocardiogr. **32**(1), 1–64 (2019)
19. Narang, A., et al.: Utility of a deep-learning algorithm to guide novices to acquire echocardiograms for limited diagnostic use. JAMA Cardiol. **6**(6), 624–632 (2021)
20. Oquab, M., et al.: DINOv2: learning robust visual features without supervision. arXiv preprint arXiv:2304.07193 (2023)
21. Ouyang, D., et al.: Video-based ai for beat-to-beat assessment of cardiac function. Nature **580**(7802), 252–256 (2020)
22. Roth, G.A., et al.: Global, regional, and national burden of cardiovascular diseases for 10 causes, 1990 to 2015. J. Am. Coll. Cardiol. **70**(1), 1–25 (2017)

23. Touvron, H., Cord, M., Douze, M., Massa, F., Sablayrolles, A., Jégou, H.: Training data-efficient image transformers & distillation through attention. In: International Conference on Machine Learning, pp. 10347–10357. PMLR (2021)
24. Wang, L., et al.: Temporal segment networks: towards good practices for deep action recognition. In: European Conference on Computer Vision, pp. 20–36. Springer (2016)
25. Wang, T., et al.: UltraHit: a hierarchical transformer architecture for generalizable internal carotid artery robotic ultrasonography. arXiv preprint arXiv:2509.13832 (2025)
26. Yang, L., Zhang, R.Y., Wang, Y., Xie, X.: MMA: multi-modal adapter for vision-language models. In: Proceedings of the IEEE/CVF Conference on Computer Vision and Pattern Recognition, pp. 23826–23837 (2024)
27. Yue, Y., Wang, Y., Jiang, H., Liu, P., Song, S., Huang, G.: EchoWorld: learning motion-aware world models for echocardiography probe guidance. In: Proceedings of the Computer Vision and Pattern Recognition Conference, pp. 25993–26003 (2025)
28. Zhang, S., et al.: BiomedCLIP: a multimodal biomedical foundation model pretrained from fifteen million scientific image-text pairs. arXiv preprint arXiv:2303.00915 (2023)

VDSB-GWSyn: Diffusion Schrödinger Bridge for Controllable and Anatomically Feasible Guidewire Synthesis in Coronary Angiography

Haoyuan Tang, Zhuo Zhang(✉), Jialin Li, Shuai Xiao, and Jiachen Yang

Tianjin University, Tianjin, China
z_zhuo@tju.edu.cn

Abstract. Coronary guidewire endpoint localization is a fundamental capability for computer-assisted PCI, and its importance increases as robot-assisted PCI is progressively adopted to reduce operator radiation exposure. However, the scarcity of annotated CAG images with guidewires and the limited adaptability of existing guidewire synthesis models remain key bottlenecks for guidewire endpoint localization. To address this issue, we propose VDSB-GWSyn, a Diffusion Schrödinger Bridge (DSB) model-based framework, enabling synthesis of controllable, high-fidelity guidewire samples under complex anatomical backgrounds. VDSB-GWSyn first uses our shape prior algorithm to learn the basic guidewire geometry. It then generates guidewire masks under constraints imposed by the vessel segmentation masks and outputs the corresponding endpoint coordinates. Finally, it synthesizes realistic guidewire samples on real CAG images using DSB conditioned with SPADE. Experimental results show that the guidewire samples synthesized by VDSB-GWSyn achieve favorable ROI-FID and ROI-KID, as well as high IPR scores. In addition, incorporating our synthesized data for synthetic pre-training followed by real fine-tuning substantially improves downstream guidewire endpoint localization, reducing MPE from 16.01 px to 7.71 px and increasing PCK at 3 px from 52.63% to 86.27%, leading to more clinically reliable deployment of robot-assisted guidewire delivery systems. Moreover, the core design philosophy of controllable device synthesis with strict background preservation and anatomical feasibility constraints has the potential to transfer to other interventional device perception tasks where annotated data are scarce.

Keywords: Coronary angiography · Guidewire synthesis · Diffusion Schrödinger Bridge

1 Introduction

Reliable guidewire perception is a prerequisite for computer aided navigation in coronary angiography [14]. In fluoroscopy, the distal tip is often weakly visible

G. Yang et al. (Eds.): MICCAI 2026, LNCS 16893, pp. 585–595, 2027.
https://doi.org/10.1007/978-3-032-38236-8_56

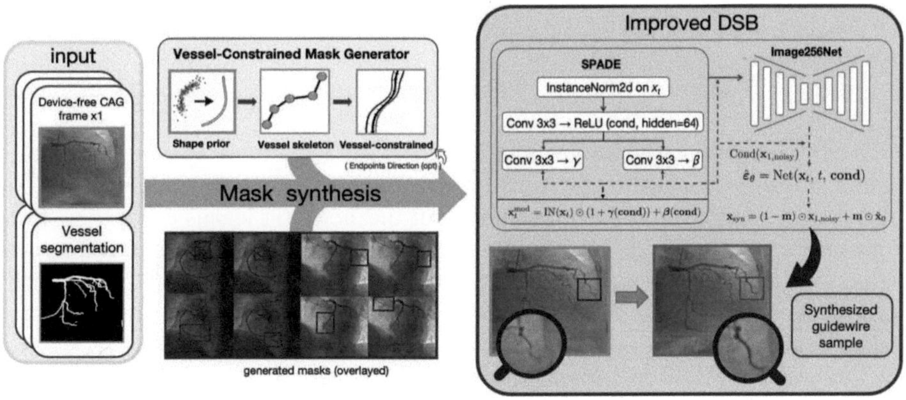

Fig. 1. Overview of the proposed VDSB-GWSyn framework for controllable guidewire synthesis.

and easily confounded by complex anatomical backgrounds [19], making endpoint localization difficult and error prone [13]. Deep learning based endpoint localization requires large scale, high quality annotations, yet labeling guidewire pixels and tip coordinates is labor intensive and privacy constraints further limit data collection and sharing [5,28]. As a result, data scarcity remains a central bottleneck for robust endpoint localization in real world fluoroscopy.

Prior work has explored learning-based catheter and guidewire segmentation under limited annotations and augmentation, and has also investigated synthetic fluoroscopic data and transfer learning to reduce labeling requirements [1,7]. For image synthesis, unpaired adversarial translation has been applied to catheter synthesis in X-ray fluoroscopy to reduce pixel-level labeling effort, and adversarial augmentation has been used to improve catheter segmentation [22,23]. More recently, diffusion-based generators have demonstrated improved controllability through mask conditioning, and have been used to synthesize labeled fluoroscopy videos for guidewire segmentation [5,6,10,19]. Despite these advances, two challenges remain for guidewire endpoint localization. First, existing conditional synthesis pipelines typically assume that a valid guidewire mask is already available as input, while the anatomical feasibility of the guidewire trajectory within coronary vessels is not explicitly enforced inside the synthesis framework [19,23]. Second, despite recent progress in conditional synthesis, it remains challenging to achieve sufficient diversity in guidewire trajectories and adequate coverage of CAG background complexity, especially under limited annotation budgets. As a result, current augmentation pipelines may not sufficiently cover real CAG examples with complex vessel context and low guidewire visibility. In addition, cost-efficient and scalable generation of guidewire CAG data with directly usable supervision, for example guidewire masks and endpoint coordinates, is still underexplored, limiting the effectiveness of synthetic augmentation for guidewire endpoint localization. Recent CAG-specific studies have further explored geometry-aware data synthesis for stenosis editing and auto-annotation generation for multi-view translational correction, highlighting the growing importance of controllable data generation in coronary angiography [3,12].

To address these gaps, we propose **VDSB-GWSyn**, a vessel-constrained diffusion Schrödinger bridge framework for controllable guidewire data synthesis on real coronary angiography backgrounds. Our method first learns guidewire shape priors and then synthesizes guidewire masks under vessel segmentation constraints, while directly producing endpoint coordinates. We formulate guidewire synthesis as a targeted inpainting problem so that generation is confined to the masked region and the anatomical background remains undisturbed. We further integrate SPADE to better preserve spatial conditioning information that can otherwise be weakened by normalization layers, improving local alignment between synthesized guidewire appearance and background texture [20]. Finally, we redesign the training objective with region normalization to mitigate gradient dilution caused by extreme guidewire pixel sparsity. Experiments demonstrate that pre-training with VDSB-GWSyn synthetic data greatly improves downstream endpoint localization on real-only evaluation sets.

2 Methods

The proposed VDSB-GWSyn framework is an end-to-end controllable synthesis pipeline designed for coronary angiography (CAG). As illustrated in Fig. 1, the framework consists of an Anatomical Mask Generator that samples plausible guidewire geometries and a Mask-Guided Diffusion Schrödinger Bridge (DSB) Engine that performs targeted rendering to ensure background consistency.

2.1 Controllable Mask Generation with Anatomical Constraints

To enable large scale synthesis of anatomically feasible guidewire masks under vessel constraints, we propose a geometry controllable mask generation algorithm.

Shape Prior and Radius Modeling. We learn a global shape prior from clinical masks. Let $\theta \in \mathbb{R}^{2N}$ be a vector representing N skeletonized control points. We extract a low-dimensional manifold $z = \text{PCA}(\theta)$ and model its distribution using a Gaussian Mixture Model (GMM). During sampling, the guidewire radius r is derived from a log-normal prior, $r = \exp(\mathcal{N}(\mu_r, \sigma_r^2))$, and capped by the local vessel diameter to adapt to distal branches.

Vessel-Constrained Path Sampling. Given a vessel mask ν, we construct an 8-connectivity graph G on its skeleton. We utilize Dijkstra's algorithm to search for a base path P, where a penalty term is applied to junction nodes (degree ≥ 3) to suppress unrealistic bifurcations. The algorithm supports precise J-tip control by allowing users to specify a tip location (x, y) and orientation ϕ. Sampled paths are projected into the vessel lumen using a distance-transform (DT) field. To simulate clinical diversity, we introduce a "wall-hugging" parameter $\rho \in [0, 1]$ that controls the target DT value during projection:

$$D_{\text{target}} = (1 - \rho) D_\nu + \rho d_{\min}, \tag{1}$$

where D_ν denotes the local vessel DT value and $d_{\min}$ is the minimum clearance to the vessel boundary. Thus, $\rho = 0$ keeps the guidewire closer to the vessel centerline, while larger ρ moves it toward the vessel wall without leaving the lumen. This module naturally supports multi-wire synthesis by iteratively sampling disjoint paths within the same anatomical domain.

2.2 Targeted Inpainting via DSB and SPADE Modulation

Standard diffusion models tend to redraw the entire image, which can cause texture drift in complex anatomical backgrounds. We therefore formulate guidewire synthesis as a targeted inpainting problem, using the original CAG anatomy as a hard background anchor [4,17].

Mask-Directed Noise Injection. Given a device-free background frame x_{bg} and a generated guidewire mask $m \in \{0, 1\}^{H \times W}$, we construct a noisy conditional endpoint x_1^n by confining the perturbation strictly within the mask region:

$$x_1^n = (1 - m) \odot x_{\text{bg}} + m \odot (x_{\text{bg}} + \sigma\epsilon), \qquad \epsilon \sim \mathcal{N}(0, \mathbf{I}). \tag{2}$$

By keeping the $(1 - m)$ background region noise-free, the model treats the surrounding anatomy as a fixed reference. The diffusion Schrödinger bridge (DSB) [4,16] then learns an evolution path that renders guidewire appearance only within the mask m.

Spatial Feature Alignment. To achieve seamless integration between the synthesized guidewire and the original background, we incorporate Spatially-Adaptive Denormalization (SPADE) [20]. Specifically, for a normalized feature map $\hat{h}$ at an intermediate layer, SPADE modulates it with spatially varying parameters predicted from the conditioning signal:

$$\text{SPADE}(\hat{h} \mid x_1^n) = \gamma(x_1^n) \odot \hat{h} + \beta(x_1^n), \tag{3}$$

where $\gamma(\cdot)$ and $\beta(\cdot)$ are learnable functions producing per-location scaling and bias. This modulation encourages the diffusion network to align synthesized guidewire edges with local contrast and noise statistics of the specific CAG frame, while avoiding undesired redrawing of the underlying vascular structure.

2.3 Region-Normalized Objective for Sparse Structures

Guidewires are extremely sparse in CAG frames, often occupying $< 1\%$ of the pixels. To prevent the background from dominating the gradient, we redesign the training objective using region-normalization. The total loss is partitioned into instrument and background components:

$$\mathcal{L} = \lambda_w \mathcal{L}_{\text{wire}} + \lambda_b \mathcal{L}_{\text{bg}}, \tag{4}$$

where

$$\mathcal{L}_{\text{wire}} = \frac{1}{\sum_i m_i} \sum_i m_i \left\| \hat{y}_i - y_i \right\|_2^2. \tag{5}$$

By setting $\lambda_w \gg \lambda_b$, we force the model to focus on the high-frequency textures of the guidewire. Furthermore, we introduce a Masked Total Variation (TV) regularization term, acting only on the mask boundary, to enforce structural continuity and mitigate wire fragmentation in low-contrast regions.

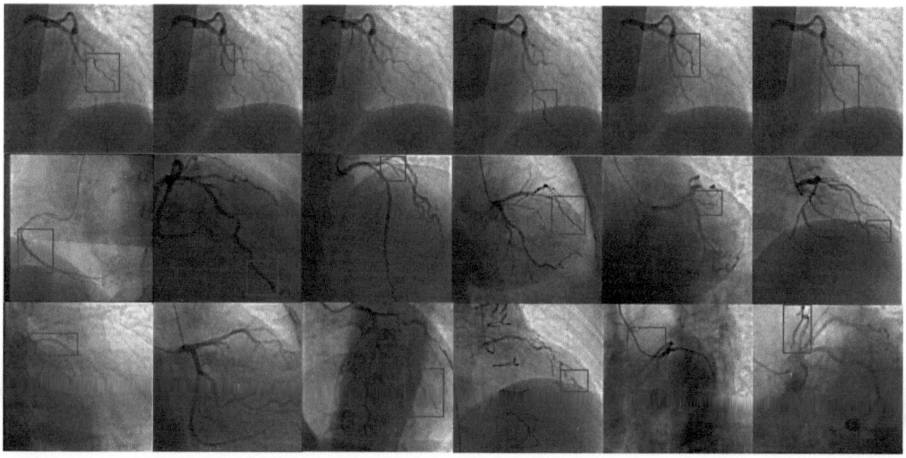

Fig. 2. Qualitative visualization of controllable guidewire synthesis in coronary angiography (CAG). Top row: Using the same device-free CAG background, we synthesize guidewires at different vessel locations to demonstrate spatial diversity while preserving the underlying anatomy. **Middle row:** Synthesized guidewires under different camera angles, showing robustness to view-dependent appearance variations in CAG. **Bottom row:** Synthesized guidewires across backgrounds with different levels of anatomical and noise complexity, illustrating background preservation and realism under challenging fluoroscopic conditions.

3 Experiments

3.1 Datasets

Internal Real Dataset. We curate an internal coronary angiography (CAG) dataset consisting of 1,125 frames in total. Among them, 283 real frames containing clinical guidewires are manually annotated with pixel-level masks and endpoint coordinates (tip and tail). This annotated subset serves three purposes: (i) extracting guidewire geometry for the shape-prior algorithm, (ii) providing paired samples to train the diffusion renderer, and (iii) acting as the training and evaluation set for the downstream endpoint localization task. For the downstream task, the 283 annotated frames are split into 182/50/51 for training/validation/testing.

Vessel Segmentation. The CAG images with vessel segmentation masks used for synthesis are drawn from two sources: (i) 955 internal clinical frames whose vessel masks are obtained using U-Mamba [18], and (ii) 832 high-quality frames selected from the ARCADE dataset [21] (released under the CC0-1.0 license), where vessel masks are generated using the same model and manually filtered for anatomical accuracy. The vessel masks are used exclusively to constrain guidewire mask sampling and to enforce anatomical plausibility; they are not used as inputs to the downstream endpoint localizer.

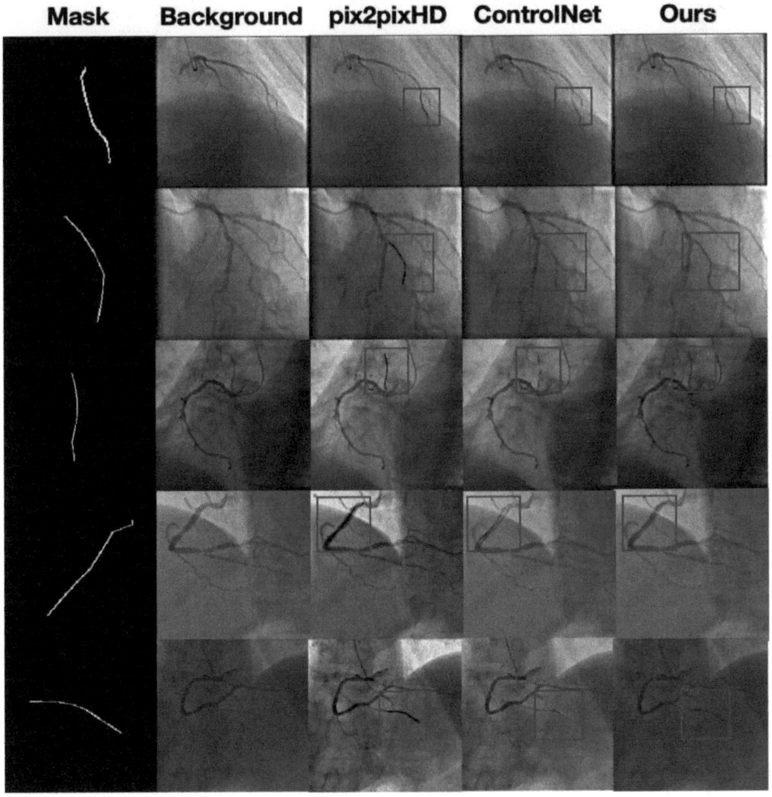

Fig. 3. Qualitative comparison of guidewire synthesis. Given the same device-free CAG background and the same input guidewire mask, we compare pix2pixHD, ControlNet, and our VDSB-GWSyn. Red boxes indicate the synthesized guidewire regions.

Synthesis Training Set. Using 1,787 CAG frames paired with vessel segmentation masks, we first sampled 7,148 candidate guidewire masks (four per frame) and then retained 3,506 for rendering after filtering out anatomically implausible cases, where the sampled trajectories deviated from the vessel course or extended outside the vessel lumen due to segmentation inaccuracies. Then we constructed a 3000-image subset for downstream pre-training via manual quality control, excluding cases where the synthesized guidewire is missing, severely blurred, or strongly fragmented. This screening is applied uniformly and uses only image-level inspection with no downstream model feedback. The synthetic set covers diverse guidewire locations within the same CAG frame, varying clinical camera angles and different levels of background complexity. Representative examples are shown in Fig. 2. Following the same uniform image-level screening procedure, we also construct a 2,000-image subset for baseline synthetic pre-training to ensure a fair comparison.

3.2 Experimental Setup

All images are resized to 512×512. We first fit a guidewire shape prior by skeletonizing clinical masks into 8 control points. The coordinates are compressed via PCA to a 4-dimensional latent space, and the latent distribution is modeled with a 5-component GMM. Our diffusion renderer follows a diffusion Schrödinger bridge with 1,000 discretization steps, noise levels from $t_0 = 10^{-4}$ to $T = 1.0$, and a symmetric beta set to 0.3. During training, Gaussian noise is injected only inside the guidewire mask regions to enforce localized inpainting. We optimize with AdamW ($\text{lr} = 5 \times 10^{-5}$), batch size 8, for 20k iterations, using EMA 0.99. We additionally apply a masked TV regularizer with weight 0.05 to preserve thin-structure continuity. For the downstream task, we adopt the RTMPose-S estimator with SimCC label encoding [9,15]. The model is pre-trained on three synthetic sets (1,000, 2,000, and 3,000 images) and then fine-tuned on real data (Table 2).

Table 1. Comprehensive comparison with baselines and ablation study on ROI-based generative quality metrics. Lower is better for ROI-FID / ROI-KID; higher is better for IPR (Precision/Recall). Bold indicates the best performance.

Method	ROI-KID (%) ↓	IPR (P/R) (%) ↑	ROI-FID ↓
Baselines			
pix2pixHD	5.5668 ± 0.1681	31.75 / 45.39	72.6365
ControlNet	2.1479 ± 0.1029	35.43 / 50.71	53.1129
Ablation			
w/o SPADE & w/o loss	2.7071 ± 0.1693	76.35 / 55.72	58.4721
w/o SPADE	2.5614 ± 0.1860	76.93 / 57.01	51.6956
Ours (DSB + SPADE)	$\mathbf{1.6181 \pm 0.1033}$	**78.74/65.87**	**49.1371**

Table 2. Downstream guidewire endpoint localization results of our VDSB-GWSyn. Lower is better for MPE; higher is better for PCK.

Pre-train data	MPE ↓	PCK@3 ↑	PCK@6 ↑	TIP MPE ↓	TAIL MPE ↓
0	16.0136	52.63	78.95	19.7241	12.3032
1,000	9.7175	77.45	84.31	9.6383	9.7966
2,000	**7.7126**	**86.27**	**91.18**	**5.8726**	9.5526
3,000	7.7781	85.29	88.24	6.7834	**8.7727**

3.3 Generation Evaluation

We evaluate the synthesis quality using both distribution alignment and local structure fidelity. Since coronary guidewires are extremely slender, global metrics such as standard FID [8] and KID [2] exhibit negligible variation. Following instance-level evaluation [24,26], we compute FID and KID on mask-centered ROI patches, which are extracted by cropping a tight bounding box around the synthesized guidewire mask, to focus evaluation on guidewire appearance rather than background. We also report IPR [11] to quantify manifold-based precision and recall, reflecting realism and coverage of the real ROI distribution. As shown in Table 1, our method achieves the best ROI-based performance compared to representative conditional generation baselines, including pix2pixHD [25] and ControlNet [29]. These quantitative trends are consistent with the qualitative comparisons in Fig. 3. Both baselines are prone to noticeable background drift and inconsistent local contrast, while pix2pixHD often produces overly thick wires with unnatural device-background blending, and ControlNet frequently yields fragmented or vanishing wire segments with weak structural continuity. In contrast, our method preserves background statistics while generating more coherent, anatomically plausible guidewire trajectories with fewer blending artifacts. Ablation results in Table 1 show that ROI-KID improves markedly when incorporating SPADE, indicating that spatially adaptive normalization enhances local feature alignment. Moreover, the proposed region-normalized objective mitigates background-dominated gradients, reducing wire fragmentation and improving structural continuity in synthesized samples.

3.4 Downstream Tasks

We adopt a synthetic pre-training followed by real fine-tuning protocol to evaluate the effectiveness of synthetic augmentation. RTMPose consistently benefits from the synthetic data. With the largest gain achieved at 2,000 synthesized images, it shows that MPE is reduced from 16.01 px to 7.71 px, and PCK at a 3-pixel threshold increases from 52.63% to 86.27% [27]. For a fair comparison, we apply the same protocol to the baseline methods. We first pre-train RTMPose on 2,000 synthetic images generated by pix2pixHD or ControlNet and then fine-tune the model on the same real training set using identical settings. Both baselines transfer poorly and yield large localization errors, with pix2pixHD reaching an MPE of 34.71 px and PCK@3 px of 5.88% and ControlNet reaching an MPE of 41.68 px and PCK@3 px of 9.86%. This gap aligns with their typical synthesis artifacts, where pix2pixHD commonly alters the wire width and local contrast, whereas ControlNet often exhibits instability on slender regions, leading to incomplete wire traces in challenging frames.

4 Conclusion

We presented VDSB-GWSyn, a controllable guidewire synthesis framework for coronary angiography, which enables large-scale generation of vessel-constrained guidewire samples under complex coronary backgrounds. The synthesized guidewire samples generated by our model substantially improve endpoint localization on real CAG images. Despite these encouraging results, several limitations remain. In particular, the quality of automatically generated guidewire masks still depends on the accuracy of vessel segmentation. In cases of spatially overlapping vessels or imperfect lumen delineation, sampled trajectories may enter anatomically inconsistent branches, leading to implausible masks that require manual rejection. Our future work will focus on topology-aware constraints and uncertainty-aware sampling to improve robustness and scalability.

Disclosure of Interests. The authors have no competing interests to declare that are relevant to the content of this article.

References

1. Ambrosini, P., Ruijters, D., Niessen, W.J., Moelker, A., van Walsum, T.: Fully automatic and real-time catheter segmentation in X-ray fluoroscopy. In: International Conference on Medical Image Computing and Computer-Assisted Intervention, pp. 577–585. Springer (2017)
2. Bińkowski, M., Sutherland, D.J., Arbel, M., Gretton, A.: Demystifying MMD GANs. arXiv preprint arXiv:1801.01401 (2018)
3. Cao, Y., et al.: Automatic translational correction of multi-view coronary angiography based on auto-annotation data generation. In: Proceedings of the AAAI Conference on Artificial Intelligence, vol. 40, pp. 2652–2660 (2026)
4. De Bortoli, V., Thornton, J., Heng, J., Doucet, A.: Diffusion schrödinger bridge with applications to score-based generative modeling. Adv. Neural. Inf. Process. Syst. **34**, 17695–17709 (2021)
5. Dorjsembe, Z., Pao, H.K., Odonchimed, S., Xiao, F.: Conditional diffusion models for semantic 3D brain MRI synthesis. IEEE J. Biomed. Health Inform. **28**(7), 4084–4093 (2024)
6. Du, Y., et al.: ArSDM: colonoscopy images synthesis with adaptive refinement semantic diffusion models. In: International Conference on Medical Image Computing and Computer-Assisted Intervention, pp. 339–349. Springer (2023)
7. Gherardini, M., Mazomenos, E., Menciassi, A., Stoyanov, D.: Catheter segmentation in X-ray fluoroscopy using synthetic data and transfer learning with light U-Nets. Comput. Methods Programs Biomed. **192**, 105420 (2020)

8. Heusel, M., Ramsauer, H., Unterthiner, T., Nessler, B., Hochreiter, S.: GANs trained by a two time-scale update rule converge to a local nash equilibrium. Adv. Neural Inf. Proces. Syst. **30** (2017)
9. Jiang, T., et al.: RTMPose: real-time multi-person pose estimation based on MMPose. arXiv preprint arXiv:2303.07399 (2023)
10. Konz, N., Chen, Y., Dong, H., Mazurowski, M.A.: Anatomically-controllable medical image generation with segmentation-guided diffusion models. In: International Conference on Medical Image Computing and Computer-Assisted Intervention, pp. 88–98. Springer (2024)
11. Kynkäänniemi, T., Karras, T., Laine, S., Lehtinen, J., Aila, T.: Improved precision and recall metric for assessing generative models. Adv. Neural. Inf. Process. Syst. **32** (2019)
12. Li, J., et al.: Geometrically constrained stenosis editing in coronary angiography via entropic optimal transport. arXiv preprint arXiv:2605.08851 (2026)
13. Li, R.Q., et al.: Real-time multi-guidewire endpoint localization in fluoroscopy images. IEEE Trans. Med. Imaging **40**(8), 2002–2014 (2021)
14. Li, R.Q., et al.: A unified framework for multi-guidewire endpoint localization in fluoroscopy images. IEEE Trans. Biomed. Eng. **69**(4), 1406–1416 (2021)
15. Li, Y., et al.: SimCC: a simple coordinate classification perspective for human pose estimation. In: European Conference on Computer Vision, pp. 89–106. Springer (2022)
16. Liu, G.H., Vahdat, A., Huang, D.A., Theodorou, E.A., Nie, W., Anandkumar, A.: I^2SB: Image-to-Image Schrödinger Bridge. arXiv preprint arXiv:2302.05872 (2023)
17. Lugmayr, A., Danelljan, M., Romero, A., Yu, F., Timofte, R., Van Gool, L.: Repaint: inpainting using denoising diffusion probabilistic models. In: Proceedings of the IEEE/CVF Conference on Computer Vision and Pattern Recognition, pp. 11461–11471 (2022)
18. Ma, J., Li, F., Wang, B.: U-Mamba: enhancing long-range dependency for biomedical image segmentation. arXiv preprint arXiv:2401.04722 (2024)
19. Pan, S., et al.: Label-efficient data augmentation with video diffusion models for guidewire segmentation in cardiac fluoroscopy. In: Proceedings of the AAAI Conference on Artificial Intelligence, vol. 39, pp. 6308–6316 (2025)
20. Park, T., Liu, M.Y., Wang, T.C., Zhu, J.Y.: Semantic image synthesis with spatially-adaptive normalization. In: Proceedings of the IEEE/CVF Conference on Computer Vision and Pattern Recognition, pp. 2337–2346 (2019)
21. Popov, M., et al.: Dataset for automatic region-based coronary artery disease diagnostics using X-ray angiography images. Sci. Data **11**(1), 20 (2024)
22. Ullah, I., Chikontwe, P., Choi, H., Yoon, C.H., Park, S.H.: Synthesize and segment: towards improved catheter segmentation via adversarial augmentation. Appl. Sci. **11**(4), 1638 (2021)
23. Ullah, I., Chikontwe, P., Park, S.H.: Catheter synthesis in X-ray fluoroscopy with generative adversarial networks. In: International Workshop on PRedictive Intelligence in Medicine, pp. 125–133. Springer (2019)
24. Wang, D., Zhang, Y., Bai, B., Yu, X., Shu, X., Dai, Y.: Grade: a generalization robustness assessment via distributional evaluation for remote sensing object detection. Remote Sensing **17**(22), 3771 (2025)
25. Wang, T.C., Liu, M.Y., Zhu, J.Y., Tao, A., Kautz, J., Catanzaro, B.: High-resolution image synthesis and semantic manipulation with conditional GANs. In: Proceedings of the IEEE Conference on Computer Vision and Pattern Recognition, pp. 8798–8807 (2018)

26. Xu, J., et al.: Decouple distortion from perception: region adaptive diffusion for extreme-low bitrate perception image compression. In: Proceedings of the Computer Vision and Pattern Recognition Conference, pp. 18051–18061 (2025)
27. Yang, Y., Ramanan, D.: Articulated human detection with flexible mixtures of parts. IEEE Trans. Pattern Anal. Mach. Intell. **35**(12), 2878–2890 (2012)
28. Yazdani, M., Medghalchi, Y., Ashrafian, P., Hacihaliloglu, I., Shahriari, D.: Flow matching for medical image synthesis: bridging the gap between speed and quality. In: International Conference on Medical Image Computing and Computer-Assisted Intervention, pp. 216–226. Springer (2025)
29. Zhang, L., Rao, A., Agrawala, M.: Adding conditional control to text-to-image diffusion models. In: Proceedings of the IEEE/CVF International Conference on Computer Vision, pp. 3836–3847. (2023)

Vision-Based Force Estimation Using Brain Surface Deformation Models

Chakib Heraoui[1,3], Nazim Haouchine[2], Nazim Ouadahi[3], Amir Hooshiar[4], D. Louis Collins[4], Rolando F. Del Maestro[5], and Houssem-Eddine Guezir[1,4](✉)

[1] Université TÉLUQ, Montreal, QC, Canada
[2] Harvard Medical School, Brigham and Women's Hospital, Boston, USA
[3] École Supérieure des Sciences et Technologies, Algiers 16104, Algeria
[4] McGill University, Montreal, QC, Canada
houssem.gueziri@teluq.ca
[5] Neurosurgical Simulation and Artificial Intelligence Learning Centre, Montreal, QC, Canada

Abstract. Haptic feedback is critical for neurosurgical training simulators, yet measuring contact forces in soft tissue interaction remains challenging. This paper presents a deep learning framework that estimates tool-tissue interaction forces directly from brain surface deformations captured by a monocular surgical microscope. A realistic dataset was generated using finite element method simulation in SOFA. The dataset contains ground-truth force magnitudes derived from tool-tissue interactions in neurosurgical scenarios. We developed D2FNet, a multi-scale convolutional neural network trained using a novel anti-ghost loss function that incorporates an asymmetric weighting scheme applying a penalty to over-predictions in low-force regions. This minimizes false high-force estimates likely to induce erroneous haptic responses. The model processes spatial features from normalized displacements, magnitude, brain mask, and divergence field. Our method enables non-invasive estimation of interaction forces using only 2D video sequences. Cross-validation on simulated data achieved R^2=0.788±0.039 and mean absolute error (MAE)=6.4±0.8 mN. The anti-ghost loss reduced spurious force predictions by 73% compared to standard MSE training, particularly in low-force regions. We demonstrate feasibility through an ex vivo calf brain experiment and quantitatively compare estimated global forces with ground-truth measurements from an external force sensor. Results showed good agreement between the predicted forces and ground-truth measurements (MAE=0.071 N, Corr.=71.1%). Frame-independent force estimation from monocular surface deformation is feasible and clinically relevant for real-time force feedback rendering in realistic surgical simulators, with potential applications in intraoperative force monitoring.

Keywords: Neurosurgery simulation · Force estimation · Deep learning · Finite element method · Brain biomechanics · Surgical training

G. Yang et al. (Eds.): MICCAI 2026, LNCS 16893, pp. 596–605, 2027.
https://doi.org/10.1007/978-3-032-38236-8_57

1 Introduction

Neurosurgical procedures require extreme precision due to the delicate nature of brain tissue. Excessive tool-tissue contact forces can cause irreversible injury, while insufficient contact limits surgical performance. Cadaveric studies with force-sensing bipolar forceps have shown that neurosurgical forces are remarkably low with maximal peak at 1.35 N, and over 70% of measured forces fall below 0.3 N [4]. Yet, force application remains a largely qualitative skill taught through years of apprenticeship. Haptic-enabled virtual surgery simulations offer risk-free training environments, but require accurate force models for realistic feedback [10,12], and animal-based simulation models [1,16,18] lack the quantitative force feedback needed to develop advanced tactile skills.

Early neurosurgical force sensing used strain gauge–based tools [4], requiring specialized hardware and calibration, and cannot estimate forces in purely computational simulations where only virtual deformation is available. Software-based approaches instead use biomechanical modeling with FEM, such as the SOFA framework [3], which enables real-time simulation using experimentally validated brain tissue properties [2,7]. However, FEM methods solve the forward problem—computing deformation from known forces—rather than the inverse problem of inferring forces from observed deformations, which requires accurate material parameters and limits real-time inverse force estimation. Vision-based deep learning methods offer a promising alternative [9], but have been mainly validated on silicone phantoms rather than brain tissue. In this work, we focus on force estimation for ex vivo neurosurgical training, where biological tissue specimens are used as physical models to replicate surgical manipulation in a controlled setting. We propose a data-driven method that predicts spatially resolved contact forces directly from 2D surface displacement fields captured by standard surgical microscopes, using FEM-based brain tissue simulations to train convolutional neural networks for the inverse deformation-to-force mapping.

Contribution. Our contributions are three-fold: 1) we introduce a framework for generating visually realistic neurosurgical simulation data with ground-truth force measurements to enable the training and validation of machine learning models; 2) we introduce a novel Anti-Ghost Loss Function with asymmetric penalty for over-predictions in low-force regions, directly addressing surgical safety requirements where false positive high forces could lead to tissue damage; 3) we develop D2FNet with pyramid pooling, attention mechanisms, and divergence field features that capture tissue compression patterns, enabling accurate force prediction across diverse surgical scenarios. The neurosurgical force data generation methods in the SOFA simulation framework[1], as well as all trained models[2] are publicly available.

2 Methods

[1] Data generation: https://github.com/D3MIA/SOFA-NeuroSim-Recorder.

[2] Force estimation: https://github.com/D3MIA/D2FNet.

Brain Biomechanical Modeling: The brain was modeled using a co-rotational finite element method (FEM), in which the stress–strain relationship is evaluated locally within each element's own reference frame, keeping the constitutive behavior linear while rigid-body rotations and geometric nonlinearities are handled globally through continuous frame updates. This formulation thus captures large deformations without requiring a fully nonlinear material model, offering a computationally efficient alternative to nonlinear viscoelastic approaches for large-scale dataset generation while still yielding physiologically plausible deformations, [2,7,8]. The model includes a 12 mm radius craniotomy and four boundary conditions simulating dura attachments at the falx cerebri and skull. These constraints prevent rigid-body motion while allowing localized deformation within the craniotomy. A linear elastic model was used, with isotropic stress-strain relationship:

$$\boldsymbol{\sigma} = \lambda \mathrm{tr}(\boldsymbol{\epsilon})\mathbf{I} + 2\mu\boldsymbol{\epsilon} \tag{1}$$

where $\boldsymbol{\sigma}$ is the Cauchy stress tensor, $\boldsymbol{\epsilon}$ is the infinitesimal strain tensor, $\mathbf{I}$ is the identity matrix, and $\lambda = \frac{E\nu}{(1+\nu)(1-2\nu)}$ and $\mu = \frac{E}{2(1+\nu)}$ are Lamé parameters derived via standard elasticity relations [15]. Using the DejaVu simulation SOFA plugin [5], tissue deformation was induced by applying spatially distributed forces centered at randomly sampled surface locations within the craniotomy region, producing diverse tissue displacement patterns across the dataset.

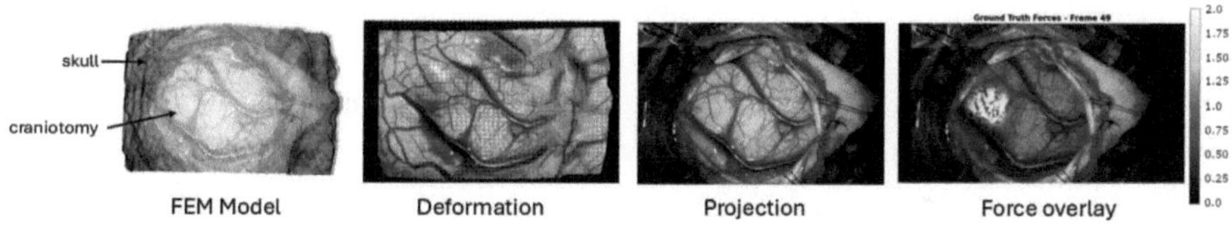

Fig. 1. Illustration of the proposed data generation framework, from left to right: FEM model is used to to simulate brain tissue biomechanics, forces are applied generating deformations, which are projected on camera view to produce 2D displacement fields, along with corresponding ground truth force maps.

Data Generation: An overview of the proposed data generation framework is shown in Fig. 1. Volumetric reaction forces $\mathbf{f}_j^{\mathrm{vol}}(t) \in \mathbb{R}^3$ were computed at each node of a sparse tetrahedral mesh representing the mechanical response to tool-tissue interaction.[3] These forces were interpolated to the dense surface mesh using k-nearest neighbor (k=8) spatial averaging with inverse distance weighting:

$$\mathbf{f}_i^{\mathrm{surf}}(t) = \sum_{j \in \mathcal{N}_8(i)} w_{ij}\mathbf{f}_j^{\mathrm{vol}}(t), \quad w_{ij} = \frac{d_{ij}^{-1}}{\sum_{j'} d_{ij'}^{-1}} \tag{2}$$

[3] Forces were extracted from SOFA's constraint solver at each timestamp using a multi-stage pipeline implemented via custom *AnimationRecorder* components.

where $d_{ij} = \|\mathbf{x}_i - \mathbf{x}_j\|_2$ is the Euclidean distance between surface node i and volumetric node j, and $\mathcal{N}_8(i)$ denotes the 8 nearest volumetric nodes to surface node i. This scheme ensures spatially smooth force reconstruction while preserving local force gradients at tool contact boundaries.

To simulate computational noise arising during deformation estimation, a two-stage noise injection strategy was implemented. First, Gaussian noise with a constant bias of 0.02 N was introduced at recording time. Second, post-processing geometric noise applied to 5% of low-force surface points far from tool contact, inducing displacement perturbations of ±10% relative to the per-frame displacement range. Finally, force magnitudes $F_i(t) = \|\mathbf{f}_i^{\text{surf}}(t)\|_2$ were projected onto the 2D craniotomy plane via camera transformation matrices.

This complete simulation and projection pipeline generated a comprehensive synthetic dataset with diverse surgical manipulation patterns. The video sequences are composed of repeated single-direction deformation events applied sequentially in different orientations, which closely resemble the pulling actions commonly performed with forceps during surgical interventions.

D2FNet Architecture: We developed D2FNet, a multi-scale U-Net [13], to estimate forces from sparse, noisy deformation data (Fig. 2):

1. *Multi-Scale Attention Mechanisms.* We integrated spatial and channel attention modules [11] at 9 network levels (encoder stages 1–4, bottleneck, decoder stages 1–4). At each decoder level, dual attention gates compute spatial attention $\alpha_{\text{spatial}} = \sigma(W_s * \text{Conv}(x))$ and channel attention $\alpha_{\text{channel}} = \sigma(W_c * \text{GlobalPool}(x))$, with combined weighting $x_{\text{out}} = x \odot \alpha_{\text{spatial}} \odot \alpha_{\text{channel}}$ applied before feature concatenation. This enables selective focus on force-relevant spatial regions while suppressing background noise.
2. *Pyramid Pooling Bottleneck.* We use pyramid pooling at 4 spatial scales [1×1, 2×2, 4×4, 8×8] to capture contextual information [20], enabling the network to integrate local force gradients and global deformation patterns.
3. *Multi-Head Adaptive Fusion.* We employed three specialized prediction heads targeting low (0–0.5 N), medium (0–1.5 N), and high (0–3.0 N) force regimes. Each head produces sigmoid-bounded predictions that are combined via attention-based soft weighting learned during training to optimally fuse predictions across force magnitudes, ensuring non-negative force outputs.

The network takes 256×256 pixel grids with five input channels derived from bilinearly interpolated 2D surface displacements from video, and predicts a single-channel map corresponding to the total 3D force magnitude rather than only the in-plane force component. The input channels encode: 1) normalized d_x/s_x and d_y/s_y displacements, with s_x, s_y as training-set 99.9th percentiles. 2) displacement magnitude $\sqrt{d_x^2 + d_y^2}/s_x$ clipped to [0, 5], where we intentionally use s_x rather than a separate magnitude scale to extend the dynamic range for large deformations while preventing outlier influence, 3) binary brain mask to exclude regions outside craniotomy, and 4) divergence field $\nabla \cdot \mathbf{d} = \frac{\partial d_x}{\partial x} + \frac{\partial d_y}{\partial y}$ computed via finite-difference on Gaussian-smoothed displacement fields (σ=1.0

pixel). Divergence encodes tissue volume changes, distinguishing compressive (negative) from tensile (positive) deformation patterns correlated to force distribution.

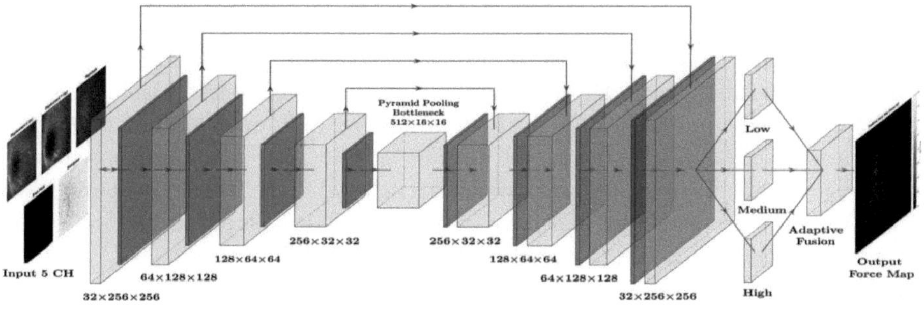

Fig. 2. D2FNet architecture overview. The network takes a 5-channel input (normalized d_x, d_y, magnitude, brain mask, divergence) processed by a U-Net encoder-decoder with pyramid pooling. Three heads predict low (0–0.5N), medium (0–1.5N), and high (0–3.0 N) force ranges, fused via adaptive attention to produce the final 1×256×256 force map. Skip connections preserve spatial detail across scales.

Anti-Ghost Loss Function: Standard regression losses (MSE, MAE) treat over-predictions and under-predictions symmetrically. In surgical applications, false high forces are considered more harmful than missed low forces. Haptic devices rendering these *phantom* forces may train surgeons to apply excessive pressure, potentially causing tissue damage. We designed an *asymmetric anti-ghost loss* with 3 times stronger penalty for over-predictions in low-force frames, inspired by focal loss for hard example mining [6]:

$$\mathcal{L}_{\text{ghost}} = \frac{1}{N}\sum_{i=1}^{N} w_i \cdot (F_i^{\text{pred}} - F_i^{\text{true}})^2 \tag{3}$$

where weights w_i are defined as:

$$w_i = \begin{cases} 3.0 & \text{if } \bar{F}_{\text{frame}} < \tau \text{ and } F_i^{\text{pred}} > F_i^{\text{true}} \\ 1.0 & \text{otherwise} \end{cases} \tag{4}$$

with frame mean force $\bar{F}_{\text{frame}} = \frac{1}{N}\sum_{i=1}^{N} F_i^{\text{true}}$ and threshold τ=0.05 N.

Finally, we use a linear weighted combination of R^2 objective function and ghost penalty:

$$\mathcal{L}_{\text{total}} = \lambda_{R^2} \cdot \mathcal{L}_{R^2} + \lambda_{ghost} \cdot \mathcal{L}_{\text{ghost}}, \tag{5}$$

where $\mathcal{L}_{R^2} = 1 - R^2$, $R^2 = 1 - \frac{\sum(F_i^{\text{pred}} - F_i^{\text{true}})^2}{\sum(F_i^{\text{true}} - \bar{F})^2}$ and λ_{R^2} and λ_{ghost} are hyperparameters controlling the relative weighting of each term with $\lambda_{R^2} + \lambda_{ghost} = 1$.

Training, Validation and Hyper-Parametrization: The network was trained on an NVIDIA A100 GPU (40 GB) using the AdamW optimizer with weight decay $\lambda = 10^{-5}$ and initial learning rate 5×10^{-4}, reduced by 0.5 upon validation plateau (patience=5). A batch size of 8 was used due to memory constraints, with gradient clipping (max norm=1.0) for stability. Each fold was trained for 50 epochs, saving the best model based on validation R^2. We performed 3-fold cross-validation at the scenario level (26,000 frames training, 12,000 frames validation). Data generation used a volumetric mesh of ∼4096 tetrahedral elements and 40,652 surface nodes for force measurement. Young's modulus was set to $E = 500$ Pa and Poisson's ratio to $\nu = 0.4$, consistent with reported brain tissue properties at low strain rates [14, 19]. Total tissue mass was 1.0 kg. Velocity-proportional damping (coefficient 2.0) ensured numerical stability and convergence. Lamé parameters were $\lambda = 714.29$ Pa and $\mu = 178.57$ Pa [15].

Experiment: We conducted a feasibility study on an ex vivo calf brain to evaluate applicability under more realistic conditions. The brain was manipulated with bipolar forceps while an external force sensor (SensONE, Bota Systems, Zürich, Switzerland) continuously measured the resulting ground truth forces. Synchronized videos were recorded with an endoscopic camera at 23 fps and 680 × 480 resolution. To mitigate instrument-induced occlusions, the forceps were manually segmented on each frame and inpainted using mean intensity. Dense tissue deformation was then estimated using frame-to-frame total variation registration method [17] with 6 pyramid levels and 0.3 grid regularization factor. Pixel-to-millimeter conversion was obtained by comparing small displacements of tracked forceps measured with an external optical tracking system (Polaris VEGA, Northern Digital Inc., ON, Canada) to corresponding tool motion in the video, assuming a camera axis normal to the brain surface. The resulting deformations were provided as inputs to the proposed model to predict the applied forces, which were then compared with the ground-truth sensor measurements.

3 Results

Table 1 summarizes cross-validation results. The method achieved consistent R^2 score ranging [0.756–0.843]) with mean 0.788±0.039 and MAE=6.4±0.8 mN. The low coefficient of variation (CV=4.97%) demonstrates good model stability and reproducibility across surgical scenarios. To evaluate the anti-ghost loss, we conducted an ablation study by training a baseline model with standard MSE on Fold 2 using identical settings. Anti-ghost loss reduced false positives by 73% (31.2%→8.4%) and mean over-prediction by 73% (18.4→4.9 mN) in low-force frames, while improving R^2 by +2.7% (0.821→0.843), suggesting asymmetric penalties improve safety-critical force prediction for haptic rendering.

Table 1. Cross-validation results on simulated data.

Metric	Fold 1	Fold 2	Fold 3	Mean ± SD	Coeff. of variation
R^2 Score	0.756	0.843	0.765	0.788 ± 0.039	4.97%
MAE (mN)	7.1	5.3	6.8	6.4 ± 0.8	12.5%
RMSE (mN)	10.3	8.1	9.8	9.4 ± 0.9	9.6%

MAE: mean absolute error; RMSE: root mean square error; mN: millinewton.

Figure 3 shows qualitative performance on representative validation frames across different force regimes. Top row shows results for a low-force palpation (peak 0.46 N). Despite reduced force, the model remains highly accurate (R^2=0.970, MAE=3.7 mN) with good spatial localization of the contact region and low absolute error (RMSE 6.7 mN, max error 98 mN). Bottom row shows high-force retraction scenario (peak 2.0 N), where the model demonstrates near-perfect spatial agreement (R^2=0.934, MAE=15.4 mN). The predicted force map accurately captures the contact hotspot's extent and magnitude. The absolute error map shows errors concentrated near force gradient boundaries, with minimal error in uniform force regions. The scatter plot shows strong linear correlation over the full magnitude range with little systematic bias.

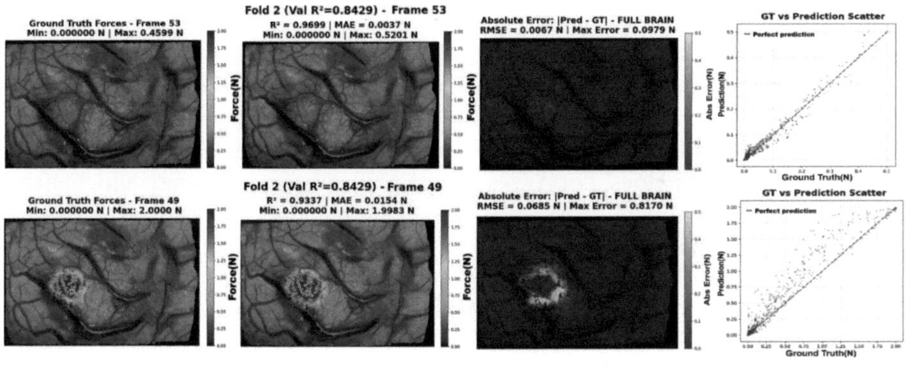

Fig. 3. Qualitative results: on low-force palpation scenario (top) and on high-force retraction scenario (bottom). From left to right: ground-truth, predicted, absolute error and scatter plots of ground truth vs. predicted forces.

Figure 4 shows the results of the ex vivo experiment. We achieved 0.076 N MAE, 0.108 N RMSE, and 71.1% correlation between the estimated and ground-truth forces. The estimated displacement fields exhibit good spatial consistency (Fig. 4c and d). Errors increase near image boundaries as the instrument enters or leaves the field of view, causing occlusions and misregistration.

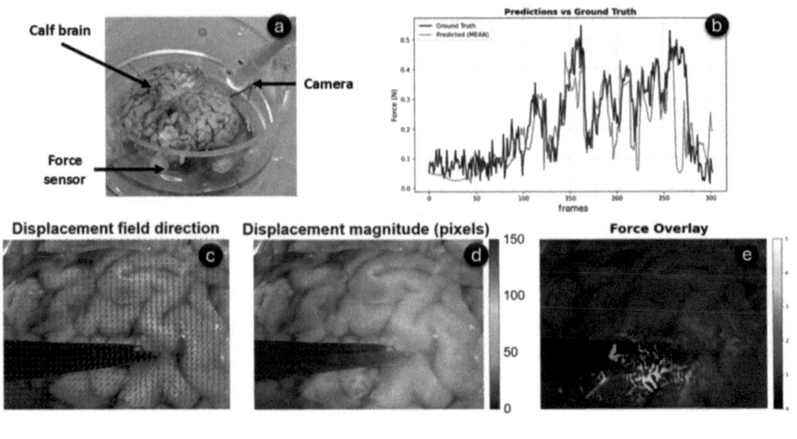

Fig. 4. Ex vivo experiment: (a) experimental setup, (b) predicted force (red) vs. ground-truth sensor measurement (black), (c) estimated displacement field directions, (d) displacement field magnitude, (e) overlay of force predictions. (Color figure online)

4 Discussion

The ex vivo calf brain experiment demonstrated promising results, with a strong correlation between the estimated forces and the force sensor measurements. The MAE of 0.076 N represent less than 5.7% of typical neurosurgical peak forces 1.35 N [4], approaching the perceptual threshold for haptic rendering systems. However, the current implementation still requires further improvement. In particular, instrument segmentation was performed manually, and the image registration approach does not yet support real-time processing, which limits immediate clinical applicability.

The frame-independent design processes each timestamp without temporal history, enabling deployment in real-time systems without frame buffering. This approach is justified by the rest-state displacement representation, in which each frame contains complete geometric information and implicitly encodes temporal coherence through the recovered tissue deformation field. Nevertheless, incorporating explicit temporal modeling could further improve prediction stability and temporal consistency across consecutive frames. Incorporating spatial divergence in the input provides explicit encoding of tissue compression/expansion patterns that complement raw displacement information. The model achieved good stability and robustness in simulated data. The proposed approach shows promise across neurosurgical applications. It could improve surgical training simulators with real-time, high-fidelity haptic feedback from optical motion data, support intraoperative monitoring via quantitative video-based force visualization to prevent excessive tissue manipulation, and enable patient-specific planning through fine-tuning on individualized FEM simulations.

Limitations: This study has several limitations related to biomechanical realism, generalization, sensing, and clinical deployment. Training data were generated using finite element simulations with simplified linear elastic properties, which do not fully capture the nonlinear, viscoelastic, anisotropic, and patient-specific behavior of real brain tissue or physiological responses such as inflammation or vascular changes. The model was also evaluated using a single force application pattern and tissue stiffness, limiting generalization to other instruments, interaction modes, and anatomical variability, although the framework can accommodate more diverse training data. Additionally, the monocular 2D approach estimates only force magnitude and does not capture the full 3D force vector. Finally, although force prediction can be run in real time, the current end-to-end pipeline is not fully automated: instrument segmentation and displacement estimation still need manual input and extra computation. More validation is needed in real surgical conditions, including occlusions, lighting changes, and camera motion.

5 Conclusion

We presented a complete framework, from data generation to tool-tissue contact force estimation, for monocular neurosurgical microscope. We achieved clinically relevant accuracy ($R^2 = 0.788$, MAE $= 6.4$ mN) on simulated data through a multi-scale U-Net architecture with anti-ghost loss function and divergence field features. The asymmetric penalty approach reduced false high-force predictions by 73%, directly addressing surgical safety requirements for haptic rendering applications. Preliminary results on an ex vivo brain showed good agreement between the predicted forces and the ground-truth sensor measurements, with an MAE of 0.071 N and a correlation of 71.1%. Future work will focus on validating the framework on additional ex vivo surgical data and expanding the dataset to include diverse tissue properties and instrument geometries, enabling broader coverage of clinically representative neurosurgical scenarios.

Acknowledgments. This work was funded by grants from The Canadian Institutes of Health Research (CIHR 195899). C. Heraoui received support through Mitacs Globalink Research Award (IT 45437). N. Haouchine was supported by the Grants from NIH (K25EB035166 and R03EB033910).

Disclosure of Interests. The authors declare that they have no competing interests.

References

1. Almansouri, A., et al.: Continuous instrument tracking in a cerebral corticectomy ex vivo calf brain simulation model: face and content validation. Operat. Neurosurg. **27**(1), 106–113 (2024)
2. Budday, S., et al.: Mechanical characterization of human brain tissue. Acta Biomater. **48**, 319–340 (2017)
3. Faure, F., et al.: SOFA: a multi-model framework for interactive physical simulation. In: Soft Tissue Biomechanical Modeling for Computer Assisted Surgery. Studies in Mechanobiology, Tissue Engineering and Biomaterials, vol. 11, pp. 283–321. Springer, Berlin, Heidelberg (2012)

4. Gan, L.S., Zareinia, K., Lama, S., Maddahi, Y., Yang, F.W., Sutherland, G.R.: Quantification of forces during a neurosurgical procedure: a pilot study. World Neurosurg. **84**(2), 537–548 (2015)
5. Haouchine, N., Stoyanov, D., Roy, F., Cotin, S.: DejaVu: intra-operative simulation for surgical gesture rehearsal. In: Medical Image Computing and Computer Assisted Intervention - MICCAI 2017. Lecture Notes in Computer Science, vol. 10434, pp. 523–531. Springer, Cham (2017)
6. Lin, T.Y., Goyal, P., Girshick, R., He, K., Dollár, P.: Focal loss for dense object detection. In: 2017 IEEE International Conference on Computer Vision (ICCV), pp. 2999–3007 (2017)
7. Miller, K., Chinzei, K., Orssengo, G., Bednarz, P.: Mechanical properties of brain tissue in-vivo: experiment and computer simulation. J. Biomech. **33**(11), 1369–1376 (2000)
8. Miller, K., et al.: Biomechanical modeling and computer simulation of the brain during neurosurgery. Int. J. Numer. Meth. Biomed. Eng. **35**(10), e3250 (2019)
9. Neidhardt, M., Mieling, R., Bengs, M., Schlaefer, A.: Optical force estimation for interactions between tool and soft tissues. Sci. Rep. **13**(1), 506 (2023)
10. Okamura, A.M., Verner, L.N., Reiley, C.E., Mahvash, M.: Haptics for robot-assisted minimally invasive surgery. In: Robotics Research. Springer Tracts in Advanced Robotics, vol. 66, pp. 361–372. Springer, Berlin, Heidelberg (2010)
11. Oktay, O., et al.: Attention U-net: learning where to look for the pancreas. In: Medical Imaging with Deep Learning (2018)
12. Pacchierotti, C., Sinclair, S., Solazzi, M., Frisoli, A., Hayward, V., Prattichizzo, D.: Wearable haptic systems for the fingertip and the hand: taxonomy, review, and perspectives. IEEE Trans. Haptics **10**(4), 580–600 (2017)
13. Ronneberger, O., Fischer, P., Brox, T.: U-Net: convolutional networks for biomedical image segmentation. In: Medical Image Computing and Computer-Assisted Intervention - MICCAI 2015. Lecture Notes in Computer Science, vol. 9351, pp. 234–241. Springer, Cham (2015)
14. Su, L., et al.: Compressive response of white matter in the brain at low strain-rates. Int. J. Mech. Sci. **277**, 109415 (2024)
15. Timoshenko, S.P., Goodier, J.N.: Theory of Elasticity, 3rd edn. McGraw-Hill, New York (1970)
16. Tran, D.H., et al.: Quantitation of tissue resection using a brain tumor model and 7-T magnetic resonance imaging technology. World Neurosurg. **148**, e326–e339 (2021)
17. Vishnevskiy, V., Gass, T., Szekely, G., Tanner, C., Goksel, O.: Isotropic total variation regularization of displacements in parametric image registration. IEEE Trans. Med. Imag. **36**(2), 385–395 (2016)
18. Winkler-Schwartz, A., et al.: Creating a comprehensive research platform for surgical technique and operative outcome in primary brain tumor neurosurgery. World Neurosurg. **144**, e62–e71 (2020)
19. Zhang, C., Liu, C., Zhao, H.: Mechanical properties of brain tissue based on microstructure. J. Mech. Behav. Biomed. Mater. **126**, 104924 (2022)
20. Zhao, H., Shi, J., Qi, X., Wang, X., Jia, J.: Pyramid scene parsing network. In: 2017 IEEE Conference on Computer Vision and Pattern Recognition (CVPR), pp. 2881–2890 (2017)

When Tissue Speaks: Vibroacoustic Monitoring of Tissue Response During Electrosurgery

Nazila Esmaeili[1](✉), Robin Urrutia[2,3], Diego Espejo[2,4], Axel Boese[5], Philipp Horvath[6], Christian Hansen[2,3], Jannis Hagenah[1,7], and Alfredo Illanes[2,3]

[1] Center for Digital Surgery, Department of General, Visceral and Pediatric Surgery, University Medical Center Göttingen, 37075 Göttingen, Germany
nazila.esmaeili@med.uni-goettingen.de

[2] Faculty of Computer Science, Otto von Guericke University Magdeburg, Universitätsplatz 2, 39106 Magdeburg, Germany

[3] Research Campus STIMULATE, Otto von Guericke University Magdeburg, Otto-Hahn-Str. 2, 39106 Magdeburg, Germany

[4] Innovation Center Computer-Assisted Surgery (ICCAS), Faculty of Medicine, Leipzig University, Semmelweisstraße 14, 04103 Leipzig, Germany

[5] Innovation Laboratory for Image Guided Therapy, Otto von Guericke University Magdeburg, Leipziger Str. 44, 39120 Magdeburg, Germany

[6] Department of General, Visceral and Pediatric Surgery, University Medical Center Göttingen, 37075 Göttingen, Germany

[7] Fraunhofer Research Institution for Individualized and Cell-based Medical Engineering (IMTE), 23562 Lübeck, Germany

Abstract. Electrosurgical coagulation is widely used in laparoscopic surgery; however, intraoperative assessment of tissue response remains indirect and largely reliant on visual cues, increasing the risk of insufficient coagulation or excessive thermal damage. In this work, we investigate vibroacoustic (VA) sensing as a non-invasive modality for monitoring electrosurgical coagulation. VA sensing captures structure-borne mechanical vibrations generated at the tool-tissue interaction point without requiring modifications to standard surgical instruments or workflows. Using a bipolar electrosurgical setup, VA signals were acquired under two complementary scenarios: prolonged coagulation of ex vivo porcine liver tissue to analyze temporal signal evolution, and coagulation of ex vivo porcine liver, muscle, and fat to investigate tissue-specific responses. The signals were analyzed using time- and time-frequency-domain signal processing methods. Results show that VA signals evolve systematically throughout coagulation, revealing distinct phases up to carbonization. In addition, tissue-specific analyses demonstrate reproducible differences in temporal dynamics and spectral content, enabling clear separation of tissue types in a non-linear embedding space. These

Supplementary Information The online version contains supplementary material available at https://doi.org/10.1007/978-3-032-38236-8_58.

G. Yang et al. (Eds.): MICCAI 2026, LNCS 16893, pp. 606–615, 2027.
https://doi.org/10.1007/978-3-032-38236-8_58

findings indicate that VA sensing captures reproducible state-dependent and tissue-specific characteristics during electrosurgical energy delivery, highlighting its potential to address the clinical challenge of perceiving and controlling tissue response during electrosurgery.

Keywords: Vibroacoustic sensing · Tissue monitoring · Electrosurgery

1 Introduction

Electrosurgery is an integral component of laparoscopic surgery, where conventional monopolar and bipolar modalities remain the most used tools for tissue dissection, coagulation, and vessel sealing [1,12]. Effective electrosurgical treatment, while minimizing the risk of lateral thermal spread, depends on the surgeon's ability to accurately perceive and control tissue response during energy delivery [5]. However, this remains challenging in laparoscopic settings. Tissue response can only be inferred from indirect visual cues, such as surface color changes and the release of water vapor, which do not reliably reflect subsurface tissue state. Visual assessment is further constrained by the camera-mediated field of view, where parts of the instruments and surrounding tissues may lie outside the visible area, and by electrosurgical smoke that can degrade image quality. Moreover, accurate interpretation of these cues depends on the surgeon's experience and understanding of electrosurgical principles, which often require dedicated training. Together, these limitations increase the risk of under-treatment, resulting in insufficient tissue coaptation, incomplete coagulation, and persistent bleeding, or over-treatment, leading to carbonization and increased lateral thermal spread [9,13]. To mitigate these risks, advanced systems such as LigaSure ™, EnSeal™, Plasma Kinetic Gyrus ™, and ultrasonic technologies have been shown to reduce lateral thermal spread, operative time, and intraoperative blood loss. However, their clinical integration remains limited; therefore, conventional electrosurgical devices continue to be widely used due to their familiarity, cost-effectiveness, and adaptability across diverse surgical scenarios [12]. Modern electrosurgical units commonly incorporate impedance-based feedback mechanisms that modulate energy delivery according to tissue electrical properties. However, these systems control electrical measurements and do not provide direct information about the local tissue state or the progression of thermal effects. Moreover, this feedback is not explicitly conveyed to the surgeon during the procedure. Consequently, perceiving and controlling tissue response during electrosurgery remains challenging in current setting [2,16,20].

Electrosurgical tissue effects are not purely electrical or thermal phenomena. Tissue heating induces a sequence of thermally driven biological and structural changes that are accompanied by mechanical processes, including vibrations generated at the tool-tissue interaction point [3,4]. These mechanically induced responses represent a natural but largely underexplored source of information that can provide insight into tissue state during electrosurgery. Vibroacoustic (VA) sensing enables access to this structure-borne vibration information. By placing a sensor on the proximal part of the surgical instrument, vibrations generated at the tool-tissue interaction that propagate along the instrument shaft can be acquired outside the body. This enables passive sensing without the need for active components inside the body, without modifying standard instruments, and without interfering with existing surgical workflows. This modality provides simple and non-invasive access to a rich source of information with high dynamical range. The feasibility of VA sensing has been demonstrated in various applications, including pedicle screw loosening and breach detection during spinal pedicle drilling [10,18], tissue characterization in needle-based procedures [8,17], and audification of laparoscopic surgical tasks [6]. In parallel, airborne acoustic signals have also been explored in laparoscopic procedures, where microphones capture sound generated during surgical activity in experimental setups. These studies have demonstrated that airborne audio contains informative features for perception enhancement and high-level classification tasks, including differentiation of cutting and coagulation modes [14,15]. However, they rely on sound transmitted through the air and do not provide direct access to structure-borne vibrations at the tool-tissue interaction point.

As the ability to directly monitor tissue response during electrosurgical energy delivery through structure-borne vibrations remains largely unexplored, this work investigates VA sensing as a novel modality for monitoring electrosurgical coagulation by capturing state-dependent and tissue-specific responses during energy delivery. The main contributions are:

- We introduce VA sensing as a non-invasive and tool-agnostic modality for capturing state-dependent and tissue-specific responses during electrosurgical energy delivery.
- We demonstrate that VA signals evolve systematically throughout the prolonged electrosurgical coagulation process, revealing distinct phases up to tissue carbonization.
- We analyze tissue-specific VA responses during electrosurgical coagulation and show that different tissue types exhibit distinct signatures, enabling discrimination based on thermal response.

2 Method

In accordance with the stated contributions, the experimental setup and analysis framework were designed to investigate VA behavior during electrosurgical coagulation using two complementary acquisition scenarios, where all coagulations were performed by an experienced surgeon: scenario I addressing the evolution of VA dynamics during prolonged coagulation up to carbonization, and scenario II examining tissue-specific responses under comparable conditions. The signal processing strategy enabled structured analysis of temporal evolution and inter-tissue variability in VA signals and was implemented in MATLAB R2024b and Python. The data and code supporting the findings of this study are available at https://gitlab.gwdg.de/cds/va-electrosurgery.

2.1 Experimental Setup and Data Acquisition

All experiments used a unified setup and predefined protocol to record VA signals during electrosurgical coagulation.

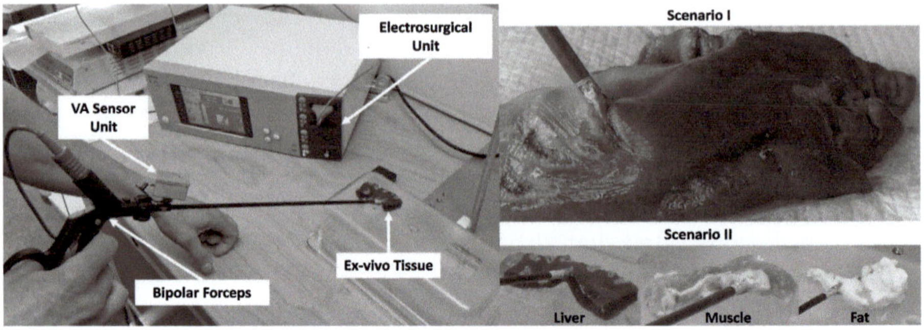

Fig. 1. The overview of experimental setup with the experiments of scenario I and II.

A schematic overview of the experimental setup is shown in Fig. 1. Electrosurgical energy was delivered using a high-frequency electrosurgical unit (VIO® 300D, Erbe Elektromedizin GmbH, Tübingen, Germany), which generates and modulates electrical current for different surgical effects. Bipolar energy was applied using a standard rotating bipolar grasping forceps (RoBi®, KARL STORZ, Tuttlingen, Germany). VA signals were acquired using a VA sensing system (SURAG Medical GmbH, Leipzig, Germany). The add-on sensor was mounted proximally on the bipolar forceps using the instrument's existing Luer-lock connection, without any modification of the surgical tool. VA data were transmitted wirelessly in real-time to a laptop. Dedicated software enabled signal acquisition, optional real-time audification, and storage for offline analysis. VA signals were recorded at a sampling frequency of 44400 Hz. In addition, an external video recording of the entire experiment was acquired.

A standardized acquisition protocol was applied in all experiments. Each trial began with the instrument placed on the table while VA recordings captured background noise for 5-10 s. The surgeon then picked up the instrument, and a reproducible synchronization event was generated by three taps on the instrument shaft, producing distinct peaks visible in both VA and video modalities. The surgeon subsequently grasped the tissue and performed coagulation. After task completion, the instrument was placed back on the table and all recordings were stopped.

In scenario I, a whole ex vivo porcine liver was used. This scenario comprised a total of 15 VA recordings. In each trial, the surgeon performed coagulation continuously on the tissue until visual cues indicated complete carbonization. In scenario II, three ex vivo porcine tissue types (liver, muscle, and fat) were investigated. Samples were prepared with comparable dimensions ($\approx 10 \times 3 \times 1$ cm) to ensure experimental consistency. For each tissue type, 10 VA recordings were obtained (30 total). This design enabled direct comparison of tissue-specific VA characteristics while minimizing geometric and procedural variability.

For all experiments, the recorded video and its audio track were used to synchronize video and VA recordings. The start and end of each coagulation event were manually annotated in the synchronized video data, and the corresponding VA signal segments were extracted using these annotations for subsequent analysis.

2.2 Vibroacoustic Data Analysis

Figure 2 illustrates the overall VA signal analysis strategy. The acquired signals were divided into two datasets corresponding to scenarios I and II. All recordings underwent a common processing pipeline, followed by specific analyses for each scenario.

The common signal processing pipeline began with pre-processing of each raw VA segment. First, the DC component was removed. Background noise was then attenuated using spectral gating by computing the spectrogram and estimating a frequency-dependent noise threshold. A binary mask was constructed to suppress spectral components below this threshold to provide the denoised time-domain VA signal. The resulting signal was used for subsequent analysis in scenario II. In the final step of this pipeline, a time-pseudo-frequency representation was computed using the Continuous Wavelet Transform (CWT) with a Morse mother wavelet. The resulting CWT matrix captures VA energy over time and pseudo frequency and forms the basis for the analyses in scenario I and II.

For scenario I, the CWT spectra were first visually inspected to identify frequency bands showing consistent dynamical changes during prolonged coagulation. For each selected band, an instantaneous band-energy contribution indicator $C(t)$ was computed. At each time point, total spectral energy $E_T(t)$ and band-specific energy $E_B(t)$ were calculated from the CWT matrix. The relative contribution was then defined as $C(t) = (E_B(t) \div E_T(t)) \times 100$. Repeating this procedure over time yielded a band-specific time-series indicator reflecting the relative energy contribution throughout coagulation. These indicators were analyzed to evaluate changes in VA dynamics during prolonged coagulation.

In scenario II, four indicators were extracted to characterize tissue-specific VA behavior. Two indicators were derived from the pre-processed time-domain VA signal. Indicator 1 captured energy evolution using a homomorphic envelope, followed by applying a low-pass filter to isolate the slow-varying amplitude component, yielding a time-series reflecting coagulation dynamics. Indicator 2 quantified transient activity by detecting peaks in the signal and applying a moving average filter to obtain a smoothed peak density time-series. Two remaining indicators were computed from the CWT representation. Indicator 3 was obtained by first scaling the CWT matrix to $[0, 1]$ and then averaging over time, emphasizing relative frequency structure independent of absolute energy. Indicator 4 was computed by averaging the original CWT matrix over time, providing information about the spectral energy distribution. In the final stage of data analysis in scenario II, the four indicator vectors from each trial were jointly embedded using Uniform Manifold Approximation and Projection (UMAP) as a descriptive visualization method, without label information [7]. UMAP was configured to generate a compact low-dimensional representation that preserves local structure in the data, using 3 nearest neighbors, a minimum distance of 0.1, and *Euclidean* metric. The resulting coordinates were then used as input to a k-Nearest Neighbors (kNN) classifier to assess supervised local label consistency and visualize class separation [21].

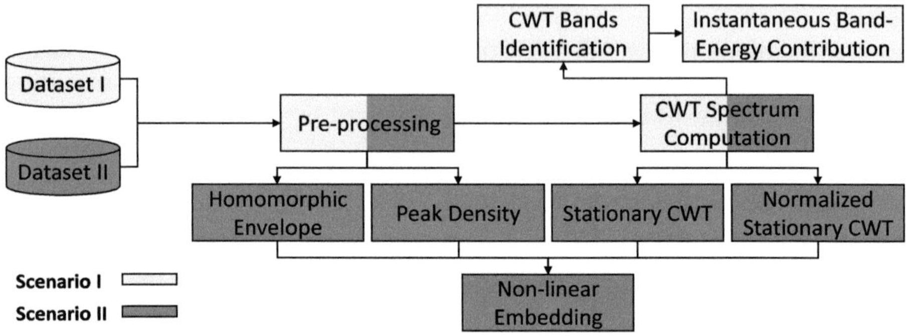

Fig. 2. The block diagram of VA data analysis for scenario I and II.

3 Results and Discussion

Figure 3 presents the results of scenario I, illustrating the temporal evolution of VA signals during prolonged liver coagulation. Figure 3(a) shows the CWT time-pseudo-frequency spectrum of a representative VA signal from the onset of electrosurgical activation to visually confirmed completion of tissue carbonization. The spectrum reveals systematic dynamical changes across three pseudo-frequency regions: low-frequency (LF, 1-200 Hz), mid-frequency (MF, 250-3000 Hz), and high-frequency (HF, 5000-12000 Hz). Figure 3(b-d) show the instantaneous band-energy contribution indicator (%) of the identified LF, MF, and HF bands. Joint inspection of these indicators and the CWT spectrum identifies two transition points (approximately 2.3 s and 7.5 s; marked red lines), dividing the signal into three phases (Ph) with distinct band dynamics. Ph1 is characterized by dominant LF activity and low HF contribution. In Ph2, HF increases markedly with strong LF attenuation while MF remains consistently active. In Ph3, HF decreases, LF increases again, and MF reduces relative to Ph2.

To evaluate whether these observations generalize across all 15 recordings in a quantitative way, each trial was manually and independently segmented into three phases based on the transition points observed in its CWT spectrum and band-energy contribution indicators. For each phase, the CWT spectrum was averaged over time to obtain a phase-specific stationary spectrum.

The spectral energy contribution of the LF, MF, and HF bands was then computed as the ratio between band-specific energy and total spectral energy (%). Figure 3(e) presents boxplots of these band-energy contributions, confirming consistent phase-dependent dynamics across trials, including HF increase in Ph2, dominant MF activity peaking in Ph2, and reduced LF contribution during Ph2. Additionally, total spectral energy within each phase was computed by integrating the segmented CWT spectrum over time and frequency. The boxplots in Fig. 3(f) demonstrate comparable total spectral energy levels in Ph1 and 2, whereas Ph3 shows a consistent reduction in overall VA energy, indicating a distinct change in signal behavior.

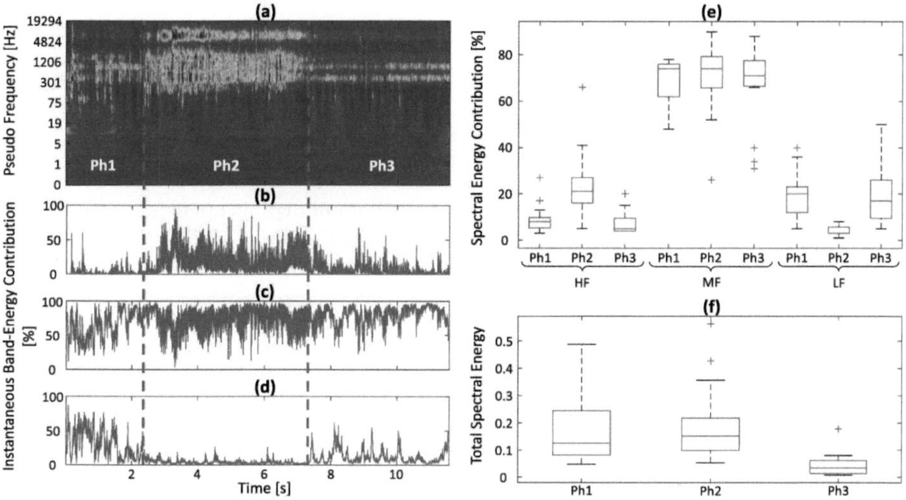

Fig. 3. Results of scenario I. (a): CWT spectrum, Instantaneous band-energy contribution indicator for (b): HF band, (c): MF band, (d): LF band, (e): Boxplot of spectral energy contribution, and (f): Boxplot of total spectral energy.

These findings confirm that VA signals evolve in a structured and reproducible manner during electrosurgical coagulation, exhibiting consistent transitions in band-specific dynamics that delineate distinct phases up to tissue carbonization. The observed phase-dependent changes appear consistent with thermally induced tissue transformations during electrosurgery, where heating can progress from early fluid-related effects to desiccation and protein coagulation and, with continued energy delivery, carbonization [3,11,19]. In Ph1, the clear transients reflect mechanically unstable events that could be associated with rapid water vaporization in highly hydrated tissue, such as liver. The marked increase in MF and HF contributions in Ph2 could correspond to tissue desiccation and coagulation, where progressive drying and structural stiffening alter the interaction dynamics and redistribute spectral energy. Finally, Ph3 aligns with direct visual inspection of the recorded video data confirming the onset of carbonization. This phase is accompanied by reduced total VA energy and altered band dynamics, indicating a distinct interaction regime once the tissue becomes carbonized.

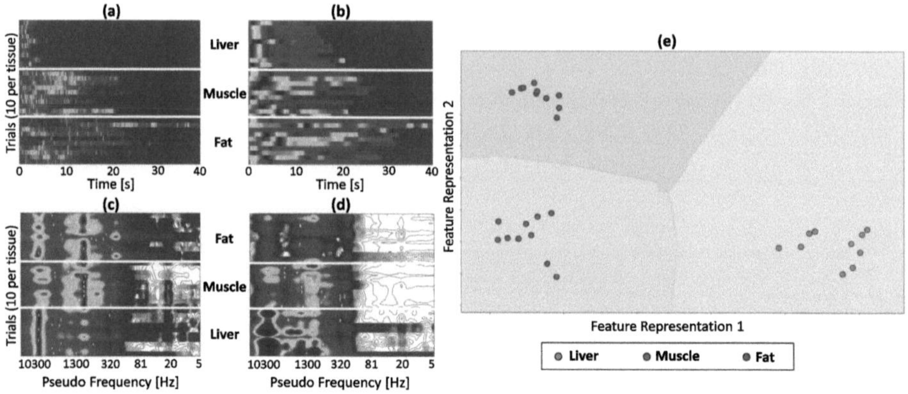

Fig. 4. Results of scenario II. (a): Indicator 1 (homomorphic envelop), (b): Indicator 2 (peak density), (c): Indicator 3 (normalized stationary CWT), (d): Indicator 4 (stationary CWT), and (e): UMAP visualization with kNN decision boundaries.

Figure 4 presents the results of scenario II based on all 30 VA signals acquired during electrosurgical coagulation of three tissue types. Each matrix corresponds to one indicator and consists of vectors from repeated trials per tissue, enabling global qualitative assessment of tissue-specific behavior. Indicator 1 (Fig. 4(a)) shows a rapid rise followed by fast decay for liver, indicating a short temporal response with most variation occurring early in coagulation. Muscle and fat show more gradual changes with longer-lasting signal intensity and slower decay. This suggests faster VA dynamics in liver compared to the more prolonged responses observed in muscle and fat. Indicator 2 (Fig. 4(b)) confirms this behavior. Liver shows concentrated transient activity early in coagulation, whereas muscle and fat display more distributed activity over time. These indicators reveal distinct temporal characteristics across tissues, with faster dynamics for liver, intermediate for muscle, and slower for fat. Indicator 3 (Fig. 4(c)) shows a narrow-band response dominated by a single frequency component for liver, indicating a relatively homogeneous vibration pattern. Muscle and fat exhibit broader spectra with mainly two dominant frequency components, indicating more complex vibration behavior, while fat shows slightly higher dominant frequency content than muscle. Indicator 4 (Fig. 4(d)) further reveals higher overall energy levels for liver compared to muscle and fat which is consistent with the faster and more concentrated signal activity observed in the time-domain indicators.

To further assess tissue differentiation, Fig. 4(e) shows the UMAP embedding of all indicators along with the corresponding kNN decision boundaries. The embedding reveals three compact, well-separated clusters corresponding to the three tissues. Clear decision boundaries without overlap indicate complete separability in the learned latent space, demonstrating that the extracted VA indicators enable robust tissue differentiation during electrosurgical coagulation. These results demonstrate that VA responses exhibit distinct and consistent tissue-specific patterns, reflecting reproducible signal characteristics of the tool-tissue interaction during electrosurgical coagulation that enable discrimination between tissue types based on their VA signatures.

4 Conclusion

In this study, we introduced VA sensing as a non-invasive, tool-agnostic modality for capturing state-dependent and tissue-specific responses during electrosurgery. We demonstrated that VA signals evolve systematically during prolonged coagulation, exhibiting reproducible phase transitions as response to tissue thermal changes up to carbonization. Furthermore, different tissue types generated consistent and distinct VA signatures, enabling discrimination based on their thermal response. Together, these findings position VA sensing as a promising approach to address the clinical challenge of perceiving and controlling tissue response during electrosurgery by providing objective information on tissue state progression and interaction dynamics. Although the observed VA phases align with expected thermally induced tissue changes, the biological interpretation is based on indirect evidence and requires validation. Future work will address this limitation through controlled thermal correlation studies, followed by extension to in vivo settings and evaluation of real-time clinical integration.

Acknowledgments. The authors would like to thank KARL STORZ SE & Co. KG (Tuttlingen, Germany) for providing the bipolar laparoscopic instrument and SURAG Medical GmbH (Leipzig, Germany) for providing the VA sensing system.

Disclosure of Interests. Nazila Esmaeili, Axel Boese and Alfredo Illanes are shareholders of SURAG Medical GmbH.

References

1. Abi Antoun, M., et al.: Outcomes of conventional and advanced energy devices in laparoscopic surgery: a systematic review. Minimally Invasive Ther. Allied Technol. **33**(1), 1–12 (2024)
2. Bao, C., Mazumder, S.K.: Output power computation and adaptation strategy of an electrosurgery inverter for reduced collateral tissue damage. IEEE Trans. Biomed. Eng. **70**(6), 1729–1740 (2022)
3. Bianchi, L., Cavarzan, F., Ciampitti, L., Cremonesi, M., Grilli, F., Saccomandi, P.: Thermophysical and mechanical properties of biological tissues as a function of temperature: a systematic literature review. Int. J. Hyperth. **39**(1), 297–340 (2022)
4. El-Sayed, M.M., Saridogan, E.: Principles and safe use of electrosurgery in minimally invasive surgery. Gynecol. Pelvic Med. **4**, 6 (2021)

5. El-Sayed, S., Saridogan, E., El-Sayed, M.: Complications of electrosurgery: mechanisms and prevention strategies. Facts Views Vis. ObGyn **16**(4), 473 (2024)
6. Esmaeili, N., et al.: Laparoscopic surgery augmentation through vibro-acoustic sensing of instrument-tissue interactions. Curr. Dir. Biomed. Eng. **9**(1) (2023)
7. Healy, J., McInnes, L.: Uniform manifold approximation and projection. Nat. Rev. Methods Primers **4**(1), 82 (2024)
8. Heryan, K., Serwatka, W., Rzepka, D., Fuentealba, P., Friebe, M.: Exploratory analysis and framework for tissue classification based on vibroacoustic signals from needle-tissue interaction. Int. J. Comput. Assist. Radiol. Surg. **20**(9), 1795–1806 (2025)
9. Lin, X., Fan, Q., Li, R., Chen, R., Yang, Z., Li, Y.: Enhancing laparoscopic visibility: efficient surgical smoke clearance innovatively using nebulization technology. Biomed. Eng. Online **24**(1), 65 (2025)
10. Massalimova, A., et al.: Automatic breach detection during spine pedicle drilling based on vibroacoustic sensing. Artif. Intell. Med. **144**, 102641 (2023)
11. Massarweh, N.N., Cosgriff, N., Slakey, D.P.: Electrosurgery: history, principles, and current and future uses. J. Am. Coll. Surg. **202**(3), 520–530 (2006)
12. Meneses Alves, T., Ferreira De Castro, L., Tomé, A., Ferreira, H.: Applications of different energy devices in laparoscopic and robotic gynecological surgery: a systematic review. Arch. Gynecol. Obstet. **312**(3), 691–719 (2025)
13. Messenger, D., Carter, F., Noble, E., Francis, N.: Electrosurgery and energized dissection. Surg. (Oxf.) **38**(3), 133–138 (2020)
14. Ostler, D., et al.: Acoustic signal analysis of instrument-tissue interaction for minimally invasive interventions. Int. J. Comput. Assist. Radiol. Surg. **15**(5), 771–779 (2020)
15. Ostler-Mildner, D., Wegener, L., Fuchtmann, J., Feussner, H., Wilhelm, D., Navab, N.: The sound of surgery-development of an acoustic trocar system enabling laparoscopic sound analysis. Int. J. Comput. Assist. Radiol. Surg. **19**(12), 2389–2397 (2024)
16. Rafiq, M.M., Ibeas, A., Ullah, N.: Expert knowledge-based peak current mode control of electrosurgical generators for improved output power regulation. J. Electr. Bioimpedance **14**(1), 32 (2023)
17. Sayahkarajy, M., Römer, F., Witte, H.: Vibroacoustic detection of inclusions in elastomer tissue phantom using MLP: a proof-of-concept. J. Mech. Behav. Biomed. Mater. 107279 (2025)
18. Seibold, M., et al.: A new sensing paradigm for the vibroacoustic detection of pedicle screw loosening. Med. Biol. Eng. Comput. **63**(4), 1001–1011 (2025)
19. Taheri, A., Mansoori, P., Sandoval, L.F., Feldman, S.R., Pearce, D., Williford, P.M.: Electrosurgery: part i. basics and principles. J. Am. Acad. Dermatol. **70**(4), 591–e1 (2014)
20. Tomov, V., Tabakov, S., Panov, G.: Modern advances in energy based electrosurgical devices. Electrotech. Electron. (E+ E) **52** (2017)
21. Wu, Y., Ianakiev, K., Govindaraju, V.: Improved k-nearest neighbor classification. Pattern Recogn. **35**(10), 2311–2318 (2002)

Where Is the Needle Tip? VA Sensing Reveals Hidden Needle-Tissue Transitions During US Guidance

Robin Urrutia[1,2(✉)], Nazila Esmaeili[3], Axel Boese[4], Sasan Matinfar[5,6], Nikolaos Davaris[7], Christoph Arens[7], Christian Hansen[1,2], and Alfredo Illanes[1,2]

[1] Faculty of Computer Science, Virtual and Augmented Reality, Otto von Guericke University Magdeburg, Universitätsplatz 2, 39106 Magdeburg, Germany
[2] Research Campus STIMULATE, Otto-Hahn-Str. 2, 39106 Magdeburg, Germany
robin.urrutia@ovgu.de
[3] Center for Digital Surgery, Department of General, Visceral and Pediatric Surgery, University Medical Center Göttingen, 37075 Göttingen, Germany
[4] Innovation Laboratory for Image Guided Therapy, Otto von Guericke University Magdeburg, Leipziger Str. 44, 39120 Magdeburg, Germany
[5] Chair for Social Affective Touch, Technische Universität Dresden, 01069 Dresden, Germany
[6] Computer Aided Medical Procedures (CAMP), Technical University of Munich, 85748 Munich, Germany
[7] Department of Otorhinolaryngology, Head and Neck Surgery, and Plastic Surgery, Justus Liebig University of Giessen, 35392 Giessen, Germany

Abstract. Reliable identification of tissue transitions during ultrasound-guided needle insertion remains challenging, particularly when needle-tip visibility is degraded by imaging geometry or acoustic artifacts. Most prior work focuses on spatial localization, while fewer approaches address mechanically meaningful events such as boundary crossing between adjacent tissues. This study investigates whether proximal vibroacoustic (VA) sensing can detect tissue transitions during insertion. VA signals recorded at the needle hub were analyzed using a time-frequency representation, and statistical similarity to tissue-specific reference segments was quantified using the first-order Wasserstein distance. Transition time was derived from a log-distance ratio signal indicating regime change. Experiments were conducted on 42 controlled insertions in a layered ex-vivo biological phantom with synchronized ultrasound (US) video. Results show consistent regime shifts at tissue boundaries and temporal agreement with US-based annotations across different visibility conditions. These findings indicate that proximal VA sensing captures mechanical interaction changes associated with tissue transitions and may provide complementary feedback during US-guided procedures.

Supplementary Information The online version contains supplementary material available at https://doi.org/10.1007/978-3-032-38236-8_59.

G. Yang et al. (Eds.): MICCAI 2026, LNCS 16893, pp. 616–625, 2027.
https://doi.org/10.1007/978-3-032-38236-8_59

Keywords: Vibroacoustic · Ultrasound needle guidance · Needle tracking

1 Introduction

Ultrasound-guided needle insertion is widely used in minimally invasive procedures such as biopsy, regional anesthesia, vascular access, and percutaneous therapy [6]. During these interventions, clinicians advance a needle toward a target under real-time ultrasound (US) imaging. Although US guidance is well established, accurate needle navigation remains technically demanding and strongly dependent on operator experience [9].

A critical moment during insertion is the crossing of a tissue boundary. As the needle traverses layered anatomical structures, it transitions between tissues with different mechanical properties [7,11]. Correct identification of these transitions is important for maintaining orientation, avoiding unintended structures, and safely reaching the target. However, reliable visualization of the needle tip in US is not always possible [10]. Tip visibility depends on insertion angle, imaging conditions, and artifacts such as speckle or shadowing [12]. In out-of-plane insertions or low-contrast settings, the exact transition moment may not be clearly visible, increasing reliance on indirect visual cues and haptic perception [1].

Most technological solutions for needle guidance focus on spatial localization [3]. Image-based methods attempt needle detection or segmentation in US images but may degrade under challenging imaging conditions. External tracking systems, including electromagnetic or optical navigation, provide additional spatial information [5], yet require dedicated hardware, calibration, and workflow integration [3], increasing setup time and procedural complexity [13]. Instrumented needles with embedded force sensors have also been explored [4,17]. While these approaches improve geometric tracking, they do not directly capture mechanical interaction changes occurring at tissue boundaries.

From a mechanical perspective, tissue transition involves altered interaction conditions at the needle tip [11]. Differences in stiffness and structure influence insertion dynamics and may generate vibrations that propagate along the needle shaft as structure-borne waves. These mechanically induced signals can be measured proximally, away from the contact point.

We refer to vibroacoustic (VA) sensing as the measurement of such signals at the needle hub, outside the patient's body. Because sensing occurs proximally, the distal needle geometry remains unmodified. The recorded signal reflects interaction dynamics and may provide information complementary to US imaging [8].

Previous studies have reported VA responses during needle insertion, demonstrating distinct signal patterns associated with structural transitions such as peritoneum puncture in cadaveric models, material changes in layered phantoms, and puncture or cavity events in layered synthetic phantoms [14,15]. Beyond needle insertion, VA tissue-instrument interaction signals have also been used for biological tissue differentiation during computerized palpation [16]. However, prior work has not systematically analyzed tissue-to-tissue transition events during continuous US-guided needle insertion in biological tissues, nor evaluated temporally localized changes in proximal VA measurements under varying US needle-tip visibility. It therefore remains unclear whether VA sensing can provide consistent information about boundary crossings during US-guided procedures.

In this work, we investigate proximal VA sensing as a complementary modality for tissue transition awareness during US-guided needle insertion. Synchronized US and VA recordings were acquired during controlled insertions into layered ex vivo tissues. A multiscale time-frequency representation and a regime-change detection framework were applied to identify transition points. The main contributions are twofold. First, we demonstrate that tissue-to-tissue transitions can be identified from proximal VA measurements, including cases with limited US needle-tip visibility. Second, we show that the VA signal exhibits stable intra-tissue regimes and distinct dynamical changes at boundary crossings. These findings support proximal VA sensing as a complementary perception channel and provide a foundation for interaction-based tissue characterization.

2 Methods

2.1 Experimental Setup and Data Acquisition

A total of 42 US-guided needle insertions were performed. Experiments were conducted using a multilayer phantom composed of two ex vivo biological tissues: bovine liver and chicken breast. The tissues were embedded in gelatin (Platinum Bloom 240) to provide structural support. The two tissue samples were positioned in direct contact with each other to create a defined tissue-to-tissue transition interface, allowing controlled insertion through consecutive biological layers. All insertions were performed using a 20G SPROTTE needle (Pajunk GmbH, Germany). VA signals generated during needle-tissue interaction were recorded using a proximal VA sensing module and acquisition system (SURAG Medical GmbH, Germany). The sensing module was connected directly to the needle hub via a standard luer-lock interface, without modification of the distal needle geometry (Fig. 1 - Components). The module communicated wirelessly via Bluetooth with a tablet computer (iPad, 10th generation), which served as the acquisition and storage unit of the system. Signals were visualized in real time and stored in WAV format at a sampling frequency of 16 kHz.

US imaging was performed using a B-mode system (GAMPT mbH, Germany) equipped with a 5 MHz linear probe. US videos were recorded at 60 frames per second. Synchronization between US and VA recordings was achieved by generating a common physical event visible in both modalities. At the beginning of each experiment, the needle was tapped three times against the US probe. These taps produced visible artifacts in the US image and corresponding peaks in the VA signal, enabling temporal alignment of both recordings.

From the recorded US videos, three time points were manually annotated: the time of first contact between the needle and the first ex vivo tissue (t_{entry}), the time of transition between the two biological tissues (t_{tc}), and the time at which

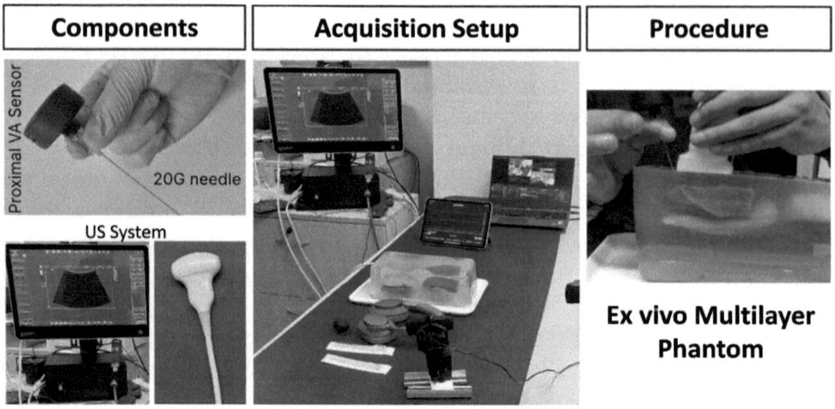

Fig. 1. Experimental setup for synchronized US and VA data acquisition, representing the components, acquisition setup, and procedure.

the needle exited the second ex vivo tissue (t_{exit}). Annotations were performed frame-by-frame using the recorded US videos.

2.2 Data Processing

The data processing strategy is to take needle insertion procedure as a transition between two interaction regimes corresponding to the two tissue types. VA signals are transformed into a time-frequency representation, and an interaction-sensitive frequency band is extracted to compute a one-dimensional indicator. The statistical behavior of this indicator within each tissue is characterized using reference segments. To track regime evolution over time, a sliding window is compared to these references using the first-order Wasserstein distance, which quantifies differences between empirical signal distributions and measures similarity to each tissue-specific regime [2]. The resulting log-ratio signal reflects similarity to either regime and enables identification of the tissue transition. In parallel, US video data are processed independently to derive a motion-based visibility indicator. This allows evaluation of VA-based transition detection under varying levels of needle-tip visibility. A schematic overview of the complete workflow is shown in Fig. 2. The VA signals were first preprocessed to remove DC components and reduce background noise. The DC component was removed by subtracting the signal mean. Noise reduction was performed using spectral gating: the spectrogram was computed, a frequency-dependent noise threshold was estimated, and a binary spectral mask was applied to suppress components below this threshold, yielding a denoised signal. A continuous wavelet transform (CWT) with a Morlet mother wavelet was applied to obtain a time-frequency representation. From the CWT spectrum, a pseudo-frequency band showing strong dynamical variations during insertion was selected. The corresponding CWT coefficients were averaged across scales to derive the one-dimensional temporal indicator $I_{\text{CWT}}(t)$.

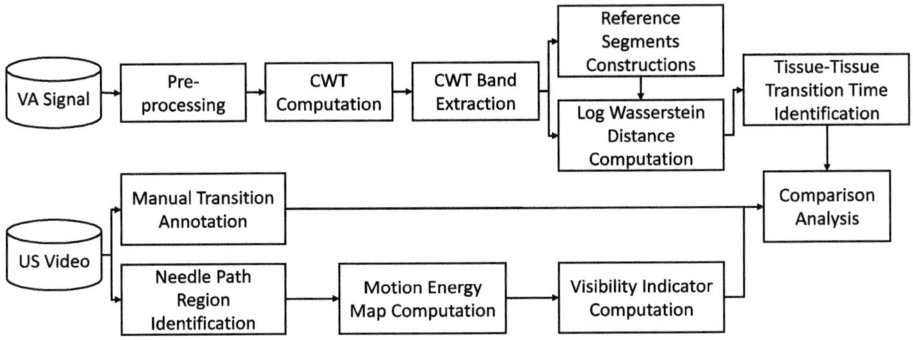

Fig. 2. Overview of the proposed processing framework.

Transition analysis was performed using a reference-based Wasserstein distance framework. For each recording, two reference segments were extracted from $I_{\mathrm{CWT}}(t)$. The first segment, denoted S_1, was selected within the interval $[t_{\mathrm{entry}} + 100\,\mathrm{ms}, t_{\mathrm{tc}} - 100\,\mathrm{ms}]$, corresponding to insertion within the first tissue. The second segment, denoted S_2, was selected within $[t_{\mathrm{tc}}+100\,\mathrm{ms}, t_{\mathrm{exit}}-100\,\mathrm{ms}]$, corresponding to insertion within the second tissue. Each segment had a duration of 300 ms. Prior to distance computation, segment values were normalized. A sliding window of 300 ms with 90% overlap was applied over $I_{\mathrm{CWT}}(t)$. For each window $W(t)$, two first-order Wasserstein distances were computed as $D_1(t) = \mathcal{W}\big(W(t), S_1\big)$ and $D_2(t) = \mathcal{W}\big(W(t), S_2\big)$, where $\mathcal{W}(\cdot,\cdot)$ denotes the Wasserstein distance between empirical distributions. A log-ratio signal was then defined as $R(t) = \log\left(\frac{D_1(t)}{D_2(t)}\right)$. Negative values of $R(t)$ indicate higher similarity to the first-tissue reference segment, while positive values indicate higher similarity to the second-tissue reference segment.

The transition time t^* was defined as the time instant at which $R(t)$ crossed zero with maximum slope in the vicinity of the regime change. For population-level analysis, each $R(t)$ signal was temporally aligned at t^* and normalized to the interval $[-1, 1]$ prior to averaging. To quantify agreement with US-based annotation, the absolute timing difference was computed as $|\Delta t| = |t^* - t_{\mathrm{tc}}|$ for each insertion.

Needle-tip visibility was quantified independently from the US video using motion analysis along the insertion path. First, the needle path was defined by manually annotating the initial and final visible tip positions and constructing a central insertion axis between them. A corridor of $\pm$ 35 pixels around this axis was retained to account for slight needle bending, while regions outside the corridor were excluded. Within this corridor, a motion energy map was computed to capture temporal intensity changes along the insertion direction. The corridor was divided into 200 equally spaced patches along the axis. For each frame, squared frame-to-frame intensity differences were calculated within each patch, yielding a time-resolved spatial distribution of motion energy that highlights localized motion along the needle path. From this motion energy map, a visibility indicator was derived by extracting, for each frame, the maximum motion energy value across all patches.

When the needle tip is clearly visible and advancing, localized motion energy is concentrated along the axis, resulting in higher indicator values. When the tip is poorly visible, motion energy decreases and the indicator correspondingly drops. For each insertion, the median value of the visibility indicator over the insertion interval was used to assign the recording to one of three visibility groups (high, medium, or low) using empirically selected thresholds. These visibility groups were subsequently used to analyze the consistency of VA transition detection under varying levels of US visibility.

3 Results and Discussion

Figure 3 presents qualitative examples from three insertions with good, medium, and low needle-tip visibility in US. The three columns correspond to individual recordings, and the five rows show different signal representations. Row (a) displays the time-position motion energy map within the predefined needle corridor, and row (b) the corresponding visibility indicator. Row (c) shows the VA CWT spectrum, with dashed white lines marking the pseudo-frequency band used to compute the CWT-band indicator $I_{\mathrm{CWT}}(t)$ in row (d). Row (e) presents the log-ratio signal based on the Wasserstein distances to the two tissue reference segments. Green dashed lines indicate the US-based manual annotations t_{entry}, t_{tc}, and t_{exit}. Rows (a-b) demonstrate the variability of US visibility across recordings. In the good-visibility example, a clear diagonal motion-energy trace is visible throughout the insertion. In the medium-visibility case, the trace weakens around the expected transition region. In the low-visibility example, motion energy remains low across the entire insertion, indicating poor needle-tip visibility. Despite these differences, the VA analysis shows consistent behavior around the tissue transition.

The CWT spectra in row (c) indicate that the main excitation changes occur in the low pseudo-frequency range (5-120 Hz), used to compute $I_{\mathrm{CWT}}(t)$. The indicator in row (d) shows a clear change around t_{tc} in all cases. The log-ratio Wasserstein signal in row (e) reveals two distinct regimes separated by an abrupt change near t_{tc}, even when the transition is not clearly visible in US. Small temporal differences between the annotated t_{tc} and the detected time t^* (black dotted line) are expected under uncertain US-based tip annotation and are further analyzed in Fig. 3.

Figure 4 shows a population-level comparison of US visibility and VA regime behavior across all 42 insertions. The left heatmap presents the visibility indicator for each insertion, sorted from highest to lowest visibility, with time normalized between needle entry and exit. Visibility decreases from top to bottom, and several recordings show very low motion energy throughout. The right heatmap displays the corresponding log-ratio Wasserstein signals in the same order. Signals were temporally normalized and aligned so that the detected transition time t is centered at zero.

A clear regime separation is visible across all recordings, with negative values before and positive values after the transition. The sharpness and contrast of this change remain comparable even in low-visibility cases, indicating that the VA regime transition is consistently identifiable independent of US visibility. Figure 5(b) presents the absolute timing difference $|\Delta t| = |t - t_{tc}|$ between VA-based transition detection and US-based manual annotation, grouped by visibility level. Timing differences are smallest in high-visibility cases and increase for medium and low visibility, consistent with greater uncertainty in US annotation when the needle tip is poorly visible. Importantly, the VA regime change

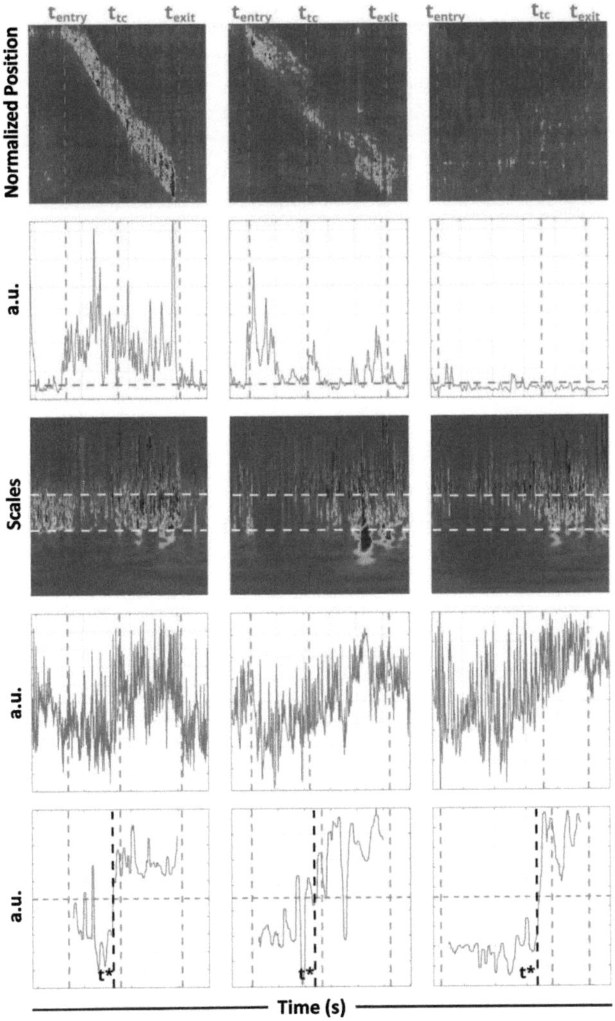

Fig. 3. Qualitative results of three US-guided insertions with good (left), medium (middle), and low (right) needle-tip visibility. Each row represents one indicator.

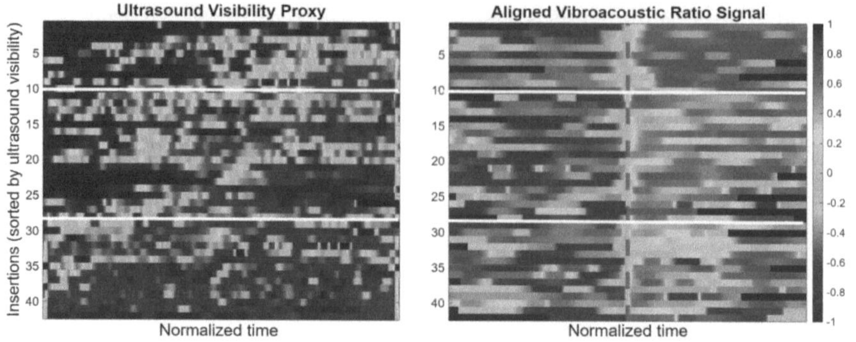

Fig. 4. Population-level comparison of US visibility and VA regime behavior. Left: visibility indicator. Right: corresponding log-ratio Wasserstein signals for the same insertions.

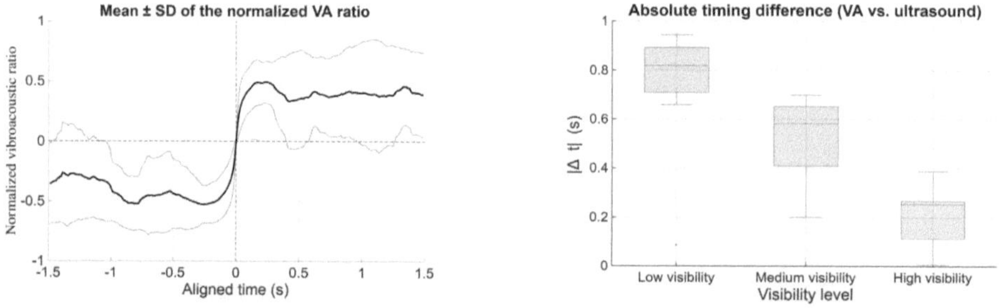

(a) (b)

Fig. 5. Timing agreement between VA transition detection and US-based annotation. (a): Signed timing difference across all insertions. (b): Absolute timing difference grouped by US visibility level (low, medium, and high).

remains identifiable across all visibility levels (Fig. 5(a)), indicating a consistent change in interaction dynamics even when visual confirmation is limited.

4 Conclusions

This study investigated VA sensing as a complementary modality for tissue-transition awareness during US-guided needle insertion. By modeling the VA signal as a sequence of interaction regimes and quantifying distributional similarity using the Wasserstein distance, we showed that distinct dynamical behaviors occur in different tissue types. Tissue transitions were consistently reflected by abrupt regime changes in the log-ratio indicator. The VA regime change remained identifiable across varying US visibility levels. Although timing differences between VA detection and US annotation increased under low-visibility conditions, this is consistent with greater uncertainty in manual tip identification. These findings indicate that proximal VA sensing provides mechanically derived transition information independent of visual contrast. Overall, VA measurements can augment needle guidance by providing complementary transition awareness when visual feedback is limited. Future work will focus on tighter integration of VA and US modalities. In particular, combining motion-energy analysis with VA regime indicators may allow compensation for visibility gaps and improved estimation of needle progression.

Acknowledgments. The work presented in this paper was funded by the European Regional Development Fund under operation number ZS/2023/12/182010, as part of the initiative "Sachsen-Anhalt WISSENSCHAFT Schwerpunkte" and was also supported by ANID (Chile) through its scholarship program Becas Chile/DAAD 2023-62230039. The authors would like to thank SURAG Medical GmbH for providing the vibroacoustic sensing system.

Disclosure of Interests. Nazila Esmaeili, Axel Boese and Alfredo Illanes are shareholders of SURAG Medical GmbH.

References

1. Arif, M., Moelker, A., van Walsum, T.: Needle Tip Visibility in 3D Ultrasound Images. Cardiovasc. Intervent. Radiol. **41**(1), 145–152 (2017). https://doi.org/10.1007/s00270-017-1798-7
2. Cazelles, E., Robert, A., Tobar, F.: The wasserstein-fourier distance for stationary time series. IEEE Trans. Signal Process. **69**, 709–721 (2020). https://doi.org/10.1109/TSP.2020.3046227
3. Cheng, Z., Koskinopoulou, M., Bano, S., Stoyanov, D., Rajeeth Savarimuthu, T., Mattos, L.S.: Sensing technologies for guidance during needle-based interventions. IEEE Trans. Instrum. Meas. **73**, 1–15 (2024). https://doi.org/10.1109/TIM.2024.3441017
4. Elayaperumal, S., Bae, J.H., Daniel, B.L., Cutkosky, M.R.: Detection of membrane puncture with haptic feedback using a tip-force sensing needle. In: 2014 IEEE/RSJ International Conference on Intelligent Robots and Systems. pp. 3975–3981. IEEE (2014). https://doi.org/10.1109/IROS.2014.6943121
5. Franz, A.M., Haidegger, T., Birkfellner, W., Cleary, K., Peters, T.M., Maier-Hein, L.: Electromagnetic tracking in medicine–a review of technology, validation, and applications. IEEE Trans. Med. Imaging **33**(8), 1702–1725 (2014). https://doi.org/10.1109/TMI.2014.2321777
6. Fukui, S., et al.: Current evidence and practical knowledge for ultrasound-guided procedures in rheumatology: Joint aspiration, injection, and other applications. Best Practice & Research Clinical Rheumatology **37**(1), 101832 (2023). https://doi.org/10.1016/j.berh.2023.101832
7. van Gerwen, D.J., Dankelman, J., van den Dobbelsteen, J.J.: Needle-tissue interaction forces-a survey of experimental data. Medical engineering & physics **34**(6), 665–680 (2012). https://doi.org/10.1016/j.medengphy.2012.04.007
8. Illanes, A.: Novel clinical device tracking and tissue event characterization using proximally placed audio signal acquisition and processing. Sci. Rep. **8**, 1–11 (2018). https://doi.org/10.1038/s41598-018-30641-0

9. Marhofer, P., Chan, V.W.: Ultrasound-guided regional anesthesia: current concepts and future trends. Anesthesia & Analgesia **104**(5), 1265–1269 (2007). https://doi.org/10.1213/01.ane.0000260614.32794.7b
10. Neal, J.M.: Ultrasound-guided regional anesthesia and patient safety: update of an evidence-based analysis. Regional Anesthesia & Pain Medicine **41**(2), 195–204 (2016). https://doi.org/10.1097/AAP.0000000000000295
11. Okamura, A.M., Simone, C., O'leary, M.D.: Force modeling for needle insertion into soft tissue. IEEE transactions on biomedical engineering **51**(10), 1707–1716 (2004). https://doi.org/10.1109/TBME.2004.831542
12. Quien, M.M., Saric, M.: Ultrasound imaging artifacts: How to recognize them and how to avoid them. Echocardiography **35**(9), 1388–1401 (2018). https://doi.org/10.1111/echo.14116
13. Scholten, H.J., Pourtaherian, A., Mihajlovic, N., Korsten, H.H., A. Bouwman, R.: Improving needle tip identification during ultrasound-guided procedures in anaesthetic practice. Anaesthesia **72**(7), 889–904 (2017). https://doi.org/10.1111/anae.13921
14. Spiller, M., et al.: Enhancing veress needle entry with proximal vibroacoustic sensing for automatic identification of peritoneum puncture. Diagnostics **14**(15), 1698 (2024). https://doi.org/10.3390/diagnostics14151698
15. Steeg, K., et al.: Vibroacoustic signatures: proof of concept for simple material characterization during needle interventions. Int. J. Comput. Assist. Radiol. Surg. **20**(9), 1807–1815 (2025). https://doi.org/10.1007/s11548-025-03492-0
16. Sühn, T., et al.: Vibro-acoustic sensing of tissue-instrument-interactions allows a differentiation of biological tissue in computerised palpation. Comput. Biol. Med. **164**, 107272 (2023). https://doi.org/10.1016/j.compbiomed.2023.107272
17. Trejos, A., Patel, R., Naish, M.: Force sensing and its application in minimally invasive surgery and therapy: a survey. Proc. Inst. Mech. Eng. C J. Mech. Eng. Sci. **224**(7), 1435–1454 (2010). https://doi.org/10.1243/09544062JMES1917

Wrist Camera Pose-Guided Multi-view Fusion for Occlusion Reconstruction in Robot-Assisted Microsurgical Anastomosis

Xinyao Zhou[1,2], Yuxuan Liu[1,2], Yating Luo[1,2], Yunfei Luan[1,2], Guang-Zhong Yang[1,2], and Yao Guo[1,2](✉)

[1] Institute of Medical Robotics, School of Biomedical Engineering, Shanghai Jiao Tong University, Shanghai, China
{zhou_xinyao,20000905lyx,gzyang,yao.guo}@sjtu.edu.cn
[2] Shanghai Key Laboratory of Flexible Medical Robotics, Tongren Hospital, Shanghai Jiao Tong University, Shanghai, China

Abstract. Precise visual perception is a cornerstone of safety and efficacy in embodied robot-assisted surgery. However, the intricate operations of microsurgical anastomosis solely through the global vision system are often plagued by severe occlusions of frequent instrument-tissue interactions, which severely hinder the visibility of micro-scale structures like suturing threads. To tackle this challenge, we introduce the Pose-Guided Geometry-Aware Transformer, a novel framework for occlusion-aware reconstruction by leveraging a wrist-mounted camera configuration for surgical robots. Specifically, we first curate a multi-view dataset with well-calibrated wrist camera poses. By introducing an implicit camera pose encoding mechanism, our proposed method is able to effectively fuse geometric priors into the framework, facilitating robust cross-view alignment and feature aggregation. Such design exhibits superior robustness to diverse occlusion ratios and numbers of multi-view inputs, enabling the reconstruction of occluded regions with complementary wrist perspectives. Our method establishes a new multi-view benchmark for suturing thread recognition in microsurgical anastomosis and significantly outperforms the current state-of-the-art approaches. This work emphasizes the importance of the wrist-camera pose in multi-view fusion, providing a paradigm-shifting approach to occlusion recovery and fine-grained visual perception for surgical robotics.

Keywords: Multi-view Fusion · Occlusion Recovery · Surgical Robotics

1 Introduction

Precise visual perception of fine anatomical and interventional structures is a prerequisite for safe and effective robot-assisted surgery [1,11,24]. In microsur-

X. Zhou and Y. Liu—Equal contribution.

G. Yang et al. (Eds.): MICCAI 2026, LNCS 16893, pp. 626–636, 2027.
https://doi.org/10.1007/978-3-032-38236-8_60

gical anastomosis, the accurate segmentation of suturing threads is of particular importance. Unlike large, well-defined organs, surgical sutures are thin, highly deformable, and exhibit complex topological configurations. High-quality segmentation of such small structures is critical not only for awareness of intra-operative situation awareness [9] but also for enabling downstream capabilities such as autonomous suturing [13,29], motion planning [22]. However current segmentation approaches, ranging from general large foundation models [15] to task-specific frameworks [8], are often inadequate for surgical sutures shown in Fig. 1-(b), as their slender morphology and complicate topology frequently lead to fragmented predictions or a complete failure to infer the geometry of occluded segments. With the rapid evolution of embodied artificial intelligence [10], surgical embodied robots have featured hardware configurations similar to general-purpose humanoid agents with dual-arm and primary global views [4,6]. However, the strategic utilization of wrist-mounted perspectives remains fundamentally under-explored. In this work, we address this gap by focusing on the microsurgical anastomosis paradigm, where we harness complementary visual streams from wrist cameras to achieve robust perception and fine-grained segmentation of sutures under challenging occlusions. Leveraging multiple wrist views [2] makes the segments occluded in the primary view easily captured by them, thus enabling the reconstruction of self-occluded structures, shown in the Fig. 1-(c).

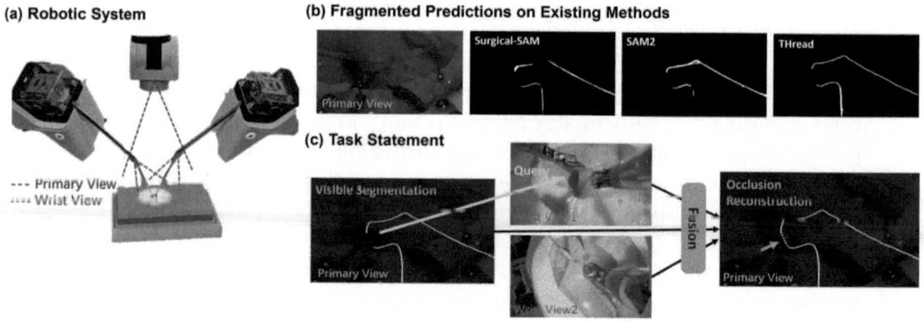

Fig. 1. (a): The surgical robot configurations with one primary camera and two wrist cameras. (b): Performances with methods Surgical-SAM [8], SAM2 [15], THread [30]. (c): The overview of our task to reconstruct the occluded segments.

Existing occlusion-handling strategies can be broadly divided into single-view completion and multi-view fusion. Single-view approaches, whether leveraging geometric priors [21,30] or generative inpainting [25,26], remain fundamentally limited by the information available in one perspective and degrade rapidly under large-scale occlusions. Multi-view reconstruction offers a principled alternative by aggregating complementary information across viewpoints [17]. However, unlike the fixed camera arrays in autonomous driving [7,28], wrist-mounted cameras on surgical robots undergo arbitrary 6-DoF motions, introducing extreme pose diversity that renders naïve feature alignment ineffective. A pose-aware fusion mechanism is therefore essential.

In this paper, we investigate the potential of integrating camera pose encoding within transformer architectures to facilitate robust wrist-view fusion. We propose cross-view alignment module, leveraging camera pose priors to simultaneously inject 3D perspective cues and 2D geometric information into each patch embedding. This enables the network to learn cross-view correspondences, thus significantly enhancing the performance of occlusion reconstruction. We curate the first multiple wrist-view occlusion dataset and evaluate our proposed method across different occlusion ratios and perspective counts, where our method demonstrates leading performance. To the best of our knowledge, this work represents the first attempt to explore multi-view information fusion specifically from the wrist-mounted perspectives, showing potential in wider applications for surgical robotic manipulation and perception tasks.

2 Methods

The proposed model accepts an input set of $\{(\mathbf{V}_i, \mathbf{K}_i, \mathbf{R}_i, \mathbf{t}_i)\}_{i=1}^{M}$, where $\mathbf{V_i} \in \mathbb{R}^{H\times W\times 3}$ denotes the input wrist-camera image, $\mathbf{K}_i \in \mathbb{R}^{3\times 3}$ and $[\mathbf{R}_i|\mathbf{t}_i] \in \mathbb{R}^{3\times 4}$ represent the associated camera intrinsics and extrinsics for M views, respectively. In order to simulate the occlusion in the primary view, we implement Proactive Occlusion Masking to manually impose masking. Our objective is to leverage $M-1$ complementary wrist perspectives to perform surgical suture segmentation and reconstruct occluded structures within the primary view. As shown in Fig. 2, the framework is structured into a two-stage pipeline: feature-level alignment pre-training, followed by fine-tuning for the downstream task. We employ DINOv3 [19] as the backbone, capitalizing on its pre-trained fine-grained perceptual capabilities for feature extraction. Within the Cross-view Alignment Module, both camera intrinsic and extrinsic parameters are encoded and injected into the Transformer architecture alongside Rotary Positional Embedding (RoPE) [20], facilitating the implicit learning of geometric feature alignment. This cross-view alignment capability provides significant potential for generalization across segmentation and other visual perception tasks.

2.1 Proactive Occlusion Masking

In practical surgical scenarios, instrument-induced self-occlusion is typically centrally localized within the operative field and varies in scale, posing an inherent paradox for ground-truth acquisition. Since occluded regions are unobservable by the hardware setup, obtaining accurate training labels is fundamentally impossible. To circumvent this challenge, we propose a Proactive Occlusion Masking strategy, where we apply deliberate masks to occlusion-free target images and force the network to reconstruct features within these regions. It ensures absolute label fidelity by allowing us to annotate raw images before simulating occlusion, and it also enables us to manipulate various mask ratios to make

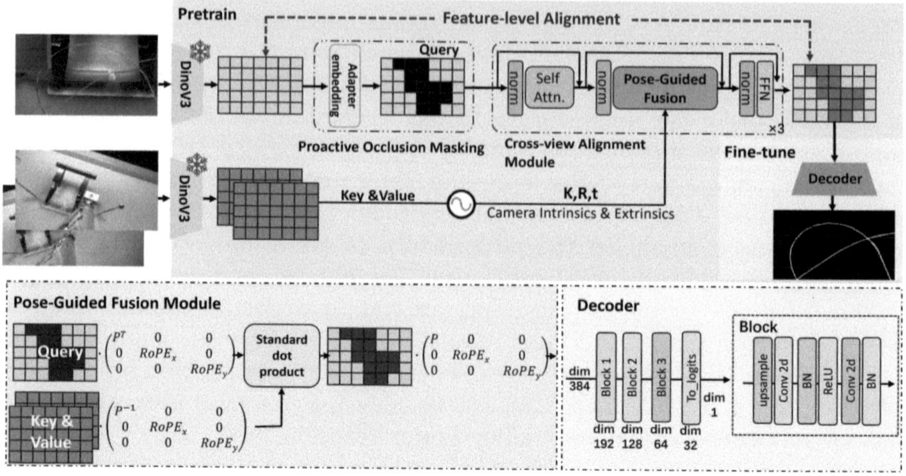

Fig. 2. Overview of the model architecture. During the pre-training phase, features of the primary view via proactive occlusion masking serve as the Query, while concatenated features from wrist views constitute the Key and Value. Cross-view Alignment Module incorporates encoded camera intrinsics and extrinsics to achieve occlusion reconstruction. The final high-fidelity segmentation masks are generated during the downstream fine-tuning stage.

the network learn robust correspondences across various viewpoints. Proactive masking can be implemented at either the image or feature level. Given that we utilize DINOv3 pre-trained weights, imposing rigid image-level masks would cause a distribution shift from natural images and introduce undesirable artifacts at feature boundaries. Thus we adopt patch-level masking scheme within the feature space where, unlike the discrete and scattered patterns of masked image modeling [3,14,16], our generated masks are spatially contiguous and centrally clustered to emulate the surgical instrument interference.

2.2 Revisiting the Camera Parameters

In contrast to conventional multi-view fusion and occlusion completion methods that rely on fixed viewpoints, the relative spatial relationships between our 6-DoF wrist perspectives vary arbitrarily across diverse poses hence relative camera pose guidance is indispensable for robust perception. Both intrinsics and extrinsics of each image are represented as the projection matrix $\mathbf{P}_i = \mathbf{K}_i[\mathbf{R}_i|\mathbf{t}_i] \in \mathbb{R}^{3\times4}$. For notational convenience, these 3×4 projection matrices can be made invertible by lifting to $\tilde{\mathbf{P}}_i \in \mathbb{R}^{4\times4}$ with the standard basis vector. It can be used to compute 2D image coordinates from world coordinates $[\tilde{\mathbf{x}}_i \ 1]^T \propto \tilde{\mathbf{P}}_i\tilde{\mathbf{X}}_{\text{world}}$, where $\tilde{\mathbf{x}}_i \in \mathbb{R}^3$ and $\tilde{\mathbf{X}}_{\text{world}} \in \mathbb{R}^4$ are homogeneous coordinates in the image and world respectively. Consequently, the geometric correspondence between the image coordinates in two distinct viewpoints can be easily established as: $\left[\tilde{\mathbf{x}}_i\ 1\right]^T = (\tilde{\mathbf{P}}_i\tilde{\mathbf{P}}_j^{-1})\left[\tilde{\mathbf{x}}_j\ 1\right]^T = \mathbf{M}_{i,j}\left[\tilde{\mathbf{x}}_j\ 1\right]^T$, where $\mathbf{M}_{i,j} \in \mathbb{R}^{4\times 4}$ denotes the relative projection matrix. It can be easily proved that $\mathbf{M}_{i,j}$ remains independent of the choice of world coordinate, as it exclusively encapsulates the relative geometric relationships. Given the inherent permutation invariance of the Transformer architecture [23], positional embeddings like RoPE are essential for the model to perceive the 2D spatial arrangement of image patches. Inspired by [5], we propose to integrate the relative camera pose $\mathbf{M}_{i,j}$ with RoPE, thereby injecting 3D spatial-geometric priors into 2D patch embeddings. Standard dot product attention is $\text{Attn}(Q, K, V) = \text{softmax}\left(\frac{Q^T K}{\sqrt{d}}\right)V$, where $Q \in \mathbb{R}^{s\times d}$, K and $V \in \mathbb{R}^{(M-1)s\times d}$, $M-1$ denotes the number of wrist views. In this work, we formulate a projection matrix $\mathbf{D}_i$ by integrating the normalized camera projection matrix $\mathbf{P}$ and the RoPE parameters: $\mathbf{D} = \begin{bmatrix} \mathbf{I}_{d/8}\otimes\mathbf{P} & \mathbf{0} & \mathbf{0} \\ \mathbf{0} & RoPE_x & \mathbf{0} \\ \mathbf{0} & \mathbf{0} & RoPE_y \end{bmatrix}_{d\times d}$, where $RoPE_x, RoPE_y \in \mathbb{R}^{\frac{d}{4}\times\frac{d}{4}}, \mathbf{I}_{d/8}\otimes\mathbf{P} \in \mathbb{R}^{\frac{d}{2}\times\frac{d}{2}}$. We denote the batched matrix-vector product as $\circledcirc$, the Kronecker product as $\otimes$, and the identity matrix of size k as $\mathbf{I}_k \in \mathbb{R}^{k\times k}$. The total dimensionality of $\mathbf{D}$ is defined to align with the feature dimension d. $\mathbf{D}_i$ is subsequently injected into the Query, Key, and Value representations within the attention layers and further incorporated into the final output for numerical stability:

$$\begin{aligned} \text{Attn}^r(Q, K, V) &= \mathbf{D}_w \circledcirc \text{Attn}(\mathbf{D}_o \circledcirc Q,\ \mathbf{D}_w^{-1} \circledcirc K,\ \mathbf{D}_w^{-1} \circledcirc V) \\ &= \mathbf{D}_w(\text{softmax}\left(\frac{Q^T(\mathbf{D}_o^T\mathbf{D}_w^{-1})K}{\sqrt{d}}\right)\mathbf{D}_w^{-1}V), \end{aligned} \tag{1}$$

where $\mathbf{D}_o, \mathbf{D}_w$ denote the matrix for the occluded perspective and wrist perspectives, respectively. $(\mathbf{D}_o^T\mathbf{D}_w^{-1})_{\frac{d}{2}} = \mathbf{I}_{d/8}\otimes\mathbf{M}_{o,w}$ plays a crucial role in relative pose guided fusion.

2.3 Training Framework and Loss Functions

Our training procedure follows a two-stage training strategy, including multi-view feature alignment pre-training and task-specific fine-tuning for the downstream segmentation. Throughout the entire training process, the DINOv3 backbone weights are kept frozen. During pre-training we optimize our framework using a composite loss function containing Cosine Similarity Loss ($\mathcal{L}_{\text{cos}}$), InfoNCE Loss ($\mathcal{L}_{\text{nce}}$) [12] and Gradient Constraint Loss ($\mathcal{L}_{\text{grad}}$). $\mathcal{L}_{\text{cos}}$ is employed to enforce directional consistency between the reconstructed feature vectors and the pristine features extracted from occlusion-free target images. $\mathcal{L}_{\text{nce}}$ prevents feature collapse by contrasting masked patches against a dictionary of global context. $\mathcal{L}_{\text{grad}}$ explicitly penalizes inconsistencies in structural details and edge gradients, ensuring the network maintains sharp boundaries for fine-grained suture segmentation. During the fine-tune stage, the pretrained encoder is frozen for one epoch to allow for initial convergence of the decoder module, after which the encoder except backbone is fully unfrozen. To ensure the topological connectivity and width consistency of the fine-grained suture structures, we employ the clDice loss [18], which implements a cross-constraint between the soft-skeleton and the volume. The topology precision T_{prec} measures the fraction of the predicted skeleton that aligns with the ground-truth region, whereas the topology sensitivity T_{sens} assesses how well the ground-truth skeleton is captured by the predicted volume. By focusing on centerline alignment, clDice effectively enhances the reconstruction of slender sutures under challenging occlusions. The combined loss functions are formulated as the weighted sum of individual terms:

$$\mathcal{L}_{\text{pretrain}} = \lambda_{\text{cos}}\mathcal{L}_{\text{cos}} + \lambda_{\text{nce}}\mathcal{L}_{\text{nce}} + \lambda_{\text{grad}}\mathcal{L}_{\text{grad}}, \; \mathcal{L}_{seg} = 1 - \frac{2 \cdot T_{prec} \cdot T_{sens}}{T_{prec} + T_{sens}}. \quad (2)$$

3 Experiments and Results

3.1 Dataset and Settings

Given the absence of specialized datasets for fine-grained surgical sutures occlusion recovery, we have meticulously curated and annotated a novel Multiple Wrist-view occlusion dataset from a robotic suturing platform, featuring fine-grained suture segmentation masks and well-calibrated camera poses. The dataset comprises 12 video sequences corresponding to 12 static top views and approximately 17,000 wrist-camera images at a resolution of 1280 × 720. This collection is partitioned into validation and testing sets, each consisting of two sequences and totaling roughly 3,000 images per set. Camera poses were rigorously calibrated using either calibration patterns or robotic kinematics, ensuring the reprojection error less than 0.5 pixels across all sequences. The dataset is accessible at https://github.com/Zoeric80/Multiple-Wrist-view-Microsurgical-Anastomosis-Occlusion-Dataset.

While our architecture is capable of processing high-resolution images, we resize the input images to 640×352 to balance computational efficiency with the architectural of DINOv3. Based on our empirical evaluations, we set the weight $\lambda_{\text{cos}} = \lambda_{\text{grad}} = 1, \lambda_{\text{nce}} = 0.1$. We pretrained on the Realestate dataset with a batch size of 4 for 35 epochs. All experiments are implemented on an NVIDIA RTX A6000 GPU. For the segmentation, we report five metrics, including the Dice coefficient (Dice↑), Peak Signal-to-Noise Ratio (PSNR↑), Intersection over Union (IoU↑), L1 distance (L1↓), and centerlineDice (clDice↑).

3.2 Comparison Results

Table. 1 compares the performance of proposed method with several state-of-the-art baselines under various mask ratios. Among these, AOT-GAN [26] and CRFill [27] represent inpainting-based approaches, while THread [30] leverages spatial context and geometric topology. Our method consistently demonstrates superior performance across all occlusion levels. At lower masking ratios, THread achieve favorable results, particularly in the clDice metric. However, their efficacy degrades rapidly as the occlusion area expands. Conversely, while AOT-GAN maintain higher image similarity under heavy occlusion, they often yield inaccurate geometric structures. While our framework ensures higher geometric fidelity, the predictive confidence for fine-grained details naturally decreases as the masking ratio increases. Qualitative results are visualized in Fig. 3. As occlusion levels increase, inpainting-based approaches tend to produce significantly more erroneous geometric structures, but our method demonstrates remarkable robustness in maintaining topological fidelity.

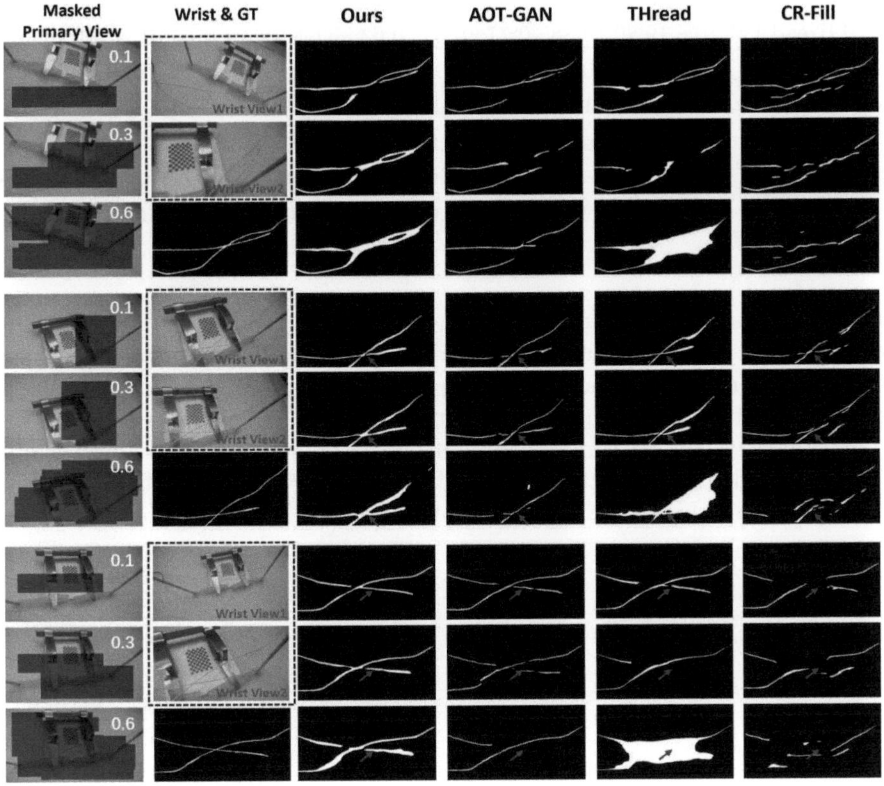

Fig. 3. Qualitative comparison results of our proposed method and other state-of-the-art baselines under various masking ratios. We utilize a dual-view fusion setup, which achieves the optimal performance.

3.3 Ablation Studies

As illustrated in Fig. 4, two sets of ablation experiments were conducted to validate the impact of view count and the camera pose encoding module. The vanilla

Table 1. Quantitative Comparisons of the Proposed Method With State-of-the-Art Models on the Dataset. The **bold** and <u>underline</u> results reported in the tables indicate the best and the second best performances. η denotes the mask ratios.

Methods	η	PSNR ↑	Dice ↑	IOU ↑	L_1 ↓	clDice ↑
AOT [26]	10%	19.08±1.30	0.68±0.12	0.52±0.12	0.64±0.24	0.76±0.15
	30%	<u>18.16±1.37</u>	0.60±0.14	0.44±0.14	<u>0.80±0.29</u>	0.66±0.18
	60%	<u>16.74±1.26</u>	<u>0.43±0.15</u>	<u>0.28±0.13</u>	<u>1.08±0.31</u>	0.46±0.17
CR-Fill [27]	10%	18.15±1.54	0.61±0.13	0.45±0.13	0.80±0.30	0.69±0.16
	30%	16.87±1.43	0.49±0.13	0.34±0.12	1.06±0.33	0.55±0.16
	60%	15.47±1.16	0.32±0.11	0.19±0.08	1.43±0.35	0.35±0.12
THread [30]	10%	<u>19.80±0.88</u>	<u>0.77±0.04</u>	<u>0.63±0.04</u>	<u>0.52±0.12</u>	**0.87±0.03**
	30%	17.83±0.84	<u>0.67±0.07</u>	<u>0.51±0.08</u>	0.82±0.20	**0.79±0.06**
	60%	11.19±1.04	0.33±0.06	0.19±0.04	3.86±1.30	<u>0.55±0.07</u>
Ours	10%	**20.15±0.32**	**0.77±0.03**	**0.64±0.06**	**0.46±0.06**	<u>0.86±0.03</u>
	30%	**19.16±0.45**	**0.71±0.03**	**0.55±0.04**	**0.58±0.07**	<u>0.78±0.05</u>
	60%	**17.15±0.56**	**0.55±0.06**	**0.38±0.05**	**0.92±0.10**	**0.59±0.07**

baseline adopts the same architecture and two-stage training strategy, with only the pose-guided encoding removed (RoPE retained). Results show that integrating pose encoding consistently outperforms the vanilla baseline across all view configurations, with peak performance at two wrist views. Insufficient views fail to capture occluded targets, while excessive views introduce noise, leading to coarser predictions. Furthermore, a dual-view setup aligns with mainstream embodied robotic hardware configurations. Conversely, the vanilla model's per-

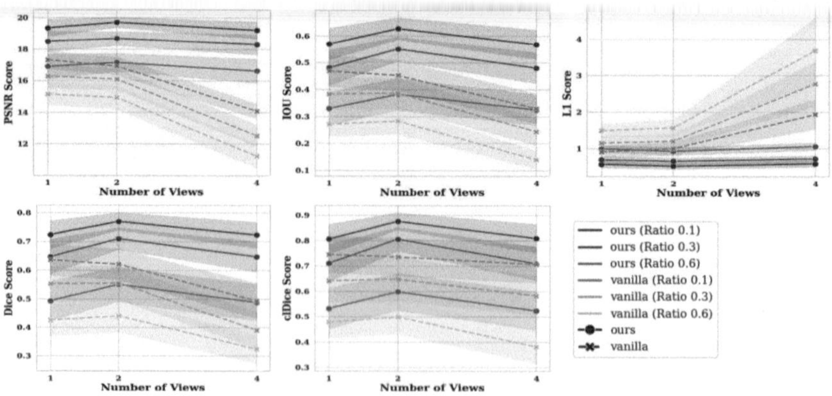

Fig. 4. Ablation study metrics for our proposed method and the vanilla baseline across varying masking ratios and numbers of viewpoints.

formance declines as view count increases due to its inability to learn view-dependent geometric relationships.

4 Conclusion

We propose a camera pose-guided multiple wrist-view fusion framework for the occlusion reconstruction and segmentation of surgical sutures. To support this fine-grained task, we meticulously curated a novel dataset, establishing the first benchmark for micro-scale flexible object reconstruction under multi-view occlusion. Our approach robustly demonstrates that wrist-mounted perspectives significantly enhance fine-grained perception, underscoring the transformative potential of wrist cameras in microsurgical anastomosis procedures.

Acknowledgements. This work was supported by Shanghai Municipal Science and Technology Major Project 2021SHZDZX. This work was supported by National Natural and Science Foundation of China under grant 62203296.

Disclosure of Interests. The authors have no competing interests to declare that are relevant to the content of this article.

References

1. Cao, S., et al.: Robot-assisted osteotomy and reconstruction with AR guidance in maxillofacial reconstructive surgery. Cyborg and Bionic Syst. **7** (2026). https://doi.org/10.34133/cbsystems.0590
2. Cuevas-Velasquez, H., Li, N., Tylecek, R., Saval-Calvo, M., Fisher, R.B.: Hybrid multi-camera visual servoing to moving target. In: IEEE/RSJ International Conference on Intelligent Robots and Systems (IROS), pp. 1132–1137. IEEE (2018)
3. He, K., Chen, X., Xie, S., Li, Y., Dollár, P., Girshick, R.: Masked autoencoders are scalable vision learners. In: Proceedings of the IEEE/CVF Conference on Computer Vision and Pattern Recognition, pp. 16000–16009 (2022)
4. Kim, J.W., et al.: SRT-H: a hierarchical framework for autonomous surgery via language-conditioned imitation learning. Sci. robot. **10**(104), eadt5254 (2025)
5. Li, R., Yi, B., Liu, J., Gao, H., Ma, Y., Kanazawa, A.: Cameras as relative positional encoding. arXiv preprint arXiv:2507.10496 (2025)
6. Li, S., Zhou, J., Jia, Z., Yeung, D.Y., Mason, M.T.: Learning accurate objectness instance segmentation from photorealistic rendering for robotic manipulation. In: International Symposium on Experimental Robotics, pp. 245–255. Springer, Cham (2018). https://doi.org/10.1007/978-3-030-33950-0_22
7. Li, Z., et al.: Bevformer: learning bird's-eye-view representation from lidar-camera via spatiotemporal transformers. IEEE Trans. Pattern Anal. Mach. Intell. **47**(3), 2020–2036 (2024)
8. Liu, H., Zhang, E., Wu, J., Hong, M., Jin, Y.: Surgical SAM 2: real-time segment anything in surgical video by efficient frame pruning. arXiv preprint arXiv:2408.07931 (2024)

9. Liu, Y., et al.: Simultaneous surgical stereo depth and motion estimation via brightness-aware self-supervised learning. Pattern Recogn. **179**, 113510 (2026). https://doi.org/10.1016/j.patcog.2026.113510
10. Long, Y., et al.: Surgical embodied intelligence for generalized task autonomy in laparoscopic robot-assisted surgery. Sci. Robot. **10**(104), eadt3093 (2025)
11. Luan, Y., et al.: Autofocusing with 3-D tracking for robot-assisted microsurgery. IEEE/ASME Trans. Mechatron. **31**(1), 220–231 (2026). https://doi.org/10.1109/TMECH.2025.3585533
12. Oord, A.v.d., Li, Y., Vinyals, O.: Representation learning with contrastive predictive coding. arXiv preprint arXiv:1807.03748 (2018)
13. Ostrander, B.T., Massillon, D., Meller, L., Chiu, Z.Y., Yip, M., Orosco, R.K.: The current state of autonomous suturing: a systematic review. Surg. Endosc. **38**(5), 2383–2397 (2024)
14. Pan, W., et al.: Semi-supervised semantic segmentation meets masked modeling: fine-grained locality learning matters in consistency regularization. Pattern Recognition p. 112586 (2025)
15. Ravi, N., et al.: SAM 2: segment anything in images and videos. arXiv preprint arXiv:2408.00714 (2024)
16. Seo, Y., Kim, J., James, S., Lee, K., Shin, J., Abbeel, P.: Multi-view masked world models for visual robotic manipulation. In: International Conference on Machine Learning, pp. 30613–30632, PMLR (2023)
17. Shen, W., et al.: Multiview integration network for multitask robotic surgical scene analysis. In: IEEE Transactions on Instrumentation and Measurement (2025)
18. Shit, S., et al.: clDICE-a novel topology-preserving loss function for tubular structure segmentation. In: Proceedings of the IEEE/CVF Conference on Computer Vision and Pattern Recognition, pp. 16560–16569 (2021)
19. Siméoni, O., et al.: Dinov3. arXiv preprint arXiv:2508.10104 (2025)
20. Su, J., Ahmed, M., Lu, Y., Pan, S., Bo, W., Liu, Y.: Roformer: enhanced transformer with rotary position embedding. Neurocomputing **568**, 127063 (2024)
21. Tran, M., Vo, K., Yamazaki, K., Fernandes, A., Kidd, M., Le, N.: Aisformer: amodal instance segmentation with transformer. arXiv preprint arXiv:2210.06323 (2022)
22. Wang, X., Guo, S., Xu, Z., Zhang, Z., Sun, Z., Xu, Y.: A robotic teleoperation system enhanced by augmented reality for natural human-robot interaction. Cyborg and Bionic Syst. **5** (2024). https://doi.org/10.34133/cbsystems.0098
23. Xu, H., Xiang, L., Ye, H., Yao, D., Chu, P., Li, B.: Permutation equivariance of transformers and its applications. In: Proceedings of the IEEE/CVF Conference on Computer Vision and Pattern Recognition, pp. 5987–5996 (2024)
24. Yang, G.Z., et al.: The grand challenges of science robotics. Sci. Robot. **3**(14), eaar7650 (2018)
25. Yu, Y., Zeng, Z., Zheng, H., Luo, J.: OmniPaint: mastering object-oriented editing via disentangled insertion-removal inpainting. In: Proceedings of the IEEE/CVF International Conference on Computer Vision, pp. 17324–17334 (2025)
26. Zeng, Y., Fu, J., Chao, H., Guo, B.: Aggregated contextual transformations for high-resolution image inpainting. IEEE Trans. Visual Comput. Graphics **29**(7), 3266–3280 (2022)
27. Zeng, Y., Lin, Z., Lu, H., Patel, V.M.: CR-FILL: generative image inpainting with auxiliary contextual reconstruction. In: Proceedings of the IEEE/CVF International Conference on Computer Vision, pp. 14164–14173 (2021)
28. Zhou, B., Krähenbühl, P.: Cross-view transformers for real-time map-view semantic segmentation. In: Proceedings of the IEEE/CVF Conference on Computer Vision and Pattern Recognition, pp. 13760–13769 (2022)

29. Zhou, X.-Y., Guo, Y., Shen, M., Yang, G.-Z.: Application of artificial intelligence in surgery. Frontiers of Medicine **14**(4), 417–430 (2020). https://doi.org/10.1007/s11684-020-0770-0
30. Zhou, X., Liu, Y., Zhang, M., Li, J., Guo, Y., Yang, G.Z.: Deep coarse-to-fine networks for robust segmentation and pose estimation of surgical suturing threads. In: 2025 IEEE/RSJ International Conference on Intelligent Robots and Systems (IROS), pp. 520–526. IEEE (2025)

Author Index

G. Yang et al. (Eds.): MICCAI 2026, LNCS 16893, pp. 637–641, 2027.
https://doi.org/10.1007/978-3-032-38236-8

R

S

T

U

V

W